THE

GREAT

POWERS

&

EASTERN

EUROPE

John A. Lukacs

CHESTNUT HILL COLLEGE AND LA SALLE COLLEGE

AMERICAN BOOK COMPANY

• *New York* •

COPYRIGHT ACKNOWLEDGMENTS

In addition to the copyright acknowledgments listed below, the author and publishers of *The Great Powers and Eastern Europe* gratefully acknowledge permission to quote from copyrighted material granted by the persons, publishers, and periodicals named in the Explanatory Notes: References section at the end of this volume.

Brandt & Brandt, for selections from *I Was There*, by William D. Leahy, published by Whittlesey House, Copyright, 1950, by William D. Leahy.

Cassell & Co., Ltd., for extension to Canada of permission to quote selections from *The Gathering Storm*, copyright, 1948, *Closing the Ring*, copyright, 1950, *The Grand Alliance*, copyright, 1950, and *The Hinge of Fate*, copyright, 1950, all by Winston Churchill.

Doubleday & Co., Inc., for selections from *Defeat in Victory*, by Jan Ciechanowski. Copyright, 1947, by Jan Ciechanowski, reprinted by permission of Doubleday & Company, Inc.

Macmillan & Co., Ltd. (London), for extension to Canada of permission to quote a selection from *Munich, Prologue to Tragedy*, by John Wheeler-Bennett, copyright, 1948.

Pearn, Pollinger, & Higham, Ltd., for extension to Canada of permission to quote a selection from *The Second World War*, by J. F. C. Fuller, copyright, 1949.

To the memory of my grandfather:
a better man of a better age.

PREFACE

&

ACKNOWLEDGMENTS

The reasons why men occasionally try writing history are curious and varied: and very personal emotions certainly do rank among them. Thus an account of a few personal dates is perhaps not out of order here. The city where I was born, where I lived and studied, was occupied by the German Armies on March 19, 1944; by the Russian Armies on January 18, 1945. I escaped from my country on July 26, 1946, walking across the frontier to Austria. I arrived in the United States on October 26, 1946. More than five years have passed since: they have been years of paradox. Never has the American and Western European public been as aware of and indignant about happenings in Eastern Europe as in these years; on the other hand, never has that unfortunate half of Europe been as segregated, chained, abandoned as it is today. To write this book I had to overcome serious doubts: was it worthwhile to try and describe the recent, tormented past of small nations now out of the range of the West and at the present remoulded, recast by the East? Finally — and perhaps not without some wilful self-delusion — I cast these doubts aside. There were causes to be served, after all. There was my conviction that the failures of peacemaking in 1919 and 1945 were due to Allied misinformation about central and eastern European realities. There was my knowledge of how much of that misinformation remains with us in the form of hasty formulae and superficial clichés, more harmful than ever today, in this age of "the terrible simplifiers." There was my resulting belief that the tragedy of Europe in the three most fateful phases of its recent past, 1915–20, 1934–39, 1942–47, was due to a more or less conscious

Western underestimation of central-eastern Europe's international importance.

The reader may notice that in a number of instances my interpretation does not conform with certain widely held versions of contemporary history. This, however, does not mean that I wished to write a "revisionist" book. The somewhat vague concept of historical revisionism is applicable only when there is an abundance of well-documented historical writing which, because of its unilateral emphasis or perspective, needs to be counterbalanced. There is no abundance of well-documented historical writing on the international history of central-eastern Europe.

In the Introduction which follows, I have tried to explain the geographical and chronological limits of my work. I find no need to comment on the recognized difficulties of writing contemporary history. They are tremendous. I would remark, however, that the responsibilities of the contemporary historian are also very great: to note but one example, I am convinced that many unwarranted illusions current during the last war about the Soviets' character and international behavior were due to a misreading of the record of Soviet foreign policy in the thirties, especially before and around Munich. On the other hand the somewhat curious techniques of contemporary documentations give us access to papers and documents with sometimes astonishing frequency and speed. It is remarkable that the full story of the Munich period may be written today with reasonable finality; here, incidentally, was much room for "revisionism"! Concerning the variety of sources consulted and concerning certain rather inevitable limitations, I refer the reader to my Bibliographical Note; here I wish to remark that the written record alone is not all and that parts of my book have been based on reminiscences, conversations, and personal correspondence, especially where I intended to present hitherto unavailable information. For technical reasons I have not followed the precise rules for transliteration from eastern European and Slavic languages. The reader is referred here to the excellent orthographic guide issued by *The American Slavic and East European Review*.

.   .   .   .   .   .

There are three persons without whose aid this book could not have been written. They are probably unaware of the nature and degree of my indebtedness. Rear-Admiral William F. Dietrich, USN, Ret., was the man who got me out of prison and helped me escape, ultimately to the United States. Ross Hoffman of Fordham University will hardly remember a talk we had on a hot June day in 1948 at Fordham. Yet it was his kind words then which made me shake off despair and finally decide to write this book. The kindness of Sister Maria Kostka, President of Chestnut Hill College, made it possible for me to find time and opportunity to write by generously arranging teaching schedules. Moreover, her understanding, together with that of the other Sisters of Chestnut Hill's administration, helped produce the atmosphere of relative peace needed for the writing of this book.

Many others have helped me. Cornelius Francis Sullivan of La Salle gave me full benefit of his literary criticism for the entire manuscript. Felix Gilbert of Bryn Mawr, Jack Howard and Robert Strausz-Hupé of the University of Pennsylvania read parts of the first draft. The constant assistance of Sister Ann Xavier, Librarian of Chestnut Hill College was very valuable; she as well as the whole staff of the University of Pennsylvania Libraries were ever charitable and patient with me. I am indebted to His Imperial and Royal Highness J. Otto Habsburg, and Their Excellencies Nicholas de Kállay and Tibor Eckhardt for their permission to consult the papers in their safe-keeping regarding the secret Hungarian armistice negotiations of 1943–44. Ambassador William C. Bullitt, Dr. Tibor Eckhardt, Sabin Manuila, the late Minister H. F. Arthur Schoenfeld, Chester Wilmot, Professor Mario Toscano, Historical Consultant to the Italian Ministry of Foreign Affairs, gave me valuable information or counsel. In the summer of 1951 Sister Clare Joseph helped me to arrange a small seminar in diplomatic history among the advanced history students of the Sisters of St. Joseph; the work done there was useful in the classification of materials for the second part of my appendix on Munich. Of my other students John Fillmore, Class of 1952, La Salle College, Felix Moletteri, '52, and James F. Sullivan, '54 worked with me in organizing the bibliographical entries. John Warren, '50, did some of the early typing. Miss Rosemary P. Haigh was far more than a typist. Her intelligence, literary knowledge and wit assisted me in surmounting many obstacles.

J. A. L.

CONTENTS

PART I (1917-1934)

PART II (*February 1934-October 1938*)

PART III (*October 1938-June 1941*)

PART IV (1941-1944)

[xi

PART V (*January 1944-July 1945*)

PART VI (*1946-1952*)

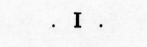

. I .

INTRODUCTION:

THE ILLUSION

OF

INDEPENDENCE

An introduction

In history, unlike in drama, the actors need not be identified in advance; they speak for themselves. The scene alone requires definition; however, this can be a most complex and formidable task. Formidable, indeed, here: for the scene of this volume begs an unequivocal definition even by geography. Clever pamphleteers fought and ignorant armies clashed by night to decide where this scene was to belong: to the East; to the West; to the Center; to Europe; to Asia. We deal with a stretch of Europe from the Arctic to the Aegean Seas. Lately thirteen nations existed there. But this is not enough for a description. What is the scene, then? Central Europe; Central-eastern Europe; Eastern Europe; Mid-eastern Europe; Eurasian Europe; South-eastern Europe; Danubian Europe — these are but the most frequent terms.

·   ·   ·   ·   ·   ·   ·

European history is conditioned by the sea: we must not let the awful sights of great land migrations, land Powers and land battles obscure our vision. Europe is a peninsula of many peninsulas, full of mountains and bays, virtually a rocky, rugged promontory of Asia, that great land-mass. Greece, Rome, North Italy, Spain, France, the Lowlands, England — the great areas and focal centers of European history — were all made, protected, succoured by surrounding

[3

seas. At the present time, in this era of national states, but three or four of the thirty-odd European states are land-locked. All others touch the seas.

Moving from West to East in Europe, however, there is less and less sea: the continent and its peninsulas broaden, the mountains and bays drop behind. Europe is surrounded by seas on all sides, except in the East, where there is no real, natural frontier. Only thousands of miles away, on the big, flat chest of Russia, rises the dull crest of the Ural Mountains; these mountains are not very high, nor do they stretch long enough to form a complete border between "European" and "Asiatic" Russia. Thus throughout the vast stretches of Russia and the flatlands of Eastern Europe the great plains of Asia silently, ominously melt into the contracted and nervously undulating body of Europe. Through these big plains marched hordes of Germanic tribes, Vandals, Huns, Tartars, Turks, Russians against Europe: the raw, fermenting hordes of Asia. For Asia is mostly plains, steppe, desert, except for its peninsulas; Europe is seas and mountains: peninsulas. The typical Asiatic is plainsman or valley-dweller; the typical European, mountaineer or sailor. There was no frontier to defend the Western European peninsulas from the East; but there were the people who lived in the eastern half of Europe, people who, albeit unwittingly, often shed their blood to save the West. Here was the zone of transition.

Thus the main trend of European history was in an East-West direction. Never was Europe threatened from the West; almost always from the East. History moved, however, from West to East also, as Western culture and civilization constantly expanded eastward. For frontiers are not only geographic. Europe has, of course, her geographic frontiers which have existed since the geological formation of the continent. But there is a much more vague, social-political frontier, a line within which nations and states are of the European community and beyond which the respective societies are of a non-European character. There is, also, an even more vague and oscillating frontier of culture: a borderline between areas predominantly infused with Western-Christian culture and lands which belong to other civilizations where neither Christian religion nor Western civilization predominates.

Since about 1000 the geographic, political, and cultural frontiers of Europe largely coincided in the West. After the last Arabs left Spain, the same fortunate circumstances prevailed in southern

Europe. About 1500, the three frontiers were essentially coterminous everywhere except in the East. The Center, Germany, then broke up in the wars caused by the Reformation, and new Powers rose in the east: Prussia and Russia. Both expanded westward; but their expansion was made possible only by an eastward movement of Western culture. Prussia and, to a much lesser extent, Russia, then went through a rough process of grammar-school education in the ways of Europe. Had Russia remained an essentially eastern-type state, challenging and battling not only her bordering states but also Western-Christian civilization in eastern Europe, her expansion would have been halted and she herself defeated by a continent united in danger before the spectre of a new Asiatic invasion. Peter 1 of Russia saw this: he began to transform Russia into a western-type state (and Russia expanded further). About 1800 the political frontier of Europe included Russia and thus coincided with the geographic frontier in the east. During the next century Western culture, arts, and industrial capitalism penetrated Russia. By about 1900 Europe was a unit: except for the decaying crumbs of the Ottoman Empire in the Balkans, the geographical, political, and cultural concepts of Europe coincided.

This almost ideal picture was destroyed by the events of 1917. The new Bolshevik régime rapidly isolated Russia from Europe; with the October Revolution a thousand-year process came to an end. The political and cultural westernization of the East stopped; indeed, the political and cultural frontiers of Europe retreated at first to the western borders of Russia; another war, and in thirty years these boundaries were pushed back another five hundred miles to the west. Thus in 1947 they stood in the middle of the continent, roughly along the Stettin-Trieste line, at points which, by a curious historical coincidence, had marked the frontiers of Europe eleven hundred years before, when Western Christianity started to move east. For the "iron curtain" line almost exactly coincides with the eastern frontiers of Charlemagne's empire.

.   .   .   .   .

This alone may account for the importance of the regions east of Germany and west of Russia. When this area — central-eastern Europe — belongs to Europe, the continent is safe from Asia. When this region is lost, the continent is in mortal danger, saved perhaps by miracles — or other, miraculous continents. The only all-European war in the Hundred Years' Peace (1815–1914), the Crimean War (1853–56), started in central-eastern Europe. The First World War started in and largely because of central-eastern Europe. So with the Second. And, were it not for the Russian occupation of central-eastern Europe, it is questionable whether the danger of a Third World War would exist in its present acute form: after all, the world-wide appeal of Communism is not much greater than it was in 1939. But it is Russia's present strategic position, her control over central-eastern Europe (and perhaps China) which counts: without it our present crisis would be far more limited, far less dangerous.

The finest and most concise discussion of central-eastern Europe's rôle in European history can be found in Professor Oscar Halecki's book, *The Limits and Divisions of European History* (1950). He deals with definitions, an inspiring endeavor, for definitions are more often dangerous than necessary. Here our definitions are necessarily arbitrary, made for the sake of drawing the frontiers of this volume. The actors of modern history are national states (alas, for the worse!). Let us, then, take those nations between Germany and Russia which have had some modern experiences with statehood: Finland, Estonia, Latvia, Lithuania, Poland, Czechoslovakia, Austria, Hungary, Rumania, Yugoslavia, Albania, Bulgaria, Greece. Their statehood became a tangible reality when, in 1917–18, Russia and Turkey retired and Austria-Hungary crumbled. The Russo-German frontier in 1918 ceased to exist. In the now inevitable gap between Germany, Austria, and Russia lay the future of Europe; but too few of the Western Allies saw this. In vain did a British geographer, Sir Halford Mackinder, speak of vague-sounding "geopolitical equations" in 1919, stating that whoever rules eastern Europe, rules the world. By then the central-eastern European states were here, some born in blood, more amidst clouds and confused tears.

They did not seem to belong together, not even by geographical definitions. If, for the sake of simplicity, one considers five European regions: North, South, West, East, Center, then Finland and the Baltic States can claim that they belong to Northern Europe, but they are also Eastern Europe; Lithuania may claim to be Central; Poland Central or Eastern; Czechoslovakia, Austria, Hungary Central, Austria even Western, Hungary South-eastern; so with Yugoslavia; Albania, Greece again Southern; infinite varieties these. Thus "central-eastern Europe" is but a convenient definition to delimit our scene.

There are, however, a few geographical realities. For these nations are bound to the Center and to the West; they have little, if any, of the Asiatic background or the hinterlands which Russia has. Thus they are not really Eastern, but central-eastern. (It may be said that Eastern Europe = European Russia.) Although they are vastly different, they also have certain common characteristics. Western Europe is largely overpopulated and industrialized. Central-eastern Europe is predominantly agricultural: except in Austria, parts of Czechoslovakia, Finland, Poland, and Hungary, the industrial revolution had just begun in recent decades. The density of population is reasonably slight: indeed, almost everywhere in central-eastern Europe the population is steadily rising, overtaking the West. Excepting the British Isles and Spain, the Holy Roman Empire gave an imprint of cultural unity to Western Europe which even withstood the split caused by Protestantism. The peoples of central-eastern Europe have less experience with statehood; their literatures are newer, their culture more folkish and rural. Their Christianity is deep and often unmarred by secular and other influences, yet, here again they are not united; unlike Southern, Catholic and Northern, Protestant Europe, there are patches of religious minorities here and there. Wholly Catholic Poland and Austria, wholly Orthodox Greece and Bulgaria, wholly Lutheran Finland and Estonia are the exceptions. There are Catholics in Lutheran Latvia, Unitarians, Catholics, and Uniates in Czechoslovakia, Calvinists in Catholic Hungary, Mohammedans and Catholics in Orthodox Yugoslavia, etc., etc. This brittle mosaic of religions, languages, and nationalities seems further complicated by the aggregation of the Jews: whereas in no Western European nation does the Jewish population exceed about two per cent, in pre-war Poland more than ten per cent of the people were Jews, in Rumania more than seven, and the percentage was also high in Lithuania, Latvia, Czechoslovakia, Austria, and Hungary. In most of these countries there was no trading or industrial class; except for the civil servants, the Jews (in some places, the Germans) were the urban middle-class. This was again unusual and unbalanced.*

---

* These remarks apply to the pre-World War II situation. The last war and its wake brought immense changes in society. Nine-tenths of the central-eastern European Jews were liquidated; the only countries where substantial Jewish minorities remain are Rumania and Bulgaria where about two-thirds, and Hungary where one-third, of the Jewish population survived. The rest of the middle classes is presently being eliminated by the Communists. Most of the German settlers were expelled and Russian settlers brought into other areas.

When in 1917–18 the independence of many central-eastern European nations was at hand, unity and strength were missing. Of all these nations Poland was largest, and there were not more than about 21 million Poles, hemmed in between 70 million Germans and the 170 millions of the Russian Empire. There were many illusions and much undue optimism.

.   .   .   .

The experiment of independence ultimately failed because of this lack of unity and insight. Much blame falls on the hot and unruly heads of the new central-eastern European states themselves. Yet the blame must be at least shared by the Great Powers and not in the least by the Western Allies, France, Britain, and the United States, the creators of the 1917 illusions and the makers of a bad peace. The fate of these small nations was, in the long run, influenced much more by the Great Powers than was at any time expected. In the last century the Great Powers often felt compelled to intervene and, if with sour temperaments, act in concert to stamp out dangerous sparks around Balkan and other central-eastern European powder kegs. Even if one of the Great Powers, such as Russia, stirred the fire under Balkan cauldrons, it was the other Great Powers whose action redressed the balance. Now, after 1917, there were thirteen independent nations in central-eastern Europe and it certainly seemed that with national self-determination and this sudden increase in independent units, the Great Powers' influence in this area would be less decisive.

This turned out to be an illusion: a paradoxical development. For, although the independent behavior of the central-eastern European states grew (by the end of the 1920's all federation plans were shelved and Western alliances and commitments watered down), they imperceptibly turned out to be less independent than ever. Unlike heretofore, by the 1930's it was the Balkans which were generally quiet and the war drums rolled in other quarters, Italy, Germany, Russia: in 1934 the Diplomatic Revolution began with Germany and Russia returning to the scene as First Powers, while France and Britain fell far back. Then the illusions of independence came to an end, and this point sets the limits of this volume. From 1934 on, the fate of central-eastern Europe well-nigh exclusively depended on the moods, attitudes, and actions of the Great Powers. And here all the central-eastern European states were involved: notwithstanding the great differences between nations such as Finland and Greece, Estonia and Bulgaria, all the peoples between Germany and Russia can be included in a great central-eastern European scene. Hence, after a short survey of the period of illusory independence, a detailed treatment of eleven years, 1934–45, will follow: a most eventful and terrible period, with an awful continental war. Germany rises first, ominously, swiftly, and dominates all. Then Russia takes over. Central-eastern Europe — and the world — suffer.

. . . .

What follows, therefore, is not a central-eastern European chronicle, but a threefold history: how did the nations of central-eastern Europe act toward each other? what were the relations of the Great Powers with each other, relations concerning central-eastern Europe? how did the Great Powers treat directly with the central-eastern European nations? Altogether, this is more than a segment of European and Russian diplomatic history, and at least a slice of American diplomatic history is involved. Complexity and limits of space partly account for the lack of contemporary political conclusions drawn; yet conclusions, if any, are inherent in the story itself.

The illusion of independence: 1917–34

[*1917.*] The First World War became an ideological war in 1917.

> A war which is preeminently revolutionary in character is . . . an ideological war. It is much more than a collision between States motivated by limited purposes which can be only achieved by force. There is in it a challenge to all the world; on one side or both, there is an effort to vindicate or propagate universally an ideological purpose. The *rationale* of a better world has been revealed, and there is an apocalyptic vision of the world remade and man reborn. A militant party obtains commanding power and acts in the firm conviction that it possesses the truths necessary to the temporal salvation of mankind . . .*

The character of the war, which started out in 1914 as a struggle for territories and spheres of influence, changed with the entrance

---

* Ross J. S. Hoffman, "Peacemaking after Ideological Wars," *Thought* (October 1945).

of the United States into the war and into European politics. Her entry was made plausible to the American people by ideological arguments. Russia withdrew from the war and from Europe; this withdrawal also had an ideological basis. With America, the war became a struggle for global democracy and national self-determination. With Russia, the war became a phase of the ideological struggle for international Communism.

These were momentous developments. The First World War lost its hitherto almost exclusively European character. For the first time in history a European war was to be decided by two non-European powers: one, Russia, temporarily withdrawing from the European scene, the other, America, temporarily entering it. Thirty years later this development reached its logical conclusions: by 1947 the fate of all Europe exclusively depended on the actions of Russia and America.

[*Independence movements: the Allies' commitments.*] The Russian revolutions of 1917 had vast political and military consequences in central-eastern Europe. In the Balkans the nuclei of national states had existed since the previous century; although not all Serbs lived within Serbia and not all Rumanians were united within Rumania, Bulgaria, Greece, Serbia, and Rumania had been in existence for several decades; by 1914 small Albania had also emerged. Further north, along the great frontier between German and Slav, there were none of these national states. Several mature nations lay, oppressed in one way or another, on the western borders of Russia. Finns, Estonians, Latvians, Lithuanians, Poles, Ukrainians, and other minor groups were about ready for independence; Germany's eastern marches also had a goodly number of Poles, and the unique Habsburg monarchy harbored Czechs, Slovaks, Poles, Ruthenians (or Carpatho-Ukrainians), Rumanians, Serbs, Croats, Slovenes, Italians. Most of these people were Slavs; most of the Slavs, except for the Poles, cast their hopes on a Russian victory when the war began in 1914. Some of the Slavs (certain Czechs), a few Italians* and most

---

* A dramatic and new piece of evidence of certain Italians' historic foresight was recently revealed in the correspondence of the Italian envoys to Vienna and Berlin in late 1914. (Carteggio Avarna-Bollati, in the *Rivista Storica Italiana*, 1949 — III–IV.) They were against the pro-Allied, interventionist policy of Salandra and Sonnino. Avarna told Sonnino that an Entente victory would be worse for Italy than a victory of the Central Powers. Avarna again, on December 15, 1914: if Russia wins, "we shall have to fight in the Balkans and the Adriatic with Serbia, a young power, ultimately more frightful than Austria-Hungary and supported by Russia [against us] . . ." Bollati, on December 23, feared

of the others, were wary. For the Western Allies, partly due to their plight, partly due to their want of interest and intelligence concerning central-eastern Europe, made dangerous, unreasonable promises and commitments when the bleak clouds of the war years weighed down on them: forerunners of Moscow, Teheran, Yalta, Potsdam! In 1915–16 France and Britain practically acquiesced in a Russian domination of the eastern Balkans and the Straits; a vague agreement between France and Russia in February 1917 went even further; in April 1915 the Treaty of London promised Trieste, Istria, the Dalmatian and Albanian coasts, and South Tyrol, among other territories, to Italy; in August 1916 Rumania was promised Transylvania; in February 1916 the French committed themselves to the establishment of a Czechoslovak state; in July 1917 Britain and France agreed to create a South, "Yugo"-Slav state after the war.

[*Independence movements: German advance and withdrawal.*] The Bolshevik Revolution, then, was in a way politically fortunate for the Allies: it automatically freed them from their central-eastern European territorial commitments to Russia. But it opened new military dangers. While these dangers developed, the independence movements of central-eastern Europe were on their way. Estonia reacted quickest, almost simultaneously with the abdication of the Tsar in March. Poles, Finns, Latvians, Lithuanians followed in due course. The new Russian provisional, would-be democratic government promised independence to the border peoples, but these were singularly wary of Russian promises, not without reason. Presently there came another development. To Finns and to some Latvians and Poles in 1916–17 it seemed that the key to their independence lay with Germany, which promised them statehood at Russia's expense; but it became increasingly clear that the Germans had not much more than satellite status in mind. (Austria, especially concerning Poland, had more humane and liberal designs, but her power was limited.) Thus, notwithstanding Baltic and Finnish reliance on German arms against the danger of incursions by the new, aggressive Bolshevik Russian régime, by early 1918 the nationalities' polit-

---

"possible rancor and vengeance" of the Central Powers. "For, even if [Germany] were defeated by the immense numerical preponderance of her enemies . . . a people with the power and magnificent qualities of the Germans cannot be destroyed, nor annihilated: and this people would never pardon Italy for what would be considered abandonment and treason . . . the revenge shall be awful!"

ical sympathies were with the Western Allies. Germany, with a
mixture of arrogance and ignorance, threw most of her chances away,
especially as events momentarily weighed in her favor. Soon after
the Bolshevik revolution, Latvia and the Ukraine proclaimed complete independence. A "Ukrainian Republic" signed a "separate
peace" with the Central Powers, while Trotsky, the Russian delegate, argued with the Germans in Brest-Litovsk about a separate
peace. The German demands were great. "We are out of the war but
refuse to sign a peace treaty," Trotsky announced; but, as Lenin said,
the Russian army "voted with its legs," that is, went home, and the
Germans pushed forward. To save their régime in face of a developing civil war and Allied intervention, the Bolsheviks decided to submit
to the German demands, and the Brest-Litovsk Treaty was signed on
March 3, 1918. It had provisions for a separate Ukraine; an "independent" Poland, Latvia, Lithuania, and Estonia; Caucasian cessions to Turkey; and economic and commercial concessions to Germany."* Although "discontinuation of external Bolshevik agitation"
was also numbered among the terms, it was soon evident that (just
as General Ludendorff had helped Lenin return to Russia the year
before) Brest-Litovsk helped the Red régime survive. For, although
in July and August Allied intervention against the Bolsheviks began,
Moscow saw the coming defeat of Germany by the Allies and the
subsequent evacuation of central-eastern Europe. On August 27 an
often forgotten supplementary treaty to Brest-Litovsk was signed
between Russia and Germany which was more favorable to the
Russians and foreshadowed the coming German withdrawal. Six
weeks later Germany asked for an armistice; ten weeks later the
European war ended. The grey stream of German soldiers poured
home from north-eastern Europe, and in their wake the Red Army
trickled in. In about a month, the Baltics were fighting overwhelming
Red Russian forces; Finland's borders were raided, and general
chaos reigned on the western borders of Russia, where the newly-
born independents had to stave off the new Russian threat alone,
without German armies to assist them and with only sporadic and
indirect Allied help. The short independence period came to an end.†

_____

* At Brest-Litovsk the Austro-Hungarians vainly tried to mitigate the German demands. The Peace of Bucharest, which in January 1918 was imposed by the Central
Powers on the defeated Rumanians, was harsh and economically oppressive, yet only very
insignificant territorial demands were presented by Austria-Hungary.

† Thus the general pattern was this: Phase i: 1917. Progress toward complete independence. Phase ii: 1918. End of first, short independence period by Bolshevik incur-

[*National self-determination.*] But we are running ahead of our main story. Although released from their political commitments to Russia — a not immediately evident fact — the Western Allies were immensely worried by the Bolsheviks' seizure of power, which realized their worst fears (and best German dreams): a one-front war for Germany. Now the Allies began to support politically the central-eastern European independence movements, as these movements were anti-Russian and, with the exception of Finland and perhaps Latvia, also anti-German. Militarily the Allied crisis was indeed grave. It was not solved by the meager amphibious landings along the vast, hostile, undefended coasts of Russia. It was ultimately eased by the arrival of a million Americans and the internal weaknesses of the Central Powers. For American intervention had its dramatic effects in central-eastern Europe. In January 1918 from one side of Europe, from the grey eastern plains echoed the treacherous bugle of the Brest-Litovsk cease-fire. From across the western oceans sounded the inspired message of an American President.

In January 1918, President Wilson announced his Fourteen Points. The underlying principle was national self-determination, the relative novelty of which obscured its very questionable value. To President Wilson this was a great chance to give the nations of central-eastern Europe the 1776, indeed, the 1787 denied to them by the historic trickeries of others. Wilson erroneously thought that nationalism and democracy do necessarily go hand in hand: a tragic mistake. About half of the Fourteen Points directly concerned central-eastern Europe: the Polish question, the nationalities of the Habsburg monarchy, etc. Their effects were immediate: the nationalities responded at once (especially the Czechs and the Lithuanians who had remarkably able connections in Washington and were influential with Wilson's entourage); within the Central Powers themselves more and more people began to believe that the Fourteen Points harbored the saving germs of a just peace, largely free from blind rancor. Thus Wilson was instrumental in the final collapse of the Central Powers, although the Fourteen Points rather expedited than generated this collapse.

———

sions and subsequent German military occupation: reduction of national sovereignty to satellite status. Phase III: October–November 1918. Second, brief period of temporary independence as Germans withdraw westward, ending with Bolshevik invasion from the east. Phase IV: 1919–20. Independence wars ending with Russian withdrawal and conclusion of treaties with Russia.

In September Turkey and Bulgaria collapsed; in October the Austro-Hungarian Monarchy began to disintegrate (the benevolent Emperor-King proclaimed the Monarchy to be a federation, but his reasonable terms came too late). The nationalities revolted; even Hungary, the junior partner, proclaimed herself an independent Republic by the end of October. Emperor Wilhelm fell on November 9; by Armistice Day a dozen new republics claimed existence in central-eastern Europe. There was widespread fighting within Austria-Hungary: "Yugoslav," Rumanian, "Czechoslovak," Polish "national armies" appeared from nowhere, sometimes led by petty potentates, sometimes by able generals such as Poland's Pilsudski. Fifteen or sixteen nationalities came thus into their own, but instead of looking into the future, they battled with infantile wrath and fury for the misery-ridden spoils of the present. There was but little to control them. In theory, the Allies were victorious. In the House of Lords on November 18, 1918, Lord Curzon spoke with assurance and pride: "The British flag has never flown over a more powerful or a more united empire. . . . Never did our voice count for more in the councils of nations; or in determining the future destinies of mankind." "Curzon had always possessed a sense of occasion," wrote Harold Nicolson in 1934. "On that 18th of November the dream (and not to Lord Curzon alone) seemed a reality. Now that it has dissolved we are able — with painfully acquired knowledge — to examine the wrecks."

.   .   .   .

[*Western chances.*]   Now peacemaking seemed to be the main, and perhaps the only task. In all of Europe, Asia, Africa, the Allies reigned supreme. Tiny British and French brigades ruled in such unlikely places as Baku, Salonika, Archangel, Memel, Corfu; the Allies alone seemed to sway the destinies of Europe. They seemed to be in possession of the continent.

But, to cite Harold Nicolson again,

> There was one thing, however, which the Allied democracies, and especially the British Empire, did not possess. They did not possess an enlightened or continuous will for power. It was not many weeks before this lack of unity, determination and enlightenment became apparent.

Perhaps never had the Allies had such a chance. The arch-villains of modern Europe, Russia and Prussia, were shorn of arms, sulking in defeat; a vast stretch of new Europe's marchland lay ahead for Allied manoeuvres and plans; central-eastern Europe from the Arctic to the Aegean was without Germans and Russians now. The Allies misused their chance. They allowed the monarchies, seats of stability, to be destroyed; here American anti-monarchist traditions and feeling had an important rôle. On the other hand, France, Italy, Britain were already committed to processes considerably less lofty than the American ideals of self-government and self-determination. The secret files of their Foreign Offices guarded documents which were concerned with something more realistic than ideas of a Europe to be made safe for democracy, documents which dealt with boundary changes and territorial occupations, and which contained provisions incompatible with Wilsonian principles. This was tragic. But it could have been rectified somehow on the old principle of European balance of power. Yet this was not done either.

[*The peace treaties.*]   Compared to what was happening in 1945–51, the peacemakers assembled and worked with unusual rapidity; within two years, all peace treaties were signed. With Germany at Versailles in June 1919, with Austria at St. Germain in October, with Bulgaria at Neuilly in November, with Hungary the next June in Trianon and with Turkey the next August at Sèvres, the paper work of the Congress of Paris was done. It was done badly. We could cite again Harold Nicolson, whose incomparable *Peace-making 1919* makes short shrift of the inaccuracies, stupidities, and faulty inclinations of the victors. Instead, let us cite the venerable Austrian Socialist Karl Renner, certainly no monarchist or upholder of any old order, who, looking back, wrote in July, 1948, in *Foreign Affairs:*

> In retrospect, what lessons can we draw from the lost opportunities of the Paris Peace Conference of 1919–1920? The Conference might, I think, have proceeded in one of two other ways. If it desired to adhere strictly to the principle of the creation of national states, under the slogan of the Self-Determination of Nations, it might have permitted the Italian territories to seek annexation to the Kingdom of Italy, the Jugoslav territory to Serbia, the Rumanian to the Kingdom of Rumania, and the German territory to the German Reich. This would have resulted in the dissolution of the Danubian mon-

archy, but would have checked the formation of international states. The prohibition of *Anschluss* [Union with Germany] was intended as a safeguard against German aggression. But had the Catholics and the Socialists of Austria voted in the German Reich . . . German democracy would not have capitulated to Hitler.

The other possible course for the Peace Conference would have been to decide that this well-balanced economic territory with its unified system of money and credit and communications should remain an entity. That would have meant that the national components, while not enjoying complete sovereignty, would have the highest possible measure of national autonomy within a federal constitution . . . and would continue to work and live together as they had for centuries. Such a commonwealth would have been a Great Power of the small nations, located between the hostile expansionist appetites from the northwest (Greater Germany), from the northeast (Russia), from the southeast (Pan-Slavism) and from the south (Italy), making Austria a larger Switzerland. Happily, it could not have entertained offensive ambitions, but it would have been eminently well made for defense, and a prototype for a Balkan Federation in the eastern Mediterranean . . .

. . . new states were created in the north, east and south, on the principle of nationality and *Anschluss*. But federation with the German Reich was forbidden to the Germans in Austria. The purpose was to safeguard France against a new attack, but the effect was to pave the way for it.

Often the peacemakers had to face accomplished facts; while the terms were being discussed, Rumanians, Serbs, Czechs, Poles, and irregulars were often in possession of the territories being considered in Paris and would not budge. Often reliable information failed to appear at the peacemakers' tables; bad "victor's peaces" resulted. Often the principle of self-determination turned out to be a deliberate farce when new states with wilfully drawn irregular frontiers were burdened with millions of frightened, seething, new inhabitants.* In some instances, the Wilsonian principles were duly honored, but this to the detriment of inter-Allied relations because of previous deals or present contingencies, thus sowing discord and hatred among the victors (for example, in the case of the Italian-Yugoslav frontier). In other instances the principle was largely flouted (as in the case of the Hungarian frontiers). In other instances again, flimsy settlements were made, honoring no ethnic principle but also

* See Table 1 in Appendix to Part I (following p. 31).

no previous agreement. By 1920 Britain cast a wary, suspicious eye at France; Italy was chafing and jealous of both France and Britain; America withdrew; France was unsure and worried. Unity among the victors was vanishing.

[*Chaos and petty wars.*]   The national revolutionary idea was on the march. While the chaos and proletarian revolutionary atmosphere of 1918–20 slowly dissipated (there were short-lived Communist experiments in Hungary and Bavaria), petty and furious nationalisms remained the main political forces in central-eastern Europe. Bitter skirmishes, even minor wars occurred in central-eastern Europe before, during, even after the conclusion of the peace treaties. Six of the new nations dreamed and acted in the spirit of unreal national expansion and grandeur. The St. Germain and Trianon Treaties consummated the establishment of three "successor" states of the Austro-Hungarian Monarchy: Greater Czechoslovakia, Greater Yugoslavia, and Greater Rumania came into existence almost unchallenged. Finnish nationalists wished to make Finland a great Baltic power and to include Finnish and Russian Karelia, the Kola Peninsula, the Baltic archipelagoes, and Estonia within a Greater Finland. Advocates of a greater Poland pressed for the frontiers of 1772, with most of Byelorussia and the western Ukraine included. Pan-Hellenes rejoiced in the territorial prospects of a Greater Greece, to extend into Asia Minor.

Thus the post-war years saw a series of central-eastern European civil wars, some between the new victors and the losers, some between the victors themselves, some even between the losers themselves — Finns and Russians fought in Karelia. Finland disputed with Sweden over the Aaland Islands. There was war between Russia and the new Baltic republics throughout 1919. Skirmishes continued on the Polish-German frontier, in Silesia until 1921. Czechoslovaks and Poles disputed three small frontier regions. Latvians and Estonians clashed over the province of Walk. Poles and Lithuanians tricked each other and fought over Wilnó. From December 1918 to November 1919 the Rumanians pushed into eastern and central Hungary. Hungary and Czechoslovakia battled on Slovakian territory. Yugoslavs and Hungarians fought a guerrilla war in southwestern Hungary; Hungary and Austria in Burgenland and Sopron. There was civil war between Whites and Reds in Hungary, in Lithuania, in Latvia; there was fighting between Baltic forces and German adventurers wandering in the

Baltic area. Yugoslav and Austrian irregulars skirmished in Carinthia; Italy intervened in Albania, only to be rebuked sharply by a somewhat belated admonition from Wilson; Yugoslavia and Albania battled continuously until 1921; the Italian poet, D'Annunzio, seized Fiume ahead of the Yugoslavs. Rumanian troops occupied Bessarabia and held it against Reds, Whites, Ukrainians, and Russians; Bulgarians and Serbs fought Macedonians in the dark valleys of Balkan mountains. And there were regular wars between Greece and Turkey; between Poland and Russia.

In addition to embattled frontiers, bloody incursions, storm troops moving through the night into foreign territory, the new states also faced great internal difficulties: Slovak-Czech, Croat-Serb, and Polish-Ukrainian distrust ran deep, and often erupted in armed conflict. Already the first post-war years indicated the weakness of the League of Nations' authority. This international organization in some instances could provide for some mutually acceptable compromises, but unsuccessful attempts to solve such problems as, for example, Fiume, Wilnó, and Eastern Karelia indicated the fictitious character of the League's alleged international power. Against an effective force there was not much that could be done, and thus many a forceful military coup, often contrary to elementary ethnic rights and international law, met with silent acquiescence; facts. brought about by force alone, received international recognition, often resulting in unjust and unrectified situations.

[*The Russian-European border.*] The case of Russia's new western boundaries was different. By 1920 the new Soviet régime had withstood the mortal threat of her enemies in the Russian Civil War, yet on the other hand, the chances for European Communist revolutions were receding. Except for temporary and sporadic attempts, no Communist government could establish itself in Europe beyond the territories which the Red Army then controlled. A normalization of Russo-European relations was now due; the first diplomatic task was that of fixing the Bolshevik boundary, especially in the Baltic, where Britain was gradually abandoning her support of rather unreliable White Russian generals and admirals. In February 1920 the (First) Treaty of Tartu was signed with Estonia, in July the Treaty of Moscow with Lithuania, in August (the First) Treaty of Riga with Latvia. These were generally (and territorially) reasonable treaties.*

---

* See Table 3 in Appendix to Part I (following p. 31).

[*The Polish-Russian war.*] Of course, they were also meant to influence the West; the Soviet Foreign Commissar, Chicherin, called the Estonian treaty "a dress rehearsal . . . for an understanding with the Entente . . . the first attempt to break through the blockade . . . the first experiment in peaceful cooperation with bourgeois States." Also, the Soviet Union was preparing to push her conflict with Poland to a full conclusion. As, under Lloyd George, British resolution to help the White Russians slowly waned, as British disgust with many of the freebooting central-eastern European nations became more and more evident, the Soviets counterattacked the patrolling Poles in force, after the latter had unwisely penetrated beyond Kiev in the Ukraine. (Pilsudski pursued a great Eastern Federation plan, but he found egotism among his neighbors, lack of understanding among the British and also among the French, in spite of their *cordon sanitaire* plans in central-eastern Europe.) By July Tukhachevski's Red Cossack legions had broken into central Poland. Here, then, was extreme danger (and certain Germans were now ready to jump on Poland's back, join with the Russian legions, and thus defiantly strike the Allied order down). Lloyd George was worried and ready to mediate with the Russians on the basis of a Polish-Russian frontier running roughly from Lwów straight north to the Lithuanian border — a price which he thought would prevent a Red excursion into the middle of Europe. (This proposed frontier was later called the Curzon Line, although the British Foreign Secretary had little to do with it. It was the creation of Lloyd George, who was pathetically ignorant of central and eastern European affairs.) The Russian negotiators suddenly hedged when the first Russian patrols in late July saw the spires of Warsaw. But there occurred the Miracle of the Vistula, as it was later called; Pilsudski, with some French help (General Weygand was there), defeated the Russians in one decisive battle on August 15, a battle which the later British Ambassador to Berlin called The Eighteenth Decisive Battle of the World. Pilsudski pursued the Russian hordes back toward Russia; the two-year-long Russian endeavor to spread Bolshevism by the sword in eastern Europe had to be abandoned. The Polish victory made Lenin drop military plans against Finland, and after some litigation the (Second) Treaty of Tartu between Russia and Finland was concluded in October 1920. The (Second) Treaty of Riga in March 1921 established peace and a Polish-Soviet frontier considerably east of the Curzon Line. This was the last — and most important — postwar treaty settlement in central-eastern Europe. Now peace could reign.

· · · · · ·

[*The lack of federations.*]   British foreign policy was hampered by narrow Prime Ministers and a very sluggish home opinion. The Foreign Secretaries, furthermore, quarreled with France; France in turn quarreled with herself in true Latin parliamentary fashion. Thus there was no real Western leadership, no stabilizing factor in a very unstable Europe, while there was but very little goodwill among the nations of central-eastern Europe.

Federations, the logical solution, were lacking. In 1922 there existed a wise plan for a great Baltic bloc from Poland to Finland, a joint defensive alliance; discussions culminated at a conference held in Warsaw. But political squabbles within Finland and Poland, the two anchor states, and Lithuanian-Polish enmity made all plans dissolve into thin air; only a frail Estonian-Latvian Alliance remained. Farther south, in the Balkans, there was much fervor for a "Green Alliance," a gradual federation of peasant states; the idea was carried forward by a remarkable person, the Bulgarian peasant statesman Stambuliski. But Croats fought Serbs, Serbs Macedonians, Macedonians Bulgars, and then Stambuliski was murdered and the Croat leaders were persecuted. (The Croat Peasant Party in its desperation even associated itself temporarily with the Third International of Moscow.) Thus vanished another noble plan.

[*Little Entente.*]   France, irked by British aloofness and suspicion, tried to erect an alliance system of her own. But her *cordon sanitaire* idea never really developed. Anxious to restrain Bolshevik Russia and an eventually renascent Germany, France in 1921 made alliances with Belgium in the West and Poland in the East; the Polish alliance was later supplemented by a military convention. At that same time the so-called Little Entente emerged. Rumania, Czechoslovakia, Yugoslavia, the successor states, allied themselves against Hungary and Austria in 1920-21. It was a frail and myopic structure. Its mere existence was a constant obstacle to Danubian reconciliation and fanned the flames of violent nationalism in Hungary, against whose resurgence the Little Entente was primarily directed. Neither was the strategic situation of this Little Entente good: a flabby ring of three states, unconnected by good routes, sparsely populated, harboring more than ten million people belonging to unfriendly national minorities. The interests of the members often clashed: Czechoslovakia did not support Rumania against Russia; Yugoslavia disagreed with Rumania on many points; the remark had been made that the Little Entente was so named because there was so little *entente* among its members. Neither was the Little Entente safely anchored to France. For France was wary of Germany, whereas the Little Entente aimed to contain Hungary and Austria (its only success occurred in 1921 when Little Entente threats frustrated the attempts of King Charles IV to return to the Hungarian throne). There was no link between Poland and Czechoslovakia, indeed, these two were jealous of each other. France and Czechoslovakia signed an alliance in 1925 which was an indirect French tie with the other members; France and Yugoslavia allied themselves in 1927 but this again was due to mutual fears of Italy. There was an important 1921 treaty between Poland and Rumania, which was extended into a military alliance in 1926, yet it was mainly directed against Russian intervention. Thus the Little Entente, instead of constituting a dependable eastern collateral of the French alliance system against Germany, ultimately proved to be of no value whatsoever: indeed, by 1938, it became a liability.

There were but slight attempts to improve relations between the victorious and the defeated states. Bulgar-Yugoslav rapprochement culminated in a treaty signed at Niš in 1923, but much goodwill disappeared with Stambuliski's death. Normal relations between Hungary and the Little Entente were virtually nonexistent until in 1922 a commercial treaty was made between Budapest and Prague. Republican Austria and republican Czechoslovakia had somewhat better relations: a friendship treaty was signed at Lana in 1921.

[*Italy and Turkey: growing revisionism.*]   In 1922–23 two important developments occurred which were to influence central-eastern Europe considerably. A victorious nationalist revolution in Turkey openly defied the Sèvres peace treaty and the Western Allies, and in a violent war destroyed the Greek armed forces. A conference assembled in Lausanne in November 1922 (there British diplomacy, with Curzon in the chair, perhaps showed its last glimmer of genius), and by March 1923 had replaced the Sèvres Treaty with a considerably better one. Here, a mere three years after the Congress of Paris, a defeated state had revolted and tore up an unjust treaty with ultimate success. Mustafa Kamâl's success deeply impressed the Balkans (not to speak of its effects in Greece, whose always turbulent politics now whirled in a tornado of protest which unseated the King in 1924; a ten-year-long republican experiment followed, replete with chaos and dictatorships).

More significant was the appearance of Mussolini on the scene. In October 1922 the Fascists gained power in Rome. Italy, frustrated by and angry with the high-handed manners of France and Britain, who disregarded many of their wartime commitments, was now bent on a more energetic Balkan policy. Mussolini at once exploited an incident and tried to wrest the island of Corfu from Greece in 1923, but international repercussions and the League made him abandon that plan. Yet Italy established herself in Fiume so strongly that in 1924 Belgrade found it necessary to cede that port in a treaty. Italy intervened in the Albanian frontier disputes with the Yugoslavs, and in 1925 the "Premier" of that tribal mountain state, Ahmed Zog, became the virtual dictator (three years later, King) of Albania; Italian economic and commercial concessions then made Albania wholly dependent on Rome, in which development Yugoslavia anxiously saw encirclement. Not without reason. In 1927 Mussolini offered his friendship to Hungary, somewhat later to Austria and Bulgaria; and these isolated states eagerly accepted. In the same year Mussolini stated that

> . . . between 1935 and 1940 we shall find ourselves at a point which I should call crucial in European history — we shall be in a position to make our voice felt, and to see at last our rights recognized.

What these rights were, was open to question. But all this spelled no favorable augury for the *status quo;* a year later Mussolini exclaimed that the peace treaties were not made for eternity. He aligned Italy with the revisionist states.

[*The climax of peace: Locarno.*] In central-eastern Europe "the zenith of peace" lasted from about 1924 to 1929. There was hope and prosperity in these years. Foremost was the economic recovery: Germany, Austria, Poland, Hungary stabilized their battered currencies; many commercial treaties were made between individual nations; high tariffs were slowly reduced; the Communist movements were rapidly losing ground. Also, Germany was re-entering the European comity of nations as an equal and again respected member. The fears of a "proletarian alliance" between Germany and Russia which three times had reached a climax — in August 1920 when the Russians stood before the walls of Warsaw, in April 1922 when a surprise treaty of friendship was signed between Russians and Germans at Rapallo, and in January 1923 when the French occupied the Ruhr and German economy crashed — were dissipating. In October 1925 at Locarno a new French Premier, Briand, grasped the hands of the German Foreign Minister, Stresemann, with full sincerity; Germany renounced her claims against Belgium and France. She was to enter the League of Nations. On the other hand, there was no "eastern Locarno"; Poland and Czechoslovakia were worried: was Germany to get a free hand in the east on some distant, future day? German nationalism was by no means dead, and, to reassure Russia, the Rapallo Treaty was extended into a Non-Aggression Treaty, signed in Berlin in April 1926. Yet with Stresemann in the Foreign Ministry, the Western orientation of Germany seemed secure; there was no crisis.

.   .   .   .

[*The authoritarian governments.*] Almost all of the new or rewritten central-eastern European constitutions were parliamentary and democratic, after republican French, federal Swiss, or other western models. The democratic experiments lasted for a while. Free elections, not untainted by corruption but largely free from coercion, were held in the first half-decade of newly-found independence. But no house can be built by putting the roof up first: the mere adaptations of western-type constitutions and political institutions did not provide for the missing foundations of democratic, liberal societies. Those essentials of Western democracy, strong and self-conscious middle-classes, were missing. Instead, there were clamoring parties and much parliamentary chaos; slowly the democratic experiments were abandoned.

The first series of dictatorships arose in 1926. In that year Pilsudski cut the Gordian knot of Polish parliamentary politics and established a semi-authoritarian, semi-parliamentary government. A more ambitious and less scrupulous man, Voldemaras, gained dictatorship in Lithuania with the help of the then President, Smetona (or, rather, with the help of the latter's wife). In that year also, Ahmed Zog of Albania transformed his rule into a full-fledged dictatorship. When in 1928 Croat-Serb enmity carried murder into the very heart of Belgrade's parliament (Radič, the Croat peasant leader, was shot by a Serb deputy), King Alexander I, facing civil war with Croatia, had to recur to dictatorship: in January 1929 the Serb-Croat-Slovene parliament was suspended and a royal-authoritarian Yugoslav state came into existence.

In view of the later, amazing history of the 1930's it is easy to brand all these changes "Fascist" dictatorships, and this was often done by British and American writers. Yet this is unjust and over-simplified, for in most cases the authoritarian governments of central-eastern Europe were actually safeguards against other, vicious, extremist mass movements. Such movements were ample in number and size. Paramilitary organizations, springing partly from the post-war chaos, partly from juvenile impatience and disgust with parliamentary lassitude and corruption, developed: "Lapua" in Finland, Estonian "Liberators," Latvian "Aizsargi," Lithuanian "Iron Wolves," "Heimwehr" and "Schutzbund" in Austria, "Arrow-Cross" in Hungary, "Iron Guard" in Rumania, Croatian "Ustaši," Bulgarian "Peasant Guards" and "Rodna Zaštita" and other, unpronounceable and innumerable varieties. The France of the 1870's and of the Boulanger era has been defined as a republic without republicans; now central-eastern Europe was replete with democracies without democrats. There also grew and spread a feeling against the West. The impoverished losers were apt to regard western democracy as hypocritical, and later the first attempts of German propaganda to portray Britain, France, and the United States as corrupt, rotting, inert, materialistic, and decadent were eagerly accepted by a bitter adolescent generation. Even in the new victor states popular feeling for the West waned as the constant drumming of nationalistic propaganda exaggerated the importance of their national efforts in the winning of independence; all this washed away much of the initial gratitude which Czechs, Slovaks, Croats, Poles, Rumanians, and others felt toward the Western Allies. (Later economic factors also entered: in the depression and after, Germany began to mean the West to many in the Danube Valley, dependent as they were on German industrial products.)

Under such circumstances many an authoritarian attempt in central-eastern Europe could be justly termed an escape to dictatorship. The second series came in 1934 when Estonia, Latvia, Austria, and Bulgaria (Greece in 1936) resorted to authoritarian government. Often this was a development favorable to the West: in Estonia, Latvia, and Austria the dictator-Presidents or Chancellors acted in the face of growing and threatening Nazi-type mass movements; as the Greek Social Democrat, Papandreou, put it in 1934, "a dictatorship may, in certain conditions, constitute a historical necessity when the supreme law of the country's salvation demands it."* It ultimately transpired that many of the authoritarian leaders (whom Western writers and politicians unjustly dubbed "Fascists") turned out to be the real opponents of the totalitarians: whatever their initial mistakes and ambitions, men such as King Alexander of Yugoslavia, Premier Metaxas of Greece, Admiral Horthy of Hungary, Chancellors Dollfuss and Schuschnigg of Austria, Presidents Ulmanis of Latvia and Päts of Estonia turned out to be more courageous and more formidable opponents of Hitler and Stalin than many so-called democrats: a Czech Beneš, a Rumanian Tatarescu, for example. But this is another story.†

[*The Communist parties.*] From 1921 to 1934 the foreign policy of the Soviet Union was characterized by isolation from Europe: a policy partly dictated by distrust and fear, partly by expediency and long-range calculations. Between 1923 and 1934 there were but two significant Communist coups in central-eastern Europe: in Estonia and in Bulgaria, both singularly unsuccessful and subsequently disavowed by the Soviet Foreign Commissariat. Except in Bulgaria, Greece, and parts of Yugoslavia the Communist parties were not significant. In Czechoslovakia alone the Communists lost 25 per cent of their votes from 1925 to 1929. Because of constant fears of communistic agitation, by 1938 the Communist parties were outlawed in every state excepting Czechoslovakia; but in the Baltic states and Bulgaria they operated for a while under a cover name, "Labor party." Completely insignificant in the mid-thirties, their only show of force occurred in 1932 when the "Bulgarian Labor Party" unexpectedly gained a majority in the municipal elections

---

* In Greece the 1936 elections put the small Communist Party in a decisive position, holding the parliamentary balance between an equal number of royalists and republican deputies.

† A definite difference between authoritarian and totalitarian governments could be detected in their respective evolution. All authoritarian governments gradually eased political restrictions and after some time even proceeded with a substituted constitution or some kind of parliament. Totalitarian governments, on the other hand, are forced by necessity to grow more ruthless, restrictive and monolithic. Cf. Table 2 in Appendix to Part I (following p. 31).

of Sofia. The party was promptly dissolved and the election results annulled.

It was certainly surprising that the depression which in 1930–34 shattered the economies of agrarian central-eastern Europe and smashed the renown of bourgeois capitalism did not spell out gains for the Communists. Instead, the appeal of Fascistic and National Socialist ideologies rose. This was the situation in Germany also; therefore in 1934–35 the direction of global Communism was revised. The Seventh Congress of the Communist International, which met in Moscow in 1935, issued the new strategy for united fronts of the Left: national Communist parties were to help form and eventually lead "popular fronts" against "international Fascism."

[*Russia and central-eastern Europe 1921–34.*] Meanwhile, Russian diplomacy in Europe concentrated on the German position. Only with Germany did Russia pursue secret military conventions for training and experiment; the Soviets strove for a German-Russian balance of power in central-eastern Europe which eventually might re-design that sphere; after all, both Germany and Russia had their primary ambitions in that region, the control of which they had lost after 1917. Yet Stresemann went to Locarno in a spirit of Western reconciliation. Russia became anxious lest Germany, ultimately at Russia's expense, draw irrevocably close to the West. Moscow immediately introduced negotiations for Friendship and Non-Aggression Treaties with those neighbors of Russia which were not aligned with the Western Powers. There were three such states, all of them nurturing some grievance against the Western-imposed *status quo:* Turkey, whose dictator, Kemâl, the West still regarded with some suspicion and who had established the earliest and friendliest ties with the Soviet Union in 1921; Afghanistan, where there was a glimmer of hope that her ruler Amanullah might pursue an actively anti-British policy; Lithuania, whose enmity against Poland made her sulk and refuse to join in a Baltic Entente. Between December 1925 and September 1926 these treaties were concluded. A multilateral Non-Aggression Treaty was offered to all Baltic states in 1926 (but not to Poland, which country the Russian-Baltic treaties were designed to isolate).

The negotiations were unsuccessful, as the Baltic states in their counterproposals raised the issue of binding and clear-cut definitions of aggression, an issue on which the Soviets did not wish to commit themselves. Moscow then proposed individual treaties instead. Only Latvia accepted, in March 1927.

In the meantime the international position of the Soviet Union deteriorated. Italy declared her support of the Rumanian incorporation of Bessarabia (although this declaration was less directed against Moscow than it was meant to weaken France's Balkan position). Because of alleged Bolshevik conspiracies in England, the British government severed relations with the Soviet Union in 1927. This evoked considerable interest throughout central-eastern Europe, and in Moscow a fraction of the Comintern actually saw a forthcoming Western attack on the Soviet Union. But this was not the case; eventually, in 1929, the British re-established full diplomatic relations with Moscow.

The Briand-Kellogg Pact, signed in Paris in August 1928, was immediately seconded by the Soviet Union, which moved for an eastern European counterpart of this academic renunciation of war. This was the so-called Litvinov Protocol, which, exactly because of the Pact's lack of any concrete meaning, was extended to all the western neighbor states of Russia, including also Rumania, with whom the Soviet Union had no diplomatic relations but did have a burning territorial dispute. As the Litvinov Protocol contained virtually no practical obligations, it was signed in the early spring of 1929 by Poland, Lithuania, Latvia, Estonia, and Rumania. (Turkey, Persia, and the Free City of Danzig signed in July 1929.) Only Finland refused, as the Finnish government was bent on considering the Finnish state as belonging to the Scandinavian sphere.

In 1930, when Litvinov followed Chicherin in the Foreign Commissariat, the international position of the Soviet Union was considerably better than in 1927. Moscow maintained very good relations with both Fascist Italy and with the conservative German régime. Stalin overestimated the potential of the German Communists. In 1930, the Communists and especially the Nazis registered great gains in the German elections, when unemployment drove the masses to extremes. The German Communist party continued its policy of trying to weaken the bourgeois parties and the Social Democrats; it was Hitler who reaped all the benefits of these strategies. In four elections of 1932 the Communists still polled an average of four million votes at each election. Only the Nazis exceeded them. But Stalin somehow believed that the trend was toward ultimate Communist victory and expected the Nazis to eventually collapse.

Meanwhile, Russia campaigned for eastern peace and security. She again pressed for meaningless Non-Aggression Treaties of propaganda value with her neighbors, and she succeeded in convincing Finland, Poland, and Estonia, also France, to sign in 1932. The treaties with Lithuania and Latvia were renewed.

Until February 28, 1933, the very day of the Reichstag fire, that is, almost a month after Hitler's coming to power, the German Communist party declined to collaborate with the Socialists, who frantically tried to forge an "Iron Front" against the Nazis. When Socialist-Communist collaboration in late February 1933 was finally decided upon, it was too late. Immediately afterwards the German Communist movement was stamped out by Hitler.

Now came a change in the direction of Soviet foreign policy. The long-range plans, based on a German-Russian domination of central-eastern Europe, were now useless. The bitterest enemy of Russia, Alfred Rosenberg, sat in Berlin and the long chapter of alliance attempts from Rapallo to the Reichstag fire was closed. In May 1933 a series of articles by Radek in *Izvestia* indicated the reversal of Soviet policies. Russia, which had hitherto condemned the Versailles Treaty and the subsequent European order, now proclaimed her willingness to align herself with those powers which stood for the preservation of the *status quo*. The urge to form a front with the *status quo* powers, in order to block a German eastward expansion as planned and expounded by Rosenberg and *Mein Kampf*, seemed elementary, the imminent goal, the security aim of the new Soviet foreign policy; in late 1933, the Kremlin seemed to fear an eventual German-Polish-Japanese attack on Russia. There is, however, some indirect evidence, substantiated by later experience, that Stalin also foresaw a situation in which the West, to secure the active aid of Soviet land armies in an anti-German war, would be compelled to compromise at the expense of the central-eastern European neighbor states of Russia.*

The new position of the Soviet Union — often wrongly considered as a new attitude — finally crystallized during the summer and fall

---

* Although his German plans failed, Stalin did try to prevent an ultimate deterioration of German-Russian relations. Not until Hugenberg had delivered an extremely pro-British and anti-Russian speech did Radek's article appear. Stalin and Litvinov often emphasized their desire to maintain good relations with Germany, notwithstanding the "sufferings of the . . . Marxist comrades." Hitler took note of this attitude with a certain satisfaction. Commercial relations between Germany and the Soviet Union were continuous and extensive. In May 1933 the Berlin Treaty of 1926 was renewed.

of 1934. When France sent her Foreign Minister, Barthou, travelling to form a new eastern alliance against a resurgent Germany, it was clear that such plans would very much depend on Russia. And when, after courteous negotiations, the Soviet Union entered the League of Nations on September 18, 1934, the statesmen of central-eastern Europe felt that, despite the virtually extinct Communist movements in that region, they would be — as they had been before 1917 — compelled to reckon anew with Russia.

.   .   .   .

[*The rise of Germany.*] Stresemann died in 1929. Depression struck in 1930; the National Socialist movement jumped ahead not only in Germany, but in Austria also: to that little country the economic crisis wrought immeasurable harm. The German and Austrian conservative régimes now planned for a bold remedy; although two Articles in the Versailles and St. Germain Treaties prohibited such a decision, the German Finance Minister, Curtius, and the Austrian Vice-Chancellor, Schober, somewhat undiplomatically announced that a German-Austrian Customs' Union Plan was under consideration. The Little Entente vehemently protested and France reacted with uncharitable and unnecessary rigor. The plan was halted and ultimately declared a breach of treaty by an 8 to 7 decision of the Hague International Court of Justice in 1932. By that time, however, National Socialism was ready to sweep Germany and Austria: the elections of 1932 showed further gains for Hitler, and words like Churchill's at that time: ". . . the removal of the just grievances of the vanquished ought to precede the disarmament of the victors" went completely unheeded. Germany was secretly rearming, showing more and more impatience with and defiance of the international disarmament conferences; France, rocked with scandals of corruption, did not arm, while Britain disarmed. On January 30, 1933, Hitler became Chancellor of Germany. On March 21 the Era of the Third Reich was officially inaugurated. A few days later Churchill spoke in the House of Commons:

> I will leave Germany and turn to France. France is not only the sole great surviving democracy in Europe; she is also the strongest military power, I am glad to say, and she is the head of a system of states and nations. France is the guarantor and protector of the whole crescent of small states which runs right round from Belgium to Yugoslavia

and Rumania. They all look to France. When any step is taken, by England or any other Power, to weaken the diplomatic or military security of France, all these small nations tremble with fear and anger. They fear that the central protective force will be weakened, and that then they will be at the mercy of the great Teutonic Power.*

"I remember particularly the look of pain and aversion which I saw on the face of Members in all parts of the House when I said, 'Thank God for the French Army,' " reminisced Churchill in 1948. "Words were vain."

[*The Austrian crisis.*]   There was, however, one favorable and new factor in the central European scene. Mussolini, who previously had had some sympathy with the idea of a German-Italian alliance, decided now to support the Austrian government against Hitler's pressure. Soon the originally Fascist-sponsored *Heimwehr* was battling Nazi legions in Austria. Not all of Mussolini's decisions were that fortunate: in 1932 secret and very personal messages from King Alexander could not influence Mussolini to make friends with Yugoslavia and constitute a factor of stability in the Balkans. It was Mussolini's rather personal request to Chancellor Dollfuss which led to the suppression of the restive Socialist Party in Austria. Dollfuss struck at the Socialists in February 1934; a four-day civil war was the result. Five months later the Austrian Nazis rose, murdered Dollfuss, and failed but by a hairbreadth to capture Austria. The courage of the Vienna police who acted on the spot and the immeasurably more important threat of Mussolini to throw Italian divisions into the balance stopped Hitler on July 25, 1934. No one else was to stop him in the six years which followed.

[*The German-Polish pact.*]   For Hitler had his clear-cut military plans, independent of Austrian Nazis and local police. His army was rapidly rebuilding. He flung his determination in Europe's face when he left the League in October.† Pilsudski thought in terms of

---

* *The Gathering Storm* (Boston, 1948), Houghton Mifflin, p. 76.

† There were vague German offers made to Czechoslovakia for a Non-Aggression Pact in September–October directed against Poland. Beneš later made some moral capital out of the Czechoslovak refusal. However, Hitler's general plans were to deal with Austria and Czechoslovakia before Poland. The first detailed German Army directive in the Hitler era was issued in November 1933. It directed that the line of the Oder and Neisse rivers be held against a Polish attack; it also directed a very slow retreat before the Czechs in the mountain region.

preventive war against Germany, but his French allies refused even to consider such eventualities. Aware of such considerations the German Ambassador to Poland dramatically offered a German-Polish Non-Aggression Pact to Pilsudski on November 27, 1933. This was Hitler's direct message: Germany was not opposed to Poland, only to Bolshevik Russia. Pilsudski hesitated for a while, sounding the French again: in vain. Rumors of the German offer turned up in Prague; Warsaw, however, denied the truth of such rumors and kept the Pact negotiations secret from everyone, including her ally France. When the French Ambassador had a routine dinner with his friendly eastern European colleagues in Berlin on January 25, 1934, the Polish envoy was queried, but Lipski, with a touch of ridicule, brushed the question off. Yet within twenty-four hours the German-Polish Non-Aggression Pact was signed. The world was over-awed. It was Hitler's first great diplomatic victory: a considerable stroke at the French alliance system. To counterbalance the Pact, Russia immediately offered a joint German-Russian "guarantee" of the Baltic states in March 1934, but Germany refused with a light heart. She did not need to negotiate with the East now that her movements were beginning to be less and less impeded by the West.

(Table 1) *THE RESULTS OF THE PARIS PEACE*
NEUILLY AND LAUSANNE — READJUSTING —

State	Territory in sq. mi. 1914	Territory in sq. mi. 1923	Population in thousands 1914	Population in thousands 1923	Minorities: approximate per cent of total population 1914
Germany	208,780	182,271	64,926	59,858	5% Poles 2% Others
Italy	110,659	117,982	35,239	38,836	Insignificant
Austria	115,982	32,352	28,996	6,428	22% Czechs, Slovaks 17% Poles 12% Ruthenians 7.5% Southern Slavs 3% Italians 1% Rumanians
Hungary	125,609	35,790	20,886	7,946	15% Rumanians 10% Germans 9% Slovaks 9% Croats 6% Serbs 3% Ruthenians
Czechoslovakia	—	54,241	—	13,610	
Poland	—	146,821	—	27,100	—
Serbia (Yugoslavia)	33,891	96,134	4,548	12,017	Insignificant
Rumania	53,489	122,282	7,516	17,594	4.5% Jews 3% Various
Bulgaria	43,305	39,841	4,753	4,910	10% Turks 2% Various
Albania	10,750	14,500	825	832	12% Serbs, Greeks, Turks
Greece	41,933	50,146	4,363	5,537	Insignificant

Minorities: approximate per cent of total population 1923	Territorial gains to the detriment of:	Territorial losses to the advantage of:	Plebiscites, Free States, or other post-treaty changes 1919–1923:
1.5% Various	—	France, Belgium, Denmark, Poland, Lithuania, Czechoslovakia	Plebiscites: North Schleswig 1919, Marienwerder 1920, Upper Silesia 1921. Free States: Memel 1919–23, Danzig, 1919–39.
1.1% Slovenes 0.6% Austrians	Austria-Hungary	—	Fiume Free State 1919–24.
2% Czechs 3% Various	Hungary	Czechoslovakia, Poland, Italy, Rumania, Yugoslavia	Plebiscites: Klagenfurt 1920, Sopron 1921.
5.5% Germans 2% Various	—	Rumania, Czechoslovakia, Austria, Yugoslavia, Italy, Poland	—
24% Germans 16% Slovaks 8% Magyars 3.8% Ruthenians 1% Others	Austria-Hungary, Germany	—	Teschen occupation 1920, Orava, Zips settlement 1924.
16% Ukrainians 11% Jews 5% Russians 4% Germans	Russia, Germany, Austria-Hungary, Lithuania	—	Wilnó occupation 1920.
22% Croats 9% Slovenes 4% Germans 4% Magyars 4% Albanians and others	Austria-Hungary, Bulgaria	—	Rapallo Treaty 1920. Albanian border settlement 1920–21.
9% Magyars 7% Jews 4% Germans 2% Bulgarians 5% Russians, Ukrainians 4% Others	Austria-Hungary, Russia, Bulgaria	—	—
10% Turks 2% Others	—	Greece, Rumania, Yugoslavia	Population exchange w. Greece 1923. Border settlements 1921–25.
13% Serbs, Greeks, Turks	—	—	—
7% Turks 0.7% Albanians	Bulgaria, Turkey	—	Greek-Turkish War 1922; population exchange w. Turkey 1923.

(Table 2) *EXTREMISM AND AUTHORITARIANISM IN CENTRAL-EASTERN EUROPE: 1921–1938*

	Communist revolution	Counter-revolution	Peak of post-1921 Communist strength	Unsuccessful Communist coup d'état	Communist Party outlawed	Socialist Party outlawed	Local Fascist movement	Local Nazi movement
Finland	1918	1918	late '20's	—	1923; 1930	—	Suomen-Lukko	Lapua
Estonia	1918	1919	mid-'20's	1924	1924; 1930	1934	Liberators	Estonian Lapua
Latvia	1918	1919	Communists insignificant	—	1922; 1923	1934	Aizšargi	Pehr Konkrusts, etc.
Lithuania	1918	1919	Communists insignificant	—	1923	1929	—	Iron Wolf
Poland	Polish-Russian War 1920		mid-'30's	—	1926	—	Polish Phalanx, NARA	Iron Wolf
Czecho-slovakia	—	—	mid-'20's	—	—	—	Gayda, Slovak Hlinka Party	German Nat. Soc. Party
Austria	—	—	Communists insignificant	—	1933	1934	Heimwehr	Austrian Nat. Soc. Party
Hungary	1919	1919	Communists insignificant	—	1919	—	Ébredök, Fajvédök, etc.	Arrow-Cross, etc.
Yugoslavia	—	—	mid-'30's	—	1920	1929	Lyotić group	Croatian Ustaši Rodna Zashtita, Kunčev
Bulgaria	—	—	mid-'20's '30's	1923	1923; 1932	1929	Tsankov group	Iron Guard
Rumania	—	—	Communists insignificant mid-'20's	—	1924	1938	—	—
Albania	—	—		—	1927	1927	Albanian National Front	
Greece	—	—	'30's	—	1936	1936	EEE (Greek Fascist Party)	—

	Fascist or semi-Fascist régime before 1938	Nazi or semi-Nazi régime before 1938	Peak of post-1921 Fascist or Nazi strength	Unsuccessful Fascist or Nazi coup d'état	Legal restriction of Fascism or Nazism	Resort to authoritarianism	End or relaxation of authoritarianism	Second or extended authoritarianism	Relative standing of middle class
Finland	—	—	1930–32	1930, 1932	partial 1931–32	—	—	—	substantial
Estonia	—	—	1932–34	—	1934	1934	1938	—	substantial
Latvia	—	—	1930–34	1927	1934	1934	—	—	substantial
Lithuania	1926–29	—	1927–34	—	1931	1926	1929	1935	weak
Poland	—	—	1937	—	—	1926	1938	1935	weak
Czecho-slovakia	—	—	1937–38	—	—	—	—	—	geographically varying
Austria	1933–36	—	1931–34	1931, 1934	1934, 1936	1933	1936	1934	weak
Hungary	—	—	1937–38	—	—	—	—	—	weak
Yugoslavia	—	—	insignificant	—	1929	1929	1935	—	—
Bulgaria	—	—	insignificant	—	1935	1934	1938	—	—
Rumania	1937–38	1937–38	1933–37	—	1938	1938	—	—	weak
Albania	—	—	insignificant	—	—	1928	—	—	—
Greece	—	—	insignificant	—	1936	1925	1926	1936	weak

(Table 3) *THE NEW WESTERN NEIGHBORS OF RUSSIA, 1917–21*

	Finland	Estonia	Latvia	Lithuania	Poland	(Ukraine)
Part of the Russian Empire since:	1809	1710	1710–1795	1795	1795	1654
First Russian recognition of independence:	July 1917	Apr. 1917	July 1917	—	Mar. 1917	—
Declaration of national independence:	Dec. 1917	Nov. 1917	Nov. 1918	Dec. 1917	Nov. 1916	Feb. 1918
German occupation during World War I:	—	Feb.–Nov. 1918	1917–1918	1915–1918	1914–1918	Jan.–Oct. 1918
First Soviet occupation:	Jan.–Mar. 1918	Nov. 1918–Jan. 1919	Jan.–May 1919	Jan.–June 1919	June–Aug. 1920	1919–
Other, external forces:	German assistance — 1918	British naval assistance — 1919–20				Scattered French, British assistance — 1918–20
German efforts to reduce to satellite status:	Apr.–Oct. 1918 —	Mar.–Sept. 1918 1919–20	Mar.–Sept. 1918 1919–20	June–Oct. 1918 1919–20	Nov. 1916–Sept. 1918	Feb.–Nov. 1918
Post-war German intrusions: Peace treaty with Russia signed:	Oct. 1920	Feb. 1920	Aug. 1920	July 1920	Mar. 1921	—
De jure recognition granted by:						
Great Britain	May 1919	Jan. 1921	Jan. 1921	Dec. 1922	Feb. 1919	
United States	May 1919	July 1922	July 1922	July 1922	Feb. 1919	
France	Jan. 1918; May 1919	Jan. 1921	Jan. 1921	Dec. 1922	Feb. 1919	
Germany	Jan. 1918	Apr. 1921	July 1920	Aug. 1921	June 1919	
Italy	May 1919	Jan. 1921	Jan. 1921	Dec. 1922	Feb. 1919	
Soviet Russia	Jan. 1918; Oct. 1920	Feb. 1920	Aug. 1920	July 1920	Mar. 1921	

· 2 ·

THE DIPLOMATIC
REVOLUTION

The Diplomatic Revolution: Phase I

In the course of human life associations, affiliations, friendships frequently occur; with the passing of time these relations change; they are terminated, renewed, subject to substitutions. Often the drama of a man's life is revealed to us by an unexpected revolution in his affiliations and friendships; it is what the poets call the dramatic break with the past and the sudden search for a new future; this intriguing spectacle is less a premeditated change of direction than a surrender to the inscrutable and inward laws of that individual's life.

Such sudden reversals also occur in the relations of peoples, nations, and states. Between 1739 and 1748 the Great European Powers were involved in an interrupted world war in which, among others, Britain and Austria fought against France, Spain, and Prussia. The peace treaty of 1748 nevertheless was no more than an armistice: not one of the Great Powers was satisfied with the arrangement. The diplomats were entrusted with the task of seeking new alliances with more favorable constellations for their nations. In one or two years the bases for reversed alliance systems were created, and when general warfare broke out again in 1754–56, France and Austria were fighting Britain and Prussia; Russia, which previously had been allied with Britain against France, now stood by an Austrian alliance which ranged her on the side of France against Britain. This spectacular rearrangement has been called the Diplomatic Revolution.

This Revolution was not merely the result of statesmen's whims nor of their transitory appraisal of positions. There were deeper currents present, currents that had determined the history of centuries. Such a current was the British desire to maintain the European balance of power and secure unperturbed time in the colonies; such was the century-old aim of France to exercise supreme influence in the geographical center of Europe; these constant aims, pursued through different avenues, were diverted but seldom by temporary inclinations.

[*The Diplomatic Revolution.*]   Between 1934 and 1937 another Diplomatic Revolution was discernible. These were strange years indeed. The map of Europe was not yet redrawn; no changes were yet made. Outwardly, 1937 seemed to be an improvement over 1934: there were no great internal crises troubling the nations between Germany and Russia; there was a spurt in international trade and some economic prosperity. Wars, international crises, conspiracies, political assassinations, coups did not occur in central-eastern Europe throughout the two years 1936 and 1937. Yet the Diplomatic Revolution ran its full course: Germany, weak and practically isolated in 1934, became the Giant of the continent three years later; in 1937 it was France who was nearly powerless and all but deserted by her allies.

All this was more than just the product of Machiavellian manoeuvrings of the German and Italian and the fumbling of the French and British diplomats. All this had been in the air for almost a decade, portended by the apparently decreasing Western influence on central-eastern European life and attitudes; the change in trend went back to almost a decade before the Diplomatic Revolution. Yet the moment when the process of crystallization started, when the tiny colored specks of the diplomatic kaleidoscope began to move and, often misleadingly, fall into position, was the year 1934. François-Poncet wrote masterfully of that year:

> In the life of nations, there are years when events, having reached a kind of crossroads and still in flux . . . suddenly veer in a definite direction — may this be due to their implicit logic or to the impact of certain men or to that of certain incidents or of accidents which themselves are the results of these imponderables which one calls "chance" or "destiny." These are the crucial years: the future is inscribed in them; one should be able to see it and predict it, were it not for the lack of a rare lucidity of mind, an insight of the spirit which is seldom common. 1934 is one of these fateful years . . . (1)*

[*The West and central-eastern Europe.*]   1934, then, brought central-eastern Europe to the foreground as the crucial region of the

---

* See numbered notes at the end of the book.

continent. The contacts of the West with central-eastern Europe as well as the spiritual affinity between the central-eastern European nations and their erstwhile Western political traditions were considerably impaired by 1934: the emergence of nationalism, the bankruptcy of central-eastern European parliamentarianism on the western model, the economic troubles, and the growth of the German and Nazi political, economic, and spiritual impact were ominous signs. As the Western democracies grew weaker, so fell their political prestige, and the non-Western concept of political behavior based solely on the measuring of relative power gained currency. It is perhaps more than coincidental that the Hungarian Premier Gömbös emphasized his nation's Asiatic origins. Above everything, the incapacity and apathy of the Western Powers were the greatest asset Germany and her central-European friends had in their arsenal of propaganda. France and Britain and the United States seemed in these years to be as far away from Bucharest, Belgrade, or Bratislava as they had been decades before, despite the fact that *Imperial Airways* and *Air France* flew passengers between these cities and the Western capitals in a few hours.

Many of the statesmen of central-eastern Europe were vaguely conscious of all this; some of them saw it more clearly; a handful of them expressed it. The contrast between throbbing German dynamism and Western inertia was dangerous enough in itself; the mere sight of such a startling paradox made people think in new terms. Twice in 1933 Poland made suggestions for a preventive military operation against Hitlerite Germany, suggestions rejected by France; and while the *Manchester Guardian* and the London *Daily Herald* reported, for example, most unfavorably on the authoritarian régimes of Poland and Austria, the British government led by the ex-Socialist MacDonald hastened to sign a Four-Power Pact in 1933 with France, Fascist Italy and Nazi Germany. This pact, meaningless as it was, failed to take into account the position, tribulations, and fears of a hundred and forty million Europeans east of Germany — and left the task to Mussolini to be the sole defender of Austrian independence. British stock was falling (2) and so was that of France. That great Republic exchanged and shuffled Ministries in rapid succession, a spectacle which not only suggested the fallacy and decay of Western-type democracy to many thinking central-eastern Europeans, but prevented France from the pursuit of a steadfast foreign policy during the important period when Hitler rose to power.

[*A revival of French foreign policy.*]   But slowly Paris now composed herself, seeing the threatening new balance of power in the east, in the south, and in the center of Europe. France was handicapped by many factors, yet she planned to follow her traditional foreign policy. Twelve years before, on January 4, 1922, Lloyd George wrote to Briand: "The British people understand the claim of France to be guaranteed against invasion, but it is not willing to be committed to military enterprises in central and eastern Europe . . ."; and, in the words of the *Survey of International Affairs for 1934*, the French experience at Locarno, although it "convinced them that it was useless to expect Great Britain to help in maintaining the stability of Eastern Europe," nevertheless "did not cause them to abandon the hope of fortifying the security of France's eastern allies as a contribution toward the security of France herself."

True, France had concrete ties with Poland and the Little Entente. Yet the practical value of her pacts was open to question. General Gamelin saw it in 1930:

> . . . in the final analysis there are no precise military dispositions which would bind us to our eventual allies or which would bind them to us. . . . Moreover, the Little Entente may be allied against Hungary — or Poland and Rumania against Russia — yet there is no text which would be specific in mentioning Germany . . . (*3*)

Thus, after the Polish-German Pact, France and Russia were to come together. Very soon after the advent of Hitler to power, Moscow harped on the theme of collective security; simultaneously, the Soviet Government indicated its eventual willingness to enter the League of Nations. In 1933 the popular Herriot visited Moscow and conducted preliminary talks on that subject. On January 26, 1934, the news of the German-Polish Pact broke.

[*Barthou's plans and travels. Poland.*]   On February 9 Barthou became Foreign Minister of France and he immediately proceeded to "pick up the thread left in 1925." Two months later, when the Rumanian Titulescu visited Paris, Barthou confided to him his plans for a great European Alliance to contain Germany. In another ten days, the old French statesman, whose goatee was already familiar to Europeans and whose strange manners and buckling posture and conversational habits had begun to impress his statesmen colleagues, was engaged in the eastern journeys which characterized the early summer of 1934. "For the next ten months Europe was treated to a display of diplomatic virility emanating from Paris which recalled the robust policies of Clemenceau and Poincaré." (*4*)

Barthou went to Warsaw first to assay the situation and repair what was possible; he had a dramatic meeting with Pilsudski but the old marshal would not budge; Pilsudski was unwilling to arouse the ire of Germany by aligning himself with the other traditional enemy of Poland, Russia, merely for the sake of a questionable eastern European Locarno and the love of France. Nor was there any great desire in Warsaw for a binding alliance with Czechoslovakia and Lithuania, two other neighbors with whom Poland had most unsatisfactory relations. From the perspective of historical experience it is perhaps unwise to criticize the Poles' attitude in 1934, but it cannot be disputed that their subsequent game of balance between the German and French alliance systems was to be to the tragic detriment of Europe as a whole.

[*Czechoslovakia and Russia.*] Disappointed, Barthou left Warsaw for Prague; there Masaryk and Beneš received him with much cordiality; the first visions of a Czech-Russian-French Triangle emerged, with the Czechs hoping less for direct assistance from Russia and France than for the indirect effect which such an alignment would have upon Poland and the revisionist powers. Having secured Czechoslovak adherence to his plans, Barthou returned to Paris. In a few weeks the rhythm of diplomatic activity accelerated. Early in May, at the League session in Geneva, Barthou met Maxim Litvinov. Russia had not risked very much by agreeing swiftly to the French plans and her return into the European comity of nations was arranged; then Barthou revealed his attractive plan for an Eastern Locarno of Mutual Assistance, which would invite Germany to renounce revisionism or else be confronted by formidable alliances. Stalin concurred in the presentation of this "Eastern Pact," and now Barthou was wont to regard the winning of Moscow as his personal achievement. Yet, the change of the Soviets' foreign policy from *anti-status quo* to *pro-status quo* had been evident since May 1933 when Radek's series of articles in *Izvestia* pointed to that change.

Barthou now requested the Little Entente to recognize the Soviet government at once. This it did in June, with the exception of Yugoslavia, where the royal house was prejudiced against the Soviets. However, even Belgrade committed herself to support the membership of Soviet Russia in the League of Nations.

Barthou was still under the impact of the rapid success of the Litvinov talks when news of Latvian and Bulgarian *coups d'état* exploded
in quick succession. Both were momentary setbacks to Germany: the
Latvian change deprived the Nazi-sponsored "Liberator" group of
a chance to take over the government in Riga; the coup in Bulgaria
brought about by the *Zveno* group was against pro-Fascist tendencies
and elements in Sofia; the new Bulgar régime was now friendly to
Belgrade and Paris, and cooler toward Rome and Berlin.

[*The meeting at Venice.*]   Early in June a cloud appeared
when Hitler and Mussolini met in Venice. But Mussolini took a file
of evidence of German-sponsored terrorist actions in Austria with him
and he was not impressed by the Hitler he saw clad in a square-
shouldered gabardine raincoat: "I don't like him," he said to his
coterie. There were a few sharp exchanges but Hitler was mild,
unusually mild, towards Mussolini, whom he admired — this attitude
saved Hitler from the worst. Yet there was one area of agreement;
neither of the two dictators wanted to see "regional alliances" and
especially not in eastern Europe.

Again, the danger of a Nazi coup in Austria drew Italy away from
Germany. Barthou was relieved, although some fear was felt in Paris
that a Russophile policy of France would make Mussolini resort to
a central European "Christian" alliance system rather than adhere
to collective security together with the Soviet Union. Yet relations
between Rome and Moscow were good. Italian shipyards were
delivering for the Soviet Union, and the Italian-Soviet Non-Aggression Pact, which Litvinov signed in Rome in September 1933, seemed
to be holding. In February 1934 Mussolini advised Hungary to recognize the Soviet Union, half a year before France advised the Little
Entente to do so. The Zagreb meeting of the Little Entente Foreign
Ministers met with but minor criticism from the Fascist press, while
in July 1934 the *Popolo di Roma* and the *Völkischer Beobachter* were
engaged in a violent polemic in which the former newspaper employed rather startling adjectives to describe the Nazi state and
system.

In mid-June Barthou set out for the second round of his eastern
travels and at the end of that month he visited Bucharest and Belgrade. In these capitals he was greeted with significant enthusiasm;
he secured full Rumanian and Yugoslav adherence to his Eastern
European Plan.

But was this enough? There were no pacts signed which would have finally extended the commitments and responsibilities of the Little Entente. The enthusiasm with which Balkan capitals greeted Barthou was directed not so much at a man who stood for European peace and security as at a symbol of a France irrevocably opposed to the slightest changes in the *status quo*. In other words, the Little Entente was pleased with France's eastern plans because these seemed to exclude any possibility of success for Hungarian (and, to a lesser extent, to Bulgarian or Austrian) revisionism.

[*New chances. France and Italy.*] When Louis Barthou travelled to Bucharest through Austria, Austrian Nazis planned to dynamite his train. (5) The day he left Paris a speech of Papen at Marburg indicated forthcoming changes within Germany. On the day he returned to Paris from Belgrade the Röhm massacres occurred, and with them the first internal crisis of the National Socialist state. Twenty-five days later the Austrian Nazis struck, and assassinated Dollfuss; but the Austrian government, with the support of Italy, crushed Hitler's attempt to win Austria. Because of Hitler's storm-troopers and their brutality, Mussolini — at least in the case of Austria — was forced to concur in the idea of all-European security. Thus, in the mid-summer of 1934, Italy became aligned with France and those other powers which stood for the preservation of the European *status quo*. This was perhaps France's Grand Hour.

. . . .

Most of the writers who have tried to recapitulate the diplomatic history of the 1930's agree on the great merits of Barthou and regard him as one of the greatest statesmen of that period. He is pictured as representing all the virtues of France and Western parliamentary democracy with energy, ambition, courage, and clearsightedness. He chose, it is said, the only right avenue; he pursued a straight path, it is maintained, which his successors deliberately abandoned in the spirit of cowardice or even of treason.

No doubt Barthou was great, perhaps greater than any other French statesman in the era between Poincaré and De Gaulle. Calumny of his person comes from subjective, ideological sources; those who regarded Barthou as the French Mephisto of Europe were looking at him from a parochial, nationalistic, anti-French and probably pro-

German angle. There are few such spectacular opposites as Barthou and his successor at the Quai d'Orsay, Pierre Laval. Yet, while an apologia for Laval is difficult to construct, it would be wrong not to criticize Barthou's policies merely because he presents such a contrast with other men of his era.

In the summer of 1934 Europe really stood at the crossroads and there were two men who had much to do with her fate: Barthou and Mussolini. This was a period of transition: Britain was in a schizophrenic mood, isolating herself from Europe's affairs; Germany was internally disturbed; the external forces of the Soviet Union, the European Communist parties, were very weak, and the foreign policy of Moscow was concentrating upon the task of returning with prowess to the European scene.

Neither Italy (6) nor Germany or the Soviet Union seemed to have even the remotest interests in the western, southern or northwestern parts of the European continent. The center of gravity lay in central-eastern Europe, where, in one way or another, the interests of the three, and those of France, the fourth, were conflicting.

Barthou's unquestionable merit lay in recognizing in the yet weak Germany the potential menace of the forthcoming decade. The elementary laws of politics therefore offered him the choice of allying himself either with Italy or with the Soviet Union, both of whose interests were threatened by the growing power of Germany. The primary question therefore was, which? and it seems that Barthou made two mistakes. First, in his overambition, he wanted both. And he chose to approach Russia first, in precedence over Italy.

General Gamelin, who, in contrast to General Weygand, thought optimistically about the potentialities of military collaboration with the Soviet Union, in 1947 described Barthou's essential line of thought as follows:

> . . . a double task of essential importance and very difficult to enforce: to rally Italy to our side and to make the USSR enter the European concert on our side . . .
> . . . I [Gamelin] agreed with [Barthou] . . . that Russia "represents the only great eastern counterweight against Germany."
> . . . Before and above everything, a German-Russian collusion is to be avoided, which would mean first of all a new partition of Poland and subsequently a rearrangement of central Europe and the Balkans, that is, a complete transformation of the European situation . . . (7)

But, was this "double task" possible?

True, the common distrust of Germany made Italy and France agree and act concordantly in Austria. Yet, the ties which bound Rome with Austria were laid down in the Rome Protocols, the Rome-Vienna-Budapest Triangle which was directed also against Yugoslavia, and with her, against the Little Entente. And as long as France labored to use the Little Entente as a potential ally against Germany and as a bridge toward Russia, she would find herself opposed by Italy, by Hungary, and to a lesser extent, by Austria.

It seemed in the summer of 1934 that Italy was losing ground in the Balkans. The outlines of a Balkan Alliance, including Bulgaria, were visible. Bulgaria now had a pro-Yugoslav and not a pro-Italian government; Rumania and Yugoslavia were at rest, anchored in the waters of the French system. The latter state, since the abruptly ended secret negotiations between King Alexander and Mussolini in 1932, was often granting refuge to Austrian Nazi terrorists, indicating thus her dislike of the Italian-Austrian front. (*8*) Even Albania, that virtual satellite of Italy, showed remarkable signs of recalcitrance and in June 1934 the demonstrative presence of Italian warships before Durazzo was required.

Whether because of the ancient French superiority complex toward the Italians, or for the sake of temporizing, Barthou seemed to regard these events as indicating the weakening of Italian interests in central-eastern Europe. The events of July 1934 and the Italian position against Hitler made him confident that Italy's return to the *status quo* front was, if not an accomplished fact, inevitable; Italy could not come to terms with Germany.

Barthou did not or could not see that the temporary Italian acquiescence in the central-eastern European *status quo* existed merely because Mussolini was preparing for a war elsewhere; the Duce had to adhere to a peace policy in Europe in order to free his hands in Africa: according to the memoirs of Marshal De Bono, Mussolini planned already in 1932 to launch the Abyssinian invasion by early 1935. In 1934, his eyes were turned in that direction. . . .

[*Barthou's choice.*] Perhaps Barthou knew that sooner or later he would have to choose between Italy and the Soviet Union. But he was over-optimistic and eventually he chose the latter. There is no evidence that France would have undertaken steps in the direction of reconciling the Little Entente with the Italo-Austrian-Hungarian system; this negative attitude indicates that Barthou put a greater emphasis on winning Moscow than Rome. His error was, therefore, that he thought the Soviet Union had to be convinced of the advantages of the French Eastern Plan and lured into it, while Italy would follow automatically because of her strategic position. Actually the situation was reversed: it was Italy which should have been convinced and lured and it was Russia who had made up her mind beforehand.

[*Polish doubts and excursions.*] There was, then, Poland, whose leaders were apt to regard her as the Sixth Great Power of Europe; no Frenchman could have convinced them of the advantages of a Russian alliance against Germany. As long as Pilsudski did not know exactly what the Western Powers were intending to do in face of an emerging Hitler-Germany, he endeavored to have good relations with Russia; indeed, never were Polish-Soviet relations as satisfactory as in 1932–33, when cultural and military conventions between the two nations were scrupulously observed. It is not impossible that had Hitler not approached Poland with the sudden friendly offer of a pact in 1933, Pilsudski would have sounded Stalin on Russia's position in a "preventive war" against Germany, such a sounding having been cast aside previously by Paris. But Hitler did approach Poland and the German-Polish Non-Aggression Pact was signed on January 26, 1934 — after that, Poland had nothing to gain from a new alliance which would have merely reaffirmed her previous ones with France and Russia and, at the same time, which would have burned her bridges to Germany.

Wheeler-Bennett summarized the situation very ably:

> Pilsudski suspected Barthou of wishing to maintain Poland in the position of a junior ally. . . . he suspected France of wishing to subordinate Polish interests to her own; he suspected the part which Dr. Beneš was playing as *entrepreneur* between Paris, Moscow and the capitals of the Little Entente. Above all, he suspected Russia of having designs of her own upon Poland and believed that an anti-German structure, of which Poland was an advanced blockhouse, could only result in driving Hitler to return to the Rapallo policy and to tempt Russia out of the new combination at the expense of Poland. He therefore refused to be a party to this alignment.

Here was an interplay of suspicion and chagrin similar to that which played so tragic a rôle in Anglo-French relations. Daladier's refusal of Poland's offer in 1933 and his failure to inform the Poles of the Four-Power Pact negotiations had resulted in the Hitler-Wysocki interview and German-Polish Treaty. This, in its turn, had been largely responsible for Barthou's proposal for an Eastern Locarno, and these proposals were consequently wrecked by Pilsudski's suspicion of what lay behind them.   (9)

It is, of course, true that Pilsudski and Beck were too ambitious. Also, had they perceived the full extent of the dynamic menace of Nazi Germany, they would have improved their relations with the Western Powers and explained Polish difficulties in more understandable terms, perhaps directing the attention of the French to the Danubian problems and Italy, instead of brusquely disassociating themselves from the Eastern Plan. On the other hand, Barthou was underestimating the importance of Polish reluctance and overestimating the value of Russia's new friendship. Therefore it is not entirely unreasonable to believe that Barthou was not at all interested in central-eastern Europe's problems; he was exclusively occupied with the creation of a French-Russian alliance system to the disadvantage of Germany, in the spirit of the 1892 Dual Alliance. While this aim was certainly patriotic and honorable, it was also insufficient; it did not solve any problem by itself; it left the clashing forces of the new central-eastern European nationalisms, the question of Italy, and the impact of Bolshevist and National-Bolshevist ideologies — questions which had not troubled Delcassé thirty years earlier — without consideration. Had Barthou had an overall settlement in eastern Europe before his eyes, his first step would have been to improve Polish-Czech (and, to a lesser extent, Polish-Lithuanian) relations and to bring about a solution by aligning the members of the Rome Protocol states with the states of the Little Entente — a task which in 1931 André Tardieu had hesitatingly tried without success — instead of casting Warsaw's objections aside in his hurry to meet Litvinov in Geneva.

[*An Eastern Locarno.*]   It may be that Barthou wanted to do all this too but, alas, his time ran out. Poland continued to harass him. The Foreign Ministers of the Baltic republics prepared to go to Moscow to discuss their eventual adherence to an Eastern Locarno. Beck rushed to Riga and Tallinn to make the Estonian and Latvian governments refrain from joining the plan. The Baltic Foreign Ministers nevertheless did travel to Moscow and declared that they had no objections to the general system of the plan. But Beck continued his intrigues, and then in September he and Barthou met in Geneva, where the old French statesman jumped upon his Polish colleague and remonstrated stormily. Beck remained adamant. The Germans watched with satisfaction. Although on September 13 — two days before the invitation was sent out to the Soviet Union by the League of Nations — Beck proclaimed in Geneva that Poland refused to submit in the future to the supervision of her minority policies by the League, and this announcement was naturally received in Berlin in bad humor, a few months later the German press practically stopped all propaganda about the "oppressed" Germans in Danzig, Silesia and the Polish Corridor. Berlin expressed the opinion that the Polish step was satisfactory, as minority problems were the mutual concerns of Poland and Germany and, in all justice, had to be withdrawn from the ineffectual atmosphere and jurisdiction of the League. In January 1935 a book published in Warsaw by a Professor Studnicki called for an alliance between Poland and Germany, their common domination of central and eastern Europe, and mutual action in pushing back Russia. The Studnicki "thesis" was naturally also directed against Lithuania, Czechoslovakia, and France, which latter country the author called a "corrupt, decaying and immoral nation." (*10*) This Studnicki Plan was exercising a certain influence among leading Poles, while in Yugoslavia certain leaders of that nation, charmed by Göring and other men, were also veering in a direction diametrically opposed to the course charted by Barthou.

Meanwhile Barthou's plan advanced, and on September 18, 1934, the Soviet Union became a member of the League of Nations. Although the Eastern Locarno plan was not moving because of the German and Polish resistance, it was not clear that it would be replaced, for practical reasons, by a series of bilateral treaties, among them a most important French-Soviet Pact to insure a lasting check on German expansion.

[*The Marseille murders.*]   But fate willed otherwise. The Yugoslav King was sailing for France; Barthou welcomed him at Marseille on October 9. While they drove to the railway station, a Macedonian terrorist (*11*) jumped from among the crowd and shot both of them.

In Yugoslavia Alexander was followed by a Regent, the Russophobe Prince Paul, and not much later the Germanophile Stoyadinovič became Premier. Barthou in Paris was succeeded by Pierre Laval, who thought little of Russia and even less of Poland and who probably still subconsciously felt jealous and malevolent toward Britain (*12*); this successor of Barthou went about changing the order of precedence: he deliberately failed to follow up the Eastern Plan and instead concentrated on Italy; as became evident soon, this reversal of procedure was due to his ideological sympathies. But the moment was too late, as Mussolini was already arranging for the first incidents on the Ethiopian frontier.

Thus, the great French Plan, the Eastern Locarno, the grand design to secure European peace from aggression, remained what it was in the beginning, ". . . a plan," theoretically seductive, as François-Poncet was to say, "yet so difficult to realize in practice, and, how fragile! . . ."

.   .   .   .

[*A Yugoslav crisis with Hungary.*] The Marseille assassinations immediately resulted in international calamities. It was established that the murderers had come from Croatian extremist centers existing in Italy and Hungary. It was not proven that the Marseille murders were organized with the silent acquiescence of Italy or Hungary, but it was a relatively well-known fact that Mussolini and Gömbös had tolerated the existence of these Croatian *Ustaši* in Italian and Hungarian territory. Consternation and shock followed October 9. In Yugoslavia all the reasonable opponents of the régime, even most of the Croats, rallied around the throne and demonstrated remarkable unity in that hour. The Belgrade government brought its case before the League and concentrated troops on the Hungarian frontier, beginning overnight to expel a few thousand Hungarian families; a crisis was in the making.

The hurried sessions in Geneva brought a solution, as it was proven that the organizers of the murders were neither subsidized nor directly supported by the Hungarian government, while there was some evidence that at least part of their arms was furnished by Germany through the media of certain Austrian Nazis. Interestingly enough, the Hungarian-Yugoslav tension brought France and Italy momentarily closer. Laval was intent on constructing a French-Italian Pact by all possible means, and he spared no effort to lessen the tension between Italy and the French-Yugoslav system; indeed, in an exemplary act of Machiavellian diplomacy he pressed the Yugoslavs to exacerbate their case against Hungary but refrain from displaying that part of their evidence which showed the Italian support to the Croat *émigré* movement. In this he succeeded, and for a moment Italy and France seemed to be moving toward each other; two leaders of the *Ustaši*, Pavelič and Kvaternik, were arrested in Italy (although not extradited), and Mussolini advised Hungary to refrain from a partial mobilization.

Yet Laval's success was ephemeral. That French-Italian relations improved was due to the desire of Mussolini not to be disturbed in Europe. While Hungarians and Yugoslavs were restricted to battling with words in Geneva and Laval waited, Mussolini looked to the south, where two thousand miles away, on the Abyssinian-Somali border, the Wal-Wal incident on December 6, 1934, was to initiate the Abyssinian War. Thus the easing of the European tension was but illusory, and Yugoslavia, because of the attitude of her rulers and also ". . . disgusted with the French attitude to the murder, began to listen to the sweet blandishments of the Third Reich." (*13*)

Two *blocs* were also created during the months of 1934. Efforts toward a Balkan *bloc* had been made since October 1930 and were manifest in a series of inter-Balkan conferences. Finally the Balkan Entente was formed in February 1934. This quadrilateral pact was signed by Yugoslavia, Rumania, Greece and Turkey (*14*), and while Bulgaria and Albania were not included, it was said that these two could join the Entente when they were willing to subscribe to its mutually binding conditions. After May 1934 it seemed that the *Zveno* government of Bulgaria might adhere and make the Entente one of the encouraging realities of eastern European politics. But the assassination of King Alexander and its international consequences and, finally, the royal elimination of the *Zveno* régime in Bulgaria a few months later were events which, fortunately for Germany and also Italy, began to deprive the Balkan Entente of all its efficacy.

[*The Baltics in 1934.*]　The Balkan events, the German-Polish Pact and other international moves were seriously watched in the little Baltic capitals. So in February 1934 the Latvian-Estonian Pact of 1923 was transformed into a Treaty of Defensive Alliance; in April the Lithuanian régime expressed its desire to adhere to such a Pact; and somewhat later, having noticed the difficulties of Barthou in Warsaw, the Estonian Foreign Minister made it clear that the Estonian-Latvian Alliance would not provide for mutual obligations if Lithuania should be threatened by Germany over Memel (*15*) or if she should be involved in a conflict with Poland over Wilnó (*16*). Lithuania's adherence was therefore secured with important reservations and the Tripartite Treaty — which was much less of a Baltic Entente than what it was originally called, a "Treaty of Good Understanding and Coöperation" — was signed in Geneva in September 1934. Its most important provision was to regularize contact between the Estonian, Latvian and Lithuanian Foreign Ministers. The first such Baltic Conference met at Tallinn in December, where the three states agreed to act in concert regarding any Eastern European Mutual Assistance Pact and manifested their common interests by maintaining a single representative with the League of Nations.

But this was not much, especially as the northern neighbor, Finland, was also reluctant to be entangled by treaties with and obligations toward more inflammable states of central-eastern Europe. Finland emphatically broadcast her intentions to pursue an absolutely neutral policy, and Helsinki drew closer to the Scandinavian capitals. On December 5, 1935, the Finnish Premier Kivimäki officially announced Finland's "Scandinavian orientation."

.   .   .   .   .   .

From the perspective of fifteen years, it is not too difficult to discover the seeds of European catastrophe in the year 1934. And such a perspective is necessary. Anybody who foresaw the shape of things to come back in 1934 must have based his prescience on intuition rather than on facts, on feelings rising from the dark tides of the heart rather than on clear calculations of the brain. Germany was still alone. True, Barthou died and the plans of an Eastern Locarno faded away; yet, all the great states of Europe seemed to share, in one way or another, the French desire to contain Germany within reasonable limits; the *status quo* cause was outwardly stronger than before; France had, after all, reinforced her eastern alliances; had improved her relations with Russia and Italy.

The observer of 1934 could hardly see the three major factors which were bringing about the Diplomatic Revolution. He could not see the ultimate effects of all those stirrings within central-eastern Europe which favored Germany; he could not know how fictitious the real value of France's new Russian tie was; he could not be aware of the true causes of Mussolini's presently placid behavior in Europe. The import of the two first factors did not show itself until 1937–39, indeed, in some cases until 1940. It was in the relationships of Italy that the first generally observable signs of the Diplomatic Revolution appeared.

[*Laval goes to Italy; the British to Berlin.*] The ideas of the French Ambassador in Rome, Chambrun, and of pro-Fascists such as De Monzie influenced Laval: these two often said in 1933–34 that in Europe horizontal alliances worked for peace but vertical ones for war. Laval was interested in but one horizontal alliance: that with Italy. Early in January he went to Rome and signed the French-Italian Pact with Mussolini. In order to win Mussolini to his plans, he went far to please Italy in Africa. (*17*) While Ethiopia kept protesting in Geneva against Italian military preparations, Laval did not bother too much about Ethiopia and League prestige. The Franco-Italian Pact also caused considerable uneasiness in Belgrade and in Budapest, the former an ally of France, the latter having based its foreign policy upon the assistance of Italy. Subsequently Mussolini had to soothe the apprehensions of Hungary, and Laval those of Ethiopia and Yugoslavia.

In the meantime Germany was girding her loins and scoring not unimportant successes. Göring undertook his third hunting trip to Poland, where not all his suggestions met with success; the subtle suggestions to Pilsudski about German-Polish collaboration against Russia were rejected; the Marshal said that Poland was not interested in her pre-1772 frontiers, as it would be impossible for Poland to maintain such extended borders. Nonetheless Polish-Russian relations were not as good as in 1932–33. (*18*) Then, in February 1935, Germany scored an overwhelming psychological success in the Saar plebiscite, and on March 16 Europe was startled to hear from Hitler that Germany was doing away with the Versailles treaty clause limiting her army and armaments. A day later another urgent Abyssinian appeal to the League was heard. But Britain and France were going in opposite directions. The French Ambassador in Berlin suggested strongest diplomatic protests after the March 16 German armament announcement; France protested, so did Italy, but Britain only faintly. Indeed, by some quirk, the British government decided to talk directly with Hitler. On March 25 the Foreign Secretary, Sir John Simon, and Anthony Eden appeared in Berlin on a rather sudden visit. (*19*)

Much did not come of the talks but Berlin was impressed, just as was Moscow, whereto Eden — without the Foreign Secretary — travelled from Germany. It was becoming evident that Britain was trying to please Germany because she was displeased with the French-Russian alliance plans. Psychologically Hitler profited from the inconclusive Simon visit and, indeed, he had some grounds to deduce false conclusions from its circumstances. (*20*) In the meantime Ethiopia was crying to Heaven for help, and France watched Italy anxiously lest she go astray and France remain alone. Laval tried to arrange for a French-British-Italian meeting, which came about in Stresa on April 11. MacDonald, Flandin, Laval and Mussolini met at the Italian spa. The two Latin nations were worried about the Germans' underhand actions in Austria, but the British announced that Great Britain could not take part in eventual armed sanctions against Germany; at the same time practically nothing was said at Stresa about Abyssinia. A communiqué gave the impression to Europe and the world that the Great Powers were unanimously agreeing to keep Germany in check, thereby guaranteeing the independence of Austria. But this was not true; Stresa was but ". . . a spirited display of finger-shaking," and this became evident in the next few months when the flimsiness of the Stresa "Front" was revealed. The subsequent conclusions of Mussolini were only too natural. (*21*)

[*Russia and Laval's doubts.*] There was a duty in the heritage left by Barthou which Laval had to fulfill; against his convictions he had to go and sign the Mutual Assistance Pact with Soviet Russia.

Unless all the available archives of the period are opened, it is very difficult to pronounce final judgment on Pierre Laval; we are too much influenced by the stealthy and dubious rôle which he performed during the last war and this may prevent us from exercising good judgment on his earlier actions. There is no direct evidence that, prior to his Moscow journey, Laval would have acted in bad faith or that he secretly held treasonable thoughts. Breaking away from the course which his predecessor charted, he favored Italy over Russia. This in itself was no mistake; indeed, perhaps Barthou should have done the same. But there are, nevertheless, certain signs of Laval's early ill will: his all too evident dislike and distrust of the British, his handling of the Hungarian-Yugoslav affair, his connections with Ribbentrop, dating back to 1934, and some of his dealings immediately preceding the Saar plebiscite; also, there is the indirect evidence of his papers, which, although consisting of so much arranged documentary *apologia pro vita sua*, do not refer in detail to 1934–35. First of all, the ambiguity of Laval's bearing makes him liable to criticism. If he felt so bad about the prospective results of Barthou's Russophile policy, why didn't he say so openly? The martyr of 1945 would have performed a much more painless martyr rôle in 1935 had he emphasized to his colleagues and the French and British cabinets the necessity for an Italian alliance. But he did not do this; instead he gave indications of servility and homage to Mussolini — just what a man like the Italian would be wont to take seriously, misinterpret and exploit. When it became clear that Mussolini wanted Abyssinia at all costs, it was not only ambiguous but useless to continue the unilateral appeasing of Mussolini — unless Britain would have been willing to capitulate before the Italian demands in Africa. Evidently Laval was too cowardly to face a sceptical Britain and a hostile public opinion; he continued his underhand manoeuvres.

In Geneva in April Beck still condemned Germany's rearmament as a repudiation of her treaty obligations. Was this Polish stand a favorable sign? It may have been, but certainly Pierre Laval was not the man who would have been willing to exploit it. A few weeks later he travelled to Moscow; the French-Russian Mutual Assistance Pact was signed, (*22*) Laval affixing his signature with ill feeling in his heart.

That the Pact had but little real value was clear. Any military action of Soviet Russia depended on what attitude her neighbors would take. Poland was definitely opposed to any Soviet Army entering her territory, and the only nation which perhaps would have been willing to accept direct Russian assistance, Czechoslovakia, had no direct frontier with Russia. The whole argument of Soviet-European relations between 1933 and 1936 has been well presented by Professor Beloff:

> . . . there were considerable obstacles in the way of inducing other powers to accept the Soviet thesis that security could be best assured by automatic commitments to mutual assistance, combined with a formal definition of aggression. Without minimizing the importance to her neighbors of avoiding action provocative to Germany, it remains true that a vital factor of their attitude was the fear that close association with the Soviet Union would be bound to have repercussions on the international situation of the country concerned. It was one thing to exchange with the Soviet Union assurances of peaceful

intentions, and promises not to support an aggressor. It was quite another to enter into pacts, which, if they were to mean anything, meant close collaboration of the defence forces of a non-Communist state with the Red Army. In addition nearly all the States involved in the negotiations had once been wholly or partially within the Russian Empire and this gave further weight to their objections to opening their frontiers for the passage of Soviet troops . . . (*23*)

In the long run the Pact was to the advantage of Germany. Hitler used it as a shining argument in his "anti-Bolshevist crusade," and as an aftermath of its protracted ratification he marched into the Rhineland, saying that the conclusion of the Pact had automatically violated Locarno. The Pact also alienated the Russophobe British government, which in June 1935, to the surprise of the world and to the anger of France and Italy, signed a Naval Treaty with Germany; this, and other significant phenomena, among them a statement of the British Legion that it was a mistake to fight Germany in 1914–18 and this mistake would not be repeated! were interpreted, rightly or wrongly, as signs of British reluctance to oppose Hitler in Europe. Hitler himself was strongly influenced by such British attitudes. The series of tragic and short-sighted misunderstandings which led to 1938 and beyond were there in the early summer of 1935: the Diplomatic Revolution had begun — there was Laval, and later Bonnet, who favored the winning of Italy first over any other European nation, including Russia and Germany; there was Baldwin, and later Chamberlain, who favored the winning of Germany first and Italy only afterwards and who left the others and Russia out of their calculations. Mussolini and Hitler could only profit from such divergences. (*24*)

But let us go back to central-eastern Europe. Laval learned before leaving Moscow that Marshal Pilsudski had died. He decided to stop on his way home in Warsaw and Geneva. In Warsaw he and Marshal Pétain met the affable and ostentatiously conservative Göring. That he might soothe Polish apprehensions about the French-Russian Pact, Laval was reported to have said in Warsaw:

> The object of France in signing the pact with Russia was less to secure assistance to herself in the event of a conflict than to forestall the possibility that Russia and Germany might come to terms with one another . . .

But this was not sincere. To Göring Laval disparaged the Soviets and said that he distrusted them — and when Göring returned to Berlin the German Foreign Ministry found a way to communicate to Moscow what Laval had said. (25)

Laval also suggested to the Poles that "the Russians can come on an alternative route" to help France; the "alternative route" was a hint to the Czechs who, while engaging in mutual diatribes with the Poles to the joy of Hitler, were sensing their later doom and were pressing for a Czechoslovak-Russian Pact. This was the idea of Beneš, whom neither the Yugoslavs nor the Rumanians trusted (especially the Yugoslav royal family thought very little of him). The missing hypotenuse of the lopsided triangle was then put down on paper; in May, ten years after the Czechoslovak-French Treaty and simultaneously with the French-Russian Pact — but also coinciding with Laval's disparaging remarks at Warsaw — a Czechoslovak-Russian Treaty of Mutual Assistance was concluded.

But Russia and Czechoslovakia had no common frontier; between them lay no roads — only a stretch of narrow territory within hostile Poland and disturbed Rumania. Politicians in Bucharest, with their traditionally sensitive noses, sensed the breezes of the Diplomatic Revolution; they had already begun internal moves to throw Barthou's friend, the Francophile and moderately pro-Russian Titulescu, out of the Foreign Ministry. This was but the beginning. On May 21 Hitler spoke and assured his neighbors, including France, Czechoslovakia, and Austria, that Germany had no territorial designs on any of them, and that he was embarking upon plans of peaceful construction. Both the British-German Naval Treaty and Laval's manoeuvre of deliberately toying with antiquated constitutional procedures to delay the ratification of the Franco-Soviet Pact made the Russians feel "snubbed." In July Beck went to Berlin, where he was received with much cordiality. To such depths had Barthou's Grand Plan fallen!

In Czechoslovakia President Masaryk was about to resign because of his advanced age, and the 1935 elections brought great gains to the Sudeten-German-Nazi party. Early in November Hodža took office; this new Premier had a much more realistic picture of the international scene than President Beneš. Yet, although Beneš believed in the Paris-Prague-Moscow triangle and Hodža thought more of a Budapest-Vienna-Prague one with the support of Italy, which could have eventually developed into a good, solid anti-German bastion in the Danube Valley, not much happened. Polish-Czech relations did not improve. In November 1935 a diplomatic crisis occurred because of Polish-Czech controversies regarding consular procedures in Teschen, and Beck tried to influence the Presidential elections against Beneš. Only relations with Vienna were improving, and early in 1936 Schuschnigg visited Prague.

[*Effects of the Abyssinian War.*] However, Italy and Britain were involved in a greater game, for, exactly a month before Hodža became the new Czech Premier, on October 2, 1935, rounds of salvos fired in the Ethiopian valleys heralded the launching of the Abyssinian War. Laval was willing to abandon the League and Russia, just to preserve the friendship of Italy — but it was now too late. In Britain a new Conservative government headed by Stanley Baldwin was confronted by a wave of public indignation which followed the revelation of the controversial Laval-Hoare Plan (*26*) — a project to keep Italy on the side of the Western Powers at the cost of sacrificing the territorial integrity of Abyssinia and somewhat impairing the remaining moral capital of the League — and swept the Italophile Sir Samuel Hoare out of the Foreign Office. In came the young Anthony Eden, who proceeded at once with impressive but also ineffective economic sanctions against Italy. The British Ambassadors in Athens and Ankara and the Minister in Belgrade let it be known that Britain would intervene if Italy attacked Greece, Turkey or Yugoslavia, yet this was about as far as Britain went. Thus was Italy lost to the Western cause; late in 1935, even before the failure of Laval and Hoare, Mussolini had spoken for the revision of frontiers in Europe, speeches obviously directed against France and the Little Entente. Disillusioned, Yugoslavia and many others felt bewildered; in Belgrade the cunning and thoroughly anti-French Stoyadinović had been Premier since June, and even such a staunch pro-Western statesman as the old Greek Venizelos expressed his opinion in 1935 that in view of Western incapacities it would be better if Greece tried to get along favorably with Italy.

But Italy and the Western Powers were now hostile to each other and hopes for a Danubian reconciliation faded out; with them went the memories of Stresa and the European *status quo.*

The great dilemma of central Europe and the world, whether to save peace by containing Germany with the help of Italy or with that of Russia, was therefore "solved." Outwardly it seemed that France had rallied both, but the sad truth was that due to half-measures she had lost the assistance of both. The original aims of Barthou, or even those of Laval may be subject to praise or disapproval on a hypothetical basis, yet the fact is that Laval in 1935 reduced the Russian Pact to a half-measure, while his "success" with Italy was never more than a half-measure. So were the British sanctions. (27)

This was the situation at the end of 1935. In central-eastern Europe the stock of the West continued to fall. (28) The Diplomatic Revolution was not yet completed, but it was in central-eastern Europe where the strange new ways of the future were most clearly indicated. The American Minister to Austria remembered in 1946:

> As early as the fall of 1935, I learned . . . that France was preparing to abandon its commitments in the south-eastern part of Europe in exchange for promises of security within her own borders. The Nazis appeared to have equal success in undermining British sentiment. The "conversion" of Lord Lothian and the attitude of the London *Times* beginning in 1935 are a matter of historical record . . . (29)

In the space of one year, approximately from October 1934 to October 1935, Mussolini turned about to favor Germany rather than France or Britain; Stalin was quietly preparing for the great changes within Russia and looked with disdain upon France and Britain. The Italo-German Axis was in the making; in 1936, Germany won over Italy, three years later she won over Russia. And in central-eastern Europe by the end of 1935, Poland, Bulgaria, Yugoslavia and Rumania had governments with more or less strong pro-German taints, often in great contrast to even a few months before, while German influence was increasing in Turkey, Hungary and Greece and was being felt everywhere between Petsamo and the Peloponnese.

The Diplomatic Revolution and Austria

Austria's pivotal rôle in European history can be easily seen. In 1809 and 1938 *finis Austriae* showed that the order of Europe was upset; in 1683 and 1945 the flood of the East swelling at the Austrian dam was endangering Vienna as well as the whole of the West; in 1797 and 1918 the disintegration of Austrian power brought about an era of European flux and instability. When in 1866 Austria's defeat by Prussia degraded her to the Second Germanic Power, Europe hardly considered the fatal elements of that position; when in 1933 Hitler reconstituted the First Germanic Power and set out to liquidate the remnant of Prussia's erstwhile contestant for the body and soul of the Germanies, the danger was perceived, but not much was done.

[*After the July revolution.*]   After the Nazi revolt was quashed in July 1934, there was relative calm; Papen, the new German Minister, was very civil: he said to the Austrian Foreign Minister, Berger-Waldenegg, early in 1935: "Yes, you have your English and French friends now and you can have your independence a little longer." (*1*) Except for minor conspiracies, internal peace came back; Schuschnigg's curious liberal authoritarianism worked; financial affairs improved; foreign visitors streamed into the Austrian mountains, and valleys, and cities; the world's attention was often captured by the glimpse of a Toscanini conducting a Mozart symphony in Salzburg or by the repeated visits of the Prince of Wales, later Edward VIII of Britain. (*2*)

The Austrian Nazis and the Socialists were on the defensive, the first temporarily, the latter in a permanent way. There was a not very significant underground Socialist organization (the so-called Revolutionary Socialists' Front) but there was a well-organized and widespread Nazi network. From the Socialist émigré centers of Brno (*3*) and Prague some propaganda trickled into the suburbs of Vienna; from Munich and Berlin tons of printed material came. As to the Socialists, the continued inadequacy of their émigrés' tactics (*4*) made even the best and oldest Socialists shrug their shoulders, a situation from which the Nazis profited. Schuschnigg once in a while contacted released Socialist leaders and the liberal wing of his Fatherland Front; and the remnants of the Christian Socialists organized a program to win the workers' support for the government with a mild and reasonable campaign which met with some success. The Chancellor, obviously influenced by the conservative demeanor of Papen and the, on the surface, juvenile and irrational fluctuations of Nazi activity and propaganda, had released not only most of the Socialists, but also several thousand imprisoned Nazis by the end of 1934.

Schuschnigg's main fear was that one of his continental supporters might be forced to adopt different views on Austrian independence at a later time. Austrian security was therefore primarily dependent on Italian-French understanding, which on the other hand was dreaded and effectively sabotaged by Hitler and Stoyadinovič.

[*Austria further isolated.*]   When in September 1934 the semi-official *Le Temps* of Paris pointed out in an article the possibility of

the consent of France to a Habsburg restoration in Austria, the Little
Entente Foreign Ministers hurriedly met in Ljubljana (5) on their
way to Geneva and sent a protest to Paris, hinting, especially at the
insistence of the Yugoslavs, that such a French stand would result in
the Little Entente turning to Berlin for assistance. Previously, at
Florence in August, Schuschnigg not very adroitly had confessed to
Mussolini that an Italian military intervention assisting Austria in
the case of a Nazi coup would help the Germans' cause, as the Austrian
people would be united and hostile to the presence of Italian soldiers
on Austrian soil. (6) From the minutes of the Florence conversations
it may be deduced that in August 1934 it was Mussolini who favored
a restoration of the monarchy, and that it was Schuschnigg, although
an avowed monarchist, who felt chary about the practical possibilities
of restoration.

It was also known that Gömbös, the Hungarian Premier, nurtured
dangerous sympathies toward the Third Reich. According to the
then American Minister to Hungary, Gömbös and Foreign Minister
Kánya assured the German Minister in Budapest on the day after
the signing of the Rome Protocols in March 1934 that these agreements did not go beyond the measure of mutual consultations and
that they fell definitely short of being a mutually binding defensive
alliance. Schuschnigg undoubtedly knew this and also knew that the
close relations between Italy and Hungary were directed mainly
against Yugoslavia. (There was a secret and very vague military agreement between Rome and Budapest, the aim of which was less the
defense of Austria than the outflanking of Yugoslavia; the agreement
provided for a linkup of the Hungarian and Italian armies somewhere
in southeastern Austria in the case of a war between Hungary and
Yugoslavia, or between Hungary and the Little Entente.)

In the fall of 1934 Mussolini said to Schuschnigg that it was possible "that you must stand on your own feet because we will be busy
in East Africa." During the following months the Austrian government became increasingly aware of this fact.

The Franco-Italian Agreement stipulated that efforts be made
toward a Danubian multilateral pact of non-intervention which was
to be signed by Austria and all her neighbors; but this stipulation
remained on paper and practically nothing was done to follow it up.
Instead, the stock of Göring and Germany rose in Belgrade. Also, to
the unpleasant surprise of Vienna and, especially, of Budapest, the
Italian Minister to Yugoslavia, di Campalto, gave a speech in March

1935 in which he emphasized Italy's understanding of Yugoslav problems, the integrity of Yugoslav territory, and the inviolability of Yugoslav frontiers. This friendly speech was an indirect gesture of Rome toward Berlin. It showed the theoretical value of the Rome Protocols and of Italy's Austrian and Hungarian alliances. Although Germany's brusque announcement of rearmament and the brief spell cast by Stresa seemed to set back plans for an Italian-German rapprochement (7), this was less important than the fact that, in spite of some halfhearted moves in July, nothing came of the Danubian Pact either. (8)

With the outbreak of the Abyssinian War Austrian difficulties increased. A few months before, on July 11, 1935, Papen gave a draft to Berger-Waldenegg for a German-Austrian Friendship Treaty, the provisions of which were vague and imprecise. Vienna politely refused. Italy was now busy with her war. Vienna needed French friendship almost as much as that of Italy, yet, loyal to Rome, the Austrian government (together with Hungary and Albania) voted against the sanctions in the League. Although Schuschnigg was showered with expressions of Italian gratitude that combined Latin emotionalism with the theatrical sentimentality of Mussolini, by the end of 1935 there were certain straws in the wind which once again pointed to an Italian-German understanding.

[*Countermeasures, plans.*] Schuschnigg saw the danger and began to proceed, alas, too cautiously, in three different ways: in addition to the Italian ties, he sought a tie with Czechoslovakia and thereby with the Little Entente; he tried to get a direct and written and unequivocal commitment of non-aggression from Germany; he endeavored to eliminate the unreliable elements of the Fatherland Front and made uneasy moves toward a restoration of the monarchy.

The Austrian-Czech rapprochement began in January 1936 when Schuschnigg went to Prague on the pretext of an unofficial invitation. This visit was followed by a Hodža visit to Baden. Thus, during 1936, and at least the first part of 1937, interesting, if unfortunately ill-organized and sporadic diplomatic conversations were going on between Vienna, Budapest and Prague. These conversations tended to explore the possibilities of forming a new triangle of the three Danubian states, a new tie which would have strengthened European security from aggression and literally linked together the hitherto incompatible (yet both originally anti-German) Triangles

of the Rome Protocols and the Paris-Prague-Moscow Mutual
Assistance Pacts. Schuschnigg, certain monarchists, Hodža, and
the Hungarian opposition leader, Eckhardt, acting with the silent
consent of Horthy, worked in that direction; unfortunately their
plans were not realized. Mussolini was not satisfied, and in March
1936 he made the Rome Protocol states sign the so-called Supplementary Protocols, with the clause that no one of the signatories
should engage herself in negotiations with another Power without having previously consulted her co-signatories. Thus Mussolini
wished to avoid serious Austrian-Czechoslovak talks. Soon afterwards he fully changed his Austrian policy. With Ciano, his new
Foreign Minister, Mussolini late in 1936 became interested in the
greatest of all triangles: Berlin-Rome-Tokyo.

[*Yugoslav and Czech shortsightedness.*] Stoyadinovič contributed
much to Mussolini's and Hitler's success in destroying the Vienna-
Prague-Budapest plans. He was using the bogey of Habsburg revival
as a pretext; nothing could be more illustrative of this than an excerpt
from a speech of his given on March 6, 1936, that is, twelve hours
before Hitler marched into the Rhineland:

> The restoration of the Habsburgs would inevitably lead to conflict
> and be of grave consequence to the peace of Europe. As a real friend
> of peace, Yugoslavia must a second and a third time say "No!" to
> this . . .

Neither were the Czechs enthusiastic about the return of Otto
Habsburg, but Hodža at least was not against restoration in principle.
He regarded it as the lesser of two evils, yet he was opposed by Beneš
and Yugoslavia. On April 1, 1936, Schuschnigg decreed rearmament
in Austria and subsequently was condemned by the Little Entente
Foreign Ministers meeting in Bratislava (9) in September; the ministers, although expressing their desire to come to good terms with
Italy and Poland were as rigid as ever in their uncompromising attitude with respect to the *status quo* and Austrian and Hungarian rearmament. At the same time Schuschnigg tried to bring about a simultaneous Austrian-Czech and German-Czech rapprochement and several
times recommended Hodža to Papen. (*10*) On the other hand, when
Stoyadinovič expressed his wish to meet Schuschnigg, the Chancellor
consulted the Italians first, who counselled him not to grasp the occasion offered. (*11*) When in February 1937 Kobr, the Czech Minister

to Hungary, told the Hungarian Foreign Minister, Kánya, for the first time that Prague would decidedly prefer Habsburg restoration in Austria to an *Anschluss* with Germany, it was already too late, as the Axis was in existence by then and the Little Entente was not much more than a fiction.

[*Italy begins urging Austria to accommodate Germany.*] Some time in September–October 1935 Mussolini began to hint at the desirability of revising German-Austrian relations. Schuschnigg resisted these suggestions awhile. In the winter of 1935–36 the Austrian régime did not take heed of the Italian advice, as press controversies with Germany were again bitter. Also, somewhat to the surprise of many, friendly words were said of France and Britain in the Austrian press, while not too much sympathy was wasted on the Italians' campaign in Africa; there was also a minor press scuffle over the treatment of the Austrian minority in Italian South Tyrol. In March 1936 Mussolini allegedly said that only Austria stood in the way of a close alliance between Germany and Italy. Schuschnigg's Czecho-slovak policy again failed to please Mussolini, nor did he like internal developments in Austria. (*12*)

Schuschnigg dismissed Fey, his unreliable lieutenant, in October 1935; then, in April 1936 the Vice Chancellor and *Heimwehr* chieftain, Prince Starhemberg, left the cabinet. This Mussolini definitely resented, although Starhemberg supported the foreign policy of Schuschnigg. (*13*) Starhemberg was not a serious factor anymore: in April he bombastically announced that the *Heimwehr* could only be done away with "over his dead body," yet in October 1936 Schuschnigg quietly dissolved the *Heimwehren*.

But in the meantime momentous developments rocked the continent. In March the Germans violated Locarno and occupied the Rhineland without the slightest opposition. In May, the Abyssinian campaign was over and Italy achieved complete victory. Although on May 18 Neurath told Bullitt that he "could see no way to reconcile the conflicting interests of Germany and Italy in Austria," (*14*) Italy and Germany drew nearer and nearer; and in the words of Schuschnigg:

The rapprochement between Rome and Berlin put before Austria a difficult but clear task: We had to keep the active interest of the Western Powers alive, secure the continued assistance of Italy, and maintain such relations with Germany as to make it at least difficult for Hitler to solve the "Austrian question" by force . . .

[*The German-Austrian agreement.*] Rome urged Austria to become a bridge between Italy and Germany and on June 5 Mussolini approved a German-Austrian Agreement draft, on which his Minister to Vienna, Suvich, was then set to work. It is evident that the draft was the Germans' idea, as it was very similar to the one which Papen had presented to Berger-Waldenegg the year before. The Western Powers perked up but only half-heartedly: early in July they invited Schuschnigg to come to Geneva to meet Delbos and Eden. Schuschnigg declined. It was a mistake. At the same time the French Ambassador in Rome told the Austrian Foreign Minister to ask for a betterment in Italian-Czechoslovak relations and make Italy extend her protection to Prague also. But Berger-Waldenegg reported this French suggestion and its origins to Ciano, the new and "dynamic" Foreign Minister, who registered it scornfully and thumbed his nose at the French. (*15*)

So the German-Austrian Agreement was signed on July 11. It contained, among other vague terms, mutual promises of non-intervention in internal affairs; Austria recognized herself as a culturally "German" state, and the Treaty stated that it did not affect Austrian relations with Hungary or with Italy, or the Rome Protocols in general. (*16*) Mussolini "expressed lively satisfaction over the event" to the German Ambassador in Rome, "which," continued the Duce, "would finally remove the last and only mortgage on German-Italian relations."

.   .   .   .

[*Germany and Austria in the following year.*] Six days after this signature the revolt of two garrisons in Spanish Morocco marked the beginning of the Spanish Civil War; on October 20, 1936, an Italo-German Treaty was signed in which Berlin recognized the Ethiopian conquest; on November 1, Mussolini spoke in Milan, pronouncing the magic word "Axis," that "vertical line Berlin-Rome . . . an Axis around which all European states can collaborate."

Hitler received the Austrian Foreign Minister, Guido Schmidt, on November 19 and played violently on the anti-Bolshevik theme; he wished to convince the Austrians that this was his sincere, construc-

tive and only policy. He said that France was about completely Bol-
shevised: "Blum . . . is [for France] what Kurt Eisner was for Bavaria
and Kerensky for Russia." (This statement is an interesting illustration of Hitler's principles: a few months later he permitted Schacht
to conduct extensive talks in Paris with Blum.)

Hitler feared the restoration attempts more than ever. Three days
after the signing of the July 11 Agreement, Berlin told Schuschnigg
that, "for the functioning of the German-Austrian Agreement," it
would be desirable if he refrained even from mentioning the issue of
restoration when interviewed by the foreign press. Schmidt was
repeatedly told by Papen and Neurath and others that Germany was
absolutely opposed to a restoration under any circumstances. Yet the
monarchist movement was still strong in Austria and was gaining
power within influential Hungarian circles. On June 16 Hassell said
to Ciano that "the only cloud in the sky" was the doubt of Berlin
whether Italy perhaps worked for a Habsburg restoration in Austria.
(*17*) At the same time Berlin tried to turn Italy and Austria against
each other; Hitler was pleased that in the summer of 1937 a clash
between players during the international Italy-Austria soccer game
developed into a popular, angry demonstration in Vienna and
that during a cross-country bicycle race in Styria the tires of the
Italian cyclists were found punctured. Göring turned to Schuschnigg at the funeral of Gömbös in Budapest on October 6: "We two
won't need those Italians," he said. (*18*) In November the organizer
of the Austrian Monarchists, Baron Wiesner, went to Rome and was
received by Mussolini; then he travelled to Budapest, and diplomatic
circles reverberated with rumors about impending steps toward a
Habsburg restoration. On New Year's Day, 1937, Archduke Otto
sent a hopeful and interesting message to the 1,456 Austrian munici-
palities of which he was an honorary citizen. Yet at that time the
Germans had already torpedoed all such hopes and dreams. Hitler
on November 19 said things to Schmidt which led to a further relaxation of the already weak contacts between Vienna, Prague and Budapest. (*19*) He especially wanted to prevent too close Austrian-Hun-
garian contacts and common policy. Schmidt was pleased with his
Berlin visit; according to Papen: "He evidently expected to receive
rather 'sabre-rattling' impressions in Berlin and the remark therefore
escaped him with great relief that 'in Rome they play with fire much
more than in Berlin!' " (*20*) On November 27 Schuschnigg delivered
a speech at Klagenfurt which strongly emphasized the independence

theme, whereupon Berlin rudely attacked him. Neurath said that in view of the "tone" of the speech, a return visit of the German Foreign Minister to Vienna "is out of the question for the time being." (*21*) Thus, in the wake of Wiesner's trips, a crisis in German-Austrian relations was in the making. Göring was now rapidly dispatched to Rome where on January 15, 1937, he told Mussolini that the prime requirement of German-Italian collaboration was that Mussolini completely disassociate himself from the support of the Austrian monarchists; if not, then the Rome-Berlin Axis might not stand, after all. Ciano hesitated somewhat. But Mussolini quickly complied: he reminded Göring that on July 11 he had already told the German Ambassador of his advice to Schuschnigg to drop the monarchist idea. (*22*) The Germans were not yet sure about the Italians; after all, it was the Italian Minister in Vienna who brought about the Wiesner journey. But now Mussolini gave definite orders, and in February the journalist Gayda began to criticize the Austrian monarchists and their plans. At the same time German official criticism of Schuschnigg's foreign policy became gradually more overt and brutal.

[*Schuschnigg's Italian hopes reduced.*] When for the next — and last — time Schuschnigg met Mussolini, in Venice on April 22, 1937, the Austrian wished to show his good faith; he knew that Mussolini had made up his mind not to support an anti-German Austria; he told the Duce how well army contacts between the Austrian and German Armies were developing. (*23*) He said that "authoritarian Austria cannot orient herself toward the ultra-democratic Paris-Prague axis" and discounted rumors of any excessive Austrian-Czech friendship. He feared, of course, a German attack on Czechoslovakia, but said that Hodža wanted the friendship of Italy. (Undoubtedly this was a message indirectly conveyed.) Schuschnigg concluded by saying that a Habsburg restoration would not be made now, but in principle he could not renounce it. Mussolini warned him not to do it, and when Schuschnigg spoke about the misdeeds of the Austrian Nazis, Mussolini said that he had emphasized to Göring the necessity of Austrian independence. To Göring Mussolini belittled the Wiesner visit and to Schuschnigg he said that he had refused to receive the pro-German Austrian Prince Rohan. There were substantial differences between Fascism and Nazism, among them racial and religious questions, said the Italian, but they might have to confront the democracies together.

On the day Schuschnigg left Venice, Gayda wrote an article forecasting the inclusion of the Austrian Nazis in an Austrian "nationalist" government. Vienna at once denied this, but it was now clear that Gayda in the *Giornale d'Italia* was little less than an official Italian mouthpiece hinting to both Vienna and Berlin that, notwithstanding the supposed effects of the Schuschnigg visit, Italy more or less agreed with what Berlin wanted. The Germans now struck while the iron was still hot. Neurath went to Rome in early May, and Göring paid a secretive short visit to Venice a fortnight later. At the same time in London, on the occasion of the coronation of George VI, Eden told the Hungarian Foreign Minister Kánya to go ahead and try hard for a Hungarian-Czech-Austrian *bloc*, as Italy was unreliable. He wanted good relations between Italy and Britain but felt that Mussolini was impossible. Notwithstanding the traditionally good Hungarian-Italian relations, Kánya himself doubted Italy's good intentions, and when the Italian royal family visited Budapest between May 19 and 22, Ciano had to reassure the Hungarian Foreign Minister that Rome still insisted on Austrian independence. (*24*) Yet anti-Monarchist and pro-Nazi hints continued to appear in the Italian press, and when Mussolini went to Berlin in September 1937, "amidst all the fanfare and splendor the Third Reich could muster," (*25*) he sent a notice to Schuschnigg that Austria had no reasons to worry.

[*German agitation against Austria.*] This was not true. Austrian-German relations were, and remained, rather insecure, (*26*) in spite of the mutual non-intervention clauses of the July 11 agreements. Incidents continued to occur, and Austrian workers were divided in loyalty. (*27*) Only two weeks after July 11 the Viennese Nazis organized a large pro-Hitler demonstration on the occasion of the Olympic torch passing through Vienna en route to the Berlin Olympics. There were "flag incidents" when Austrian authorities protested against the display of swastikas and were fiercely resisted by the displayers. In February 1937 Neurath finally came to Vienna, but when the local Nazis exploited the occasion of his arrival and arranged a great political demonstration, the government organized in turn a less spontaneous but very conspicuous counter-demonstration, drowning the *Heil Hitler!* shouts with *Heil Schuschnigg!* and *Österreich!* exclamations as Neurath drove to the railway station. A Nazi engineer, Woitsche, was found to be involved in a serious plan of railroad sabotage in the autumn of 1937. He was but one of many. In the grey suburbs of Vienna, in the hollow staircases of the great flathouses under the bleak, eerie twilights of the autumnal evenings, disillusioned workers, hoodlums, frustrated students and half-educated engineers met German couriers, and distributed firearms and bundles of pamphlets from the other side of the border. (*28*) In November 1937 the Austrian police were on the trail of a secret Nazi plan containing details for a Nazi coup or the eventual coercion of the Austrian government into submission. There was now direct and indisputable evidence of connections between the Nazis and German authorities in Berlin, and on January 25, 1938, the so-called Tavs memorandum advocating the German invasion of Austria was seized.

Schuschnigg missed the chance of exploiting the Tavs papers; he did not reveal this document to the world or even to other governments — perhaps because of Schmidt, or because of the pledges of Papen, or, most likely, because of his fear of Mussolini's reaction. Undoubtedly Schuschnigg committed a major tactical error here, the avoidance of which, however, would not have helped him — we know now what he did not know then: his fate was already sealed.

·   ·   ·   ·   ·   ·

The "Austrian Legion," *SS Standarte 89*, sent a New Year's greeting to Hitler in 1937, and Hitler, obviously moved, angrily demanded their release from Austrian prisons and camps. On January 12 Papen sent a "balance sheet" report to Hitler, (*29*) summing up the situation as it presented itself at the beginning of the new year: it was altogether favorable to the Nazi cause.

[*Diplomatic soundings.*] When Neurath was in Vienna, he strongly urged Schuschnigg to shelve the Habsburgs. He angrily protested against the influence and the tactics of Wiesner. "A Habsburg restoration would be the best way for Austria to commit suicide," said he; Schuschnigg responded that he was aware of this, and later added confidentially that in case of a Habsburg coup, he would not hesitate to have Otto arrested before the Pretender arrived in Vienna. (*30*) Papen drew intelligent deductions from the Neurath visit; on March 3 he reported to Hitler, with whom he had direct communications, that it was now unmistakable: the Axis worked. Italy had the Mediterranean area, and Germany the Danube region. Ten days later Papen reported to Hitler orally: "The Berlin-Rome Axis can only be injured at its weakest point, Vienna, and there with the maximum help of the Austrians themselves." He noted the influence which the British Minister in Vienna had with persons who might make Schuschnigg take a more aloof, anti-German course. Papen therefore asked Hitler to issue orders to the German press: Schuschnigg should not be criticized too much. There were now divergences between Papen, the German Legation, and the Austrian Nazis and Nazi refugees in Germany; Papen complained to his Führer that there were "too many offices in the Reich concerning themselves with Austrian policy."

At the same time Hodža tried vainly to convince Schuschnigg to align himself with Paris and Prague. The German chargé d'affaires, Stein, was informed of these moves through certain people within the Austrian Foreign Office (*31*); similar reports were given to Papen, who on April 17 wrote directly to Hitler again: "It is an open secret, confirmed by many other sources, that with the German-Italian ties growing ever closer, the Austrian Government considers itself in a more than uncomfortable situation." And he enclosed some interesting — perhaps false — instructions from the Austrian Foreign Ministry to the Austrian envoys in London and Rome. (*32*) Meanwhile Papen was uncomfortably busy with the bickerings of the Nazis and intrigues against himself; Göring in May told the Nazi leader, Captain Leopold, to adopt a more aggressive line of action in Austria, which course Papen opposed on tactical grounds. (*33*)

Schmidt, that strange Foreign Minister, visited London and Paris during the Coronation ceremonies and returning therefrom saw Papen. He told the German that he had not done much. He certainly did not seek a pro-Western policy, but he was surprised how much interest, however academic, there was to be found in London about central European questions. Papen's answer: "He should not depend on the possibility that . . . the British Government would actively intervene in Austria's behalf. Although [Schmidt's] impressions in this connection were very encouraging, the Reich Government considered the evolutionary solution of the central European problem a question in which it would tolerate no interference from England." (*34*) Two weeks later Rome informed Berlin that what Schmidt said to Papen was not true, for he had asked for a French-British guarantee during his journey. The Germans soon checked this, and Papen took Schmidt secretly to task. After this Schmidt changed: he became extremely anxious to make a good impression in Berlin when he visited there, (*35*) and he did his best to obtain a good German press.

[*A military directive.*]   In the meantime, on June 24, a *Wehrmacht* directive was issued in Berlin, providing for the following military eventualities:

a) *Case Red*, a two-front war with the main effort in the West.
b) *Case Green*, with the main effort in the south-east
Special *Case Otto:* Armed intervention if Austria tries to restore the Monarchy. (*36*)

The directive added that the invasion of Austria could come also as part of *Case Red*, but not simultaneous with *Green* (Czechoslovakia); if *Red* should come, then *Otto* should be undertaken after *Green* were finished; inasmuch as *Green* might develop, on the other hand, as a result of *Otto*, preparations to cope with such a case should also be made.

[*Again, soundings.*]   On August 8 Schmidt met Neurath secretly in the mountains but without much success, due to renewed German interference with the Austrian Nazis; there were now increasing incidents, and some Austrian singers greeted Hitler as their Führer at a German Song Festival held in Breslau. The international scene was rapidly shifting in favor of Berlin and the extent of the Diplomatic Revolution was perceived by Papen, who now saw that he could openly support the Nazis in Austria. On September 1 he informed Neurath that perhaps the previous policy of trying to get along with the reasonable Schuschnigg should be abandoned, because the careful policies of Schuschnigg seemed to work, in the long run, to the disadvantage of the German-Nazi cause. (*37*) Neurath had returned not long before from a visit to Belgrade and Sofia and Budapest, where he found satisfactory sentiments. Stoyadinović especially pleased the Germans, and when Schmidt in September proposed a hunting-trip meeting with the Yugoslav, Stoyadinović informed Neurath of that suggestion and then evaded and postponed the invitation.

During his visit in Germany Mussolini clearly indicated that he agreed with the German interpretation of the Danubian Basin; Italy's interests were in the central Mediterranean, said he; Sicily was the geographical center of the Italian Empire. (*38*) Papen's private visits to Paris and Berlin in October–November convinced him that Austria could be absorbed by Germany without foreign intervention. As long as Neurath was Foreign Minister, however, peaceful, evolutionary absorption was the order of the day.

[*The decisive directive.*] But not to Hitler, who on November 5, 1937, summoned the high chiefs of the Third Reich and revealed his immediate program for eliminating an independent Austria and Czechoslovakia: "The German question can be only solved by force," said he. (*39*) The others listened silently.

The Diplomatic Revolution: Phase II

The Second Phase of the Diplomatic Revolution began on March 7, 1936. In the morning hours of that day, Hitler's new German army marched into the Rhineland. By the evening of March 7, the bulk of the inmarching *Reichswehr* troops had crossed the Rhine in the northern sector; the whole world was agog, waiting for tremendous repercussions.

[*The Rhineland effects.*] When the first news of the German action reached Paris, a restricted council of ministers and generals was called. Sarraut, the Premier, presided; Flandin, the Foreign Minister, attended for a limited time. They had just begun to discuss countermeasures when Paul-Boncour turned to Gamelin: "I should like to see you in Mayence as soon as possible." To which the general answered, "Yes, but there is another thing: that is exactly what I want to do myself but I need the means to do it, indeed I do." (*1*) And, in assaying the possibilities of an isolated French-German war, Gamelin said that in the beginning the advantage would be on the French side, but the industrial capacity and greater manpower of Germany would possibly play a decisive rôle in the long run. Here were the tragic effects of the Diplomatic Revolution: France could not count on Italy; neither could she count on Britain. Here were the results of Laval's policies: Mussolini, alienated from Britain, sought the friendship of Hitler; Britain, still smarting from what was called in London the ambiguous French foreign policy under Laval, did not wish to be embroiled in a French-German war, as she was fully unprepared to support France in Europe while probably fighting against Italy in the Mediterranean and Africa. (*2*) Thirty-six hours after the Rhineland coup, the cables coming into the French Foreign Ministry confirmed the fears of many Frenchmen, first of all, Flandin: the possibility of a France fighting alone loomed large; it was indicated by London and Brussels that Britain and Belgium would acquiesce in the accomplished fact. Poland, the Eastern European ally, suspected that France would not march.

And France did not march.

Her generals told her ministers that the prerequisite for any successful move would be general and not partial mobilization; this the ministers did not like; in turn, they said to the generals that it would be dangerous to jump upon Germany at once and convey a picture to the world of France's being the bloodthirsty Cerberus of Europe. A compromise was drafted: it was decided to bring the Rhineland case before the League of Nations, and Flandin was sent to London to prepare a joint stand with the British which would result in a League ultimatum to Germany. To back up the ultimatum, it was decided that the French Army would undertake a limited operation, a preventive occupation of Luxembourg and the partial occupation of the Saar region, and the Belgian General Staff would be asked to collaborate with the French if and when German armed resistance resulted.

The draft remained a draft. Flandin returned from London with the news that the British did not intend to use force; neither did the intimidated Belgians. Thus did Locarno go; with it sank the chance to stop Hitler.

> "This completely changed the European situation" said Flandin. "The French alliance with the Little Entente was now valueless. In the future France could not hope to give effective assistance to Poland, Czechoslovakia, Yugoslavia or Rumania, in the event of German aggression. So far as I am concerned. . . . this means a fundamental reorientation of French policy. In my opinion, the last chance of saving central and eastern Europe from German domination has been thrown away. So far as France is concerned, we shall have to make the best terms with Germany we can get, and leave the rest of Europe to her fate." (*3*)

Flandin "spoke with a cold passion," recorded one of his British conversants, "which impressed us all . . . he meant what he said." (*4*)

Immediate were the results in central-eastern Europe. The German pretext for the Rhineland action was that Locarno had been automatically annulled by the ratification of the French-Soviet Pact ten days before the German move, a pretext which was willingly accepted by those states who never favored the French-Soviet Pact. On the other hand, there were Frenchmen, and not only Flandin, who, impressed by Hitler and disillusioned by the British, felt that *mort Locarno, mort l'accessoire de Locarno* (*5*); this stand led down the road to Munich. The inevitable waning of French prestige set in.

[*The Polish position.*] The Poles in the winter of 1935–36 moved nearer to France, influenced especially by German revisionist manifestations; an extremely aggressive speech was given by Schacht in the Upper Silesian Beuthen in February 1936. The Poles offered to attack Germany with France, but Paris did not grasp this most favorable opportunity. And now that the Warsaw régime saw the West both unwilling and unable to check German expansion, Beck and his colleagues felt justified by events and continued the ambivalent policy they had followed since 1933. Beck also suspected that the excellent German intelligence apparatus had known about the secret Polish offer of March 9 to stand by France. Now he ordered government press organs to publish articles praising the restraint of the Great Powers for not having launched a general war, and ten days after March 7, a Polish newspaper assailed the system of regional alliances again, thus reverting to the 1934–35 line.

On April 5, Beck put a straight question to France: did the French government regard the 1921 French-Polish Alliance as valid still? That this question was at all asked indicates in itself the depths of incertitude and mistrust from which France was being regarded in the spring of 1936. The French answered in the affirmative; subsequently, visits were exchanged between the military leaders of the two governments: first Gamelin visited Warsaw, then, in July, Marshal Smigly-Rydz went to France, where he signed an agreement at Rambouillet, providing for a large French credit for Polish military furnishings. (*6*) But concerning the practical and ultimate values of the French alliances, not many nurtured great illusions. In spite of French efforts of mediation in August–September 1936, Polish-Czechoslovak relations remained parlous, (*7*) while Hitler was hesitating over which country to jump on first. (*8*) Of course, neither inner events in Russia nor the successful conclusion of the Anti-Comintern Front later in 1936 contributed to the realization of the Polish-Russian rapprochement desired by Paris. Instead, Beck approached Rumania to prevent closer cooperation between that state, Czechoslovakia and Russia (*9*); Polish-Italian relations grew more cordial, as Beck was one of the first to announce solemnly in Geneva, on June 30, 1936, that Poland regarded the sanctions as out-of-date.

[*Yugoslavia; Rumania.*]   Although in the summer of 1936 the Yugoslav and Rumanian Chiefs of Staff visited Paris, there was no doubt that the ties of the Little Entente with France were relaxing. Stoyadinovič on September 23 and Mussolini on November 1 pompously spoke of Yugoslav-Italian amity, and Göring said to Comnen (then Rumanian Minister to Germany and in 1938 Foreign Minister) on December 4: "We have a quite clear agreement (*Abmachung*) with Yugoslavia." (*10*) Nazi internal agitation in Rumania and Stoyadinovič in Belgrade impaired the Little Entente ties to such an extent that when the time of troubles came in 1938, they vanished. Titulescu ran into trouble because of a verbal battle he had with Italian journalists during a League session in early July; in August he resigned, and in his stead came a new Rumanian Foreign Minister, Victor Antonescu (not related to the later Antonescus), about whose first speech Arnold Toynbee wrote: "The extreme catholicity of Monsieur Antonescu's benignity made it difficult to translate its meaning with any precision into terms of current international politics." (Antonescu had spoken kind words about almost every Great Power, with scarcely varying emphasis.)   Germany now began to let Bucharest know that if she only behaved well, Germany would support Rumania rather than Hungary, and these suggestions were conveyed through various media, the Liberal leader, Bratianu, as well as the Iron Guardists.   Late in 1936 German criticism of Hungary pleased the Rumanians no end, while the pro-German Hungarians simply did not take notice of Berlin's steadfastness. Only six days after the Rhineland occupation, the Greek Premier Demertzis denied the existence of Greek commitments to the Little Entente "in regard to Central Europe"; in other words, the Balkan Entente became a frail instrument, replete with reservations, a mere eighteen months after its inauguration.

The system of French security received a final blow on October 14 when the Belgian king declared the "absolute neutrality" of his country, implicitly denouncing the Belgian-French military alliance of 1921. This made all the eastern allies of France reconsider the practical value of their pacts and seemed only to confirm the course of a

Tatarescu or a Stoyadinovič. In Vienna in November (*11*) Ciano
told Kánya to be friendly with the Yugoslavs, more friendly than
with the Czechs. Kánya said, very well, but he regarded the Czech
situation with anxiety, Göring having said recently that in two or
three years Czechoslovakia would cease to exist. Ciano told him not
to worry but go ahead with Stoyadinovič. (*12*)

[*The Axis structure nears completion.*] While Germany and
Italy, having generally agreed about Austria, were further driven
together by British-French differences in the Mediterranean and in
Spain, (*13*) France herself presented a sorry picture, writhing amidst
strikes and dulled by eternal parliamentary manoeuvres of Popular
Front governments. Moreover, the lag in French production delayed
the promised armament shipments to the Polish and Rumanian governments to an extent which made even the most Francophile army
circles seriously doubt the willingness and effectiveness of France's
assistance. Finally, on November 25, the German-Japanese Agreement gave the "Axis" a superstructure of a Grand Triangle, Berlin-
Rome-Tokyo, adorned with a shiny banner which read, "Anti-Comintern Front." The cause of Hitler and Mussolini was further advanced
by the "anti-Comintern" argument, putting them into a good bargaining position concerning not only Europe's body, but also her soul.

.   .   .   .

Of the year 1936, Arnold Toynbee wrote that ". . . the most conspicuous and widespread movement was a retreat — which at times
and places almost quickened to a rout — of the forces that, since the
peace settlement of A.D. 1920–1, had been supporting a collective
system of international relations." But on the surface, nothing conspicuous happened throughout Europe in the year 1937. Indeed, this
was the last year of full European peace; the capitals and spas of
central-eastern Europe received foreign tourists by the thousands; it
was a year with a good crop, a beautiful summer, and international
festivals. But decisions were nevertheless made and that their results
were not visible only made their impact more grave. One secret
decision was Hitler's declaration of November 5 that he would solve
the "German question", Austria and Czechoslovakia — by force, if
necessary. Another decision was less dramatic and perhaps it does
not qualify as a "decision": it was a perceptible change in the course
of Britain.

[*A new British policy toward Italy.*] During the Second Phase
of the Diplomatic Revolution, Britain perceived European uneasiness and the French-Russian "system" or "half-system" —
of which London never thought much — counterbalanced by the
formidable central European Axis. Throughout 1936, the balance
began to weigh in favor of the Axis, and this German diplomacy
skillfully exploited. The uneasy squirming of France's central-
eastern European allies, her serious domestic troubles, and the
Russian purges weighed heavily in the considerations of the British
statesmen. Pursuing her age-old — and perhaps already antiquated
— balance of power policy in Europe, the Baldwin and later the
Chamberlain governments began altering the course of British foreign
policy, approximately from February 1935 and then again from the
fall of 1936 onwards. When London tried mediating between Paris
and Berlin, the result was the weakening of French prestige and interests to an extent which drove many otherwise responsible French
politicians to take up a bitter and almost negative anti-British attitude; when Paris endeavored to reconcile London and Rome, British
suspicions rose, and it became easier for Hitler to win Mussolini.
And now, early in 1937, Neville Chamberlain began to favor the
Germans:

> If only we could get on terms with the Germans, I would not care
> a rap for Musso. (*14*)

And he sent a very friendly Ambassador to Berlin.

At the other end of the Axis, Eden was instructed to make friendly
gestures to Italy. Britain was on the way to recognizing Italy's new
Abyssinian Empire, and in January 1937 a Mediterranean agreement was signed between Italy and Britain, a so-called "Gentleman's
Agreement," indirectly recognizing Mussolini's Ethiopian conquest
and establishing that Italy's rôle as a great Mediterranean power
was not incompatible with British interests.

The unusual sight of a Britain asking for the friendship of Italy (*15*)
had its unfortunate effects in central-eastern Europe. The most
responsible conservative statesmen were inclined to think that behind
the British-Italian Agreement there lay a secret understanding that
both would oppose German penetration in south-eastern Europe;
others thought that Britain was already quietly consenting to a German-Italian economic, (*16*) if not political, domination of the Bal-

kans. Neither of these hypotheses was correct, although the second had, unfortunately, a grain of truth within it.

These uncertainties of the West continued to destroy the remaining reservoir of prestige which the West had in central-eastern Europe. The masses, lured by dynamic and radical ideologies, saw absolutely nothing in the West to attract them in the least; many politicians, industrialists, and a considerable number of army men felt likewise. (*17*)

[*A new Italian policy toward Yugoslavia.*] In January 1937 a Friendship and Non-Aggression Pact was signed between Bulgaria and Yugoslavia, and on March 25 a similar Pact was being negotiated in Belgrade between the former arch-enemies, Italy and Yugoslavia. Yugoslavia, bound by her new ties and the crafty Stoyadinovič' policies, could now be practically discounted by France. We have Ciano's record of the talks he had with Stoyadinovič in Belgrade. It is a startling record. It reflects the end of democratic prestige. It reflects the end of an era.

Stoyadinovič told Ciano about French suggestions that the Little Entente conclude a military alliance; the Serbian said that he had deliberately delayed and sabotaged this idea; at the next meeting of the Little Entente he would reject the proposal as he could not delay answering much longer.

Stoyadinovič then began to explain the motives of his new policies to Ciano:

> "We did not receive and are not receiving anything from France. Her economic assistance for Yugoslavia is worth nothing . . . [we pay] loans back at an usurer's interest rate. Militarily, [France] and Czechoslovakia were until lately our main armament providers. But [France] did not give us a single bayonet. What we received we had to pay for, just like we shall pay Italy, given that in the future we intend to order our war matériel primarily from Italy and Germany.
>
> "I should add that the moral and cultural influence which France exercises in our country has become . . . disgusting: both press and letters are expressions of the Jewish, Masonic and pro-Communistic mentality of Blum's France.
>
> "As to the rest, when we were bound to a military policy of collaboration with France, the situation was fully different. One foresaw then that if Germany attacked Czechoslovakia, Italy would have reacted in an anti-German sense and would have permitted French

troops — at least this is what was being told us in Paris — to cross the Po Valley to fight in Austria against the German armies. All this has now dissolved into thin air. If Germany should attack Czechoslovakia now, we would have to invade Hungary with the weak and uncertain military help of the Rumanians, in order to get to the aid of the Czechs. But, even conceding that it would be possible for us to occupy Hungary completely (and I consider this very difficult) we would arrive at the Czech frontiers but in time to meet with the remnants of the defeated Prague armies. Behind us we would have Hungary, occupied and hostile. Before us the victorious German armies. A most unfortunate situation, this, and a risk which we cannot let the Yugoslav people undertake; especially not as this people has no hostile sentiments for the Hungarians and nurtures no solidarity for Czechoslovakia. . . . [There will come soon] a further cooling off in relations between France and Yugoslavia, perhaps even an open clash. They will accuse me of egoism. The French always accuse people of being egotistic who are not disposed to let themselves be murdered for the sake of the French. All this leaves me completely indifferent, as I have now succeeded in concluding an agreement with Italy which I consider fundamental for our policy.

". . . The Little Entente . . . will not be transformed formally . . . but while relations between Yugoslavia and Rumania will remain the same, that is, loyal and cordial, relations between these two on one side and Czechoslovakia on the other will be reduced to empty formalities.

"Beneš has told me that if he should not be able anymore to count on the Little Entente, on France and on the League of Nations, he would always find a way to make an agreement with the Germans. I advised him to do so and shall continue advising him. Those, and I mean the French and the English, who counsel implacable resistance in the face of Hitler, are the same people who counseled the Negus to resist Italy by arms. Without them Haile Selassie would probably be in Addis Ababa today. Mussolini would have left him there. . . . With Czechoslovakia the situation is the same: if matters became really serious and Germany took action, those who are now encouraging the hostility of Prague against Berlin, would retreat and Beneš would find himself alone."

Passing to the examination of Yugoslav relations with Austria, Stoyadinović told me that he considers the *Anschluss* inevitable. Austria as she is today, has neither moral nor material bases for an [independent] life. Nevertheless [the union with Germany] should be delayed as much as possible. But this delay should be expedited by such means which would not provoke a conflict or only a tension with Germany.

. . . Of the great foreign Powers, Stoyadinovič spoke of Britain only, as [Britain], without any direct reason, pretends or aspires to exercise considerable influence on Yugoslav policies.

"During the sanctions Britain tried to push Yugoslavia further from Italy. . . . After the sanctions Britain continued to lure us and promise her help in the Mediterranean. We do not need it. I even ask myself whether Britain is in the position to help us or to help any other nation in the Mediterranean, as she herself had to solicit our help when she was at odds with you. The game of poker is an Anglo-Saxon game and we all know that they use the "bluff" very often in order to save at least a part of their own money. Even if Britain should complete her material rearmament, it would not mean that she assumed again her rôle in the world. Men count more than arms. And I nurture many a doubt about the will and fighting spirit of the British people of today. . . . I have the honor of never having been in Geneva and I intend to maintain this honor forever. [I shall] formally recognize . . . the Italian Empire [in Abyssinia]. Then the French and British will protest . . . and if they will lament the fact that I took that decision without informing them in advance, I shall answer that neither London nor Paris informed me when they disestablished their Legations in Addis Ababa. Thus shall I answer France, France which, notwithstanding the Havas communiqués, I have informed of my dealings with Rome, [and] the suggestion of our seeking an accord with Italy came from their Premier. Then it was Laval, now it is Blum. It isn't my mistake that in France governments and ideas change so often."

My talks with Stoyadinovič reflect his personality which made a real, profound impression on me. Stoyadinovič is a Fascist. If he is not affirming this publicly or by party affiliation he is certainly one by his conception of authority, the State and of life. His position in his country is eminent . . . *(18)*

. . . .

[*German diplomatic profits.*] These developments were most pleasing to Hitler; the fruits of his Italian alliance were ripening sooner than expected. But Neville Chamberlain did not know this; he possessed no special psychological gift for sizing up men outside his circle. He had no inkling of the disdain and hatred, stemming from the Latin inferiority complex, which Mussolini, who began to speak in 1937 of the "bleating democracies," felt against Britain. During the whole of 1937, Britain was most careful not to offend

Italy in the international disputes centering around the neutrality question of the Spanish civil war.

The result was that on August 25, 1937, Ciano began to think of the Italian occupation of Albania (and on the same day a book on the Peace of Amiens of 1802 induced him to reflect on Britain's allegedly analogous situation), and when, next month, Mussolini visited Hitler, Ciano could confirm to Neurath

> . . . the irrevocable decision of the Duce not to deviate, whatever may happen, from the line Rome-Berlin . . . All efforts to separate Germany from Italy, undertaken first of all by the English, will have no results . . . It [is] indispensable that in the years to follow Italy should not be engulfed by armed conflict. For this reason, whatever could serve as a pretext to war to the other side, above all, to Britain, should be avoided . . . Rome, for the sake of appearance, would listen to the British tentatives of a rapprochement. [Germany] will be constantly kept informed of events . . . (19)

Germany did not need much information. After the Mussolini visit to Munich and Berlin, Chamberlain decided to send an important British statesman to Germany to meet leading Germans and, if possible, have a detailed conversation with Hitler. Against the objections of Eden (and notwithstanding Mussolini, who did not trust Henderson and still feared a German-English alliance to the detriment of Italy) it was decided that Lord Halifax, then Lord President of the Council, should go. (20) He left Britain on November 16, 1937, (21) and returned a week later.

[*The Halifax-Hitler meeting.*] Although for more than a decade nothing was revealed, the full story of the Halifax-Hitler talks is fairly clear now. In answer to the State Department's publication of Nazi-Soviet Relations in January 1948, the Soviet government countered by publishing two volumes entitled *Documents and Materials Relating to the Eve of the Second World War.* (22) The first document of the first volume reproduces the German minutes of the Hitler-Halifax conversation. (23)

Halifax began by saying that in Britain, the "great services of the Führer [are] recognized," although public opinion was influenced by the sometimes exaggeratedly critical press. But he could assure Hitler that he was expressing the views of the entire Cabinet when he said that "the Führer had not only performed a great service in Germany but also . . . had been able, by preventing the entry of Communism into his own country to bar its passage further West." Undoubtedly, this was an appeal to Hitler's favorite complex.

The British statesman continued by saying that Chamberlain was willing to seek solutions "by an open exchange of opinions" and preferred a German-British understanding; "at the appropriate time" France and Italy could be included in this German-British friendship scheme. Now Halifax got to the main point. "Britons were realistic and perhaps more than others, convinced that mistakes had been made in the Treaty of Versailles which had to be put right. . . ." He "pointed to Britain's rôle with regard to the re-occupation of the Rhineland. . . . On the English side it was not necessarily thought that the *status quo* must be maintained under all circumstances. . . . It was recognized that we might have to contemplate an adjustment to new conditions, a correction of former mistakes and the recognition of changed circumstances when such need arose." Halifax nevertheless mentioned a reservation. He had to stress "in the name of the British Government, that no possibility of changing the existing situation must be precluded, but that the changes must take place only on the basis of a reasonable arrangement."

Hitler answered so undiplomatically that the others present in the room must have shuddered. He expressed his dislike of democracy: he was glad that Halifax conceded the existence of a hostile press and certain hostile British circles, and he then took off on a lengthy diatribe against the evils of democratic politics. The gaunt Halifax perceptibly stiffened for a moment and said, "If the Chancellor was really of that opinion, it was clear that he [Halifax] had wasted his time. . . ." British democracy intended to survive. But Hitler dropped his ideological sally as rapidly as he had started it. The atmosphere mellowed and Halifax could continue. Was Hitler sure "that the hostile circles were confined to England?" Then he asked Hitler to consider a return to the League and contemplate general disarmament of the European nations on the basis of equality. "All other questions could be characterized as relating to changes in the European order, changes that sooner or later would probably take place. To these questions belonged Danzig, Austria and Czechoslovakia." He finished with a gentle admonition: "It would have considerable effect upon the reestablishment of confidence between the nations . . . that any alterations should come through the course of peaceful evolution."

Hitler answered in a general sense, emphasizing that the "grave problems" of Czechoslovakia and Austria were internal. "Germany," said the Führer, "was deeply interested in maintaining good relations with all her neighbors." And, at the end, he uttered his standard anti-Bolshevik argument: "Only a country like Soviet Russia could gain by a general conflict. All others were for the preservation of peace from the bottom of their hearts." Halifax could not know that a mere two weeks before, Hitler had given orders to his military chiefs to prepare for a war and a forceful solution of his problems. A few days after Halifax returned, Chamberlain privately noted: "I don't see why we shouldn't say to Germany, 'give us satisfactory assurances that you won't use force to deal with the Austrians and the Czechoslovakians, and we will give you similar assurances that we won't use force to prevent the changes you want, if you can get them by peaceful means.' " (24) Nevile Henderson (25) recorded that Hitler was very favorably impressed by Lord Halifax and his message, a reaction which the Chancellor did not usually have toward people who dared to raise objections to his plans. Not very much later, the *Survey of International Affairs, 1937* philosophized brilliantly:

> To the average Englishman's eye Mr. Gandhi and Herr Hitler were two hardly distinguishable specimens of the same species of foreigner in virtue of their being, both of them, superlatively exotic; and the average member of a British Cabinet may have reasoned in November 1937 that the guileless tamer of Gandhi had at any rate "a sporting chance" of taming Hitler likewise. Were not both these political "mad-Mullahs" non-smokers, non-drinkers of alcohol, non-eaters of meat, non-riders on horseback and non-practisers of blood-sports in their cranky private lives? And did not the German Führer, like the Indian Mahatma, have some bee in his bonnet about the importance of being "Aryan"? Whether, however, when it came to the point, Lord Halifax did succeed in establishing the same sympathetic relations with the Führer as he had once established with the Mahatma, was a question which the historian had no means of answering at the time of writing; for the outcome of the Halifax-Hitler conversations of 1937 — unlike that of the Irwin-Gandhi conversations of 1931 — was kept a closely guarded secret. (26)

The historian might venture to answer today. The benignity of Chamberlain conveyed through Halifax was misinterpreted by Hitler. (27) Hitler was now convinced that he was right in his plans, that Britain would not fight when he remade central-eastern Europe, and subsequently, without British assistance, France would not go to war either. (*28*) The publication of the minutes of the Halifax-Hitler talks disproves the theory, once widely held, that Britain actually gave a blank check to Hitler in regard to Austria and Czechoslovakia; but, of course, there is a grain of truth in these implications. For, after Hitler won the acquiescence of Italy to his plans in the First Phase, he had reason to think that he had Britain's; and thus in November 1937 the Second — and final — Phase of the Diplomatic Revolution came to an end. (*29*) The last part of the story, leading to Munich and the defection of France, is not a phase in itself but the inevitable consequence of this catastrophic chain of events.

Chautemps and Delbos visited London at the end of November and the British now told them officially that "a closer connection between Germany and Austria would have to come sometime." They asked Delbos to intervene with the Czechs in favor of the Sudeten Germans. (*30*)

[*German analyses.*] The German Foreign Ministry nevertheless warned Hitler not to misinterpret the attitude of Britain; Weizsäcker, the canny Swabian counselor, prepared this memorandum on December 20, 1937:

> We ourselves are not yet strong enough to engage in European conflicts and shall therefore not seek any. Italy can and must be restrained from engaging in any adventures if she should be so inclined. . . . England is today still undecided as to whether or not she should buy peace in Europe by making concessions to Germany. It must be doubted whether a suitable price can be agreed on. But our attitude will have to be decided independently of these doubts. Keeping England in a state of vacillation as long as possible is certainly to be preferred to a condition of definite British hostility toward us. (*31*)

And a similar picture was drawn by Ambassador Mackensen the next day, noting the definite French trend of writing off as much of central-eastern Europe as was reasonably possible. His analysis was also remarkable and correct:

> If there are certain indications today of a dawning understanding in England and France that the path toward the realization of every political aim of ours in central and eastern Europe can no longer simply be blocked, this is attributable essentially to our regained freedom of political action.

But Ribbentrop saw the year of great decisions coming. On January 2, 1938, he gave the following evaluation to Hitler in the form of a memorandum:

> England . . . is playing for time. . . .
> Conclusions to be drawn by us:
> 1) outwardly further understanding with England
> 2) formation under great secrecy but with wholehearted tenacity of a coalition against England . . . also the winning over of all nations whose interests conform with ours directly or indirectly. . . .
> The particular question whether in event of a war by Germany in Central Europe, France and thereby England would interfere, depends on the circumstances and the time at which such a war commences and ceases and on military considerations which cannot be gone into here. . . . (32)

Other international developments

[*Effects of the Spanish war.*]   The issue of the Spanish civil war was cleverly exploited by Germany and Italy; the experiment which most of central-eastern Europe had with Communism between 1918 and 1921 assured a good reception for such propaganda. The Spanish affair turned out to be an internationally spectacular affair, with its crystallized front of "nationalist Powers" battling against a gloomy coalition of "Internationalists–Masons–Liberals–Marxists–Democrats–Anarchists–Bolsheviks." It was not yet realized that both Italy and Germany used Spain with supreme egotism for their very special purposes (or that as early as 1937 Mussolini voiced his distrust of Franco). There stood the picture of a new chivalry, the "heroic" Powers, Germany and Italy, aiding the good against the evil and decadent, the latter assisted by the France of the Jew Blum and by the Soviets, while "mercantile" Britain stood aloof, believed to be afraid of or, in her heart, sympathetic to the "dynamic" Powers of a new Europe. (1)

By mid-1937 most of the central-eastern European governments recognized *de facto* — and some *de jure* — the Franco régime. (2) The only nation expressly friendly with the Republicans was Czechoslovakia; elsewhere and especially in the Catholic countries, sympathies were overwhelmingly with Franco. Volunteers seldom appeared on the Spanish battlefields, but from Rumania a number of Iron Guardists went — uninvited — to help the cause of the Nationalists. Two of these were killed and the return of their bodies was exploited by Codreanu and his Guardists into a spectacular pro-Axis demonstration in the streets of Bucharest. On the other side, among the members of the International Brigade were quite a few refugee Communists from central-eastern Europe, mostly Poles, Letts, Czechs and Hungarians. (Among the latter was a Russian-Hungarian named Zalka who figured for awhile as a general under the assumed name of "Lucas.")

[*Communists and Soviets.*] The Anti-Comintern Front of 1936–37 — which in the long run was more anti-English than anti-Russian — fitted well into the pattern of the Spanish affair. In July–August 1935 the Seventh (and up to now the last) Congress of the Communist International met and the Comintern ordered the united-front tactics of Communist parties throughout the world. While this decision had but little effect in view of the general insignificance of Communist movements in central-eastern Europe, it again served as a good argument for Axis propaganda, as it was often very hard to explain that considerable differences existed between the Spanish *Frente Popular*, the French *Front Populaire*, and the British Laborites. The Germans put all of these into the same category, and the Soviets aided the German propaganda here by constant proclamations of Communist solidarity with democrats, Socialists, Liberals and Radicals "in the fight against Fascism."

Ten days after the German march into the Rhineland the Soviet régime announced that it would be willing to participate in countermeasures; in June 1936 the Soviets expressed their interest in naval affairs at the Montreux Conference dealing with the Dardanelles; on July 17, the Spanish civil war began. The Russians furnished material aid to Republican Spain, but they never regarded themselves as fully committed, and they were hampered by the distances between the nearest Soviet port, Odessa, and Valencia and Barcelona. Moreover, the route of ships led through the Mediterranean, and Italian submarines torpedoed Soviet merchantmen on several occasions. The previously very correct Soviet-Italian relations thus deteriorated seriously.

[*The Russian purges.*] Only a few days after the outbreak of the Spanish War, the first wave of the Great Purges rose in Russia. We know very little of the story; in certain instances we can do no more than conjecture. The reliability of the suggestions of Davies, Beneš (*3*) (it is a pity that the personal account of the latter was accepted by Mr. Churchill as worthy enough to be included in his memoirs) and others, that the purges were the result of a careful investigation after Stalin and his friends found a vast network of pro-German and pro-Japanese organizations within high Soviet civil and military circles can hardly be ascertained. The irrational and psychic elements of the Soviet régime, with all its Byzantine characteristics and Tartar cunning, should be taken into consideration. There is no doubt that great numbers were "liquidated" for personal reasons; every dictatorship strives for a constant internal *tabula rasa* and this desire probably guided Stalin in his frightful decisions.

[*Russia and Germany.*] There is some evidence, however, that Marshal Tukhachevski (widely thought of in 1936 as a friend of France) may have had some contact with Germany, or that Stalin himself was still pursuing his pre-1934 aim to get along with Hitler and was merely frustrated by his failures. In February 1937 Göring visited Warsaw and said to Smigly-Rydz:

> Until Hitler came to power, the policymakers of Germany committed numerous and grave errors. In regard to Russia the dangerous policy of Rapallo was pursued. In consequence of this policy, Germany helped Russia militarily by arming her, by furnishing instructors to her, by helping Russia in building her war industry. The old Reichswehr had a great many partisans of friendship with the Soviets. (*4*) This has been terminated now by the exclusion of these elements from the Army. General Schleicher, it is true, affirmed his will to fight Communism within Germany, but this did not stop him from searching for contacts with the Soviets. These were the heavy mistakes which should not be repeated. The Chancellor has once and for all reversed the situation by adopting the thesis that any contact with Communism is out of the question. He clearly expressed this viewpoint of his when Marshal Tukhachevski was passing through Berlin. Not only did he (Hitler) decline to receive him but he also refrained to permit any of the military to enter into contact with him. (*5*)

This was not the first or the last time that Göring argued thus; as late as August 24, 1939, he expressed his regret to the Polish Ambassador that things developed in such a way as to make a German-Soviet Treaty necessary.

But Göring was not the main actor. Stalin was more important. The Russian dictator talked with the German journalist-writer Ludwig in 1934 and said that he had a high opinion of Americans and Germans. "If we sympathize with anyone, either as a nation, or with the majority of the nation, it is the Germans. The friendly feelings we have for America cannot be compared with our sympathy for the Germans." Laval found no real anti-German sentiments or anti-German plans in Moscow and he so informed Göring in 1935; and in a speech he gave on January 10, 1936, Molotov hinted that the Soviet Union desired better relations with Germany. There were, in 1936, still important elements among the German military who favored a German-Russian alliance. There were von Twardowski and Niedermeyer, who played a rôle similar to that of a special Prussian military liaison officer, a *Pruski Fligeladjutant* of the last century in St. Petersburg. In September Hitler spoke to his Labor Front in Nuremberg and said among other things:

> If we had at our disposal the immeasurable wealth and the treasure of raw material of the Ural Mountains; moreover the fertile plains of the Ukraine, to be exploited under National Socialist leadership, then we could produce and our German people would swim in wealth . . .

And curiously enough, this passage of the Hitler speech was censored in later editions of the German papers and removed from Army mess halls. The text was emended and appeared in the newspapers two days afterwards thus: "If the treasure . . . lay in Germany, the German people would swim in plenty."

Early in 1937 the Chief of the German General Staff, Beck, sent the National-Bolshevist writer, Niekisch, to Moscow in order to establish contacts with Radek. The Rumanian Minister in Berlin wrote on April 27, 1937, to his government that a German-Russian entente was not impossible (6); the new American envoy to Moscow, Joseph E. Davies, reported the same on February 19; rumors of a German-Russian rapprochement were current in Berlin among foreign diplomats in the summer of 1937.

(In late 1948 a German publication reproduced a statement of an anonymous German writer who claimed that most of the documents incriminating the Soviet generals in the Moscow trials of 1937–38 were secretly manufactured in Germany, under SS directives, and disseminated among the Soviet counter-espionage agencies. One of the alleged means of dissemination was said to have been through

Prague. There has come forth no further evidence of documentation since, but there is some reason to believe that Beneš was crudely fooled, and that the story according to which Stalin was indebted to him for having revealed pro-German military conspiracies was the product of his own conjecture; instead, it might be that the German or the Russian secret services fooled the Czech President. There is also some evidence that Papen in Vienna had a hand in all this and that he used his old General Staff contacts to Russia in 1936–37.)

From July 1936 to December 1937, the purge spread from the Politburo through the civil service and then reached the Army and the diplomatic corps. The timetable coincides in certain instances with the dates given for the alleged SS operations and for Beneš' communication; also, Niedermeyer was suddenly arrested on a special order by Hitler and sent to a detention camp.

Although embroiled in Spain, Russia still had enough occasion and enough time to court Italy in secret. On August 30, 1937, the Soviets indicated to Rome their eventual willingness to recognize the Italian Empire in Abyssinia, but their counterprice was that the Axis be somewhat less aggressive. Ciano rebuffed the Soviet chargé in Rome, who two weeks later complained that the Italian Foreign Minister treated Russia as if she were a small state like Lithuania: a mild complaint, and without any real demand for rectification. (7) In the meantime, on September 6, a Russian note accused Italy of having torpedoed a Soviet merchantman in the Adriatic (the sinking had taken place several weeks before), and Moscow waited until November 8 to state that Italy's plans to adhere to the Anti-Comintern Pact seemed "incompatible" with the previously very correct Italian-Russian relations and agreements. Then, on November 25, the Anti-Comintern Pact was signed between Germany and Japan. (8)

The Soviets were worried. They ratified the new Montreux Convention in November — a gesture of understanding toward Britain and France; in December they failed to ratify the Fisheries' Treaty with Japan — an indirect gesture toward the United States. A new Soviet "democratic" constitution, a reasonable stand in the Brussels Far Eastern Conference, and gradually-assumed moderation during the discussions on non-intervention in Spain were means to indicate the Soviet willingness to make some kind of common cause with the Western Powers against a growing and ominous Berlin-Rome-Tokyo Triangle. When the Sino-Japanese War broke out again in 1937 and Japan and Russia were becoming very inimical to each other, an

increasing community of Soviet-American interests was perceived
and eagerly interpreted as a sign of Soviet sincerity by Joseph F.
Davies, the new American Ambassador to Moscow who had replaced
the stern William C. Bullitt: a development which had certain echoes
in Washington, and which a few years later was to have a tremendous
effect on central-eastern Europe and the world.

The Soviets were worried. They stated to Poland that they did
not wish to embroil themselves with Italy, and the Foreign Commissariat seemed to fear Germany foremost. The Russian Counselor of
the Embassy at Rome said to his German colleague in the autumn
that ". . . it was quite obvious that the [Anti-Comintern] Agreement
was an aggressive alliance against Russia; primarily, however, against
England." (*9*) This was supreme realism, a fact confirmed by Stalin,
who was to say in August 1939 to his new friend Ribbentrop that the
Anti-Comintern Pact never had frightened Russia, but rather the
merchants of London. (*10*)

The usually well-informed Soviets correctly gauged the importance
of the Halifax-Hitler talks, and by November 25, *Pravda* and *Izvestia*
were commenting upon the talks as a definite sign of England's
appeasement of Germany. According to the German Ambassador in
Moscow: "The comments reflect the alarm over ignoring of the Soviet
Union and are obviously made for the purpose of influencing
France. . . ." (*11*)

[*Russia, Poland and the Baltics.*] Due to the manifest strength
of the Axis and the weakness of Russia shown by the Purges, relations
between the Soviet Union and the states of central-eastern Europe
were generally developing for the worse. Poland, however friendly
with Germany, did not intend to embroil herself with Russia. In
July 1936 the Polish Ambassador to Moscow, Grzybowski, when
presenting his credentials, was reproached because of Poland's foreign
policy. But by the end of the year Polish-Soviet relations were improving, and in November 1937 Beck sent a circular message to Polish
diplomatic posts, denying categorically that Poland had been asked
to adhere or would consider adhering to the Anti-Comintern Pact.
With Finland, relations had been bad since July 1935, when the
Soviets deported great numbers of Finns from Soviet Karelia; in 1936
a Soviet citizen had disappeared during the trial of one Antikainen,
a Finnish Communist who had illegally re-entered Finland. But in
February 1937 the Germanophile Svinhufvud was followed in the

Presidency by the more liberal Kalliö and Finnish-Russian tension slowly began to subside. Somewhat later the Finnish Foreign Minister, Holsti, visited Moscow.

On November 2, 1936, Zhdanov made an aggressive speech in Leningrad, which city he termed the "window to the world." The Baltic States, he said, should not allow themselves to be used by the aggressors:

> . . . if these [small nations] are not satisfied to mind only their own business, we may be forced to open our windows a bit wider, and they will not be comfortable if we have to call upon our Red Army to defend our country.

A serious crisis in Baltic-Russian relations was looming, but in a month the tension relaxed after the Soviet Ministers to Latvia and Estonia — strangely enough, the Minister to Lithuania did not make a similar statement — assured the Baltic states that Zhdanov did not mean any harm. In February 1937, then, the Soviet Marshal Yegorov visited the three Baltic capitals, returning the visit of the Baltic Chiefs-of-Staff to Moscow which had taken place in 1936. The Latvian and Swedish Foreign Ministers also visited Moscow in 1937. The fact that Poland, the European nation which stood most in the way of the Soviets, nevertheless declined to adhere to the Anti-Comintern Pact in November 1937 was duly registered in the Baltics. Neither did Italy wish to broaden the Anti-Comintern Pact too much. On November 17 Ciano said to the German Ambassador in Rome that he did not press for the adherence of Poland, Hungary, or Austria at the moment. And when Delbos, passing through Berlin to Warsaw, was greeted by Neurath at the railroad station, the exchange of amenities was called "a grave fact" by Mussolini; of this Berlin was duly informed.

The Hungarian Foreign Minister made an interesting remark to Ciano on November 12:

> Although Hungary is staunchly anti-Communist and it is evident that the Hungarian government cannot regard [Russia] with much sympathy, nevertheless a Communist government in Moscow, until it tends to distribute its ideological and political influence beyond its national frontiers, is preferable to a Tsarist regime which forms the nucleus and source of a brutal and incontrollable pan-Slavism.

Yet the Czech Minister in Berlin assured the German Foreign Ministry in the same month that relations between Prague and Moscow were by no means so close as was generally thought.

. . . .

[*The Little Entente disintegrates.*] Neither were the ties of the Little and Balkan Ententes unimpaired. The Diplomatic Revolution corroded them. There was now inter-allied friction; in November 1936, the Czechoslovak Minister to Rumania, Šaba, published a book, *The Rôle of the Little Entente in World Politics*, dealing mainly with inter-Little Entente relations and criticizing the developing new trends in Rumanian and Yugoslav foreign policies. The book caused some sensation and created a perceivable uneasiness in Czechoslovak-Rumanian relations which did not subside throughout 1937, especially as the book pointed at the necessity of a Czech-Russian common frontier. A visit of King Carol to Poland in late 1937 and the reciprocating journeys of Polish statesmen led instead to a strengthening of ties between Bucharest and Warsaw, ostensibly to the disadvantage of Czechoslovakia. Beneš tried to approach Hungary now, but it was well-nigh too late. Krofta and Kánya, the two Foreign Ministers, talked in Geneva in September, and during a hunting visit of Carol to Czechoslovakia in November, Beneš asked him to be understanding with the Hungarians. But it was the Germans now who intrigued Rumanian imaginations! (*12*)

There were other international events in 1936–37 which were either too spectacular to be significant or too insignificant to be noticed. A diplomatic crisis between Austria and Peru developed because of a brawl which started during an international football match (*13*); Portugal severed relations with Czechoslovakia in August 1937 because of a dispute concerning deliveries of faulty Czech machine-guns. Picturesque events occupied the attention of Europe for awhile: the visit of Horthy to Austria and Italy in 1936 and the return visit of the Italian King and his family to Budapest in 1937 gave a false impression to the world as to the practical validity of the Rome Protocols; this impression continued to exist even after December 12, 1937, when Italy left the League of Nations. (*14*) The Coronation in London and the opening of the International Exposition in Paris made it possible for many diplomats to conduct interesting and informal talks, yet without apparent results; the "quarantine" speech

of Roosevelt in Chicago in October 1937, which may be regarded by
future historiographers as an outstanding event in the shaping of
Europe's destinies, was scarcely noticed at all. *(15)*

[*American diplomacy.*] While the reaction to the President's
speech within the United States was not too encouraging, *(16)* American diplomatic activity was nevertheless slowly increasing. Certain
ambassadors, like Mr. Bullitt in Paris, were more active than the
less adequate Mr. Kennedy in London. The Germans noted, for
example, how Bullitt tried to smooth the way for a Polish-French
understanding during his visit to Warsaw in November 1937. On the
other hand, Mr. Gilbert, the American Counselor of the Embassy
in Berlin, dropped some undiplomatic remarks about the French
which were eagerly registered by German ears. The inconsistencies
and the lack of unity in American foreign policies were evident —
and thus almost everybody disregarded America. *(17)*

Other, internal events

Here was the new, dynamic Germany, and she provided more
than mere symbolic encouragement to the central-eastern European
National Socialist movements. With a few exceptions, the German
Foreign Service was not yet involved in the network of the German-
Nazi clandestine contacts; the main tasks were carried out by the
Party and the SS, and even these two organizations acted independently; sometimes they challenged the jurisdiction and counter-
manded the directives of the German diplomatic representatives.
Only when Ribbentrop assumed full control in the Wilhelmstrasse
did these divergencies subside somewhat (although in many instances
they continued to exist during the entire war period).

[*Native "Fifth Columns."*] Finland, the Baltic republics,
Austria, and Hungary passed restrictive measures against their local
Nazis between 1932 and 1934; partial restrictions were applied in
Rumania, Yugoslavia, and Poland. To halt the emergence of other
Nazi-type parties and to deprive them of their potential appeal to
the young, the wearing of party uniforms was prohibited in Austria
and Hungary in 1934; Poland and Latvia took similar measures in
1936. It was, of course, impossible to prevent the existence of National

Socialist movements by parliamentary or semi-parliamentary methods. According to National Peasant sources, six hundred million *Lei* were given to the Iron Guard by the Germans in 1936; in the same year there were no less than six Nazi "parties" existing in Hungary, where they gained among the agricultural proletariat and among the less capable of the university youth. In Bulgaria, Kunčev's National Socialists, Tsankov's group, and another Nazi-type organization, "Rodna Zaštita," carried the Nazi banner; in Greece there was the Fascistic EEE; in Poland a segment of the Government *bloc* played with fire for awhile, and in 1937 a Fascist-type NARA and a "Union of Young Poles" existed, their heyday coinciding with a wave of minor anti-Semitic demonstrations in Galicia.

The German minorities were, then, the best lever with which the Third Reich could operate. The sympathy of foreigners was often with these minorities, to wit the Lloyd George memorandum in the early twenties:

> I cannot conceive any greater cause of a future war than that the German people should be surrounded by a mob of small States, many of them consisting of peoples who have never previously set up stable governments for themselves, but each of them containing large masses of Germans. . . .

In 1919 Masaryk had not wished to have too many Germans within the confines of his new state, but he had nevertheless accepted them. After the 1935 elections the Sudeten German leader, Henlein, sent a telegram of loyalty to Masaryk, but this was almost the last of such gestures.

[*The Sudetens.*] On September 16, 1937, the new Premier, Hodža, met Henlein for the second time. Hodža saw things clearly: he told Henlein that the "Sudeten German question was not the primary factor, but the relationship of Prague to Berlin" was, and hinted at the possibility of a British mediation for the first time. (*1*) About two weeks later Henlein went to London — a strange experience to a *Turnvereiner* it must have been — and met people like Vansittart, who expressed sympathy with the Sudeten German desire for autonomy. This was, indeed, as Vansittart said, "in accordance with the British policy of eliminating points of friction in Europe in such a way as to avoid raising the major problems which lie behind them."

The moderate German Minister from Prague reported on October 22:

> It cannot at the moment be foreseen what tactics the Government here will employ toward the Sudeten German Party in the immediate future. It will depend whether their fear of Germany or their hope of support from the Western Powers is the greater.

The German Minister, Eisenlohr, asked Berlin to give press orders not to attack the reasonable Hodža. And, as the Halifax visit was coming, Göbbels actually gave such orders early in November.

But, as T. S. Eliot once noted in an essay: "People can be persuaded to desire almost anything, for a time, if they are constantly told that it is something to which they are entitled and which is unjustly withheld from them." And Henlein felt the sweet breezes of power. He intrigued for leadership with other angry-eyed Sudetens, and on November 19 (Halifax was just about to return to London) he wrote a long letter to Hitler, inciting him to and asking him for "action." This was the meat of his letter; the rest was the customary, if unusually rich garnishing of attacks on the Vatican, Jewry, Freemasons, Bolshevists, and so on.

.   .   .   .

[*German minorities.*] When pan-German propaganda abated in Poland, it was due to the temporary exigencies of German foreign policy, and elsewhere the *Volksdeutsch* question was developing into the main lever of German pressure. Originally there existed difficulties; in Danzig, for example, elections as late as February 1935 increased the votes of the Catholic Center Party (although the Nazis had an absolute clear majority); the Socialists lost only slightly, and Greiser, the Nazi leader, broke off his contacts with the Catholics. In Hungary, where German Catholic sentiment was strong, the Nazi Basch and the Conservative Gratz fought for the leadership of the German minority; in 1935, Basch received Gömbös' silent support: the respected old Gratz lost out, and retired to write excellent history. The young German generation in the *Schwäbische Türkei*, the Banat, and in Transylvania veered more and more toward the Nazis. Roth, the leader of the Transylvanian Saxons, was a Nazi now and gained the confidence and following of the German minority in Rumania by 1936. The entire Lutheran clergy of German-Transylvania supported him.

In the same year the Lithuanian government discovered a clandestine Nazi network, *Baltische Bruderschaft*, and brought the leaders to trial in April (*2*); in August, Estonia clamped down on the reviving "Liberators" when their close contact with the *Auslandsdeutsch* organizations was ascertained. So there was now friction between Germany and certain Baltic States; during the winter of 1936–37, the Nazi press often charged that secret and extensive plans of a Lithuanian-Soviet military collaboration were laid, charges which were naturally without foundation.

[*Opposition.*] The composition of the anti-Nazi opposition was unorthodox; the forces of the Left were so small and ineffectual that the burden of opposing the nationalist radicals fell upon Conservatives, Catholics and Liberals (the latter in the European sense of the term): traditionalist parties but without strong organizations, circles of a select few rather than gatherings of the masses. The anti-Nazi papal encyclical, *Mit brennender Sorge*, on Passion Sunday of 1937 had its effects among Catholic leaders, but too few bothered to read encyclicals in a "dynamic age." Only where the German danger was not directly evident, in Finland, Bulgaria, and Greece, did the Communist movement hold its ground. An internal crisis tore the Polish Communists apart in 1937; the party was then practically dissolved by Moscow's orders. (*3*) In Yugoslavia, some groups of the young intelligentsia were receptive to Communist ideas; a man named Corkič was expelled from the post of Secretary-General of the Yugoslav Communist Party in 1937 and another, named Broz-Tito, got the post. Only in Greece did Communism gain among radical elements; in January 1938 a Communist plot to assassinate Metaxas was discovered and many leading Communists were arrested.

Meanwhile the economic orchard of Hjalmar Schacht bore many fruits. From 1933 to 1936, Germany more than doubled her imports from Greece, Turkey, Hungary, Bulgaria, Rumania and Yugoslavia; the value of her exports to these countries rose from 155 to 175 million Reichsmarks. Thus the Western Powers' influence decreased. The allies of France, Yugoslavia, Rumania, Poland, were often the primary economic targets. Schacht was told by Göring in 1936 to get control somehow over the Bor copper mines in Serbia, vitally essential for the German war effort, which were in the hands of a French company. (*4*) Stoyadinovič at the same time tried to make himself a Balkan condottiere, a Serb renaissance man doing a Machiavelli; he thereby cut a strange figure and also brought about some strange results. Internal Serb-Croat difficulties still prevailed, and plans for a Concordat with the Vatican were obstructed by the Serb Orthodox opposition. In late 1937 the national opposition got together, and friendship between the Croat and Serb opposition leaders, Maček and Budisavljevič, bloomed into a realization of Croat-Serb fraternity. Indeed, Maček was hailed in Belgrade by a Serb crowd, a demonstration intended to show spontaneous and common Croat-Serb sentiment against Stoyadinovič and his régime. Similar demonstrations occurred when Delbos visited the Yugoslav capital: the cheering thousands on the street were meant to be a warning for Stoyadinovič to stay away from a pro-Axis foreign policy.

While the Friendship Pacts between Italy and Yugoslavia, Yugoslavia and Bulgaria, and Bulgaria and Turkey in 1937 outwardly stabilized Balkan peace, in reality their value depended upon the relations of the Great Powers — and Italy was already preparing for the occupation of Albania and an eventual war on Greece. (5) However strongly Yugoslav-French amity manifested itself in the cheers of the Belgrade populace, the fact remained that serious German inroads were made there and that France was incapable of strengthening the armed forces of the Little Entente, as she herself was in dire need of rearmament. The German military planners knew this. Further German possibilities loomed when, incensed by the stubborn resistance of the Hungarian Interior Minister against external attempts to Nazify the German minority in Hungary, Alfred Rosenberg and other members of the German hierarchy began to support Rumania against Hungarian revisionism. From November 1936 on, German-Rumanian relations steadily improved, until a year later a pro-German government sat in Bucharest. In Bulgaria, German economic and political penetration was similarly evident, but King Boris was cautious enough not to ask the pro-Nazi Tsankov to participate in any cabinet. In Bulgaria and Poland municipal elections held in early 1937 showed the strength of the democratic opposition. King Boris subsequently lifted press restrictions, and in Warsaw, where under the weak and colorless presidency of Moscicki, the Koscialkowski government was followed by Skladkowski's in 1936, freedom of the press was partially restored early in 1938. In Estonia a constitutional reform took place in February 1938 and non-party elections followed; in a strange, and rather paternalistic policy, the government put opposition leaders as individual candidates on the single slate, among them men so far to the Left as to be virtual crypto-Communists. About 25 per cent of the votes fell to opposition candidates and the assembly then re-elected Päts as President.

A certain realization of a common European destiny still prevailed in that year before the storm broke. Cultural contacts continued to exist between the states of central-eastern Europe and the West. In the Hungarian Parliament the Foreign Minister, Kánya, could refer to the concept of Europeanism by citing that great European Spaniard, Madariaga, and the kings of Rumania and Greece visited the Western capitals. Yet these were but symbolic gestures. When the military leaders of the Little Entente — the Czech General Syrový, the Yugoslav Marič and the Rumanians Sicitiu, Samsonovici and Antonescu — went to Paris in 1936 and 1937, the ties which bound France to her eastern allies were theoretically reaffirmed; actually they were weaker than ever before. (6) Nor did any happier results come from the eastern European tour which the French Foreign Minister, Delbos, undertook in November–December 1937.

[*Delbos' 'travels.*] The Delbos journey was fruitless, but it brought to light significant symptoms. In Warsaw, Delbos tried to help Hodža, and argued about the merits of a Polish-Czechoslovak rapprochement. But Beck was not to willing to align himself thus; he did not want to provoke the wrath of Hitler. The American Ambassador to France, Mr. Bullitt, carried his convictions to Warsaw in the same month and said there that the French did not trust the Soviet Union anymore, and as Poland was France's only and natural ally in the East, a reshaping of French-Polish relations was imperative. . . . But he was not successful. On December 11, talking to Moltke, the German Ambassador, Beck belittled the French and the importance of the Delbos visit. In Rome, the Polish Ambassador told the Italians two days later that the Delbos-Beck talks only revealed the profound differences existing between the Polish and French concepts of European politics. Beck was so cocky at that time that he intimated that Polish interests should be taken into consideration in case of a general revision of colonial allotments.

And at the same time Stoyadinovič told Mussolini that Czechoslovakia was a "sausage state," an expression which pleased the Italian, who freely used it afterwards. Delbos' visit to Belgrade was industriously being discounted by Stoyadinovič and only cool handshakes and Balkan smiles greeted the French visitor in Bucharest. In Prague,

Delbos wanted to make it clear that what France desired was an improvement in Czech-German relations: France was not backing Czechoslovakia unconditionally anymore; the exigencies of France's program required that there be no dangerous friction now between Czechoslovakia and Germany. His attitude was apparent to everyone. At a state dinner given for Delbos, Hodža made some allusions to Czechoslovak friendliness toward Germany; Beneš a few days later told the German Minister that France insisted on good relations between Prague and Berlin. Eisenlohr reported to Berlin: "But what was unusual about it and completely novel for the visit of a French Minister to Prague was the fact that this demonstration of friendship and loyalty to the alliance was not accompanied by any anti-German note."

.   .   .   .

[*The Soviets take notice.*]   In the wake of the Soviet worries raised by the Halifax-Hitler talks came the unpleasant realization that Delbos ignored Moscow and Litvinov's invitation. He did not visit that capital. An attitude of disillusionment was very noticeable in the Russian press, while for tactical reasons (and psychological ones, too) the press did not complain openly about the fact that the French Foreign Minister had not come to Moscow. Soviet diplomacy and the press attacked Beck and Poland instead. That excellent observer, Count Schulenburg, remarked, "These and other insinuations directed at Polish foreign policy are no doubt calculated to discredit Poland in the eyes of France and of the French reader . . . [this is an] effort to recommend the Soviet Union, in contrast to unreliable Poland . . ." (7)

Soon afterwards Stalin directed Molotov (8) to blast France openly, on the pretext of White Russians' activities in Paris. This happened in January 1938 and signified the beginning of the end for the policy of collective security, for the efforts towards an unconditional French-Russian alliance — and, incidentally, for Litvinov also.

The Rumanian dictatorship and its meaning

Delbos was not yet back at his desk on the Quai d'Orsay when a pro-German government sat in Bucharest, the establishment of which was interpreted throughout Europe as further proof of the disintegration of the French alliance system and another evidence of the Little Entente fiction.

[*Rumanian politics.*] After 1933 the ranks of the Rumanian Iron Guard swelled, and the King, while occasionally enacting energetic measures, could not bring himself to proceed with the ruthless liquidation of Codreanu and his coterie. The different governments tried to outbid the nationalist radicals by adopting extreme nationalist measures of their own; thus, in 1934, a Law for the Defense of National Labor established a "numerus valachicus" which provided that at least fifty per cent of the companies' directors and eighty per cent of the employees must be born Rumanians. Corruption, as always, made it possible to circumvent these measures; the successes of Nazi Germany meanwhile continued to exercise great influence, especially among the young radicals. Anti-Semitism was one of the main arguments, and spectacular press campaigns against the evaders of the "numerus valachicus" law fanned the flames. The forces of the extreme right were strengthened in 1935 when the party of Cuza, the "Christian National Defense League," (*1*) merged with Goga's National Christian Party. A report of the Foreign Bureau of the Nazi Party in Germany established that the Bureau's efforts were extremely important in achieving this merger. (*2*)

The first weak tremors of the Diplomatic Revolution unseated Titulescu, a development which had been in the making since 1935. Bucharest could not rejoice at the sight of a Czech-Russian alliance, the efficacy of which depended on Rumanian permission for the passage of Soviet troops; because of Bessarabia and also for other reasons, the fact that such a passage was at all contemplated was intensely disturbing. Rumania's other allies, Yugoslavia and Poland, gradually assumed entirely new positions in the international arena, a development which also had to be taken into account. Thus, when the French De Monzie visited Bucharest in October 1935, he could predict to "Titu"· "Take care! You will be liquidated at the first opportunity. . . . [The amity with] Prague will cost you much!" (*3*) After Titulescu left, a year of uncertainties and hesitations followed. The King's position was strengthened by a split among the Iron Guardists: but the latter was still strong and menacing to Carol. From the other side, Maniu and his Peasants continued to assail the duplicity and corruption of the monarch and his circle.

In April 1936 Goga went to Berlin; his contacts with German circles were very satisfactory, and shortly after his return, Rosenberg and others began alluding to German friendship towards Rumania. This was sweet music, intended to lure the Rumanians away from the

Little Entente by implying that Berlin had no real preference for
Budapest over Bucharest and, that if the latter were willing, even the
contrary could be expected . . . This attitude was carefully noted by
Tatarescu in Bucharest, while the inter-party struggles continued.
The Cabinet was reorganized after the Iron Guard demonstrations
of February 1937; in local elections the Maniu forces proved to be
strongest and Titulescu, now a sick man, joined the National Peasants.
The parties girded their loins for the scheduled national elections.

[*The 1937 elections.*] The Rumanian constitution and its
parliamentary arithmetics provided for a bonus system, so that if a
party won forty per cent of all votes cast, it was assured of a clear
majority in Parliament. Seldom did a Rumanian government lose an
election, and it seemed that the government coalition of 1937 would
win as usual. But, strangely enough, Left and extreme Right now
faced the government together. Maniu with his Peasants, the so-called
Dissident Liberals, and Codreanu's Iron Guardists were creating an
"electoral police" to avoid large-scale cheating by Tatarescu. There
was fraudulence, nevertheless; yet, the government coalition fell short
of the desired goal of forty per cent. It polled thirty-nine per cent,
while the Peasants won twenty-one and the Guardists sixteen per cent
of the votes. The opposition defeated the government.

[*The Goga régime.*] Fire and water would not mix; a Maniu-
Codreanu coalition was impossible; also, the King had his personal
fears. Thus his choice fell upon Goga, whose "National Christians"
had polled somewhat less than ten per cent. This appointment surprised the extreme Right at first; then it was hailed. Goga, a mystic,
Transylvanian nationalist, announced broad and sweeping revisions
in the existing social order; he enacted by decree crudely restrictive
measures against the Jews. A panic shocked the financial circles of
Bucharest. While Goga announced no change in the direction of
Rumanian foreign policy, there was no doubt that the new course
would be set in the direction of Berlin. On January 7 a visiting Rumanian senator told Ciano in Rome that the Goga régime was Papen-like;
Codreanu was to follow.

Yet the Iron Guard did not fully support Goga; of course Maniu
was against him too, who never thought that his somewhat unorthodox
electoral tactics would result in a Goga government. With Maniu in
opposition, Carol's hand was strengthened. Violent altercations took

place when Goga dissolved Parliament, and the French and British diplomatic representatives protested against the measures which the Goga government took against Englishmen and Frenchmen employed in Rumanian industries, notably in the oil industry. With the exception of the extreme Right, the majority of the politically conscious obviously desired some return to normalcy; Goga himself was ailing. Finally Carol decided to act. In January he began negotiating with various Rumanians, and on February 10, Goga fell. Carol announced the formation of a "national ministry" under the Patriarch Miron Christea. (*4*) The King then proclaimed the creation of a "Front of National Rebirth," a royalist-authoritarian organization which was to transform Rumania into a corporative state. While Goga left office with the hoarse cry, "Juda has won!" the most varied Rumanian personalities rallied under the Front's new banner: the chameleon Tatarescu, such pro-Westerners as Calinescu and Argetoianu, and opportunists such as Ghelmegeanu and Ralea. (*5*) A new Rumanian constitution was submitted to a "plebiscite" and won overwhelming majority on February 24. Three days later the constitution was proclaimed and Rumania became a royalist-authoritarian state, the last of the central-eastern European states to become a dictatorship before World War II. It was just two weeks before the day that the first of such states, Austria, was to be absorbed by Hitler.

. . . .

[*Russia and Rumania.*] The Rumanian elections and the attitudes of the subsequent Goga régime indicated how the system of the Little Entente was undermined by that time. With the exception of Czechoslovakia, all the other allies of France were veering away. Poland was anxious lest Paris should bring about a Czechoslovak-Rumanian-Russian alliance, and Titulescu had fallen because he had been identified with such ideas. Early in 1937 Carol and Tatarescu told Stoyadinovič that they would never permit a Russian passage through Bessarabia, for the Russians, once in there, would stay there. Stoyadinovič at once told this to Ciano. When in the autumn of 1937 Carol and Moscicki met, the Poles endeavored to exact a promise from the King that he would never permit a Russian crossing, even if Czechoslovakia might be vitally endangered.

This question of Russian-Rumanian relations was the moot point in Rumania's foreign affairs. Early in 1937, the Soviet Minister to

Bucharest, Ostrovsky, indirectly admonished the Rumanian government: if in the event of a German attack in the Danubian area,
Rumania stayed neutral, Russia would help herself to Bessarabia.
Doubts about Bucharest's Russian policy increased to such an extent
that during the electoral campaign of late 1937, Titulescu found it
necessary to give an interview to a leading newspaper and declare
that during his tenure as Foreign Minister he never made any secret
arrangements allowing for an eventual passage. (6) A few months
later, according to Gamelin's recollections, King Carol told him that
France could count on his *secret* permission to let the Soviet troops
pass; but the purely hypothetical value of such an indirect promise was
evident. Even before the Goga government, and immediately in the
wake of the Delbos visit, the Rumanian Foreign Minister repeatedly
assured the German Minister in Bucharest "that the question of a
treaty of alliance between Rumania and the Little Entente on the one
hand, and France, on the other hand, was definitely disposed of." And
that "the French statesmen were well aware of this." (7) Fabricius, the
German Minister to Rumania, reported: "I believe, however, that
the King is too shrewd and cautious, (8) simply on the basis of encouragement from England, to decide on a policy differing from that of
Prince Paul of Yugoslavia; he would at least demand that England,
too, enter the pact and England will not do that under present circumstances." Here was the whole central-eastern European situation in
a nutshell: admiration for the West and especially for Britain had
long been cherished by the elite and higher circles ("The King likes
to listen to British advice"), by the Polish and Hungarian aristocracy,
the Czech political class, the Anglophile Prince Paul, the respectful
Boris, the Greeks — and then the sudden, awful realization that those
gaunt, tall, admirable, and noble Englishmen wouldn't or couldn't
help them.

The Poles were, of course, violently opposed to any Rumanian-
Russian rapprochement; their extreme uneasiness was reflected in
the spring of 1938, when, after seven Czech aircraft manufactured in
Russia were delivered to Czechoslovakia by air, Beck asked the Ruma-
nian Foreign Office in a démarche how Rumania could permit such
flights to take place over her territory. To his satisfaction, Rumanian-
Russian relations deteriorated in February, when a predecessor of
Kravchenko, a secretary of the Soviet Legation in Bucharest by the
name of Butenko, deserted the Soviet service and left for the West.
The Soviet government accused Bucharest of complicity in Butenko's

escape, and the ensuing acid diplomatic correspondence most certainly did not contribute to Rumanian-Russian amity.

First two months of a terrible year

[*The military plans for 1938.*] The outline of Hitler's time-table was set up in 1934: it scheduled Austria and Czechoslovakia to be dealt with before Poland; the military plans and diplomatic develop-ments of 1937 caused the agenda to be set down in detail. *Case 2,* as put by Hitler at the "Hoszbach" Conference, called for a move against Czechoslovakia at once if internal troubles developed within France. *Case 3:* "If France is so embroiled by a war with another state that she cannot 'proceed' against Germany," Hitler would prefer a French-Italian war: "The time for our attacks on the Czechs and Austria must be made dependent on the course of the Anglo-French-Italian war and would not necessarily coincide with the commencement of military operations by these three states." Then he would descend upon the Czechs with "lightning speed." He also thought that in that case, Britain would not go to war with Germany, as she would not want to increase the number of her enemies. (*1*)

As to Austria, Hitler, Göring, and Papen agreed on December 16, 1937, that "the Führer wishes to think the situation over thoroughly . . . and will see Papen after the New Year in Obersalzberg to decide the Austrian timetable."

.   .   .   .

[*Yugoslavia's importance.*] Poland had no particular ties with Austria. Rumania had her internal troubles; moreover, her foreign policy depended on the interplay of possible Russian, Polish and French actions. Therefore her rôle did not require clarification. But it was vital to Hitler that an eventual concerted action of the Little Entente be precluded, and thus the position of Yugoslavia assumed great importance.

Yugoslavia under Stoyadinovič was now moving away from the Powers whose action could contain Germany; what could be expected from Austria and Hungary if Yugoslavia went that way? Stoyadinovič' conduct was not unequivocal; but Ciano and Mussolini, and prob-ably Neurath also, knew where he stood and what could be expected from him. In September 1937 the Yugoslav Premier visited Prague. In an allegedly very dramatic conversation with Beneš, he was exposed

to the reproaches of the Czech President; consequently Stoyadinovič
mellowed, even if he did not break down. (2) Stoyadinovič confessed
that Hitler asked him to come to Berlin, and, according to Beneš, he
also said that he knew what the German had in mind. "But I won't
go," said Stoyadinovič. And so two months passed. On November 25,
1937, a few days after the Halifax talks, Hitler received the Hungarian
Premier, Darányi, and the old and canny Foreign Minister, Kánya.

Hitler began by referring to his then favorite bogey of an Austrian-
Czech collusion; he knew that the revisionist Magyars were not too
eager to see such an entente. Against the wishes of Kánya, Darányi,
the obtuse Premier, responded that Schuschnigg told him that he
did not contemplate such an alignment. Thereafter the Hungarian
spoke of the question of the national minorities. Hitler advised that
Hungary should seek a worth-while solution with Rumania and Yugoslavia and brought up German-Polish relations as an example of a
minority settlement satisfactory to both parties. But, he continued, it
would be advisable that with Czechoslovakia no flexibility and no
spirit of compromise should be shown. Kánya said that this was in
accordance with the plans and intentions of Budapest, and then he
turned to report on his contacts with Stoyadinovič: Hungary was
willing to renounce her territorial aims in Yugoslavia if Belgrade
would grant cultural autonomy to the Magyar minority there. Hitler
responded with emphatic interest. He made it clear that Germany
desired a Hungarian-Yugoslav friendship policy: "Given that the
Little Entente cannot be broken up," he said, "it is indispensable that
every effort be made to weaken her interrelations." He himself would
propose the Yugoslav rapprochement with Hungary during the next
visit of Stoyadinovič to Berlin which was expected to take place soon.

Kánya probably felt that he had gone too far; the revisionist aims
were not meant to serve Hitler as a means of furthering his European
supremacy. The old Hungarian insisted that his country "did not
plan to realize her revisionist exigencies by arms"; he wished to avoid
a war and asked the Führer to take note of this fact. Hitler, with an
hypocritically serious air, acknowledged this. (3)

In the meantime Stoyadinovič had been in Paris for two days
(October 12–13), where he did nothing. Now he was preparing to go
to Rome; before he left, Hodža asked him to bring about a Czecho-
slovak-Italian rapprochement. He arrived in Rome on December 6;
at once he told Mussolini that he had a message from Prince Paul:
Whatever the future might bring, Yugoslavia would never find her-

self in a camp opposed to Italy. He also showed his "clearest aversion" to Great Britain and spoke of French machinations and the material and psychological crisis of the French army; he had made no commitments to France. As to his rôle of a broker between Rome and Prague, he deliberately defaulted, telling Mussolini that he was transmitting the Czech communication without recommending it. Mussolini answered that Italy neither could nor did desire to intervene for Prague. (4)

Kánya, before going to Germany, had urged an Italian-Hungarian-Austrian meeting in early November; but Ciano told him that he could come only in January. And on November 16 Hassell told Ciano he had information that Schuschnigg was searching for a way to secure himself by binding ties anew with Prague, Paris, and London. A month later Papen talked with Schuschnigg; the usually suave German Minister was now rude. He knew from his previous talks with Hitler that the days of Austria were numbered; Papen's new tone was significant.

[*Austrian hopes in Britain.*] On December 22 the Austrian Minister to London, Baron von Franckenstein, sent a brilliant summary report to Vienna:

> . . . the British Government is not so interested as the German or Italian Governments in educating the masses along political lines, but only keeping them in good spirits. This can only be done by means of somewhat ambiguous answers from which everyone may select what happens to strike his fancy. Of course, one should not forget that the Cabinet reflects more or less accurately the mood of the nation: On the one hand, there are the Ministers friendly to Germany, on the other, those antagonistic to Germany. The result of their discussions: the formula of the Covenant of the League of Nations. . . . [Lord Rothermere] is the British peddler of the Hitler slogan that Germany had saved Western Europe from Bolshevism. . . . (Beaverbrook was more restrained, and the Astor group was more dangerous because of their personal influence in British politics and with the London *Times*.) The latest masterstroke of this group was Lord Halifax's visit to Berlin . . .

But Franckenstein drew too optimistic a conclusion: "That British leaders," he wrote, "have become aware of the necessity of the absolute maintenance of Austria's independence, and are willing to support it, is evident."

This was not so. The Germans' agents got the full Franckenstein report and sent it to Berlin. The men there knew that the analysis was correct; but the conclusion was not.

.   .   .   .

[*Italy and the Danubian states.*]   On January 5, 1938, Count Bethlen, the confidant of Horthy and an early friend of Italy, went to Rome. He foresaw troubles in Austria and wanted to secure strong Italian support in view of the imminent advance of the German frontier southeastward. To Mussolini, he conceded that public opinion in Austria was strongly pro-Nazi but told the Duce to be careful with Germany: after all, "Hungary's only chance is Italy." Bethlen also spoke of the necessity for a Polish-Hungarian frontier, deeming it possible that Prague would also fall, and then only a Warsaw-Budapest-Belgrade-Rome line could stop Hitler. He also tried to sound out Mussolini on the chances of a close Italian-British friendship, but, instead, Mussolini spoke of the chances of an Italian-British war. (5)

The routine Rome Protocol conference of the Austrian, Hungarian and Italian foreign ministers took place in Budapest on January 10–12. The Austrian and Hungarian ministers expressed their sympathy with the Rome-Berlin Axis, but the Austrian at the same time wanted to get some joint expression dealing with Austria's independence, and this Ciano refused to do. Instead, he informed the German Minister to Budapest thereof, an act which was not only base, but stupid. The only encouragement he gave to the Austrians was a comment he dropped to the Minister to Hungary: the question of Austrian independence was a point of cardinal importance to Italy, "yet, for the moment, we cannot help you." Before Ciano left for Budapest, Mussolini, in one of his periodic outbursts, ranted against the Austrians and Hungarians and told Ciano that after the Spanish affair was liquidated, he would tell Göring to nazify Austria. Even Ciano was somewhat set back by this statement, although he knew that Mussolini could not always be taken literally.

Hungary was also afraid of closer Italian-Rumanian relations in the wake of Goga's establishment. Kánya told Ciano in Budapest that he did not trust either Goga or Stoyadinovič, who were Balkan scoundrels. Ciano was, however, impressed by a spontaneous demonstration of Hungarian students and cadets when he attended a gala performance; they gave him the Fascist salute, whereupon he deduced that Kánya and Bethlen and the old, feudal Hungarians were not representative; the youth was with Fascism, "a clear sign of the times." (6)

[*Stoyadinovič in Berlin.*] On January 17, 1938, Stoyadinovič arrived in Berlin and turned out to be more noncommittal than Hitler had expected him to be from the reports of Göring and Mussolini. The Yugoslav Premier said that he would guarantee the rights of the Hungarian minorities and pleased Hitler no end by stating that neither he nor Prince Paul was willing to see the Little Entente transformed into a system of mutual assistance pacts. But he made a cardinal reservation. "The Hungarian question is still the capital point in the union of the Little Entente states." (7) Machiavellian as he was, Stoyadinovič was no quisling, nor was he a hireling of Göring, a charge so often trumpeted later. With the earthy realism of his Serb peasant stock, he endeavored to play an unsentimental, immoral, but at the same time cautious and double rôle. He left Hitler with the impression that probably Yugoslavia would not fight to aid the Czechs . . . *alone*. But there was yet no talk of a Hungarian-Yugoslav treaty, and neither was there an answer to the question of what Yugoslavia would do if and when France fought. After Stoyadinovič departed from Berlin, German counterintelligence intercepted a telegram which he sent to Paris, calming French rancor and assuring France that he "would still fight with France." Thus Hitler could say, angrily exaggerating, that "everything communicated to Stoyadinovič is known in Paris and Prague forty-eight hours afterwards."

Immediately after the Stoyadinovič conversations, Hitler ordered Bohle, Gauleiter, a State Secretary of the Foreign Office and confidant of Ribbentrop, to Budapest. From January 23 to 27 Bohle talked in detail with Kánya, who was, as always, cautious. But the German made great progress in his talk with the young Csáky, Chief of Cabinet in the Hungarian Foreign Office. (8) Csáky went much further than had Kánya in Berlin. He envisaged war. He told Bohle that Berlin should direct all efforts to bring about a commitment by Belgrade, thus assuring Yugoslav neutrality in the case of a Hungarian attack on Czechoslovakia. Since the fall of 1937, exuberant members of the Hungarian General Staff had held talks with General Blomberg about Hungarian-German military collaboration against Czechoslovakia. Sztójay, the very mediocre and Germanophile Hungarian Minister to Berlin, gave his benevolent blessings to these talks (which were obviously conducted without Kánya's knowledge), and now Csáky went into military considerations with Bohle. He even hinted — what a stupid remark to make to a Bohle! — that Hungary would be glad to see the *Anschluss* come, provided that Germany did not plan to annex Hungary too. . . .

[*Changes in the German régime.*] Hitler received the Bohle report at the time he was deciding to bring Schuschnigg to Berchtesgaden. In these first weeks of February great events took place. The Führer, in a gradually executed stratagem, eliminated the influence of Fritsch and the more conservative generals and virtually assumed complete control over the German Army: purely military considerations would not hamper the politico-military plans of Hitler from now on.

Foolishly, Ciano also took pleasure that the Neurath era was gone. On February 5, he wrote in his Diary: "Very good, Ribbentrop is Foreign Minister." (*9*) Very good, because Ribbentrop was anti-British. But soon Ciano was to be sorry, very sorry. . . .

.   .   .   .

[*Chamberlain and Roosevelt.*] And now an important episode: a spark foolishly smothered by the Prime Minister of Britain. On January 11 the American President sent a secret message to him, proposing some kind of collaboration, even an international conference. But Chamberlain did not think much of Americans, and refused. "That Mr. Chamberlain, with his limited outlook and inexperience of the European scene, should have possessed the self-sufficiency to wave away the proffered hand stretched out across the Atlantic leaves one, even at this date, breathless with amazement. The lack of all sense of proportion, and even of self-preservation, which this episode reveals in an upright, competent, well-meaning man, charged with the destinies of our country and all who depended upon it, is appalling." In all his writing, this is Churchill's harshest criticism of Chamberlain. Churchill knew that even if not much could have come out of the American move, the mere hint of intervention and solidarity with the Western democracies would have wrought portentous results. But Chamberlain — not unlike some other Anglo-Saxons who later dealt with Russia — although well enough imbued with the liberal propensity for taking middle-of-the-road courses and for thinking idealistically of international law and neighborly love between countries, had at the same time a suspicious, unaristocratic aversion for faraway European races and peoples. This provincialism contributed to the ruin of the locust years. (If only his attitude had been reversed; if only people of Chamberlain's ilk had nurtured a healthy scepticism rather than an unrealistic idealism concerning international relations, and, at the same time had had a human understanding of the problems of faraway countries!)

[*Chamberlain and Grandi.*] A week after Schuschnigg's lugubrious Berchtesgaden visit, Anthony Eden was removed. On February 16 Ciano wrote to Grandi: "What will England do in face of new Nazi moves? what new errors will she commit?" Ciano thought that it would be well to talk with the British now, not later, when the pressure of events might force Italy to go to London "as to Canossa" because of German preponderance.

On the next day Chamberlain met Grandi, who cleverly noted the exacerbating conflict between Chamberlain and Eden; for four days previously the Foreign Secretary had tried to speak with Grandi, but the latter had excused himself with all kinds of tricks — golf games, previous appointments, etc. (Grandi to Ciano: "I hate golf but I pretend playing the game; I have to.") Grandi wanted to make Eden understand that he was unwilling to talk with him in the Foreign Office and thereby furnish eager observers and journalists with the awaited news that, after Berchtesgaden, Italian-British consultations were going on. In the meantime Grandi was also in contact with a secret emissary of Chamberlain, Sir Joseph Ball, for the past month almost a daily visitor at the Italian Embassy; now Ball intimated that Chamberlain would be present at a conversation between Grandi and Eden; then Grandi told Ball why he objected to talking with Eden alone, but added that he would always be glad to meet Chamberlain. Within a few hours Ball returned with Chamberlain's invitation to Grandi to visit Downing Street on the next day.

The Chamberlain-Grandi conversation was classic (and tragic). Chamberlain: "What has been happening now in central Europe is very disturbing, isn't it?" Grandi: "What has been happening in Europe not in the last days but for some time is disturbing." Grandi and Chamberlain were lining up against Eden; when Grandi made a good point, Chamberlain looked directly, sternly at Eden. Eden tried to pin the Italian down on specific points. Austria was most important, the Foreign Secretary said, and in all negotiations between London and Rome the Austrian question should now take precedence. "But now Ambassador Grandi," Eden remarked, "refuses to discuss this problem." When Eden said this, Chamberlain "gave visible signs of disappointment and irritation while he did not say a word." Thus do stubborn, narrow men spoil great opportunities. As Grandi reported the matter to Rome:

> Chamberlain and Eden were not a Prime Minister and a Foreign Minister who discussed delicate matters of international portents with an Ambassador of a foreign state; they . . . revealed themselves to be two enemies facing each other, two cocks in a true and proper fighting position. The requests and questions posed to me by Chamberlain were all, without exception, put intentionally to me in order to bring forth answers [to defeat Eden]. . . . I took account of this at once and sought naturally to give Chamberlain all the ammunition which could be utilized here. There is no doubt that the preceding contacts with Ball proved very valuable. (*10*)

Grandi thus could inform Mussolini that Chamberlain gave the impression that he was unwilling to take steps to save Austria; he predicted that the British attitude towards a forceful German solution there would be one of "indignant acquiescence."

[*Eden resigns.*]   On the next day Lord Perth indirectly confirmed the Chamberlain-Eden tension when he spoke to Ciano, and on that same day, February 19, Chamberlain wrote a personal letter to Mussolini which he did not show to Eden. Twenty-four hours later, the crisis in London was on, and Mussolini telephoned excitedly from Terminillo to Rome every half-hour to find out what was happening. By evening Eden had resigned, and Mussolini went to bed contentedly, saying a hearty good night to Ciano. (*11*) Winston Churchill's heart was heavy and, as he recorded, this was the first night in many, many years that he lay long awake, and could not sleep.

Lord Halifax was the new Foreign Secretary. He, being a peer, could not speak in the Commons; and thus as the German chargé to Berlin reported, "the defense of foreign policy there, is, to a very large extent, placed in the hands of the Prime Minister." On February 21 Sir John Simon confirmed the fact in the House of Commons that there was no British guarantee of Austria.

.   .   .   .   .   .

After the Berchtesgaden events France tried at once to rally British support against Germany, but this support Chamberlain refused to give. This stubborn stand, according to the very well-informed German Ambassador to France, was a factor in Eden's resignation. François-Poncet in Berlin let it be known that he was disappointed, predicting that Chamberlain would "try to bring about an understanding with Italy and Germany, without regard for French interests." "To restore the balance," M. Poncet declared, "France would again have to lean more on Russia." (*12*) But Paris bound herself instead more closely to London.

[*Hungary's plans and her fate.*] Stoyadinovič informed the German Minister in Belgrade on February 22 that he had flatly refused a French suggestion about a joint protest against German intervention in Austria. A few days later the Italian intelligence organs intercepted certain Czech telegrams in which Beneš called Rumania and Stoyadinovič disloyal; Ciano, of course, sent copies to Belgrade. On February 27, Kánya went over to Vienna for a hurried visit and learned the true state of things from Schuschnigg; back in Budapest, he had to adapt himself to the new and unforeseeable circumstances. Early in March it was he who, through the German Minister, Erdmansdorff, asked Berlin to consider a German guarantee of the Hungarian-Yugoslav frontier. Kánya and Horthy toyed now with the idea of a real *entente* between Budapest and Belgrade; with Austria about to disappear, this *entente* would provide neutrality in a European war for both countries; there would be no fear of a Yugoslav attack on Hungary and at the same time no Hungarian attack on Czechoslovakia. Such an alignment, which before Berchtesgaden would have pleased Hitler, now could gradually become a defensive bond against him.

But all was in vain, and too late. On March 4 Sztójay transmitted to Ribbentrop the wish of a few impatient young Hungarian generals to get in touch with Keitel about preparations for a German-Hungarian offensive against Czechoslovakia (*13*) and the radical nationalist press in Hungary was whipping up hatred and scorn for "reactionaries" in Austria and "plutodemocrats" of Paris, London, and Prague, who conspired against the "young nations of Central Europe." On the same day Darányi spoke in Győr. He announced a million-*pengő* plan for armaments and — "to take the wind out of the extremists' sails," as it was put later, he declared that the government would introduce legislation in Parliament to curb the disproportionate number of Jews in certain occupational branches. The Darányi government and behind it the majority of the vast and heterogeneous National Unity Party had obviously decided to take the German course with but few reservations.

. . . .

[*Soviet observations.*] Russia was far away, cool and unfriendly. She spurned France in January. Then, late in January or early in February, the Soviets received from their agents in Washington a copy of an important telegram in which Mr. Bullitt reported from Paris on an important talk he had on January 25 with Delbos.

Delbos had spoken with the Soviet Ambassador on the twentieth:

> [The Ambassador] complained that the French Government seemed to be working for a reconciliation with Germany and had intimated strongly that if France should begin serious negotiations with Germany, the Soviet Union would come to terms with Germany at once. Delbos . . . replied that he was quite certain that Germany would much prefer to come to terms with France rather than with the Soviet Union and any such attempt on the part of the Soviets would be anticipated by France . . .

This is one of the few documents from the restricted files of the State Department which were introduced by the Government as evidence in the trial of Alger Hiss. Its photostat was reproduced in the New York *Times* on December 2, 1949. (Strangely enough, no interest has yet been shown in this most important document. (*14*))

At the same time, President Roosevelt instructed the eager Davies to explore the possibilities of closer Soviet-American collaboration, especially in the Far East. Then, on February 11, *Pravda* published a letter which Stalin wrote to the young Comrade Ivanov concerning the victory of socialism in a single country. This "letter" indicated that Stalin was definitely turning away from his European policy, especially in regard to France. The French Ambassador in Moscow, Coulondre, reported his suspicions of such a change.

[*French alarms and ambiguities.*] Britain, Russia, Italy were silent; France had to speak nevertheless, as Czechoslovakia, her ally, was in danger. As long as Neurath was Foreign Minister, he thought of political pressure but not of war: in October 1937 he told the French Ambassador that French intervention with Beneš to make the Czechs grant certain autonomy to the Sudetens would be welcomed. But under Ribbentrop both tone and emphasis were changing. Even before his taking office, Nevile Henderson asked his predecessor about German plans in Czechoslovakia and Austria. Neurath recorded: "As far as Austria was concerned, I could only tell him — and with the request that it be repeated in London — that we could not permit England, either, to interfere in the settlement of our relations with Austria. This settlement was an exclusively German-Austrian question, and we would reject any interference." This categorical statement was evidently made to sound out British reactions; but these did not come. Acquiescence was in the air. From Paris the German Ambassador reported on February 11:

> Regarding the treatment of the Austrian question in the press here, it appears significant that the rôle which France *herself* will be called upon to play in a crisis is hardly mentioned at all. This fact clearly shows how uncertain and hesitating the French are on the Austrian question in its present stage of development. They really have no clear conception of how France should behave in case of a political upheaval in Austria. . . . I should like to state that in certain circles of the Diplomatic Corps here the opinion is held that France would offer no military resistance to a "German solution" of the Austrian question. (*15*)

A report of Osuský, Czechoslovak Ambassador to France, to his Foreign Minister on March 4, 1938, gives a fine analysis of the schizophrenic mood of France in the first two months of 1938. "Conflict between Two Political Trends" (*16*) is the title of the report, and the accuracy of Osuský's observation has been well proven since.

Only a part of the French Left, even fewer nationalists, and Paul Reynaud and his group among the Radicals asserted that war was coming and asked for concrete military conventions with Britain and Russia. On February 17, Delbos requested the British government to define Britain's position concerning further German pressure on Austria and Czechoslovakia. Then came the resignation of Eden and an unusual delay: the British noncommittal answer arrived only on February 26, a day after the Foreign Affairs' Committee of the French Senate met; and, although Delbos and Chautemps declared that France would fulfill her obligations to Czechoslovakia, powerful groups of the Right, headed by Bérenger and Caillaux, advanced the thesis which the French journalist, Joseph Barthélémy, phrased as *mort Locarno, mort l'accessoire de Locarno.* (*17*) Thus, for the first time since its conclusion, the French-Czechoslovak Pact seemed to be weakened because of the hesitations of one of its signatories. Osuský correctly remarked in his report that "the technical question is secondary." Important only was "whether France declares war or not." And, because of the two basic political trends in France, this previously nonexistent question began to shape up as a big, complex problem.

On March 2, Delbos appeared before the Senate Committee and, to the great anxiety of the Czech Ambassador, it was now clear that the French Foreign Minister expressly refrained from mentioning in the committee communiqué "that France remained sincere in her pledges." "The Committee makes an express distinction," Osuský noted, "between the continuation of close collaboration with England in the policy of national security and European peace and the affirmation that the French government will remain true to its commitments."

[*Henderson's remarks.*] Neither Osuský nor Delbos knew that on the next day, March 3, Henderson, the Carlylean, narrow-minded, snobbish, and stubbornly Germanophile Ambassador of His Britannic Majesty to Germany, thought it well to remind Hitler in a private conversation that he, Nevile Henderson, had often expressed himself in favor of *Anschluss.* . . . (*18*) The Ambassador was later rebuked by Halifax for this statement; the Ambassador himself denied that this was more than his personal view and informed Ribbentrop to this effect in a note on March 4. But the harm was done.

Anschluss *and its consequences*

The diplomatic prelude to the liquidation of Austria lasted exactly five weeks. On January 29 the Austrian Minister in Berlin was instructed to complain because of intensified activities of the Nazi "Austrian Legion," but on February 2 Seyss-Inquart, the Austrian Nazi, told Berlin that Schuschnigg did not seem to be in a mood unfavorable to concessions. Intrigues among the leading Austrian Nazis were far from subsiding, and on February 4 Papen suddenly had to report to Berlin. Ribbentrop received an Austrian Nazi report on Schuschnigg on the 7th: "His [Schuschnigg's] chances of escaping the pressure from the Reich by diplomatic measures are dwindling. . . ." On February 10 Papen returned to Vienna with Hitler's message to Schuschnigg: the Chancellor should go to Berchtesgaden at once, on the twelfth.

[*The Berchtesgaden journey.*] Schuschnigg undertook the trip, as he received assurances from Papen that nothing else but the interpretation of the 1936 Agreement would be discussed. Schuschnigg was surprised somewhat by the precipitate departure of Papen on the 4th, but the friendly spirit in which Papen called on him when he returned seemed to allay the worst fears of the Chancellor. (*1*) The incoming cables at the Austrian Foreign Office were not unduly disturbing, although from Prague came news of certain German military measures. (*2*)

The horrible hours which Schuschnigg spent in Berchtesgaden have often been described, and Schuschnigg in his memoirs has left an almost verbatim account for posterity. (*3*) He was confronted by a furious, brutal, yelling Hitler; Schuschnigg, whose personality was anything but dynamic, could not withstand the incredible psychological pressure put upon him. The sly Papen, commuting between dwellings and anterooms, gave the false impression that Hitler's rage was temporary and that the Führer was less incensed than he seemed to be. Thus Papen mediated and meddled. After the negotiations were twice interrupted by Hitler, the first draft of an agreement was presented to Schuschnigg. It stipulated, among other things, a complete amnesty for the Austrian Nazis and the appointment of two of them, Fischböck and Seyss-Inquart, to the Vienna Cabinet, the latter to be Minister of Police and Security. It was, in Schuschnigg's mixed metaphor, "the trap . . . which, once signed, was to be used as a club against the weaker partner. It was intended to cloak the treacherous blow with a thin remnant of so-called legality." (*4*) After protracted talks between Papen, Ribbentrop and Schuschnigg, minor changes were made; then Hitler asked for Schuschnigg and heaped a torrent of abuse on the latter's head, shouting that "not a single iota" would be changed in the draft. He left again and came back again. The document was finally signed, embodying some of the meek reservations of Schuschnigg; more important, the press release, on Hitler's insistence, was cryptically short:

Today the *Führer und Reichskanzler* conferred with the Austrian *Bundeskanzler* at the Berghof.

[*After the meeting.*]   The second stage of developments lasted ten days, from February 14 to 24. After his somber return, Schusch nigg conferred with President Miklas, offering his resignation, but Miklas asked him to stay and save what was possible. Thus Schusch nigg remained; with bitterness in his heart, he began executing the terms of Berchtesgaden; hundreds of Nazis were released; they found their way into the police. Glaise-Horstenau, who in 1936 had been the first pro-German appointed to the Cabinet, came into it again. Measures were taken to exchange Austrian officers with the German Army. The Nazis received admission into the Fatherland Front. Now, perhaps for the first time, in central-eastern Europe the classic methodology of modern totalitarian aggression from within could be observed. It corresponded with the procedure which the Russians followed when they occupied most central-eastern European states in 1945.

[*Foreign reactions.*]   Hitler told Schuschnigg at Berchtesgaden that he had the agreement of Lord Halifax and the British; this Schuschnigg did not believe, but the aftermath brought a bleak report from Franckenstein in London: circles close to Chamberlain actually were describing Berchtesgaden as "an easing of the German-Austrian tension." On the evening of February 14 Hitler agreed with the suggestion presented to him that "false but credible" news should be distributed about German military movements towards Austria. (5) The German Embassy at Paris reported two days later that the press was noncommittal, and that on the previous day Delbos had been informed by Sir Eric Phipps, the British Ambassador, that Britain had no obligations whatsoever in regard to Austria: "In many places they are saying: *Finis Austriae.*" The Austrian Nazis meanwhile paraded delightedly; Hitler's pictures appeared in the windows, and improvised "Austrian SA" marches were held, especially in Styria, the stronghold of Austrian Nazidom. Veesenmeyer, the tough Austrian Nazi, reported to Berlin on the evening of the 18th that although Schuschnigg was under "heavy pressure from Jews, and, especially the Catholics," and that although the Nuncio intervened to strengthen Schuschnigg's position in many quarters, the Legitimists abandoned all hope. "On the basis of a detailed and comprehensive four-day observation, it must be stated that the breakthrough succeeded absolutely and is much deeper than is assumed in many quarters of the Reich."

[*Hopes.*] But Schuschnigg still hoped. Archduke Otto sent a letter urging him to stand fast: Schuschnigg pinned much hope on special messengers whom he thought Mussolini would send; through Salata, a former Italian Minister to Austria, he had heard that the Duce approved of his behavior. The unfortunate Austrian attached exaggerated importance to such vague words; also Kánya sent word to Vienna that, in his personal view, Hitler was bluffing.

Hitler now broke another promise. In his long-awaited speech on February 20 he did not refer to Austria in a friendly tone; violating his Berchtesgaden pledge, he finished Austria off with two brusque sentences. (6) Schuschnigg now acted; he convoked the *Bundestag* for February 24. Full of hope, he sent the draft of his speech to Rome for approval, where Ciano noted privately, "What could I do? . . . no external guarantee can save Austria. . . . A state whose independence is assured by a third power is virtually finished." Schuschnigg did not know that in Rome this was the mood; Salata was scheduled to arrive on the 24th, and a debate in the Paris Chamber of Deputies showed an unusual French preoccupation with the Austrian crisis. While the still loyal elements of the police supplied Schuschnigg with irrefutable evidence of Nazi subversive plans (Papen was not in Vienna anymore, but Keppler gave a steady stream of revolutionary instructions to various Nazis in Papen's stead), (7) the remnants of the Socialists emerged; they were willing to let bygones be bygones and support resistance against the common Nazi enemy in a patriotic manner.

Schuschnigg spoke before the *Bundestag*. He welcomed the "magnanimous settlement" with Germany, and with somewhat curious phraseology emphasized the "true German" essence of Austria. Yet, with much courage, he said that he would go as far as the July 1936 agreement but no further. It was a brave speech, and a friend of Papen asked the German Ambassador, just returning from Berlin: "Did he deliver it in order to die gracefully?" "The developments of the immediate future will show," answered Papen. With the speech Hitler was naturally dissatisfied, and the last phase of the diplomatic prelude began.

[*The crisis opens.*] On February 26 Papen called upon Schuschnigg and told him rather brutally that he should not delude himself with the hope of getting aid from "non-German European alliances." Referring to the French parliamentary debate, Papen said that "for Germany an Austrian independence supported by French and Czechoslovak crutches is intolerable." Schuschnigg agreed and went so far as to show Papen his press directives suppressing news of the French parliamentary demonstrations. Then Papen, along with Keppler, who travelled aboard Ribbentrop's personal airplane, vanished again into the German night, not knowing that a decision was in the making which might have upset the German plans.

[*Schuschnigg's counterplan.*]   When news reached Schuschnigg that in wake of his *Bundestag* speech the Styrian Nazis had taken virtual control over Graz and had hoisted the swastika flag on most public buildings (*8*), he began to consider a decisive step, an heroic gesture to call the world's attention to Austria. He himself says in his memoirs that the thought of holding an *Anschluss* plebiscite came to him first at the end of February; it must have come after the Papen visit, some time on the 27th or 28th, when further news from Styria reported that the Nazi crowds there planned a gigantic German Day demonstration later in March. Here was something which had to be averted. During February 28–March 1 he was still telling Kánya that a plebiscite would be too dangerous. On March 2, he nevertheless decided on the plebiscite. He postponed its announcement to the latest possible date in order to prevent a Nazi coup between the date of announcement and the actual day of the referendum. But how about external intervention? Did he count on that? Obviously he did, but he did not find it possible to believe that Germany could attack Austria within four or five days. And, to make sure, he sent his military attaché, Colonel Liebitzky, to Mussolini. After twenty-four hours, Liebitzky flew back from Rome, reporting that the Duce was "optimistic," and had "expressed his satisfaction," but at the same time thought that the plebiscite idea was a mistake. With a sort of desperate gallantry, and not without a fortifying dose of wishful thinking, Schuschnigg decided to go ahead with the plebiscite, notwithstanding Mussolini's admonition. "Above all, it was too late now. I gave all . . . reasons to the Duce through Colonel Liebitzky. I never heard from Mussolini again." (*9*)

[*Britain undecided; Hitler decided.*]   The British Minister to Vienna, who caught Papen during the latter's brief *séjour* there, dramatically reproached him, warning him of the consequences of Germany's ruthless behavior. This worried Ribbentrop a little. Yet, at the same time that Schuschnigg was making his grave decision about the unpledged and unsupported plebiscite, the grey shadow of the tall Sir Nevile Henderson appeared on the scene again. On March 2 Chamberlain left an Opposition question about Austria unanswered in the Commons, and openly disassociated himself from the French; Henderson did the same during the March 3 conversation with Hitler and Ribbentrop. But this was not all. When Ribbentrop asked Henderson, in reference to the talk between the British Minister in Vienna and Papen, "If the British Minister protested in such a dramatic way to . . . Papen, then how would he have talked to [the] Austrian Foreign Minister?" Henderson reassured the German that "the views of the Minister do not necessarily represent the views of the British government"; and after this inopportune disavowal of his colleague, he added the already cited personal reminder on his own: he always had favored *Anschluss*. (*10*)

We know today that the British government did not even consider a gesture to encourage the resistance of Schuschnigg; Alexis Léger of the French Foreign Ministry anxiously confirmed the truth of this negative attitude to General Gamelin. (*11*) Ribbentrop reported the Henderson conversation to Keitel on March 4. By March 5 the Nazis controlled the police and some of the army barracks in Styria, and Keppler reported to Berlin: "In Austria the Party is now in fine shape." On March 7 Schuschnigg sent a courier to Belgium to inform Archduke Otto of his decision, and on the evening of March 8 he told Seyss-Inquart about the plebiscite; twelve hours later, at Innsbruck, he officially announced that a referendum on *Anschluss* would take place on the following Sunday, March 13. (*12*) The afternoon newspapers carried the surprise news in banner headlines; the loudspeaker propaganda of the Fatherland Front began to swing into action; for a moment the Nazis seemed to be taken aback; Socialists and Fatherland Front members appeared on the densely packed sidewalks of Vienna; under the clear and cool March sky, patriotic songs reverberated in the night. At 10:18 P.M., a laconic order from Hitler was dispatched to the High Command of the German Army, where General Jodl recorded it in his War Diary for posterity. "Prepare *Case Otto*," said the order. (*13*) The invasion of Austria was to begin.

. . . . . .

[*The Great Powers stand by.*] The next day, March 10, was one of hope and excitement. As the Fatherland Front seemed to be maintaining its control all over Austria, Schuschnigg and Miklas ex-

pected to hold out until Sunday. Some people in Berlin were disturbed, but their worries proved to be exaggerated. Italy did not
move. Mussolini ruled supreme (*14*) and Italian diplomacy was
wantonly ineffective. Attolico, the Ambassador to Berlin, on March 9
asked to see Ribbentrop but could not get an audience, and when on
the next day he got to see Weizsäcker, the latter, in spite of his usual
loquacity, was rather close-mouthed.

Neither Henderson nor Ribbentrop was close-mouthed, however.
Henderson called the plebiscite "Schuschnigg's folly" when he talked
to Göring privately, and he telegraphed Halifax on March 10: "Both
in wording of the question and in manner in which plebiscite is to be
carried out, Dr. Schuschnigg seems to have taken a leaf out of the
Nazi book." (*15*) On March 10, Ribbentrop appeared in London —
he was Foreign Minister now — ostensibly to finish up business left
over from his Ambassadorship. That evening German divisions were
moving into positions, and all along the Austrian frontier the Germans
were gradually restricting traffic. At five o'clock on Friday morning,
March 11, the Germans closed the frontier. Schuschnigg received the
message at six. With the morning hours, the aim of the German
military measures became increasingly evident; then the ultimata
began to arrive, delivered by telephone or personally by Glaise-
Horstenau, and later Seyss-Inquart. Schuschnigg tried to get in touch
with Mussolini, but the Palazzo Venezia remained mute; there was
no answer on the other end of the line; after waiting for awhile,
Schuschnigg cancelled the call to Rome. A few minutes later came a
message that the Italian Government "could not give any advice."
By noon, France was without a government, as Chautemps had
resigned and the new cabinet of Blum was not installed until two
days later. And in London, Ribbentrop was lunching with Chamberlain and Halifax. Shortly after luncheon, the Vienna telegrams were
handed to Halifax. There was a terse discussion; Halifax thought it
"exceedingly serious . . . that the Germans brought the threat of
invasion against Schuschnigg." Ribbentrop retorted that the telegrams did not show this to be the case — and Chamberlain sided
with him. The German Foreign Minister then left, promising to communicate with Berlin. There was not much to be said; previously,
just before the last telegram came, Chamberlain told Ribbentrop that
"once we had all got past this unpleasant affair [of Austria] . . . it
was to be hoped that we could begin working in earnest toward a
German-British understanding." (*16*)

At half past two in the afternoon Schuschnigg asked for immediate
advice from the British and French governments. The French Minister urged him to gain time. Halifax telegraphed to the British envoy
shortly after he and Ribbentrop parted:

> His Majesty's Government cannot take responsibility of advising the
> Chancellor to take any course of action which might expose his coun-
> try to dangers against which His Majesty's Government are unable
> to guarantee protection.

The Nazis paraded now on the Vienna streets; no help was forthcoming from without, and as the day progressed, resistance from
within seemed to be more and more futile. Schuschnigg could not
count on the police; the Army against the Germans was worthless.
Miklas and Schuschnigg were still negotiating with Glaise, Seyss, and
Muff, the brutal little German attaché (*17*); Hitler, after having
spent an anxious forenoon milling around in his rooms, sent an order
to Jodl a few minutes after noon: "If other measures prove unsuccessful, I intend to invade Austria with armed forces. . . . The whole
operation will be directed by myself . . ." (*18*)

[*The last hours.*]   But the "other measures" proved successful.
The trampling of the Nazi stormtroops on the Vienna cobblestones,
the silence of the outside world, and the helpless gestures of the police
officials convinced Schuschnigg of the obvious uselessness of further
resistance. At noon, he let it be announced that the plebiscite was
cancelled. At six o'clock he went on the air. His resignation speech,
short, noble, and dramatic as it was, brought but one moment of
awed silence; then the thunderous echo of victorious Nazi *Heils*
shook the air; the droning calls penetrated the inner rooms of the
Chancellery; half an hour later a provisional Nazi government was
appointed under Seyss-Inquart. (*19*) At that time, Austrian and
German customs guards were busily hacking apart the frontier barriers as the first German trucks began to roll toward Vienna.

They did not reach Vienna until very late in the night; Jodl's
instructions were careful. "If Czech troops or militia" were encountered, the troops were to oppose them by arms; if Italian troops
showed themselves, the attitude was to be "friendly." (*20*) Of course,
no troops came. By midnight the green-gray German Army uniforms
were to be seen mingling in increasing numbers among the frenzied,
spasmodically laughing and crying, happy-go-lucky, irresponsible

Viennese crowds. Former *Heimwehren*, Fatherland Fronters, *Schutz-bündler* — there was no distinction now. *(21)* The "modern man" of a "new Europe" hailed his democratic freedom from freedom with masochistic frenzy before the spectre of Power.

[*Immediate effects: the Czechs.*]   The consequences of *Anschluss* were strategical, political, and moral. Germany had now a common frontier with Italy *(22)*; from Schleswig to Sicily the solid block of the Axis stood, dividing Europe. Hitler gained another seven million Germans for his plans, with Austrian mines and heavy industry. The military position of Czechoslovakia changed overnight; another few hundred miles of frontier had to be defended, mostly without the great circle of mountains which elsewhere separated Germany from Czechoslovakia.

Hitler was determined to destroy the Czechs; but he needed a little time. On March 12 and 14, Göring assured Mastny, the Czech Minister to Berlin, that Germany had no designs on Czechoslovakia. *(23)* But notwithstanding these pious assurances, even Hitler's March 11 letter to Mussolini contained indications of a future German attack on Czechoslovakia, and when the Italians asked for Hitler's permission to publish the letter, he requested Rome to omit the two passages dealing with Czechoslovakia.

[*Yugoslavs.*]   On March 11 the Yugoslav Minister in Berlin informed the German Foreign Office that "the Yugoslav Government held the point of view that the Austrian question was an internal German affair; Yugoslavia placed particular importance on good relations with the German Reich." On March 14 Beneš confidentially proposed that the Little Entente meet at Bucharest, but Stoyadinovič promptly refused; indeed, on March 14 he publicly declared that Yugoslavia was not concerned with Austrian events.

[*British, French, Americans.*]   Chamberlain did not say much and did not want his envoys to say much either. On March 12 Ciano and Lord Perth conversed and almost failed to mention Austria at all; only brief note was taken thereof at the end of their talk. *(24)* The French were taken aback, but it was evident that démarches did not mean much. In Bonnet's words, "The *Anschluss* . . . was absorbed by

French public opinion as lightly as the Rhineland occupation. . . . One could ask why public opinion remained so indifferent to events of such heavy consequences. The historian will wonder by what contradiction all those Frenchmen who were to react violently — and, with reason — to the misfortunes of the Czechs, did . . . without a word accept the occupation of the Rhineland, and without shedding a tear, the fate dealt out to unhappy Austria." The American attitude was even less realistic. The State Department's reaction to the plebiscite news of March 9 was indicated by a comment heard in the Department and quoted verbatim by the German Ambassador: "That fellow [Schuschnigg] is asking for trouble!" (*25*) — scarcely a diplomatic remark. Washington was obsessed with democratic procedure, and the New York *Times* criticized Schuschnigg because of the practical inadequacies of the election preparations. Surely, this was no New England township ballot! In a later report, Ambassador Dieckhoff stated:

> It was striking that the Congress took no stand on the German action in Austria and that neither Representatives nor Senators made use of the popular method of expressing their opinions on everything between heaven and earth. Only Senator Borah, in a really classical radio and press statement, elucidated the Austrian problem and its development, and he may to a certain extent have promoted an understanding of the German action among wide circles. (*26*)

On March 12 Dieckhoff reported that Mr. Hull "was obviously still thoroughly impressed by the [*Anschluss*] proclamation. He thanked me for the information. From a few questions which he asked, it was apparent that he thoroughly understands our action." (*27*) Not until about March 14 did the attitude of the American press and officials change, a change which Dieckhoff attributed to President Roosevelt's personal intervention; on March 15, Under-Secretary Welles, in a routine conversation with Dieckhoff, spoke bitterly about events in Austria. The outrages and persecutions of the first few days of *Anschluss* had undoubtedly left their mark on the American spectators.

The Austrian diplomatic stations were now liquidated everywhere (a year later, in March 1939, Paris and London tacitly recognized the dissident Czech diplomatic representatives). A few Austrian diplomats resigned, among them Baron Franckenstein in London, who thus unwittingly became the first in a subsequently long list of *émigré* diplomats. Unlike him, the Austrian Minister to Berlin shouted *Heil Hitlers!* with the crowds.

[*Within Austria.*] The psychological implications were serious. Poland's Minister, impressed by the mass jubilation, said to Papen in Vienna that he never thought such a thing were possible. The picture of mass enthusiasm annihilated moral and spiritual resistance for the present; in some instances the German invaders had to restrain Austrian Nazis from excesses against the cowed and unfortunate Jewish inhabitants. The old Cardinal Innitzer (of Sudeten German origin) (*28*) himself experienced a momentary breakdown: on March 13 he appeared at Hitler's place in the Hotel Imperial and incomprehensibly raised his arm to a meek *Heil Hitler!* Soon, however, relations between the Austrian Church and the Nazi government deteriorated (*29*); in April Innitzer was called to Rome, where Pope Pius xi reproached him for having appeased Hitler. By the summer many priests were imprisoned, while a great number of the clergy were busily trying to help the persecuted; in July, Hitler decided that the Austrian incorporation should automatically invalidate the Austrian Concordat; many convents, among them the famous Kremsmünster, were expropriated, and tension between Church and state developed to a climax in October, when, after a courageous antitotalitarian sermon by Cardinal Innitzer, the Nazi mob stormed his palace and beat up some of his priests. (*30*)

Yet, during the spring and the summer the image of "happy," "rejuvenated" Austrian masses impressed the spectators: the Catholic opposition in the Sudetenland was practically liquidated, and the Henlein movement was the supreme force to which the great majority of Sudeten Catholics adhered. (*31*) In Hungary and Rumania and Bulgaria the German success gave wings to local Nazis; unrest in Hungarian souls was great and Admiral Horthy himself decided to calm the nation in a radio speech on April 3, a speech in which he referred to *Anschluss* in a tone of melancholy acceptance. A week later, on April 10, an "all-German plebiscite" sanctioned *Anschluss* by a majority vote of 98.5 per cent; but even if we take the rigged character of totalitarian elections into consideration, there remains no doubt that the German and Austrian peoples would have confirmed the annexation in a free referendum. (Records found after the war in Koblenz, a traditionally conservative and non-Nazi city, showed that "No" votes there ranged from 5.6 to 13.1 per cent.) (*32*)

The Czech government wanted to please the Germans; the Foreign Minister was suave; on February 16 Beneš said to Eisenlohr that "his pact with Russia was the relic of a former epoch, but he could not just throw it into the wastepaper basket." (*33*) The Prague régime, in order to show its good intentions, organized ten special trains to carry German and former Austrian nationals resident in Czechoslovakia to partake in the plebiscite, and provided for a special fifty per cent fare reduction. Everywhere in central-eastern Europe the policy was to "take the wind out of the Nazi sails"; yet the effects of the dynamic German successes were evident: cabinet ministers began dreaming of high, windswept balconies, military parades, and patent leather boots; foreign ministers, imitating the former champagne salesman, Ribbentrop, created military uniforms of their own, with glittering medals and tight waists, thus shedding the morning coat together with all other vestiges of the "decadent bourgeois past." (*34*) Was Europe finished? To many it seemed so. A few months later, after Godesberg, Reynaud said to a group of French politicians: "Godesberg is the end of Czechoslovakia. Now . . . it is Europe." No, said Anatole de Monzie, "Europe . . . that was Vienna." (*35*) Behind this correct assumption lurked the Machiavellian conclusions of de Monzie, and, alas, of so many others. (*36*)

The Polish-Lithuanian crisis

During the hectic days of *Anschluss* another crisis developed; a week after the German ultimata were handed to Schuschnigg, a Polish ultimatum dispatched to Kaunas almost resulted in a war between Lithuania and Poland.

The Polish-Lithuanian frontier had been closed since 1920, when, in a coup, the Poles occupied Wilnó. Normal relations between the two countries lapsed and the border regions became one vast no-man's land; rail and personal traffic did not exist. In 1927 Pilsudski submitted the dispute to the League; a rude debate ensued, but Lithuania defied the League authority. In 1928, the Lithuanian Voldemaras and the Polish Foreign Minister, Zaleski, met in Königsberg to discuss an eventual resumption of frontier traffic, but their meeting was not successful; later talks between the diplomats Beck and Lozoraitis in 1935 in Geneva were equally fruitless.

On March 10, 1938, a Lithuanian frontier patrol shot and killed a Polish soldier; on that day Beck returned to Warsaw from Rome. He acted with quick determination; his reasons were not simple. He feared Russia's designs; in February, Litvinov had sent an unusually friendly telegram to Kaunas on the twentieth anniversary of Lithuanian independence. And the successful gain of Hitler in Austria made it imperative that Poland reduce the number of her eventual enemies. The anniversary celebrations resulted in a resurgence of anti-Polish demonstrations in Lithuania; there were the frontier incidents, and the extraordinary sensitivity of the Poles about their national pride is well-known.

[*The crisis.*] On March 18, an ultimatum was sent to Kaunas; its harshness again reduced the sympathy with which the West regarded the Poles. The French wanted a compromise solution of the Polish-Lithuanian conflict, and this disappointed Warsaw. Beck was in no mood to accept counsels of moderation. The Lithuanian government then tried to ask for Russian advice or help, and the Lithuanian envoy travelled in vain between Moscow and Kaunas: neither advice nor help came. This was a very significant development. For Russia, which in the twenties often took advantage of the Lithuanian-Polish dispute to pose as the eventual ally of the little Baltic republic against the "Polish aggressors," now withdrew into her shell, just as Italy had done a week before in the case of Austria. (*I*) The Russians' refusal to commit themselves meant a resurgence of Russian isolationism; the indirect contradiction between the gesture of Litvinov's February telegram and the Soviet caution in March should have been noticed by those who took it for granted that Russia's stand on "collective security" — and her alliance with the Czechs — was firm.

[*The solution.*] On March 18 Hitler ordered the German armed forces to march into Memel in the event of Polish-Lithuanian hostilities. But on March 19 the Lithuanian government accepted the Polish ultimatum. After his unduly crude threat, Beck spoke to Kaunas with a certain magnanimity, an attitude which seems to confirm the Polish thesis that his action was aimed at securing Poland's northeastern flank against Hitler. (*2*)

Western doubts

[*Forty days.*] The breathing-space which Hitler required after *Anschluss* did not last longer than the diplomatic prelude to his

Austrian endeavor. On March 12, Göring gave his word to the Czech envoy, and the German Foreign Office assured Prague of German goodwill. On March 16 the Czech General Staff reported minor German troop concentrations in Saxony. On April 21 the German High Command drew up the definite plan for the attack on Czechoslovakia: *Case Green.* (*1*)

During these forty days the Western Powers failed to demonstrate any strength or any determination to regain the diplomatic initiative. Only Mr. Churchill spoke anxiously in the House of Commons about the real threat of force. None of the central-eastern European capitals was able to see a rehabilitation of the West's faded diplomatic prestige. The French and British envoys were either silent or non-committal; many of them could but grit diplomatic teeth and hope some kind of miraculously wise new course would be charted in their respective Foreign Ministries. Important Tories in England were now revealing themselves as sympathetic to Hitler's cause; such attitudes could not fail to impress many a central-eastern European statesman. (*2*) Meanwhile, parliamentarians and politicians in London and Paris, who knew but little about the peoples and plains beyond the Rhine, were dazzled and stupefied by events; they were carried away by sentiments, emotions and fears, often considering foreign matters on the plane of internal politics and personal relations.

1938 thus became the year of "Western doubts"; disbelief in the moral and intellectual values of the West, long evident, was now to reach its climax, while, at the same time, the intentions of the Western leaders seemed uncertain and vague.

[*Chamberlain after* Anschluss.] It is true that the British Foreign Office watched the impending transformation of central-eastern Europe with anxiety, but the mood shown by London in March 1938 was not different from that of March 1937, when Lord Halifax had said in the House of Lords: "We are unable to define beforehand what might be our attitude to a hypothetical complication in Central or Eastern Europe."

On March 20, in a private letter, Chamberlain indicated that he could not see how Czechoslovakia could be helped. (*3*) Four days later he rose in Parliament with a statement on foreign policy. This statement, in Wheeler-Bennett's words, was a "masterpiece of obfuscation. While re-stating the old and obvious, it left the world in complete uncertainty on the essential issues involved in the new situation created by Germany in Central and Eastern Europe. It made crystal-clear what Britain was not prepared to do, but was singularly unclear as to what she might do if faced with certain circumstances." (*4*) In essence, Chamberlain said that Britain might fight; after enumerating ridiculously evident cases of "we might," he added that one such case "might, for example, include Czechoslovakia." (*5*) On the same day, Henderson reported to Halifax in detail. He referred to Hitler in the text of his telegram as a "constructive genius"; yet the essence of his report was coldly realistic:

> In his speech on the 18th March Hitler was able to refer to the sympathetic attitude adopted in the Austrian crisis, not only by Italy, but by Poland, Hungary and Yugoslavia. The three last are still members of the League of Nations, and their haste in welcoming the rape of their fellow-member Austria is sadly symptomatic of many things. However immoral Germany's next action may be, it would be the height of unwisdom to count on the cooperation of a single small Power in Europe against her. . . . What . . . matters at the moment is that German hegemony east of the Rhine, down to the Brenner and the Balkans in the south and as far as the Russians in the east, is a fact, however unpalatable it may be to admit it. . . . After Hitler, and once normalcy is restored, Germany may change her face again, but so long as he is there, with Goebbels and the radio behind him, the threat of foreign intervention before him and an army ready to do whatever it is told, Central and Eastern Europe will in general have to dance as Hitler pipes. (*6*)

The Russians proposed Great Power talks, but the British refused: "In present circumstances, however, it would not appear that such a meeting could be arranged."

Neville Chamberlain wanted only peace; while his concept of space was faulty — he refused to understand the implications of a German-ruled central-eastern Europe — his concept of time was not; he re-armed, often in the face of Fabianist tirades of the Labor parliamentarians. After all, Britain had no direct obligations in central-eastern Europe; but France did.

[*France considers her commitments: the Russian alliance.*] France was considerably dissatisfied with the Chamberlain statements. On March 16, the Permanent National Defense Committee met in Paris; certain things had to be clarified. Paul-Boncour, then Foreign Minister, spoke first, pointing out that the English were, in effect, saying,

"You say that you shall assist Czechoslovakia, but in practice what do you plan to do?" Daladier, then War Minister, answered that France could not furnish any direct assistance to Czechoslovakia; her aid would be indirect and would tie down the bulk of the German Army in the West. Léon Blum declared that Russia would intervene. But General Gamelin, not doubting that Russia would come in, stated that she could not effectively assist the Czechs. (7) Russian mobilization, said Gamelin, would probably result in renewed Polish and Rumanian hesitations; a Russian passage through the only and poor rail line leading through Rumanian territory would be practically impossible; only motorized troops could be sent and the efficacy of these was doubtful.

General Vuillemin added that neither could Russian air aid to the Czechs be very effective, in view of the few airports in eastern Czechoslovakia and of the expected rapid mastery of the air by the Germans. These analyses were obviously correct. Premier Blum now summarized the discussion: it was possible to tie down a part of the German Army, but France could not prevent German action against Czechoslovakia; this state of things should be pointed out to the British to make them intervene in Bucharest and Brussels. (8)

Thus the secret session did not resolve much; meanwhile the French press and public opinion were divided. Thus did the "Western doubts" extend unto France. (9) The French were more interested than the British in the Litvinov proposal of Great Power talks but did not commit themselves; Chamberlain had, on his part, no confidence in the French, as a private letter of his on March 20 shows. He also described the Russians as

> stealthily and cunningly pulling all the strings behind the scenes to get us involved in war with Germany (our Secret Service doesn't spend all its time looking out the window) . . .

At the end of March the German chargé in Moscow informed Berlin that diplomats in Moscow regarded French-Soviet relations as "the worst imaginable." A report of the German Embassy from Paris on April 14 essentially confirmed this fact.

. . . .

There were now substantial differences in the views of certain diplomats. Two of Britain's envoys saw things differently. (10) Henderson

in Berlin believed that Hitler's ultimate intentions were decent; he
concurred with the German theories of national behavior and generally disliked eastern Europeans. While he did not comment too much
on the Czechs after Halifax reprimanded him, he expressed his disdain of the Poles, an attitude which he did not fail to voice even in
the summer of 1939. (*11*) Newton in Prague, however, saw the
German danger more clearly. On March 15 he telegraphed Halifax,
weighing two sides of the question:

> If . . . His Majesty's Government feel justified in accepting such com-
> mitments or risks as will enable Czechoslovakia, when the test comes,
> to preserve her complete independence against brute force or eco-
> nomic strangulation, the sooner Germany can be convinced that if
> she tried to intimidate Czechoslovakia she will be barking up the
> wrong tree, the better.
> At the same time, I feel bound to draw attention to the misgivings
> that fill my mind as to the practicability of such a policy. . . . Should
> war come, nothing that we or France could do would save Czecho-
> slovakia from being overrun. . . . From the point of view of personal
> sympathy, I should be only too pleased, if, on a review of wider con-
> siderations than those with which I am here concerned, His Majesty's
> Government found it possible to adopt a policy which would maintain
> Czechoslovak independence without any impairment. For the Czechs,
> unlike the Austrians, know what they want, and, if sufficiently backed,
> would probably be prepared to fight for it. But I am anxious that in
> framing the policy of His Majesty's Government the foregoing con-
> siderations shall be given due weight in the long view.   (*12*)

[*British-Czech conversations.*]   Next day Henlein received secret
instructions to break away from the Czechoslovak state and act only
on orders of the German Legation in Prague or other Berlin instructions. (*13*) On April 4, Sir Alexander Cadogan of the Foreign Office
advised the Czech Minister to London, Jan Masaryk, to tell his
government to start negotiations with Henlein. (*14*) The Masaryk
report on this talk compares in importance with the Osuský report
from Paris exactly a month before: Cadogan's remarks exactly reflected
the Foreign Office attitude; his words reflected a certain distrust of
France, especially of Paul-Boncour, and a "deep distrust" of Russia.
Cadogan said that it was doubtful whether Russia "would effectively
intervene outside her borders. This did not mean that Russia could
not be utilized politically; on the contrary, it was in Czechoslovakia's

interest to keep the danger of Russian intervention before the eyes of the Germans, because, notwithstanding all assurances, Germany was afraid of Russia . . ." (*15*)

On the next day, April 5, Newton conversed with his German colleague in Prague. Eisenlohr made it clear to Newton what the Germans wanted — this elderly German career diplomat did not know that one of the plans hatched in Berlin to provide a *casus belli* against Czechoslovakia was his arranged assassination "by a rabble of Czech nationalists." When Newton later asked him about certain Czech compromises to satisfy Germany, Eisenlohr cynically said that "nothing was ever final." (*16*)

[*The Italo-British agreement: a false impression.*] Yet, there were not even faint signs of a Western diplomatic counteroffensive. On April 13, in a letter to Halifax, Henderson unwittingly echoed the argument which Mussolini had expressed: "In a sense Czechoslovakia today is a sort of miniature Austrian Empire" (Mussolini had said, "a caricature of the Austrian Empire"). On April 16, upon Chamberlain's insistence, a provisional agreement was signed between Britain and Italy dealing with Mediterranean problems. Most of the central-eastern European capitals thought that this was the first step in a diplomatic campaign wherein Britain and France were to regain the initiative; some of them, Belgrade for example, did not think so. (*17*) The latter were proven right in their estimations. For Mussolini regarded all treaties with England as meaningless; on April 16 France informed Italy that she desired French-Italian negotiations similar to those going on between Britain and Italy, but Ciano rejected the offer. On April 27 a German Foreign Office memorandum stated: "From the point of view of German policy, the Italian-British Agreement is advantageous. . . . (*18*) Not quite two weeks after the Italian-British paper was signed, Hitler entered Rome on a triumphant goodwill visit. Under the blue Latin sky, which had smiled centuries ago on Caesar and Barbarossa, the chant of thousands of youngsters and the roar of hundreds of tanks and airplanes was heard by the two happily smiling dictators.

[*The attitude at Downing Street.*] Meanwhile, to a Birmingham audience Chamberlain said in mid-April that it would be indeed a noble ambition to a British statesman to mediate in Europe and to "make gentle the life of the world." On April 22 the German chargé d'affaires had a talk with Stewart, Chamberlain's new Parliamentary Under Secretary, who said, in the words of his German conversant,

> . . . that he knew from close association with Chamberlain and Lord Halifax that both, now as in the past, held fast to the idea of a real understanding with Germany and that the events in Austria had not altered this in any way. He made himself the spokesman, as it were, of the younger generation in England — that is, a spokesman, as he said of the intelligent, not the intellectual class. In contrast with the actual intellectuals, among whom there was now as in the past a strong antipathy to the authoritarian states, the circles close to him fully understood that Germany had to pursue her national aims in her own way. The German and the British peoples were of the same blood — which in itself meant a bond of unity. To the circle close to him it was inconceivable that Germany and England should meet again on the battlefield. . . . England was aware that Germany would attain "her next goal." The manner in which this was done, however, was decisive for the reaction in England . . . (*19*)

[*Hitler's plan to strike.*]   On the same day the basic memorandum on *Case Green* was drawn up by Hitler:

1. Idea of a strategic attack out of the blue without cause or possibility of justification is rejected. Reason: hostile world opinion which might lead to serious situation.
2. Action after a period of diplomatic discussions which gradually lead to a crisis and to war.
3. Lightning action based on an incident (for example, murder of the German envoy at Prague).

The German Foreign Office instructed all misssons abroad on April 25 to assume a state of readiness.

The Czechoslovak crisis: Phase I

Thanks to the voluminous diplomatic papers published since 1948, we are now in a position to dispose of a number of legends and to revise many judgments concerning Munich and the great crisis of 1938; it is possible now to reconstruct significant details.

[*The Sudeten Germans among themselves.*]   There were considerable differences between the Sudeten German agitators on one side and Eisenlohr, the German envoy to Prague, on the other. While in February Eisenlohr suggested negotiations with the Czech President, who was in a willing mood, the Party and the Sudeten leaders carried on with conspiratorial and secret talks: they clandestinely conferred with Slovaks, Magyars, and Ruthenians. These confabulations went so far that the German Minister himself had to take a stand against them on February 17. But then came the Austrian avalanche, and overwhelming emotions. By the middle of March all the important German-speaking groups rallied under Henlein's flag: only Jaksch's German Social Democrats stood apart. Yet perhaps not more than half of all the Sudeten people envisaged full incorporation into the Reich: most of them demanded regional autonomy. Henlein, however, had an inkling of Hitler's ultimate plans. (*1*)

On March 17 Henlein turned to Hitler with a begging, unctuous letter; a day later he complained about Eisenlohr to the German Foreign Ministry. Hitler answered him ten days later. "In the not-too-distant future" he would settle the Sudeten question and Henlein would be his Governor. On March 29 a report by Eisenlohr cited the fanatic enthusiasm of the Sudeten groups; he gave some credit to the restraint of the Czechs. (*2*) The agitation went on, unrestrained by diplomatic admonitions. Other ears perked up. The pro-German Hungarian Minister to Berlin inquired on March 31 about German guarantees against Yugoslavia **if and when** Hungary attacked the Czechs: Sztójay lacked confidence in his own government, which, in his eyes, was unduly cautious and hesitating.

There were others, who counted on British and French resistance to Germany. They counted wrong. Certain Germans knew better. On March 29 a conference of Sudeten and Wilhelmstrasse men met in Berlin to chart the best course: because of British indecision, it was decided to proceed full speed ahead.

[*The Anglo-French conversations of April.*] The British did not lack information: Mr. Newton from Prague and their excellent Consuls in the Sudeten area told them of trends and plans in detail and made intelligent interpretations. (*3*) Yet, when on April 28–29, the heads of the British and French governments met in London, Chamberlain let it be known that, in his view, "the moment was not favorable" (*4*) for stopping Germany.

Here, according to Chamberlain's biographer, were Daladier: "the taciturn peasant of the South, on whom were pinned expectations of a French revival, and with him his foreign minister Bonnet, with his vast nose, his voracious ambition, and a political reputation slightly soiled." But these Frenchmen were better than the British: at least Daladier argued courageously. On the first day of the conference the British presented gloomy military estimates ("assistance mainly by sea and air") and Chamberlain next day even envisaged defeat. As the British minutes recorded his words:

> We must therefore consider with the greatest care whether, if the at-
> titude [M. Daladier] had just outlined towards Germany were
> adopted, we — and in this connexion he was thinking of His Maj-
> esty's Government and the French Government, since we could not
> count on any outside support — were sufficiently powerful to make
> victory certain. Frankly, he did not think we were. . . . a time [could]
> come when a gamble on the issue of peace or war might be contem-
> plated with less anxiety than at present.

The British persisted against further commitments: it was agreed that pressure be brought upon Prague to bring about maximum con-cessions from Beneš. If these efforts failed it could be said to Germany that Britain and France had done their best; if the Germans would still resort to arms, "they would be doing so in full knowledge . . . that France would be compelled to intervene by virtue of her obliga-tions and that His Majesty's Government could not guarantee that they would not do the same . . ."

[*The Germans aware of the British trend.*]   Within an hour after the talks with the French ended, Halifax asked for the German chargé and told him that there were no commitments, no new obligations made. (5) The Germans noted the developing British attitude with much satisfaction; they noticed the absolute omission of Russia; (". . . there are indications that the British have suggested to the French that they become more aloof from the Russians"), and they learned, partly from French sources, that while the Italians were informed of the content of the Anglo-French talks, the Soviets were not. Not until May 5 did Halifax ask for the Soviet Ambassador.

Chamberlain, who, chasing illusions, still thought that the Anglo-Italian agreement gave the Axis "a nasty jar," noted on May 1 that "fortunately the papers have had no hint of how near we came to a break [with the French] over Czechoslovakia. . . ." (6) On May 3 Henderson wrote to Halifax:

I fear that I am unprincipled, but I must say that I love my country more than Czechs or Sudetendeutschen, or Austrians or even Schuschnigg, or Poles, or even Frenchmen. And it distresses me to see how we throw away our opportunities for the sake of international mirages. I cannot say "principles," for they are not always basically sound or straightforward enough for that. . . . If I may do so, I would suggest for your consideration that on some favourable occasion in the House of Commons or House of Lords we should say quite openly that we have no intention of trying to hamper Germany's *legitimate* freedom of action in Central or Eastern Europe. . . . I admit that personally I am only too glad to wish that [Germany] should look eastwards instead of westwards.   (7)

Three days later in another telegram he accused the French; in his view their London stand, however moderate, amounted to advocating preventive war. Meanwhile the German Ambassador in London received, as a courtesy by the editor, the proofs of a forthcoming *Daily Mail* editorial entitled "Czechs Not Our Business." (8)

On May 9 Halifax rebuked Henderson for having gone so far as to state British preference for the transformation of Czechoslovakia into a state of nationalities: the Germans should not know this, "at the present stage at any rate." Yet, when two days later Henderson talked to Ribbentrop, he said that he was already convinced of the justice of the German viewpoint: "Ribbentrop was, therefore, preaching to one already converted . . ."; it was hoped that Beneš would listen to reason. (9)

[*The Karlsbad "points" and the Henlein journey.*]   Planning for *Case Green* was introduced on April 21. (10) Hitler said to Keitel that quick action was necessary, before "the others" would intervene. Three days later the Sudeten Germans published their Karlsbad program to preclude any compromise with the Czechs, whose Premier, the Agrarian Hodža, planned for a Minorities' Statute to be enacted in the autumn at the occasion of the twentieth anniversary of the Czechoslovak Republic. Although one of the alternative plans for *Green* was provocation of war by arranging a "Czech" assassination of Eisenlohr in Prague, Konrad Henlein was sent to London, where he arrived on May 14. He was instructed to give the impression that he was acting quite independently of Berlin and that he was a reasonable man. He appeared at the Foreign Office, spoke at Chatham House, won a minor propaganda battle; his proposals seemed reasonable even to the Czech Ambassador, Jan Masaryk. But reality was different. Sudeten representatives talking with German journalists at the same time admitted that the autonomy demand was indeed out of date. Even if the Czechs were willing to give full autonomy to the Sudeten regions, the Sudeten German Party would no longer accept it. And before Henlein arrived in London, Bonnet suggested to Halifax at Geneva on May 12 that Britain

> should put as much pressure as possible on Dr. Beneš to reach a settle-
> ment with the Sudeten Deutsch in order to save France from the
> cruel dilemma of dishonouring her Agreement or becoming involved
> in war. (*11*)

[*Italy.*] The position of Italy assumed great importance: it was now an index of the European situation. To the French Chamberlain predicted that Italy would stay neutral. On May 7 Lord Perth, the British Ambassador to Rome, informed the Italian government in confidence about the British and French steps at Prague. But then Mussolini's speech at Genoa a week later was very disappointing for the Allies. (*12*) It is true that on May 22 Ciano told Perth that Italy was expected to stay neutral and that certain conservatively inclined Italian newspapers, such as *La Stampa*, showed a degree of reserve about the Sudeten claims, (*13*) but the general tenor of the Italian press, radio, and official announcements definitely gave the small nations of central-eastern Europe the impression that the Axis stood firm and was bound to come out victorious. If Russia was neutral, noted a German Foreign Office memorandum early in June, Italy could be expected to be neutral in the case of a Czech war. But neutrality had its variations.

Strangely, more was widely expected from the French and the British than they intended to do. It was thought that due to the direct French alliance with Prague, the time had come now when the strength and determination of the Western Powers would balance the scales against Germany. The anxious tone of the British press was misinterpreted as a sign of Albion's doggedness in the face of any attempt to upset the European balance of power. Thus, in the month of May the Hungarian and Rumanian political scene showed a cautious shift toward the center. In Hungary Darányi, who introduced the program of Nazi appeasement, resigned, and the Regent appointed to the Premiership Imrédy, a man who was known to have had strong Conservative leanings and who had good contacts with British financial circles. In Rumania, the royal-authoritarian régime acted with dispatch and determination against the underground Iron Guardists and jailed their leaders. While certain Hungarian generals were impatiently asking for military talks with the Germans, Imrédy instructed the Hungarian Minister to Berlin not to heed such ambitious voices; also, the visit of Keitel to Budapest was postponed. Still, the extreme Right was agitating for a more aggressive course and it was obvious that any Hungarian régime which would have neglected to exploit a favorable occasion to redeem lost territories from Czechoslovakia would have had to face a popular revolt. Thus, government propaganda placed emphasis upon a revamped Army; the government press continued to assail Prague, while negotiations went on to assure, with the cooperation of Berlin if necessary, the neutrality of Yugoslavia in case of a Czech-Hungarian war. On May 16 the Hungarian government asked an Italian secret guarantee on the same issue, but Ciano was sceptical: he knew how Stoyadinovič would act. . . . Indeed, about this same time the Serb Premier informed Kiosseivanov, his Bulgarian colleague, that in his opinion the Czechs would not be helped. The Bulgar shared this view.

A Rumanian emissary arrived in Rome on May 19, but Ciano wasn't impressed by his long-winded talks. ("Among all diplomats, the Rumanians are the greatest liars," he wrote.) He was influenced by other portents: rumors flew that the German attack on Czechoslovakia was imminent and he had heard that Paul-Boncour's answer to the question whether France had mobilized was "almost." "In that 'almost,' " noted Ciano, "there is plenty of democracy, but not anymore the greatness of France." (*14*)

[*Poland, Russia.*] In spite of protracted and anxious French efforts, Beck did not intend to join hands with Czechoslovakia. (*15*) He continued to believe that an anti-Czech stand would once and for all ingratiate his country with Germany; moreover, he feared nothing more than the armed intervention of Russia in central-eastern Europe. Warsaw also had a small territorial demand to raise concerning the territory of Teschen, or the Olza, as the Poles called it, where Poles lived and which the Czechs took away in 1920. He wished to show that he, too, could act as ruthlessly and aptly as the contemporary Machiavellians, and could manoeuvre his nation through all dangers, only to emerge later as the Great Statesman of the Sixth Great Power of

Europe. Yet on May 22 a vague Polish statement was communicated to Bonnet by Lukasiewicz, the Polish Ambassador, containing an allusion to closer Polish-French collaboration — a statement which, because of its vagueness, has since evoked a minor historiographical debate. (16)

The ties between the Little Entente members (17), France's eastern allies, were very loose. Yet there was Russia. Two days after the *Anschluss*, Kalinin greeted a visiting Czech trade mission to Moscow in an unusually friendly spirit; four days later Litvinov assured the Czechoslovak Minister of the continuing validity of the Russian-Czechoslovak Mutual Assistance Pact. The British then spurned the Russian plan to confer. There is no doubt that the personal ill feelings which Chamberlain and his circle had toward Russia contributed to the Czechoslovak catastrophe. There is, however, ample evidence today to shatter the almost universally accepted thesis that in 1938 everybody but Russia betrayed Czechoslovakia and that, consequently, the German-Russian Pact was the direct outcome of Munich. The evidence which is now available points to the contrary: in all probability Russia, just as Britain, would have left the Czechs alone in the case of an isolated German-Czech war.*

The record of Soviet diplomacy from May to September 1938 indicates a steady tendency to evoke technical reservations concerning the Russian treaty obligations. On May 12, Bonnet and Litvinov met at Geneva. Litvinov reiterated that Russia would assist Czechoslovakia; because of the lack of a common frontier, however, active assistance would be forthcoming only if Poland and Rumania consented to the passage of the Red Army. But this permission was evidently impossible to obtain. Bonnet turned to the Rumanian Foreign Minister, Comnen, who refused unhesitatingly; the attitude of the Poles was even more obvious. (18)

[*The May 22 crisis.*] Municipal elections were scheduled in Czechoslovakia for May 22; after the 15th, violence grew in the Sudeten regions. All this coincided with previously scheduled troop manoeuvres in southeastern Germany; the European newspapers saw a major crisis in the making. On May 20, partial mobilization was suddenly declared in Prague. (19) The critical day of May 21 passed and the elections were postponed; no German attack came and the tension slowly lessened. (20) In May it was yet too early for Hitler

---

* See "Munich in Retrospect: The Russian Rôle" in Appendix to Part II, p. 166.

to act; but, as British diplomatic activity was considerable on that unusual week-end, it has been erroneously stated that a show of Western determination made Hitler recoil. The great Liberal newspapers of Paris, London, and New York rejoiced, and the mobilization of the few Czech divisions was hailed as a magnificent counterblow to Hitlerite plans. But this was not the case: the result was that Hitler's pride was outraged; he assailed the "Western liars," and on May 28 he made his decision: the Czech problem must be liquidated in 1938. He ordered the immediate construction of heavy fortifications along the western borders of Germany: the Siegfried Line. He said: "We must do it this year." October 1 was set as the final date. (*21*)

The Czechoslovak crisis: Phase II

The British Ambassador reported from Prague on June 2:

> I think it very desirable that we should continue to show sympathetic appreciation of the fact that Czechoslovak Government have hitherto accepted very far-reaching and doubtless unpalatable advice and appear to have been doing their utmost of late at any rate to cope with the problems which might well baffle the wisest statesmanship.

That Hodža had serious intentions of coming to an agreement was not to be doubted, wrote Eisenlohr to his government a week later: this the Sudeten Party itself had to recognize. (*1*) But, he added, even with the happiest outcome, "the thousand-year-old conflict in the Bohemian region would not be ended, nor would old wounds be closed."

London was veering toward German viewpoints and mediation. Newton disagreed with Henderson, and Bonnet did not fully trust his envoy in Prague, M. Lacroix; Kennard from Warsaw reported that the Poles were more and more anti-Czech, that they feared the Russians and were for a Polish-Hungarian common frontier after the partition of Czechoslovakia. The German envoy on June 8 estimated sentiments in London very ably: the idea of a plebiscite was gaining ground, and an influential Englishman gave this advice to a German friend: "Don't shoot Czechoslovakia, strangle her." Henderson saw Ribbentrop on the 10th and showed his sympathy again with the Sudeten cause. On the same evening he drafted a concrete proposal of mediation: he and Hitler, in case of a final deadlock, would decide on terms which would then be imposed on both sides. And Bonnet praised Henlein's restraint to the Czech envoy. (2)

[*The United States and Germany.*] If the reports and attitudes of certain British diplomats seemed to be inconsistent, the American inconsistencies were far worse. On one hand the American press and radio turned more and more sharply against Germany; on the other the positions of the American diplomats were widely divergent. Bullitt in Paris was deeply worried, while Kennedy in London and Wilson in Berlin were not unsympathetic to German views. All this momentarily impressed Hitler, who gave his assent to better German-American relations: Captain Wiedemann was sent to tell Kuhn of the German-American Bund to make the Bund drop its aggressive and conspicuous rôle. On May 13 Henderson reported to Halifax that his views closely coincided with those of his American colleague in Berlin. About a week later Kennedy in London offered to assist his German colleague there. The German Ambassador in Washington did not think much of Kennedy, but Dirksen wrote on May 31: "Regardless whether Kennedy possesses the influence which he ascribes to himself, I should consider it wrong to rebuff him and not take advantage of his offer." (3)

The same day came Dieckhoff's report from Washington: Roosevelt could not openly side with France and Britain, however much he would like to do so, as "after the setback which he suffered with the Chicago speech and the Brussels conference, he has become somewhat more cautious, and Hull, who thinks in quieter terms, has succeeded in preventing him from taking unnecessary risks." Dieckhoff thought that in a world war, the United States would nevertheless side with Britain:

> Feeling here has become much more acute and bitter in recent months and the few friends we still have are so timorous and dumb that there is little to prevent the entry of the United States into war against us.

On June 13 Kennedy had a talk with the German Ambassador in London, during which — showing a curious misunderstanding of ambassadorial duties — he inveighed against Britain, the country to which he was accredited. (4) Not even the Germans could take him seriously, as Dieckhoff had reported from Washington that Kennedy was known for his poor judgment.

The lack of coordination in American diplomacy strikingly emerges from a memorandum which Davies drafted in Moscow three days later and which ended with the following summary:

> If Japan should go berserk by any chance, the fact that Russia is at her back door is of consequence to us.
>
> The Soviet Union is more friendly to the United States than to any other foreign power. That is quite clear.
>
> If the [Soviet Union] should be excluded from the proposed Four Power Pact and become isolated (as it now seems to be convinced it will be) there is reason to believe that it may continue to live unto itself and develop indefinitely. It may develop into a very potential threat to world economic and political stability.
>
> Communism holds no serious threat to the United States. Friendly relations in the future may be of great general value.

Three days later, very unexpectedly, Stalin personally appeared at the Foreign Commissariat when Davies was paying his farewell visit, and an unusually cordial talk on Russian-American relations ensued. Perhaps Stalin knew the contents of Davies' memorandum; perhaps not. He was at any rate aware of the departing Ambassador's sympathies.

[*Henderson in Berlin.*]   At least the British envoy to Germany was unmistakably consistent in his opinions and advice. He assailed "Czech extremists" in his dispatches to Halifax, although the Foreign Office did not always agree with his opinions. Halifax gave a speech at the end of June in Chatham House, showing sympathetic comprehension of the Sudetens' cause; but Henderson went further and on July 3 intimated to Ribbentrop that the present British government understood Germany's aims in Central Europe. Newton in Prague saw things more clearly, especially since his conservative German colleague once in awhile honestly told him that Germany's aim was to do away with all of Czechoslovakia. Newton pointed out:

> When it suits them, German spokesmen talk of splendid and meritorious discipline of Sudeten German population . . . On other occasions, however, it is suggested . . . that Sudeten Germans are an undisciplined mob out of their leaders' control. Either may be credible but not both.

Henderson kept insisting. On July 18 he said, "The moment has come for Prague to get a real twist of the screw. And something that the Czech nation as a whole will appreciate. It is a French job, but if they won't face it, I believe that we shall have to." He made similar statements to German officials, and failed to challenge their criticism of Newton. (5) Around July 18–20 there arose some controversy between Henderson, Newton, and Sir Orme Sargent of the Foreign Office: Henderson's new argument was that even in case of war, Czechoslovakia "would have to be redrawn." On the same day, obviously to strengthen his position, he said that the French envoy to Berlin intimated to him that the French themselves might like to get rid of Beneš. "But," he added, "I fear that the Czechs as a whole are an incorrigibly pig-headed people." On July 21 the Foreign Office informed him that intelligence pointed toward German plans for an autumn war. (6)

[*Calculations about war.*]   In spite of the warnings given to the British envoy by his own Foreign Office, Weizsäcker could note on July 28:

> The British Ambassador yesterday happened to speak to me about our present military preparations, giving them, however, the description: "understandable defense measures." (7)

This position was, of course, highly encouraging to Berlin; nevertheless there was some divergence there too. In mid-June Albrecht Haushofer, the noted geopolitician's son, visited Britain and upon his return wrote a memorandum advising caution against underestimating Britain's will and capacities. But on the margin of this memorandum Ribbentrop wrote: "Secret Service propaganda!" (8) Weizsäcker shared Haushofer's fears. His memorandum said that the Czech fruit could not yet be plucked: the risks were too great. (9) Dirksen from London informed Berlin that there was much good will, and an "essential part of Chamberlain's program is agreement with the Rome-Berlin Axis." (10) He nevertheless warned that Britain would probably side with France if it came to war.

At that time Göring and other members of the Nazi hierarchy became especially violent against Czechoslovakia in their conversations with foreign diplomats: ("the abdominal appendix of Europe"; "let them be deported where they belong, to Russia"). On July 21 Ribbentrop had an important conversation with Weizsäcker; with considerable courage the latter warned him. A postponement was necessary, he said. But Ribbentrop insisted that the risk of a war with the Western Powers could be taken: the German Air Force and the Army were so good that it was a good gamble. On July 31 Weizsäcker repeated his arguments, and subtly used some of Hitler's previous statements to attribute to Hitler the opinion that at present an act of direct aggression against Czechoslovakia should not be made. (*11*) On August 19 Ribbentrop explained to Weizsäcker, who still expressed a certain caution, that Hitler "was firmly resolved to settle the Czech affair by force of arms" by mid-October at the latest and would himself head an armored division. At the same time a British intelligence report from Germany indicated that Hitler and the High Command were anxious to find out how Britain would react militarily in case of a Czech war. (*12*) On August 21 Lady Chilston, the wife of the British Ambassador, asked the German Ambassador in Moscow: "Come and tell me: will you be naughty?" (*13*)

Three days later Dirksen from London noted:

1) The growing British comprehension of the Czech problem,
2) the increasing British readiness to take our demands into consideration, always providing that peace be maintained.

A week before, Stewart, Chamberlain's confidant and press secretary, had told a German friend of his that "the British Government were prepared to demand the most far-reaching sacrifices from Czechoslovakia if only Germany would adhere to peaceful methods in settling the Czech question." (*14*) But the wheels were slowly turning towards war. An Estonian diplomat forecast that the end of September would be the date of Czechoslovakia's invasion; on August 23 and again four days later Attolico asked the Germans, at Mussolini's request, for the projected date, but upon Hitler's instruction this information was not given. There was still Neurath, jealous of Ribbentrop, who called on Henderson on August 26 and told him that the generals were not for war, and neither was public opinion. There was Weizsäcker, who on August 30 wrote a summary memorandum for Ribbentrop:

> Germany is keyed up for war with Czechoslovakia and is completely prepared for it. . . . Hungary's readiness for war is . . . conditional. . . . Italy seems at present neither to desire a European war nor entirely to shun one. . . . Czechoslovakia is playing for high stakes and would not avoid a war, in view of her confidence in receiving assistance from the outside. . . . Great Britain and France wish to pre-

vent war as far as they can. . . . Poland is on the alert and wants to keep all roads open for herself. . . . The only certainty is that, in event of war, Poland will not permit the Russians to set foot in their country . . .

His conclusion was:

> The coalition of the Western Powers can, if it will, decide the war against Germany without any great bloodshed by the mere employment of siege tactics. The consequences of such a defeat for Adolf Hitler's reconstruction work are obvious.

But there were others, Forster, Gauleiter of Danzig, for example, who a day later chatted with the horrified Burckhardt, the League's High Commissioner there: war was certain and immediate. "There would not be much time wasted, but matters would be settled by brute force. For a start, 1000 aircraft would be sent over Prague, which would be razed to the ground." And four days earlier a secret document had been drafted in the German Foreign Ministry: "it will be generally assumed that Poland will be the next in turn. But the later this assumption sinks into international politics as a firm factor, the better." (*15*)

     •   •   ·   ,   •   ·   •

[*The Runciman mission; mediation proposals.*]   The British ideas about mediation began to crystallize in mid-June (*16*); the Czechs were none too happy about this development, feeling that whatever the mediator's recommendations might be, the issue would not be decided by demographic arguments but by the actual balance of power. The choice fell on Lord Runciman in London to be the mediator; Newton foresaw the possible academic nature of Runciman's recommendations: "The real reason why Germany was making such difficulties was because she wished to force Czechoslovakia into her orbit." Chamberlain's final decision was taken when Hitler sent his well-mannered emissary, Captain Wiedemann, to London on July 18 on a secret visit; Wiedemann made a good impression.

Runciman's mission is excellently portrayed in Wheeler-Bennett's monograph; there is no need to dwell upon it here. It meant a further step in Chamberlain's personal diplomacy, with Henderson's opinions and Sir Horace Wilson's background advice (*17*) heeded. At the same time it encouraged the Sudeten considerably. (*18*) Few had illusions about the mission's efficacy, and as early as July 30 Henderson and others in London envisaged a Four Power Conference (with Italy included) as the last resort. (*19*) On August 2 Henderson proposed concrete conditions under which a Four Power Conference would be convoked. Halifax was not yet decided: he received some intelligent suggestions from Lord Tweedsmuir of Canada, who on August 5 advised, "perpetually telling Beneš of what we might *not* do in the event of trouble: and tactfully reminding the Germans of what we *might* do. And meanwhile use every effort to coerce the two sides, by joint pressure and persuasion, into agreement." He was against the idea of a plebiscite and against "doing over Czechoslovakia if I can avoid it." Meanwhile Runciman wearily trod the stony yards of the Sudeten castles and inns (*20*); the Czechs were now fearful and cooperative; on August 19 Hodža informed Runciman that he was ready to appoint Sudeten leaders to internal administrative posts. But the mission had already failed. Not that this fact changed the British attitude; Henderson telegraphed on August 22:

> I feel so strongly also on the big British issue. Have we or have we not got to fight Germany again? The followers of the Crowe tradition in your Department argue and have long argued that it is inevitable. I regard that attitude as nothing short of disastrous. It may prove to be inevitable, but it seems to me a suicidal policy fatalistically to accept it as so. If we fight Germany this year or next over the Sudeten question, we shall probably beat her but it will mean that we shall have to go on fighting her again and again, until one day we may be ourselves beaten. . . . That is not defeatism. Defeatism to my mind is saying that we must fight Germany again, when there is still a chance and a big one that we need never do so. It is repugnant to me to run bad horses and back losing ones all the time. I would fight Germany tomorrow for a good cause but I refuse to contemplate our doing so for the Sudeten. If they were Hungarians or Poles or Roumanians or the citizens of any small nation, all England would be on their side. They are Germans, so we shut our eyes to realities and are influenced by other considerations, some honourable, some chivalrous but many egotistical or inspired by fear. (*21*)

On August 24 Henderson was summoned to London for consultations; on August 27 Sir John Simon made a conciliatory speech at Lanark. But mediation faded: the crisis grew.

[*End of the Little Entente: Rumania.*]   In the meantime Czecho-slovakia's erstwhile allies completed their tenuous and circuitous routes toward desertion. Not that the Little Entente could have been directly effective: of the 2550 miles of Czechoslovak frontiers only 125 bor-dered on a friendly state, Rumania. But Rumania's indirect impor-tance was great: if what King Carol told Gamelin in 1937 was true, the Russians could come through and help the Czechs. King Carol was cautious, however: he saw no signs of a Western diplomatic counteroffensive; he did not want to sacrifice eventual German sym-pathies for antiquated notions about honoring contracts and respect-ing neighbors. Instead, he decided to approach Italy, especially as the main Rumanian concern was with Budapest, not Berlin.

In June the Rumanian Minister in Berlin asked the Italian Ambas-sador to find out whether Germany planned to use Hungary against the Czechs. Attolico went to the Foreign Office, where Weizsäcker assured him that there were no such plans; the German rightly deduced from the conversation that Italy may have indicated to Rumania that she would probably remain outside of the conflict. (*22*)

Now Carol and his Foreign Minister urged Beneš and Krofta to try to solve the Sudeten conflict peacefully, and on August 17 the German Minister to Bucharest gave a summary report on Rumania's position. His opinion was that Rumania would not aid the Czechs; she would also prevent the eventual passage of Russian troops,

> and, like her ally Poland, will, in theory, resist the passage of Soviet aircraft. The fact that she does not possess the necessary anti-aircraft defenses . . . is quite another matter, as is also the fact that, out of fear of being involved in the conflict, she might not have the courage to take open belligerent action by employing fighter squadrons against Soviet aircraft violating her territory. (*23*)

Nevertheless, during the last Little Entente Foreign Ministers con-ference at Bled on August 22, the Rumanian Comnen confidentially told Krofta that he had decided to inform Litvinov that Rumania would not interfere with Soviet aircraft flying high over her territory into Czechoslovakia. Of troops there was no word.

[*End of the Little Entente: Yugoslavia.*]   Stoyadinovič and Ciano met at Venice on June 18. The Yugoslav wanted to find out what the Italians would do: he himself, recorded Ciano, "does not, in the least, want to drag his country into a conflict with Germany to save the artificial and unfriendly Czechoslovakia, nor to please France which is openly hostile to him." Stoyadinovič asked the Italians to make Hungary abstain from an attack on Czechoslovakia: for thus he could evade all obligations. Ciano subsequently informed Berlin that Stoyadinovič was more pro-Axis than ever. (*24*)

Similar anxious queries were addressed to Rome by the Hungarians. There the power of the extremists was increasing and the German minority openly supported the local Nazi Arrow-Cross movement, opposing the heterogeneous government party. The Minister in Berlin finally brought about Keitel's visit to Budapest in June and urged staff talks with the Germans. Imrédy's position was not very strong. Sometime in July he perceived the contours of British appease-ment. On the 18th he went to Rome with Kánya, inquiring about Italy's stand and asking Mussolini to sound out Belgrade and Bucharest: what would they do if Hungary went to war with the Czechs? Kánya said that he had no confidence in Stoyadinovič and ruled out a unilateral Hungarian attack on Czechoslovakia. It was Mussolini who was impatient now. He told the Hungarians that France and Britain would not fight: they were old and tired. He was irked that Hungary had not adhered to the Anti-Comintern Pact as yet; he advised Hungary to exploit the favorable occasion which would occur when Czechoslovakia would start to fall apart, and he promised to make certain of Rumanian and Yugoslav neutrality. At a state banquet he toasted good relations with Yugoslavia, and the courtesy call of Italian warships at a Yugoslav port was announced while the Hungarians were in Rome. (*25*)

Ciano now asked Stoyadinovič and received a classic answer from which it could be deduced that Yugoslavia would not go to war with Hungary if only the latter provoked a Czechoslovak war declaration; Stoyadinovič thus indirectly invited the Hungarians to produce a fake attack upon themselves in the best totalitarian manner. But it did not come to this.

[*The Horthy visit to Germany; the Bled conference.*] Months before, it had been arranged that the Hungarian Regent would pay a state visit to Hitler in August. For a time, Horthy hesitated whether he should go in such critical times and manifest his alignment with the Germans. But now Imrédy, previously hesitant, pressed him, and Csáky intimated to the German Minister in Budapest that the latter should make the Regent undertake the journey, for in person Hitler would undoubtedly be able to influence him greatly: then all Hungarian hesitations would be over. At the same time Kánya and the opposition leader Eckhardt insisted that something be done to counterbalance the effect of the Regent's German trip. It was agreed that a Hungarian diplomat would be sent to Bled in Yugoslavia, where the Little Entente Foreign Ministers were to gather at the same time as the Horthy-Hitler meeting.

From August 19 to 23 Horthy was in Germany. His talks with Hitler were not at all successful; Hitler was angry and Horthy was reserved. Hitler assailed Kánya's duplicity: Why did Hungary have to negotiate with the Little Entente at Bled? According to the German minutes, "the counterarguments of Kánya were little convincing." Ribbentrop inquired what Hungary would do in case of war. Horthy presented obstacles: not only must Yugoslav neutrality be unconditionally assured, but "if Hungary marches towards the north and perhaps the east," she will need more arms and equipment; as Hungarian rearmament was in its very early stages, two more years of development were needed. Nevertheless, Horthy "wished to put Hungary's intention to participate on record." Hitler was rude. (26) He told the Regent: "whoever wants to join the meal would have to participate in the cooking as well"; he could not eat words, Hitler complained, and the time of an eventual Hungarian intervention was not even mentioned. Kánya, unaware that the same date had been set in the *Case Green* plans, finally said to Ribbentrop that the Hungarian armed forces would be "ready to march" by October 1. Somewhat mollified, Hitler bid farewell to Horthy on the 23rd; to the deeply impressed Imrédy two days later he stated that he demanded nothing of Hungary and that this fact had better be taken into account. (27)

At the same time the three Foreign Ministers met in Bled. German notes were sent to the Little Entente capitals after August 15, notes which sowed discord and hesitancy at Bled; but that was hardly necessary. The conversants decided to declare their willingness to acquiesce in Hungarian rearmament. Thus, months behind accomplished facts, they demonstrated some good will toward Hungary: a joint agreement was signed, lifting the respective restricting clauses of the Trianon Treaty of 1920. After this, the ministers proceeded to discuss Czechoslovakia; Krofta, however, could not succeed in committing his Yugoslav colleague.

[*Poland.*] And all French efforts to make Poland budge were in vain. Public opinion in Poland was pro-French and on June 18 the Czechs invited Warsaw to enter into direct talks, but Beck rather preferred a neutral bloc further east, and approached Hungary and the Baltic states. Not that Berlin was happy. On June 23 Moltke, the German Ambassador to Warsaw, spoke with Beck, showing German dissatisfaction because of Polish designs on Slovakia and the creation of a Polish-Hungarian common frontier; a new *cordon sanitaire* this was to be, between Germany and Russia. In July the Poles asked that Runciman investigate the grievances of the small Polish minority in Teschen also, insisting, however, that they acted quite independently of Germany. The Polish opposition tried to do its best, and in July the exiled leader of the Peasant Party, Witós, and one of the party leaders, Kukiel, met secretly in the Tatra mountains to discuss eventual action against the foreign policy of Beck. But the opposition could not influence Beck, who could only feel that his policies were justified when on August 11 Lipski reported from Berlin that Henderson had told him privately: "The Germans were right when they asserted that, owing to the intransigence of the Czechs, the only effective measure was force."

[*And the Russian "enigma."*] Litvinov and Maisky, the "old school," of course remonstrated with the Western Powers, and if nothing else, this had some propaganda value. On August 17 Maisky told Halifax that the Soviet Union would "certainly do its bit" if Czechoslovakia were attacked. Suritz, the Soviet Ambassador in Paris, tried to intervene with Bonnet against the sending of Runciman (Bonnet told the German Ambassador of this intervention); Litvinov on July 7 told the Italian envoy to Moscow that he was displeased with Italy's new foreign policy, which was not sufficiently wary of Germany. Yet there was no one who could gauge what exactly the Soviets would do: even Beneš himself asked Bonnet in July to find out how Russia could help the Czechs. (He chose the right man to ask such a question!) The Germans themselves did not seem to be unduly anxious about prospects of Russian intervention. (*28*) It was, rather, their opponents who were. On August 22 the French Ambassador to Moscow said to his German counterpart: "I hope from my heart that it does not come to a German-French conflict. You know as well as I do for whom we are working if we get at loggerheads." Even Beneš saw this: on August 27 he told a group of Sudeten dele-

gates that he was "afraid of two things only: a war and then Bolshevism." (29) The American Ambassador in Paris, Bullitt, agreed
with such views. He said to Sir Eric Phipps:

> Russia's great wish is to provoke a general conflagration in which
> she herself will play but little part, beyond perhaps a little bombing
> from a distance, but after which she will arise like a phoenix, but out
> of all our ashes, and bring about a world revolution. (30)

Bonnet, pressed by Soviet diplomats for a more energetic French
stand against Germany, distrusted them and agreed with Bullitt; a
British Embassy official in Moscow expressed himself in the same vein
to a German colleague, and this, of course, was reported back to
Berlin. Schulenburg, the German Ambassador, was quiet and undisturbed. On August 28 he even ventured to tell Litvinov in a routine
conversation that he thought a German-Soviet war to be unlikely,
for Poland and Rumania would not grant crossing rights to Russian
troops. Litvinov answered that he was not so sure, especially as
Rumania seemed to be much alarmed by the Czech crisis. More,
however, he did not — or could not — say.

Then on August 31, the French Embassy at Moscow was instructed
to ask the Soviet government directly about its position in a possible
German-Czechoslovak war; a telegram from Lacroix in Prague confirmed that Rumania would "close her eyes" and merely protest, and
not interfere with Soviet flights over her territory. On September 2
Litvinov received Payart, the French chargé. The Russian Foreign
Commissar himself cited what Comnen had said to Krofta at Bled;
he also said that Rumania had improved relations with the Soviets.
Yet this was not sufficient authorization for the 'Soviet Union.
Rumania — or Poland — must officially declare the right of passage,
and as both Litvinov and Payart knew that this was impossible, the
Russian added that perhaps the League of Nations could intervene.
(31) It was evident that the League, with its slow machinery and
public discussion was entirely unsatisfactory, nay, impossible: there
was no doubt that no gentle hint emanating from Geneva could make
Rumanians or Poles accept what they feared with all their souls,
namely, the spectre of a Red Army in Galicia, Bukovina, Bessarabia,
Volhynia.

Now the French Minister to Bucharest spoke to Comnen, who
merely reaffirmed what he had said about the Russians flying through,

and, at the same time, he invoked the Polish-Rumanian Pact of 1926, a treaty directed against eventual intervention of Russia; even if the Rumanian government would not object to the Soviet passage, this treaty categorically forbid such permission without the consent of Poland. Here was the vicious circle; the imperfections of the French alliance system were revealed now at the most critical time. But then Russia herself was not at all eager to be called to the field by a Rumanian's permission. On September 11 Bonnet met Litvinov and Comnen at Geneva. Litvinov reaffirmed what he had said nine days before. "We examined the Czechoslovak question," writes Comnen. "Litvinov did not make any allusion to technical possibilities of assisting Czechoslovakia." After they separated, Bonnet went into conference with the Rumanian, who pointed out on a map the technical impossibility of transporting any significant number of Russian troops through the narrow corridor of Rumanian territory into Czechoslovakia within a reasonable time. Comnen also surmised that the Russian demand for passage permission probably harbored the hidden design of occupying Bessarabia without an armed conflict: with their armies once inside, the Soviets would expect to stay there.

Thus, as early as September 2, Paris came to know definitely that unconditional Russian assistance would not be forthcoming. At the same time other grave events were taking place.

[*Two decisions.*] Although on September 2 Bonnet asked for the German Ambassador and uttered honeyed and unctuous words of peace ("the Führer the greatest statesman," etc.), this was merely an evasion of critical realities. For it was now clear that mediation had failed and the time had come to put the utmost pressure on the Czechs. Bonnet's words about Beneš when he spoke to Phipps were less honeyed: " . . . if Beneš would not accept Lord Runciman's verdict, France would consider herself released from her engagements to Czechoslovakia." On the 3rd, Newton was ordered to tell Beneš "in the name of His Majesty's Government what might be the fate of Czechoslovakia in the event of hostilities." On the same day Neville Chamberlain decided to make a dramatic move: he would fly to Hitler, if necessary, a decision which he kept to himself for ten more days.

Almost in the same hour another decision was taken in Hitler's mountain castle: "0 Hour" and "X Day" for the invasion of Czechoslovakia were set — noon, on September 27.

Phase III: Berchtesgaden, Godesberg, Munich

Beneš made up his mind the next day. He asked for two of the Sudeten leaders, Kundt and Sebekovsky; when they entered his office, the President told them to write their full demands on a piece of paper: they would be fulfilled. Beneš wanted to call the Sudeten bluff by acceding to their original demands, to make them commit themselves to a regional autonomy plan which still would fall short of the German aim of detaching the whole territory from Czechoslovakia. (*1*)

But all this was too late: Beneš did not succeed. Ashton-Gwatkin of Runciman's mission described Henlein's personal staff thus: "gray uniforms, high black boots, clean, decent-looking fellows." Henderson wrote Cadogan the same day, September 6:

> If I am right I do wish it might be possible to get at any rate "The Times," Camrose, Beaverbrook Press, etc., to write up Hitler as the apostle of peace. It will be terribly shortsighted if this is not done. Cannot the News Department help?

It could. Next morning the stately London *Times*, regarded widely as reflecting the views of Whitehall, appeared with an editorial which stated, among other things, "the cession of that fringe of alien population who are contiguous to the nation with which they are united by race" would be desirable. Immediately a cold chill fell upon Prague. Later in the day, the Foreign Office denied that the editorial represented official British views; but the Germans were told that this denial should not be taken too seriously. (*2*)

[*The United States.*] Ambassador Bullitt made a strong pro-Allied speech at a commemoration ceremony at Point-de-Graves on the 4th, but later he told a French friend: "You may count on us for everything except troops and loans." President Roosevelt at his press conference five days later termed it "100 per cent wrong" to say that the United States would eventually join Britain and France. On September 10 Kennedy appeared at Whitehall and asked Halifax "whether over the weekend it might not be possible for the Soviet Government to make some movement that would compel attention, such as concentration of aeroplanes near the frontier." In view of Kennedy's evident pro-German and anti-Russian sympathies, it is probable that this query was made at Roosevelt's instructions. (*3*)

[*France and Poland; France and Britain.*] Roosevelt apparently did not know how ambiguous the Soviet position really was; neither did he know that the Poles had informed Bonnet of their probable neutrality and had added that they would fight Russia if her army attempted passage through Polish lands. The French Ambassador at Warsaw requested Paris to influence Russia not to take measures "which might determine Poland to throw herself into the German camp." (*4*) Kennard from Warsaw reported essentially the same. The British envoy from Belgrade telegraphed that Yugoslavia would almost certainly not aid the Czechs, and the Rumanian Minister on the 9th directly informed Berlin for the first time that "Rumania, too, would do [its] best not to be involved" and was requesting Germany's help merely to keep the Hungarians out.

There was now a divergence between the French Premier and his Foreign Minister. While Bonnet was vague, hesitant, afraid, Daladier forgot his anxiety and lost his patience for a moment; on the 9th he told Sir Eric Phipps that France would march if Germany attacked. Halifax was worried; he said to the French envoy in London that "not only His Majesty's Government but British public opinion" were unprepared to enter a war on account of a German attack on the Czechs; with diplomatic casuistry he almost turned the French arguments into advocacy of a preventive war.

The definite question was raised next afternoon. Bonnet asked the British Ambassador directly: "Will you march with us?"

Almost forty-eight hours passed before Halifax gave his answer:

> So far, therefore, as I am in a position to give any answer at this stage to M. Bonnet's question, it would have to be that while His Majesty's Government would never allow the security of France to be threatened, they are unable to make precise statements of the character of their future action, or the time at which it would be taken, in circumstances that they cannot at present foresee. (*5*)

[*The Nuremberg Congress; the day of September 13.*] While, in the words of Churchill, the British and French cabinets presented a picture of "two overripe melons crushed together, whereas what was needed was a gleam of steel," the Nuremberg Party Congress began, with dignitaries and Ambassadors gathered and listening to Hitler make (*6*) a ranting, war-like speech. On September 13 a strange, depressing tension was palpable in Berlin. The Counselor of the

British Embassy wrote about the absolute absence of any deep public animosity to the Czechs or West Powers. "The people are like sheep being led to the slaughter. If war breaks out they will march and do their duty for some time at least. Their subsequent behavior will depend on developments." Some conservative German generals conspired against Hitler; even opportunistic diplomats, Weizsäcker and others, seemed to waver away from allegiance to the Führer and Ribbentrop. Just before his return to Berlin, Henderson dined with high German diplomats (Ribbentrop was not present) and characteristically described their mood: "Some of them talked a lot of treason to my colleagues." Nevertheless, the British envoy himself saw the German uncertainties now; although he had some praise for Hitler's speech, he said that if, after all the British warnings, Britain still did not take up arms when Germany deliberately provoked war with Czechoslovakia, she would be regarded by the Germans

> with universal contempt. The opponents of the régime will hate us for our cowardice whilst the Nazi, far from thanking us for our neutrality, will be infuriated at our impotent reprobation.

On this September 13th "the opponents" were indeed active within Germany. In the evening came the news that Henlein had abruptly broken off all negotiations with Prague. (7) Weizsäcker, in a desperate mood, told Attolico that the Czech proposals almost completely satisfied the original German desires. Within an hour, all these uncertainties were abruptly suspended. For Chamberlain's message was flashed to Hitler: tomorrow morning he would fly over to meet him at Berchtesgaden. (8)

[*Chamberlain with Hitler at Berchtesgaden.*]   To the lion's den, then; but the eagle was old and tired and carried an umbrella.

The impression which Hitler received was about the opposite of that which was needed: a peaceful old merchant instead of a stern British negotiator. Worse, Chamberlain flattered Hitler; there were some pleasant exchanges and for a time the German was touched by Chamberlain's goodwill and celestial journey. But that was about all. Chamberlain gained some time; he promised to make the Czechs accept concrete territorial demands, and Hitler agreed to wait for a few days. The time won, however, did not make up for the tremendous psychological victory Hitler had gained. (9)

[*International repercussions.*] The Italians gloated. Mussolini congratulated Hitler and asked for his suggestions for a contemplated speech. On September 19, at Trieste, he demanded plebiscites. It was now clear that Italy planned to partake fully in the diplomatic game, and it was intimated that Italian troops would be available to police and occupy the contested areas in the case of plebiscites. Immediately on the return of Chamberlain, Poland asked for plebiscites; Hungary, which on the 14th requested in a circular note that there should be no discrimination in handling the Hungarian minorities, followed suit. On the 20th Imrédy wrote Hitler that Hungary would oppose a solution merely between Germans and Czechs; on the same afternoon large revisionist demonstrations were held in Budapest and Warsaw; on that evening Hitler promised the Polish and Hungarian envoys full German support for their territorial demands. (*10*) As early as August 31 Stoyadinovič had let the German Minister to Belgrade know that Yugoslavia would stay out even if Hungary were involved, unless Hungary made an "unprovoked" attack on the Czechs. (*11*) The Yugoslav Minister in Rome reaffirmed his country's "benevolent neutrality" toward the Axis on September 13, and added another, new reservation: If Hungarian participation in the German attack was *only of a temporary character*, Yugoslavia in all probability would not intervene. (*12*) Stoyadinovič told Heeren, the German Minister, that he regarded the Sudeten question as he did the Austrian problem: both were internal affairs of the German people. The Little Entente sank quietly but swiftly: without a ripple.

[*The Sudeten disturbances.*] Immediately after Hitler's Nuremberg speech and Henlein's breaking off of negotiations, the Sudeten Germans attacked Czech police, civilians, and military posts; a grave riot at Moravska-Ostrava (*13*) served as a pretext. The German Minister conceded that the Czech press was relatively calm, and the German consulate at Brno reported on the 17th that great masses of the Sudeten Germans were somehow losing faith. He felt that the Reich radio broadcasts about non-existent incidents impaired Sudeten morale. A subsequent report established that there were more Czechs dead in the riots than Germans; on the 20th the German chargé wrote: "There can be no doubt that the departure of the leaders of the Party [into Germany] is viewed as flight by the Sudeten German population remaining behind in the country." On that day a virtual state of war prevailed in the German-inhabited territories of Czechoslovakia; in the border town of Asch — a minuscule salient of Czechoslovakia jutting into Germany — the frontier posts were hacked away and a few German troops entered, setting up a line well inside Czech territory.

[*The Anglo-French Plan: its birth and acceptance.*] Beneš informed the Western Powers on the 17th that he would discuss the cession of certain mountain salients which had about 850,000 Sudetens. (In 1919–20 President Masaryk had thought of such a redrawing of frontiers.) This, however, was not enough now. On the 18th it was arranged that the French statesmen should go to London and discuss a "new plan," which, in substance, amounted to granting Hitler's Berchtesgaden demands. (*14*) The tone of the London talks was sad: each party tried to pass responsibility along to the other. The British were evasive, as always: "Nothing was further from [their] thoughts than that the French Government should fail to honor their obligations to the Czechoslovak Government," but it was France's business how she carried out her own obligations. The French were against plebiscites; at the end Chamberlain went so far as to say that even after a victorious war against Germany, Britain would not restore Czechoslovakia with her present boundaries. Chamberlain was "still against any British engagement in Central Europe." He said that neither America nor Russia would help. "You shall be alone. Will you reconstitute Czechoslovakia as it is?" (*15*)

Only with great difficulty could Daladier bring about a Western guarantee of the new frontiers as defined by the Anglo-French Plan. In the early hours of September 19 this plan was telegraphed to Prague, where Beneš, according to Newton, was "very receptive to any reason which will help him to justify acceptance to his people." Now very great pressure was put upon Prague. Intelligence there feared a sudden German attack, and the Czechs began to mobilize, although the British had asked them not to (and this request was communicated to the Germans). Beneš could not procrastinate for more than a few hours. (*16*) For a moment he turned to Moscow (in spite of the objections of his Premier and Chief of Staff, who were chary of any Russian move, seeing therein but an ineffective gesture and one sufficient to furnish a pretext for a German attack). But Beneš saw Alexandrovsky, the Soviet envoy: once more he asked what Russia would do. The answer was that Russia would help *if* France did. (Litvinov had told Comnen the same thing the day before.) *If* amounted to a new excuse, and Beneš' circle thus closed. (*17*) At five in the afternoon of September 21, the President informed the Western Ministers that he submitted to their plan. In Prague, indignation was grave and ran deep with the people.

[*Chamberlain with Hitler at Godesberg.*] On September 21 Kordt reported from London:

> I have it on the best authority that Chamberlain is going to Godesberg with such a fund of good will toward Germany as no British statesman before him has had. Should he succeed in settling the Czech question, and thereby lay the foundation stone of an Anglo-German understanding, he will then wield a weapon which will enable him to defeat any opposition in this country.

Yet Hitler's strange mind did not ponder upon such long-range, pacific prospects. His active information sources revealed to him that Beneš would accept the Anglo-French Plan (*18*); he made war plans, assailed the Hungarians for their caution and slowness, and ridiculed the Poles. On the 22nd the British Premier again took to the skies and descended upon a bleak Germany: now it was at Godesberg, a town on the Rhine. Hitler met him with restrained cordiality. Soon he received official confirmation of territorial cession from the mouth of the British Prime Minister and then pronounced this famous utterance: "It pains me terribly, but this will not work any more." He wanted to have more.

Meanwhile a frightened continent watched the hours clicking away. The new German demands were swiftly transmitted and decoded, and now Czechoslovakia mobilized; Chamberlain sat for a few more hours in Godesberg, separated by a river from Hitler. Hitler's new ultimatum demanded not only the immediate cession of those areas with a German-speaking population of more than 50 per cent — the rest was to be determined by a plebiscite — but he brought up a map and pointed out the areas which he had to have unconditionally. If not, he would march in on October 1. (*19*) His last statement amounted to an ultimatum: the Sudeten territory had to be evacuated before the 28th. Even now, Chamberlain's departing gestures were not unfriendly. His press adviser told a German friend that the Premier's position

> . . . had been made extremely difficult by latest events in Godesberg. Persons friendly to Germany . . . are beginning to be afraid that the

Prime Minister will not be able to hold out in face of the revolt of
public opinion which is brewing in England . . . The consequence
would be the formation of a Cabinet under Eden and Churchill,
which could only be described as a War Cabinet. (*20*)

[*Repercussions; international plans and fears.*]   Hodža resigned in
Prague. A new semi-military government was set up under the Inspec-
tor-General of the Army, Jan Syrový, who unconditionally rejected
the Godesberg demands. (*21*) A day later France partially mobilized;
several Hungarian and Polish divisions were put on war footing;
preparations were made for the mobilization of the British fleet.

Rumania reinforced her western borders against Hungary; she
was very much afraid of a Polish-Hungarian attack and partition of
eastern Slovakia and the Carpathian Ukraine. When the Anglo-
French Plan left the Hungarian and Polish minorities unmentioned,
Poland and Hungary took diplomatic steps which indicated their
intention to partake immediately in any territorial settlement. (*22*)
Especially Italy supported them. Again a Rumanian envoy was
rushed to Ciano to say that Hungary could regain territories but that
Rome make Budapest abstain from any "gesture of impulsiveness"
which would force Rumania to intervene. Ciano noted: "I do my best
to encourage the Rumanian to betray the Little Entente. I do not have
to exert myself, as he does not desire otherwise." (*23*)

On September 21 Litvinov cried out aloud in Geneva for "collective security"; *Pravda* blasted London, and a Geneva dispatch of
Izvestia dated September 20 depicted the consequences of appeasement
with unusual clarity. Yet there were no appreciable Russian military
moves; the Russian envoy in Prague did not promise anything new (*24*),
and Russian attentions slowly turned toward Poland.

On September 23 (when Bonnet decided once more to mediate
between Warsaw and Prague) the Soviet government notified Poland
in a stern note that Russia would immediately denounce her 1932
Non-Aggression Pact with Poland if the latter attacked Czechoslovakia. There were Russian cavalry concentrations on the Polish
frontier — in the direction of Brest-Litóvsk and Warsaw, but not in
the direction of the Czech Carpathians! Whatever might be said of
Georges Bonnet — and an appeaser he surely was — he sized this
up correctly; he foresaw a probable Russo-Polish conflict which would
put France and Britain into an impossible situation. In a conflict
between Germany and Poland on one side and Czechoslovakia and

Russia on the other, the Western Powers would have to sacrifice their principles, even their professed war aims; if, on the contrary, they would back Poland, this would lead to collusion between Germany and Russia and to a later and inevitable partition. Bonnet asked the Soviets not to take any action in regard to Poland without notifying Paris in advance; at the same time he pressed Beneš to cede Teschen for the sake of gaining Polish tranquillity. On the 25th, Beneš accepted, with a vague condition: he would give Teschen up at once if Poland would change her general position in the all-European crisis. But Beck refused curtly, and although President Moscicki answered in a not unfriendly vein a letter which Beneš had written him four days before, the Polish position did not change. (25) Göring in Berlin was delighted to hear from a Polish conversant that Poland would under no circumstances cooperate with the Soviets; Ribbentrop asked Lipski whether Poland would join in the attack. The Polish diplomat, at first noncommittal, said that "resort to force was not precluded."

Using intermediaries to avoid German tapping of the wires, General Gamelin sent two urgent messages on the next day. One went to General Syrový, advising him to fall back into Moravia instead of leaving flanks open to German attacks from three sides by joining battle around Prague. During the Munich hours, this letter was being misinterpreted by Bonnet, who allegedly told French parliamentarians that "the best proof of our incapacity is the advice General Gamelin gave to the Czechoslovak High Command: retreat." (26) The other message went to Marshal Smigly-Rydz of Poland, who in 1936 had said to him that "Poland would never find herself in a camp opposite France." Gamelin asked the Marshal to exercise restraint over Teschen; Smigly-Rydz had also promised him in 1936 that Poland would never attack the Czechs. Now Gamelin invoked this pledge; he received only a noncommittal answer. Both the Polish message and that of Syrový arrived in Paris on the 29th; by that time Munich had begun.

· · · · · · · ·

[*The last Western deliberations.*] The French flew to London again on the 25th; but beforehand Phipps sent a strange report to his government:

All that is best in France is against war, *almost* at any price. . . . To embark upon what will presumably be the biggest conflict in history with our ally, who will fight, if fight she must, without eyes [Air Force], and without real heart must surely give us furiously to think. (27)

The French were divided, and only Daladier fenced with Chamberlain, at times courageously. "Perhaps formulae of conciliation might be found," but this was "only preparing for the destruction of Western civilization and of liberty in the world." But Daladier was over-optimistic about the Russians. Finally, exasperated, he raised three questions: Did the British accept Hitler's new demands? Did they intend to press the Czechs to accept these? Did they think that France should do nothing? Chamberlain tried to explain the questions away and pointed to the impossibility of effective French military action. The meeting adjourned, and it was arranged that the French Chief of Staff should come over next morning. (28) September 26: fog and overcast over most of Europe. Amidst drizzling rain, the French, laden with doubts and uncertainties, flew back to Paris; in Berlin, trucks and tanks rolled eastward on the rainy pavements. A sullen and somewhat disheartened populace watched. (29)

[*The Horace Wilson letter and mission.*] Attempts at mediation abounded: Pope Pius XI, President Roosevelt, Lord Rothermere (who contacted Ribbentrop "in the name of our old friendship"), and Chamberlain, who asked Hitler to receive the President of the British Legion. Now, on the morning of the 26th, Chamberlain sent Sir Horace Wilson with a letter, a friendly one in which he merely cited the Czech view, without commending the Czechs for their demonstrated willingness to make unusual sacrifices. At 4:10 in the afternoon Halifax telegraphed Wilson to make it definitely known to Hitler that, should he attack, France and Britain would fight.

Wilson made his call. At 7:20 he wired. "Very violent hour. He is clearly determined to make great passionate speech tonight and most impatient." A passionate speech it was; of all Hitler's orations this reached perhaps the highest pitch of hysterics. "German patience has come to an end! . . . If Beneš decides so," there would be war by October 1. (30)

In the same hour of the Sportpalast speech, a serious communiqué was issued by the Foreign Office, later attributed to the Germanophobe Vansittart: France would assist the Czechs "and Great Britain and Russia will certainly stand by France." On the grounds that it had not the full authorization of the Foreign Secretary, Bonnet disavowed the communiqué when he spoke to the anxious journalists in Paris: it had "no confirmation." London did not insist. (*31*)

Wilson waited and Henderson wired in the morning:

> If His Majesty's Government do not at this eleventh hour advise Czechs in the name of humanity and of the Czechs themselves, since we cannot in practice help them, to make the best terms they can with Berlin, we shall be exposing Czechoslovakia to the same fate as Abyssinia. Moreover, if we do not seize this last chance of pinning Herr Hitler down to his public statement yesterday that Sudetens are the last of his territorial aims in Europe, we shall be exposing Central Europe to even worse things in the future.

Wilson called on Hitler again, who was determined: he did not care for Sir Horace's flatteries, who "had followed the Führer's speech at the Sportpalast with interest."

> He could not but congratulate him on the magnificent reception accorded to him. It must have been a great moment for him. Both the Prime Minister and he himself had noticed with appreciation various references in the speech to points raised by Chamberlain. (*32*)

Hitler did not seem to care what France and Britain would do. "Today is Tuesday," said he. "By next Monday we shall be at war." (*33*)

[*News from Rome.*] An interesting telegram came from Rome in the early hours: Lord Perth saw willingness there to mediate. He suggested that Mussolini be asked to intervene (*34*); indeed, this thought lingered with the Italian dictator. In the early afternoon Mussolini sent a message to Hitler, asking him to postpone mobilization and arrange a Four-Power Conference: he could get what he wanted.

At 5:45 P.M. Chamberlain wired Beneš: if he did not accept the German conditions by 2:00 P.M. next day, Germany would attack.

> This means that Bohemia would be overrun by the German Army and nothing which another Power or Powers would do would be able to save your country from such a fate. This remains true whatever the result of a world war might be. His Majesty's Government cannot assume the responsibility of advising you what you should do, but it believes that this information should be brought to your notice without delay.

Two hours later a second message followed: inconsistent with the first, it did give advice to the Czechs. Chamberlain envisaged a compromise plan between the Anglo-French provisions and the Godesberg demands and stated that

> . . . the only alternative of this plan would be invasion and the dismemberment of the country by force, and that Czechoslovakia, though a conflict might arise which would lead to incalculable loss of life, could not be reconstituted in her frontiers, whatever the results of the conflict may be.

The Fleet mobilized. The Premier then went on the air, tired and filled with a dated Carlylean disdain for the non-western inhabitants of the continent: "How horrible, fantastic, incredible it is that we should be digging trenches and trying on gas-masks because of a quarrel in a faraway country between people of whom we know nothing." Scarcely had he finished with his speech, when a message came from Hitler to whom he had written once more a few hours before. Hitler's answer was solemn and dramatic. The Sudeten problem was his last demand; he added that he would not interfere with the independence of the "new" Czechoslovak state. This was an inflexible letter, but at least the tone was moderate. Now night fell.

[*Last-minute international alignments.*] Chamberlain's biographer, Keith Feiling, in 1946 commented with acid precision on President Roosevelt's peace appeal: ". . . but moral opinion was not marketable in central Europe, and these very statements made it explicit that the United States assumed no obligation." Yet, on the 28th, Roosevelt in a last-minute, desperate, and most unrealistic attempt, asked that the head of the Soviet government make an appeal to Germans and Czechs; as if Hitler would care! As if Stalin would try! The Soviet press continuously concentrated fire on Poland. Moscow informed Washington that instead of a direct appeal it would prefer an international conference, (35) acutely noting that Russia was about to be left out of a prospective Four-Power meeting. Ciano asked the Hungarians to restrain themselves, and so did Stoyadinovič, whose position seemed to be momentarily difficult. Nationalist Spain announced her neutrality in Berlin, which made Ciano and Mussolini cry out with indignation: this was "a direct betrayal of the common cause."

[*St. Wenceslas' Day.*] The day of the Czechs' national saint dawned.

In Berlin, Sir Horace Wilson spoke with a representative of Ribbentrop: "if [Germany] were to give way *on the form* [Britain] would be prepared to push through all [German] demands with the Czechs and French. But if [Germany] marched today, everything would, without a doubt, be at an end." Göring and Finance Minister Schwerin-Krosigk were with Hitler, pleading caution, foreseeing economic difficulties in a protracted war, when it was Mussolini who swung the balance for peace. His message for a concrete Four-Power Conference was received shortly after ten by Attolico, who telephoned the Chancellery and obtained an immediate audience. (With undiplomatic haste, the Ambassador ran down the steps of his Embassy, looked in vain for his chauffeur and then impatiently hailed a taxi.) Hitler nodded to Attolico: he agreed. Half an hour later came the French Ambassador, who was informed of Hitler's willingness to consider a Four-Power Conference at Munich. Another half hour and a joyous Henderson heard from Hitler that German mobilization had been postponed.

Unaware of Mussolini's success, Chamberlain telegraphed a last, desperate message to Hitler that morning: "After reading your letter I feel certain that you can get all essentials without war and without delay," and offered the same Four-Power conference proposal in Berlin, with Italians and Czech representatives included.

Shortly after three o'clock a weary, though silently hopeful Chamberlain stood up to speak in the House of Commons; not very much later the well-known historic scene took place: the message came from Hitler, acquiescing in a Four-Power Conference. A frenzy of jubilation swept through the British parliament; in an hour, all was over. Daladier, Chamberlain, and Mussolini were packing their bags for Munich.

[*Munich.*] There they arrived in the late morning hours of the 29th: in twelve hours, all business was finished. Not only Russia, but Czechoslovakia was not invited. Two Czech diplomats, Mastny and Masardjik, travelled to the Munich ante-rooms to eavesdrop on their country's fate. Their report describes the atmosphere: "The reception we met with at the airdrome was roughly that accorded to police suspects." (*36*)

The agreement, signed in the morning hours of September 30, was rather simple:

Germany was to receive the areas she demanded. Occupation was to begin on October 1 and proceed gradually until October 10.

A few disputable areas were to be determined by an international commission (which, incidentally, never met).

Czechoslovakia was to evacuate the ceded lands without any effort to dismantle or damage installations therein.

A right of option was provided for, extended to Sudeten nationals imprisoned and those serving in the Czechoslovak armed forces.

The question of Polish (37) and Hungarian minorities was to be settled between the respective states and Czechoslovakia within a period of three months, pending which, another international conference was to be convoked.

In a meaningless appendix to the agreement, the Western Powers guaranteed the new boundaries of Czechoslovakia "against unprovoked attacks."

Chamberlain, Daladier and Mussolini were well on their way home when the Czech Foreign Minister met the Italian, French and British envoys a few minutes after noon on September 30. The fog of the last week was disappearing; a golden sunshine broke through the clouds and glittered on the domes of the Hradčany Palace. "After us, many others will meet with the same fate," said Krofta, not without dignity.

· · · · · · · ·

Halifax, in order to explain Munich, asked for the Soviet Ambassador on the morning of the 29th: he was anxious that the Soviet Union "should not misinterpret the fact that this Conference did not include a representative of the Soviet Government." Maisky thanked him for the invitation and information. He said "that he hoped that we should keep his Government as closely informed as possible of what passed at Munich." "This I undertook to do," noted Halifax. "His general attitude seemed to me, as indeed, it was likely to be, one of some suspicion, but not one of resentment in face of facts, which he was perforce obliged to admit. And, as our conversation proceeded, he seemed to discard some of the suspicion."

Indirect effects of the Czechoslovak crisis

In the Baltic area and in the far Balkans the Czechoslovak crisis had but indirect effects. Finland, Estonia and Latvia were greatly impressed by the prowess of Hitler; they were also relieved when

armed conflict was avoided. The main preoccupation in these countries was Russia; they knew that if Russia intervened, the Baltic area
would be sealed off, a prey to the Russian land armies and, at best,
the scene of a German counter-offensive. If the Soviets — as many
indications showed — remained neutral and watched the European
struggle from the sidelines, there was again no doubt that sooner or
later their intervention would be invited, with the Baltic area figuring
preeminently in the great bargain. A special Soviet emissary, Yartsev,
appeared in Finland in March (without the knowledge of the Soviet
Minister there) and asked for a Finnish island in the Gulf, offering
at the same time a kind of military alliance. (*1*)

Lithuania, remembering the March crisis and her previous vexa-
tions, nurtured a second thought that she might be able to take
advantage of any complication in which Poland was to be involved.
However, the government in Kaunas did not yield to the extreme
nationalists, and the news of Munich was greeted there with satisfaction, restrained only by sympathy for Czechoslovakia, with which
state Lithuania always had had excellent relations.

[*The Balkans and Italy.*] The Balkan nations drew somewhat
closely together during the dangerous summer of 1938, despite the
duplicities of Stoyadinovič and the fears of Carol. Regent Paul tried
to strengthen the Yugoslav state by bringing about an agreement
with the Croats; early in 1938, Belgrade also announced her efforts
to sign a Concordat with the Vatican, a long-expected pledge to the
Catholic Croat population. Yet during the summer these efforts were
abandoned.

The Bulgar Premier, Kiosseivanov, said to the German Minister in
the early summer that the Czechs were unpopular in Bulgaria; they
were "the Jews among the Slavs." But the Balkan monarchs still
nurtured admiration for Britain. As the German Minister to Sofia
reported in August:

> Bulgarian policy will shun any commitment which brings her into
> opposition with Britain. Alien as British ways, culture, and speech
> are to the Bulgarian — he does not know what to make of the British
> — even today he still respects British world power which, backed by
> American help, he considers would be decisive in any future war.
> The King [Boris III] has spoken with me quite frankly and repeat-
> edly on this subject. . . . It may be that historical memories of the

past and of the Gladstone era play their part in the Bulgarian attitude to Britain. In any case this is an attitude which will have to be taken into account. (*2*)

All of the Balkan states were under the impact of German might, but the preoccupation of most was either with Italy (*3*) or with the Soviets. The aggressive voice of Italy disturbed Turkey, Greece, and the whole Middle East, where Mussolini's Arab propaganda made certain strides. Especially Turkey felt that in the event of a European war, Italy might embark on a minor Aegean conquest of her own, and the Anglo-Italian Agreement of April worried Ankara as well as Athens considerably. While Litvinov lashed out against the Agreement, no Soviet assistance was desired in view of the growing military might of the Red Army weighing upon Turkey's Caucasian frontier and the relatively strong Communist movement in Greece.

A friendship treaty was signed between Greece and Turkey on April 8 and between France and Turkey on July 2 (*4*); the leaders of Turkey voiced their strong attachment to the Western Powers in order to impress Italy. The Turkish Foreign Minister, Aras, eulogized Britain: "Britain showed she has faith in us; we will show her that this faith is not misplaced. . . . Britain may lose a battle but never a war!" In July, a Balkan naval conference met in Athens, where Italian eventualities were discussed. It was decided also to take advantage of King Boris' flexibility and invite Bulgaria to the Balkan "Club." Subsequently, on July 31, in Salonika, a Greek-Bulgar Treaty of friendship and non-aggression was signed. The Salonika conference lifted the clauses of the Neuilly Treaty limiting Bulgarian rearmament at the same time. Thus the military equality of Bulgaria was restored in principle; and a month later, in Bled, the same was done for Hungary.

The spectre of an aggressive Italy continued to haunt the Balkan statesmen. And not without reason. The Germans themselves were aware of this. In May, Ciano went to Tirana to represent Italy on the occasion of King Zog's marriage, after which he noted privately: "I do not think that a few rounds from machine-guns sent into the necks of a few Albanians would move a world which was not even moved by the explosion of torpedoes between Malta and Tunis. The agreement, or better, the complicity of Yugoslavia is a condition both sufficient and necessary." Indeed, Stoyadinovič had certain designs on Salonika and seemed willing to conspire against Albanians and

Greeks with Rome. By the end of August, it seemed that while Italy would not enter an eventual German-French war, she might turn eastward. Italian naval concentrations were anxiously being watched by Greece during September; the Munich settlement then brought momentary relief to the Balkans and to the Aegean.

All over central-eastern Europe, the greatest indirect effect of the Czechoslovak affair was the rise in Nazi prestige, especially among the Nazi-type movements of the central-eastern European states. With the exception of Yugoslavia, where wide indignation against the foreign policy of Stoyadinovič was growing, people cowered while the Nazis crowed. In the economic and financial field, 1938 witnessed the peak of German penetration both in the Baltics and in the Balkans. After Munich, many of the disillusioned were to turn to the Communists: as the prestige of the West fell to great depths, the glorious image of the "Eastern Defender" rose again on the horizon. In Bulgaria, Yugoslavia and in Greece, the underground Communist party was rapidly increasing its strength. (*5*)

MUNICH
IN RETROSPECT:
THE
RUSSIAN
RÔLE

I

To justify the Munich settlement on moral grounds is hardly possible. That its psychological effects on Europe in general and on the small states of central-eastern Europe in particular were especially disastrous was immediately evident. As Pope Pius XI on October 3, 1938, put the case: "In the past nations had been offered as matrimonial presents; today they are being traded away without their consent, animal-like." And Churchill on October 5: "the terrible words have for the time being been pronounced against the Western Democracies: 'Thou art weighed in the balance and found wanting.' And do not suppose that this is the end." Yet because of these prophetic words Churchill almost faced a resolution of censure by his constituents, for, as Namier later put it, the Munich era was "a failure of

European morality." Today there is practically no one who would defend Munich on an ideological plane and dispute its immediate consequences. These were psychological as well as international. The Director of Artillery of the Czech War Ministry to the British Military Attaché at the end of August 1938: "In the meantime, and before you are ready, you English possess a powerful weapon to a degree which no other country enjoys and that is your national prestige. That prestige is only partially based on your resources; it derives its real strength from your high moral standards in public life and policy. A single departure from these standards would mean moral suicide for you and disaster for the rest of the world." The British attaché: "Lest he should be inferring that Great Britain was already in some way compromised with the fate of his own country, I quickly retorted that precisely because we were as good as our word we were most careful not to get lightly committed, and as regards Central Europe, as he no doubt knew, our hands were entirely free." The Czech officer: "that, indeed, was the case at present and that any action [Britain] might decide to take if the occasion arose would be dictated by [her] own interests and not by reason of the *beaux yeux* of the Czechs." (*Documents on British Foreign Policy, 1919–1939*, Series III, volume II — further: *BD*, II.) François-Poncet blushed for a moment at Munich: "Thus does France treat her only allies who had remained faithful to her." (Ciano, *Diario 1937–38*, further: *CD*.) Churchill in the Commons: "We are in the presence of a disaster of the first magnitude which has befallen Great Britain and France. Do not let us blind ourselves to that. It must now be accepted that all the countries of Central and Eastern Europe will make the best terms they can with the triumphant Nazi power." They indeed did. Gafencu masterfully described how Munich was tantamount to an actual partition of Europe, a virtual acquies-

cence in the German domination of the Danubian area and of most of the Balkans. Churchill: "a total, unmitigated defeat" with gravest psychological repercussions; to mitigate the Czechs' tragedy, the French and British Ambassadors in Warsaw called on Beck to request that Poland refrain from aggressive action against Czechoslovakia, and on October 1 this protest of Britain and France was met with a flippant gesture by a central-eastern European Foreign Minister: ". . . the door was shut in their faces." (Churchill.) And the great door to the southeast flung open to Hitler.

Even if the certainly unsatisfactory conditions of a minority state are being considered, even if Beneš' cruel expulsion measures of 1945–46 accompany October 1938 in the annals of infamy, there is no moral excuse. In face of continued totalitarian maneuvers of international blackmail, the Western Powers should have manifested their determination to halt German aggression even if they did not have all the means to do so. Instead the peoples between Germany and Russia witnessed Western weakness, weariness, and hypocrisy. This should not have been.

II

However, in view of the evidence and documents since available, a discussion seems to be in order about the *practical* expediency of appeasement at Munich.

Against Munich it can be stated that:
(*1*) *With his new provinces, Hitler gained valuable territories, industries, and manpower for his empire.* As a potential opponent, Czechoslovakia ceased to exist; her mountain fortresses and many of her natural resources passed into German hands. Another reservoir for German manpower: more than 3,000,000 new in-

habitants (among them more than 700,000 Czechs). Ribbentrop to Ciano on October 28: "Czechoslovakia one can consider finished. In September two weeks were needed to overrun her; now 48 hours are enough. In certain frontier points German artillery posts had to be moved back to avoid that from the other side of the Czechoslovak frontier German batteries should hit them." (*L'Europa verso la catastrofe*, further: *CLD*.) On determining the frontier, "the Germans acted on strategic rather than ethnic considerations." (Coulondre, French Yellow Book.) In vain did the Czechs plead with the French to take into account the last remaining Czech forts at the drawing of the final frontier line; Bonnet did not wish to intervene in another boundary dispute. In November a German-Czech frontier agreement added another batch of square miles with more than a hundred villages to the Reich territory. Chamberlain's letter to the Archbishop of Canterbury on October 2 thus seems maudlin: "I am sure that some day the Czechs will see that what we did was to save them for a happier future. And I sincerely believe that we have at last opened the way to that general appeasement which alone can save the world from chaos." (Feiling.) (2) *Hitler gained additional military advantages for a campaign against Poland.* This was evident, especially when Slovakia became a German protectorate: the Polish defences were outflanked. The British military attaché to Prague in 1938 stated that given another year, the Czechs could defend themselves better against Germany. (*BD*, I, 122.) Czech arms were better than Polish arms, said Hitler to Burckhardt in August 1939. (3) *German public opinion was less prepared for a war against Czechoslovakia in 1938 than it was a year later against Poland.* This has been abundantly confirmed. Besides, the average German did not feel strongly against Czechs, while he had a historic disdain for Poles. Before the British delegation left for Munich, Halifax told them that he had information from "moderate" (that is, anti-Nazi) German circles that British firmness had had and would continue to have considerable effect on German public opinion. "This may, if true, assist you in negotiation." (*BD*, II, 620.) (4) *In view of (3), there is evidence that the German generals intended to rebel, but Chamberlain's attitude and actions foiled this movement.* Churchill, for one,

emphasizes this point. It was also brought out in various German testimonies, e.g. at Nuremberg (*International Military Tribunal Documents,* further: *IMT*, 388–PS); also later (Halder, Kordt). On August 30 Brauchitsch expressed his fears to Hitler about a war against an anti-German coalition. Gisevius wrote of plans which were ready for a generals' coup against Hitler around mid-September and which failed only when the stupendous news of Chamberlain's trip to Berchtesgaden came. On August 7 a Rittmeister von Koerber called on the British military attaché in Berlin, stating that he belonged to the military opposition to Hitler: "War cannot be avoided except through the overthrow of the Hitler régime from within." (*BD*, II, 64–6.) The British were informed of the military-conservative opponents also through Burckhardt and Switzerland. On August 16 a von Kleist, stating that he was the emissary of the anti-Hitler elements within the German General Staff, arrived in London. (*BD*, II, 683 ff. on his conversations.) He assured the British that opposition to Hitler was very strong among the generals. Yet Chamberlain wrote to Halifax on August 19: "I take it that Von Kleist is violently anti-Hitler and is extremely anxious to stir up his friends in Germany to make an attempt at his overthrow. He reminds me of the Jacobites at the Court of France in King William's time and I think we must discount a good deal of what he says." (*Ibid.,* p. 686.) On September 8 the German military attaché in Belgrade intimated to his British colleague there that Hitler was "bluffing" and that the Army was not behind him. (*Ibid.,* p. 268.) Hitler to General Beck during a stormy interview in September: yes, war might come but he, Hitler, while ready for it, vaguely denied that he wanted it to come. (See also the German resistance literature,

Rothfels, Gisevius, Schlabrendorff, Dulles, Pechel, Mourin. However, a certain comparison of the documents dealing with the anti-Nazi emissaries in London in *German Documents on Foreign Policy, 1918–1945*, series D, volume II (further: *GD*) with *BD*, II, suggest that some of these men were planted in London by German intelligence.) (*5*) *Munich confirmed Mussolini in his disdain of France and Britain and in his rather unconditional favoring of Germany.* (*CD, CLD,* Anfuso, Favagrossa, Donosti, Mussolini confirm this.) On one hand, Hitler on August 23, 1939: "Our enemies are little worms; I saw them at Munich"; on the other, Mussolini upon the Berchtesgaden news: "There will be no war. But this is the end of British prestige." (See also his views just before Munich in *CD*, p. 251.) To Ciano on September 17: "I made my decisions"; he would remain neutral but if Britain intervened and the war assumed an ideological character, he would enter: "Italy and Fascism cannot be neutral." (*Ibid.,* pp. 239–40.) Ribbentrop sensed this attitude and greeted Mussolini at Munich with the proposal of a German-Italian-Japanese alliance. (Nevertheless, Mussolini was happy, perhaps even relieved at the fact that a settlement was made at Munich.)

The main sin of the British and French in September 1938 was that they gave Hitler a wrong impression: the impression that they had really acquiesced in Germany's rule over central-eastern Europe. Although Munich nearly amounted to such acquiescence, the impression was basically a wrong one and it ultimately furthered the causes of misunderstanding and war. Another false impression with a long-range consequence flowed from Munich: (*6*) *Disillusioned with the democracies, many people saw in Russia the only apparent bulwark resisting Nazi or Fascist aggression.*

. . . .

There is, however, some evidence that Munich was expedient.

(*1*) *From October 1938 to September 1939 the Allies gained relatively more by arming than Germany did.* True, in absolute numbers German war production grew much in a year, but Britain and France were infinitely better off in 1939 than they had been in 1938. If nothing else, they had won some time at Munich: from complete military unpreparedness they progressed to the stage of relative debility. Not only Chamberlain argued this, but Attlee conceded it in 1940. (Also see Henderson to Halifax on August 12, 1938, when he foresees the Twilight War of 1939–40: "If the worst happens I fail completely to see what the French can do. Mobilize yes, but is it conceivable that they will attack the Siegfried Line? I cannot believe it . . . There can only be stalemate in the west on the ground . . ." *BD*, II, 86; see also the fear-ridden opinions of General Vuillemin and Colonel Lindbergh about the overwhelming German Air Force, in Bonnet, Gamelin, etc.) (*2*) *There was a clearer case of aggression in Poland than in Czechoslovakia,* both from the viewpoint of international law and from that of ethnic principle. And the sequence of events had a tremendous impact on world opinion, not least in the United States. (See especially *GD*, IV, 633–679.) (*3*) *The British people, who were disturbed and divided in 1938 faced war with more unity and determination in 1939.* There is little doubt that, given the same military circumstances, a Chamberlain government and the British people in the summer of 1939 would not have fought a Churchillian Battle of Britain. There is also some evidence that the Commonwealth Nations would not have fully supported a British war government in 1938. The High Commissioner of Australia to

Chamberlain on May 11, 1940: "War apparently had to come, but by your resolute personal action you gained for us a year of preparation and brought into the conflict a united British Empire." At the height of the Battle of Britain, on October 6, 1940, the Archbishop of Canterbury to Chamberlain: "You enabled your country to enter the war with a clear conscience and a united will." (Feiling, p. 463.) Malcolm MacDonald in the same vein to the sick Chamberlain on November 8: ". . . and long, long after all the scribblers who have attacked you are forgotten, your name will be amongst the most honoured in the dynasty of our Prime Ministers." (*Ibid.*, p. 465.) Namier in 1950: "Few . . . will accept M. Bonnet's elaborate explanations. But the crowds which acclaimed M. Daladier and Mr. Chamberlain (especially the latter! See the British press on October 1 [my remark]) on their return from Munich showed once more that these Prime Ministers represented the spirit of the period." A close examination of British and French public opinion in the last days of the crisis is also instructive. (See the unpublished paper of Sister M. Alberta, S.S.J., in my possession.) Wheeler-Bennett's statement is true, "The bulk of the British public were deeply shocked at the rapacity of the German demands and were united in applauding their rejection by the British Government. With reluctant determination, the British man-in-the-street again faced the prospect of war and did not flinch from it"; but, it must be added, the man-in-the-street was by no means convinced that any deal with the new Germany was useless or impossible. Namier rightly judged the British Foreign Office: "Within the Foreign Office even in this period, one of the saddest and most depressed in its history, there was no lack of sound knowledge of European

affairs, or of sane insight into them. And the willingness which they have shown to allow all their material to see daylight does them honour now" (1949). But the Foreign Office and the masses were not the same.

Even in the very last days of the crisis "the issues were still clouded on a very essential point — How far would Britain go in support of France?" (Sister Alberta.) (*4*) *The French attitude was a moot point, although it seems that, like Britain, France was not prepared psychologically to go to war, united, in 1938.* Sir Eric Phipps cited ambiguous reports on September 25; Herriot, for example, said: "There is no kind of enthusiasm for war in the country but a firm and melancholy determination to resist." The French Financial Adviser "finds that while there is no enthusiasm for war, people are resigned but resolute . . . There is also a fatalistic feeling that war is inevitable now or later." Jeanneney, the President of the French Senate, on September 26: ". . . feeling in the whole country, though grave and even sad was absolutely firm. Realization was general that it was either war now or a little later and that now we had a much better chance of victory." Similar was the opinion of Blum. But Phipps reported "that in the opinion of Cardinal Verdier, apart from the Communists, nobody in France wants a war over the present issues. The French are prepared to fight and will obey without exception if honour demands. But they do not consider it opportune or necessary and still refuse to believe that war will come." The nationalist and anti-German Louis Marin: "The heart of the great majority of the French would not be in the game from the start. French preparations are very imperfect and many shortcomings have been revealed, not only in the air." (See also all Phipps' telegrams in *BD*, particularly Nos. 1146, 1160); Bräuer, the German chargé in Paris drew similar conclusions on September 25: "Situation can be described by saying that the state of preparedness has been intensified, although the basic trend of mood, which in Government and people is set on the preservation of peace, is unchanged." Two days later, however, the German Embassy reported that "the population is growing accustomed to the idea of war despite an inherent strong aversion and is becoming reconciled to it." While the cleverest of the *munichois*, de Monzie, wrote in October about the *anti-munichois:* "... *une fureur de l'élite contre la paix*" and "I tremble before their propaganda which corresponds so well to the temperament of many Frenchmen," it seems reasonable to deduce from all evidence that the broad fabric of French society would not have withstood the strains of war better in 1938 than it did a year later. And there is also no question that (5) *British-French diplomatic and military liaison was closer and more efficient in 1939 than it had been a year before.*

More important among the arguments supporting the expediency of Munich are (6) *those remarks and statements by Hitler which show his dissatisfaction that it did not come to war in September 1938.* Was Hitler bluffing? The evidence points to the contrary. He often and definitely indicated his dissatisfaction with the settlement; as early as October he indicated this mood to François-Poncet and to some of his generals. He felt frustrated that it did not come to a showdown. At times he contradicted himself, but, to say the least, this was not unusual with him; at times he gloated over his Munich success, on other occasions he brooded, gloomy and angry, saying that Chamberlain and Mussolini had deprived him from exploiting an unusual chance in history. Even within one conversation he could

state two fundamentally contradictory views. On January 16, 1939, he assailed Hungary to Csáky: Why did not Hungary act with determination when they both could have "marched" and he, Hitler, instead of "talking ... could have laughed in Chamberlain's face." (*Documents secrets ... Hongrie,* p. 78.) Yet a few minutes later he calmed down and said to the cowed Csáky: "The impossible has happened. Do you think that even I could have thought six months ago that Czechoslovakia would be presented to me, so to say, on a plate, by her very friends? What happened cannot occur but once in history. We should congratulate ourselves ..."

Hitler was ready for war in 1938. He, who in 1939 did not hesitate to attack Poland even at the price of signing a most dubious pact with Russia, could have appeared in 1938 as the champion of anti-Bolshevism by posing as the defender of Central Europe — and of Poland — against any eventual Russian intervention. Important persons who believe that in 1938 Hitler would have fought are many: among them, Attolico, Halifax, Chvalkovsky, Bonnet, François-Poncet, Mussolini, Daladier, D'Avignon, the Belgian Minister to Berlin, and Papée, the Polish Minister to Prague. (See also the two contradictory letters of Halifax and Vansittart in Comnen, Appendix.) This leaves Vansittart, Keitel, and the French Communists (see also the record of Daladier's testimony and the debate in the Assemblée Nationale on July 18, 1946) alone in their conviction that Hitler was bluffing — a strange combination, indeed. Anfuso recounts how Hitler, when he went to meet Mussolini's train, described to the Duce how he would attack in the West: not the Sudeten map was spread before him but maps of the German-French frontier. True, his Siegfried-Wall was not yet quite completed, but his Air Force had full superiority in the West. It is true that he sometimes envisaged difficulties; for example his military estimations on June 18 and September 4 (*IMT*, 388–PS) reflect a certain amount of caution. When on September 25 he witnessed the indifference of the Berlin population while a troop unit passed, he spoke out angrily: "With this people I cannot yet wage a war." But such hesitations constantly occurred with him; it would be mistaken to overestimate their importance. On October 14 he said to Chvalkovsky that Britain and France would not have intervened: supposing they did, they would have done so without success, for the German Army was far stronger than those of the adversaries. Thus Keitel's Nuremberg testimony (*IMT*, 1954–PS) cannot be taken seriously. Along with the now decreasing assertions of the violent *anti-munichois* who argued that Hitler was in no position to go to war in September 1938, it cannot stand up against the mass of contrary evidence; it should be discounted.

III

But the factor on which virtually all the theories concerning Munich hinge is the rôle of Russia. The main thesis, hitherto generally accepted, is that it was due to Munich that Russia turned away from the policy of "collective security" and became responsive to eventual German gestures; that in 1938 Russia definitely would have fought against Germany.

Yet a note of caution is already detectible in what the earliest diplomatic historian of Munich wrote in 1945–46 in his fine volume: "That Russia was prepared to fight at the time of Munich is more than a strong probability, it is only the effectiveness and capacity of her intervention which are in doubt." With an apology to Mr. Wheeler-Bennett, I would reword his sentence as follows: "That Russia was prepared to fight at the time of Munich is possible but not probable; and the capacity of her intervention is very doubtful."

"Capacity": where, when, and with what aims would Russia have intervened? She seems to have prepared an attack on Poland; this the Western Powers dreaded. Let us, however, suppose that what the post-Munich wishful thinkers argued was true: somehow, with or without Polish and Rumanian consent, the Russian armies would have passed through the Carpathians to the aid of the Czechoslovak Republic, thus associating Russia with the Western Powers in a grand alliance. Yet who would dare to state today that the Russian move into central-eastern Europe would have had the sole, unselfish aim, identical with the aim of the Western Powers: to liberate Europe from the menace of Hitler-Germany? Europe's experiences with Russia since 1944 and the record of German-Russian relations from March 1939 onward leave but little doubt that Stalin was far from formulating such unselfish aims in 1938: he had concrete, territorial designs which he was out to realize. Any Western-Russian coalition would have been necessarily frail: the Russian bargaining position in 1938 would have been not less excellent than that which Stalin actually assumed in 1939. Very soon after the eventual appearance of the Red Army in central-eastern Europe, Soviet territorial plans would have been unfolding: and if the Western Powers had paid with their silent consent to Russian conquests for the undoubtedly valuable assistance of Soviet arms, they would have lost all moral grounds in their war against Hitler; moreover, British public opinion, which was far less anti-German in 1938 than in 1939, would have assisted Chamberlain in making a settlement with Hitler, after the latter's policy and arguments would have seemed to have been vindicated by Russian behavior. On the other hand, had the Western Powers been unwilling to pay the territorial price to Russia, Stalin could have come to terms with Hitler over Poland and central-eastern Europe along the exact lines of the secret Protocol of August 1939; it would have been only too logical that Stalin do so, and Hitler would not have had excessive pangs of conscience either. The settlement of August 22, 1939, would have happened earlier, entering the annals of history under another date.

. . . .

Speculation, however, seriously impairs the historian's craft. Let us turn, therefore, to the cornerstone of the argument: the clear supposition that Russia would have intervened to aid the Czechs — and we might conclude that such intervention was perhaps entirely out of the question.

Before and throughout the Czech crisis, (1) *the Soviet Union cautiously avoided any definite statement as to HOW she would fulfill her treaty obligations to Czechoslovakia.* The whole tone of the German documents in *GD*, I, dealing with direct relations between Germany and the Soviet Union in the period November 1937– July 1938 indicates that Russia was impressed with the power of Germany; the government used measures to inculcate a strong spirit of Russian patriotism on one hand and to limit relations with other countries on the other. German

diplomats had noted this carefully, despite Hitler's anti-Bolshevist statements which temporarily seemed to outrule any possibility of German-Russian coöperation. As early as March 17, 1938, the German chargé, Tippelskirch, commented on a Litvinov statement which indicated that the Soviet Government would more actively participate in European politics: Tippelskirch thought, however, that Russia would not intervene, for Litvinov had said nothing definite about *how* Russia would fulfill her mutual aid obligations to the Czechs. Schulenburg termed the Litvinov statement a classic example of "Russian double talk." Soviet statements containing generalities abounded in March, April, May (before the crisis ripened), and Coulondre, at that time French Ambassador to Moscow, seems to have been a bit optimistic on May 15 when he said to the British chargé: "Whereas before M. Litvinov might have been likened to a soldier marching gaily to the front with a posy in the barrel of his rifle, he, Litvinov, now gave [Coulondre] the impression of the same soldier, just returned from the trenches, brought face to face with the realities of a situation which the Soviets had up till now endeavoured to shirk." (*BD*, I, 304; also Coulondre.) In June the German Army directive "Extended Case Green," which envisaged Italy, Hungary, Nationalist Spain, and Japan as "benevolent neutrals," stated that the German Supreme Command thought direct Russian aid to the Czechs improbable; ". . . the active participation of Russia will be largely restricted to the prosecution of the war in the Baltic." (*IMT*, 325–PS.) By the end of August Schulenburg as well as the Baltic and Finnish envoys in Moscow were convinced that Soviet Russia "would do as little as possible" in a general conflict involving Czechoslovakia. Schulenburg regarded his exchange of views with the Baltic diplomats important enough to write a third, additional report about them to Berlin on August 26, after having referred to these conversations twice previously. (*GD*, II, 629–31.) In session with his military and naval attachés he reached the following conclusions: "(1) Whereas the Soviet Union is attempting to force France and Great Britain to take the initiative against Germany, she herself will hold back. This does not exclude the possibility that France and Czechoslovakia may agree, or have already agreed with the Soviet Union on how help is to be rendered. (2) The Soviet Union will not attack Germany, because she has no common frontier with Germany. However, she will at least mobilize the Western Military Districts . . . (6) The Soviet Union will make use of every opportunity to supply Czechoslovakia with war material in considerable quantities, in particular with aircraft. The sending of troops to Czechoslovakia is difficult to accomplish and is also not in the interests of the Soviet Union . . ." (The memorandum mentioned the possibility of Soviet naval activities in the Baltic, propaganda efforts, and the dispatch of missions of military technicians.) Nothing happened in September to change these opinions of Schulenburg; rather, his views were confirmed.

(2) *The Soviet Union consistently set forth the lack of a common frontier with Czechoslovakia as a pretext for her eventual nonintervention.* The main line running through this theme was that Russia demanded formal consent for passage through Poland and Rumania, consent, which was almost certainly not obtainable; and even when Bucharest agreed to "close its eyes" to the passage of Russian planes, Litvinov rejected this as "insufficient." Never during the French-Russian conversations did Litvinov allude to technical measures with which Russia would aid the Czechs, and it was felt in Paris and London (although, strangely enough there was no really detailed examination of the circumstances and eventuality of Russian intervention) that the Western Powers were running a grave risk of becoming engaged in a war while Russia might slip out by invoking the need of Polish and Rumanian coöperation, certain to be denied.

The report of the French General Schweissguth who had returned from an official visit to Moscow in September 1936 was sceptical and wise. In the event of an attack by Germany on herself, Russia would wish to have France for an ally, wrote Schweissguth, but Russia would prefer that "the thunderbolt strike France rather; she prefers to play the second card." A war between France and Germany would have two advantages: Russia, in view of the nonexistence of a frontier with Germany, could presumably emerge uninjured and also the sole arbiter of an exhausted Europe. To win this play, Russia must make two moves: tempt Germany — by indicating that France was easy prey; tempt France — by showing that she would be the first victim of German rearmament and by persuading France of dangers inherent in any collaboration with Germany. (See Bonnet, the crucial Appendix IV: *L'opposition de vues russo-roumaine en 1938.*) In February 1937 the Blum-Potemkin negotiations revealed Russian evasiveness; they evoked the pretext of Rumanian and Polish non-coöperation; thus, in practice, if not in theory, the Russians disassociated themselves from "collective security" and were not at all specific about concerted plans of defense against German aggression. Welczeck, the German Ambassador, wrote from

Paris on March 16, 1938: "French Government wants concrete proof of assurance from military quarters concerning Czech-Soviet Treaty of Mutual Assistance." Welczeck again on April 8: "There is particular skepticism about effective Russian help which would permit Czechoslovakia a longer, serious resistance. It is maintained in many quarters that this is not to be reckoned with at all, as neither Poland nor Rumania would permit passage of Red aircraft and troops." On March 14 the German Legation in Prague received a report from a "reliable Ukrainian source" (but the Ukrainians were notorious for their unreliability) that the Czech General Staff had lost confidence in the Russian General Staff; the Czechs had turned down a Russian request for staff talks, as they were not certain whether the military information given there would not ultimately reach German ears. (*GD*, II, 165.) Welczeck wrote to Berlin that on March 14–15 the Soviet Ambassador had informed the Quai d'Orsay that the Soviet Union was standing by her treaty obligations to the Czechs and that three Soviet military districts, White Russia, Kiev, Odessa, had been put on a war footing, ready for action; two days later, however, the able Tippelskirch from Moscow stated that there was no Odessa Military District and nothing special had been observed in the two other cited places either. On March 17 Litvinov stated to the press: "Tomorrow it may be too late, but today the time has not yet passed if all the states and especially the Great Powers will adopt a firm and unequivocal stand in regard to the problems of the collective salvation of peace." He added that "means would be found" to get Russian aid to the Czechs; but the Soviet censor struck out the reference to a corridor for the passage of Russian troops from the

dispatch of a foreign journalist. Tippelskirch: "[Litvinov's] statement demonstrates intention of Soviet Government to take a hand in European politics once more. At the same time it deliberately avoids committing the Soviet Government and makes everything further dependent on attitude of remaining powers . . . " (Tippelskirch also thought that the Litvinov statement was intended to influence the United States.) The British chargé in Moscow saw the situation rather well: "We must not, however, forget that the Russians were Asiatics, more so now than at any period since the time of Peter the Great and that with the present Byzantine régime in the Kremlin anything might happen . . . I felt, however, that even a partial military adventure or demonstration on their part was improbable . . ." Chamberlain on March 20 about the Grand Alliance idea, suggested by Churchill: "It is a very attractive idea; indeed, there is almost everything to be said for it until you come to examine its practicability. From that moment its attraction vanishes . . ." (Feiling; see also Churchill's comment.) At the end of March various rumors arose about secret negotiations between Russia and Rumania concerning the troop passage issue, but in Moscow the German Embassy believed that any such talks would have to be introduced and conducted by Paris. A Rumanian provincial newspaper reported that on April 12 a Russian bomber flying to Czechoslovakia had made an emergency landing in Transylvania, but the report was found to be untrue. All rumors of Russian-Rumanian negotiations were denied by Rumania; especially to Poland the Rumanians vehemently denied even contemplating such talks. When the French questioned them, the Rumanians were more ambiguous and evasive, but then the Russians never pressed Rumania for a definite reply. And in the numerous German dispatches from Bucharest and Warsaw during the whole crisis — two excellent observers represented Germany there — significantly little mention of the Russian passage issue occurs. Throughout April the Soviet press treated the Czech question with great reserve; only the French obligations to Czechoslovakia received mention. When Alexandrovsky, the Soviet Minister to Prague, returning to Moscow, met Comnen in Bucharest on April 16, he was singularly noncommittal and discussed only routine diplomatic matters with the Rumanian Foreign Minister. And on April 19 the British Ambassador, Lord Chilston, wrote lengthily to Halifax, commenting upon a memorandum by Colonel Firebrace, the British military attaché to Moscow: "... in these circumstances the Red Army, though no doubt equal to a defensive war within the frontiers of the Soviet Union, is not capable of carrying the war into the enemy's territory with any hope of ultimate success or without thereby running the risk of endangering the régime, and that it would therefore be contrary to reason for the rulers of this country to involve the Soviet Union in war unless vital national interests were involved ... I personally consider it highly unlikely that the Soviet Government would declare war merely in order to fulfill her treaty obligations or even to forestall a blow to Soviet prestige or an indirect threat to Soviet security, such, for example, as the occupation by Germany of a part of Czechoslovakia ... the Soviet Union must rather, for the time being, be counted out of European politics in so far as the exercise of a decisive influence one way or the other is concerned, though there is no reason why, with time and in changed circumstances, it should not play an extremely important rôle in

world affairs." (*BD*, I, 161–3.) Rumors and counter-rumors: Newton learned on April 23 that a Russian general and a colonel arrived in Prague for staff talks but this was not confirmed; Paul-Boncour heard from Russian diplomats in Paris that *if* France fought, Russia, too, would fight and that the Soviets would have welcomed a slight French-Italian rapprochement. But on April 30 Comnen gave his word to Fabricius that there were absolutely no negotiations going on between Russia and Rumania. (*GD*, II, 249.)

The reputation of the Czechoslovak Communists was not untarnished. Until late 1933 they had agitated for self-determination and supported the German minority with anti-Versailles and self-determination slogans; even a writer of Leftist leanings could state later: "The list of Czechoslovakia's 'guilty men' would be incomplete, were the Communists omitted; for many years they have incited the minorities of Czechoslovakia by the slogan 'self-determination unto separation!'" (Kolarz.) Yet from February 1938 onwards the Czech Communist Party turned to support the government. On May 1 *Rote Fahne*, the official German-language organ of the Czechoslovak Communist Party, displayed this sentence on its first page in a streamer head: "Thirty thousand Soviet bombers will appear over Berlin on the day when the first German soldier crosses the Czech frontier." At once TASS stated that this sentence and the accompanying assertion that it was broadcast from the Comintern radio station in Moscow was "a falsehood throughout." A significant denial! All that happened in early May was that the Czechs purchased twenty Russian bombers. Henderson from Berlin on May 9: the German Foreign Ministry did not believe that Russia would intervene in Czechoslovakia, except perhaps by air. "They reckon that if Germany marches into Czechoslovakia, Poland will follow suit, a displeasing but inevitable contingency." (*BD*, I, 265.) On May 11 Kalinin referred to the Czech Treaty: "The Soviet Union has invariably fulfilled all its treaties concluded with other states in all their consequences, and will do so in this case also. It will, if called upon, fulfill to the last letter all its obligations to Czechoslovakia and France . . ." (But Kalinin, the figurehead atop the Soviet Empire, was not an important person, and general opinions expressed by him were known to be not necessarily synonymous with Kremlin views: for example in July 1936 he spoke in a rather friendly vein to the new Polish Ambassador, Grzybowski, while the latter was received coolly by the Soviet Foreign Commissariat.) On the same day of this Kalinin statement, Litvinov in Geneva told Bonnet that Russia could not do much for the Czechs unless Rumania and Poland coöperated. Even the ever hopeful Beneš told Newton on May 18 that he was reserved concerning Russia: "Czechoslovakia would refuse to be an instrument of Russian policy"; she counted first and well-nigh exclusively on the Western Powers. (*BD*, I, 314. If only Beneš had remembered these words in 1942–45!) He was clever now. Newton: "[Beneš] had been, he said, always opposed to a Pan-Slav policy and to excessive Russian influence in Central Europe. He was a Westerner but did not wish to exclude Russia from Europe where she might be a useful make-weight against German pressure. Similarly he believed that France and England needed Russia as a balancing factor. An attempt to exclude Russia completely from Europe would, he believed, be disastrous and would only force her to make an agreement with Germany against the rest of

Europe." During the May crisis no word of the treaty obligations appeared in the Soviet press, which consistently avoided even the suggestion that under certain circumstances Russia would help Czechoslovakia. Neither did the Soviet press reproduce the Kalinin statement: a rather unusual procedure. And on May 16, the day on which the anniversary of the signing of the Soviet-Czechoslovak Mutual Aid Pact had, in the past, been enthusiastically celebrated, the Soviet press and radio remained completely silent. The British chargé from Moscow to Halifax on May 22: "I feel bound in the present circumstances to record once again the opinion . . . that it is unlikely that Soviet Union will go to war in defence of Czechoslovakia, except possibly in the event of a general European conflagration, and I consider, even in the latter event, possibility of Soviet Union standing aloof cannot be excluded." (*BD*, I, 346.) After their May 1 *faux-pas*, the Czech Communists became suddenly quiet, and the Prague government thought that such were their orders from Moscow. (See Newton to Halifax on May 25, *ibid.*, pp. 377–8.) Yet in the Prague municipal elections the Communists made some gains. Coulondre in Moscow was also convinced that the Soviet Government had instructed the Czech Communists to be quiet, "whose attitude up to date seems to have been exemplary." (Vereker to Halifax, May 28.) Schulenburg on May 27: "I share the opinion of the Bucharest Legation that the Rumanian Government will not grant right of troop transit to the Russians . . . Neither can I believe that the Russians are making great efforts to obtain this privilege. One is constantly seeing signs here of how little the Soviet Union wants war. I enclose a short report which shows how reserved the Soviet Press is in regard to the Sudeten German question. It is obviously no pleasant thought for the Soviet Union to have to go to war on account of Czechoslovakia." (*GD*, II, 348.) Only after the May crisis did the Russian press revert to the alliance; *Izvestia* on May 26 and *Pravda* on June 5 expressed themselves with typical Stalinesque phraseology (Stalin's statements are often interspersed with remarks on touchy subjects introduced by phrases such as "it is well known," "as is known," "as it is universally recognized," etc.) *Pravda:* "The fact that nobody doubted the loyalty of the Soviet Union to the obligations undertaken by it naturally played a considerable rôle [in the passing of the crisis.]" Schulenburg now reiterated his opinion that the Soviet régime was entirely unwilling to commit itself: ". . . in the event of a German-Czech war the Soviet Union will at first limit her assistance to a minimum; for which the absence of a common frontier between the Soviet Union and Czechoslovakia could at any time be put forward on the Soviet side as a convenient excuse." (On May 30. *GD*, II, 363. Yet the *Case Green* directive on that day: "In all probability attempts by Russia to give Czechoslovakia military support, particularly with her air force, are to be expected.") At that time the consensus of the diplomatic corps at Moscow was virtually unanimous and agreed with the views held by Schulenburg. The Russian prospects were especially well gauged by the Baltic envoys and by the German and British military attachés; generally speaking, eastern Europeans usually saw Russian tendencies more realistically than Western diplomats did. Only the loquacious Czech Minister, Fierlinger — who seemed unusually depressed and lonely during the May crisis — began to voice loudly to every diplomat his belief that Russia would aid the Czechs, but the character of Fierlinger was such that but few took him seriously. (After 1945 he turned out to be one of the key Soviet stooges in Czechoslovakia.)

On May 31 Krofta told Comnen that he understood Rumania's caution and fears concerning Russian plans; all the Czech Foreign Minister could get from the Rumanians was their most secret consent that those planes which the Czechs had *bought* from Russia could fly over a stretch of Rumanian territory and be delivered by air, if equipped with Czech markings. Immediately afterwards, however, General Ionescu, the chief of the Rumanian General Staff, went to Warsaw (May 30–June 5) to reassure the Poles: there would be no Rumanian permission for Russian passage. Information both from the Warsaw Embassy and the Prague Legation reached Berlin to the same effect. (On June 12 the German consulate at Cernauti reported, however, that a Soviet plane had made a secret emergency landing in Bukovina, and there were rumors of Russian troop concentrations on the Rumanian frontier. *GD*, II, 431.) The Rumanian chargé in Moscow emphatically denied to Schulenburg on June 18 that a Russian-Rumanian transit agreement existed. Urdureanu, the Rumanian Court Minister, violently denied the same to Fabricius; the argument was somewhat overdone, however, in typical Balkan fashion, for when the Rumanian insisted that any plane coming from Russia toward Czechoslovakia would be immediately fired upon, Fabricius asked if the Rumanian Army had sufficient and effective anti-aircraft guns. Urdureanu: no. (*GD*, II, 434.) On July 10 the German chargé from Warsaw wrote Berlin that 40 aircraft had passed from Russia to Czechoslovakia in the previous six months; according to Japanese intelligence, twelve Czech pilots were waiting in Kiev for planes to be put at their disposal. The Rumanian military attaché informed his German colleague in Warsaw on July 19 that Rumania would militarily oppose Russian passage, which, however, was not at all probable. (*Ibid.*, p. 500.)

The German Undersecretary of State, Woermann, sent a confidential telegram to the Legations in Bucharest and Belgrade on July 25: "We have learned confidentially that . . . the French Foreign Minister . . . in order to stress as strongly as possible the difficulty of Czechoslovakia's political situation . . . told Osuský that Comnen had informed him personally, Rumania would never tolerate Soviet passage through her territory. Bonnet is said to have added that Rumania made such declarations in Berlin and Warsaw. Thereupon Krofta . . . understood the Rumanian attitude but . . . was surprised that he found it necessary to make such a declaration in Berlin . . ." (*Documents and materials . . .*) The telegram added that Comnen had denied having made any such declaration and that Berlin was "confidentially informed" that at the coming Little Entente conference, at Bled, Stoyadinović was expected to advise Comnen in favor of such a declaration. (Despite such German expectations, there was no such Rumanian declaration at Bled, where, to the contrary, Comnen suggested to Krofta that Bucharest would not actively oppose a Russian air lift into Czechoslovakia.) In July the Polish and Baltic envoys in Moscow did not think Russian ground intervention probable; only the Hungarian Minister thought so. Early in August Italian intelligence reports from Odessa indicated the movement of not more than a dozen Czech purchasing agents, military technicians and pilots to Russia and back, through Rumania. Beneš, who occasionally made fantastic statements for domestic consumption about large numbers of Russian aircraft being ready to help the Czechs, in August did not seem to regard the Russian Pact as either very helpful or unusually effective. (See his statements of August 24, *GD*, II, 640.) While on August 30 Hencke, the German chargé in Prague — a man not very reliable in his observations and considerably more sanguine than his chief, Minister Eisenlohr — reported information received by a confidential agent concerning transit talks in Bucharest (at most 100,000 Soviet troops involved, in civilian clothes; prerequisite: agreement with Poland about all this), these reports were untrue; and at the same time Bucharest informed London of Rumanian opposition against Russian transit. Litvinov and Schulenburg talked on August 28, at which time the Soviet Foreign Commissar was non-specific and obscure. To allay French suspicions, Payart, the French chargé, was told of this conversation; on August 30 Payart talked with Schulenburg and expressed his views that, at best, Russia would aid the Czechs with some air action, otherwise not at all. "France had a treaty with Czechoslovakia. There was no point in discussing whether this treaty was good or bad. It existed and France must keep her word, otherwise she would cease to be a Great Power. In case of war the Soviets would have the last laugh. Having no common frontier, they had no need to expose themselves to any danger . . ." (*GD*, II, 666-7.)

On September 2 Litvinov asked for Fierlinger and Payart. He told them of the Soviet determination to help Czechoslovakia. But he did not say how, and Chilston rightly called the Russian remarks "somewhat half-hearted assurances." Litvinov's statements were again conditional on the question of passage.

Neither Poland nor Rumania was un-duly anxious to be coöperative, but the Russians did not press them at all. Be-fore leaving for Geneva, Comnen found it necessary to assure the German chargé on September 6 (the record of this conversation casts a somewhat dubi-ous shade on the picture Comnen had painted of himself in his two memoirs) that there were no Russian-Rumanian staff talks; the very inadequate facilities for ground passage were not being dis-cussed; no Rumanian promises were made to the Western Powers either; the situation was very critical; "sole benefi-ciaries of a conflict would be Bolshevism and international Jewry." (*GD*, II, 701.) Information about air passage was con-tradictory, however. The Polish envoy in Bucharest believed that there would be no transit agreement, except for a few tacitly condoned flights; the Italian Min-ister there thought, however, that upon British requests, the Rumanians would permit Russian ground passage. (*GD*, II, 855; *CD*, p. 231.) But the Rumanian en-voy in Rome energetically denied all transit, ground or air, to Ciano on Sep-tember 16 and 23, "even though Ru-mania was under the strongest pres-sures." The Italian military attaché in Prague on September 7 reported that Rumanian permission for Soviet flights existed and that 45 planes had been lately flown into Czechoslovakia over Rumania. The German chargés in Bu-charest and Prague (on September 9 and 14, respectively), contrary to opin-ions held by better balanced and more informed German envoys, reported that the Rumanian General Staff agreed not to interfere with the delivery of Russian planes to the Czechs; estimates of the German War Ministry showed that the maximum number of such deliveries was about 300 planes (*GD*, II, 724; see also the two Bullitt telegrams cited in Langer-

Gleason, *A Challenge to Isolation*, p. 56, *n.* 9); this estimate was later pared down considerably. It is my belief that *all* Soviet deliveries, including regular pur-chases, did not amount to more than 80 planes in 1937 and 1938. The Poles underestimated Russian plans and capa-bilities: General Stachiewicz told an Englishman that all Russian troop con-centrations on their western frontiers were due to undue fears of invasion, an age-old Russian *idée fixe*.

On September 11 and 12 Litvinov in Geneva brought to the attention of Bon-net and Comnen the Russian pretexts: Rumanian official consent was neces-sary. Litvinov did not go into technical questions, after Comnen had indicated that Rumania might not interfere with aerial passage. The Foreign Commissar actually stated that Russia would come in only *after* France did and then she would request the League of Nations Council to "recommend" that Rumania allow the passage of Russian planes and troops. The Geneva talks thus did not alter anything and Comnen found it necessary to let the Germans know in-directly, through a Yugoslav diplomat in Geneva, that all speculations about Rumanian permission were untrue. On September 19 Schulenburg summarized his information and views: there would be no passage through Rumania; at most, some limited aerial transgression. (*GD*, II, 847.) Similar were the views of the British military attaché in Moscow. Now, when it was clear that at least Rumanian consent to aerial passage could be expected, Russia slowly, gradu-ally began to employ another pretext: the issue of the primary French obliga-tions. (See below, (*3*).) To Lord De La Warr, the British representative in Ge-neva, Litvinov was unwilling to say any-thing of Russian military plans or dispo-sitions: he limited himself to stating that if *Poland* attacked Czechoslovakia, Russia would take action against *Poland*. He also delivered a thundering anti-aggression speech at Geneva on the 21st, dropping, however, the remark that Soviet aid to Czechoslovakia would be given "by ways open to us."

Truly, some Russian preparations against Poland were now under way: early on September 23 the Polish chargé was asked to call on the Foreign Commissariat and was sternly informed in a note: if Poland attacked Czechoslovakia, Russia would renounce the Non-aggression Pact of 1932 with Poland. The Russian note emphasized Polish troop concentrations, and some indications pointed towards eventual Russian plans to attack Poland even if Poland did not join Germany in the invasion of Czechoslovakia. (Interestingly enough, the Soviets had informed France on September 20 that they would not force a passage through Poland; this information the French communicated to Warsaw at once. There is a slight possibility that this Russian statement was misinterpreted by either Paris or Warsaw, and when subsequently Poland made it known that she would intervene for Teschen if the Germans got the Sudetens, this may have led to the corresponding Russian pressure on Poland and the September 23 note. It is, however, exaggerated to state that on September 23 Poland was massing troops against Czechoslovakia (Namier).) The Rumanian Minister in Rome now informed Ciano (on the 25th) that there would be no Russian passage; indeed, that Rumania would be inclined to seek a rapprochement with Hungary if only the latter "would not be impulsive." "The Rumanian alliance with Poland would have precedence over any obligation to Prague." (*GD*, II, 936; also *CD*.) In these last days of the crisis the Soviets did not send planes into Czechoslovakia, and their press made no allusions to the Soviet-Czechoslovak Treaty at all. Hitler used his famous Bolshevik bogey argument at Godesberg and later at Munich with Chamberlain: he screamed against untold numbers of Russian aviators on Czech airfields in readiness, but the Anglo-French delegations called these statements "a legend." (Even Churchill, in his anti-Munich argument, is entirely too optimistic about the eventual passage through Rumania, and in his memoirs he writes, strangely enough, of Rumanian and Hungarian [?] railroads.) On September 25 at the Anglo-French conference, Chamberlain asked "what assurances France had received from Russia? Great Britain had received very disturbing news about the probable Russian attitudes. . . . Russia possessed a large number of aircraft but the question was, would she come in with the full force of her aviation?" In order to influence Chamberlain, Daladier answered that Russia would come in, in the air, but the action would be slow and Czechoslovakia would be occupied before the impact of Russian aid was felt. (Of course, this was evident: even if Russia intervened in full strength, the poor communications in eastern Czechoslovakia and Rumania — which had but one, weak railroad line — could not have prevented the swift occupation of the country by the Germans.) On September 26 Gamelin analyzed the situation correspondingly — he mistakenly thought, however, that if Hungary attacked the Czechs, Rumania "in her own interests" would give airports in Transylvania to the use of the Russians. Back in Paris, Gamelin immediately contacted Voroshilov through the French Embassy in Moscow; but the reply of the Russian marshal was characteristically vague: he envisaged merely that Russia would go to war against Poland if the latter attacked the Czechs. Bonnet now said to Daladier: Russia will not fight. Gamelin urgently requested the Russian military attaché who was leaving for Moscow next day to convey a friendly message to Voroshilov: Russia should not attack Poland without consulting France beforehand. (Gamelin, p. 348.) (After all, had Russia really wished to stand by her agreements, she could have attacked Poland upon the October 1 ultimatum of the latter, concerning Teschen.) Comnen on September 28 officially informed Fabricius that Rumania would not grant anything to the Russians, and Litvinov did not request aerial passage — Comnen's explanation aimed to ingratiate himself with the Germans: Litvinov did not request it of him, he said, "because he knew that the answer would be in the negative" — nor would Rumania intervene, except *perhaps* in the extreme case, if Hungary *without provocation* attacked Czechoslovakia. (*GD*, II, 980–1; italics mine.) The German Minister was pleased.

No word about the question of Russian passage or even about Russian intervention was said at Munich (see the note of Wilson in *BD*, II, 630 *ff*.) except on one occasion, after the settlement, when Hitler made a fantastic statement to Chamberlain during their private talk, using his staple anti-Bolshevik arguments to impress the Premier: "Unlike Germany, whose ideology is confined to herself (a strange statement in view of Codreanu, Szálasi, and others), Russia's ideology is an article of export. Poland intervenes geographically between Germany and Russia but he [Hitler] had no very clear idea of her power of resistance. The same was the case with Rumania. As to Czechoslovakia . . . they had only got to prepare a few landing grounds and it would be possible for Russia to land from 2000

to 4000 machines in a space of from two or three hours." This ridiculous statement requires no comment.

(*3*) *The Soviet Union stressed the French obligations to Czechoslovakia and stated that she would fulfill her treaty obligations to the latter only if and when France did.* This "French pretext" developed only gradually and came into the open when (a) the Soviets found out that France might renege on her alliance with the Czechs (b) when finally some Rumanian consent to Russian passage seemed to be forthcoming. However, Soviet calculations concerning France were present throughout the crisis. Already on May 8 Kalinin stated to a visiting Czech trade union delegation that the Soviet Union would fulfill her obligations; he ended with these remarks: "if the Treaty of Friendship [?] between the Soviet Union, France, and Czechoslovakia were as strong as we wish it to be, then it would influence Britain also to choose other directions for her policy than those so far followed, and the Treaty would have greater international significance and weight."

The definite French question was put to Russia on September 1: *How* would Russia intervene? Litvinov did not answer until the 5th, suggesting that Russia would *follow* France and also wait until the League condemned German aggression. Litvinov offered a British-French-Russian conference to Bonnet, but Phipps wrote Halifax: "M. Bonnet feels that Russia is showing much more caution in this matter than she wishes others to show." (*BD*, II, 255.) In Moscow, Vice-Commissar Potemkin to Chilston on the 8th "repeated what is already well known, that the Soviet Union was not obliged to intervene unless and until France were actually engaged; and I gathered the impression that he [Potemkin] doubted whether France was politically in a position to make an immediate or powerful move." (*Ibid.,* p. 266.) At that time Alexandrovsky told a neutral diplomat in Prague that Russia would not help the Czechs if France remained neutral (this remark then reached German ears). The Poles shared this opinion. This was also the gist of Litvinov's Geneva statements, both to Bonnet and Comnen on September 11–12 and to the British delegates later; and it was reflected in his speech of September 21 in full session. (It is thus not quite correct to say, as Wheeler-Bennett did, that "Bonnet deliberately misrepresented the assurances given him recently by Litvinov," as these assurances were so conditional and vague that they had scarcely qualified as "assurances." But the Bonnet and Comnen accounts were published, of course, after the Wheeler-Bennett book.)

The crucial moment came after the presentation of the Anglo-French Plan to the Czechoslovak Government, when Prague, feeling deserted by the Western Powers, turned to Russia. On September 19 a Czechoslovak note was presented to Russia, and Beneš met the Soviet envoy on the 20th. There are two main versions of the Alexandrovsky-Beneš interview. Wheeler-Bennett's account is based on information he had received from Beneš during the war; but Beneš at that time was very anxious to give the impression that he could have depended on Russia in 1938. (In the published volumes of his memoirs Beneš maintains — flying in the face of facts particularly known to him — that Russia was ready to keep its word before Munich; see the review in the *Journal of Modern History,* September 1948, by a sympathetic compatriot.) According to the first version, Alexandrovsky, in a personal message from Litvinov, said to Beneš that "in the event of war, Russia would stand by Czechoslovakia whatever the Western Powers might do." The League was invoked by the Soviet envoy but only thus: "The Soviet Government would come to the support of Czechoslovakia . . . as soon as Moscow was informed that the League had . . . the case and would not wait for a decision to be reached at Geneva." Two years after this was published, Táborsky, a Czech refugee who had been close to Beneš, stated a contrary version in *Foreign Affairs,* January 1949: that Alexandrovsky evoked the French pretext and did not promise unconditional Soviet help. The Soviet-published *Documents and Materials* neither gives the text of the Czech note which asked for Soviet assistance, nor the Soviet answer; evidently the record of the Alexandrovsky-Beneš talks contains something which Moscow intended to hide. On September 21 Litvinov stated in his Geneva speech: "Two days ago . . . the Czechoslovak Government addressed a formal inquiry to my Government as to whether the Soviet Union is prepared, in accordance with the Soviet-Czechoslovak Pact, to render Czechoslovakia immediate and effective aid *if* France, loyal to her obligations, will render similar assistance, to which my Government gave a clear answer in the affirmative." Yet everything points to the fact that the Czech question did not contain that "if." The Soviet document collection refers in a footnote to the instructions sent by Litvinov to Alexandrovsky on September 20, and the Soviet editor in 1948 states: "The position of the USSR on this question may be seen from [this telegram] instructing [Alexandrovsky] to communicate to [Beneš] the following: (1) To Beneš' question whether the USSR will, in accordance with the treaty, render immediate and effective aid to Czechoslovakia *if France remains loyal to it and also renders aid* [italics mine], you may in the name of the Government of the Soviet Union give an affirmative answer. (2) You may also give an affirmative answer to Beneš' second question: Will the USSR assist Czechoslovakia, as a member of the League of Nations, in accordance with Articles 16 and 17 if, in the event of attack by Germany, Beneš requests the Council of the League to apply the above-mentioned articles? (3) Inform Beneš that we are simultaneously advising the French Government of our answer to his questions." There is no record of Beneš' questions elsewhere. But it is, to say the least, rather unlikely that his questions were worded and formulated thus, replete with conditions. It is also unlikely that Litvinov could have given such grave and decisive answers directly from Geneva, without having consulted the Kremlin.

It is true that when in the evening of September 26 a British communiqué, approved and drafted by a few Tories who were against appeasement and certain men of the Foreign Office, intimated that France, Britain, and Russia would go to war if Germany attacked Czechoslovakia, this communiqué was suppressed by Bonnet and the French government press denied it; yet Schulenburg wrote on the same day: "It appears that the Soviet Union is making her support absolutely dependent on the French rendering help first." (*GD*, II, 946.) Not even the Russian note to Poland (of the 23rd) was reproduced in the Soviet press until the 28th (on that day the Czech Minister in Belgrade said that Russia would intervene with a great aerial attack against Poland). When, on the morning of the 28th a German General Staff deputation prepared to give Hitler a written memorandum, warning him of the dangers which Germany faced in a European war, the memorandum did not mention Russia; neither was Russia mentioned at the plenary sessions of Munich.

On October 10 the Polish Ambassador said to Sumner Welles in Washington that Russia, at best, would have sent a few planes to the Czechs and that there had been but few preparations in the Russian frontier regions. A more authoritative observer, Tippelskirch, writing from Moscow on the same day, recalled how little prominence the Soviet newspapers had given to the Czech crisis and that the Soviets "also neglected to take such preliminary measures of mobilization as was considered necessary, for instance, in Holland, Belgium and Switzerland. Considering that the Soviet Union was under an obligation to render assistance to Czechoslovakia, this attitude must seem particularly striking." (*GD*, IV, 604.) (From all this Tippelskirch concluded that an amelioration of German-Russian relations could be expected and he recommended the offer of new economic agreements to the Soviets. Such talks actually began in Berlin on December 23.)

(4) Several indirect suggestions and veiled hints were given about the possibility of a German-Russian alignment. From the contemporary record of Soviet diplomacy it clearly transpires that the foreign policy of the Kremlin is never unduly hampered by ideological considerations. And thus the German-Soviet Pact of 1939 cannot be regarded as a sally, a surprise, a reaction. The record of Russian diplomacy in 1938 bears this out; it is discernible even earlier. On the one hand Stalin, of course, knew how certain circles in England were thinking (Lord Lothian to Blomberg and Hess in 1935: "Germany would cut through Russia as a knife cuts through butter"); on the other hand Litvinov and other Russian leaders in Moscow often made it known

to Schulenburg and other German diplomats how difficult it was for the Soviets to have "reasonable relations with petty-bourgeois French and greedy Anglo-Saxons." (Kordt; also Dirksen.) On his visit to Germany, Schulenburg addressed the Academy of the Wehrmacht on November 25, 1937, about Soviet Russia: in this profound speech he cautioned German officers not to underestimate the new Russia and mentioned the great Russian "conviction, born partly of respect, partly of fear . . . that of the fearful strength of the German people." (*GD*, I, 898.) Upon his return to Moscow the Ambassador found some rumors current that a German-Russian rapprochement was in the making; at the same time (December 1), Beneš spoke in confidence to Marek, the Austrian Minister to Prague (the conversation was then secretly recounted by Schmidt to Papen); Beneš said that Czech policy in regard to Russia "had nothing whatsoever to do with any similarity of ideologies; [it] arose from the necessity of the balance of power in Europe and from the realization that Russia represented a political reality, regardless of the régime which was in the saddle there. [Beneš] hoped that no agreement between Germany and Russia would materialize for a very long time, since such an understanding would be the worst possible thing that could happen to Europe, for it would mean neither more nor less than a division of Europe into spheres of interest." (*GD*, II, 63-4.) In January 1938 — in the wake of the purges — the Soviet Foreign Commissariat requested several European governments to close their Consulates in European Russia; among them the Czechoslovak Consulate in Kiev was closed. Schulenburg: "Particularly amazing . . . established only a year and a half ago as the only Czech Consular office . . . in spite of the close

relations between Moscow and Prague." (*GD*, I, 903.) And later: "The Soviet Government's action shows very clearly that foreign policy has to give way to domestic policy. Litvinov has to accommodate himself to this predominance of domestic policy." In a letter to Mackensen, Schulenburg followed up his views and reported Russian foreign policy trends as favorable to Germany (this was not published in *GD*, as the letter had not been found). The yearly summary report of Eisenlohr from Prague on January 12: "The [Czech] treaty relationship with Soviet Russia has not mellowed: on the contrary, it has paled." (*GD*, II, 99.) When in January, during the Fritsch crisis, a number of old-school generals were purged by Hitler, *Pravda* stated that the crisis "traces back to June 30, 1934," indicating dissatisfaction that a number of the Seeckt-type, pro-Russian generals were disposed of. Coulondre from Moscow indicated in February the possibilities of secret German-Russian contacts; according to Barmine, such actually existed through Ribbentrop's friends. A German Foreign Ministry circular at the end of February stated that French diplomatic circles saw the French-Russian alliance having very problematical value; France only entered it to prevent a Russian-German rapprochement, said certain Frenchmen; Litvinov actually used the bogey of such a rapprochement to bring France closer to Russia; on the other hand the official Soviet statement that the Soviet generals executed in the purges had been pro-German and had had contacts with German intelligence was untrue. (Circular, *GD*, I, 150; see also the Wilhelmstrasse memorandum of February 22, *ibid.*, p. 915 and Ribbentrop's directive of March 29: "In Moscow purge of the Army, the German defendants were interrogated under oath and you are to place a false picture of Russia before France for the purpose of keeping Russia out of the international picture as desired by Germany. The Führer's speech of February 20 would dispel any belief in the possibility of political coöperation between Germany and the Soviet Union.") The Counselor of the Polish Embassy in Paris told his German colleague on March 28 that in a European conflict "Russia would not move a man," because of geographical, political, and internal reasons: at most, the Soviet Air Force would intervene on a limited scale. (*GD*, I, 202.) These estimates seemed confirmed by the hesitant and cautious Soviet attitude during the Polish-Lithuanian crisis. Newton to Halifax on April 12: "I note and agree with (Henderson's) opinion that the abandonment of Czechoslovakia's alliance with Russia is likely to be one of the conditions of a definite and peaceful solution, unless indeed Germany itself one day makes friends with Russia, when an altogether new situation would arise." (*BD*, I, 153.) On April 2 the Moscow Embassy and on April 14 the Paris Embassy informed the Wilhelmstrasse that Soviet-French relations were very bad. Weizsäcker to the German Ambassador to China on May 30: "Russia hardly exists in our calculations today. As long as Stalin makes himself as useful as now, we need not particularly worry about him as regards military policy." (*GD*, I, 864.)

In June the Soviet press made some direct references to German warlike attitudes and military preparations. Yet Merekalov, the new Soviet Ambassador to Germany, had called on Schulenburg before his departure and, for a Soviet diplomat, he was unusually affable: he "hoped" that German-Russian relations "would be expanded and strengthened." He spoke emphatically of commercial relations: this is significant, as the stand-

ard practice of Soviet diplomacy was to inaugurate political rapprochement by commercial negotiations. He arrived in Berlin on June 16. Of course, his words might have been purely conventional. But on June 21 the American chargé in Moscow told Schulenburg of the fact that the Soviet censor of the Foreign Commissariat, when dealing with an American news dispatch, had suggested the following version: "Any proposal by Germany that promoted world peace would presumably be favorably received by the Soviet Government. Any proposal by Germany amounting to a weakening of world peace would be rejected by the Soviet Government, since new unrest in the world would be thereby created and the front of the peace-loving powers would be weakened." Next day a secretary of the American Embassy told Schulenburg that this revision seemed significant, "since it indicated that the Soviet Union on its part did not intend to close the door to negotiations with Germany definitely . . ." (*GD*, I, 920-1.)

On June 23 Litvinov made a rather obscure speech in Leningrad which, precisely because of its length and repetitive Soviet phraseology about peace-loving, etc., did not receive much attention in the Western press; yet Litvinov did make a few very significant allusions to Germany: "if Germany were only democratic, the Soviet attitude toward the Czechoslovakian question would be completely different"; "if the Soviet Union has sided with the democracies, and the League of Nations during the last few years, it has done so because Germany aims not merely at the restoration of her prewar boundaries and the rights denied her by the Versailles Treaty but also pursues an open and mad anti-Soviet policy and a policy of unlimited aggression"; "when the proposed regional pact for the East had been blocked by Germany and Poland (thus Litvinov alluded to 1933–34), the Soviet Union concluded Mutual Assistance Pacts with France and Czechoslovakia." The Litvinov speech was excellently analyzed in two Schulenburg memoranda, on June 24 and July 5 (*GD*, I, 921–3 and 928–9): "Since the Soviet suggestions frequently fall upon deaf ears among the Western Powers, Litvinov absolves the Soviet Union from any 'responsibility of further developments' *and thereby reserves his freedom of action.* . . . The tone of the speech has remarkably little aggressiveness and strives to leave open all possibilities. The attempt to arrive at an objective attitude toward the policy of the Third Reich is striking." Similar were the conclusions of Tippelskirch on July 5, reflecting upon rumors that Stalin had told the American Ambassador Davies of his decision to help the Czechs militarily. Tippelskirch: Russia still wants to avoid participating in a war. "It can be assumed that in the event of a German-Czech war the Soviet Union will at first adopt an attitude of wait and see. . . . Stronger Soviet intervention is only to be reckoned with if Germany, in a possible war, is faced with a coalition of superior powers, and if the Soviet Government becomes convinced that the outcome of the war will be unfavorable for Germany." (*GD*, II, 467–8.) On July 1 the influential *Revue des deux mondes* in Paris published an article about the possibilities of a German-Russian alignment in the near future.

While the Japanese, who were involved in a veritable war with Russia on the Manchurian border, with tanks and airplanes, tried to turn Germany against the Soviets (the Japanese Ambassador to Berlin presented fantastic intelligence reports there in July about the internal disorganization and troubles within the Soviet Union), somewhat later the Italian chargé in Moscow was told by a Soviet official that Japan first had limited and then stopped the border war because Germany did not promise her military assistance against Russia. This, of course, could well have been one of the Soviet trial balloons; but Massigli, a highly placed French diplomat, told Sir Ronald Campbell on August 13: "Once Germany secured the supplies which a penetration to the South-East would give her, she would be careful not to get embroiled with Russia but would then turn West again." (*BD*, II, 93.) On August 20 Schulenburg spoke to Potemkin, who "acted as if the Czechoslovak question were indeed of great interest to the Soviet Government, but did not concern them particularly. Potemkin's attitude obviously conforms to a 'mot d'ordre' given out by the Soviet Government. . . . I have the impression that M. Litvinov is postponing my visit [the Ambassador had requested an appointment] because he wished first to find out through Potemkin . . ." As so often, Schulenburg's analysis was correct. Two days later Litvinov received him, and the Soviet Foreign Commissar, while verbally firm, again and again avoided saying whether and how Russia would assist Czechoslovakia. Litvinov naturally defended the latter, but he also added: "The Soviet Union considers the Sudeten German question to be the domestic concern of Czechoslovakia. The Soviet Union had not interfered in any war or given advice, whether in the one or the other direction. Neither will she do it in the future. . . . If the old democratic Germany still existed, the Czechoslovak question would have had quite a different aspect for the Soviet Union. We have always espoused the cause of self-determination of peoples." (*GD*, II, 604.) Here was a clear indication that the Soviet would like to approach a receptive Germany; this was also Lord Chilston's conclusion. (*BD*, II, 141, n. 2.) The Soviet chargé in Rome, Helfand, saw Ciano on August 28 and intimated "in veiled terms" that Russia would not seriously intervene in a German-Czech war; a day later the Italian Ambassador confirmed this view from Moscow. (*CD*, pp. 228-9.) A few days later Hitler told his generals: Russia was not worth considering.

On the day when war seemed inevitable — September 27 — the Polish Ambassador was told by Weizsäcker that Ribbentrop was "very optimistic" in regard to Russia; on the day of Munich Potemkin bitterly remonstrated with Schulenburg, not against the German aggression against Czechs, but against the exclusion of the Soviets from the Munich Conference, and he concluded with an interesting hint to the German Ambassador: Germany, said Potemkin, better beware of Mussolini, who intervenes in central-eastern Europe to prevent German gains and to build up his own bases in Poland and Hungary. This, noted Schulenburg, was a definite indication of Stalin saying to Hitler: I am a better friend than Mussolini. (*GD*, II, 998-9.)

.   .   .   .

After Munich, Western political thinking developed a veritable guilt complex, which manifested itself in the intellectual argument that it was Russia which was about to take a most righteous course and defend Europe in 1938 but which was spurned and shunned and discriminated against by the Western Powers and henceforth became disillusioned and distrustful. This tendency was especially manifest in the United States, where the press indignantly criticized Britain after Munich. Moscow was quick to exploit this American tendency; she needed the trust of the United States in 1938, when American military and diplomatic circles were largely distrustful of the Soviets. As early as September 28, the Soviet Union issued a communiqué supporting and welcoming the academic peace message of President Roosevelt of the day before. The Kremlin correctly foresaw the coming ascendancy of the United States in world politics; it also envisaged a growing community of interests between Russia and America in face of Japan and in view of the probability that both would be non-belligerents in the first phase of a future European conflict. At the same time Moscow wished to make it clear that she was untainted by what had happened at Munich: on October 3 Tippelskirch referred to some Russian depression in Moscow, but added that the Soviets were also "anxious to avoid any appearance of direct or indirect participation in the Munich Agreement." (*GD*, IV, 602.) This was the tenor of the first TASS statements after Munich and was kept up for a while. On October 9 TASS denied "rumors" that Daladier had been authorized to speak on behalf of Russia at Munich; this denial was made "in the name of the Soviet Embassy in Washington"; the Soviet Embassy in London at the same time assailed the British correspondent, Winterton, for his alleged statement that Russia, like the Western Powers, had also refused to aid Czechoslovakia in the crisis. The Kremlin exploited this undue Western "guilt complex" brilliantly throughout the Second World War; perhaps, had the truth about the Soviet attitude in 1938 been known and not clouded by propaganda, the road might not have led to Yalta. There Stalin said to Churchill and Roosevelt that it was Munich which had made him consider dealing with Hitler, as Russia's exclusion from Munich had affronted him. But neither his own broadcast of July 3, 1941, to the Russian people, when he justified his pact with Hitler by stating that thereby he had won a year and a half for military preparations, nor the diplomatic record, nor Potemkin's words to Coulondre immediately after Munich (October 4: "My poor friend, what did you do? This may lead to the fourth partition of Poland") bear out Stalin's Yalta statement. Indeed, while he wished to profit from a European war from which Russia would be absent (see also the secret Comintern document of 1939, cited by Bonnet, Appendix), he played into Ribbentrop's hands (the latter to Ciano on October 28: "In the East Russia is weak and will remain so for many years; all our dynamism may be directed against the western democracies." *CLD*, p. 375. At the same time the American chargé reported from Moscow that Litvinov's influence seemed to be waning). The usefulness of the Munich argument continued to impress Stalin even after the Second World War; in reply to the State Department's publication of German documents which revealed the main story of Nazi-Soviet relations between 1939 and 1941, the Russian government countered by publishing two document collections, the larger part of which refers almost exclusively to the Czechoslovak crisis, and the editing and composition of which indicate the Russian desire to appear as the only angel among the devils in 1938 and to profit from this image as much and as long as possible. But this image is a false one.

· 3 ·

BETWEEN

GERMAN

HAMMER

&

RUSSIAN

ANVIL

The results of Munich

If at first you don't succeed, try, try, try again," said the sedately triumphant Chamberlain on his return from Munich — to which Winston Churchill bitterly retorted, "If at first you don't concede, fly, fly, fly again." The flights were ended, but the trials continued: from Munich to Prague, from October 1, 1938, to March 15, 1939, France and Britain endeavored to preserve the peace of Europe in concert with Hitler — but all in vain.

[*The twilight of the Czechs.*] With Munich sank most of Czechoslovakia's independence. Sýrový, the Czech Prime Minister, confided to his French and British visitors that only one aim guided him now and that was to make the very best possible terms with the victorious Germans. On October 1, the day after Munich, Göring told Mastny that Germany could not tolerate Beneš in the Presidency. The latter resigned on October 5 and later during the month he flew to London. Yet even Beneš did not expect the transformation of Czechoslovakia into a German satellite state. For months he continued to believe that the new situation did not necessarily mean complete subjugation by the Germans. Indeed for a while it seemed that the new Czech government would somehow hold its own. There were, of course, grave problems, internal and external. The minorities of Czechoslovakia demanded a post-Munich solution. (*1*) Poland took care of her own by marching into Teschen on October 1, and Hungary demanded a rectification of the Trianon frontier. In addition, Slovaks and Ruthenians suddenly discovered the sweet arcanum of power and pressed Prague for concessions. Semi-autonomous "régimes" and new "statesmen" were popping up in Bratislava; in Ruthenia, national committees and even a Ruthenian autonomous government were introduced under the leadership of the pro-Magyar Brody, who was demoted by Prague on October 26. (*2*) On November 22 almost complete autonomy was granted to Slovakia and Ruthenia. The name of the latter was officially changed to Carpatho-Ukraine and the name of the mother republic itself became hyphenated: Czecho-Slovakia. The new Slovak and Carpatho-Ukranian "governments" were soon playing the German game. The moderates disappeared, and in Slovakia a "Hlinka Guard," resuscitated by German money, was rapidly transforming itself into a hopeful Fifth Column. In the Carpatho-Ukraine similar people, the "Sič-Guardists," were Greater Ukrainians, and in the winter of 1938 it seemed that the Carpatho-Ukraine might play the rôle of a Piedmont in relation to the Greater Ukraine, an idea encouraged by Hitler until he changed his mind and, abandoning his Ukrainian plans, decided to come to an agreement with Russia.

[*The Hungarian problem and the First Vienna Award.*] Budapest emphatically demanded settlement of the problem of Hungarian minorities. Strong notes were delivered to Prague; partial mobilization was ordered and slowly increasing pressure was put all along the southern frontier of Slovakia. After some delay Hungarian, Czech and Slovak delegates met at Komarno (*3*) on October 9. The Czechs did not desire a war with Hungary, and yet their Slovak partners, especially Tiso, rabidly fought against any concessions. The Komarno meeting broke up. The Czechoslovaks had proposed the cession of 1840 square kilometres with a population of about 100,000, whereas the minimum demands of the Hungarians were almost ten times greater. To show their goodwill, the Czechs ceded two localities to Hungary as "tokens": the town of Ipolyság (*4*) and the railroad station of Sátoraljaujhely (*5*), both located one or two miles beyond the Trianon frontiers. Around the middle of October, the situation became more dangerous; Hungarian free troops entered Southern Slovakia and Carpatho-Ukraine, dynamiting Czech military installations. A second Komarno meeting also was unsuccessful, although by the end of the month, Prague increased her offer, first four-, then sevenfold. Finally, after having ascertained that the Western Powers had no desire whatsoever to intervene in the dispute, Chvalkovsky, the new Czechoslovak Foreign Minister (6), asked Hitler and Mussolini to arbitrate. On October 27 Ribbentrop arrived in Rome to prepare for the arbitration. He now favored the Czechs, and Ciano noted:

> This is ugly. Very ugly. And perhaps instructive. After having for twenty years cultivated the friendship and illusions of the Hungarians, they abandon them; moreover they obstruct them when support would mean but a little sacrifice. I fought with much energy. If the arbitration will take place, I hope to succeed and snatch from the Germans the three eastern cities [which Hungary had requested]. But it will be a hard battle. (7)

Ribbentrop also brought a message to Mussolini about the formation of a German-Italian-Japanese military alliance. Hitler was convinced that in three or four years a war with the democracies was inevitable; he was convinced of American isolationism. Mussolini assured him of the sincere pro-Axis sentiment among the broad masses in Italy, but he added that the people were "not yet ready" for a military alliance.

On November 2, the delegates met in the Belvedere Palace of Vienna and meted out the so-called First Vienna Award: twelve thousand square miles of southern Slovakia and Carpatho-Ukraine were returned to Hungary, with about a million inhabitants, of whom about eighty per cent were Magyars. (8) The Czechs were dejected, the Slovaks bitter, the Hungarians somewhat dissatisfied.

.   .   .   .

[*Liquidation plans and faint Western reactions.*] Hitler recognized at once the possibilities which Munich opened to him. He decided to liquidate the remnants of Czechoslovakia as soon as possible; on October 5 he spoke to Weizsäcker in this vein, and on the 11th, he conferred with him at Godesberg: the International Commission should be made to disappear from "the scene" at the earliest date possible; an extraterritorial motor-highway should be planned, cutting across Czech territory and connecting Breslau and Vienna; the economic aims of Germany should be pursued unconditionally; at the same time Warsaw should be told that Germany was interested in the steel centers of Vitkovice and Moravska-Ostrava. In a month, all these instructions were carried out.

Meanwhile, on October 21, a directive was issued by the German High Command: "The Armed Forces should be prepared for the liquidation of the remainder of Czechoslovakia . . . [and Memel.]" (9) Where, then, was the Munich guarantee of Czech frontiers? Chamberlain, in a rather clumsy, nineteenth-century materialistic gesture, tried to sweeten the bitter pill of Munich: on his return he announced that Britain would give a ten-million-pound sterling loan to Czechoslovakia. But this was all. At the Vienna arbitration, the Western Powers did not have a word, because they did not desire to have any. On November 6, Chamberlain and Halifax explained to Daladier and Bonnet in Paris that the Czechoslovak guarantee could only be upheld jointly with Germany and Italy. The Czechoslovak statesmen asked for a concrete definition of the Munich guarantee. Even when Sýrový resigned on November 30 and the new Czechoslovak President, Hácha, installed the Agrarian Beran as Premier, the latter still tried to reap at least some benefits from the remains of Western ties. Nonetheless, on December 10, Newton told Chvalkovsky that Britain could not give any guarantee alone, hinting that Germany was the sole guarantor acceptable to the British, "who would not put themselves in the position in which France was in last October." (10) At the end of December, the new French Ambassador in Berlin reported that Germany had new, further designs on Czechoslovakia, and when in the second week of January 1939 Chamberlain and Halifax made a pilgrimage to Rome, they brought up the question of a Czechoslovak guarantee with Mussolini. He, sensing what Hitler had in mind, refused to commit himself and spoke only in very vague terms about the interpretation of the guarantee. (11) On January 21, Hitler received Chvalkovsky in Germany. The Czech pleaded his nation's goodwill, pointing to the complete absence among Czechs of a desire for revenge against Germany. But Hitler was not satisfied; he harped on charges that the new Czech régime did not enact radical measures against the remnants of the Liberal opposition, that it maintained a semblance of a parliament, that it was not sufficiently anti-Semitic. It is "impossible to conduct a foreign policy, A and a domestic policy *B*!" shouted Hitler. *(12)* From that moment on it was clear to Chvalkovsky that Hitler would not tolerate even a partially independent Czecho-Slovakia; he wanted all of it for himself.

With the destruction of Czechoslovakia, the Ukrainian question came into the foreground.

[*The Polish-Hungarian barrier idea.*] During the whole crisis, Poland and Hungary wished for the incorporation of Carpatho-Ukraine into Hungary. Poland preferred that Ukrainian Piedmont disappear, absorbed into the non-Slavic Hungarian state; Hungary had a thousand-year-old historical claim to Ruthenia. There was, besides, the sentimental issue of the traditional friends, Poland and Hungary, grasping hands at the crest of the Carpathians. As long as German foreign policy was dogmatically inimical towards Russia and Czechoslovakia, there seemed to be no controversy. Especially did Göring, the sportsman, hunter, and would-be aristocrat, who thought of himself as a great Master of Foxhounds together with his "friends," Henderson and Beck, nurture the typical German "Western complex." He wished to make a grandiose agreement with the "aristocratic" states of Europe, Poland and Britain, well-nigh monopolizing Europe for themselves: Russia would then not count. In August 1938, Göring spoke favorably of the Polish-Hungarian frontier, saying that a Polish-dominated Ukraine would always be favored by Germany.

But Hitler and Ribbentrop saw further. They saw that the conservative leaders of central-eastern Europe, especially those of Poland, Hungary and Yugoslavia, would not be altogether glad at the prospects of German domination of the Danubian area after a complete disappearance of Czechoslovakia. The establishment of the Polish-Hungarian frontier would result in a strong bloc of anti-Communist, but not necessarily pro-German states, an independent *cordon sanitaire*, an uninterrupted tier of three states, Poland, Hungary and Yugoslavia, extending from the Baltic to the Adriatic seas. *(13)* Hitler had no desire to see this happen.

During his interview with Hitler on September 20, Lipski brought up the question of a common frontier with Hungary, but Hitler was noncommittal. Concerning Teschen, Ribbentrop could tell Beck on October 1 of Germany's "complete understanding of the Polish point of view," (*14*) but Carpatho-Ukraine was different. On October 5 a German High Command memorandum stated that "for military reasons a common Hungarian-Polish frontier was undesirable" and "the creation of a compact bloc of succession states on Germany's eastern frontier, with lines of communication to southeast Europe, will not be to our interest." To François-Poncet, Hitler on October 18 spoke impatiently of the "excessive demands of Hungary" concerning the common frontier. Six days later the first gun of the German diplomatic offensive against Poland was fired.

On October 24, Ribbentrop saw Lipski and a broad discussion ensued on a surprising variety of matters. Ribbentrop proposed a joint German-Polish stand on the colonial question; a joint endeavor to "solve" the Jewish question of central-eastern Europe; a joint front against Russia; he recapitulated the fruitful four years and common benefits of Polish-German amity (*15*) — then he played out his trumps. All would be well, if only Poland would agree to Danzig's return to the Reich and not object to an extraterritorial highway and railroad line connecting metropolitan Germany with East Prussia through the Polish Corridor. In addition to these thinly disguised demands, Ribbentrop asked the Poles to counsel the Hungarians to moderation in regard to the Polish-Hungarian common frontier.

The diplomatic overtures for the winning of Poland lasted from October 1938 to March 1939. Hitler believed that the winter months were not suitable for great overt actions; he preferred to make diplomatic preparations in the winter and "act" in the summer. From the Ribbentrop-Lipski talk in October to the German entry into Prague in March, Hitler tried to bring the Poles in line by diplomatic means. On January 5 to Beck, and on January 18 to Csáky he emphasized the importance of concerted, aggressive German-Polish-Hungarian-Italian cooperation. Csáky was very much impressed ("finally, we now have a free hand in the Danubian basin . . . the West shall not dare to intervene with us. . . . The future belongs to the states of central Europe . . ."). Beck was not impressed; he felt he could not discuss the German demands about Danzig and the corridor.

[*The Polish game of balance: Russia.*] While he spared no efforts to assure Hitler of Poland's unbroken friendship, immediately after the Lipski-Ribbentrop conversations Beck set out to improve relations with Russia. After Polish-Soviet relations had reached an almost unprecedented low in the September crisis, Beck approached

Litvinov. In October, a rail traffic agreement was signed between the two nations, and Soviet assurances were given to Poland concerning the restoration of the Polish military cemetery in Kiev, which the Soviets had razed a few weeks before. Moscow was very anxious, suspecting that Britain may have given a blank check to Hitler in regard to the Ukraine. Despite the clearly anti-Bolshevik character of the new Czech régime, on November 6 Molotov said that the Soviet Union would still be willing to fulfill her obligations toward Czechoslovakia, if called upon. It was a move excellently geared to the aftermath of the Vienna Award, at which time no Czechoslovak nurtured very friendly feelings toward Germany and Italy, or toward Britain and France, either. On November 26, a joint Polish-Soviet communiqué was issued, reaffirming the Polish-Soviet Non-Aggression Pact of 1932. On December 9, Sir William Strang of the Foreign Office expressed his satisfaction to Raczynski, the Polish Ambassador: "The British Government certainly does not want Poland to abandon the balance of power policy pursued till now." (*16*)

But this "balance of power policy" was not exactly what Russia wanted. Stalin had estimated Hitler's plans very well, and the well-known Comintern leader, Dimitrov, in a 1938 autumn issue of *Bolshevik* had predicted the German "timetable" with admirable accuracy. It also transpired that Bonnet was thinking about concluding a French Non-Aggression Pact with Germany. On November 22, Bonnet showed the entire draft of the German-French declaration to the Polish envoy, but withheld the full text from the Soviet Ambassador, who had also asked for it. (On the same day, the French Ambassador in Poland wrote to General Gamelin complaining about the Poles: ". . . such an impressionable nation . . . her intransigence hampers us in regard to Russia.") In December, Poland was still very friendly with the Axis (*17*); Bonnet and Ribbentrop signed the German-French Non-Aggression Pact on the 6th in Paris (*18*); and although Chvalkovsky on the 14th reiterated the continued validity of the Czechoslovak-Soviet Pact, the Soviet press and radio began to attack Czechoslovakia and Russia made a diplomatic protest because of the "Greater Ukrainian" activities in Prague and in the Carpatho-Ukraine. And Neville Chamberlain illustrated his Christmas cards with the airplane which had flown him to Munich. Mussolini, answering a question by Chamberlain on January 12, 1939, said that he was sure Hitler would not attack the Ukraine. But both Hitler and he were against the Polish-Hungarian frontier idea.

There occurred now a highly interesting development. Somehow —
probably due to faulty security within the British Embassy at Rome —
the record of the Chamberlain-Mussolini conversations transpired to
Moscow, where Chamberlain's question about German intentions in
the Ukraine was immediately and thoroughly misinterpreted. Stalin
and Russian diplomacy saw in this query the quest of an anxious
Britain trying to enlist the aid of Italy to turn Hitler eastward. Two
consequences arose out of this Muscovite misunderstanding. In view
of Mussolini's answer, Russian diplomacy suddenly warmed toward
Italy and hinted at a rapprochement. The second effect was more
decisive. Stalin thought his suspicions thoroughly confirmed now, and
this belief directly led to the speech he was to give on March 10, the
speech in which he put Britain and France in the van of "imperialist"
powers and sounded the first hint of the desirability of better German-
Russian relations.

Meanwhile, Poland: until March she could continue her balancing
game, but not a minute later. When Czechoslovakia was finished, it
would be her turn. When winter passed without bringing full completion of the necessary diplomatic framework for a summer offensive,
Hitler immediately considered military action against Poland. (*19*)
Therefore, when he marched into Prague on March 15, he did not
object to the realization of the common Hungarian-Polish frontier
anymore, *because the whole Ukrainian issue became irrelevant to him from the
moment he decided to liquidate Poland — if need be, with the cooperation of
Soviet Russia.* (*20*)

.   .   .   .

[*Independent efforts of some small states.*]   In the winter there was
some stiffening of anti-German sentiment in Yugoslavia, Poland and
Bulgaria. The Yugoslav opposition polled 44 per cent of the votes in
rather primitive municipal elections, a fact which weakened the position of Stoyadinovič. Regent Paul travelled to Rome, Paris, and London in November and December. When he returned, he decided to
put an end to the Stoyadinovič régime; action was taken two months
later. In Bulgaria, Prime Minister Kiosseivanov labored for better
Bulgar-Yugoslav relations and met Stoyadinovič at Niš in October
1938. (At the same time Kiosseivanov predicted to the French Minister in Sofia the probability of a future German-Russian alliance.)
In November, King Carol of Rumania likewise went to Paris and

London; he also visited Hitler. In the same month, the arrested Iron Guard leaders, including Codreanu, were shot "in an attempt to escape"; almost the entire leadership of the Iron Guard was eliminated. Hitler was furious. He could never forget the duplicity of Carol, who had been most affable and understanding during their visit (after having been previously admonished by Bonnet not to count too much on French support). In December Gafencu replaced Comnen as Rumanian Foreign Minister. Also, Horthy of Hungary tried to remove the now extremely pro-German Imrédy from the Premiership. (*21*) In November, Imrédy was voted down in Parliament, but after the liberal wing of the National Unity Party was unable to form a cabinet, he was requested to continue in office. In December, Csáky replaced Kánya in the Foreign Ministry — a move to the Right; in February, by pointing, ironically enough, at one of his Jewish ancestors, it was finally possible to make the anti-Semitic Imrédy resign. Count Teleki succeeded him in the Premiership — a move back toward Center. Meanwhile, an armed intrusion of Carpatho-Ukrainian troops into Hungarian territory at Munkács (*22*) in January, and Csáky's signing of the Anti-Comintern Pact, followed by the subsequent Soviet decision to break off diplomatic relations with Hungary on February 3, did not leave Hungarian diplomatic waters unruffled.

Hitler's fatal step: the occupation of Prague. Memel

[*The German timetable.*] Around Christmas, the Slovak-language program of the Vienna radio began to attack the Prague government; through Bratislava, Nazi leaders established contact with Tiso and his Hlinka-Guardists, Karmasin, the leader of the German minority group in Slovakia, playing the rôle of middleman.

France was informed of these developments through Coulondre, to whom Ribbentrop, encouraged by the Franco-German Pact of December 6, hinted at the desirability of a clear division of spheres of interest. When on December 22 the French Ambassador asked Weizsäcker about the four-power guarantee to Czechoslovakia, the German retorted, "Could not this matter be forgotten?" and, hinting at the Christmas season, jovially added that there was no urgency to discuss it. Coulondre waited for further developments. They came rapidly. On January 5, 1939, Beck stopped at Berchtesgaden on his way home from the French Riviera. Hitler expressed his disinterest in the Carpatho-Ukraine and carefully but affably, approached the question of Danzig and the Corridor, the issue which had lain practically dormant since the Lipski-Ribbentrop conversation of October 24. But Beck was a clever seer of souls. He switched topics, assailing the "criminal" policies of Beneš and the Czechoslovaks, and thus opened an issue dear to Hitler's heart, who took great joy in the fact that the elegant Polish visitor so fully agreed with him. Thus Hitler let Beck go, without reverting to the subject of Danzig.

Hitler decided to "liquidate" Czechoslovakia before broaching the ticklish Polish issues. (1) On January 18, he spoke to Csáky of the possibility of occupation of the Czecho-Slovak remnants; a few days later, he railed at Chvalkovsky, and gave orders to the press and the radio gradually to increase their pro-Slovak propaganda. The intimidated Chvalkovsky returned to Prague, where it was decided to take another step to appease Hitler. At the end of January, a high officer of the Czechoslovak Foreign Ministry, Masardjik, was sent to Berlin with almost full powers: his orders were to inquire about possible German demands and to grant them. But just as in September 1938 Beneš could not goad the Sudeten leaders into committing themselves, neither could Masardjik get the Germans to list their demands. Instead, on February 5, definite and detailed military plans for the subjugation of Czechoslovakia were issued.

[*French-British questions.*]   All this did not escape the attention of Coulondre. As a result of his observations, a joint Franco-British note was sent on February 8 to Berlin: What were the German intentions in regard to Czechoslovakia? For a moment, Bonnet thought of playing Berlin against Rome; Coulondre stated in Berlin that "it was difficult for France to forego her interests in the east and at the same time to make concessions in the Mediterranean. France would, however, naturally not pursue any policy in the east which would disturb Germany." Yet it was now clear to Hitler that the Western Powers — incredible as it seemed to him — did not intend simply to write Prague off. He decided not to reply to the February 8 note. He asked Karmasin to bring the Slovak leaders to him; the old Tuka trembled before the Führer and unctuously said: "I entrust the fate of my people to your care." (2)

The Tuka visit, secretive as it was, did not escape the attention of Chvalkovsky, who informed the French envoy. On February 18, Lacroix's extensive report reached Paris, substantiating the evaluations of Coulondre. (*3*) Now the German Foreign Ministry's answer to the February 8 note was again requested, but not until March 2 was the German reply given. The answer rejected the Western note, stating that the Czechoslovak guarantee was out-of-date. By that time, preparations for the final occupation of Czechoslovakia were progressing rapidly. The Vienna radio increased its propaganda and the ominous stories of Czech "atrocities" against Germans began to crop up; meanwhile, from cafés in Engerau (*4*) and in Vienna Nazi leaders were directing the Slovak "autonomists." The first explosion occurred on March 6; in some backwoods districts of the Carpatho-Ukraine, the Sič-Guardists began to eject Czech officials. On the evening of that day, it was announced that the Carpatho-Ukrainian "autonomists" were dismissed; two days later they suddenly appeared in Berlin. Here was the pattern. The Slovak Durčansky fled to Göring next morning and the Germans now promised direct and rapid aid. On the ninth, Hlinka-Guardists brawled in Bratislava and a Slovak "parliament" was formed, whereupon Tiso was arrested by the Czechs, but Tuka and Durčansky slipped over the bridge to Austria. A few conservative Slovak leaders rallied around Prague, but their voices were drowned out by the rising wind. Operations were directed by the German SS chief, Keppler, who felt put upon by the passive attitude of the Czech militia: "We scarcely succeeded to provoke the necessary incidents," he complained.

[*The last phase.*] Alone, helpless, torn, menaced, the remaining Czech leaders tried to brave the storm. Yet at the same time (on March 10) Chamberlain was envisaging a Europe "settling down to a period of tranquillity" and Sir Samuel Hoare spoke to his constituents about a forthcoming "Golden Age," in which the leaders of Europe in 1939 "working together might make themselves the eternal benefactors of the human race. . . ." Halifax energetically protested against the speech, but the effects of such statements by responsible Englishmen on Poles, Hungarians, and Rumanians could well be imagined.

Tiso was quickly "liberated," and on March 13 he flew to Hitler and entrusted Slovakia to his care. (*5*) Sztójay, misinterpreting a remark of Hitler's, wired Budapest that the whole of eastern Slovakia and the Carpatho-Ukraine could be occupied, if Horthy so wished. Thereupon Horthy sent a message to Hitler on the same day: "My sincere thanks. . . . I can hardly tell you how happy I am because of this . . ." He said that on Thursday, March 16, a "frontier incident" would be arranged, after which would come the "big blow on Saturday." (6) (It was later pointed out that Slovakia had not been mentioned.)

There is no need to record again the cunning, duplicity and terror which Hitler used to force Hácha and Chvalkovsky to come to Berlin on the night of the 14th. While Hácha and his daughter were on their way, German troops had already entered Vitkovice and Moravska-Ostrava — to forestall the Poles, as Göring later put it. The Nuremberg documents have confirmed how the old man was harassed during the night and threatened by arguments of a merciless air attack on Prague. Finally, as the grey dawn broke, he signed the proffered German document, (7) and at that moment, Czechoslovakia ceased to exist. Next morning, under a rainy, bleak sky, the swastika appeared on the Hradčany Palace; and in Slovakia the "independent Slovak republic" was established. The situation was obscure for days in eastern Slovakia, where Guardists, Czechs under General Prchala, German advance formations, and the left flank of the Hungarian divisions which slowly moved into the Carpatho-Ukraine were clashing with each other. Not until the last week of March was order restored in Slovakia. On March 23, Hitler and Tiso signed a German-Slovak Protection Treaty, a secret protocol of which provided for German right to keep garrisons in "independent" Slovakia. (8) Thus, not only "Czechia" (Bohemia and Moravia), but also Slovakia became a German protectorate. (9) Coulondre could report to Paris, "Germany is still the nation of scraps of paper."

.   .   .   .

[*Memel.*] Poland, obviously the next target, felt somewhat comforted when, after two days' fighting against Sič-Guardists, Hungarian detachments reached the Carpathian border in a heavy snowstorm. (*10*) The common frontier now came into being, yet Poland could feel but little satisfaction over this fact. She was now outflanked in the south, where the Slovak mountains could be manned by German divisions, and all the mountain passes were in German hands.

Four days after Prague, Germany demanded Memel. On December 10, 1938, the German Foreign Ministry had denied to Coulondre that Berlin had designs upon the Memelland; yet a short time later, Weizsäcker boasted that the conquest of Memel called but for "a registered letter to Kaunas." The "letter" was registered and dispatched immediately after a haggard-faced Hitler had driven up the castle hill of Prague. The able Lithuanian Foreign Minister, Urbsys, who in February had tried to make the Germans commit themselves and had also tried to muster some Western assistance, was unsuccessful in both efforts; on March 19, he travelled to Berlin and signed. Four days later a warship carried Hitler to Memel for another triumphant entry. The Baltics trembled.

. . . .

[*The great change; reaction in Britain.*]   Only eight days elapsed between Prague and Memel; yet, the whole scene changed in these days. On March 15, appeasement had still been the password. Neville Chamberlain clung to the Slovak independence declaration: "The effect of this decision put an end by internal disruption to a state whose frontier we had proposed to guarantee. His Majesty's Government cannot accordingly hold themselves any longer bound by this obligation." But the mood of Britain now changed. Lord Halifax wrote a long letter to Chamberlain, who was to speak at Birmingham on the 17th; the latter, finally taken aback by the unmistakable breach of the promise which Hitler gave to him in person, understood the argument and yielded to the Foreign Secretary's viewpoint. (*11*) Two days after Prague, a speech by Great Britain's Prime Minister officially terminated the era of appeasement.

There is no doubt that the course of Hitler's career turned with his entry into Prague: had he waited somewhat longer, acted elsewhere, or at least with more circumspection, he could have perhaps avoided the abrupt collapse of appeasement. Perhaps Prague was his greatest mistake. Immediately plans for a Western diplomatic counteroffensive rose. It was expected that Hitler was soon to raise the question of territorial demands with Poland; a day or two after Prague, rumors came of a German "economic ultimatum" to Rumania. While the Rumanian Minister to Paris was more cautious and the Poles sceptical, the Minister in London, Tilea, hurried to Halifax and asked for immediate assistance. (*12*) Halifax had already asked the French and Russian Ambassadors what their countries would do in case of further German aggression, notably in the direction of Rumania; on March 18 the Soviet envoy in Berlin protested against the annihilation of Czechoslovakia; the Memel action added to Russian worries.

(*13*) In answer to the British overture, the Soviets proposed a Six-Power Conference: with Britain, France, Poland, Rumania, and Turkey. Although London declined the conference idea, a diplomatic counteroffensive seemed to be in the making, and for the first time since 1934 there seemed to be a definite will to stop Hitler. That it might turn out to be a case of too little and too late was hardly noted in the West; in central-eastern Europe, people were more sceptical. But there were some hopes and some superficial optimism.

Mussolini's Albanian venture

Two weeks after Memel, another little country of central-eastern Europe fell: on April 6, 1939, Mussolini invaded Albania. This Italian conquest was the last of the Axis' "pacific" victories; when Poland's turn was to come, the guns were destined to speak.

[*Psychic origins.*] Mussolini's behavior had always been subject to deep, subconscious elements; now, in direct ratio with Hitler's mounting successes, his jealousy increased. He sought to demonstrate his equal capacity for leadership by equal acts of ruthlessness. Not so much power itself as its external manifestations seemed to inspire him; the same feeling of inferiority which gripped him whenever he considered British naval power in the Mediterranean, now made him want to awe his Teuton allies by a great show of Latin prowess. Deep in his soul, he must have known the real truth. As his critic, Donosti, later put it: "The Germans liked the Italians much, and esteemed them little; the Italians liked the Germans little, and esteemed them much."

[*First preparations.*] Back on May 10, 1938, Ciano and Mussolini had discussed a paper setting forth Italy's position on Albania; it was then decided that, on "local and international grounds," about a year of preparation would be needed. On June 13 the German Embassy reported from Rome that Mussolini and Ciano planned to annex Albania "as soon as the international situation permitted," and in August Ciano spoke of these plans to the Italian military attaché to Athens. (*1*) At the end of October Ciano bribed a number of Albanians, calling this procedure "economic moves to prepare the action"; and for awhile he considered buying a tribal leader there, who was to assassinate King Zog for a price of ten million *Lire*. On

December 6 Mussolini approved Ciano's Albanian plan, saying that he did not fear Greece, Britain, or France, but only Yugoslavia. On January 8, 1939, Ciano and the Duce again conferred. Italo-Yugoslav relations were good; Stoyadinovič was drawing slightly away from the Germans and moving toward Rome. It was decided, therefore, that "the liquidation of Albania" would proceed by agreement with Belgrade; Italy, envisaging also a "settlement" with Greece in the long run, would support a properly timed Yugoslav claim to Salonika. (*2*)

[*The fall of Stoyadinovič.*] Stoyadinovič now played a card which had often been used in the game of Balkan politics: he began to curtail and mistreat the Albanian minority in Yugoslavia (in the Kossovo region). Thereupon, on January 16, King Zog contacted Rome and asked Italy to mediate in the Kossovo case. That evening, Ciano recorded in his Diary: "If everything goes well and if Stoyadinovič is able to march ahead with determination, I shall certainly give Zog his mediation!" (*3*) Then he left for Belgrade.

But the Yugoslav visit of Ciano was not as successful as he had hoped. Regent Paul, admonished by the strong opposition, enraged by Stoyadinovič' Albanian game, by financial corruption around the Premier, and provoked by the lavish hunting party which the latter arranged for Ciano in the castle of Belye, had already decided to make him resign. Stoyadinovič, sensing this, did not go into details about the expected partition of Albania — much to the surprise of Ciano. Using a psychological trick similar to the one which Beck had played on Hitler, Stoyadinovič charmed Ciano by shouting "Corsica, Tunis, Nice!" (*4*) when a telegram confirming Italian-Nationalist successes on the Barcelona front was handed to the Foreign Minister. Ciano returned to Rome, reporting that the Salonika issue had to be abandoned (to the sorrow of Mussolini, who was especially incensed at the Greeks when he heard that their military attaché in Berlin had made some disparaging comments on the Italian Army).

Then, on February 4–5, in a quiet coup, Stoyadinovič was removed; Prince Paul appointed Tsvetkovič, a colorless person, to the Premiership, and Mussolini had to speed up his plans. On February 6, he ordered final preparations for the venture and he set the actual time: Easter Week. Ciano complained that after Stoyadinovič' removal, "the Yugoslav card lost for us ninety per cent of its value. . . ."

Meanwhile, the war in Spain neared its end; Barcelona fell; the

Franco forces drew closer to Madrid, and the day was soon to come when the Italian troops would be leaving Spain. While the Albanian invasion was being prepared and the Spanish victory being completed, Hitler made his Czech coup. (With strange logic, he justified it to Mussolini by writing to him saying that "the action" had been necessary because the Czech government continued to keep contacts with the Soviets.) Before Prague, Ciano had protested to the German Ambassador against developing German attempts to get control over Albanian petroleum. On the aftermath of Prague, Ciano wrote:

> This concerns and humiliates the Italian people; it is necessary to give them a satisfaction and compensation: Albania.

[*An historic moment of hesitation.*]   For two or three days Mussolini himself considered swinging over to the anti-German front. Chamberlain's Birmingham speech had impressed Ciano, but the supremely opportune moment passed on the twentieth, when a letter from Chamberlain, sweet and pleading in tone, arrived on Mussolini's desk. Its effects, like those of the Berchtesgaden trip, were the worst possible. Here was "another proof of the democracies' inertia," Mussolini told Ciano; a few minutes later he added that Italy would not change fronts now: "We are not prostitutes." (5) Ribbentrop, somehow aware of Italian hesitations, sent on the same day an affable letter to Ciano, pointing out that as Italy showed disinterest in the Czechs, so Germany had no interests in Croatia. A few weeks earlier Croats had approached him for German protection, but he had refused, telling them that they were within Italy's competence. (6) All this seemed to have allayed Mussolini's worries; this great friend of Hungary now seemed very pleased, and told Ciano that he would not object if Germany took that country over.

[*Executing the plan.*]   The first Albanian rumors came, strangely enough, from Moscow. On March 17, the Moscow radio broadcast a report that Italian troops had landed at Valona (the well-organized Communist Balkan underground may have been at work). The rumor was soon substantiated. On March 25, a virtual ultimatum in the form of a "treaty" was given to King Zog; he was requested to transform Albania into an Italian protectorate. The King tried to play for time, but the British envoy told him that he could not be helped. Britain did not desire to have her relations with Italy deteriorate. Thus Mussolini was given a free hand. (7) King Victor

Emmanuel III was by no means enthusiastic. On the 27th he turned to Mussolini and asked why Italy should "risk such a venture in order to grab four rocks?" but this royal admonition only increased the Duce's ambition. Next day, Madrid fell and the Spanish war was over. The book would now be opened to another page, said Mussolini.

The Albanian crisis broke on April 3. A second, urgent ultimatum was dispatched to the Albanian capital, and Ciano disclosed this fact to the "friendly" envoys, including Christič, the Yugoslav Minister. (*8*) To secure Yugoslav acquiescence, Ciano asked that Hungary send a division to the Yugoslav frontier, a request which Hungary carried out. But Yugoslavia did not move; neither did Greece, to whose Metaxas Mussolini sent a friendly letter of explanation. On the fourth, Zog's son was born; on the seventh — Good Friday — he had to escape through the mountains into Greece, while Italian planes droned overhead and troops which had landed at Valona and Durazzo were marching toward Tirana. There were but a few skirmishes. On the ninth, the Roman Easter was over. The full entry in Ciano's Diary for the 10th reads as follows:

> We examine with the Duce the project drawn up yesterday which is approved, except for a few formal variations. Program: the electoral body at Tirana on the twelfth, the Grand Council at Rome on the thirteenth, my speech to the Chamber on the fifteenth, and Sunday, the sixteenth, a great national celebration of the event. (*9*)
>
> Reaction abroad begins to lessen. It is clear above all that the British protests are more for domestic consumption than anything else. (*10*)
>
> News from Albania is good; military occupation is carried out according to plans and without obstacles. (*11*)

The origins of the Moscow pact

Not until May 30, 1939, did Hitler definitely decide to negotiate the partition of central-eastern Europe with Soviet Russia; yet, the groundwork of such negotiations was laid long before that time.

[*The choice falls against Poland.*] To Germans, a Polish war would always be more popular than a Czechoslovak one; and a German attack on Poland necessitated some clarification of German-Russian relations. The German Ambassador in London, Dirksen, (*1*) who as Ambassador to Moscow in 1931 had advocated a German-Russian alignment, disliked the Poles very much. His position was important, for, in spite of the inherent disdain Hitler felt for the "old school" diplomats, he occasionally checked with them in 1938–39. When the Poles tried to bring about a common frontier with Hungary, Dirksen detected the designs of Beck and Kánya for a great anti-German and anti-Russian "quadrangle" of Warsaw, Bucharest, Budapest and Belgrade, with a possible tie-in with Rome. Of course, Budapest and Warsaw emphasized the "anti-Russian" issue in order to evade German suspicions, which arose nevertheless; Dirksen therefore advised Berlin not to permit the common Polish-Hungarian frontier. For once, Hitler could find comfort in the fact that the "old school" was in full agreement with him. At the same time in London Dirksen tried to influence the British against the Polish-Hungarian demands, pointing at "German moderation" in the face of "excessive Hungarian nationalism." Rumania was also bitterly opposed to the Polish-Hungarian idea, (2) fearing any increase in Hungarian power because of its potential impact on Transylvania; and even Italy ceased her support of Hungarian demands. '

[*Improvement in the Soviet diplomatic position.*] Russia watched the Carpatho-Ukrainian issue with great interest. After the Galatz meeting between Beck and King Carol on October 20, 1938, the Soviet chargé in Bucharest, Kokoliev, appeared at the Foreign Ministry for the first time in months and asked about the issues of the Rumanian-Polish conversations, which had been left unrevealed by a laconic communiqué. Although Russia feared Hitlerite designs on the Ukrainian "Piedmont," she feared even more the new *cordon sanitaire* idea of the Polish-Hungarian-Rumanian-Yugoslav *bloc.* The completion of this *bloc* might have helped to restore the European balance of power in favor of the West without the participation of Russia, lessened the chances of a European war, and strengthened the hand of the pro-Westerners in Germany. Thus Stalin rejoiced in the fact that the Galatz talks were unsuccessful. There was no *bloc;* instead, Budapest, Belgrade, Warsaw and Bucharest each went on its own narrow way, a development desired by Berlin as well as by Moscow. This community of interests was perceived by the clever Beck; for after the Vienna Award failed to give Carpatho-Ukraine to Hungary, he speeded up his attempts to approach Moscow, which attitude led to the joint Polish-Soviet declaration of November 26, 1938. The Soviets could not lose by this declaration. By it, they again manifested to the Western world and particularly to the United States their "willingness" to partake in any defensive alignment against Germany, while Chamberlain had assured Daladier, Halifax assured King Carol, and the Radical Socialist Party assured the French people that Germany would have to be allowed a dominant rôle in central-eastern Europe.

[*German approaches toward Russia.*] In 1934, Hitler had said to Rauschning: "Perhaps I shall not be able to avoid an alliance with Russia"; only between 1935 and 1937 — with prospects of a German-British alliance — did he profess extreme anti-Russian views but not until the Anglo-German Naval Pact did he order the disestablishment of the secret German military mission to Russia. The party radicals were always more favorable to Stalin than to the Western statesmen; the earliest entries in Göbbels' youthful diary are indication enough of that. (*3*) Ribbentrop, who had been snubbed by the British — this feeling of social inferiority remained with him until the last day of his life — was only too eager to punch "*die Klub-gentlemens*" in the nose and crush the Anglo-Saxons by forging an alliance between Germans and Russians, the "young races." Göbbels and Ribbentrop, under Hitler, were the most important members of the Nazi hierarchy after Munich. Hitler saw that even Chamberlain was playing for time; he felt now that the Englishman, although aware that Britain no longer carried a voice in European matters comparable to the days of a Pitt or a Beaconsfield, (*4*) was not willing to acquiesce in a permanent domination of Germany in Europe. Hitler told his confidants — and repeated it later to Csáky — that "the danger is the West." Not the East! But the West was reluctant to believe that Hitler's military calculations were leading him to press for war. The East knew better: Stalin saw the coming of war in Europe, and now his Russian isolation policy could begin to bear fruits and he slowly began to prepare for the picking.

Few saw the situation with more clarity than Count Schulenburg in Moscow. The dean of the diplomatic corps there, an old conservative gentleman whose idol was Bismarck, he perceived the nationalistic course Russia was taking under Stalin. Only a man such as Schulenburg could despise a Trotsky and admire a Stalin — only a man such as Stalin could respect a Schulenburg and ridicule a Cripps.

[*The turning of the year.*] After Munich, Soviet diplomatic activity increased in the Baltic. Secretly, Finland was sounded out concerning a military alliance, and an offer was even made to exchange

Eastern Karelia for Soviet lease of certain island bases in the Baltic. But the Finnish government rejected the proposals and instead agreed with Sweden in January 1939 upon the remilitarization of the Aaland Islands. This Soviet move and attempts to bring about an increased rapprochement with the United States were in contrast to Russian inactivity elsewhere in central-eastern Europe and in Germany, a contrast which did not escape Schulenburg's attention. In October 1938 he made a private agreement with Litvinov that neither the German nor the Soviet radio broadcasts would indulge in personal attacks on the respective leaders of the two nations. In December, a minor German-Russian agreement on trade payments was extended.

But these were insignificant developments. At the end of 1938, Schulenburg stood alone, presumably without any instructions from Berlin which would have indicated new "possibilities." Indeed, the Soviet consulate in Milan was closed in December after Soviet-Axis relations had been troubled by an Italian move to block certain Soviet funds in Italian banks. On January 4, 1939, Schulenburg cabled Berlin about a new oath now being taken by the Soviet Army: the soldiers no longer swore to the "proletariat of the world," but to the Soviet "fatherland." During that month, Hitler began to push the Polish issue, but the astute Beck won a month's time by his verbal manoeuvres. Thus, when it was proposed that a German trade mission go to Moscow and undertake economic negotiations, Hitler did not at first raise objections; but at the end of January, after he had sent Ribbentrop to Warsaw, he changed his mind. On January 30, the German delegation was recalled after their train had already crossed the German border. In those days, Hitler was still influenced by Göring and Mussolini (although the tone of Mussolini's statements in 1938 revealed that he favored a "proletarian front" against the "capitalist democracies"). Hitler thought that instead of depending upon Britain he could secure the active help of Italy and Japan, and perhaps the aquiescence of Poland. While Ribbentrop was in Warsaw, the Germanophile Japanese Ambassador told Hitler tales of motorboat-conveyed "missions" inciting anti-Bolshevist elements in the Crimea and about propaganda leaflets which the Japanese Intelligence Service transported to Russia by balloons. (5)

[*The first, vague reports.*]   Yet as early as November 26, 1938, a dispatch of the American Ambassador Biddle from Warsaw suggested the possibility of a Russian-German alignment; the Moscow dispatches of Davies on January 18, February 9, and March 21 made similar suggestions. A situation was developing in which Washington turned out to be an unusually well-informed capital, and American diplomatic ears were bound to hear more and more interesting confidences, especially in Moscow where, among others, a German diplomat gave a lot of valuable information to the American Embassy. In Professor Langer's view, "virtually every step leading to the Nazi-Soviet Pact was therefore known in Washington almost as soon as in Berlin, and President Roosevelt was far better informed on these matters than Paris or London." (6)

On January 13 Litvinov, talking to Grzybowski, the Polish Ambassador, said that Paris and London wished to persuade Hitler that Germany's future lay to the east, "but Hitler is less convinced of this than are the French and English." This interesting statement was due to Russian intelligence gathered about the contents of the Mussolini-Chamberlain talks in Rome, from which the Kremlin deduced that the British Premier wished, through Mussolini's help, to induce Hitler to leave the West alone and turn against the Ukraine. Yet this was not the case.

The Soviet press remained significantly silent about the en route recall of the German commercial mission, a recall which Schulenburg attributed to Polish and French machinations. And on February 14 Berlin turned down a Hungarian suggestion that all anti-Comintern states should withdraw their envoys from Moscow. On February 22 Litvinov talked with the British and French Ambassadors; the French envoy seemed to have caught a glimpse of a Russian threat of a pact with Germany. Kirk, the American chargé in Moscow reported the same, and added that Litvinov's star might be waning. On the same day the Rumanian Minister to Berlin informed his government that for some time a number of reliable reports had been circulating there concerning an improvement in German-Russian relations. On February 28 Japanese diplomats in Berlin and Rome informed the German and Italian governments that Japan wished to concur in previous German plans and to elevate the Anti-Comintern Pact to a military alliance. They added, however, that the alliance should be directed against one front only, preferably Russia. This stand left some questions open: What would the Axis do in the case of a Russo-Japanese war? What would Japan do in the case of an Axis-British war? A few days later Ribbentrop intimated to Weizsäcker that Hitler had recently been considering the restoration of reasonable relations with the Soviet Union, and Attolico tele-graphed Ciano on the 9th that Ribbentrop had mentioned the pos-sibility of a Non-Aggression Pact with Russia. (7) Sir William Seeds occasionally warned London of overoptimism regarding Russian intentions, and the situation was neatly summed up on February 20 in a letter from the Chancery of the British Embassy in Moscow to the Co-ordination Section of the Foreign Office: "It would thus be a grave mistake to suppose that sympathy for the 'so-called democ-racies' or dislike of the 'fascist aggressor' *bloc* would necessarily influ-ence the Soviet attitude in the event of a conflict between the two *blocs*."

Now, Stalin made one of his rare speeches, on March 10 at the opening of the eighteenth congress of the Communist (Bolshevik) Party. What he said was clever and seemingly self-evident: he did not intend to pull chestnuts out of the fire for the selfish Western "imperialist" Powers. He spoke of a "suspicious uproar . . . for the purpose to arouse Soviet anger against Germany to poison the atmos-phere and to provoke a conflict with Germany without visible reason." And although a week later Litvinov strongly denounced the German occupation of Prague in a note to Berlin, Hitler could not fail to perceive the import of Stalin's words. On March 17 the Italian Ambassador to Moscow was told by Vice-Commissar Potemkin that Russia sought a rapprochement with Italy; Potemkin stated that the Russian diplomatic position had become very strong, as Russia feared no attack from any Power, while many Powers — and he cited France, Britain, Poland, *and Germany* — were trying to gain sym-pathies in Moscow.

[*The economic pretext.*] With the German occupation of Czechoslovakia there developed an economic issue between Berlin and Moscow: Russia had put orders with the Plzen Skoda works and she wished to know how the new political situation would affect deliveries. The Soviet Ambassador to Germany, Merekalov, asked Director Wiehl of the Commercial Policy Section of the German Foreign Ministry to consult with him. They met late in March and to the Russian's satisfaction, Wiehl told him — upon Ribbentrop's instructions — that the Skoda contracts were not affected by the German occupation of the Czech protectorate; moreover, Germany was willing to improve economic relations with Russia. This declara-tion, coming not quite two months after the recall of a German delegation en route to Moscow, evidently aroused interest in the Kremlin, where at the same time the first contacts with France and Britain concerning the Western-desired great anti-Hitler coalition were being pondered upon. *(8)* About the end of March, the Soviet press began to temper its attacks on Germany and "the Fascists." On April 17, the Soviet Ambassador — for the first time since his arrival in Berlin — decided to call upon Weizsäcker. With their talk, the preliminary phase of Russian-German negotiations began. *(9)*

. . . .

[*April 17: first important contact.*] The conversation started with "practical matters"; but Weizsäcker felt that Merekalov wanted to speak with him on issues more important than the Skoda deliveries. Right he was. He recorded in his memorandum:

> Toward the end of the discussion, I casually mentioned that . . . a favorable atmosphere for the delivery of war materials to Soviet Russia was not exactly being created at present by reports of a Russian-British-French air pact and the like. Herr Merekalov seized on these words to take up political matters. . . .

After a careful sparring, the Ambassador came out in the open:

> Russian policy had always moved in a straight line. Ideological differences of opinion had hardly influenced the Russian-Italian relationship and they did not have to prove a stumbling block with regard to Germany either. Soviet Russia had not exploited the present friction between Germany and the Western democracies against us, nor did she desire to do so. There exists for Russia no reason why she should not live with us on a normal footing. And from normal, the relations might become better and better. *(10)*

[*Stalin takes stock.*] While these statements were eagerly being recorded by Ribbentrop, on April 19 the first concrete Soviet proposal was conveyed to London: a guarantee to Rumania, Poland, Latvia and Estonia with the hidden thought of acquiring Russian control of part of these countries. The Soviet Union began to assume an ideal bargaining position. At the same time the Italian Ambassador reported from Moscow that Stalin was sincere in seeking a rapprochement with Italy, and Mussolini mentioned to Göring on April 14 that in view of Western intransigence, a Russian-German rapprochement could perhaps be indeed propitious. Ten days later Ribbentrop made the same point to Attolico; on April 28 Hitler spoke, denouncing Roosevelt's plan of an international guarantee against aggression, the Anglo-German Naval Treaty, and the German-Polish Non-Aggression Treaty, but he kept significantly silent about Soviet Russia and the hitherto eloquently evoked spectre of Bolshevik danger.

In April, both Hitler and Stalin were still very careful. The former spoke to Gafencu, who visited him with a message from Beck; Germany had nothing to ask from Rumania (and this a few days after the latter accepted the British guarantee!) but requested Bucharest to refrain from signing a pact with Russia; Gafencu agreed. Stalin contemplated possible bargains; at the end of April he sent Potemkin, an Assistant Foreign Commissar, on a tour of central-eastern Europe. To Turkey, Bulgaria, Rumania and Poland Potemkin went; Beck was surprised how well this Russian seemed to understand Polish foreign policy; and Gafencu recorded that "the messenger of Moscow spoke as people were speaking in London, Paris and Bucharest." (11)

[*The replacement of Litvinov.*]   By that time Litvinov was out; as Churchill put it: " . . . the eminent Jew, the target of German antagonism, was flung aside for the time being like a broken tool, and without being allowed a word of explanation, was bundled off the world stage to obscurity, a pittance, and police supervision." The removal of Litvinov was in all probability decided by the Kremlin in the afternoon on May 3; a midnight radio communiqué followed; next day a buried notice in the Soviet press announced his dismissal, and Molotov was appointed in his stead. The Soviet Ambassadors and travelling envoys such as Potemkin hastened to announce that the change at the helm did not mean a change in the course. But this was not the truth.

As early as May 4, the London *Times* reported that "the tactics of Litvinov . . . were approved only halfheartedly by the Politbureau." In Berlin the Soviet chargé d'affaires, Astakhov, was informed that the Russian request had been granted: Skoda was to fulfill its Soviet contracts as soon as possible. Astakhov, the German record says, "was visibly gratified . . . and stressed the fact that for the Soviet Government the material side of the question was not of as great importance as the question of principle." He also asked whether the economic negotiations could not be resumed; and, like his Ambassador who had previously used the economic issue for a springboard into deeper waters, the Russian chargé "touched upon the dismissal of Litvinov and tried without asking direct questions to learn whether this event would cause a change in [the German] position toward the Soviet Union." (*12*)

Another day: on the 6th, Ribbentrop met Ciano in Milan; "the opportunity should be exploited . . . to prevent Russia's adhesion to the anti-totalitarian (*13*) *bloc*, but this [should be done] with great discretion and absolute sense of proportion." (*14*) Coulondre reported from Berlin that a Herr "x" (*15*) mentioned to him preliminary negotiations toward a German-Russian Pact. Two days later, Astakhov, whom Namier calls "a singularly talkative Soviet diplomatist," gave himself away unwittingly in a talk with a French diplomat. He also called on the Foreign Ministry to introduce a new TASS representative in Berlin and while he was cautious ("for the time being one could not speak of a reorientation of policy") and indulged in the obscure semantics so dear to the Russians, he said that he was "happy that Herr Filipov (the TASS man) could start his work under new conditions which were completely different from the past."

Schulenburg was in Teheran in the first part of May, unaware of all the important developments which had taken place in his absence until he was urgently — and secretly — called to fly from Teheran to Munich to confer with Ribbentrop; the rest of the world, meanwhile, was anticipating progress in the Western-Russian negotiations. But there was none. On May 17, Astakhov remarked to Schnurre that "under the present circumstances the result desired by England could scarcely be achieved"; on the 20th, Maisky sent from London a pessimistic report to Moscow concerning the chances of Western-Russian agreement.

[*After some caution, the German decision is made.*]   The same day, after having studied the new reports, Schulenburg called on Molotov. The latter was cautious, canny and chary of any commitments: "The Soviet government could only agree to a resumption of economic negotiations if the necessary political bases for these had been constructed." More he did not say. There developed now some misunderstanding: in Berlin it was at first believed that Molotov did not wish to go further at the moment; yet the Russian statement could be construed as an indirect invitation to the dance. Schulenburg was instructed to sit tight and wait. On the 23rd, Hitler gave a hint to

his generals: "It is not impossible that Russia will show herself disinterested in the destruction of Poland" (*16*); and Göring said to
Henderson four days later that out of self-interest Russia would not
give any assistance to the Poles. The German Ministry acted with
great caution. On the 27th, supplementary explanations were sent to
Schulenburg from Berlin in a letter, stating that "the possibility of
success [concerning Russo-German negotiations] is considered here
to be quite limited." This letter was not dispatched to Moscow until
the 30th, and meanwhile, significant changes had taken place. While
Schulenburg was drafting a letter in Moscow (he did not send it until
June 5), stating that the reluctance of Molotov to say much was being
completely misinterpreted by Berlin, Hitler, on the 30th, decided to
give his august consent "to a distinctly limited exchange of views"
with the Russians. This information was relayed to Schulenburg as
a postscript. On the same day another message was sent to the German
Ambassador: "*contrary to the policy previously planned, we have now decided
to undertake definite negotiations with the Soviet Union.*" Weizsäcker also
informed Astakhov to this effect; the Russian assured him, "on his own
account," that "Herr Molotov had, to be sure, talked with the customary Russian distrust, but not with the intention of barring further
German-Russian discussions." Both Astakhov and Weizsäcker, in
characteristic Byzantine fashion, recounted instances to prove the
benevolence of their respective governments. The German further
pointed out that "Beck's interpretation of the German policy toward
the Ukraine was refuted by the German conduct in the case of the Carpathian Ukraine," a reference which in itself showed that the slate
had been cleared; with Hitler's consent of May 30, 1939, the preliminary phase was ended; a more decisive phase of German-Russian
negotiations, directed at the partitioning of Poland and most of central-
eastern Europe, was to begin. (*17*)

Development of the Polish crisis

Hitler wanted to deal with Poland in Frederick the Great's manner,
which required the previous reduction of Austria, the securing of
Russian collaboration, French weakness and British acquiescence. He
succeeded only in part. His military aims seemed limited at first (on
November 24, 1938, a German Army directive planned for a surprise
attack on Danzig) but then Beck talked with him glibly at Berchtesgaden. On January 25, Ribbentrop travelled to Warsaw, with the

avowed aim of bringing Poland into the Anti-Comintern Pact. The territorial issues were again lightly touched upon, but Beck dodged a clear-cut discussion with considerable success. In those days, Hitler still hesitated between Poland and Russia. (While Ribbentrop was in Warsaw, Weizsäcker told Hassell on January 26 that "the diplomatic barometer stands on peace in the East . . . perhaps [on] Poland," and that "surely Czechoslovakia is next.")

Beck was worried and tried to lean on Italy. At the end of February, Ciano visited Warsaw. Beck felt rather sure of himself and disparaged the French on one hand, while on the other he maintained caution and reserve concerning an alignment with the Axis. (*1*) Two weeks later, Hitler ordered the march into Prague; another week and the diplomatic offensive against Poland opened with a speed which was unusual even for the "new" German diplomacy.

. . . .

[*From Prague to the British guarantee.*] Ribbentrop called the Polish Ambassador on March 21 and presented him with the German demands to Danzig and to "the settlement of the Corridor issue." In return, Germany would be ready to guarantee Poland's new frontiers. This was Memel Day; Lipski asked what Germany intended to do with Lithuania, but a haughty and disdainful Ribbentrop brushed him aside; the Pole inquired about German plans in Slovakia, and his question was left unanswered. At once, the envoy departed for Warsaw to report; on the way home he learned of the final establishment of the German "protectorate" over Slovakia.

After conferring with Beck, the pessimistic Lipski returned to Berlin in great haste. There were divergences between Hitler's thoughts and those of his Foreign Minister. Hitler was anxious over Chamberlain's angry change at Birmingham, while Ribbentrop rejoiced that Hitler was at last irrevocably turning against Britain. Hitler weighed possible deals with Russia which a Polish crisis might necessitate, and Ribbentrop anticipated such talks with considerable pleasure. Hitler had not yet made his final decision. He told General Brauchitsch on March 25 that although the necessary preparations regarding Poland were to be made, he did "*not* want war with Britain" and there was as yet no word of a concrete military timetable for a Polish campaign. Neither had Beck decided on final alignments, except that Poland would resist German territorial demands. He received warning messages from Lukasiewicz, stating that all British offers would be worthless unless

Britain decided unequivocally to fight. These uncertainties did not
last for long. On March 31, the British guarantee brought about an
altogether new picture.

Fourteen days elapsed between Prague and the British guarantee
to Poland — crucial days these were. For, after the Birmingham
speech, the image of an anti-German Grand Alliance had emerged
for many, not as a vision but as a tangible reality. Rumanian alarms,
(2) the Ribbentrop-Lipski talks, and Memel now spurred the British
and French. Beck was asked what Poland would do if Germany
attacked Rumania, and hints were made to him of a Western
guarantee and perhaps a military pact. After some hesitation Beck
answered that Poland would assist Rumania if Britain would also extend her guarantee to that country. At the same time Bonnet, through
the French Minister in Budapest, asked Count Teleki, the Conservative
Hungarian Premier, not to provoke any incident with Rumania:
Hungary complied.

In the background loomed the initiation of the Western-Russian
talks, and Beck's main problem was Russia. The French politicians
were divided on the Russian issue; many still thought as Franklin-
Bouillon had in 1932: "The French frontier is on the Vistula." But
what did this mean now? In 1920, Weygand stood at the Vistula: then
it was the frontier of Europe and France — against the Russians. In
1939, the Vistula "frontier" was to be defended against attack from
an opposite direction, perhaps with the assistance of the same Russians who had been driven away from there nineteen years before.
However, the French military was constantly reminded by the Poles
— as Gamelin in 1936 had been told by Rydz-Smigly — that the
Russians were worse than the Germans. In spite of Noël's profuse
assurances about the expected rôle of Russia, on the 24th, Beck telegraphed to London and Paris: he would not sign an Eastern European
alliance or guarantee pact which included Soviet Russia.

On March 26 Lipski brought a rejection of the German proposals
for the cession of Danzig. There is little doubt that it was during
these days that Ribbentrop began planning for his Russian alliance
and thus he received the Polish diplomat more coolly than ever
before, complaining incessantly, and adopting a generally menacing
tone. Two days later, Moltke spoke with Beck in Warsaw. Their
conversation was much more friendly, but obviously the German
diplomat could not deviate from the instructions of his chief in
Berlin, instructions which surely were not very flexible.

The great and unprecedented step came next day. Beck in Warsaw met Kennard, the British Ambassador; while they talked, the message came from London that the British government consented to give a full guarantee to Poland: Beck accepted it at once. The stakes were set.

[*The British guarantee; causes and effects.*]

> And now, when every one of [the previous] advantages had been squandered and thrown away, Great Britain advances, leading France by the hand, to guarantee the integrity of Poland — of that very Poland which with hyena appetite had only six months before joined in the pillage and destruction of the Czechoslovak State. There was sense in fighting for Czechoslovakia in 1938 when the German Army could scarcely put half a dozen trained divisions on the Western Front, when the French with nearly sixty or seventy divisions could most certainly have rolled forward across the Rhine or into the Ruhr. But this had been judged unreasonable, rash, below the level of modern intellectual thought and morality. Yet now at last the two Western Democracies declared themselves ready to stake their lives upon the territorial integrity of Poland. History, which we are told is mainly the record of the crimes, follies, and miseries of mankind, may be scoured and ransacked to find a parallel to this sudden and complete reversal of five or six years' policy of easy-going placatory appeasement, and its transformation almost overnight into a readiness to accept an obviously imminent war on far worse conditions and on the greatest scale. (3)

Thus Mr. Churchill, writing in 1948. Morally, he approved of the gesture: "God helping, we can do no other" he had said in the Commons. Professor Namier's analysis is only partly different:

> The British guarantee was thrust on [Poland] on March 30 — a hasty and ill-considered move . . . unnecessary — for Poland would have anyhow resisted German territorial plans or attempts to chain her to the Axis . . . (4)

No need to contest Mr. Churchill's evaluation of Munich, nor Professor Namier's hypothesis. There remains, in any case, one incontestable truth about the British guarantee: illogical as it may have been, it was above all a moral gesture meant to terminate officially the era in which Britons were prone to appease the evildoers. The British point of view concerning the guarantee is not without interest, but there are more far-reaching considerations to be taken into account. What were its effects on central-eastern Europe? And why and in what manner did Poland accept the guarantee? Throughout her history, Poland continually emphasized her "Western" characteristics, and hence her irreconcilable conflicts with Eastern Russia. Irrational Polish statesmanship has often been erroneously attributed to the Slavic dream-element in the Polish psyche; it may much more correctly be attributed to a deeply Catholic and "Western" desire to show the extent of Polish capacity for sacrifice in the interest of good causes. Undaunted and always hopeless, the Polish hero could make wonderful sacrifices in the face of insurmountable obstacles, to a point far beyond the realm of logic. Thus it may be said that while Russia seldom chose the path of war unless she had a good chance to win, Poland often deliberately went to war when all odds were against her — on the basis of a foolish "Western" rationalization of chances non-existent.

If the British offer of March 1939 stands in strange contrast to British behavior in the preceding autumn, there is even a greater contrast in Polish attitudes. Beck in 1938 rashly disassociated himself from the Western democracies to prove that he understood "new" political ideas and had a realistic awareness of the twentieth-century statesmanship which put a premium on ruthless power and prestige gained by conquest. He thought he understood the soul of Europe; he did not. Then, in March 1939 the voice — nothing but the voice — of the West called to him to be an ally in a great Western European partnership: he immediately accepted. If London's offer was strange, Warsaw's spontaneous acceptance was even more so. But whatever her previous faults, whatever her previous follies, Poland found now her soul once again. Unswervingly, proudly, gallantly, she withstood German threats and Russian encirclement. And when the end came she was to go down in battle with a noble dignity rarely to be found in our century.

The British guarantee was decisive. Hitler's hesitations came abruptly to an end. On April 3, a directive was issued by Keitel to the General Staff to prepare for the attack on Poland: "Operation White" was drafted, with a time schedule establishing September 1 as the first possible date for the Polish war. (5)

[*Beck's logic.*] Beck went to London thinking there would be no war, that the Western guarantee system would prove an active deterrent rather than an incentive to Hitler's martial plans. (*6*) He went so far as to try to assert his unduly rigid logic on Hitler. Gafencu, who made a tour of Germany and Western Europe in April, was met by Beck on his train and was asked to convey to Hitler a message of his continued goodwill. "What can Germany's interest be in making war on Poland?" Beck asked Gafencu. "To weaken Poland would be to play Russia's game. If the Polish bastion were to fall, the gates of Europe would be open to the Soviets' forward drive. Do you believe that Hitler wants that? I know that he does not." (*7*)

Perhaps Beck knew what Hitler did not want; perhaps he did not want to know Hitler. For on the same day that he spoke thus to Gafencu — on April 17 — the Merekalov-Ribbentrop conversation in Berlin opened a new chapter in the history of his nation, of central-eastern Europe, and of the world.

Beck and Daladier were instrumental in persuading the British to extend their guarantee to Rumania on April 13. Due to the Albanian coup, Greece was also offered a guarantee on the same day. (The Bulgarian Government had already declined a British guarantee offer of March 22.) Beck and the Rumanian government for all practical purposes rejected Russian alliances, stating on the 20th that the crossing of Russian ground troops or aircraft through Polish or Rumanian territory would be unwelcome. Probably Beck thought that his position, together with Gafencu's message, would serve to prove again his goodwill to Hitler. The latter's speech at Wilhelmshaven eight days later must have shattered this belief. Hitler lashed out against the Poles, who, according to him, had spurned even the best occasions for an understanding. (He also mentioned that he had offered to share with them a "triple condominium" in Slovakia.) (*8*) The 1934 Non-Aggression Treaty, Hitler said, was now abrogated.

[*His vain hopes.*] Beck kept on trying. His answer to Hitler, on May 5, was surprisingly moderate, and he instructed Grzybowski, his Ambassador to Moscow, to be cautious. Litvinov's dismissal Beck seemed to discount and when on May 7 he was informed of the official Soviet alliance terms — the Russian armies would enter Poland along two routes to join against Germany and the Polish-Rumanian alliance would be nullified — he refused to accept them. (*9*)

He seemed satisfied by Potemkin's assertion on May 13 that in case of a German-Polish conflict the Soviets would adopt a "benevolent attitude" toward Poland. Beck continued to think wishfully, believing that Hitler, like he himself, would be basically unwilling to partake in a deal with the East. Around May 20, he instructed Arciszewski (*10*) of his Foreign Office to talk matters over with the German Ambassador, while Lipski was instructed to make a parallel call on that "old friend of the Poles," Göring. Arciszewski also told Troyanov, the Bulgarian Minister in Warsaw, that the British alignment was not a final goal and, in fact, "the whole policy goes against Beck's grain." These talks took place on May 23, in what seemed to Beck to be a hopeful atmosphere. He did not know that on the same day instructions had been sent out by Hitler and Keitel *to attack Poland at the first suitable opportunity.* "If there were an alliance of France, England, Russia against Germany, Italy and Japan," Hitler said, "I would be constrained to crush England and France with a few annihilating blows. I am only afraid that at the last minute some swine-dog will make a proposal for mediation . . ." (*11*)

. . . .

Meanwhile the Polish General Kasprzycki began military talks with the French in Paris, but he did not succeed in bringing about a clear political agreement. Still, general optimism prevailed in Warsaw, and a few of the Polish military even envisaged a glorious Polish march on Berlin. The mediation attempts of the newly invested Pope Pius XII failed and May came to an end. On the 31st, Molotov spoke with great caution and reserve; his speech was certainly not encouraging to the West, yet, at the same time, neither was it unfriendly to Poland. On June 14, Charonov, the newly appointed Soviet Ambassador to Warsaw told Beck that he did not expect a European war in the foreseeable future.

Broadening of the Polish crisis: the international scene

[*Russia courted.*]   The six weeks from the middle of April to the end of May, during which Hitler and Stalin began to understand each other, revealed at the same time the divergence between the aims of Western Powers and the Soviets. The West was striving to maintain peace and the *status quo;* Russia was seeking territorial gains and conquest.

The Russian note to Estonia on March 28 (a similar note was handed to the Latvian government) was of a somewhat threatening character; Moscow stated that it would be "intolerable if Estonia gives semblance of compromising her economic or other sovereignty." Superficial observers might have thought that the note showed Russian will to defend the small states of central-eastern Europe against Germany; instead, Moscow was preparing to use the pretext of a partial "loss of sovereignty" to her own advantage. Throughout 1938 and early 1939 secret Soviet overtures were made in the Baltic area to obtain bases which would be "leased" to Russia to provide a "common" defense against Germany. (*1*) Now the Kremlin claimed the right to determine the circumstances under which the sovereignty of her small neighbor states would be impaired. The Baltic states knew what lay behind the Soviet notes; their statesmen explained them to the Western envoys, who in turn reported it to Paris and London and Washington. Here was the Russian Trojan horse.

The Western-Russian talks met their first obstacles. The British were wont to overestimate the importance of Poland and underestimate that of Russia; Neville Chamberlain could not refrain from expressing intimately his distrust of the Soviet Union, which in turn had its own designs. Now Russian diplomacy enjoyed the pleasant prospects of being courted, after two decades of segregation from Europe, by the Great European Powers. On March 31, Lord Halifax announced the Polish guarantee in Parliament; on the same day he called Maisky and explained to him the "new course" of Britain. Halifax, who was to act with admirable zeal and energy and with almost un-British speed in the next two weeks, obviously wished to capture the last and most important stake in this spectacular diplomatic contest: he asked Maisky "whether the Prime Minister could say in the House of Commons that afternoon that the Russian government would associate itself with the guarantee of Britain and France?" "But for this unexpected situation," as Hugh Dalton later wrote, "the Ambassador — not unnaturally — had no instructions." (*2*)

Throughout April and May, the Western-Russian talks went on, dominated by occidental anxiety and impatience and oriental evasiveness and caution.

[*Poland and the small states chary of Russia.*]   As it had been a year before, the main question was: where, how, in what capacity, would the Soviets join an anti-German military front? Moscow did not wish to join in a theoretical guarantee to Poland which would make Stalin recognize the integrity of that state and thus automatically exclude any eventual Russian action against Poland. In Warsaw, Ambassador Noël, seeing that rigid Western support of Poland could alienate Moscow, was willing to loosen French-Polish ties if necessary for the winning of Russia. By the middle of May, British desire to win Russia even at high cost had become more and more evident, and Lukasiewicz complained to Bullitt in Paris: "Britain exploits Poland . . . it is supremely rash to start such action publicly and give prominence to the participation of the Soviet Union . . . frivolously dangerous." (*3*)

Even though Poland was not, would Rumania be willing to accept Russian aid? Rumania was fortunate in 1939 in having a Foreign Minister of exceptionally keen insight and diplomatic ability. Grigore Gafencu steered the Rumanian ship of state through the Scyllae of the German trade pact (March 23) and the Charybdis of the British guarantee (April 13), and three days later he embarked on a European journey. Travelling through Poland, he visited Berlin, Brussels, London, Paris, and Rome, then on to Turkey, Greece, and Yugoslavia. He listened rather than spoke, but he listened well. Rumania did not wish to anger Hitler; neither did she want to alienate British sympathies. She wished to be friendly with the Russians, but she did not wish to invite them into her own house. If only Stalin would join in the British guarantee! But he did not; instead, in the first week of April, the Soviet Ambassador in Paris asked Bonnet why Poland and Rumania would not accept Soviet aid? The old question of 1938! It was not France's fault, Bonnet replied, that these two neighbors of Russia refused to invite Soviet military assistance, but every effort would of course be made to bring about Russian-Polish and Russian-Rumanian cooperation against the common German danger. A few days later, the French military attaché in Moscow was instructed to enter into military conversations with Marshal Voroshilov.

On April 14, the day after the British guarantee to Rumania, to the pleasant surprise of London and Paris, Maisky told Halifax that Russia would be ready to assist Rumania in case of a German attack. Halifax informed Bonnet at once, and the latter drafted a common declaration affirming that a German attack on Rumania — or Poland (*4*) — would mean immediate intervention by Britain, France, and the Soviet Union. But two days later, to Bonnet's surprise, Chamberlain proposed a much less precise and specific plan and Moscow informed London that Maisky's statement had been "misunderstood," that it did not correspond with the views of Moscow. (This immediately after the Merekalov-Ribbentrop conversations: a coincidence?) Next day, the Soviet government rejected the French declaration draft and came out with certain counter-proposals, the most important of which was the inclusion of the Baltic states and Finland in the French-British-Soviet mutual assistance and guarantee system — *if necessary, even without the consent* of these small nations.

The French in their dire need were willing to accept this rather ominous Soviet stipulation; the British were not. After all, the British guarantee to Poland had been a moral gesture, and acceptance of the Soviet proposition would have at once deprived Great Britain of the advantage of being considered the guarantor and defender of small states against aggression. On April 7 the Estonian government answered the Soviets, reserving the right to decide what constituted aggression against itself, and maintaining its freedom of action; on April 25 the Turkish Government notified France and Britain that it preferred to wait with a treaty until the Western-Russian negotiations got ahead. The Soviet note to London was not answered until May 8, and on May 19 Churchill and Lloyd George accused Chamberlain in the Commons of undue diffidence towards Russia. (5) Next day, returning from Geneva and Paris, Halifax became finally convinced that a pact with Russia was so imperative that, perhaps, it had to be made on Soviet terms.

The Soviets now suggested that the Polish-Rumanian Treaty, originally directed against Russia, be transformed into a mutual assistance pact dealing with aggression coming from whatever side. Gafencu and King Carol were none too eager for such a change, which would have automatically embroiled them in a war with Germany upon the latter's attack on Poland. Beck told Potemkin that such an extension would not be possible because of Poland's friendship with Hungary, for in case of an accidental Hungarian-Rumanian conflict, Poland could not attack Hungary. Later, the Soviets themselves dropped the issue. As their designs on Poland became more definite, they lost all desire to see Bucharest and Warsaw welded closely together by a newly-revamped mutual assistance pact.

Thus were all kinds of obstacles standing in the way of a great Western-Eastern alliance when on May 30 Hitler decided to approach the problem of central-eastern Europe's partition with Stalin. It was a weighty decision. During the time he had pondered upon it, he had been nervous and capricious. The central-eastern European statesmen who met him during April and May found him unusually unsure of himself. A strange picture it was — Hitler vacillating. He had made up his mind months before to deal with Russia if necessary, but he had not known how far he should go. Ribbentrop prodded him to go ahead. When Gafencu called on him with Beck's message, Hitler was relatively pleasant; only once during his long tirade against the Poles did his unusual calm leave him. "In the end, all of us, victors and vanquished," he cried, "will be lying under the same ruins and only one person will benefit from this, that man there from Moscow." Nevertheless, he had no desire to come to any understanding with "the slovenly Poles." (6)

[*Italy and the Balkans.*]   Hitler had another worry: in 1939, Italy could not go to war, for she was not yet prepared. Ciano emphasized this fact when he spoke to Ribbentrop. Hitler acknowledged without comment Ribbentrop's communication to this effect, and Mussolini made the mistake of misinterpreting this silence.

Mussolini did not want to participate in a European war; he wanted but a little war for himself, to further his prestige and power in the Mediterranean. Yugoslavia and Greece were his primary targets. He had had to assure both countries before and during his Albanian coup that he had no designs on them; Yugoslavs and Greeks were troubled and angry, but they remained passive. Indeed, the Greek government was glad to get rid of King Zog, who had escaped to Greece from Albania and whose presence on Greek soil might have given Rome a pretext to charge Athens with an anti-Italian conspiracy. In Milan, Ribbentrop invited Ciano to proceed against Greece, and Hitler tried to lure Mussolini by "offering" him a free hand in Yugoslavia. (7) On May 10 — between the Milan meeting with Ribbentrop and the Berlin signature of the "Steel Pact" — Ciano suggested to Regent Paul and Tsintsar-Markovič, who were visiting Rome, the possibilities of an Italian-Rumanian-Yugoslav-Bulgar (8) Balkan *bloc* (the primary object of such an alliance would have been to isolate Greece and Turkey). On May 22, Germany and Italy signed their "Steel Pact."

Gafencu asked the Turks to work for good relations between the Balkan Entente and the Soviet Union; but as German-Soviet relations improved, that Turkish-Russian amity which Kamâl and Lenin had initiated in 1921 was nearing its end. Ciano also tried to bring Bulgaria into the Axis system, but in spite of all promises, King Boris was cautious. (9) Chamberlain and Knatchbull-Hugessen, the

British envoy in Ankara, believed on the other hand that a minor
Rumanian territorial concession to Bulgaria in the Southern Dobrudja
would align Sofia with the Balkan Entente, but such British mediation
resulted only in increasing Bulgarian nationalist appetites. In June,
while Greece was watching Italy uneasily, Turkey signed a political
agreement with France and Britain. De Monzie noted cynically in
his diary: "Instead of Russia, Turkey . . ." (*10*) For — as he rightly
saw it — prospects for a French-British-Russian agreement were
indeed frail.

[*The Baltic bid.*] Neither De Monzie nor any of the other
well-informed men in Paris and London were, of course, aware of the
secretly proceeding Russian-German conversations. A few Western
diplomats, such as Coulondre, suspected them; a few statesmen of
central-eastern Europe expected them sooner or later. After Hitler's
decision to negotiate with Moscow, Ribbentrop scribbled a big red
"settled" on the margin of Schulenburg's explanatory letter. But
was it "settled"? Now, noting German willingness, the Soviets again
recoiled somewhat. On June 2, Molotov, suddenly reverting to the
previous Soviet proposals, demanded again that Britain and France
agree that a Russian-French-British alliance should lend its "military
support" to the Baltic states if deemed necessary, even if these small
states refused such assistance. The Western Powers were hesitant. The
Soviet press presaged Russian aims by attacking the Finnish-Swedish
agreement remilitarizing the Aalands; if Moscow did not wish to in-
trude into the Baltics but merely defend them, why these protests? The
Baltic envoys in London and Paris were aware of the main lines of
Western-Soviet negotiations; now Germany found it advantageous to
convince the world of her peaceful conduct, and therefore offered to
sign Non-Aggression Pacts with the Baltic states. Lithuania had already
signed such a pact after having ceded Memel on March 22; now
Estonia signed on May 31 and Latvia on June 6. (The latter kept in
close touch with Poland throughout the summer.) Referring to their
traditional neutrality, Finland, Norway, and Sweden excused themselves from signing, but Denmark, however, concurred. Immediately
after signing the Pact with Germany on June 6, Latvia, Estonia, and
Finland protested against external guarantees imposed upon them
against their will.

[*First Soviet suggestion for a Pact with Germany.*] In a turgid speech to the Supreme Soviet on May 31, Molotov stated that the Soviet Union was not committed in any way in her foreign policy: all roads were open to her — an obvious hint that not even a preliminary Soviet-Western agreement existed. Especially the French were disturbed. They pressed the British to be more flexible toward Soviet wishes, and Lord Halifax now decided to send a direct negotiator to Moscow. He still refused to include the unwilling Baltic states among those the Great Powers were to guarantee. The representative, William Strang, left for Moscow on June 12. At that time the German-Russian talks were at a momentary standstill, although the German-Latvian and German-Estonian Non-Aggression Pacts were indication that Hitler had no designs in the Baltic beyond Memel. (*11*) The Russian response was enigmatic: Molotov did not call Schulenburg again; the economic conversations proceeded very slowly, very cautiously; Hitler felt "disillusioned," recorded Kordt.

Then, Strang arrived in Moscow: here was the other suitor. Was he willing to go all the way? Perhaps, but it was time to make him wait . . . a little. On the day of his arrival, *Pravda* shrilly insisted that the Baltic states must be guaranteed; Strang had not yet unpacked his diplomatic baggage when on June 15 a TASS communiqué announced that "circles close to the Foreign Commissariat note that the 'new' Anglo-French proposals do not show any progress compared with the previous ones." The same day, in Berlin, the Soviet chargé, Astakhov (*12*), called unexpectedly on Draganov, the Bulgarian Minister there. They scarcely knew each other: they had met but once or twice during dreary diplomatic social functions. To the immense surprise of Draganov, Astakhov spoke for two hours to him. Among other things, the Russian said this:

> . . . if Germany would declare that she would not attack the Soviet Union, or that *she would conclude a Non-Aggression Pact with her*, the Soviet Union would probably refrain from concluding a treaty with England . . . (*13*)

There was but little doubt in Draganov's mind that Astakhov was using him as an indirect channel of communication to Ribbentrop. The Bulgarian went to the German Foreign Ministry at once and reported diligently.

. . . .

[*The British calculate.*] There still were influential men in Britain who desired an agreement with Germany. Around June 20, the Western press reported that significant economic conversations were being held between the British Hudson and the German Wohltat, commercial delegates of the respective Foreign Offices; and the memoranda of Dirksen reveal that from mid-June on, circles close to Chamberlain, especially Sir Horace Wilson, and even certain Laborites (Buxton) were having secret talks with the German Ambassador. (*14*) Stalin expressed his fear of an Anglo-German Alliance when he spoke to the American Ambassador to Moscow; but he need not have feared such a possibility — for Ribbentrop was with him. (*15*)

On June 17 the German Counselor of Legation, Hilger, called on the Soviet Commissar, Mikoyan, who received him at once, which, in the opinion of the German chargé d'affaires, Tippelskirch, showed that Mikoyan was "anxious not to lose contact."

> That Mikoyan would immediately accept the German [economic] proposal could hardly be expected, considering the mentality of the Soviet Government, which at present is riding a high horse, and its known methods of negotiation. The continually repeated statement of Mikoyan that he suspects a political game behind our offer of negotiation may not be due only to tactical motives but may partly reflect his true opinion. Mikoyan seems to believe that we had deliberately chosen the present time for economic negotiations. This becomes clear from his remarks that we expected an advantage from a resumption of the economic negotiations just now.

"It is a remarkable nuance," Tippelskirch continued, "that Mikoyan in his answer uses the same formula as the communiqué published on June 16 on the first conversation of Molotov with the British and French Ambassadors and Strang. In this as well as in the other case the result is called 'not entirely favorable.' "

Around the end of June, Ribbentrop and Weizsäcker asked Gaus, Head of the Legal Division of the German Foreign Office, to Ribbentrop's country estate, where they began to draw up the first draft of a German-Russian Non-Aggression Treaty. (*16*) On June 28 Molotov received Schulenburg: he was amiable, but extremely cautious. Schulenburg reported: "Although a strong distrust was evident in everything that Molotov said, nevertheless he described normalization of relations with Germany [as] desirable." The impatient and somewhat disillusioned Ribbentrop-Weizsäcker team now instructed Schulenburg that enough had been said (on the political level) "until further instructions." Meanwhile, on the 29th, the British government — upon the desperate insistence of Paris — finally accepted the demand which Russia had made in April that the states guaranteed by the Great Powers should be included in a secret list even without their concurrence.

[*The Russians procrastinate.*]   It seemed that the long-awaited agreement was at hand. But no. Five days later, Molotov raised a new demand, disguised in the issue of "indirect aggression."

Moscow wanted to force Britain and France to accept what Russia had not been able to push down the throats of the Baltic states in March. As Ryti, the Finnish President, was to put it during his trial in 1945, this insistence that she be allowed to define "indirect aggression" meant that Russia would get a free hand in the Baltics, that she would be free to march into Finland, Estonia or Latvia whenever an editorial writer in *Pravda* or *Izvestia* or *Red Fleet* cared to label the government of any of these countries "pro-German"; and it meant that the Aalands, the islands of the Finnish Gulf, Hangö, Tallin, Dagö, Ösel, Baltiski, Riga, Tartu, all would be at the Soviets' disposal. (*17*)

The patience of the British government was nearly exhausted, a fact which was manifest in their note to Moscow on July 13. Paris was equally distressed. Come what might, Britain decided to stand loyally by her Polish guarantee. An Anglo-Polish financial agreement was signed and General Ironside visited Warsaw. From July 4 to July 23, nervous and protracted negotiations continued between Paris and London and Moscow; it was mainly due to French insistence that Halifax finally compromised on many of the issues in dispute.

[*Agreement at hand.*]   Stalin now decided to slow down momentarily the pace of German-Soviet soundings. On July 12, the chargé Tippelskirch wrote to Schulenburg: "I told [Schnurre] that the Embassy and particularly you yourself had done everything possible, but we could not drag Molotov and Mikoyan through the Brandenburger Tor . . ." On July 24, the British and the Russian negotiators came to report almost complete agreement. It was agreed that a secret protocol would be applied to Estonia, Finland, Latvia, Lithuania, Poland, Belgium, Turkey, Greece, and Rumania (due to the demand of the Soviets, Lithuania was included while Yugoslavia,

Switzerland, and Holland were excluded), a protocol which would provide for the immediate intervention of Russia, France, and Britain in the case of aggression against any of the enumerated States. Only minor nuances in regard to the precise definition of "indirect aggression" remained unsettled. It was agreed that military negotiations between the three Powers should begin immediately; thus, on July 27 the Western diplomats announced to Molotov that military missions would be sent to Moscow at once. True, the British missions set out from a Scottish port in a boat so slow that their journey took about a week. But Molotov himself had agreed that a delay of eight or ten days would be "equally convenient to him."

[*The Germans act.*]   As a matter of fact, he was in no hurry whatsoever. He was quite willing to wait to see what the Germans would now have to offer. On July 22, a short notice in the Soviet press reported that economic negotiations had begun between Russia and Germany. (On the 8th the Soviet Ambassador to Poland had denied that such talks were even contemplated.) On the 27th, Schnurre invited Babarin, the Soviet economic negotiator, and Astakhov to dinner at an elegant Berlin restaurant. The "economic experts" talked for several hours. The Russians did not commit themselves, but indicated that they approved of the German plan to bring about a full rapprochement in gradual stages. At once Weizsäcker instructed Schulenburg to tell Moscow that in Poland as well as in the Baltic, Germany was prepared to safeguard Soviet interests. On August 1, when London and Paris thought that now that Franco-British-Soviet political negotiations had been concluded, military talks were to begin, a TASS communiqué reverted to the political talks, stating that "difficulties arose" due to the definition of "indirect aggression." This was obviously a hint to Germany that there was room for extending the field of German-Russian talks — "gradually," as Astakhov had said in Berlin four days before.

[*Elsewhere. The Balkans.*]   The summer of 1939 was unusually warm in central-eastern Europe, yet enough rain fell to secure bountiful crops. There was some upsurge of economic prosperity; people hoped for an undisturbed future and could not bring themselves to believe that Germans and Russians would soon divide their countries into spheres of influence. The position of the extremists was gradually weakening: in Greece, Bulgaria, Rumania, Hungary, and Estonia a conservative-liberal tendency was perceptible. The Yugoslavs were near to solving their troublesome Serb-Croat differences. In Poland, national danger welded parties and groups together; exiles returned; the opposition forgot its grievances and joined the colors with patriotic fervor. Politics were quiet in Finland, Latvia, and Lithuania. Only the already subjugated Austrians, Czechs, democratic Slovaks, and patriotic Albanians, were suffering.

In June, Tsintsar-Markovič and Regent Paul visited Berlin, where Ribbentrop demanded, among other things, that Yugoslavia leave the League of Nations and abrogate her remaining Little Entente alliance with Rumania. The Yugoslavs courteously refused. Ribbentrop could not force their hand, as he needed friendly economic relations with the Balkans during that summer and the coming autumn. (*18*) In July, the Bulgarian Premier, Kiosseivanov, visited Berlin; in August King Carol sailed his yacht to Istanbul to meet the Turkish President, Inönü. Meanwhile a crisis in Hungarian-German relations developed. Premier Teleki, worried about reports of German plans to use Hungary as another springboard in the war against Poland, sent two letters each to Hitler and Mussolini on July 24. One affirmed Hungary's full adherence to the Axis camp, the other stated that "in order to avoid any misinterpretations," and due to moral considerations, Hungary could not participate in a war against Poland. This courageous but clumsy diplomatic manoeuvre threw Hitler into a rage; Mussolini was also displeased and remonstrated so strongly with Budapest that two weeks later Csáky found it necessary to inform Berlin and Rome that Teleki's second letter was to be disregarded.

[*The United States in the summer of 1939.*] As Britain had now committed herself to stop further German aggression, a new picture of the United States was developing: that of an important mediating power. The first request for direct American mediation came, interestingly enough, from Finland after Russia had put some pressure on her as early as March 1938; Secretary of State Hull was, however, noncommittal so far as direct American action was concerned. But Washington was becoming an important information center concerning the affairs of central-eastern Europe. The State Department was aware of the contacts between Russia and Germany. Ambassador Bullitt in Paris, while chary of Russia, readily recognized the German

danger; he was very active. In January 1939 Potocki, the Polish Ambassador to Washington, and in February Lukasiewicz in Paris heard
Bullitt say that, sooner or later, America would intervene in a European war on the side of France and Britain. Impressed by the German
march into Prague, on March 14 Bullitt telephoned Roosevelt, asking
the President to consider a public denunciation of aggression and go
before Congress with a request for the repeal of the Neutrality Laws.
The White House deemed such steps premature. Bullitt, very anxious
and friendly to Poland, joined Beck between Calais and Lille for a
talk as the Polish Foreign Minister was returning from London. The
eager Beneš, who in his memoirs later claimed that in May 1939 Roosevelt told him that the United States would ultimately enter a war
against Hitler, toured the United States in "unpolitical exile," keeping some contact with Maisky in London and the Soviet Ambassador,
Oumansky, in Washington. The latter was also told by President
Roosevelt in August 1939 to inform Stalin not to join with Hitler:
for if Hitler conquered France, he then would turn against Russia.

American trade with central-eastern Europe significantly increased
in the summer of 1939. As the great European Powers were stocking
up their arsenals, there developed a growing dependence on the
United States for industrial and military material; in August the
Yugoslav Ambassador in Washington inquired about the possibilities
of buying airplanes from the United States. Thus the prospects of a
European war brought American realities to the serious attention of
central-eastern Europe. The far western and the far eastern outposts
of Western civilizations were discovering their interdependence —
not quite eight years before the United States was to move into Greece
in 1947 and establish a potential defense of what was then to be the
easternmost ramparts of the western world.

.　.　.　.　.　.　.　.

[*August 3–14: decisive days.*]　The British and French military
missions were at sea when, on August 3, Ribbentrop received the
eager Astakhov again. "I dropped a gentle hint," noted the German,
"of coming to an agreement with Russia on the fate of Poland."
Ribbentrop then went on to point out that the choice now lay with
Russia. He did not have to wait for long. Next morning, Molotov
received Schulenburg. The Foreign Commissar "abandoned his usual
reserve," reported Schulenburg (this was in strange contrast to the

exhausting tactics and oriental cunning which the Russian adopted in his talks with the Western diplomats; a Frenchman later exclaimed: "Thank God that fellow [Molotov] will not participate in the military negotiations"). However, Molotov was still cautious. Then, in Danzig, an incident occurred which accelerated the march of events.

Continuous German provocations in and around Danzig had made the Polish civil positions almost intolerable there, (*19*) and on August 4 the Polish customs guards in a frontier sector were forcibly prevented from doing their duties. A crisis developed, but after some negotiating, the matter was temporarily settled. Unfortunately — just as they had done on May 21, 1938 — the great Western newspapers declared that not only the Danzig authorities but the whole cause of National Socialism had been defeated and that Germany had given in all along the line "to the threat of Polish reprisals." Back in 1938, such an interpretation had made the neurotically proud Hitler roar out a promise to smash his insolent opponents, and the same thing happened now. On August 11, Hitler received Carl Burckhardt, the Swiss High Commissar of the League of Nations, in Danzig. "I shall crush Poland in three weeks!" he cried. The whole content of the Burckhardt-Hitler talks was communicated to Bonnet in Paris.

There is, however, a debatable point in Bonnet's interpretation thereof. Because Hitler told Burckhardt that Germany was not afraid of Russia's might and that an Anglo-French-Russian alliance did not intimidate him, Bonnet deduces that on August 11 Hitler still considered Russia an adversary. However, the very next day, when Ciano told Ribbentrop at Salzburg that Italy would not fight, Hitler gave orders to bring about an immediate agreement with Russia. There is no doubt that the German-Russian conversations had by August 11 advanced far beyond the point where Hitler had to consider an Anglo-French-Russian alliance. On the other hand, the fact that Italian participation was doubtful must have been evident to Hitler before August 12; Ciano's communication was certainly not a totally unexpected surprise. (*20*) More probably, Hitler, aware that what he said to Burckhardt would soon be known in London and Paris, wanted his Swiss conversant to believe that Germany had no contacts with Russia. (*21*)

On August 10, Astakhov called on Schnurre to discuss economic matters, and, as usual, their talk rapidly developed into a broadly political conversation. (According to Kordt, Astakhov got full instructions on the 7th, and on the 10th was ready for all-embracing discussions, a timetable which seems to have been synchronized with the arrival of the Western military missions in Moscow.) Schnurre again confirmed the fact that Germany was willing to make an agreement with the Soviets concerning Poland. Astakhov said that he had no instructions on that subject, but went so far as to say that, in his opinion, the new German friendship made the outcome of Western-Soviet negotiations "uncertain," and that "it was quite possible that his Government likewise considered the question as completely open." Two days later, on Saturday, August 12, Astakhov called again: he had received instructions from Molotov that the Soviets would welcome a German negotiator in Moscow to deal with all political issues in gradual stages — *Poland included*. Ribbentrop was away from Berlin, meeting Ciano in Salzburg. (*22*) Schulenburg in Moscow evidently felt that something was in the making there, for on Monday, the 14th, he wrote to Weizsäcker, asking to be released from the obligation of going to the Nuremberg Party Congress, pointing out that he preferred to stay in Moscow at such an important time. The correctness of Schulenburg's instinct was confirmed when Schnurre telegraphed him that Monday afternoon about the Saturday talks with Astakhov. After sending the telegram, Schnurre went over to Ribbentrop. A few minutes before eleven o'clock that night, the German Foreign Minister sent a "most urgent" telegram to Moscow, instructing his Ambassador to see the Soviet Foreign Commissar immediately and to inform Molotov that "a historic turning-point" in German-Russian relations had come and that Ribbentrop, in the name of Hitler, was ready to visit Moscow at once to confer with Molotov and Stalin.

Conclusion of the Nazi-Soviet Pact — The last ten days

It was a quarter to five in the early morning of August 15 when the code clerk on duty in the Moscow German Embassy recorded the receipt of Ribbentrop's telegram. It was about three o'clock in the morning, when a telegram from General Doumenc, the French chief of the Anglo-French military mission to Moscow, was received at the Quai d'Orsay. After having decoded the message, the clerk on duty decided to awaken the sleeping Georges Bonnet. "About five in the morning I heard somebody knocking at my door," writes Bonnet. There is but two hours difference between Moscow and Paris clocks in the summer. It is very likely that in the same hour that Bonnet was reading Doumenc's telegram in Paris, Count Schulenburg was perusing Ribbentrop's message at seven o'clock, Moscow time.

[*The partition offer.*] Ribbentrop's *most urgent* message was long, turgid, florid. He expatiated on the historic turning-point to which German-Soviet relations had come. He did not mention a non-aggression pact; instead, he went considerably further. Having reaffirmed that Germany had no aggressive intentions against the USSR, he then declared: "The Reich Government is of the opinion that there is no question between the Baltic and the Black Seas which cannot be settled to the complete satisfaction of both countries. Among these are such questions as: the Baltic Sea, the Baltic area, Poland, Southeastern questions, etc. In such matters political cooperation between the two countries can only have a beneficial effect." (*1*) Here, in essence, was the proposal to partition central-eastern Europe.

General Doumenc's telegram was short, dry, dramatic. He informed the French government that during the night session of August 14–15, Marshal Voroshilov had suddenly requested that passage of Russian troops through Wilnó, Galicia, eastern Poland and, if necessary, through Rumania be the first question taken up by the negotiators. When the British and French delegates answered that without the consent of the Polish and Rumanian governments they had no authorization for such discussions, Voroshilov coolly retorted that in that case the military discussions were of no value, for all further negotiations were conditional on the permission of passage.

[*Proof of Soviet duplicity.*] The exact coincidence of Ribbentrop's decision and Voroshilov's bombshell excludes the hypothesis that it was the German offer which made the Russians raise conditions which they knew the French and British were in no position to fulfill. While it had been decided as far back as mid-summer that in case of a German attack, the Polish government would enter into talks with the Soviet Union to determine the conditions under which the Red Army could participate in the defense of Poland, it was also obvious that the Anglo-French mission was not prepared to deal with this specific question. Instead, the mission was but to define the capacities and capabilities of joint Anglo-French-Russian military action. German willingness to share territorial spoils with Russia — so important to the territory-conscious Russian hearts — had been clear since early August. On the other hand, the Western Powers could not have offered Russia anything comparable to such an agreement. Stalin considered the possibility that Britain and France might some day be willing to pay for a Soviet alliance by tacitly acquiescing in Soviet control over certain parts of central-eastern Europe. Yet the Soviet Union would certainly gain in power and prestige from a European war between Germany and the Western powers, if she herself could only remain neutral. In fact, any eventual Western territorial concessions to Russia could not really counterbalance the advantages of a German-Russian overall settlement in August, 1939. Thus Stalin decided in the first ten days of August to invite a settlement with Germany, blocking meanwhile a military agreement with the Western powers. That the dramatic results of these parallel manoeuvres came during the same night as the final offer of Germany and in the painful realization of the Western powers' impossible situation was but a spectacular coincidence.

Here, however, arises a consideration of fundamental importance. Unsuccessful as the Western-Soviet negotiations were, their failure exonerated France and Britain from direct responsibility for the war. Although their very fate depended upon it, they would not, for moral reasons, consent to a Russian occupation of parts of central-eastern Europe: a price which Germany willingly paid. In view of this first Bolshevik admission into Europe, and the consequent unleashing of the war, later German recriminations concerning the Western Powers' tragic wartime mistakes are on singularly shaky moral ground: and this is an historical fact.

[*The journey arranged.*] In the evening hours of August 15, Molotov received Schulenburg, who gave him Ribbentrop's message. The Russian listened tensely to the words of the interpreter; a look of satisfaction appeared on his face. The Soviet Union, said Molotov, warmly welcomed Germany's intentions of improving relations between the two countries "and now believed in the sincerity of these intentions." He asked about the concrete possibilities of a German-Russian Non-Aggression Pact, and spoke about a joint Baltic "guarantee" by Germany and Russia. He also welcomed the idea of Ribbentrop's trip but suggested that the important issues should be clarified first, for "a trip required adequate preparation in order that the exchange of opinions might lead to results." Next day, Ribbentrop instructed Schulenburg to see Molotov again and tell him that Ribbentrop and Hitler agreed to the Non-Aggression Pact as well as to the Baltic guarantee. The Ambassador was to tell Molotov that Ribbentrop was prepared to fly to Moscow any time after Friday, August 18. Molotov welcomed this message. Ribbentrop's willingness to come, noted Molotov, "stands in noteworthy contrast with England, who . . . had sent only an official of the second class [Strang] to Moscow." Yet, his cunning and caution did not leave him. He suggested that the economic negotiations should be concluded first; only then, "after a short interval," should the Non-Aggression Pact be announced, (2) and after this, Ribbentrop's journey, which required "thorough preparation," could be considered. The time element, thus, was to remain again in the hands of Molotov who would use it to his advantage! Schulenburg was impatient, but in vain; Molotov was still distrustful. Within twenty-four hours, however, Russian distrust was dispelled by another message from Berlin, announcing that the economic negotiations were completed and communicating at the same time the draft of a Non-Aggression Pact. At first, Molotov, although amiable, insisted that the time of Ribbentrop's journey could not yet be determined; but after conferring with Stalin, he called the Embassy scarcely half an hour after Schulenburg had left the Kremlin. The Ambassador was asked to return to Molotov's office: there he was told that the Soviet government was agreeing to the Non-Aggression Pact as well as to the visit from the German Foreign Minister a week after the signature of the economic agreement, that is, around August 26 or 27.

Ribbentrop wished to come earlier. The original army directives planned to open the Polish war in the dawn hours of the 26th. (3) He now had with him the Soviet draft of the Non-Aggression Pact and he was in a hurry. Already on the 18th, Molotov had grasped the meaning of the "from the Baltic to the Black Sea" sentence in Ribbentrop's historic message and had spoken of a "supplementary protocol" defining the exact sphere of German and Russian interests in central-eastern Europe. To further convince Moscow of his goodwill, Ribbentrop intervened with Hitler, who sent a personal telegram to Stalin on the afternoon of the 20th:

> The supplementary protocol desired by the Government of the Soviet Union can, I am convinced, be substantially clarified in shortest possible time if a responsible German statesman can come to Moscow himself to negotiate. Otherwise the Government of the Reich is not clear as to how the supplementary protocol could be cleared up and settled in a short time.

And, after hinting that the German attack on Poland was imminent, Hitler continued:

In my opinion, it is desirable, in view of the intentions of the two states to enter into a new relation to each other, not to lose any time. I therefore again propose that you receive my Foreign Minister on Tuesday, August 22, but at the latest on Wednesday, August 23. The Reich Foreign Minister has full powers to draw up and sign the non-aggression pact as well as the protocol . . . *(4)*

Molotov received the telegram at 3 P.M. on the 21st. Two hours later, he handed Schulenburg Stalin's somewhat laconic but friendly reply: Ribbentrop would be welcome on the 23rd.

[*British-French pressure put on Poland.*] Through the Polish Ambassadors in London and Paris, through the French and British Embassies in Warsaw, through General Doumenc and through General Musse, the French military attaché to Poland, came frantic efforts between August 15 and 20 to make the Poles accept the Soviet passage. After all, it was argued, if war came, Poland would have to rely on the Russian armies anyhow. But the Poles did not budge; how could they? They foresaw a new, fourth partition of their country. As Lukasiewicz put the case to Bonnet after the latter had demanded the Polish acceptance of the Soviet request, "Would you consent to put Alsace-Lorraine under German protection?" Beck told Noël: "There is nothing to convince us that the Russians, once they are installed in the eastern districts of our country, will take an effective part in the war." Rydz-Smigly told Musse: "With the Germans we risk losing our freedom. With the Russians we shall lose our soul."

There is no doubt that undue confidence and blind rashness governed the doings of Beck and of many Polish military leaders. Yet this unfortunate attitude is at least understandable. Soviet diplomacy employed expert timing in order to put the blame on the Poles, but the published evidence of the German-Russian negotiations refutes the argument which Voroshilov later voiced to General Doumenc that it was only due to Poland's unyielding attitude that Moscow found it necessary to sign a Non-Aggression Pact with Germany; the published documents show that this was not true.

From August 15 on, more and more danger signals pointing toward the conclusion of a German-Russian political agreement were being received in London and Paris. On the 15th, Weizsäcker expressed his private opinion to Henderson that not only would Russian aid to Poland be negligible, but that Russia would ultimately join in sharing the Polish spoils. (Weizsäcker, Göring, and the German would-be conservatives were momentarily frightened in those days by the spectre of a proletarian coalition against Britain; while Ribbentrop and his cohorts wished to partition central-eastern Europe by agreement with Russia, Weizsäcker, Göring, and the others wished to do the same with the consent of Britain.) Then, on August 19, came the news of the conclusion of a German-Soviet economic agreement. On the same day, *Pravda* published an article attacking British conservative circles as negotiators of a new Munich; it was significant that *Pravda* published these charges as late as August 19, charges which had appeared in the London *Daily Worker* a fortnight before.

The French now undertook a desperate step, one to which Lord Halifax halfheartedly gave his consent. Upon his government's instructions, General Doumenc told Voroshilov on the 21st that the Soviet Army was authorized to pass through the territories designated by Voroshilov. But this was not enough for the Marshal, who said that nothing could be done without Poland notifying Moscow of her direct acceptance; Paris could not speak in Warsaw's name. (It is noteworthy that this stern Russian demand was communicated to Doumenc at a time when Stalin had already telegraphed to Hitler and just a few hours before the official announcement of Ribbentrop's scheduled arrival, the pact, secret protocol and all.)

There is little use to recapitulate the last, tragic efforts with which the French tried to gain Poland's acquiescence. Daladier maintained that he actually gave an ultimatum to the Polish Ambassador on the morning of the 21st, but Lukasiewicz has denied this assertion in a series of articles which he wrote in 1946. During that day it nevertheless seemed that Warsaw was about to consider the French requests at least in part, but it was not until the 23rd that the Polish government indicated her vague consent (5); then it was too late. (6)

.   .   .   .

[*Ribbentrop and Stalin meet; the Pact.*]   The news of Ribbentrop's journey to Moscow broke upon the world at midnight. It was announced by a nocturnal communiqué from Moscow and a simultaneous release of the German DNB news agency; by dawn, foreign ministers were being shaken from their sleep, press attachés were hurrying through empty streets to their desks, and fifth-column Nazi and Communist chieftains were alertly waiting for new instructions. In central-eastern Europe's capitals, feelings were varied. In the

Baltics, people were aware that the German-Russian Non-Aggression Pact meant, one way or the other, the end of their independence; elsewhere, those Europeans who were inclined to underestimate the doggedness of the Anglo-Saxon race believed that under these new circumstances a new Munich was inevitable. (7) The Polish leaders pretended that they were not surprised and, to assure themselves, tried to minimize the importance of the event. (8) But in Rumania, Calinescu and Gafencu were deeply worried. (9)

The true import of the German-Soviet agreement was not primarily ideological; indeed, the alignment of extreme Right and extreme Left against the pro-Western Center was not an unexpected or even a new development in central-eastern Europe. What people did not know was that Ribbentrop and the Soviet leaders were signing a paper in Moscow which dealt with entire countries as though they lay on the counters of a gigantic bargain sale. This was the so-called Secret Protocol added to the German-Soviet Non-Aggression Pact.

[*The Secret Protocol.*]   Before his departure, Ribbentrop had been instructed by Hitler to express general German disinterestedness in south-eastern Europe, if necessary, as far as Constantinople and the Straits. (*10*) Seven years later, just before he was to be hanged, Ribbentrop sent a letter through General Montgomery to "Mr. Vincent Churchill," claiming that the Russian Pact was exclusively the result of his influence. Indeed, he was very happy with these instructions. He was willing to pay almost any price for a smashing defeat of British diplomacy. Thus in Moscow he and Stalin and Molotov agreed with unexpected swiftness (Schmidt calls it "a diplomatic speed record") on the territorial lines along which central-eastern Europe was to be partitioned. Stalin was pleasantly surprised by the understanding, generosity, and broad views of the Germans, and felt that his secret admiration for Teutonic talent and racial qualities was being confirmed. (Ribbentrop, nervous, stiff, and blinking-eyed, did not impress Stalin very much, but he would always esteem men like Schulenburg and Hitler.)

The Secret Protocol (*11*) dealt with the Baltics first: "In the event of a political rearrangement in areas belonging to the Baltic states," the northern boundary of Lithuania was to constitute the line of partition between German and Soviet "spheres of influence." (*12*) Both parties recognized the claims of Lithuania concerning Vilna.

In Poland, the line of the three rivers, Narew, Vistula, and San, was to be the partition line; a Polish buffer state was to follow the defeat of Poland, the boundaries of which were to be determined later by common consent.

Upon request of the Soviets, Germany expressed her "lack of interest" in Bessarabia, while maintaining that she had certain economic interests throughout south-eastern Europe.

As Ribbentrop had said in his telegram ten days before, no question remained unsettled from the Baltic to the Black Sea. The line of the future German-Russian frontier was established; it was only a question of time until the world would experience the establishment of a common German-Russian frontier along the partition line, a circumstance which would mean the eventual disappearance of a number of unfortunate nations.

Stalin was greatly pleased, and enjoyed himself cracking jokes with Ribbentrop at the expense of the British. Ribbentrop let him know of Britain's last desperate attempts to come to an agreement with Hitler; Stalin said he knew all along about these. (On August 23, Henderson had delivered a letter from Chamberlain to Hitler and had used the occasion to say: "If an agreement be made with Moscow I had rather Germany make it than ourselves" — a revealing statement.) The German made a joke out of the Anti-Comintern Pact; Stalin retorted that the Anti-Comintern had in fact "frightened principally the City of London and the small British merchants." The two also discussed Italy. Stalin raised the question whether Italy had aspirations of gaining Greek territory; Ribbentrop assured him that Mussolini was very much satisfied with the conclusion of the German-Russian Pact. Then both agreed that something should be done with Turkey, whose politicians were corrupt, bought by the British, and whose foreign policy was vacillating. Other questions were also briefly touched upon.

Then came the usual Soviet toasts: an ordeal to the weak-stomached Ribbentrop. But his physical discomfort must have left him when he saw Stalin rise to toast Hitler: "I know how much the German nation loves its Führer; I should therefore like to drink to his health."

And they drank.

.   .   .   .

[*Hitler speaks to his generals.*]   While he was being toasted in faraway Moscow by the man whom he some time ago had discovered to be "very sympathetic," Hitler spoke to his generals and to Keitel at Obersalzberg. This extemporaneous address on August 22, 1939, should be recorded here, at least in part: it is one of the great documents of our great century.

After recapitulating recent events, he announced that his decision to attack Poland had been made in the spring. Then he continued:

> Since Autumn 1938, and since, I have found out that Japan does not go with us without conditions and that Mussolini is menaced by the weak-headed King and the treacherous scoundrel of a Crown Prince. I have decided to go with Stalin. On the whole, there are only three great statesmen in the world: Stalin, myself and Mussolini. Mussolini, the weakest, has not been able to break either the power of the crown or that of the church. Stalin and I are the only ones that see only the future. So I shall shake hands with Stalin within a few weeks on the common German-Russian border and undertake with him a new distribution of the world.
>
> Our strength is in our quickness and in our brutality. Ghenghis Khan had millions of women and children killed by his own will and with a gay heart. History sees only in him a great state leader. What weak Western European civilization thinks about me, does not matter. . . .
> Thus for the time being, I have sent to the East only my "Death's Head Units," with the order to kill without pity or mercy all men, women and children of the Polish race and language. Only in such a way will we win the vital space that we need. Who still talks nowadays of the extermination of the Armenians?
> . . . My pact with Poland was only meant to stall for time. And besides, gentlemen, with Russia will happen just what I have practiced with Poland. After Stalin's death . . . we shall crush the Soviet Union.
> . . . I saw our enemies at Munich . . . they were miserable worms.
> The occasion is favorable now as it has never been. I have only one fear and that is that Chamberlain or such another dirty swine comes to me with propositions or a change of mind. (*13*) He will be thrown downstairs. And even if I must personally kick him in the belly before the eyes of all the photographers.
> No, for this it is too late. The invasion and extermination of Poland begins on Saturday (*14*) morning. I will have a few companies in Polish uniform attack in Upper Silesia or in the Protectorate. (*15*) Whether the world believes it doesn't mean a damn to me. The world believes only in success.
> Be hard. . . . Be without mercy. The citizens of Western Europe must quiver in horror.
> The new warfare corresponds to the new border status. A wall from Reval, Lublin, Kaschau (*16*) to the Danube estuary. The Russians

get the rest. Ribbentrop has received instructions to make any offer
and to accept any demand . . . (*17*)

.   .   .   .

[*The Western reaction: a courageous one.*]   On August 22, the
French and the British cabinets met to face the new order of things
brought about by the Russo-German alignment; on August 23 the
French called a Supreme War Council. It was decided that the Western Powers would continue their previous Polish policy, despite the
new developments. In order to manifest the continued validity of this
position — and, also, to impress Hitler with British determination —
the British government signed an alliance with Poland. (*18*)

For awhile it was still hoped that all was not lost in Moscow: Naggiar, the French Ambassador, was quoted as believing that in three
months the Soviets and the French would get together again; he had
been impressed by Voroshilov's cordiality when bidding good-bye to
the Anglo-French military missions. Also, Molotov was putting the
blame on Poland, pointing out that "a great country like the USSR
could not go and beg Poland to accept help which she did not desire
at any price." When Naggiar asked whether there were any secret
clauses to the German-Soviet Treaty, Molotov evaded the question,
but insisted again that it was due to Poland's delay in accepting the
Soviet "offer of help" that Ribbentrop had come to Moscow. (*19*)
(Stalin's own statements in 1941, and the secret directive to the south-
eastern European Communist parties found by Calinescu and
transmitted to the French in September 1939, explaining that Russia
did not wish "to reinforce the Western European bourgeoisie" but
preferred to profit from a Western-German war, refuted this thesis
even before the found German documents revealed the full extent of
German-Soviet negotiations. Stalin in 1941 acknowledged that he
needed the Pact to gain time, a statement which indicates that he
would not have gone to war in 1938 either.)

That Hitler ultimately would not be able to control his greed and
would therefore force a war with Russia was foreseen by many Western statesmen, especially those who knew history well. (In 1768, de
Vergennes wrote to Louis xv: "It does not seem that France should
be alarmed. The cooperation established between the Kings of Prussia
and Russia for their respective aggrandisement, cannot be of long
duration. Their aggrandisement, by making them close neighbors,

will also make them more redoubtable in each other's eyes; it will engender jealousy between them and jealousy soon degenerates into enmity.") But in the bleak days of August 1939, diplomatic parallels out of the past were but small consolation.

The Anglo-Polish alliance, in which a small but certain sparkle of Western honor now gleamed, was announced on August 25. Ten days had passed since Ribbentrop had telegraphed his offer to divide central-eastern Europe with Russia. Now it was partitioned from the Baltic to the Black Sea. What would be the fate, then, of the vast Balkan triangle and its northern approaches? What was to happen between the Black Sea, the Aegean and the Adriatic? The Moscow line of partition ended where the northern arm of the Danube delta reaches the Black Sea and forms the southern border of Bessarabia. South of that line, there were no arrangements between Berlin and Moscow, a situation which, a year later, was to serve as one of the primary causes of Russian-German misunderstandings. Here lay a vast sphere where another Power, Italy, pursued its own interests.

[*Italian deliberations and the Balkans.*] On that same day of August 25 a letter sent by Mussolini to Hitler unmistakably established Italian non-belligerence, a development which had been expected for some time. Mussolini's letter had two effects: First, it led Hitler to hear the pleas of a few frantic last-minute negotiators while he postponed the date of his attack on Poland for six days. (*20*) Second, it secured a breathing space for Hungary and the Balkans for about nine months, until Hitler had eliminated his opponents in Poland and Western Europe and until Mussolini, envious and impatient, had decided to go to war himself. (*21*)

In spite of his dissatisfaction with Greece, in spite of Fascist desires and ambitions (as early as August 1938, Ciano, speaking to the departing new Italian military attaché to Athens, could tell him not much more than a Sicilian saying: "If you encounter a wolf and a Greek, murder the Greek and let the wolf go." (*22*); in spite of his Albanian propaganda (a great industrial enterprise — AMMI — was to make a forward bastion out of that backward country and Albanian "claims" against the Greeks in Epirus, in the so-called Čamuria region were being pressed), Mussolini now had to give up his Greek plans. On August 21, Grazzi, the Italian Ambassador, met General Metaxas who, although he complained about certain Italian measures, assured Rome of Greece's desire not to provoke Italy. (*23*) A similar assurance was given eight days later by General Papagos to Mondini, the Italian military attaché in Athens. On September 12, Mussolini assured the Greek government of his benevolence.

The Yugoslav issue was even more luring than the Greek prospects, but here again Mussolini had to wait. He planned to disrupt the Yugoslav state from within, and incredible amounts had been paid to dubious Croat agents to bring about a revolt in Croatia, a revolt which would have resulted in the establishment of an Italian duchy there. But the Croat extremists, Pavelič and others, were flirting with Hitler; and the majority of the Croats had rallied around the peasant leader, Maček. When in July the Belgrade government began seriously to consider reconstructing the partial autonomy of Croatia, Italian bribery lost out.

Thus the possibilities for Mussolini's "little war" were none too good. Yet he hated to turn away from the fat prize of a Yugoslavia offered to him in return for his participation in a "great war." Throughout the summer of 1939 he hesitated; finally it was the advice of the military which made him decide against the "great war." On June 3 he sent a letter to Hitler in which he assured himself of a certain latitude for his own interpretation of the Steel Pact. (*24*) On July 4, he signed an ethnic agreement with Germany concerning the rights and transfer possibilities of the German-speaking population in the South Tyrol province (Alto Adige) (*25*) — a problem which later troubled him considerably. On July 7 he threatened the British Ambassador in Rome that if England helped Poland, Italy would help Germany. But these were only words.

Ciano knew of the Russo-German contacts; Rosso in Moscow was well-informed and in June the Italian Foreign Minister even hinted to the Soviet chargé d'affaires in Rome that Germany wished to achieve a rapprochement with the Soviets. (Molotov received due notice of this hint, and he mentioned it to Ribbentrop in August.) Attolico in Berlin kept insisting from mid-July on, that a sudden decision would be made by Hitler around August 15, a prediction which proved to be very accurate although Attolico refused to believe that a German-Russian Pact was in the making. In spite of his presentiments, when, on August 11, Ciano went to see Ribbentrop and Hitler at Salzburg, he was taken aback as he heard Ribbentrop declare flatly: "We want war."

Ciano rushed back to report to Mussolini. The latter still continued to weigh the risky imponderables of the "great war" against the temporary impossibility of the "little war." The Ciano Diaries record how hesitant Mussolini was on August 13: he could not get away from the luring prospects of Croatia and Dalmatia. (26) Only on August 21 did he finally make up his mind. The German Finance Minister, Schwerin-Krosigk, met Ciano in Rome on the 23rd and noted the Italian's anxiety; but Hitler had already counted out the possibility of Italy's participation. On the 25th Hitler wrote to Mussolini excusing himself for not having informed the Duce previously about the Russian negotiations; he then went on to emphasize the advantages of the Russian pact, especially concerning Rumania, which country had become practically paralyzed by the new pact and need no longer be counted as a possible adversary of the Axis. Hitler committed an error in sending a letter with an explanatory tone to the Duce — he felt guilty for having made an agreement with the East without having spoken with his Fascist friend — for Mussolini, slightly ashamed of still remaining outside of the war, would have perhaps been frightened or at least uneasy if he had received a stern letter from Hitler. Instead, this kind of communication relieved him. His answer of the same day reiterated his reasons for not entering the war right away, although he had "complete understanding" for Germany's war plans regarding Poland, approved completely of the agreement with Russia, and agreed with Hitler's estimation of Rumania's new situation.

[*The last days of peace.*] On the same evening Ciano confidentially told the British Ambassador that Italy would keep out of the war, and Sir Percy Lorraine was deeply moved and grateful. From August 30 to September 3, Mussolini tried to mediate between Germany and the Western Powers; he thought that perhaps a second Munich was in the cards, which would have further increased his prestige.

At seven in the evening of August 31, Attolico called on Hitler again with one of the usual mediation proposals, but the Führer was unyielding. "To the question of Attolico whether herewith everything is at an end, the Führer answered yes." (27)

The Polish war and central-eastern European repercussions

Germany attacked Poland at 4:40 in the morning of September 1, 1939; sixty hours later Great Britain and France were at war with Germany. The Second World War had begun.

[*The first days of the war.*]   There were many who had thought that a second Munich was in the offing. The hasty, last-minute letters exchanged between the British and French Premiers and Hitler and Mussolini's attempts (*1*) had given a false impression. In central-eastern Europe a certain calm and restraint was noticeable in these critical days. There was an almost universal hope of neutrality, and most governments hurried to express their desire to remain outside of the conflict. There was also a sense of common destiny, especially in the Balkans, where it was thought that a close grouping of neutral states could provide for common security. On the day when the last threads between Germany and Poland were breaking, in Belgrade, after ten years of trying, an agreement was finally made between Croats and Serbs. Maček and Tsvetkovič reached a temporary understanding on August 26, a so-called *Sporazum* which was to bring about Yugoslav unity; this was regarded as one of the few hopeful signs in those bleak and frightening days.

On August 31, Beck and others were still overestimating the value of Poland's traditional military virtues in the face of mechanized giant armies. . . . A few hours later, dark-bodied German planes roared off into the turquoise dawn sky; steel-helmeted infantry ripped the frontier barriers apart; iron and steel ground heavily through the melancholic Polish landscape.

Early in the morning of September 1, while Polish cities were under air attack, Hitler announced his war on Poland and the re-incorporation of Danzig into the Reich. An anxious Europe watched the Western Powers. These did not go to war at once; there was yet another last-minute mediation attempt by Ciano. But the minimum condition of the West that the German spearheads in Poland be stopped and withdrawn to the frontier or that they at least effect a "symbolic withdrawal" (*2*) was not even considered by Hitler. Thus, after a delay of two days, during which the main figures were a reluctant Bonnet, an ambitious Ciano, a sad Chamberlain (and many impatient men with Munich memories, among them Churchill and Beck, anxiously inquiring about the delay), the British and French final ultimata were delivered: on Sunday, September 3, Britain went to war with Germany at 11:00 A.M.; at 5:00 P.M., France followed suit.

In resolving to fight Poland, Ribbentrop and Hitler had also planned to confront the Western Powers with accomplished military facts, after which they expected peace proposals — the image of "the old" Chamberlain was still strongly impressed upon their minds. Thus could Göbbels and Dietrich of the Foreign Ministry assure officials on the night of September 2–3 that there would be no world war. (*3*) Hitler was incredulous and Admiral Raeder recorded that during his September 3 interview, Hitler was downcast and embarrassed; Göring said to Schmidt, "If we lose this war, then may Heaven help us!" Molotov was also somewhat surprised. When on September 2 Grzybowski in Moscow had told him that he expected the Western Powers to go to war at any moment, the Foreign Commissar was sceptical. Yet within twenty-four hours the French and British declarations of war were in effect.

[*The German victory.*] On that September 3, the German armies crashing into Poland had already made spectacular advances and achieved decisive results. Complete air superiority had been gained; the German motorized attack brought a new and unexpected kind of warfare; the old technique of linear defense proved to be useless and tanks pierced the Polish lines, roaming the plains at will. The north-south riverlines of Poland formed no defense fronts against the encircling German armies; indeed, there was nothing to fall back upon until the Vistula line. The Poles fought valiantly. But the Corridor was cut in two on the third day of the campaign, the few Polish cavalry which had penetrated into East Prussia were driven out, and by the 6th the tentacles of German armor revealed themselves menacingly. There was an outer tentacle, formed by the German armies pushing down from East Prussia and up from Slovakia, which was to meet somewhere around Brest-Litóvsk; there was an inner tentacle, operating from Pomerania to encircle the Polish armies before Warsaw in the Vistula bend. The southern arm of the outer tentacle was temporarily halted by desperate Polish counterattacks around Lwów (*4*) and because of the relatively light armor of the right flank of the German Fourteenth Army. Thus a gap remained through which the Polish Government and some of the army could flee; the exodus began around the 10th. For by that date Poland was beaten, definitely, totally, irrevocably; the Germans had reached the outskirts of Warsaw and encircled the bulk of the resisting Polish armies around Kutno; the capital was heavily bombed. No longer was there an organized front, only broken-up segments and pockets of resistance.

This astonishing spectacle bore a great influence upon neighboring states. Everyone was impressed by the tranquillity which reigned on the western front, a circumstance which gave vent to fantastic peace rumors of an Anglo-French-German armistice deal after Poland's defeat. Gamelin, irresponsibly and against the expressed views of the French Foreign Ministry, had promised the Poles in May that the French would start a large-scale operation against the Siegfried Line sixteen days after a German attack on Poland; yet the actual condition of the French Army and the ridiculously small number of British troops in France made even the mere consideration of such a relief operation entirely unwarranted. (Gamelin in his memoirs, however, maintains that in September 1939 an attack against the Germans in the West could have been made.) The Western Allies, due to their unpreparedness, remained on the defensive — and Poland bled away. (5)

[*Slovakia and Hungary.*] Slovakia had been practically taken over by the German Army before the Polish war started, and from the Tatra mountains and passes, German troops surged down upon the hills and plains of southern Poland. The extremists and the Hlinka-Guardists agitated against the Poles; with some success, for, after the campaign, the Čaca and Orava sectors on the Slovak-Polish frontier — a few square miles, which had been the subject of sporadic litigations between Slovaks and Poles in 1924 and 1938 — were transferred to the Slovak Republic. Intensification of radio propaganda from the British Broadcasting Corporation, however, began to foster a growing spirit of Czecho-Slovak resistance. (6) Even among Slovak nationalists there were symptoms of dissidence: there was Szatmáry, the Slovak Minister to Warsaw, who on September 1 announced his resignation and joined the fight against Germany from Poland.

Hungary, bound to Poland by traditional ties of sympathy, watched the war with anxiety, and except for the notoriously pro-German young officers and Arrow-Cross extremists, Hungarian sentiment was distinctly pro-Polish. On September 5, the German Legation protested against Hungarian newspapers, whose reports from Warsaw had been sympathetic toward Poland's gallant struggle. Then, on September 8, the crisis which Teleki had feared since mid-July broke. A message from Ribbentrop demanded that Hungary permit the passage of German troops on her railroads through the Carpatho-Ukraine. (At that time the first Polish refugees had already begun streaming into Hungary through the Carpathian passes.) Worse, the Slovaks, whom the Magyars heartily despised, sent a note to Budapest on the 9th, asking for the same concessions. Teleki went into conference with

Horthy. It was decided courteously to refuse the German demand and to leave the Slovak note unanswered. The rapid defeat of the Polish armies then outmoded the German request, but Ribbentrop did not forget Teleki's refusal.

[*Rumania and Lithuania.*] Now Hungary and Rumania were to become the great receiving centers and transit-camps for Polish refugees. The Rumanian government feared the Germans and was troubled by the new danger of a Russian intrusion into Bessarabia. On September 19, Gafencu went to a small frontier station on the Yugoslav border to meet Tsintsar-Marković; but the Yugoslavs could offer no advice; they had their own fears. The Germans spared no efforts to make use of Rumania's bewilderment while the Russians were busy with the Polish spoils: on September 22, a bloody burst of Iron Guard terrorism flared up; the strong man of Rumania, the pro-Western Armand Calinescu, was brutally murdered. Carol avenged the murder by equal ruthlessness: the bodies of slain Iron Guardists were allowed to decompose upon the streets of Bucharest to give an example to future plotters. The police and the gendarmerie quelled what was to have been a potential rebellion.

Two other neighbors of Poland, Lithuania and the Soviet Union, were of course far less sympathetic to the Polish cause than was Hungary or Rumania. Some Lithuanians were worried about the rapid German advance, but Vilna, the great prize, was looming, and German diplomacy made hints to Kaunas that a Lithuanian occupation of Vilna was a possibility after Poland's defeat.

[*The Soviet moves.*] The policy of the Soviet Union was more shrewd. The men in the Kremlin — although having *in theory* partitioned Poland with the Germans — were anxious *in practice* lest an altogether too rapid Polish defeat should result in a German military occupation of those territories which the Secret Protocol had allotted to the Soviets. The land-minded Russians could not believe that the Germans would ever evacuate such territories once they had overrun them; they also feared that a quick defeat of Poland might result in a Polish pro-Nazi government, which, after concluding a peace or armistice with the Germans, (7) would again render the disposition of the lands east of the Narew-Vistula-San line subject to discussion. Therefore, Moscow thought it well to strengthen the Polish government temporarily. An article in *Izvestia* as early as August 27 let it

be known that the Soviet Union felt free to sell war materials even
to nations with which she had no mutual assistance pact. On September 2, the day after the German attack, the Soviet Ambassador
called on Beck and asked him why Poland did not negotiate with the
Soviets concerning armament deliveries. Beck was pleasantly surprised by the Soviet offer, but this Indian Summer of Polish-Russian
relations did not last long. Time was now pressing, and on September 8, Warsaw was told that the Soviet offer to sell armaments
no longer stood. Nine days later, her army fighting her last battles,
her capital invested and bombarded from all sides, her western and
central provinces overrun by the Germans, who had already begun
to set up their strange and barbarous satrapy, (8) the rest of Poland
was invaded by Russia. (9) The Polish state, as such, practically
ceased to exist on that September 17th when a telegram from the
Polish government, sitting in a wretched little village on the Rumanian
border, requested the Rumanian régime to grant asylum; in return,
Rumania was released from her treaty obligations which otherwise
would have demanded that she declare war on Russia upon the latter's
invasion of Poland. It was obvious that the execution of such a commitment was not to be expected; the era of treaties was gone.

The Russian intervention and the Baltic area

On September 17, 1939, Russia invaded Poland from the east;
within a month, eastern Poland was practically incorporated into the
Soviet Union; Lithuania, Latvia and Estonia fell under Russian military domination, and the last remaining independent Baltic state,
Finland, was expecting an attack from her eastern neighbor any day.
The bill of August 23 which Germany had underwritten was being
filled with astonishing eagerness and speed.

[*The Soviet invasion prepared.*]   Moscow followed the development of the Polish campaign with quick and eager interest. Her intentions were vaguely indicated in a speech which Molotov made on
August 31: "Russia and Germany are the two states which suffered
most after World War I." On September 3, a communication from
Ribbentrop (1) invited the Russians to advance to the demarcation
line established in the Secret Protocol; his argument was that within
a few weeks the Polish Army would be definitely beaten. Molotov
answered on September 5 with considerable caution:

We agree with you that at a suitable time it will be absolutely necessary for us to start concrete action. We are of the view, however, that this time has not yet come. It is possible that we are mistaken, but it seems to us that through excessive haste we might injure our cause and promote unity among our opponents. We understand that as the operations proceed, one of the parties or both parties might be forced temporarily to cross the line of demarcation between the spheres of interest of the two parties; but such cases must not prevent the strict execution of the plan adopted.

These were not arguments intended to excuse; the telegram exactly reflected the calculations of the Soviet government. However, the rapidity of the German advance upset all calculations. On September 8, as the Germans reached the outskirts of Warsaw, Molotov told the Poles that the negotiations for war matériel were closed, and on the same day he sent a congratulatory message to the German government. Soviet Russia, whose troops had been defeated before the gates of Warsaw nineteen years before, now hailed the entry of the German Army into the Polish capital. On September 9, at 5:00 P.M., Molotov summoned Schulenburg and told him that "a Soviet military action" would be forthcoming in the next few days. The German successes had surprised the Soviet Union, and now the men in Moscow were in a hurry. Quick preparations were made, reservists were called up, pretexts were raised. On September 12, *Pravda* violently attacked the Polish record of handling her minorities; on September 14 the same paper editorialized on the internal reasons for "corrupt, effete" Poland's defeat. The same day *Izvestia* raised a well-timed protest against "violations" of the Soviet frontier by Polish aircraft.

[*Diplomatic caution.*] Yet these were pretexts for internal consumption. Stalin had still to find some argument for the outside world that Soviet invasion of eastern Poland would not be a stab-in-the-back, but a precautionary measure; also, the Soviet Union had treaties with Poland, and for propaganda purposes had to find a way in which these pacts could be declared void. Thus on September 10 Molotov told Schulenburg that he was worried about possibilities of a German-Polish armistice. The Soviet Government, he said,

. . . had intended to take the occasion of the further advance of German troops to declare that Poland was falling apart and that it was necessary for the Soviet Union, in consequence, to come to the aid of the Ukrainians and the White Russians "threatened" by Germany. This argument was to make the intervention of the Soviet Union plausible to the masses and at the same time avoid giving the Soviet Union the appearance of an aggressor.

Even the Poles, ever distrustful of Russia, did not expect an imminent Soviet attack. The Polish Army was retreating into eastern Poland; the peasants and the forest-people were gathering arms in hideouts; rumors were circulating about colossal German defeats or an impending Russo-Polish alliance.

On September 14 the military situation was fluid: Warsaw was invested but not yet taken; the central German armies were engaged in liquidating the great Kutno pocket; south and north of Warsaw, however, the front line ran well beyond the Secret Protocol partition line, and in some instances German spearheads were reported operating a hundred miles beyond the Vistula River. The elimination of the Polish Army made it possible for the Russians to invade Poland with relatively weak forces, but the German advance eastward made the territorially-minded Stalin rack his peasant brains. Thus, while on September 14 Molotov informed Berlin that the Soviet "action" was imminent, he added that "for the sake of political motivation," he was anxious to know when Warsaw would fall; only then would he wish to start with the invasion. Ribbentrop answered next day, stating that the fall of Warsaw was to be expected "in the next few days" (actually the defenders of the capital were to hold out until September 27). He invited the Soviet invasion as most welcome, requested that German and Russian military missions meet at Bialystok, and proposed a joint German-Russian communiqué explaining the Soviet attack. On September 16, Molotov thanked Ribbentrop but said that a joint communiqué was not necessary; the Soviet Government intended to "motivate" the invasion by claiming that the Polish State had ceased to exist and therefore all agreements concluded with Poland were void. Further, Russia "considered itself obligated to intervene to protect its Ukrainian and White Russian brothers." To Schulenburg, "Molotov conceded that the projected argument of the Soviet Government contained a note that was jarring to German sensibilities but asked that in view of the difficult situation of the Soviet Government we [Germany] not let a trifle like this stand in our way. The Soviet Government unfortunately saw no possibility of any other motivation, since the Soviet Union had thus far not concerned itself about the plight of its minorities in Poland and had to justify abroad, in some way or other, its present intervention." Thus it happened. At dawn on September 17, the hand that concealed the dagger struck.

. . . .

[*Stalin's worry: the partition line.*]   Only sporadically did the Red Army encounter strong Polish resistance. The Government fled to Rumania; Lwów fell to the Germans; forty-eight hours after the Soviet invasion, Poland was cut in two: around Brest-Litóvsk and Lwów the spearheads of the German and the Russian armies met. On September 19, Russian troops entered Wilnó in the north and reached the Carpatho-Ukrainian border around Lawočne in the south. (*2*) This advance necessitated a diplomatic sequence. On September 17, Moscow recognized Slovakia as an independent state — only a few months after she had protested against the partition of her erstwhile Czechoslovak ally. Hungary, with whom the Soviets had broken in February, now approached Russia to re-establish diplomatic relations. On September 24 an agreement was concluded, and the Soviets proceeded to send a Minister to Budapest.

Notwithstanding the hurry with which the Russian armies jumped forward to secure the Polish spoils, the fact remained that the German front line in Poland stood considerably east of the Secret Protocol line. True, the military missions were about to meet in Bialystok, but Stalin was still worried. On September 18 he expressed his doubts to Schulenburg, pointing out that he believed it likely that the German High Command would not abide by the Moscow agreement and would fail to withdraw to the partition line. "Military men are loath to give up occupied territories," said Stalin; later, in the Suwalki issue, the Russians themselves were loath to part with even the most insignificant, few square miles, and for the sake of occupying a few deserted patches of territory were willing to pay incredible prices, political or financial. Indeed, the behavior of Stalin in September 1939 proves that Russian territorial expansion in Europe was and is something more than just a phase of the grand design of Communist world revolution, a fact significantly obscured and forgotten by our ideology-ridden world.

However, the German military attaché and Schulenburg assured Stalin that his doubts were unfounded. The Bialystok liaison meeting was being discussed, and the question of a joint German-Soviet communiqué came up. A German draft was rejected by Stalin as "too sincerely relating the facts." He himself wrote out a draft which was accepted by Ribbentrop next day and subsequently broadcast. On September 20 an agreement was reached: there would be no residual Polish state but the partition line would constitute the final German-Russian frontier. Ribbentrop was asked to come to Moscow for the final discussion on this point. Meanwhile Stalin proposed — again conscious of actual territorial realities — that instead of the Narew-Vistula-San line (which would have, among other things, reduced Warsaw to a frontier city and probably caused some friction between Germans and Russians), the partition should be drawn further east, along the rivers Narew, Bug and San. Thus the province of Lublin and the greater part of the Warsaw province would go to Germany, in exchange for which, Stalin asked that Lithuania be transferred to the Soviet "sphere of influence." He also intimated that he would "take up the solution" of the Lithuanian, Latvian, and Estonian "problems" at once, Germany consenting. All this was acceptable to Ribbentrop, who left Berlin early on September 27. (*3*)

[*The Moscow Agreements.*] The Moscow agreements of September 28 formed a vast supplement to the August 23 treaty and protocol.

There was a German-Soviet Boundary and Friendship Treaty, establishing the final line of partition along the four rivers, Pissa, Narew, Bug and San, that is, along the lines proposed by Stalin. Thus 76,500 square miles of the Polish State, with a population of more than twelve million inhabitants, was allotted to the Soviet Union. (Except in the south, this Ribbentrop-Molotov line largely coincided with the Russo-Polish frontier proposed by Lord Curzon in 1920.)

A Confidential Protocol arranged for the population exchange of Germans and Ukrainians and White Russians. Thus the gigantic task of the German "national integration" in the East was begun. (*4*) Under this and subsequent supplementary agreements, about 437,000 Germans were repatriated into the Reich from Soviet-occupied territories. (Separate arrangements were made for Baltic Germans, Bessarabian Germans, and others.)

A Secret Supplementary Protocol reaffirmed the Boundary and Friendship Treaty and amended the August 23 Secret Protocol in order to incorporate the new changes. Also, although under the new arrangement Lithuania went to Russia, a pocket of Lithuanian territory around Suwalki was allotted to Germany. A second Secret Supplementary Protocol declared that both parties agreed to suppress any kind of Polish agitation in their territories. Undoubtedly, this was a Russian demand.

A Common Declaration of the two governments said that "after [having] definitely settled the problems arising from the collapse of the Polish state and [having] thereby created a sure foundation for a lasting peace in Eastern Europe," both governments were sincerely expecting the cessation of the European war; "should, however, the efforts of the two Governments remain fruitless, this would demonstrate the fact that England and France are responsible for the continuation of the war, whereupon, in case of the continuation of the war, the Governments of Germany and of the USSR shall engage in mutual consultations with each other." (5)

Two other agreements were reached between Ribbentrop and Molotov: one preparing a vast coordinating of mutual trade and production, the other providing for Russian permission giving the Germans easily accessible transit facilities on the vital railroad line running from Lwów to Rumania and for German transit traffic to Iran, Afghanistan and the Far East. The Germans were also to profit from Soviet production in the newly acquired Drohobycz oil fields in southeastern Poland.

[*The end of Poland.*] The surrender of Warsaw took place while Ribbentrop was in Moscow. On September 22, a last heroic message from the Mayor of Warsaw was heard in London — whose Lord Mayor answered by a solemn declaration — then, to the strains of Chopin, Radio Warsaw faded out. Polish troops holding out on the Hela peninsula did not surrender until October 2. The Polish campaign was at an end; German losses had been significantly small. The unfortunate Polish statesmen made their way to France, (6) where the Polish government-in-exile was set up. There on September 30, President Moscicki resigned and Raczkiewicz was elected in his stead, with the democratic patriot, General Sikorski, becoming Premier. Nobody knew how long the road to Poland's liberation would be. The Soviets expelled the Polish Ambassador, violating the most elementary diplomatic conventions; they hesitated not at all to abduct the Polish diplomat Matusinski from his train.

On October 6, Hitler spoke and offered peace to France and England. (7) He did not chastise any nation in particular, but instead heaped a torrent of abuse upon the Jews which was unusual even with him. Molotov expressed his agreement with the speech, and on October 8, *Izvestia* supported Hitler in an article which was an almost verbatim copy of a speech which Molotov was to deliver on October 31. While the Soviets rapidly bolshevized eastern Poland, the NKVD took over and the first preparations for large-scale deportations were begun. The Germans began their systematic eradication of the Poles in western Poland with such incredible brutality that it evoked a stern protest from Pope Pius XII. On October 19, Hitler ordered the incorporation of the formerly western Polish territories into Germany and set up the Polish "General-Gouvernement" with its seat in Cracow. The Russians held "elections" in eastern Poland on October 23; on November 1 the lands east of the Four-River-Line were incorporated in the Soviet Union by "joining" the Ukrainian and the Byelorussian Soviet Republics.

[*Germany and Russia in October.*] Aside from Poland, four other issues were testing Russo-German cooperation during October. These were: Suwalki, naval questions, Ribbentrop's statements, and Soviet policy in the Baltic States.

In 1920, the lands around the village of Suwalki had been claimed by Lithuanians and Poles alike; finally, they were left to Poland. The Four-River-Line and Secret Supplementary Protocol allotted the Suwalki pocket to Germany in order to avoid an undue bulge in the German-Russian frontier. The German incorporation of the Suwalki-Augustów region, however, did not eliminate all problems resulting from an impractically drawn border line, and therefore it was agreed on September 28 that when the Soviets occupied Lithuania, a small southwestern strip of Lithuanian territory around the towns of Kalvarija and Seštokai would be added to the German lands. Immediately after Ribbentrop's departure, the Lithuanian Foreign Minister — the last of the unfortunate Baltic visitors — was asked to Moscow. On October 3, Molotov suggested to Schulenburg that he, Molotov, would inform the Lithuanian Foreign Minister of the Soviet decision to award Wilnó to Lithuania, while suggesting that the Kalvarija strip be ceded to Germany. Schulenburg deemed this unacceptable, for "in the eyes of the world it would make [Germany] appear as 'robbers' of Lithuanian territory, while the Soviet Government figures as the donor." Ribbentrop agreed with his Ambassador and suggested that Molotov keep silent about the Kalvarija issue; if and when the Soviets occupied Lithuania, they would leave that strip unoccupied, whereafter the Germans could take it over at a suitable time. Molotov, however, said that, unfortunately, he had already informed the Lithuanian statesmen of the German demand; an hour later he called Schulenburg and stated that Stalin personally requested Germany not to insist on the Kalvarija cession for the time being. The same day, Ribbentrop informed the Lithuanian Government in a confidential message that the German Government was not now requesting the Kalvarija strip; on October 8, Molotov informed the German Government that the territory "shall not be occupied in case forces of the Red Army should be stationed (in Lithuania)." Nevertheless, when in June–July 1940 the Soviets incorporated Lithuania, they occupied the Kalvarija strip, which then became the subject of protracted Russo-German negotiations. It finally remained within the Soviet Union, when for these few insignificant square miles, the Soviets were willing to pay seven and a half million gold dollars to Germany (*8*) — more than the purchase price of Alaska! — another indication of the Russian land-mindedness which bordered on obsession.

Naval cooperation between Germany and Russia was growing. To prevent any chance of Franco-British naval assistance reaching Rumania, Berlin and Moscow simultaneously put pressure upon Turkey and the Straits. The *Bremen* successfully fled from New York to Murmansk; on October 10, Russia offered a base near that port for the use of the German Navy. One auxiliary cruiser was stationed in Murmansk for outfitting, and an offer was made to the Germans to build or buy submarines in Russian shipyards. For political reasons, however, Hitler left this offer open. (*9*)

Ribbentrop, gloating over his Russian success, now prepared an address to refute Western rumors of eventual Russo-German misunderstandings. He wished to quote from the conversation he had had with Stalin on August 23rd, and, observing diplomatic procedure, sent the draft of the speech for Stalin's approval. On October 19 Stalin edited the proposed draft:

Ribbentrop draft	*Text edited by Stalin*
. . . Germany was taking a proud attitude by rejecting at the outset any armed assistance from the Soviets. The Soviet Union, however,	The attitude of Germany in declining military aid commands respect. However, a strong Germany is the absolute prerequisite

Ribbentrop draft — (*continued*)

was interested in having a strong Germany as a neighbor and in the case of an armed showdown between Germany and the Western democracies the interests of the Soviet Union and of Germany would certainly run parallel to each other. The Soviet Union would never stand for Germany's getting into a difficult position.

Text edited by Stalin — (*continued*)

for peace in Europe, whence follows that the Soviet Union is interested in the existence of a strong Germany. Therefore the Soviet Union cannot give its approval to the Western Powers creating conditions which would weaken Germany and place her in a difficult position. Therein lies the community of interests between Germany and the Soviet Union.

Germany was largely indifferent to Soviet methods in the Baltic states, so long as the German Balts were protected as Hitler wished. (*10*) Early in October, German-Latvian and German-Estonian agreements were signed, which provided for the evacuation and compensation of the German-speaking population. There was something diabolical and tragic in the speed with which the evacuation was completed. The German Balts, whose ancestors had settled in the towns and villages of these countries eight hundred years before, in cities whose buildings and monuments bore witness to their long tradition, were forced to leave within two or three weeks. Most Estonians and Latvians were not especially sorry to witness the departure of their erstwhile ruling class; still there was a strange air of sullen sadness hovering over the winding streets leading to the Baltic harbors and the tumultuous quays, at whose side white German ships were being loaded to capacity with uprooted human beings. The atmosphere was more than that of the end of an era; it was like the end of a world.

.   .   .   .   .   .

[*Estonia's turn.*]   For a few weeks after August 23 little happened in the Baltic states; as late as on September 10, the Estonian Foreign Ministry did not believe that a German-Russian partition agreement existed. The Russian Ministers were queried about what the German-Russian Treaty meant, but the envoys remained pleasantly noncommittal, repeatedly spoke of the unalterable Russian will to maintain peace, and continued to invite the small neighbors to go on with trade negotiations. Thus, on September 15, an Estonian delegation arrived in Moscow; but to the surprise of Selter, the Estonian Foreign Minister, instead of a commercial agreement, he was presented with a Russian demand for naval bases in Estonia and the draft of a Mutual Assistance Pact on September 23. Selter tried to gain time; he flew back to Tallinn, consulted the Germans, who refrained from giving him advice other than that he comply with the Russian demands. Meanwhile the Soviet press began to attack the foreign policy of Estonia, and notice came from Riga that Selter's Latvian colleague, Munters, had also received an "invitation" to Moscow. A Polish submarine, setting out from Gdynia on the 11th, roamed the Baltic for a few days and then, its fuel and supplies exhausted, the *Orzel* reached Tallinn. The Estonians dealt with the submarine according to the neutrals' duties as prescribed by international law; however, after the Polish crew had learned of the Soviet invasion of Poland, they broke away from the harbor police and set out to sea. Immediately the Soviet press accused the Estonian government of a "military conspiracy" and even claimed that the *Orzel* had sunk a Soviet vessel in the Baltic. (The Polish submarine eventually ploughed her way to a British port.) The Estonian government hoped to satisfy the Soviets by punishing the responsible harbor officials, but this did not help. Selter had to fly back to Moscow again, while on September 25 and 26, Soviet aircraft began to undertake extensive flights over Estonian territory. On September 28, Selter signed. Tired, sad, exhausted, he accidentally met Ribbentrop on one of the Kremlin staircases in the dawn hours.

[*Latvia; Lithuania.*] The Soviet-Estonian Treaty provided for "Mutual Assistance," Soviet armament supplies to Estonia, and the granting of Soviet air and naval bases on the islands of Dagö, Ösel, and in the port of Paldiski. (*11*) Article v established that the pact did "not affect to any extent the sovereign rights of the contracting parties, in particular their economic systems and State organization. The sites allotted for bases and aerodromes shall remain the territory of the Estonian republic." The Estonian Pact was to serve as a model for the other Baltic treaties. On October 5, the Latvian Foreign Minister, Munters, had to sign (to him Stalin was frank enough to reveal that a sphere of interest agreement existed with Germany); on October 10 the Lithuanian Urbsys had his turn. (The Lithuanian negotiators tried to appeal to the Georgian in Stalin; didn't he come from a small, non-Russian nation? But in vain: he was not a Georgian anymore, Stalin said, but a Russian.) In return, Lithuania received

Wilnó, which was evacuated by the Soviet Army and turned over to Lithuanian occupation on October 27. By October 30, the Russians had completed their occupation of the Estonian and Latvian bases. *(12)*

It was evident that the independence of these countries was at an end; but, peculiarly enough — perhaps due to a Russian "guilt complex" — the terms of the treaties were scrupulously observed; there was no intervention in the internal affairs of these small republics; the Russian garrisons remained aloof and reserved in their contacts with the population. The only visible change was the voluntary elimination of any news material in the Baltic press dealing adversely with Russia and a gradual relaxation of cultural, economic, and political ties with France, Britain and the United States.

[*Finnish forebodings.*] The geographical situation of Finland being different than that of the other Baltic states, that country decided to resist the Russian demands, demands which she fully expected to come in due course. During the summer, the Soviet press attacked Helsinki for the remilitarization of the Aaland Islands; in August, Molotov protested to Idman, the Finnish envoy to Moscow, against the "hostile attitude" of the Finnish press. Soviet pressure increased in September, and on September 24 a curt Soviet note struck a blow against Finnish trade: it withdrew the rights of Finnish vessels to use the Neva River between the Baltic and Lake Ladoga. Yet, conscious of her favorable geographical situation, and with a strong faith in her moral resources despite her evident helplessness — Germany had advised her to comply with the Russian demands — Finland resisted.

Efforts toward a Balkan consolidation and the uncertain position of Italy

[*Italian chances.*] Throughout central-eastern Europe the news of Italy's non-belligerence was greeted with unmitigated joy. The prestige of Italy was increasing: qualities of moderation and sagacity were attributed to Mussolini and to Ciano; friendly notices and sincere proposals were communicated to Rome; it was thought by many that the Cavourian traditions of Italian diplomacy were being resuscitated. Some even recalled 1934 and looked upon Italy as a potential opponent of Germany.

These expectations could last for about seven months, from September 1939 to March 1940. In March 1940, Mussolini began to consider the timing of his entrance into the war. Insight, logic, cultural heritage, not to mention common sense, would have demanded that Italy remain neutral. Had Mussolini stayed out of the war, the fortunes of Italy, of central-eastern Europe, and perhaps of the whole continent might well have been far less tragic. Even if one considers the worst, namely, that continued Italian neutrality might have resulted in a close German-Russian alliance or a separate peace after an inconclusive campaign, the present division of Europe might still have occurred; nevertheless, Italian neutrality would have kept the ideological slate clear, and the spiritual forces of Western civilization would not have been so utterly rent . . .

Throughout the Balkans in September–October 1939, neighbors drew closer to each other and ancient antagonisms faded. In the background of the whole pleasant picture was Italian neutrality and Italian opposition to Russia. The preservation of the *status quo* in the Balkans also met with favor in London, and the cordial exchange of letters between Ciano and Lord Halifax in mid-September indicated the present harmony of British and Italian interests. (*1*)

[*Italy and the Polish defeat.*] As Poland disappeared, Mussolini felt uncomfortable; he would have preferred the existence of a Polish rump-state. The King, the aristocracy, as well as the common people of Italy, first of all, the Pope, were horrified at the brutal liquidation policies of Hitler. And, aside from the moral implications of the Polish "settlement," Mussolini was extremely conscious that two giant states, Germany and Russia, now had great land masses weighing down upon the Balkans in a tremendous northern arch. Speaking to Ciano, Mussolini on September 15 envisaged a neutral Danubian-Balkan *bloc*, led by Italy; Cardinal Maglione, the Vatican Secretary of State, also heard such a suggestion from the Rumanian Ambassador to the Vatican. Just before Ribbentrop left for Moscow on September 26, Attolico asked to see him, but the German — probably suspecting what the Italians wanted to ask — excused himself. After he returned, he telephoned Ciano to come; Ciano was in Berlin on October 1. He mentioned the Italian desire to see a residual Polish state, but Hitler spoke only of the planned "General-Gouvernement," at best a Polish state under complete German tutelage, comprising about ten million Poles, leaving three or four million more in the lands occupied by the Soviet Union, and Hitler assured Ciano that he felt "completely disinterested what happens behind the Bug." (2) (Ciano noted in his report to Mussolini that times had certainly changed: in August, Ribbentrop had spoken to him of twenty million Poles, by October the number had shrunk to fourteen . . .) Hitler was convinced that Germany would quickly win the war and gently hinted that Italy had better enter the conflict soon; Ciano reminded him of Italian loyalty to the Axis cause, and asserted that Italy had really never made a neutrality declaration. Ribbentrop eulogized the Russians: the Comintern and Politburo people resembled the old party-members or the early Fascists, he said. Ciano was not particularly impressed.

[*Italy and Rumania.*]   During these talks mention also was made of Rumania — the second from among the states guaranteed by the Western Powers which now also sought Italian help. On September 16, François-Poncet told Ciano that he expected a German attack on Rumania and that Weygand's Army assembling in Syria would be ready to execute a Balkan counteroffensive. To this French communication — obviously meant to sound out Italy on Rumania — Ciano replied that he did not expect a German invasion of that country, a cautious remark which proved to be temporarily accurate.

Rumania also drew close to Turkey; strategic questions surrounding the eventual passage of the Weygand Army through the Balkans closely linked these two states. Gafencu, who in his extensive summer tours had tried to establish a Balkan neutrality system, now asked the Turkish Foreign Minister, Sarajoglu, who was departing for Moscow, to sound out the Soviet stand on the Balkans. When Gafencu met Tsintsar-Markovič at the frontier station of Jebel on September 19 (already his third meeting with Yugoslavs since May), it transpired that Yugoslavia would hardly assist Rumania if the Russians moved on Bessarabia. Yet it was decided that formation of a Balkan bloc should be speeded up by inviting the Bulgars and offering Sofia concrete proposals after Sarajoglu had reported what he heard in Moscow.

[*The Turkish Foreign Minister in Moscow.*]   But Gafencu did not know then that he scarcely could have chosen a worse medium than Sarajoglu for such inquiries, for the Turkish Foreign Minister, instead of being cordially received in Moscow, was treated coldly and even somewhat threateningly. (*3*) As early as September 2, Molotov told Schulenburg that Russian and German interests ran parallel in Turkey; the Kremlin had decided to force the "permanent neutralization" of that state. (*4*) With Sarajoglu in Moscow the question of a Mutual Assistance Pact between Russia and Turkey was raised, but Stalin insisted that a restrictive clause should be inserted stating that a German attack on Turkey would not call for invocation of that Pact. This, of course, would have deprived the treaty of its main value for the Turks, who in return insisted on a similar restrictive clause with regard to France and Britain. Sarajoglu stayed in Moscow for more than three long weeks. No pact was concluded; instead, both Germany and Russia tried to influence Turkey against Britain and France. (These machinations were unsuccessful: after a bitter Sarajoglu returned from Moscow, he signed a fifteen-year treaty of Mutual Assistance with France and Britain on October 19.) It was now clear that the Soviet Union was not interested in a Balkan consolidation. She had her own designs. Hence, Sarajoglu's inquiries were in vain; he received vague hints from Molotov about the primary Soviet aim being to re-establish the 1914 frontiers of Russia — and within these lay Bessarabia.

On the day of Sarajoglu's arrival in Moscow, the Calinescu murder took place in Bucharest; three governments (led by Argeseanu, Argetoianu, and Tatarescu) were inaugurated in rapid succession by Carol, who knew of Hitler's desire to make him pay for the blood of Codreanu. On October 1, while Sarajoglu sat in the Kremlin anterooms and Gafencu anxiously marked time, Hitler told Ciano that if Rumania abandoned her neutrality — and it was known how liberally Hitler could interpret such an "abandonment" — Germany would encourage Soviet or Hungarian or Bulgarian aggression against her.

[*Russia lures Rumania's neighbors.*] This Ciano did not like, for it was Italy's main concern that Russia should not gain more territory and that the Balkan *status quo* should remain unchanged. Only later, when the fat prize of Yugoslav lands beclouded Fascist visions, did this policy undergo a change. Ciano did not inform Bucharest of what Hitler had said, but instead began to intimate that Italy would support Rumania against an eventual Russian aggression. Rumania's position was further alleviated when on October 7, Budapest and Bucharest agreed to reduce the number of troops along the

Hungarian-Rumanian frontier — a beneficial agreement brought about by Yugoslav and Italian mediation. The Soviet Union, which barely a few days before had re-established diplomatic relations with Hungary, now began to hint at Russian support of Hungary if the latter evoked her never-abandoned claims concerning the Hungarian-inhabited lands of Transylvania. "The Russians see in the Hungarians comrades in peace and war," said Kalinin to the Hungarian Minister on October 19. The Hungarian government, although it could only have gained by such support and action, refused to discuss the matter.

Similarly pacific was the Bulgarian attitude. The new anti-Turkish foreign policy of Russia necessitated that Moscow, in the age-old tradition, base her Balkan plans upon Sofia. Early in October, Molotov suggested a Soviet-Bulgarian Mutual Assistance Pact, which King Boris declined, but he in turn was willing to discuss a Non-Aggression Pact with the Soviet Union. This was not enough for Stalin and Molotov; they aimed for more, wishing to encircle Rumania, and offered full Soviet assistance if Bulgaria helped herself to the Dobrudja; they envisaged a common Soviet-Bulgarian frontier which would advance the Muscovite-Slav bloc almost to the gates of Constantinople, where it had stood in 1878. But Bulgaria was loyal. Sofia informed Bucharest about the Soviet offers. From that moment on there could be no doubt about the Russian designs on Rumania and the Balkans.

[*All bound to Italian neutrality.*] That Rumania's neighbors, in spite of their justifiable territorial claims, showed this loyal solidarity which rarely existed among these small nations by refusing to plot against her with the Soviets, was naturally reassuring. But it was also evident that Rumania alone could not withstand a Russian attack. The Rumanian government consequently decided to ask London whether the British guarantee was to cover aggression by Russia as well as by Germany. The text did not explicitly deal with such an eventuality; and nobody in London and Paris wished to declare war on Russia for the sake of Bessarabia. Thus, sometime in mid-November, Bucharest received notice that the British government was "not in a position to give public clarification" on the question of whether the guarantee specified the eventuality of Soviet aggression or not. (5) On December 14, however, Sir Reginald Hoare, the British Minister to Rumania, explained that the guarantee would stand *if*, in the case of a Russian attack, Turkey aided Rumania and Italy remained neutral.

These reservations were to be expected if only for strategic reasons: without Turkish collaboration and Italian neutrality no Western aid could get to Rumania. In December, the Soviet Ambassador asked Sarajoglu what Turkey would do if Russia undertook "military measures" in Rumania; the latter answered that she would stand by her obligations under the British-French guarantee. (*6*) But it was also evident that all this depended in turn on Italy's non-belligerence; so long as Italy was not a military partner of Germany, there was hope for security and peace in the Balkans. This satisfactory situation prevailed throughout the winter, until in March–April 1940 Mussolini's jealousy and folly started him on a road wherefrom there was no return. While the partition of northern central-eastern Europe was consummated by Germany and Russia in a rapid two months between August and October 1939, the partition of the Balkans began a somewhat slower development with Italy's entry into the European war in June 1940 and was consummated finally in May 1941.

[*Italy and Greece.*]   In the winter there still was peace in the Balkans. Although in August Italian troop concentrations had taken place on the Albanian-Greek frontier and Greece had ordered partial mobilization, Mussolini decided early in September not to provoke Greece; the Italian Minister conveyed assurances of Italian friendship, and on September 30 it was agreed that the troops on both sides of the Albanian-Greek border would withdraw to a distance of twenty kilometres. (*7*) Now friendly messages were being exchanged between Rome and Athens; and this betterment in Italian-Greek relations coincided with the first signs of Italian displeasure with the Soviets' successes and intentions.

[*Italy turns against Russia; Germany displeased.*] *Izvestia* attacked the Turco-Western Pact two days after its conclusion; about the same time an article by a Bulgarian Communist, Stefanov, in the periodical *Communist International* advocated a Russo-Rumanian Mutual Assistance Pact similar to that which Moscow had concluded with the Baltic states. In November Lavrentiev, the new Soviet envoy to Bulgaria, when presenting his credentials, spoke lengthily of the "historic affinities" linking Russia and the southern Slav sister nation. (The High Command of the German Navy at the same time considered the Black Sea as waters exclusively Russian (8).) Italy had already brought about a certain Hungarian-Rumanian rapprochement; now Rome decided in a gradually broadening manner to manifest her assistance to the Balkan states, in the first place, Rumania, against Soviet pressure and eventual aggression. Ciano and many other members of the Fascist hierarchy felt that Italy would profit from the image of Italy's constituting the only determined bulwark of anti-Communism. On November 30, Russia attacked Finland in the north. It was suggested that Stalin had intended to invade Bessarabia on December 6, but the unexpected resistance of the Finns forced him to postpone this plan. Although early in December the German Minister suddenly began to insist at Bucharest that Rumania "improve" her relations with Russia, on December 9 a TASS communiqué denied that the Stefanov article represented the views of the Soviet government.

More important was that (and mostly because of Ribbentrop's haughtiness and Russophilia) Italo-German relations were significantly cooling off. Ciano protested against interpretations current in Berlin which were emanating from Ribbentrop's circle: according to these views, Britain entered the war only because she knew that Italy would remain outside of it. German economic and trade tactics in the Balkans continued to hurt Italian interests there. (9) The outbreak of the Finnish War further accentuated German-Italian misunderstandings. At once the Italian press and radio embarked on a violent anti-Soviet campaign, despite German advice and requests to the contrary; Italian volunteers and war materials were sent to Finland; Balbo's newspaper, the *Corriere Padano*, daily attacked the Soviet Union with unusual force, and the Turin *Stampa* gave vent to rumors of Soviet Balkan designs; the Soviet Ambassador, Gorelkin, left Rome, and his Italian counterpart, Rosso, was temporarily recalled from Moscow. On December 6 the German Labor Front leader, Ley, called on Mussolini and Ciano in Rome. The arguments he used in support of the Russophile policy of Ribbentrop were transparent: it was Finland who had provoked the war with the Soviets; the Nordic nations were always anti-Axis; wasn't it the Swedish Sandler who first proposed the sanctions against Italy in 1935? He, Ley, did not think that the Russians contemplated an invasion of Bessarabia. The fatuous arguments of Ley only confirmed the Italian leaders in their belief that the time had come for the formulation of Italy's Balkan policy. On December 8, the Fascist Grand Council agreed that Italy had primary interests in maintaining peace in the Danubian area. The report which Ciano made to the Council was secret; however, whether because of the unexpected Finnish campaign, or because of the growing manifestations of Italian support of Rumania, or because of both, the Soviet chargé d'affaires in Bucharest informed the Rumanian government that Russia had no aggressive intentions toward Bessarabia. On December 16 Ciano delivered a speech in the Fascist Chambers. After having overcome, not without difficulty, the objections of Mussolini, Ciano made a speech which constituted a broad attack against Russia, to the great relish of all central-eastern Europe, the British, and the French (and of Ciano himself who — somewhat overenthusiastically — considered it as an almost heroic dig against Ribbentrop). (*10*) A week later, a Rumanian special emissary, the former Foreign Minister Victor Antonescu, (*11*) arrived in Rome to find out what Italy could do to help Rumania in case of a Soviet attack. Ciano could not clearly commit himself because of geographic and strategic difficulties, but promised to take the matter under serious consideration. On January 6–7, 1940, Ciano asked Csáky to come to Venice, and in their talks the Soviet problem again figured pre-eminently. Ciano asked what Hungary would do if she were invaded by Russia; for, lacking direct connections between Hungary and Italy, it was hard to see how the Italians could help. Csáky answered that he feared no such attack; moreover, the experiences of the Finnish war showed that Hungary would not require outside help in order to halt the Russians in the Carpathians. He also promised, to the great satisfaction of Ciano, that in case of a Soviet attack on Rumania, Hungary would remain benevolently neutral. She would not march into Transylvania unless a Soviet-Rumanian war should result in anarchy or Bolshevist revolution, or unless Bucharest should cede territories to the Soviets and to Bulgaria without fighting. Ciano, satisfied, returned to Rome and assured the Rumanian Minister on January 10 that if the need arose, Italy would furnish Rumania with all possible assistance against the Soviet Union. (*12*)

[*Mussolini writes to Hitler.*] But now Mussolini decided to intervene more actively in the conduct of Italian foreign affairs. On January 3 he wrote to Hitler:

> I think it is my duty to add here that a further advance in your relations with Moscow would have catastrophic repercussions in Italy.

...The solution of your *Lebensraum* is in Russia and not elsewhere.

and complained of seeing no end to the European war. On the other hand, his letter was weak, without nerve and vigor; he meekly made excuses for Ciano's December 16 speech; he gave profuse and friendly assurances of his loyalty to the Axis.

Attolico discussed Mussolini's letter with Ribbentrop on January 10 and again spoke of a "Congress-Poland," (*13*) arguing that the establishment of such a state would eventually deprive the Western Allies of a basis for their avowed war aims. Ribbentrop asked Attolico whether, if Germany created such a Poland and the Western Powers would still not negotiate a peace, Italy would then announce that she would join Germany militarily? This was not what Mussolini meant, retorted Attolico. But Mussolini soon abandoned his Ambassador, duly heeding German complaints against that sick and honest man. (*14*) Mussolini was again thinking of a Yugoslavian expedition. There Ciano was ready to go along all the way; with his chief Croat agent, Bombelles, he plotted in January about insurrections in Zagreb and conferred with the Croat *Ustaši* leader, Pavelič. Gradually, Italian-German relations began once more to improve; as the warm winds of the spring flurried in, Mussolini thought of glorious spring and summer campaigns. He, like all the plebeian dictators, required opposing force and determination to remind him of his limitations, but during the winter months, when Italian stock was rising, the Western Ambassadors kept complimenting him, and other important people throughout the world rendered him distinct homage. These things filled him with pride and disdain and he believed himself bigger and stronger than he really was.... Throughout central-eastern Europe the "Italian honeymoon" was coming to an end. The word "Axis," which had scarcely appeared during the winter months and was left unmentioned in Ciano's December 16 speech, was again reiterated with increasing frequency in the Italian press and by Italian representatives throughout central-eastern Europe.

[*The Belgrade Conference.*]   On February 2, the Balkan Foreign Ministers met in Belgrade. No mutual assistance provisions were discussed, for at that time each of the participating states calculated on attacks from different directions: Rumania and Turkey feared Russia most, Yugoslavia and Greece feared Italy — and all of them had to provide against an attack by Germany. It was decided to invite Bulgaria to join the consolidated group of Balkan states, and suggestions were made concerning political or even territorial concessions to Sofia. On his way back to Ankara, the Turkish Foreign Minister stopped there and tried to influence the Bulgarian régime. During the Belgrade Conference, *Izvestia* attacked the participants and hinted at Soviet support of Hungarian and Bulgarian revisionism. Noting the displeasure of Russia as well as that of Germany, and observing the developing pro-German trend of Italy's foreign policy, King Boris did not wish to sacrifice his liberty of action by joining a group of states caught in such a diplomatic crossfire; on February 15 the pro-Western Kiosseivanov resigned and Filov became the new Bulgarian Premier. In spite of official affirmations that the change in the Prime Ministry did not mean a subsequent change in policies, both Russia and Germany registered the event as a defeat for the Western cause and a subsequent victory of their own.

Germany was not happy to see a strong and united Turkish-Balkan bloc, an obstacle to her eventual plans in the Near East. In Belgrade, the Balkan Ministers were unduly cautious about an alignment with Turkey. As the Turkish diplomat Acikalin was later to write:

> The then Turkish Foreign Minister tried again to persuade responsible statesmen of the Balkan States of the "necessity of a common decision and attitude" in the face of the common danger. But again, in spite of the crude reality, no decision was reached. This curious attitude of some of the Balkan statesmen was a matter of concern, but it was difficult to diagnose it. We again attributed their vacillation, while considering it a very dangerous game to play, to an excess of caution. Much later we learned that some statesmen and, by a curious coincidence, those belonging to countries which were the first objective of German aggression, considered the Turkish endeavours as provocative manoeuvres undertaken with the object of driving the Balkan States into the Anglo-French orbit. In their suspicion they went so far as to think seriously of creating a new Balkan Entente, including Bulgaria, against Turkish menace.
>
> I may as well confess that we had really hoped to create a link between the Balkan Pact countries and our efforts with the French and the British to resist aggression. How great is the sin of those who prevented this possibility, history alone can judge. (15)

Acikalin's reminiscences may be somewhat exaggerated, but there is no doubt that a chance had been missed. Still, it was Italy which now counted most.

[*Ribbentrop brings Hitler's answer; Mussolini's decision.*] On March 10, Ribbentrop arrived in Rome. He brought a message from Hitler, a somewhat late answer to Mussolini's January 3 letter. Ribbentrop came to prepare a meeting between the two Axis dictators on the Brenner. On that day, the peace negotiations of the Finnish-Russian War were about to be concluded. The sudden end of that war and the coinciding European tour of Sumner Welles gave vent to peace rumors and raised hopes throughout central-eastern Europe. It was not known that Mussolini was to cast Welles' arguments lightly aside; neither was it known that Ribbentrop's main mission was to convince Mussolini of the righteousness of Hitler's Russian policy. On the first day — March 10 — the ideological sallies of Ribbentrop did not yet produce full results: when the German said that he thought Stalin had renounced the aim of world revolution, Mussolini was somewhat sceptical. Next day, however, his mood changed, and he began to listen more and more attentively to an exposition of Hitler's war plans and Britain's "impossible" situation. When Ribbentrop reverted to the topic of Russia again, arguing forcefully that there was no Russian danger in the Balkans, Mussolini nodded in agreement. He now began to talk and reminisced how satisfactorily Soviet-Italian relations had developed in the past. He decided now to re-establish normal relations with Russia.

Ciano still hoped in Mussolini's habitual hesitations. But a week later they were on their way to meet Hitler on the Brenner; three months later Italy was at war.

The Finnish War and central-eastern Europe

The Winter War of 1939–40 stands as an independent episode in the long-drawn military history of the Second World War. But this does not mean that it was an illogical excursion of Russian foreign policy; it organically fitted into great designs and discernible developments.

[*Why Finland fought.*] That Finland resisted Russia was first of all due to geographical factors, then to political calculations. In spite of Finland's awful inferiority, three million Finns against the mass of one hundred and eighty million Russians, the Finnish statesmen thought they had a meager chance: perhaps the forest terrain and similar strategic conditions would provide for an effective resistance. There was also the political gamble: if Finland resisted successfully for awhile, the pressure of external opinion might force the Russians to modify their demands, notwithstanding their military superiority in the long run. These calculations were courageous and wisely taken. While they did not spare Finland from mutilations and sufferings in two wars, they nevertheless saved her from being absorbed into the Russian orbit in 1940 — and again in 1945, when Finland's previous record and the subsequent attention of the world made Stalin, all-powerful and victorious after the Second World War, refrain from any drastic absorption measure. The Finnish decision of October–November 1939 to fight rather than to submit deserved the heartfelt gratitude of their Scandinavian neighbors in 1939–40. It continues to deserve it today.

[*The Soviet demands presented.*]　　The first phase of the Soviet diplomatic offensive against Finland began in September; the Soviets offered treaties of mutual assistance to Helsinki exactly like those accepted by the smaller Baltic states. From Finland, Russia demanded naval bases in the Finnish Gulf and the Fisher Peninsula around Petsamo, in order to close the last westward windows of the Baltic and northeastern Europe.

[*Finland and Germany.*]　　Distance prevented Britain from helping Finland, while Germany, Finland's former anti-Bolshevik ally, refused to help. In the summer, Finnish statesmen and the Finnish press showed pro-British sympathies; also, Helsinki refrained from signing a Non-Aggression Pact with Germany. Hitler and Ribbentrop felt justified in taking the Russian side in the dispute; they instructed German officialdom to adhere to a new line: full support of the Russian diplomatic offensive.

On October 2, the Finns were still being told in Berlin that they had no reasons to be worried, but by October 9, a sinister tone of warning was beginning to creep into the conversations there; Weizsäcker curtly told the Finnish envoy that he personally hoped and wished "that Finland might settle matters with Russia in a peaceful manner." (At the same time Churchill was convinced — and made his conviction known in a somewhat undiplomatic speech on October 1 — that the Russian advance in the Baltic was "clearly necessary for the safety of Russia against the Nazi menace . . . an Eastern front has been created which Nazi Germany does not dare assail.")

On October 11 direct Soviet-Finnish negotiations opened in Moscow: they lasted until November 13. The Soviet demands were such that the Finnish delegates could not and would not accept them. The Germans warned the Finns not to resist; they nevertheless resisted. On October 18, the Scandinavian monarchs and the President of Finland met in an emergency conference in Stockholm.

At that time the first facts about the Russo-Finnish negotiations transpired: a Mutual Assistance Pact had been brought up again, one which demanded "assurances" that relations between Finland and the Soviet Union should be as close as possible. This was but a resuscitation of the diplomatic trap of "internal aggression" which had obstructed the agreement between Russia and the Western Powers during the summer. In addition to islands in the Finnish Gulf, the Soviets demanded territories in the Karelian Straits and the "lease" of a base on the small peninsula of Hangö.

These were impossible demands. While the Scandinavian Kings and statesmen pondered upon them, a special Swedish emissary returned from Berlin and reported what Hitler told him about the Finnish issue: Hitler did not believe in the imminence of a war between Russia and Finland, for, according to him, the Russian demands were definitely more limited than those presented to the other Baltic states. If, however, a conflict should break out, Germany would be strictly neutral. At the same time, Hitler warned Sweden not to interfere in such a conflict and to leave Finland strictly alone. After this menacing allusion, the Scandinavian states spared no efforts to intervene with Molotov, but it was obvious that these efforts were to fail. There was, however, another attempt at mediation: that of the United States.

[*The United States.*]   On October 11, 1939, President Roosevelt sent a mild and conciliatory message to the Soviet President, Kalinin, offering the good services of the United States (a week later he cabled the same offer to King Gustav v of Sweden). This was neither the first nor the last of Roosevelt's proposals to mediate in a critical European dispute: from 1938 to 1944 he often endeavored to intervene, with much goodwill and, as such mediations go, with little success. The American mediation proposal of October 1939 is nevertheless significant from a historical viewpoint. At that time Russia, the United States, and Italy were the three non-warring Great Powers. Franklin Roosevelt spared no efforts to establish a community of interests among the three and thus avoid spreading of the war and, indirectly, hamper the movements and chances of Hitler. Since 1938, and especially since Munich, there was a growing community of interests between Russia and America in the Far East; moreover, an influential segment of American public opinion, disgusted with British "duplicity" before and after Munich, developed a "liberal," and Russophile tendency of its own. Despite the German-Soviet Pact, the community of interests remained and the American mediation attempt in October was that of a friendly Power trying to help two friends in their dispute. Although outbreak of the Winter War was to destroy a good deal of American friendship toward Russia, Roosevelt's proposal to mediate between Soviets and Finns in October 1939 was an important milestone on the long and broad avenue of American-Russian relations, the development of which was so characteristically unique and significant during the Second World War.

[*The Russian threats.*] The mediation failed. Later in October the movements of Finnish vessels were arbitrarily restricted by Russian naval authorities; frontier sectors were sealed, and a steady flow of Russian troops trickled westward on new strategic roads and trunk rail lines leading toward Finland. Meanwhile in Moscow the negotiations dragged along; for awhile the Russians seemed willing to abandon their demand for a Mutual Assistance Pact, yet they insisted on forcing indirectly some kind of an "internal guarantee." Most important were their unceasing claims to Hangö; it was primarily on this subject that the negotiations failed. (1)

On October 31 Molotov broadcast an uncouth speech in which he violated all accepted diplomatic standards by giving an almost complete account of the proceeding negotiations and the difficulties involved. All this, naturally, from the Soviet viewpoint. Thereby, Molotov made the position of the negotiators practically impossible.

Other classic elements of Molotov's speech were contained in these often-quoted sentences:

> One swift blow to Poland, first by the German Army, then by the Red Army and nothing was left of this ugly offspring of the Versailles Treaty which existed by oppressing non-Polish nationalities . . .

> One may accept or reject the ideology of Hitlerism; that is a matter of political views. But everybody could understand that ideologies can-

not be destroyed by force . . . [it is] not only senseless but criminal to wage such a war camouflaged as a fight for "democracy" . . .

He also denounced the intervention of the United States. On November 9, the negotiations were broken off; four days later the Finnish delegation left Moscow.

When in 1945 the ex-President, Ryti, Tanner, and other Finnish politicians were tried before a Helsinki court, Ryti claimed to have known that the Germans were aware of the demands of the Russians and supported them. According to him, the August 23 Secret Protocol, allotting Finland generally to the Soviet sphere, provided in detail for the October–November demands: Viipuri, Petsamo, and so on. If the Russians were to advance beyond these points, the Germans would have had the right to adjust the Baltic balance of power by helping themselves to the Aalands, or, eventually, to Western Finnish ports. (2) *Nazi-Soviet Relations* does not clear up this point; perhaps Ryti knew more. (3) At any rate, the Soviet communiqué broadcast in July 1941 which stated that "it was Germany that the Soviet Union fought in Finland in 1940" was a hopeless falsehood.

[*The war breaks out.*] On November 26, the Soviets provoked a "frontier incident" around Mainila; on November 28, Moscow denounced her 1932 Non-Aggression Pact with Finland; on November 30 Russia attacked Finland without having declared war on her. (4)

Stalin, who during the previous negotiations had addressed a quiet threat to the Finnish delegates: "Look what happened to Poland," did not adopt the same procedure which he had followed there. While the Soviet Air Force dropped bombs on Helsinki, and Russian flame-throwers broke into the Finnish frontier outposts, he pretended that the Soviet Union was not at war with Finland, but that this was a civil strife between the "reactionary" Helsinki government and "the representatives of a people's Finland." As early as November, Moscow tried to set up a Finnish Communist counter-government, which was to serve as a stooge in the war against Finland; but the Finnish Communist, Tuominen, to whom the "Premiership" was offered, refused to accept this honor. Another, Otto Kuusinen, nevertheless accepted. On November 30, the Moscow radio announced that a Finnish "popular government" sat in the frontier village of Terijoki, and on December 2, the Soviet Union and Kuusinen's "régime" signed a Mutual Assistance and Friendship Pact. With such clumsiness was the ideological pretext for the war presented.

[*The international scene.*] The Finnish people received the news of the Russian attack with expected calm. The Cajander government resigned, and Ryti formed a new Finnish régime, (5) which could count, however, on nothing but moral support from the outside. (In many instances it could not even count on that.) Although there existed some little friction between Germany and Russia at that time, (6) Berlin firmly continued with her policy of hostile neutrality toward Finland. Hitler was glad that "Holsti (7) and his Anglophile gang" got "what they deserved"; he personally saw to it that a Helsinki representative of the German news agency, DNB, who had volunteered to serve in the Finnish Army was deprived of his German citizenship. General Jodl disparaged the value of the Finnish army in a newspaper article; German naval authorities hampered the movements of Finnish ships. To the Norwegian Quisling, who visited him in mid-December, Hitler expressed his full sympathy with the Russian cause and, as General Halder recorded it, Hitler was glad to see that Stalin had begun "indicating interest in Afghanistan and India." Immediately after the outbreak of hostilities, a circular instruction was sent to all German diplomatic missions ordering them not to support the Finnish cause and to refrain from indicating the least sympathy for the Finns, even in personal conversations.

Germany put obstacles in the way of Italian shipments to Finland. The rest of central-eastern Europe was intimidated. The policy of the Baltic states was to impose a strict voluntary censorship on their newspapers. Thus the brother Estonians — whose naval bases were being used by the Russians in their attack upon Finland and whose port of Paldiski was in retaliation bombed by Finnish aircraft in December — the Lithuanians, and the Latvians had to remain silent witnesses to the Bolshevik juggernaut's advance on their neighbor. When the Finnish Legation left Moscow upon the outbreak of the war, neither the Baltic envoys nor their Rumanian and Bulgarian colleagues dared to see them off at the railroad station. Only Hungary endeavored to show sympathy for the Finnish cause; a small number of Hungarian volunteers left for Finland, travelling in a roundabout way via Britain; yet even Budapest, in spite of popular sympathy for the linguistically and racially related Finns, did not venture far: Hungary wished to avoid the wrath of her new Soviet neighbor, and, moreover, that of Germany.

On December 14, the League of Nations expelled the Soviet Union from its membership. France, Britain, and the United States proclaimed their sympathy with the Finnish cause; the State Department, for a moment, even considered breaking relations with the Soviet Union. But these states were far away; shipments were slow and had to pass the German blockade.

[*Finnish military successes.*]   To the great surprise of the world, the first reports of the Winter War were not unfavorable to Finland; in a few weeks it became known that the Russian invasion was not only halted but in some sectors, decisively beaten. How was this possible? It was suggested after 1941 that the Russians had deliberately fought badly; they had wanted, it was said, to trick the world into believing that the Russian Army was worthless. This, however, was not the case. From the very beginning, the Russians had underestimated the strength of Finnish resistance. They did not count on a war until late; the first operations were conducted under the direction of the Leningrad Army Region ("*Raion*"). A more general Russian mobilization developed only later. The Soviets also made a strategic miscalculation. Instead of breaking through the long and undefendable Finnish frontier at various points and executing pincer-like operations, they stuck to the old technique of linear advance which had proven satisfactory when they invaded crumbling Poland on September 17, 1939. But Finland was not crumbling, and instead of the wide Polish plains, there were forests and lakes along the lengthy Finnish-Russian frontier. The Russian plan was to exercise pressure all along the Finnish front and thus make the small defense force spread itself thin; their main advance was planned in the Repola-Suomossalmi sector, along the "thin waistline" of Finland, where the Russian generals hoped to cut across Finland to the Baltic around Ulea. Knowing that the main Finnish defenses were along the so-called "Mannerheim Line" on the Karelian Isthmus, they massed their artillery there and took it for granted that after a deep advance in the "waistline" sector, the rules of elementary strategy would compel the bulk of the Finnish Army to withdraw from the Karelian Isthmus, whereupon the main Russian Army, operating from Leningrad, would march against Helsinki. A not unreasonable strategy; but its main premise failed to be carried out. The Finnish frontier troops easily stopped the relatively thinly-distributed Russian attack formations along the "waistline"; by Christmas, the Russians were driven back across the frontier, out of Suomossalmi, and Finnish ski troops were harassing Russian troop movements and rail communications well within Soviet territory. Thus the Soviet master plan fell through (*8*); the Leningrad Army had to wait and prepare under duress; more effort was required.

[*Diplomatic repercussions.*] The unexpected success of Finland's resistance brought important diplomatic developments. As the conflict threatened to develop into a long war, Germany, who had previously silently encouraged the Russian "settlement," now tried hard to put an end to the Finnish campaign. She had multiple reasons for that. She had to pledge her moral support to the Russians and thus she was apt to alienate herself from Italy; she could but lose from a continued strain on Russian economic resources; she felt that a lengthy Finnish-Russian war would bring the Western Powers some way or another into Scandinavia. Thus, around mid-December, Berlin began to try for mediation. In order to evade serious Italian apprehensions, Italian shipments for Finland were unevenly, yet slowly trickling through Germany; on December 9 this resulted in the first slight rift in Soviet-German relations since August, as TASS published a report about German shipments going to Finland. Here was the German quandary; Ribbentrop now had to complain to the Soviet Ambassador about the "inappropriateness" of the Soviet allegations. The German denial quieted Russian fears and, obviously in order to win further German sympathies, Moscow announced the withdrawal of Russian recognition of the Czechoslovak government-in-exile (after she had already recognized "independent" Slovakia in September) and on Christmas Day Fierlinger, the Czechoslovak Minister, was virtually expelled from Moscow. (*9*)

On December 15, in a radio speech, Tanner offered peace to Moscow. The Ciano speech of December 16 provoked an intense Russian propaganda campaign against Italy, and Ciano went so far as to establish a special Office of Finnish Affairs. *Pravda* and *Izvestia* criticized the Italian attitude with harsh words, and the Kiev radio and Balbo's *Corriere Padano* fought a little propaganda war between themselves. But Italy, of course, could not be very effective in aiding the Finns; meanwhile Hitler took care to prevent Rome from getting too

friendly with London and Paris. (*10*) Yet the growing interest of
the Western Powers in the Finnish War increasingly worried Hitler
as well as Stalin. While the Russian Army was regrouping, Moscow
intimated through Sweden that she would be willing to drop the
Kuusinen fiction and deal directly with the Helsinki government in
negotiating a peace. The Soviets obviously had gotten wind of certain Allied plans to undertake a military operation against Russia.
The documents found in 1940 at La Charité by the Germans revealed
that some kind of obscure talk was going on in Ankara between the
French Ambassador there and Sarajoglu concerning preparations
for an aerial and eventual land attack of the Franco-British army in
the Near East upon Baku and the Soviet Caucasus (*11*); in the north,
the Russians as well as the Germans dreaded the appearance of an
Allied expeditionary force in Scandinavia and the penetration of the
British into Arctic and eventually into Baltic waters. (*12*) On January 20, Winston Churchill delivered a magnificent, resolute speech
in favor of Finland. Ribbentrop told the Italian Magistrati on that
same day that he did not see any possibilities of a German mediation
between Russia and Finland; he termed the Russian attitude as
"reasonable," stemming from an aim of "modest revisionism." On
January 26, *Izvestia* labelled Winston Churchill as "the greatest
enemy of the Soviet Union"; a week later the entire Soviet press
attacked the Balkan Conference sitting in Belgrade, where Turkey
in vain tried to mould the Balkan states into a strong anti-totalitarian
and pro-Western, independent bloc.

.   .   .   .

[*The Western intervention.*] We know today that Britain and
France had decided to intervene and help Finland, and thus create
a second front against Germany, even if such an action should result
in a war between Russia and the Western Powers.
     In Ryti's words:

> In the last phase of the war the Western Powers offered us military
> assistance. Their aim was to wage war against Germany also in the
> north. . . . *In our hands lay then a historical decision of global range.* An
> acceptance of their help would have led the Western Powers into
> war with Russia, thus making Russia and Germany allies in (the
> Second) World War. Very serious considerations led us, however, to
> the conclusion that the offered assistance could not save us but in-

stead transform our country into the battleground of a war between the Great Powers, resulting in infinite sufferings for our people. While the peace, our only alternative to the acceptance of the military aid, was hard, we still chose it and could henceforth remain outside of the war. Russia had probably had the chance to annihilate us despite our heroic resistance; yet, in spite of the fact that during the negotiations she presented us with harder demands than those whereof we were previously informed . . . Russia's interests then required a conclusion of peace . . . *(13)*

The first Russian peace proposals were communicated to Finland at the end of January. On January 29 Sweden was officially informed by Moscow that the Soviet Union was ready to negotiate; the requested Finnish answer came on February 2. Tanner arrived in Stockholm and contacted the Soviet Embassy there. On the same day, the expected Soviet offensive against the Mannerheim Line began. The superiority of Soviet artillery finally resulted in a breakthrough; subsequently, the Soviets made their peace conditions more difficult. There was now a virtual race between German and Franco-British diplomacy. The Germans employed every possible means to terminate the war; even anti-Bolshevist friends of Göring, the pro-German Swedish industrialist, Wenner-Gren, for example, were used to mediate between Finnish and Russian representatives in the United States.

While persistent, if sporadically interrupted peace negotiations were going on in Moscow and Stockholm, the French and British were aiming to convince the Finns of the advantages of continued resistance. As early as December 27, 1939, the Swedish envoys in London and Paris received parallel notes which requested Swedish (and Norwegian) cooperation:

> His Majesty's Government and the French Government . . . are for their part disposed to afford unofficially to Finland, for the defence of her national independence, all the indirect assistance in their power. The details of this assistance . . . are at present under examination. In any case, however, it will be put into effect with all possible speed . . . *(14)*

Throughout January, negotiations with Sweden went on. But the Swedes (more so than the Norwegians) were against the passage of Allied troops to aid Finland. For their own security, they preferred to see the end of the Finnish War; official persons as well as non-official ones mediated between Russians and Finns. This unfavorable Swedish attitude and the development of the Russians' Karelian offensive then called for an acceleration of Allied plans.

" 'Round the Finnish question . . . gathered tendencies of great future import," wrote Chamberlain's biographer; and there were a number of people gathered around Chamberlain trying to make him sound out peace with Germany. He was, of course, anti-Russian, and when the War Council met on February 5, this timid man seemed strangely eager to send three or four divisions into Finland through Norway and Sweden: the Narvik route. Churchill was not eager at all; he sensed ideological leanings. (15) Neither did he think the expedition practical. "The issue of what to do if Norway and Sweden refused, as seemed probable," he later pointed out, "was never faced."

Yet in mid-February French Alpine brigades made ready to embark for Finland; the British Admiralty made preparations to cut the Scandinavian iron ore route to Germany by securing Narvik and blockading the Baltic; most of the material help given to the Finns came from Britain.

On February 13 Tanner again appeared in Stockholm; this time he came to ask for Swedish help for Finland, but this was refused on the 16th. As this Swedish reprisal transpired to Moscow, when on February 20–22 the Finns received a new set of Soviet peace terms, they were harsher than the previous ones. Rather desperate, the Finns asked Sweden on February 23 to permit the passage of Allied troops; the request was refused. Not that the Soviets weren't worried: on February 26 Maisky called on Halifax and asked him to transmit rather unreasonable Soviet peace terms to Finland; behind this move was the Soviets' desire to find out if France and Britain really planned to intervene in the Finnish War. It seemed so. On February 28 the Swedish military attaché from London reported full details of the planned British-French expedition; in Britain, volunteers were assembling from the four corners of Europe, navigation plans were being made, troops were gathered for embarkation. A stiff German note was handed to Sweden that day, demanding that under no circumstances should Sweden assist the Finns.

The Soviets had now pounded holes into the main Finnish defence lines and Finnish resistance weakened. On March 2 (without having consulted the British) Daladier made up his mind to send 50,000 volunteers and 100 planes to Finland which were to be followed by

50 bombers. This action was planned "soon after March 20." On the same day a French-British note was handed to Stockholm:

> The Allied Governments understand that the military position of Finland is becoming desperate. After carefully considering all the possibilities, they have reached the conclusion that the only means by which they can render effective help to Finland is by the despatch of an Allied force, and they are prepared to send such a force in response to a Finnish appeal. The force with its full equipment is available and could sail at short notice. In order to render help to Finland where help is needed, the force would have to cross Norwegian and Swedish territory, and His Majesty's Government will in due course formally request leave for its passage.

And the note to Oslo stated, among other things:

> The forces for Finland, and those destined for the support of Sweden, could begin arriving in Norwegian ports on the 20th March . . .

But Sweden could not and would not abandon her neutrality; King Gustav personally appealed to Daladier (on March 4 came another threatening German note). Stockholm's refusal evoked a bitter remark from Mr. Mallet, the British Minister:

> I will forward this reply to my Government who will be extremely disappointed. You abandon the Finns to their fate.

Meanwhile the Finnish-Russian negotiations reached a point where agreement was in sight; the visit of Sumner Welles was being interpreted as a sign for general peace (*16*); the Finnish elder statesman, Svinhufvud, who had always had excellent German relations, travelled to Berlin where he was promised full German goodwill and benevolence if Finland proved to be "reasonable" and signed a peace with Russia. British-Italian relations were meanwhile deteriorating because of the British blockade on German coal shipments to Italy. On March 10, Ribbentrop said in Rome that having frustrated all British designs, the Finnish-Russian War had come to an end. (He also said that the whole war had been started by the Finnish Free Masons and by Tanner, the chief warmonger and Menshevik — Ribbentrop obviously preferred the Bolsheviks — and that Russia had been pushed into the Finnish War. Another fabrication of Ribbentrop's mind.) The Swedish representatives in London and es-

pecially in Paris (where the Swedish financier, Marcus Wallenberg, Jr.
(*17*), exercised his personal influence in high French financial circles)
tried to convince the Western Powers of the impossibilities of a successful Finnish campaign in order to dispel "Finlandsromantik."
Nevertheless, on March 7 Finland was informed that, upon her
request, the Allied army would be ready to proceed into Scandinavia;
on March 12 another urgent note was handed to the Swedish government by Mr. Mallet. In the evening the British Minister announced
in Helsinki that the Allied army was ready to sail now even if Sweden
and Norway did not consent. But it was too late. Radio Moscow
broadcast a hurried and somewhat premature announcement about
the armistice; at midnight the peace treaty between Russia and Finland was signed in Moscow.

It remains to the reader to ponder how the world and Europe
would look today if, either due to more Swedish flexibility or Russian
inflexibility, Allied troops had arrived in Finland and a gigantic
war of Britain, France, Poland, and Finland against Germany and
Russia had been the result.

.   .   .   .

[*The settlement.*] The terms of the Moscow peace were accepted by the Finnish Parliament on March 15 by a vote of 145
against 3. The Soviet Union received the Karelian Straits, including
the coveted Viipuri, the adjacent islands, territory around Lake
Ladoga, and the three cities, Kexholm, Suojärvi, and Sortavala, a
stretch of territory in and north of the "waistline," and most of the
Fisher Peninsula (*18*) around Petsamo. In addition, Russia received
transit rights to Sweden and Norway, and the Finns were obliged
to build a railroad trunk line between Kandalaksa and Kemijärvi
for Soviet transit purposes. The peninsula of Hangö was "leased"
to the Soviet Union for thirty years. A new and uncertain period of
Russo-Finnish relations had opened.

Russia, central-eastern Europe and the German victory in the West

[*Cordial contacts.*] During the winter of 1939–40, relations
between Germany and Russia were developing to the quiet satisfaction of the men in Berlin and Moscow. The German position during
the Finnish War was punctilious and correct; there was no change in

the cordial reports between the newfangled "proletarian allies."
When a bomb attempt on Hitler's life took place in November,
Molotov congratulated him on his escape; on Stalin's birthday anniversary, Hitler and Ribbentrop dispatched flowery good wishes.
A German-Soviet transit and railroad agreement was signed in
December. True, on November 23 Hitler spoke to the German generals and told them how things would be settled with Russia after
his task in the West was done, but it should be remembered that he
was always excitable and emotional, carried away with himself,
whenever as supreme warlord he addressed a gallery of his military
commanders. Although he underestimated the Red Army, he foresaw an extended period of collaboration: "For the next year or two
the present situation will remain." On February 11, an extensive
economic agreement was signed between the Soviet Union and Germany. The supplies from Russia flowed in a steady stream; Ribbentrop and Hitler could point with pride at the results achieved by
the Russian Pact.

[*Russia weighs her German relations.*]   Some time in February,
Stalin and Molotov began to find themselves in a quandary as their
war with Finland threatened to develop into a continental conflict
with France and Great Britain. The cordiality of Russo-German
relations now abated slightly; Moscow assumed a somewhat more
reserved attitude. On January 29 the usual medium of a TASS denial
was used to indicate that there was absolutely no truth in the rumors
that German troops or military missions had arrived in the Ukraine.
There were certain obstacles put in the way of the population exchange agreements; great projects of naval cooperation at "Basis
Nord" near Murmansk were reduced; the Governor-General in
Poland reported minor frontier incidents along the demarcation
line. (*1*)

[*The fear of Allied intervention.*]   While Moscow was making
parochial attempts to prove her freedom of decision, the last phase
of the Finnish War brought the Western Allies dangerously near to
intervention. The Germans again behaved in the best interests of
Russia, as they left no stone unturned to promote the quick conclusion of the Finnish War. The community of German and Russian
interests in Scandinavia seemed so extensive that on March 9 Admiral Raeder suggested that Moscow be informed of the German

plans against the northern Norwegian ports during the highly secret
Operation Weserübung (invasions of Denmark and Norway). "Better
the Russians sit in Tromsö than the English," wrote Raeder to Hitler,
who nevertheless rejected the idea as unnecessary. He was proven
right: within a few days the Moscow Peace had been signed.

Momentarily it seemed that even the newly concluded peace had
not altered the plan of the Western Allies to establish themselves in
Scandinavia and menace both Russia and Germany therefrom. The
fears of Moscow were great. Finland, reduced in size and in strength,
wished to assure her second and permanent neutrality and planned
to join a Swedish-Norwegian-Finnish *bloc:* a mutual defence alliance. Russia, however, raised vehement protests against such plans.
She knew that such a *bloc* would be in the interests of Britain in the
long run; at the same time she wished to continue to confront a weak
and lonely Finland. Thus nothing came out of the reasonable plans
for a Scandinavian alliance. The Western Powers were frustrated
and irritated, angry with Russia; the French government requested
that the Soviet Ambassador be recalled from Paris; Soviet protests
against the detention of Russian vessels in French, British and American ports were numerous. In Moscow, strenuous attempts were made
to appease the United States; on March 26 Maisky even called on
Halifax and cordially proposed a Russo-British trade agreement.
Ribbentrop was aware of the Soviets' uneasiness. Consequently, he
again tried to convince the Russians of the advantages of their German
alliance; he instructed Schulenburg to approach Molotov and, if
possible, Stalin himself with a majestic invitation to Berlin. On
March 30, Schulenburg answered extensively; such an invitation
would not be propitious at a time when Stalin was perhaps more
bent than ever on emphasizing the absolute neutrality of Russia.
On the same day, Hitler ordered that, "so far as necessary," delivery
of war materials to Russia should have priority over German Army
deliveries. This directive remained unchanged until August 14. (2)

Meanwhile, on March 28, the Allied Supreme Council met. Among
other things, it was decided, to study "at once . . . the project for
bombing the Russian oil area in the Caucasus." Detailed preparations were ordered. Another decision was to send a note to Stockholm and Oslo on April 1, which stated:

> The Allied Governments cannot permit a new attack on Finland,
> either by the Russian or the German Government. If a new aggres-

sion did take place and if the Norwegian and Swedish Governments refused to facilitate the efforts of the Allied Governments to help Finland, under such conditions as they deemed appropriate and, *a fortiori*, if those governments [Norwegian and Swedish] tried to prevent such aid being given, this attitude would be considered hostile to their vital interests by the Allies and would provoke an appropriate reaction. *(3)*

Sweden and Norway were also warned not to sign political agreements with Germany, even for the defence of Finland; Norway was warned not to lease or cede any coastal bases to the Soviet Union.

These stern resolutions and rigid demands coincided with a speech on March 29 by Molotov, who, while again needling France and Britain, was nevertheless moderate in his praise of Germany and tried to give an overall picture of peaceful relations with as many neighbors as possible. *(4)* The only unfriendly allusion to future actions was directed at Rumania: Molotov stated that the Bessarabian question remained open and demanded a solution.

[*Instead, the Germans in Scandinavia.*] In ten days, however, the whole picture changed. The nebulous projects of the Western Allies were swept away by the unexpected windstorm of the Germans' daring descent on Scandinavia. When, on the morning of April 9, Schulenburg informed Molotov of the German invasion of Denmark and Norway, the Russian was serene and friendly. He "understood the measures forced upon Germany." Russia, he said, wished Germany "complete success in her defensive measures." All Molotov asked was that the Germans respect the neutrality of Sweden; and on the 15th, Germany promised to do so. The German successes had changed the Russian attitude; Stalin and Molotov were once again impressed by German might and prowess; as the chances of a Franco-British Scandinavian victory vanished, the Russians' paramount aim was once again to assure the Germans of Soviet friendship. TASS denied that Germany had ever requested passage through Murmansk for her troops going to Norway; TASS denied that there was any tension between Berlin and Moscow; TASS denied that Russian-French-Rumanian conversations were going on in order to guarantee the present Rumanian-Russian frontier. On April 26 *Pravda* attacked British plans in the Middle East. The whole changed attitude of the Soviets was well summed up in a memorandum of Schulenburg, who added: "I must honestly say that I was completely

amazed at the change . . ." The German Ambassador, who had
called at the Kremlin on the morrow of the German attack on Scandinavia with some anxiety, was much more at ease on May 10 when
he made a similar call to announce the invasion of Holland, Belgium
and Luxemburg. His expectations were confirmed by Molotov, who
appreciated the news and understood.

. . . .

[*The Western campaign.*] While the German armies were
rushing forward in the West with unexpected speed, central-eastern
Europe was quiet. Under the glittering blue sky of Athens, in the
kafanas of Belgrade, in defeated Warsaw, bombed Helsinki, fearful
Bucharest, people watched the terrible defeat of the West with incredulity. The spring of 1940 was unusually beautiful; three weeks
of undisturbed sunshine followed the German invasion in the West;
people simply refused to believe that all this could be true. Even those
sympathetic to the Germans did not give full credit to the Berlin
victory announcements; only in the end, after Italy had entered the
war, did they come fully to believe them. Then — with the exception of local Nazis, Arrow-Cross, *Ustaši*, and Iron Guardists — the
men and women of central-eastern Europe were sad and broken.
They saw the crumbling of the culture and the world in whose ideals
they believed; considerations of their security, that there remained
now nothing to counterbalance the might of Germany, was but one
source of their sorrow. More important was the spiritual shock.
Those living in the eastern half of Europe now witnessed the
miserable defeat of France, the ideal and inspiration of so many
central-eastern European nations, and the unexpected weakness of
Britain, that revered and misunderstood rock of world order. The
effect of 1940 on the souls of the then young generation of central-
eastern Europe was such that it survived the war and it now aids
the Soviets in their postwar efforts which aim at the complete eradication of Western memories, traditions and values.

[*Soviet reactions: Rumania.*] During the Battles of Belgium,
Flanders, and France, Soviet foreign policy was active in three fields:
the Baltics, Rumania, and Yugoslavia. Final preparations for incorporation of the unfortunate Baltic republics were made. After
Molotov's March 29 speech, Rumania could nurture no doubts in

regard to immediate Soviet intentions. The German envoy hinted to Bucharest that perhaps it would be advantageous if Rumania abandoned Southern Bessarabia; in April, significant frontier incidents occurred along the Bessarabian border. Not much later, certain reports indicated that the Russians wanted more than just Bessarabia proper; rumors spoke of Soviet designs on adjacent territories, Bukovina, for example, but these rumors were discounted by Hitler, who told Halder on May 5 that he believed the Russians would limit themselves to Bessarabia. (5) Russian pressure increased. Day after day, the Soviet press attacked Bucharest; at the same time the Soviet newspapers were conspicuously silent about the war in the West. As Gafencu remarked: "The Russians pushed, the Germans pulled Rumania into the system of the Axis." Acutely aware of the growing importance of America, he asked Washington to intervene in Moscow lest Stalin attack Rumania while Hitler was busy in the West; but his solicitations brought but a general statement by the American chargé in Moscow that the United States stood against "a further extension of hostilities."

On April 19, the Rumanian crown council reaffirmed previous decisions to resist either a German or a Russian attack. A month later, the Germans broke through at Sedan; on May 28, Belgium capitulated. The crown council met again. Against a minority of ministers, King Carol decided to "acknowledge the facts" and change the course of Rumanian foreign policy, announce a close collaboration with Germany and thus eventually strengthen Rumania's position against Russia. Gafencu resigned. The German course was taken; but it did not save Rumania.

[*Soviet reactions: Yugoslavia.*] The third field in which Soviet diplomacy was very active was Yugoslavia. Since the Secret Protocol did not cover the Balkans, Germany regarded that area as entirely within the Axis sphere; the Soviets, on the other hand, interpreted the lack of a concrete, "sphere of interest" agreement concerning the Balkans to mean that a kind of partial vacuum existed there, that it was open to a cautious and not necessarily hostile balance of power game. Both Germany and Russia rejoiced that Yugoslavia refused to go into a Balkan alliance of neutral states; both Germany and Russia disliked the idea of an Italian invasion of Yugoslavia — the former because she wished Italian armor to be directed against France and Britain and did not want to trouble the, to her, temporarily convenient peace of the Balkans, the latter because she wanted to profit from being considered a potential protector of Yugoslavia.

Because of the Yugoslav dynasty's Romanov connections, Yugoslavia was the only Balkan state which did not have diplomatic relations with the Soviet Union. About March–April 1940, negotiations began through Sofia and Ankara. (6) At the end of April the Yugoslav Finance Minister visited Moscow, and in May a trade treaty was signed. The very active Soviet Minister to Sofia, Lavrentiev, visited Belgrade; both German admonition and Soviet hostility were paramount in Mussolini's decision to turn against France instead of Yugoslavia. As late as June 6, Moscow Radio warned Italy; on June 10, Mussolini went to war against the Western Allies; on June 24, two days before the Soviets' Bessarabian ultimatum to Rumania, Yugoslavia and the Soviet Union established diplomatic relations. The leader of the left-of-center Agrarian Party, Gavrilovič, was sent to Moscow as the first Yugoslav Minister; his first reports and the careful statements of Plotnikov, the Soviet Minister to Belgrade, left no doubt that Russia intended to play a gradually increasing rôle in Balkan affairs.

Italy, central-eastern Europe and the victory of Germany in the West

Mussolini decided upon war in March, when the coaching of Ribbentrop in Rome and Hitler on the Brenner gave the final impetus to that decision; however, from March 18 to May 30, he vacillated between two alternatives. He could make war on Yugoslavia (this was the alternative supported by Ciano, who preferred a "little war" instead of plunging into a vast and incalculable conflict with France and Britain). But if the Duce wished to have an equal share in making the new world together with Hitler and possibly Stalin, he would have to participate in the actual wresting of the spoils.

[*Italy yet preoccupied with the Balkans.*] For awhile Ciano's "little war" plan was gaining with Mussolini. On March 21, Politis, the Greek Minister, asked Ciano what had happened at the Brenner? Ciano said that there the Balkans had been discussed only in passing. This was true. Politis also asked him whether he knew anything of Bessarabia, whereupon Ciano replied: "Our relations with the Soviets are not of such a nature as to enable me to know their intentions." He also denied rumors of an Italian-Soviet rapprochement now that the Finnish War was over. Yet from the record of the

Mussolini-Ribbentrop talks, held ten days before, it transpires that Mussolini had already decided to better Italian relations with Russia. On March 23, the Hungarian Teleki visited Rome. Ciano asked him not to press against Rumania, as the Soviets would unquestionably profit therefrom. (Exactly a year before, on March 22, 1939, it was the French who requested the same from Budapest.) Teleki promised this; while they played golf together amidst the placid hills of the Campagna, he turned to Ciano: "I do not want to go to war; I do not want to attack Rumania, in spite of the two million compatriots of mine; I do not want minorities; I do not want to help Russia within Europe's gates; the Germans might do that, but not I; I fear their victory which would result in the national-bolshevization of Europe and the world." (*1*) Later Teleki asked Ciano whether he knew how to play bridge "for the day when we are together in the Dachau Concentration Camp." That Ciano recorded these words in detail shows his anxiety and fears; but he also recorded that during this time Mussolini was in very good humor and "growing every day more definitely pro-German."

[*Mussolini weighs a double campaign.*] In the first week of April, the pro-Nazi elements of the Hungarian General Staff told the Teleki Government about a communication from the German High Command requesting the free passage of German troops through Hungary "to protect" the Rumanian oil fields in case of a Russian move against Bessarabia. (It turned out later that the German request was not official, but a trial balloon sent up either by the German military attaché or by a German officer friendly with the pro-German Hungarian Minister to Berlin.) If such permission were granted, reported the Hungarian General Staff, Hungary could reoccupy most of Transylvania. Teleki was very much alarmed and sent a friend, Baranyay, the President of the Hungarian National Bank, on a secret mission to Rome, where he arrived on April 8. But — in contrast to his advice exactly seven months before, when Mussolini had told Teleki to refuse, very politely if need be, the German request for troop passage through Hungary into Poland — the Duce now had nothing to say; he could offer no help. (*2*) Next morning news of the Germans' Scandinavian invasion broke.

The German military successes in the North and in the West made Mussolini shelve Ciano's plan for a "little war." For awhile, he thought he could conduct operations against France and Yugoslavia at the same time. At the end of April, he explained this strategy to Marshal Graziani: "Defensive in the west [France] and offensive in the east [Yugoslavia]." But there were now obstacles in his way. The Soviet Union, increasingly pro-Yugoslav, was cagey, and jealous of Italy's Balkan ambitions. Neither was the Italian army well enough equipped for a two-front war in Europe. And Germany kept expressing her wish to maintain the Balkan *status quo*. The Germans were supporting the politicians of the moderate Right in Yugoslavia — with Stoyadinovič in the background — while Italy was supporting the Croats and Pavelič. How times had changed! In May 1939 Hitler had lured Mussolini into the Steel Pact and towards war by telling him to invade Yugoslavia; now, a year later, Mussolini wanted to do just that and Hitler was holding him back. (*3*)

Early in May the situation changed: Mussolini had to abandon his plan for a two-front war. The German armies were surging down on Western Europe; three days after their launching, Mussolini decided definitely to enter the war and attack France. (*4*) He had to hurry; the Germans were advancing through Belgium and France with surprising speed. The situation in the Balkans was not favorable. The German Ambassador kept urging him to seek a rapprochement with Moscow, and now Mussolini did so. But Stalin did not want to commit himself before he saw how the war in the West was going; Yugoslavia's armies were ready to repel any Italian attack; it was discovered that Ciano's chief Croat agent was playing a double game. Nevertheless, Ciano argued for an attack on Yugoslavia; he still hoped that Mussolini would come to the conclusion that a "little war" was preferable. As late as May 26, Ciano advised his new Berlin Ambassador, Alfieri, to emphasize "Yugoslav duplicity and anti-Axis sentiments" with all his power. Ciano calculated that, in her present plight, Britain would not declare war on Italy if the latter invaded Yugoslavia. But the whole picture changed within a week. Dunkirk was going on in the West, and on May 30, Mussolini made his final decision to attack France within ten days. Subsequently, Mr. Churchill decided on June 6 to regard an Italian "little war" as a *casus belli:*

> . . . [the] situation has changed. . . . We are so near a break with
> Italy on grounds which have nothing to do with Yugoslavia, that it
> would seem that our main aim might well be now to procure this
> Balkan mobilization . . . (*5*)

[*War on France.*]   Another "little war" possibility loomed in the prospect of an attack on Greece, but such plans were also shelved for awhile. (The Germans themselves were angry with Athens for the continued Anglophile demeanor of the Greek government and press; Berlin often protested against Piraeus' rôle as the main port of embarkation from whence Polish refugees, trickling through the Balkans, finally departed for France and England to join the Polish Army there.) Britain made preliminary plans to secure Crete if Italians invaded the Greek mainland. There was no such invasion, however. On June 10, Mussolini declared war on the Western Powers (6); in the same short speech, he assured Italy's neighbors, first of all Yugoslavia and Greece, that they had nothing to fear from Italy.

[*Italian attempts to divide the Balkans with Russia.*]   This was, of course, a "strategic lie." As soon as the French war was over, Mussolini (especially after he learned that Hitler's aim was to woo the "new France" and that Italian share of the French spoils was to be small indeed) began planning to swoop down upon his Adriatic and Aegean neighbors. In mid-June the Italian press was instructed to attack the Greek government, a policy which glibly reached a quick crescendo. More important was the diplomatic game. Mussolini decided to settle things together with Stalin — a full-scale reversal of Italy's previous Balkan policy.

On May 25, Mackensen in Rome told the Soviet chargé d'affaires that all Balkan problems should be solved by mutual cooperation among Germany, Russia, and Italy. (7) This communication pleased Molotov and Stalin no end: they were beginning at that time to worry about how they should adapt themselves to the situation caused by the unexpectedly rapid collapse of France, a development which made them fear Germany more than ever but which at the same time necessitated a new pledge of Soviet sincerity toward the Axis cause. Molotov at once asked Schulenburg whether Mackensen's statement was a personal opinion or an official Axis interpretation. Meanwhile, early in June, it was agreed that the Italian and Russian Ambassadors, absent from their posts since the Finnish War, should return to them at once. Italy's new policy was also evident from the fact that on June 10 she announced the break of relations with Poland; whereas previously the continued existence of Italian consulates in Poland had been a constant cause of German protests and a sign of hope for the Poles, now Mussolini announced his consent to the German-Soviet new order there.

It was now Germany which did not desire a "sphere of interest" agreement in the Balkans. On June 16, Ribbentrop instructed Schulenburg to tell Molotov that the Soviet diplomat in Rome had probably misinterpreted what Mackensen had said to him: the Axis policy was *to prevent the spreading of the war to the Balkans*. When, two days later, Mussolini, Hitler, Ciano, and Ribbentrop met at Munich to discuss the vast problem of the French armistice, the Germans again expressed their desire temporarily to maintain the *status quo* there.

On June 25, however, Molotov received the returning Italian Ambassador, Rosso, and said that Soviet-Italian relations should be very friendly, for they could produce the same excellent results as had Soviet-German relations. Russia considered certain Hungarian and Bulgarian claims on Rumania "reasonable," while she herself was determined to wrest Bessarabia from Rumania even at the cost of war; Molotov also declared his displeasure at Turkey's "unfriendly attitude" toward Russia, Germany, and Italy. Rosso was pleased at Molotov's concluding remark:

> In the Mediterranean, the Soviet Government would recognize Italy's hegemony, provided that Italy would recognize the Soviet Government's hegemony in the Black Sea. (8)

However, on June 22, Ciano received the Soviet Ambassador and said that Italian policy in the Balkans was to preserve the *status quo*. In his diary he summed up Soviet policy well:

> . . . it is clear that Russian policy is increasingly anti-German. The capital in which there is the greatest amount of conspiracy against German victory is Moscow. The situation has appeared quite otherwise when, in August and September (1939), the Bolsheviks signed pacts with the Nazis. At that time they didn't believe in a German triumph. They wanted to push Germany into a conflict and Europe into a crisis because they were thinking of a long and exhausting struggle between the democracies and Hitler. Things have moved fast, and now Moscow is trying to trouble the waters. (9)

This analysis was essentially correct, except that Moscow did not necessarily want "to trouble the waters," but to secure further spoils and territories: a more limited aim. Italian foreign policy wished something of the same kind. On July 3, Ciano received the Greek Ambassador and assailed him for alleged Greek-British cooperation: "The Greek Minister tried weakly to deny it, but he left with his tail between his legs." (The account of the same talk in the Greek White Book uses different words, of course.) On July 7, Ciano went to Berlin to ask Hitler's permission to attack Greece and carve up Yugoslavia. Hitler declared himself in full accord with the "liquidation of the [Yugoslav] problem in an Italian sense" but requested that Italy wait until all was over with Britain; he also feared that Russia might intervene; the present Yugoslavia "had no citizenship rights" in the new, Axis-created European community. Italy, it was decided, would postpone her intervention until a more propitious moment, but would go on with military preparations for an immediate action against Yugoslavia in the case of "Balkan complications" or at the time of "the British collapse."

Once more, in August, Mussolini thought of concluding a sensational pact with Russia covering the Balkans and then turning against Yugoslavia. At that time, however, Germany was definitely opposed to such a plan and nothing came of it.

Summer 1940: I. The Soviet occupation of the Baltics and the quandaries of Finland

"But Mussolini was not the only hungry animal seeking prey" — reminisced Mr. Churchill in his inimitable manner. "To join the Jackal came the Bear." During the ten days from the fall of Paris to the cease-fire on all French fronts, Russia eagerly annexed Estonia, Latvia, Lithuania, Bessarabia, and part of the Rumanian Bukovina.

[*The Baltics from October 1939 to June 1940.*] Relations between the Baltic states and the Soviet Union were very unusual while the twilight war lasted in the West. Soldiers, grim-faced Russian sailors, and blue-uniformed airmen lived in the Baltic cities, went shopping in the streets, but did not speak to the citizens; there was no visible Soviet interference with the affairs of these countries. Presidents Smetona, Ulmanis, and Päts of Lithuania, Latvia, and Estonia respectively, all hardened dictators of the anti-Communist variety, continued to rule; their governments were slightly altered by the inclusion of moderate Leftist elements, as in Estonia, where the Uluots cabinet included the Liberal

Piip; in Lithuania the soldier-Premier Cernius was succeeded by
Merkys; in Latvia there was even less change. The Soviet envoys
assured the Baltic governments of Stalin's desire to abide by the
non-intervention clause of the Mutual Assistance Pacts; especially
Nikitin, the Minister to Estonia, considered it his duty to voice
such assurances frequently. Relations between the population and
the Soviet soldiery stationed in Estonia were scrupulously correct;
during the Finnish War there was no interference at all, and when
in February an Estonian plane was mistakingly attacked by Soviet
anti-aircraft batteries and fighters, the Soviet general commanding
the air base openly apologized. Only in one case did very minor and
practically unavoidable friction occur: in January the Soviet Minister to Latvia protested against alleged Latvian failure to supply
goods to Russia, delivery of which had been agreed upon by a commercial treaty. But that was all. The Soviet press drew the world's
attention to Russia's peaceful relations with her neighbors; on February 24, TASS denied foreign reports that the Soviets had presented new demands for naval bases in the Baltics.

These were strange but reassuring symptoms; yet, under the surface, people knew that these were but twilight days. It remains now
to ask, why did Russia employ this silk-gloved policy in territories
which were allotted to her in a clear agreement? Why did she
change suddenly from a policy of careful abstinence to that of
brutal subjugation? There were a number of reasons. There was
the factor of prestige: the Russians first wanted to show how well
states which put themselves under their "protection" fared, hoping
thereby to influence states such as Finland, Bulgaria, and, probably,
Rumania. Another reason was the known and almost pathological
Soviet urge for "security"; after the German victory in the West,
the Russians feared that if they did not incorporate their holdings,
these might eventually convert themselves into buffer states. Finally
the land-minded Stalin had to show something to his people to
counterbalance the effects of the great German victories in the
North and in the West; Molotov's speech on August 1, 1940, proudly
enumerated the new dozens of thousands of square miles which increased the territories of the Soviet Union and noted the impressive
Soviet population of 193 million.

When, after the end of the Winter War, Finland and Sweden tried
preliminary talks for a Northern Defensive Alliance, the Russians
angrily protested. Yet at this time the usual meeting of the Lat-

vian, Estonian, and Lithuanian Foreign Ministers took place and a neutrality communiqué was jointly issued and Russia did not protest against this harmless and pacific Baltic meeting. At that time, she faced an organized and unfriendly Western Europe. Two months later the West was crumbling under German blows and the Soviets raised the pretext that the Baltic states were secretly conniving in a "military conspiracy" against Russia.

[*The Russian absorption.*] In September, 1939, it was Estonia which had "conspired" first against Russia. Now the order was reversed: Lithuania came first, Latvia, and Estonia followed. At the end of May, Molotov began to hint to the Lithuanian envoy at "reprisals" which were necessitated by "attacks" against individual members of the Russian garrisons in Lithuania. On the first day of Dunkirk, May 30, the first outward and ominous sign appeared: TASS published a list of anti-Soviet activities in Lithuania. The Lithuanian Premier, Merkys, was summoned to Moscow. (*1*) While he was facing an artificially wrathful Molotov there, the Lithuanian government arrested some of their own state security officers to convince the Russians of Lithuanian sincerity, despite the fact that nothing warranted the arrest of these men: the Russian officer, Butaev, whose disappearance served as the Russian cause of complaint, was beyond doubt a suicide; he was neither kidnapped nor murdered. Merkys returned to Kaunas, and on June 14 and 15, Soviet troops poured across the Lithuanian frontier. On the 15th, President Smetona and a few others escaped into Germany. They were not easily admitted; they were interned at once upon Ribbentrop's orders. Excepting these men and a few soldiers, no one else could escape; the frontier remained closed. On the same day, Latvia was served with a Soviet ultimatum; next day one was served on the Estonians. (Estonia's demanded an answer within *nine* hours.) The ultimata accused these nations of having violated their Mutual Assistance Pacts with Russia and demanded the substitution of their governments by régimes "honestly willing" to collaborate with the Soviet Union.

[*The Powers' reaction.*] The world was shocked by these developments. Germany did not raise a finger. It was only the unexpectedly swift timing of Moscow which worried Hitler; but when Ribbentrop reminded him of the Secret Protocol's exact wording, it was decided to instruct all German diplomatic posts and military authorities to acknowledge the Baltic events and refrain from making any anti-Soviet comment. (2) Only Britain and the United States expressed dissatisfaction with the Russians; but the British protest was studiously formal and not very strong. But Sumner Welles, in a strongly worded note, announced that Washington did not recognize the change in the Baltics. (3) Thereby America became the center of the Baltic movements-in-exile, whose position — especially that of the Latvians — was strengthened by a last-minute decision to transfer emergency powers of sovereign representation to their envoys in the West; the Latvian Minister to London, Zarins, received these *pleins pouvoirs* as the visible head of a submerged state.

[*Incorporation.*]   Like three black angels descending from the bleak eastern heavens of Muscovy, came three men, equipped with more *pleins pouvoirs* than a million of Zarins' ilk. Dekanosov landed in Kaunas, Vishinsky arrived in Riga, Zhdanov went over from Leningrad to Tallinn. The Lithuanian government was made to resign on June 16; a curious crypto-Communist cabinet was installed, the most important member of which was a Soviet stooge, Paletskis. On June 20, Ulmanis resigned in Latvia; in came a fellow-traveller, Professor Kirchensteins. Two days later, Päts and his Premier Uluots were deposed; a poet by the name of Vares became the new Prime Minister of Estonia.

All these developments occurred after carefully organized "demonstrations" in Kaunas, Riga, and Tallinn; yet the newly organized "governments" were not fully Communistic. Like the Groza government in Rumania, the Bulgarian Georgiev, the Polish Osóbka-Morawski, and the Hungarian Dinnyés in 1944–1947, they were composed of a few cleverly "back-seat-driving" Communists (all the Communists were at once released from prisons and previously nonexistent Communist newspapers appeared), but the leading government posts were held by Leftist, "progressive" scholars, writers, and politically inexperienced persons who combined soured idealism and intoxicating opportunism. As the British expert on Estonia wrote: "Altogether it was a Government of the Bloomsbury or Greenwich Village stamp." For awhile, the new régimes, while proclaiming unswerving loyalty to the Soviet Union, assured the people of their continued independence. This play was maintained for about four weeks. In mid-July, all three governments (some members of which had already been forced to resign) announced "modification" of the existing election laws and organized single-slate elections. By July 20, all the new Assemblies were elected and, naturally, the "Working People's Front" or "Union" received more than ninety per cent of the vote. *(4)* When the new Assemblies met, they were surprised to see that the chambers of their Parliaments were adorned with the Soviet flag and the well-known gigantic portraits of Lenin and Stalin. Only then were they told to "request" the incorporation of their nation into the Soviet Union. Soviet armed guards — in Kaunas, they were crouched with their tommy-guns under the green cloth of the conference table — saw to it that the reliable candidates of the "Working People's Front" did their task quickly and without hesitation.

The final act took place in Moscow, where the Supreme Council of the Soviets generously "considered" the request of the Lithuanian, Latvian, and Estonian delegations and between August 1 and 6 "admitted" the Baltic States as member republics of the Soviet Union. On September 7, a Supreme Council decree granted Soviet citizenship to the former nationals of these states.

[*Russian calculations; German reactions.*]   Later, Soviet apologists were wont to state that all this was dictated by strategic necessities *(5)*: essentially a defensive measure. But this argument is unacceptable. The frantic haste wherewith the Russian armies abandoned the Baltics after the German attack on June 22, 1941 — in a week they retreated more than two hundred miles; Lithuania was occupied by the German spearheads in thirty hours! — is evidence to the contrary. Furthermore, if the Soviet argument stands, why was there need for the suppression, deportation, and liquidation of anti-German elements in these states? The more or less independent, and traditionally Germanophobic Baltic republics would certainly have proven a greater obstacle to Germany in 1941. Probably the Soviet leaders thought just as Schulenburg supposed:

> Some things are not yet completely clear, as for instance the question, as to why the Soviet Union *just at this time* proceeded or allegedly will yet proceed against a number of countries. Most of my colleagues are of the opinion that the Soviets, who are always very well-informed, know or at least assume the end of the war to be imminent.   *(6)*

It was on June 18 that Molotov first officially informed Germany of the Soviet action. For obvious psychological reasons, he expressed "the warmest congratulations of the Soviet Government on the

splendid success of the German Armed Forces." (It was the day of
Bordeaux and the French armistice request.) He said that "it had
become necessary to put an end to all the intrigues by which England
and France had tried to sow discord and mistrust between Germany
and the Soviet Union in the Baltic States." Tacitly, the Germans
understood. Five days later, on the eve of the Soviet invasion of
Bessarabia — whose manner of execution irked Hitler considerably —
a classic TASS "denial" was broadcast and published in Moscow.
TASS categorically denied that any cause for Soviet-German disagreement existed or that the Soviets were concentrating troops in
Lithuania against Germany. Schulenburg thought that the communiqué was worded by Stalin himself; reassuring Germany of full
Soviet friendship, this TASS statement was to serve as a diplomatic
preparation to expedite the ease of the Soviet action in Bessarabia.
Throughout July, the problem of the Baltics faded into the background. Ribbentrop even refused to receive the notes of the unfortunate Baltic envoys in Berlin; only with difficulty could the more
humane elements of the German Foreign Office prevent their expulsion or eventual deportation to Russia. There was, nevertheless, some
minor friction between Germany and Russia. First, there was the
problem of the Kalvarija territory. Now the land-hungry Soviets had
all of Lithuania, and they did not intend to cede this unimportant
patch to Germany. On August 13, Molotov offered first 3,800,000
dollars for the strip; on January 10, 1941, a final Secret Protocol
was made and Germany sold the strip for 7,500,000 gold dollars.
Five months and eleven days later, the Germans retook it practically
in the first hour of their invasion of Russia.

A minor friction occurred when an article with an anti-German
undertone was published in a Latvian Communist newspaper, for
which the Russian Ambassador in Berlin dejectedly apologized. Some
misunderstanding prevailed from the German refusal to grant the
same privileges to the Soviets which Lithuania had had in the Free
Port Zone of Memel. (7)

Meanwhile sovietization of the Baltic states proceeded rapidly. The
leading statesmen were taken to Russia. Only in introducing the
collective farm system did the Russian occupiers proceed slowly, in
order to assure continuous production from these agrarian states
whose fruits they reaped. The pattern was the same in all three countries: the Catholic clergy in Lithuania and the Lutherans in Estonia
and central and northern Latvia were persecuted, the great majority

of their Bishops imprisoned, deported, killed. A carefully executed
policy of deportations, reaching its climax just before the German
attack in June, 1941, carried out by local commanders, such as
Guzevitsius in Lithuania (*8*), and supervised by the Russian NKVD
chieftain, Serov, was primarily designed to extirpate all possible
seeds of anti-Soviet resistance (underground organizations existed
throughout 1940–41, and in Estonia, students and peasants sporadically demonstrated against the Communist régime during 1940), and
to make place for future Russian settlers of the Baltic countries. (*9*)
This ruthless Russification policy was stopped on June 22, 1941, by
the German war: however, it began anew in 1945 and has probably
partly achieved its goals at the time of this writing.

.   .   .   .

[*Again, Finland.*] After the signing of the Moscow Peace,
the Soviet Union did everything to draw Finland within her sphere,
but the methods which she employed were far too clumsy. The new
Russian demands were territorial, political, and economic. Issues of
minor territorial adjustments along the new Russo-Finnish frontier
were raised and remained a continuous source of friction. The Soviets
also requested the rapid demilitarization of the Aalands. The patient
and shrewd Paasikivi, the new Finnish envoy to Moscow, was sub-
jected to lengthy verbal attacks by Molotov, who said to him: "One
cannot negotiate with you . . . with the Germans one can settle even
big matters in a few days." (*10*) There was considerable Soviet espionage activity in the Aalands; their consulate in Mariehamn swelled
with a number of "officials" sufficient for a virtual Fifth Column.
Finally, on October 11, an agreement was reached; the Aalands were
to be demilitarized, and not to be placed at the disposal of any third
Power.

Political pressure was exercised during the whole summer. The
Russians demanded that the "Menshevik" Tanner relinquish his cab-
inet post; after a continuous barrage, Tanner resigned in August.
When the Finnish Presidential elections came up in December, the
Russians informed Helsinki of the "impossibility" of four Presidential
candidates. (After this crass interference in Finnish internal affairs,
Ryti, no friend of Russia, was elected President.)

While Molotov continuously warned Paasikivi not to cultivate relations with such "imperialists' agents" as the Swedish Sandler or the
Norwegian Hambro, the Soviets shut down dams to impede the work

of plants dependent on hydroelectricity on the Finnish side of the new Karelian border; in the summer a dozen new strategic highways were built leading toward Finland. The Russian intentions were clear (*11*); only the occasion was lacking. Their occupation of the Baltics brought increased Soviet naval and air activities in the Finnish Gulf; the first Soviet ultimatum had not yet been handed to Lithuania when on June 14 a Soviet warplane shot down the Helsinki-Tallinn passenger plane over the Gulf. The Russians demanded increased transit facilities to and from Hangö, a request which the Finnish government was in no position to refuse. Finnish restraint continued to prevail; on August 18, Ryti, now Premier, broadcast to the nation, affirming his government's desire to live in friendship with all neighboring nations.

[*But Germany intervenes.*]   By that time, however, important changes were in the making. Late in July, Hitler ordered preparations for an eventual war with Russia. These were, however, most secret, and for a long time, German-Russian relations remained unperturbed. But around August 15, secret negotiations began between the Finnish and German military concerning the transit rights of German troops through western and northern Finland to Norway; the Germans naturally hinted at the possibility that some of these troops would constitute a symbolic deterrent against Russia. On August 26 Hitler said for the first time in a private conversation that he had decided to support Finland against a new Russian attack. On September 6 at his High Command conference Hitler nebulously spoke of a North Germanic Union, with Norway, northern Sweden, Finland included, "in which the individual states would have a certain sovereignty [diplomatic representation, etc.] and have armed forces trained and equipped by them but organized on the pattern of the German Armed Forces." On September 12, the secret agreement providing for transit of the Germans through Finland was signed. (Ryti later claimed that for reasons of naval security, he was not informed of the agreement until the first German troopship had entered Finnish waters.) On September 21, a German vessel docked at Vaasa, where the German troops debarked and then departed for Norway. Berlin did not hesitate to inform Moscow of the transit agreement. (Since July 5, Germany had had a transit agreement with Sweden, (*12*) against which the Soviet government did not protest.) There is no doubt, however, that the arrival of German troops in Finland marked a milestone, if not a turning-point, in German-Russian relations. From that time on, Germany slowly encouraged Finnish resistance against further Soviet advance.

[*Union plans with Sweden; British reactions.*] On September 26, Britain protested to Finland against the transit agreement. Now the Finnish government was in a quandary; but there loomed a favorable solution. Sweden was willing to resume the discussion of a Northern Defensive Alliance which had been suspended in March. With Norway under German occupation, a Swedish-Finnish alliance would clearly be bound to neutrality; negotiations began, and even a personal union of the two states under the crown of King Gustav v was envisaged. The Finns were willing finally and fully to disavow any claims to the territories lost by the Moscow Peace. Especially the United States favored such an alliance or union, knowing that it would have considerable prestige and would be strong enough to remain permanently neutral. But Russia opposed it. *Pravda* and *Izvestia* assailed the Finns as "violators of the peace treaty"; a "Society of the Friends of the Soviet Union," *(13)* formed in the summer of 1940 under the aegis of the Soviet Legation in Helsinki, protested; from September 27 to December 13, Molotov threatened and menaced Paasikivi in Moscow; upon the latter's advice, the project was finally shelved. A Swedish-Finnish Alliance or Union would have terminated Germany's transit facilities through both countries; it would have prevented Germany from using Finland, her army and her territory, in a war against the Soviet Union; how much easier the Russians' military position would have been in 1941 if they had not had to defend a thousand-mile long northwestern front! But Russia feared that she might miss the prize of the Finnish lands today, instead of fearing the German attack of tomorrow.

For the same strategic reasons, Berlin was bitterly opposed to the Finnish-Swedish plans; Hitler did not want to see any "American meddling" in Scandinavia. *(14)*

On the other side it was intimated that, despite Western protests, Finland's difficult situation was understood. Britain was alone, battered, without any allies on the European continent, hoping only to gain in the diplomatic battle by Hitler's follies. In November 1940, a high official of the British Foreign Office was said to have expressed his opinion thus: "Britain can do nothing for Finland, as she does not want to drive Russia into Germany's arms." *(15)* This was logical.

[*The Petsamo case.*] The outstanding economic dispute between Russia and Finland centered around the Petsamo nickel mines, owned by the Canadian Nickel Company, whose concession the Soviet government wanted to abrogate. But there they met with the opposition not only of the Finns, but of Britain, Canada . . . and Germany, whose Göring Works had had interests in the mines. For long months, negotiations dragged on. The Russians constantly argued how "generous" they had been in having left Petsamo with Finland; in 1920 and in the Winter War they could have taken it, they said. However, despite many Soviet threats and much Soviet cunning, (*16*) the Finns did not give in. An excerpt from a memorandum of Paasikivi, referring to one of his talks with Vishinsky, is instructive:

> I pointed out that under our laws we could not take away the concessions from the British. Vishinsky paid no attention to my explanations about conception of law in the Northern countries, but answered that if the requisite law did not now exist, we should go ahead and pass one. . . .

Such difficulties continued to color Finnish-Russian relations throughout the fall and winter of 1940.

Summer 1940: II. Rumania, Hungary, Bulgaria

On June 23, the Soviet Union turned against Rumania. That evening, Molotov informed Schulenburg that the "solution" of the Bessarabian issue would not be delayed anymore; Russia furthermore claimed the province of Bukovina with its "predominantly Ukrainian population." (*1*) Schulenburg feigned surprise; he had not expected the "problem" to be so acute. However, there was nothing to do. The Secret Protocol had awarded Bessarabia to the Russian sphere. An unusually harsh ultimatum was presented to the Russian Minister to Moscow, Davidescu, late in the night of June 26: it demanded that Rumania abandon the territories claimed by the Soviet Union within forty-eight hours.

[*Threat of war.*] The full extent of Russian aims was, however, not quite clear. The abruptness with which the Soviets handled the Bessarabian issue stemmed, of course, from their desire to incorporate their Secret Protocol holdings as rapidly as possible at the time when Germany had won her astonishing military victory in the

West. However, a difference existed between the Bessarabian and the Baltic actions. In the Baltics Stalin acted when the doomed states could not resist; the whole execution of the rapid but nevertheless gradual absorption of these states showed that he wished to avoid the semblance of an external invasion. But when broaching the case of Bessarabia, Stalin did not exclude the possibility of a Russian-Rumanian war; indeed, Molotov envisaged such a possibility to the German and Italian Ambassadors. Furthermore, the Soviet Union made it known that she demanded not only Bessarabia, but the (formerly Austrian and since 1918 Rumanian) province of Bukovina, unmentioned by the Secret Protocol. It is not impossible that Moscow wanted to present harsh terms in a well-nigh unacceptable manner: war would then have resulted, and after its rapid and victorious conclusion the Soviets could have established their frontiers well beyond the Danube Delta, appeared as an impressive Balkan Power, probably contiguous with Bulgaria and thus have been in immediate sight of the eternal Russian objective, the Straits.

There was no war, however. Ribbentrop was willing to acquiesce in the incorporation of Bessarabia, although after the first communication of Molotov, he exclaimed that Bukovina was certainly "something new." He also asked that the German minority of Bessarabia be protected and transferred later, with full security, to Germany; above all, he insisted that there be no war. Ribbentrop's note strongly emphasized German economic interests in the rest of Rumania. (*2*) These were forceful arguments which Stalin had to consider.

On June 25, Molotov, still desiring to interpret the Secret Protocol in a way which would have left room for a Balkan "sphere of interest" policy, spoke to the Italian Ambassador:

> The Soviet Union would prefer to realize her claims to Bessarabia without war, but, if that was impossible because of Rumanian intransigence, *she was determined to resort to force. Regarding other areas of Rumania*, the Soviet Government would communicate with Germany. (*3*)

A laconic statement. But a few hours later Schulenburg called on him with Ribbentrop's note. Subsequently Molotov had to inform Schulenburg that Russia had dropped her demands concerning the whole of Bukovina; she was limiting herself to the northern part of that province. He also promised to honor all German interests in the rest of Rumania. (*4*)

[*Bucharest submits.*] Rumania was scarcely in a position to resist. Bewildered by the defeat of France in the West, internally unstable, militarily weak, the crown council decided to submit to the Russian demands, after it was ascertained that neither Germany nor Italy would aid Rumania. The German Minister received instructions from Ribbentrop through a telephone message which reached him by courier when he was in the Royal Palace facing King Carol. It was obvious that neither Britain nor France could assist Rumania; their help was not even asked. The Rumanian parties acquiesced; only the old Professor Iorga argued in the crown council that military resistance should be endeavored. Even Maniu was against war; he, a Transylvanian, foresaw Hungarian demands on Transylvania, and he wished to save the Rumanian armed forces for an eventual conflict with Hungary.

After Ciano had advised the Rumanians to give in, he wrote in his Diary: "In fact, Rumania yields rather sadly, but also with a rapidity worthy of Rumanian traditions as a belligerent people." Surely unjust words, these, from a Ciano: one might well ask what he would have done in a position similar to that of the Rumanians in June 1940.

.   .   .   .

[*The Hungarian and Bulgarian demands: their unexpected support by Russia.*] It was evident that in the wake of the war in the West — where the German occupation of Versailles symbolized the end of the European order created by the Congress of Paris in 1919–20 — Hungary and Bulgaria would press for a revision of the Trianon and Neuilly peace treaties. The Russian move only accelerated these expected developments, especially since the Hungarian and Bulgarian demands regarding Transylvania and the Dobrudja were far more justified than was the Russian ethnic claim to Bessarabia.

As early as October 1939 the Soviet Union intimated to Sofia that she would support Bulgarian claims to the Dobrudja. The Soviet desire to align Bulgaria on her side was great; her aim was to resuscitate ancient, spiritual pan-Slav and Russian imperial tendencies. Molotov told Rosso on June 26 that Soviet-Hungarian relations were also improving (5); he thought certain Hungarian and Bulgarian claims justified; not only the Dobrudja claim but also Bulgarian demands for an access to the Aegean were reasonable, he said. Thus, on the eve of the Bessarabian invasion, Russia hinted to Italy at the partition of Rumania as well as at the partition of Greece.

Mussolini, however, could not go along without the consent of his Axis partner; also, neither King Boris nor the Hungarians were willing to arraign themselves on the side of Moscow. Both Hungary and Bulgaria thought that their pro-German and anti-Versailles past would bring full German support for their claims against Rumania, a former ally of France and at best a neophyte among the pro-Axis nations. But no. On June 18, Hitler, in Mussolini's presence, showed himself unsympathetic toward Hungary as opposed to Rumania (6); King Carol appreciated this situation. He saw that Rumania's fortunes depended now on Hitler; only with German assistance could Rumania continue to exist in the face of Hungarian, Bulgarian, and, eventually, further Russian demands. He decided therefore to turn and run for Hitler's favors — a somewhat disgraceful sight.

[*Germany shows her interest in Rumania.*] From June 26 to July 15 Hitler did not quite know what to do with Rumania. He did not wish to arbitrate between Rumania and her neighbors. But in the meantime Rumania turned a full circle. As early as May 29 the crown council had decided that a "reorientation" was necessary. A general amnesty released thousands of Iron Guardists, who thereupon began violently agitating for a German-Rumanian alliance. A new Rumanian Tatarescu-Gigurtu government conducted affairs in June, and the King profusely assured the German Minister of his sympathy for the ideals of "the new Europe." The Government newspapers conducted a campaign of the basest vituperation against Britain; the cocky German minority and the almost exclusively pro-Nazi heads of the German Evangelical Lutheran church in Transylvania did their share of the work. (7) Came the Bessarabian débâcle. On July 2, the "new orientation of Rumania" was officially announced; Tatarescu praised the Germans and the "new European spirit" in a radio broadcast; the Iron Guardist, Sima, returning from exile in Germany, entered the cabinet as Minister of Religion. A clever and corrupt politician, Manoilescu, who was very friendly with Fabricius, the German envoy, was appointed to be Foreign Minister. Bucharest officially renounced the Franco-British guarantee. The British managers and engineers were dismissed from the Rumanian oilfields and expelled from the country; British and French ships were detained on the Danube; on July 14, Rumania announced her departure from the League of Nations; all this to satisfy a violent and irresponsible segment of public opinion and to appease Hitler. (*8*) On July 7 Hitler said to Ciano that the Hungarians were rash and impatient; he did not wish to intervene in the Hungarian-Rumanian strife. The new Rumanian position nevertheless made him change this attitude. As early as July 1 German bombers arrived at the Brasov (*9*) airfield; on July 15, Rumania requested Germany to send a military mission to "instruct" the Rumanian Army in the methods of modern warfare. At that time, Russian diplomatic overtures to Bulgaria and frontier incidents on the new Russo-Rumanian frontier indicated that the Soviets would be glad to profit from a partial political vacuum existing in a harassed and weak Rumania. Consequently, Hitler decided to accept King Carol's gesture, patch up Rumania's territorial problems with Bulgaria and Hungary, and move into Rumania finally as the guarantor of a new, pro-German and anti-Russian state, whose somewhat diminished but more homogeneous territory would then provide a great strategic garrison area for German troops, whence they could at any time turn northwards — against Russia — or southwards — against Greece or Turkey through Bulgaria. Hitler wrote a letter to Carol on that day, advising him to commence direct negotiations with Budapest and Sofia and assured him at the same time of Germany's interests and efforts to bring about modest and reasonable solutions. (*10*)

[*German mediation.*]   In July, Hitler received the visits of the Hungarian, Rumanian, Bulgarian, and Slovak leaders in succession — a gradual pilgrimage, which, until 1944, was to be characteristic of the "new Europe." Hungarians, Bulgarians and Rumanians argued their own cause, while Hitler listened, without too much interest, in Berchtesgaden; he was preoccupied with the problem of defeating Britain and had little thought to spare for the petty litigations of new satellites. To the Hungarians he advised modesty, to the Rumanians flexibility, especially in regard to the Bulgarian claims, as he feared an eventual Russo-Bulgarian alliance. To the Bulgarians he said that Russia had nothing to seek beyond the river Pruth. On July 20, he told Ciano that he would bring about direct negotiations between Rumania and her neighbors, but he wanted to avoid arbitrating, if possible.

[*Italian arbitration.*]   At the end of the month, Hungarians and Rumanians went separately to see Mussolini. On July 27 Gigurtu and Manoilescu arrived in Rome in newly-designed totalitarian uniforms, and delivered melliferous homage to the Axis and to the "new order"; Ciano wrote: "I received the Rumanians. They are simply disgusting"; the Italian King said that they reminded him of hotel porters in their uniforms, if not bootblacks. Mussolini advised the Rumanians to deal directly with the Hungarians: he told them of Teleki's stand; the Hungarian Premier was willing to make compromises on an ethnic basis. Hungary did not demand all of Transylvania, but only those territories whose majority was inhabited by Hungarians. He also admonished the Rumanians to reach an agreement in view of the dangers of Pan-Slavism — in Yugoslavia the Communists had already made important advances; he finally asked the Rumanian visitors to take drastic measures to eliminate the remnants of Jewish influence in Rumania.

[*Genesis of the Second Vienna Award.*] Thus direct negotiations began between Hungary and Rumania at Turnu-Severin and between Bulgaria and Rumania at Craiova. The first led nowhere; the latter were more fruitful. The tactics of Bucharest were to agree to the limited claims of Sofia and to resist Hungary, if necessary, by armed force. Both nations undertook measures of partial mobilization. Agreement was reached with the Bulgarians by mid-August, and the Turnu-Severin talks broke off on August 24. Carol spoke with an emissary of Göring, saw Fabricius, and decided to ask the Axis Powers to mediate. On August 26, Ribbentrop telephoned Ciano, asking him to come to Vienna where the Second Vienna Award was to be administered.

[*Stalin and the Rumanian troubled waters.*] At that time Russia appeared on the scene again. After Stalin on June 26 dropped his claim to Southern Bukovina due to German insistence, he continued to maintain his interest in developments affecting Rumania as well as the entire Balkan peninsula. On July 29 Molotov invoked the consultative clause (Article III) of the Non-Aggression Pact; he asked Berlin what had been discussed during the visits of the Balkan statesmen to Hitler in the preceding two weeks. In Bulgaria, German diplomacy was already active in opposing Russian influences. Stalin was also aware of Italian intentions. On August 6, Mussolini again planned to invade Yugoslavia and said to Ciano that such an attack must be precluded by an Italian-Soviet agreement: perhaps

Ciano could go to Moscow? While nothing came of this plan, it was clear that Mussolini was aware of the new order of things: Russia could no longer be neglected when dealing with Balkan affairs. The Yugoslav and Bulgar envoys in Berlin, Andrič and Draganov, informed their governments of this newly evolving Russian rôle. Germany, however, was not officially notified thereof until the Second Vienna Award.

During the month of August, the Soviet radio kept sniping at Rumania. Gafencu in Moscow, trying very ambitiously to bring about good Russo-Rumanian relations in his new capacity as Rumanian Minister there, was stunned by daily reports of "frontier incidents." Russian troops were making short sallies into Rumanian territory; Soviet gunboats occupied uninhabited islands in the no-man's-land boundary formed by the rivers Pruth and Danube; monitors fired at Rumanian positions. Yet, Molotov repeatedly told Gafencu that Russia had no territorial designs on Rumania once the Bessarabian issue was settled. Why this military pressure along the border then? On August 29 it was announced that Germany and Italy would arbitrate in Vienna. On the same day, Dekanozov, Assistant Commissar for Foreign Affairs, urgently requested that Gafencu come to see him at midnight, although but a few hours before he had excused himself when the Rumanian Minister requested an interview upon receipt of news from Bucharest reporting strange Russian troop concentrations along the Bessarabian border. Now, in this midnight hour, Dekanozov assailed the Rumanian on the pretext of a minor frontier incident: the Soviet Union certainly could not tolerate such Rumanian "provocations." Next morning — the day of the Vienna Award — an unusually sharp TASS communiqué informed the world about this Soviet "protest" against Rumanian frontier incidents. Russia was showing her teeth again; but why? For a moment it was thought that here again was a play of Russian-German collusion, that the Russian pressure was meant to contribute to an easy Rumanian acquiescence in the German-proposed arbitration terms. This was, however, not the right interpretation; for, on August 31, Molotov protested against the fact that the German-Italian arbitration had not been communicated to the Soviet Union until the last moment; this he regarded as a "violation" of the consultative clause of the Non-Aggression Pact. (11) Ribbentrop later answered in a detailed memorandum, but Molotov again insisted that Germany acted "not quite loyally." This German-Russian dispute concerning the Vienna Award procedure subsided a few weeks later.

Here, then, the first concrete misunderstanding had arisen between Germany and Russia since August, 1939. The show of Russian force, aimed to impress Rumania and Germany, achieved but negative results, for at Vienna, Ciano and Ribbentrop made the Rumanians sign the Award by using the argument of the Russian menace. The Vienna Award was accompanied by a solemn declaration of the Axis Powers to guarantee the new frontiers of Rumania. It was rather apparent that this guarantee was directed against the Soviet Union. Stalin had suffered a diplomatic defeat.

[*The second Vienna Award administered.*]   The new Hungarian-Rumanian frontier in itself was far from perfect. The Hungarians wanted to split Transylvania along a vertical line, annexing mostly contiguous, Hungarian-inhabited territories. Hitler was angry at the Hungarians' "illogical and exaggerated" demands; he used harsh words against them. Finally, Transylvania was partitioned along a fairly straight east-west line; the northern part went to Hungary, with important cities such as Kolozsvár and Nagyvárad. (*12*) The line was slightly indented south-east of Kolozsvár; here was the so-called "Göring Gulf," where Göring's economic interests in this small territory, rich with natural gas, demanded that it remain with Rumania. Altogether 19,300 square miles were allotted to Hungary, with a population of 2,200,000 inhabitants. Hungary had to pay heavily for the new territories: she was now doubly obliged to the Axis by the two Vienna Awards, a fact which the Hungarian Nazi extremists could exploit indefinitely. Furthermore, while Rumania got her guarantee, Hungary had to sign a minority agreement providing for the new status of the German-speaking Hungarians, giving them privileges and rights hitherto unheard of in a sovereign state, permitting them, for example, to join the German Army and the SS instead of serving under Hungarian colors.

[*Its wake: the Rumanian revolution.*]   The cession of Northern Transylvania provoked a violent reaction in Rumania. The Rumanian constitution was suspended; King Carol, after he had appointed a coalition government of Iron Guardists and military figures led by General Antonescu, had ignominiously to flee his country on September 6. The young king, Michael I, was a figurehead, while Antonescu became the Rumanian Duce, "Conductor," announcing that the Iron Guard would constitute henceforth the one and only legal political group, party, or movement in Rumania.

[*Bulgaria; long-range international implications.*] The final agreement with Bulgaria was signed at Craiova on September 7; Bulgaria received the southern part of the Dobrudja, which she had lost in 1913, a territory of 2700 square miles with about 400,000 inhabitants. It is interesting to note that while the Axis preferred the methods of direct negotiations, the Soviet Union openly supported Bulgaria's demands. And, in order to weaken the Axis in the Balkans by any possible means, Britain indirectly associated herself with the Soviet stand by terming the Bulgarian claims reasonable. Bulgaria therefore expressed her gratitude to Moscow as well as to London for their friendly attitude shown during the Dobrudja affair. Although at that time the Yugoslav Minister in Moscow asked Molotov in vain what the Soviet Union would do if Germany entered Bulgaria, and although Soviet coolness toward Britain and friendliness toward Germany continued, it nevertheless may be detected how even in the late summer of 1940, a community of British and Russian interests developed in the cases of Bulgaria, Rumania, and Yugoslavia: a very important development, foreshadowing the decade to come when the fate of the Balkans and south-eastern Europe was to depend on Russia and the Anglo-Saxon Powers, Germany excluded. (*13*) Churchill perceived this community of interests at an early stage; justly, he must have felt that his prophecies were to be proven right: somewhere, some time, Russia and Germany would come into conflict. But Stalin refused to recognize this state of things.

Early autumn 1940: The impasse in German-Russian relations

[*After the fall of France: Stalin and Hitler.*] At the moment when Britain's fortunes had reached the lowest point of her history (notwithstanding 1586, 1756, and 1797) Winston Churchill wrote a personal letter to Stalin on June 25, 1940. He pointed to the danger which the German domination of Europe spelled out for the two remaining Powers on the fringes, Britain and Russia; he was willing, at any time, to consult with Russia. Sir Stafford Cripps carried the letter to Stalin. It remained unanswered.

Stalin received him on July 1: we have two versions of their conversation. One is the version of Cripps' biographer, Esterick; the other is that culled by Professor Langer from the State Department archives. It seems that Cripps overestimated his success with Stalin. Of course, in those days it was a vital matter for the British to convince Washington that Britain had a good chance to pull through — for exactly in those days Washington was hesitating as to whether an American investment in Britain was worth while: was it not an investment in an irrevocably lost cause? According to the American archives, Stalin was "frank and outspoken" with Cripps; he agreed that Germany "was the only great threat to the Soviet Union" but explained that the best Russian policy remained

> ... to avoid conflict with the Nazis. Russia, he alleged, was not aiding Germany more than absolutely necessary, but could not afford to change the existing policy for fear of inviting attack. Prophetically he ventured the opinion that Germany might take Russia on in the spring of 1941, provided Britain had been subdued. Nonetheless, he preferred to run the risk, if Britain went under, of having to fight the Germans singlehanded; for in his opinion the Germans, even if victorious over Britain, would be seriously weakened and the Nazi leaders might in fact find it difficult to persuade the German people to embark on yet another war. (*1*)

Yet Churchill, in his memoirs, remembered this interview as having been of a "formal and frigid character."

Meanwhile the Russian occupation of Bessarabia took place, together with an increasing activity of the Soviets in the Balkans. On July 7, Hitler asked Ciano to let Yugoslavia alone for the moment, for he feared that Russia might intervene there. Ciano noted that Hitler generally avoided speaking of Russia, yet a few indirect remarks indicated his diffidence toward the Soviets. On July 13 the Counselor of the Italian Embassy in Berlin noted that a slowly growing animosity toward Russia was noticeable in German official circles.

On the same day, in order to assure Hitler of Russia's best intentions, Stalin instructed Molotov to hand over to the Germans the memorandum of the conversation he had had with Cripps. (*2*) Suspicion is the mainspring of dictators' minds. While Hitler anxiously watched for signs of a rapprochement between London and Moscow, Stalin feared that Britain and Germany might successfully negotiate a peace. He knew Hitler well; he understood that his German colleague always desired an alliance with Britain, on the condition that Germany got a free hand in eastern Europe. So long as Britain was strong, this was impossible; but now Britain was weak, very weak. Perhaps it was possible, reasoned Stalin. So did Hitler. Neither knew the British. (*3*)

[*Peace rumors and attempts.*]   When, on June 19, Hitler, Mussolini, Ribbentrop, and Ciano met at Munich at the peak of German
might, Ciano was surprised to find a placid Hitler and a peaceful
Ribbentrop. This was not the Ribbentrop who in August 1939 had
told him: "We want war." Now he said: "We want peace" and
embarked on a long discourse upon the necessity of maintaining the
British Empire as a cornerstone of world order. To Mussolini, Hitler
ironically deprecated Russia. A week later, the first in a series of
many official, semi-official, and unofficial German peace proposals
reached London through the Papal Nuncio in Switzerland. On June
28, Churchill refused it in an unmistakable manner. Stalin suspected
how Hitler and Ribbentrop were thinking in those days, and he was
not convinced that Churchill was determined to fight it out to the
bitter end. He could not recover from the surprise of how the armies
of France — Russia's great ally in 1757 and 1914, formidable and
glorious enemy in 1799, 1805, 1812, 1854 — were rapidly defeated
(and how the new French Ambassador to Moscow, Labonne, by a
coincidence presented his credentials in the Kremlin on Compiègne
Day). (4) Anyhow, he marshalled his forces. On June 27, a Soviet
decree introduced an actual seven-day-week in Soviet factories; the
workers' freedom of movement was also severely restricted; the
famous Order No. 1 of the October Revolution was abolished: Soviet
soldiers were now ordered strictly to observe minute distinctions of
rank; officers were to be saluted again; "Mother Russia" and not
the "red proletarian kernel of the world" was the password.

Unofficial German peace feelers continued throughout the rest of
the year. There were talks through Sweden and through the Netherlands Legation in Stockholm; Göring and a Dutch businessman,
Plessen, had interesting contacts which were only stopped later by
the Dutch Foreign Minister in exile, Van Kleffens. (5) Many German diplomats saw some significance in the fact that the Munich
agreement was not officially disavowed by the British Government. (6) On June 25 Alfieri, the Italian Ambassador, approached
the American chargé in Berlin, and the State Department was not
wholly averse to taking steps with the British Government to facilitate
peace negotiations. The American Secretary of War said on July 31
that in his opinion it was possible that Britain might fall in thirty
days. In August, King Gustav v of Sweden tried to mediate; throughout the fall and winter German conservatives — and not only the
anti-Nazi von Hassell but also Hjalmar Schacht and Wohltat of 1939

fame — were probing toward peace through the media of the Swiss Burckhardt and his Finnish friend, Borenius, a resident of London; the mediation of the United States was tried through "Stallforth," an American businessman in Berlin with noted pro-German sympathies. Schacht even went to Hitler and asked permission to go to New York and Washington, where he claimed to have had certain ties with President Roosevelt's circle; but Hitler did not want him to go. It was, then, another segment of the German hierarchy which approached the West. On September 23, Professor Haushofer sent a letter to the Duke of Hamilton, requesting that they meet in Lisbon, but nothing came of this. In December, therefore, Haushofer and Hess prepared the first attempt of the latter to fly to England; this had to be postponed, however.

[*The turning-point of the war.*] These attempts were unfruitful, belated, and unimportant. Although Hitler was master of Europe, his armies ruling the continent and his only antagonist ejected, expelled, punished, Britain was refusing to talk with him. She was, however, willing to talk with Russia, as Churchill's June 25 letter clearly showed. The Russian move into Bessarabia seemed to Churchill a confirmation of the timeliness of his approach. Consequently, he may have sent supplementary instructions to Cripps, for, when the Ambassador called on Stalin on July 9, he made a veiled offer to the Soviets concerning the Balkans; this was an official communication which had not been hinted at in the June 25 letter and which was probably motivated by the significant south-eastern European developments occurring between June 25 and July 9:

> The British Government was of the opinion that the unification and leadership of the Balkan countries for the purpose of maintaining the *status quo* was rightly the task of the Soviet Union. Under present circumstances this important mission could be carried out only by the Soviet Union.

The historical significance of this communication is indeed great; for the first time in history, Britain was hinting at her acquiescence in Russia's overlordship of the eastern part of the continent as the only possible alternative to the German domination of the whole of Europe. That in July, 1940, during her desperate plight, Britain made such a statement — this was understandable; that Britain and America (7) continued this policy in 1943, 1944, and 1945 — this was tragic.

Stalin's falsely pious answer to this communication — carefully handed over to Schulenburg — was this:

> In [Stalin's] opinion no power had the right to an exclusive rôle in the consolidation and leadership of the Balkan countries. The Soviet Union did not claim such a mission either, although she was interested in Balkan affairs.

Thus did Russia refuse to talk with Britain. Ten days later, Britain unequivocally refused to talk with Hitler. This was the turning-point of the war. On July 19, Hitler made his grandiose speech, summarizing the fantastic victories achieved by German arms. While three days before he had given orders to prepare for the invasion of Britain, on July 19, for a last time, he offered peace to the British. They knew what Hitler's "peace" terms would be and how he would keep them. Within twenty-four hours, the reaction of the British press and radio made it clear that Churchill's Great Britain had no intention of listening to what a Hitler had to offer.

Then Hitler asked himself not a technical but a political question: how could Germany remain the master of Europe *without* invading England? He continued invasion preparations, of course. But he did not stake everything on that card; perhaps, deep down, he did not really think that the invasion would be feasible. On June 18 he had said to the Italians that the war would be over quickly; now, on July 20, he foresaw a bloody and long conflict. Two men watched him carefully, anxiously. In these days, Mussolini and Stalin wished that he would not get a favorable answer from the British. Both wanted more war, and they got it, too, each in his own way. But not until the very day of the German invasion of Russia could Stalin bring himself to believe that Hitler wanted to defeat Britain not through the Channel, not through Gibraltar and North Africa, not through Egypt and the Middle East, but through Russia. The peasant logic of Stalin's mind could not imagine that Hitler, whom he respected, could ever make this incredible blunder.

For the blunder was made. Between July 19 and 29, 1940, Hitler made up his mind to invade Soviet Russia.

.   .   .   .

[*First German plans against Russia.*]   At that time there were no clear-cut invasion plans but projects to cover eventualities. Keitel heard of them for the first time on July 22. During the following week, Hitler told his plans to Jodl and Keitel, who convinced him that by no means could Russia be attacked before the spring of 1941 — for Hitler was toying with the idea of turning eastward as early as the fall. On July 29, Jodl ordered the High Command Operations Staff to prepare the first outlines of an operation plan against Russia. The code-name was then *Construction East*. The same day Hitler told General Warlimont that "if it was not his decision, it was at least his intention" to wage war on Russia. Two days later, Hitler spoke to his commanders:

> In the course of this conflict Russia must be disposed of. Spring 1941. The sooner we smash Russia the better. The operation makes sense only if the Russian state is shattered at one blow. A gain of territory is not enough. To have to halt during the winter is a questionable business. Therefore it is better to wait, but the decision to dispose of Russia is definitive.

On August 2 the Swedish Minister to Berlin reported to his government certain military preparations against Russia. Between August 6 and 8, General Halder, the German Chief of Staff, communicated these plans to General Köstring, the German military attaché in Moscow. (*8*) On August 13, Hitler said to Admiral Raeder that he wanted the northern Norwegian fjords strengthened so that a Russian (!) attack against them would be hopeless. Yet he kept the plans for the Russian war within a close circle and did not disclose them to Raeder: a strange diffidence. (In January, 1944, Raeder, who was never convinced of the necessity of a war against Russia and who assessed Russian plans and Stalin very well, wrote a memorandum to his confidant, Assmann: "The Führer described the moving of troops to the eastern front in August [1940] *to me* as a large scale camouflage measure for *Sealion* [invasion of Britain].") Raeder did not quite believe this. On August 14, a Hitler directive cancelled the priority of war matériel deliveries to Russia and ordered that punctual deliveries should be kept up only until the spring of 1941.

On August 3, Winston Churchill mildly rebuked the Foreign Office for having drafted a too flexible — "too clever" — rebuttal of the German peace offer conveyed to London through King Gustav of Sweden: according to Churchill, the British prerequisite for any basis of negotiations was the "restoration of the free and independent life of Czechoslovakia, Poland, Norway, Denmark, Holland, Belgium and above all, France." (It is interesting to note that neither Austria nor the Baltic states were included then.) On August 6, Ciano informed Berlin that the Russians told him of existing "British-German negotiations" (but Ribbentrop "limited himself to declare" to the inquiring Alfieri "that the British are idiots and Churchill a fool"). On that day, Mussolini told Ciano to bring about the mutually desired Italian-Russian rapprochement. But on August 17 a nervous Ribbentrop told Alfieri that Germany did not desire closer Italian-Russian relations; Rome was requested not to engage in talks with the Russians concerning the Balkans. Mussolini abandoned his plan, and on September 7 told Ciano that in his opinion a war between the Axis and Russia was due between 1945 and 1950. (9)

On August 1, Molotov complimented Hitler in a speech; there followed a series of TASS denials of Soviet plans in the Balkans; on August 23, the Soviet press paid a glowing tribute to Germany on the first anniversary of the Moscow Pact. The economic negotiations were also undisturbed. Yet, on August 26 *Abwehr* (German counter-intelligence) passed down an informative directive to the army, which recorded it on September 6:

> The Eastern territory will be manned stronger in the weeks to come. . . . These regroupings must not create the impression in Russia that we are preparing an offensive in the East. . . . The impression is to be created that the center of the massing of troops is in the southern part of the General-Gouvernement, in the Protectorate and in Austria and that the massing in the North is relatively unimportant.

And a High Command directive stated on August 27:

> The present forces in Poland are to be strengthened immediately . . . 10 infantry and 2 armored divisions to be transferred to south-eastern Poland to be ready in case of "intervention" in Rumania.

On September 3, General Paulus, who had no inkling that a little more than two years later he was to be the battered hero of Stalingrad, received orders to prepare in his capacity as Quartermaster-General a logistical plan for the marshaling of 130 to 140 divisions against Russia. The secret could not be held any longer from the Navy; soon the new code word *Case East*, supplanting *Construction East*, began to appear in the documents of the German Naval Command.

At that time an Italian observer in Berlin saw that Germany was going to force a two-front war against her very interests:

> The truth is that war, like every human passion, has the power to make men often turn against their own wills.

[*Diplomatic frictions.*] While the slow and extensively camouflaged eastward movement of German divisions was taking place, Soviet-German relations reached an open impasse. This lasted from August 29 to September 25, 1940. Friction had been negligible during August. But on August 29 it became clear that Russia regarded Axis arbitration in Vienna and the subsequent German penetration into Rumania as a breach of the Moscow Pact. Misunderstandings increased. On August 29, Hitler told Ciano in Vienna that he was very wary of Russian tactics; in his view, Russia was ready to go with Bulgaria and Yugoslavia to the Straits, the Aegean, and the Adriatic. This was perhaps exaggerated in order to persuade the Italians not to make a deal with Russia; but the Soviet protest against the Vienna Award clearly showed that conflicts existed. While on September 5 a minor agreement was signed concerning the evacuation and repatriation of Germans from Bessarabia and Bukovina, on the same day the German Navy decided to abandon its "North Base," which the Soviets had accorded to the Germans in Murmansk. And when Molotov asked Schulenburg why Germany guaranteed Rumania, "You knew that we did not intend to attack Rumania," Schulenburg answered: "therefore"; i.e., that was the very reason. Through Hungarian railroads at night, the silent descent of German troops into Rumania went on. A Russian countermove was necessary. Molotov brought up the question of the Danube Commission again. Russia was now a Danubian state; she had the right to participate in regulating Danube navigation. There were two Danubian commissions: an "international commission" dealing with navigation questions from Ulm to Braila, and a "European commission" responsible for the sector of the delta from Braila to the sea. The Germans proposed a meeting in Vienna to exclude France and Britain from their commission seats, bring Italy in, and merge the two commissions into one. On September 11, Schulenburg was asked by Vishinsky why the Soviet Union was not invited to the Danube commission talks. On September 14, Molotov gave a note to Schulenburg in Moscow and Ribbentrop received a note from Ambassador Shkvartsev (*10*) in Berlin containing a Soviet proposal: there should be a united European commission on which the Soviet Union would have a seat together with the other Danubian states; the non-riparian states, Britain, France and Italy, (*11*) should be excluded. Molotov reminded Ribbentrop that the old commissions had originated with the Paris Treaty of 1856, after the Crimean War.

The note was duly acknowledged and Russia was invited to participate in the discussions which were scheduled to begin in Bucharest in October; this at least was a limited Russian success. Yet, meanwhile, the German military plans went ahead. On September 18 an intelligence report mentioned growing anti-German propaganda within the Red Army; on September 20 a top secret Keitel directive explained to commanders why Germany was sending troops into Rumania:

> Since the Rumanians asked for German instructors and instruction troops, military missions [were sent to Rumania]. To the world their tasks will be to guide friendly Rumania in organizing and instructing her forces. The real tasks — which must not become apparent either to the Rumanians or to our own troops — will be: (a) to protect the oil district against seizure by third powers or destruction; (b) to enable the Rumanian forces to fulfill certain tasks according to a systematic plan, worked out with special regard to German interests; (c) to prepare for deployment from Rumanian bases of German and Rumanian forces in case a war with Soviet Russia is forced upon us. (*12*)

[*Broader visions: the Tripartite Pact.*] On that day Ribbentrop was in Rome; he assured Ciano that Britain was decisively beaten. He brought a surprise: "Japan," which he "had all in his bag." He said then, hinting at the Vienna Award controversy: "The Russian dream vanished forever in the rooms of the Belvedere of Vienna," but he did not think that "Russia will be thrown in the arms of the democracies . . ." Surely there might be complications. "But this does not mean that the Axis intends to or should develop a policy of hostility toward Russia." He and Hitler had in mind a Tripartite Pact among Germany, Italy and Japan, intended to contribute to Britain's defeat and impede the delivery of American help to Britain as well as to divert American public attention and strengthen isolationist sentiment there. The Tripartite Pact was, therefore, in no way directed against Soviet Russia. The Italians consented.

[*Stalin's reactions.*]   While Ribbentrop was unfurling the tripartite banner in Rome, two important events occurred. One was the landing of the first German troops in Finland on September 19; Moscow had been officially notified thereof on the 16th, but the note spoke only of the transport of one anti-aircraft battalion to northern Norway which was to be landed near Haparanda at the northernmost sector of Finland's Baltic seacoast. In reality, the German troops landed at Vaasa and in other ports too; and, after the first transport, others were to follow.

The other event took place in Moscow on the afternoon of September 21. For the first time in many months, Schulenburg was to travel to Berlin and report there in person. Stalin and Molotov knew that his journey would be of utmost importance; German-Russian relations had reached a critical phase. Since early September, the Soviet newspapers, especially the organs of the armed forces, had begun gradually to mention the communiqués of the Battle of Britain and to give limited praise to the war potential of Britain and America. Stalin knew what the German guarantee to Rumania meant; he knew of the slow concentration of divisions in German Poland. Now Molotov received Schulenburg before the latter's departure for Berlin: a long memorandum was handed to the Ambassador, a long explanation insisting that the German procedure in Vienna had essentially violated the Moscow Pact. (*13*) The essence of the note, drafted presumably by that crafty, cautious, canny and consistent man, Molotov, was that Russia would be willing either to abrogate the consultative clause (Article III) of the Moscow Pact or to amend it.

The note, at a time when Germany was not expected to conclude the war victoriously during the year, served its purpose: to impress Hitler with Stalin's determination to be reasonable, but not to bow. If Germany wanted Russia's friendship, she should not try to outflank her in Finland and in Rumania. Schulenburg knew this. He arrived in Berlin at a propitious juncture, when he could convince Hitler and Ribbentrop of the necessity for restoring good German-Russian relations. The invasion of Britain was already partially called off and Ribbentrop faced a double task which would have taxed the resources of far greater men. He had to explain the Tripartite Pact both to the world and to Russia in an unequivocal manner, to make people believe that it was not directed against Russia; he had to soothe Russian suspicions when German troops were moving through Finland and Rumania.

[*Molotov invited.*] Thus Ribbentrop and Hitler made up their minds to negotiate with Russia again. The Tripartite Pact was broadcast to the world on the evening of September 27; it had a special article stating that it was not directed against the Soviet Union, nor did it affect existing relations and treaties between the signatories and the Soviet Union. A day before, Ribbentrop sent a special message to Molotov which explained the Tripartite Pact and added:

> . . . I had taken cognizance of the memorandum handed to Count Schulenburg on September 21 and . . . I intended shortly to address a personal letter to Herr Stalin in which I would reply to the memorandum in the spirit of German-Russian friendship, but beyond that would frankly and confidently set forth the German conception of the present political situation. I hoped that this letter would contribute anew to the strengthening of our friendly relations. Besides, the letter would contain an invitation to Berlin for Herr Molotov, whose return visit we were expecting after [Ribbentrop's] two visits to Moscow and with whom on this occasion I should like to discuss important questions relating to the establishment of common political aims for the future. (*14*)

This met with Molotov's "evident satisfaction." At that time, Russia was carefully sounding out Japan about an eventual rapprochement. If the Tripartite Pact was really directed against the United States, all was well; but first this had to be ascertained. Therefore Molotov insisted that the Pact's full text, including secret clauses, be shown to the Soviet Government in accordance with the often invoked Article III. He also insisted that the text of the German-Finnish transit agreement and its "secret portions" should be given to Moscow. On October 2, a full interpretation of the Tripartite Pact was sent by Ribbentrop, together with the text of the Finnish transit agreement.

[*Suspicions around Rumania.*] The world did not know of these developments. It was suspected that a new Russo-German deal was in the making, but no one knew how things really stood. The Rumanian government asked to be admitted as a co-signatory of the Tripartite Pact, but Berlin (and Rome) had not yet decided whether the Pact would be open to other, minor powers. Europe saw only a series of carefully published TASS denials. Early in October TASS denied that negotiations were going on concerning Russia's adherence to the Tripartite Pact; TASS denied that Soviet-German talks were being held concerning new territorial adjustments in Poland. On October 10, the German chargé in Moscow assured Molotov on Ribbentrop's instructions that the number of the German "instruction units" in Rumania was very small and that their presence constituted nothing but a protective measure against the British. Molotov received this communication dryly and said that "England now had other worries and ought to be glad to save her own life." Nevertheless, on October 15 TASS denied that the Soviet Union was discussing Balkan affairs with Britain, Turkey, Yugoslavia, and Greece, and this denial was accurately counterbalanced by a new one on the following day: "it was falsely reported" that the Soviet Union had been initially informed of the arrival of German troops in Rumania. The last report of an incident on the Russian-Rumanian frontier had been dated September 13; on October 19 TASS denied that there had occurred a Russian-German clash along the Bessarabian border.

[*The invitation accepted: the quadripartite plan.*] These Russian fears concerning her flanks seemed indeed parochial to the Germans. For Ribbentrop's letter to Stalin had invited the Soviet Union to participate with Germany, Italy, and Japan in a quadripartite division of the globe. The date of Ribbentrop's letter was October 13 — the day after Hitler had to issue a directive abandoning his plans to invade Britain during that year. Schulenburg carried the letter to Moscow himself.

On October 21, Stalin answered and accepted this invitation. Molotov was to arrive in Berlin on November 12. The diary of the German Naval High Command noted on October 23: "In view of the current situation, a war with Russia no longer seems probable."

Between October 21 and November 12, however, significant events occurred which greatly conditioned the atmosphere of the forthcoming talks in Berlin. To Stalin it became more and more clear that England was not beaten. The American presidential election amounted to another British victory. Between Stalin's acceptance of the invitation and Molotov's arrival in Berlin, Hitler met Franco at Hendaye, Pétain at Montoire, Mussolini at Florence. All three were friendly and willing to give promises; but Spain was not yet ready, Vichy-France convincingly hesitant, and Italy upset all Mediterranean plans by attacking Greece on October 28. Stalin noticed that Mussolini's rash action in-

conveniently diverted German attention; by the time Molotov arrived
in Berlin, it was also apparent that an easy Italian victory over the
Greeks was out of the question.

True, Stalin was still unwilling to talk with the British. The TASS
denials were proof of that; Russian economic deliveries to Germany
were punctual; in September, a Russian icebreaker cut the way to
the Pacific for a German raider through the perilous Arctic passage.
Cripps was becoming more and more frustrated; on the other hand the
Soviets were adopting friendly tones and gestures towards the United
States and reported news of the Battle of Britain with some objec-
tivity in their press. Hitler continued to be sceptical. On October 4
Hitler told Mussolini at the Brenner that he did not have much faith
in the Russians but that Stalin could not do much in view of the
German armor massed against his western borders. During October
the Quadripartite Plan, sponsored by Ribbentrop, was developing,
and Hitler revealed the plan to Mussolini for the first time in Florence
on October 28: "It has to be admitted that my diffidence in regard
to Stalin is equalled by his in regard to me." But he could not permit
a new Russian penetration into Finland, not only for sentimental but
also for political reasons. He had released five Finnish ships which
had been detained in Bergen, vessels loaded with arms destined for
Finland during the Winter War. (*15*) He had to take care in Rumania
also; that country was completely "demoralized." (*16*) Mussolini
agreed with Hitler, but said that new and closer relations between
Russia and the Axis were indeed necessary. Hitler acknowledged the
truth of this: he added that if the Molotov visit resulted in a new Pact,
this would be not a German-Soviet, but a German-Italian-Soviet
Pact.

These ideas were further expounded to Ciano by Ribbentrop at
Schönhof in the Sudetenland, where the two men met on a hunting-
party on November 4. Ribbentrop explained that he would propose
secret protocols to the Quadripartite Pact, but would not mention
the Balkans, which were purely Axis *Lebensraum*. However, the Black
Sea would be recognized as Russian, and the abrogation of the Montreux Convention, giving Russia and the Axis the right of free passage through the Dardanelles, would also be proposed.

A week later, Molotov set out for Berlin. He arrived there on a
grey, rainy, colorless autumn day; the German capital on such days
leaves doubly bleak impressions on its visitors: the surprisingly large
number of security people accompanying Molotov, the suspicious air

with which they surrounded the delegates and handled their valises did not impress the hosts too favorably. There was no glamor. There was no drama. There was no success. (In Gafencu's words, this was not Tilsit — this was Erfurt.)

Molotov in Berlin

On November 12 and 13, Molotov and Hitler met twice; on two other occasions, the Russian conversed with Ribbentrop.

[*The first day.*] The first meeting took place between the two Foreign Ministers. Ribbentrop embarked on a very long discourse: Britain was beaten, he said; the time had come to divide Europe, Asia, Africa, and Oceania into spheres of influence. What he said about China and Japan met with Molotov's full accord. But,

> Molotov replied that precision was necessary in a delimitation of spheres of influence over a rather long period of time. . . . Particular vigilance was needed in the delimitation of the spheres of influence between Germany and Russia. The establishment of these spheres of influence in the past year was only a partial solution, which had been rendered obsolete and meaningless by recent circumstances and events, with the exception of the Finnish question, which he would discuss in detail later. It would necessarily take some time to make a permanent settlement. In this connection, in the first place, Russia wanted to come to an understanding with Germany, and only then with Japan and Italy, after she had previously obtained precise information regarding the significance, the nature, and the aim of the Tripartite Pact. (*1*)

An hour later, Molotov and Hitler met for the first time. In his usual manner, Hitler began with a lengthy historical-philosophical exposé. He said, among other things:

> In the case of Russia and Germany . . . two very great nations were involved which need not by nature have any conflict of interests, if each nation understood that the other required certain vital necessities without the guarantee of which its existence was impossible.
> . . . probably neither of the two peoples had realized its wishes 100 percent. In political life, however, even a 20–25 percent realization of demands was worth a good deal . . .

Molotov emphatically expressed his agreement. Hitler wound up his very, very long talk, arguing not so much that England was definitely beaten, as had Ribbentrop, but emphasizing rather the need for a new world order of the proletarian nations. Now it was the Russian's turn to speak. He said that Germany gained much from the German-Russian Pact. But he insisted stubbornly that "the Finnish question was still unsolved," and he asked the Führer to tell him "whether the German-Russian agreement, as far as it concerned Finland, was still in force."

He also pointed out that "in the opinion of the Soviet Government, the German-Russian agreement of last year represented only a partial solution. In the meanwhile, other issues had arisen that also had to be solved."

This was a reply to Hitler's offer to "effect an improvement for Russia in the régime of the Straits." But Molotov covered more than just the Dardanelles and the Bosphorus. He insisted that "there were issues to be clarified regarding Russia's Balkan and Black Sea interests with respect to Bulgaria, Rumania and Turkey."

This clarification was his main aim. It must have just dawned on Hitler how land-minded these Russians really were: he was offering them hundreds of thousands of square miles in the Indies, in Persia; and they were haggling over a few hundred square miles and wretched ports in Finland and the Balkans . . . At that moment, when both agreed that the mercenary Anglo-Saxons were to be excluded from Europe once and for all, a few British aircraft were reported flying high above the nocturnal German landscape toward Berlin; thus, necessarily, the talks of the great world deal were postponed until the following day.

[*The second day.*]   The conversation of November 13 between Molotov and Hitler was the decisive event of the Berlin visit. On that day, the Quadripartite Pact vanished into the background; instead, a nervous Hitler was forced by a cold-blooded Russian to abandon history, philosophy, plans in Asia, Africa, the Indies, and wrangle instead for hours about issues such as Finland and Bulgaria.

Hitler argued that Germany had "lived up to the agreements, which was not quite the case on the Russian side," thus reversing Molotov's argument of the previous day. They sparred for half an hour whether in 1939 the province of Lublin had been or had not been just compensation for Lithuania. Molotov reduced the transcontinental horizon of the conversation to indeed pedestrian areas: in rebuttal to Hitler's arguments he asked why Germany did not definitely answer the Soviet request concerning the Kalvarija strip, and then went on to point out that as "Russia had at first confined her demands to Northern Bukovina, under the present circumstances . . . Germany had . . . completely disregarded Russia's wishes in regard to Southern Bukovina."

Hitler rejected the Southern Bukovina claim. He was angry at this parochial Russian attitude, and when Molotov persisted that "the revisions desired by Russia were insignificant," Hitler said:

> . . . the Soviet Government would have to understand that Germany was engaged in a life and death struggle . . .

Were Russia involved in such a war, he would show much understanding. But Finland should not be disturbed. There should be no Baltic war. Moreover,

> . . . much greater successes could then be achieved, provided that Russia did not now seek successes in territories in which Germany was interested for the duration of the war. . . . there was no power on earth which could oppose the two countries.

Molotov said that it was Stalin's particular wish that Germany and Russia should be close allies; however, he had to return to Finland:

> . . . the Soviet Government considered it as its duty definitively to settle and clarify the Finnish question.

At that point, even Hitler began to yield and said that no further troop transports would be sent to Finland:

> . . . the decisive question for Germany was whether Russia had the intention of going to war against Finland.

But Molotov evaded this question. And, in addition to the difference existing between the broad German and the parochial Russian concepts of space, a similar difference was being revealed now in the concept of time:

Hitler

> . . . repeated that entirely different results could be achieved in future collaboration between [Germany and Russia] and that Russia

would after all, on the basis of the peace, receive everything that in her opinion was due her. It would perhaps be only a matter of six months or a year's delay.

Molotov

. . . persisted in the opinion which he had previously expressed: that peace in the Baltic Sea region could be absolutely insured, if perfect understanding were attained between Germany and Russia in the Finnish matter. Under those circumstances he did not understand why Russia should postpone the realization of her wishes for six months or a year . . .

The Russian admitted that

. . . he imagined the [Finnish] settlement on the same scale as in Bessarabia and in the adjacent countries, and he requested the Führer to give his opinion on that.

Hitler replied

. . . there must be no war with Finland, because such a conflict might have far-reaching repercussions.

And Molotov stated that thus

. . . a new factor had been introduced into the discussion by this position, which was not expressed in the treaty of last year.

For a while, Molotov debated with Hitler about Finland and the chances for a Baltic war. In view of the Swedish-Finnish alliance plans, Hitler also asked whether Russia "would declare war on the United States, in case the latter should intervene" through Sweden in a Finnish conflict. Molotov evaded answering, saying that "this question was not of present interest," and Hitler retorted acrimoniously that "it would be too late for a decision when it became so." Whereupon it was Molotov who retreated and said that he "did not see any indication of the outbreak of war in the Baltic." In that case, said Hitler, "everything would be in order anyway and the whole discussion was really of a purely theoretical nature." Now Ribbentrop came to patch up this "agreement"; he, in the background, had been anxiously squirming and waiting for a possibility of adjustment. In a lengthy summary, he made Hitler agree "in principle that Finland belonged to the Russian sphere of influence."

Instead, therefore, of continuing a purely theoretical discussion, they should rather turn to more important problems.

And Hitler continued to draw up plans for the division of the world out of the "gigantic world-wide estate in bankruptcy" after the conquest of England. While he spoke, enraptured, his Russian conversant must have realized how this daydream was the "purely theoretical discussion" and how the, to Russia, "more important problems" were left unsolved and hanging in mid-air. Thus, after Hitler had finished his grand speech of global visions, Molotov confined himself to a Balkan scale and began to enumerate Soviet wishes there:

The Rumanian guarantee of the Axis, which Bucharest had accepted "without consultation with Russia" was aimed against Russia and therefore "the question had arisen of revoking this guarantee."

Hitler answered that this was not possible. That Molotov obviously expected. Now he turned southward. He knew that the Germans were to propose a joint Axis-Russian action to modify the status of the Straits. But did Russia want this at a time when the Italians were in Greece and when, from an Axis-controlled Balkans, Germany could grasp at the Straits? Stalin could control the Straits from Bulgaria, maintain a pressure on Turkey, and at the same time counterbalance the German occupation of Rumania. Therefore Molotov, to condition Hitler psychologically, called the Straits "England's historic gateway for attack on the Soviet Union" and referred to the menace of Britain, who had "now gained a foothold in Greece." For this reason, he asked what Germany's reaction would be

> . . . if Russia gave Bulgaria, that is, the independent country located closest to the Straits, a guarantee under exactly the same conditions as Germany and Italy had given one to Rumania. Russia, however, intended to agree beforehand on this matter with Germany and, if possible, with Italy too.

Furthermore, he

> . . . gave the assurance that the Soviet Union did not intend to interfere in the internal order of the country under any circumstances. "Not a hairbreadth" would they deviate from this.

Hitler parried the issue by stating that Bulgaria would first have to request such a Russian guarantee and that Italy would have to be consulted too. Molotov now argued in vain. The conversation, which had lasted for many hours, was once more directed by Hitler to the great Quadripartite Plan for dividing the British "bankrupt estate." Hitler was now tired. He

> . . . pointed out that he was not, of course, absolutely sure whether these plans could be carried out. In case it was not possible, a great historical opportunity would be missed, at any rate . . .

He envisaged a later conference of the four Foreign Ministers in Moscow. Then the talks were broken off; the hour was late, supper was ready for Ribbentrop at the Soviet Embassy, and air raids were due.

[*The Grand Plan: its secret protocols.*]   Shortly after supper, the sirens sounded; Molotov and Ribbentrop went down to the latter's deep and great air raid shelter. There, if we can believe Stalin, who told this story to Churchill in 1942, Ribbentrop shut the door and said: "England is finished." Whereupon Molotov: "If that is so, why are we in this shelter and whose are these bombs which fall?" At any rate, it was again Ribbentrop who started to talk about the phrasing and meaning of the Quadripartite Pact. He presented a draft of three articles, the two most important passages of which were:

> Germany, Italy, Japan and the Soviet Union undertake to respect each other's natural spheres of influence.

And

> Germany, Italy, Japan, and the Soviet Union undertake to join no combination of powers and to support no combination of powers which is directed against one of the Four Powers.

Ribbentrop brought up two secret protocols. One was to define "the focal points in the territorial aspirations of the Four Countries":

> As to Germany, apart from the territorial revisions to be made in Europe at the conclusion of the peace, her territorial aspirations centered in the Central African Region.
> The territorial aspirations of Italy, apart from the European territorial revisions to be made at the conclusion of the peace, centered in North and Northeast Africa.
> The aspirations of Japan would still have to be clarified through diplomatic channels. Here, too, a delimitation could easily be found.

possibly by fixing a line which would run south of the Japanese home islands and Manchukuo.

The focal points in the territorial aspirations of the Soviet Union would presumably be centered south of the territory of the Soviet Union in the direction of the Indian Ocean.

The second secret protocol was to deal with the abrogation of the Montreux Convention and with the new status of Turkey and the Straits.

Ribbentrop also planned a Non-Aggression Pact between Russia and Japan. This idea met with Molotov's approval. Russia was interested in discussing the Straits question in detail, but her interests, as Molotov had earlier mentioned to Hitler,

> . . . concerned not only Turkey, but Bulgaria, for instance . . . the fate of Rumania and Hungary was also of interest to the Soviet Union and could not be immaterial to her under any circumstances. It would further interest the Soviet Government to learn what the Axis contemplated with regard to Yugoslavia and Greece, and, likewise, what Germany intended with regard to . . . the future form of Poland. . . . The Soviet Government was also interested in the question of Swedish neutrality. . . . Besides, there existed the question of the passages out of the Baltic Sea. . . . As to the Finnish question, it was sufficiently clarified during [Molotov's] previous conversations with the Führer.

Ribbentrop answered that he had no comment other than Hitler's previous refusal concerning Bulgaria. He touched superficially on the other countries mentioned by Molotov, and said that "he felt he had been queried too closely." His most important statement was that "as soon as England conceded her defeat and asked for peace," Germany would withdraw from the Balkans. Germany had, "as the Führer had repeatedly declared — no territorial interests in the Balkans."

The main question was, concluded Ribbentrop, whether Russia was willing to cooperate "in the great liquidation of the British Empire."

Molotov casually hinted at his doubts whether Britain was actually beaten and the war won. However, Russia was willing to collaborate. "A delimitation of the spheres of influence must also be sought." His Berlin visit had been very worthwhile, but he would have to ask Stalin's opinion about the great spheres of influence program.

However, he had to state that all these great issues of tomorrow could
not be separated from the issues of today and the fulfillment of existing agreements. [Again a hint at Finland.] The things that were
started must be first completed before they proceeded to new tasks.

It was mutually reiterated that the conversations had been very useful and then the participants "cordially bade farewell" to each other.
Next day, Molotov left Berlin.

[*The Soviet counterdraft.*] On November 26 the Soviet comment on the draft of the Quadripartite Pact was given to Schulenburg. Soviet Russia accepted the draft "subject to the following conditions":

Provided that the German troops are immediately withdrawn from
Finland . . .
Provided that within the next few months the security of the Soviet
Union in the Straits is assured by the conclusion of a mutual assistance
pact between the Soviet Union and Bulgaria . . . and by the establishment of a base for land and naval forces of the USSR within range
of the Bosphorus and the Dardanelles by means of a long-term lease.
Provided that the area south of Batum and Baku in the general direction of the Persian Gulf is recognized as the center of aspirations of
the Soviet Union.
Provided that Japan renounces her rights to concessions for coal and
oil in Northern Sakhalin.
. . . the draft of the protocol or agreement between Germany, Italy
and the Soviet Union with respect to Turkey should be amended so
as to guarantee a base for light naval and land forces of the USSR on
the Bosphorus and the Dardanelles by means of a long-term base, including — in case Turkey declares herself willing to join the Four
Power Pact — a guarantee of the independence and of the territory
of Turkey by the three countries named.
This protocol should provide that in case Turkey refuses to join the
Four Powers, Germany, Italy and the Soviet Union agree to work
out and to carry through the required military and diplomatic measures, and a separate agreement to this effect should be concluded.

The Soviet draft added three protocols to the two mentioned by Ribbentrop: one dealing with Finland, one with Sakhalin, and one with
Bulgaria.

The Soviet draft was transmitted to Berlin; it never received an
answer.

As Gafencu wrote, in the wake of Molotov's journey to Berlin,

> . . . the charm of the Soviets, so *en vogue* in Germany after the Moscow Pact, just like the Slavic charm in Paris after the Russian Alliance, was gone . . .

[*Signs of German dissatisfaction.*] The impasse soon became evident. While a Foreign Ministry circular ordered all German diplomatic posts to emphasize the friendly character and success of the Molotov conversations, Admiral Raeder recorded as early as the day Molotov left Berlin that Hitler was "still inclined to instigate the conflict with Russia," although the Admiral asked him to put it off until England was beaten. On November 16, TASS denied that Soviet-Japanese political conversations were going on; on December 5, a TASS communiqué stated that good relations between the Soviet Union and China continued to prevail. (This was designed also to reassure the United States, after Sir Stafford Cripps had protested in vain against Molotov's Berlin journey.)

The absence of a new German-Russian agreement became clear to Italy and the Balkans. On November 18, Ciano and Ribbentrop met at Salzburg. Ciano noted that the Germans "did not speak of Russia anymore"; this was a different atmosphere from the hopeful one in which Ribbentrop had received him at Schönhof two weeks before. (2) On November 20, Hitler complained to Mussolini in a letter: it should be tried "with all means" to divert Russia's attention from the Balkans to the Near and Middle East. At the same time, he asked the Italians to help persuade Hungary to permit the passage of more German troops to Rumania, in order to build up a reservoir of German forces there. On the same day, Hungary announced her adherence to the Tripartite Pact (in Parliament, the Conservatives, the Small Holders, the Liberals, and the Social Democrats — Bethlen, Eckhardt, Rassay and Peyer — opposed this step). On November 23, Rumania and on the 25th, Slovakia signed the Pact. (3)

[*Russian manoeuvres refuted: Bulgaria, Rumania, Finland.*] But as early as the 23rd came a thinly veiled Russian move: TASS emphatically denied a report in the German *Hamburger Fremdenblatt* on November 13 (when Molotov was in Berlin), which stated that Hungary's adherence to the Tripartite Pact had been approved by the

Soviets. On November 25 a high Soviet diplomat, Sobolev, appeared in Sofia and requested an audience with King Boris. Sobolev offered a Mutual Assistance Pact; he hinted at Stalin's request to obtain bases in Bulgaria and the prospects of a joint Russo-Bulgarian attack on Turkey, whereafter the Bulgars would receive Thrace and the Soviets the Straits. But Boris, having just returned from a visit to Hitler, was aware of the Soviet plans concerning Bulgaria. He received Sobolev cordially but he courteously declined to sign such a pact, and pointed out Bulgaria's desire to stay neutral (and confidentially informed Ankara).

Meanwhile the Danube conference which had convened in Bucharest on October 28 dragged on endlessly; the Soviet delegates could not realize their claims. Moscow refused a British protest against Russian participation, but even this did not convince the Germans and Rumanians that they should give in to the Soviets, who had already penetrated the Danube Delta beyond the Bessarabian frontier. As Gafencu remarked: "The Danube was for Russia more than a frontier — she was a barrier!" On December 21, the Bucharest conference adjourned without having reached an agreement. Russia, in vain anger, flexed her muscles at Rumania. On January 2, 1941, Soviet torpedo boats appeared before Sulina and fired shots; Soviet attempts to gain possession of a few deserted islands in the Danube Delta by unilateral action continued.

Neither was Russia successful in Finland. Göring wrote a letter to his brother-in-law on November 21, explaining how German-Finnish relations had changed after the Molotov visit to Berlin. With the presence of German troops, the Finnish attitude was stiffening; Russian threats were in vain. (4)

[*The military directive: Barbarossa.*]   While Russia was still unwilling to engage in conversations with Britain or the United States — on December 13, the Soviet Ambassador Oumansky told his Yugoslav colleague Fotitch in Washington that the Soviet policy was "not to be involved in the present conflict" — Hitler (probably against the wishes of Ribbentrop) pushed ahead with his military preparations. On November 29, a German Army directive stated: "No orders are expected in case of *Case East*. At the moment the [possibility of] Russian action against Rumania is dismissed as a trifling matter." But on December 5 the Operations Staffs reported to Hitler about the planned operation against Russia (5); on December 11 planning for *Operation Felix* (against Gibraltar and North Africa) was postponed; on December 13, planning for *Operation Marita* (towards Greece and Turkey through Bulgaria) was introduced and the codename *Case East* was changed to *Operation Barbarossa.*

Directive No. 21 — *Operation Barbarossa* — was issued on December 18:

> The German Armed Forces must be prepared to crush Soviet Russia in a quick campaign . . . even before the conclusion of the war against England.

The document mentioned Rumania and Finland as probable allies "on the flanks." (In December, the Finnish General Heinrichs, who was visiting Germany, was first informed of eventual German support for Finland in case of a war against Russia, and the German General Buschenhagen went to Finland in order to prepare a liaison between the two armies.) The "ultimate objective of the operation" was to establish a "defense line against Asiatic Russia from a line running approximately from the Volga River to Archangel." The document, which was signed by Hitler himself, ended, however, with this warning:

> All orders to be issued . . . on the basis of this directive must clearly indicate that they are *precautionary measures* for the possibility that Russia should change her present attitude toward us. . . . the date of [our preparations'] execution has not even been fixed . . . (6)

On December 27 Raeder spoke to Hitler of "Italy's serious blunders" and said that there ought to be no *Barbarossa* until after Britain was defeated. On December 31, Hitler wrote to Mussolini that he did not put many hopes in Russian sincerity, but that he did not expect a war with Russia so long as Stalin lived; perhaps the remaining points of difference could be resolved: ". . . in fact, the only two questions which still divide us are Finland and Constantinople." (Hitler also complained of Boris, but praised Antonescu.) On the same day, however, the Finnish Minister told Weizsäcker in Berlin: ". . . people in Finland [were] now reassured because they thought that they knew that in a future conflict with Russia they would not stand alone . . ."

[*Russian-Italian plans renewed.*] During the last two weeks of 1940, a short-lived but interesting diplomatic episode opened between Russia and Italy. The reader will remember how in the summer attempts at a Russian-Italian rapprochement were begun and then abandoned upon German requests. On December 13, a surprisingly great number of high Soviet officials appeared together with Molotov at a dinner given by the Italian Ambassador and showed quite unusual cordiality toward their host and his nation. About this same time, the Russian representative at the Bucharest Danube conference was significantly friendly to the Italian delegate, supporting him in various matters. Ciano decided to pick up the handkerchief dropped by Stalin. On December 28 he instructed Rosso to start talks with Molotov at once. Probably due to his ire at Ribbentrop, who never failed to insert into his communications a few acrid remarks about the failure of the Italian military in Greece, Ciano did not notify Rosso that Berlin had not been previously consulted. Rosso called on Molotov on December 29. The Foreign Commissar was very friendly. He asked for continued cooperation in the Danube commission, and the two men discussed such questions as Rumania, Bulgaria, and the Straits. When Molotov asked whether Italy was ready to acknowledge that the Soviets had special interests in the Straits, Rosso answered in the affirmative.

[*Germany intervenes.*] On January 6, Alfieri informed Ribbentrop about the Russo-Italian negotiations. Ribbentrop was in "worst humor" and very angry; he complained that he should have been notified in advance. (The full content of the Molotov-Hitler-Ribbentrop conversations and the extensions in the Soviet draft of the Quadripartite Treaty had never been communicated to Rome by Berlin.) On January 10, Weizsäcker asked Alfieri to the Wilhelmstrasse to receive the German answer to the Italian note concerning the Rosso-Molotov talks, but later in the day the appointment was cancelled, as Weizsäcker was to receive further instructions. Ribbentrop's note, delivered six days later, strongly requested that the Italian-Russian negotiations be suspended at once. (7) When he met Ciano on January 19, Ribbentrop explained that he was most sceptical of the Russians: they wanted Italy's agreement to requests which Germany had already refused them. He asked Ciano to answer Moscow in a dilatory manner and to keep Berlin constantly informed of the general development of Russo-Italian relations. Thus did Germany frustrate Italian-Russian plans for a second time, before the negotiations between Rome and Moscow could advance beyond their preliminary phase.

The Greek War and central-eastern Europe

In the summer of 1940 Mussolini experienced a double frustration. Hitler wrought victories immeasurably greater than his; Mussolini had entered the French campaign with too little, and almost too late. He was halted on the frontier of Egypt. Except in British Somaliland, there were no Italian victories in sight. Italian martial zeal was tempered; it flagged. The second frustration was more acute. Military necessity had forced him to concentrate on the western front alone, but after France was beaten, Hitler asked him not to advance territorial claims. Worried because of the new German policy aimed to "win France's soul," Mussolini feared every rumor of a German-British peace also. As long as Hitler planned to bring Spain into the war and march into French North Africa, all was well; but Mussolini doubted whether this was the main line of German strategy; furthermore, he rightly evaluated the difficulties of such an undertaking, especially with Spain. The Duce therefore plotted to advance against Yugoslavia and Greece again, but in June and again in July Hitler asked him to wait. Italy should temporarily postpone her Balkan projects. Thus did his Axis loyalty limit Mussolini in the Eastern and the Western Mediterranean. And the problems of the two were closely interwoven. They determined his course.

[*The diplomatic offensive.*] Hitler's requests to Mussolini, Ribbentrop's stand against a Russo-Italian Balkan agreement, the new development of Russo-Yugoslav relations, and the Bessarabian invasion definitely bound the hands of Italy in regard to Yugoslavia. With Greece things were slightly different. The first gun of the Italian diplomatic offensive against that country was fired on July 3, on the occasion of the Ciano-Politis interview. On the same day, however, the British showed that, regardless of the French defeat, their Fleet did not regard the Western Mediterranean as a vacuum; Britain crippled the capital ships of her ally at Mers-el-Kebir. It was a Greek tragedy, sad but impressive. While in 1939 Mussolini had said to Ciano that the statesmen of Britain were no longer "made of the same stuff as the Francis Drakes and the other magnificent adventurers who created the empire," Ciano now wrote that "the fighting spirit of His British Majesty's fleet is quite alive and still has the aggressive ruthlessness of the captains and pirates of the seventeenth century."

It was, therefore, in the Eastern Mediterranean that some kind of action was desirable, and on July 6–7 Hitler's talk with Ciano left a door open. Hitler thought it possible that Britain would occupy the Ionian Islands and use them as a base against Italy; he asked Mussolini that nothing should be done against Greece without having previously reached a full agreement with the Yugoslavs. Thus, while action against Yugoslavia was not to be excluded, a carefully prepared diplomatic offensive against Greece, to be followed up later by a military advance, was a possibility. (*1*)

The diplomatic offensive moved ahead. The Italian representatives in Sofia, and in Belgrade, tried to reach a partition agreement among Italy, Yugoslavia, and Bulgaria against Greece. But these first soundings ran into difficulties from the very beginning; taking note of growing British resistance and Russian interests, Yugoslavia and Bulgaria remained aloof. Direct action was necessary. The task was allotted to one leading Italian daily, the *Giornale d'Italia*, which began to attack the Athens government for "British conspiracies"; Italian planes began to fly over Greek territories; the Greek warships *Orion* and *Hydra* were bombed by Italian naval aircraft. Athens remained quiet; the Greek press showed remarkable restraint in commenting upon the war news, and Metaxas even requested the notoriously Anglophile upper crust of Athens to abate somewhat its usual snubbing of the Italian set there; only a certain typographical emphasis manifest in the headlines in the Athens dailies indicated faintly and indirectly where the Hellenes' sympathies lay. This correct neutrality was, however, no defense. On August 1, the Greek Minister in Rome received a severe note complaining of Greek "unneutrality and unfriendliness"; a week later a similar protest followed. Meanwhile Athens was forced to recall the Greek Consul from Trieste because of alleged "anti-Italian remarks"; on August 2, Mussolini told the visiting Manoilescu that Italian-Greek relations were at a delicate stage.

Then it was decided to resort to direct provocations. On August 11, an Albanian newspaper and a communiqué of the Italian Stefani Agency told the world of the "murder" by Greek "bandits" of the Albanian "patriot," Daut Hodja, and two of his comrades in Albanian territory. The charge was fabricated, but its significance was evident. The Italian-controlled Albanian newspapers began a campaign for the "liberation" of the Čamuria territory. On August 15, a brilliant feast day of the Holy Assumption, the population of the small Greek island of Tenos streamed to and fro in the narrow streets

around the church and the flag-bedecked market place. Suddenly a
series of gigantic explosions rocked the harbor. An unknown submarine
had torpedoed the cruiser *Helle*, the pride of the Greek Fleet. She sank
immediately with many aboard; one of the torpedoes narrowly missed
the pier full of Sunday strollers. The black cloud of oil and smoke rising
above Tenos and besmirching the radiant blue Mediterranean sky was
clearly a portent.

[*German reactions.*] Everyone knew that the torpedoes were
fired from an Italian submarine. On August 16 the Italian Embassy
in Berlin was informed by Ciano: ". . . provoked incidents might
bring their fruits in September." (2) About this the German Foreign
Ministry was not too happy. On July 23 and August 9, Italy requested
German consent to the passage of Italian troops through Carinthia
and Styria against Yugoslavia; these requests were first shelved, then
finally refused by Hitler on August 15. On August 17 Ribbentrop
remonstrated with Alfieri, reminding him that Italy had promised not
to attack Yugoslavia while the main task, the defeat of Britain, was
still to be achieved. This remonstration was sourly acknowledged
by Ciano, who on August 18 told his Berlin Embassy that no action
against Yugoslavia was now pending. On August 22, he wrote to
Jacomoni, the Albanian Governor-General, that plans against Yugoslavia and Greece had to be slowed down. The German Minister to
Athens, an old diplomat of the Schulenburg type, von Erbach-Schön-
berg, was friendly to the Greeks; Metaxas was encouraged by the German attitude, and asked Berlin what to do after this Italian provocation. The Greeks were counseled to remain quiet and not to offer a
pretext for Italian action. They did not mobilize, and even refrained
from publishing later the findings of the naval commission, which,
from the fragments of the fired torpedoes, established beyond doubt
that the "unidentified submarine" torpedoing the *Helle* had been
Italian. On August 24, the Greek Minister to Germany was received
by Ribbentrop, who assured him of Germany's friendly feelings.

However, Hitler received from Mussolini an explanatory letter
which patched up diplomatic misunderstandings and explained that
Italy would refrain from doing anything in the Balkans which would
not be strictly of a precautionary character. Probably this letter made
Hitler order his Foreign Minister to assume a more pro-Italian attitude; on August 26, Ribbentrop spoke to Ciano by telephone, telling
him that he had cold-shouldered the Greek envoy. Next day he said

to the Greek Minister, who tried to call on him again: "We regard
Greece as a country which has opted for Britain . . ." On August 28,
Churchill, wrote to President Roosevelt about the requested American
destroyers and supported his request with the argument of "the recent menace which Mussolini is showing to Greece." On August 31 a
brutal article by Gayda of the *Giornale d'Italia* was meant to cow the
Hellenes into submission:

> And if [Greece] wishes in 1940 to recall the glorious memory of Ther-
> mopylae and its spears, we must again remind her that today war is
> waged and won with tanks, aircraft and heavy guns . . .

But the threats of the *Giornale d'Italia* were not enough. On September 19, the Greek "problem" was again presented to Ribbentrop
in Rome by Mussolini and Ciano. Ribbentrop reaffirmed that in
Germany's opinion Yugoslavia and Greece belonged to the Italian
sphere; Germany had no territorial interests whatsoever except for
some Slovene territory around Maribor in Yugoslavia. But the main
effort of the Axis should be directed against England and England
only. When Mussolini heard this, he already knew that there would
be no invasion of Britain in 1940; it was too late. Consequently he
emphasized the need for a Balkan "solution," as "Greece was to Italy
what Norway was to Germany." He had five hundred thousand men
on the Yugoslav frontier and two hundred thousand in Albania; these
were "precautionary measures." Eight days later, Ciano was in Berlin
to sign the Tripartite Pact and noted the absence there of the glittering *Blitzkrieg* atmosphere: the grey, ominous air of a long-drawn out
war set down on the city, there was no longer talk of an invasion of
Britain. Another meeting came on October 4 between Mussolini and
Hitler at the Brenner. The Führer spoke about France and Spain,
and although he castigated the French, it was clear to Mussolini and
Ciano that with Britain left uninvaded, the Germans were compelled
to broaden the Axis into a great anti-British coalition and bring
France and Spain into it. Since the latter was not yet ready to enter
the war (as Suñer's Berlin journey showed), Hitler had to play a little
private game for Pétain's sympathies, a development which Mussolini
feared. He was happy that not a word was spoken of Greece during
the Brenner meeting; the lack of a reiterated German request for continued Balkan tranquillity seemed to free his hands.

[*The October 15 council.*]   His final decision to attack Greece
was therefore made some time between October 4 and October 15,

1940. The Duce was irritated by German high-handedness; just as with Albania in April, 1939, he wanted to show that he was an equally important warlord and European master. Then it had been the German march into Prague which made him finally decide to "compensate" with Albania; now his final decision was provoked partly by French, partly by Rumanian developments. At the end of September Ribbentrop asked Ciano to intervene with the Hungarians, who seemed dissatisfied with the Vienna Award, and Ciano promised to do this. Then, when Mussolini returned from the Brenner, he learned of the impending announcement of the arrival of German "instruction units" in Rumania. Here was another accomplished fact, another country taken by Hitler without having consulted him previously. Mussolini also heard that the German Consul in Tirana had spoken deprecatingly about the Italians; Rome asked for his recall. On October 10, Ribbentrop reported to Rome that Hungary wanted to join the Tripartite Pact. If so, retorted Mussolini, then the Rumanians should join the Pact too. The Italian Minister to Bucharest was instructed to emphasize Italian interest in Rumania's welfare; Mussolini wished to solicit a Rumanian invitation of Italian "instruction troops" also. (A few Italian Air Force officers were quickly sent to Bucharest.) On October 12 Mussolini said to Ciano: "He [Hitler] will find out from the papers that I have occupied Greece." The council of war met on October 15.

After having heard the reports of Jacomoni and of Visconti-Prasca, the commanding general of the Italian Army in Albania, it was decided to attack. According to Visconti-Prasca, superiority was about two to one on the side of the Italians. (*3*) The objective of the campaign was then discussed. By a strange irony of fate it was Badoglio who explained that in order to assure command of the Greek peninsula against British invasions, the whole of Greece should be occupied (previously more limited war aims were planned). (*4*) Mussolini wound up the discussion: he commanded that the invasion of Greece was not to be postponed after October 26, even by an hour.

[*Greece: her army and neighbors.*]   Greece was meanwhile in a state of half-preparation. Her mule-drawn artillery and small army was put toward the Albanian frontier, but there was no real mobilization, not least because of diplomatic reasons. Strict neutrality was proclaimed and preserved; on September 30, British planes made an emergency landing in Crete, and General Metaxas forbade local authorities to permit the planes to take off again: the airmen were interned. Greek diplomacy was anxious to secure the good will of the northern neighbors because Belgrade and Sofia told Athens of the Italian overtures; it was clear what an Italian-occupied Greece would mean to Yugoslavia and Bulgaria. Turkey felt somewhat comforted by this Balkan solidarity; in September she proposed a common defensive front with Yugoslavia and Bulgaria, if necessary, confirmed by a military alliance. But Prince Paul and Boris knew that this would incense Hitler and Mussolini (and perhaps also Stalin), and Turkey's valiant offer was not accepted. On October 13, the Greek Minister in Budapest wired Athens that he had authentic information of an impending Italian attack on Greece.

At the October 15 meeting, Mussolini said that Yugoslavia and Turkey would "keep quiet," but he added that "Bulgaria can play a part in our game . . . ," due to Bulgarian aspirations in Greek Macedonia and her long-desired access to the Aegean in Western Thrace. He sent a personal letter to Boris on October 17, but Anfuso, his messenger, reported from Sofia on the 19th that Boris was clever and "evasive"; he said that due to technical factors he could not attack Greece.

On the same day Mussolini wrote Hitler (he obviously had decided that it would nevertheless be better if the Germans were not to "find out from the papers") and informed him of the Greek War. But the letter did not reach Hitler, who was setting out on a circular journey to meet Franco at Hendaye and Pétain at Montoire. The letter wandered after the Führer and reached him only after Montoire. Consternation was great. (5) Hitler urgently asked Mussolini to meet him at Florence on the morning of the 28th. On August 25, 1939, partly due to Mussolini's message, Hitler postponed his Polish invasion plans by six days; now the Italian postponed the Greek War by two days — but no more — as he waited impatiently for Hitler's delayed answer. Yet nothing could have stopped him from attacking Greece, especially at a time when the seemingly cordial Hitler-Pétain talks added to his worries. And, when Hitler arrived in Florence, the world got the false impression that a prearranged war council of the Axis chiefs was taking place there; for on that morning, Italy had already attacked Greece.

[*The attack.*] The war preparations were so secret that the Italian military attaché in Athens did not hear of them until October 23, when an Italian airline pilot touching down at the Athens airport told him that war was impending. The attaché and the Italian Minister, Grazzi, were sceptical; they had been saturated with false rumors for months. The Italian governorship of the Dodecanese Islands and Italian counter-intelligence organs in Albania were constantly being fooled by "agents" claiming to have corrupted high Greek military men and producing absolutely baseless information, most of which was conjecture and mere prevarication. Into this comic-opera atmosphere burst a melodramatic Italian communiqué on October 26, reporting that "Greek and British agents" had made a bomb attempt in Santi Quaranta (which the Italians had named Porto Edda after Mussolini's daughter). Also "serious frontier incidents" were mentioned. The Greek General Papagos immediately protested to the Italian military attaché and demanded a rectification of these false statements. By that time, however, the war was but a question of hours.

These last hours are still debated by Italians and Greeks. On the evening of October 27, a reception was given by the Italian Legation in Athens in honor of a Puccini production. Some Greeks maintain that the reception was a deliberate and dishonest Italian attempt to deceive the Greek Government, just as the German Minister to Norway staged a reception in Oslo on the evening of April 8, 1940; the Italians, on the other hand, say that this social event, planned and announced long before the Legation had had an inkling of the war plans, could not simply be called off. Thus the reception took place, the guests placidly conversed with the hosts, and quite a few noticed a symbol of friendship, a large chocolate cake, whose icing was adorned with sugared letters: "Viva la Grecia." However, as Mondini writes, the hosts thought it best not to cut the cake.

The final instructions and ultimatum text arrived from Rome at midnight. In the quiet night, Grazzi descended into an automobile and raced through the dreamy Attic plains to the residence of Metaxas, where, then, the crowning act of the melodrama took place. The Greek Premier appeared in a dressing-gown, sleepy, rumpled, disturbed. It was a perfect *petit-bourgeois* scene. Metaxas greeted Grazzi with surprise: "Oh, Mr. Minister, how do you do?" His surprise increased when Grazzi read to him the impossible terms of the Italian "ultimatum." It was scarcely an ultimatum, as there was no practical time limit set; Metaxas had to answer within three and a half hours. The Greeks claim that he rejected the ultimatum proudly, and the

word "no," *ochi!*, appeared as a defiant gesture on the white walls of
Greek houses throughout the war. The Italians maintain that Metaxas
wanted to consult with King George and was disturbed mainly because the ultimatum had left him practically no breathing-space for
that. In any case, he rejected it.

[*The military surprise.*] The Italian plan was to advance
through Ioannina and northern Epirus onto the plains. They did not
even reach their first objectives. While the Italian Air Force conducted
hit-and-run expeditions against Athens (followed by ridiculously boast-
ing communiqués), the Army, despite its numerical and air superiority
(in October 1940, Greece had but 140 planes, most of them antiquated
French Potez types), was defeated. The Third Alpine Division was
beaten in the Pindus Mountains and by the middle of November, the
Greek Army crossed into Albania. Koriza fell on November 22; before
winter made large-scale operations impossible, General Papagos' sixteen Greek divisions pinned down about thirty Italian ones. Argiro-
castro, Pogradetz, Tepelini, Delvino, and Santi Quaranta fell to the
Hellenes; British planes bombed Durazzo and Valona; on December 6 Marshal Badoglio resigned from his position as Chief of the
Italian General Staff.

[*Other Italian defeats.*] These events had their natural impact throughout central-eastern Europe. Italian prestige fell low.
Nor could the Germans hide their feelings. On November 9, a few
old torpedo-planes of the British Mediterranean Fleet Air Arm attacked the Italian naval base of Taranto in a daring raid in which
battleships and cruisers were sunk; the pride of the Italian Fleet was
crippled. Added to these misfortunes, the British established themselves in the harbors of Crete and began to build a great base in the
well-protected Suda Bay there. From a few Greek airports — the
Greeks were cautious not to ask too many British into Greece, wishing to impress the Germans with the isolated character of the Italo-
Greek War — the RAF could harass Mediterranean shipping.

[*Hitler's anger.*] It was evident that the Italians had made
a mistake: Hitler was angry at Mussolini and called the Italians
"foolish": at best, he said, they should have attacked Crete and not
invaded Greece from the north. Hitler told Molotov that he did not
like "Italy's war against Greece, as it directed forces to the periphery

instead of concentrating them against England at one point." On November 19, Hitler addressed a remarkable letter to Mussolini:

> Duce! Allow me at the beginning of this letter to assure you that my heart and my thoughts have been in the last fourteen days, more than ever, with you. Be further assured, Duce, of my determination to do all what I can in the present situation to be of aid to you. When I asked you to receive me in Florence, I began the journey in the hope that I could make my thoughts known to you before the threatening conflict with Greece, of which I had received only general knowledge.
>
> I wanted to ask you first of all to postpone the battle, if possible, to a more favorable time of year, in any case, however, until the American presidential election.
>
> In any case, however, I wanted to ask you, Duce, not to undertake this battle without a previous lightning-like occupation of Crete, and for this purpose I wanted also to bring along . . . a German parachute division and a further airborne division. . . . Yugoslavia must become disinterested, but if possible . . . cooperate in cleaning up the Greek question. Without security on the part of Yugoslavia, no successful operation in the Balkans is to be risked.
>
> I must, however, unfortunately observe that conducting a war in the Balkans is not possible before March. Therefore, any threatening move towards Yugoslavia would be useless, since the impossibility of a materialization of such threats before March is well known to the Serbian General Staff. Therefore, Yugoslavia must be won, if at all possible, by other ways and means . . . (6)

Hitler repeated the same arguments to the visiting Ciano on the same day. Then he had a wonderful idea:

> Do you think that Mussolini would be willing to make a Yugoslav Pact based on three points: Axis guarantee for Yugoslavia's frontiers; Salonika offered to Yugoslavia; the Adriatic coast of Yugoslavia demilitarized?

Ciano thought that Mussolini would agree, for Rome was now anxious to secure her flank, and afraid of Yugoslavia. Whereupon Hitler replied that if Mussolini were willing,

> I am sure that we can make Yugoslavia join us. . . . Yugoslavia should have Salonika, Bulgaria, her outlet to the Aegean and Italy the rest of Greece.

Mussolini agreed of course. On November 22, he answered Hitler's letter: "I had my black week, but the worst is over." (His answer, full of pedestrian excuses, was called "an ignoble document" by Simoni.) But the Yugoslavs did not agree, and all was not well in the Balkans.

[*Yugoslavia's position.*] Yugoslavia declared her neutrality in the Greek-Italian War on November 1. (According to a document allegedly in the possession of the Yugoslav politician, Knežević, on October 28 a council at Regent Paul's was considering a Yugoslav occupation of Salonika.) Yugoslav public opinion was strongly pro-Ally and becoming increasingly pro-Soviet; the popularity of the régime and of Prince Paul was very weak now. In early November, Italian planes bombed the Serbian city of Bitolj, which they mistook for Florina; despite Italian apologies, anti-Italian feelings were bitter. (7) In regard to Yugoslavia, Berlin and Rome acted independently of, nay, somewhat jealously of each other. German economic pressure was put on Belgrade: Göring tried to extend his economic empire into the Balkans with the aid of persons of dubious character, first among them his Belgrade "emissary," Neuhausen, whom Kordt aptly called "a bankrupt German purchasing agent."

[*The Soviets.*] The Soviet attitude concerning the Greek War was cautious, but not unfriendly to the Hellenes. On November 1, TASS denied a report that Soviet aircraft had been offered to Greece; later, however, the Russian authorities showed surprising cordiality to Greek purchasing agents in Russia; the Soviet press gave limited but nevertheless significant space to the Greek communiqués of military successes. The Italians noticed this; as a prelude to the subsequent attempts at direct Soviet-Italian talks, Ciano ostentatiously appeared in person at the reception which the Rome Soviet Embassy gave on November 7, 1940, the twenty-third anniversary of the Bolshevik Revolution.

[*Rumanian troubles.*] The growing prestige of Soviet Russia and the returning prestige of Great Britain were important developments, when the Nazi cause was further weakened by internal troubles in Rumania. There Antonescu, "Conducator," ruled, heading generals and Iron Guardists, a constellation which he named the "National-Legionnaire" régime. But it soon became clear that the Iron Guardists were as irresponsible when they ruled as when they were underground. They infiltrated into army and police, extorted bribes by threats of assassination, conspired among themselves and against Antonescu, and came very close to plunging Rumania into complete anarchy. In November, a double disaster rocked Bucharest. First, an unprecedented earthquake shook the city. Then, a mixed "police" force of Guardists and terrorist storm troopers swept through Bucharest on the pretext of "curbing the Jews," and while many Jews were killed, the Iron Guard took this favorable occasion to revenge themselves on their former political opponents. Many Liberals, Conservatives, Carolists were murdered in cold blood, among them the historian and former Prime Minister, Iorga. It was now clear to Antonescu that sooner or later he would have to curb the "Legionnaires." He succeeded in convincing the Germans — who, because of their economic and military interests in Rumania, needed stability there more than anywhere else — and gradually began to restrict the Guardists. At the end of November Antonescu visited Rome and complained there against the Vienna Award. This was the first act in a subtle diplomatic game which he was to continue until 1944: he wanted to convince the Axis that he was the most faithful ally, much more so than Hungary, and thus obtain aid or, at least, silent permission to eventually revise the Award and regain Northern Transylvania.

[*Boris' quandaries.*]   King Boris visited Hitler on November 18. When he returned to Sofia, he was confronted with a Russian request for a pact and eventual leasing of naval bases; he refused; on the other hand, he also refused to attack Greece, in spite of continuous Italian requests. As long as he could, Boris tried to curb pro-German extremists: the pro-Nazi Tsankov was defeated in the Bulgarian Parliament by Filov and Popov in December. Churchill foresaw that due to the impact of the German armies assembling in Rumania, Bulgaria would have to give in sooner or later. (*8*) On November 26, Churchill told the Foreign Secretary to try to bring about a Turkish-Yugoslav alliance which would move against Bulgaria if the latter became hostile to either of these two or to Greece. Nevertheless, Churchill did not wish to provoke the Germans into offensive action. On November 27, he wrote to Halifax:

> I should not like these people in Greece to feel that, for the sake of what is after all only a parade, we had pressed them into action which could be cited by Germany as a justification for marching . . .

While Eden (then Secretary of State for War) deliberated with General Wavell whether, in case of necessity, troops from the British Army of the Nile should be withdrawn for Greece or not, the British armed forces in Greek metropolitan territory were being kept at a minimum upon the request of the Greek government; only air and naval cooperation (9) proceeded without limitations.

[*Mussolini's crisis: his request for German intervention.*] The world press described in detail the amusing spectacle of Italian prisoners-of-war in the streets of Athens, shouting words of admiration, "*Bella Grecia!*" and saluting half-humorously, half-seriously, the strolling British sailors and airmen; Mussolini was immensely worried because of the loss of his prestige. The Vichy press took a certain quiet satisfaction in his misfortunes; only his loquacious friend, Serrano Suñer, remained loyal (he also requested the recall of the Greek Minister to Madrid, who had made a few jesting remarks about the Italians). On December 4, Mussolini urgently asked Alfieri to come to Rome and there told him to request Hitler's intervention. The scene, with typical Latin theatricality, is described by Alfieri:

> I found the Duce extremely broken down, such as I never saw him before. His face was pale and drawn, his eyes swollen and tired, his expression sad and preoccupied. He looked even more depressed as he wore a shirt with wilted collars, excessively large, and had a beard of two or three days.

Mussolini was ready to ask the Germans to mediate between Greece and Italy. Ciano convinced his eternally hesitating chief that to ask Ribbentrop to "mediate" at that juncture would be worse than to ask Keitel to direct the Albanian war. Hitler was somewhat moved and proposed a meeting with Mussolini for the next week. However, war news was better the next day and Ciano could convince Mussolini to postpone the meeting. Thus, when Alfieri, back in Berlin, called on Ribbentrop on December 8, his request was not diplomatic but military. He asked that the German armies make movements in the direction of Greece. Ribbentrop retorted that this was impossible; when Alfieri asked that perhaps Germany could exert pressure on Bulgaria in order to procure the mobilization of the latter, Ribbentrop answered that this also was out of the question. However, Ribbentrop did say that he expected the adherence of Yugoslavia to the Tripartite Pact with but little delay. (He could not refrain from adding in an acid manner that the delay was surely due to the "Italian-Greek situation.") Yet, Yugoslavia's signature was far from being as imminent as Ribbentrop envisaged it. Instead, the Yugoslavs negotiated a Non-Aggression and Friendship Treaty with Hungary.

[*The Hungarian-Yugoslav Pact.*] The Pact between Budapest and Belgrade was signed on December 12. To the world it seemed that it was truly an indirect move of Hitler's: Kordt records that the pact came into existence "at Hitler's inducement," and Churchill expresses a similar opinion in his memoirs. But Teleki and Tsvetković had more subtle designs. Both had just cracked down on their local Nazis; both watched Germany with anxiety. Both regarded the Yugoslav-Hungarian Pact as a preliminary move toward a later neutrals' *bloc*, together with Bulgaria and Turkey and, possibly, Greece, after the Greek War — not unlike the Finnish War — ended with a negotiated peace treaty. On December 15, Tsintsar-Marković assured the anxious Yugoslav Minister to Washington that the pact with Hungary was not quite in accordance with Axis designs and wishes.

[*Operation Marita.*] Notwithstanding all this, on December 13 the plan for *Operation Marita* was set up in Berlin. The German directive left the question of Yugoslavia's future position unanswered, while it spoke of the gradual transformation of Bulgaria into a base from whence the German Army could attack Turkey or Greece.

At the same time, General Wavell routed Graziani at Sidi-el-Barrani; Italian armor in North Africa was wrecked, and the British were pursuing Mussolini's hastily retreating legions. The Libyan campaign had a great effect on the Balkans; yet, paradoxically, British victories contributed to the doom of Greece. While the German Minister in Athens continued to be correctly neutral (on December 20 he conversed with Metaxas himself, and the Minister's wife participated in Greek Red Cross activities), it was daily more evident that Hitler would strike against Greece at a propitious time. He made up his mind some time after Christmas. His decision was expedited by the hesitancy of Franco, which temporarily bound his hands in the western Mediterranean. Now, for once, Spanish duplicity and the uncertainties of Vichy-France worked in Mussolini's favor. In his December 31 letter Hitler wrote Mussolini that he was dissatisfied with Franco, who would not give a precise date for Spain's entry in the war; he, Hitler, had had his troops ready to enter Spain in January and planned to invest Gibraltar in February. At the same time, General Jodl conferred with an Italian military mission in Berlin and told them that in March Germany would attack Greece.

Thus ended the year 1940 and the Greek drama developed into a Balkan tragedy.

The Germans in Bulgaria

The first diplomatic event of the year 1941 was the journey of the Bulgarian Premier, Filov, to Germany in the first week of January. The Filov-Hitler conversations were decisive. Previously King Boris had bided his time with German offers, refused Russian enticings firmly but in a friendly manner (*1*); he tried to satisfy Hitler without incurring the wrath of Churchill (and Stalin). While German troops in Rumania were few, and so long as they performed the function of a thin but significant protective screen facing the incalculable Soviets, Bulgaria's neutral position could be maintained. But when the Filov journey took place, it became more and more evident that Rumania was to be a springboard instead of a screen, a springboard whence the German armies could jump southward and reach the Aegean in one gigantic leap. In-between lay Bulgaria.

[*Bulgaria consents.*] Forty German staff officers were sent to Bulgaria as early as December 8 to prepare a German advance through that country; a suspiciously great number of German businessmen applied for and received tourist and business visas; in early January there were almost half a million German soldiers in Rumania, and the number of German agents in Bulgaria increased correspondingly. Boris and his ministers welcomed the staff officers indifferently. Boris could hardly refuse the Germans' military demands; and public opinion was not uninterested in the prospects of a German-Bulgarian advance on Salonika and Western Thrace, which would mean regaining the Bulgar outlet to the Aegean, lost since 1913. On January 3, Filov half-heartedly and orally agreed to Ribbentrop's request for the passage of German troops and said that shortly Bulgaria would consider joining the Tripartite Pact nations. On January 5 — belatedly — the Italian Embassy in Berlin was informed of the Ribbentrop-Filov accord.

Very soon afterwards a significant strategic move was made, when around January 10, German troops began to cross the Danube in

Rumania over the great Cernavoda bridge. The Danube forms most of the Bulgar-Rumanian frontier, except in the Dobrudja, where the borderline continues in an approximately straight line to the Black Sea coast while the Danube turns northward. It was here that the German crossing took place: an unmistakable evidence that the troops were ready for a southward march after covering the full length of the Bulgar-Rumanian border.

On January 19 an important Hitler-Mussolini meeting took place at the Obersalzberg. For the first time since October, Hitler could promise Mussolini military support (at that time, Bardia and Tobruk had been lost to the British and Derna and Benghazi were about to fall). Mussolini knew already that Hitler would support him in Greece. Thus the atmosphere of the conference was pleasant. Ribbentrop reported that "difficulties" in Bulgaria, which were primarily due to the temperament and certain pro-British sympathies of Boris, had been overcome; at the end of February Bulgaria would adhere to the Tripartite Pact. Turkey would not interfere, said Ribbentrop, "but if yes, a word of the Axis to Moscow would be sufficient to make Turkey disappear from the map." He was not particularly worried about Yugoslavia.

Hitler also assured Mussolini that there was nothing to fear from Yugoslavia or from Turkey. Mussolini asked him not to send German troops to Albania, but rather to North Africa. This Hitler promised, adding that, due to technical difficulties, German military action against Greece would not be possible before the end of March.

[*The Rumanian revolution.*] There remained an urgent issue which required discussion; this was the Iron Guard revolution in Rumania. On January 19–20 the four month-old Iron Guard-military coalition came to an end. Antonescu cracked down on the Iron Guardists, after having learned of an imminently pending Legionnaire *coup d'état.* For three days violent civil war raged in Rumania, accompanied by the usual political assassinations, lootings and minor pogroms. On January 22, Antonescu had the situation firmly in hand. The Iron Guardists were crushed; their leader, Horia Sima, fled to Germany. This was one of the rare occasions during the war when German action was dictated by factors of purely military expediency, superseding politico-ideological factors. The German commanders needed peace in Rumania, and it could have been very detrimental to their Balkan campaign plans to base their armies in a country seething with revolution and agog with the wildest social experiments. Local German commanders helped Antonescu in the civil war, in Brasov, for example, where a German major was killed during the street fighting and where the radio station was held by the Legionnaires for five days. More important was the personal sympathy which Hitler had for Antonescu. The Roman profile and almost Prussian-like military bearing of the "conducator" deeply impressed Hitler in 1940, who had previously thought of Rumanian statesmen in Carolist clichés only. (2) He told Antonescu to deal with the Guardists as he had done with Röhm and the SA in 1934; and there certainly was a parallel here. (Throughout the war, Hitler believed in Antonescu — even when German intelligence told him of Antonescu's armistice attempts. Himmler, on the other hand, supported Sima to the bitter end.) Mussolini asked Hitler whether Antonescu might have been too harsh with the Legionnaires, but Hitler heaped scorn on them and said that he had full trust in Antonescu. (It is indeed strange that, notwithstanding differences on the ideological scale, Mussolini, throughout the Balkans, toyed with the explosive idea of supporting the wild extremists, Pavelič, Sima, and the like while the Germans often considered men like Stoyadinovič and Antonescu to be their main assets.) (3)

Dated January 29, 1941, the concrete results of the Obersalzberg talks appeared in the planning papers of the German High Command: next to the final plans of *Operation Marita* (Bulgaria), *Operation Sunflower* (transport of German troops to Tripoli) was mentioned, and also *Mountain Violet* (transport to the Albanian front).

[*Russia disturbed.*] Molotov was waiting for the Italian answer to his suggestions concerning a Russo-Italian Balkan understanding, (4) as reports of the German troop movements in Rumania began to accumulate. The Germans themselves had no intentions of concealing these movements. On January 7, a limited Foreign Ministry circular advised German envoys to emphasize that the movements of the German forces were directed against possible British actions in Greece.

The Russian Minister in Sofia now tried to gain some information about the Bulgarian position after the Filov journey, or rather, he tried to win a Bulgarian reassurance and commitment to further neutrality. But he did not succeed. Therefore on January 12, TASS "denied" alleged reports that the Soviet Union had given her consent to the arrival of German military units in Bulgaria. Molotov and Stalin waited for the reaction, but this was faint: the German press reproduced the TASS communiqué without any comment. On January 13 Boris met Hitler again. On January 17, a Soviet protest note was delivered in Berlin.

The Russian memorandum took cognizance of "all reports" according to which Germany was "prepared to march into Bulgaria, having as [her] goal the occupation of Bulgaria, Greece and the Straits." It mentioned the chances of a British-Turkish countermove which would "turn Bulgaria into a theater of operations," and added:

> The Soviet Government has stated repeatedly to the German Government that it considers the territory of Bulgaria and of the Straits as the security zone of the USSR and that it cannot be indifferent to events which threaten the security interests of the USSR. In view of all this the Soviet Government regards it as its duty to give warning that it will consider the appearance of any foreign armed forces on the territory of Bulgaria and of the Straits as a violation of the security interests of the USSR. (5)

On January 20, a speech by Stalin was reported by German Naval Intelligence, in which the Soviet leader was supposed to have said: "The international situation is complicated and confused, even Russia is threatened by war." That day, Hitler told Mussolini that "a *démarche* of the Russians on account of our massing of troops in Rumania has taken place and will be duly rejected." Then, hinting at the winter conditions, he pointed out that the Soviets "always become insolent at a time when they cannot be harmed. . . . As long as Stalin lives, there is probably no danger, he is intelligent and careful . . ." (6)

On January 22 and 23, the German answers were handed to Dekanosov and Molotov, stating that the German troop movements in Rumania were aimed solely to impede British plans and that this was also to the interest of the Soviets. Dekanosov and Molotov repeated that Russia considered Bulgaria to be within her "security zone." Molotov sourly acknowledged the facts: he "understood the communication of the Government of the German Reich to mean that the transit of German troops through Bulgaria was in itself a matter that was definitely decided on, but only in the event that England should expand her military operations on Greek soil beyond their present scope." On January 25 the German Twelfth Army in

Rumania was made ready to cross into Bulgaria at twelve hours' notice; secret German-Bulgar staff conversations were taking place in Predeal, for the Bulgars had requested that the Rumanian mountains would be preferable for security reasons. Presently there was another Bulgar request: that the Germans should be ready to advance rapidly along the Bulgarian sea-coast, to forestall an eventual Russian move on Varna which Sofia suspected.

[*Churchill's Balkan plans.*]   Churchill overestimated the Russians' pluck:

> Fear only will restrain Russia from war [against Germany], and perhaps a strong Allied front in the Balkans, with the growing prestige of the British Army and sea and air power, may lessen that fear. But we must not count on this,

he wrote in a memorandum on January 6. (7) Greece and spring in the Balkans preoccupied him:

> It is quite clear to me that supporting Greece must have priority after the western flank of Egypt has been made secure (to General Ismay on January 6).

And,

> Destruction of Greece will eclipse victories you have gained in Lybia (to General Wavell on January 10).

Wavell and Air Chief Marshall Longmore flew to Athens on January 13 and conferred with Metaxas and Papagos; the Greeks insisted that Britain should not land troops in Greece until a sufficient number could be sent to eventually counterbalance a German onslaught. Churchill agreed. He had to shelve (just as he did later, in 1943) a plan of wresting Rhodes and the Dodecanese from the Italians. On January 31 he proposed to the Turkish President that Britain be permitted to take the same measures in Turkey which the Germans were taking in Bulgaria, that the Royal Air Force be allowed to use Turkish airfields. He also hinted that this might favorably influence the position of Russia. But the Turks were cagey and cautious.

[*The Donovan mission.*]   At that time the United States appeared unexpectedly on the Balkan scene. President Roosevelt felt relieved in January 1941 when his Lend-Lease Bill had fought its way through Congress and the British military successes in Africa promised the opening of a tactical second front against the Axis. The prospect of this second front had to be realized. The President looked forward to chances of a serious German-Russian rift (to the Soviet Ambassador in Washington he gave information concerning Hitler's aggressive plans; on January 21, 1941, the State Department announced the lifting of the so-called "moral embargo" which the United States had imposed upon Russia during the Finnish War). The President also considered the time ripe enough to support potential Balkan resistance against Germany. (This policy bore his personal imprint — it is known how he and Mrs. Roosevelt had always been greatly interested in the Balkans and had kept up their interest by reading interpretative works thereof and were influenced by Rebecca West and Louis Adamic alike.) (8) Thus, after Lend-Lease had cleared its obstacles, an unprecedented, and historically very significant American note was sent to Turkey, Bulgaria, and Yugoslavia, informing their governments that the United States intended to support Britain in her anti-Axis war by all possible means.

On February 12 Churchill wrote Wavell:

> If Turkey and Yugoslavia would tell Bulgaria they will attack her unless she joins them in resisting a German advance southward, this might create a barrier requiring much larger German forces than are now available in Rumania. But I fear they will not do this, and will fool away their chances of continued resistance, as was done in the Low Countries.

On February 14 the Yugoslav Premier and the Foreign Minister went to Hitler at Berchtesgaden. Hitler received them in a friendly manner. He requested that Yugoslavia join the Tripartite Pact, but he promised that there would be no mass passage of German troops; he only needed Yugoslav railroads and highways for his supplies. On that day, President Roosevelt sent a personal message to Prince Paul, warning him against joining with the Axis. The President reiterated the active American interest in the European war and said that Lend-Lease would be open to any country which decided to withstand the diplomatic or military threats of the Axis. A friendly answer was sent through the Yugoslav Minister in Washington, Fotitch; and when another journey of the Yugoslav Premier to Germany was impending, a second message from Roosevelt followed on February 22.

Meanwhile a personal emissary of the American President had already arrived in the Balkans and caused considerable speculation by his unusual journey. Colonel (later Major-General) Donovan visited Athens, Sofia, and Belgrade in January, conducted political talks with leading people there and examined the diplomatic and military situation. His mission was ostensibly secretive, yet it was clear that Donovan had been sent by Roosevelt to prod Balkan resistance against Hitler's demands and to promise in turn material help. His journey could not be kept wholly secret and this naturally hampered the results. He nevertheless succeeded in pooling a lot of important information, and this, together with the very important symbolic token aspect of America's interest in southeastern Europe which characterized his trip, made it worthwhile.

[*A long-range view.*]   While the British were ready to write off Bulgaria and concentrate rather on a Macedonian-Thracian defense line, the Americans thought that something still could be done with the Bulgars. This Donovan examined. Then there was the long-range view of Axis strategy. There were a few cool-headed leaders in the Balkans who thought that perhaps it would be better if Yugoslavia and Bulgaria made the best possible terms with Mussolini and Hitler, if a German-Russian war was to come; by no means would Yugoslavia and Greece be able successfully to resist a German invasion, while during a German-Russian war, Hitler, just as from September 1939 to late 1940, would be both unwilling and unable to concentrate an important part of his armed forces against the Balkans. This point of view, which Maček, the Croat Peasant leader, explained to Donovan, was a reasonable one. The Yugoslavs and Bulgars knew that Hitler's enticements were entirely dishonest (for example, in February the Japanese Ambassador in Ankara informed his Yugoslav colleague there that Hitler had offered Salonika both to the Bulgars and to the Yugoslavs at the same time), yet they could have played for time. While the Bulgars joined the Axis and aggravated their culpability later by sharing spoils with the Germans in Serbia and Greece, the Yugoslavs acted more impetuously and more heroically and with tragic results. In the long run, both became victims of Russia's ascendancy in the Balkans.

.   .   .   .

[*Marita: the final timetable.*] While these all-round deliberations were taking place, the final plans for *Barbarossa* were accepted
by the German High Command on February 3. (*9*) The same document spoke of *Marita* and *Operation Felix* (German-Spanish invasion
of Gibraltar and establishment of German forces in Spanish Morocco
and in the Canary Islands) as subsidiary measures. But, due to
Franco's diplomatic hesitations, *Felix* was doomed. *Marita* came into
the foreground. On February 5, a German document reported the
connection between *Barbarossa* and *Marita* (one as a camouflage of
the other). On February 8 a secret German-Bulgarian military
protocol was agreed upon: the German Army would at once pass
through Bulgaria if Turkey entered the war on Greece's side. The
German report nevertheless cautiously stated: "Bulgaria [is] not yet
directly committed . . ." On February 9 it was established that the
construction of a Danube pontoon bridge between Rumania and Bulgaria was to begin on February 28 over which the German armies
were to pass into Bulgaria from March 2 onwards. This timetable
was punctually adhered to.

[*Russian protest.*] Diplomatic repercussions followed in due
course. On February 9, Winston Churchill warned Bulgaria in a
speech; on the 12th, Britain severed diplomatic relations with Rumania. It was clear that Stalin was equally preoccupied with the
Balkan situation. (*10*) In Belgrade, Sofia, Ankara, the Soviet envoys
began to speak again of "collective" security; the Soviet Ambassador
to Turkey, Terentiev, who was reported to have had too friendly
connections with Papen, was recalled, and Vinogradov became the
new Russian envoy. (*11*) To be sure, no official or even unofficial
Soviet announcement made the Soviets' displeasure with the Germans known to the outside world. But there were signs. In the north,
Vishinsky spoke bitterly to Paasikivi on February 12: "We are already in a trade war with each other!" (*12*) In the south, the Soviet
envoy in Sofia feverishly tried to impress public opinion there by
staging exhibitions, arranging an unprecedented visit of the Moscow
soccer team to Sofia, which turned into a minor pro-Russian demonstration, and generally seeking to reconstruct and fortify the image
of Mother Russia as the traditional and strong protectress of the Slav
Bulgarians. With Slovakia, Rumania, and Hungary, the Soviet government signed fair and profitable trade agreements; Moscow also
decided to impress the non-Slavic, and traditionally anti-Communist,

but history-minded Hungarians with a gesture: the Hungarian Army banners which the Tsarist expeditionary forces had captured in 1849 were ceremoniously returned to Hungary — and the population of Budapest could witness the strange spectacle of a ceremony in which a military band of Horthy's Army intoned the Hungarian national anthem together with the *Internationale*.

On February 17, the situation seemed to be momentarily complicated by the sudden announcement that Bulgaria and Turkey had signed a Neutrality and Non-Aggression Treaty. Bulgaria offered the Neutrality Treaty to Turkey in early February. After some hesitation, the Turks accepted it. (The treaty was not unlike the Hungarian-Yugoslav Treaty of December 1940.) But it was neither anti-German, nor was it Russian-sponsored, as had been first thought (especially when Sobolev paid a hurried, secretive visit to Sofia on February 5. Yet on the 10th the Bulgarian Ministry of the Interior suddenly acted against certain Bulgarian Communist and cover organizations). The Soviet displeasure was duly communicated — again through a TASS "denial" — on February 23, when the Soviet news agency denied "reports" that the Soviet Union had participated in bringing about the Bulgarian-Turkish Treaty.

There was no need to camouflage German intentions any more. Indeed, it was decided to impress Moscow with the strength of the German Balkan armies. On February 22 Schulenburg was instructed to let it be known in Moscow that

> In Rumania there are 680,000 (six hundred eighty thousand) German troops in readiness. Among these troops there is an unusually high percentage of technical troops with the most up-to-date military equipment, especially armored units. Behind these troops there are inexhaustible reserves in Germany, including the permanent units stationed at the German-Yugoslav border.
>
> I request the members of the mission and any available trusted persons to start, in suitable ways, to let this strength be known in an impressive manner — indicating that it is more than sufficient to meet any eventuality in the Balkans from any side whatever . . . and to do so not only in Government circles there but also in the foreign missions concerned. I leave it to your discretion not always to mention the exact figure given above. On the contrary, innuendo and circumlocution may also be used, as, for example, "almost 700,000," and the like.

[*The German entry.*] A week later, the sad procession of Filov and his entourage appeared in Vienna and signed the Tripartite Pact. The German and Bulgarian envoys in Moscow informed the Soviet Government of the signing a day in advance; Hitler, somewhat worried by the chances of Turkish intervention, wrote a friendly letter to President Inönü. On March 1, Bulgaria became an Axis satellite; immediately the grey masses of German infantry began streaming over the Danube pontoon bridge into Bulgaria. This military entry was explained officially to Moscow as "a precautionary measure to prevent the British from gaining a firm foothold in Greece." Molotov received this communication with dismay and "with obvious concern," as Schulenburg reported. A Soviet note was handed to Schulenburg at once, protesting against the German action:

> It is to be regretted that despite the caution contained in the *démarche* of November 25, 1940, on the part of the Soviet Government, the German Reich Government has deemed it possible to take a course that involves injury to the security interests of the USSR and has decided to effect the military occupation of Bulgaria.

An even stronger note was handed to the Bulgarian envoy. The German motorized units rapidly advanced through Bulgaria and took up positions along the Yugoslav and Greek frontiers, especially in the vicinity of the highly important Rupel Pass leading from Bulgaria into Western Thrace. Bulgarian popular opinion was dumbfounded and the great majority of the population remained calm. (*13*) Twenty courageous members of Parliament, however, openly dared to vote against the Tripartite Pact. To satisfy Bulgarian nationalism, the Aegean claims of Sofia were acknowledged in a secret German-Bulgar protocol signed on March 2. On March 5, Great Britain broke off diplomatic relations with Bulgaria, and on March 8, another of those ambiguous TASS "denials" said that there was no truth in reports according to which the Soviet Union was seeking naval bases on the Rumanian Black Sea Coast. German-Russian relations had now reached a full and ominous impasse (*14*); but because of the Yugoslavs' pluck, *Marita*, developing a month later into a full-scale Balkan war, upset the German timetable and instead of remaining the subsidiary measure of *Barbarossa*, considerably retarded it.

[*The Tatoi conference.*] Now, as the outlines of *Marita* became visible, the Greeks' position changed. They could deal alone with the Italians, but they desperately needed help against a joint German-Italian attack. The tragedy of Greece was aggravated by the sudden death of Metaxas on January 29. He was succeeded in the Premiership by Korizis.

On February 11 Churchill decided to send Anthony Eden (who on December 22 replaced Halifax as Foreign Secretary) and Field Marshal Sir John Dill to Greece and Turkey; the "principal object" of this tour "will be the sending of speedy succour to Greece." Eden pondered the military chances; there were days when he thought that it would be better to leave Wavell strong and not send troops to Greece. The decisive meeting was at Tatoi, near Athens, on February 22 with the Greeks and their King. It was agreed that, as the Germans were to enter Bulgaria at any moment, the British would send troops into Greece; next day the military details were discussed: in case of a German invasion, the Greek-British forces would withdraw to the Aliakhmon River line and meet the challenge there. (*15*) Now Churchill put everything on a broader plane: he suggested forging a last-minute Turkish-Yugoslav-Greek defense coalition. Eden flew to Turkey, but the Turks were unwilling. (In Ankara he also met Cripps who flew down from Moscow to meet him.) Back in Athens, Campbell, the British envoy to Belgrade, awaited Eden and explained the Yugoslavs' situation. (Campbell carried back a confidential letter to Prince Paul from Eden.) In the meantime the Germans occupied Bulgaria, and there was no defense front, no coalition. Prospects were dark again.

[*A sudden British hesitation overcome.*] The British Chiefs of Staff now changed their views and on March 5 presented their estimate to Churchill: it might be better not to send troops to Greece. The Premier telegraphed Eden:

> Situation has indeed changed for worse. . . . We have done our best to promote Balkan combination against Germany. We must be careful not to urge Greece against her better judgment into a hopeless resistance alone when we have only handfuls of troops which can reach scene in time. Grave Imperial issues are raised by committing New Zealand and Australian troops to an enterprise which, as you say, has become even more hazardous. . . . We must liberate Greeks from feeling bound to fight, we must to some extent share their ordeal.

But rapid German advance will probably prevent any appreciable British Imperial forces from being engaged . . .

Palairet, the British envoy to Athens, was distressed by these estimates and sent three urgent telegrams to Eden at Cairo:

> This seems to me quite unthinkable. We shall be pilloried by the Greeks and the world in general as going back on our word. 2. There is no question of "liberating the Greeks" from feeling bound to reject the ultimatum. They have decided to fight Germany alone if necessary. The question is whether we help or abandon them. (*16*)

Eden and Dill re-examined the situation in Cairo with Wavell; they decided to concur with Palairet's views and the Tatoi decisions. Churchill and the War Cabinet agreed on the 7th.

From March 4 on, British reinforcements seeped into Greece through Crete and the harbors of the mainland, but ultimately they proved insufficient to stem the German onslaught, while their withdrawal weakened the Wavell Army in Libya, where early in April the German-Italian forces with General Rommel attacked the British beyond Benghazi and drove them back to Tobruk and the Egyptian frontier belt.

The Greek government tried to impress Berlin with her continued neutrality in the German-British war and desperately emphasized the separate character of the Italian-Greek "little war"; but these "frequent Greek assurances, intended for German ears," were rejected by Ribbentrop as false and fictitious. The Bulgarian occupation, then, fully beclouded the already swiftly darkening Greek horizon. Once more the Greeks endeavored to cast off the worst: on March 8 a clever and restrained "open letter" to Hitler was published by the Athens newspaper *Kathimerini* from the pen of G. Vlachos, which explained how the acceptance of the very limited British help was thrust upon Greece by the Italian invasion. The Vlachos letter appealed to Hitler's "sense of justice": a somewhat pathetic appeal.

The Yugoslav Revolution

[*Berchtesgaden again.*] Prince Paul visited Hitler in Berchtesgaden on the day of the Bulgarian occupation. (*1*) His visit was secret; the Yugoslav people were told that the Regent had left the capital for his country estate. Again, Hitler was pleasant. Aware of Paul's Russophobia, Hitler told him of his intention to attack the

Soviets in the future. (Two weeks earlier Hitler had told the Yugoslav Premier that German-Russian relations were good.) Hitler went so far as to point out the danger of Mussolini and of Italian aggression to a neutral Yugoslavia not included in the Tripartite group. (A curious manifestation of Axis loyalty.) By pointing at the Italian danger he wanted to make Paul think that Yugoslavia, once having joined the Pact, could play Berlin against Rome. Then, Hitler demanded nothing more than a mere signature: no German troops would pass through Yugoslavia, no territorial cessions would be demanded. On the contrary, he promised that eventually the Yugoslavs could have Salonika. Hitler had no special sympathy for the Yugoslavs. But *Marita* against Greece was pending, and the prospect of a lengthy Balkan campaign in which the Greek forces would be bolstered by the divisions of the Yugoslav Army, creating a new lengthy front stretching from the Carinthian border to Turkey could be dangerous not only for *Marita* but also for *Barbarossa*, calculated Hitler. (2) Therefore he was willing to pay — temporarily — a high price for a friendly Yugoslavia.

Paul knew this and he returned from Berchtesgaden with grave thoughts; the horizon was dark; his soul stirred with black forebodings and tragic dilemmas. The Serbs were violently against the Axis; in the cafes of Belgrade the gypsy bands were more than once asked to play *Tipperary* while a patriotic Serb audience cheered and sang with tears in their eyes; when Mussolini appeared on the newsreel screens, the audiences booed, laughed, and yelled delightful insults. On March 3, a dramatic telegram from the envoy Fotitch from Washington begged Paul not to give in to Hitler. The Prince-Regent consulted his friends and talked with his Ministers; but there remained little time for deliberations.

[*Greece and Italian jitters.*] Much depended on the military situation of Greece. That the Germans would attack from Bulgaria was known; but would there be a short campaign, ending with (or, perhaps, forestalled by) a negotiated armistice or peace, or would there be enough British troops forthcoming to make permanent resistance possible in Greece? The Germans, of course, planned for a quick war — so quick and astute that they clashed with their Italian allies on this point. On March 3, the Italian Embassy in Berlin received a confidential communication from the German General Staff which stated that during *Marita*, German troops would move against Salonika only very slowly in order to give the Greeks enough time to deliberate and, in face of a desperate strategic position, make them cede without further resistance. The Italian generals were furious. General Guzzoni sent a message to Alfieri: "It is inadmissible that the Germans should seek to enter Greece peacefully while our troops are fighting and dying there." All this was further aggravated by the premature and unsuccessful Italian offensive which started in Albania during the second week of March. In Berlin, Simoni noted that the men in Rome "had completely lost their nerve." On March 15, Rome telephoned urgently, saying that a Yugoslav attack against Italy was impending, ". . . there were no sufficient Italian forces to meet the Yugoslavs"; Rome requested that Berlin, either by diplomatic or military means, should immediately counteract this "menace." Two days later, Rome telephoned again: the previous reports were false; there were no aggressive Yugoslav intentions but, instead, Belgrade would surely join the Tripartite Pact if the Axis would guarantee her territorial integrity. The Italian Counselor at the Berlin Embassy noted sadly: "Often it seems that one has to deal [in Rome] either with children or imbeciles."

[*A non-committal Stalin; an anxious Roosevelt.*] While these Italian jitters rose and died, nothing happened to increase Yugoslav prospects for a successful resistance against the Axis. British manpower, scarcely enough for a Libyan campaign, was insufficient for a large-scale "second front" in the Balkans. The Yugoslav Minister in Moscow, Gavrilović, kept up a close friendship with Cripps there, but he was unable to report signs of a Russian diplomatic intervention; even after the Bulgarian affair, Stalin, while recording his displeasure, remained aloof and unwilling to bolster an anti-Axis Yugoslavia. This became clear on March 10, when *Izvestia* "denied reports" according to which a Soviet-Yugoslav agreement existed providing for Soviet aid if Yugoslavia were attacked.

On the same day Churchill informed Roosevelt on Greece and the Balkans: "At this juncture the action of Yugoslavia is cardinal. No country ever had such a military chance. If they will fall on the Italian rear in Albania there is no measuring what might happen in a few weeks." (*3*) This was, of course, exaggerated; but the United States continued to influence Prince Paul against the Axis. Early in March, the Yugoslavs prepared the transfer of Yugoslav assets from the United States to Brazil, fearing that — as was the practice then — the American government would "freeze" these assets when Yugoslavia declared her adherence to the Tripartite Pact. This financial action clearly indicated that joining the Pact was more than a strong probability. A message from President Roosevelt and the desperate attempts of Fotitch made Belgrade cancel the transfer orders on March 19. But the cancellation was only a gesture; for on that day Prince Paul returned from Berchtesgaden again — he had gone there for a second, secret talk with Hitler on the 15th — and on March 20 a Crown Council decided in principle on the acceptance of the Axis demand. (*4*)

[*The decisive days.*] Internal discontent suddenly rose to previously unexpected heights. Three important ministers had resigned on the aftermath of the Crown Council. While wild rumors circulated in Belgrade, on March 22 a severe German note was handed to Tsvetkovič by the German Minister: the Yugoslav representatives were expected to appear in Vienna not later than the 25th to sign the Pact there. British intelligence did some work, however. On March 20, Stoyadinovič was arrested and quickly spirited away to Greece: ultimately he wound up as an isolated, well-treated prisoner on Mauritius Island, in the Indian Ocean. On March 22 Churchill directly telegraphed Tsvetkovič; he used wonderful arguments:

> We know that the hearts of all true Serbs, Croats, and Slovenes beat for the freedom, integrity and independence of their country, and that they share the forward outlook of the English-speaking world. If Yugoslavia were at this time to stoop to the fate of Rumania, or commit the crime of Bulgaria, and become an accomplice in an attempted assassination of Greece, her ruin will be certain and irreparable. . . . I trust Your Excellency may rise to the height of world events. (*5*)

Except for a few Croats (*6*) and the Communists, the nation protested in a frenzied, dramatic mood. This national protest was felt by the best Yugoslavs abroad too: Fotitch in Washington contacted Gavrilovič in Moscow to consider a joint action of retirement-in-protest and thus form the core of a Yugoslav external resistance movement. On March 24, Fotitch wired Belgrade his intentions to resign. Many other diplomats acted likewise, and the crews of Yugoslav ships in foreign ports moved to consider a break with the government and remain in exile.

On the evening of the 24th, Tsvetkovič and Tsintsar-Markovič left for Vienna. Fearing hostile demonstrations, the exact time of departure for their train was not announced. Still, there was trouble at the frontier station with a group of locomotive crewmen who staged a protest strike of their own. Rarely has there been such unity, such determination, such fiery courage, such pride; rarely has the will of an independent people manifested itself so unequivocally and defiantly. However, on March 25, the Yugoslav delegates signed sadly. Many statesmen of the neighboring countries felt relieved, and even complacent: so now it was the Yugoslavs' turn, they said. (The nationalists in Bulgaria were disappointed — the Bulgarian industrial magnate, Balabanov, said to the visiting Hassell that the Yugoslav adherence to the Tripartite Pact made twenty per cent of the previously pro-Axis Bulgarians turn against Hitler — an indication of how nationalism turns countries into satellites.)

[*Revolution.*] Early on March 26, Tsvetkovič and Tsintsar-Markovič returned to a grey country and a silent, hostile capital. That day passed in ominous silence (*7*) — until midnight. Then, a group of Yugoslav army and air force officers set out in a lightning *coup d'état* and seized all government buildings, the radio, the barracks; in an hour and a half, the coup was completed. Prince Paul resigned. Early in the dawn hours the young King Peter was proclaimed Peter II of Yugoslavia, and a military-liberal government was announced under the leadership of General Dusan Simovič, the main chief of the military "rising." (*8*) Here occurred one of the most heart-lifting demonstrations in the history of modern Europe: a flag-bedecked capital greeted the news with roaring, spontaneous, enraptured joy. (*9*) The British and American Ministers were cheered by crowds wherever they appeared; in March 1941, in the midst of Axis-occupied Europe, hand-made British, French, and American flags were flying, the national anthems of Britain and Yugoslavia were being sung, and home-made pictures of Winston Churchill and Franklin Roosevelt were being carried throughout the streets. (*10*) Seldom was there such a sincere meeting of East and West; never did this magnificent and tearful spectacle repeat itself: the heartbeats of millions of Anglo-Saxons of the Atlantic World and those of the Balkan mountain-dwellers were mysteriously synchronized in those days.

Public enthusiasm reached its heights when King Peter II was solemnly crowned and a glorious *Te Deum* followed in the Orthodox

Cathedral of Belgrade. (Prince Paul and his wife chose "retreat into detention" in African Kenya.) All the oppressed of Europe took hope from this spectacle; their hearts rose as they saw the Yugoslav David ready to defy the might of Goliath Germany. In Marseille, the monument of King Alexander I was overnight covered with flowers; throughout occupied and unoccupied France, Frenchmen greeted their old Serb comrades-in-arms. The spirit of World War I was found again and new hopes rose throughout Europe.

[*The German reaction.*]   Hitler must have had some inkling of what was brewing in Belgrade, for on March 25 he expressed his fears of an eventual Yugoslav-Turkish "intervention." The excellent Soviet intelligence system also gathered valuable information from Belgrade, for on that same March 25 a joint Soviet-Turkish Declaration stated that if one of them were attacked, the other would remain benevolently neutral and friendly. Thus, in face of the common German danger, a two-year period of Russo-Turkish hostility came to an end. Hitler was angry. "Russia becomes ever more hostile," he said to Ciano; "our good relations with Russia are guaranteed more by the divisions assembled on the frontier than by Pacts in vigor . . ." The Yugoslav revolution further incensed him against Russia.

[*Italy: new alarms.*]   The launching of the German attack against Greece was but a matter of days when the Yugoslav coup upset the timetable. The Germans had already asked Rome for an enumeration of Italy's territorial aims in Greece; on March 23, Mussolini telegraphed these to Berlin: total occupation of Greece in two zones — one Italian, one German; Čamuria and the Ionian Islands to be incorporated into Italy. (Interestingly enough, Mussolini did not mention Bulgarian claims.) On March 25 Hitler said to Ciano that the Greeks had made a great strategic mistake by concentrating their troops in Western Thrace. But now all had to be newly examined, prepared, reshuffled; new doubts, new uncertainties appeared. The news of the Yugoslav revolution threw Rome into consternation. On March 27, Mussolini telephoned several times to Berlin, where Simoni recorded: "Alfieri . . . had completely lost his head. Rome asks . . . what do they say in Berlin? What should we do? And if the Yugoslavs attack us? We aren't ready . . . ask for help . . . obtain promises . . ."

In Britain, Mr. Churchill announced to a jubilant House of Commons: "Yugoslavia has found her soul." Undoubtedly, the broadcasts of the BBC (a wonderful speech by Lord Amery to the Yugoslav nation was heard on the critical night of March 25) contributed to the success of the *coup d'état*. But the British could offer very little military help to the Yugoslavs now. (*11*) Also, the new Yugoslav government, unwilling to furnish Hitler with a suitable pretext for invasion, declared that it adhered to all previous Pacts, assumed a correct policy of neutrality, and professed that it would not effect any changes in Yugoslav-Axis relations. Thus General Simovič did not consult with Sir John Dill on the aftermath of the revolution, and Foreign Minister Ninčič continued to maintain friendly ties with the German and Italian Ministers.

[*The military directives; prospects of Italian mediation.*] On the very day of the Belgrade coup, Hitler switched his plans and summoned his military chiefs: on March 27, he ordered preparations for the immediate invasion of Yugoslavia "to destroy Yugoslavia as a national unit . . . with unmerciful harshness." Yugoslavia was an uncertain factor anyhow, stated Hitler, potentially dangerous on the flanks of *Marita*, and likely to be even more dangerous when *Barbarossa* would be launched. He, therefore, welcomed the chance to wipe Yugoslavia off the slate. The chronological schedule was this: attack against Greece on April 2–3, against Yugoslavia on April 3–4, at the latest on April 12. Next day, Hitler wrote to Mussolini to arrange for the Italian entry into the Yugoslav War. The Italians hesitated for awhile. The Yugoslav government tried to secure its own neutrality and proposed a joint policy of Yugoslav-Italian understanding. The German press and radio began to attack Yugoslavia with increasing fervor, and the usual atrocity stories were concocted; on March 30, the German Minister left Belgrade, and the German chargé d'affaires openly insulted the Yugoslav Foreign Minister when the latter called on him with an inquiry. On the other hand, the Italian press refrained from reporting atrocity stories, and on April 1, Mussolini suggested that the First Vice-Premier, Yovanovič, come to Rome and undertake a joint attempt at mediation with the Italians between Belgrade and Berlin. (*12*) Yovanovič left for Rome on April 3.

By that time it was too late. The final German High Command directive was issued on March 30: "The Führer and Supreme Com-

mander has decided . . . to destroy Yugoslavia as quickly as possible." The Yugoslav invasion received the code-name *Action 25.*

[*Hungary's misfortune.*] It was necessary for Hitler to secure
Hungary for his plans: from the broad Hungarian plains German
armored divisions could outflank the Yugoslav armies and pierce defense lines easily. On March 28 Hitler summoned Sztójay, the pro-
German Hungarian envoy, and explained to him the need for
Hungary's joining in the Yugoslav "kill." He gave a special plane
to Sztójay to fly to Budapest at once and return with Hungarian
concurrence; he promised to be generous about Hungary's territorial
claims — he went so far as to speak about Fiume, Hungary's ancient
port, which she had lost in 1918. (*13*) Hitler sent an extremely
friendly message to Horthy.

Sztójay had his best contacts not with Horthy or with Prime Minister Teleki (who despised him), but with the pro-German War Minister, Bartha, and General Werth, the German-born Chief of the
Hungarian General Staff. These three men made Horthy face accomplished facts. The Regent — not quite aware of the implications
of his step — answered Hitler on March 29 and agreed that at a suitable time, Hungary would concur. But what would this concurrence
mean in reality? Hungary had signed a Non-Aggression and Eternal
Friendship Treaty with Yugoslavia not quite four months before . . .
This Premier Teleki knew. Nevertheless, General Bartha left on
April 2 to call on Hitler. The rift between the General Staff and the
Teleki group seemed to be critical; the Germans requested immediate permission for their troops to pass through Hungary. From
March 31 to April 2, Horthy and Teleki deliberated — they secretly
consulted Count Bethlen and other conservative leaders. Should
Hungary resist — and share the fate of Poland? Could Hungary resist? The auspices were bad. Hungary could count on no outside help,
and public opinion was wholly unprepared for an heroic leap into
the Allied camp. Thus, on the night of April 2–3, German troops
began to stream across the Hungarian borders; on the quays of the
Danube the silent, curious populace of Budapest watched the thundering German tanks and trucks rolling southwards. During the same
night Count Teleki shot himself. The Premier wanted to call the attention of the world to Hungary's tragic dilemma and fate by dramatically putting an end to his life. This was pure heroism. It did
not change the course of events. Britain broke off relations with Hun-

gary at once, while Bartha and Hitler agreed that a fake "bombardment" of the Hungarian town of Szeged by "Yugoslav" planes
would furnish the pretext for a Hungarian declaration of war against
Yugoslavia.

[*Croat prospects.*] The Germans were busy stirring up discord also within Yugoslavia. The Croats were not too happy with the
Belgrade coup, for the military government of Simović was clearly of
a Serb-Orthodox character. (*14*) Pavelić, Kvaternik, and the other
Croat quislings were readying themselves for the Great Secession. (*15*)
The March 30 German High Command directive of *Action 25* stated
that no air raids should take place in Croat areas. Maček himself
deliberated and did not enter the Simović cabinet until April 3. On
the same day another High Command directive drew up the partition
of Yugoslavia: there would be a satellite Croatia; the Medjomurje as
well as the Bačka would go to Hungary (*16*); the fate of the Banat
was "pending," while "the Italian territories . . . will be prepared
by a letter from the Führer to the Duce."

.   .   .   .

[*Russian bungling.*] There was also another group in Yugoslavia which expressed its discontent with the March 27 revolution:
the Communists. During the frenzied parade days of Belgrade, Communist groups occasionally appeared, shouting against the "imperialist warmongers"; a secret meeting of the Yugoslav Communist Party
Politbureau on March 30 decided to continue its anti-British propaganda. They thought this to be the Moscow line . . . But the policy of
Moscow was dangerously fluctuating. (*17*) The Soviet-Turkish Declaration of March 25 was a step away from Germany; yet, at the same
time, Soviet deliveries to Germany, which had lagged somewhat
when German-Russian relations were cooling off, now "rose by leaps
and bounds," reported Schnurre in Berlin. "The grain contract,
which we had struggled so hard to get, was closed . . . at relatively
favorable prices, for delivery by September of this year. . . . Transit
traffic through Siberia is proceeding favorably as usual. At our request, the Soviet Government even put a special freight train for
rubber at our disposal at the Manchurian border." Gavrilović was
still shunned by Molotov, and on April 1, *Pravda* denied reports that
the Soviets had sent congratulations to Belgrade when the new Yugo-

slav government was installed. It was a classic piece of diplomacy-
via-journalism:

> The Yugoslav people doubtless have a glorious past and deserve con-
> gratulations and there would be nothing astonishing in such congrat-
> ulations, had there been any. But no such congratulations were sent
> because the Soviet government did not think of sending them. (*18*)

We know today that the Yugoslav Revolution not only postponed
Barbarossa but that the delay may have been instrumental in bringing
about the Germans' defeat at Rostov and Moscow in November–
December 1941. (Thus Simovič and his friends contributed to the
saving of Stalin, who was certainly not thankful; he and his agents
later torpedoed the Serb Royalists, while pushing to the fore those
Yugoslav Communists who in March 1941 agitated against resisting
the Axis.) One might ponder what would have happened had Stalin
grasped the favorable occasion and joined the Yugoslav-Greek-
British front in April 1941, forestalling the German invasion of Greece
and Russia. But Stalin closed his eyes and could not believe that Hitler would attack him. Exactly 70 years before, Mazzini had written
of Napoleon III:

> . . . a deceiver, he was deceived . . . he found himself . . . condemned
> to the defensive, as incapable of marching on Mayence, as of operat-
> ing from Strasbourg against South Germany; incapable too of de-
> stroying the neighbouring centres where the German railways met.
> Inert and unable to move, he awaited the attack and was exposed to
> it. The traditional valour of the French soldier was not enough in the
> unfavourable conditions . . .

Substitute Warsaw for Mayence, Jassy for Strasbourg, and South
Germany for Rumania: the positions of the "French soldier" in 1870
and of the Russian in 1941 are obviously similar. (*19*)

[*Finally, a pact with Yugoslavia.*] The German entry into
Hungary then made it clear to Stalin that a German attack against
Yugoslavia was impending. During that week, Soviet diplomatic
stock rose, as the Japanese Foreign Minister Matsuoka stayed in
Moscow on his way to Berlin and Rome as well as on his return and
expressed his desire for a treaty with the Russians. Meanwhile Britain
again defeated the Italian Navy at the Battle of Cape Matapan, off
Greece, on March 31; on the same day the Italian defenses gave way

all along the Abyssinian front. Gavrilović, prodded by his British colleague, kept on asking the Russians for eventual assistance, but Molotov and Stalin were, at best, willing only to negotiate a Neutrality and Non-Aggression Pact. The negotiations were proceeding very slowly, alas, too cautiously for the Yugoslavs, who, remembering the Soviets' desire for a Bulgar Pact during the previous month, had thought that Moscow would gladly take up their proposal. But there was no alliance, no mutual assistance pact. Finally, on April 4, Molotov summoned Schulenburg to the Kremlin (Gavrilović was still sitting on tenterhooks) and informed the German Ambassador:

> The Yugoslav Government had proposed to the Soviet Government the negotiation of a treaty of friendship and nonaggression, and the Soviet Government had accepted the proposal. This agreement would be signed today or tomorrow. In its decision to accede to the proposal of the Yugoslav Government, the Soviet Government had been actuated solely by the desire to preserve peace. It knew that in this desire it was in harmony with the Reich Government, which was likewise opposed to an extension of the war. The Soviet Government therefore hoped that the German Government, too, in its present relations to Yugoslavia, would do everything to maintain peace. . . . relations of the Soviet Union to other countries were not affected by the agreement with Yugoslavia . . .

Schulenburg replied that "the moment chosen by the Soviet Union for the negotiation for such a treaty had been very unfortunate. . . . the policy of the Yugoslav Government was entirely unclear, and its attitude, as well as the behavior of the Yugoslav public toward Germany, was challenging." Whereupon Molotov tried to assure the German Ambassador: ". . . the Yugoslav envoy [in Moscow], who was at the same time a member of the new Cabinet, had assured the Soviet Government that the new Yugoslav Government was observing the [Tripartite] Treaty":

> . . . under these circumstances, the Soviet Government had thought that it could, for its part, conclude an agreement with Yugoslavia that was not even as far-reaching as the German-Yugoslav Treaty.

The Soviet Union was, therefore, apologizing, a bearing not likely to create that impression upon Germany which the Balkan peoples as well as the Atlantic Powers wished Russia to make. Nevertheless, Schulenburg's objections did not make Stalin and Molotov change their minds. Throughout April 5, Gavrilovič impatiently waited; then, suddenly at eleven at night, the Yugoslav diplomats were asked to the Kremlin, where Stalin received them. All was set for a banquet; the tables were bedecked and it was announced that the signature of the Soviet-Yugoslav Friendship and Non-Aggression Treaty would be signed there, on the spot, at once. It was signed after midnight, although predated back to April 5; the canny Stalin obviously wished to have it signed *before* the Yugoslav-German War broke out. After the signature ceremonies, everybody ate and drank copiously; a benign Stalin smiled while diplomats and officers mingled in a happy-go-lucky spirit of Slav defiance, an ancient fraternal response to the new German challenge. Gavrilovič and the other members of the Yugoslav mission returned from the Kremlin in the dawn hours. They could not rest for long. At six o'clock in the morning a radio message announced that the German invasion of Yugoslavia and Greece had begun.

The Balkan campaign and the mysteries of Soviet diplomacy

[*The campaign.*] The Balkan campaign opened with the violent air bombardment of Belgrade. Simultaneously, the German Air Force swept over the whole of Yugoslavia and northern Greece in one great tactical operation, gaining complete mastery of the air. Within twenty-four hours, the few and therefore very important rail centers of Yugoslavia were crippled, and the Yugoslav General Staff could dispose of no important reserves to be moved to the dangerous sectors of the fronts. British air power in Greece was not strong enough to conduct effective tactical operations against German armored spearheads; instead, the RAF bombed Sofia by night, a strategic operation which had some psychological effects but did no harm at all to the Germans. (*1*)

The Germans made the best use of their enormous tactical advantage. They concentrated in Macedonia and pushed rapidly against the flanks of the Yugoslav armies in Serbia. The military key to Serbia and northern Greece is the Skoplje Gap; forty-eight hours after the war had broken out, Skoplje was in German hands. On that day — April 8 — the Germans also broke through the Rupel Pass, and their spearheads reached the outskirts of Salonika. The Greek Army fell rapidly back from Western Thrace; on April 9, the German capture of Djevdjeliya cut the last link between Yugoslavia and

Greece. On April 10, Niš fell, and the armies of Marshal List began to fan out from the Macedonian mountains to the north and south while an armored column cut its way through Slovenia and northern Croatia; three other columns were converging on Belgrade from the direction of the Rumanian Banat and from Hungary.

The Yugoslav armies were therefore strategically beaten on the fourth day of the Balkan campaign. This rapid development brought rapid political events. The Yugoslav state began to disintegrate. As Belgrade was being physically annihilated, a vacuum set in. The Germans, since they were sparing Croat cities from air raids, could count on an hourly increasing tendency of the Croats to regard them as "liberators." German-operated radio stations were inciting Croat regiments to revolt against Serb leadership. As early as April 8, sporadic mutinies occurred (for example, two Croat regiments fired on their Serb comrades at the rail center of Vinkovci). Croat soldiers deserted and revolted at many minor points and in the cities of Mostar and Zara; the Yugoslav Fleet, predominantly manned by Croat seamen, was slowly paralyzed. On April 9, the Germans pushed to the outskirts of Zagreb and a "Croat national government" took over in the city. The red and white checkered flag of Croatia was raised and the *Ustaši*, Pavelič, Budak, Kvaternik, triumphantly marched in amidst the impressive roar of German tanks. The real leader of the Croat nation, Maček, did not participate in the somewhat artificial celebrations; he retired to the country. But this reticence did not change the facts: the Yugoslav state was dissolving with astonishing rapidity.

[*Italy enters.*]   Now Mussolini also joined in for the spoils. (2) Had the Yugoslavs had a chance to stop the German onslaught, the Italians' situation in Albania would have been disastrous. Hitler almost frantically warned Mussolini in a letter on April 5: "Before everything I hold one thing important, Duce: your front, Duce, in Albania, must not give way under any circumstances." On April 7, a Yugoslav force broke into northern Albania, by-passed Skutari and advanced toward Tirana. Another Yugoslav sally was prepared against Fiume and Zara. But the rapid German advance and the defection of the Croat units forced the abandonment of these operations; on April 12, the Yugoslavs' Adriatic front collapsed; five days later, the Yugoslav fleet surrendered to the Italians. Only two submarines and a few other minor craft escaped to British-held ports.

[*And Hungary.*] On April 7 and April 8, "Yugoslav" planes dropped half-a-dozen light bombs on villages in southern Hungary; this was arranged between the Hungarian and German General Staffs. Horthy, however, deeply impressed by the Teleki suicide and by the British decision to break diplomatic relations with Hungary, did not declare war on Yugoslavia. He waited until April 10 and used the dissolution of Yugoslavia as a pretext for intervention. On April 10, the Hungarian army attacked in the Bačka, and on April 14 the objective was gained: the Danube had been reached all along the line. Against the opinion of the new Premier, Bárdossy, Horthy did not wish to enter Croatia; therefore the Drava river line was not crossed, *(3)* while further to the east, it was the German High Command which specifically prohibited a Hungarian advance into the Banat territory, east of the Tisza river.

Belgrade fell to the Germans in the morning hours of Easter Sunday, April 13: that evening strange things happened in Moscow; it is there and not in Belgrade that the historic significance of April 13. 1941, ought to be sought.

. . . .

[*Calculations — with Japan.*] Adolf Hitler knew that the ominous silences and the periodic growls of the Russian giant were eagerly noted in the Balkans. He correctly sized up the Yugoslav coup to Schulenburg a month later:

> . . . the British pulled the strings behind the Yugoslav coup, but the Balkan peoples will think that the Russians were behind it . . . *(4)*

The Soviet-Yugoslav Friendship Treaty, then — however cautious its timing and announcement — definitely established before the eyes of the world that a conflict of Russian and German interests existed. Berlin received the treaty announcement with cold hostility, while Molotov, when he received the German note informing him of the outbreak of hostilities, "repeated [to Schulenburg] several times that it was extremely deplorable that an extension of the war had thus proved inevitable after all." (Yet Molotov did not speak of the Soviet-Yugoslav Pact.) On April 6, 1941, the friction between Germany and Russia, which had been slowly increasing since August 1940, reached its climax.

This was not against the interests of Germany, for *Barbarossa* had definitely been decided upon. There were, however, complications. Ribbentrop's original plan was to induce Japan to attack Britain in Asia during 1941. In 1940, he hoped for an Axis-Soviet-Japanese alliance and knew that the southward advance of the Japanese in the Pacific and in China would not be against Russian interests. In the spring of 1941, however, the *Barbarossa* plans required that Japan tie down a considerable number of Soviet troops in eastern Siberia. The journey of the Japanese Foreign Minister, Matsuoka, who set out in March 1941 for a visit to Moscow, Berlin and Rome, seemed to be a favorable occasion for Ribbentrop to discuss this new implementation of the Tripartite Pact.

Ribbentrop's plan did not materialize, for Matsuoka paid but verbal tributes to the Tripartite Pact. He followed an independent, exclusively Japanese course, which only partly coincided with that planned by Ribbentrop. The European conversations of Matsuoka, highly interesting and suggestive, revealed this divergence of concepts (ultimately fatal for Germany):

> In the spring of 1941, Hitler already regarded Russia as his enemy no. 1, Britain as enemy no. 2, and the United States as enemy no. 3; while the Japanese were regarding the United States as their enemy no. 1, Britain as enemy no. 2, and Russia was regarded as not inevitably, only potentially inimical. Thus, while the enemies of the Tripartite Pact Powers were the same, the strategic order was reversed. (Mussolini also regarded the Anglo-Saxon Powers as the main enemy — he agreed with the Japanese.)

Thus Ribbentrop labored for an Axis-Japanese alliance directed against Russia, an alignment accompanied either by the optimal premise of a defeated Britain and an isolationist America or by the probable premise of a Britain reduced to the defensive and shrinking in power and an America stagnant in power and not in a position to intervene.

Matsuoka also labored for an Axis-Japanese alliance, directed, however, against Britain and the United States, an alignment accompanied either by the optimal premise of an Axis-Soviet-Japanese alliance or by the probable premise of a Russia neutral to Japan.

Ribbentrop did not succeed in realizing either of his premises, and his Reich was defeated in 1944. Matsuoka succeeded in realizing his probable premise for awhile; his empire collapsed in 1945.

Matsuoka's conversations revealed the actual state of German-Russian relations. The Japanese Foreign Minister first passed through Moscow on March 25. His talks with the Russians were friendly and gave promise of further developments. Stalin was not in an easy position. On March 20, Sumner Welles gave the Soviet Ambassador in Washington authentic intelligence about German plans for an attack on Russia. Yet, Stalin still hoped that he could come to a long-term deal with the Germans. He therefore used Matsuoka as a diplomatic messenger of love, and when the eager Japanese (who said to Stalin, "the Japanese are moral communists") asked him what he thought of the Anglo-Saxon Powers, "the common foe of Japan, Germany and Soviet Russia," Joseph Stalin stated that "Soviet Russia had never gotten along well with Great Britain and never would."

This statement, however sincere and spontaneous, was noted in Berlin without further comment. On the other hand, Matsuoka heard from Ribbentrop and Hitler such utterances as: "[Germany's] relations with Russia are correct but not very friendly . . ."; "it was possible that Russia would set out on the wrong road, although [Hitler] did not really expect this from Stalin . . ."; "closer collaboration with Russia . . . absolute impossibility," and the like.

This lack of German response was not known to Stalin when he made up his mind to sign the Yugoslav Treaty, for Matsuoka had not yet arrived in Moscow on his return journey. Nevertheless, Stalin saw to it that neither Berlin nor London should interpret the Treaty as a move toward a Russian alignment with the anti-Axis Powers: for six days, the British Ambassador was unable to secure an interview even with Molotov's deputy.

For on March 31 a British intelligence report had excited Churchill. This report noted that when the Yugoslavs signed the Tripartite Pact, three German armored divisions moving southward through Rumania were sent back north to the Cracow area. After the Belgrade revolution these divisions were, however, sent south again. "To me it illuminated the whole Eastern scene like a lightning flash," wrote Churchill in his memoirs. On April 3 he instructed Cripps to inform Stalin personally of this piece of news. There occurred a series of delays, and the message did not reach Stalin until about April 21–22. (5)

Meanwhile, for a few days the Yugoslav Treaty was played up in the Soviet press, and the first Yugoslav war news was given con-

spicuous space. Moscow capitalized now on Russia's rôle as champion
of Balkan peace; on April 9, Vishinsky had a routine talk with
Gafencu, and to the great surprise of the latter, the Russian voiced
sincere friendship toward Rumania, praised Antonescu, and made
significant economic promises. On April 12, after the Hungarian
attack on Yugoslavia, Vishinsky summoned the Hungarian Minister
to the Kremlin. The Russian remonstrated in a serious tone against
the Hungarian aggression, "especially in view of the fact that Hungary had signed a Non-Aggression Pact with Yugoslavia only months
ago . . ." And when the Hungarian envoy ventured to say that, after
all, the Soviet Union had employed the same policy of "defending
the Russian and Ukrainian brethren" when she marched into eastern
Poland in September 1939, Vishinsky dismissed this argument with
an angry gesture.

On the same day, however, Matsuoka was back in Moscow. Back,
indeed, to conclude a Neutrality and Non-Aggression Treaty with
Russia — vitally necessary before Japan could venture to start a war
in the Pacific. But there were difficulties in the way of the Japanese-
Russian Treaty: territorial and other disputes which had stood between Tokyo and Moscow for decades. Stalin saw two facts. First,
Matsuoka said nothing about any indications of Hitler's friendship;
Matsuoka's mission of reconciliation had evidently been unsuccessful.
Secondly, Matsuoka was nevertheless eager to sign a pact with him.
This meant that Russia's back would be secured if a German invasion came, and also that Japan was preparing for an Asian War, and
soon Germany, Italy and Japan would be fighting Britain and America. The prospect of such a war and a neutral Russia pleased Stalin
to the utmost; he could only gain. The only problem was whether
Russia *could* remain neutral, whether Hitler would, foolishly enough,
attack him.

[*Stalin: a treaty and a gesture.*]   Then, on April 13 — the day
when Matsuoka was to leave Moscow on his long eastward train
journey to Tokyo — the news came that Belgrade had fallen; Yugoslavia was collapsing. This impressed Stalin immensely. From now on,
his task was to secure German goodwill at any price: Russia must not
be attacked, Russia must remain neutral. The Balkans in any case
were now within the German sphere; any kind of direct or indirect
diplomatic demonstration of Russian displeasure or resistance was
useless. (While a few Yugoslav planes sought refuge in Russia after

the débâcle, the Yugoslav Minister in Moscow, who had been showered by tokens of friendship during the previous week, was no longer
received at the Kremlin.) In the morning Stalin gave in to Matsuoka
on points where previously the Soviet attitude had been inflexible; in
the afternoon the Soviet-Japanese Treaty of Neutrality and Non-
Aggression was signed, to the great surprise of the world. The
ceremonies of the signing necessitated a slight delay in Matsuoka's
schedule; the departure of the Trans-Siberian Express was postponed
by an hour.

This was not all. To the joyous and pleasantly surprised Matsuoka,
Stalin's parting words were that "he was a convinced adherent of the
Axis and a foe of England and the United States." Matsuoka then
drove to the railroad station, where occurred the greatest surprise,
the historic gesture which made this April 13 a really noteworthy
Easter Sunday. To the great astonishment of the officials, diplomats
and other people present, Stalin himself appeared at the platform.
He personally bade farewell to the enraptured Japanese diplomats;
then he turned around: he looked for somebody in the crowd. Everybody watched him carefully. Suddenly, Stalin smiled; he detected
the tall Count von der Schulenburg in his dark coat. He went over
to the German Ambassador, stopped, then put his arms on Schulenburg's shoulder and, looking straight into his eyes, said in a clearly
audible tone: "We must remain friends and you must now do everything to that end!" A murmur rose from among the crowd. A few
minutes later Stalin turned to the group of military attachés and
greeted some of them with unusual cordiality. When he got to Colonel
Krebs, the German acting military attaché, he looked at his uniform
and half-amusedly, half-seriously asked the officer whether he was
German. Krebs, his face flushed, stood straight at attention and
answered "Yes!" Stalin then threw his arms around him and said
loudly, so that everybody could hear his ringing words reverberating
under the cupola of the station: "We will remain friends with you —
in any event!"

The Soviet dictator might have been — perhaps — in a slightly
exuberant condition; but this was as immaterial as the meaning of
his gestures and his words was obvious.

⋅   ⋅   ⋅   ⋅   ⋅   ⋅

[*Conclusion of the campaign.*]   The decisive phase of the Balkan campaign was completed between April 13 and 23. The Yugoslav

government made its way to the coast, and on April 16, General Simovič authorized General Kalafatovič, the leader of the remaining Yugoslav army groups in Bosnia, to surrender. A number of troops, led by Serbian colonels, one of them named Mihailovič, disappeared in the mountains of Old Serbia. On April 17, King Peter and the government took off from the port of Kotor in a British seaplane for Athens; thence to Jerusalem; thence later to London, the seat of all émigré governments and the hope of all free Europeans.

The Greek military situation was somewhat less impossible; perhaps, had the Greek General Staff not changed its mind and decided to defend Western Thrace, the sixty thousand British and colonial troops together with the Greek Army could have held the Germans for a considerable time. King Boris was careful enough not to appear as a potential aggressor; like Horthy, he postponed his operations until *after* Yugoslavia — and Greece — were beaten. Bulgaria broke diplomatic relations with Yugoslavia only on April 15, and Bulgarian units began to advance into Macedonia; a few days later, Sofia broke with Athens also, and on April 24 the Bulgarian Army moved into Western Thrace. (6)

The Epirus defenses were broken into on April 16: the Mount Olympos line was abandoned and the Greek, British, and New Zealand divisions retreated toward the Attic plains. On April 19, another central-eastern European Prime Minister took his own life: Korizis, appalled at the rapidly approaching tragedy of the Greek nation, for whose victory and welfare he had labored day and night, quietly committed suicide. King George II was, curiously enough, his own Premier for four days; then he nominated Tsouderos to the Premiership. On that day Athens could already hear the gunfire, and the "second Dunkirk" was beginning in Piraeus, Patras, and in the ports of the Peloponnese. In the north, the half-encircled Army of the Epirus surrendered on the same day. The surrender was arranged by the Greek General Tsolakoglu — who later was to become a quisling Premier of Greece — and the German Marshal List; neither the Italians, nor the British were consulted; both had to face accomplished facts. The surrender of the Epirus Army practically concluded the Balkan campaign; what remained was the occupation of the rest of Greece and of the Aegean "appendices." On April 26 German parachutists captured the Corinth Canal. The Greek government had moved to Crete, never dreaming that the Germans, despite their complete lack of naval craft, would try to invade that great island by air, undertaking one of the most daring and unorthodox military operations of the war. (The German High Command directive for the planning and necessary reconnaissance concerning the Cretan invasion — *Operation Mercury* — had been issued as early as March 21, 1941.)

Even before the Aegean campaign was completed, the complicated political task of partitioning Yugoslavia and Greece had to be dealt with. Here lay grave conflicts of interests among Italy, Germany, Bulgaria, and the new Croatian state.

Ciano went to Vienna on April 21 to meet Ribbentrop. Rome planned on having complete control over the puppet state of Croatia, but the way the Germans handled the "liberation" indicated a developing tug-of-war there. The SS plenipotentiary, Veesenmayer, supported Kvaternik, while the Italians backed Pavelič; but Pavelič himself was not unwilling to play the German game, for his gratitude to his Italian keepers was overwhelmed by his desire to make an independent Croatia and not to be simply the head-of-state of an Italian province like Albania. The Croats also had territorial disputes with Italy, for Ciano and Mussolini were out to annex almost the whole Adriatic littoral of Yugoslavia, while Croatia aspired to have her own seacoast. (King Victor Emmanuel III had no desire to gain new territories; he said to Ciano, ". . . the less of Dalmatia we take, the less trouble we will have" — an honest and farsighted statement.)

The German meddlings in Zagreb were well-known to Ciano when he met Ribbentrop. Further unpleasant surprises awaited him. Although Hitler and Ribbentrop had previously told Rome that Germany had no territorial demands in Yugoslavia except for the narrow strip of Yugoslav Carinthia, the map which Ribbentrop produced in Vienna showed that the new frontier of Germany was to run a bare two miles north of Ljubljana, the capital of Italy's new Slovenian province. Ribbentrop was also against plans for a Croat-Italian personal union. When Ciano mentioned the Adriatic frontier problem, the German Foreign Minister remarked that Dalmatia was ethnically Croat; Ciano retorted that the Italian claim to the Dalmatian coast was not based on ethnic arguments. Ribbentrop went to consult Hitler while Ciano waited in Vienna. Finally the Germans agreed to the Italian requests. Thereafter Ciano met Pavelič on April 24 and had a "convincing" talk; a frontier "conference" was hastily summoned. On April 30, Ciano wrote a friendly letter to Pavelič; on May 7 Pavelič, Mussolini, and Ciano met at Monfalcone for a short conversation. The Croats got a small stretch of the coast, but the

Italians retained the port of Split. A controversy between Rome and Sofia had also arisen, for the Bulgarian army advancing in Macedonia had reached the Lake Ochrida region on the former Albanian-Yugoslav border, a territory which Ciano and Mussolini had claimed for their Albanian province. The Bulgar occupation of that territory was then silently acknowledged by Rome.

[*The partitions.*] The partition of Yugoslavia thus occurred along these lines:

Germany got the Slovene territories of Maribor and Celje, thus annexing the majority of districts which Yugoslavia received from Austria in 1919; (7)
she maintained full military and civil control over the territory of the Banat which was eventually to serve as the core of a great German *Südgau;* (8)
she maintained full military control over Serbia, where in August 1941 a "national" Serb government was installed, led by the Serbian General Nedič. (The quisling rôle in that government was not played by Nedič — who had fought well in the Balkan campaign and tried to save what was possible after the collapse — but by the Serbian Fascist leader Lyotič.)
Italy annexed the southern part of Slovenia, with the capital of Ljubljana, and (9) the Dalmatian seacoast south from Split to the Albanian border; she added the Kossovo territories of Yugoslavia to Albania; she established her "protectorate" over a resuscitated Montenegro. (10)
Croatia was formed out of the Croatian territories of Yugoslavia and received the Dalmatian seacoast from Susak to Split; her territory was enlarged by the "incorporation" of Bosnia and Herzegovina.
Hungary annexed the Bačka, the small Danube-Drava triangle (Drávaköz), and the Medjemurje territory, thereby making the entire length of the line of the rivers Drava and Danube serve as the southern frontier of Hungary;
Bulgaria received the whole of Yugoslav Macedonia except for the Upper Vardar Valley above Skoplje, and the Tetovo-Gostivar region, which went to Italian-Albania. Yet Germany did not allow Bulgaria to annex Macedonia formally (in the words of Miss Elizabeth Barker, Germany "was holding the card of Macedonian autonomy up her sleeve for future contingencies").

Athens fell on April 27. In a few days the German occupation of the Greek mainland was completed. Again, there were controversies.

General Tsolakoglu, who had surrendered with the Epirus Army, was willing to make a deal with the Germans behind the backs of the Italians. He gambled on Hitler's sympathies (an astute calculation. Hitler expressed himself to Schulenburg after the Greek campaign thus: "he [Hitler] regretted exceedingly that he had been forced to have to strike down, against his natural impulse, this small plucky nation.") (*11*) The Italians meanwhile planned to get Salonika, but they were not awarded with that prize (neither were the Bulgars). Simoni at the Berlin Embassy noted bitterly on April 29 the "German hypocrisy . . . the Germans are working now clandestinely against us in Greece and in Croatia." (*12*) Friction among Italians, Germans, and Bulgarians continued in Greece throughout the war.

Greece was partitioned thus:

> *Bulgaria* received Western Thrace (her 1913 frontiers), Greek eastern Macedonia, and the districts of Florina and Kastoria.
> *Italy* annexed the Ionian Islands and added the Čamuria territory to Albania as well as other parts of Greek Western Macedonia and Epirus, thereby pushing her frontiers to the port of Preveza and to the Ioannina region.
> The Salonika area was put directly under the German General Löhr's administration.

The rest of Greece remained under joint Axis military occupation. (It is interesting to observe that the Germans wanted to install a republican, anti-Royalist Greek government; the republican exile, General Plastiras, was invited back to Greece, and Damaskinos was installed as Orthodox Archbishop of Athens. But both men refused to serve the Germans.) By May 11, all of the main Aegean islands were occupied by the Axis, and the campaign of Crete, which began on May 19, was successfully terminated on June 2 when the last British and Greek troops were forced to abandon the island.

On May 4, Hitler spoke triumphantly, announcing that all German casualties during the entire Balkan campaign amounted to not more than 5,500. Germany's lightning victory had important effects abroad. Stalin was the first to take stock of the new situation; also, isolationist sentiment in the United States received momentary support from the all-too-clear fact that the Balkan peoples' sudden resistance against Germany had been stimulated by President Roosevelt and his personal emissary. In May, the *Saturday Evening Post* published an impressive account, accusing the makers of American foreign policy of downright and irresponsible interference: Can America have her frontier on the Danube? asked the article, at a time when America is not "yet" at war? (Six years later, America — well after the war — established her frontiers, if not on the Danube, then in northern Greece.)

Hitler overrode Ribbentrop — and did not raise objections against the planned close dynastic ties between Italy and Croatia. It was decided in Rome that the Duke of Spoleto should become King of Croatia, under the name of Aimone I. The new monarch had to be notified first; but to the great dismay of the authorities, he could not be found for some time, until on May 8 it was discovered that he was hiding out in a Milan hotel with a young lady friend. On May 18 he was proclaimed King in Zagreb (a Croat-Italian treaty of collaboration was also signed on the same day and Ante Pavelič became the Croat *Poglavnik*, another petty Führer, with Kvaternik as his Prime Minister). Yet the Duke of Spoleto really had nothing to fear, for the continuous chaos in the "Kingdom of Croatia" was to make it forever preferable that he remain in Italy; consequently, he never went to Zagreb and never occupied his "throne."

.   .   .   .   .

[*Schulenburg and Hitler.*]   A few hours after the Trans-Siberian Express had left Moscow eastward with Matsuoka, Count von der Schulenburg stepped on the Berlin train, which speeded him westward. There he was to report in person to Ribbentrop and to Hitler.

From April 13 to April 30 Schulenburg was away from Moscow. The men in the Kremlin hoped that his journey would be successful. The atmosphere of those days was masterfully described by Gafencu; the parallel between Schulenburg and the French ambassadors of 1811–12, Caulaincourt and Lauriston, was almost perfect. But Napoleon, while angry with Caulaincourt's opinions, never doubted his sincerity; in an amicable manner, he plucked the Ambassador's ears: "You Russian!" said he, half-angrily, half-amusedly. Hitler was no Napoleon. Schulenburg reached him on April 28, at Hitler's favorite Hotel Imperial in Vienna. The Ambassador's arguments were useless, as those of his French predecessors had been 129 years before; but — unlike Napoleon — Hitler was not even willing to listen. He could not bear the gaunt, aristocratic Schulenburg, nor the arguments whereby the Ambassador explained the basic loyalty of Stalin to the

German Pact, excused the Russians for the Yugoslav Pact, for troop concentrations, in short, for everything which Hitler might have interpreted as signs of unfriendliness.

> I [Schulenburg] could not believe that Russia would ever attack Germany. The Führer said that he had been forewarned by events in Serbia. What had happened there was to him an example of the political unreliability of states. . . .

After Hitler's arguments, Schulenburg continued:

> In 1939 England and France had taken all conceivable means to win Russia over to their side, and if Stalin had not been able to decide in favor of England and France at a time when England and France were both still strong, I believed that he would certainly not make such a decision today, when France was destroyed and England badly battered. On the contrary, I was convinced that Stalin was prepared to make even further concessions to us. It had already been intimated to our economic negotiators that (if we applied in due time) Russia could supply us up to 5 million tons of grain next year. Citing figures, the Führer said he thought that Russian deliveries were limited by transportation conditions. I pointed out that a more thorough utilization of Russian ports would obviate the difficulties of transportation. The Führer then took leave of me.

This was Hitler's answer: interrupting the conversation with a cool farewell. He closed his ears to arguments which clashed with his plans, plans, however, which he did not reveal, nor even indicate, to his Ambassador. Such was his foolish distrust. (*13*)

[*Signals; rumors; Schulenburg's return.*] During Schulenburg's absence, Stalin's new pro-German policy became increasingly evident. On April 15, the German Embassy was informed that the Soviet government had unconditionally accepted the German requests concerning minor problems of the German-Soviet boundary line which a mixed commission had been discussing for long months. The Soviets' compliant attitude was most remarkable: Stalin gave permission to the German military attaché to visit the most modern Soviet airplane factories: an unprecedented step. The new Vichy Ambassador, Gaston Bergéry, was sympathetically received in Moscow; it was known that he was an adherent of the idea of a "new Europe" under a German-Italian-French-Russian leadership and directed against interferences from external, naval powers. (*14*)

But there were disturbing signs on the Axis side. On April 21, Marshal Pétain told the American Ambassador Leahy that a German-Russian war was due to come. An article in the Italian weekly, *Oggi*, at the end of April called for the revival of the Anti-Comintern Pact. On April 22, a Soviet note protested against frontier violations by German planes: from March 27 to April 18, about 80 violations occurred, and a plane landed at Rovno, where it was discovered that the pilot was doing extensive aerial reconnaissance of Soviet territory. Nevertheless, the Soviet note was not made public; it was neither menacing, nor strong in tone; it merely deemed it necessary

> . . . to remind the German Embassy of the statement that was made on March 28, 1940 . . . according to which [the USSR] made an exception . . . and gave the border troops the order not to fire on the German planes flying over Soviet territory so long as such flights do not occur frequently.

On April 23, the German High Command reported to the German Foreign Ministry 20 border violations by Soviet planes between April 11 and 19, adding that the High Command

> . . . now find that the steadily mounting number of border trespass flights can only be regarded as the deliberate employment of the air force of the USSR over the sovereign territory of the Reich . . . we have to reckon with increased danger of grave border incidents.
> The orders of the High Command of the Armed Forces for the exercise of utmost restraint nevertheless continue in force.

Schulenburg was still away on April 24 when the German Naval Attaché in Moscow reported about circulating rumors of an impending German-Russian war — Cripps was said to have predicted June 22 as the day of the outbreak, and May 20 was mentioned by other people. The attaché added that he was doing everything "to counteract the rumors, which are manifestly absurd." (*15*) The German Ambassador arrived back in Moscow on the eve of the great May 1 military parade. He watched the gigantic show with grave thoughts, ill forebodings — to the spectators, his feelings were hidden by a serene diplomatic smile. On May 2, he sent an energetic message to Berlin; he urged the Foreign Ministry to help him combat the rumors of an imminent war, the continuous source of which were travellers coming from Germany: ". . . it is natural that rumors of that kind constitute a great hazard for the continued peaceful development of German-Soviet relations."

Seven weeks were yet to pass before the day which Schulenburg dreaded and of whose exact date he was left uninformed until the very end.

Beginnings of the central-eastern European resistance movements

[*The status of central-eastern Europe.*]   By the early spring of 1941, Hitler ruled most of central-eastern Europe. Greece and Finland were the only two countries which at that time did not face an immediate German occupation. (Exactly the same situation prevailed in 1945 in regard to Russia.) In April, Yugoslavia and Greece fell in battle, and thus, when the great turning-point came on June 22, 1941, the only fully independent nation in central-eastern Europe was Finland.

Then came the three Tripartite Pact adherents: Hungary, Bulgaria, and Rumania. Of these, the first two preserved most of their sovereignty, and the last was nearest to what Allied propaganda was beginning to call "satellite status." (*1*)   Two full-fledged satellites were the puppet states of Slovakia and Croatia. Albania was a province of the Italian crown; Austria a gau of Germany (*2*); the three Baltic states were member republics of the Soviet Union; Finnish Karelia, eastern Poland, Bessarabia, and northern Bukovina were respective parts of the Karelo-Finnish, Byelorussian, Ukrainian, and Moldavian Soviet Socialist Republics.

[*Poland.*]   The rest of central-eastern Europe was German "colonial" territory: the Czech Protectorate, the Polish General-gouvernement, Greece, and the unannexed parts of Yugoslavia. Of these "colonies," the Protectorate, Greece, and Serbia had some kind of a German-sponsored "national" pseudo-government, made up of a mixed group of anti-Bolshevik (and not entirely dishonest) patriots, adventurers, German spies, and quislings — the latter greatly preponderant. Poland's case was the worst: she had no "government," no "committee," no status at all in the New European Order.

Thus the history of Poland during the Second World War was unique. The German treatment of the Poles was as incredible as it was illogical; its origins were truly psychopathic. None of Germany's enemies on the continent fought more bravely and more hopelessly;

none of Germany's enemies was handled with such a frightful mixture of brutality, torture and truly inhuman contempt. The whole Polish nation was regarded as racially inferior. (*3*) Polish men and women were taken to Germany for slave labor; millions were branded cattle-like. The worst — and most stupid — SS leaders sat in Poland and dictated there over life and death. The German Army did not participate in these atrocities; many high officers expressed their criticism, but, alas, only among themselves. Nor did the majority of the German people know of the Nazis' Polish policies, and those who did, disbelieved the reports. The German people did not realize how great was the sin of their Nazi leaders, a sin which made, perhaps for decades, a future German-Polish reconciliation well-nigh impossible.

This colonial policy bore its fruits from the very beginning. Even the worst foreign tyrant can find a good number of native servants — a truism very evident in the history of our century. Yet, there was no Polish "quisling" group. Ribbentrop wished to abide by the Moscow agreements; he knew that no Polish "national" group could be at the same time pro-Russian and pro-German; he wanted to avoid anything which might have contained potentialities of friction with Russia. But Ribbentrop's strange mind kept to this line of thought even after German-Russian relations deteriorated and war had resulted. Thus, Germany faced a universally hostile Polish and Russian nation at the same time, a catastrophic course, as Hassell noted, against the elementary rules of any German Eastern policy. There is some evidence that Göring and Himmler did not always support Ribbentrop's ideas; their idea was to set up a Polish Regency or something similar. But German overtures to Cardinal Hlond and to the conservative statesman, Bartel, were rejected. The Germans failed to find Polish satellites. Meanwhile, with his plebeian, *nouveau riche* retinue, Frank, the SS "Gouverneur," was enthroned above the ancient city of Cracow, sowing death with one hand and collecting epicurean treasures with the other.

Briefly stated, the main lines of the German colonial policy in Poland were these: establishment of a special legal order; meting out justice on two levels, one for "superior" Germans, the other for "inferior" Poles, Jews, etc.; concentration in ghettos, followed by labor exploitation and final liquidation of the three million Polish Jews; labor exploitation of Poles for the German labor market; complete stifling of Polish cultural and spiritual activity; total curbing of the "degenerate" Catholic Church in Poland.

In the Polish territories which were incorporated into Germany, a forced population "exchange" was made; tens of thousands of Baltic Germans were transported and settled in the "Warthegau," while the Poles were driven out of their homes, segregated, the majority of them ultimately shipped back into the General-gouvernement territory. (4)

[*Resistance.*]   Out of these dark portents grew a wonderfully genuine "resistance movement." It became visible within months after the Polish downfall. By 1940, the Polish Home (Underground) Army — *Armia Krajowa* — began to carry out minor operations, directed by a central command. An underground political "council" had been in existence since late 1939. The organizers of this invisible state were exposed to the greatest dangers. Nothing illustrates their situation more than the fact that almost all of the original national council leaders were discovered and executed by the Germans in 1940; even so, the political branch of the resistance continued to exist.

Every resistance movement has two branches, an internal one and the external branch of émigré activities abroad. Here, too, Poland was unique. The Polish government fled the country after the military collapse, but it continued to exist. In the eyes of the world — except for Germany, Slovakia, and Russia (5) — the Polish government-in-exile represented the Polish nation. There was no lapse, no break in constitutional continuity. There was contact between the Polish underground state and the government-in-exile. Tens of thousands of young Poles left their country through Rumania, Hungary, Yugoslavia, and Greece, making their way to France to join the free Polish Army. Secret emissaries travelled to and fro on this perilous transcontinental route; from the end of 1940 onwards, liaison men were dropped by parachute.

[*Abroad.*]   The Polish national government reached Paris at the end of September. There a thorough reorganization took place; as with every national catastrophe, some scapegoat-hunting was involved. Beck, ill, remained in Rumania (where he died in 1944) — he was not granted an exit visa, probably due to some French pressure. President Moscicki resigned; after his candidates for Prime Minister were courteously rejected by the French, a broad coalition government-in-exile, led by General Sikorski, was formed. The French hosts provided a seat for the Polish government at Angers; in November, the first cabinet meeting took place there. Preparations were made for a free Polish university-in-exile; and, most important, an "army-in-exile" was forming. The government gained by a cooperative agreement which the representatives of the four major political parties (Peasant, Socialist, National Democrat, and Christian Labor) reached in Paris in February 1940. The programs of the Free Polish radio services in London and Paris and the Polish underground radio transmitter *Swit* were also coordinated.

Polish troops fought valiantly in the Narvik campaign in April–May. When the French collapse came, there were more than twenty thousand Polish troops in France, many of them in the Maginot Line, commanded by the able generals Duch, Prugar-Kettling, Szyszko-Bohusz, and Maczek. On June 15, the French Premier received the Polish Foreign Minister, Zaleski, and told him of the necessity for the request of a Franco-German armistice; he suggested that the Polish government-in-exile follow the same policy. Zaleski refused, while Reynaud said that due to psychological reasons France would receive a better deal from the Germans than had the Poles. Subsequently, the Sikorski government prepared to move to England; there seemed to be no hope for a North African resistance. Polish units, fighting in the Maginot Line, stood in heavy battle; some sustaining losses up to 30 per cent (6); some cut through northeastern France and joined other units. France was sinking, and a grim little foreign army worked its way through the clogged roads to the Atlantic ports. The last troops, accompanied by some Polish statesmen, left the little Basque port of St. Jean-de-Luz on June 22 aboard the Polish ocean liner *Batory*, the last liner which left France for England. A Polish Brigade crossed into Palestine from French-held Syria.

Thus, for the first time in history, the government of a central-eastern European nation was set up on British soil — a symbol, perhaps, of the coming Anglo-Saxon Age. The Polish President, Raczkiewicz, arrived in London on the evening of June 21, and King George VI went to Victoria Station to greet him in person. The significance of this royal gesture went beyond mere courtesy and protocol. In those days of the French Armistice, Poland's repute and her future prospects were glorious. This fortunate condition continued to exist until it became suddenly complicated by the German attack on Russia.

The political conduct of the émigré usually requires exceptional tact, intelligence, restraint, and sagacity. Especially when there are two different groups among the exiled, the elimination of their differences becomes virtually impossible and later, furthered by jealousy, petty politicking and personal intrigues, this situation produces interminable worries for the host nation. Even if later, for the sake of appearance or because of temporary national exigencies, a coalition is achieved, this coalition turns out to be temporary only, as it does not bear within the seed sown by the spirit and procedure of compromise. The émigré himself is an uprooted person, often irresponsible and usually bewildered by the political and social procedures, concepts, and mannerisms of the host country. Added to this, his daily existence hinges upon a thread. Unless he adapts himself to manual labor — which politicians seldom practice — or unless he is a known scholar, specialist, or multilingual journalist, he is dependent on some kind of an allotment which he receives from the émigré council or government or, sometimes, from the foreign service of the host nation. As many individuals vie for such support, controversies and mutual recriminations are almost inevitable.

Fortunately, the Poles in exile did not operate in a vacuum; the Polish government in London had real tasks ahead and the successfully saved cadres of the Polish Army absorbed the energies of many people. These units had to be equipped, organized, and kept in good shape — soon they were to appear in the four corners of the world. (7) There was but little time and there remained but a few little men for scheming, intrigues, and ideological quarrels. There were, of course, disagreements. Sikorski — due to his Western Polish origin — was prone to underestimate the Russian danger; for this he was criticized by quite a few Poles. Also, former adherents of the Polish extreme Right formed little groups among themselves and published one or two silly periodicals; their conduct was sometimes questioned by the British press and in Parliament. The Polish government and the body of the Polish nation-in-exile remained unified, however, until the outbreak of the Russian War brought about a great national dilemma.

.   .   .   .

[*Czechoslovaks abroad.*] A Czechoslovak National Council was formed in Paris in November 1939; Britain recognized it in December. Not until July 23, 1940, was a provisional Czechoslovak government-in-exile recognized by the British Foreign Office; full recognition was granted only on July 18, 1941. (*8*)

The Czechs, unlike the Poles, were split into two groups: pro-Beneš and anti-Beneš; in view of the fact that Beneš had resigned in October 1938 in a perfectly constitutional manner, there were arguments concerning the constitutional basis of councils and governments-in-exile. These are delicate problems, when the constitutionality of émigré organs comes up. The sponsoring Powers have to find a golden mean between an opportunistically flexible and a mechanically rigid adaptation of principles to all cases. Then, these principles, if adopted, must be carried out with a certain consistency — a task even more difficult. It is during the evaluation of public opinion within the external and internal resistance groups that various arguments of various émigré groups arise to unduly influence the policies of the Great Powers. Theoretically it may be argued that while tolerating or even encouraging the presence of various groups within the political body of the émigrés, the "sponsor nation" — and this is especially true of the United States — is unwilling to interfere in the internal development of that political body. Unfortunately, full adherence to this principle is impossible to practice. The administrators of foreign policy cannot waste valuable time trying to keep their contacts with each of the émigré groups calculated to a regular and meticulous equality. Thus frequent personal, social, and (in the case of former diplomats) traditional contacts develop into regular consultation, which, in some cases, may lead to lack of impartiality on one side and exaggerated influence on the other. Jealousy on the part of those who have lesser contacts with the official organs of the "sponsor nation" is always a regrettable and unfortunate factor. This jealousy is furthered by the ever more extensive technical faculties of communication, for modern press and radio give ample opportunity for the publicity and ideas of a certain émigré group to overshadow that of another.

When Beneš left Czechoslovakia, he wished to retire from political life; he lived in London from October 1938 to February 1939, at which time he left for the United States to accept a university chair. Shortly after his arrival, the German occupation of Czechoslovakia took place. Time had come to establish the external branch of Czechoslovak resistance.

Many patriots rallied, however, around Hodža, the former Premier, and Osuský, the former Czechoslovak Minister to Paris. These two statesmen regarded the superficial Beneš as one of the authors of the Czechoslovak catastrophe. Osuský and Hodža put their faith in plans for a great Austrian-Hungarian-Polish-Czechoslovak federation and maintained contacts with various émigré leaders of these countries. Both Osuský and Hodža were favored by the French Foreign Ministry, and the ex-President seemed not to command too much influence in London; only in the United States did he seem favored. Osuský continued to believe, even after March 1939, that Hácha and Chvalkovsky were not traitors but had tried to save what was possible, had taken a reasonable stand which enabled the French and British governments to build up the framework of the Czechoslovak resistance organization; and as the Germans discovered in 1941, many of the leaders of the Czech "government," dubbed "puppets" by journalists, were implicated in a vast anti-German conspiracy.

[*Resistance at home.*] The internal resistance of Czechoslovakia was conditioned by the fact that Germany's treatment of the Czechs was far better than that accorded to the Poles. To distinguish, of course, between the Czech (Bohemian-Moravian) Protectorate and Slovakia is necessary; the latter was an independent state under the ambitious and perhaps unduly unscrupulous Monsignor Tiso. There the Hlinka Guards ruled, strongly aided by the local German national elements; and although as early as December 1939, the German minority leader, Karmasin, reported the existence of resistance attitudes, most of the Slovaks seemed to enjoy their "independence" from Czech rule. Economically they were not unfortunate, as the industries of Slovakia (all former Czech or Jewish properties) were "Slovakized," and Slovakia traded freely with Hungary, Russia, and Germany. Not until 1943 did a Slovak "resistance" movement show itself. The parochial character of the Tiso dictatorship satisfied most Slovaks; Slovak Catholicism, although Roman in rite and name, had always had a certain Orthodox tinge: personal and power-conscious, in contrast to the traditions of Austria and of lands further to the south and west, where the visible body of the Catholic Church stood for western ideals.

In "Czechia," the Reich Protector was Neurath, a man regarded as a German Conservative. He ruled severely and often complied with the cruelest Nazi directives; yet, his rule was far better than the tyrannies of Frank and others in Poland. Tranquillity in that vitally important industrial region of the New Europe was essential to Germany. (9) There were, of course, vast restrictions. The Czech press became "government" controlled, under the pro-German propaganda politician, Moravec, while the Germans oppressed the nation spiritually and intellectually. As in Poland, wide discrimination was made in favor of the German inhabitants; slave labor was exploited, although more gradually than in Poland; the Jewish population was deported. Neurath tried to give a legal aspect to German rule, until SS influences made Hitler consider Neurath a weakling; in October 1940, a Hitler directive ordered the abolishment of the remnants of legal procedure in which Neurath's Czech legislation was clad. The resisters, saboteurs, Czech nationalists, should be summarily shot, said the directive; there was "no need . . . for martyrs." On October 1, 1940, a complete customs' union was declared to exist between the Reich and the Protectorate territory.

The formation of the Czech underground began after the National Council was created in Paris in November 1939. The last open demonstration against the Germans took place on October 28, 1939, when students of Charles University in Prague celebrated the Czechoslovak Republic's anniversary. The students were dispersed and many of them arrested; a month later, a second demonstration took place. The German police then cracked down and forced the resisters to go underground.

[*Foreign policy.*] The external branch of the resistance formed a Czechoslovak Legion, which fought well in France and parts of which succeeded in making their way to England. By the fall of 1940, the so-called Foreign Corps of the British Army had four thousand Czechs in its ranks, together with three thousand anti-Nazi Germans. (*10*) Polish and Czech airmen excelled themselves in the great air battles over Britain during the autumn.

By that time, the Czechoslovak government-in-exile was in existence; Beneš had the provisional presidency, while Monsignor Šramek headed a coalition government. But there were important differences between the Beneš group and Osuský and Hodža in their concept of foreign policy. Hodža, for example, was not opposed to plans for an Austro-Hungarian monarchy and a Czechoslovak-Central-European federation, of which the Monarchy would be one pillar and Czechoslovakia the other. Beneš, on the other hand, was anti-Habsburg and wished to restore the Little Entente system, leaning rather on Russia. Especially after the fall of France, Beneš envisaged Czechoslovakia as playing a rôle of a great European power after the war, perhaps the

"gendarme" of Britain in central Europe, and a great "bridge" between the East, Soviet Russia, and the Western world, the Anglo-
Saxon Powers. Beneš foresaw the coming Russian-German War, but,
with exaggerated idealism, he hoped that it was to be Stalin who
would attack Hitler. He continuously tried to approach Soviet diplomats but was shunned by them; yet, even an attack by Czech Communist manifestoes as late as December 1940, which criticized his
Munich stand and his "warmonger" policies, did not convince Beneš.
In the spring of 1941, he sent the Czechoslovak General Pika to Russia via Turkey, but even at so late a time, the Russians did not want
to listen to Beneš's emissary, who waited in vain for a Russian visa
until after Hitler attacked Stalin. (The same General Pika was
condemned to death by the Czech Communists as a pro-Western
conspirator in 1948.)

However, not until 1941 did these differences become vitally important. In 1940, despite the great German victories and the seemingly
very, very long, unsure and tiring road to victory, post-war plans
were already being hatched. Ironically enough, these premature plans
of 1940 were much more realistic than the hurried and incomplete
ones that were to be made during the months and years when victory
was in sight. (11) First in Paris, then in London and in Washington,
plans for a central-eastern European federation were sympathetically
received. On November 11, 1940, a Czechoslovak-Polish Declaration was issued in London, which not only provided for mutual consultations and put an end to all previous Polish-Czech differences,
but proclaimed a mutual interest in a central-eastern European federation. All the émigré diplomats, including Austrian, Hungarian,
and Rumanian dissidents, welcomed the idea. President Roosevelt
expressed his full agreement with the federation plans when he received the new Polish Ambassador, Ciechanowski, in March 1941.
Neither was Britain willing to return to the Little Entente system and
the World War I peace treaties, and this could be seen from the fact
that in 1940–41, the British Government still had not committed
herself as to whether she regarded the Munich Pact as invalid or not.
(These "silences" of the Foreign Office concerning Munich were
meant not so much to encourage German proposals for a negotiated
peace as to indirectly encourage Austrians, Hungarians and Slovaks
to put their faith in British victory and British peacemaking. (12))

The Russian War, then, changed everything; Beneš set out at once
to win the sympathies of Stalin and to assume the image of a great

statesman, building his Czechoslovak bridge "between East and West." A tragic concept; a futile attempt! Early in 1942, the first signs of Stalin's aggressive and anti-Polish foreign policy became visible, and Beneš tried to accommodate himself to the Soviets. He saw that Stalin was against any kind of central-eastern European fed-eration, which, however friendly to Russia, would be an obstacle to the Soviet advance into Europe. Consequently, Beneš (although in January 1942 the November 1940 Declaration was embodied into a Czechoslovak-Polish Agreement) drew away from the Poles, and in October 1942, he actually denounced the idea of a central-eastern European confederation. By that time, he was the undisputed leader of the Czechoslovak exile movement, as he had full support of both Washington and London; also, Hodža became very ill during the crucial year 1942 and died shortly afterwards.

.   .   .   .

[*The others.*]   In the other central-eastern European states, anti-German resistance was just beginning; the external branches were more visible than the internal ones. Baron von Franckenstein, the Austrian Minister to London who resigned in protest against *Anschluss*, was the first of a long line of central-eastern European émigré diplomats. In 1940–41, a number of Hungarian and Rumanian diplomats stationed in Britain and in the United States resigned and thereby formed the core of Hungarian and Rumanian émigré move-ments. Practically the whole corps of the Lithuanian, Estonian, and Latvian foreign envoys resigned in protest against the Soviet occupa-tion of their countries. One Slovak Minister, Szatmáry, surprisingly resigned in Warsaw on September 1, 1939, and declared himself for the Allied cause.

The bulk of Hungarians, Rumanians, and Bulgarians nevertheless continued to serve. There was no popular discontent against the pre-vailing régimes in these countries. Indeed, anti-German resistance appeared only among the upper classes: the aristocracy and the *grande bourgeoisie;* apart from them, only the small intellectual cadres of the small democratic peasant parties stood fast against the imple-mentation of a German-made New Europe. Great influence was ex-ercised by the British Broadcasting Corporation, whose broadcasts were avidly listened to. In 1938, the BBC had instituted a Euro-pean newscast service in several languages, and although from political and psychological viewpoints the programs were often wanting, these British broadcasts, with their reliable news services and reports, became the daily fare for tens of thousands throughout central-eastern Europe.

It is interesting that the origins of anti-German resistance were to be found almost entirely among the conservatives. The Social Democratic movements in central-eastern Europe had long before lost their vigor; besides, their parties, except in Hungary, were illegal. Almost all the radicals were in the Nazi camps; only a few educated ones were secretly pro-British and generally unpopular. The Communist parties were virtually non-existent, except in Yugoslavia, Bulgaria, and, of course, in the newly acquired Soviet territories. They commanded no following elsewhere. While until June 1941 they had campaigned against the "capitalist warmongers" (in December 1940, for example, the Central Committee of the Czechoslovak Communist Party praised the effort of the "German workers" while it assailed Beneš and the Anglo-American "imperialists"), even after the Russian War broke out, the Communists were incapable of gaining much influence among the masses. (However, in Hungary and Yugoslavia, British intelligence sometimes worked with local Communist intellectuals.) The only interesting developments in the history of the central-eastern European Communist parties were personal changes within the parties themselves. A secret conference of the Yugoslav Communist Party met in October 1940 (*13*) when, under the nose of the Royal Yugoslav Police, more than a hundred party representatives met and elected several central committee members, candidates, and seven Politburo members. The mysterious organizer of that conference was a Comrade Valter, who was to appear a year later under the pseudonym, Tito. . . . In November, 1940, a prisoners' exchange agreement between Hungary and the Soviet Union enabled the Hungarian Communist leader, Rákosi, to transfer his residence from a Hungarian prison to Moscow. In March 1941 the Rumanian Ana Pauker was freed and deported to Russia in a similar manner.

In Hungary the Regent and his Premier, Teleki, secretly tried to form an external branch of Hungarian resistance. Intellectual circles in Hungary — except for the strong group of Imrédy and the National Socialists — were largely anti-German, but their support was not enough. Teleki himself hesitated, as he was uncertain of the Allies' plans and failed to see what Otto Habsburg was doing in the United States, where, in 1940, the Archduke seemingly had the ear and support of President Roosevelt. (*14*) His hesitations were at last overcome, and it was decided that the opposition leader, Eckhardt, who had Horthy's sympathy, would go to the United States and start a Hungarian émigré movement there. Eckhardt arrived in New York in 1941. For awhile he could keep up his secret contacts with Horthy, but in 1942 the Hungarian government condemned him *in absentia* and deprived him of his Hungarian citizenship. This was the fate of the few Rumanian and Bulgarian dissidents too.

Thus, when the Russian War broke out on June 22, 1941, the situation of the external resistance branches of the central-eastern European nations was this: Poland, Czechoslovakia, Yugoslavia, and Greece had governments-in-exile, while the organization of Free Austrian, Free Hungarian, and Free Rumanian groups in Britain and in the United States had just begun on the committee level. The envoys of the Baltic states continued to function as honorable symbols of an independent Lithuania, Latvia, and Estonia in London and Washington.

At this time the relative strength of anti-German resistance in central-eastern Europe (not including, of course, the nations incorporated by the Soviet Union) ranged approximately as follows, from the strongest to the least strong: Poland, the Czech parts of Czechoslovakia, the Serb, Macedonian and Montenegrin parts of Yugoslavia, Greece, Albania, (*15*) and the Slovene and Dalmatian parts of Yugoslavia. In Slovakia, Hungary, Croatia, Rumania, Bulgaria, and Austria direct anti-German action was only sporadic; resistance was indirectly exercised mainly by outstanding persons, the churches (particularly certain Catholic churchmen), and through the writings of certain intellectuals.

The last phase of Nazi-Soviet peace

Adolf Hitler was considered a talkative individual; thus his silences usually had ominous significances. On April 28, 1939, he made a speech, and although he touched upon almost every point of the European horizon, he failed to speak a single word about the Soviet Union. Five days later, the dramatic Litvinov-Molotov change occurred: the Wilhelmshaven silences brought their rewards. They were understood. Exactly two years later, Joseph Stalin anxiously waited in Moscow. The German Ambassador had returned from Berlin; his long-delayed personal report to Hitler had been made. What was the message which Schulenburg brought back with him — or, rather, was there any message? For five days, Stalin and Molotov expected the German Ambassador to call at the Kremlin; but no such call was made. Then, on May 4, Hitler spoke; but, as at Wilhelmshaven, he kept ominously silent, not a word did he say about Soviet Russia.

[*Stalin at the helm.*]   From that day on, Stalin could no longer doubt what was behind the ominous silences. It was now clear that neither the new Soviet attitude after April 13, nor Schulenburg's report had convinced Hitler that he should relinquish his suspicion and hostility. From the western borders, report after report spoke about German troop concentrations. Countermeasures had to be taken. On May 5, Stalin addressed the graduates of the Soviet War Academy; his speech was not made public but it was reported that he admonished the young officers to ready themselves for future tasks with extraordinary alertness, for the danger of war was there. Dekanosov was recalled from Berlin: Stalin wanted to hear a direct personal report from the German capital. On May 7, the Soviet radio stations and newspapers surprised the 193 million Soviet citizens with the grave and important announcement that Joseph Vissarionovich Stalin had taken the post of Chairman of the Council of People's Commissars. To the query of foreign diplomats, the highest Soviet officials stated that undoubtedly this was the greatest historic event in the life of the Soviet Union since Lenin died.

Schulenburg explained the great event thus:

> . . . the reason for it may be sought in the recent mistakes in foreign policy which led to a cooling off of the cordiality of German-Soviet relations, for the creation and preservation of which Stalin had consciously striven, while Molotov's own initiative often expended itself in an obstinate defense of individual issues. . . .

And the German Naval Attaché: "Stalin is the pivot of German-Soviet collaboration," an essentially correct interpretation. While in the placid May nights, truck after truck rumbled westward on the dirt-covered Russian highways, division after division moved slowly, inconspicuously toward the frontier; on May 8, a TASS communiqué "denied reports" that Soviet troop concentrations were taking place. Nevertheless, on May 9 a Finnish intelligence reported a quiet evacuation of civilians in some Russian frontier areas, and the German

Consul in Harbin, Manchuria, intercepted a circular instruction sent out by the Soviet Foreign Commissariat on that same day:

> Although German-Russian negotiations are proceeding normally, it has become imperative for the Soviets, in view of Germany's dictatorial attitude, to warn Germany that the Soviets are prepared to protect their interests if . . . they are violated. Under the circumstances it is very important to learn the attitude of all other countries in the event of a German-Russian conflict. It is necessary to proceed with the greatest caution. A survey of the situation and prompt report are requested. (*1*)

About the same time, Madame Kollontay, the known Germanophobe Soviet Ambassadress in Stockholm, was reported to have said that "at no time in Russian history have there been stronger troop contingents assembled on Russia's western border than now."

Yet all this did not mean that the Soviet leaders were now willing and ready to face war, come what might. The Russian sense of security made it imperative that extensive military preparations should proceed. But Stalin was still unwilling to consult with Churchill or with Roosevelt; he was bent upon the task of convincing Hitler of his goodwill. Another, April 13-like diplomatic demonstration came. Just before the Iraqi government of Rashid Ali-el-Qailani attacked the British at Basra and Baghdad, the Soviet Union announced its decision to establish diplomatic relations with the state of Iraq. More temerity was needed for the next step. On May 7 it was announced that the Soviet government withdrew her recognition from the Belgian, Norwegian, and, last but not least, the Yugoslav governments. The same Gavrilovič who a month before was being feted as the truest brother of Russia was shown the door: together with his colleagues, he was expelled from Moscow.

Stalin had to take into account, however, the feelings of the Russian public: even in his phalanster-like state, morale would suffer if exposed to seemingly ever-varying changes in foreign policy, the underlying consistency of which could not be openly explained. Thus the expulsion of the three legations was not mentioned by the Soviet press, and it became known in diplomatic circles that General (the later Marshal) Zhukov bade a cordial farewell to Colonel Popovič, the Yugoslav military attaché, and said with a twinkling eye that all this should not be taken too seriously.

Berlin failed to respond to these obvious gestures of sincere friendship. The diary entries of Simoni are illuminating:

> *May 7:*   German political circles judge the war against the Soviet
> Union more and more as inevitable, while military circles
> are not so convinced of its inevitability. (2)
>
> *May 15:* There is no doubt anymore that the Russians are trying the
> impossible to evade the war. They shall not succeed. The
> Führer has made his decision.

[*Hess, Ribbentrop, Mussolini.*] Meanwhile the diplomatic scene had been stirred to the depths by the Hess bombshell. Rudolf Hess, equipped with visiting-cards of Professor Haushofer, as well as with hazy ideas and a frail memory, descended by parachute on May 10 upon the green pastures of Scotland. Here was the specter of German-British negotiations . . . perhaps. Stalin and Mussolini, the two arch-opponents of such a development were, however, promptly reassured by Hitler's disavowal of his deputy and by the amused and complacent attitude with which Britain greeted the unexpected arrival. (3) Despite all contemporary speculations, the Hess "mystery" harbored no germs of diplomatic surprises. The sensation fizzled out in a few days, while Ribbentrop rushed to Rome to reassure Mussolini and Ciano, and also to discuss with them the pending Mediterranean plans of the Axis. These centered around Crete, Iraq, and Syria. Mussolini insisted upon the capture of Cyprus, which he regarded as "the anteroom of Syria." (Cyprus was not invaded; and on June 7, after the Iraqi rebellion had been quashed, British and Free French forces moved against Syria.) But in Crete, the Axis won full victory. (There the Italian armed forces contributed considerably to the military success. Operating from the Dodecanese, they undertook an amphibious landing in eastern Crete in the last phase of the campaign. The campaign in Crete, however, somewhat delayed the Germans in their shifting of military equipment to Russia.) Important was, however, Ribbentrop's distrust; he wanted to mislead the Italians in regard to the Russian War, although as early as May 1 a military directive had fixed "B-Day" to be on June 22. (4) Ribbentrop had no faith in the Italians, much less in their sense of secrecy. He mentioned that relations with Russia were not too good, but that was about as far as he went. When Mussolini hesitatingly interjected that collaboration with Russia seemed to him to be advantageous, the German Foreign Minister said with a stiff face that he did not

believe "that Stalin would undertake anything against Germany . . .",
and that "the Führer would certainly not look for any quarrel. . . ." (5)

[*Germany's small allies.*] Italy's eventual participation in
Barbarossa was of negligible importance; but the nations which bor-
dered Russia on the west, Finland, Hungary, and Rumania, (6) had
to be included in the German calculations. The first and the last of
these had been robbed of their borderlands by Stalin in 1940; they
would likely be willing to grasp the occasion for reconquest. Hungary's
position was different. The German High Command conference of
February 3 envisaged Rumanian and Finnish participation, but was
doubtful of what Hungary would do. Therefore the High Command
planned a trick. "If Hungary is not to participate," said the *Barbarossa*
paper, the passage of German troops through Hungary will be requested as usual and subsequently undertaken. "The destination of
the march will be given as Rumania. At the last minute the direction
will change toward the Russian frontier." On March 17 Hitler
expressed himself against any Hungarian participation. But after
the death of Teleki, the Hungarian situation changed, as the new
Premier Bárdossy (7) was more prone to listen to the enthusiastic
pro-Germans of the General Staff and to the War Minister.

The care and secrecy of the German military planners could still
not be abandoned, whether the dealings were with trustworthy allies
or not. The same care prevailed in regard to Japan. The "B-Day"
plan of May 1 said that "conversations with Hungary and Rumania
[should be undertaken only] at a very advanced date. . . . [these] are
only possible in the last third of May. The Führer believes that the
Hungarians will be prepared to carry out defensive operations on the
Russian border but they will not allow any German attack from Hungary." The directive added that, for the "concealment of conversations with friendly countries," it should be argued that the eastern
front must be covered in the event of a "projected German assault
in the West." That Antonescu would participate in the reconquest
of Bessarabia was clear. But there were differences of opinion about
the scale of Rumanian participation. On March 20, Göring expressed
his views that Rumania should supply at least twenty divisions; this
number was then whittled down considerably. On May 23, a top
secret military directive "on the orders of the Führer" went out to
the German liaison commander in Rumania, Col. Gen. Ritter von
Schobert, telling him of the coming of *Barbarossa*, adding that "large-

scale Rumanian mobilization is, however, undesirable" and that "any
questions in regard to a German-Russian war [should] be avoided."
On that day the British Joint Intelligence committee estimated that
a German attack on Russia was not yet a certainty.

Finland was the first ally to be concretely informed of the German
war plans. Early in May, President Ryti heard somewhat conflicting
predictions by the German Minister Blücker, but on the 8th the Minister said that there would be no war with Russia in the near future
— anyhow, not until the spring of 1943. Then, on May 20, Schnurre,
a German emissary, appeared in Helsinki, called on Ryti, and informed him that Hitler had expressed his desire that staff talks with
the Finnish military should begin, since a "forestalling" Soviet attack
in the direction of Finland or the Balkans had to be taken into account. Ryti therefore summoned his Premier, Rangell, Field-Marshal
Mannerheim, Foreign Minister Witting, and the War Minister,
Walden. It was decided to send a military mission to Germany, and
the German General Buschenhagen (8) was dispatched to Finland.
Despite these liaison talks, the Germans were nevertheless unable to
wrest an unequivocal promise of Finnish participation in the coming
operation against Russia. The Ryti-Rangell régime, while not unwilling to plan for a prospective Finnish war of reconquest, was still
hesitant to abandon Finnish neutrality in the conflict of the Great
Powers. (9)

Thus ended the month of May.

.   .   .   .

The final timetable for *Barbarossa* was issued on June 1. This said
that Rumania had already started mobilization; Bulgaria had been
requested not to weaken her Turkish frontier; Hungary was not yet
to be informed; Sweden was not to be consulted at all; consultations
with the Finnish General Staff had been proceeding since May 25.
A camouflage *Operation Harpoon* was to be undertaken: all naval
movements were to be disguised as precautionary measures in northern Norwegian waters. On June 5 the German naval mission in
Leningrad, where a number of German engineers and technicians
were constructing a cruiser, was to be recalled, the recall to take place
"in groups and by stages." On May 22 Kesselring's Air Force headquarters had been moved to Poznan in Poland; on May 15 Italian,
on May 31 British Intelligence estimated the German attack on Russia

to be at hand; on June 5 this was reaffirmed; on June 12 British Intelligence was certain. On June 14 Churchill informed Washington thereof.

[*Conflicts and rumors: Soviet reactions.*] However, the diplomatic picture was far from being correspondingly clear. The German-Italian conflicts in Croatia necessitated a meeting on the Brenner. Mussolini and Hitler met on June 2. The former was angry because of the German meddlings in Croatia and in Greece; this the latter suspected, hence he was very cordial. Both he and Ribbentrop were, on the other hand, misleading. Mussolini pleaded for a "radical solution" to the Russian problem, preferably a military alliance or, as a last resort, war. Hitler said that "Balkan events showed that the first alternative was to be excluded." But this was all. Ribbentrop said to Ciano that rumors of a Russian war were "excessively premature," and he did not divulge anything to the Italians. Thus, nineteen days before the greatest war in the history of Europe was to begin, the Axis partner was left groping in the dark!

While the German silence continued and the dark silhouettes of the lean German guns could be seen across the frontier in the light Polish evenings, while the deadweight of Hitler's divisions on the borders of Stalin's empire was increasing day by day, Russia continued her diplomatic game to convince Hitler that she was a sincere friend. (*10*) The Rumanian and Hungarian Ministers in Moscow were now amazed by a sudden Russian spirit of courtesy and cooperation with which their problems were treated. Finland was spared all adverse propaganda by radio and press; on June 1 Stalin received Paasikivi smilingly and spoke of goodwill and good relations. He spoke of the necessity for a Russian-Finnish collaboration; he also said that the Soviet Union was considerably to augment grain deliveries to Finland (a most important item in the balance of Finnish economy, which had undergone a very grave crisis during the previous winter).

On June 3, the Soviet government withdrew her recognition from the Greek government-in-exile. On June 4, the correspondent of the London *News Chronicle*, who was eagerly predicting the coming break, was expelled from Russia. On June 6, Schulenburg repeated his arguments, again and again the same, ever reasonable, ever sincere:

Russia will only fight if attacked by Germany. . . . Russian policy still strives as before to produce the best relationship to Germany. . . .

> All observations show that Stalin and Molotov, who alone are re-
> sponsible for Russian foreign policy, are doing everything to avoid a
> conflict with Germany.

But Berlin's silence remained uninterrupted. On that day, instructions
went out to the entire German press not to reproduce the news of the
British correspondent's expulsion. Two days later, German troops
began to land in Finnish ports. On June 9, President Ryti spoke to
his cabinet council in Helsinki:

> Should a war break out between Germany and the Soviet Union,
> this would be to the gain of the whole world. Germany is the only
> state which is presently able to defeat Russia or, at least, weaken her
> — and the world would not suffer if Germany would be simultane-
> ously weakened.

This June 9 was a Monday. On that day and during the subsequent
week not only did the most irresponsible rumors circulate, but the
reports, communiqués, and announcements from which the Foreign
Offices made their estimates were wholly confusing.

The Hungarian War Minister, Bartha, was in Rome on Monday
and expressed his opinion that the German-Russian War was imminent, adding that the campaign would be over in eight weeks.
That same afternoon the First Secretary of the Italian Embassy in
Moscow arrived in Berlin, reporting that there could be no war, as
the Russians were ready to accede to every possible German request.
On Tuesday Sir Stafford Cripps, who previously had predicted the
outbreak of the war with precision, left Moscow for London. Everybody knew that this was no simple trip of a diplomat who went to
report. Sir Stafford was tired. He had lost his patience; he felt that
he could do nothing with the men in the Kremlin; as he left, his colleagues in Moscow doubted whether he would ever return or whether
Churchill would try to send a new Ambassador, less sensitive and
more astute. That Tuesday evening the Russian Minister in Budapest, Charonov, told his Finnish colleague there that relations between Berlin and Moscow were "excellent." Meanwhile the Finnish
envoy was informed in Berlin that day that a "satisfactory preliminary reply" to Finland's requests had been received from Russian
officials.

Throughout Wednesday, fantastic rumors of an impending German-Russian alliance were increasing. Perhaps to fool the Italians,
the SS leader, Lutze, told the Italian Embassy in Berlin that a broad

German-Russian agreement was to be expected and that Stalin was to come to Berlin. The Finnish Minister in Berlin reported that the Soviet attachés there were surprised when a deterioration in German-Russian relations was mentioned to them. On Thursday, even Washington abated its certain belief in a war between Germany and Russia, as Sumner Welles told Procopé, the Finnish Minister, that he thought a German-Soviet compromise was forthcoming. That evening, however, Hitler decided to inform Antonescu of the impending war. The Rumanian was happy.

On Friday evening at seven o'clock the Soviet radio stations broadcast the most classic "denial" which TASS had ever produced, a communiqué which may long be studied by students of diplomatic history. It deserves to be reproduced in its entirety:

> Even before the return of the English Ambassador Cripps to London, but especially after his return, there have been widespread rumors of "an impending war between the USSR and Germany" in the English and foreign press. These rumors allege:
>
> 1. That Germany supposedly has made various territorial and economic demands on the USSR and that at present negotiations are impending between Germany and the USSR for the conclusion of a new and closer agreement between them;
>
> 2. That the Soviet Union is supposed to have declined these demands and that as a result Germany has begun to concentrate her troops on the frontier of the Soviet Union in order to attack the Soviet Union;
>
> 3. That on its side the Soviet Union is supposed to have begun intensive preparations for war with Germany and to have concentrated its troops on the German border.
>
> Despite the obvious absurdity of these rumors, responsible circles in Moscow have thought it necessary, in view of the persistent spread of these rumors, to authorize TASS to state that these rumors are a clumsy propaganda maneuver of the forces arrayed against the Soviet Union and Germany, which are interested in a spread and intensification of the war.
>
> TASS declares that:
>
> 1. Germany has addressed no demands to the Soviet Union and has asked for no new closer agreement, and that therefore negotiations cannot be taking place;
>
> 2. According to the evidence in the possession of the Soviet Union, both Germany and the Soviet Union are fulfilling to the letter the terms of the Soviet-German Nonaggression Pact, so that in the opinion of Soviet circles the rumors of the intention of Germany to break

the Pact and to launch an attack against the Soviet Union are completely without foundation, while the recent movements of German
troops which have completed their operations in the Balkans, to the
eastern and northern parts of Germany, must be explained by other
motives which have no connection with Soviet-German relations;

3. The Soviet Union, in accordance with its peace policy, has fulfilled and intends to fulfill the terms of the Soviet-German Nonag-
gression Pact; as a result, all the rumors according to which the
Soviet Union is preparing for a war with Germany are false and pro-
vocative;

4. The summer calling-up of the reserves of the Red Army which is
now taking place and the impending maneuvers mean nothing but a
training of the reservists and a check on the operations of the railroad
system, which as is known takes place every year; consequently, it
appears at least nonsensical to interpret these measures of the Red
Army as an action hostile to Germany.

The Russian government handed the text of this communiqué to
the German Ambassador at once. Was the silence of Berlin to break
now at last? Gafencu described the atmosphere well: "Stalin . . . was
waiting in the solitude of the Kremlin, waiting on a foreign decision,
somebody else was to decide his fate. He was no more the master of
events. His will had to conform to a force without; his immense
might was of no use anymore. He could but wait — wait, silently
wait, as Finland and the Baltic states, Poland and Rumania had done;
wait until a mighty and ruthless neighbor, who would not even
deign him a word — as he himself had not deigned these small neighboring states a word — decided to strike."

Two days were yet to pass before the pattern revealed itself with
more clarity; meanwhile it could be ascertained that Russia was taking certain precautionary measures. On the night of June 13-14,
Finnish naval intelligence reported increased Russian patrol activity
at the western exit of the Gulf of Finland. On the same night the
great wave of deportations of "socially dangerous elements" took
place in the Baltic states, which, however senseless and brutal, nevertheless proved that the Muscovite chieftains were aware that soon the
Baltic states might be the battleground where the German and Soviet
armies would come to grips.

[*The last weeks of peace.*]   On Sunday, June 15, Ribbentrop
and Ciano held one of their seemingly regular meetings. (*11*) The

two Foreign Ministers came to Venice to witness Croatia's adherence to the Tripartite Pact. Ribbentrop could hide but little now. He said that in view of a steady worsening of relations with Russia, a "clarification" would be made by Hitler before the end of the month. Before leaving Venice, Ribbentrop telegraphed the German Minister to Budapest to inform Bárdossy along the same lines. (The Hungarian and Rumanian War Ministers had been notified by the German High Command during the previous night.) To Ciano Ribbentrop mentioned the end of June; the communication to Bárdossy spoke of "the beginning of July at the latest," and both statements spoke of "negotiations." But "B-Day" was already set for Sunday, June 22, and there were no negotiations — although a German intelligence report on the same day reported that Stalin was prepared to "make extreme concessions," while the leading Soviet army circles were against a "further policy of compliance" — indeed, nothing was asked from Moscow, nothing was said to Moscow.

The last week dawned. The military preparations had entered their very last stage. Late during that June 15, the German High Command granted a request of the Naval High Command of the same day: "1. The use of weapons against Russian U-Boats [is] authorized *with immediate effect*, south of the . . . Aaland area. 2. Ruthless annihilation is to be the aim." (The Naval Command had requested the authorization of "annihilation of Russian submarines without any trace including their crews.") "Reason to be given up to B-Day is that our naval forces [are] believed to be dealing with penetrating British submarines." (*12*)

Churchill informed Roosevelt that Sunday: "I do not expect any class political reactions here, and trust a German-Russian conflict will not cause you any embarrassment." (*13*) Monday and Tuesday passed. The German press failed to comment on the TASS communiqué; it was not even reprinted or rebroadcast in Germany. Stalin was not the only one who was waiting, anxiously waiting: Count Schulenburg waited with him; the German Ambassador had indications but no concrete knowledge of what was coming. (*14*) He was left uninformed by Hitler — he could only hope, while he feared that the worst was due at any moment.

On Wednesday, June 18, the world learned that the clever Papen had succeeded in reassuring Turkey that Germany had no aggressive intentions against her; Berlin wanted Turkish neutrality now that a war with Russia, as Papen hinted, was to be expected. Germany and

Turkey signed a Treaty of Neutrality and Non-Aggression. That
evening, Finland began to call up her reservists and Hitler officially
invited Antonescu to participate in the Russian War. The *Barbarossa*
timetable established that from Wednesday on the "intention to attack need no longer be camouflaged."

Thursday was a day of relative quiet. On Friday morning, Finland
broke her relations with the Yugoslav government-in-exile and Hungary broke with Greece. That afternoon, the American Ambassador
in London stated that any British statement supporting Russia in the
case of the outbreak of a German-Russian War would be agreeable
to Washington. Later in the evening the families of the Italian Embassy officials arrived in Berlin from Moscow, loudly expressing disbelief that a war was in the offing: the Russians were ready to discuss
whatever the Axis might request. A usually very well-informed neutral
diplomat in Berlin expressed his views to the Finnish Minister there
that a war between Germany and Russia was improbable; instead,
he foresaw a broad and historic German-Russian agreement.

On Saturday morning Orlov, the Russian Minister in Helsinki,
said to the Finnish Foreign Minister, Witting, that there was absolutely no possibility of a war. (Yet the Finnish envoy in Berlin reported that decisive events could be expected within hours.) The
diary of the German Naval High Command on Saturday noon established that "reconnaissance of the Baltic theatre shows no Russian
readiness, no symptoms that the Russians are set for imminent German operations." Yet the *Barbarossa* schedule put 1 P.M. of that day
as the last hour after which the planned attack on B-Day could not
be stopped or postponed; from that hour on, "complete absence of
camouflage [is] to be reckoned with. . . ."

Stalin now felt that he had to break the deadly silence. At half past
nine on that Saturday evening, (*15*) Molotov summoned Schulenburg
to his office in the Kremlin. Dekanosov was instructed to call on Ribbentrop at the same hour in Berlin. He only got to see Weizsäcker.
The Russian Ambassador handed a note to the German State Secretary, protesting against the numerous border violations of German
aircraft. Weizsäcker was cool and accused Dekanosov of "wholesale"
border flights on the part of the Soviets. The Russian Ambassador
was very amenable. He "tried to prolong the conversation somewhat."
Of course, Weizsäcker could not go into this; he promised a "forthcoming" reply from Ribbentrop. Dekanosov "agreed to [this] procedure."

Neither was Molotov aggressive with Schulenburg; on the contrary, he was meek and friendly. The German minutes reproduce his words:

There were a number of indications that the German Government was dissatisfied with the Soviet Government. Rumors were even current that a war was impending between Germany and the Soviet Union. They found sustenance in the fact that there was no reaction whatsoever on the part of Germany to the TASS report of June 13; that it was not even published in Germany. The Soviet Government was unable to understand the reasons for Germany's dissatisfaction. If the Yugoslav question had at the time given rise to such dissatisfaction, he — Molotov — believed that, by means of his earlier communications, he had cleared up this question, which, moreover was a thing of the past. He would appreciate it if [Schulenburg] could tell him what had brought about the present situation in German-Soviet Russian relations.

Schulenburg was honest in his reply:

I could not answer his question, as I lacked the pertinent information . . . I would, however, transmit his communication to Berlin.

It was telegraphed at a quarter past one that night. By that time, Schulenburg had in his hand the radio message from Ribbentrop containing the German declaration of war of which he was to inform Molotov immediately. The declaration ended with this passage:

To sum up, the Government of the Reich declares, therefore, that the Soviet Government, contrary to the obligations it assumed,
1) has not only continued, but even intensified its attempts to undermine Germany and Europe;
2) has adopted a more and more anti-German foreign policy;
3) has concentrated all its forces in readiness at the German border. Thereby the Soviet Government has broken its treaties with Germany and is about to attack Germany from the rear, in its struggle for life. The Führer has therefore ordered the German Armed Forces to oppose this threat with all the means at their disposal.

Schulenburg saw Molotov again in the same hour that Dekanosov was summoned to Ribbentrop. (*16*) Four A.M. on Sunday, June 22 — the longest day of the year. In Berlin Ribbentrop repeated the arguments of the war declaration to the Soviet Ambassador and "regretted not to be able to add anything to these remarks, especially since he himself had had to conclude that, in spite of earnest efforts, he had not succeeded in creating sensible relations between the two countries."

To this one allusion to a friendly past which broke through the icy hostility of Ribbentrop's words, Dekanosov clung:

> . . . for his part too, he exceedingly regretted this development, which was based on a completely erroneous conception on the part of the German Government . . . (*17*)

In that hour, the guns were already speaking. (*18*)

.   .   .   .

It was a sunny day. From the Arctic to the Aegean, the soil of central-eastern Europe was baking in the sun under the same unbroken blue sky, while the earth trembled from the Baltic to the Black Sea, from Tauroggen to Tulcea, from Suwalki to Jassy. Millions heard of the war with relief, other millions with astonishment, others in a mood of anticipation, others again with fear. In Rome, both Mussolini and the Soviet Ambassador were not to be found; they had gone to bathe in the sea. Only after the Duce had returned did he receive the Führer's historic letter, the last passage of which explained the psychological origins of the blundering decision due to which Adolf Hitler was ultimately to lose his war.

> Since I struggled through to this decision, I again feel spiritually free. The partnership with the Soviet Union, in spite of the complete sincerity of the efforts to bring about a final conciliation, was nevertheless often very irksome to me, for in some way or other it seemed to me to be a break with my whole origin, my concepts and my former obligations. I am happy now to be relieved of these mental agonies.

The day advanced slowly; dusk and a light summer evening came. Then night fell, a night in which the Kremlin was silent, while "Russia and the world waited on the voice of the British arch-'imperialist,' Winston Churchill." (*19*) He had shared with Hitler the happiness of relief.

· 4 ·

THE
WAR OF
WARS

The Russian War, the "satellites" and Finland — 1941

Operational code-names serve but one aim: to disguise. But *Barbarossa* was different. The plans for the invasion of Russia bore the name of the great German crusader-emperor; it was to be the war of the new Europe, a new crusade. This was the main line of German propaganda. But in reality there existed no real plan for the mobilization of the "new Europe." The greatest reservoirs of anti-Bolshevik manpower — those in eastern Poland, the Baltics and in the Ukraine — were left untouched, as the population of these territories was to be reduced to colonial status within the German eastern empire; on the other hand, loud huzzahs and spectacular celebrations greeted appearing Spanish Blue Divisions, "Wallon" and "French" SS-Legions, etc.

[*The war declarations. Finland's case.*] The lack of political planning could already be detected from the different ways in which Germany's "allies" entered this new phase of their history. Italy, Rumania and Slovakia declared war on Russia on June 22. Croatia followed with a declaration during the night. Finland, however, did not enter the war until the 25th, and Hungary not until the 27th.

The Finnish entry into the war was mostly due to Russian misunderstanding. Stalin believed that Finland would exploit the occasion to jump forward with Germany and regain the territories lost in 1940 — indeed, to go beyond. The appearance of German troops in Finland from September 1940 on convinced him that the Helsinki régime had decided to take this course; he prepared for a war with Finland.

[415

Finnish and German intelligence were, of course, closely cooperating. On June 15 the Fifth Finnish Army Corps, stationed around Rovaniemi in the extreme north of Finland, was put under German command. The Norway Corps of General Dietl crossed the Russian frontier on June 22; German planes bombed the Soviet base at Hangö. There is, however, no evidence that on June 22 the Finnish government intended to attack. Finnish mobilization was regarded as mainly defensive, and the phrasing of Hitler's declaration, broadcast at six o'clock in the morning of June 22, came as a mild shock to the Finnish government:

> United with their Finnish comrades, the warriors who won the victory of Narvik are manning the shores of the Arctic Ocean. German divisions commanded by the conqueror of Norway, together with the champions of Finnish liberty commanded by their Marshal, are protecting Finnish territory. From East Prussia to the Carpathians fresh formations mass along the German Eastern Front. Along the lower regions of the Danube down to the shores of the Black Sea, German and Rumanian soldiers are united under the Rumanian Prime Minister Antonescu.

German troops under General Dietl crossed into Soviet territory on the Arctic Front early on June 22; but Finnish units did not participate. Later during the day, the German Minister in Helsinki was told that Finland would protect her interests but would also try to stay neutral. Molotov, in a speech in the morning, had taken note of the Hitler declaration: he mentioned that Finnish armed forces were participating in the aggression against the Soviet Union.

But at dawn Soviet aircraft and artillery in the Finnish Gulf and in Hangö had already begun to bombard Finnish ships, and a few shells were fired on the Karelian frontier. Therefore the Finnish Foreign Minister called the Soviet envoy and asked for explanations; Orlov said that he would ask his government.

On the evening of June 22, a circular instruction from the Finnish Foreign Ministry went out to all diplomatic posts abroad: it established the desire of the Finnish government to remain neutral, and slightly depreciated the importance of the Soviet bombardments, the news of which had been excitedly broadcast by the Finnish radio during the day. Berlin was worried by this attitude. On the morning of June 23, the Finnish Minister in Berlin was urgently requested to establish Finland's final attitude toward the Russian War. Later

Molotov received Paasikivi in Moscow with similar questions. What was Finland's position? Was Finland the ally of Germany or not? Paasikivi promised to give a full answer after consulting his government; late in the night he sent an extensive telegram to Helsinki, but due to the interruption of normal telegraph service, this vitally important despatch reached Helsinki only after twenty-four hours. (*1*) An official Finnish statement was given to the Swedish press: Finland would remain neutral unless she were attacked by Russia.

On June 23, Finnish and Russian batteries around Hangö sporadically fired at each other. The Russians insisted that Finnish planes were flying over Leningrad that day; it was established later that the planes were German. Moreover, all German planes operating in the northern sector of the front took off not from Finnish but from East Prussian aerodromes.

Another circular to the Finnish diplomatic posts was sent abroad on June 24. It affirmed that "it was Finland's intention to continue her previous course as long as possible," and that a government declaration on foreign affairs would be given in Parliament the next day. In the House of Commons Anthony Eden said that day that, according to his best knowledge, Finland was neutral. Finland's name was now omitted from German broadcasts which spoke of Germany and her allies in the "eastern crusade."

Yet next morning the Soviet Air Force began extensive bombing operations all over Finland; Russian artillery fired across the border and the first skirmishes between advanced posts took place. Twenty-six Russian aircraft were shot down by Finnish anti-artillery during that day. On that evening, the government announced that Finland had been forced into a "defensive war." Two days of relative silence on the fronts followed, until June 28, on which day Finnish troops began to advance, crossing the border in various sectors.

That the Finnish government did not intend to fight unless attacked is clear. What is not quite clear, however, is what Helsinki would have done had the Russians not attacked at all. The Helsinki government, while very much aware of the favorable occasion which a German-Russian war presented to Finland, tried to be, if not strictly neutral, at least non-belligerent. A confidential political survey made by the Finnish Foreign Ministry a month later established the events of June 25 thus: ". . . it was known to us that the military leadership of the Soviet Union had issued a series of orders which expressly indicated that the war against Finland had begun. . . . Had Russia

not attacked, we would have stayed out of the war and had we only
been able to remain outside for one or two months, the danger would
have greatly subsided and our chances to remain a non-belligerent
country to the end of the war perhaps could have been realized." (2)

[*Rumania.*]   As to Hungary and Rumania, Stalin and Molotov wanted to keep them out of the war. Rumania attacked on the
morning of June 22, after a rather bombastic proclamation by
Antonescu; Rumanian public opinion, on the whole, favored the war;
Maniu and the opposition did not protest against seizing the occasion
to re-occupy Bessarabia and Northern Bukovina. Maniu wanted to
see a "little war" with limited objectives, separate from Germany's
campaign, as Finland did. But Antonescu decided to push deeply
into Russia, commit Rumanian manpower, and annex territories beyond those which Rumania could rightfully reclaim. When Molotov
bid good-bye to the Italian, Rumanian, and Hungarian envoys, he
was friendly. To Gafencu he seemed tired, pale as he spoke of Russia's
friendly intentions toward Rumania: why did the Rumanians have
to join the German "bandits"? Gafencu could only say that he, like
Schulenburg, was sorry that his sincere efforts had failed. During the
conversation he reminded Molotov that the brutal Russian ultimatum
concerning Bessarabia was cause enough to create ill feeling on the
part of Rumania; Molotov's answer was not that of frigid dialectics.
The Foreign Commissar "remarked that perhaps there would have
been another way to settle the Bessarabian question. . . . Yet, as I
[Gafencu] made an inquisitive gesture, he declined to express his
thoughts more clearly . . ." (an episode which should be noted by
those who are or will be responsible for the present and future international contacts with the Russians).

[*Hungary and the war.*]   To the Hungarian Minister Molotov
explained that Russia wanted nothing from Hungary, that there
were no disputes; Hungary could only gain from assuming a neutral
or, at least, a non-belligerent position in the German-Russian War.
The Soviet Union had expressed her displeasure with the way the
Vienna Award was meted out by the Axis in 1940, but this protest
had not been directed against Hungary; and should Hungary remain
outside of the Russian War, the Soviets would recognize the Hungarian
incorporation of Northern Transylvania, said Molotov, adding a hint
that other Hungarian territorial claims could also count upon Soviet

support. Kristóffy promised to report all this to Budapest; the telegram was duly sent, but Bárdossy withheld it from Horthy and from others in the government. (*3*) The Prime Minister had already decided that Hungary should join in the "crusade"; he and his War Minister raised the threat of their resignation to other, cautious members of the government. On June 26, two German planes with Russian markings dropped a few bombs on the cities of Kassa and Munkács (*4*); on June 27, without having consulted Parliament, the Bárdossy government declared war on the Soviet Union.

Wishing to avoid internal repercussions in that country, Hitler did not require Bulgaria to declare war on Russia: Bulgaria continued to maintain diplomatic relations with the Soviet Union throughout the war and the existence of a Soviet diplomatic post in Sofia (as did the one in Tokyo) proved to be of inestimable value to Moscow.

[*Germany's allies and the 1941 campaign.*] The participation of satellite troops in the Russian campaign was at first limited. The Germans themselves had no particular desire to be bothered with unequipped and uncertain allies. Also, Stalin was prone to deride the efforts of the satellites: in September 1941, he said to Harriman and Beaverbrook that he had respect for the German soldiers only; their allies were not to be feared, the best of them still being the Finns, then came the Italians, Rumanians and Hungarians, in that order. The Italian army corps, CSIR (*Corpo Spedizionario Italiano in Russia*), (*5*) under General Messe had fought well in 1941 in the southern Ukraine. South of the Italians stood the Rumanians; in the southernmost sector of the front, Antonescu had nominal command. The Russians rapidly retreated from Bessarabia, and the German-Rumanian armies had crossed the Dniester everywhere by early August. This reconquest was, however, not enough for Antonescu, who decided to push forward; and subsequently the territory between Dniester and Bug was officially incorporated into Rumania under the name Transnistria. The city of Odessa, which fell in October, was temporarily named "Antonescu." This "conquest" was not only useless — partisans as well as local German commanders frustrated all Rumanian attempts to integrate Transnistria into Rumania proper — but it also put an end to all Rumanian hopes for a "little war." The ruthless butcheries by certain Rumanian commanders and Iron Guardist police chiefs in liberated Bessarabia contributed to the further sinking of Rumanian prestige. Hungary sent a light armored division, a few infantry bataillons, and labor cadres to the Russian front. The light armored division operated in the central Ukraine; the rest of the Hungarian forces were employed in construction work and policing behind the lines. At the end of 1941, the armored division returned to Hungary, and only a very small number of troops remained in the Russian theatre until, early in 1942, strong German demands necessitated the dispatch of a full army group. A "Slovak Expeditionary Army," a Croat corps, and a Croatian SS-Legion, also participated in the war.

Finland meanwhile tried to stick to her "little" and separate war; except in the extreme north, the Finnish armies did not cooperate with the German armed forces. (6) The aim was to establish a security line along the river Svir and the western shores of Lake Onega. This line included most of Eastern Karelia and its capital, Petrozavodsk (7); once the line was reached, the Finns did not advance further. On August 24, the President of Finland, the Supreme Commander of the Armed Forces, and the Minister of War reached a fundamental decision: in spite of a German request, the Finnish forces would not advance beyond the 1939 frontiers in Karelia and would not cross the Svir nor start an offensive against Leningrad. The German spearheads reached Schlüsselburg on the southern shore of Lake Ladoga on September 22, thus cutting Leningrad off from the rest of Russia, yet, in spite of a siege which lasted for two years, the German armies could not take the metropolis. Had the Finns not restricted their operations and had they continued to advance, Leningrad would very probably have fallen.

.   .   .   .   .   .

[*Ostland.*] Hitler's political conduct of the Russian War was a series of great blunders. Just as part of his success in the Western European campaigns lay in his mixing political devices with military ones, part of his failure in Russia lay in his almost complete neglect of political considerations. He fought an ideological war in Russia, with only vaguely defined military, political, territorial aims. The political organization of the Russian War was entrusted to the Nazi ideologist, Alfred Rosenberg. His plans for creating a great German *Ostland* — which Göbbels later cynically dubbed *Chaostland* — were well known. On June 20, Rosenberg lectured to the highest German staff officers. He set forth the outlines of the new eastern order: a greater Finland, autonomy granted to certain Caucasian states, and three German Commissariats, one in the Baltic States, one in White Russia, and one in the Ukraine. *(8)*

The great Rosenberg Plan thus envisaged three gigantic German satrapies in the East, instead of mobilizing and using the local anti-Bolshevik elements. When the German armies forged ahead in the Baltics — on June 24, Brest-Litóvsk, Vilna, and Kaunas were already occupied; on July 1 Riga and Lwów fell — they were greeted with relief by the destitute Lithuanians, Latvians, and Estonians. For two weeks it seemed that the German commanders would cooperate with local national committees, in which conservative and pro-German elements mingled; soon, however, it was clear that the Baltic States were destined to be made German colonies; Nazi High Commissioners were appointed, and instead of encouraging the respective national movements, the Germans suppressed them. The former German expatriates were also coming back. On July 17 a high-level political conference was called at the Führer's headquarters, Hitler, Rosenberg, Göring, Keitel, and Lammers participating. Rosenberg again carried the day with his catastrophic plans. The subordination of the whole Baltic territory into his *Ostland* was accepted. Except for supporting local German hirelings, Lithuanian, Latvian and Estonian SS-Legions, pro-Nazi leaders such as the Latvian General Dankers and the Estonian Mäe, and "native anti-Semitic forces," the political fruits which the Germans could have reaped with their armies appearing in the Baltics as liberators were not even considered. *(9)* By the end of August practically all of the Baltic lands were in German hands, and the Axis armies were beyond Smolensk and near Kiev, which latter eventually fell on September 19.

Broadly stated, the launching of the Russian War — however "crusade"-like — instead of simplifying, had made the central-eastern political scene more complicated. To the international implications of this new situation I shall now turn.

The international position of the central-eastern European states — 1941

> Any State who fights Nazism will have our aid. . . . It follows therefore that we shall give whatever help we can to Russia.

Eighteen hours after the Russian War was declared, the ringing words of Winston Churchill made it clear that, due to the unrelenting efforts of Adolf Hitler to gain mental comfort (*1*) and to the immutable laws of geography, Great Britain and Soviet Russia were already *de facto* allies.

This was an inevitable and logical development. In the future, however, loomed the great question: how would the British-Russian alliance develop? There was much wishful thinking in central-eastern Europe. It could be discerned along these lines:

> *Nazis and pro-Germans:* Germany would crush Russia and then direct her forces against Britain, who subsequently would be compelled to sue for peace. *The majority of this group held a more moderate viewpoint:* After the German victory in Russia, Britain and Germany would sign a negotiated peace, Britain acquiescing in the German domination of most of Europe.
>
> *Conservatives (anti-Russian):* Russia would be defeated but Germany would also be exhausted in the campaign. Britain would gain the upper hand and a non-Churchillian régime would establish a new balance-of-power in central-eastern Europe, Russia excluded and Germany considerably less aggressive.
>
> *Conservatives (pro-British) and Liberals:* Hitler would break his back in Russia like Napoleon. The British would invade Europe from the south, Wellington-like, and dictate peace in Europe. The British alliance would force Stalin to behave according to European rules and manners.
>
> *Radical Democrats; the Left:* Russia with British help would and should defeat Germany. The only aim and logical conclusion of the Second World War should be the defeat of the Axis.
>
> *Communists:* Russia would defeat Hitler: the only aim and logical conclusion of the Second World War should be the political and military victory of the Soviet Union and her subsequent and exclusive mastery of central-eastern Europe, to be achieved by whatever means. (*2*)

.   .   .   .

[*Britain and Russia.*] Only parts of Churchill's speech were printed in the Soviet press. "The silence on the top level was oppressive," Churchill later wrote, "and I thought it my duty to break the ice." (*3*) On July 7 Churchill sent his first message to Stalin. On July 12 Great Britain and Russia announced conclusion of an Agreement of Mutual Assistance against Nazi Germany, which mutually obliged the signatories not to conclude a separate peace. The states of central-eastern Europe — with the exception of Finland — had already broken off relations with Great Britain. While the Soviet régime was busy mending fences, on July 18 diplomatic relations had been re-established between Russia and the Czechoslovak government-in-exile; on July 30 an agreement was signed with the Poles; on August 5, a communiqué stated that the Soviet-Yugoslav Pact of the previous April was still considered unbroken and valid by the Soviet government — the mutual obligations of Britain and Russia gradually assumed more concrete forms. The deadly torrent of German steel and fire and the metallic prongs of the German armored divisions cutting through the black Russian soil called for more and more British help. On July 17 Stalin answered Churchill: he excused his delay and asked for British help, a landing in Norway. "The Soviet Government," wrote Churchill, "had the impression that they were conferring a great favour on us by fighting in their own country for their own lives. The more they fought, the heavier our debt became. This was not a balanced view . . ." On the other hand, Britain could ill afford to disillusion her new ally; it was necessary to convince the cunning and suspicious Stalin that Britain was steadfast and sincerely loyal. The day, therefore, was looming not far ahead when Britain was to declare war on Hungary, Finland, Rumania (and Bulgaria).

[*The American position; some central-eastern European illusions.*] Under these circumstances the position of the United States assumed a curious and exceptional importance in the eyes of the statesmen of these countries. America was, of course, helping Russia with matériel as well as by an involuntary distraction of Japanese attention, a distraction which spared the Soviet Union a second front. On July 10 the German government requested Japan to attack the Soviet Union, but the Japanese High Cabinet council had already rejected the idea on June 28, and Japan politely refused Germany: she needed her forces for the Pacific. (4) Despite the apparent community of Russian-American interests — often and loudly acknowledged in Washington — the fact remained that in the summer of 1941 America was not yet at war.

Therefore — except for the wholly puppet states, Slovakia and Croatia — the allies of Germany began to intensify their contacts with America during the year 1941. They saw in America a potential power whose voice would be decisive in the coming peacemaking; they saw in America a more stable and, for their purposes, hopeful factor of world order than Churchill's Britain. (5) There were many reasons for such views. There was American non-belligerency. There existed a common belief that American public opinion was considerably more pro-German and less pro-Russian than that of Britain — a calculation not without foundation, but one excessively furthered by the social contacts and expressed opinions of many American diplomatic representatives in central-eastern European countries before the war and during its early period, personal opinions which sometimes gave a false impression of the trends of public opinion prevailing in the United States; the calculation was also furthered by the exaggerated reports of the German press and radio services about the impact of the non-interventionist sentiment in America, by the isolationist senators, and by Lindbergh and the America First movement.

Such beliefs held by the Foreign Ministries in Bucharest, Helsinki, Sofia, Budapest — to a limited extent in Berlin and Rome also — were of course not very realistic; but they had some justification. Only after 1941 was the direction of American foreign policy transferred from the State Department to the White House. The State Department, with which the diplomats of the Axis countries were in professional contact, was, after all, an official organization handling formal relations. There was a slight divergence discernible in the ways in which the State Department and the White House viewed world affairs. During the winter of 1940–41, for example, it was intimated to the Ambassador of the Polish government-in-exile by the State Department that propaganda activities among Polish-Americans should be somewhat curtailed in view of the fact that the United States was a non-belligerent nation. In March 1941, during an interview accorded to the Polish Premier-in-exile, President Roosevelt brushed this interpretation aside with great vigor and exhorted General Sikorski and the Polish Ambassador to carry on their activities unrestrictedly. (6) When some members of the Yugoslav government-in-exile were about to come to Washington in 1941, it was courteously hinted to them that they should establish their center of activities in Canada instead of Washington. Even after August 1941, when the principles and terms of the Atlantic Charter were jointly announced by the British Premier and the American President, the United States continued to be regarded as the more conservative, more "Rightist," more flexible of the two Anglo-Saxon Powers. The European statesmen not only saw actual divergences in American and British foreign policy (the Franco and Vichy cases were eagerly scrutinized in the "satellite" capitals), but they were aware that President Roosevelt's freedom of action was hampered by potentially hostile segments of public opinion and by an uneasy Congress. It was also known that very high American diplomatic and military officials estimated the probability of successful Russian resistance to the Germans to be very low.

[*The American change.*]   We know today that there was much wishful thinking in these estimates of American foreign policy. After Pearl Harbor, it became increasingly clear that it was America who was the more ideologically-inclined of the two English-speaking Powers; the policy of Washington suited Moscow much more than that of London. To be sure, the United States planned ahead for peace. The White House, the State and War Departments bristled with plans, committees, experts' papers. Within the State Department a "special sub-committee on problems of European Organization" examined regional federation plans, a European customs' union, a Balkan federation, etc.; within this worthy committee

> . . . the functioning of multinational states such as Yugoslavia and Czechoslovakia was examined in connection with the foreseeable problems involved in such neighborhood groupings. The subcommittee also appraised possible Soviet programs and attitudes with respect to Eastern Europe so far as they were then known or could be conjectured.

But committees, however worthy or numerous, do not make, nor direct, foreign policy.

That Britain made necessity-dictated deals with Russia was due to evident reasons of temporary political and military expediency. But the position of the United States was primarily conditioned by ideological calculations, the foremost of these being the belief that America was destined to appear as an honest young broker, between the two polar systems of old Victorian imperialism, represented by Churchill's Britain, and Communism, represented by the roughshod but in many ways admirable young Russia of Stalin. This concept, upheld and maintained by a benevolent but unduly optimistic President, had originated and been formulated in the somewhat antiquated, stale, and rather confused climate of the American demo-liberal and so-called "radical" Left. (7) As early as January 1941, it was Washington's decision to lift the "moral embargo" against Russia; at that

time, London was against such a step. On June 26 Roosevelt wrote
Leahy:

> Now comes this Russian diversion. If it is more than just that it will
> mean the liberation of Europe from Nazi domination — and at the
> same time I do not think we need worry about any possibility of Rus-
> sian domination. (8)

On September 3 the President wrote a letter to Pope Pius XII, expressing his view that Russia was less dangerous than Germany, for
Russia used only the weapon of Communist propaganda outside of
her borders, while Germany was a military aggressor. There is no
doubt that on the second anniversary of the outbreak of the Second
World War, Russia was less dangerous than Germany; but the subsequent distinction could be easily challenged by the record of Russian
action in central-eastern Europe between 1939 and 1941.

. . . .

[*The Finnish position; the break with Britain.*]   Significant and
eventful were Finland's foreign relations. On July 4, Ryti talked with
Schoenfeld, the American Minister, who stated that the United States
understood Finland's difficult position. The United States at that
time hoped to exercise American influence at some favorable opportunity to end the "separate war" between Finland and Russia. Eight
days later the British-Russian Agreement was announced. The Germans consistently pressed Helsinki to join the Tripartite Pact, but
the Finns refrained from doing so. However, Ryti and his government
(not quite unanimously) felt that Finnish-British relations should be
re-examined. On July 22 Ryti instructed the Foreign Minister to
summon Vereker, the British envoy, who was told that as a result of
the British-Russian alliance normal diplomatic relations between Finland and Great Britain could not be maintained any longer, and
Finland was ready to abolish her diplomatic representation in London. (9) The British answered with a note on July 28. On July 31,
the Royal Air Force bombed German and Finnish ships in Petsamo,
and on August 1 Finland severed her relations with Great Britain.

Yet Finnish public figures consistently tried to impress the public
of the Western Allies with Finland's "separate war" concept; Finnish
Trade Union leaders sent confidential letters to British labor leaders
and to the chiefs of the American Federation of Labor. On August 18
Sumner Welles told Procopé, the Finnish Minister to Washington,

that he thought the Russians would be willing to negotiate with Finland. The American note remained unanswered until November 11. The Finnish Government obviously did not wish to commit itself during what seemed to be the decisive phase of the Russian campaign. Certain diplomatic steps were taken to impress Germany: for example, Finland broke diplomatic relations with the Polish and Yugoslav governments-in-exile and in November 1941 she joined the revived Anti-Comintern Pact in Berlin (Denmark's joining the Pact and German wheat shipments were influential in the Finnish decision); yet caution prevailed — Helsinki consistently refused to enter the Tripartite Pact and, for example, refrained from recognizing the puppet Chinese government of Nanking; in two speeches Tanner refused to consider alleged plans for a "Greater Finland." The manner in which the severance of diplomatic relations with Britain was handled revealed that this step was regarded as an uncomfortable and necessity-dictated measure by both Helsinki and London. The Finnish note did not even mention severance of relations, but maintained that, "in consequence of events," the Finnish government "had reached the conclusion that the Finnish Legation in London should, until further notice, terminate its functions." Before Vereker left Helsinki, he made a friendly farewell call at Ryti's place, and Witting gave a farewell luncheon for the whole staff of the Legation.

On September 22 — the day that Schlüsselburg fell — the Norwegian government-in-exile transmitted a British communication to Helsinki, which contained this passage:

> Should the Finnish Government continue her advance in Russian territory, the situation would arise in which Great Britain would find herself compelled to regard Finland openly as her enemy; not only for the duration of the war but also at the conclusion of peace.

[*The prospect of war: British attempts to evade it.*] It was now evident that Britain was being forced by Russia to declare war on the allies of Germany. The Finnish answer of October 8 established that as long as there were former Finnish lands in Russian hands (at that time, Russian forces still held Hangö and parts of the Petsamo region), and until Finland's security could be guaranteed beyond doubt from a military point of view, Finland would continue the war. There were rumors of Russian-Finnish peace possibilities. A Soviet-inspired hint was dropped at the Finnish Legation to Vichy. The Soviet Ambassadress in Stockholm looked upon such possibilities with benevolent eyes, conceding in a talk with the Swedish Foreign Minister that it would be very difficult for the Finns to successfully negotiate a separate peace.

According to Ryti, the British government — in spite of the alliance with Russia — was unwilling to declare war on Finland, while from October 1941 on, it was, surprisingly enough, the American government — in spite of its uninterruptedly maintained friendly relations with Finland — which advised Britain to conform to Russian wishes. (But Mr. Schoenfeld, whom I queried about this, was kind enough to write me: "I know nothing that justifies the reported statement of ex-President Ryti to which you refer to the effect that American pressure was exerted on Britain to declare war on Finland . . .") Procopé saw Hull on September 8, at which time the American Secretary of State emphatically declared that the view of the United States was: Germany the greatest danger, all other issues of secondary importance. On September 17, the British chargé d'affaires in Washington requested Hull to find out about concrete terms which Russia and Finland could eventually submit and which could then form the basis of peace discussions. Hull answered that he would not undertake such a step. (This refusal was symbolic of the attitude of the United States, which country, although neutral and maintaining friendly relations with Finland, was already enclosed in the haze of the ideological war, committed by her own ideology but unwilling to deal with concrete questions and limitations, although in the position of a potential mediator; Britain, on the other hand, more dependent on and allied with Russia, fighting a life-and-death struggle, bound by no ties or special sympathies to the Finns, wished to find out *what constituted the concrete territorial ends of the Finnish-Russian War and what the subsequent territorial problems and limitations would be.*)

Somewhat later, when Lord Halifax in Washington asked the Secretary of State for advice as to whether or not Britain should declare war on Finland, Hull said that he could not give any advice on this matter. Britain waited, however, for another two months. There was much suspicion between Russia and Britain. On November 4 Churchill wrote Stalin:

> Will you however consider whether it is really good business that Britain should declare war on Finland, Hungary and Rumania at this moment? It is only a formality . . . our extreme blockade is already in force against them. My judgement is against it . . .

He brought forth two arguments: Finland had many American friends; Rumania and Hungary were "full of our friends [and one day] they might turn to our side. A British declaration of war would only freeze them all and make it look as if Hitler were the head of a grand European alliance solid against us."

Stalin answered very rudely on the 8th. Churchill was angry and refused to answer. Maisky then called on Eden on the 20th with Stalin's apologies: "It had certainly not been M. Stalin's intention to cause any offense. . . ." Stalin was restive only because the Finnish affair had received undue publicity, which fact he had regarded as humiliating.

There followed two weeks in which Churchill tried to gain time. On November 28 the American Minister in Helsinki transmitted the British note to Finland, which note requested that the Finnish government cease her military participation in the war before December 5; otherwise His Majesty's Government would be compelled to declare that a state of war existed between the two countries. Similar ultimata were communicated to the Hungarian and Rumanian governments on November 30, through the media of the American Ministers in Budapest and Bucharest.

That Britain regarded Finland's case as different from that of the others transpires from the private letter which Churchill addressed to Marshal Mannerheim on November 29 in which he said:

> I am deeply grieved at what I see coming, namely that we shall be forced in a few days out of loyalty to our ally Russia to declare war upon Finland. Surely your troops have advanced far enough for security during the war and could now halt and give leave. It is not necessary to make any public declaration but simply leave off fighting and close military operations immediately for which the severe winter affords every reason and make a *de facto* exit from the war. (*10*)

Mannerheim answered the Premier on December 2 and expressed his grief at the inevitable. "It was very kind of you to send me a personal message in these trying days, and I have fully appreciated it." The official Finnish note was given on December 4; it was rather flexible and stated that "the Finnish forces were not far anymore from their strategic goals." But this declaration did not contain enough material for London to demonstrate to Moscow a change in the Finnish attitude. Consequently, Britain declared war on Finland on December 6. Somewhat later, the Swedish financial magnate, Mar-

cus Wallenberg, Jr. (with the knowledge of the Swedish Foreign
Minister, who, due to the delicate situation of his neutral country,
did not want to participate in the conversations directly) tried to
establish contact between Finnish personalities and Ambassadress
Kollontay in Stockholm. Ryti asked Wallenberg to Helsinki in January 1942. The possibilities of peace were examined in detail, yet it
was concluded that the solitary opinions expressed by the Soviet Ambassadress and the vagueness of her allusions to a separate peace
were not sufficient. At the same time an American request to Finland not to attack in the direction of the Murmansk railroad was
silently acknowledged in Helsinki.

[*Rumania and Hungary.*]   The relations of the other allies of
Germany with Britain and America were naturally less eventful and
significant. In Hungary, Horthy — whose son, Nicholas Jr., was
Hungarian Minister to Brazil — and the conservatives secretly looked
hopefully upon Eckhardt's clandestine mission in America, not knowing, of course, that adverse propaganda from the American Left had
already begun to undermine the position of this extraordinary envoy.
The Hungarian Minister to Madrid, General Andorka, also maintained connections with the Western Allies. Mihai Antonescu, the
Rumanian Foreign Minister (only distantly related to the Conducator), was cautious about the war prospects and tried to make
Rome consider a Spanish-Portugese-French-Italian-Rumanian "Latin
Axis, horizontal in every respect . . . a barrier against pan-Germans
and pan-Slavs" — so he explained it to the Italian Minister Bova
Scoppa. Ciano was invited to Bucharest to hear such plans, but he
could not come. (*11*) Antonescu himself nurtured certain hopes in
regard to the United States. His envoy informed Hull in September
that Rumania would eventually stop offensive operations after the
fall of Odessa. Hull did not attach too much importance to this communication.

[*Turkey and Bulgaria.*]   Meanwhile Papen was busy trying
to bring about an anti-Russian Balkan alliance, with Turkey participating. Certain members of the Greek "quisling" government
were not adverse to his suggestions, and certain Turkish "pan-
Turanians" listened to his inducements. (*12*) The German-Turkish
Pact of June 18 worried Stalin. On July 11 a dispatch of the New York
Times quoted Russian official circles in Turkey as denying that Rus-

sia would put any pressure on Ankara; in regard to the Kars and Ardahan territories the Russians said: "We do not want Kars back again." (*13*) On July 28, Stalin addressed a special letter to President Inönü. But in spite of these sudden manifestations of Russian friendliness, important Turkish persons — among them Menemenčoglu, who was to be the Foreign Minister of Turkey from 1942 to 1944 and General Čakmak, the Chief-of-Staff until 1944 — were in contact with the Germans in regard to an eventual Turkish entry in the war against Russia. Vague plans for a new Turanian-Mohammedan state, comprising Azerbeidjani, Turkmens, Crimean Tartars, etc., were drawn up. The Germans also hinted at an eventual rectification of the Turkish frontier in Europe at the expense of Bulgaria (the final delimitation of the Balkan frontiers was not yet regarded as fully settled by the Germans in spite of a Frontier Agreement with the Italians on July 8.) The Soviet Union was aware of all this. She continued to be grateful for Bulgarian neutrality, and while occasional protests were made against restrictions imposed on the Russian Legation in Sofia, in September 1941 a friendly Russian message assured the Bulgar government of Soviet understanding and amity. The Bulgarian Foreign Ministry answered with similar correctness and affirmed Bulgarian neutrality in the German-Russian War.

[*Inter-European attempts.*] The allies of Germany were eager in 1941 to strengthen their relations with other European nations and establish some feeling of European solidarity. Where there were territorial aspirations — as in the case of Rumania and Slovakia against Hungary — there could be, of course, no sense of solidarity, despite the fact that these three states were "allies" in the "crusade" against Russia. But inter-European connections increased. French literature was rediscovered; the number of foreign translations published and foreign plays adapted was steadily increasing. Polish exiles found a safe haven in Rumania and in Hungary, where a Polish high-school was established for the exiles' children. (*14*) Rumania and Hungary shipped wheat to Belgium and Greece, and the British blockade was lifted so that wheat ships of the Turkish Red Cross could get to Greece. Hungary supplied most of the wheat for the Vatican during the war; Helsinki, Budapest, Sofia and Bucharest widened the scope of their political, cultural and economic relations with Sweden, Switzerland, and, to a lesser extent, with Portugal — the neutral nations of Europe; before his suicide, Count Teleki sent a number of young Hungarian scholars to the United States. Yet, when on November 26, 1941, its fifth anniversary, the Anti-Comintern Pact was resuscitated, Germany's allies adhered without exception; significant were the words of Ribbentrop, who regarded the United States and Britain as the "real targets" of the Pact.

[*War with the West.*] The final British notes of November 30 to the Rumanian and Hungarian governments were, naturally, without avail, and thus Britain declared war on Rumania and Hungary on December 6. Not quite forty-eight hours later, the news of Pearl Harbor shocked the world.

Hastily and without much consideration, Hungary declared war on the United States on December 12, following the Axis declarations. For this measure, Bárdossy alone was responsible. Rumania did the same on the same day. Bulgaria joined by adding her own declaration of war against Great Britain. (*15*) "Slovakia" and "Croatia" followed suit by declaring war against Britain and America simultaneously; Bratislava announced her tragicomic declaration on the 12th, Zagreb on the 14th.

. . . .

[*Russian dangers: the Beaverbrook mission.*] On the evening of September 4 the Soviet Ambassador called on Churchill. Maisky brought Stalin's quick reply to a letter which Churchill had written on August 29, explaining the present impossibility of mounting a second front. The Russian message was rude and ominous; there was an "underlying air of menace in it." Churchill severely rebuked the Russian Ambassador; next morning he telegraphed Roosevelt: "We could not exclude the impression that they might be thinking of separate terms . . ." On September 15 Stalin in his dire need again asked Churchill for 25 to 30 British divisions: for a moment the curious prospect of Northumberland Fusiliers milling and marching amidst Bolshevik Ukrainian mud-huts arose. But Britain could not spare divisions. Churchill gave detailed directives to Lord Beaverbrook, who was to leave for Moscow (*16*); Averell Harriman went with him. Thus, at the very first high-level conversation between Russia and Britain, the Americans were represented and involved: a development which ultimately turned out to be a most favorable one for the Soviets.

Now Stalin knew that he could exploit British and American fears of a Russo-German separate peace. There was, of course, nothing in 1941 to indicate such a desire on the German side — although in September Hitler said to Papen that when a certain line was reached in Russia, approximately from Murmansk to Maikop, he would perhaps consider negotiating with Stalin, who was, after all, "a great man, who had accomplished deeds hitherto unheard of." (*17*) In September Laval also told Rahn, the German envoy extraordinary, to urge Hitler to make peace with Russia: this was most important.

The Beaverbrook-Harriman mission arrived in Moscow on September 28, when the military situation was dangerous and unpredictable. "The reception was bleak," and Stalin levelled charges of halfheartedness at the British. Beaverbrook suggested that British troops be sent to the Caucasus (in August a joint British-Russian occupation cleared the way in Persia for a land connection and supply route between the British and Russian armies), but Stalin rudely interrupted him: "There is no war in the Caucasus, but there is one in the Ukraine." (*18*) Nevertheless, the atmosphere improved in the end, and the Anglo-American promises of supply were accepted in good stead. There were no political discussions of major import.

[*The Battle of Moscow; political consequences.*] Beaverbrook and Harriman were still in Moscow when on October 3 Berlin announced that the Russian armies were defeated and virtually finished. For about two months, this announcement could not be entirely discounted. German armor crept nearer and nearer to Moscow; in the south, the Germans held the whole northern shoreline of the Sea of Azov. Then, on November 28, the Russians recaptured Rostov. A few days later, the German advance posts near Moscow were attacked and some of them taken. On December 3 it was reported that the Russian winter had set in all along the two-thousand-mile eastern front with unusual speed and rigor. On the same day, a Yugoslav communiqué from Cairo announced that fighting between German and Yugoslav partisans was going on in Serbia and Bosnia — the first notice of organized military resistance within occupied Europe. On December 11, Winston Churchill referred to Hitler's attack on Russia as "one of the outstanding blunders in history." A week later, General Brauchitsch resigned and Hitler took over the supreme command of the German armed forces.

The lightning war of 1941 thus failed, and political speculations arose. Especially the Italians hoped for a German-Russian peace which would liberate all available Axis forces against the Anglo-Saxon Powers. The only Axis newspaper which even cautiously expressed its belief in October 1941 that the Russian campaign, despite German announcements, might yet harbor considerable surprises, was Farinacci's *Regime Fascista* — and the newspaper of that notorious pro-Nazi extremist was thereupon rebuked by the *Völkischer Beobachter*. On November 6 Stalin stated, in his usual clumsy Russian style: "Can the Hitlerites be regarded as nationalists? No, they cannot. Actually, the Hitlerites are now not nationalists but imperialists" — a not uninteresting allusion to possible peace chances with a nationalist Germany. On December 28, the Italian Ambassador reported from Tokyo that Japanese circles were alluding to the desirability and possibility of a German-Russian separate peace. Others hoped for a German-British compromise. In February 1942 a Russian agent attempted to assassinate Papen in Istanbul; Moscow was worried about the German Ambassador, who, assisted by the Turks, could perhaps bring about negotiations with Britain.

Papen himself saw, however, that with the entry of America into the war, chances for a separate German-British settlement scarcely existed. (*19*) The unexpected successes of the Japanese in the first months of the Far Eastern War resuscitated hopes for the defeat of Britain, while the winter checkmate seemed to strengthen rather than weaken Hitler's resolution to annihilate the Russian armies during 1942. While in Helsinki, Budapest, Bucharest, Sofia — and in Ankara — it was not believed that the present alignment of the warring powers would continue to prevail until the very end of the war, the exiles in London and Washington as well as many of the Axis' opponents in central-eastern Europe, could, for the first time, envisage the possibility that the alliance between Britain, the United States and Russia would remain steady in purpose and in its context, defeat the Axis, and carry the war eventually to Berlin, where it would dictate the peace. These expectations — indeed remote at the end of 1941 — were fulfilled forty months later. Therefore it is important to examine the goals of Britain, the United States, and Russia in central-eastern Europe in 1941, and to see how they changed as the war progressed.

[*The disturbing problem of war aims.*] There was a basic difference between the British and American views. The American concept of a "democratic" foreign policy, unduly dependent on the tempers and changes of public opinion, resulted in the presentation of the war to the American people as an ideological conflict; and, although this concept contributed much to the idealism with which young Americans went into battle, it prevented the general public from realizing the political and territorial problems which the warring alliance inevitably would have to face. The British, on the other hand, preferred to set concrete political goals and form the strategic conditions of the war in accordance with them. The military problems of the Allies were, however, so urgently paramount at the end of 1941 that the British had neither the opportunity nor the will to fully reveal their concept to the Americans, on whom at that time Britain's military and economic dependence was greater than ever before. As the military picture was dark with Axis and Japanese advances, and as the fronts were far beyond Europe's frontiers, Churchill thought it better to postpone the strenuous and delicate task of concretely formulating the war aims of the English-speaking nations. During the "Arcadia" conference of Christmastime, 1941, in Washington, the invasion of Europe by the Anglo-Saxon Powers was concretely planned for the first time; it was tentatively set for sometime during 1943. (*20*) Strategic and political implications of the European invasion had not yet been examined: thus it was mentioned that the invasion could take place either in the Balkans — across the Mediterranean and from the direction of Turkey — or in Western Europe. But already the abrupt manner in which the so-called United Nations' Declaration of New Year's Day, 1942, was handled by Washington protocol — hurriedly gathering the signatures of the minor allied governments to the historic document drafted exclusively by President Roosevelt and Mr. Churchill without having consulted the representatives of the minor Powers — was something of an indication of how the noble principles of the Atlantic Charter were to be applied to future problems arising between minor and major states when relative power, it seemed, was to be the dominant factor.

The pure and distilled American ideological conception of the war could also be seen from the fact that the American government — by clinging to the concept of "satellites" — simply refused to take notice of the Hungarian, Rumanian, and Bulgarian war declarations (*21*); only when Molotov mentioned the subject in Washington during a luncheon with President Roosevelt on May 30, 1942, did the American President decide to comply with the Russian request, and on June 5, 1942, the United States Senate "accepted" the Hungarian, Bulgarian, and Rumanian declarations of war on the United States. It is noteworthy that neither the war declaration of Slovakia nor that of Croatia was "accepted," for the American government refused to complicate its concept of the war by taking notice of the existence of these puppet states, which, notwithstanding their undoubtedly "satellite" character, were nevertheless indicative to some extent of central-eastern European realities.

While the English-speaking nations found it difficult, inopportune, or unnecessary to clarify and formulate their aims in central-eastern Europe, the ambitions of Joseph Stalin revealed themselves more and more clearly; and an unmistakable indication of these ambitions was the development of relations between Russia and Poland.

Britain, Poland and Russia — 1941

[*The Polish quandary.*]   1812 repeated itself; yet, in 1941, there was no Duchy of Warsaw, no Napoleon to march on Russia, accompanied by Polish soldiers and Polish hopes. The pledge of a free Poland now lay with Britain, ally of Russia. Anthony Eden spoke in the Commons on June 24, 1941:

> At a time like this our thoughts go out with heartfelt sympathy to our Polish Allies. Once again their soil is a battlefield; once again their people suffer for no fault of their own. The Polish people have had a hard history. By their courage in a time of unparalleled ordeal they have earned and they will redeem their freedom. That remains our pledge.

These were reassuring words. But in those days the body politic of the Polish nation, represented by the sovereign government in exile, was badly rent. It was evident that a totally new situation had arisen with the German attack, that the relations of Poland with Russia would have to be necessarily re-examined, and that Britain was destined to mediate there. When the Polish Premier, General Sikorski, adopted a friendly tone toward Russia in his broadcast on the evening of June 23, he faced much opposition. Sikorski was prone to underestimate somewhat the Russian danger: the Polish Premier was born and raised in western Poland, and thus his background and traditions lacked the bitter experiences which the eastern Poles had had with the Russians, experiences which produced distrust, but which also bred caution and skill in dealings with them.

Immediately the British government approached Moscow to bring about negotiations for a Polish-Russian Agreement. The British Foreign Office was on the heels of Maisky in London, and Sir Stafford Cripps (back in Moscow since June 25) continually reminded the Foreign Commissariat officials of the urgent necessity of dealing with the Polish problem. Moscow gave its consent to direct contact only on July 4. In Whitehall on July 5 Sir Alexander Cadogan, Maisky, Sikorski, and the Polish Foreign Minister, Zaleski, met for the first time.

[*The British position.*] It now became more and more apparent that the British government urged the conclusion and publication of an Agreement with undue haste. The British view — and Cripps made it known to the Russians — was that the fact of the agreement was now of more importance than concrete terms were. In Washington Lord Halifax showed no particular sympathy for Polish viewpoints. Interestingly enough, in the Polish-Russian problem it was, at first, the United States which adopted a more cautious attitude toward Russia, in spite of the fact that it was Britain who had concrete obligations to Poland, dating back to August 1939. A succinct explanation of this situation was given in the memoirs of the wartime Polish Ambassador to the United States:

> . . . in America the reaction to the German campaign in Russia was less immediate, less complete than in England, and the United States was still studiously wary.
>
> From the Polish angle, it was regrettable that Churchill had not taken advantage of the Soviet-German war to condition the British attitude on an immediate Soviet declaration re-establishing the *status quo ante* in Soviet-Polish relations by nullifying the Ribbentrop-Molotov pact partitioning Poland.
>
> In my conversations of that period at the State Department and with political friends I sensed a certain apprehension and even regret that Churchill had not seen fit to attach any strings to Britain's declaration of friendship and support for the Soviets. . . .
>
> I deeply regretted that at that time the requirements of what still remained of American neutrality prevented the creation of an openly united policy of the two English-speaking democracies, for I knew that for the time being America was not prepared too easily or unconditionally to unite her democratic destinies with those of totalitarian communist Russia.

It was becoming evident, however, that Mr. Churchill's haste in professing unconditional support of Russia was in no small measure dictated by the then current apprehension that after initial defeats inflicted by Hitler, Stalin might see his advantage in making a separate peace with Germany and turn against the democracies which for twenty-odd years he had so continuously and forcefully denounced as the main capitalist menace. . . .

Through my many years of close association with British diplomacy I knew how difficult it was for British statesmen to understand the Russian mentality and methods of negotiation. Apart from that, in this particular case the Ribbentrop-Molotov line ran uncomfortably close to the famous "Curzon Line" which we Poles had learned to know as the British "sword of Damocles" hung over Poland by Lloyd George in 1920. (*1*)

[*Disturbing symptoms.*]   Stalin was aware of Churchill's tendency — which the Premier had revealed in a 1939 speech — to appreciate certain Russian territorial ambitions. On July 18, in his first wartime message to Churchill, Stalin stated:

> It is easy to imagine that the position of the German forces would have been many times more favourable had the Soviet troops had to face the attack of the German forces, not in the regions of Kishinev, Lwów, Brest, Kaunas and Viborg, but in the regions of Odessa, Kamenets-Podolski, Minsk and the environs of Leningrad.

This was a questionable view, craftily addressed to a man who had said ". . . I have never underrated this argument." From all this the Curzon Line was ultimately to result again.

After three weeks of nervous talks, the Polish-Soviet Agreement was concluded to the great satisfaction of Britain and of all who believed that the German War had brought a drastic change in the behavior of Russia. The Agreement called for the resumption of diplomatic relations, the annulment of the Soviet-German agreements concerning Poland, and the establishment of a Polish Army in Russia. There were two disturbing symptoms. One was the rift within the Polish government: three ministers, Zaleski, Sosnkowski, and Seyda resigned in protest. The other was the attitude of the British government, which, in Churchill's words, was

> . . . in a dilemma from the beginning. . . . There was no way out. The issue of the territorial future of Poland must be postponed until

easier times. We had the invidious responsibility of recommending General Sikorski to rely on Soviet good faith in the future settlement of Russian-Polish relations, and not to insist at this moment on any written guarantees for the future. I sincerely hoped for my part that . . . the major Allies would (later) be able to resolve the territorial problems in amicable discussion at the conference table. (2)

While Eden officially reassured the Poles that Britain did not recognize any territorial changes in Poland made after August 1939, he was compelled to say in an answer to a question raised in Parliament — and he later repeated it to the Polish government — that this British assurance did not involve a guarantee of Poland's 1939 frontiers.

On August 12 the Soviets decreed amnesty for Polish prisoners; two days later a military agreement providing for the establishment of a Polish Army in Russia was signed. But the disturbing signs increased. The Polish press in Britain and in the United States, perhaps not too tactfully, dwelled upon the frontier question, stating that the Polish-Russian Agreement had to mean a Russian recognition of Poland's 1921–39 frontiers. Whereupon the Soviet press and radio began to deny such an interpretation of the Agreement; and the British attitude could be discerned as early as August 1941, when the London *Times* and the *Manchester Guardian* cautiously began to hint at the desirability of re-examining the pre-war Polish-Russian frontier. (3)

Another problem was that of the Polish deportees in Russia, who numbered between one and one-and-a-half million. A Polish military mission arrived in the Soviet Union, General Anders was suddenly released from a Moscow prison, and the Soviet authorities, in a surprising departure from their traditions, gave considerable freedom to the Poles in their efforts to establish camps and assemble the 1939–41 deportees and prisoners of war. (4) But the Russians, as could be expected, were not very cooperative; soon it was discovered that most of the Polish commissioned and non-commissioned officers were missing; the civilian deportees told horrible tales of their misery in some of the worst slave labor camps of the Soviet Union, from Magadan to the Solovetski Islands in the Arctic. Also, the Russian leaders were none too eager for the appearance of an independent Polish Army in Soviet territory, even when the tremendous blows of the Germans threatened to bring Russia to the brink of military disaster.

Sikorski had to face disagreements, continued disagreements, and troubles with his fellow countrymen, (5) as all the bitterness and frustration of émigré life was present in the spectre of Poland's tragic future; an immensely sad chapter of Polish history was to begin. The skilled diplomats of Poland tried to present their case as successfully as was possible. Ciechanowski in Washington kept reminding Americans of the great danger which compromises or imprecise dealings with Russia harbored; he closely followed the manoeuvres of the Russian Ambassador Oumansky there; he even succeeded in making President Roosevelt ask Harriman to bring up the Polish "problem" with Molotov and Stalin in Moscow. But the Harriman-Beaverbrook mission was burdened with a strenuous and far too extensive agenda; upon his return, Harriman confided to the Polish Ambassador that he could find no occasion to discuss Poland with Stalin. (6)

Meanwhile their military dangers seemed to make the Russians somewhat more flexible. On September 24 the Soviet Union signed a document at St. James's Palace in London, concurring in the principles of the Atlantic Charter — a long-forgotten document, a long-forgotten date, a long-forgotten signature! — and on October 6, Stalin declared:

> We have not, and cannot have any war aims such as the seizure of foreign territories and the subjugation of foreign peoples — whether it be peoples and territories of Europe or peoples and territories of Asia, including Iran. . . . We have not, and cannot have, any war aims such as that of imposing our will and our régime upon the Slavonic or other enslaved nations of Europe, who are expecting our help. Our aim is to help these nations in their struggle for liberation which they are waging against Hitler's tyranny and then leave it to them quite freely to organise their life in their lands as they think fit.

Yet it was clear that the Soviets had entirely different intentions. On September 27 a Soviet-Czechoslovak Agreement was signed. In direct ratio to the increase of difficulties between Russia and Poland, Beneš' relations with Stalin became more close; the Russian press and radio adopted a friendly tone toward Czechoslovakia, which indicated that Moscow accepted the aid of Beneš in her planned diplomatic game, while Hodža and other Czechoslovaks in exile vainly opposed Beneš' concept and policies.

[*Anders and Sikorski in Moscow.*] In November 1941 reports reached London from Poland that the Soviets had begun to build the framework of a great Communist underground there. This was evidence that, beyond their territorial aims, the Russians wished to install their own men in Poland, and, after a period of skillfully conducted rivalry, to reach a position where Polish Communists would be put in power when eventually the Germans retreated from Poland. Within the Soviet Union Polish Communists and NKVD agents were constantly spying on Anders and his people, whose actions and movements began to be officially obstructed. But Stalin was as yet undecided how to handle the problem of the Polish army-in-exile. Anders had a more or less favorable interview with him in November. The bald, fiery-eyed, towering Pole commanded Stalin's interest and respect; he promised to accelerate the process of equipping the Polish soldiers.

On December 3 — forward German guns were audible in Moscow then — Prime Minister Sikorski flew into Moscow. He was immediately escorted to the Kremlin; he had two long and highly instructive talks with Stalin. The Soviet dictator tried to extract an anti-British statement from Sikorski, but the Polish visitor stood fast by his British allies and praised Churchill and the British people and army. Most of the conversation dealt with the problems of the Polish army-in-exile. The presence of the Polish soldiers in Russia seemed to be a burden to Stalin. He arranged with Sikorski for the partial evacuation of the army-in-exile to Iran and Iraq; the great, indescribable trek of the civilian deportees, children, women, cripples, and old men, from the vast Asiatic plains of the Soviet Union to the Near East and India was to begin. At the end of the conversations, Stalin, employing the subtle medium of joking, then brought up the frontier problem. "Should we not now talk about the frontier between Poland and Russia?" The Polish Premier stiffly refused to talk about something he did not consider to be a topic for discussion. Perhaps this was a mistake; for Stalin indicated — it was December 1941 and the Germans were *very* close to Moscow — that he desired "a little" rectification only. (7) Sikorski was not a diplomat but an honest, very straightforward soldier. He did not grasp the occasion to commit Stalin, or even to sound out Stalin on what his ambitions were at that time. He nevertheless succeeded in impressing the Russian dictator of his goodwill — a considerable achievement, one, however, without very permanent results. Sikorski broadcast to the Soviet people, and before his departure, a Soviet-Polish Declaration of Friendship and Mutual Aid was signed and announced to the world. (8)

[*Eden and Stalin: the Russian aims first revealed.*]   On December 7 Sikorski was on his way back to London. Other history-making airplanes flew on that day. Twelve thousand miles away, the fliers of Admiral Nagumo roared off the decks of Japanese carriers bound for Hawaii. In another hemisphere Anthony Eden sailed toward Russia. On December 5 Hull had sent him a message; in the opinion of the American Government it was inadvisable to make any commitments with respect to specific terms: "therefore . . . it would be unfortunate if we were hampered at the peace conference by prior commitments to individual countries, which might jeopardize the realization of our common aims with respect to an enduring peace. Above all . . . there must not be any secret agreements." (9)

This was a most important warning. Originally Eden was to deal with the problem of British supplies to Russia and to dispel Russian suspicions that Britain was not a true-hearted ally. Stalin also wanted to discuss a Russian-British amphibious landing in the Petsamo area; he insisted on full Russian command at the higher level and complete Russian responsibility for the planning, stipulations which Eden could not accept. Then, at the very first meeting, Stalin turned to territorial questions. First of all, the Soviet Union was to be reconstituted within her 1941 frontiers.

He also had other, highly interesting proposals: Rumania should give special bases to the Soviet Union, to which contract Britain should give secret consent; on the other hand, it would be just if Britain received bases in Western Europe, Norway, and Denmark. Rumania could receive compensation "from territories presently occupied by Hungary; Turkey could get northern Syria and eventually rectify her European frontiers to the detriment of Bulgaria." (10) Stalin, who in a previous letter to Churchill in November had mentioned the aim of preventing Germany "and in the first place, Prussia," from provoking aggression once more, proposed that Poland be compensated in East Prussia, that the Sudeten region be restored to Czechoslovakia, that Austria be independent, and that possibly there should also be a separate Rhineland and Bavaria. He had "no objection to certain countries of Europe entering into a federal relationship, if they so desired." Yugoslavia and Albania were to be restored, the former to receive some Italian territories. Greece would receive the Dodecanese. All this was a clear-cut sphere-of-interest proposal. Eden refused to commit himself, although Stalin pressed for a British recognition of the 1941 Soviet frontiers, even stating that this was to be a prerequisite of any Anglo-Soviet Agreement. But he pressed in vain.

Churchill was duly informed, and on the 20th he sent a message to Eden:

> Naturally you will not be rough with Stalin. We are bound to United States not to enter into secret and special pacts. To approach President Roosevelt with these proposals would be to court a blank refusal, and might cause lasting trouble on both sides. (*11*)

The Premier was at sea, on his way to a most important conference with the Americans; in Washington he was to present his war plans for 1942. He continued to support Eden's refusal to enter into territorial discussions. He wired Attlee:

> Stalin's demand about Finland, Baltic States and Rumania are directly contrary to the first, second and third articles of the Atlantic Charter to which Stalin has subscribed. There can be no question whatever of our making such an agreement, secret or public, direct or implied, without prior agreement with the United States. The time has not yet come to settle frontier questions, which can be only resolved at the Peace Conference when we have won the war.
> 2. The mere desire to have an agreement which can be published should never lead us into making wrongful promises. Foreign Secretary has acquitted himself admirably, and should not be downhearted if he has to leave Moscow without any flourish of trumpets . . . (*12*)

Yet such Russian demands, communicated at a time when the Germans were but a few dozen miles from Moscow, in the suburbs of Leningrad, and holding a line which cut European Russia almost in half, were a bad augury for the future. Soon the year 1942 dawned, a year in which Stalin was to progress with his central-eastern European plans and to meet with more understanding, fewer obstacles.

The national resistance movements during 1941 and 1942

[*Poles.*] Shortly before *Barbarossa*, Hitler was quoted as saying: "The Poles are not Europeans but Asiatics who can be handled only with the knout."

There were also millions of Poles and Ukrainians under Soviet rule. The *Chaostpolitik* of Rosenberg doomed these people too. On

May 14, 1941, a Führer order was issued on the exercise of "martial jurisdiction and procedure in the area of *Barbarossa*," a document of monumental brutality. (*1*) An order on July 27 required that all available copies of the May 14 order be destroyed (this was merely a security measure in face of eventual enemy propaganda). On July 16 a Hitler-Rosenberg conference confirmed the latter's policies, and on July 23 Keitel issued this directive:

> In view of the vast size of the occupied areas in the East, the forces available for establishing security in these areas will be sufficient only if all resistance is punished not by legal prosecution of the guilty, but by the spreading of such terror by the occupying forces as is alone appropriate to eradicate every inclination to resist among the population.

Thus a preventive war of terror was launched against a population, elements of which had originally been inclined to receive the Germans with friendly feelings. Ukrainian villages in eastern Poland and in the western Ukraine had greeted the first German troops with wretched little celebrations, and the local German commanders were surprised by the swelling number of young Ukrainians willing to serve with them. Some of the volunteers were accepted, assigned to police duties, and trained by the SS for the rôle of bloodhounds around and within the ghettos established in Poland and in the Ukraine. But this was about all. Very soon the slightest pro-German sympathies vanished; subsequently a Communist partisan army began to appear in the eastern marshes of Poland and in the Ukraine. On September 16, 1941, Keitel was forced to admit the failure of the political terror warfare; supplementary directives were issued in November. (*2*)

[*Some German reforms.*] Around the middle of 1942 a slight change in German policies became perceptible in Poland. In the summer of 1941 the Russian radio had lauded the Polish underground and continuously appealed for a (militarily senseless) revolt of the Slav brethren behind the German front. In the autumn, the framework of a rival Communist underground was emerging in Poland; within Russia, the Polish "General" Berling organized Russian-Polish formations, a counterpart of the Polish Home Army; a "Kosciuszko Radio" (*3*) began to operate from somewhere in the Soviet

Union, beaming Polish "national" programs, lauding the Communists, and occasionally delivering broadsides against the London exile government. "Gouverneur" Frank, the snob and poor imitator of renaissance princes, (*4*) decided — on his own initiative — to exploit these differences. From June 1942 on, he slightly relaxed the iron grip of the SS on Polish cultural and spiritual activities, and in July 1942 he delivered a speech evoking the principles of law and order, an address which was a minor milestone on the sad calvary of Poland's German era. But Frank's subtle appeals met with no success. Polish resistance continued, notwithstanding the different concepts held by Frank and some of the SS leaders (*5*); the latter were also tainted with corruption, as the case of Lausch, the "Governor" of Galicia, showed. Because of his fantastic black-market activities — it was well known that in Galicia all kinds of weapons were directly purchasable from German civilians and from Axis troops — Lausch was brought before a military court and executed in Breslau in 1942.

Frank and all the other satraps, however, proceeded to act together in the unabated and wholesale extermination of the Jewish population. Frank planned also to stimulate a native anti-Semitism among the Poles, but he was generally unsuccessful. Neither the German-sponsored anti-Semitism, nor the evident divergence between the two branches of the Underground, one national, the other Communist, produced good grist for Frank's mills. Meanwhile other mills were erected, the death-mills for the Jews in Majdanek and Oswiecim. (*6*) By the end of 1942, most of the city ghettos had been evacuated, the inhabitants having been decimated and the remainder transported to these horrible death factories. In May 1943 the liquidation of the largest ghetto in Warsaw met with a futile effort of last-ditch resistance; the Jews fought with stones, pistols, and a few rifles against the SS forces, who were finally compelled to bring up artillery and tanks and level the whole of the ghetto city.

[*Czechs.*]   In September 1941 the relatively peaceful life of the Protectorate suddenly changed for the worse, as it was discovered that many members of the Czech "government," led by General Elias, the Premier, were part and parcel of the resistance movement. A violent purge swept through Prague and a wave of executions followed. The relatively mild Reich "Protector," Neurath, resigned; his successor was the SS chieftain Heydrich, whose brutality was to become legendary. A new puppet government was installed in January

1942, in which the propagandist Moravec played the only relatively
important rôle. Göbbels could note in his Diary that the Protectorate
was quiet. There is no doubt that among the subjugated eastern
peoples the Czechs fared relatively best. Yet, while there was no secret
state or underground army comparable to those of the Poles, the
Czech resistance operated with gradually increasing effectiveness. On
May 27, 1942, the SS overlord, Heydrich, was attacked in a daring
fashion and killed; an unprecedented wave of terror roared now
through "Czechia," one of the results of which was the tragic and incredible extermination of the village of Lidice on June 10, 1942. (7)

[*Slovaks.*] While the Protectorate was being thrown about
by the sinister waves of her masters' blackening temper, the former
sister, Slovakia, was plodding along a curiously independent course.
The Slovak state, a half-Nazi, half-Fascist one, was led by a group
of unscrupulous, parochial, and non-western politicians, first among
them that narrow-minded priest, Tiso. Aided by the local SS and the
leaders of the German national group, Tiso ruled with the Hlinka-
Guardists, fat and complacent, from Bratislava. Here was the perfect
operetta state, with an operetta army, a sallow-faced group of mousy
civil servants, corrupt and cowardly, wearing martial uniforms, and
with busybody *parvenu* functionaries fluttering to and fro. Two Slovak
army bataillons were sent to Russia; and the climax of Tiso's life
came perhaps on that day in the summer of 1942 when he, the Slovak
Catholic "leader," travelled eastward behind the mighty armies of
Germany and visited the capital of the Ukrainians, the altar-city
of Russia's Orthodoxy, Kiev; there, notwithstanding his professed
Roman religion, lay his Byzantine and essentially anti-western
origins.

All this does not mean that the Slovak satellite state was built on
nothing but sand: indeed, most Slovaks enjoyed their independence
from Prague, and grumblings against the Tiso régime were neither
frequent nor too significant. While Slovak anti-German resistance
was very weak until about 1944, and not comparable to that of the
Czechs, the pressure of the bishops and clergy and of certain intellectual circles made the Tiso régime refrain from imposing a cruel
terror such as the Pavelič government exercised in Croatia. The warnings of Pope Pius and the silent threat of an eventual open rebuke or
excommunication by the Vatican was a strong restraining factor in
the conduct of Tiso; the existence of that factor manifested itself

in more than one way. (Slovakia was, for example, the only place in central-eastern Europe where Jewish converts to Christianity were left largely unharmed; in 1944, however, the German SS took Jewish affairs out of the hands of the Tiso government and the death-mills swallowed Slovakia's Jews.)

[*Abroad: Beneš.*]   On November 10, 1941, the Polish-Czechoslovak Declaration was enlarged by the formation of a "coordination committee" to which, upon Polish suggestions, the later invitation of Austria, Hungary, and eventually Rumania was envisaged; on January 23, 1942, the Czech-Polish preliminary Agreement based on the Declaration was signed in London. But despite all the lip service given to the federation plans, it became clear during 1942 that friendship with Russia, nothing but friendship with Russia, was Beneš' guiding star. Austrian, Hungarian and Polish "Leftists," among them a goodly number of crypto-communists, were encouraged and supported by Beneš and his circle. During 1942 it was still possible for Otto Habsburg and Edvard Beneš to publish parallel articles on the subject of a post-war Danubian federation in *Foreign Affairs*, but by the end of that year the stock of the Danubian conservatives, of the Czechoslovak Hodža, Otto Habsburg, Walter Schuschnigg (the ex-chancellor's brother), of the Hungarian Eckhardt, and the Rumanian Davila, had fallen deeply because of clever adverse propaganda. In 1942 Otto suggested the formation of an Austrian bataillon to serve with the American Army. When, in November, Secretary of War Stimson addressed his acknowledging letter to "Otto of Austria, President, the Military Committee for the Liberation of Austria," the Beneš group and the whole central-eastern European Left, ranging from Louis Adamic to clever journalists and commentators in the *New Republic*, the *Nation*, and even The *Atlantic Monthly*, let out a well-timed cry — a cry which exactly coincided with the great controversy over Darlan in North Africa — and this cry was carried by their accomplices, OWI functionaries and columnists, into the White House itself. At that time Beneš began to plan his visit to Moscow, a trip which the British consistently tried to oppose, but the myth of Beneš' 1938 martyrdom and his personal contacts duly impressed, and the rosy ideological picture of a Czechoslovakia constituting the bridge between East and West duly pleased, President Roosevelt and his circle; thereafter, with American encouragement, Beneš went ahead with preparations for his Moscow trip and for the

Czechoslovak-Soviet Treaty. What Professor Kolarz had written about American policy in 1917 could be repeated in reference to 1942, that is, that policy "was strongly moulded by the programmes and aspirations formulated on American soil by immigrants from Central and Eastern Europe, aspirations which, however, had nothing in common with the requirements of a stable world policy or with American interests." (8)

There were very few Slovaks in Slovakia who had particular sympathies for the exile government, and the war, instead of easing, aggravated the misunderstandings between Czechs and Slovaks — just as it aggravated the very acute Serb-Croat differences. This increased misunderstanding was as evident in the columns of the immigrants' primitive newspapers in the mining towns of Pennsylvania, in Pittsburgh, Detroit, and Chicago as it was at home. Shallow optimism nonetheless continued to be pursued for the sake of the wishful thinkers, and the obvious ambitions of Russia were encountered by nothing more than this figleaf of propaganda, tremblingly covering truly naked issues. In the formulation of this partly wistful, partly hypocritical, and, in its consequences, catastrophic policy, a large number of central-eastern European émigrés had a share, a share big enough to make it morally impossible for them to put the blame later solely on the leaders of the English-speaking nations who in their grave business of carrying global destinies could not always do their charting faultlessly.

[*The Baltics.*]   By the end of 1941, Rosenberg's projects and his misrule eradicated most pro-German sympathies in the Baltics. Once more Lithuanians, Latvians, and Estonians were reduced to political and economic serfdom. A veritable iron curtain descended upon the Baltics, which were exploited with shortsighted haste by Rosenberg's *Chaostministerium.* A Gauleiter, Lohse, sat in Riga; a High Commissioner, Litzmann, ruled over Estonia. The Soviet nationalization decrees were kept by the Germans and the collective farms were made to continue; almost nothing was done to restore private property. Civilian movement was also very much restricted: only a number of Estonian Swedes who were repatriated to Sweden in 1942–43, and only those Latvians, Lithuanians, and Estonians who were willing to do slave labor in Germany were able to leave their unhappy countries. Employment of Baltic slave-labor was intensified during 1942. (9) Local politics were supervised by the SS and consisted exclusively of

the recruiting and marshalling of native extremists. Even such collaboration was, however, rather short-lived: by the end of 1941 an
SS report mentioned that among the "native anti-Semitic forces" the
"inducement to act against Jews" was becoming more and more difficult. Late in 1942, many Lithuanians, Latvians, and Estonians,
whose only hope and encouragement was the voice of London with
the miraculous short-wave seeping through the dark and mystic
Baltic forests and the existence of their respective exile committees
in Britain and in the United States, took to the forests again to defend themselves against the dangers of forced slave labor for the
Germans. By 1943, an anti-German resistance network with independent national liberation committees existed throughout the three
Baltic republics. As was the case almost everywhere else in central-
eastern Europe, the Communist underground was still insignificant
and its activities only sporadic.

[*Serbs and Croats, Slovenes and Montenegrins.*]   On August 25,
1941, Mussolini went to see Hitler in the latter's field headquarters
and the two reviewed the general war situation. Hitler (who, as usual,
spoke well-nigh incessantly) said that the Russians were proving a good
bit tougher than he expected from the intelligence he had previously
been given. This sudden modesty and self-criticism of Barbarossa
Hitler was only partly due to an amicable mood: he had had his second thoughts. The Germans needed more and more troops in Russia:
Hitler wanted the Italians to relieve German divisions wherever
feasible. In theory this could be done in three areas: France, North
Africa, and the Balkans, but political reasons ruled out the first, and
Rommel's presence was indispensable in the second area. Only in the
Balkans was a partial withdrawal of German forces and their replacement by Italians advisable. At the end of August an Italian division
arrived in Crete, whence a German Alpine division left for the southern sector of the Russian front. On August 30, 1941, the Nedič "government" was installed in Belgrade by the Germans to alleviate their
task of policing Serbia; during September, the reduction of the German occupation forces in Yugoslavia and Greece began. The consequences soon became apparent. On September 25 — exactly a month
had passed since the Mussolini-Hitler meeting — a German High
Command communiqué surprised the world with the acknowledgment that partisan warfare existed in Serbia: it stated that dive-
bombers had been employed against "irregular troops" there. Thus

the partisan phase of the Balkan War began. But before looking at
the forces involved, a glance at the confusing political situation in
occupied Yugoslavia and Greece is necessary.

[*The Croat-Serb fratricide.*]   The unexpected rapidity and zeal
with which the Croats seceded from a crumbling Yugoslavia in the
very first week of the Balkan campaign left grave and indelible impressions in its wake, notably within the ranks of the Yugoslav government-in-exile, in which, three days after its flight from Yugoslavia,
the first rift between Croats and Serbs showed itself because of a
statement issued in Athens. The Serb Fotitch gives a most interesting
account of these differences in his book. By the middle of 1941, it was
clear that the grave Croat-Serb controversy, intensively furthered by
the redoubtable dissensions among the Serb and Croat and Slovene
minority groups in the United States, where President Roosevelt himself was not immune to anti-Serb influences, was bound to be the
greatest obstacle in the way of the Yugoslav exile movement. The
Croat representatives in the government-in-exile, Krnyevič, Subasič,
Sutey, were accused by the Serbs of secretly casting glances back
toward "independent" Croatia; and while these accusations should
have been taken with a grain of salt, they also bore a grain of truth
within them. The situation was then made even more difficult by the
inevitably sanguinary reaction to the sad news coming from Yugoslavia.

In May–June 1941, the Croat *Ustaši* embarked on a series of St.
Bartholomew's Nights against the Serb and Orthodox population in
Bosnia and other Serb-inhabited regions of the new Croatian republic. The massacre was done in the worst Balkan fashion; blood literally flowed in the ditches and on the streets. The Croat governor of
Bosnia, Gutič, together with his accomplices, Puk, Žhanič and the
official propagandist, Budak, openly incited to murder. The outrage
reached such limits that the German plenipotentiary, Glaise-Horstenau, found it necessary to intervene: he angrily remonstrated with
Kvaternik in Zagreb. The Bishops of Serbia protested to General
Dankelmann, the German commander there, and the Metropolitan
of Sofia also conveyed a solemn protest to the Croat government;
but all this came too late; the killing spree wiped out entire villages
in a manner similar to the German massacre at Lidice, which, however awful, was but a mere single punitive sally compared with the
Yugoslav horrors of 1941. (*10*)

Immediately the smoke of vengeance rose from the Serbian valleys. The passion of revenge glowed white among the Serbs; the Chetniks in the mountains and the still-intact small army units organized under Colonel Mihailovič rallied and launched a counter-crusade against invaders and Croat traitors alike. When later in the summer of 1941 the Communist partisans under Broz-Tito appeared on the scene (Tito hid incognito in Belgrade until August, when he left for Valjevo), they had the relative advantage of being able to demonstrate to the natives and to the world alike in their propaganda that they were truly intra-national, fully Yugoslav in their composition. Meanwhile the Croat-Serb controversy caused angry headaches in the Foreign Office in London and the State Department in Washington, presenting quandaries from which the more convincingly and spectacularly "Yugoslav" Tito was ultimately to profit.

[*Italian troubles and settlements.*]   Intrigues between Germans and Italians in Croatia continued uninterruptedly, notwithstanding Ribbentrop's reiterated "assurances" to Ciano. German and Italian hirelings of the Croatian cabinet fought daily political battles among themselves, with financial assistance being supplied by their respective keepers. When Hungary annexed the Medjemurje (*11*) in July 1941, Pavelič announced that he wanted the Novibazar region for compensation, but the German military command in Serbia opposed this cession. There were serious troubles in Slovenia and Montenegro. The Italians in Slovenia were rather easygoing, and soon the local partisans supplied themselves almost exclusively with weapons bought from the soldiers of the Italian Second Army (Glaise-Horstenau later said that "he had never known anything like it"), while in Montenegro the high mountains became a veritable partisan stronghold — the strategic nucleus of the guerrilla warfare. Despite the wishes of Queen Elena of Italy, none of her Montenegrin relatives wanted to occupy the "throne" in Cetinje, and the Italian military governor of the province, General Biroli, tried to make the best of the situation by maintaining reasonably good terms with the Mihailovič forces.

In early August 1941 the Italians asked Ribbentrop again for a frontier rectification around Ljubljana, the suburbs of which town actually contained German frontier posts; on August 11, Ribbentrop rudely answered that if Italy would barter with Germany and cede a small crescent of territory around Tarvisio, the Ljubljana deal could be discussed; this the Italians were unwilling to do. Thus things stood when, in the wake of the general *Barbarossa*-New Europe spirit, Pavelič announced that according to historical evidence lately unearthed the Croats were not Slavs, but descendants of the Gothic tribes. This incensed Mussolini. Then Hitler instructed Ribbentrop to be somewhat more pliable, and when Ciano went to Berlin in November, Ribbentrop acknowledged that certain German officials "on the lower level" might have been difficult with the Italians, but he himself had spoken to the Croat Foreign Minister, Lorkovič, and now everything would be ironed out.

Pavelič himself pretended to be a true friend of Italy, grateful to and humble toward his former Italian keepers. On December 16, he and Ciano met at Venice, and while he proudly announced that the Jews in Croatian territories had been already "reduced" from thirty-five to twelve thousand, he complained about the exaggerated demands of the German minority, whose leader, Krafft, was a close confidant and collaborator of Kasche, the German SA envoy in Zagreb. (*12*) (Pavelič also spoke bitterly against some of the Croatian Catholic bishops, who were "openly hostile" to his régime.) Ciano was, of course, sceptical, and rightly so: having returned from Venice, Pavelič called on Kasche to complain about the Italians. In January 1942, Croats were sniping at Italians in Split, and open anti-Italian demonstrations were taking place in Zagreb, secretly sponsored by university friends of Kasche. At the same time Göbbels remarked in his Diary that the Croatian situation was very rotten: "The Italians already had cost us many sympathies in this world." In May, the Germans arrested a great number of Catholic priests in Slovenia, in whose favor the Italians intervened, largely in vain. By June 1942 the Partisans were shooting and raiding at the very outskirts of Ljubljana, and the Italian-held Dalmatian port of Knin had to be temporarily abandoned to them. Now the Italians, betrayed by their Croat, German "allies" and the Chetniks, menaced by Germans and Communist partisans alike, came to a patchwork truce "agreement" at Doboi. This agreement, wrongly called a treaty between the two supreme commanders, Roatta and Mihailovič, was in reality a Non-Aggression Pact. It strengthened the hand of the Italians for awhile; subsequently they could regain some of their influence in Croatia (the Germans officially incorporated Northern Slovenia on October 1, 1942, not having paid attention to Pavelič' requests that they refrain from officially announcing this incorporation in view of his waning popularity in Zagreb). Now, in October, Pavelič turned somewhat away from Berlin and towards Rome: he threw the chief German hirelings, Kvaternik and "General" Laxa, out of his government (Budak was kicked upstairs: he became Minister to Berlin), while he and his friends extended their personal control.

[*Nedič; Mihailovič; Tito.*] Added to the German, Italian, Hungarian and Bulgarian occupation forces and the Croat national army, there were three private armies forming in the summer of 1941: the Communist partisans of Tito, the Chetniks of Mihailovič, and the Civil Guards of Nedič. General Nedič, trying to save what could be saved under the bleakest of circumstances, organized these Guards in Belgrade and other Serb towns as a semi-military police force to be used against bandits, Macedonian terrorists and Communist partisans. For awhile the German military commander of Serbia did not intervene; later in 1941, however, mainly due to Croat and SS pressure, the Germans demanded that Nedič abolish the Guards. But then it was too late, and most of the Guard members flocked into Old Serbia where they joined the Mihailovič forces.

Milan Nedič played the rôle of a Balkan Pétain, essentially anti-German; through some of his lieutenants, he maintained contact with Mihailovič. Both were sincere patriots, stubborn, egocentric, fierce and narrow nationalists, unwilling to compromise Serb national interests for the sake of continued cooperation with Britain (Mihailovič) or with Germany (Nedič). Nedič procrastinated when the Germans demanded that he set up a Serbian Legion to join the other "volunteer" corps on the Russian front. Yet he was not strong enough to prevent the rise of a few German-paid opportunists in Belgrade, nor was he blunt enough to withdraw from his post when the Germans, after a momentary lapse, again began to treat the Serbs as inferior slaves. He committed many errors and perhaps a few sins: but he did not deserve to pay for them with his life. (*13*) He and Tito were bitter and irreconcilable enemies, while the Chetniks and the Partisans sporadically cooperated until the late autumn of 1941. The Mihailovič forces operated throughout Serbia, while Tito's bands appeared only in the western part, their strongholds being in Montenegro, Slovenia and southern Croatia.

[*The break between Mihailovič and Tito.*] In October 1941 a small group of British officers, the so-called Hudson mission, arrived in Serbia after a perilous air journey in order to establish contact with Mihailovič. Somewhat later the Soviet radio and certain "clandestine" Yugoslav radio services — it was then discovered that these stations operated from Tiflis in the Caucasus — began to assail the Chetniks and praise the Tito forces. The initial skirmishes between Mihailovič and Tito did not at first result in an all-out hostility. Twice the two leaders, the witty, blond, heavy-set Communist chieftain, a man of the modern, mechanical twentieth century, and the dark, lean, burning-eyed and bearded man of the forests, who seemed to have stepped out from a romantic nineteenth-century atmosphere, met in the mountains of the Ravna Gora, at first in the house of the retired Serbian General Misič. But their meetings were unsuccessful: here two worlds, two loyalties, two entirely different conceptions of honor were colliding. On November 2, 1941, Mihailovič and Tito forces clashed for the first time outside the city of Uzhice, occupied by the Partisans. After two bloody skirmishes, Communists and Royalists separated. Both Germans and Italians took careful notice of the developing fratricidal conflict; the Axis tried to exploit the situation but the Chetniks did not give in (*14*); they retired sullenly to the high forests in the impenetrable rocky fastnesses of Mother Serbia, while the Germans launched minor counterattacks in December and tried to smoke out the valleys.

The perils of the Yugoslav peoples were thus deepened by more shedding of blood under ideological stars. Added to these sufferings, Lidice-like "punitive expeditions" were undertaken by the German SS in the regions of Kralyevo and Mačva, while at Kraguyevac and in the Kopaonik mountains the Bulgarian occupation troops went off and murdered in worst Balkan fashion. In January 1942 a detachment of Nazi-trained Hungarian field gendarmes conducted a three-day orgy of murder among the Serb and Jewish residents of Novi Sad (*15*) in the Bačka, thereby badly compromising the previous relatively good reputation of the Hungarian occupants. However, the Arrow-Cross commanders of the massacre were to be tried before a military court in Budapest, but they then fled to Germany, whence they returned in March 1944 when a Nazi-type régime took Hungary over.

Of the future and international implications of the Chetnik-Partisan civil war the Yugoslav government-in-exile was intensely aware. On November 13, after the Uzhice battle, the envoy Gavrilovič was instructed to request the Soviet government to admonish the Yugoslav Communists so that civil war in Yugoslavia might be averted; on

November 24 the British military mission in Moscow made the same request to the Russians. But the Soviets had no intention to intervene: Gavrilovič was piously told that Russia did not wish to interfere in internal affairs which the Yugoslavs "should work out among themselves." (*16*)

[*Britain supports Tito.*] In the spring of 1942 the British appeasement of Russia made itself felt in Russo-British-Yugoslav relations just as it had in the contacts between Poles, British, and Soviets. Aware of the Poles' experiences, the Yugoslav government-in-exile was reorganized; in January 1942 Yovanovič followed Simovič in the Premiership and Mihailovič was named War Minister; the latter decided to run a bolder course, more independent of British advice and suggestions. Thereby, Mihailovič' position and prestige was strengthened, and the Chetniks, contrary to British desires, continued with their local agreements with Italians and Civil Guards. This irked the British considerably, who were impressed by the opinions and papers of certain academic "Balkan experts" and by what seemed to them the uncompromising, anti-Axis Tito. (*17*) The Yugoslav exile government now pinned some hopes on the United States, and some military intelligence contact between American and Mihailovič forces was established. By the summer of 1942, however, the British radio services began to pay somewhat unilateral homages to the Partisans, and it was even discovered that certain officials with the British High Command in Cairo were deliberately trying to frustrate direct contact between Mihailovič and the Americans. (*18*)

The usual amount of émigré personal intrigue prevailed among the Yugoslavs in Cairo, London, and Washington (this, of course, did not help mitigate Mr. Churchill's somewhat authoritarian views nor dispel his Kipling-like distrust of non-western European politics and statesmen); and the Yugoslav government once more tried to make the Soviets commit themselves on the side of the Royal Yugoslav government. Surprisingly enough, relations between Tito and Stalin were not quite smooth. On March 5 Tito was instructed by Moscow to collaborate with all parties and to stress the "popular front" idea rather than the proletarian character of the Partisan revolution. Moscow stated: "It is difficult [for us] to agree that London and the Yugoslav government are collaborating with the invader — there must be some misunderstanding." (*19*) The first "Titobuses" — slow transport planes which were to fly nightly, high over Rumania and Hungary from Russia to Tito — were not yet in operation, but the unbroken diplomatic relations between Bulgaria and the Soviet Union made the Russian legation in Sofia a most important center of Soviet intelligence in the Balkans. When the Yugoslav government again asked the Russians to intervene in the Yugoslav civil war, Moscow coolly stated on April 29 that the Soviet Union did not feel authorized to intervene. The Yugoslavs had one more card to play. The Yugoslav-Soviet Treaty of April 5, 1941, was not yet ratified by the Supreme Council of the USSR because of the turmoil of pre-war manoeuvres and early war events; then, in early 1942, the Soviets were notified of the Yugoslav desire to see the pact ratified. Foreign Minister Ninčič also planned that King Peter II should visit Moscow and pay a symbolic homage to Slav unity there. But the Russian government answered that it preferred the signing of a new treaty to the ratification of the "old" one. (*20*)

In May, Bogomolov, the Soviet Ambassador accredited to the assembled governments-in-exile in London, repeated to Yovanovič that no Soviet "interference" in the Yugoslav civil war could be expected, and Molotov, in London at the end of May, learned that the Yugoslavs had postponed the idea of negotiating a new treaty with Russia. Instead of Moscow, King Peter therefore visited the United States in June, where the atmosphere was, of course, open-hearted and friendly, but where also the undermining by propaganda of his government, of the Chetniks, of Mihailovič, indeed, of the entire Yugoslav Royalist cause, was already proceeding full blast.

[*Albanians.*] In 1941–42, Albania was relatively fortunate, compared with her neighbors. The Italian rulers were neither cruel nor wholly unscrupulous, and the Albanian conservatives, Kruia, Kupi, and Frasheri, could continue their daily activities under the Italian era and prepare for the future of a free Albania; also, the popularity of these men had some influence on the Italian-imposed Albanian administration of Verlači and others.

The key Italian administrators in the eastern Adriatic, Bastianini in Dalmatia, Jacomoni in Albania, and Geloso in Greece, could neither prevent nor suppress the strong national resistance movements; but the Italians were also preoccupied with the conflicts they had with their own allies, with Germans and Croats almost everywhere, and with the Bulgars in western Macedonia. The Bulgar government was partially transformed in April 1942; Filov, whom Berlin trusted, became Foreign Minister. Somewhat later the Bulgarian occupation troops in southern Serbia moved toward the Albanian frontier and penetrated the Ochrida-Prespa Lake region, which the Italians claimed for Albania after the Balkan campaign. The Italian-Bulgarian crisis reached a climax in August; thereafter tension between Sofia and Rome receded and attempts were made to reach a clear delimitation of the Albanian-Bulgar frontier, but the activities of the local partisans and the increasing troubles of Italy elsewhere prevented a permanent settlement.

[*Greeks.*]   The Greek situation was not unlike the Yugoslav: early in 1942, two private guerilla armies appeared, one Royalist and one crypto-Communist, EDES and ELAS, the nuclei of the forces of the Greek Civil War of 1944–49. *(21)* The strength of ELAS was in northern Greece, and the Macedonian Communists, aided by the Soviet Legation in Sofia, instructed and informed the ELAS bands. (Supplies came only later, and not a few of these supplies came from the British.) Greece had her own brand of collaboration with the enemy: again, it was more like that of Nedič and Pétain than that of Quisling. There was Tsolakoglu, an opportunist soldier, Rhallis, a calculating financier, and Logothetopoulos, perhaps the only one sympathetic with German ideology. With their usual lack of tact, the German occupants (despite the fact that there were no SS units in Greece) crudely gambled away the initial sympathies of certain Greeks who favored the victorious and, it was hoped, more generous Germans over the despised Italians. (Tsolakoglu's surrender to the Germans was part of such Greek calculations.) By the end of 1941, the original sympathies were revised and reversed: the occupation experiences taught the Greeks to appreciate the perhaps more corrupt but essentially human, Mediterranean, and mellow qualities of the Italian occupants.

The Greeks faced a terrible winter in 1941: their food stocks were completely depleted and a catastrophic famine was in the making. Neubacher, the German economic chief, met with a few Greek economic experts, first among them the clever Gotzamanis; but there was nothing to do: in spite of the few Red Cross and Turkish wheat ships which the British had allowed to pass the blockade, many thousand Greeks were destined to certain starvation. The head of the German political mission, Plessen, now requested that Italy (whose masses lived on black bread and soggy, brown *pasta* that winter) should feed Greece, a request received with ill humor in Rome; and when Ciano went to Berlin in November 1941, he took the issue up with the Germans, who then promised to assist the Italians by sharing their burden somewhat. Göring said to Ciano that he would not be opposed if "that self-appointed angel of humanitarianism," President Roosevelt, would arrange for some South American grain to be shipped to the Greeks. "On the other hand," continued Göring, "we should not preoccupy ourselves too much with the Greeks . . . certain people are destined to be decimated . . ."; he jokingly referred to reported instances of cannibalism among starving Russian prisoners-of-war, "with a cynicism which betray[ed] the fame of his relative *bonhomie*," noted Ciano.

In July 1942, flying back from an inspection tour of the Libyan-Egyptian front, Mussolini stopped in Athens and talked with Ghigi, the Italian Ambassador there; this able man was exasperated by the daily increasing difficulties and misunderstandings with the Germans. Mussolini then wrote another of his honey-toned letters to Hitler, requesting him to help the Italians in their economic endeavors in Greece. Hitler's reply was equally proper, full of general promises, but he did not specify exactly what he intended to do; in September Neubacher, Gotzamanis, Clodius, the German economic plenipotentiary in the Balkans, and the Rumanian, Bulgarian, and Croatian Ministers of Economy met in Berlin, where the discussions again had a slightly anti-Italian tinge and produced but little results to alleviate the food crisis. Thus Greece remained the sun-drenched land where dry leaves and dry bones rattled, a land where more and more hungry and bitter people fled from their daily perils and miseries to join the Communist forces in the mountains. (22)

[*Futile plans.*] The Greek government-in-exile shared the preoccupations of the Yugoslavs; it was well aware of the increasingly unstable domestic situation. Its necessary peregrinations did not raise its prestige: the Egyptian government, due to Axis pressure, persuaded King George II to leave for Capetown in May 1941, where the government remained until September. Striving for a future Balkan confederation, the Greek exiles collaborated closely with the Yugoslavs, and on January 15, 1942, an extensive Greek-Yugoslav Agreement was signed which contained the basic lines of a future Balkan federation. Eight months later Mihailovič sent a message, written in French, to Zervas, proposing cooperation between the Yugoslav and Greek

Royalist guerrilla forces. The Greek-Yugoslav Agreement was the exact counterpart of the Polish-Czechoslovak Agreement and Declaration, but just as the latter became worthless with Beneš' default and the growing trials of the Polish government-in-exile, the Allies' support of Tito in 1943 reduced the Greek-Yugoslav agreement to mere theory. As Woodhouse, the brilliant British intelligence officer, wrote: ". . . January 1942 was already too late for the policy which that Greco-Yugoslav agreement implied. To succeed, the policy had to be a Balkan policy: but Britain had no Balkan policy; still less had the USA." Thus did the promising federation plans for central-eastern Europe vanish into thin air even before the decisive military phase of the war, the Allied liberation of Europe, had begun.

[*Resistance within the "satellites."*]   In Bulgaria, Hungary and Rumania life was less tragic but equally dramatic; less fortuitous but equally flavorful; less intense but equally tortuous. There were restrictions, but political opposition, if one lay low, was at least personally safe. Indirect action against the Axis and its local partisans was taken through subtle media: finely chiselled articles citing historical parallels in the conservative newspapers, a few courageous sentences on the stage, in books and elsewhere. (*23*)

[*"From above."*]   Direct resistance was threefold. First, and of primary importance, was "resistance from above," in which the anti-German elements in the highest circles of the "satellite" states quietly tried to divert urgent German demands, to de-radicalize internal policies and to steer the vessel of state in line with those precious moral traditions which formed their piloting instincts rather than with those continually blinking signals of the mighty German man-of-war closely standing by, nudging them day by day, night by night. Thus Horthy in Hungary and members of the royal families in Rumania and Bulgaria tried to follow a more-or-less independent policy of their own, aided by a very close circle of faithful conservative accomplices.

In January 1942 the Germans pressed Budapest to send more Hungarian troops to the Russian front. Berlin even asked that Finland intervene with Hungary, and the Finnish Minister to Berlin requested his government to instruct the envoy to Budapest to request there a more extensive Hungarian participation in the Russian War. On January 19, Ciano arrived in Budapest and noted the apparent easy and pacific atmosphere of the Hungarian capital. His talks with Horthy convinced him that the Hungarians were sceptical about Hitler's statements according to which 1942 was to be "a year of great victories again." Ciano also asked Horthy to send troops to Russia; the Regent made excuses; he "was disposed to intensify the [Hungarian] participation in the war, but he did not intend to arrive at a general mobilization." (24)

[*The Hungarian Vice-Regency.*] Yet more Hungarian troops went to Russia; and the Second Hungarian Army was equipped and sent "out," and participated throughout the 1942 campaign. This was done to appease the Germans: it was imperative that they should find no pretext to intervene in Hungarian affairs at a time when an important and subtle political design was approaching its first stage of execution.

This was the creation of the office of a Hungarian Vice-Regency, the Vice-Regent to be the "Hungarian Umberto." Horthy, who carefully watched the Italian dynasty, knew that in the case of a Fascist defeat, the Italian monarch was prepared to step to the fore. Horthy thus agreed with his closest advisers, and it was decided that his elder son, Stephen Horthy, be brought before the nation and that the office of Vice-Regent be created for him. The Germans were angry, for it was known that Stephen Horthy was a dashing and easy-going young man with certain Anglophile sympathies. During the winter of 1941–42, the Vice-Regency question was officially opened. The Arrow-Cross newspapers at first fulminated, but the wet blanket of censorship doused their sparks, while more serious was the personal jealousy of the unbalanced Archduke Albrecht Habsburg, a noted hope of pro-Nazi circles. In February and March Gestapo reports fluttered to and fro between Budapest and Berlin. Fortunately for the Regent's plans, even the Himmler crowd in Berlin knew the irresponsibility of their Arrow-Cross informers and the motives of personal jealousy involved; also, Jagow, the German Minister, was, unlike his colleagues in Bratislava, Zagreb and Bucharest, conditioned by the mellow atmosphere of Budapest and the comfortable life of his Hungarian hosts and friends, and thus the German envoy emphatically denied that Horthy was "a hireling of the Jews." (25)

On February 19, 1942, Stephen Horthy was proclaimed Vice-Regent, and Ciano wrote:

Through this gesture Hungary tries to take out an insurance policy of an anti-German sort. I don't know if they have guessed right. In Berlin there is much coolness and I am told they will not send congratulations to the Vice-Regent.

On March 10, Horthy dismissed the pro-German Bárdossy and appointed Kállay to the Premiership, a man much nearer to him in his personal traits and in his political outlook. There were no other changes in the cabinet and Kállay introduced himself with a very pro-Axis speech in Parliament. It was nevertheless clear that a gradual change in Hungary's policies was occurring. Berlin, keenly aware of this "resistance from above," began to prepare countermeasures.

[*Democratic resistance.*]   Another form of resistance was that sporadically undertaken by various democratic organizations. In Bulgaria and in Hungary, where Parliaments still existed, remnants of the pre-war opposition could occasionally voice thinly veiled and courageous attacks against the "New Order"; men like Petkov in Sofia and Bajcsy-Zsilinszky in Budapest, groups like the former Zveno and the Agrarians in Bulgaria, some of the Liberals and the National Peasants in Rumania, the Small Holders and Social Democrats in Hungary prepared for future tasks and carried out their propaganda activities effectively, if with care-dictated reservations. (*26*) There was also some intellectual resistance; members of the Hungarian pro-democratic opposition organized a small group of anti-German intellectuals, "March Front," on the occasion of the Hungarian national festival day on March 15, 1942; an unduly loquacious actor, working for the British, was discovered during that summer directing industrial sabotage. In Bulgaria, two pro-German generals were assassinated. In Rumania a number of anti-German Rumanians were in contact with that retired grand old man, Maniu, whom even the Iron Guard and Antonescu did not dare to harm. Late in October 1941 it was discovered that a young engineer, Georgescu, had radio contacts with British intelligence: he was arrested, but due to the conveniently corruptible nature of Rumanian courts, he was later released; Maniu wrote a letter to Antonescu, stating that he himself assumed full responsibility for what Georgescu had done.

[*Rumanian complexities.*]   Rumania also had her "resistance from above" in court circles and among the Anglophile aristocracy.

Antonescu himself became slightly sceptical of the chances of German victory, and among members of his régime, there were known grafters and neo-Byzantine epicureans for whom the Germanic "New Order" became more and more uncomfortable. The severe winter of 1941–42 had a grave effect on the once so rich, agricultural Rumania, and in January 1942 Berlin for the first time learnt that Antonescu was not always flexible and pleasing: he declined to send more wheat to Germany. (This Göbbels attributed to the "impertinent influence" of Mihai Antonescu.) There were other reasons for friction between Germany and Rumania. Despite the zeal of certain local Rumanian commanders to outdo the Germans in cruelty and arrogance, the German military acted in Bessarabia and Transnistria as if it were their own territory; only after difficulties could Rumania and Germany conclude an "Agreement on the administration, security and economic exploitation of Transnistria and the Bug-Dnieper territory." (27) This Tatarnu-Hauffe Agreement (named after the respective signers, a Rumanian and a German general) displeased Rosenberg, who on December 14, 1941, took the problem to Hitler and suggested that the Rumanians abandon their control over southeastern Transnistria. The Rumanians, explained Rosenberg, were standing across the river from Nikolayev, where "they can look into all our shipbuilding installations." But Hitler let the agreement stand, probably because of his personal goodwill toward Antonescu.

Yet three months later the reports of Killinger from Bucharest clearly showed the differences between him and the Conducator, and Hitler sent a message to the latter: Why did he not collaborate with the "sincere elements" of the Iron Guard? Antonescu answered lengthily and it was even thought in Berlin that he was turning against Mihai Antonescu, but Göbbels remained sceptical: "much will certainly not come from this." The travel notes of Hassell, who visited Rumania at that time, give an illuminating insight into the Bucharest atmosphere: everybody intriguing against everybody, the Queen opening her heart to Hassell on the first occasion and pouring out typical Balkan gossip to this private German traveller, complaining that Antonescu kept everyone away from the young King except Bratianu, who was permitted to visit Mihai weekly as his "professor." Hassell, the rigid German gentleman-visitor, regarded Mihai Antonescu, who was supposed to have had close romantic ties with the wife of his chief, a "rascal . . . like Ciano." The main grafter was the widow of Goga, "a woman without scruples," worse than the

Lupescu woman had ever been. There were also troubles within the German-Saxon minority. The young neo-pagan, Andreas Schmidt, a protégé of Killinger, attacked the more conservative, while still avowedly Nazi, Vicar Müller in Sibiu. (*28*) Partly fearing the resurgence of the Iron Guard, partly due to Schmidt, who ruled in the Saxon parts of Transylvania almost as if he had a medieval Teutonic duchy of his own, Antonescu issued a decree in May 1942 which forbade the wearing of any kind of non-army uniforms. Ribbentrop was angry and protested. (*29*)

So the "unity sacred with blood" of the first *Barbarossa* days between Germany and her allies was no longer the same. The seeds of doubt were sprouting and there was now increasing evidence of resistance among the people.

The third kind of resistance, that of the underground Communist parties, was of sporadic nature in Bulgaria and virtually non-existent in Rumania and in Hungary.

The Hungarian-Rumanian crisis of 1942: the "new Little Entente" idea

[*The origins of enmity.*]   Four times between 1938 and 1941 Hungary had increased her territory to the detriment of her neighbors, and the extreme pro-Nazi policies adapted by the new Slovak and Rumanian régimes in 1939 and 1940 were at least partly due to calculations of Tiso and Antonescu, who aimed to ingratiate their countries with Hitler by proving better and truer allies than the Hungarians and thereby later to facilitate an eventual German-supported revision of the Vienna Awards. Bitter enmity prevailed between Hungary, Rumania and Slovakia, the "united" Axis allies. In Berlin at the solemn sanctification of this "unity," the signing of the Anti-Comintern Pact in November 1941, Ciano noted: "With each of their conversants, Bárdossy, Tuka and Mihai Antonescu intensively pursue a lively campaign of reciprocal denigration." Soon Pavelič joined the anti-Hungarian front, as he was irked by the Hungarian occupation of the Medjemurje and by reports that the Hungarians had some contact with his enemies, Nedič and Mihailovič; in Venice, in December 1941, Pavelič complained to Ciano about Hungary.

[*The new Little Entente idea and German responses.*]   Horthy a month later told Ciano that Hungary could not send many troops to

Russia as long as Rumanian hostility against Hungary prevailed. Secret negotiations between Bucharest, Bratislava and Zagreb began in January 1942 to exploit the German dissatisfaction with Hungary's war attitudes, the extent of which dissatisfaction may be seen from a few entries in Göbbels' Diary in the month of March 1942:

> March 6: "(But) all of us are longing for that coming moment when we can bring the Hungarians again to account . . ."
> March 11: "At the moment we cannot intervene in the Hungarian government forming. But later . . ."

Commenting upon the young Horthy's new position: "catastrophic . . . a hireling of the Jews. But today is not the time to occupy ourselves with so delicate a question . . . there will come a reckoning after the war . . ." On the handling of the German minorities and the personal attitude of Kállay: "impertinent."

In February, Antonescu went to see Hitler and pleaded for the return of Transylvania. Hitler liked Antonescu and disliked Hungary; he indicated a promise of an eventual revision of the Vienna Award. Subsequently the Antonescus delivered two violently anti-Hungarian, revisionist speeches. In April 1942 Slovakia took measures against the Hungarian minority, and the Hungarian-Rumanian frontier was partly closed: a crisis seemed imminent. (1) The intrigue proceeded in true Balkan fashion: Rumanian diplomats in Switzerland informed the German intelligence service there that Hungary was conducting secret conversations with British agents at neutral points; in turn, Hungarian consuls directed German attention to the ambiguous activities of certain Rumanians in Switzerland, among them the clever Gafencu, who had settled there after his diplomatic mission in Moscow had come to an end.

When Hitler, Mussolini, and their coterie met again in Salzburg on April 30, 1942, Ribbentrop requested Ciano to intervene and at least make the Hungarians understand that no Hungarian-Rumanian war would be tolerated by the Axis before the World War came to an end. (2) The Germans were now exasperated with Budapest and Bucharest. (With Sofia they had relatively less trouble at that time: King Boris, who visited Berlin in March 1942, was an astute diplomat, and complimented the vain Göbbels who therefore found him "very sympathetic.")

In May Hungary won some German confidence by dispatching her Second Army to Russia, passing new restrictive decrees against the Jews, and conscripting Jewish labor bataillons, which were sent to the Russian front; she also sent more wheat to the Axis. Increasing caution and independence in Antonescu's policies and the neutral impression which Kállay made on Hitler in June on his first visit to Germany contributed to the German coolness towards the idea of a Rumanian-Croat-Slovak alliance against Hungary. Also, in June German counterintelligence reported that the British Secret Service operating from Lisbon allegedly tried to further the possibilities of an open conflict between Rumania and Hungary. (*3*) The Hungarian-Rumanian crisis remained acute, and in July the German Minister reported from Finland that the government there was worried about the possibilities of a war between the two Danubian Axis "allies."

Early in August growing Hungarian anti-Axis opposition and contacts which Horthy and certain influential Hungarian aristocrats had with Eckhardt in the United States were reported by German counterintelligence, resulting in increased German suspicion and ill will toward Hungary. The cabinet position of the narrow Germanophile War Minister, Bartha, was tottering; early in September, the known anti-German and anti-Rumanian Nagy de Nagybaczon became War Minister, and later incensed Hitler by referring in Parliament to the Jewish labor bataillons as "equally soldiers of the fatherland." On August 20, the sudden news broke upon Budapest that Stephen Horthy, the Vice-Regent, who was serving with a fighter squadron in Russia, had been killed at dawn in an airplane accident. The rumor spread that he had taken to his plane in an intoxicated condition, but a week later when Count Imre Károlyi, a relative of the Regent, and another confidant perished in another accident, there was ground to believe that German agents had caused the death of these two men, potential obstacles in Hitler's path. At Stephen Horthy's funeral it was intimated to the Italians that King Victor Emmanuel might be offered the Hungarian Crown; but Mussolini rejected the idea; he saw that this could be construed as an anti-German move and could bring about a crisis within the Axis.

[*German difficulties.*] There were now considerable divergencies among the makers of German foreign policy themselves. The more conservative officialdom of the Wilhelmsstrasse, Weizsäcker, Kordt, and others, believed that it was foolish to alienate Horthy, who, in their eyes, was an honorable old gentleman. On the other hand Göbbels and the SS were extremely anti-Hungarian and made their own policy. Early in September, Killinger in Bucharest indicated German acquiescence in the "new Little Entente" talks, and military staff conversations took place between Slovakia and Rumania. The Hungarians were upset and angry; what helped them was the general war situation. For the Germans began to be involved in a fierce and unpredictable battle of attrition around Stalingrad, and the canny Antonescu himself, as Horthy had done eight months before, began to concentrate power in his own hands and transfer some of Rumania's precious eggs from their German basket. On September 23 a decree announced that the Conducator was thereafter the sole source of Rumanian law. The Little Entente talks continued but with less German support; certain German circles even listened to the personal enemy of Antonescu, the Iron Guard leader Horia Sima, living in Italy; Sima, instead of the Little Entente plans, proposed a forceful overthrow of the Horthy régime with German assistance, whereby his Hungarian counterpart, the Arrow-Cross leader Szálasi, would come to power in Budapest. (4) With the beginning of the Soviets' winter counter-offensive in November and the evident change in their war fortunes, all German support for the Little Entente idea ceased: in Berlin as well as in Budapest and Bucharest the greater questions of an uncertain future occupied all attention. (5)

Russian developments — 1942

The Declaration of the United Nations was issued on January 1, 1942; it introduced those mystery-laden four years during which the Atlantic Powers, the champions of the Western world, to use the words with which Tawney pithily depicted other great historical junctures, "walked reluctantly backward into the future." The ideological character of the war grew steadily throughout 1942 and reached its full expression in the unconditional surrender declaration of Casablanca in the early days of 1943. But 1942 was also a great military year during which the war fortunes turned; and one should not forget: it is easy to criticize decisions, not so easy to scrutinize desires. Paramount and all-embracing was the desire of the Atlantic Powers to achieve victory, an end so homogeneous in its psychic texture that it left virtually no room for the examination of what long-range, postvictory advantages the heterogeneous means might provide. On January 1, 1942, the strategic position of the Axis-Japanese alliance seemed formidable; even the "end of the beginning" seemed far away. The problems were military and not political. So were the aims.

[*The Anglo-American attitude concerning Russian ambitions.*] Churchill informed the Americans in Washington of what Eden had learned in Moscow of Russia's ambitions. But the "Arcadia" conference was overloaded with an awful and pressing military agenda and there was, alas, not enough time and opportunity to discuss and coordinate what common policy the English-speaking Powers should follow in regard to Russia's territorial aims.

Churchill wrote Eden on January 8:

> We have never recognized the 1941 frontiers of Russia except *de facto.* They were acquired by acts of aggression in shameful collusion with Hitler . . . In any case there can be no question of settling frontiers until the Peace Conference. I know President Roosevelt holds this view as strongly as I do, and he has several times expressed his pleasure to me at the firm line we took at Moscow . . .

But all this was based on the following assumptions, so tragically neglected later:

> . . . No one can foresee how the balance of power will lie or where the winning armies will stand at the end of the war. It seems probable, however, that the United States and the British Empire, far from being exhausted, will be the most powerfully armed and economic *bloc* the world has ever seen, and that the Soviet Union will need our aid for reconstruction far more than we shall then need theirs. (*1*)

Somewhat later London nevertheless pressed for Washington's opinion. The Russians were requesting that a Russo-British Treaty be signed, incorporating the territorial requirements of the Soviet Union either openly or in secret clauses. Early in February President Roosevelt received a memorandum from Secretary Hull on the subject, which insisted that all territorial problems should be excluded from war-time discussions and treaties. The idealist Hull smelled an eastern European compromise and in February 1942 the President supported his memorandum: he even refrained from discussing with the British the problem of the Baltic states, whose incorporation into the Soviet Union the United States had never recognized.

[*The first compromise.*]   At the end of the month, Cordell Hull became ill and did not return to his office until April 20. Meanwhile the British were troubled by the American approach, which they regarded as not very helpful, even though basically constructive. A State Department Sub-Committee on Political Problems met first on March 7, and on the 14th a Territorial Sub-Committee chose Poland "as a test case." On March 28 this group reported that it "had also selected the major problem areas in order of their priority for study, concluding that most of the territorial questions of greatest concern in Europe lay in the belt of populations and land faced by the Soviet Union, extending from the north of Finland to the Aegean."
But:

> A fixed conclusion of the subcommittee . . . was that the vital interests of the United States lay in following a "diplomacy of principle" — of moral disinterestedness instead of power politics . . . (2)

Notwithstanding American opinions, Churchill, in the words of Hull "seemed reluctantly determined to go ahead with the Russo-British accord and Stalin continued to press for an immediate signature." Also, the British had some fears. Certain Russophile members of the German military and middlemen such as Niedermeyer were reported to have been moving freely in Eastern Europe. (When in 1946, during his Nuremberg interrogation, Fritzsche — of known pro-Russian sympathies in 1939–41 — mentioned the name of Niedermeyer, the Russian member of the prosecuting staff interrupted his testimony before Fritzsche could continue.)

Were there any peace soundings between Russia and Germany in the spring of 1942? There may have been. The well-informed Italian observer in Berlin, Simoni, quoted one of his high German conversants, "very much *au courant* with the situation," on April 2:

> In his last speech Hitler, for the first time, gave the impression that among the war aims of the Reich the total annihilation of the Stalinist régime does not figure but only its keeping away from Europe. It is hoped that Stalin, when beaten in the Caucasus and faced with the incapacity of his allies, would give proof of his political realism and show himself disposed to come to a deal. If this should happen, why should Germany not listen to such soundings (perhaps through Turkey), in order to seek a way out of this inextricable conflict?

At the same time, the Russians feared that through Papen and Turkey, the Germans and British might talk. Hitler, while confident of final victory, seemed to vacillate. Stalin was still far more sympathetic to him than Churchill was, yet, he took pleasure in portraying himself as a defender of Europe against Oriental Bolshevism. In April at Salzburg Hitler said to Mussolini: "Churchill will make peace. . . "

Churchill had, of course, no intention of talking peace with Hitler; he subordinated everything to the cause of supreme victory. Late in March 1942 the Combined Chiefs of Staff in Washington drew up the first concrete plans for an invasion of Western Europe (*Sledgehammer*), to obtain a "toehold" in France. This was to be followed by a major cross-Channel operation (*Roundup*), probably in 1943. Churchill was still not sure about the American determination to defeat Hitler first; in April Hopkins admitted to him, "If public opinion in America had its way, the weight of American effort would be directed against Japan."

At the same time the British government was very anxious to reach some kind of an agreement with the Russians; the London *Times* in March indirectly hinted at the acceptance of Russia's 1941 frontiers; *Life*, the American magazine, published an interview with Sir Stafford Cripps in which the former Ambassador left the question of Russia's western frontiers open, and while he did not commit himself, he seemed to lean toward accepting Russian viewpoints. Thus the British appeasement of Russia continued while Mr. Hull was away from his office; when he returned, other unpleasant surprises awaited him. President Roosevelt, previously adamant against the discussion of territorial problems, was now veering toward the British point of view. On March 7 Churchill wrote the President (he already had explained this argument to John Winant, the American Ambassador):

> The increasing gravity of the war has led me to feel that the principles of the Atlantic Charter ought not to be construed so as to deny Russia the frontiers she occupied when Germany attacked her. (*3*)

Two days later Churchill informed Stalin of this message to the American President. Roosevelt now learned that Molotov was to visit London in order to discuss there the Russo-British Treaty. The President, eager and idealistic, wished to exploit this occasion and pictured himself able, with his genial cordiality, to eliminate all shreds of Russian suspicion and to bring about a happy entry of Russia into the sincere, hard-working and august society of the anti-Axis crusaders. A dangerous illusion! Late in March he wrote Churchill: "I know you will not mind my being brutally frank when I tell you that I think I can personally handle Stalin better than either your Foreign Office or my State Department. Stalin hates the guts of all your top people. He thinks he likes me better, and I hope he will continue to do so." (Roosevelt wanted Molotov to come to Washington *first*, before London.) Then he was made aware of the serious implications of such a gesture; on April 11, he cabled Stalin and asked him to send Molotov to Washington after the London visit. Stalin gladly complied. When Stalin's reply came, Hull was back at his desk and learned that Roosevelt's view now was that perhaps it would, after all, be necessary to consider Russia's territorial demands in the Baltic and in eastern Finland: in a somewhat ill-fitting, Yankee trading spirit, Roosevelt suggested that, as a form of compensation, the Baltic and Finnish people living in the lands to be re-annexed by the Soviets might be allowed to leave freely with their properties. Here was the first American compromise. (*4*)

[*Molotov in London. A commitment avoided.*] Now Molotov arrived in London on May 20 and insisted upon the incorporation of territorial clauses in the Russo-British Treaty, a demand which kept the Foreign Office in a dither. The British counter-drafts contained no mention of frontiers and territorial issues. Two issues helped Eden (and Churchill): first, the Americans were still adamant against the incorporation of territorial clauses in important inter-Allied treaties. Second was the beginning of the Germans' 1942 offensive. While Molotov was in London, the German tanks broke through the Russian defense positions in the Kertch peninsula in the eastern Crimea, and Timoshenko's forestalling offensive in the eastern Ukraine was also broken. A situation now developed where Russia needed the treaty with Britain as badly as did the latter; on May 22 Molotov even asked Churchill "what, if the Soviet Army failed to hold out during 1942, would be the position and the attitude of the British Government." Molotov wished to make a favorable impression (especially in Washington), and expedite the Allied decision to open a second front in Western Europe as soon as possible. On the evening of the 23rd Molotov began to give way; to the great relief of the Americans and British, Molotov dropped his insistence on the territorial clauses, and on May 26, 1942, the twenty-year Russo-British Treaty was signed, providing for "full collaboration" during and after the war.

[*Molotov in Washington: a good impression.*]   In Washington, Molotov was friendly and generally made a good impression on Roosevelt and on other leading Americans. Sherwood, in *Roosevelt and Hopkins*, gives a detailed account of how Hopkins reacted during the Molotov visit: there were no territorial discussions. But Russophilia was then fashionable in America, and the belief in a new order, a new kind of world democracy was swelling. In the published Hopkins papers occasional allusions are made to the Russian-Baltic problem, but no word on Poland appears in the papers concerned with the Molotov visit. (A touchy subject was thus carefully avoided.) (5) On June 13, Molotov was back in Moscow, and on June 17, Sumner Welles, in a speech at Baltimore, said that the final terms of peace should wait until the most important post-war tasks were dealt with.

Truly, until Yalta, February 1945, there was not one occasion when the Western Allies made definite territorial commitments to Russia. The elimination of the territorial problems from the agenda of Russian-Western talks was mistakenly considered a pleasant and successful achievement by Mr. Hull and other Americans. . . . Molotov's anxiety and the arguments during his visit to the Western capitals showed that at that time Russia was eager not to forfeit the aid and sympathies of her Allies. This was the time to secure Russian commitments. If at that time it was considered impossible or diplomatically undesirable to achieve or to press for such commitments, then it was imperative that the Western Allies should at once formulate their strategic plans with the post-war political picture in mind; in other words, they needed to plan their occupation of Europe in a manner which would reduce the chances of Russian *faits accomplis* in the areas which the Soviet armies were to overrun in the last stages of the war.

It must be said in all fairness, however, that the adoption of these policies, while running counter to the optimistic and benign ideological trends which prevailed in London and especially in Washington in 1942, would also have necessitated a measure of such prescience, especially among the military leaders of the English-speaking Powers, which seldom appears in history. Such prescience was notably absent in the political-military decisions of the First World War, when the needs and dangers with which the Western Allies were confronted were immeasurably less than those in the Second. It could not be demanded of the leaders of the English-speaking Powers that they grope with nebulous post-war political issues during the awesome and dark days of 1942, at a time when they were on the brink of the

greatest military decisions and had to keep the possibility of an eventual series of gruesome defeats in mind. They could neither envisage,
nor even adequately sense, the time of the end of the war. The silent
demands of history are strong, but the pleas of contemporaries are
not so silent and are more harsh — therefore these leaders may be
severely criticized but not unequivocally damned. Yet it was in their
decisions that the future fate of a hundred million central-eastern
Europeans lay. (6)

.   .   .   .

[*Russian-Polish relations grow worse.*] Ominous symptoms
were increasing. By January 1942 Lwów, Wilnó, Brest-Litovsk were
repeatedly listed as Soviet cities in Russian radio announcements and
other communiqués; the inhabitants of Poland who lived east of the
Molotov-Ribbentrop line were claimed as Soviet citizens; the small
Baltic states continued to be referred to as member Soviet republics
despite indignant protests of their exiles in Britain and America. It
was clear that his 1941 frontier constituted, at best, Stalin's minimum
territorial aims.

The new Russian propaganda appealing to the "fraternal Slav
peoples" was now in full swing, yet the existence of a Polish Army
(and the Polish Red Cross) within the borders of the Soviet Union
proved to be more and more undesirable to Stalin. Only a few weeks
after the Sikorski-Anders-Stalin talks in Moscow, the formation of
the army-in-exile was systematically obstructed by the Russians; in
April–May it was decided that the Polish Army should assemble outside the Soviet Union, in Iran and Iraq, and serve under British
command. The long and incredible trek of the Polish soldiers and
civilians through the most barren regions of the Soviet Union has
been described by many — surely, this was one of the strangest migrations in modern history: volunteers of an ally ordered out of the
territory of another ally because their presence might eventually
prove to be an obstacle to the plotting for the subjugation of their
homeland by their ally. Altogether 115,000 Poles left Russia; but more
than 1,300,000 who had been deported were unaccounted for. Until
mid-July Sikorski was against the evacuation; the official Soviet
agreement to the departure of the remaining 44,000 soldiers for the
Middle East was given to Anders on July 8. Thus ended a chapter in
the strange and glorious history of the Polish Army in the Second

World War. About that time the advancing Sixth and Fourth German Armies had moved across the Don, pushing steadily eastward.

.   .   .   .   .   .

[*The German 1942 offensive.*] The local offensives and counter-
offensives in the southern Ukraine and on the Kertch peninsula
developed into a full-scale German offensive in the last week of June
when the Soviet attack on Kharkov collapsed. At the end of June,
178 German, 31 Rumanian, 17 Hungarian, 10 Italian, 2 Slovak and
1 Spanish division were ranged for what was generally expected by
the Axis to be the second and final chapter of the *Barbarossa* crusade.
Sevastopol fell on July 1, and on July 7 the German-Hungarian armies
operating in the Don sector reached that river and crossed into the
city of Voronezh. Here Hitler made his great strategic mistake. Instead of pushing beyond Voronezh to cut into the central defense
area around Saratov and Kuybishev, he restricted himself to a bridgehead around Voronezh itself and directed that the great push be
made in the direction of Stalingrad and the Caucasus. Meanwhile
the oppression of the Ukrainian and Russian nationalistic movements
continued, and over the military mistakes hovered this portentuous
political one. (7)

That the 1942 campaign did not promise decisive victory in Russia
was seen earlier by the neutrals and by Hitler's allies than by Britain
and the United States. Despite the rapid advance of the German
motorized troops on the northern slopes of the Caucasus, Turkey,
which in February seemed to waver, was again studiously neutral (8);
neither would Japan, although in the prime of her power, enter the
war against Russia when Ribbentrop requested this in July. On
August 24 the German spearheads reached the outskirts of Stalingrad — soon the battle of attrition was to develop, a battle in which
the Axis Powers, against whom time was working, could only lose.
Early in September, General Halder, the chief of the German General
Staff, proposed a withdrawal to the Kiev-Riga line, where the
Russians could be successfully held and later decisively beaten. This
suggestion incensed Hitler, who decided to dismiss Halder on September 25.

.   .   .   .   .   .

[*The Allied strategic decisions.*] During and after the Molotov
visit to the Western capitals, the propaganda for the immediate cre-

ation of a second front in Europe was intensified by the Soviets, and soon the whole orchestra of the world-wide Communist and extreme Leftist movements, aided by many illusionists and impatients, carried this theme, roaring unabatedly with but few variations.

The Russian arguments for a second front impressed the somewhat naive and as yet militarily unhardened Americans more than the British; from May 1942 on, Washington pressed for a speedy offensive, while London grew more cautious. Churchill was aware of the tremendous risks and losses which the creation of a second front, particularly in Western Europe, could mean. On May 1 he drafted a plan for *Operation Jupiter*, a landing in northern Norway and the Petsamo area in Finland; by the end of June he had to drop it. In the summer of 1942 the manpower of the British and Commonwealth forces was already stretched to dangerous extremes on the seven seas and in five continents. Another catastrophe struck on June 21 when Tobruk fell and the tanks of Rommel rattled toward Alexandria. The Joint Chiefs of Staff now gave generous help to the British. Yet on July 15 Sir John Dill reported to Churchill: "I have a feeling . . . that there are highly placed Americans who do not believe that anything better than a stalemate with Germany is possible." Nevertheless, definite plans were drawn up in Washington for an invasion of Western France in October 1942; they were presented in detail on July 19. Three days later Churchill and the British Chiefs of Staff rejected them emphatically: they were convinced it was impossible to gain a toehold on the continent with limited forces and at so early a date. After a decisive meeting of the Combined Chiefs of Staff the Americans reluctantly agreed on July 22: the invasion of France was to be postponed until 1943. (9) Instead, the invasion of French North Africa was planned.

Yet the ideological temper of the war steadily mounted. The honest Hull himself conceded in his *Memoirs* that when in July 1942 the United States abrogated her consular representations in Finland, this was done solely in order to please the Russians. On August 6 Eden announced in the House of Commons the long-awaited denunciation of the Munich settlement. (10) Churchill was already packing his bags for a grand trip to the Egyptian front and Moscow; before his departure, he received a message from Roosevelt; a message which departed considerably from the previously upheld American policy concerning post-war territorial questions. Roosevelt suggested that Stalin be coaxed into agreeing that after the war "another plebiscite" be held in the three Baltic republics, a suggestion communicated in a way which virtually meant that the United States acquiesced in the Soviet incorporation of the Baltics; for the sake of public opinion this should be legalized by a second, and perhaps more fair, plebiscite. (Yet in 1940 no "first" plebiscite had taken place, merely a Soviet-executed "election" in each country, after which the local Soviet governments requested incorporation into the Soviet Union.) While the nervous queries of the Polish government-in-exile were, at best, courteously listened to by the Department of State, ever unwilling to commit itself, the Roosevelt message to Churchill also suggested that a new Russian-Polish frontier be drawn, somewhat east of the Curzon Line, and that Lwów remain with Poland. (*11*)

[*Churchill in Moscow.*]　Stalin gauged the situation correctly. Here was America, vigorous and strong, wishing to be the arbitrating power, the young conciliator, portraying herself as standing somewhere in the middle between the respectable but somewhat antiquated system of Churchill's Victorian British Empire and that ragged, uncouth, attractive, mighty adolescent, Soviet Russia. The British had more reason to be grateful to Russia than the Americans had (German air raids on Britain were now sporadic and infrequent), yet it was in America that the fashionableness of Russia, in the moving pictures, in the press, and in high American society was more and more apparent. This Stalin knew. He was cool, canny, crude, and he duly impressed Churchill as well as Harriman, whom he often tried to play against the British Premier. (*12*)

The Moscow Conference lasted from August 12 to August 16. "A relationship [was] established," and Churchill very skillfully administered the bitter pill to Stalin: there was to be no second front in 1942. But the plans for the North African invasion were revealed to the Russian. (*13*) There were no significant political conversations; Churchill was to dine with the Polish Anders on his last evening in Moscow, but Stalin invited the Prime Minister to his private dwelling within the Kremlin; an interesting and long evening followed. Only minutes were left for Anders when Churchill returned, exhausted, very late at night.

[*Russian suspicion: separate peace attempts and rumors.*]　Churchill, returning to London, referred to the Russians jokingly as "land animals," to whom the difficulties of Allied strategy where naval power was involved, were hard to grasp. The raid on Dieppe on August 19 demonstrated the British determination to make an heroic plunge over the Channel, at the same time proving the need for overwhelming forces if the German defenses were to be penetrated. A certain amount of carefully calculated bitterness was dropped now into the tone of Soviet announcements, and Communist radio propaganda to central-eastern Europe was intensified; the Soviets now came out openly for Tito and attacked the Polish, Yugoslav, and other "reactionaries." In Finland, Bulgaria, Rumania, Hungary and Greece new instructions were given to the local Communists. (*14*) All efforts were directed at impressing central-eastern Europe with the sole and impressive might of the Soviets; in symbolic operations, a handful of Russian planes raided Budapest, Bucharest and Vienna early in September, although the Russian Air Force seldom made strategic bombings, especially not when these required fourteen-hundred mile round-trip flights over enemy territory (and at a time when the front-line lay near the Caspian and in the Caucasus). These were the first Russian moves in their expected and slowly developing contest with Britain for the control of the Balkans.

Early in September the Japanese made certain steps to sound out the possibilities of a German-Russian truce. Japan offered to send an "important negotiator" around September 10 to Moscow to mediate between Russia and Germany. Molotov rejected the proposal on September 13; he knew that the Japanese suggestion had no direct authorization from Berlin. He informed the American and British Ambassadors. All this was very disturbing. Two days after Molotov's information, on September 15, a revived draft of the "toehold" operation in Western France (*Sledgehammer*) was accepted: an Anglo-American landing to be undertaken only if the Russian situation became desperate or if Germany suddenly became critically weakened by internal events.

On October 5 Roosevelt informed Churchill that the American Ambassador had asked to return from Moscow with a very important personal message and that he had "some fears of what that message might be." Churchill answered that he did not now fear a Russian separate peace; yet on October 9 he wrote Stalin about the plans for an Anglo-American air force to be put into southern Russia. Stalin was not responsive to gestures of friendship now. The Moscow press ominously brought up Rudolf Hess and accused "certain British circles" of conspiring for a British-German separate peace. (*15*)

[*British reactions: the future of Europe.*] Churchill was angry, and wary of the Russians. He thought of Europe, forecasting its federation in a memorandum to Eden on October 21:

> I must admit that my thoughts rest primarily in Europe — the revival of the glory of Europe, the parent continent of the modern nations and of civilisation. It would be a measureless disaster if Russian barbarism overlaid the culture and independence of the ancient States of Europe.

He looked forward to a United States of Europe, a Council of Europe with various units, an international police, Prussia disarmed, a Scandinavian, Danubian, Balkan confederation.

> Of course we shall have to work with the Americans in many ways, and in the greatest ways, but Europe is our prime care, and we certainly do not wish to be shut up with the Russians and the Chinese when Swedes, Norwegians, Danes, Dutch, Belgians, Frenchmen, Spaniards, Poles, Czechs and Turks will have their burning questions, their desire for our aid, and their very great power of making their voices heard. It would be easy to dilate upon these themes. Unhappily the war has prior claims on your attention and on mine.

Again to Eden, six days later:

> I am sure it would be a great mistake to run after the Russians in their present mood; and still less to run around with them chasing a chimera. . . . Meanwhile I should treat the Russians coolly, not getting excited about the lies they tell, but going steadily on with our task. You must remember the Bolsheviks have undermined so many powerful Governments by lying, machine-made propaganda, and they probably think they make some impression on us by these methods. (*16*)

Yet Roosevelt wrote the Premier that very day that he was not "unduly disturbed" by Stalin's attitude: "I have decided they do not use speech for the same purposes as we do." A correct statement; but surely no cause for mental comfort. . . .

[*British reactions: the Balkans.*] On October 25 the Battle of El Alamein began; seven days later the Axis' African armor was smashed beyond repair. On November 8 General Eisenhower's expeditionary forces landed in French North Africa. The Allied campaign in the Mediterranean was on. Aware of its portents, the British took certain political steps. Time and other factors seemed to work against them: Beneš made a speech late in October in which he ranged himself with the Soviets, as he carefully took a stand against the Polish-Czech confederation scheme; Communist guerrillas were gaining power not only in Yugoslavia but also in Greece.

A British Military Mission flew secretly into Greece on October 1 to establish contact with the guerrillas; a high intelligence command, similar to the American OSS, SOE (Special Operations Executive) was set up in Cairo. Churchill aimed to give British coordination and guidance to all guerrillas, with an eye cast upon the political future; yet this aim never developed into a clear policy. On one hand, as Woodhouse stated,

> There was no such thing as [British] policy towards Greece, in the sense of a fixed set of objectives laid down in advance. British foreign policy has never been something that is laid down in advance, to be achieved regardless of what may happen between its formulation and its execution; it is rather of an emergency character which can gradually be detected amongst the welter of *ad hoc* decisions. It has principles by which the problems are to be solved, but it does not boast a programme which announces what the problems are to be. It cannot be precisely defined in advance; it can only be recognised in retrospect. (*17*)

On the other hand, the head of the SOE Balkan section was an expert on Baltic affairs, and the British officials in Cairo were not given specific political directives, except to try to bring the Greek guerrilla forces together for better military efficiency. The British mission succeeded in making EDES and ELAS, Zervas' and Ares' forces, cooperate with them, and in November the very important Gorgopotamos railroad bridge along one of the most important German supply routes was dynamited.

In these days Churchill looked to the future with rare prescience. The Russian armies were defending barren Asiatic steppes around Stalingrad, two thousand miles to the east; but the British Premier saw that when the German armies would reel back — as he said to his people, this was but "the end of the beginning" — the Russians would take the Germans' place in central-eastern Europe and establish their own order and never leave again. When Pitt the Younger said before he died that "England saved herself by her exertions and saved Europe by her example," the self-exertions and the shining example were almost enough; not so one hundred and forty years later. The future of Europe was bound to the undisputed victory of the English-speaking Powers and to the well-nigh ubiquitous presence of their armies at the time of victory. It was something of the "white man's burden" in a more tragic, European version.

[*The idea of a Balkan invasion first raised; its shelving.*] Not quite twenty-four hours passed after the successful landing at Algiers, and Churchill urged his Chiefs of Staff to plan for the exploitation of the campaign: North Africa meant more than just Sicily and Sardinia; it was to be "a springboard and not a sofa." (*18*) The sudden blaze of victory impressed Roosevelt, who wrote Churchill on the 12th: it was right to make a survey of further possibilities, "including a forward movement directed against Sardinia, Sicily, Italy, Greece and other Balkan areas, and including the possibility of obtaining Turkish support for an attack through the Black Sea against Germany's flank." The Prime Minister now sent an urgent message to General Eisenhower along these lines, in order to consider and revise the European strategy of the Anglo-Saxon Powers. Yet to Eisenhower these seemed far-fetched plans: he was groping with great logistic and equipment problems which held him down before Tunis for six months. Moreover, he depended on his Chiefs-of-Staff and his President — and other winds were blowing in America: Hopkins advised the President to invite Stalin to the next inter-Allied meeting. Stalin excused himself on December 17; he was very busy with the winter campaign and requested that the Allies continue planning for the opening of the second front in Western Europe.

He had very good reasons to divert the main Allied offensive from the Mediterranean. For on November 19 came the turning point of the Battle of Stalingrad: through a remarkably well-planned and executed operation the German Sixth Army was encircled; within a week the strategic phase of the battle was decided; 330,000 Axis troops and their commander were trapped. Soon the last German counterattacks failed and the vast retreat of the German armies along the whole length of the Russian front began.

Hitler and Mussolini were far more aware of the Allies' Balkan chances than any Allied leader, perhaps even Churchill. As early as December 29, 1941, Mussolini wrote Hitler that he feared an Anglo-

American invasion of the Balkans in 1942: their chances of success were great. In January 1942 Hitler feared a British descent on Norway, "a zone of destiny in this war"; later he again anxiously turned to the Balkans. At his military conference of November 19 he correctly projected Balkan invasion possibilities. He even admitted that the Allies could penetrate the Black Sea: a landing in Rumania would be disastrous to Germany, he said.

But the Allies were bogged down before Tunis and debated islands: Sicily, Sardinia (unwilling even to contemplate Crete). (*19*)

·   ·   ·   ·

When Sikorski visited the United States in November–December 1942, he could not secure any American re-affirmation of the Atlantic Charter concerning central-eastern Europe. He was forced to notice the rapidly growing ideological propaganda and pro-Russian attitudes. Of such inclinations Ambassador Davies' *Mission to Moscow* was indicative. Influential columnists and writers now spoke of the necessity of giving the Soviet Union a decisive rôle in European affairs after the war; the book of the British historian, E. H. Carr, *Conditions of Peace*, argued for the impossibility of the continued existence of small and independent states in central-eastern Europe; Walter Lippmann's important book, *U.S. Foreign Policy — Shield of the Republic*, was less sympathetic to the Soviets but argued that not much could be done by the Atlantic Allies to influence the fate of eastern Europe after the war. (*20*)

Russia, on the other hand, did not conceal her designs any longer with the same caution she had used a year before. On January 16, 1943, the Soviet government in a curt note informed the Polish envoy in Moscow of a Soviet citizenship decree which automatically recognized the Polish deportees still within the Soviet Union as Soviet citizens, inasmuch as they were born "within the confines of the USSR." This declaration opened a new phase in the history of central-eastern Europe.

Efforts toward a Finnish-Russian separate peace — Phase II

[*Finnish foreign policy and the 1942 campaign.*] In the early summer of 1942 the Finnish government began to be intensely worried about the emotional outburst of Russo-American amity which the Molotov visit to Washington seemed to have brought about.

When Roosevelt mentioned the Finnish question to Molotov on June 1, the Russian took good note of the extreme sensitivity of American public opinion concerning Finland (*1*) (something which the cautious Russians constantly kept and continue to keep before their eyes); nothing definite was achieved, while the possibilities of American mediation remained open. When the great German offensive was launched, Keitel (and later General Dietl) invited Mannerheim again, but all German requests for a more intensive Finnish participation in the campaign were courteously rejected. Hitler, who respected Mannerheim (the latter's aristocratic, Nordic stature impressed him), met with the Marshal on his 75th birthday, but the Finnish government immediately informed the United States that the meeting was not significant. On June 16 the Finnish Foreign Minister again suggested to the American envoy that the Finnish Army had *almost* reached its strategic objects all along the front, and hinted that, notwithstanding German demands, the Finns would not advance against the Murmansk Railroad. To Minister Schoenfeld these assurances, however reasonable, were not enough if the United States was to assume the delicate and important position of a mediator between Helsinki and Moscow. Thus, while the Germans' fire and steel was blazing across the plains of southern Russia, the Soviets were nudging Washington to impress the world with signs of American-Russian solidarity, and on August 16, the United States announced the disestablishment of American consular representation in Finland: a gesture to appease Russia.

The Finnish government, of course, wished to bide its time until the results of the Germans' 1942 campaign became visible. On the other hand, efforts were made to establish stronger ties with neutral and non-Axis countries and thus expedite indirect contacts between Finland and the United Nations. (*2*) The eyes and ears of Finnish diplomacy worked primarily through Stockholm; also previously insignificant Finnish-Swiss, Finnish-Portuguese, Finnish-Spanish, Finnish-Turkish relations increased in scope, and in July 1942 Lutheran Finland, for the first time in her history, appointed an envoy to the Vatican.

[*The Yartsev episode.*]   An episode now occurred: in October 1942 a Soviet attaché in Stockholm, Yartsev, let it be known to a Swedish middleman that Russia was ready to negotiate with Finland on the basis of the 1939 frontiers. Helsinki tried to measure how authentic all this was, but seems to have failed to obtain satisfactory results. The whole Yartsev case is not quite clear. During their postwar trial, Ryti and other members of the Finnish government were accused of deliberately having let the Yartsev "offer" lapse, but Ryti retorted that the offer was communicated through the Swedish middleman in "such a vague and unreliable form" (*3*) that, despite instructions given to the Finnish Legation in Stockholm to try to keep in touch with Yartsev and his conversant, nothing came out of this.

[*Finland approaches the United States.*] The second phase of the efforts toward a separate peace began with simultaneous reports pouring into Helsinki in the last days of January 1943 — the time of the Stalingrad capitulation. In November 1942 the Finnish Minister in Berlin began to urge Helsinki to examine any reasonable peace soundings; on November 30 the Finnish Government officially asked Germany whether she would object if Finland made preliminary explorations concerning negotiations toward a separate peace. On December 8 the German envoy naturally stated Germany's thorough objections. Stray and variously reliable reports of soundings and peace attempts came during December and January. On January 17 Ryti asked Witting to inform Washington through and with the help of Stockholm of the Finnish desire to bring about closer relations between Finland and the United States. Before Söderblom, the chief of the Political Section of the Swedish Foreign Ministry, spoke with the American Minister in Stockholm, a report from Assarson, the Swedish envoy in the Soviets' temporary capital, Kuybishev, reached the Swedish Foreign Ministry. Assarson wrote that the Czechoslovak Minister there told him he was certain that Russia was intending to reach a separate settlement with Finland. The Czech Minister was very close to the Soviets; thus this amounted to a Russian signal. The Assarson report was corroborated by Ankara, whence it was reported that a similar assertion was made to the Turkish Minister by Vishinsky. Söderblom told this to the American envoy on January 25. The Swedish Minister in Helsinki now informed Ryti of the Assarson report; on the same day Boström, the Swedish envoy to Washington, had a rather satisfactory talk with Sumner Welles.

In possession of this news, Helsinki informed the Swedish government that after the presidential elections (on February 15 Ryti was re-elected President) a transformation of the Finnish government would take place — an indirect gesture toward the United States — and after a crucial conference in the Finnish Army Headquarters, Ryti and Mannerheim participating, it was definitely decided that the government should strive toward a separate peace with Russia and Britain.

While through Stockholm and through a series of conversations between the Swedish and American Ministers to Russia the Swedish mediation continued, direct contact between Finland and the Allies now began. On February 13 Tanner sent a personal letter through the Swedish Foreign Minister to Alexander, the First Lord of the Admiralty, an old acquaintance of his. Alexander's answer did not, however, satisfy Finnish wishes, as apart from a general statement of benevolence it did not contain specific answers concerning an eventual Finnish peace treaty. (*4*)

On February 15 the Council of the Finnish Social Democratic Party issued a declaration which strongly emphasized the "separate war" concept and ended with this sentence:

> . . . Finland maintains the liberty to decide herself about her withdrawal from this war at a given moment and when her independence and freedom are guaranteed . . . (*5*)

and this, of course, incensed Berlin.

[*The American offer of* bona officia *a failure.*]   On February 8 the Finnish government communicated to the United States the Finnish desire to come to a reasonable agreement which would end the hostilities between Finland and Russia. Five days later an American note acknowledged the Finnish memorandum. After another exchange of memoranda an American note on March 20 finally stated that the United States was ready to offer their good services, *bona officia*, to facilitate a contact between Finland and the Soviet Union. At that time Finland had a new government: the cabinet changed on March 5 when Rangell resigned; the conservative Linkomies became Prime Minister and the well-known Anglophile, Ramsay, had Foreign Affairs. There was a silent understanding that, especially in view of the serious Axis defeats everywhere on the peripheries of Europe, the paramount aim of this government was to lead Finland out of the war with what would seem a just and honorable peace settlement. The American *bona officia* offer put the new cabinet immediately in the midst of these delicate efforts.

For four days they deliberated. Then it was decided that, knowing
how territory-conscious the Russians were, it would be best again to
find out what their basic conditions were. Such concrete information
was requested by way of the United States; this Ramsay told Schoenfeld on March 24. Immediately afterwards the Foreign Minister took
the train for Germany, where he — somewhat naively — tried to get
a German commitment to withdraw their troops from Finland if
that country should reach a separate peace agreement. Ribbentrop
was not at all willing to make such a commitment; instead, he assailed
Ramsay with bitter words and said that rather the Finns should commit themselves not to make a separate peace without the consent of
Germany. This, then, Ramsay could not promise. The two Foreign
Ministers parted, Ramsay aware that the halcyon days of 1941 were
over and that Finland faced now, besides her enemies, a bitter and
suspicious Germany.

The Ramsay journey was very short, and when the Foreign Minister returned to Helsinki, he expected to have the American note
containing the first concrete proposals, the answer to his March 24
request. But no such note was on his desk. Not until April 10 did the
American answer come, which, in Ryti's words, "clearly indicates
that in the meantime a discussion had taken place between Russia
and the United States concerning the answer." Ryti also claimed to
know from a reliable diplomatic source that on March 27 — after
the Ramsay journey to Berlin — the American Ambassador in Moscow
told Molotov about the Finnish note and asked for Russian specifica-
tions; these, however, were not given. Anyhow, the late American
answer, instead of containing the desired information on specific
points, was but a statement that the American government was not
in a position to furnish the required information, as its intention was
not to mediate, but only to establish a contact between Finland and the
Soviet Union. This was, undoubtedly, an American withdrawal. The
Finns were disillusioned and indignant (6); on April 27 Ryti told
Schoenfeld that Finland would conclude peace with Russia only if
the Anglo-Saxon Powers guaranteed the peace terms. Thus, as the
Russians found it better not to commit themselves in regard to their
peace aims at a time when their military successes provided them with
a set of high diplomatic trump cards, and as the United States, conforming to the Russian wishes, stopped short of her originally envisaged position of mediator, the second part of the second phase of
the efforts toward a separate peace between Finland and Russia came

to an end. Four months elapsed before, in the wake of the Italian armistice, the third phase began.

The returning prestige of the West

Now the charm of the "New Europe," so appealing to hearts in 1938 and so luring to the eyes in 1940, was gone.

In vain Laval said to Hitler: "You want to win the war to make Europe — but instead, make Europe and win the war."

The dull and strenuous distant war of the Russian plains inspired more fear than awe, even among the totalitarian hotheads of the Germans' followers; in the so-called satellites, only those continued to believe in the message of a Hitlerian New Order who, with their monies, brutal or sly actions, or their scratching pens had inalterably committed themselves and their spiritual fortunes to the Germans' side; while these people were loud, they were few in number and intellectually well-nigh insignificant. Curiously enough, the masses (especially the industrial workers) in Hungary, Bulgaria, Rumania, Slovakia, and Croatia were still widely infected with the Nazi virus through reading the brutal columns and rantings of the totalitarian tabloid press; also the New Order and its ideology provided a vent for the previously subconscious hatred of the aristocracy and the bourgeoisie (where Jews remained) — the two "Western"-type classes. While political resistance started from above, spiritual resistance germinated from the thin layer of the intellectual middle-class, some of whom were torn by the high waters, but most of whom were spiritually anchored to their humanitarian beliefs and European traditions.

[*Spiritual and intellectual endeavors.*]   By the middle of 1942 it was evident that, except for the irresponsible, the stubbornly pro-German, and the very few Communists, the thinkers and citizens of central-eastern Europe sought for a rediscovery and formulation of basic ideas which were essentially and typically Western in their context. This was reflected in segments of the Conservative and Liberal press — in Hungary and Bulgaria Liberal press organs existed until 1944 — as well as in art, in the universities, in the theater, and in the churches, especially the Roman Catholic. In Rumania, the idea of Latin spiritual unity was extolled in the form of an intellectual protest against the Teutonic order. Previously insignificant Rumanian-

Spanish and Rumanian-Portuguese relations were eagerly broadened; cultural exchanges between Rumania and Italy, and Rumania and France, multiplied in depth and in volume despite wartime conditions. Similar ties were sought with Switzerland. Historical allusions to Rumanian Latinism were constantly made by clever and cautious columnists; in 1942, translations and adaptations of French literary works already dominated the Rumanian stage and the book market. In Hungary during 1942 less than twenty per cent of books translated were from the German (and these included the writings of émigré authors: Mann, Werfel, Zweig, etc.), while twice as many British and American translations were published. (*1*)

[*Political trends.*] Except for Finland, Switzerland, and Sweden, Hungary was the only country in Europe where, until 1944, a legal Socialist party existed, with a Socialist daily and weekly; a Liberal-Conservative newspaper — *Magyar Nemzet* — in 1943 published Allied war communiqués and news in a thinly disguised form. French and Polish prisoners-of-war remained undisturbed in Hungary, Rumania, and later in Bulgaria. All this does not mean that a truly democratic-liberal atmosphere prevailed in these countries; suppression of the Jews was severe in 1941–42; some consciences were still badly rent; knowledge and propaganda concerning Britain and America were often mistaken and faulty. The annual reports of the Hungarian Supreme War Council lightly depreciated the qualities of the British and American armies and soldiers, tersely stating in 1943, for example, that in contrast to the heroic military leadership of Germany, the English-speaking Powers' military leadership was conditioned by "a mercantile way of thought."

The weary "satellites," Hungary, Rumania, and Bulgaria — Finland, of course, even more so — became sensitive to the change of the war fortunes beginning in November 1942, and thereafter the returning prestige of the West was manifest in political changes as well as in spiritual trends. From November 1942 on, the cabinets and Foreign Ministries scanned the Western skies and gathered reports from Berne, Ankara, Stockholm, and from newspaper fragments and radiocasts coming from the Western world. Speeches like that of the British Professor Seton-Watson, who in December 1942 called upon the British government to declare that Rumania's pre-war territorial integrity (with the reservation of population exchanges) be numbered among British war aims, found eager listeners and wide-

spread echoes in Bucharest and elsewhere. A new and strangely uncertain year was coming: 1943, in which the "satellites" were to
undertake their first concrete steps to detach themselves from Germany. There was an indescribably vague, but strangely widespread,
irrational, curious optimism in the air; more and more prominent
people dared to speak and write about common European destinies. (2)

Only a few people sensed the new dangers; only a few were consciously aware of the alternative perils of Europe, which Mr. Churchill
so clearly saw when in October 1942 he wrote his memorandum to
Eden about the post-war Russian dangers; the territorial ambitions
of Russia were known; but then everybody expected Britain and
America to have a decisive influence in Moscow. (3)

The strange spring of 1943: I — Rome, Budapest, Bucharest

[*The "satellites' " position.*] We have arrived at the turning
point of the war, November 1942, the month of El Alamein, Algiers,
and Stalingrad. Now came the dramatic period when, due to the
military changes, the political fortunes of Europe became ever more
important; but first a myth should be dispelled and the approach
clarified. From 1942 onward Germany's central-eastern European
allies sought a way out of the war with increasingly anxious activity.
Contemporary political comment and historiography has hitherto
been practically unanimous in condemning these efforts for one
reason or another: but this criticism has been inconsistent.

The main line of the criticism chides the "satellites," together with
Italy, for having been and having continued to be the allies of Hitler
until the bitter realities of the war brought about their secession from
the German side. This is accompanied by a secondary charge, suggested and expressed with increasing frequency: how base and mercenary it was for Germany's allies to stick with her while the going
was good and thereafter desert the tottering German ship, rat-like.
Even when this second line of criticism is not expressly mentioned, it
underlies the emphasis of the first. Here is the inconsistency. For, if it
was originally sinful and despicable for these states to have joined
with the Germans — which interpretation largely excludes the basic
factor of central-eastern Europe's geographic position, and also for-
gets the truism that politics is the art of the possible — then any
change in their attitude, at whatever time and for whatever reasons,

should have been welcome and seen as a commendable jump from the camp of the devils to that of the angels. On the other hand, if their attempts to desert the Germans at the time of defeats and ill prospects smack of Machiavellianism, then their original adherence to the German side can not be condemned, for if desertion was dishonorable, adherence could not have been.

Trite as this expression may sound, reality and truth are somewhere in the middle; there is more than just a grain of truth in both inconsistent judgments but not enough to swing Clio's balance. While the original adherence to the Axis may be academically criticized on grounds of national or international morality, this kind of criticism cannot refer to the separate peace attempts. These attempts form a very interesting chapter in diplomatic history (and a rewarding field of inquiry for the analyst of what may be called contemporary statesmanship). What can be criticized in these efforts is rather the sometimes amazing lack of realism and the curious optimism of some of the "satellites' " statesmen, once underestimating German reactions to their attempts, then again overestimating their personal stock with the Allies, hoping for their personal survival. Here were practical defects in statecraft, though it is true that often this lack of vision stemmed from their previous misreading of morality: some of these people did not know or did not want to know how far their previous actions had committed them.

．　　．　　．　　．　　．　　．　　．

[*Alfieri's "plan."*]　When in 1847 the British Cabinet decided to send the Earl of Minto on a mission to Rome, Disraeli made a jocular remark: Minto was eventually going to "teach politics in the country in which Machiavelli was born": a pleasant and airy observation. Who would have thought that ninety years later, clumsy Germans would join up with the Italians and earnestly try to teach them new political ideologies and Machiavellianisms? Yet this is what happened. One of the men whom the Germans thought sufficiently untouched by Latin political finesse to qualify as their true adherent was Dino Alfieri, Ambassador of Italy to Berlin, a loquacious and lovable Axis bumpkin, arch-Fascist and orator, charter member of the 1940 New Europe days.

They should have known better. More, they should have known what El Alamein and the North African invasion spelled out for all Italians alike.

On November 24, 1942, the counter-attacking Russians completed the encirclement of the German Sixth Army at Stalingrad. On the same day Alfieri summoned his confidants in the Berlin Embassy. With utmost secrecy, he placed a "jumping-off" plan before them, a master plan which, if successful, would result in Italy's withdrawal from the war, together with Hungary, Bulgaria, and Rumania.

The plan first called for the establishment of a special service of Italian diplomats to make most secret and cautious soundings in Sofia, Budapest, and Bucharest, and also in Ankara and Madrid, which were to serve later as contact points with the Allies. After this preliminary task of ascertaining the general feasibility of the plan was completed, the Italian government, with Hungary, Rumania and Bulgaria, would present a memorandum to Germany calling for a reorganization of the Axis forces and for the creation of a supreme common command in which the highest military representatives of all these countries would participate. To please the Germans, this joint military board would be headed by a German general. Now came the truly subtle part of the plan: in exchange for this German military leadership, the Italians would move that a similar, supreme political command be established. There the non-German delegates would ask Germany to present her plans: how did she envisage the termination of the war? As the German answer to such a question would certainly be unsatisfactory or evasive, the Italians and their Danubian allies would seize upon this answer as a pretext and subsequently communicate through the already established and prepared channels their desire to contact the Allies concerning a separate peace settlement.

This Alfieri Plan never went beyond the planning stage; yet its existence and the time of its appearance make it significant. Semi-official private soundings of Italian diplomats in the Balkan capitals were sporadically made from September, 1942, on; Ciano established tentative contact with such anti-Germans as Generals Ambrosio and Castellano as early as April. In October the previously strained Bulgar-Italian relations became more friendly, and by November the cordiality of the contacts of Rome with Budapest, Bucharest, and Sofia had a definite political significance: the Hungarian, Rumanian, and Bulgarian governments, or better, their leaders, Kállay, Antonescu, and Boris III, watched Italy's course with expectant eagerness.

[*Mussolini's attempts toward a separate peace with Russia.*] But that course was yet jagged and unpredictable, despite the tremendous pressure of waves beaten up by the Western winds which steadily pushed the Italian ship toward the rocky shore. The seasick captain, Mussolini, was the victim of his own hesitations. Before 1942 he took some comfort from the German retreats in Russia; they favored his own balance of power. But now he saw that there was no other way out for him other than German victory or a compromise peace together with Germany. He had developed a blind hatred of the Anglo-Saxons now; he favored a German-Russian separate peace, in contrast to the majority of his cabinet and the Italian governmental hierarchy. (1) Around December 20 he planned to go to Hitler and discuss this great diplomatic coup; according to his information, said Mussolini to confidants, the Russians would be willing to consider such a possibility.

His sickness then prevented him and he decided to send Ciano and Cavallero in his stead. He wrote a long letter to Hitler, advising him to reach a separate peace settlement with Russia in the quickest possible way. Ciano and the Italian mission arrived at the Führer's headquarters on the 19th. It was a gloomy December day and both sides were nervous and depressed. Nothing concrete was discussed except at a minor side-conference where Ciano, Ribbentrop, Keitel, and Cavallero presented their conflicting views as to how to deal with the Yugoslav guerrilla forces. (2) Hitler was verbose and changed from moods of peculiar, and, to his guests, unprecedented gloom to airy moods of "historical optimism." Ciano spoke again of Mussolini's wish to get an agreement with the Russians, when Hitler suddenly fell into that latter mood and, pretending to see the future with his glassy, hazy eyes, announced that "he was certain of winning the war." Thus Ciano returned to Rome, empty-handed.

On December 29 an interesting piece of information came from Ankara through the person of an intelligent Italian officer, Colonel Lucca, who for years had been on friendly terms with Sarajoglu. When Lucca bade farewell to the Turkish Premier, Sarajoglu gave him his own estimates of the general situation, indirectly entrusting Lucca with a message to Rome: Turkey was very much worried by the Soviet military successes and rapid advances, said Sarajoglu; he saw definite possibilities of negotiating an Axis-Soviet separate peace. This, from the Premier and, until lately, Foreign Minister of Turkey, that Grand Bazaar and Oriental clearing-house of political information, was important news indeed. On January 2, 1943, Ciano presented Lucca to the Duce. Mussolini, however, bearing the Hitler refusal in his mind, said that because of the great Russian successes of the day, the discussion of an Axis-Soviet separate peace seemed temporarily inopportune to him: Stalin would surely present impossible terms.

It is indeed probable that Mussolini was right in this estimate, while it is highly interesting that a person such as Sarajoglu regarded such contacts in December 1942 as possible. The year 1943 now opened. Mussolini notwithstanding, the whole structure of Italian society was bending in the wind, away, away from Germany.

.   .   .   .

[*Collapse of the Don front.*]   In the area of Stalingrad only a small number of Rumanian troops and a few Croatian legionnaires were involved in the battle. Then, on the cold, wintry, black Russian dawn of January 11, 1943, the Russian armies struck on the middle Don front, where the Second Hungarian Army and the bulk of the Italian expeditionary forces stood. Within twelve hours the defense lines were wrecked. Back streamed tens of thousands of half-frozen soldiers, trodding the icy snow of the dead, inimical steppe. Within twelve days the middle Don front, as such, ceased to exist.

Altogether more than fifty thousand Hungarian, Italian, and Rumanian soldiers perished here — the remnants fled westward. There were some bitter skirmishes between the better equipped German soldiers and their allies; the Russian campaign was stripped of all its glory. (No wonder that during this war in Russia not one Italian, Hungarian or Rumanian folk-song was born — and these peasant nations traditionally produced dozens of soldier songs in previous wars and campaigns.)

On January 24 Voronezh was given up and the last of the Stalingrad defenders surrendered a week later.

[*Bastianini's plans.*]   Now a new protagonist appeared on the diplomatic scene: Giuseppe Bastianini, former Italian Ambassador to Warsaw and to London, former Governor of Dalmatia, now Under-Secretary of Foreign Affairs. Disillusioned with Mussolini and only partly relying on the unsure Ciano, Bastianini believed that Italy and the small states of central-eastern Europe could and should reach a separate agreement with the English-speaking Powers. He had good sources of information and contacts. In 1939 and 1940, he had saved the lives of many Poles who had fled before the German onslaught; he maintained good relations with influential individuals among these Poles, and thus Bastianini occasionally had some indirect information from the circles of the London Polish government. He also had had a few good friends among the English Conservatives; finally, through Ciano, certain members of the Roman aristocracy, and a few generals, he had his most valuable contacts with the Italian King and his circle. When Governor of Dalmatia, he was no satrap, but a half-closed-eyed, tired, elegant Roman proconsul, under whose "rule" Serbs, Jews and other persecuted quietly survived. Bastianini could not imagine that the British and the Americans would look with equanimity at the upset of the balance of power in central Europe and especially in the Balkans; he was aware of the great divergence between the Soviet and Western postwar goals. But he mistakenly believed that this preoccupation with central-eastern Europe was in the forefront and shared by all concerned in London and Washington; he also expected the British and Americans to collaborate with a seceding Italy, notwithstanding unconditional surrender declarations. He underestimated the prevailing ideological anti-Fascist temper and overestimated the European knowledge and vision of the Anglo-Saxon policymakers and military leaders.

[*And Rumania.*] Bastianini proceeded cautiously; in his labors he was aided by the able Bova Scoppa in Bucharest, who developed close relations with Mihai Antonescu. The relations of Bova Scoppa with the Mother Queen, Helena, were also good. (*3*) Shortly before Christmas Mihai Antonescu and Bova Scoppa agreed that Italy "should grasp the initiative." At the same time Salazar and the Turks offered to sound out the Anglo-Americans (especially Tanriover, the Turkish envoy to Bucharest, a very able man, was important in these clandestine preparations). On January 15, 1943, Bova Scoppa left for Rome to report there in person. It seemed a routine journey, but before he left Bucharest, Mihai Antonescu depicted the future in darkest colors to him: the war against Russia was lost, Italy and the Danubian "satellites" (*4*) would have to get together and seek a solution, get out of the war and impress the Western Allies with the Bolshevik danger; this would facilitate their withdrawal. Bova Scoppa went to Ciano and Bastianini. The latter was glad to learn of this Rumanian view, as he already had made broader plans: he wanted Mussolini to announce a European Charter of small nations, returning to Fascist "conservatism," re-establishing Poland, granting limited rights to the subjugated nations, Greece, Yugoslavia (and Belgium), first of all. These were plans which the Germans would probably reject, yet the subsequent announcement of which would lead directly to Italy's secession from Hitler's Germany.

[*Mussolini's reaction; the Soviet offensive halted.*]   On January 20 Ciano took Bova Scoppa's report to Mussolini. The Duce rejected the idea: "The Danubian 'channel' is certainly not the one along which we should proceed." (*5*) He nevertheless brooded and hesitated over the report for a day, but then he said to Ciano that he still trusted the Germans' capacity to defeat or halt the Russians. He was now angry; he said that there was no need for such defeatism. He was probably impressed by Hitler's arguments; furthermore, he wished an agreement with Stalin and not with Churchill or Roosevelt. On February 5 the Rome régime was shaken up: Ciano had to resign and relinquish Foreign Affairs to Mussolini. With Ciano went Grandi, Bottai, and a host of others, and there is some evidence that Mussolini finally decided to remove Ciano from his post in consequence of the latter's presentation of the Bova Scoppa report.

At that time the Soviets had reoccupied Rostov, Millerovo, Kharkov and the whole Donets Basin; certain spearheads in the steppe were a mere twenty miles from the great Dnieper bend, near Dnepropetrovsk. Then, on February 24, the Germans counter-attacked (on the same day Ribbentrop arrived on a routine visit to Rome (*6*)). The Russians were still advancing around Rzhev in the north, but the dangerous southern salient was reduced by the Sepp Dietrich's Sixth SS Army; by March 7 the Russians were definitely beaten there and they withdrew throughout the southern front. On March 14 the Germans re-entered Kharkov. About a week later the lines stabilized all along the front from Rostov to Leningrad. The danger of a German collapse passed; Antonescu breathed more freely and the plans to seek a way out of the war together with Italy seemed to be momentarily inopportune. Distrust now grew between the two Antonescus. Ribbentrop informed Ion Antonescu that Germany did not contemplate any separate peace contacts with the Anglo-Saxons (he did not mention the Russians). Göbbels, who knew or rather suspected something of the Bastianini-satellite contacts, praised Ion Antonescu for a "definitely anti-aristocratic" speech which the latter made in March. While Bova Scoppa kept in close contact with Mihai and others in Bucharest, the Rumanian-Italian plans lapsed for awhile.

[*Attempts in Budapest.*]   Not so with Hungary. Even in December, independent from what Bova Scoppa heard and said, Anfuso, the Italian Minister in Budapest reported the secession attempts of the Kállay government. (The two men were made of different material and had very different concepts.) (7) Through neutral capitals, tentative contacts were made by the Horthy-Kállay régime; it was decided that certain Hungarian diplomats in Switzerland should be furnished with a considerable fund to be devoted to later diplomatic tasks, notably the preparation of a Hungarian separate peace and the support of the Hungarian cause abroad, should the Germans capture Horthy and frustrate his attempts. (8) The catastrophe of the Hungarian troops on the Don front intensified the anti-German trend within the régime: Kállay and his pro-Allied War Minister decided to withdraw as many troops from Russia as was possible. This withdrawal continued when the Germans stabilized the frontline in March; unlike the Rumanians, who now felt less menaced by the Russian advance, the Hungarian régime continued its clandestine secession efforts.

[*Hitler puts pressure on Hungary.*]   On March 20 Germany confronted the Hungarian Government with a sudden request. Three Hungarian divisions were demanded by the Germans to be sent to Serbia and aid the Axis in its occupational duties. Hitler had a double motive in mind: to alleviate the strain on the German Balkan Command; also, to commit the hesitant Hungarians in a theatre where they might get in combat contact with Anglo-American forces, which contact Hungary had hitherto studiously avoided. On March 30, Kállay and Nagy made the Council of Ministers refuse the German demand. Other urgent requests came in May and September, and Kállay, against some members of his government and against the opinion of the General Staff, refused again. (9)

Meanwhile Hitler, Ribbentrop, Göbbels, and SS leaders decided not to tolerate any longer the "impertinences" of the Hungarians and began to undermine the Horthy-Kállay régime. The Hungarian Arrow-Cross movement was clandestinely aided with arms, intelligence and money, while certain members of the General Staff, usually of German origin, were wooed and courted by different confidential

German agents. At the end of March, a top level SS conference in Berlin revised the Hungarian situation, deciding that sooner or later intervention would be necessary there. "The suggestions of the Hungarian government are always only patchwork." (*10*)

[*Kállay in Rome; Mussolini in Klessheim.*] On April 1 Kállay suddenly left for Rome: a hurried visit, which lasted four days and was not announced until after his return, a novel procedure. He wished to convince Mussolini of the necessity of an Italian-Danubian *bloc* and withdrawal from the war. (On the same day Mihai Antonescu said to Bova Scoppa that in view of Germany's negative attitude, Italy should at once seek contact with the Anglo-Saxons.) But Kállay came at an inopportune time. Mussolini had just written to Hitler, and a meeting between the two was set for April 7 at Klessheim Castle near Salzburg. The Duce was again obsessed with the idea of a Soviet-Axis separate peace and he prepared himself to discuss this with Hitler in detail. Touched by Kállay's clever flattery (he even asked the Hungarian what he thought of an eventual Italian-Hungarian partition of Croatia, but Kállay evaded the issue), Mussolini did not reproach him for having brought up the secession idea. Kállay was wont to misinterpret this lack of reproach as a partial, silent understanding, for upon his return he delivered an extremely pro-Italian speech in Parliament on April 10 which evoked great interest and comment in every quarter.

What Kállay did not know was the amazing degree of influence which Hitler still exercised upon Mussolini. The two met from April 7 to 10 and Mussolini achieved nothing. He went, sure that he would have the occasion to convince Hitler of the necessity of concluding a peace with Stalin; but he hardly spoke. Hitler had the floor and ranted through the three days of the "conference." After the first day, Mussolini said to Ambrosio and Bastianini that he had listened enough: it would be his turn now to speak. But nothing happened, except that, due to Bastianini's continuous proddings, he brought up the idea of an Axis European Charter for small nations, to which Hitler's reaction was noncommittal and negative. More significant was a side conference between the military, Ribbentrop and Bastianini. Here acrimonious words were uttered. Ribbentrop let it be known that Berlin was informed of the Italian-Danubian secession plans: "In this small Europe we know everything that goes on." When Bastianini cautiously asked for German opinion concerning the establishment of a more independent Greek government and of a small Greek state, Ribbentrop rejected the idea with such scorn that the Italian Under-Secretary's more important project — the establishment of an independent rump-Poland — was not even mentioned.

[*Other visitors.*] The usual array of south-eastern European state-chief visitors then followed Mussolini. Between April 13 and 25 came Antonescu, Horthy, Tiso, and Pavelič. Of these Antonescu was the best diplomat: he asked Hitler to try to make peace with the West and concentrate everything against the Soviets, but Hitler assured him of victory (while accusing the Rumanian royal family and Maniu: "I have killed my opponents!" To which Antonescu allegedly answered, "I didn't!"). But this erect soldier — "so un-Rumanian," said Hitler, Göbbels, and Kaltenbrunner — again impressed Hitler with his steady loyalty, and hence he was not called down. Not so with Horthy. Hitler was extremely rude to his old visitor, assailing him for Kállay's infidelities (he mentioned several times the relatively undisturbed life of the Hungarian Jews as an indication of Hungary's treacherous unwillingness to be a true ally of the Axis. "What should I do with them? Kill them?" burst out the irritated old Admiral to his sympathetic entourage). For six hours Hitler pestered Horthy, finally exacting a promise that the Hungarian government would not engage in "subversive" activities or inquiries. Hitler was also somewhat dissatisfied with the leader of his "model protectorate," Tiso, and asked him to be more energetic against his internal opposition. Of the canny Pavelič, Schmidt wrote, "never before was the mayor of a city received with such ceremony by the head of a state," inasmuch as at that time the Pavelič régime controlled not much more than the immediate environs of Zagreb. The Croat brought up the idea of a German-Soviet separate peace, and hinted at the foreseeable defection of Italy from the Axis camp. Hitler indicated his silent agreement, and Pavelič went home to Zagreb, plotting to take over most of the Italian heritage in Croatia, Dalmatia, and Slovenia at the moment Italy fell out of the war.

[*The Hungarian crisis.*] Hitler continued to be very angry with Hungary. Early in May, to the circle of Nazi leaders he again expressed his disdain of the satellite armies: in Russia the Rumanians fought best, said he; then came the Italians, the others, and last of all, the Hungarians, "because in Hungary there is no social equilibrium, nor any sight of a social solution"; he raged against the remaining Jews. At the same time, Kállay and Horthy took a decisive step. Confronted by a formidable pro-Nazi movement in Parliament, the Imrédy-Rainiss Party, which was preparing to present a memorandum criticizing the Kállay régime for laxity in the war effort, Horthy adjourned the House on May 10 before the memorandum could be presented. The reaction of the pro-Nazi forces was violent. Something had to be done to appease the Axis, and notes were sent to the German and Italian Ministers, assuring them of continued Hungarian loyalty. Hitler and Ribbentrop now demanded the dismissal of Nagy de Nagybaczon from the War Ministry; the Germans now also mobilized Mussolini, who similarly pressed Kállay to remove Nagy. Finally, in June, Kállay made Nagy resign. The leader of the small pro-Allied opposition, the gallant Bajcsy-Zsilinszky, sent a memorandum to Horthy, in which he asked the Regent to take decisive measures for the restoration of full Hungarian independence. But Nagy had to go.

[*Alfieri writes a letter; the Italian catastrophe looms.*]   In the meantime, Alfieri sent an important letter to Mussolini on May 14. This dealt with Pavelič' success with the Germans, and enumerated evidences of German-Croat collusion against Italy. He also informed Mussolini of the latest German request: the Axis envoys in Budapest and Bucharest were henceforth to deal with the respective heads of state directly, neglecting Mihai Antonescu and Kállay. This was a most embarrassing request, opined Alfieri, for such a form of coercion would certainly do no good in Budapest and Bucharest. He also let Mussolini know that Ribbentrop and the German Foreign Office were opposed to the Axis' European Charter idea proposed at Klessheim by the Italians. The Alfieri letter ended thus:

> There remains nothing but to wait for the first German military successes in order to grasp the favorable situation in that moment and try to undertake then a decisive step toward a negotiation of peace.

Worried and uncertain about Mussolini's reactions, Alfieri changed the last part of this sentence at the last minute before sending it: ". . . try to undertake then another step toward the formulation of a European Charter."

When this letter was written, the last Axis soldiers in Africa had capitulated. On May 25, Hitler cried out angrily to his generals about his allies: "I shall finish off definitely those small states, God help me!" On June 11, Ribbentrop asked Alfieri to Fuschl and explained there his "full confidence" in the Finns, Hungarians, and Rumanians. There was nothing to fear; there was to be no desertion from the Axis ranks in spite of people like Kállay, said the German. "And at the moment the Anglo-Saxons would undertake an invasion of the Balkans, Bulgaria would jump in line with us with 28 divisions." These surprisingly optimistic statements were, of course, transparent: they were intended to reassure Italy, whose hour of decision was rapidly approaching — on that very day, June 11, Pantelleria surrendered.

Friends of Bastianini had been contacting Allied representatives in Lisbon since November 1942; now it was planned that an influential Italian banker would travel to America; it was quite evident that Italy sought her salvation. Already the first mass strikes in Axis Europe had broken out in Turin and Milan.

[*The Antonescu mission.*]   The Antonescu-Bova Scoppa-Bastianini plans now matured.

Mihai Antonescu was irked with the Conducator, who had issued a very pro-German communiqué after his visit to Hitler, thundering determination "to fight against the plutocracies to the end." On May 5, "after many sleepless nights," Bova Scoppa drafted a letter to Mussolini. He did not send it yet. The Germans were protesting at Bucharest; they discovered that certain Rumanian diplomats in Lisbon and Berne had made some contact with Allied agents; German intelligence also claimed to have caught and deciphered a telegram which Hull sent to the American Legation to Lisbon. On May 7 the Turkish envoy had a very important talk with Bova Scoppa ("after long hesitation, I came to tell you something which seems to me . . . of historic importance . . ."); here was the time for a contact with the Western Allies, said the Turk; a German-Russian separate peace seemed to him out of the question. On May 29 Bova Scoppa arrived in Rome. He had transformed his letter to Mussolini into a memorandum which he showed first to Count Acquarone of the royal household on June 4, to Bastianini on June 5. King Victor Emmanuel III was impressed. All agreed that here was the time for Italian intervention, "the Munich of the war." Another copy was given to

Ciano (and when Bottai entered the room, Ciano turned to him, pointing at the paper: "Hear what this fool [Antonescu] had to say; he wants to change the ideas of that other madman [Mussolini]"). Yet Bastianini could not get to Mussolini for more than a week; meanwhile Bova Scoppa wrote in his diary, "I am jittery, I bite my fingernails, I walk up and down in my room. . . . Every hour we lose may be fatal!"

On June 14 Bastianini succeeded in presenting the Bova Scoppa-Antonescu memorandum to the Duce so cleverly and subtly that Mussolini said he largely agreed with many points, but he wanted to wait for another two months. He nevertheless agreed to a secret visit of Mihai Antonescu to Italy.

This was exactly what the Rumanian wanted. On June 27 he secretly left for Italy with his military aide, Colonel Turtureanu. (*11*) During the journey Antonescu advanced the somewhat Levantine idea that Mussolini could be influenced favorably if he offered ten thousand carloads of Rumanian grain to Italy. Bastianini travelled to Venice to meet the Rumanians and prepare everything. On July 1 Antonescu arrived in Mussolini's summer place, Rocca delle Cam-minate. The Duce listened silently and said of Antonescu, "a coura-geous man; he says many true things." But he put his faith in time again, and fled from a decision:

> We have to wait for another two months with this action, for we can-not give the impression that Italy cedes before the Anglo-Saxons' threat of extermination. . . . In two months, I shall ask Hitler to con-voke a conference of all the Axis allies and the neutral states, and if Hitler does not want to do it, I shall do it without him.

When the Rumanian asked whether during these two months he could go ahead with his own preparations, Mussolini agreed: "Yes, do; I authorize you."

This last chapter of the Italian-Danubian secession attempts never came; for Mussolini, even if sincere and consistent in his promise to Antonescu — which, considering his then frequent hesitations, could be doubted — did not have his two months. The Antonescu mission (after paying a visit also to the King) left Rome on the evening of July 3. A week later the Allies landed in Sicily; once more Mussolini tried to make Hitler resort to some kind of a miraculous political settlement, and the two met at Feltre on July 19, but again only Hitler spoke. (*12*) Three weeks to the day after the returning Antonescu mission pulled into Bucharest's Banasea Station, Benito Mussolini was a political prisoner as Italian Fascism was coming to an ignoble, strange and sudden end.

The strange spring of 1943: II — Berlin, London, Washington, Moscow

When, by November 1942, the prospect of military victory began to fade, this was certainly bound to change the political situation of the globe. Now who was to get together with whom, and for what purposes, and how?

[*German inclinations.*] This was the point after which most of the thinking Germans believed that a political deal, a negotiated agreement, was needed to prevent the loss of their war. But here they were divided: one man believed in a deal with the Russians, another in a negotiated peace with the Western Allies. Opinion cut sharply across the relative "Right" and "Left" of the Third Reich's hierarchy. The England-haters, the National-Bolshevists, Ribbentrop, Göbbels, Koch, Bormann, favored a separate peace with Stalin, and in this they were joined — of course, with different ends in mind — by the Russophile conservatives and the General Staff, such men as Schulenburg, Fritzsche, Niedermeyer. On the other side were the Russophobes and men obsessed with the pleasant memories of the mid-thirties; extremists such as Streicher and Rosenberg, neo-epicureans such as Frank and Schirach, and also such conservatives as Weizsäcker and Schacht, and such anti-Nazis as Hassell and the Bishops. Somewhere between those holding these two general opinions (who never crystallized into perceptible groups or camps) stood Göring and Papen, hesitating, and before them marched Hitler, driven by unreason and foolish instinct, with the artificially rigid and straight steps of the mad and blind who look but do not see.

Three times before had Japanese attempts to bring Russians and Germans together failed, when, on the day of the American landing in French North Africa, Ribbentrop turned to Hitler in the forenoon of November 8, 1942. The Führer train was standing in Bydgoszcz, (*1*) in the former Polish Corridor, where the war had started. Ribbentrop asked Hitler: "Allow me today, give me full power to treat with Stalin to make peace with Russia at any sacrifice!" (*2*) But Hitler turned the idea down, "very flat"; he could not imagine losing; he continued to gamble on his military prowess. Mussolini asked him to make peace with Stalin, but Hitler reaffirmed his belief in ultimate, sudden victory. Then, in December, a Madrid newspaper interpreted a Tokyo dispatch to the effect that German-Russian negotiations were due; in January Russian-Polish relations took a turn for the worse, and Stalin did not accept the invitation of Roosevelt to go to Casablanca: indeed, no Russian representative was present when the "unconditional surrender" formula was announced. At the time of the Italian cabinet shake-up, in February, Hassell noted: "But would there still be anyone to make peace with Mussolini? Perhaps. Certainly not with Hitler, with the exception of Stalin — but this could be done only at the cost of completely relinquishing any German claims on Russian territory or influence, and Hitler could hardly do this."

Hassell was right. On February 22 Ribbentrop, echoing Hitler, told Alfieri that "it would be impossible to reach an agreement with Moscow. The solution of the conflict is going to be found on the battlefield." He nevertheless indicated to Alfieri that certain Soviet overtures had recently been made, but the German policy was to reject them. Two days later the first successes of the southern German counteroffensive were reported, and Hitler issued a proclamation dealing with "the mobilization of European labor against Bolshevism." (*3*)

[*Mussolini tries to convince Hitler.*] On March 6 Ribbentrop and the Japanese Ambassador conferred; the latter confirmed again that Japan could not enter the war against Russia. On March 8 Mussolini wrote another epistle to Hitler who answered on March 14: Mussolini worried unnecessarily, for the Eastern front was now consolidated.

On March 25 Mussolini wrote again, with a more insistent tone. To deprive Hitler of his previous arguments, Mussolini began with a flattering note: there existed no Russian danger now, as the German Army had succeeded in eliminating it.

Therefore I tell you that the Russian chapter should be closed with a peace treaty if possible — and I see such a possibility — or else with a systematic defensive measure, an imposing East Wall, which the Russians will never be able to break. The viewpoint which directs me to this conclusion is that Russia cannot be annihilated . . . even

in the case of the very improbable intervention of Japan . . . due to
the enormous distances. Therefore, in one way or another, the Russian chapter must be closed. (*4*)

Meanwhile relations between Russia and the Anglo-Saxon Powers
were becoming more obscure and less friendly. On March 8 Admiral
Standley in Moscow openly complained of the silence with which the
Soviet Government handled American Lend-Lease supplies. Three
days later Moscow quickly patched up the affair by broadcasting the
volume of American aid and Litvinov publicly expressed his thanks.
Eden now arrived in Washington for an extensive survey of the military and diplomatic situation. Rumors of German-Soviet contacts
were in the spring air. On March 12 German intelligence intercepted
a report of the Turkish Minister in Washington which, as Göbbels
recorded, was "full of fear and grief concerning the advance of
Bolshevism not only in the military but also in the propaganda and
political fields." Sarajoglu, always sensitive toward murmurs and
signals of a German-Russian understanding, reformed his cabinet on
March 15 and made a strong pro-British speech in the Turkish Parliament. Other neutrals were also worried. On March 28 the Swedish
Defense Minister Sköld advocated the formation of a strong Scandinavian military alliance "after the war."

[*Lull on the front: March 15–May 7.*] By March 15 the German counteroffensive had spent its fury, and five days later an almost
complete lull, except in the Kuban region, set in along the entire
Russian front. In certain sectors this state of affairs amounted to a
de facto armistice, lasting for several weeks.

Central-eastern Europe seethed with rumors. Were there secret
negotiations between Soviets and Germans in that period? Göbbels'
Diary indicates something. He often tried to catch an elusive Ribbentrop and an evasive Hitler between March 20 — the beginning of
the front-line lull — and May 7, when Hitler spoke again strongly
to him concerning the Russian military situation. On May 6, the lull
on the fronts was interrupted by the first large Russian tactical air
raid on the central front. If there were contacts and talks, it is thus
likely that they occurred some time between March 15 and May 5,
for the prerequisite of the Soviets to any negotiation had always been
a *de facto* cessation of major hostilities on the battlefront, to wit, in
the case of Finland.

If there had been any negotiations, there is no doubt that Göbbels did not know of them. But Göbbels was never fully informed of what was going on; in 1939, for example, he did not know of the concrete German-Russian Pact talks until August 15, that is, until their very · last stage of completion. Hitler did not tell him everything; neither did high officials of Ribbentrop's entourage. (5)

There were vague contacts with the Japanese through the German Naval Attaché in Tokyo. A Soviet Embassy Counselor in Stockholm had contacted Kleist and Clauss, Ribbentrop's agents. Kleist and Clauss also knew a German Jew residing in Stockholm, whom they used as a middleman, but it was suggested that Hitler could not make up his mind whether to use that individual or not. (6) The Japanese military attachés in Berlin and Stockholm and the German aristocratic resistance also had some Russian contacts. Now the old Schulenburg turned to action; early in March he proposed to Field-Marshal Kluge that the latter get him through the front to the Russians. (For a moment after the fall of Cherbourg in the West and a new Soviet offensive in the East, around June 25, 1944, Hitler himself toyed with the idea of parachuting Schulenburg into Russia to contact Stalin.) Kluge did not dare to make up his mind. On March 10 and April 25 Vlassov, the Russian general who deserted in 1941, talked with Schulenburg about Russian-German separate peace chances; Vlassov claimed to know that Ribbentrop had offered Russia the 1914 frontiers, a Russian sphere of interest in the Balkans and a new régime of the Straits; but Stalin was yet undecided. (There is also some evidence that one of Vlassov's main aides, Kozlovsky, was simultaneously in the service of the German and Russian intelligence organs.) Vlassov's information coincided with what Antonescu had told Bova Scoppa in May about Russo-German peace terms and attempts.

On April 12 a German communiqué informed the world of the discovery of a mass grave of Polish officers murdered by the Russians at Katyn, near Smolensk. Göbbels was jubilant. But, to his great surprise, strange measures temporarily prevented his utilizing the Katyn item. For a few days Hitler refused to give permission to publish the discovery; after its publication Göbbels continued to encounter difficulties from the military. He noted on April 28 that "the military at the Führer's headquarters succeeded again in withdrawing the Katyn pictures from the weeklies"; it seemed that the military were strongly against exploiting the Katyn discovery or anything else which would be an unnecessary obstacle in the way of eventual German-Russian contacts. Frank was told not to encourage Polish anti-Soviet nationalism in the wake of Katyn; this would have decisively diminished possibilities of a German-Russian understanding. The Katyn find only furthered strong pro-Polish sympathies (7) among the Italians; Hitler delayed its publication; on the 15th, he "could not be influenced to publish an *"Ostproklamation"*; on the 17th Hitler received Quisling of Norway, who begged the Führer to make "positive politics" in the East and contact Stalin. On April 22 Göbbels commented on rumors concerning another Japanese mediation between Moscow and Berlin. "Perhaps Shigemitsu, who is a Chinese expert . . . has the task of bringing a contact between Berlin and Moscow. Anyhow, I could not, at this moment, imagine how this mediation would look . . . [Yet] certain facts seem to point thereto. . . . Would this be feasible in whatever manner, the war would then assume a basically different face." (8) Four days later the news of the break between the London Poles and Moscow reached Berlin, and Göbbels decided to "wait for awhile with this sensational news. . . . I shall wait for future developments for another day, in order to see what can be done here." Next day he again encountered the opposition of the military against the exploiting of Polish-Russian differences. Early in May two generals, Manstein and Kleist, decided to curb the brutal methods of the SS in purely Russian and Ukrainian territories; there exists a curious letter from Manstein, dated May 9, to the retired Ambassador Dirksen, who was on very good terms with Schulenburg: reference is made to a visit which Dirksen paid to Niedermeyer concerning the eventual organization of non-Russian minorities, especially Crimeans and Caucasians, into auxiliary military formations with the German Army (this was a pet idea of Schulenburg for awhile); nonetheless, the letter is curt, courteous, and alludes to Manstein's opinion that such organizations would perhaps be contrary to broader political aims. (9)

By that time, however, the situation had changed; if there were any Russian-German negotiations in late March or April, by May 6 they dwindled to insignificance; on that night, with the Russian air raids, the frontline quiet was broken. Next day Hitler ordered the military to prepare a "limited offensive" in the Kursk sector, while his general orders dropped the plans for a general 1943 summer offensive. On May 8 he said to the assembled bigwigs and Göbbels: "There exists practically no possibility of compromise with the Soviets" and added that now diplomacy would not have as much to say as in previous wars: "After this war there will be no Talleyrand." His ideological anti-Bolshevik zeal returned; significantly, a few days later he ordered that the previously suspended forming of an "anti-Bolshevik legion" among British prisoners of war should proceed. Hitler, Rosenberg, Keitel, and Zeitzler on June 8 disposed of the idea of forming an anti-Bolshevik force among Soviet prisoners and non-Russian nationalities in the occupied areas: "We will never build up a Russian army." In the meantime Stalin had announced the dissolution of the Communist International. Admiral Raeder, who generally assessed Stalin very well, gave his estimate of this event:

> Was the announcement of the dissolution of the Comintern perhaps a hint to Germany that an understanding between Germany and Russia would have been possible even then, and that, after the Russian territories had been regained, a peaceful relationship would have been possible between the two states who, taking the longer view, are both threatened by the United States of America?

However, Ribbentrop, speaking to Alfieri on June 11, regarded the dissolution of the Comintern as a sign of Russian weakness. The German Foreign Minister, while reluctant and secretive about German military plans in Russia, also added:

> Anyhow, today an agreement with the Russians is impossible because both parties retain their vital claims to the Ukraine. In six months perhaps the situation would be different.

He was thereby suggesting that not ideological incompatibilities but practical and territorial differences prevented an agreement between Berlin and Moscow — another indication that some contact had existed between the two in the spring of 1943.

. . . . .

A "cool period" in American-Soviet relations threatened to prolong itself, but Roosevelt suddenly decided in May to send the well-known friend of the Soviets, Joseph Davies, to Moscow on a secret and special mission. The former Ambassador left for Moscow on May 18; yet by that time the most propitious moment for Russian-German negotiations had passed. On July 5 the tank battle at Kursk opened the summer campaign of 1943.

[*The Polish problem; mistaken Anglo-American calculations.*]
Fears of a German-Soviet separate peace had, however, grave effects
upon the foreign policies of the English-speaking Powers. The Polish
Ambassador to Washington ably summarized the atmosphere of these
months:

> Both Britain and America appeared to understand fully the danger-
> ous trend of Soviet policy and were probing the possibilities of in-
> fluencing Stalin. Neither of them really trusted him. Both were
> considerably frightened at losing Soviet Russia as a partner in the
> war. Each was passing the buck to the other. The American govern-
> ment contended that Britain, as Poland's ally, was in a better posi-
> tion to defend Poland's interests. The British government was inclined
> to believe that the United States could intervene more effectively,
> being less directly interested in European issues.
>
> As a result, Poland was becoming the subject of pending Power-politi-
> cal discussions regarding her ultimate fate. She was practically aban-
> doned by her Allies and left alone to face her destiny of becoming the
> first victim of Soviet imperialism. Her government was paralyzed,
> having been promised Anglo-American support which was not forth-
> coming, on condition that it remain silent and make no attempt
> to enlist the powerful support of public opinion for its righteous
> cause. (*10*)

When in May 1942 Molotov presented the Soviet territorial claims
to the British in London, the Poles were not informed of the scope
and content of these exploratory conversations. And when Churchill
(and Harriman) in August 1942 found no time to talk with Stalin in
Moscow about the Polish question, this, as Kot, the Polish Ambassador
(an otherwise rather timid and impractical professor) telegraphed to
his government at that time "was immediately understood by the
Russians to be a proof that the Anglo-Saxons had deserted us . . ."

By 1943 it was clear that both the British and American governments wished the Curzon Line to be the future frontier between Poland and Russia, and they were also confident that the
acceptance of this frontier would basically solve the Russian-Polish
problem.

Alas, this was not the case; for, almost simultaneously with the
official Soviet announcement of territorial aims, the first steps were
taken to reduce Poland to a Soviet dependency, a satellite. On February 20, 1943, the Ukrainian Communist writer, Korneichuk, whose

wife Wassilewska was a prominent Polish Communist, published an article stating that "the present Polish ruling circles do not reflect genuine Polish public opinion." Exactly at the same time, upon Eden's proddings, Maisky revealed that, in his opinion, the Soviet government "would not look with favor on the re-establishment of governments like the Polish government-in-exile." Yet, the American and the better informed British government continued to believe that, had the Sikorski government accepted the Curzon Line in the beginning, Soviet interference in Polish internal affairs could have been avoided (Churchill insisted on this point to Mikolajczyk as late as October 1944). It is fairly clear that even at Yalta, Churchill and Roosevelt hoped for a democratic Poland in exchange for the eastern Polish territorial concessions. (The additional price then was the establishment of a new, half-Communist Polish government, similarly agreed to at Yalta, which they hopefully regarded as an indefinite and temporary concession.) Thus, for almost two years, London and Washington thought the Soviet aims in Poland — and in the other border states — to be essentially and perhaps exclusively territorial: a fatal mistake. On the other hand, it might be conceded that had the Polish government-in-exile in London reluctantly accepted a territorial settlement earlier than 1944, it could have counted on much stronger British and American support when the Russian-created puppet Communist "governments" appeared on the scene; but whether this strong Western support would have effectively helped the London Poles is again very questionable. Also, a territorial compromise would have brought a fatal crisis to the Polish government-in-exile: such things went against the grain of the heroic Polish national psyche, unrelieved and at the same time, unburdened by realism. There were noteworthy differences within the government. The usual émigré intrigues prevailed; deep differences of opinion separated those who were more flexible in their attitudes: Mikolajczyk, Grabski, and Ambassador Kot, from the majority, who, like General Anders, saw mortal danger in Russia and her designs. Sikorski stood somewhere in the middle; in the winter of 1942–43 intriguers succeeded in creating misunderstanding between him and Anders; important Polish newspapers turned against Sikorski. The Premier, however, possessed the advantage of great personal charm, straightforwardness and, most important of all, he understood somehow the ways and manners of the Anglo-Saxons, a knowledge which was lacking in most of the other Poles. (*11*)

[*The Russian break with the Polish government.*]   On March 1,
1943, a Russian note addressed to the Polish government directly
claimed the recognition of the Soviets' right to eastern Poland. The
Poles were indignant, and on the 4th General Anders issued a fiery
Order of the Day to the Polish forces assembling in the Middle East
(the proud and undiplomatic tone of which Order made him unpopular with the Foreign Office and an anxious State Department,
afraid lest Stalin consider an eventual separate peace with Germany).
On April 12 came the German announcement of Katyn. The Polish
Minister of Defense in London somewhat inadvertently issued a com-
muniqué in which the Polish government asked the International
Red Cross in Switzerland to investigate the Katyn murders "in view
of the abundant and detailed German information." (*12*) The rash
Polish announcement on Katyn furnished the welcome pretext to the
Soviets. On April 25, 1943, the bombshell burst: Russia severed dip-
lomatic relations with the Polish government.

The British and American governments sincerely believed that,
with good will and mediation, the rift between Poles and Russians
would be bridged somehow, but Göbbels was more of a realist. He
wrote on April 15 (before the break between Russia and Poland),
when an American press agency reported that Roosevelt and Eden
had resolved to restore Poland within her pre-war frontiers:

> As if Roosevelt and Eden could restore anything concerning that
> matter! Those who shall resolve it are exclusively the Axis Powers
> and the Soviet Union and with the Soviet Union we still shall have
> to have a word of authority.

The Americans, as Göbbels saw them, were unduly naive. The State
Department continued with its subcommittees; the "study of Central
European territorial problems was intensified" in 1943. One of these
subcommittees, on the 1941 frontiers, stated on March 26:

> Should the Soviet Union desire to play an active rôle in Central
> Europe, it would prefer [this] line to the other suggested boundaries.
> Central and Western European nations may look with some appre-
> hension on the extension of Soviet territory so far to the West.

And, about a Soviet frontier on the Carpathians:

> The strategic position of the Soviet Union in the face of a potentially
> hostile Polish-Rumanian bloc or larger Eastern European grouping

would be very strong. The possibility that any of the nations of Eastern Europe, singly or in combination, could defend themselves against the Soviet Union, would be small. *(13)*

which statement indicates that the State Department, while somewhat concerned with Russia's frontiers, did not as yet envisage potential Soviet plans of reducing the central-eastern European border states into satellites.

British official circles were, in contrast, cool and ugly with the Poles. On April 28 a *Times* editorial attacked the Polish government. *(14)*

On May 2, on the occasion of Poland's national day, President Raczkiewicz and Premier Sikorski spoke of the Poles' unfaltering loyalty to the Allied cause, at the same time assuring the nation that no territorial compromise would be considered by the government. Meanwhile the Polish diplomats leaving Russia were accused of espionage; Beneš was now invited to address Congress in Washington; he kept studiously away from his former Polish friends, and was exceedingly anxious to ingratiate himself with Stalin. The dissolution of the Comintern was announced on May 22, but Soviet agitation was evident everywhere; there were troubles with Yugoslavia, where the usual émigré clashes, gravely abetted by the civil war between Tito and Mihailovič brought about the fall of successive Yugoslav governments-in-exile, first Trifunovič, then Purič. In Greece, June brought renewed fights between Communist and Royalist Partisans, and the Supreme Allied Commander in the Mediterranean vainly ordered all Greek partisans to come under his command; upon strong British advice King George II promised elections in Greece six months after the liberation.

On July 9 a tragic piece of news came: General Sikorski perished in an airplane accident at Gibraltar. A few months earlier trouble had developed with the airplane on which Sikorski was to fly from Montreal to Washington; an American investigation then established that foul play might have existed. Whether the Gibraltar disaster was an accident or whether the long arm of Stalin reached to the Rock, Sikorski's death was disastrous to the Polish cause. On July 14 a new government was formed by Mikolajczyk, the leader of the Polish Peasant Party; the participation of Stanczyk, Grabski, and Kot aroused great anxiety among the Polish military and those who believed that further flexibility shown toward Russia would be tantamount to surrender. (Yet two staunch anti-Russians were appointed: Romer as Foreign Minister and General Sosnkowski as Commander-in-Chief.) The government-in-exile was less and less master of Poland's fate. Moscow, which on July 21 announced the formation of a "Free Germany Committee" in Russia, showed no worry over the breaking of relations with the London Polish government nor any desire to resume them.

. . . .

[*Casablanca.*]   Churchill and Roosevelt met at Casablanca on January 14, 1943; neither Stalin nor Molotov came. Their absence did not unduly worry the British Premier, as he wanted to find time and occasion at Casablanca to discuss not only the military but the political aspects of Europe's liberation.

"Unconditional surrender" was announced at Casablanca, and this was one of the major mistakes of the Allies' political warfare. Churchill, who agreed to it, considered it of not much more than propaganda importance, largely devoid of practical implications. (Stalin, the great realist, was not in favor of the unconditional surrender formula; he also expressed his understanding of the Darlan deal.) Behind the formula lurked, however, the adopted ideological image of the war, so popular in America: the war had but one aim, the total defeat of the Nazi-Fascist-Japanese totalitarian alliance. The singular concentration of all available forces upon this aim obscured the fact that the defeat of the Axis-Japanese alliance was not an end in itself, but only a means to the end — the re-establishment of reasonable political conditions throughout the world and especially in Europe.

[*Churchill's Balkan and Turkish plans.*]   Moreover, the unconditional surrender principle, although accepted by both, resulted in a growing divergence of feeling and opinion between the American President and the British Prime Minister. In Roosevelt's view, the ideological character of the war was increasing; yet Churchill saw that the growth of the ideological concept could favor only Russia, whose very practical and imperialistic war aims would thereby be obscured; Churchill hoped and planned for decreasing the ideological spectre, and with a more realistic approach he kept the uncertainties and the dangers of the post-war situation in mind.

The concentration of everything for the most rapid and total military defeat of Hitler without present and future political considerations earmarked also the strategic planning of the American Chiefs of Staff. They planned to invade Europe via Northern France, the shortest route to Berlin. Churchill, on the other hand, was champion of a Balkan invasion to attack "the soft underbelly of Europe"; but he could not have his way for, by 1943, Britain was definitely the minor partner in the Anglo-American coalition: two-thirds of the invasion armies, three-quarters of their equipment came from the United States. Britain was not in a position to decide where American blood should be shed in the liberation of Europe; she could not suggest more military sacrifice and a longer American route, especially not for what seemed subtle political considerations to the Americans. (*15*) Churchill could but hope to influence his allies.

This he again tried to do at Casablanca. But he could not convince Roosevelt that the main war against Germany should continue to be fought in the Mediterranean area. The Combined Chiefs of Staff reaffirmed their basic plan to invade Germany through Northern France; the cross-channel operation was envisaged for the spring of 1944. But, to Churchill's great satisfaction, at least it was decided to exploit the Mediterranean campaign after the ejection of the Axis forces from Tunisia, and on January 18 the invasion of Sicily, *Operation Husky*, was decided upon.

At that moment Churchill returned to his pet idea: Turkey. Because of logistic difficulties, the Americans in November 1942 were unconvinced of the feasibility and advantages of creating an Anglo-American-Turkish front at the gates of southeastern Europe. (*16*) The rapid winter advance of the Russians and the daily increasing evidence of their post-war designs in central-eastern Europe made Churchill revert to the Turkish issue at Casablanca. The Turks were worried about the speed of the Russian advance; as they very much feared to see the Germans in Suez, they abhorred the sight of the Russians in the Balkans. In October 1942, the Turkish envoy in Bucharest told Mihai Antonescu that Turkey continued to consider Soviet Russia as its Enemy Number One, and on December 9 the German Consul-General in Istanbul reported thus to Berlin:

> Turkey, who does not desire to see the British ejected from the Mediterranean [Suez Canal], wishes us [Germany], on the other hand, success in our campaign against Russia. She is anxious whether our

forces would prove sufficient to defeat the Russians for a more or
less lengthy period.

Actually, she [Turkey] is less ready than ever to help us in this campaign as the Turks see the question of ultimate victory being very
doubtful . . . (*17*)

The report then cited the Anglo-American desire to utilize Turkey
as a great air base against the Germans in the Balkans and the Rumanian oil fields, while it established that Menemenčoglu's earlier
declaration to Papen ("Turkey shall not abandon her neutrality,
even in the case when the Axis might find itself on the verge of collapse") was probably sincere. But the German diplomat concluded
by quoting the widespread view that if a strong American (not British)
army appeared in the Near East, it was doubtful whether this absolute neutrality would be upheld by the Turks.

[*The Adana meeting.*]   Yet it was America which did not contemplate sending an army there, while the British planned to do so.
From North Africa, Churchill on January 30 flew east. In the southern
Anatolian town of Adana he met the Turkish President, Inönü. Their
conference lasted two days; a frank exchange of views occurred.

Churchill brought a grand Balkan plan, envisaging the opening of
a long front with Mihailovič in Serbia and the Partisans in Slovenia.
Inönü said that Turkey should be prudent. Churchill assured him
that Britain and the United States would be on their guard if Russia
proved too dangerous later; but the Turks would not enter the war,
nor give bases. Churchill returned to Cairo and communicated some
of his "morning thoughts" to Cordell Hull, "more on post-war
security," in which he envisaged post-war European confederations,
"among which a Scandinavian Bloc, a Danubian Bloc, and a Balkan
Bloc appear to be obvious . . ." (*18*)

On the same day Churchill informed Stalin on Adana; he said
that he had defended Russia's record, and he asked for a friendly
Russian gesture toward Turkey. Stalin answered coolly on February 6. On February 13 the Turkish Foreign Minister told the Soviet
envoy that Turkey wished to enter into political negotiations with
Russia, but this offer was spurned. On the 23rd Stalin declared that
the Soviet Union was bearing the full weight of the war (although by
January three million tons of American lend-lease had arrived in
Russia). Russian-Allied relations cooled now. On March 15 Stalin

wrote Churchill angrily about the delaying of the Second Front and again sounded Britain and America on the subject of the Soviets' postwar frontiers. In another exchange, the American mediation with Finland was discussed and Churchill supported the American approach. Nevertheless, on March 30 Stalin had to be told that because of the German attacks the Allied supply route to Northern Russia had to be temporarily abandoned. There was now much mutual suspicion.

[*Eden in Washington.*]   On March 12 Eden arrived in Washington. He had very important conferences with Roosevelt and Hopkins. (*19*) Eden said that the very first Russian demand would be the absorption of the Baltic states; Roosevelt thought that American and British opinion would be repelled by a new Russian absorption, but "realistically" speaking, the Russian Army would be there anyhow when Germany was defeated. He again contemplated asking Stalin to hold a new plebiscite in the Baltics. Eden thought that Stalin would not agree to this, whereupon Roosevelt said that it at least could be used as a "bargaining argument."

Then Eden expressed his opinion that Russia did not want much territory from Poland and spoke of the Curzon Line; they agreed, however, that Poland should be eventually compensated with East Prussia. (*20*) Neither the Americans nor Eden yet envisaged a Russian attempt to establish a satellite government in Poland. Eden also complained of Sikorski's "bargaining" with the little Balkan powers. Roosevelt deemed the March 1940 boundary between Finland and Russia "reasonable" and Eden agreed, with the provision that the Hangö base be retained by the Finns. All agreed to accept the Russian incorporation of Bessarabia. As to Yugoslavia, the American President put great emphasis on Croat-Serb difficulties, and spoke of some kind of an inter-Yugoslav trusteeship for Croatia. Eden and Roosevelt saw no real difficulties with Czechoslovakia, Rumania, Turkey, Bulgaria, or Greece "from a geographical point of view." An independent Austria and Hungary were also agreed upon, and Eden remarked that Stalin was biased against the Hungarians.

Expressing his purely private opinion, Eden thought that Stalin would prefer a continued British-American-Russian cooperation after the war, instead of an American withdrawal from Europe; for, in his view, Stalin was not prepared to face the implications of an extensive Russian control over Europe, while Britain would probably be too weak to face Russia alone. Eden believed that "it was a fixed matter of Russian foreign policy to have both British and American troops heavily in Europe when the collapse comes."

Next day the always agile Hopkins tried to sound out Litvinov on Soviet post-war intentions, but without success; soon Litvinov's trunks were to be packed, and the Ambassador, a universally exalted "symbol" of an era when Russia and the West seemed to have understood each other, was to go back to Moscow, as was Maisky from London. In the place of these two elderly Jews came young and largely unknown representatives of a new Russian diplomatic generation, Gromyko to Washington and Gusev to London: a cool whiff from the air of the steppes. These diplomatic changes coincided with the rumors of German-Russian negotiations (and with a new trend in Soviet propaganda, which, since November 1942, spoke "soft" toward Germany and insisted that there was a fundamental difference between the "Hitlerite Fascists" and German nationalists).

.   .   .   .

The Allies were now winning the last battles in Africa. In view of this, and also in view of the rather evident Allied difficulties with Russia, there was practically no German strategist who did not expect the Anglo-Americans to land in the Balkans. A report from German counterintelligence in mid-April repeated this thesis, in which Göbbels and Hitler concurred. On April 30 Göbbels wrote that if the Anglo-Americans would land in south-eastern Europe,

> . . . we have to fear popular revolt. The Balkans is still the powder keg of Europe. Let us hope that the English and Americans are not clear about the opportunities awaiting them there . . .

The hopes of Göbbels came true.

[*The American decision: Churchill in Washington.*]   Churchill wrote to General Ismay on April 2:

> In any case, it must be considered a most important objective to get a footing on the Dalmatian coast, so that we can foment the insurgents of Albania and Yugoslavia by weapons, supplies, and possibly Commandos. I believe that, in spite of his present naturally foxy at-

titude, Mihailovic will throw his whole weight against the Italians the moment we are able to give him any effective help. Evidently great possibilities are open in this theatre. *(21)*

Yet the Americans were unwilling to realize these great possibilities. Their Joint Chiefs of Staff, wary of Churchill's Balkan plans, on May 8 definitely decided to commit the British to the unalterable invasion plans of 1944 in Northern France. (Admiral Leahy had a hand in this decision.) *(22)* On May 12 Churchill arrived in Washington, to fight the second round of his Mediterranean battle; Roosevelt told him of the military decision, a decision which also meant that the Americans were against any operation in Italy which would aim beyond the capture of Sardinia and Sicily.

[*Churchill and Marshall; lack of understanding and lost opportunities.*]   Again and again, Churchill argued against the decision. He was distressed. *(23)* His final arguments were presented on May 24, when he fought forcefully for an invasion of Italy, to extend into Yugoslavia and Greece. But the plan was rejected. He accepted the American arguments with extreme reluctance; however, he set a price for his acceptance. From Washington he planned to fly to North Africa (Tunis had fallen on the 7th and the last Axis forces in Africa surrendered on the 12th) and he requested General Marshall to go with him. He hoped that on this long tour he would be able to convince Marshall of the validity of the arguments for a strong Mediterranean campaign with a Balkan invasion. Churchill was bound to fail here; for throughout the war, General Marshall indicated singularly little, if any, understanding of political implications. The aide of General Eisenhower noted in his diary:

> . . . the Premier openly and avowedly is seeking to influence Ike to pursue the campaign in the Mediterranean area until the Italians are out of the war. Presumably, he then wants the Allies' effort to continue in the Mediterranean area rather than across the Channel as already agreed by the Combined Chiefs at their Washington meeting. He makes no bones of his point of view and apparently regards the decision already taken as quite open to review and change. *(24)*

Presumably to sweeten his pill for the Americans, on May 30 Churchill, in a memorandum, stated that he thought in terms of Commando-size troops and not armies in the Balkans.

We should not have the troops to engage in any serious operations
there, and His Majesty's Government do not contemplate or desire
the provision of any organised armed force for the Balkan theatre,
either this year or in any period with which we are now concerned.
Nevertheless, the aiding, within the limits proposed, of the patriot
bands in Yugoslavia, the fomenting of revolt in Greece and Albania,
are measures of high importance, all of which, together with our
main operations, will influence the action of Turkey. In this way the
utmost aid in our power will be given to Russia and also to "Bolero"
[preparations for the invasion of France]. It is only if and when these
prospects are decisively closed to us that we should consider secondary or minor alternatives for Mediterranean action.

He was courteously refused. He was worried. Eden reported on
Turkey, which, Churchill believed, "would become much more
friendly . . . when our troops had reached the Balkan area . . ."
"Eden and I were in full agreement on the war policy," wrote
Churchill, "but I feared that the turn of his phrase might mislead
our American friends. The record states, 'The Prime Minister intervened to observe emphatically that he was not advocating sending an
army into the Balkans now or in the near future. Mr. Eden agreed
that it would not be necessary to put an army into the Balkans, since
the Turks would begin to show favorable reactions as soon as we were
able to constitute an immediate threat to the Balkans.' "
Thus everything had to be watered down, and Göbbels' hopes were
realized. Hitler said to Admiral Dönitz on May 14 that he did not
think that Sicily would be invaded, as this excluded the element of
surprise; he thought that rather Sardinia or southern Greece would
be the place of the Allied landing. On June 10 a German military
estimate, communicated to the Italian Embassy in Berlin, stated that
the Germans did not believe that the Allies would land in Sicily and
subsequently fight northward through the hard mountains of the
Italian peninsula. The Germans thought that the Anglo-American
armies would rather land in Sardinia and Corsica, which was relatively easy to do, and that from there they could jump on to central
Italy, to the Livorno-Rome coastal sector (the Maremma region)
"whenever they wanted." (25)
The Germans had again credited the Allied leadership with too
much imagination; for the only invasion of the Italian mainland after
Sicily, *Avalanche*, was planned for the Salerno region, its sole aim
being the securing of the port of Naples. As late as July 24, 1943,

Admiral King and General Marshall argued even against this Salerno operation. The dramatic fall of Mussolini did not change these limited plans: a most amazing fact; notwithstanding the Italian armistice and military opportunities, the Mediterranean area began to be regarded as a secondary and merely diversionary theater of operations.

On July 26, 1943, when the news of Mussolini's fall reverberated throughout the globe, Secretary of War Stimson, just returned from London, sent a message to General Eisenhower which was recorded by Captain Butcher, and requires no comment:

> [Stimson] felt that the Prime Minister was obsessed with the idea of proving to history that the invasion of the Continent by way of the Balkans was wise strategy and would repair whatever charge history now records for Churchill's misfortune at the Dardanelles in the last war. (*26*)

Effects of the Italian armistice: the Great Powers

[*American misunderstandings.*]   On the exciting night of July 25, 1943, the basic differences between the official American and British concept of the war was apparent in the radio broadcasts of the BBC and the "Voice of America." The BBC greeted the fall of Mussolini as jubilant tidings, deeming the Italian events an example to the other "satellites." The "Voice of America," on the other hand, was taking a different stand: the director of the OWI drafted a directive that night, assailing the "clique," Badoglio and the King, who overthrew Mussolini: they were not true democrats, patriots, liberals, said the Voice of America, but just another group of militarists and Fascists. It took days before the State Department succeeded in curtailing the ideological fervor of the OWI. The effects of the Italian armistice were immediately evident on the battlefronts, and in the Balkans in particular — on the same night of July 25 commanding officers of five Italian divisions in Yugoslavia informed British intelligence agents that they were willing to negotiate their surrender to the Allies. The divergence between the British and American views on war aims grew. As Mrs. Roosevelt wrote of 1943:

> I remember very well his [Roosevelt's] irritation at Churchill's determination that we should attack through Greece and the Balkans. Franklin said that would mean the loss of many men, though strategically it might be a help to Great Britain and get us to Berlin before the Russians. However, he did not think that was important . . .

Neither did Secretary of War Stimson think it important. On August 4 he wrote another memorandum, accusing the British of harboring dark second thoughts, and stating that the American conception of the Italian invasion was entirely different from the British one. "The Italian effort must be strictly confined to the objective . . .": in other words, the armistice must have no effect whatsoever on the scope of the military operations. Harry Hopkins fully agreed. On August 10 Stimson sent another memorandum to the President:

> The difference between us is a vital difference in faith. . . . the British theory (which cropped up again and again in unguarded sentences of the British leaders with whom I have just been talking) is that Germany can be beaten . . . in Northern Italy, in the Eastern Mediterranean . . . in the Balkans and other satellite countries. . . . To me, in the light of the postwar problems which we shall face, that attitude . . . seems terribly dangerous. . . . None of these methods of pinprick warfare can be counted on by us to fool Stalin into the belief that we have kept . . . our pledge.

Roosevelt answered and assured Stimson that the Allies would not proceed beyond Rome in Italy. (Yet on August 6 Ribbentrop, ill-humored, told the new Italian Foreign Minister, Guariglia, at Tarvisio: "if Italy should capitulate, it would also mean the ruin of Germany.") On August 12 Marshall cabled to Eisenhower, stating that in Italy "we will go as far as we can" and that then the Allies would withdraw seven divisions, from November 1 on, and plan instead for the invasion of Southern France in 1944. These were terrible mistakes, showing a lack of military and political insight which served the Germans' and Russians' purposes in the long run, and reduced the stature of the Western military leaders in the esteem of future historians. (1)

[*Quebec.*]   Under such circumstances the First Quebec Conference assembled on August 17 and deliberated for a week. Again Churchill — across the Atlantic for the fifth time in two years — fought a united front of Marshall, Hull, Stimson and Roosevelt, who were all against his Balkan invasion plans. Hopkins brought a document to Quebec entitled "Russia's Position"; according to Sherwood, it was quoted "from a very high-level American military strategic estimate":

Russia's postwar position in Europe will be a dominant one. With Germany crushed, there is no power in Europe to oppose her tremendous military forces. It is true that Great Britain is building up a position in the Mediterranean vis-à-vis Russia that she may find useful in balancing power in Europe. However, even here she may not be able to oppose Russia unless she is otherwise supported.

This hitherto clear and correct estimate continues, however:

The conclusions from the foregoing are obvious. Since Russia is the decisive factor in the war, she must be given every assistance and every effort must be made to obtain her friendship. Likewise, since without question she will dominate Europe on the defeat of the Axis, it is even more essential to develop and maintain the most friendly relations with Russia. (2)

If there be a Third World War, then this was its birth certificate.

In Quebec the final military decision was made concerning Normandy, and also in regard to *Anvil-Dragoon*, the "D–Day plus 90" invasion of Southern France. Churchill, having been forced to acquiesce in the Normandy plan, now began his second uphill fight: he argued against the need for such a secondary invasion, and pressed instead for his Balkan invasion project again. The preliminary round of this bout was at Quebec; the bout continued in Cairo, Teheran, London, until the very day of *Anvil-Dragoon*, August 15, 1944 (indeed, even a few days after), but without success. Marshall and Roosevelt overruled Churchill. (3)

In Quebec news arrived of the first contact between the Badoglio armistice negotiators and the Allies. Roosevelt and Churchill decided to notify Stalin — who had excused himself from coming to Quebec. He was also told of the impending invasion of the Salerno area (*Avalanche*), the extent, place, and scope of which operation was left unchanged by the Allied military planners, notwithstanding the sensational Italian developments. (4)

[*The armistice: unexploited chances.*] On September 3 the secret Italian armistice was signed, to be published five to eight days later. At dawn on that fateful September 8 German planes spotted ships of the Allied armada heading towards Salerno. They could not believe their eyes. Admiral Canaris and the German counterintelligence service immediately regarded the moving of the Allied battlecraft toward Salerno to be a feint; notwithstanding armistice rumors, they were so sure in their estimates that they communicated their opinion even to the Italians; it seemed impossible that the Allies would undertake a landing at a point of "so little strategic importance." Again the Germans overestimated the ingenuity of the Anglo-American planners; the dull butchery of the Salerno Battle followed. (5)

At half past six in the evening the Italian armistice was announced through hundreds of radio transmitters. This was the moment when throughout central-eastern Europe, and especially in the Balkans, the political stock of the Western Allies stood highest; their movements were scanned with extreme eagerness and anticipation. The Balkans rumbled. In the summer the more moderate Bozhilov had succeeded Filov in Bulgaria; Rhallis instead of Logothetopoulos headed the Greek satellite government; five times the Italians had to reshuffle the Albanian "cabinet." The Hungarian General Staff estimated in early September an Allied invasion of the Balkans to be imminent; in accordance with a thesis which the German Field-Marshal Mackensen had expounded in a book in 1924, the General Staff expected one of the decisive battles of the war to develop around Lake Balaton in the southwestern Hungarian plains. In Greece the sporadic appearance of small British Commando parties and a speech by King George II in July were parts of a great British intelligence manoeuver to deceive the Germans into expecting the Allied landings in Greece and the Balkans instead of Sicily and Italy. "The Germans were successfully deceived," wrote Woodhouse, "but almost everyone in Greece was deceived as well, with incalculably important results . . ." King Mihai and Boris, Admiral Horthy, Kállay, Mihai Antonescu, Bozhilov, Mihailovič, Nedič, Tanner, and Ryti, many of the German generals, and many persons in the Foreign Ministry were ready to desert Hitler and make peace with the Western Allies. But the military policy of the Allies ruined all chances; as Miss Elizabeth Wiskemann correctly stated:

> The anti-German parties in Rumania and Hungary and, indeed, throughout Axis Europe, were stimulated to such a degree that if the Allies could have followed up their advantage in Italy, the war might have ended in 1943. (6)

[*The German reaction: dramatic dilemma and unexpected relief.*]
The Italian armistice had tremendous repercussions in Germany too.

The Germans, including Hitler, overestimated the Allies' political vision. On August 11 at his military conference, Hitler spoke of

> . . . indications which show Anglo-Saxon-Russian differences. . . . The Anglo-Saxons do not wish to see Russia in Finland, nor, under any circumstances, that Russia should improve her sea communication in the North. Poland is to be restored; the Russians will not be allowed to come near the Bosphorus, and they will be kept out of the Balkans as well as Iran and Iraq. These reasons are enough to nettle Stalin . . .

Göbbels fell to such depths of pessimism that on September 10 he considered the search for a separate peace inevitable, "The only question was with whom (Russia or Britain)?" And this in his Diaries, written with an eye upon later publicity. On the same day Hitler told him that, at best, he counted on a line running "considerably north of Rome"; thus Hitler anticipated the Allies by about a year. Göbbels told Hitler his views concerning the desirability of a German-Russian separate peace, and Hitler answered: "At this moment nothing can be done with Stalin," but he hoped that "in the long run the English would recover their reason"; whereupon Göbbels cautiously opined that he saw more chance in coming to a deal with Stalin, who was a *Realpolitiker*, than with Churchill, "a romantic phantast." Hitler turned Göbbels down, and explained that as the British now had Sicily and Calabria, possibly also Sardinia, the balance of the war was, from a territorial point of view, already favorable to them. (Thus he intimated to Göbbels that, as it had sometime in the 1930's, a British-German deal aimed at Italy seemed possible to him.)

Now came stark, cold reality, which doused all optimism, dynamic hopes, and central-eastern European eagerness. The Allies landed at Salerno and nowhere else. They failed to capture Rome — they did not even try. Every armchair watcher of maps complacently and confidently looked at the northern neck of the Italian peninsula, the Genoa-Venice or the La Spezia-Rimini line; but the Allies did nothing. Indeed, they were almost hurled back into the sea by the German divisions hurried to Salerno; only relief by the Eighth Army assured their foothold. And to this anticlimax came the additional cold shower: the celestial liberation of Mussolini. A handful of German paratroopers achieved a success greater than that of thousands of English and American soldiers cranking jeeps, carrying crates

ashore, stirring up dust, and churning the waves off Salerno. The
Mussolini rescue

> ... had the right basic coloring that Hitler had wished. The democ-
> racies had been fooled again and still more fooled were all those who
> had had faith in them. (7)

It also influenced Berlin; according to Ribbentrop's testimony at
Nuremberg, he went to Hitler after the Mussolini liberation, trying
to convince him again to deal with Stalin. "The Führer at first was
willing; he stretched out a line to the Russians. But the next day he
said: 'No'." The "line" was probably the Japanese one: on September 10, Sato, the Japanese Ambassador, called on Molotov and
informed the Russian that the Japanese government was ready
to send an envoy to travel to Moscow and Berlin to mediate for a
German-Russian peace. The Kremlin was silent for three days: only
on the 13th did Molotov call Sato again and very courteously refuse
the Japanese offer, adding that " 'under different circumstances the
Soviet government would have considered it its duty to accept the
Japanese offer of mediation' — a remark full of implications." (8)
On September 23 Hitler told Göbbels that he now favored a separate
agreement with Stalin. Göbbels asked whether, generally speaking,
Hitler would be willing to deal with Churchill, or would he reject
such a contact on principle. Hitler's answer was classic, an answer
to those who dubbed and are still dubbing him an idealist: "When
it comes to personal problems, there are no principles in politics."
He now believed that with the realistic Stalin there was a better
chance of agreement than with Churchill; but not at that moment,
for "what he [Hitler] wished to secure in the East, Stalin could not
renounce." On that day Hitler also expressed his respect for the
Russian dictator and he said to Göbbels that Mussolini was "no true
revolutionary in the sense of a Hitler or a Stalin." (9)

.   .   .   .

[*Russia: a favorable situation.*]   But a deal with Stalin did not
come about; Stalin was aware of the Washington and Quebec decisions; Italy was not the second, but the third front; as to the second,
the Anglo-Americans were to land in Western, not Southeastern
Europe; this suited him very well. And the Russian armies victoriously advanced. The time was approaching when Russia could not

gain very much by a separate peace with Germany. The "soft line" of the Russian propaganda aimed at the German military, the "Free Germany Committee," and the general Russian policy which wished to goad the German military leaders into overthrowing Hitler and signing a peace treaty or armistice with Russia (a decent and honorable treaty, no "unconditional surrender") was gradually abandoned; although for propaganda purposes the Moscow radio kept this line up until about after Teheran. Then it was no longer needed: the original purpose of a Soviet-German armistice would have been to bring about the Germans' voluntary evacuation of the Balkans and Poland and withdrawal to the approximately 1938–9 frontiers of an intact Germany, leaving behind Poland, Finland, the Baltic states and most of the Balkans — a vast vacuum which Stalin planned to fill quickly.

But now, when there was no Balkan invasion (nor peace chances between Germany and the West), the Soviet could see the vacuum forming without a Russian-German arrangement. Germany's defeat was approaching, and then there would be no power which would challenge Russia's plans in central-eastern Europe. At the Moscow conference in October, the Allies' political and military plans were first officially revealed to Stalin and Molotov; all this was confirmed in Teheran. From January 1944 onwards neither Russian propaganda, nor Stalin himself raised any more objections against the "unconditional surrender" formula, which now, for the first time, began definitely to favor the political aims of the Soviet Union, primarily in central-eastern Europe.

This was a development of tremendous significance. The Communists in central-eastern Europe now began to regard the Anglo-Americans as potentially inimical to their ultimate designs, while previously all of them, except for the few Polish, Finnish and Baltic comrades, eagerly banked on and hoped for Anglo-American victories in their areas. In Greece Communist and anti-Communist guerrillas now fought; ELAS refused to obey British orders. Skirmishes between different resistance groups occurred in Bulgaria, Albania, and in eastern Slovakia and the Carpatho-Ukraine; in Poland and Yugoslavia the struggle between the rival guerrilla organizations flared up. Expediency still reigned supreme: in Yugoslavia, Tito continued to depend on British supplies and illusions; in Hungary and Rumania, where the Communists were very insignificant, Moscow made them continue with their "popular front" policies, collaborating with the

other anti-German parties of the moderate Left and Center. But the
coming struggle between East and West, between Churchill and
Stalin, between the Atlantic and the Asiatic world slowly began to
cast its shadow upon central-eastern Europe. (*10*)

[*The Mediterranean campaign of 1943 comes to its end.*] On
September 16 Captain Butcher noted:

> Britain has only reluctantly acceded to *Overlord* [Normandy], but
> really has its heart in the Mediterranean and therefore prefers to go
> all-out in Italy and thence at the so-called "soft underbelly."

The German High Command paper on the "strategic position in
the beginning of the fifth year of the war" was indeed pessimistic
about the "soft underbelly"; it estimated 100,000 Tito-troops, 30,000
Mihailovič Chetniks, 15,000 Greek EAM, and 10,000 EDES partisans
in the Balkans; the report was also very ill-humoured about Hungary,
Rumania and their soldiery, and only slightly hopeful about the
Finns' and Bulgars' fighting qualities. But the campaign against the
"soft underbelly" came to a halt after the capture of Naples early in
October; the mountains, rocks and rapids of the Apennines were
difficult terrain and the advance was halted for long months. The
Allies were not even able to occupy the Dodecanese and the unde-
fended Italian islands of the Aegean; a heavy blow to Anglo-American
prestige fell in October–November when the three islands Cos, Leros,
Samos, which were taken by British Commandos in September, were
lost again to the Germans. The poor picture of the Aegean campaign
decisively influenced Turkey to remain out of the war. In Italy
Rommel favored a German retreat to the Po line even as late as
October 12 in a talk with the rescued Mussolini, and on October 11
Churchill urged, nudged, pestered Eisenhower again ". . . to exploit
our advantages throughout the Mediterranean as rapidly as possible." (*11*) But Eisenhower, aware of his limited strength and of the
orders, plans, and directives of his Commander-in-Chief and Chief
of Staff in Washington could only feel with his staff "that every atom
of our strength will be required to beat the Germans in Italy." On
that day the Allied thrust beyond Naples had finally bogged down in
the rain, mud, and the Germans' fire. A week later the Moscow
conference opened, with Eden, Hull and Molotov.

Effects of the Italian armistice within central-eastern Europe

[*Preliminary developments.*] Months before July 25 the eventual consequences of an Italian secession from the German side were apparent in the parts of the Balkans which since 1941 had belonged to the Italian sphere of influence. Here sporadic contacts between anti-German resistance groups and the Italians became routine; there were actual working agreements between some of the Chetnik and EDES commanders and the Italians; in some areas there was a silent armistice between Titoist guerrillas and Italian garrisons. On February 16, 1943, Hitler wrote Mussolini:

> Duce, I am very greatly preoccupied with the situation of the Balkans. However inviting it may seem to play one against the other of the two or three competing [guerrilla] parties, I regard this as running very grave dangers inasmuch as the three parties are unconditionally in agreement on one point: that is the limitless hatred against Italy and Germany.

Ribbentrop remonstrated with the Italian Ambassador five days later, accusing the Italian commanders, General Roatta in particular, of letting the Chetniks prosper in Montenegro. The Germans now introduced their *Weiss-Plan*, a late winter offensive against the partisans in Bosnia; the Tito forces were defeated but the Fifth Italian Army Corps did not take the important plateaux in the Bihać area fast enough, and Partisan units straggled into the Italian zones, where they felt relatively safe. Mihailović executed a similar manoeuvre in Serbia. (*1*) The German General Löhr met the Italian Robotti in Zagreb on May 5; Löhr tried to sound out Italian plans and dispositions, while he kept silent about German military projects: ten days later he suddenly attacked Chetnik forces in western Serbia and Montenegro, which offensive threw the Italian forces there off balance. The Germans now openly conspired with the Croats against Italian interests; Alfieri reported this to Mussolini. On May 19, however, Hitler wrote an indignant letter to the Duce, reproaching Biroli, the Italian military governor of Montenegro, for Germany had evidence that the latter had made various agreements with Chetniks and Partisans. Mussolini three days later ordered Biroli to attack the Mihailović forces; but all this was too late.

[*Albania.*] In Albania a change in the government in January served the resistance: the Conservatives and the Beys (the local aristocrats) dominated the "cabinet" led by Libohova, a former Foreign Minister under King Zog. This state of affairs was recommended by the Italian Governor, who reported to Rome that otherwise an Albanian rebellion would be fast forthcoming. Ciano reluctantly told Jacomoni to go ahead; yet the Albanian cabinet crisis lasted for two weeks, which was most disturbing: ". . . the government of Libohova is also up to tricks. The men who were most faithful to us are trying to abandon ship. Even Vrioni. Even Verlaci. These are signs of the times," wrote Ciano on February 1. He recommended the sending of a strong-armed general to Tirana instead of Jacomoni.

.   .   .   .

[*July 25–September 8.*]   Mussolini fell on July 25, and a few Italian soldiers went over at once to Chetniks, Partisans, EDES, EAM, Albanian units. Commanders of whole units contacted guerrillas to discuss common reconnaissance and eventual armed collaboration against the Germans. Other Italian commanders requested the guerrillas to help them contact British liaison officers; among the Italian troops themselves partisan units were being formed. The whole Balkan situation suddenly became extremely confused; in the turmoil the Germans, the Croats, and the Communists immediately made plans. (2)

The direct consequences of the Italian coup were not made officially clear to the Germans until August 5, when at Tarvisio Ribbentrop and Keitel met with the new Italian Foreign Minister, Guariglia, and with General Ambrosio, the Italian Chief of Staff. Guariglia promised that Italy would not deal with the Allies separately — tongue-in-cheek statement, tongue-in-cheek reception! — and told the Germans that the decision of the Italian government was to withdraw the Italian occupation forces from the Balkans and from southern France. The Germans now set out to plot with Croats, Bulgars and Albanians (and to a limited extent with quisling Serbs and Greeks also) to draft a new division of the Balkans, anticipating the estate which Italy was to leave behind her.

At dawn on August 27 a German division with tanks and armored cars appeared outside Ljubljana, the capital of Italian Slovenia, and demanded the evacuation of the city from the garrison commander of the Italian Fifteenth Corps. A six-hour ultimatum expired and fighting began; after several hours the Italians retreated. At other points Croatian army units and *Ustaši* attacked Italian outposts. (On that day "Tomislav II," that singularly aloof monarch, signed his "abdication" somewhere in Italy.)

The dissolution of the Italian armies in the Balkans thus had already reached its first stage when the armistice was announced on September 8. Immediately Germans and *Ustaši* attacked the Italians, while Tito's Partisans and Greek Communists took a hostile position, forcefully disarming the majority of Italian units which wished to cooperate with them.

[*The military consequences: Yugoslavia.*] From north to south, from the Julian Alps to the warm rocks of southern Greece, the armistice brought varied results. In Slovenia Germans and Croats encircled the Italian garrisons, which surrendered after fighting for a few days; some of the Italian soldiers fled to the mountains where they joined the partisans. The Austrian Nazis were jubilant; on September 10 Göbbels noted: "The Austrian Gauleiters are excelling themselves in presenting territorial claims." General Dietl, of Styrian descent and of Narvik fame, told Göbbels that his troops itched with eagerness to fight the Italians; all the buried memories of 1915 flared up again. Pavelič was glad about the Italian armistice; for a moment he considered it propitious to appeal to Croat national unity now: in a flair of enthusiasm he contacted the grand old man of Croat democracy and peasantry, Maček. But then the extremists of the *Ustaši* and the German envoy rebuked him. Nevertheless a wave of optimism swept Zagreb; except in the Adriatic sector, where the Partisans took full advantage of the flux, the Croats gained all those coveted territories which Italy had corralled before them in 1941. In the towns the Germans discriminated against the Italians, conscripted them for labor; in Zagreb the whole staff of the Italian Legation, which had declared itself for the King and for the legal government, was interned.

The Yugoslav government-in-exile was largely optimistic in regard to the situation; it moved from London to Cairo in September. But soon it was clear that, despite the excellent chances which the situation offered, the Anglo-Americans did not contemplate taking advantage of it, although they could have virtually walked into Fortress Europe through certain gaps. With the exception of the little equipment and few soldiers which the Mihailovič forces gained from the armistice, the pro-Allied group won but little. On September 11 the

Partisans took the port of Split (*3*) and held it until September 27;
they occupied almost all of Istria and southern Slovenia, where the
local population assisted them in outrages against the Italian inhabitants. On September 23 the Tito forces almost broke into Gorizia;
in Pisino the Croat Partisans "declared" the union of Istria with
Yugoslavia. The islands of Veglia, Cherso, and Lussino were occupied
by Tito forces in November. The Croats entered Zara, in agreement
with the Germans. (*4*)

Late in September General Nedič personally tried to persuade
Hitler to take a more lenient policy toward Serbia; he partly succeeded, as Hitler was considering the establishment of a somewhat
larger, more independent, yet pro-German Serbia. In Albania,
guerrilla bands roamed, and it took weeks before the Germans and
Bulgarians could control the situation, at least in the most important
towns and along the most strategic roads.

[*Greece.*] In Greece, where the relative mildness of the
Italian occupation had preceded the armistice with a strangely re-
appearing mutual benevolence between Italians and Greeks — these
two brothers of the sunny Mediterranean felt the common factor of
Hellenic humanism in their tradition — the Italian army immediately dissolved among the Greek partisans; only a few Black Shirts
and artillery units went over to the Germans. But this did not solve
the Italians' problems. The Pinerolo division which contacted EAM
in the Epirus was suddenly surrounded and disarmed, its soldiers
miserably interned or put to forced labor under awful conditions,
despite the agreement which their commanders had made with the
EAM representatives; there the EAM openly and brazenly disregarded the orders of the (British) Supreme Commander of the Eastern
Mediterranean. (*5*) The Acqui division, which was stationed in the
Ionian Islands, immediately turned on the Germans on September 8,
took prisoners and interned the German military technicians on the
islands, in accordance with the radio instructions of the Allies. A
German ultimatum to this division was unheeded. The Italians sent
signals to the Anglo-Americans for help; they held the islands and
requested the Allies to land, but no help came; all radio messages
were in vain. Then the Germans, many weeks later, back on their
feet again in Greece, attacked the Acqui: the German wrath was
murderous, and those who escaped death were herded into deadly
slave-labor camps.

The same pattern repeated itself in most of the Italian-occupied Aegean Islands and the Dodecanese, whereto, notwithstanding Churchill's desires, Allied forces did not penetrate. In Greece the important Italian holdings and mine concessions were taken over by the Germans; most of the Italian military and civilian officials, excepting those who returned to North Italy to join the Neo-Fascist Republic, were interned and transported to Germany.

[*Political consequences: division of the Italian sphere.*] The bankrupt Italian estate in the Balkans was divided by the Germans along these territorial lines:

A Hitler order on October 5, 1943, annexed Trieste, Istria and the adjacent regions and islands under the name of *Küstenland* — this was allotted to the eager Gauleiter of Styria. South Tyrol, under the name of *Alpenvorland*, was annexed to the *Gau Tirol-Vorarlberg*. Minor frontier regions in Italian Slovenia were also taken by the Germans. (6)

Croatia received Italian Slovenia and Dalmatia, but the most important coastal sectors were put under German administration. (7) The new German policy of befriending Serbia resulted in the fiction of an "independent" Montenegro (doubly fictitious as practically all of that mountain-state was in the hands of Partisans and Chetniks). There was no "independent" cabinet, but three German-sponsored Montenegrins entered the Nedič "government," whereupon it was promised to grant "Serbia" access to the Adriatic.

While Albania was also granted a semblance of "independence," the Kossovo district was taken from the Albanians and "allotted" to Serbia in a somewhat obscure manner. For the first time since 1941, the rights of Serbia to the Banat were recognized, with the proviso that the German ethnic group in that territory had special, extra-territorial, "master race" privileges. In this clumsy juggling with their satellites, the Germans also made vague promises to Nedič concerning Bosnia to the detriment of Pavelič-Croatia.

The Bulgarians gained further territories in Macedonia, concerning which the previously cautious German policy changed: the Bulgarian incorporation of Macedonia was encouraged. The Bulgarian government tried to set up a Bulgarian "University" at Skoplje, and pressed the Macedonians to opt for Bulgarian citizenship. Italian-occupied Thrace was "restored" to "Greece," which, like "Serbia," was promised independence, and it was hinted by the Germans that "Greece" might receive the Dodecanese and Corfu after the war.

After the war! Nobody, not even the hired men of the Germans could take these plans, projects, promises, even the actual allotments, seriously. For in October 1943 most of these territories were either already controlled by anti-German forces, or formed a vast, mysterious no-man's-land of high mountains and long valleys. Neither the Germans nor their satellites could exercise their sovereignty over their new lands — thus the interregnal period of Europe following the German defeat had practically begun in the Balkans by September 1943. From this unnecessary interregnum Hitler, partly and temporarily, and Stalin, fully and permanently, profited.

.   .   .   .

These were the direct effects of the Italian armistice in the Balkans; the indirect effects in other parts of central-eastern Europe were not less important.

[*Finland's separate peace attempts: Phase III.*]   In August 1943 Finnish efforts toward a separate peace entered their third phase. On August 23 a memorandum by thirty-three leading Finnish personalities was presented to the government, urging the continued investigation of peace possibilities with steady effort and sincerity. The United States repeated their *bona officia* offer at the same time, and a Finnish-American Society was formed in Helsinki to further cultural and economic contacts between the two countries. At the end of August the first contact between Finland and Russia was made through the mediation of the Belgian Legation in Stockholm.

Through this contact, called "The Channel," it was made known that the Soviets were ready to examine the Finnish peace proposals, dealing now with concrete territorial issues. Helsinki requested a revision of the 1940 frontier in Karelia and compensation in Eastern Karelia for territories ceded elsewhere in the Moscow Peace; she was willing to cede the islands in the Finnish Gulf, except Suursaari, to Russia. Within a week, the Soviet government rejected these proposals. On September 10 new Finnish proposals were given, among which the most important innovation was that the major differences be discussed with the help of negotiators. "The Channel," upon receiving these proposals, told the Finns that they very obviously did not furnish enough new material to provide a basis of new negotiations with the Russians, and consequently the episode came to an end.

America repeated her *bona officia* offer in September, and again in November, but the unfruitful experience with the American non-committal methods in the spring made Ryti, rightly or wrongly, let the offer pass. (Perhaps Procopé, the Finnish Minister to Washington, influenced Helsinki with dispatches reflecting his dark pessimism and strong criticism concerning American foreign policy.) Yet Finland's dilemma was regarded with considerable sympathy in London and Washington; in August and September Helsinki twice was secretly sounded out by the Anglo-American military intelligence as to what Finland would do in the case of an Allied invasion of northern Scandinavia; and Helsinki indicated that Finland would not resist, provided the Allied troops were Anglo-Americans, not Russians.

This communication impressed Cordell Hull; on September 21 he told the Swedish Minister in Washington that he understood Finland's difficult situation; Finland was merely fighting for her old frontiers. Helsinki also learned of Hull's alleged private views, according to which he did not yet regard a Finnish-Soviet peace possible. At the same time, according to Procopé, "a high British military source" even expressed the opinion that for political and post-war reasons the conclusion of a Finnish-Soviet peace did not now seem to be particularly favored by the Western Allies. And when, also on September 21, the Swedish Minister to Moscow, Assarson, said to Molotov that Finland seemed ready for a separate peace, only to receive the cold answer that in view of the "lack" of Finnish proposals to the Soviet government it seemed that Finland was neither ready for nor wished an agreement, Stockholm informed Helsinki of Sweden's own opinion: it would be better for Finland to wait a while.

It was Finland's good fortune that more than just a Brenner Pass separated her from Germany; also, German officials were divided in regard to Finland's position. The German Minister to Finland seemed to silently understand the attempts of the Linkomies government, while Göbbels, aware now of the ties and sympathies of Marshal Mannerheim, exclaimed against him and pinned his hopes on Ryti. Early in October Hitler wrote a letter to the Finnish President, requesting a direct commitment that Finland would not negotiate separately with the Allies. Ryti, after having consulted the Foreign Affairs Committee of the Finnish parliament, cautiously but firmly refused this request on October 27. On November 4 Ribbentrop repeated the German request on the Foreign Office level and in a more detailed and specific memorandum. The Foreign Affairs' Committee set out to draft an answer, delayed it, finally deciding upon it a month later; the answer was again "no"; the note was sent to Berlin on January 4, 1944.

[*The fourth phase.*]   Meanwhile the fourth phase of Finland's peace story opened on November 20, 1943, that is, after the Moscow and before the Teheran Conferences. By that time, the Soviets had begun to abandon the consideration of a Soviet-German separate peace, as they now knew that the strategic plans of the Anglo-Americans were of such scope and character that they did not interfere with the Soviet aim to overrun central-eastern Europe and reach their territorial goals in the last phase of the war. Now it seemed propitious to Moscow to conclude a "reasonable" separate peace with Finland, in order to hasten the rapid collapse of Germany, which the Kremlin now eagerly wished. The Soviets feared lest a change occur in the world situation which might revise Anglo-American plans and upset Russian ones. For political reasons it was also advantageous to Russia that she demonstrate her "Allied unity" spirit by announcing her willingness to negotiate with Finland, something which would greatly please London, Washington, and British and American public opinion in general. Thus on November 20 Ambassadress Kollontay, with unusual openness for a Soviet diplomat, told Boheman in Stockholm to communicate these three points to the Finns: first, a Finnish delegate was welcome to come to Moscow; second, the Finnish proposals should be communicated in advance; third, the Soviet Union did not wish to injure Finnish independence nor to reduce Finland to a province. On November 26 and 27 the Finnish Foreign Affairs' Committee discussed these proposals and decided to agree to them. Thus began the fourth phase of the Finnish-Russian peace attempts.

. . . .

The Italian events had far-reaching effects in Hungary, Rumania, Bulgaria and Slovakia also.

It was not yet clear what the difference between armistice and peace really was. The Italian example was confusing. It was, however, now appreciated that in contrast to previous historical practice, armistices now amounted to preliminary peace treaties. (*8*)

[*Political consequences: Bulgaria.*]   In Sofia, Tsankov, Gabrovski, and the pro-Germans bitterly fought pro-Allied groups; the highest circles of the state, led by Boris, cautiously tipped the balance in favor of the latter. Thus, by August 1943, Sofia newspapers began to express pan-Slav sentiments, and stray allusions to historic Bulgar-Russian amity appeared. Then, on August 28, Boris suddenly died. The cause of his death is still a mystery today: it was widely thought that German agents had poisoned him, but post-war German evidence does not substantiate this. The Germans had even tried to investigate the death of Boris; Hitler thought that perhaps the Italians had poisoned the Bulgar Tsar, but this was not true. The death of Boris made the Bulgar situation more confused. His little son became Tsar Simeon II; a regency was set up with three members — Prince Kyrill, and the statesmen Filov and Michov. The Bulgar government was reshuffled and gained a more conservative tinge. With tongue in cheek, the Bulgars accepted the German notes, answered them, took over occupational duties in Macedonia; but they watched with foremost interest the approaching Russian armies, while on the other flank of the Balkans they expected a British-American offensive.

[*Slovakia.*]   In Slovakia, the Germans' "model protectorate," the Tiso government also took notice of the changing times — certain Slovak newspapers and government statements emphasized the right to life of the small states of Europe; more allusions were made to the ties which bound Catholic Slovakia to Rome. (9) The Germans did not directly intervene with Tiso, who ably manoeuvred with the leaders of the German minority against the dangers of the SS. His situation was temporarily brightened by the relatively good economic situation; Slovak industry, previously hindered by the Czechs, now prospered. Nevertheless, anti-Tiso resistance grew; the Communists also appeared. There were partisans in the Slovak mountains, and in the autumn campaign of retreat on the Eastern Front two Slovak brigades went over to the Russians.

[*Hungary offers surrender to the Western Allies.*]   Most interesting, then, were the diplomatic effects of the Italian armistice. By October 1943 all three "satellites," Hungary, Rumania, and Bulgaria, had contacted the Anglo-Americans in one way or another. All three were anxious lest the other rival precede them and win points with the future victors; Hungary led in this almost fantastic race. On August 9, a representative of the Kállay government made an agreement with Knatchbull-Hugessen, the British Ambassador in Turkey, in which

Hungary committed herself not to fire at nor intercept British and American planes crossing Hungary on bombing missions from Italy; in exchange, British or American planes would not bomb Hungarian cities or targets. For the first time the American Air Force, four days later, bombed Wiener-Neustadt in daylight, crossing over Hungary without disturbance; until early April 1944 Hungary was the only state in Axis-controlled Europe which, except for two small Russian raids in 1942, was not bombed by the Allied air forces.

On August 14 the Badoglio government declared Rome an open city; next day the official newspaper *Pester Lloyd* in Budapest published an editorial which claimed that Hungary had no quarrels with the Anglo-Saxon Powers and implied that the proclaiming of Budapest to be an open city was under consideration. On August 17 Kállay, who, with other elder statesmen, thought that Allied victory was a matter of weeks now, spoke on the Hungarian radio and referred to the universally pacific desires of the Magyar people. Within twenty-four hours Kállay, through his contacts, communicated this message to the British Embassy in Turkey:

> Prime Minister Kállay, Minister of Interior Keresztes-Fischer and the leading personalities of the Hungarian Foreign Office inform the Allies that they accept unconditional surrender and are anxious to do everything to have this realized as soon as possible. They are willing to follow advice of the Allies as to when and how it can be best carried out.   (10)

The British answer came, delayed, on September 9:

> His Majesty's Government (further HMG) would like to see some more authoritative credentials which would presumably be communicated through any channel which the Hungarian Government (further HG) thought advisable . . .

The British requested a public announcement, if possible; but if this was out of the question, minor sabotage against the Germans should begin. Now the Hungarian Consul in Istanbul, Ujváry, came to Budapest, and another message was sent through him:

> The HG do their utmost in order to avoid such a situation in which Hungarian troops would be forced to fight Anglo-American troops. For this reason the HG's chief endeavor is to avoid German occupation of Hungary. . . . The HG are obliged to refrain from any dan-

gerous and premature act jeopardizing this endeavor, all the more so because Germany — due to Hungary's increasingly aloof policy and specially due to Italian events — is watching with growing suspicion Hungarian moves. On the other hand the fate of Italy had a terrifying effect on important factors of Hungarian political and public life whose disposition cannot be ignored by the Government.

The HG are moreover impelled to greater precaution by the not excluded possibility of an armistice or an understanding between Germany and Russia, or that the Russian Army might reach sooner Hungarian territory than the Allied troops. If these possibilities might find Hungary in a disarmed state then even Hungary's and the Danubian basin's internal order could not be maintained . . .

This Hungarian communication did not satisfy the British. The Hungarian government also asked them not to send a British Military Mission to Hungary as yet; the British then said that this would be "essentially a conspirational party"; they also wished to enter into discussions with Hungarian staff officers and preferred that further negotiations be carried on through Lisbon. These exchanges extended into October. Contact was now established between Hungary and the United States, through Eckhardt in New York and through Archduke Otto Habsburg, who was well known by President Roosevelt; somewhat later Baron Bessenyey, the Hungarian Minister to Switzerland, got in touch with Allen Dulles of the OSS in Berne.

Grand Admiral Raeder, who represented Hitler at the funeral of Boris, reported that complete lack of belief in the success of the German arms existed in the Balkans. Back from Sofia, Raeder delivered a present from Hitler, a river yacht to Admiral Horthy in Budapest; but on Hitler's orders he refused to dine with Kállay, and the Hungarian press gave very limited space to the visit. The new Hungarian Foreign Minister, Ghiczy, was a known anti-Nazi, of monarchist and pro-Allied leanings, and even within the notoriously pro-German General Staff changes occurred: the Chief of Staff was now General Szombathelyi, replacing the German-born Werth. The Supreme War Council meeting early in September envisaged a negotiated peace, and another German request for the sending of Hungarian occupation troops to the Balkans was refused.

[*Rumanian attempts.*] The Rumanians also acted quickly. Less than twenty-four hours after Mussolini's arrest, Mihai Antonescu contacted the new Italian Foreign Minister:

Please inquire whether His Excellency Guariglia is disposed to establish an alliance with us, if he wants to act in coordination with that united front which I for some time have offered to Italy and to lead this action of a group of States wishing to act for their own and Europe's salvation. (*11*)

Guariglia answered that his freedom of action was hampered; yet one of the first acts of his ministry was to urge a rapid rapprochement between Hungary and Rumania. Mihai Antonescu, on the other hand, pursued illusions. He told Bova Scoppa that he was convinced that the Anglo-Americans had a tremendous army in the Near East, ready to jump forward.

Early in August Antonescu learned that the British were unwilling to deal with him personally and on August 6 he complained to the Italian envoy:

We witness today the paradox that America rises to defend the eternal values of European civilization while English shortsightedness seems to destroy them.

He had established some contact with the American Embassy in Madrid; he informed Ambassador Hayes that Rumania was "willing" to cede Bukovina and Bessarabia. He also got together with Maniu, that silent grand old man of the opposition. They agreed to send a member of the Peasant Party, Cretzianu, as Rumanian Ambassador to Turkey, with full diplomatic powers to negotiate with the Anglo-Americans. Through Bratianu and other confidants, King Mihai was informed and eagerly gave his consent. (On October 17 the British government informed the Rumanians of their terms in a note similar to that given to Hungary in September.) Truly, as R. W. Markham put it:

Cretzianu had one of the strangest diplomatic missions in history; he was ostensibly to represent a pro-Nazi dictator, but actually was to help a pro-Allied opposition group that was trying to overthrow the dictator — which it eventually did.

But nothing was strange in the Balkans in those days.

[*The recognition problem concerning the two Italies.*] The strangeness was reflected in the way these governments handled the risky situation which arose with the Italian armistice and the subsequent formation of the Neo-Fascist Republic in northern Italy. Contrary to German wishes, none of the Italian residents, soldiers, workers, officials were interned in Hungary, Rumania, Bulgaria, not even in Slovakia. Throughout the Balkans, the majority of Italian diplomats and officials declared themselves for the King.

Thereafter Hungary and Rumania silently continued to recognize the Badoglio government (even after that government had declared war on Germany on October 13), and despite insistent German demands, the Legation buildings were not turned over to the Neo-Fascist representatives until later. After a furious German protest the Kállay government was forced to issue, on September 18, a flexible statement which implied that Hungary continued with the recognition of the royal government and that she was considering recognizing the new Mussolini régime — which she eventually did. Rumania watched Hungary anxiously, knowing that the Allies watched them both; a week later a not less strange and twisted communiqué in Bucharest announced the Rumanian recognition of Mussolini's "Italian Social Republic," after Mussolini in vain had put a personal telephone call through to Bova Scoppa, who nevertheless refused to be influenced by the former Duce's personal arguments. Rumania thereby ceased to recognize Badoglio, but the Badoglio diplomats remained free, as did the personnel of the minor craft of the Italian Black Sea flotilla, which also proclaimed its loyalty to the King. From September 27 there really were two separate Italian legations in Bucharest. When the Neo-Fascist "Minister," Odenigo, finally took over, the Rumanian Premier received him; his *agrément* was given, but somehow it was avoided that Odenigo present his credentials to King Michael in the routine manner. (*12*)

Bulgaria hesitated for awhile. SS leaders, Kaltenbrunner first among them, were proposing to Hitler that he abandon Germany's "soft" policy toward Bulgaria and support instead a pro-German Serbia and Albania, even taking territories away from the Bulgars if necessary; when these rumors reached Sofia, it was finally decided to recognize the Neo-Fascist régime on September 28, one day after Rumania. Weeks later the Badoglio Minister was politely asked to hand the Legation building over to his Fascist successor. Slovakia at once recognized the Mussolini "government," but even in Bratislava the diplomatic effects of the changing winds could be seen: the Tiso régime was friendly towards the Badoglio diplomats, silently dodging a German request; they were not interned.

[*German counterplans.*]   These actions were painfully and angrily noted in Berlin, and while preventive measures were not possible
in all cases, the Germans generally knew where they stood — perhaps
Rumania was an exception, for Hitler, due to emotional associations,
thought Ion Antonescu to be his truly faithful ally. On September 23,
Göbbels wrote that Horthy would like very much "to jump off," but
the Führer was taking countermeasures; Kállay was "a perfect swine"
while Antonescu was "good so far as a Balkanese is good." The Nazi
and pro-German elements in Hungary now began to plot with the
SS for the eventual overthrow of the Kállay régime, and in October
the SS envoy Veesenmeyer secretly met the Arrow-Cross leader
Szálasi in Hungary, who told him that a revolution against the régime
was not possible without German support. At the same time Prince
Kyrill and the Bulgarian regents paid a visit to Hitler; a month later
the Bulgarian Premier and his new Foreign Minister, Sismanov, paid
their homages at Klessheim, and Hitler was slightly reassured concerning Bulgaria. On October 26 Hitler had received intelligence
about Finland's peace feelers; on November 19 he heard about Hungary and Rumania. On November 10 Göbbels wrote that, if and
when the Balkan invasion came, "Hungary would jump first, with her
intact army, because of later anti-Rumanian plans. . . . Hungary's
behavior is perfidious and shameless." In the same month the Bishop
of Sofia made a strong anti-German and anti-government speech at
the mass funeral which followed an RAF bombing of Sofia, and in
Bucharest, Mihai Antonescu delivered a speech at the University
there, replete with obscure historical allusions but also discernibly
anti-German. He had established another contact with the Western
Allies through his envoy Dimitrescu in Lisbon. (*13*) Indeed, "jumping off" was the problem of those days.

The resistance movements at the end of 1943

In 1943 German policy in certain occupied territories turned toward
the extreme. Where there had been sporadic efforts to collaborate
with the nationalist-conservative elements, these were abandoned.
Collaboration with primitive movements of National-Bolshevist character — e.g., some Ukrainians, Arrow-Cross in Hungary, Iron Guard
in Rumania — began. The posts of the former Foreign Ministry
plenipotentiaries in Serbia, Greece, and Albania were abolished, and
Göring's man, the SA Neubacher, became a "special plenipotentiary

for south-eastern Europe." The SS gradually became entrusted with
independent policymaking and executive functions. (*1*)

While the influence of the British broadcasts was everywhere great,
and Allied agents' messages sparked throughout the night, the Germans
increased their interference and tried to crush the foci of resistance.
By the end of 1943, anti-German sentiment prevailed throughout the
Baltic states, and in miserable, hungry, oppressed Estonia and Latvia,
SS and SD forces began to skirmish with the national resistance. (*2*)
The Vatican protested to Ribbentrop against the cruel German treatment of the Poles and the persecution of the religious in November
1942 and again in March 1943, but to no avail. German wrath rose
to barbaric peaks. An SS order established the "collective responsibility of members of families of assassins and saboteurs" in Poland.
The "resistance from above" in Hungary, Rumania and Bulgaria
brought German counter-measures: when the Cardinal-Primate Serédi
of Hungary in a speech late in 1943 stated that racialist and totalitarian ideas were wholly alien to Hungarian traditions, Ribbentrop
was incensed. In Rumania, Maniu, although closely watched, acted
as a nucleus of resistance plans; in November 1943 the Germans demanded his "elimination." Antonescu sent Maniu a message requesting that he stop his activities, as the Germans were constantly urging
his arrest; Maniu did not commit himself and answered Antonescu in
a vein he had used before: "I find it unjust for you to engage the people
in a death struggle without their consent . . . after the recovery of
Bessarabia and Bukovina you had no right to engage Rumania on the
side of the Axis in an ideological war against Russia. You committed
a crime by engaging the Rumanian Army in a war on Russian soil."
That people like Maniu in Rumania, Bajcsy-Zsilinszky in Hungary,
Petkov in Bulgaria could speak thus without immediate danger of
arrest in November 1943 showed that much had changed.

But the whole trend of the resistance movements had changed also.
And this indicated — if not in Hungary, Rumania and Bulgaria —
that the change of the times was not in the direction which Maniu,
Bajcsy-Zsilinszky, and Petkov envisaged and on which they were so
courageously staking their fortunes.

.   .   .   .

[*The struggle within Yugoslavia.*] Events within Yugoslavia
were particularly pointing toward this change. There Tito now overshadowed Mihailovič. On November 25, 1942, the first meeting of

Tito's Communist-organized "Anti-Fascist Liberation Assembly" met at Bihać; the first "parliament" of Tito-Yugoslavia met at Jajce a year later, on November 29, 1943, a date which is still being celebrated as the birthday of the New Yugoslavia. The Jajce proclamations clearly showed the future policy and tendencies of Tito and his cohorts; in December Tito announced that it was "forbidden" for King Peter to return to Yugoslavia until after "liberation" when "the people" were to announce whether they wanted him or not.

What happened within Yugoslavia from Bihać to Jajce was definitely a reflection of the Great Powers' policies and relations. Ridden with frequent crises, the prestige of the Yugoslav exile government paled; its continuous movings from Canada to London, and again to Cairo during fifteen months in 1942–43, rendered it impossible that the government exercise even its minimal functions. There were also the sad and inevitable intrigues. Throughout 1943 the position of Mihailović weakened, notwithstanding the rather successful German counterattack against Tito from January to April 1943 (in which the latter suffered almost 10,000 casualties). Also, the Germans had reoccupied Bihać. After the worst crisis broke within the Yugoslav government-in-exile, in December 1942, Mihailović became more active; he attacked German forces steadily throughout the spring. Only when he was exhausted and saw that Britain and America were unwilling to give him unconditional support did he resume his local contacts with the Italians. The Tito-Mihailović controversy impressed the German command in Yugoslavia; at the time of the Italian armistice there were two schools of thought in Berlin: Hitler, peculiarly impressed with Nedić, decided to fight against both Mihailović-Chetniks and Tito-Partisans, while important people in the Foreign Ministry, the local Army generals and General Warlimont of the High Command wished to bring about an armistice between the Chetniks and Germans. But Hitler overruled these plans.

By the end of 1943 Tito was the supreme factor in Yugoslavia. The Germans had to concede this — after an acid controversy between different ministries, it was decided in December, among other things, that captured members of the Allied military missions to the Partisans should be treated as prisoners-of-war instead of illegal fighters, *franc-tireurs*, "for reasons of expediency." On the last day of the year, Beneš, just having returned from Moscow, met the Yugoslav Premier, Purić; the Czech expressed his optimism concerning the postwar spirit of the Soviets, and advised the Yugoslav statesman to cope with the new winds, the new climates of central-eastern Europe. Soon afterwards, to counter Jajce, Mihailovič convoked a "National Conference" on the icy, windswept plateaux of the Ravna Gora in January 1944, (3) but this was not much more than a gesture; meanwhile Tito advanced, and at the end of January occupied the Banyaluka region. True, he soon was to face a formidable German counteroffensive, threatening him with great dangers, even military annihilation, but politically Tito had little to fear. Croats were going over to the Partisans now in great numbers — even former *Ustaši* leaders, Leontič, Nazor, Pirts. By that time the real heroes of Balkan resistance, Mihailovič, Kupi in Albania, Zervas in Greece, had faded; some of them were dubbed German collaborationists; the Communists were the apparent heroes of the day.

[*Within Greece.*] Greek politics were eventful and confusing; the Greeks fought and argued on three fronts. There was the German-imposed "government," in which Tsolakoglu intrigued against Gotzamanis, and Rhallis against Logothetopoulos. General Löhr, the new German Commander-in-Chief in south-eastern Europe, was an Austrian with considerable political skill; first he put Logothetopoulos into power; then came Rhallis, who was more of a clever *attentiste* (this term was quite widespread in the Balkans throughout the war, borrowed from the political dictionary of Vichy, and denoting a person who cautiously watched and waited for the war fortunes to take their final, decisive turn).

There was the Greek government-in-exile which finally settled in Cairo (where the Soviet intelligence organs could easily profit from the formidable amount of gossip and patter which fluttered in Cairo and Alexandria, and in which the wealthy and influential Egyptian Greek community was involved). Communist propaganda had its first successes. In the spring of 1943 signs of mutiny appeared among the Greek brigades and sailors in Egypt. Meanwhile the Greek exile government was regarded with some annoyance by the British and American governments; when King George II requested advice from Churchill and Eden, he was told to return to Greece soon after liberation and hold a free plebiscite. The honest Premier, Tsouderos, appealed over the radio with his frail voice for unity, but everybody was sceptical as the Yugoslav experience unfolded before the Greek cabinet; British policy was not clear, and the BBC, while not quite in favor of the Communists, did not have a good word for Zervas'

nationalist resistance forces. The Greek government was deeply disillusioned, and in September turned to Hull and Admiral Leahy,
secretly requesting that American troops be sent to participate in the
liberation and occupation of Greece: such was their distrust of the
British. But the American attitude was not encouraging; in Woodhouse's words,

> The cynical observer would incline to stress three characteristics of
> the process by which American opinion was formed: none of them
> was reproduced in England, though there were others just as harm-
> ful. The first was a Greek minority in the USA, who might be expected
> to know their fellow Greeks, and whose collective vote was important.
> This minority was inclined sympathetically towards EAM/ELAS,
> partly because that organisation alone paid attention to propaganda
> abroad; partly because it was simplest to think of Greece's gallant
> struggle in terms of one protagonist, and the natural one was the only
> organisation that extended over the whole country. The second thing
> was the lurking remnant of the ancient grudge against England, which
> encouraged propagandists of EAM to argue that they were only doing
> what the Americans themselves had done in 1776; the more recent
> parallels of Palestine and Eire gave conviction to the argument. The
> current form of the ancient grudge was to assume that all British
> diplomats were twice as slick as the plain American, and that every-
> thing the English did in any country outside their own was another
> manifestation of their notorious imperialism. The third thing was the
> American belief that kings, however ornamental at cocktail parties,
> were out of place on thrones. (4)

And the lack of American realism concerning the Balkans was reflected in a State Department publication, the previously cited *Post-
War Foreign Policy Preparations*, which as late as 1950 described the
1943 Balkan situation thus:

> Internal political developments with respect to Greece and Yugo-
> slavia already foreshadowed the difficulties that were to be encoun-
> tered in reestablishing acceptable governments in these nations upon
> their liberation . . .

But, may we ask, acceptable to whom? Acceptable to all parties, the
phrasing indicates, including Soviet Russia and the Greek Communists.

[*The Greek civil war: the Communist manoeuvres.*] For the Greek situation, confusing as it was, moved inexorably in a Communist-inspired direction. KKE, the Communist Party, had completed the superstructure of EAM, their "national front" (in line with Soviet political strategy, the official figurehead Secretary-General, Econo-mou, was still only a non-Communist fellow-traveller); in May 1943 an unknown Greek army officer, Sarafis, surrendered to ELAS and, strangely enough, was made supreme commander a few months later. ELAS had already attacked rival resistance formations; one of these, EKKA, surrendered; the other, PAO, was ruthlessly eliminated and its leader, Psarros, killed; Zervas' nationalist guerrillas, EDES, con-tinued to resist. Yet the Communists signed limited armistices and collaborated with the Bulgarians in Thrace and Macedonia; in cer-tain instances there were truces arranged between ELAS and the Germans. (5) The Germans, who since the Italian armistice had been prepared for the evacuation of Greece, finally decided to profit from the presence of ELAS and from what they correctly deemed to be an inevitable conflict between the Communists and the British-led forces of liberation: when in 1944 the German retreat began, arms and ammunition were dumped and left behind at strategic points where they would fall into ELAS hands; the Germans knew that these arms would immediately produce skirmishes within Greece, which would impede the British pursuit of the orderly German with-drawal.

In the summer of 1943 British efforts and misleading manoeuvres indicating the immediately pending invasion of Greece brought about an abatement in the Greek civil war, but after the Italian armistice it was clear that the Allies would not come before, at best, the late spring of the following year. ELAS now planned to control the entire field. On October 8 ELAS attacked EDES and the smaller nation-alist guerrillas. Within a week, the civil war flared up all along the mountain fronts with great brutality; some British liaison officers were involved, and a New Zealand officer was killed by the Communists. These rumblings of a Third World War impressed Churchill, and, fortunately for the Greek government-in-exile, British support of ELAS abated, became conditional, and never developed into all-out aid comparable to that which Tito was receiving.

[*Within Albania.*] In Albania (where the Communist Party in 1941 numbered but fifty members), the National Republicans, the

Zog-Monarchists and the Independents, led by Frasheri, Kupi, Kryeziu, noticed the appearance and rapid success of a previously unknown individual, the Communist organizer, Enver Hoxha. By 1944 Hoxha developed into an important personage, making clever local deals with the Germans and vanishing in the mountains before his guerrilla adversaries. Julian Amery quoted an Albanian friend as saying in early 1944:

> There are three parties in Albania: the agents of Germany, the agents of Russia, and the agents of England. That is quite natural, but what none of us can understand is why the agents of Russia are paid in English gold.

[*Within Bulgaria.*]   By the end of 1943 the unimpeded activities of the Russian Legation in Sofia, the comparatively easy movement of agents coming from Russia, and the developing pan-Slav trend of Soviet propaganda produced a substantial Communist underground in Bulgaria also. While "resistance from above" still predominated with Agrarians, Liberals, Conservatives, men such as Peshev, Burov, Petkov, G. Dimitrov, and Mushanov, Macedonian-style terrorism raised its head; sabotage and assassination suddenly became more frequent: in the autumn two prominent pro-Germans, Lukov and Janov, were ambushed and killed.

[*Within Czechoslovakia.*]   Further north, German power was still strongly felt because of the geographic and strategic importance of that region. In August 1943 the government of the Czech Protectorate was reorganized. A new ministry was set up under Karl Hermann Frank, the former Sudeten German leader, who, along with Frick's "Permanent Deputy," the SS plenipotentiary, Daluege, was far more important than the new Reich Protector, Frick. Frank strongly supported the Czech quisling, Emanuel Moravec, while he maintained some suspicion concerning the "Premier," Krejči. Moravec, aware of the pro-Western sentiment prevalent among the Czech youth, late in 1943 embarked on a great educational plan, the so-called *Kuratorium*, a central fund and institution to "re-educate" the Czech youth. All this was, of course, in vain. But there was not much open Czech resistance; the Germans needed Czech agriculture and the Czech factories, and in September 1943 Göbbels reported "Czechia" as being relatively quiet, while Poland was, as always, afire.

[*Within Poland.*] The Home Army now operated openly. But it was harassed not only by German forces, but by the appearance of the Communist underground and also by Ukrainian and Lithuanian bands. While Polish defiance was mounting in the face of the Germans — by the end of 1943 about two hundred resistance newspapers and periodicals were being published — the policies of the German administration began to diverge considerably. Frank, about whom even Hitler dropped an angry remark — "too capricious" — continued with his self-imposed "Western" policies: in August he set up two "defense councils," and he spoke to the Poles at least once of the approaching Soviet danger, cautiously and surprisingly praising Polish culture and the "loyal understanding" of those Poles who were collaborating with the Germans. But the SS and Rosenberg, Himmler, and Göbbels, on the other hand, planned to support the National-Bolshevist elements in the eastern lands, and began to subsidize Vlassov and Ukrainian "Armies of Liberation." (*6*) The Ukrainian bands caused turmoil and terrorized the population in eastern Poland, but by the end of 1943 the independent, anti-German, anti-Russian, anti-Polish "Banderowci," led by the mysterious Bandera, overshadowed the importance of the German-sponsored Ukrainians, who were represented by the weakling "Professor" Kubiyovič. (*7*) The nihilistic, Eastern *Götterdämmerung* spirit of the Nazis could be detected in the declaration which Gauleiter Koch made to his officials on New Year's Day, 1944:

> The shortened front-lines confront us with new and unaccustomed duties; our tasks differ from 1942. Instead of building up, we are now winding up.

Now it was the Russians who were building up.

[*Soviet policy.*] On September 4, 1943, a Soviet decree restored the rights of the Orthodox Church in Russia; the Holy Synod and Moscow Patriarchate were reestablished; as Stalin's biographer stated, "Russia's influence in the Balkans is worth a Greek Orthodox Mass [Stalin] might have said to himself." (*8*)

The trend of Russian-Polish relations was, of course, evident. But Yugoslavia proved to be another clear example of how Soviet-directed propaganda and Russian diplomacy worked hand in hand. This is how the international implications of the Tito-Mihailovič civil war developed: on July 28, 1942, the London *Daily Worker* accused Mihailovič of collaborating with the Axis, and on August 3 the Assistant Soviet Foreign Commissar officially accused Mihailovič before the assembled foreign diplomats and the press. In November 1943 the Soviets sent a military mission to Tito. Perhaps guided also by a faint trust in true pan-Slavism, the Yugoslav exile government then decided on a subtle and clever approach. Purič proposed a close Russian-Yugoslav postwar friendship and alliance treaty to the Kremlin: a truly desperate, yet not unwise attempt! But Novikov, the Russian Ambassador to the exile governments in London, was ostentatiously rude, and on December 10 the Yugoslavs were informed of Moscow's rejection. And, when, three weeks later, Purič met Beneš, the latter told the Yugoslav Premier that the Soviets would only deal with a government which was fully in accord with their own terms and aims.

·   ·   ·   ·   ·   ·   ·

[*Anglo-American propaganda in favor of Tito.*] By November 1943 there was scarcely no great British or American daily which did not criticize the Chetniks in one way or another and which did not eulogize Tito with great fervor. The London *Times* published extreme pro-Tito editorials; the tenor of the American and British broadcasts was the same. In March 1943 a British mission was established to work with Tito; its leader, Brigadier Fitzroy MacLean, (*9*) became a friend of Tito and sent optimistic reports to London. Other Britishers were also sufficiently impressed with Tito's deeds (later Randolph Churchill arrived); Croats and Titoists influenced the BBC and British intelligence against Mihailovič. (*10*) In May an American mission under Colonel Seitz arrived at Mihailovič' headquarters, and the British Brigadier, Armstrong, was sent there in August; but by then Tito was far ahead of Mihailovič in the race for Allied favors. To be sure, Mihailovič himself contributed to his doom a bit, due to his sensitive, fiery Serb personality. He spoke to his leaders at Lipova in February 1943, bitterly criticizing the British for "betraying" him and helping Tito instead of himself; he referred to the vainly promised British help in the campaign days of 1941. Churchill was very angry about the Lipova speech and sent a reprimanding note to the exile government. On May 7, Eden strongly requested the Yugoslav government to order Mihailovič at once to stop his collaboration with the Italians and with the Nedič gendarmerie forces and to make an effort to reach an agreement with the Partisans. After some hesitation, Mihailovič agreed to these terms on June 19.

By that time, however, machine-guns, food and ammunition had been parachuted to the Tito forces, and the general directives of the British High Command, Middle East, definitely favored Tito over Mihailovič, occasionally even overruling American-Mihailovič contacts. In July the British High Command requested Mihailovič to stop his widespread guerrilla operations and withdraw his forces to the Kopaonik Plateau and its immediate area; the fighting capacities and potentialities of the Chetnik forces were underestimated. An angry radio dispute developed, after which the High Command revoked the initial dispatch.

By the time of the Italian armistice the propaganda battle of Tito's was won. Official American propaganda was dull and noncommittal and, as even one of the directors of the OWI recalled:

> Instead of encouraging the Yugoslavs to rally around Peter, Mihailovic or Tito, [official American radio propaganda] held up to them an unattainable ideal called "Unity." Strange as it may seem, the policy which worked to the temporary advantage of the right wing in France, worked to the permanent advantage of the Communists in Yugoslavia. For with his armor, Tito crushed Mihailovic and his other opponents and the American pledge of free elections, which was realized in France, proved unredeemable in Yugoslavia. (*11*)

American-Slav pressure organizations, many of them Communist-led, played an important propaganda rôle, and even President Roosevelt was exposed to such influences. When, on his way to Teheran, he met King Peter in Cairo, the President was amiable but did not promise anything. Pro-Tito propaganda also penetrated the inner chambers of the British government and the inner chambers of Mr. Churchill's heart. There was a strange feeling that Britain's Balkan prospects hinged on the understanding and true friendship with a new breed of man, a man such as Tito, in whom many saw a mixture of Keir Hardie and Dimitrov, Protestant social reformer and Communist Balkan national hero. Thus did Tito acquire a legend of glory and an aura of history. (*12*)

In September–October, after the limitations of the Mediterranean campaign were enforced by the Americans, the British computed the changes in their Balkan potentialities. Now British official propaganda began to favor Tito fully; British diplomacy began assuming a "second-best" attitude, and began to indicate that certain compromises in Poland, the Baltics, Czechoslovakia and most of the Balkans were inevitable, while in Washington American propaganda and diplomacy proudly and emphatically insisted on not having any ambitions, projects or plans in the Balkans. (*13*)

All this bore curious fruits in the short run, tragic fruits in the long run. On October 7–8, Chetnik forces successfully attacked the Germans near Visegrad; next night they were dazed to hear that the BBC broadcasts attributed the success to Tito forces. In Greece, ELAS attacked EDES. On November 6, Djilas of the Yugoslav Communist Party addressed its Politbureau; his publicized speech demanded that the Western Allies set up their second front in Western Europe, only in Western Europe. On November 29 Tito's Assembly met in Jajce, setting the pattern of future Communist-dominated, united-front, "Anti-Fascist" National Assemblies in other countries. On that day opened the Teheran Conference.

Moscow, Cairo, Teheran: central-eastern Europe and world strategy

[*Preparations for Moscow.*] Eden was to fly to Moscow immediately after the Quebec conference, but Stalin sent Maisky to London for discussions first; these discussions, in early September, revealed fundamental differences and occasionally reached points where acrimonious debate developed. The Soviets demanded zones of influence; Eden was opposed to this. There were also the news and rumors of German-Russian secret negotiations. Late in September Admiral Standley, the American Ambassador to Russia, deeply disgusted with the methods of Soviet diplomacy, resigned his post.

Yet, so far as the British and American public were concerned, radio and press propaganda continued to be optimistic and indulged in picturesque illusions of postwar Russian-Allied unity, Danubian TVA's, eastern European federations, peasant democracies; the visions of famous émigrés returning to their homelands to be greeted by white-clad virgins amidst the strains of the common man's victory march dominated the scene; in the background of all this propaganda spun dizzily the skeletons of Mazzini, Kossuth, Slowacki, Mickiewicz, and Masaryk, resurrected from their graves and clothed in pink flesh as conceived by minor propagandists in New York. Meanwhile the old and venerable Cordell Hull prepared for his global flight to Moscow.

Roosevelt briefed him on October 4, 5, 6: they went through the planned agenda in detail. The President indicated that in regard to the Baltic countries and eastern Poland he was eventually willing to move forward and meet the Russian aims. "For grounds of high morality," Roosevelt talked of plebiscites: yet Hull, while feeling a growing spirit of compromise, received no direct instructions from the President.

Before his departure, Hull wished to see the Polish Ambassador for an earnest, long talk. Ciechanowski came on October 6, grave and concise. He brought specific proposals and asked Hull to present them at Moscow. Poland asked for an American-British guarantee of her independence; her government wished to have American and British troops, or at least numerous token missions, participate in the liberation and the subsequent occupation of Poland. The government-in-exile once again reaffirmed its desire to live peacefully next to the Soviet Union; a resumption of the severed diplomatic relations was highly desired by the Polish government. Ciechanowski also had two interesting suggestions; one dealt with the Polish desire for a postwar central-eastern European federation. The earnest and naïve Hull welcomed this; he did not yet see that such a federation, however friendly to Russia, would be intolerable to Stalin, as it would counter all Soviet plans in that part of Europe. Ciechanowski also suggested that the Western Allies pay more attention to the restive German "satellites," especially Rumania, Hungary and Slovakia, and help their secession efforts (*1*); no doubt this suggestion stemmed from the Polish desire to see these countries fall into the Anglo-American zone of operations. And, in regard to Germany, Ciechanowski stated,

> The recently expressed readiness of the Soviet Government generously to support the claims of Poland to some German territories, with the view to inducing Poland to give up the eastern half of her territory to the USSR, was interpreted by the Polish Government and people as an attempt on the part of the Soviet Government to make Poland dependent on Russia, and possibly to use her as a springboard for extended Soviet domination of Central Europe, and of Germany in particular.

Hull deemed these remarks "reasonable" and said later these encouraging words:

> The Polish Government is entitled to act the part of host to the Soviets when they come into Poland. This is both just and logical and re-

quires, as your government rightly maintains, the re-establishment of direct relations between the Soviet and Polish governments.

Hull added that "he was decided to defend the cause of Poland as he would defend the cause of his own country."

[*The Foreign Ministers in Moscow: the military discussions.*] But the Moscow Conference turned out to be different. From October 18 to November 3 the Foreign Ministers and military chiefs broke the ground there for the coming Big Three meeting — and revealed the place and scope of the decisive Allied operations of 1944. At the very first meeting the British General Ismay and the American General Deane (2) explained the invasion of France to the Russians, and by speaking of "maintenance of pressure in Italy, secondary landings in southern France, guerrilla activities in the Balkans . . . all helpful to [the] plan," indirectly revealed that the Western Allies did not contemplate a Balkan invasion. Molotov wanted to be more certain. In later sessions he asked Hull and Eden about their opinions concerning the position of Turkey; the Russians knew that the American Chiefs of Staff were fully opposed to the creation of an Aegean-Turkish front and to Turkey's entry in general. According to General Deane, Eden was non-committal, saying that the entry of Turkey *might* be an unnecessary burden for the Allies, while Vishinsky, at the end of that particular meeting, showed himself to be very disillusioned and bitter about the Anglo-American reluctance to bring about the Turkish front. Was this part of an extremely clever diplomatic game? Perhaps so; for Eden wanted to smoke out Molotov. Churchill had instructed him on October 20:

You should find out what the Russians really feel about the Balkans. Would they be attracted by their idea of our acting through the Aegean, involving Turkey in the war, and opening the Dardanelles and Bosphorus so that British naval forces and shipping could aid the Russian advance and so that we could ultimately give them our right hand along the Danube? . . . It may be that for political reasons the Russians would not want us to develop a large-scale Balkan strategy. (3)

On the other hand, the Russians wanted to see what the British reaction would be. The British now wished to postpone the bringing in of Turkey because they felt that this could mean the extension of the Soviet sphere of influence to that country before considerable American-British troops and matériel could arrive in the Aegean-Turkish area. The Russians had already made references to British "interference" regarding Rumania; there arose now questions of relative authority in the Balkan theatre. (Eden also asked the Russians to cooperate with Britain in coordinating Balkan guerrilla activities and eliminating all strife there, but his request was refused.) Soon after Moscow, the rôles were again reversed: Britain pressed for the Turkish front, which the Soviets opposed — and America sided with the latter.

Apart from the military and preparatory phase of the talks, the Moscow conference had two important results. One was the creation of the European Advisory Commission, a high policy-coordinating body set up by the Three Powers. We shall hear of its functions later. The other was the Declaration on Liberated Austria.

[*The Austrian Declaration.*] Winston Churchill saw the future with pessimism now. He envisaged the possible loss of most of eastern Europe; but he wanted to save at least central Europe. It was he who pushed, through Eden, for the Declaration on Liberated Austria to be put on the agenda at Moscow; it was placed on the agenda as an item concerning which there could be no controversy, and it was accordingly accepted; it might well be that this prescient political manoeuvre saved Austria from the Soviets in the long run. On November 1, 1943, the Declaration was announced and widely broadcast. (*4*)

The final Moscow communiqué was non-specific, and immediately grave doubts arose in the minds of those who had their well-grounded doubts and fears concerning the Soviets. That a preliminary concordance of views concerning the Baltic States and eastern Poland had been reached in Moscow was now expected. That there existed now a certain tragic divergence in the British and American viewpoints concerning the political and military conduct of the war in central-eastern Europe also became gradually known. Meanwhile the pro-Russian line of propaganda was pushed further: especially the British press and the American radio fell in with Leftist and often pro-Soviet propaganda concerning central-eastern Europe (the British radio and the American press were not yet quite organized along these lines). "As matters stood," wrote Ciechanowski, "Stalin had won the first round of an uneven contest of statesmanship, and the artificially aroused public enthusiasm for the results of the Moscow conference had confirmed his belief that he was dealing with weak partners who preferred to conceal the truth from their people rather than face him squarely." (5)

[*American changes.*] There were also significant changes in the State Department. Sumner Welles clashed with Hull, who energetically demanded his resignation in August 1943; late in October, Welles' place was filled by Edward R. Stettinius, Jr. (6). Other leading persons changed positions: Ray Atherton, a man who nurtured strong doubts about the Soviets, was replaced by H. Freeman Matthews as Chief of European Affairs; in the Russian and Eastern European Division Charles Bohlen became chief in the stead of Loy Henderson. Although none of these officials was definitely Russophile, these changes had a definite bearing on the relations of official Washington with the central-eastern European exiles: these relations became cooler, less personal, more reserved, and gradually even strained; the adherents of the line of thought which planned for a Grand Two-Power American-Russian cooperation on a global scale increased in number and in importance.

The Polish Ambassador tried to see Hull immediately after the latter returned from Moscow, but he had to wait until November 19. Cordell Hull was now different and less optimistic than before his eastward flight: he gave the impression that America could not do much, as no Anglo-American troops were scheduled to be in central-eastern Europe when the Germans retreated therefrom. He asked Ciechanowski what the Poles thought would be wise to do: the Polish Ambassador again reiterated the psychological and political need to pursue a determined policy in regard to the Soviets; he again asked for an Anglo-American declaration concerning Poland's frontiers and independence. Hull said that this he could not promise, but he would suggest it to the President. And now responsibility was again evaded in the face of a precarious situation: acting in the strange Anglo-Saxon manner which shows a love of general declarations but a fear of specific commitments, (7) Hull said that, after all, Poland's interests should be defended by Britain: was not Britain Poland's ally? To the suggestion of the earnest, despairing Ciechanowski, Hull also replied that Polish statesmen should not try to meet Roosevelt or Churchill before the pending Big Three Conference, as this might further prejudice Stalin.

The Combined Chiefs of Staff now informed Polish liaison officers in Washington that the parachuting of Anglo-American weapons to the Home Army in Poland would be temporarily discontinued: immediately before the arrival of the first Soviet troops in eastern Poland, the military planners in Washington were thus considering abandoning their heroic allies rather than face the possibility of clashes between Soviet armor and British-American armor in Polish hands, clashes which would disturb all the grand designs in the making.

. . . .

But these grand designs seemed far from perfect to the designers themselves. Just before Roosevelt and the Chiefs of Staff were to leave for Cairo and Teheran, General Deane reported from Moscow that all was not well. He did not yet discern the Russian long-range plans which aimed at keeping the Western Allies in Western instead of Southern Europe; Deane signalled to his Chiefs: they should be "prepared to resist Soviet demands for more active operations in the Mediterranean area designed to draw additional German divisions from the Russian front." (*8*) About ten days later, Deane became increasingly aware of the fact that the Soviets desired not *more* but *less* active operations in that area: something that Winston Churchill knew all the time.

[*The first Cairo meeting: Churchill loses.*]   The British Premier departed from London unusually early. He prepared himself for another, desperate attempt to convince the Americans of the urgent, ultimate necessity of a Balkan invasion. On November 9 he declared that Britain supported King George of Greece. On November 15 Churchill was in Algiers and asked General Eisenhower's Chief of Staff, the far-sighted Walter Bedell Smith, to come aboard the *Renown* for a talk there under the same blue Mediterranean sky where, exactly six months before, the Prime Minister had vainly fought to convince General Marshall, ever unwilling to understand his ideas. General Smith understood him much better; yet he could do not much more than report to Eisenhower; the essence of these talks was jotted down by Eisenhower's Naval Aide:

> The PM and the British are still unconvinced as to the wisdom of *Overlord* [Normandy] and are persistent in their desire to pursue our advantages in the Mediterranean, especially through the Balkans.

Intelligence reports reached the Allied Supreme Command which seemed to assist Churchill: according to these reports, Turkey could probably be induced to decide to enter the war, provided that Anglo-American forces in the Mediterranean would guarantee her strong air protection. But on November 20 the Allies gave up Samos, their last Aegean stronghold, and two other minor islands in the Dodecanese: a fleet of rowboats carried stealthily fleeing British, Greek, Badogliano soldiers and the Greek-Orthodox Metropolitan to Turkey (wherefrom, in civilian clothes and assisted by Turkish authorities, they travelled to rejoin the British forces in the Middle East). And on November 22 opened the first Cairo conference with Churchill, Roosevelt and Chiang Kai-shek. (*9*)

The naïveté with which the Americans misread the situation clearly emerges from what Harry Hopkins said to Captain Butcher on the first day of Cairo:

> . . . there must be some non-stated reason why the British sought to have the Cairo Conference so soon after the Quebec Conference. [Hopkins] thought that probably the Russians and British had gotten together and decided the best strategy now would be to exploit our situation in the Mediterranean, with the object of opening the Aegean route through the Dardanelles to the Black Sea to hasten delivery of Russian supply. This also envisages inducement of Turkey definitely and actively entering the war . . .
>
> . . . Hopkins thought it possible that the Russians might now prefer that our efforts be redoubled in the Mediterranean and that the cross-Channel operation be delayed or abandoned, dependent upon conditions in Germany as the Russians advance and as we theoretically push through Italy into Austria or southern France. (*10*)

Thus the British policy of not having told the Americans the real motives behind their arguments for the Balkan invasion boomeranged — a great mistake in Churchill's planning. Yet it should be remembered that Churchill had had the 1940–41 experiences; he did not wish to confront American idealism again with what Americans were prone to call designs of naked "power politics."

Churchill now finally came into the open, but he faced all-round American opposition in Cairo; Roosevelt himself did not wish to stay closeted with him for too long, as the President feared that Stalin might become unduly suspicious. On November 24 Churchill strongly pressed for a new offensive in the Aegean, against Rhodes, to develop later into something in connection with Turkey; but Hopkins said that there was no landing craft available, and the American Joint Chiefs of Staff rejected the plan. To Eisenhower Churchill again proposed further landings in northern Italy and spoke for the first time of the Ljubljana Gap, through which he envisaged the breakthrough of Anglo-American armor into the plains of northeastern Slovenia, Austria, and southeastern Hungary. But Eisenhower was not too sympathetic and thought Churchill to be over-optimistic when the Prime Minister spoke of how to fan out to the left or right when, in a few months, the Pisa-Rimini line in Italy would be reached. On November 25 the British Chiefs of Staff proposed to postpone the cross-Channel invasion and plan for an Aegean offensive with Turkey in 1944; the plan was rejected; Admiral Leahy thought it alarming: "The British bulldog tenacity did not like to let go of a desire to retain a controlling hold on the Mediterranean and in the Near East." (*11*)

Ultimately the British "let go" of their "controlling hold," as Leahy wished; the Russians got in control instead.

[*Teheran: more lost battles.*] Churchill lost his fight in Cairo. His faithful friend, the gallant South African Smuts, spoke in London on November 25 to the Commonwealth officials; his speech was only released after Teheran, and indicated that Smuts sensed what was happening. He spoke of the need for a Western European Union after the war, for ". . . you will see Russia in a position which no country had ever occupied in the midst of Europe." He did not qualify this statement. But it was clear that no illusory optimism colored his words, words pronounced not far from quiet places where the earthly remains of Castlereagh, Palmerston, Disraeli were resting — but very far from the capital of Persia, where the true descendant of these men was destined to fight for and lose what these spiritual ancestors had fought for and won.

The Teheran Conference assembled on November 28.

On the very first day it became evident that Roosevelt and his delegation were sparing no effort to impress Stalin with American understanding, sympathy and friendship, even at the cost of seeming to depart from the policy of close British-American collaboration. Thus Churchill found himself alone on many important occasions, facing a strange coalition of Roosevelt and Stalin. The President stayed at the Russian Embassy building in Teheran from the very beginning; when Churchill proposed to dine with him, Roosevelt objected to an *en deux* meal, lest Stalin become suspicious. Such was the atmosphere of Teheran. (*12*)

After the first two sessions Churchill lost his great battle, and perhaps it would not be too exaggerated to say it was then that Soviet Russia won the Second World War; on November 30, 1943, the decision which had the effect of delivering central-eastern Europe to Russia was made: it was finally and irrevocably decided that the main invasion of Europe would come in northwestern France during May-June 1944, followed by a secondary landing on France's Mediterranean shores. According to Leahy, Stalin "had made . . . [a] good case . . . for a flank attack through Southern France. . . . Marshal Voroshilov pressed for a decision on this point. General Marshall and I were inclined to go along, but Sir Alan Brooke insisted stubbornly . . . "

Churchill's military arguments proved inefficient; as General Deane wrote:

> Stalin appeared to know exactly what he wanted at the conference. This was also true of Churchill, but not so of Roosevelt. This is not said as a reflection on our President, but his apparent indecision was probably the direct result of our obscure foreign policy. President Roosevelt was thinking of winning the war; the others were thinking of their relative position when the war was over. Stalin wanted the Anglo-American forces in Western, not southern Europe; Churchill thought our postwar position would be improved and British interests best served if the Anglo-Americans as well as the Russians participated in the occupation of the Balkans. (*13*)

Harry Hopkins' eyes also opened, and he prided himself for having seen through Churchill's motives:

> The U.S. Chiefs of Staff had no doubts in their own minds as to just what all this [Churchill's arguments] signified. . . . They prepared themselves for battles at Teheran in which the Americans and Russians would form a united front.

A united front, indeed, surpassing the best dreams of Stalin! As a matter of fact, it was Roosevelt who on November 29 wavered for a moment and leaned towards Churchill; the President

> . . . surprised and disturbed Hopkins by mentioning the possibility of an operation across the Adriatic for a drive, aided by Tito's Partisans, (*14*) northeastward into Rumania to effect a junction with the

Red Army advancing southward from the region of Odessa. . . . Certainly nothing would be farther from the plans of the American Chiefs of Staff. (*15*)

"We ourselves," said Churchill, "had no ambitions in the Balkans. All we wanted to do was to nail down those thirty hostile divisions." But Stalin disputed the existence of such German strength in the Balkans and he sided with the American Chiefs of Staff. These Balkan plans, to Churchill's dismay, were then abandoned.

The American Chiefs of Staff and Stalin defeated Churchill on Turkey also; the Russian now argued sharply against the Turkish plan, calling it a dangerous and unnecessary drain on Allied supplies; Hopkins noted that General Marshall was "alarmed" at the British, and said that if Turkey came in, this would "burn up our logistics right down the line." So all plans for a Turkish-Aegean front were ruled out, while it was agreed that all-out support be given to Tito's forces. Stalin went so far as to hint at the "desirability" of reducing Allied efforts in the Mediterranean even to the point of abandoning the tactical aim to take Rome in the spring.

[*Teheran: the political picture.*]   Although the Conference occupied itself primarily with military matters, its political portents were not less significant.

Throughout the conference, one primary factor emerged, and this was the almost total absence of postwar political considerations in American planning. This one-sidedness, of course, was fully to Russia's advantage.

There was also a lack of American understanding of the strategic and geographic importance of central-eastern Europe and the relative lack of interest in that area shown by the American people. There was also the growing belief among American intellectuals that the *homo americanus* and the *homo sovieticus* had something in common: youth, innocence, primitive power, primitive democracy, idealism were attributed to both. Yet that these rationalizations were not exclusively those of Russophile intellectuals was apparent in the attitude of General Arnold, chief of the American Air Force, who in December 1943, after his return from Teheran, said in Washington to his dinner neighbor, the Polish Ambassador:

He [Arnold] saw no great difference in Stalin's and Roosevelt's ideologies, and he believed it was a mistake to think that Stalin was a communist. . . . Stalin had impressed him rather as a democrat, or at least, he [Arnold] added, "he succeeded in giving me that impression."

This was the same chief of the American Air Force who late in 1949 opined in a world-circulated American magazine that "Russia has no fear of a navy, since she does not see how it can be employed against her." He was defying history — for whenever Russia had been defeated (in 1854–55, 1904–05, and in the Baltics in 1919–20) her defeat had been brought about, mainly, by naval forces.

There was, also, another consideration, important in the mind of President Roosevelt. He, correctly gauging American public opinion, was aware that his political opponents, backed by much American sentiment, were, throughout the war, for a "Tokyo first" strategy, and that they would be hostile toward and indignant about an American commitment to police much of Europe. This was one of the reasons why the President was so much against any Balkan invasion plans; Roosevelt feared popular (and Republican) reaction at home against such plans to such an extent that at Teheran a despairing Churchill and a Stalin who could scarcely believe his own ears, were unable to commit him to the future American occupation of a zone in southern Germany. Britain alone was unable to hold and occupy Europe after the war, and at the time of Teheran even Stalin could not envisage that when the war ended his troops would be in control of everything east of Lübeck, Magdeburg, Linz and Graz: early in December, Britain *and* Russia presented papers at the European Advisory Commission which provided for American-occupied zones in southern Germany and Austria. Roosevelt refused to accept these plans; only long months later, upon the urgings of the State Department, did he unwillingly agree.

This American unwillingness to make specific commitments, together with the incapacity of Britain to go ahead alone, met with some Russian surprise and incredulity. Stalin was visibly pleased by Roosevelt's stand (and with the few pinpricks which the President gave to Churchill) at Teheran; as Deutscher, his biographer, stated:

> This was a moment of Stalin's supreme triumph. Perhaps only he and Churchill were aware of its implications. Europe had now been militarily divided in two; and behind the military decision here loomed the social and political cleavage. . . . an old dream of Russian diplomacy . . . bringing the Balkans under Russian influence — was coming true.

Stalin did not need to discuss his territorial aims and commit him-self; Churchill asked him on one occasion point-blank: what were the Russian territorial interests? Stalin answered: "There is no need to speak at the present time about any Soviet desires — but when the time comes, we will speak." No, certainly he would not commit him-self — except that he opposed Churchill wherever he could do so on crucial issues; for example, at the very end of the Conference, Roose-velt proposed the dismemberment of Germany into five states and two internationally-controlled territories. Churchill then brought up his idea of a Bavarian-Austrian state, arguing that South Germans differed from Prussians. But Stalin would not agree; he also argued for the clear separation of Austria, Hungary, Rumania — no Danu-bian federation. When Churchill asked him whether he wanted bases in the Baltic States, Stalin answered in the affirmative, and added that their governments would not necessarily have to be Communistic. When Roosevelt asked him about Finland, Stalin (always keenly aware of the pro-Finnish sympathies of American public opinion) said that Finnish-Russian negotiations were already proceeding sat-isfactorily (this was not true at that particular time) and promised to be "generous." He would, however, insist that friendly Finns such as Paasikivi lead a postwar Finland. (*16*)

And when it came to Poland, he said: "If I could only find a Polish Paasikivi!" This was, of course, sheer hypocrisy, for there was the Polish Paasikivi in the person of Mikolajczyk; but all this, of course, impressed Roosevelt very much. Churchill was more cautious. He knew that the minimum concession to Stalin would have to be the Baltics and eastern Poland. He knew that sooner or later the problem of the government of Poland would come up, as he was increasingly aware of the Russian wish to supplant any independent Polish régime with Soviet satellites. Furthermore, the Premier believed — mistakenly — in his 1939 thesis that at that time the Soviets surged forward into eastern Poland and the Baltics primarily for strategic reasons. He had a certain minimum sympathy for Russian imperialism, which he thought to be the truly limiting factor of Bolshevik revolutionary ex-pansion: but here his aristocratic and historic instinct did not prove to be fully right (and the fact that he made a territorial agreement to the detriment of Britain's ally cannot be excused on ethical grounds). Yet, he wanted to save Poland; this guided him here, nothing else. But he failed to appreciate what Bismarck had written fifty years be-fore in his memoirs: "India and Constantinople can be more easily

defended from Russia on the Polish than on the Afghan frontier."
And Stalin saw through the British motive to make an agreement
on the Curzon Line, and at that price forestall more Russian penetration of and control over Poland. (*17*) Partly due to his somewhat
undue optimism on this point, partly due to the undiplomatic rigidity
of certain Poles, partly due to the continued failure of the Americans
to understand the political nature of the war, partly due to Russian
deceit and cunning on a scale which few could perceive or even
gauge, the British Premier was bound to fail here.

Thus at Teheran the Big Three orally accepted the so-called Curzon
Line; it was, indeed, Churchill who accepted it quickly and unconditionally, while Roosevelt at least mentioned the desirability of leaving Lwów and the southeastern oil district with Poland, if possible.
The Polish government was not informed of this decision; eleven
months later in Moscow, Mikolajczyk, confronted by Molotov in the
presence of Eden, Harriman, and a grumbling, uneasy Churchill,
was to hear from the mouth of the Soviet Foreign Commissar that
at Teheran Britain and America had agreed to the cession of eastern
Poland (forty-six percent of pre-war Polish territory) to Russia.

Roosevelt was hopeful. He achieved the basic coordination of military plans; this was his main aim: Stalin agreed in principle that
after the German war he would attack Japan; another Russian agreement was won in regard to the establishment of American bases in
southeastern Russia for bombers' shuttle flights.

When Metternich met Castlereagh for the first time in January
1814, he said that in spite of the Allied armies having marched to the
very frontiers of France, he was uncertain: for there was no Allied
unity; there was a divergence of views and aims; there was "no definite
object." This Churchill knew at Teheran; but Roosevelt, full of illusions, plans, and hopes, did not. In 1814, the first steps were taken to
save Europe from Russian-Prussian preponderance and to make a
good peace, a peace from which eventually a hundred years of prosperity resulted; Teheran in 1943 was the decisive step which led to
the impossibility of making peace in 1945 and after. (*18*)

.   .   .   .

[*The second Cairo conference: another plan frustrated.*] But
Churchill did not give up yet. Even before Teheran he had made
arrangements through his elegant and respectable Ambassador, Sir
Hugh Knatchbull-Hugessen, to bring the Turkish President to Cairo

to meet him and Roosevelt upon their return from Persia. So the second Cairo conference met on December 4–5: the Turks, Inönü and Menemenčoglu, the Americans, Roosevelt and Hopkins, the British, Churchill and Eden. When he had arranged for this meeting, Churchill was not yet fully aware how at Teheran the Russians and Americans would reject the idea of bringing Turkey into the war. Nevertheless, he still had some hopes: after all, if the Turks wanted to come in themselves, what could Stalin say? Thus in Cairo Eden pampered Menemenčoglu with promises: the Russians were not obsessed with revolutionary crusading ideology, one could talk reasonably with them: they were understanding. Menemenčoglu was not convinced, but he was sufficiently impressed to let a Rumanian diplomat know later what Eden had said about the Russians. The British also promised sufficient air protection if the Turks would immediately place air bases at the disposal of the Allies.

The Turks almost accepted. They were told of an agreement made at Teheran, according to which Moscow would notify Sofia that Russia would go to war with Bulgaria if the latter aided the Germans against Turkey. Inönü made an agreement with Churchill according to which a few thousand Allied specialists were to "infiltrate" into Turkey to make preparations; arrangements were also made for the establishment of a special British and American Military Mission. But during the second day of Cairo, the Turks became increasingly aware that Britain and America did not see eye to eye with regard to the Turkish plans. Thus Inönü and Menemenčoglu established the minimum amount of military supplies and air protection which would be necessary for Turkey; these demands proved to be far too high for the Mediterranean Command to meet. Turkish intelligence also had gathered some information pertaining to the decisive fact that the Allies did not plan to undertake a major invasion of the Balkans. Thus the Turks did not give the impression that they burned with great zeal to enter the war; Eden tried to get them to act as if they did, and he failed. (*19*)

The basic directives of the Allied Supreme Command in the Mediterranean thus remained unchanged to such an extent that when in December the British brought up again their plans for *Operation Hercules* (amphibious landings and occupation of the main Aegean islands, operations about which Turkey had to be informed), the Combined Chiefs of Staff instructed Eisenhower that no commitment be made to Turkey that this operation would be undertaken.

[*The Ukrainian campaign: November–December 1943.*] There
was another calculation in which the British were mistaken: but this
time it was the Germans who failed them. British intelligence noted
the continuous German withdrawal which had begun in late August
1943 on the southern Russian front and the surprisingly easy abandonment of Kiev (November 3); the Germans made troop concentrations in the western Ukraine. All reports pieced together showed that
the Germans were to make a strong stand, eventually a counteroffensive, in the Ukraine toward the middle Dnieper front. The Germans
indeed surprised Russian spearheads, and just before Teheran pushed
against them at Berdichev, Zhitomir and Korosten: their thrusts were
successful and the Russians were repulsed from two of these three
cities. This did not fail to impress London. But at that time Russian
strategy was already dictated by political expediency; there was a
master plan which continued to be rather brilliantly followed throughout 1944. Leaving the Germans uncertain and relatively free in the
central and the northern sectors of the immense front, the Russians
threw mass forces against them in the south; they wanted to get
nearer the Balkans, into the Balkans. By the time of the second Cairo
conference the Russians had repelled the German counter-thrust, and
their armies stood on the western banks of the Dnieper everywhere
north of Nikopol, a situation which made it almost impossible for the
Germans to hold the southern Dnieper alone; they were being outflanked. Consequently, around December 18 the Russians eliminated
Cherson, the last German bridgehead east of the Dnieper and on the
same day launched at Nevel the northern offensive toward Latvia.
On December 31 Zhitomir, Berdichev, and Korosten were again safely
in Russian hands.

[*The Germans' knowledge.*] At that time, however, German
intelligence had found a pot of gold. They got basic information on
the military decisions made at Teheran.

About December 20 German counterintelligence was in possession
of reports confirming that at Teheran the decision was taken against
a Balkan invasion. Just as in the case of Italy, Canaris and others
could not believe their ears; they could not see how the Western Allies
could forfeit their chances in the Balkans. Göbbels was jubilant. First,
neither Ribbentrop nor the military were inclined to believe these
reports — which were sold to the Germans in Turkey by an amateur
spy, the Albanian valet of the unsuspecting Sir Hugh Knatchbull-

Hugessen, allegedly after having been stolen from his private safe while the Ambassador was singing in the bathroom. (*20*) Then other reports substantiated the evidence and everything was pieced together. One of the reports stated (the Germans got some papers on the Moscow and Cairo conferences also) that, as the Allies had abandoned the Balkan invasion plans, Churchill had proposed, for the sake of deception and psychological effects, an intensified Allied strategic air offensive against Balkan cities, including Sofia, which offensive was to start in the middle of January. On January 15, 1944, Sofia was attacked by Allied bombers on a scale hitherto unprecedented in the Balkans. (*21*) Now the Germans believed their reports.

There were also other reports circulating: at the end of December 1943, the Japanese Minister in Stockholm told his Hungarian colleague, in order to insert doubts into the latter's hopeful mind, that there was to be no Anglo-American invasion in the Balkans.

[*Beneš' treaty.*]   In the same month, British diplomacy underwent another defeat. This was the Czechoslovak-Soviet Pact of Moscow, signed on December 12.

The agile Beneš saw the trend of events. He had always been rather optimistic about the Soviets; in the summer of 1941 he was one of the few who did not underestimate Russian power. From 1942 on he leaned more and more in a pro-Soviet direction; he abandoned and renounced his former agreements with the Poles. He encountered the opposition of Hodža, of Monsignor Šramek, of certain conservative members among the Czech exiles, of the Foreign Office and of the State Department. But this was not enough. He saw the growing divergences between Churchill and Stalin and he wishfully thought that he and his postwar Czechoslovakia could be the "Third Force." (*22*)

His trip to Moscow was arranged in a hurried, eager fashion, so characteristic of him; it was also prepared without the knowledge of Eden, who was away in Moscow, Cairo, Teheran: faced with an accomplished fact, the British Foreign Secretary could do no more than express to Beneš his displeasure with the trip. Nevertheless, Beneš flew to Moscow and signed the Russo-Czechoslovak Treaty. He was impressed by the clever compliments of Stalin and Molotov and the cordial reception with which he was received. This little man, of whom his good friend Sir Bruce Lockhart wrote that "optimism has always been his strongest virtue and overconfidence his greatest fault," was very much overawed by the friendliness and the confidences of the greatest men of the Soviet Union. And so he said that the December 12 treaty was "a guarantee of our independence and of our Republic of the kind which we had not before." This was indeed true. Such a guarantee of independence Czechoslovakia certainly did not have before. Beneš himself found that out in February 1948, and probably much earlier. (Of his memoirs, the parts published in 1946 carry the story only up until December 1943; the promised Volume II will probably never appear — unless the manuscript can one day be spirited from behind the Iron Curtain to Britain and to America where some of the Beneš papers on Munich are.)

In Moscow Beneš had long discussions with the Czech Communists, whose leader, Gottwald, pressed for a National Front which Beneš in principle accepted. The Beneš-Gottwald agreement left important points open, an arrangement from which in 1945 and later the Communists unilaterally profited. The papers which Beneš signed in Moscow were very much similar to the Allied commitments at Teheran and Yalta: broad, sweeping generalizations without technical and specific clauses. The other Moscow Czechs, Nejedly, Kopecky, and Slansky, all of whom at first looked at the petit-bourgeois Beneš with a certain amount of concealed apprehension (these Czech Communists even criticized him for his attitude in the days of Munich) became more and more friendly after being confronted with the smiling and eagerly explanative Beneš. Just as did his agreement with the Communists, his treaty with Russia left important points open — for example, the question of Ruthenia (Carpatho-Ukraine) was not mentioned, although Stalin himself revealed in 1945 that the cession of that territory to the Soviet Union (which cession gave a foothold to Russia within the Carpathian Basin for the first time in history) was discussed and agreed upon in 1943. (23) Thus, as the year 1943 closed, much of central-eastern Europe's fate had already been decided in the two months from October 18 to December 12. During this period Stalin achieved the limits of diplomatic success. The whole of eastern Poland, (24) the Baltic states, and the Carpatho-Ukraine were awarded to him in agreements of varying clarity but of unmistakable practicability; the military decisions communicated to him at Teheran meant that at least Bulgaria and Rumania would fall into Russian hands; events at Jajce meant that Yugoslavia would do the same; the agreements with Beneš meant that sooner or later Czechoslovakia would share the same fate. (25) He certainly had reason enough to be proud. The whole tone of the Soviet press reflected this; instead of using dialectical arguments, it often spoke now with force and pride. As a Soviet newspaper wrote shortly after Teheran: "In 1917 Russian weakness lost the Baltic States, but now Soviet Russia is so powerful that she simply takes them." (*26*)

On January 4, 1944, the advancing Russian troops crossed the frontier into Poland.

(TABLE 4) THE WAR STATUS OF CENTRAL-EASTERN EUROPE, AUGUST 1943

	Germany	Italy	Japan	Bulgaria	Finland	Hungary	Rumania
Recognized governments-in-exile:							
Czechoslovakia	W	Wn	Wn	Wn	Wn	Wn	Wn
Greece	W	W	n	W	npr	n	rs
Poland	W	n	Wn	rs	rs	rs	rs
Yugoslavia	W	W	Wn	W	n	W	n
The other "United Nations":							
Great Britain	W	W^d	W	W^{id}	Wn^{id}	Wn^d	W^{id}
United States	W	W^d	W	Wn	CD	Wn^d	W^{id}
Soviet Union	W	W^{id}	CD	CD	W^d	W	W
Australia	W	W	W	W	Wn	Wn	W
Belgium	W	Wn	Wn	n	n	rs	n
Bolivia	Wn	Wn	Wn	npr	npr	npr	npr
Brazil	Wn	W	n	npr	CD	n	n
Canada	W	W	W	W	Wn	Wn	Wn
China	Wn	Wn	W	npr	npr	npr	n
Costa Rica	Wn	Wn	Wn	npr	npr	Wn	Wn
Cuba	Wn	Wn	Wn	npr	npr	npr	npr
Dominican Republic	Wn	Wn	Wn	npr	npr	npr	npr.
El Salvador	Wn	Wn	Wn	npr	npr	npr	npr
Ethiopia	Wn	W	Wn	npr	npr	npr	npr
Guatemala	Wn	Wn	Wn	CD	CD	CD	CD
Haiti	Wn	Wn	Wn	Wn	npr	Wn	Wn
Honduras	Wn	Wn	Wn	npr	npr	npr	npr
India	W	W	W	Wn	Wn	Wn	Wn
Iraq	Wn	Wn	Wn	npr	npr	npr	npr
Luxembourg	W	Wn	Wn	npr	npr	n	npr
Mexico	Wn	Wn	Wn	n	npr	n	n
Netherlands	W	Wn	W	n	rs	rs	n
New Zealand	W	W	W	W	Wn	Wn	W
Nicaragua	Wn	Wn	Wn	Wn	npr	Wn	Wn
Norway	W	n	n	n	rs	n	n
Panama	Wn	Wn	Wn	n	CD	n	n
Philippines	Wn	Wn	W	npr	npr	npr	npr
South Africa	W	W	W	Wn	Wn	Wn	Wn

W — At war.
Wn — At war, but no direct fighting or bombing between the respective states as yet.
n — Diplomatic relations severed.
CD — Diplomatic relations maintained.
rs — Certain relations secretly maintained.
npr — No previous relations.
[d] — direct, secret contact for peace negotiations established.
[id] — indirect contact for peace negotiations established.

· 5 ·

C

THE

RUSSIAN ERA

BEGINS

Preliminaries to the Russian era: the ominous spring
(January–June) of 1944

[*Poland turns to America.*] With the appearance of the Russian soldier within the frontiers of central-eastern Europe's formerly independent states, the political representation of these nations became of paramount importance. Of this the Ambassador of Poland was fully aware when he called on Hull on January 4, 1944, practically in the same hour when the first Soviet patrols moved cautiously forward under the bitter, frozen Polish sky amidst the wooden houses of the dark and dreary frontier villages. Ciechanowski informed Hull of the goodwill with which the Polish nation was to receive the Russian "liberators"; the Ambassador intimated that the territorial question, the Curzon Line, was now less important than was the problem of Soviet interference with the political future of Poland.

It is questionable whether Hull clearly grasped the issue. He had a general and righteous feeling about the plight of Poland but no concrete thoughts about practical procedure. The American Secretary of State never had the slightest intention of making a deal with Stalin to the detriment of Poland, yet, with typical and supercilious aloofness, he kept referring in his Diary to "the extremely emotional state of the Polish Ambassador" (the Finnish one, Procopé, noted Hull, was "of an emotional nature, could scarcely control himself"). (*1*)

A loyal Polish communiqué greeted the Soviets' crossing of the frontier, but, as could be expected, an ugly Soviet official statement followed on January 11, which deemed eastern Poland outside of any "discussions" and insulted the Polish government. The latter now asked Britain and the United States to mediate, but within ten days the Soviets rejected the idea of any "mediation," while the United States again passed responsibility to London. The Russian offensive rolled forward in the meantime; also, in the north, the front drew near to Estonia and Latvia; on January 16 the Finnish Minister reported from Berlin that the Germans seemed thoroughly beaten in the East.

[*German politics in the East.*]   The atmosphere was changing and the Germans for the first time tried to make political capital in the East: they slightly relaxed the stifling political measures in the Baltic states and, somewhat half-heartedly, began to recruit volunteers there; the tone of their Eastern broadcasts became more amicable. On December 17, 1943, it was announced that under "Professor" Ostrovski a "White Ruthenian" council met at Baranowicze, but then nothing more was heard of these people. In the Ukrainian-inhabited regions, anti-Polish sentiment increased as the Russians approached and guerrilla bands fought: Polish, Ukrainian and Communist units fought against Germans, against Russians, and often against each other. Exasperated with the situation, Frank became his own self again, and frankly stated on January 14, 1944:

> Once we have won the war, then for all I care, mincemeat can be made of the Poles and the Ukrainians and all the others who run around here — it does not matter what happens.   (2)

[*The Anzio failure: Churchill's reactions.*]   But Germany was very far from winning the war. On January 22 Allied forces were put onto the Roman littoral at Anzio and Nettuno, upon the insistence of Churchill, who again wanted to step up the Mediterranean campaign, push well beyond Rome and eventually sweep into the northern Balkans, instead of "dragging the hot rake of war up through the Italian peninsula," slowly, very slowly. Yet the tactical planning of the Anzio landings was faulty: quick German counteraction followed, and the operation practically failed; the bridgehead was established but no advance was made. The psychological portents of the Anzio muddle were even worse than the strategic failure; German soldiery could gloat over Western slowness and incapacity: "If *we* had landed," said Field-Marshal Kesselring, "we would have been in Rome within a few hours."

Churchill was worried about the overall political picture. Moscow announced that the exercise of independence in foreign relations had been granted to three Soviet republics, a move which was aimed to strengthen Stalin's hand in international organizations but which also could be construed as aiming to help the Russian incorporation of eastern European states: the three republics involved, Ukraine, Byelorussia, Armenia, bordered on the Baltics, Poland, Rumania and Turkey. A Russian note to the Greek government on January 12 suggested that the government facilitate a "united front" of the Greek guerrillas; at that time Communist forces had almost destroyed EDES, which was saved at the last moment by a sudden British air shipment of arms. Churchill had to tell King Peter and the Yugoslav Premier of the Teheran decision to support Tito because of his "activity"; on January 8 Churchill sent a personal message to Tito; the Foreign Office now pressed the Yugoslav government to drop Mihailović from the cabinet in view of "incriminating documents." Churchill noted to General Ismay that, due to British naval superiority,

> We ought to assert domination of the Dalmatian coast. . . . We are letting the whole of this Dalmatian coast be sealed off from us by an enemy who has neither the command of the air nor the sea.

Paramount in Churchill's mind was, however, the Polish problem. He was concerned about possible Russian-German contacts which could develop from the inter-Allied disputes concerning Poland; intelligence reports indicated a mounting sentiment among leading Germans to come to an agreement with Stalin; a considerable number of the anti-Hitler conspirators had a German-Russian deal in mind. Grand Admiral Raeder spoke to his confidant Assmann on January 10, 1944, and deeply deplored the fact that Hitler had attacked Russia in 1941; Seyss-Inquart, the Gauleiter in the Netherlands, made an interesting speech during the same week with some indirect praise of Communism; on January 17 a strange Cairo cable of *Pravda*, essentially a trial balloon, reported that "contacts existed" between British diplomats and Ribbentrop. (*3*)

[*Churchill and the Polish problem.*] It was thus an anxious Churchill who asked the Polish statesmen to a most important parley on Anzio Day, January 22: Eden, Cadogan, Mikolajczyk, Romer participated. Churchill presented a five-point proposal. He requested that the Curzon Line be agreed upon; in return for this, Poland was to receive East Prussia, Danzig, and Upper Silesia to the Oder; minority problems would be solved by population exchanges. If Poland accepted, Churchill would strongly safeguard the interests of the government-in-exile; indeed, he said, only thus would he have a strong bargaining hand.

The Poles hesitated; Mikolajczyk decided to consult the Polish underground and also Roosevelt (4); Churchill was dissatisfied, as he knew that not much time remained. On January 27 Hull, talking to Ciechanowski, felt that the Poles might be eventually willing to negotiate about the Curzon Line, but soon Washington was told by Molotov that the main issue was now regarded by the Soviets to be the constitution of "the London government in its present form." On January 31 Roosevelt and Hull discussed Poland, and on February 2 the Polish Ambassador recorded,

> . . . for the first time [Roosevelt] stated that, in the case of Poland, his adherence to the American principle of non-recognition of territorial settlements in time of war did not exclude attempts to bring about "amicable settlements between countries."

[*Another American* bona officia *offer: a failure.*] While the American President offered his "good offices" (as a year before he had done in the case of Finland; this now actually meant less than mediation), he did not want to commit himself on the side of the Polish government and intimated that he would like to have the pending visit of Mikolajczyk to Washington postponed. (5) Thus Ciechanowski decided to fly to London; he was unable to secure an audience with Roosevelt before his departure.

Washington now looked at the international picture with more confidence. In Greece an uneasy armistice was being patched up between the two guerrilla armies; on February 2 — perhaps to impress Roosevelt at a moment of uneasiness — Stalin informed Harriman in Moscow that the establishment of shuttle-bombing bases for American bombers within Russia now had been finally granted; on February 11 Mount Cassino fell in Italy (here Polish troops carried the flag, just as later, in June–August, it was the Polish Army in Italy which broke into Pescara and Ancona and, in April 1945, into Bologna. They were congratulated by King George VI personally). But Churchill was more pessimistic: President Roosevelt cabled him on February 8 that he was "absolutely unwilling to police France and possibly Italy and the Balkans as well" when the war was over. The Premier was also deeply disappointed with the Anzio enterprise and the Italian campaign in general, and on February 27 told Eisenhower how he felt about the matter. (*6*) The Turks were now definitely unwilling to enter the war, and the Turkish Ambassador to London resigned in March.

Having ascertained that the Polish government would not make an unequivocal statement about the cession of eastern Poland (*7*), Churchill delivered one of his most important speeches in the House of Commons on February 22. In this speech the British Premier, in a rather rough-shod manner, trampled over Peter, Mihailovič, and Purič and came out openly for Tito. More important, he stated:

> The liberation of Poland may . . . be achieved [after] the Russian armies . . . have suffered millions of casualties. . . . I cannot feel that the Russian demand . . . about her western frontiers goes beyond . . . what is reasonable. . . . Marshal Stalin and I also . . . agreed upon the need of Poland to obtain compensation at the expense of Germany both in the north and in the west.

The Commons accepted this statement, although in the ensuing debate a few Conservatives and Liberals, wary of Russia, criticized Churchill's stand: a peer in the House of Lords added that Poland truly constituted a "test case." (*8*)

[*Churchill intervenes with Stalin: another failure.*]   The Churchill speech wrought tragic repercussions in Polish circles. Romer officially protested against it on February 24; others, like the Commander-in-Chief, General Sosnkowski — who had already clashed with Mikolajczyk in true, bitter émigré fashion — issued an abrupt statement: "We shall not sacrifice our rights" (while, on the other hand, Sosnkowski confirmed that the underground and the Home Army had received orders to cooperate with the advancing Red Army units). (*9*) Sosnkowski was now facing cold British disapproval. Early in March a new Polish proposal, not very different from the February 17 one, was communicated to Moscow through London. On that basis Churchill on March 7 proposed to Stalin that the Curzon Line be accepted for demarcation purposes and that the whole Russian-Polish frontier question be finally settled at the postwar peace conference. There came no answer. On March 21 Churchill sent another, stronger message: if Stalin refused to answer, the Premier would feel compelled to make a statement in the House of Commons that all territorial decisions were to be made later and that he could not accept anything based on force without the sanction of a peace conference.

Two days later Stalin sent an angry answer (a copy of which he speeded to President Roosevelt). He accused Churchill of having reversed the Teheran agreement on the Curzon Line; he added:

> It is difficult for me even to point out a difference between the London Polish Government and the like émigré Government of Yugoslavia, as well as between certain Polish émigré generals and the Serbian General Mikhailovitch. . . . You are free to make any speech in the House of Commons. That is your affair. But if you make such a speech, I shall consider that you have committed an act of injustice and unfriendliness toward the Soviet Union.

Here was a subtle allusion (to British policy in Yugoslavia); a subtle approach (to Roosevelt); a not-so-subtle threat, which was repeated once more.

[*The military picture.*] At that time the Russian offensive in southeastern Poland slowed down. The forward-jutting salient there could be outflanked from the north, where the frontline ran about two hundred miles back eastward from the city of Kovel, which the Germans held at the end of March; to the south the front ran somewhat west of Luck and Tarnopol (where a small German garrison was pocketed) to the region of Kolomea, where it reached the Carpathians. It became more and more clear that the armored Russian giant had turned his Martian face toward the south, toward the Balkans, where on March 18 the Russians cut the Cernauti-Lwów railroad, occupied Cernauti, crossed the Dniester and by April 1 held a line running southeast from Kolomea, Cernauti, Balta, and Ochakov. On April 2 Russian patrols of Malinowski's Second Ukrainian Front crossed the Pruth into Rumanian territory. Thus the fate of Hungary and Rumania reached a critical juncture, while in the north the Russian Air Force raided Helsinki with increasing intensity from January on; the black bells of fate were tolling for Finland also.

.   .   .   .

[*Finland's peace: the fourth phase.*] A lengthy and difficult new phase of Finnish-Russian peace negotiations opened in November and lasted until April 22, 1944. On November 20 Madame Kollontay invited Finnish negotiators to come to Stockholm with specific Finnish proposals. The first Finnish answer expressed full willingness to negotiate but generally referred to the 1920 boundaries as a basis; thus some kind of a deadlock set in in January, at which time the Russian Air Force, departing from its usual tactics, began to bomb Finnish cities. On January 30 the United States in a note half urged, half demanded that Finland approach Russia again. On February 12 the Finnish government dispatched Juho Paasikivi to Stockholm. He conferred with the Russian Ambassadress three times in the following nine days.

One group of the Russian terms was "to be accepted immediately" (of these the most important were the 1940 boundaries, severance of relations with Germany, and internment of the eventually remaining German forces in Finland). (*10*) Demobilization, reparation questions, and the problem of Petsamo were to be discussed later. The Finnish Parliament in secret session on February 29 declared the Russian terms impossible, but decided that the examination of peace possibilities be continued. The Finnish reply, carefully edited and "altered . . . slightly on the 6th at the suggestion of the Swedish Foreign Minister" was subsequently handed to Madame Kollontay. Two days later the Russian answer deemed the Finnish note unsatisfactory and demanded that within a week — by March 18 — Finland accept the Russian terms. During that week King Gustav v, the American government, and President Roosevelt intervened to influence Finland. Meanwhile the Finnish Minister from Berlin reported on March 7 that the situation was such (the Russians had finally broken the siege of Leningrad and pushed into Estonia at Narva) that "even against an overwhelming public opinion," Finnish foreign policy should be examined "realistically." Urged from all quarters, the Linkomies government went into secret session with Parliament again, and on March 17 sent a note to Moscow: Finland was willing to examine earnestly all Russian proposals in detail; on March 19 Moscow invited a Finnish delegation to Moscow and on the following day Finland agreed to its dispatch.

But in the meantime an important event occurred: Germany on March 19 occupied Hungary. The German Minister in Helsinki, who during the Finnish-Russian negotiations had accused and threatened the Finnish régime, now inquired again about the matter. The Finns shuddered; despite the geographically more favorable position of Finland, the quickness and brutality of the German occupation of Hungary made a deep impression in Helsinki. Nevertheless on March 25 the delegates Paasikivi and Enckell were sent to Moscow. There they heard from Molotov and Dekanosov Soviet terms which were even harsher than those communicated previously by Kollontay. The main point of the Russian demands now was the quick ousting (or internment) of German forces, which had to be completed within a month from the armistice. These were practically impossible terms. On April 1 the delegates returned; after having found out that American support for Finland's negotiations and proposals was not forthcoming, another secret session of Parliament was held and the Finnish reply was sent to Russia on the 18th. It ended with these words:

> The Finnish government, which earnestly desires the return of peaceful relations and lasting good relations with its eastern neighbor, regrets that the terms now proposed, which it has carefully considered, do not offer possibilities for the achieving of this goal.

[*Rumania: the second phase.*]   It was now certain that Churchill's inviting statement of September 1943: ". . . the satellite states, suborned or over-awed, may perhaps, if they can shorten the war, be allowed to work their passage home," depended on other factors than local resolution and willpower and Western Allied "permission."

Rumania, for example, had continued her separate peace attempts through three or four various channels. Spurred by the rapid approach of the Russian armies (and also to a certain extent by the example of Hungary), Mihai Antonescu contacted the American Ambassador Hayes in Madrid and on December 20 offered Rumanian surrender at the moment the Allies invaded the Balkans and Turkey entered the war. Maniu used the same channel in November 1943. These approaches now assumed a concrete pattern and became almost regular by early January 1944. It is interesting to note that Ion Antonescu himself had one or two agents in Stockholm and Berne; he sent Tatarescu, a Balkan diplomat with a wily "chameleon" past, to Berne, and through him and another envoy in Stockholm, Nano, Antonescu contacted the Russians. (*11*)

There arose now a development of unusual significance: that of secret Soviet-Rumanian negotiations. It should be pondered by those who are prone to regard Stalin an arch-Communist and world revolutionary. While propaganda from Moscow fulminated against world Fascism, among whose cohorts Antonescu, in Communist eyes, occupied a leading position, and while in the Crimea Stalin's Russians and Antonescu's Rumanians fought, in Stockholm "Communist" Russian and "Fascist" Rumanian diplomats were negotiating: and, however strange or inconclusive these negotiations were, there was no doubt that the Russians had initiated them and that they were eager to conduct them. "The Russians were clearly in a hurry," wrote Nano, "being . . . [rather] afraid of a change in the attitude of the Western Powers in the matter of allowing them a free hand in eastern Europe. . . ." On January 2, 1944, a clandestine meeting between Nano and Semyonov, the Soviet chargé, took place. The preliminary negotiations were inconclusive. Whether the Russians kept the Stockholm talks from their Allies was not known; at any rate, the Rumanians did, Maniu especially, who wished to keep the secret lest it seem that the Rumanian-Russian contacts were aimed at exploiting Allied-Russian differences (while it seems that Antonescu was not particularly averse to finding out whether chances for such exploitation existed.) On April 12 Nano met the ailing Ambassadress Kollontay at Saltsjöbaden; but by that time the scene of Rumanian peace negotiations had shifted to places where more important emissaries were involved.

The most important emissary at that time was Prince Barbu Stirbey. Early in 1944 Maniu and other opposition leaders agreed that this respectable aristocrat should be the peace envoy of Rumania. Through Allied agents it was first arranged that Stirbey go to London, but the Russians strongly opposed this and insisted to the British that this violated their "competences" in Rumania. While these clandestine background discussions lasted, external developments matured. On February 1 a British intelligence official called in Ankara on the main contact man, the envoy Cretzianu, and invited Stirbey to proceed to Cairo. Stirbey left secretly and arrived in Istanbul on March 10. On the same day Killinger appeared at Mihai Antonescu's office: the German envoy asked why Stirbey had left for Turkey. With great difficulty Antonescu tried to explain his responsibility away. On March 13, in a sudden diplomatic move, the Soviet Union recognized the Badoglio government; within twenty-four hours Antonescu requested of Bova Scoppa that Italy now facilitate contacts between Moscow and Bucharest.

[*Bulgaria.*]   Balkan politics tried, uneasily, to conform to the global realities of the day. In January even Pavelič attempted to resign and slip back to obscurity; he was not allowed to do so; Nedič tried the same in February — in vain. Early that month the first concrete Bulgarian peace feelers were sent to London and Washington; a letter was written by the opposition leaders Georgiev and Bagrianov to the Prime Minister, requesting withdrawal from the war, a warning similar to that of the Finnish "33," to the Small Holders' manifesto in Hungary, and to Maniu's letters in Rumania. The British knew that Russian difficulties in Bulgaria would be forthcoming; the Americans (Stettinius and Leahy) simply sent a message to Harriman in Moscow about the Bulgarian secession offers: according to Leahy's memoirs, this diplomatic act, revealing in its noncommittal simplicity, was done because Bulgaria was veering toward the Russian sphere anyhow. (*12*) Here was another instance of "passing the buck" — surprisingly enough, to Russia now, despite the fact that Bulgaria's secession was relatively easy; the Germans already had reduced their forces there and had begun the slow evacuation of the remaining troops.

[*The fate of Hungary.*]   Hungary, mostly due to her geographical situation, was not so successful. German intelligence succeeded in intercepting the correspondence of two Hungarian secret emissaries; it also became known that Horthy and Kállay had already taken financial measures to support Hungarian interests in neutral and Allied countries in case of extreme necessity. Early in 1944 the government-controlled press assumed more and more of a European and conservative, neutral attitude. (*13*) On February 10 the Foreign Minister instructed the Hungarian envoy in Lisbon that Hungary could not surrender to Russian, Rumanian or Slovak troops, but, aside from that, he should again try to impress on the Allies the Government's unconditional willingness to surrender. In late February Kállay, who at first believed that he could bring about the Anglo-American occupation of the country, began to be aware of the dreary fact that he had to deal with the Russians also; the British and Americans strongly advised him to do so. He prepared for steps to contact the Soviets; but it was now too late. The Russian spearheads were approaching the Carpathians, and only a few miles separated them from the vital Lwów-Cernauti railroad.

Himmler and Hitler had made up their minds as early as September 1943 to arrange a *coup d'état* in Hungary. On March 11, an SS-Army-Police meeting was held "for the absorption of Hungary." Kaltenbrunner and others presented complete plans; they decided on the most minute details, finally deeming it necessary, at the Foreign Ministry's insistence, to keep Horthy instead of "disposing of him." "I daresay," said Kaltenbrunner, "that such an attempt could . . . bring about a government of the [notoriously pro-German] people within three days. The Trojan method remains assured, but so does our reputation as well." (*14*)

. . . .

[*The Ides of March.*] To the north of Hungary stood Slovakia, whose leader was able and talkative enough to persuade Hitler that he should leave Slovakia alone and that he, Tiso, was reasonably trustworthy. To the south, in the Balkans, the time of decision was rapidly approaching, if it had not already arrived. True, on February 12, with British mediation, an ELAS–EDES truce was signed at the Plaka Bridge over the river Arakthos, delimiting their respective zones of operation. But ELAS did not really observe the agreement; it attacked other non-Communist guerrillas, and on March 17 a National Liberation Council, PEEA, equivalent to the Communist-dominated government of mountain Greece, was announced. The Soviets, who heretofore studiously abstained from giving even a semblance of intervention in Greek affairs, suddenly acclaimed PEEA. (*15*) Four days before, the Russians had suddenly recognized the Badoglio government, while the British and Americans were haggling over Italian personalities and ideological assets. (*16*)

King Peter and Purič were now summoned to London; some of the exiled Yugoslav diplomats had already swung to Tito's side; the Balkan developments made Churchill act with brutal despatch. He wrote a letter to Tito, who seemed deeply impressed. (*17*) On March 15, a British note again demanded that the Yugoslavs finally and definitely exclude Mihailovič from the exile cabinet; and when a second note was needed, two days later the British envoy brusquely stated that in British opinion, the Yugoslav government-in-exile was "no longer necessary." Next day, Churchill saw King Peter and admonished the boy-King sternly: he should conform to the British view: Tito was the only possible solution; he could not be disregarded.

The acceleration of history was frightful. If one examined the world press between March 10 and 20, 1944, these seemed rather eventless days. Yet, how much happened secretly and in the background! Let us look once more at these typical ten days:

March 10: Stirbey arrives in Istanbul. Russian ultimatum-like note to Finns: their answer unsatisfactory. Turkey's Ambassador to Britain resigns.

March 11: SS-Army conference decides to "absorb" Hungary. Peter and Purič, summoned to London, arrive. Yugoslav Ambassador to Russia declares himself loyal to Tito.

March 12: King Gustav intervenes in Finland.

March 13: American memorandum, urging and threatening Finland. Stirbey leaves for Cairo. Russia announces recognition of Badoglio.

March 14: Secret session in Finnish Parliament decides to continue peace negotiations. Antonescu asks Italy to help in contacting Russia.

March 15: British demand to Yugoslavs to drop Mihailovič. Germans mobilize divisions on Hungarian border. Russians cross River Bug. Secret German intelligence conference about German-Russian negotiated peace.

March 16: Roosevelt hint to Finland made. Admiral Horthy summoned to Hitler.

March 17: Finnish reply to Russia: negotiations welcome. British Ambassador: Yugoslav government-in-exile no longer necessary. Stirbey begins first official Rumanian armistice talks in Cairo. Hull says that he was not consulted on Soviet-Italian recognition. Greek PEEA government announced by Communists.

March 18: Horthy temporarily imprisoned by Hitler. Russians cross Cernauti-Lwów railroad. Churchill's stern talk with King Peter.

March 19: Germans occupy Hungary. Russia demands that Finnish delegates come to Moscow.

Here are twenty-eight important events: if the most careful observers, by some miraculous means, could in those days have read all the newspapers and listened to all the radio stations of the world, they would have known but eight of them.

[*The German coup.*]   I shall now return to what the SS called "the Trojan method." On Thursday, March 16, Jagow, the German envoy in Budapest, was instructed to request that Admiral Horthy

go to meet Hitler at once. (*18*) On Friday morning, Horthy conferred with Kállay: he had to go, but he told the Premier to be
extremely careful and not to obey any orders or do anything without
hearing from Horthy personally. Shortly after Kállay left the Regent,
a report from the Hungarian Consulate in Vienna confirmed previous
counterintelligence rumors about German troop concentrations on
the Hungarian border. Secretly, and with untold anxiety, the Regent
left for Klessheim. There, on Saturday, March 18, Schuschnigg's
Berchtesgaden experiences repeated themselves; this scene was even
worse: Hitler thoroughly detested the old, conservative Horthy and,
against the advice of Ribbentrop and the SS, even wanted to arrest
him. (*19*) The Regent was insulted, accused, threatened by Hitler,
who told him that orders had already been given to the German
Army to enter Hungary. He put a paper before Horthy, requesting
his signature: a common communiqué agreeing to the arrival of the
"assisting German forces" in Hungary. Horthy refused to sign. Hitler
accused him again of preparing a "Leftist *putsch*" and making a deal
with the Anglo-Saxons; this Horthy denied, but without success. Hitler now said that whether the Regent wanted it or not, German forces
had already crossed the frontiers of Hungary: he, Hitler, requested but
one thing, the resignation of Kállay and the Anglophiles from the
government; aside from this he would not intervene in Hungarian
politics, and the occupation, which would not touch Budapest, would
be of a temporary character. Horthy first refused, then hesitated,
provoking another violent outburst of rage on the part of Hitler.
Ribbentrop then anxiously summoned the simpleton Hungarian
envoy to Berlin, Sztójay, from the anteroom: "For heaven's sake, do
something!" Sztójay was virtually pushed into the room; after another talk it was uneasily agreed that he would form a new cabinet
in Budapest. At nightfall, Horthy's train left the castle; in the dark
shadows of the Alps, Horthy was alone, filled with dark thoughts and
forebodings. Then, unexpectedly, his train was halted somewhere in
eastern Austria.

Horthy wanted to return to Budapest and do things in his own way
on Sunday: discuss the situation with Kállay first and appoint Sztójay
only after having taken some mitigating measures. But Hitler tricked
him. While Horthy's train was standing in the bleak dawn of March 19
on a lonely railroad siding, a German armored division rumbled
through the Transdanubian plains toward Budapest; German parachute troops descended onto the main Hungarian airfields, and Buda-

pest was occupied by SS troops and police forces. Horthy's train was shunted onto the Budapest tracks in the morning; when it pulled into the capital, the *coup d'état* was over. Many Hungarian Conservatives and opposition leaders were arrested; the only one who could resist was the heroic Bajcsy-Zsilinszky; he was subdued after being shot and wounded. Kállay fled through an underground passageway to the Turkish Legation, where he was offered sanctuary. A complete blackout of news and radio messages was imposed upon the country, a blackout which was lifted slowly only on the 22nd; then the formation of the Sztójay government was announced, in which the only remaining conservative was Csatay, the War Minister. Meanwhile German police closed in on all possible resistance centers and took early measures for the fantastic extermination of the 500,000 Hungarian Jews, for which task the Special SS Commando Group of Wisliceny had already been activated in Vienna on March 10. Jagow was whisked away from the scene, speedily recalled: Hungary received a veritable Gauleiter, the SS envoy and "plenipotentiary," Edmund Veesenmeyer, who publicly insulted the Regent's name on March 19 and threatened the arrested Hungarian Chief-of-Staff with the partial occupation of the country by despised Slovaks, Croatians, and Rumanians if there was any Hungarian resistance to his orders.

All this, of course, changed Hungary's international situation. The advancing Russians reached the crest of the Carpathians, and the Anglo-Americans knew that the secret air agreements with Hungary were now worthless; on April 3 the first American and British air raids on Budapest and other Hungarian centers began. (20)

Ullein-Reviczky could write, from the sad perspective of 1946:

> Even if Hungary had been as heroic as Poland, as tenacious as Greece, as gallant as Yugoslavia or able like Czechoslovakia, the situation, basically, would not have been different from what it is today; for a small country, in the center of gigantic, global events can hardly make history: it suffers it. (21)

[*The Russian Army crosses the Rumanian frontier.*] Of this Rumania furnished a contemporary example. Perhaps more able, and certainly more fortunate than her neighbor, her main emissary had begun his talks with the Allies in Cairo on March 17. It was now certain that Rumania would be occupied exclusively by the Russian armies: something which Prince Stirbey did not know when he left

Bucharest. He also did not know that due to Russian pressure on Britain, the inscrutable Russian Ambassador, Novikov, sat at the middle of the Cairo table, flanked only by the British Lord Moyne and the American MacVeagh. (*22*) On that first meeting Stirbey was told that Russia wanted no concrete political commitments; a commitment by the Rumanian government and army in regard to the actual, technical execution and provisions of the armistice was enough. The political future of Rumania was thus left obscure: Stirbey did not know what to do. The dramatic news of the German move in Hungary came, and the Rumanians, as exactly four years before, were suddenly frightened by the prospects of an immediate German occupation of Rumania. Of this they informed the Western Allies; but, as in March 1939, their fears were exaggerated. To their frantic dispatches the Allied Commander in the Mediterranean, Sir Maitland Wilson, answered that Antonescu should refuse Hitler's invitation. But then Antonescu was not unduly pressed by Hitler. Meanwhile the Malinowski and Tolbuchin armies were rapidly advancing through Bessarabia and northern Bukovina. On March 22 Bucharest was officially informed through Stirbey and Cretzianu that the first Allied demand was the surrender of the Rumanian Army to the Russians. This statement was repeated on the 29th, and it was added that after the armistice, Rumanian troops would be expected to attack German forces. On April 1 the Russian Ambassadors in Washington and London officially informed the United States and Britain that the Soviet Union was to retain her 1940 borders; the note also contained the text of Molotov's generous statement which was broadcast on the next day:

> The Soviet government declares that it does not pursue the aim of acquiring any part of Rumanian territory or of changing the existing social order in Rumania. It equally declares that the entry into Rumania of Soviet troops is solely the consequence of military necessities and of the continuation of resistance to enemy forces.

This was very clever: issued on the day when the first Russian patrols advanced in territories *beyond* the 1940 frontiers, it brought a tremendous propaganda advantage; it assured the rosy optimists in Washington and London that Stalin's war aims were of limited extent — an illusion which persisted throughout this critical year, until Yalta; then it was too late. Churchill expressed his "admiration" of the Soviet statement; also Hull. There were no political assurances, however; nor did the message of Wilson on April 2 contain any. And later in April, when Cretzianu expressed his fears of Russian Communist plans and the eventual reduction of Rumania to a Soviet satellite, the political adviser of Lord Moyne wrote him condescendingly: "You are still living in cloud-cuckoo land."

The admirable Soviet communiqué of April 2, of course, also aimed to influence the surrender of Rumania and of the other satellites. Having seen what happened in Hungary, the British *and the Soviet* governments again urged the United States to soften the rigid "unconditional surrender" principle when it came to the satellites. It is strange how America clung to this principle: on April 5 Roosevelt in a memorandum stated to the State Department that he understood the practical disadvantages of this policy, but he wanted "to preserve the principle at all costs." Finally, when a Three-Power Declaration to the satellites, inviting them to secede from Germany, was broadcast on April 27, it did not mention unconditional surrender. (*23*) Meanwhile, however, the Soviet advance into Rumania stopped before Jassy (Odessa, which the Rumanians handed over to German administration in April, was not as yet reoccupied), and the front remained stationary there until August 19. The Antonescus thereupon breathed somewhat more freely, relaxed in the knowledge that some precious time had been gained; thus, although Maniu around April 15 received concrete Russian-Allied armistice proposals, action was temporarily postponed. (*24*)

· · · · · · ·

Germany showed no signs of giving up yet. Her vigorous action in Hungary showed keenness and ability to stamp out political dangers where possible, an important secondary contribution to the general war effort. Nor were primary considerations lacking, as on March 15 the top-level conference of the High Command of the Armed Forces, the SD, counterintelligence and the Foreign Ministry showed; Canaris recorded the conference as follows:

> The political and military leaders are of the opinion that Germany has nothing to expect from the Russians; on the contrary, should the war take a turn for the worse, the Slavs may retaliate the harsh treatment we inflicted upon them. Nevertheless, every alley should be explored in order to create a political state of mind which will induce the Russians to negotiate a separate peace with us.

In the event of a negotiated peace, or should we be defeated — on a long-range plan Germany has everything to gain by cooperating with the East.

Right now, the chances of a separate peace with the West are a little better, especially if we succeed, through our propaganda campaign and our "confidential" channels to convince the enemy that Roosevelt's policy of unconditional surrender drives the German people toward communism.

The opposition against Roosevelt's alliance with Stalin grows constantly. Our chances for success are good, if we succeed to stir up influential circles against Roosevelt's policy. This can be done through clever pieces of information, or by references to unsuspicious neutral ecclesiastical contact men.

We have at our command in the United States efficient contacts, which have been carefully kept up during the war. The campaign of hatred stirred up by Roosevelt and the Jews against everything German has temporarily silenced the pro-German bloc in the USA. However, there is every hope that this situation will be completely changed in a few months. (*25*)

If the Republicans succeed in defeating Roosevelt in the coming presidential election, it would greatly influence the American war policy towards us.

The KO-leaders abroad and their staff have innumerable opportunities of constantly referring to Roosevelt's hate policy.

They can at the same time hint at the danger that Germany may thereby be forced to cooperate with Russia. The greatest caution has to be observed in all conversations and meetings by those who as "anti-Nazis" maintain contact with the enemy. When fulfilling missions, they have to comply strictly with instructions.

Schmidt had recorded that at that time Hitler had rejected hints for a separate peace with Stalin with "definitely less vehemence" than suggestions that he deal with the West; and the SS leaders were not averse to creating a National-Bolshevist front with Russia against Britain, France and America. (*26*)

[*American lack of realism: the friendship with Russia.*] At the same time Washington again increased its efforts to avoid the slightest chances of misunderstandings with Russia. On March 18 Mikolajczyk wrote a long letter to Roosevelt; humbly and with warm emotion he asked the President to save the peace of the world and help Poland and Europe against the dangerous aspirations of the Soviets. The answer was disheartening. Hull stated again that the United States was offering only their *bona officia:* "We were not entering into the merits of the differences between Poland and Russia." Roosevelt answered Mikolajczyk's long letter on April 3 in a cold, curt and almost supercilious way, again requesting the Polish Premier to postpone his visit to Washington. The April visit was therefore postponed until early June.

The Poles were not the only ones disturbed: the Greek government had learned with painful surprise the Anglo-American decision to give part of the Italian navy to the Soviets. Here again was a matter which vitally concerned the interests of a central-eastern European ally: a decision was taken about which this small ally was neither consulted nor previously informed.

Washington tended now to subordinate everything to the grand plan of American-Russian collaboration. To further gain Stalin's confidence, on April 8 he was informed of D-Day, the exact date of the coming Normandy invasion. By chance, it was on the same day that the Japanese Ambassador called on Molotov and again presented a plan for mediating a peace between Russia and Germany. Molotov, *after* having ascertained from the envoy that it was not upon an official German request that the Japanese mediation offer came, rejected the proposal, and three days later Gromyko told Hull of the Japanese approach. *(27)* Yet the main German armor was still in the East: in mid-April this was the distribution of German divisions:

on the Russian front	199
in Finland	7
in western Poland	3
in Hungary	5
in the Balkans	21
in Western Europe	51

On April 25 General Antonov of the Soviet General Staff informed General Deane in Moscow that a Russian offensive was to be launched, coinciding with the Normandy invasion. About that time an interesting "incident" indicated the prevalent trend of thought in leading American circles: General Patton informally spoke before a British service club and said that Britain and America would have to rule the world after the war. General Marshall was furious, and, as Captain Butcher noted, "Our Public Relations Officer has been busy on his own getting Russia included and to some extent succeeded . . ." A noble and great effort, indeed! But the rest of Butcher's note is even more illuminating:

> . . . Republicans at home construed Patton's remarks as a general's intrusion into political affairs — political on Roosevelt's side — just why, I don't know . . . General Marshall says that [now] practically any hope of senatorial approval of the permanent promotions for a long list of officers, including Patton and Beetle [General Walter Bedell Smith], is out!

[*American lack of realism: the German and Austrian occupation.*] Not less enlightening was the fundamental and important case of the occupation zones in Germany and Austria. Vain British efforts to convince Washington of the feasibility and desirability, nay, necessity, of a joint American-British push into Austria through northern Italy (the British even gave a name to this project: Operation *Rankin*) continued. In the winter of 1943–44 even the Russians wished for a more extensive American participation in the occupation of central Europe, as Stalin could not see yet how the situation at the end of the war would develop, how and where the Russian armies would be standing. The British made a proposal as early as January 1944 at the European Advisory Commission which allocated southern Germany and Austria to the American zone of occupation. But this was rejected:

> . . . for political and military reasons the President and the Joint Chiefs of Staff were determined not to accept a zone either in southern Germany or in Austria, or to participate in the national control of Austria.
> They felt that American zones in South Germany and Austria would interfere with redeployment, because United States forces in these areas would be landlocked far from North Sea and Channel ports . . .

It can be detected here how the impact of isolationist opinion and the fear of "Japan first" and "Bring the boys back home" slogans were constantly in the background of the President's mind; but this was not all:

> . . . an Austrian zone would draw the United States into the Balkan trouble center and involve her with the long-standing rivalry between Great Britain and Russia in the Balkans. (*28*)

The fatal Third Power concept of America again! Compare this with the tragic, grumbling contemplation of Britain's rôle in the post-war world which Churchill pondered in the Commons on April 21:

> Should we draw closer to Europe — there is another question, an aim at creating . . . an entity in Europe, a United States of Europe? Or, again, should we concentrate upon our own Imperial and Common-wealth organization, or upon our fraternal association with the United States, and put our trust in the English Channel, in air power and in sea power?

Two weeks later, after the visit of the Australian Premier, Churchill wrote Eden:

> Broadly speaking, the issue is: Are we going to acquiesce in the Com-munisation of the Balkans and perhaps of Italy? Mr. Curtin touched upon this today, and I am of the opinion on the whole that we ought to come to a definite conclusion about it, and that if our conclusion is that we resist the Communist infusion and invasion, we should put it to them pretty plainly at the best moment that military events per-mit. We should of course have to consult the United States first. (29)

History's irony was no less tragic. On April 23 a Communist-inspired revolt broke out in the Greek Navy in Alexandria and among certain Greek Army units; with British assistance, the Greek govern-ment and loyal troops subdued the revolt with great difficulty. Not quite three years later the same Americans who in 1944 did not wish to be involved in the Balkans, "between Britain and Russia," were compelled to take one of the historic steps of American foreign policy: the United States extended military aid and dispatched military mis-sions to Greece and Turkey and in 1947 General Marshall, as Sec-retary of State, enunciated the "Truman Doctrine." Three years be-fore, the same General Marshall, then Chief of Staff, had disavowed America's interest in these very countries.

Winant in London was now (somewhat belatedly) aware of the fallacy of the American policy of not wishing to participate in the control of Austria; he was worried and cabled his worries home. Then in April, perceiving the growing popularity of the Third, Neutral Power concept in the United States, it was Russia which proposed the tripartite occupation of Austria instead of the original proposal which had allowed Austria to the British occupation sphere. On May 1 the State Department instructed Winant to refuse proposals which would commit the United States in Austria.

The situation was further complicated by a deadlock over Germany. The President and the Joint Chiefs of Staff instructed Winant in March to request an American Zone in northwest Germany only, just outside of Berlin: not only were their proposed boundaries most unrealistic, but the American plan also defied the confidential British suggestions that the United States take her zone in southern Germany, next to Austria. Thus an American-British deadlock arose in regard to the respective German zones.

To save the position of the Western Powers in central Europe, the British turned to the Soviets for a deal in early May: they would be willing to advocate the granting of the whole of East Prussia to Poland if the Soviets acquiesced in the control of Austria by British forces alone. In that month, the State Department also presented an important memorandum to Roosevelt advising against the eventual partitioning of Germany; it established the impracticability and erroneous concept of all projects calling for Germany's dismemberment. The lack of any concrete American planning in regard to the future of Germany became dangerously evident.

[*Churchill's sudden proposal to Russia: to divide the Balkans.*] Everything seemed to be in utmost confusion and flux; the British were bewildered. Churchill once more tried to make Eisenhower abandon the invasion plans of southern France and divert forces to the Adriatic; according to Eisenhower, "he [Churchill] did not admit that political factors were influencing him"; Eisenhower refused to budge, requesting Churchill to take the matter up with Roosevelt. (*30*) The general optimism and naïveté reigning supreme in the United States made Churchill act then; something concrete had to be done before, in the maze of hazy, general agreements, the hard facts, the hard boots of occupying Soviet soldiery, would stamp out all possible resistance to Russia in the Balkans.

Thus, on May 19 Churchill bluntly turned to Stalin and requested Russia to examine and conclude a sphere of interest agreement in the Balkans. The Soviets were taken by surprise by this astute manoeuvre: they suggested to Britain that the United States be consulted about all this; the idealistic and non-specific American statements disturbed Russian plans far less than even the smallest practical limitation of their sphere of conquest. On May 24 Churchill gave one of his most interesting speeches in the House of Commons, saying among other things that the war had lost its ideological character — a strange-sounding statement which but few understood then. (*31*)

On May 30 Lord Halifax called on Hull and asked him how the United States would feel if Britain and Russia made a "principal military responsibility" agreement, whereby Greece would fall into the British sphere of "principal military responsibility," while Rumania fell into the Soviet one — such arrangement to be only for the wartime period. The Ambassador said that the conclusion of such an agreement was urgently imperative, for already dangerous difficulties regarding their respective spheres had arisen between Britain and Russia, particularly concerning Rumania. Hull received the proposal with righteous wrath; he did not fully perceive what was behind it. (*32*) Winant now intervened on Churchill's side; next day Churchill cabled Roosevelt, urging him to agree. On May 31 Roosevelt permitted Winant to announce American "participation" in the control of Austria on the "national level," but without any commitment as to the existence or size of the American occupation forces. (The President did this without having informed the State Department or the Joint Chiefs of Staff; because of this lack of coordination, troubles later resulted.) As to Churchill's sphere of interest proposal, Roosevelt flatly rejected it. On June 8, Churchill cabled him again, trying to impress the American President with the utmost urgency of such an arrangement between Britain and Russia; in this message, aware of Russian demands, Churchill added Bulgaria to Rumania and (inasmuch as Tito had just suffered a crushing defeat by the Germans and was barely saved with the help of British and Americans) Churchill added Yugoslavia to Greece in the British sphere. Roosevelt saw now more clearly (*33*); on June 10 he answered Churchill: he again refused the proposal, but was now less unequivocal. Roosevelt suggested that perhaps a triangular or quadrangular agreement between the Great Powers might work in the Balkans. To this Churchill answered within twenty-four hours, making it clear that from any such typical American proposal to create another commission, only chaos or impotence would result. The impatient and anxious Prime Minister now urged and begged Roosevelt to consent to the sphere of interest agreement as a temporary measure, only for three months. Roosevelt then reluctantly agreed, without telling Hull about his decision.

[*The Balkan scene in April.*] Tito forces raided some of the Dalmatian islands in late April; Hitler, who at first had expressed his admiration of Tito before his generals, then ordered his best Balkan troops to stage a counteroffensive and wipe out the Partisan leader. The Germans also held out spectacular offers to Bulgarians, who, however, were unwilling and weary; to quisling Greeks, who were very few; to some Albanians about a German-dominated Albanian "national" government in late April (which Berlin quickly "recognized" and the former Counselor of the Moscow Embassy, Schliep, became the first German Minister to that "government"); and to Macedonians (the old Mihailov was flown in July to Skoplje to install an "independent Macedonian government"). Of course, it was far too late.

The British were not less impressed with Tito. On April 6 Eden, and on April 13 Churchill insisted to the Yugoslav King that a Regency of three persons, friendly to Tito, should supplant the present government-in-exile. The helpless young Peter appealed to Roosevelt for aid, who answered him in a friendly tone but did not promise support, and hinted that he agreed with Churchill. The British insisted that the Croatian Subasič, who by that time had considerable contacts with Tito, form a new government; meanwhile Tito sent a military mission, led by his "General" Terzič, to Moscow in order to get information about the Russian offensive in the Balkans; another emissary was sent to Eisenhower for more aerial aid and material supplies; a small Titoist mission went to London.

[*The Lebanon Conference.*] The British were obsessed with the idea that in the Balkans a new "progressive," national, Leftist leadership was emerging. (*34*) While they agreed with the strong measures with which the Greek government quelled the mutiny of April 23, British pressure resulted in the dismissal of the anti-Communist Liberal, Sophocles Venizelos; instead, the moderate Socialist Papandreou became Prime Minister, a man of considerable ability who at that time was somewhat obsessed with the idea that he himself could unite Right and Left in Greece. On May 5 the Russian government refused a Greek official request to intervene in the strife between the guerrillas. The British now arranged a unique conference of the Greek parties, the conferees being called from the mountains and valleys of Greece, from the hiding-cellars of the Athens apartment houses, and clandestinely transported to near Beirut in the Lebanon, where from May 17 to 23 the Lebanon Conference assembled. The Communists sent a surprisingly moderate delegation, led by the theoretical Marxist Svolos and other "front" men. (*35*) Their conduct was correspondingly mild: the Lebanon Agreement, recognizing the Papandreou cabinet, resulted. This Communist attitude was probably taken on Russian advice, for Stalin knew at that time that with or without sphere interest agreements, Greece would fall into Britain's zone of occupation. It was a masterful example of Russian-Communist tactical coordination: by the Lebanon Agreement the EAM gained certain British sympathies, propaganda advantages, the chance to enter a coalition government, and avoided the possibility that British troops, soon to land in Greece, would come supporting an anti-Communist government-in-exile and fighting an outlawed ELAS/EAM. Similar were developments in Albania, where in May, in the village of Permet, met the first Albanian "Anti-Fascist National Liberation Congress" modeled after Tito's Jajce "assembly" (it included delegates from Northern Epirus, foreshadowing trouble with Greek nationalism), and a handful of Albanian Communists under Xoxe and Hoxha formed LNC, a "united front" government which, surprisingly enough, the British began to support.

[*The Germans attack Tito.*]   German forces, scraped together from the bottom of the almost empty German war reservoir, began a general offensive against the Yugoslav Partisans around May 10 and were surprisingly successful, especially in Bosnia and in eastern Croatia. In the morning of May 24, SS paratroopers were dropped around Tito's headquarters near Drvar; general confusion and flight followed. The Germans captured several officers and almost got the prize of the expedition, Tito himself, who, together with Randolph Churchill, barely escaped. The Staff and Partisan headquarters fled to the small island of Vis, which was supported and supplied exclusively by the American and British air forces from Italy (a regular airlift was arranged, with more than 40 planes); from Vis, Tito flew several times to the Italian mainland. (*36*) It was time that the exaggerated notion of Partisan glory be dampened: when, if Churchill's statement in his February 22 speech was to be believed, 250,000 Titoists were facing fourteen German divisions, it seemed strange that a mere six hundred paratroopers could make Tito retreat, and actually expel him from the Yugoslav mainland. (*37*)

[*British pressure.*] Nevertheless, Churchill went ahead insisting on a Subasič-Tito government and in his May 24 speech actually announced that he had a message from King Peter about the Subasič government having been accepted; Churchill thus confronted the government-in-exile with accomplished facts: for even if the King gave such a notice to the British — and there are some who deny it — he did it without having consulted the government-in-exile in its entirety. This was the last phase of their tragedy. The young, weak King, carefully avoided by the influential people of the day, haplessly wandering in the May evenings of London from the political confabulations of dark, sullen Serbs to polite, unhelpful British offices, was alone, drearily alone. Pressed by the British, he asked his own Serbs whether it was true that Mihailovič was collaborating with the Germans or not. (*38*) And, when it was impressed upon him that the trend of the times demanded a transformation of Yugoslav governments and politics in a more "progressive" manner, Peter himself repeated the not so long ago treacherous-sounding argument: "If Mihailovič does not agree, his value to the country is finished." On June 1, Peter issued a declaration to all Serbs, Croats, and Slovenes for national "unity," stating that the "new Premier," Subasič, was to form a new government after having consulted all elements of the Yugoslav resistance. All this was, of course, in line with the Soviet-desired "united front" policies, the same pattern as everywhere in Europe, America, and Asia. (*39*)

The recollections of the new British Ambassador, Sir Maurice Peterson, who was sent to Turkey in the place of his unfortunate predecessor, are characteristic of these days:

> When I reached Turkey in 1944 I conceived it was my mission to reassure the Turks. I pointed out — *and the Foreign Office commended me for doing so* — that German, Italian and even French influence was disappearing in the Balkans. There was a vacuum and it was only natural that it should in part be filled by the Soviet Union. There was nothing to be alarmed about.
> The Turks listened without appearing to be convinced. The Turks were right. (*40*)

[*Hungary's trials.*] The temporary breathing-space allotted to the Danubian satellites by the halt in the Russian offensive provided but insignificant relief; for these unfortunate nations were truly between anvil and hammer. In Hungary police terror reigned throughout April and May; Horthy and those few who remained faithful to him could do nothing. *(41)* The Hungarian Army stood in the Carpathians, the Rumanian Army was at the Pruth, badly equipped, unenthusiastic, dispersed among German units and without chance of independent strategic action, while the bombs of the Western Allies plastered railroad yards, factories, plants in Budapest, Bucharest, Debrecen, and Constanta, the Weiss Manfred works at Csepel, and the Ploesti oil wells. By the end of April the Danube was mined by aerial action; Hungary and Rumania announced the suspension of fluvial shipping. The smell of death and decay was in the air; only the fanatics and the fools closed their eyes and ears.

[*Rumanian experiments.*]   Horthy, with the cooperation of a few loyal diplomats, generals, and aristocrats, began to try to gradually resist Veesenmeyer and the Nazis in early June; in Rumania Mihai Antonescu himself knew that there remained not much time to act. Many Hungarian diplomats had resigned, and those in contact with the Allies tried to request that Molotov's April statement reassuring Rumania be repeated in regard to Hungary. In Bucharest it became known around April 20 that the Rumanian armistice talks were temporarily interrupted. Ten days later the Turkish Minister left Bucharest for Ankara to facilitate a new Rumanian contact with the Allies, but then the Turks were not standing in Russian favor, and the Soviet Ambassador to Turkey was known to be anti-Rumanian. Mihai Antonescu told all kinds of things to his friend Bova Scoppa: he wanted to send Gafencu to London; the Americans were willing to deal with him; he was in contact with "certain American professors of international law." But most of this was illusionary, and only their military cataclysms prevented the Germans from taking strong measures in Rumania, as they did in Hungary. Having received a personal rebuff from the Western Allies, Mihai Antonescu momentarily returned to his former favorite idea in May: he sent a personal envoy to the sick and weary Mussolini, who presided over his shadow Italian Social Republic amidst the drying rhododendrons of Lake Garda. As he had done a year before, Antonescu wrote to Mussolini in the pretentious vein of one Latin dictator to another: peace negotiations were inevitable; as Mussolini knew it, couldn't he do something too? Mussolini was pleased with this approach, rather complimentary now (how angry he had been a year before!) but answered that he could do nothing. (*42*) Which was true.

[*Bulgarian fortunes.*] The more favorable geographical situation of Bulgaria began to show strategic consequences in early June when the Germans surreptitiously began to withdraw troops from that country; the Bulgarian statesmen put considerable hopes in the fact that Bulgaria was not at war with the Soviet Union, and Bulgarian newspapers hinted at old Slav ties. In spite of such behavior, on April 17 the first tough Russian note was sent to Sofia. It was answered with courtesy and utmost efforts at assurance. On April 26 the Soviets demanded the reopening of their consulates at Varna and Burgas. The Soviet Minister to Sofia called on the Foreign Ministry immediately in the wake of the British sphere of interest approach and presented a severe note protesting Bulgaria's alleged support of the Germans: a pretext for further intervention in Bulgaria. In the wake of the Russian note, the Prime Minister, Bozhilov, resigned, and the Conservative-Liberal Bagrianov became Premier; he immediately released a great number of political prisoners and silently relaxed anti-Jewish measures. A few days later Filov, one of the Regents, went to Berchtesgaden to promise Hitler that Bulgaria would not betray Germany: he was lucky to call on a day when the Führer was in a relatively balanced mood; thus, without having achieved much, but having gained time, Filov returned to Sofia.

Direct contact between Russia and Finland did not exist during May, except when Tanner went to Stockholm to attend the Congress of the Swedish Social Democratic Party, where a contact man arranged a meeting between him and Semyonov; but nothing came of their talk. Later in May Russia asked for British consent to and even naval assistance for the staging of raids on the northern Finnish and Norwegian coasts, whereupon Britain requested that the Norwegian government be approached first. These Russian plans were then abandoned. Finnish diplomacy vainly tried to win some official British and American understanding and assistance for Finland's plight; in the north the calm before the storm continued.

[*The Polish horizon brightens: Mikolajczyk in Washington.*] In Poland (except for the Stanisławów region where the Germans mounted a local counteroffensive around April 15 with limited success) stillness reigned on the battlefront. The Polish underground had now come out in the open, and greatly harassed the Germans. Thus indirectly the Home Army cooperated with the Russians; direct, local cooperation extended throughout Volhynia (in the Równe district for example the Home Army Commander established direct contact with Russian commanders). In May some underground leaders began to be secretly flown out from Poland, hardy, courageous men, whose arrival and stories made a strong impact on those American and British officials who met them: for example, Roosevelt was deeply impressed by the valiant young Jan Karski. Similarly impressive were the feats of the Polish troops in Italy: the Australian Prime Minister Curtin, who was visiting Britain, made a speech in which he came out very strongly for the Polish cause; in his May 24 speech, Churchill said: "I have the impression — and it is no more than an impression — that things are not so bad as they may appear on the surface between Russia and Poland." (In those days the agile Beneš offered his services as intermediary between Stalin and the Poles and actually communicated a Russian offer to Mikolajczyk containing three points: Russia requested the acceptance of the Curzon Line, a "certain reorganization" of the Polish government, and a new President in the place of Raczkiewicz.)

Then, after two postponements, Mikolajczyk finally left for Washington, where he arrived on the eve of D-Day. Suddenly, and to his great and joyful surprise, Roosevelt received him charmingly, cordially — in the words of Ciechanowski, who devoted an interesting chapter to the visit, this was "Red Carpet for Mikolajczyk." In nine days, the Polish Premier had four long and intimate talks with Roosevelt, despite the obviously pressing agenda of the American President. Roosevelt listened and seemed now to grasp the fact that the problem of the Polish Communists and the future government of Poland was now far more important than the frontiers of eastern Poland. The Polish Premier was pleased and awed. Roosevelt revealed to him that Stalin wanted to extend the Soviet frontier into East Prussia to get Königsberg (this transpired from the EAC meetings) and said that although he was personally sympathetic to the Finns, he could not help them — besides, the Soviet peace conditions seemed reasonable. Roosevelt was in his best mood, planning good things, optimistic, speaking of Polish TVA's, economic aid, and high moral principles. He said that he would surely defend Poland's interests, "but of one thing I am certain," he added, "Stalin is not an imperialist." He said that he was in contact with Stalin on the Polish issue and would ar-

range for Mikolajczyk to meet Stalin personally; thus things could
be eventually solved.

It is strange to compare these two leaders in 1944: the product of
a pragmatic society, the empirically trained Roosevelt, so supremely
idealistic, and the man of the mystic Caucasus, thoroughly steeped
in ideological training, Stalin, the supreme realist.

[*The Russian era casts its gloom.*]   There were, however, disturbing symptoms before and during Mikolajczyk's visit. Already in
the spring of 1944 influential elements among American Slavs tried,
at Russian suggestions, to make the Moscow-created Polish Communists more acceptable: a misled Polish-American priest, Father
Orlemanski, was tricked into presenting their cause in May; more
important, the new chiefs of the State Department's Eastern European
Division, Bohlen and Durbrow, requested that Mikolajczyk meet
with one of the representatives of the pro-Soviet Polish propagandists
in the United States, Professor Lange, who a few weeks before had
seen Stalin in person. Mikolajczyk and Lange actually met and had
a courteous talk, (43) nothing else; yet the State Department's action
foreshadowed the approach to a time when Washington, and to a lesser
extent London, would eagerly search for "political personalities" in
central-eastern Europe "mutually acceptable" to the peoples involved
and to Stalin, thus unwittingly playing the Russian game — as if
anybody truly independent would be "acceptable" to the Kremlin!

History was then further accelerated by four decisive events on the
European battlefronts. On June 4, Rome fell; on June 6 the Allies
were back in France. On June 9 the Russian Army launched its first
summer attack on the Karelian front against Finland and broke
through in two days; on June 22 the long-awaited Russian offensive
along the entire length of the central front, from Latvia to the Carpathians, began.

The decisive months of Russian victory: the climactic summer (June–October) of 1944

[*The Karelian offensive. Ribbentrop in Helsinki.*]   The launching
of the Russian offensive on the Finnish front took the world by surprise; the summer campaign had not been expected to start there.
The origins and aims of the Karelian offensive were clearly political.
On June 9 the Russians stormed the Finnish positions with their best

troops and with overwhelming equipment; their tactical air force
dominated overhead. Within three days the Finnish lines were broken
and the situation assumed critical proportions. Ryti consulted his
closest confidants and held three important conferences on June 15
and 16; he offered first the Premiership, then the Presidency to Field-
Marshal Mannerheim. The Commander-in-Chief refused, however,
as did General Walden, whom Mannerheim suggested; these two
leaders thought it better to remain with the armies during the military crisis. Finally Ramsay accepted the bid; during his efforts at
cabinet construction, on June 20 Viipuri fell. There followed now two
dramatic days, replete with the highest conferences; on June 21 it was
decided to examine once more Russian peace possibilities through
Stockholm; on the same day Germany was requested to furnish urgent
aid to Finland, as Mannerheim opined that without such aid a complete military collapse could hardly be avoided. (The Germans, fearing lest the lack of assistance to Finland might present a pretext or
a cause for renewed Finnish separate peace efforts, had already
previously exerted themselves to send supplies.) In the morning of
June 22 the news broke that the Russian armies had begun their great
offensive on the central front; Ribbentrop in Berlin was now more
than anxious to keep Finland in the war and avoid the release of
Russian divisions from the Finnish front to the detriment of the overwhelmed German lines in Byelorussia and Poland. Thus Ribbentrop
telephoned the German envoy in Helsinki to arrange his visit to the
Finnish capital at once; Blücher rushed to Ryti to ask the President's
agreement to the visit; Ryti, after inquiring in vain about the detailed
purpose of Ribbentrop's journey, agreed. This diplomatic journey,
probably the most hastily prepared, arranged, and executed in all
history, was subsequently undertaken: to Ryti's amazement, Ribbentrop flew from Berlin on the same afternoon, arrived in Helsinki in
the evening and called on Ryti at once. They talked until two in the
morning: with nervous eloquence, Ribbentrop spoke of German victory and forcefully insisted that it was suicidally erroneous and, anyhow, impossible for Finland to negotiate a separate peace with Russia.
He also denounced Paasikivi and the peace partisans, and spoke
angrily of existing Finnish-American relations.

Ryti did not commit himself and was reluctant to answer, while he
listened carefully. Much of Ribbentrop's argument was true. Moscow
had just answered the Finnish inquiry of two days before; it stated
that as the Soviet Government, due to previous experiences, did not

trust the Finns' sincerity, an official Finnish declaration should announce the capitulation of Finland and ask the Soviet Union to consider the Finnish peace request; only then would Moscow be ready to receive a Finnish delegation to negotiate. Such terms seemed impossible to the Finnish government. Relations with the United States also worsened. On June 16 the outspoken and somewhat undiplomatic Procopé, with three counselors of the Finnish Legation, was requested to leave Washington. On June 20 the able and active Finnish Minister to Ankara, Yrjö-Koskinen, talked with the American Ambassador Steinhardt, and the latter very pessimistically expressed his opinion that the United States could do nothing to help Finland. Steinhardt also thought that the Russians had decided to wind up the Finnish front as soon as possible, without consideration of losses in manpower and material; he professed to know that Finland would remain an independent state, (*1*) but there was the possibility that Russian forces would occupy most of the country; this the United States sought to avoid. Steinhardt also said that he personally "was ashamed to admit that the United States made a great military power factor of the Soviet Union — without American help the Soviet Union would have been defeated by Germany." And he added that in the United States it was understood that "Finland's comradeship-in-arms with Germany and her dependence on German help were solely due to the fact that Finland hated Germany less than she did Russia," concluding that, unfortunately, the acceptance of German assistance to Finland seemed natural to him. (*2*)

Ribbentrop was, however, mistaken, very much mistaken in his foolish and transparent optimism regarding the military chances of Germany. In the West and in the East the German armies were retreating, battered; Cherbourg fell and the Russians wheeled into the suburbs of Minsk, Borisov, Bobruisk; on June 24 the Finnish Minister from Berlin reported that the Germans seemed to have failed in their defense of the Normandy bridgehead; three days later Kivimäki expressed his opinion that Germany was beaten on both fronts.

On June 23 and 24 Ribbentrop tried hard to convince Ryti (who, to be sure, did not need much convincing to accept German aid) to accede to the German request and sign a commitment that Finland would not negotiate a separate peace. Otherwise Germany could not and would not assist Finland. Ribbentrop prepared a draft of such a declaration, also a draft of an official and solemn Ryti letter to Hitler, which was to confirm the declaration. On June 24 and 25 the Finns argued among themselves, conferred and hesitated, while Ribbentrop impatiently waited; he telephoned to Hitler, who ordered him not to accept any compromises but to insist on the presented texts. Aware of the expected bitter opposition of the Social Democrats and others in Parliament to such a Finnish-German agreement, but also aware of the juridical loophole which lay in the fact that a simple signature of Ryti, not presented later to Parliament, would limit the responsibility of the Finnish signature to the person of the President, the latter, without having consulted Parliament, accepted the Ribbentrop Agreement. Ribbentrop flew back to Berlin on the 26th. Ryti knew that the Germans were beaten. But he wanted to gain time. In this he succeeded. The Germans were unusually scrupulous in keeping their side of the agreement; they sent troops and equipment and also a few fighter squadrons and grain shipments to the distressed Finns. Around July 5 the Finnish lines were generally stabilized and the military situation did not take a turn for the worse for another month.

But this was the military situation only; on June 2 Kivimäki reported that with the speed of the Russian offensive westward, beyond the Latvian frontier and Minsk, the *military-political* situation was rapidly deteriorating. Within Finland, the Social Democrats and Tanner expressed their strong objection to the Ribbentrop Agreement, and a grave governmental crisis was only overcome by an earnest appeal to the Socialists to continue participating in the government for the sake of national unity. Only on July 2 did Tanner and the opposition acquiesce. Three days before, on June 30, the United States announced the severance of diplomatic relations with Finland.

.   .   .   .

From April onwards every military decision concerning the Balkans could not fail to have a political complexion. The problems of Allied military spheres and of the Allies' differing aims revealed themselves. Early in April, the American military mission in Moscow succeeded in getting the shuttle-bombing bases in the Ukraine: Poltava, Mirgorod, Piryatin. Long and useless discussions occurred with the Russians about the "bomb frontier" limiting Anglo-American air operations in the east and Russian air action in the west; experiencing delays and obstructions by the Russians, the Allies finally agreed to an indeed unpractical line, running roughly east of Constanta, Bucharest, Ploesti, and Budapest. After various and obscure delays, the first shuttle-bombing by American planes was agreed upon, and

the Americans notified the Russian General Staff of the selected targets. Suddenly on May 29, four days before the operation, the Russian
General Staff announced its disapproval of the American-selected
targets; as General Deane suspected, this was due to "the General
Staff's desire to deny us any inkling of what the Russian objectives
were to be in the Red Army offensive about to be launched." *(3)*

Two days after Rome had fallen to the Allies, the commander of
the Fifth Army, General Mark Wayne Clark, made a sincere and
respectful call on the Pope: and amidst these days of universal victory
and rejoicing the words of His Holiness were anxious as well as serene.
He asked General Clark about Allied military plans concerning Central Europe and the Danubian states; he expressed his anxiety about
Russian plans and prospects. The foresight of this reserved and saintly
man was not, however, shared by other men and organizations, pro-
fessedly very much at home with the affairs of the secular world.

[*New British Balkan plans: Sir Maitland Wilson.*] Now, immediately after the successful invasion of Normandy, the Anglo-American
conflict centering around the objectives in the Mediterranean campaign erupted again. Churchill, seeing the success of the French landings, wished to reorganize the Mediterranean effort in the direction
of the Balkans again. Probably because of his previous experiences,
he now wished that the British military chiefs impress their American
counterparts. But on June 9 — in connection with the obscure directives concerning the future of Austria — a directive of the American Joint Chiefs of Staff was passed down to the Supreme Allied
Commander of the Mediterranean Theatre which established that
no American forces were to be sent into any part of the Balkans,
Hungary, or Austria. Thereafter the Supreme Commander, Sir
Maitland Wilson, took steps of his own. On June 14 he issued
instructions concerning the formation of the American Seventh Army
(which later became General Patch's First Army): the Allies were
now well beyond Rome and climbing up on the Adriatic littoral.
The Wilson directive listed the winning of the Po Valley as the
objective of the Allied forces and also envisaged an amphibious landing in Istria "for exploitation through the Ljubljana Gap into the
plains of Hungary." On June 20 Wilson sent a message to Eisenhower
to the same effect. Eisenhower was somewhat irked, but seemed to
appreciate at least some of Wilson's points and turned to Marshall,
if not for instruction, at least for some general advice. *(4)*

[*Marshall overrules Churchill.*] In Washington the fully unrealistic illusions about global cooperation dominated the scene. The
State Department continued with the forming of its professorial committees; another *ad hoc* committee was set up to examine central-
eastern European territorial problems in June 1944 and industriously
wrote, presented, and filed some good papers (5); the United States
did not even contemplate the possibility that its recommendations
might be totally irrelevant to the realities of central-eastern Europe.
For there the Russians were arriving, with the full consent, nay, cooperation of the American Chiefs of Staff. Marshall answered Eisenhower
on June 28, informing him that the Chiefs of Staff had succeeded in
winning the President's concurrence in favor of *Anvil-Dragoon;* none
of this Balkan stuff, said Marshall, as the President was similarly
"opposed to use all our Mediterranean forces to fight on to Northern
Italy and beyond. He has so notified the Prime Minister and hopes
there will not be a deadlock in the Combined Chiefs of Staff."

Roosevelt wrote Churchill on June 29: "In view of [Teheran], I
cannot agree without Stalin's approval to any use of force or equipment elsewhere." Now Eisenhower informed Churchill on July 1 of
Washington's directives in a lengthy telephone conversation; Churchill reluctantly agreed. On July 2 Eisenhower informed Wilson of the
logistic need for a major port in France (Marseilles) and issued his
directives for the planned *Anvil-Dragoon* in southern France. A week
later Eisenhower saw Churchill at Chequers; they argued heatedly
as, according to Eisenhower's aide, Churchill "gave [Eisenhower]
hell for insisting on the *Anvil* operation, the British Prime Minister
still being wedded to pursuit of the Germans in Italy and to possibilities in the Balkans."

[*The Austrian confusion.*] The British-American differences
now extended into Austria, concerning whose future utmost confusion
reigned. Neither the State Department nor the Joint Chiefs of Staff
were informed of the Roosevelt directive which he sent to Winant on
May 31, after the latter's urging and numerous requests. This lack of
coordination resulted in the fact that although the State Department
presented two papers, on American objectives in Austria and on the
future "treatment" of that country, the Joint Chiefs of Staff kept
insisting that American armed forces were not to participate in anything concerning Austria, while Winant in the European Advisory
Commission assured the Allies that token American occupation

forces would be sent. Among such confusing circumstances the British Chiefs of Staff on July 7 officially requested the clarification of the differences existing between the Winant statements and the stand of the Joint Chiefs of Staff. Only in late July was all this obscurity clearing — and the Joint Chiefs of Staff were not at all happy about it. They continued to oppose sending American troops into Austria: only a token American garrison force should be sent into Vienna. (6) Not until September was the American standpoint fully clarified. The military were still unable to think in political terms; they were wilfully blinding themselves. No commitments! that was the word of the day. (7)

In the meanwhile both sides of the Adriatic were burning more and more with the fires of war; on the Italian coast an international army was marching northwards, in whose ranks Britons, Frenchmen, Italians, Brazilians, Americans, Canadians, Poles, Greeks fought. In Greece the civil war flared up again at the end of June. Tito fluttered from Vis to Bari to Rome and back; he met Subasič, and a new Yugoslav Government was announced on July 7 in which Subasič had included Tito delegates. (8) In Albania the nationalist guerrillas were involved in increasingly frequent clashes with the now Tito-supported forces of the Communist "National Liberation Front." In Macedonia also the Greek Communists seemed to gain ground: their secret agreements with the Bulgars began to bear fruit as the latter began to withdraw from Greek Macedonia.

[*Turkey and the Allies.*] After the successful Normandy invasion Turkey seemed to be more willing to participate in an Allied Balkan campaign; Steinhardt let Washington know that there was great distrust of the British in the Balkans, but (according to Leahy), especially the Turks had "real confidence in the integrity of the United States." If they had only known that it was due to the American military that Britain had to assume a Balkan policy which led to distrust! Leahy, for example, made another myopic remark at the end of June: "The British wished to defeat the Nazis but at the same time to acquire for the Empire postwar advantages in the Balkan States." Churchill again turned to the Turks, but they were cautious, and a Turkish-Russian diplomatic exchange took place, in which Ankara tried to gain some knowledge of Russian plans in the Balkans; instead, Moscow learned of the new British approach. Stalin expressed his supreme displeasure and took good care to notify Hull thereof on

July 10, deeming the British action a breach of previous agreements, according to which only a joint Allied bid could be made to Turkey. Stalin knew that he could count on American support against British Balkan plans; to make doubly sure, Gromyko asked the State Department whether America really concurred in the British-Russian "sphere of primary military responsibility" agreement on the Balkans; Washington answered, yes, for the duration of the three months agreed upon, but only if this was not to mean a sphere of influence agreement.

A naïve and pious wish! The example of Rumania proved that it was. On May 26 another secret emissary, Visoianu, arrived in Cairo. But in the meantime the Churchill sphere proposal had taken place, with a corresponding change in the Russian position. On June 1 the Soviets categorically refused to discuss anything until Maniu accepted their previous armistice conditions. Ten days later Maniu finally agreed. He now also asked for the eventual dispatch of Anglo-American airborne brigades into Rumania but he received no answer. Now Maniu formed an underground Democratic bloc, including the Peasants, Liberals, Socialists, and the representatives of the few hundred Rumanian Communists; this group sent another courier to the Allies on June 29, requesting the Soviets to start a vigorous drive into Rumania. But Rumania was now fixed in the Russian sphere as agreed upon by the Allies: the note was unanswered; the Russians were to drive into Rumania when they wished to, on their own terms, and bringing their own people. (9)

[*July.*]   Early in July 1944 Wilson succeeded in influencing the Commander of the Fifteenth American Air Force, General Eaker, by strong military-political arguments, whereafter Marshall said to Eaker: "You have been too damned long with the British . . ."; King George VI visited the Allied troops in Italy during July, and he himself spoke to high American officials about the desirability of trans-Adriatic operations: the Ljubljana drive, Zara, Istria — but without results. The German military situation rapidly grew worse in France, where the Americans at St. Lô and the British at Caen hammered at the last links of the German defenses; the Russians were near the frontier of East Prussia. The rockets and the V–1 weapon did not seriously alleviate the Germans' misfortunes. Their supply situation was so bad that early in July the SS leader Eichmann negotiated with Jewish circles in Switzerland, offering to spare the lives of the remaining Hungarian and Slovak Jews if the SS would receive American trucks through Portugal. This gigantic blackmailing operation then foundered, partly because of the misgivings of Hitler, partly because of the American stipulation that these trucks not be used against any one of the Allies, whereas Eichmann would only promise not to employ them in the West. In Hungary Horthy again began to summon his best advisers; having received messages from the Pope, from the Swedish King, and, through the International Red Cross, from Britain and America, he took steps to prevent the deportation of the Jews still in Budapest; he gave orders to trustworthy generals to organize crack army corps which would in moments of emergency obey his orders. On July 9 units of the German-controlled and Nazi-inspired Hungarian field gendarmerie assembled in their Budapest barracks, ready to deport the last 200,000 Jews in a coup; but armored troops pulled into the streets blocking the barracks with their tanks: the coup was avoided and the Jews of Budapest temporarily saved.

On July 13 the Finnish Minister in Berlin reported to his government that it was only in German dreams that the possibility of Russia stopping at her 1914 frontiers and of England making peace existed: it was now clear that Germany had lost the war. (*10*)

[*The July 20 coup. Churchill's new attempt.*] These were dark, obscure days, notwithstanding the magnificent, rich summer of that year. On July 16 Churchill again urgently asked Roosevelt to have the Combined Chiefs of Staff meet and consider revising their strategy. In the morning of July 20, when Mussolini arrived in the East Prussian forest to meet Hitler at his headquarters, Kivimäki cabled to Helsinki that German official circles were reflecting much anxiety. He was right. A few hours later the ill-fated German revolt of July 20 broke. Historians should refrain from speculating; yet one is tempted to consider the probable effects of July 20, had Hitler been killed and had the coup succeeded — after all, the Russians were still only at the edges of Europe. (*11*) As in Paris and Brussels, so in Athens and Belgrade the German commanders ordered the surrounding and disarming of the SS troops. (These generals then paid with their lives.) The population of these capitals, indeed, the whole of central-eastern Europe spent a breathless day and night. Then the magnificent attempt collapsed.

On July 22 the British Middle East Headquarters asked Turkey again to enter the war: in vain. Churchill cabled the influential Hopkins all his arguments for the abandonment of the southern France landing; he was worried about the Russians; he had planned to confer with Stalin about central-eastern Europe, but Stalin wanted to postpone such talks.

This new, *n*th attempt of Churchill was again bound to be fruitless. The Russian influence grew; the plot against Hitler failed, and the Russian armies entered central Latvia, and Estonia, and pushed toward Warsaw. Turkey finally decided to break relations with Germany (on August 2) but did not declare war (*12*); other neutrals were cowed: when on July 22 the democratic Estonian National Council published its manifesto in Stockholm, the Swedish press refrained from publishing it.

The preparations for the invasion of southern France went ahead in the meantime; then, on July 31, the Americans broke through at Avranches. The Battle of France was won: swinging around in an imposing half-circle, Bradley and Patton sped toward Paris. The people of Western Europe, the military, Washington, London were jubilant. But not Churchill: supremely aware of the Russian danger, the Prime Minister of Britain, the head of an ancient and glorious empire, felt desperate in those days. He could not influence the military; he was alone; the die seemed cast against him.

[*Another British idea.*]   Then he tried again. Knowing that a Balkan or north Italian invasion was now out of the question, he saw Eisenhower on August 7, determined, by dogged arguments, to make the Commander-in-Chief alter his decision: Churchill proposed that *Anvil-Dragoon* be abandoned and that the scheduled armies be thrown into the French theatre from the already gained Normandy and Brittany bridgeheads. No doubt, Churchill's idea was to gain such a decisive victory in the West as to expedite the Anglo-American advance through France and southwestern Germany into Austria and central Europe before the Russians got there; instead of a northward push from Italy, he now tried to arrange a gigantic eastward push from France. Eisenhower was unwilling: only his Chief of Staff, Walter Bedell Smith, agreed with Churchill, and when the British mission put the proposal before the Combined Chiefs of Staff in Washington, the Americans registered "their complete disapproval." On August 10 Eisenhower paid a courtesy visit to Churchill in Downing Street. According to Captain Butcher, Churchill was "still pouty over *Anvil*" and "was bemoaning the future of Alexander's campaign in Italy. He saw the Italian front drying up just when such a fine opportunity presented itself to enter Yugoslavia." His words were those of a hurt, aging man, whose whole grandiose work was endangered before his very eyes and who could not do anything about it. Bitterly he turned to Eisenhower: "I may lay down the mantle of my high office." Beyond his being impressed by the drama of fine rhetoric, the statement did not influence Eisenhower; once more they met, at which time the warm-hearted General was impressed at seeing Churchill almost in tears in his frustrated determination. All the Italian plans came up again, but Eisenhower would not and could not budge; he said to his aide that the Prime Minister wanted to go through "that gap whose name I cannot even pronounce." This was the Ljubljana Gap, of course — today seven million Austrians, ten million Hungarians, and another ten million Croats, Czechs, and Slovaks wish that the American Commander-in-Chief had known and pronounced the name of that wretched city of Ljubljana and the gap around it.

Next day, Churchill left for Italy, and on August 15 southern France was invaded without any serious resistance. General Fuller summarized the position well:

> Technically and administratively the invasion of southern France was an overwhelming success; strategically it was a blunder. . . . The defeat of Germany was now certain in any realizable set of circumstances; therefore the political problem had become paramount. Yet [Eisenhower] still thought in terms of France as the decisive theatre of the war, and of building up overwhelming strength at what, though still strategically the decisive point in the West, had long ceased to be politically the decisive area. This area was Austria and Hungary, for were the Russians to occupy those two countries — the strategic centre of Europe — before the Americans and British could do so, then the two Western Allies would have fought the war in vain; for all that would happen would be the establishment of a Russian *Lebensraum* in Eastern Europe instead of a German. (*13*)

Even after the Allied landing in southern France, instead of having pushed northward through the Rhône Valley, they could have turned eastward through the Alpes Maritimes as Hannibal and Napoleon had: they could have rushed east along the Po Valley and broken into northwestern Yugoslavia: the Ljubljana Gap.

America and Britain thus lost their last chance to shape the future of central-eastern Europe by making a military-political decision. Let us now turn to see what Stalin was doing.

. . . .

He was more able.

The Russian offensive storming ahead in Poland was daily growing in its political portents, while the military picture receded to the back of Stalin's mind. The Polish government was once more eager to assure Stalin of its goodwill, and Mikolajczyk readied himself for his visit to Moscow, a visit which Roosevelt sponsored. On July 25, the day before Mikolajczyk flew off from London, the Russians crossed the Bug in central Poland; now they operated in territories beyond the Curzon-Molotov-Ribbentrop line, and a communiqué, intended to comfort and confirm, was issued by Moscow: "The Soviet Government declares that it does not pursue the aim of acquiring any part of Polish territory or of changing the Polish social order." Didn't it? Behind the Soviet lines, in Chelm, the Moscow Poles on July 21 had already formed a "Polish Committee of National Liberation" in which the presence of Communists and fellow-travellers, Bierut, Osóbka-Morawski, "General" Berling, and Rola-Zymierski, was attenuated only by a few good-natured and unwitting peasants like the brother of Witós. All this smacked of 1793, when, in Targówica, the Russians made their Polish hirelings dig Poland's grave. Mikolajczyk left London with grave misgivings and doubts. When his plane stopped in Cairo, excited Poles surrounded him with the news of a Soviet broadcast: a few hours before, on the 26th, an "agreement was signed" between the Chelm Committee and the Soviet Union, which was "handing over the administration of the liberated Polish territories" to the Committee.

[*The Warsaw revolt.*] Mikolajczyk wanted to return from Cairo at once. (*14*) But then, partly due to Allied pressure, partly due to his knowledge of the immediately pending Warsaw uprising, he was persuaded to continue on to Moscow.

The Polish government decided to present its case to the world by a truly Polish, heroic effort: the Home Army was to revolt in Warsaw when the Russians were nearing the city; in a magnificent feat of arms the Germans would be driven out and the entering Russians would find a Polish army greeting them in brotherly spirit but determined to stay and rule the capital city, the heart of Poland. It was a worthy plan, one which manifested gallantry, devotion, courage, and a supreme will to sacrifice. Not all of the exile leaders agreed with it: Generals Anders and Sosnkowski did not. They doubted its results. Ultimately they were proven right.

Mikolajczyk arrived in Moscow on July 30. On that day the Russians had surged forward beyond Siedlce and Brest-Litóvsk; in the north they stood before Kaunas. Radio Moscow broadcast appeals to the citizens of Warsaw to revolt; the night was full of such sparkling messages. On the morning of August 1 Kaunas fell. At noon in Helsinki, Ryti offered his resignation. At two in the afternoon the population of Warsaw could clearly hear the low thunder of gunfire from the east. The Russians stood then about nine miles from the capital, and General Bór-Komorowski, the Home Army Commander, had already sent envoys to contact the advancing Russian General Rokossovski. At five P.M. Operation *Tempest*, the Warsaw revolt, began.

A few hours later the Russian advance slowed down before Warsaw; half a day passed and then the advance stopped; in a few days the Russian offensive throughout most of the Polish front came to a standstill. Except for movements on the flanks and occasional short forays, it was not resumed until January 12, 1945.

This is the tragic story of the Warsaw uprising. The Russians lured, if not invited, the Polish Home Army to come out in the open; the heroic, quixotic Poles rose, fought, and were destroyed by the Germans. The Russians folded their arms and watched the fight: except in a few cases, no Russian airplanes appeared over Warsaw; only around September 10, when the whole matter threatened to become a globally known scandal, did they send a liaison officer and advance into Praga, the eastern suburb across the Vistula — but not into Warsaw itself; a few planes then ventured over and dropped unpacked, useless supplies. To Mikolajczyk in Moscow Stalin and Molotov promised aid which never came and then accused the Poles of provoking an uncoordinated uprising — as if Radio Moscow had not urged it for three days; on August 16, Molotov called the Warsaw people "adventurers" when he spoke to Harriman. When Mikolajczyk arrived in Moscow, he found a representative of the Russian Poles, Rzymowski, occupying the Polish Embassy building there. The political proposals given to the Polish Premier were unacceptable: the Soviets requested that the Polish constitution of 1935 be replaced with that of 1921 (a move aimed to impress the Western "liberals" again) and insisted that a Polish government of "unity" be created comprising 14 Chelm Poles and only 3 London Poles. This, of course, was impossible. Meanwhile Russian army units forcefully dispersed Polish peasants and Home Army groups who had come from the provinces to help beleaguered Warsaw, where after August 9 the German SS began to counterattack, with the help of a Ukrainian-Russian volunteer brigade which later excelled itself in the awful, systematic butcheries that followed.

To General Bór-Komorowski it was a deadly shock to listen to the ominous silence after the Russian gunfire died down on the first night after the uprising. Thereafter he turned to the Allies; with the Polish Vice-Premier, Jankowski, he sent an urgent message for help on August 6. Meanwhile the entire world press, except for the Soviet and a few British and American newspapers, carried the communiqués of the Warsaw Home Army. On August 13, Sosnkowski sent a message to Eisenhower for arms, ammunition, and planes to drop Polish parachute troops into Warsaw. Eisenhower answered that Warsaw was out of his theater of operational competence, and suggested that Sosnkowski turn to the Combined Chiefs of Staff. (At the same time the Russians refused to agree to the use of their shuttle-bombing bases for such an operation.) Finally, a week later, Allied air aid began, but it was too little; and when on September 18 a mass American supply drop was made, it was already too late. After sixty-three days of incredible effort, the Warsaw rising collapsed; there perished the flower of the Home Army in Poland, the remaining hope and basis of Polish independence. On October 2, Bór-Komorowski surrendered to the SS General von dem Bach.

[*Stalin: a wise military policy.*] The lessons of all this were obvious: Stalin had now fully subordinated military aims to political expediency. On the eve of the Warsaw revolt, the Russian front at its westernmost tips stood about 325 miles from Berlin; the Anglo-American front in France was about 620 miles from the German capital; from Italy (Florence-Ancona) the distance was about the same. On January 1, 1945, the Western Allies were in Aachen, Luxembourg, Strasbourg: they were half-way through. The Russians were still before Warsaw: the same 325 miles separated them from Berlin (*15*); but in the meantime they got Bucharest, Sofia, Budapest — and Belgrade and Tirana fell to them too.

To conclude:

Stalin in August 1944	America and Britain in August 1944
Subordinated military objectives to long-range political goals;	Practically excluded political considerations from their military plans;
stopped his offensive 325 miles from Berlin, leaving the central bulk of the German armies intact in order to:	ordered their main armies to make a bee-line lunge toward Berlin, whereby they:
1. throw the bulk of the Russian armies into the Balkans, Hungary and Austria;	1. abandoned the possibilities of an advance into Austria, Hungary, Yugoslavia;
2. bring about the destruction of the Polish insurgents by the Germans;	2. did not give effective help to the Poles; were unable to assist Czech, Slovak, Serb insurgents, certain Hungarian forces ready to secede;
3. thereby indirectly enable the Germans to gain a breathing space on the main sector of their eastern front and thus delay the advance of the Western Allies into Germany.	3. were facing the bulk of the western German armies on a relatively short front; suffered three defeats at Arnheim, in the Ardennes and in Alsace, thus delaying their final advance into central Germany from September 1944 to March 1945.

. . . .

[*Decisive secession efforts: more Russian influence.*] The régimes of Finland, Hungary, and Bulgaria had now definitely made up their minds to get out of the war. On August 4 the grand old man, Mannerheim, accepted the Presidency of Finland and four days later appointed Hackzell to be Premier and Enckell Foreign Minister. This government was to establish peace with the Soviet Union. Once more the Germans sent Keitel to Finland; all he accomplished was to award an additional decoration to Mannerheim.

On August 5 the two Antonescus flew to Hitler's Prussian headquarters; their plane flew near burning Warsaw and a German turned to Antonescu: "This is the fate of those people who betray Germany." Hitler spoke of the miraculous new weapons; by October 15 the crisis would be over and Germany would resume the offensive in the East; in four days he would throw the Anglo-Americans into the ocean. Hinting that he might evacuate Greece and

Bulgaria, he said that he would not abandon Rumania and Hungary, which were necessary for Germany's defense. He asked Antonescu to break relations with Turkey; the Conducator evaded the issue, refused. The talks were short; the Rumanians flew back the same night. Next morning King Mihai called for Antonescu; the young monarch showed dissatisfaction and impatience. Four days passed but Hitler did not chase the Allies into the sea; instead, they moved fast toward Paris.

On August 9 Horthy forced the sick Sztójay to replace the Nazi Minister of the Interior with a Conservative; the cabinet was reshuffled; most members of the pro-Nazi wing were ousted. The German General Guderian was sent to Budapest, where all he could do was to speak of the German secret weapon. On August 10 Mihai Antonescu told the German envoy that he considered the situation hopeless. At the same time the new Bulgarian Foreign Minister Draganov talked with Papen, who passed through Sofia on his way home from Turkey: from this conversation the Bulgarian deduced that the Germans were definitely pulling out of the Balkans.

In the north the Russian generals Bagramian, Chernishevski, and Obukhov pushed to the sea in Latvia; the commanding German Lindemann was replaced by General Schörner, who in a counterattack retook Tukums and ordered the gradual abandonment of all of Estonia and Latvia, withdrawing through the narrow remaining corridor, but mostly by sea: a new chapter was opening in the tragic history of these people also. In the south, the Greek civil war flared up again. The turmoil was great. And on July 26 (when Mikolajczyk was off for Moscow), "at this moment of irresoluble deadlock a *deus* intervened literally *ex machina*" (*16*); a Russian plane ostensibly on a training flight took off from an Anglo-American air base in Italy, picked up two Soviet officers in Yugoslavia on the way, and dropped them in Greece. This was the Russian mission to ELAS/EAM Headquarters, led by a Colonel Popov. Churchill, who stayed in Italy from August 11 to 29, met Tito in Naples on the 12th; four days later Subasič and Tito signed an agreement, the text of which was published on the 22nd. (Aware of the gossipy nature of the Greeks in Egypt, Churchill had Papandreou meet him secretly in Italy.) On the 17th came the first visible crack in the wall of the Balkan satellites: Bagrianov announced the Bulgarian desire to withdraw from the war. This information was solemnly communicated to the Soviet Legation and, through Bulgarian emissaries, to the Allies in Cairo (*17*);

Tito was also contacted. On the 18th Stalin rejected Mikolajczyk's cabled request for aid to the Warsaw Poles; the Chelm Communists declared Lublin to be the temporary capital of Poland; upon Soviet advice — Russian armies were not going to arrive in Greece — EAM representatives suddenly decided to enter Papandreou's cabinet on that day. And in the West the Americans were in Chartres, thirty-four miles from Paris, where the revolt had already begun. Events were moving incredibly fast. (*18*)

[*The Rumanian armistice.*] Then, on the morning of August 19, thousands of Russian guns roared around Jassy: the great thrust into the Balkans was starting! That afternoon Maniu and the King decided to "jump" on the 26th; the Allies were informed by radio. But by the evening of the 21st the Russians broke through; the Germans were streaming back. In the morning of the 22nd the news came that Paris had fallen — and for Francophile Bucharest this was a decisive psychological factor. That morning Mihai Antonescu called on Killinger at the latter's suburban residence and told him that a Rumanian armistice was almost inevitable; later in the day the Foreign Minister told the King of this talk with Killinger. King Mihai was shocked, as he very much feared German countermeasures; he now summoned his advisers and decided to undertake the *coup d'état* the next day, August 23: at four o'clock the two Antonescus entered the palace. A dramatic scene took place: Ion Antonescu insisted that this was not yet the time for such a step; he even believed that a Turkish-Allied landing would be made in the next few days. (Yet the King knew that Antonescu planned to retreat into Transylvania with the Germans.) With the help of General Sanatescu and Maniu's friend, Nicolescu-Buzesti, the Antonescus were arrested on the spot. At ten P.M. the King announced the armistice on the radio. (*19*)

The armistice was a complete success and a surprise to the Germans; immediately they attacked Bucharest and cruelly bombed the city. But the Rumanian garrison under Sanatescu tenaciously held out, although far outnumbered by the Germans. A declaration of war on Germany followed; Rumania was now a co-belligerent of the Allies. Fighting continued for five days; in the end the Germans lost heart, as the Russian tank columns threateningly advanced. On August 27 Bucharest was free; everywhere the Germans were rapidly withdrawing from the Rumanian plains; the small garrison of Bucharest, faithful to the King, achieved an unexpected and astounding

success. Killinger committed suicide; Clodius, the German economic
envoy for the whole south-eastern European area, was arrested and
delivered to the Russians with the Antonescus. On August 30 Malinowski's Third Ukrainian Army entered Bucharest.

[*Its effects.*] All this, and Paris too, had its consequences.
On August 22 Bagrianov announced the Bulgarian wish to remain
"neutral" in this war; on the 26th he officially proclaimed "neutrality"; Bulgarian troops skirmished now with the retreating Germans
in northwestern Bulgaria. On August 24 the Hungarian government
ordered the dissolution of all political parties, a move aimed at a
semi-military organization sponsored by Imrédy and the Nazis, the
"Comradely Alliance of the Eastern Frontfighters"; on August 25
Horthy refused a German proposal to attack Rumania, a proposal
which also promised Hungary all of Transylvania; previously Budapest refused to sever diplomatic relations with Turkey. (On the same
day Finland asked for final Soviet peace terms through Stockholm.)
On August 29 a new Hungarian government was formed under General Lakatos, the Hungarian equivalent of Badoglio in Italy, Manner-
heim-Hackzell in Finland, and Bagrianov-Mushanov in Bulgaria.

[*The Slovak insurrection.*] Spurred by the Polish example and
anxious about the ambiguous record and status of the Slovaks, the
Czechoslovak government-in-exile decided to foment and organize a
revolt in Slovakia, to be coordinated with the Russian offensive at
the Carpathians. In mid-August a small government delegation,
headed by Nemec, flew to Moscow to coordinate the plans for the
Slovak rising: a Slovak National Council was chosen, in which Šrobar
represented the democratic parties, and Smidke the very small Slovak
Communist Party. The rising began on August 26. The Russians were
not too happy about it; if it succeeded, it would impede their efforts
to sovietize Czechoslovakia. The Communists in the revolt were few;
mostly Agrarians and Democrats fought, and the Slovak War Minister, General Čatlos, a satellite careerist, went over to the insurgents
with some Slovak Army units. For a while the insurrection was successful; it spread throughout the mountains and valleys of Slovakia,
and the rebels held Banska-Bystrica as a temporary capital. Tuka
resigned from the Slovak cabinet and Tiso seemed all alone. But the
promise of the Russian advance through the Carpathian passes did
not materialize; except for a Czech parachute brigade led by Gen-

eral Pika, no Czech troops were transported into Slovakia from Russia; indeed, outside of supplies ferried by air from Italy by American and British planes (later a small Anglo-American military mission arrived in Banska-Bystrica), no help came at all. Early in November the revolt collapsed. It was a repetition of the Warsaw experience in a somewhat more obscure manner.

[*The Bulgarian secession attempts.*] Essentially the same thing happened to Bulgaria. When on August 26 Bagrianov solemnly announced Bulgarian neutrality, Moscow, which previously had pressed Sofia for precisely that, suddenly announced her refusal to "accept" this neutrality declaration. The Bulgarians were dumbfounded. Whereas Malinowski was relatively slow in marching on Bucharest (his orders could have been to go slow so that the Royalist Rumanian Army, like the Warsaw Poles, might be wiped out by the Germans), on the left flank, on the Black Sea shores, Tolbukhin's army rapidly occupied Constanta and on August 30 reached the Bulgarian frontier in the Dobrudja; there Tolbukhin suddenly halted and waited (also Malinowski stopped the next day when his forward elements reached the Bulgarian frontier). After his communications to the Russian government remained unanswered, Bagrianov resigned on September 1: the new Mushanov government unofficially expressed its wish that the Russian armies enter Bulgaria and participate in its liberation from the Germans, but Malinowski and Tolbukhin did not move. The Bulgarian peace envoys were nervously sitting in Cairo; their government broke relations with Germany; the situation was indeed paradoxical, for now Russia stood on the borders of Bulgaria and her fate wholly depended on what Moscow had to say; yet it was not Russia but Britain and America who were at war with Bulgaria. The armistice with the Western Allies was practically completed; by September 5 the decrees and directives of the Mushanov government made Bulgarian political life fall fully in line with the democracies' requests: all political parties of the center and left were allowed to operate, and the restrictive measures of the German era were gone.

[*A Russian master-stroke.*] Then, on the morning of September 6, the Soviet Union declared war on Bulgaria: a fantastic piece of news. The Russians raised the charge that the Bulgarian government had collaborated with the Germans and facilitated their retreat, which was, of course, untrue; behind their war declaration hid the real motive: the Russians wanted to make the position of any Western-type Bulgarian government untenable. They succeeded well. Within twenty hours, Bulgaria sued for peace and the shortest "war" in history was over. Mushanov was succeeded by the even more liberal Muraviev, who declared war on Germany and invited the Communists (a definite minority) into his government; to his great surprise, they refused. Two days later, on September 9, the Communist-organized "Fatherland Front," which comprised remnants of the 1934 Zveno, the Social Democrats, and the Agrarians staged a picturesque "popular uprising" in Sofia and installed the Zveno man, Georgiev, as Prime Minister, a man governed by, guided by, and committed to the Communists; only then did Tolbukhin's tanks and trucks roll toward Sofia, entering that city on September 15. (*20*)

Thus Stalin gained the only and decisive hand in Bulgaria. Now Russia became an official participant in the armistice talks with Bulgaria (the armistice was signed only on October 28); a Soviet military mission dominated Sofia and immediately an iron curtain was rolled down: no news reached the free world of what was happening there. Although the child king, Simeon II, was temporarily (after some Communist indecision) permitted to stay in the country, a new Regency was installed; everything was done to discourage contacts with the British and the Americans; a widespread, truly orthodox-style purge followed, in which most Conservatives and Liberals were systematically eliminated from the scene by more or less violent measures. This was what the Russian interpretation of the Three-Power agreements, and of the "sphere of primary military responsibility" meant.

In Rumania, where Stalin had not yet tried to put the ridiculously few Communists into full control, the trend was somewhat less evident, but could be detected nevertheless: also there the iron curtain of communications was clamped down; as soon as the Russians entered Bucharest, the few hundred British and American airmen, former prisoners of war, who had been released and armed by the Rumanians and had played a conspicuous and significant rôle in the Battle of Bucharest, were ordered to leave the country: the Fifteenth Air Force ferried them out between September 1 and 3. (The Rumanian armistice was officially signed in Moscow on the 12th. There the American Ambassador assured the Rumanian delegates that Molotov was most trustworthy: "it is a matter of course that the Soviet forces should leave Rumanian territory at the cessation of hostilities"; and the British Ambassador added: "Rumania is needlessly worried.")

[*The Finnish armistice: Hungary's trials.*] Thus matters stood in the countries where the Russians were; in places where they had not yet arrived or where they were not supposed to go the situation was colored by some fainthearted optimism. On September 2, after the Finnish Parliament in a secret session accepted the Soviets' preliminary conditions by a vote of 108 to 45, Premier Hackzell announced in a broadcast that Finland was withdrawing from the war, and he energetically requested the Germans to evacuate the country. Mannerheim wrote a noble letter to Hitler:

> My responsibility now is to withdraw our people from the war. I cannot, nor would I ever want to turn our arms . . . against Germans. I trust that you, too, desire and will strive to settle our relations without any extreme bitterness settling over our affairs.

On the same day the Greek Premier, evidently whistling in the dark, spoke optimistically of the August 18 coalition agreement with the Communists: now complete unity prevailed, declared Papandreou. On September 1 Premier Lakatos of Hungary made a great *faux-pas* in his first radio speech: he, pointing at Finland, announced to the nation that Hungary was continuing to fight, for, as the Finnish example proved, this was the only way for national survival; thirty-six hours later the Finnish armistice was announced. (Cease-fire on the Finnish front came into effect on September 5; Hackzell and the Finnish peace delegation left for Moscow the next day; for some reason Molotov and the others procrastinated, and the armistice was not signed until September 19 in Moscow, after the Finnish Parliament gave its agreement at six o'clock of that morning.) Thus, within a fortnight, from August 23 to September 5, three of Germany's "allies" had "jumped off." The Finns were relatively fortunate: the German diplomats and military authorities left Helsinki without undue rancor and with some silent sympathy and understanding. (*21*) Not Hungary, whose geographic misfortune it was to lie within the "inner circle." The Lakatos *faux-pas* passed without consequences, for what did a *faux-pas* mean in those days? On September 4 the Supreme Council of the Hungarian General Staff admitted that in all probability Germany had lost the war, but added, showing a rather childish mood, that if shameful capitulation was inevitable, it should be made only to the Anglo-Americans. As if these generals could have had the pleasure of a choice!

Rumania had already declared war on Hungary, and while the Germans were rapidly pulling out of Rumania, they urged the Hungarian army to enter southern Transylvania and occupy the natural defense position of the southern Carpathians. Horthy was extremely reluctant to do so, and the Hungarian advance got slowly on its way only on September 5. The Hungarian government refused to accept, acknowledge, or answer the Rumanian "declaration of war," and the advance did not get very far: by September 6 the Russian spearheads were already beyond some of the Carpathians' passes, groping their way forward in southern Transylvania, where most of the land was controlled by their new Rumanian allies anyhow. Horthy then summoned a Crown Council on September 7, at which, with his characteristic lack of manoeuvring sense, he announced before two known pro-German ministers of the Lakatos cabinet that Hungary had to seek an armistice with the Allies. The pro-German elements were frightened, and they sent the former Premier, Bárdossy, and the German envoy to intervene with the Regent. Veesenmeyer and Bárdossy assured Horthy that new, German military help was forthcoming; faced with their thinly veiled threats, Horthy had to postpone the armistice plans. But preparations, now within a more restricted circle, continued, especially after General Vörös, the Chief of the Hungarian General Staff, reported his conversation with Hitler on September 12, in which the latter said that he had no confidence at all in the Hungarian government. Two days previously, Hitler and General Jodl issued an order to the SS to prepare plans for an eventual attack on Budapest and for the arrest of Horthy. (22)

. . . .

[*Russia advances: Tito in Moscow; Japanese attempts; Poland's fate.*] Immediately upon the start of the Russians' Balkan offensive, Tito, who had just returned to Vis from Naples, where he had met Churchill, disappeared from his island residence. He flew, in a Russian plane, to Tolbukhin's headquarters and to Russia; Tito, proud and optimistic, told Brigadier MacLean that he was going to Moscow "to give the Red Army his permission to enter Yugoslavia": an exaggerated statement. On August 15 two Russian military mission officers arrived in Albania from Greece. Thus, carefully fluttering from one "base" to another, Soviet military agents nudged their way into various political centers of the Balkans. The German-supported "national government" announced Albanian "neutrality," but its power waned fast; the Communists made "FNC" out of "LNC," transforming it into a broad Communist front, and began to exclude the democratic elements.

Churchill on August 26 delivered an admirable speech to the Italians about his concepts of what constituted totalitarianism and the definite conditions of political liberty; the whole tone of the speech showed that Churchill was riveting his attention to the coming time of troubles in central-eastern Europe. He also met General Anders; they spoke of the great feats of the Polish Brigade, of the incredible Russian duplicity at Warsaw, and of the general international situation. With characteristic frankness, Churchill turned to Anders: "You were right in '42"; moved, he added: "We shall never abandon you." (*23*)

Added to Churchill's ample worries were certain signs that, fostered by the industrious mediation of Tokyo, a separate German-Russian peace and an eventual German-Russian-Japanese coalition were again being considered in Berlin and Moscow. In Budapest, a German intelligence officer of Guderian's entourage hinted at such a possibility, and other vague but similar intelligence reports made the Chief of the Hungarian General Staff mention "current news about preparations of a Russian-German-Japanese alliance" in his memorandum of September 4; Papen gave such a hint to Draganov in August. The Japanese Ambassador tried to convince Hitler that he should approach Stalin, and on September 16 a concrete Japanese offer was made in Moscow. Gromyko casually mentioned this Japanese overture to Hull on September 23: all this served to delay further an energetic American-British stand against the obscure Russian plans and actions in central-eastern Europe, but Stalin did not need to reverse his alliances anymore. He was winning his game.

The German Foreign Ministry gradually abandoned hopes of sudden diplomatic reversals; in a ridiculously belated effort to win Polish sympathies, the Foreign Ministry declared on September 5 that the Polish insurgents would be treated thereafter as prisoners of war. (*24*) The Polish issue was becoming a source of grave diplomatic difficulties in London also. The Commander-in-Chief, Sosnkowski, a fiery Pole and, as such people usually are, a bad diplomat, made not only bitter anti-Soviet but also anti-British utterances in September. (*25*) After all, more than 100,000 Poles died in Warsaw, tying up five German divisions; only 11,000 surrendered to the Germans. Also, mention of the feats of a Polish parachute unit which was almost entirely sacrificed at the Arnhem operation, and the capture of Breda by the Poles was omitted or toned down in certain British and American newspapers. (26) The British protested about Sosnkowski, and on September 22 Mikolajczyk persuaded Raczkiewicz to dismiss him; Bór-Komorowski, fighting to the end in Warsaw, was symbolically appointed Polish Commander-in-Chief. Meanwhile the Russians proceeded with their political plans; on September 9 a population exchange agreement was announced between the Lublin Poles and the Soviet Ukrainian and Byelorussian "Republics"; it indicated the Soviets' long-range plans with Poland. On September 13 the appointment of the Communist Bierut as the provisional President of the Lublin Committee was announced; the Committee was now a veritable government of Soviet Poland.

[*Quebec again.*]   On the other side of the world, the Second Quebec Conference met between September 11 and 16.

The main topic of the discussions there was not central-eastern Europe but the future of the world in general, and that of Europe and its center, Germany. Churchill finally succeeded in making the Americans agree to their occupation of southern Germany and eventually of Austria also (27); the zones of Germany were now definitely fixed; in the words of an observer: "The President finally accepted the bitter South German zone pill, mildly sweetened by the Bremen enclave." (28) But Churchill, in turn, nodded to the fantastic and naïve Morgenthau Plan, which was announced in Quebec, and which was entirely at variance with the viewpoints of the State and War Departments. As to central-eastern Europe, Churchill expressed his anxiety that no clearcut arrangement existed with the Russians: the three-month trial period was coming to an end; Stalin showed no particular predilection for a Three-Power Conference in the near future. Once again Churchill intended to convince Roosevelt of the necessities of a limited push into the Balkans, but, as might be expected, he did not succeed. All he achieved was a commitment of the combined Chiefs of Staff that no troops were to be withdrawn from Italy while the offensive went on there; on the other hand, nothing would be put into the Balkans except two British brigades, which were made ready in Egypt to go to Athens and support the Greek government. (29) (A few days after the short Second Quebec Conference, the Allies suffered a decisive defeat in their plans to break into the northern German plains towards Berlin and perhaps to force the final collapse of Germany before the winter: the ingeniously planned Arnhem-Nymwegen parachute operation failed.)

[*The Russians' Balkan offensive.*] While the Quebec confer-ence was taking place, the Russians continued their unabated ad-vance. Forward elements had crossed the Yugoslav frontier on September 6, and Malinowski pulled through the important Negotin Gap on the 12th. A few days later, with the help of British com-mandoes, most of the Albanian coast, all of the Dalmatian, and the Ionian Islands were liberated. In possession of these, the Anglo-Americans in Italy could now without further difficulty set foot in Albania and Yugoslavia, but the previous high-level decisions held. There developed now an interesting situation, as in eastern Serbia Russian troops came into contact with Mihailovič forces. Just as it happened in some cases with the Polish Home Army in January–July 1944, friendly local contact developed between Russian com-manders and Mihailovič captains; indeed, for a moment it was thought that the overwhelming groundswell of Slavic amity would prevail over imposed ideological differences. Even among Yugoslavs abroad a faint resurgence of optimism occurred; while the complete disorganization of the Yugoslav body politic in exile continued (on September 12 King Peter made a pathetically infantile radio appeal, exhorting all Yugoslavs to unite behind Tito), the clever Fotitch asked Gromyko to receive him in early September. The Soviet Am-bassador at first did not answer; then, obviously on higher instruc-tions, he received the Serb diplomat: an interesting conversation ensued but one without practical results. Around September 20, the political directives of Moscow reached the armies in Serbia: a few days later three chief lieutenants of Mihailovič, in contact with the Russians, were treacherously arrested by them. Here was the Polish pattern again. (*30*)

[*Greek confusion: the Caserta "agreement."*] "The terrible blun-der made by Great Britain in Yugoslavia was nearly repeated in Greece — nearly, but not quite," wrote Voigt. (*31*) About mid-September Papandreou shed all his former optimism, as EAM–EDES warfare again developed throughout Greece, and Communist military and political representatives controlled most of the Greek towns and villages which the Germans had already partially evacuated. In view of this, on September 22 Papandreou anxiously cabled Churchill and Eden, asking that British troops occupy all Greece up to the Turkish frontier. (The seat of the Greek government was moved to Salerno then.) On that day technical negotiations conducted at Caserta between the British generals Wilson and Scobie, and Sarafis, the Communist, and Zervas, the nationalist guerrilla leaders seemed to have reached a deadlock; next day, partly due to British pressure, partly aware of his Russian instructions, Sarafis gave in and the so-called Caserta "Agreement" was born; according to the terms of this "Agreement" the rival guerrilla leaders again delimited their respective areas and put themselves under the authority of Scobie, named Supreme Allied Commander in Greece, and of the Greek Government. Sarafis protested against the wording of the Agreement which said that British troops were to arrive in Greece with the task, among others, of restoring law and order there — this statement was then omitted. To emphasize the existence of British military power in the eastern Mediterranean, an official British announcement was simultaneously issued about the presence of British forces operating in the Ionian and Dalmatian Isles and in certain sectors of Albania; but this was not much more than a gesture.

[*The Tallinn revolt.*]   Thus things stood in an area Britain was to occupy; even there all was not well for the non-Communists. At the same time the Russian armies were occupying Estonia. The narrow German policies in the Baltics prevented the existence of any kind of national army there; only in the summer of 1944 were a few meager Estonian and Latvian defense units hastily patched together, the former strengthened by about 2,000 Estonians coming from Finland. True Estonian resistance was anti-Russian as well as anti-German. On September 18 an heroic episode took place — another Warsaw rising, with the same, short-lived results. Estonian patriots, led by Otto Tief, rose in Tallinn, which the Germans were hastily evacuating, and hoisted the beautiful blue-black-white Estonian colors on the capital buildings. For three days there existed an independent Estonian government. Then on the 21st the heavy Russian tanks rumbled into Tallinn; Tief and his committee disappeared: they met the fate of the Warsaw Poles, of the Bulgarian liberals, of the Mihailovič captains, and of their Hungarian counterparts. (32)

[*Hungary offers surrender: German countermeasures taken.*]   On September 23 the Russians announced the closing of all Baltic ports to all foreign shipping; on the same day they crossed the pre-war frontiers of Hungary, quickly descending from the last Transylvanian foothills to the great Hungarian plains. The last bells tolled for Hungary now. That morning a secret military mission led by Horthy's trusted General Náday flew to Italy to offer surrender to the Allies; two days later another secret mission led by General Faraghó flew to Russia; certain members of his mission were ferried to Moscow after having walked afoot through the tortuous mountain passes of eastern Slovakia. The whole case history of Horthy's armistice efforts is extremely complicated. Otto Habsburg, who was invited by Roosevelt to sit in on the Second Quebec Conference as an observer, spoke with Eden there; the latter was angry and worried about the Russians' tricks and their high-handedness in Bulgaria; he told Otto that Hungary should go ahead and make a separate armistice with the Western Allies, if necessary. (Churchill told Otto that he was very pessimistic about the future.) The Pretender now communicated with Eckhardt in New York on September 18 to send a message to Horthy that this was indeed the last chance for Hungary to secede; Eckhardt went to the White House at once and gave the telegram to the President's secretary to transmit to the naval communications office which was using its special code and signals for such contacts; but the message never reached Lisbon, or Budapest. (*33*)

The Náday mission was welcomed in Caserta, and the request for an Anglo-American parachute brigade to assist the Hungarian armistice coup was considered (such an oral promise was made by Roosevelt to Otto Habsburg and Eckhardt); especially the British favored the plan, and in his speech on September 28 Churchill made unusually friendly allusions to Hungary. Meanwhile, however, the Germans, who had not been very cognizant of what had happened in Rumania but were rather well informed about what was going on in Hungary (they were always more suspicious of Horthy than of Mihai), planned their exact, deadly countermeasures; as no British-American forces were to appear in the Balkans, Panzer and SS troops were rushed through Hungary to keep Budapest in check and to meet the Russian armored columns in the middle of the Alföld plain. On September 20 Ribbentrop requested General Hennyey, the Hungarian Foreign Minister, to make a strong pro-German speech on the occasion of the fourth anniversary of the Tripartite Pact on September 27; when Hennyey refused, orders were immediately given to Veesenmeyer to deal with the Nazi leader, Szálasi, and his henchmen, who were already in hiding. On the 26th Szálasi concluded his pact with Veesen-meyer; the German SS was authorized to put Szálasi into power whenever it was deemed necessary and to furnish the military means for his *coup d'état* against Horthy.

On September 28 Moscow announced the conclusion of an agreement with Tito regarding the administration of Yugoslav territories in the war zone; on the same day the Soviet commander in Sofia ordered the previously flown in British and American officers to leave Bulgaria. (*34*)

[*Preliminaries to a conference: Hopkins' influence.*]   The American Assistant Secretary of State, Adolf A. Berle, on September 26 wrote a confidential memorandum warning of future troubles due to the Soviet domination of central-eastern Europe and the eastern Mediterranean; but his almost lone voice was not heeded; soon thereafter he resigned from his post. On October 1 Churchill urgently cabled Roosevelt, requesting an immediate Three-Power meeting, as the Russians were deep in south-eastern Europe and no agreement existed among the Allies concerning the future of that region. He also asked Hopkins to intervene with the President; but Hopkins professed to know that no specific agreement was desired by the Russians (which was true), and therefore he did not intervene in Churchill's favor. The latter, who was meanwhile making arrangements for a quick trip to Moscow, cabled again and asked for the minimum: that the United States should side with Britain when it came to discussing the Balkans. Indeed a minimum! But Hopkins did not understand all this and persuaded Roosevelt to agree that "there is in that global war literally no question, either military, or political, in which the United States is not interested." The way Hopkins handled this situation may be seen from his biographer's account:

> On October 3, 1944, Roosevelt had cabled Churchill implying that Churchill could speak for the United States on Balkan affairs when he next saw Stalin. Roosevelt had written a cable to Stalin to the same effect. When Hopkins heard about this, he ordered the White House map room to stop the Stalin cable. The cable officers obeyed without question. Then Hopkins went to Roosevelt's bedroom, told him what he had done, and persuaded him that the United States should always speak for itself. Roosevelt admitted that he had made a mistake and took it all back. (*35*)

Thus the American Ambassador Harriman was instructed to participate in the Moscow Conference which opened on October 9 when Churchill and Eden arrived in the cold, great Russian capital.

. . . .

[*The Moscow conference.*] This was the second political conference of the Three Powers in Moscow, the second Churchill visit there, the fifth important inter-Allied meeting in the Russian capital since 1941. The Conference now dealt with two fields mainly: Poland and the Balkans in general. Churchill achieved the participation of a Polish delegation from London: Mikolajczyk, Grabski, and Romer arrived on October 10. The first British-Polish-Russian conference took place on the 13th; after the first session, Churchill told the Poles that there existed no other alternative but that Poland definitely cede the eastern territories. The Poles objected: no Polish parliament would accept such a solution; whereupon Churchill became extremely angry:

> . . . then there is nothing to prevent Poland from declaring war on Russia after she is deprived of the support of the Powers. What is public opinion, after all? What are you fighting for, the right to be crushed? I want to save the Polish nation . . .

He insisted that the Poles had committed a fatal mistake in not having previously acquiesced in the territorial cession: this would have saved the Polish government and, with it, Polish independence. He still believed that they could be saved. In Ciechanowski's words: "If Mikolajczyk agreed on the frontier issue, continued Churchill, then certainly the Russians would withdraw their support of the Committee of Liberation. He said that when he had criticized the Lublin Poles in talking to Stalin, the Russian dictator also criticized them. Stalin evidently considered them unworthy of his support."

Notwithstanding the clever psychological approach with which he succeeded in making Stalin agree with his view about the unworthiness of the mousy Polish Communist representatives, Churchill failed to attain his main aim: no agreement was made in regard to the composition of a future, united, and mutually acceptable Polish government. The Lublin people insisted on having three out of every four cabinet posts: this was clearly impossible. Churchill himself saw it. Thus Mikolajczyk, Grabski, and Romer flew back to London; the results of Moscow on the Polish issue were negative.

There was, however, an agreement which Churchill reached with Stalin: the "sphere of principal military responsibility" deal of May was now transformed into a true division of spheres of influence, expressed, curiously enough, in percentages.

The ratio of Russian to British interests in Bulgaria, Rumania and Hungary was to be 75:25 or 80:20; in Yugoslavia 50:50 (*36*); Greece was to fall 100 per cent into the British sphere. Thus Churchill wished to save what he could.

The United States remained silent. As Cordell Hull stated later:

> Had we made such a determined fight against the Anglo-Russian agreement as we had made successfully against the proposed territorial clauses of the Anglo-Russian alliance in May 1942, it is possible that some of our later difficulties in the Balkans might not have arisen.

Not until the Hull memoirs were published in 1948 did the world gain knowledge of these sphere-of-influence deals of 1944. It was not the first nor the last time that statesmen and ambassadors of central-eastern European nations learned the truth in bitter exile, years later, about how their nations had been dissected or dealt with from the memoir installments published in the rosy, homey pages of the *Ladies' Home Journal* or the *Saturday Evening Post*.

.   .   .   .   .   .

Nothing that happened in central-eastern Europe during the Moscow Conference warranted the slightest optimism. On October 5 the first British troops landed at Patras, but with the exception of a few places in Epirus and the Peloponnese, all of Greece was overwhelmed by the Communistic guerrillas. Contact and preliminary agreement had already been made between "50 per cent" Yugoslavia and "75–80 per cent" Bulgaria for the formation of a Communist Balkan federation. (*37*) As for Hungary, Stalin now saw that, perhaps unexpectedly, this country was going to fall into his lap too; he revealed his intentions to Mikolajczyk at Moscow: "Hungary . . . will change completely when we get there." (*38*)

[*The fall of Hungary.*] On October 6 Malinowski broke through the Tisza river front, advancing almost a hundred miles in four days; in the evening of October 10 Russian forward units reached points within 45 miles of Budapest. German armored forces counter-attacked around Debrecen but had only momentary successes. On October 11 four important events occurred. Skorzeny's troopers kidnapped the garrison commander of Budapest, General Bakay, Horthy's confidant, who was to defend the capital in the case of the planned armistice coup. A few hours previously Horthy met Tildy and Szakasits, the underground chiefs of the Small Holders and the Socialists; Szakasits, who in 1945 was to become the pro-Communist leader of his party and later "President" of Communist Hungary, was overawed by Horthy's invitation, charmed: he trembled from excitement and addressed the Regent in the most flowery terms. During the same day another political meeting took place in the province of Szeged, where the Communist Révay contacted a corrupt and opportunist priest, Balogh; as Szakasits was to do with the Socialists, Balogh was destined to sell out the Small Holders to the Communists later. That same night a second Hungarian armistice delegation arrived in Moscow and signed a preliminary armistice there. Horthy's official declaration was planned for the 19th.

At this moment came another application of the Russian discretionary method. The government wanted direct military contact with Malinowski; two Hungarian officers were entrusted to cross the frontline near Szeged and request the Soviet general to march on Budapest at once. But Malinowski, on the contrary, stopped his offensive; treating his guests well, he refused to discuss military matters with them; the armistice plotters in Budapest impatiently waited for news, but none came. Meanwhile the Russians rebuffed the German counterattacks around Debrecen; Russian power could be seen from the record of that October 13, when, from north to south, Petsamo, Riga, Szeged, and Niš fell to them. (The British entered Athens that morning. Stalin still was not quite aware of the extent of his prospects: on October 13 Harriman reported from Moscow that Stalin would agree to a limited Allied advance from the Venice-Trieste area toward Vienna. Churchill naturally jumped at the proposal; but ultimately, the American military, as always, turned down such plans.) But in Hungary the Russians did not move toward Budapest, although only a few scattered units stood between them and the capital. (Their intentions were revealed by the statement which slipped from the Russian Minister, Pushkin, who said to the Premier, Nagy, in 1946 that on October 11, 1944, it was Horthy who had asked the Russians to halt their advance; whereas the contrary was true.)

On the evening of October 13 Ribbentrop ordered preparations for the formation of a Hungarian Nazi countergovernment in Esztergom; the SS hid Szálasi by clothing him in a German uniform; Veesenmeyer did not forget what happened to Killinger in Bucharest and to his colleague in Sofia who had been captured. Early on October 15 there was still no news about the Russian advance; in the morning Horthy decided to declare the armistice; a few hours later his son was lured into an SS trap, wounded and captured; at noon Horthy called a German plenipotentiary, Rahn, who was sent to Budapest to convince the Regent; at one P.M. the Budapest radio broadcast the dramatic and sincere armistice declaration of the Regent. (39) Five hours of uncertainty followed; then the SS and the Arrow-Cross stormtroopers occupied the centers of the capital; most of Horthy's German-trained young officers deserted him. By nightfall the armistice attempt had failed; after a dawn battle between loyal Hungarian troops and the SS, Horthy was captured and deported to Germany: a "government" of Szálasi and his Arrow-Cross people was set up and a nightmare reign of horror began.

Thus the Russians achieved what they wanted. (40) Now, with the fall of Horthy and an armistice government, they could proceed with their occupation of Hungary in a constitutional vacuum, as they had done in Poland, Estonia, Slovakia, Bulgaria, and establish later, directly and without any reservations, a new Russian- and Communist-dominated government. (41)

On October 22 Churchill arrived back in London; on that day the Russians reached the Norwegian frontier in the north, the Danube in Hungary at Baja; they and the Partisans entered Belgrade and Dubrovnik; in the south the British moved up to Thebes. In the west the last shattered forts of Aachen fell to the Americans. The Battle for Germany had begun. The Battle for western Hungary, Czechoslovakia, and western Poland was pending. The Battle for the Balkans was already over. Stalin had won.

From Moscow to Yalta: a winter of chaos

[*Poland: abandonment.*] After his return from Moscow, Mikolajczyk contacted Roosevelt. 1944 was election year and Roosevelt was receiving Polish-American delegations, promising his support of Poland's cause (1); Mikolajczyk hoped for American understanding and wholehearted aid. He received but a friendly and non-committal answer from the American President. Thereafter, on November 24, Mikolajczyk resigned.

[*Yugoslavia: Tito's "unity."*] Fotitch (already relieved of his Yugoslav Ambassadorship) also tried vainly to intervene with Roosevelt in October. Churchill himself now harbored doubts concerning Yugoslavia. He talked about Tito with Stalin, but he did not see clearly; when he reported on Moscow to the Commons on October 28, he was rather vague concerning Yugoslavia and concluded that "permanent agreement awaits the presence of the United States who have been constantly informed what is going forward." Meanwhile the Yugoslav non-Communist cause was going to pieces. When Belgrade was liberated, King Peter on the radio weakly greeted "glorious, intrepid Tito"; on November 1 Tito and Subasič — the latter soon afterwards departed on a visit of homage for Moscow — signed the basis of their agreement about the formation of a "united" Yugoslav government, which was not announced until January 23, 1945. Around November 10 certain cut-off German army corps, forming the bulk of the German forces in Bosnia and western Serbia, sent two messages to Mihailovič announcing their willingness to capitulate on certain terms to his forces only; Mihailovič informed the Allied Supreme Command in Caserta, which forbade him to accept such a German capitulation. (*2*)

[*Greece: preliminaries to the civil war.*] On November 21 Tirana and Durazzo fell to the Albanian Communist guerrillas; Kupri, the Albanian nationalist leader, was to share Mihailovič' fate soon. Tito now controlled Monastir and his forces were strung along the entire length of the Yugoslav-Greek frontier, south of which trouble brewed. By early November, all of Greece was free, and British units motored up to Salonika and the Macedonian frontier "to show the flag." But they were not numerous; the anomalous situation was only slightly influenced by their presence. In Athens the legal government of Papandreou sat, while throughout the country the guerrillas "governed" in their own way. The Athens government had only a very few men to represent its authority in Salonika; EAM–ELAS (their temporary headquarters were established in Lamia) ruled most of the north. There were about 50,000 Communist and 10,000 nationalist guerrillas; it was evident that the disbanding of these was of vital importance to the central government. To strengthen the position of the governmental forces, early in November two crack loyal brigades (the Third and Mountain) arrived in Greece; the Left rapidly spread rumors that they were brought to suppress the guerrillas and to impose the iron rule of an authoritarian government. As early as November 5 Papandreou agreed with Scobie that the disbandment of the guerrillas was inevitable (similar problems bothered the French and Belgian governments at that time); Papandreou included the disbanding of the nationalist EDES also, and this decision was suggested to the guerrilla leaders. Communist demonstrations — the economic condition of the hungry, robbed, and arid country helped to foment them — in Athens and other cities increased during November. Weighted by the irascible, emotional element of passionate politicking, so typical of Greeks, (3) an atmosphere seething with wild rumors, conspiracy and chaos lay heavily over Greece as the disbanding talks between the government, the British, and the guerrillas began. EAM–ELAS insisted that not only they and EDES but also the two army brigades be disbanded — this would have naturally helped the Communists, whose disbanding could neither be properly supervised nor controlled. General Scobie stuck to the previous proposal that only EAM–ELAS and EDES be disbanded; he wanted the Army to constitute a non-political national force. On November 26 a crucial meeting took place between Scobie and the Communist Sarafis, who refused to agree (while Zervas of EDES had previously expressed his willingness to comply). For a moment the EAM member Svolos, a Marxist theoretician, proposed a compromise solution which centered around a mixed division formed of elements from the two Army brigades and EDES counterbalanced by an ELAS brigade of equal strength. Scobie was reluctant, but Papandreou saw the chance of a compromise and offered a not very different proposal of his own, which Svolos was ready to accept; however, the Communist leadership of the EAM rejected it two days later.

It was now clear that the Communists had decided upon a course of revolutionary action in Greece. On December 1 a British proclamation established December 10 as the day of the final dissolution of the guerrilla armies; Zervas accepted, Sarafis did not. In the early morning hours of December 2 the EAM ministers withdrew from the government; later during the day EAM–ELAS forces in the Athens area began to mobilize and assemble in connection with the presently announced great EAM demonstration set for the following day. Late in the evening the British and the Government announced the cancellation of the permission granted for the Communist demonstration, but this no longer mattered. On December 3 the Greek civil war began.

. . . .

[*The Russian sphere: Finland.*] From within the now prostrate former "satellites" very little news reached the outside world during these months. It was nevertheless clear that the Russian military victory had its specific political consequences: in contrast to previous, wishful theories, no dichotomy existed between traditional Russian imperialism and Communist political aims. At most, the tactics were different. In Finland, Stalin upheld the semblance of non-intervention for external reasons. Finland lay now between anvil and hammer, weak and battered: after October 2, when Finnish units landed at Torneo and ejected the Germans from Kemi near the Swedish-Finnish frontier, skirmishes between Germans and Finns continued throughout northern Finland; most of the countryside there was burned and ravaged by the retreating German army of General Rendulic. The Russians now were installed off Helsinki in their naval-land base of Porkkala-Udd, acquired in the armistice agreement; their presence weighed heavily upon what remained of independent Finnish politics. Upon Russian insistence all Finnish veterans' organizations and voluntary defense societies were dissolved by decree, and on November 27 a new, evidently Russophile government was installed, with Paasikivi as Premier.

[*Rumania.*] The Rumanian Army pursued the Germans with zeal and participated with the Russians in the Transylvanian campaign, fighting as far north as the Javorina Pass in Slovakia (these military efforts were thought to strengthen Rumanian standing with the Allies and to assist Rumania in the argument for Transylvania at the future peace conference). Yet in the long run this did not alter the fate of the King, Maniu, Bratianu, and all the non-Communists in Bucharest. Within the army, the Russians turned important officers into their hirelings; by November a Communist-inspired division had been created and was being progressively indoctrinated. (4) The few Communists in Bucharest established their press and began to undermine systematically the authority and prestige of the government. (5) Late in November Maniu sent a memorandum to Vishinsky

and to the Russian Command, stating that Rumania sincerely wished
to be friendly with the Soviet Union and pleading that, for the sake
of such a continuous and earnest friendship, the Russians should not
impose Communism upon Rumania. The memorandum produced
no effects; the Communists continued with their agitation. (6) On
December 4 — the day when the Greek civil war broke out —
Vishinsky arrived in Bucharest and promptly and harshly demanded
the resignation of Sanatescu. The hero of the armistice had to go;
General Radescu was installed in his place. The Russians did not
find it advisable yet to put their own candidates to the fore — there
were still only a few thousand Communists all over Rumania. As
it turned out, Radescu was an even tougher and more determined
anti-Communist than his predecessor; nevertheless it was daily more
clear that the entire political life of Rumania was bound to be exclusively determined (notwithstanding 75:25, 80:20, and other arith-
metical games) by the Russians.

[*Hungary.*] In Hungary the awful weeks of the Szálasi
régime dragged along; the last nuclei of the resistance movement were
liquidated by Szálasi's storm troopers, the gendarmes, and the SS. (7)
The systematic extermination of the Hungarian conservative, liberal,
and democratic resistance certainly did not displease the Russians;
indeed, their whole campaign in central Hungary slowed down: they
were surely the future lords of Hungary; they now tried to conserve
as much material and manpower as was possible. On November 2 a
number of Malinowski's tanks penetrated the southeastern suburbs
of Budapest and could have easily taken the capital, where utmost
confusion reigned; but Malinowski did not press on, and the frontline
then receded, to be stabilized about 25 miles from the city. Instead
of a direct assault, the Russians decided to move into southern Trans-
danubia and ultimately encircle Budapest. Thus, in a well-executed
manoeuvre Tolbukhin crossed the Danube in the Mohács-Baja sector
on November 30 and advanced quickly northward toward Lake
Balaton along the western Danube shores. The battle for Budapest
did not begin until December 21–22 when Tolbukhin took Bicske,
moving toward Buda from the rear. Two hundred miles to the east,
in the middle of the plains, cut off from everything, in the ravaged
and shattered city of Debrecen, the Russians established the Hungarian "National Government," whose figurehead Premier was the
former Commander of the First Hungarian Army, General Miklós,

an adherent of Horthy, who had crossed the lines to the Russians when the October 15 armistice attempt collapsed. This shadow government was already well-studded with Communists and well-concealed crypto-Communists; again, the Russians operated carefully, knowing that, as in Rumania, no more than a few hundred individuals constituted the cadre of the Hungarian Communist party; most of the Communist leaders had to be imported from Moscow. On December 24 the long-awaited siege of Budapest began. (*8*)

[*Bulgaria.*]   The pattern in Bulgaria was not much different; indeed, the politics of that country were considerably more sovietized than those of Rumania, Hungary, or Finland. Bulgarian troops were participating in the campaign of Tolbukhin; some of their commanders were very eager to endear themselves to the Russians. As Bulgarian nationalism was by no means extinguished, the first postwar differences between Yugoslavia and Bulgaria showed themselves; more important, the sharpening differences of opinion existing between Tito's Yugoslav Communist Party and the Bulgarian Communists came out into the open.

[*The Macedonian dispute with Tito.*]   When in 1943 Tito gained predominant control of the Macedonian Communists, he declared his intention to incorporate an "autonomous" Macedonia within the framework of the federated South Slav republic; this aim was expressed in and confirmed by the Jajce Declaration which Moscow had approved. Yet in December 1943 the Bulgarian resistance front declared itself for an independent "Macedonia for the Macedonians," a position with which the Bulgarian Communists associated themselves, thus defying Tito's stand. In 1944 the pro-Tito "Assembly of National Liberation of Macedonia" met on St. Elijah's Day in August; across the border in Bulgaria the Pirin (Bulgarian) Macedonians expressed their willingness to join. However, Tito in Moscow was advised — or perhaps he himself deemed it advisable — to go slow, and the Macedonian question was discussed in Sofia during September by Yugoslav and Bulgarian high Communist leaders; the latter promised much, including the granting of immediate autonomy to Pirin Macedonia. But these promises were not kept; differences of opinion within the Bulgarian Communist Party itself existed concerning Macedonia; Kostov, for example (who was expelled and executed in 1949), showed himself in favor of Tito's proposals.

These Macedonian controversies were kept secret; only Britain had some notion about them. Tito now began to plan for a Yugoslav-Bulgarian federation; but the Bulgarian Communists were cagey, knowing that in such a federation Bulgaria would certainly be the junior partner and even perhaps no more than the seventh federated "republic" within a South Slav "federation" ruled from Belgrade. Stalin, who had been asked to mediate, was equally cautious and, playing one against the other, in the long run he sided with the Bulgarians. This was probably partly due to his knowledge that Yugoslavia was not yet firmly in his hand (50:50!), whereas Bulgaria was; but it is more than possible that his Russian suspicion and nationalist calculations began to make him regard Tito with a certain reserve and that he did not wish to see a further increase in the power and realm of the Yugoslavs.

By the end of 1944 the federation, customs' union plans, and even a mere watered-down proposal for an alliance between Yugoslavia and Bulgaria had lapsed; within these broader differences, the Macedonian question also remained unsolved. "Although superficially there was now the closest friendship between the new Yugoslavia and the new Bulgaria, both parties remained suspicious and unsatisfied." (9)

.   .   .   .

[*American relations with Russia: the air boundary.*]   It was in the late autumn of 1944 that the first faint discords in Russian-American relations were half-heartedly registered in Washington. In October the United States protested against the undue severity of the economic terms which the Russian draft of the Hungarian armistice contained: the reparations sum was then reduced from 400 to 300 million dollars. American objections to the procedure of the Allied Control Commissions were also raised; the Russian procedure was evident in Bucharest and Sofia, where Allied Control Commissions simply meant full Soviet command and extremely limited Anglo-American observation. In November at the International Civil Aviation Organization conference in Chicago, the Soviet delegates walked out.

More acute were the differences on the military level. (10)   In September a Russian general on Malinowski's staff requested the American Military Mission in Bucharest to bring in a high American air officer, who would establish and control direct liaison between the advancing Malinowski army and the Fifteenth Air Force operating from Italy; as soon as news of this request reached Moscow, the already established liaison was abruptly abolished by the Russian General Staff. Without such liaison, confusion and conflict between the Russian ground and tactical air forces and the American strategic air arm were bound to result; yet the Russian General Staff was unwilling to establish aerial operational zones; even in the air the Russians were jealous of the British and Americans and wanted to keep them out of the clouds over central-eastern Europe. Late in November American planes mistakenly bombed a Russian column in Serbia; elsewhere the incidence of uneasy contact between American bombers and Russian fighters was increasing; due to errors in recognition it nearly came to exchange of fire on several occasions.

The strong-willed commander of the Fifteenth Air Force, General Eaker, finally lost his patience. Through the American Military Mission in Moscow he informed the Russians that from December 3 on the Anglo-American air arm would confine its activities to the west of an operational boundary drawn up by him. The Russian counterproposal, given to General Deane in Moscow a week later, suggested an air boundary *about 450 miles to the west* of the Russian front lines; in Deane's words:

> Acceptance of the Russian proposal would have meant that all of eastern Germany, western Poland and the greater part of Czechoslovakia would have been free from attack by our heavy bombers. The area contained many of the oil refineries that were included as targets in the combined British-American bomber offensive which was then concentrated on German oil. . . . In the course of our argument [the Russian General] Slavin revealed that his proposed line was planned so far to the west in order to stop the British practice of dropping weapons, ammunition and food to Polish partisans loyal to the Polish government-in-exile . . . (*11*)

A typical example of the subordination of Russian military operations to long-range plans! Ultimately a compromise air boundary was adopted.

[*Austria's future.*] Meanwhile the Austrian issue matured within the European Advisory Commission. While on September 12 the EAC was informed of the American acceptance of the zoning of

Germany, the zoning of Austria was still undecided. *(12)* On November 23 the Soviets put forward a new proposal for the tripartite zoning of Austria, according to which the Russian zone would have encompassed the eastern part of Lower Austria and eastern Styria (a plan aimed to separate the British-American zones of Austria from the Hungarian border); the British would control the western parts of Lower Austria and Styria, together with Carinthia; the American Zone would extend to Upper Austria, Salzburg, Tirol, and Vorarlberg; Vienna would be under tripartite occupation. But the Joint Chiefs of Staff continued to adhere rigidly to their stand: no American occupation zone in Austria; only token forces should be sent there. This was indeed strange: the Russians proposing that America send troops into Austria and the highest military leaders of the United States, together with the President, refusing to do so! (At that time Roosevelt gave personal instructions to the departing American Minister to Bulgaria: he should understand that no American troops would be sent east of Trieste.) Ambassador Winant now turned to Roosevelt; for two weeks he sent desperate cables and personal messages to Washington; he also spoke to the President by radiotelephone. Winant's military adviser cited Bulgaria as a clear example of what happened to countries where Russian military forces were in control. Roosevelt then consulted an extremely reluctant Chief of Staff, and on December 8 informed the State Department that American participation in the occupation of Austria had been accepted, with the provision that the American zones should be adjacent to Bavaria.

Thus, after having steadfastly refused to participate in any commitments relative to central-eastern Europe, the Chiefs of Staff of the mightiest nation on earth, fighting their country's battle for no other aim than the avowed restoration of global freedoms and democracy, were restricting the responsibilities of this great country so much that as late as early September 1944 they refused to accept American commitments in central and southern Germany; as late as early December 1944 they still refused to do so in Austria. *(13)*

Upon the advice of Generals Eisenhower and McNarney, the Joint Chiefs of Staff accepted on January 5, 1945, the proposed agreement about the use of an American airport outside of Vienna; at the end of January Britain proposed that France participate in the occupation of Austria, with which proposal the State Department later agreed.

. . . .

[*The Greek civil war.*]

> Russia is in Europe, but not of Europe. England is of Europe, but not
> in Europe. She and Europe are one. Without her, Europe cannot be.
> Without Europe, she cannot be. Germany and Russia are Europe's
> dread. They are most dreaded by their neighbors. England is Europe's
> hope. She inspires no dread, save the dread, felt so little by herself
> and so much by others, lest she have less faith in herself than others
> have in her. Long before the Second World War was won, this dread
> came upon Europe to dim the brightness of oncoming victory. (*14*)

Voigt's words were very true in December 1944. Truths, however,
have consequences: and the consequences of these truths were difficult
to apply; the only place where British determination and power
applied them was Greece.

On December 3 the monster Communist-led demonstration in
Athens' Constitution Square led to bloodshed; in a few hours ELAS
forces began to attack government positions and police stations
around Athens. Papandreou wanted to resign; a telegram from
Churchill persuaded him to stay. The British Premier now intervened
with a strong hand. When, on the night of December 4–5, ELAS
units were within a thousand yards from the center of the Greek
government and from British headquarters at the Hôtel Grande
Bretagne, he sent orders to General Scobie to fight:

> "For three or four days, or more," explained Churchill later in Par-
> liament, "it was a struggle to prevent a hideous massacre in the centre
> of Athens, in which all forms of government would have been swept
> away and naked, triumphant Trotskyism installed . . ."

Significantly — and these words were said on January 18, 1945,
before Yalta — Churchill had clung to the concept that the Greek
Communists were not Moscow-directed; he branded them as "Trot-
skyites." But this was not the case: ELAS acted in a true, non-Trot-
skyist fashion. Even when Scobie's 72-hour ultimatum, which ordered
them to evacuate the Athens area, had expired on the 26th, ELAS
forces hesitated to get into direct combat contact with British units;
thrice (on the 9th, 10th, and 14th) ELAS sent messengers to Scobie
with an armistice offer. The Communist terms proved inacceptable
and a full guerrilla war between ELAS and the British began on the
14th, at a moment of supreme crisis, when ELAS held almost all of
Greece except a part of Athens. Yet a few British troops turned the

scales: General Hawkesworth arrived with supporting units on December 15; slowly the capital area was cleared and ELAS retreated.

The hurried arrival of the British Cabinet Minister Macmillan and Field-Marshal Alexander on December 10 did not avert the battle; the British now labored to create an acceptable government around which all non-Communist elements would gather; difficulties were latent in the differences between Royalists and Republicans. But then the indefatigable Churchill himself, taking Eden with him, flew into Athens on Christmas Day. His short, angry presence and talks resulted in a regency under the strong, virile, and apolitical Archbishop Damaskinos; it was proclaimed that King George II would not return to Greece until the nation voted whether it willed monarchy or republic. (*15*) On January 3 a government of national unity was formed under the popular and non-royalist General Plastiras. The Foreign Minister was, significantly enough, the slightly pro-Russian Sophianopoulos. (*16*)

The civil war now led to vile Communist massacres in the country, especially when ELAS' military plans seemed to founder. The Socialists and the small Leftist Agrarian Party withdrew from EAM; on January 11 ELAS delegates appeared at Scobie's headquarters and asked for an armistice. The truce was signed on January 15. The revolution had collapsed.

[*Effects abroad.*] While the Greek civil war lasted, international complexities arose An ELAS division which attacked Zervas marched through Albania to get to the rear of EDES' coastal flank; EAM also came out for a "Balkan Federation" (and the Greek Right answered with "Greater Greece"). It was significant that Yugoslavia was silent and the Soviets almost sphinx-like; Stalin remained true to his sphere commitments and, in order to be left alone elsewhere, let Britain have a rather free hand in Greece. Yet, strangely and sadly, influential circles and press organs in Britain and especially in the United States presented the Greek issue as a bitter strife waged between reactionaries and radical social reformers; no kind words were wasted on the Greek government, and the intervention of British troops was passionately chastised. (*17*) The official reports from Athens which recounted the Communists' misdeeds and cruel murders made but little impression in certain British circles. The British Ambassador to Greece, Sir Reginald Leeper, lost his patience and cabled Eden on January 15:

At the risk of being wearisome I must point out once again that British press still treat what has happened in Greece as though it were a dispute between the Right and the Left in which the Left evoked a general strike which unfortunately led to disorders. Hence the remedy they suggest of a round table conference, a fair deal for all and taming of that immoderate man General Plastiras. It is my task as you know to keep the Greek Government on the lines which reasonable people in England will think reasonable, but the kind of comments mentioned above are so utterly unreal that I find it difficult to talk to the Greeks about British public opinion, if this is what is meant . . . (*18*)

Criticism of "reactionary British generals" was even worse in America, where it was also indulged in by members of official circles. (*19*) Such ideological tendencies continued in Washington for a long time; the State Department publication, *Post-War Foreign Policy Preparations*, published in early 1950, included statements phrased as follows:

[About Albania in the autumn of 1944]: The most effective of these groups, the National Liberation Front led by General Hoxha . . .
[About Greece]: . . . strife broke out early in December when the principal local resistance group (EAM), which had come under Communist domination, resorted to force against the coalition government.

Indeed mild, ambiguous words!

Back on December 5, 1944, Stettinius at his press conference (one of his speech-writers was Dalton Trumbo, later proved to have been a Communist) openly disavowed the British and criticized their Greek and Italian policies; and, according to Elliott Roosevelt, the President angrily exclaimed against Britain when he heard the first news of the Athens fighting.

[*The end of Polish independence.*] After Mikolajczyk, whose hopes in American intervention had collapsed, resigned, the Polish émigré world entered a tragic stage of disintegration. The new Polish Premier was the anti-Russian Socialist, Arciszewski, whose régime was not favored by Whitehall. Certain Polish military figures, among them General Zeligowski of 1920 Wilnó fame, suddenly clamored for more collaboration with the Soviets; most of the others were bitter and somewhat precocious; the London *Observer* in December published a harsh critique on the Arciszewski government, an article inspired by a certain group of émigrés. Gestures, such as the presentation of the highest Polish order, *Virtuti Militari*, to General Eisenhower by the Polish Chief of Staff, General Kopanski, did not change much. The existence of the Polish forces within Allied ranks came to be regarded more and more as a diplomatic burden.

On December 10 Arciszewski made a significant declaration against the plans which called for Poland's compensation in the west for her eastern territorial losses. He suggested unwillingness to accept German territories; he was promptly assailed by the Peasant Party and the National Democrats when he stated that Poland did not want eight or ten million Germans, that she wanted neither Breslau nor Stettin. An important declaration, but its contemporary impact was but slight: what did the voice of an Arciszewski count for now? On December 15 Churchill acknowledged to Parliament that certain hopes about the solution of the Polish "problem," which had been raised during October in Moscow, had now failed. Again, publicly, he repeated the thesis that had the Poles accepted the territorial compromise, their full independence would have been assured. A short debate followed in which the Conservative Captain Graham made an important statement: "Today our frontier is the Vistula; tomorrow it may be the Dnieper."

No. It is the Elbe. Or, perhaps, the Rhine.

Ciechanowski was also worried about growing pro-German sentiment within America, where the opposition was now somewhat more courageously criticizing pro-Russian tendencies in Washington; often, however, the alternative policy which lurked behind their voices was naive and crude isolationism; some of their leaders, like Senator Vandenberg, awoke to responsibilities worthy of true statesmen, but such men were few. (20) On December 18 another noncommittal, dull American official statement was issued on Poland; on December 31 the Lublin Committee declared itself to be the Provisional Government of Poland, with the puppet Osóbka-Morawski in the Premiership and with four Communists and four Communist-sponsored Peasants, Socialists, and "Democrats" in the "cabinet."

Roosevelt now looked at Eastern Europe more pessimistically; he sensed a coming great diplomatic débâcle; disillusionment and physical discomfort began to weigh upon him. He began to discern long-range Soviet planning, which revealed itself during the United Nations' preparatory conference at Dumbarton Oaks, where the

Russians at one time demanded that their sixteen "independent" republics all be represented in the United Nations' Assembly. On January 6, 1945, Roosevelt spoke to Congress:

> The nearer we come to vanquishing our enemies, the more we inevitably become conscious of differences among the victors.
> We must not let these differences divide us and blind us to our more important common and continuing interests in winning the war and building the peace.

But he also spoke of the "misuse of power" in "power politics":

> . . . perfectionism, no less than isolationism or imperialism or power politics may obstruct the paths to international peace.

[*The Eastern front.*] He was concerned, he said, about Greece and Poland "for example." Two days later Washington made a draft for the creation of an Emergency High Commission for Liberated Europe; on January 11 the President discussed the eastern European situation with the Senate Foreign Relations Committee. Yet commissions and discussions could not change much now. On the same day, the great Soviet offensive in central Poland, halted since August 1, began. Within twelve hours the German lines were broken; Warsaw fell the next day; on the 17th the Lublin "government" entered Warsaw. The armies of Marshals Koniev and Zhukov surged forward with great speed, broke through Cracow, into Silesia, and reached the Oder river; in the north the Russian neared Königsberg. Meanwhile the Western Allied advance into Germany and central Europe was again delayed for six weeks by the Ardennes counteroffensive which Hitler launched on December 16 (something which again proved that, notwithstanding his histrionic anti-Bolshevik utterances, Hitler regarded the Western Allies as his paramount enemies). Hitler would not have used his best troops and last good weapons for an attack in Belgium had the case been different; he had just told his generals that he respected only two of his opponents: Tito and Stalin. And on December 27, 1944, he wrote Mussolini: "One thing is certain and that is that neither Fascism nor National Socialism will ever be replaced in Europe by democracy."

Budapest was now fully encircled, and its siege slowly developed. In Sopron, under German wings, sat the miserable Szálasi government; in deserted Austrian and German hotels and evacuated university classrooms the last German quislings of central-eastern Europe gathered (*21*): the Bulgarian Tsankov, the Rumanian Sima, the Greek Logothetopoulos; soon Szálasi, Tiso, and Moravec were to join them. These shadow Hungarian, Bulgarian, and Rumanian "national governments" still continued to "operate," drafting imaginary policies and decrees. In early 1945 German propaganda perked up for the last time; false radio stations, "The Voice of National Serbia," "Red Hungarian Radio," "The Bulgarian National Station," were installed by the Germans, but soon their origin became apparent and they faded out.

[*Displaced populations.*] The population displacement of central-eastern Europe was tremendous. Horded into evacuated cities and into camps, more than a million Baltic refugees shivered under the cold, grey North German skies; central Germany was full of German evacuees from Transylvania, Hungary, Slovakia, Yugoslavia, the Baltics and Poland (*22*); their number, about two million, was swelled by the mounting wave of the German refugees from East Prussia, Silesia, and the Oder lands; in the south and in Austria about 500,000 Hungarians and another 100,000 Rumanians, Slovaks, Serbs, Ukrainians, Bulgars, and Croats camped. To these many millions were added the bombed-out Germans and millions of foreign workers; the number of foreign workers in the 1938 German territory alone was officially reported by Berlin in January 1945 to be 2.5 million Russians, 911,000 Poles, 627,000 Italians, 230,000 Yugoslavs, 140,000 Czechs, 130,000 Baltics, 15,000 Greeks, 10,000 Hungarians, 5,000 Rumanians, 2,000 Bulgarians. (*23*) (And the French, Belgians, Dutch, Danes, Norwegians!) One of the bleakest scenes in the history of human suffering was unfolding itself.

[*Russia's troubles: the last German counteroffensive.*] All was not well, however, behind Russian lines either, and the statements so often repeated by State Department officials in 1949–50 (belatedly then) were certainly true in early 1945: in many instances the Soviets bit off more than they could chew.

This fact showed itself also militarily: on January 1, a German counteroffensive was launched in the Esztergom-Bicske sector which came close to encircling Budapest. (*24*) For the first time in long months, German divisions were moved from the Western to the Eastern front; early in January the 711th Infantry Division, previously in Holland, was reported to be in western Hungary; ten other divisions were moved subsequently from west to east. The German counterattack in Hungary — the first one on the eastern front in many months — was defeated after ten days of fighting, but a month later a second, more serious German counteroffensive — this was Hitler's personal idea and originated from a promise to Szálasi — was launched by the Sixth SS Army, coming from the western front.

[*Differences with Tito.*]   Also nationalistic troubles existed. In eastern Poland, typically Ukrainian (anti-Polish, anti-German, anti-Russian, anti-Jewish) guerrillas, "Banderowci" and "Bulbowci," roamed in the forests and occasionally descended upon Polish villages; even Soviet official commentators admitted their existence in January 1945 and actually used this fact to point at the necessity of a "just" frontier between Poland and the Soviet Ukraine.

More important was the Bulgar-Yugoslav controversy. On January 22 the Bulgarian Premier, his Communist entourage, and the Foreign Minister, Yugov, left for Moscow; the Yugoslav Communist Piyade left Belgrade on the same day. In Moscow Piyade learned to his dismay and the Bulgarian Communists to their joy that Stalin and the Russians were not in favor of Tito's Yugoslav-Bulgar federation plans. Only Dimitrov among the Bulgarians showed himself in favor of the federation idea in general (although not with Tito's specific plans); the other Bulgar Communists were trying to avoid discussing *any* kind of a close Bulgar-Yugoslav alignment; according to Piyade, "even certain [Bulgar] Fatherland Front politicians of bourgeois democratic parties displayed more sincerity for federation than the Bulgarian Communist leaders."

While Stalin indicated his support of the Bulgar point of view, the British probably gained some information about what was being discussed in Moscow, for on January 26 the Bulgarian and Yugoslav governments were officially informed that Britain did not approve of any Yugoslav-Bulgar confederation previous to the signature of the peace treaties, and that Britain generally favored a Balkan federation only if it was to include Albania, Greece, and Turkey also. The British note also took a stand against Tito's federal Macedonian idea and warned the Bulgarians not to tamper with Greek Macedonia. This British note, according to Piyade, helped (perhaps inadvertently) the Bulgars. Pirin was to remain within Bulgaria, said Stalin, and while (again according to Piyade's account) on January 28 he seemed to appreciate the expressed Yugoslav aim of a Balkan federation, the time was not deemed to be propitious enough; even a suggested Yugoslav-Bulgarian alliance treaty had to be abandoned "at the request of the Soviet Government. So long as the British maintained their action in Sofia, Moscow hastened us to sign the agreement. But when the British also took steps with the Soviet Government, the agreement could no longer be signed." (25)

[*The demise of Yugoslav democracy.*] What happened now to King Peter and to the Yugoslav Conservatives, Liberals, Democrats, indeed to all pro-Westerners abroad, was not much more than a tragic farce. In December Winant informed Washington of an alleged Churchill statement to the frightened, poor young Peter: "The Three Great Powers will not lift one finger, nor sacrifice one man to put any king back on any throne on Europe," and Stettinius remarked that this was indeed an amazing statement "in view of Churchill's favorable attitude toward the Italian and Greek monarchies." The young King then was influenced by his supporters to take a last stand: on January 11 Peter openly declared that he held reservations about the yet unannounced Tito-Subasič agreement: while he "basically approved," he objected to the powers of the "Veče," the Communist-ruled "Anti-Fascist Council of National Liberation," and to the suggested regency council. On January 15 Peter, Churchill, Eden, and "General" Velebit, Tito's military envoy, met in London; on the 16th, representatives of Field-Marshal Alexander signed a military supply and coordination agreement with Tito, while on the 18th Churchill in the Commons denied that a clear-cut sphere of influence agreement had been made with the Russians. Churchill summoned Peter again on the 19th, badgering him to agree with the Tito-Subasič plan: anyhow, said Churchill, it was now well-nigh irrelevant whether the King concurred or not. Three days later Peter dismissed his government, and the Tito-Subasič agreement was broadcast. On January 29 the new Yugoslav government was announced, Subasič holding the Premiership and the fictitious portfolios of Foreign Minister and War Minister; an official communiqué added that King Peter had decided to transfer his royal powers to a Regency Council.

[*The Kosice agreement.*] Meanwhile on January 20 the Soviet-sponsored Hungarian Government signed the armistice in Moscow; on January 23 in Kosice the Czechoslovak government, many of whose members, not heeding British advice, were returning to their home country via Moscow, signed with the Soviets a highly important agreement concerning the military-political administration of Czechoslovak territories. On January 31 the Czechoslovak government of Beneš announced its recognition of the Communist-controlled and dominated "government" of the Lublin Poles, sitting now in Warsaw.

On that day, all of Poland, except isolated pockets around Poznan, Bydgoszcz, and Torun, (26) was cleared of German forces. The Home Army was officially disbanded on that day; now, a few days before Yalta, Stalin could repeat what Alexander I said of Poland in Vienna, 131 years before: when one has hundreds of thousands of soldiers in a country whose fate allegedly is "pending," one does not negotiate very much.

Into Malta Winston Churchill flew on his way to the Crimean Conference.

The Russian era begins: I. Acknowledgment at Yalta

[*The attitude.*] Stalin had proposed that the Three-Power Conference be held in the Crimea. Many of Roosevelt's advisers were against the idea of flying so far again to please Stalin: also the British, led by Churchill, opposed the acceptance of the place. But in late November 1944 Hopkins and others urged Roosevelt, and the President agreed.

The usual planning staffs and committees were assembled and prepared agenda, papers, reports; the President himself made little practical preparation for the conference. Throughout January on the American domestic political front, "internationalism" (mingled with that vague and strange thing called anti-Fascism) seemed to have won its final victory, and the air of Washington once again began to be filled with optimistic expectancy. The observations of the Polish Ambassador masterfully delineated the atmosphere:

> Official America appeared to me to be going through a psychosis of misunderstood "Internationalism." I was regarded as a "perfectionist" who "put the cart before the horse." I was told that the President would certainly rise to the occasion "at the appropriate moment." Was he not a "past master at timing his moves"?
> It was considered of primary importance "to gain the confidence of the Soviets." Then, when this was achieved, "friendly coercion" would follow, and make Stalin realize he had everything to gain by

following the President's advice. "You just wait awhile. You will soon see how tough we can get, now that the war is practically won."

More precisely, Ciechanowski elaborated:

> In the course of the twenty years of the peace period following the Versailles Treaty, the democracies proved incapable of defending a sound peace, based on democratic principles, in defence of which they had not hesitated to fight with indomitable courage at the cost of untold sacrifices.
>
> At the end of World War II democratic statesmanship was once more showing weakness in its timid attempts to win a democratic peace after the victory of the totalitarian imperialism of the Axis Powers.
>
> My conversations with leading American officials appeared to confirm this paradox. In practically every discussion on American-Soviet relations, in connection with the Soviet unilateral policy of accomplished facts, they would throw up their hands and exclaim that there was nothing to be done, as "it was unthinkable for the United States to fight Russia."
>
> In my opinion nothing could better demonstrate that the American people appeared to ignore the force that American arguments would have in peaceful but determined negotiations. They still believed that there were only two alternatives: to agree to all Soviet demands, or to fight Russia.
>
> I regarded this as a sad proof of the inferiority complex of some of the high officials of the great American nation which, in the past, had steadfastly refused to assume the role of a world power. It also showed profound ignorance of Russian psychology and of Russian methods of negotiations . . . (1)

[*Malta.*]   On the way to the Crimea, Roosevelt landed in Malta and met Churchill on February 2; the Combined Chiefs of Staff also met. (2) Churchill was very pessimistic about the future of Europe and the world. Once more, for the last time, he attempted to convince the Americans of the necessity of an invasion of and concentrated push into Austria, northern Yugoslavia, and western Hungary. But the American Chiefs of Staff vigorously objected; there were also other substantial dissensions. The American Chiefs of Staff were, if possible, even more unwilling than Stettinius and Hopkins to consider anything which would eventually provoke Russian distrust: they openly stated their foremost desire to bring about the "earliest possible" entry of Russia in the Far Eastern theatre against Japan.

Roosevelt also wanted to avoid any lengthy talk with Churchill before the Crimean Conference lest Stalin and the Russians become suspicious.

So, after the Malta talk — for it did not amount to a regular conference — the chiefs of the two English-speaking Powers flew on to the Crimea. They flew in silvery planes in a big arc under the blue Mediterranean sky, avoiding Crete (still in German hands), crossing over the dark valleys of Turkey in Asia and the mythical Hellenic-Asiatic Black Sea (Churchill had designed the code-name of the Crimean Conference: *Operation Argonaut*). They landed on the same Crimean shores where, exactly ninety years before, British Light Brigades prepared their charges and off which the awe-inspiring warships of Her Britannic Majesty then had anchored to teach the Russians a lesson about how the Lion could roar when the Russian Bear upset the order and balance of eastern Europe. There was also something symbolical (if not intentional) in the Crimean accommodations: the high Western guests were housed in former Tsarist palaces; the Russian mansion was in Koreis, in the middle; on one side was the palace of Livadia, where Roosevelt was domiciled; on the other side was Alupka, where the British were housed. It was a hard and circuitous drive from Alupka to Livadia. One had to go through Koreis . . .

The participants arrived on February 4 and the conference got under way immediately.

.   .   .   .

[*Yalta: the approach.*] Notwithstanding a widespread belief that dark, mysterious, and secret deals were perpetrated at Yalta, more has been revealed of that meeting than of any other important international high-policy conference since 1941; we have today several accounts of the participants, explaining the Crimean Conference in considerable detail. There is very little, if any, secret about Yalta (but, of course, there was nothing secret about Munich either.)

A chronological sequence of the Yalta talks is unnecessary: instead, I shall try to examine the specific issues of the Conference.

There were, first of all, considerable differences in the respective compositions and also in the approaches and aims of the American and British delegations. (*3*) These differences were, of course, outweighed in number and in scope by the agreement, cooperation and general concert which existed between the American and the British representatives. They were nevertheless significant and, as at Teheran, the Russians had good opportunities to exploit them. Again American idealism and optimism could be contrasted with British realism. The Americans wilfully avoided recognizing the fact that most of central-eastern Europe was now under the heels of the Russians, while the British were aware of this fact; the British were far more tactical-minded than the Americans: they made some unsavory compromises, advanced at one point and retreated on the other in order to save what in their eyes still could be saved. Here was a fundamental difference. And this difference in temperament was in some cases wilfully emphasized by the American President: symbolically, he sat between Churchill and Stalin in the Yalta photographs; he again believed himself and the United States to be in the center, between the two antipodes of an aristocratic-liberal, Victorian Britain and a democratic-totalitarian, young pioneer Russia. (And Roosevelt was not always a loyal ally: again, and more than once, he avoided an Anglo-American talk with Churchill, if only to avoid Russian suspicion. Before the first conference session, a private talk took place between Roosevelt, Bohlen, Stalin, and Molotov (no Britons); once, during the February 7 plenary, when the Polish discussion neared its climax and Churchill rose to speak, Roosevelt whispered to Stettinius: "Now we are in for half an hour of it"; such remarks from the American President could easily be heard by Russian ears . . .)

Another already familiar recurrence at Yalta was the contrast and paradox of an embattled, depleted, war-weary Britain, trying steadfastly to extend its power to vital points throughout Europe, and a big, high-hearted, victorious America, reducing its responsibilities to minimums imposed by domestic considerations. Typical of the American position was the case of the Emergency High Commission for Liberated Europe, originally proposed by Washington on January 9, to deal with whatever critical differences of opinion and procedure were to arise among the Great Powers. Already at Malta, Stettinius had told Eden "that the President had misgivings that the proposed European high commission might prejudice the prospects of world organization"; in other words, the little and the meek had better perhaps be sacrificed for the sake of a grand world design. Just before the conference began, Roosevelt decided to drop the High Commission proposal from the Yalta agenda, a decision based on the following arguments, according to the published State Department account on postwar peace planning:

On February 4 the President expressed to Secretary Stettinius his unfavorable impression of the record of the European Advisory Commission, and said that, rather than to establish another commission, he preferred to have meetings of the Foreign Ministers to handle the necessary work regarding liberated areas. A further objection to the proposed high commission was that the United States would be loath to assume the responsibilities in regard to the internal problems of the liberated countries that such a standing high commission would unavoidably entail. This, in the circumstances, was a view applicable predominantly to Eastern European countries.

Whether we accept the somewhat naïve Stettinius afterthought, expressed in his memoirs: "The establishment of such a commission, I believe, might have forestalled some of the difficulties which arose in eastern Europe" or not, the above quotation is a documentary record of fundamental importance and shows why Yalta was to be a failure. It is most interesting to note that the editors of the State Department volume, a volume compiled and written with dryness and precision, found it necessary to insert a quite surprising footnote for such books:

> The records do not clearly show whether this view was one held by the President or represented the view of an adviser.

A most curious footnote! However, adviser or President, the responsibility remains essentially the same. (4)

. . . .

[*The Polish issue.*]   There were certain important points concerning Poland on which the United States and Britain initially agreed. Both of them opposed the transfer of large German territories to Poland; the Oder-Neisse Line, tentatively mentioned by the Russians in the autumn of 1944, was rejected. The United States, still unwilling to violate the Atlantic Charter, agreed only with extreme reluctance to the compensation of Poland with East Prussia. It was, however, now envisaged that Königsberg would go to the Russians, and some of Pomerania and Silesia to the Poles. As to the eastern Polish frontier, Roosevelt often expressed his wish that, at least for appearances' sake, the Russian-Polish frontier in some sectors be drawn east of the Curzon Line; he wanted Stalin to let Poland retain Lwów or, if not that ancient town, at least the Drohobycz oil region. Thus the American stand on the territorial question was more just and favorable to Poland than was the British. Yet on the other issue the American delegation continued to be imbued with the falsely-conceived idea of compromise: they prepared to propose a Polish "unity" government to constitute "a middle ground" between the Communist Poles and the London exile régime. (5)

The first substantial discussion on Poland took place in the third plenary session, on February 6. Here Churchill uttered the famous, forceful phrase: the Western Powers wanted Poland to be "captain of her soul." Roosevelt joined him with somewhat less vigor; he was willing to accept the Curzon Line with some concessions, but "he made it plain that his chief interest was in a satisfactory Polish government and not in the establishment of particular boundaries." Thus Roosevelt (one year after Churchill) recognized the real issue. He made a proposal to invite to Yalta some of the Communist Poles and some of the middle-of-the-road men from Poland (6); he also insisted that Mikolajczyk, Grabski, and Romer be included in the future Polish government and that the holding of free elections in Poland be guaranteed. But Stalin was supremely evasive and hypocritical and avoided being pinned down: he was a friend of Poland, he said, but this was, after all, a Polish internal affair. And in rebuttal to Roosevelt's and Churchill's suggestion that he make a "magnanimous gesture" by altering the Russo-Polish frontier somewhat, Stalin said that if he did so, the Russian people "will say that Stalin and Molotov are far less reliable defenders of Russia than Curzon and Clemenceau." Thus the momentary deadlock arose. The following plenary sessions began with the Polish issue. Molotov brought forth a proposal containing three points: 1. acceptance of the Curzon Line, 2. declaration that Poland be compensated in the west to a line running south of Stettin along the Oder and Neisse rivers, 3. a declaration be given by the Three Powers stating that it was "deemed desirable" to add to the "Provisional Polish Government true democratic leaders from Polish émigré circles." Molotov added that time would not permit the Poles to come to Yalta, as Roosevelt had suggested. (He knew that the British, and especially the Americans, had no time to lose and wished to return home.) Both Roosevelt and Churchill protested against the "émigré" adjective; Churchill insisted upon the wording: "Poles temporarily abroad." In the next plenary session the United States presented a compromise proposal for the creation of a Presidential Committee of Three, Bierut, Grabski, and Sapieha (among whom only Bierut was a Communist), whereupon Molotov retorted that the American and British proposals "ignore the existence of the present government," and Stalin insisted that the Lublin-Warsaw "government" was "extremely popular" in Poland. Here the real divergence between Stalin's concept of the Polish régime and that held by the West revealed itself.

From now on the Russians struggled to avoid any agreement on specific measures concerned with the forming of the Polish government; they tried instead to narrow the issue down to the phrasing of a mere tripartite declaration on Poland, not too binding for them and thus not uncomfortable. In this they largely succeeded. The fifth and sixth plenary sessions on February 9 saw the presentation of the American formula on Poland couched in general terms: it dropped the Presidential Committee idea and proposed that the future régime be called "The Provisional Government of National Unity." Molotov again insisted that the new government be based on the Lublin people; subsequently the American formula was reworded. Churchill now proclaimed that the Polish question was the most important one of the whole conference. (7) Sensing a gathering of British determination, Stalin affably complimented the British on Greece and suggested that Poland's case was an isolated question. The whole procedure of the conference was now somewhat disorganized, and scattered and different issues kept popping up while the important Polish issue was still on the table. After dinner on the 9th the British presented their revised formula: the Polish Provisional Government of National Unity should be based upon the government "now functioning in Poland" and on other Polish democratic leaders from the Poles abroad; Churchill also insisted that the American, British, and Russian Ambassadors in Warsaw supervise the first free Polish election; Roosevelt agreed, but Stalin rejected this proposal with a wonderfully evasive argument: such supervision would go against the pride of the Polish people, he said.

The next morning Eden brought a somewhat altered British report, and Stalin now made three minor concessions. No definite agreement on the Oder-Neisse Line was to be incorporated into the declaration dealing with Poland, as the United States and Britain refused to agree to that line; the Curzon Line was basically accepted, but in certain sectors deviations would be made, running five to eight kilometres to the east in favor of Poland. And, in its final wording, the Yalta declaration heeded the American wish, speaking not merely of the "enlargement" but of the "reorganization" of the Lublin régime.

Thus the Yalta Three-Power Declaration on Poland was finally born.
It was then that Admiral Leahy turned to President Roosevelt:

> Mr. President, this is so elastic that the Russians can stretch it all the
> way from Yalta to Washington without ever technically breaking it.

And Roosevelt answered, "I know, Bill; I know it. But it's the best I
can do for Poland at this time." That he could do little more was
true; his Secretary of State knew that because of the military situation, "it was not a question of what Great Britain and the United
States would permit Russia to do in Poland, but what the two countries would persuade the Soviet Union to accept."

But is it not the aim of war and diplomacy to avoid such situations
(especially at the threshold of victory)?

. . . .

[*Yalta and Yugoslavia.*] While the Yalta Agreement and
Declaration dealing with liberated Europe spoke of free and unfettered
elections, the Conference dealt specifically with but a few eastern
European areas and nations. One of these was Yugoslavia. Churchill
sensed the existence of certain differences between Stalin and Tito,
and a few interesting interchanges took place; during the first session,
for example, Stalin declared: "Yugoslavia, Albania and such small
countries do not deserve to be at this table." On the February 8
plenary session, when the Polish question seemed to have reached a
full impasse, it was Stalin who turned to the Western Powers, inquiring about Yugoslavia and Greece. Clearly, he wanted to return to
the sphere of interest principle, bringing the discussion to a territorial
quid pro quo level. Churchill, who knew how the Yugoslav Communists
planned to exploit unilaterally the Subasič-Tito agreement, asked
Stalin "to say two words to Tito to settle the matter," whereupon Stalin

> . . . replied that Tito was a proud man and now that he was a popu-
> lar head of a régime, he might resent advice. The Prime Minister
> answered that he felt that Marshal Stalin could risk this. Stalin ob-
> served that he was not afraid to advise Tito.

Here Stalin added that he did not intend to criticize British actions
in Greece, nor "did he have any intentions of interfering in that

country." (*8*) On February 10 Eden expressed British objections to a Yugoslav-Bulgarian alliance treaty and said that Britain wished to postpone Balkan federation talks until the armistice period was over. The United States supported the British standpoint here. Eden also made some points concerning the future Yugoslav-Italian and Yugo-slav-Austrian frontiers. Finally, he proposed his revised amendments which he wished added to the Subasič-Tito agreement: members of the last Yugoslav Parliament who had not collaborated with the Germans should be included in Tito's "Anti-Fascist Assembly of National Liberation," and the actions of the latter (the AVNOJ) should be supervised by a constituent assembly (Veče). Had these amendments been accepted, they might have altered certain internal events in Yugoslavia during 1945: but the Russians, insisting that all this would be an impossible intrusion into the affairs of an independent nation, succeeded in having the amendments dropped.

[*Other Yalta issues.*] The rest of the Yalta conference con-cerned central-eastern Europe only indirectly. Such was the post-ponement of the great political discussion over Germany to a further conference to be held after the German capitulation (although Church-ill spoke for the creation of two German states, one with Vienna as capital, where the historically-minded Prime Minister hoped to see a balancing Danubian Power. He was unwilling to partition Ger-many, unless such a partition could be bound to the creation of a strong Danubian confederation); such was the definite insistence of the American Chiefs of Staff to bring about the quickest entry of Russia into the war against Japan, a stand which indirectly influ-enced practically everything the American delegation did during the Conference; such was the mounting evidence of Russian hostility toward France as a European power and against the person of Gen-eral DeGaulle in particular, an attitude expressed by Stalin several times during the formal and informal talks (once he even went so far as to say that the Lublin Poles had a more lawful government than DeGaulle had in France; after all, the DeGaulle people were but returning émigrés). (*9*)

Three military decisions taken at Yalta concerned central-eastern Europe: One provided for the procedure of consultation within the Allied Control Commissions in Bulgaria, Rumania, and Hungary (an agreement which the Russians never observed); there was a final air agreement which established that the British and American air forces

were not to operate within 200 miles south and west of the advancing
Russian Army front without giving twenty-four hours previous notice
to the Russians (an agreement which the Allies always observed);
another air agreement provided for the erection of certain temporary
American air bases in Hungary from which the Fifteenth Air Force
could bomb Austria and southwestern Germany (an agreement whose
implementation the Russians deliberately succeeded in delaying until
a time when the establishment of these American airfields in Hungary
was no longer necessary). (*10*)

[*The immediate consequences.*]   The Crimean Conference ended
on February 11; the official communiqués were issued the next day.
These require no comment except perhaps two later quotations. One
deals with the "free, unfettered elections" declaration: five months
after Yalta, Stalin himself conceded in a remark at Potsdam that in
eastern Europe the freely elected governments would be anti-Soviet
and this he could not allow. The other is the summation of Stettinius:
"The trouble was not the Yalta formula but the fact that the Soviet
Union later failed to live up to the terms of the agreement."
    One wonders how the task of diplomacy was being understood in
1945 when politics, instead of being the art of the possible, seemed
to be the art of drafting statements about the impossible. (*11*)

.   .   .   .

A few hours after Roosevelt and Churchill had left the Crimea, a
Yugoslav announcement was made to the effect that the Subasič-Tito
government, in agreement with King Peter, was to return to Belgrade (*12*); in Greece the Communist guerrillas signed a disarmament
agreement at Varkiza with the British and with the Greek régime,
while in Rumania the Premier, General Radescu, seriously and dramatically broadcast a speech against the actions of the inordinate and
destructive Communist demonstrators in Bucharest. The contrast between Varkiza and Bucharest clearly shows how Stalin interpreted
Yalta: all over his sphere (but not in Greece, which was not allotted to him) he was establishing his new domains unhampered by
freshly issued statements of national independence and "free, unfettered elections."
    On February 14 the fall of the gutted and ravaged Buda citadel
ended the 51-day siege of Budapest. The Russians were now in the

suburbs of Königsberg, Danzig, and Frankfurt on the Oder, but not yet in Bohemia, Moravia, and Austria; the final zoning boundaries of this latter country were drawn up in the European Advisory Commission conferences in London, where the American Ambassador at the last moment succeeded in preventing the acceptance of Russian proposals which would have separated Czechoslovakia from the American occupation zones.

The Russian era begins: II. The consequences. From Yalta to the German surrender

There remained after Yalta no room for doubt about Britain and America having acknowledged *de facto* the predominance of Russia in eastern Europe. Not even for a day — for events within eastern Europe were revealing the consequences of the Crimean Conference practically within hours. Yet, most Europeans thought Yalta to be, for better or worse, the beginning of something; whereas Yalta was really the end-product, the perhaps logical conclusion of a long series of political errors flowing from a thoughtless strategy.

[*Marshall, Anders, Göbbels, and posterity.*] On February 12 General Marshall, coming from the Crimea, met General Anders in Florence. The issuance of the Yalta communiqués was only a few hours away, yet the American Chief of Staff refused to say a word to his Polish colleague about what had happened there. And when the emotional Anders painted a dark picture of Europe's future, an irritated and weary Marshall answered him: "We continue to march with Soviet Russia against the Germans; what will happen afterwards, God alone knows."

One shudders imagining what might happen if the American people, bewildered and frightened, should turn against their leaders and intellectuals with mordant, primeval fury, rising against those who unwittingly let the Second World War reach that total, dead, political impasse unconsciously admitted by General Marshall; for such a popular move in America would mean the complete repudiation of the Second World War and the raising of the brazen slogan that Hitler should have been left alone, because he was right. For, he was right in one respect: unintentionally and unconsciously his mouthpiece, Göbbels, for once came dangerously near the truth in his turgid prophecies. The following words were penned by him at the same time that Marshall made his statement to Anders — they were printed in his February 23 editorial in *Das Reich:*

> If the German people should lay down their arms, the agreement between Roosevelt, Churchill and Stalin would allow the Soviets to occupy all Eastern and South-Eastern Europe, together with the major part of the Reich. An iron curtain would at once descend on this territory, which, including the Soviet Union, would be of tremendous dimensions. Behind this curtain there would then begin a mass slaughter of peoples, probably with acclamation from the Jewish press in London and New York. All that would remain would be a type of human being in the raw, a dull, fermenting mass of millions of proletarian and despairing human beasts of burden who would know nothing of the rest of the world except what the Kremlin considered useful to its own purposes. Without leadership of their own, they would be at the mercy of the bloody dictatorship of the Soviets. The rest of Europe would be engulfed in chaotic political and social confusion which would only represent a preparatory stage for the coming Bolshevization . . .

Tragic are the consequences inherent in the circumstance that individuals, groups, perhaps entire nations and civilizations — "the terrible simplifiers," as the great Swiss historian, Burckhardt, had put it — might in the future acclaim Göbbels and Hitler as the true prophets and Christian heroes; these tragic consequences would be the result of the lack of responsibility with which the otherwise so responsible, idealistic, and courageous English-speaking nations mishandled the fate of central and eastern Europe in 1942–45. In a way it was the fate of Europe they mishandled; in a way, their own fate.

. . . .

[*Vishinsky's Rumanian coup.*] In Rumania Stalin's free-handed interpretation of the Yalta declarations showed itself first. By February 24 — just twelve days after Yalta — no doubt remained of what Stalin was doing: Communist disturbances against the legal government reached a climax; the American and British representatives on the Allied Control Commission asked for a joint meeting of that body on that day. But the Russian representative did not pay heed to this Allied request, for he knew that greater men were to do greater things. Three days later Vishinsky suddenly arrived in Bucharest and immediately called on King Mihai; in brutal fashion, menacing and threatening, he obtained the dismissal of Radescu. The American representative was unable to see Vishinsky, who stayed in Bucharest for a whole week and personally installed a new government headed by the opportunist Groza, a hireling of the Communists who was officially the head of a curious minuscule party named "Plowmen's Front." The King was on the verge of abdicating; Vishinsky several times threatened Rumania with extinction as an "independent state," and Mihai finally gave in. Also, no help came from abroad; according to Byrnes, ". . . the British heartily disapproved of Soviet actions in Rumania but they did not want to take the initiative in protesting to Stalin" (*1*); American reaction was also fruitless. On March 1, 5 and 6 Harriman protested to Molotov in Moscow, but on March 6 Vishinsky had the Groza régime accepted by the King, and thus a day later Molotov could tell Harriman that the entire question was solved and the American protest was no longer pertinent. (*2*)

Here was the same pattern which repeated itself all over central-eastern Europe in the following years. In addition, Stalin enhanced the standing of the Groza régime by a clever diplomatic move. As he did not know at the time how well he might succeed in Rumania and Hungary, he had previously left the Transylvanian issue pending. But now Hungary was firmly in his hand too; there was no need to lure the Hungarians any more, and the Russians won certain Rumanian politicians to Groza's side by dangling the forthcoming Russian support for Rumania's claim to Transylvania before them. Consequently, on March 8 Stalin declared by way of a letter that the Soviet Union supported the restoration of northern Transylvania to "friendly Rumania"; thus did Stalin gain advantages by playing various vainly and senselessly surviving central-eastern European nationalisms against each other.

[*The Polish agony.*] Roosevelt now thought and said that Poland constituted a better "test case" of American-Soviet relations than Rumania did. This, in a certain way, was true: but his argument, which, according to Byrnes, stated that in Rumania the Soviets could better argue that their intervention was due to the necessity of protecting their communication lines, was faulty. For the same communication issue existed in Poland — Stalin himself used it as a pretext to Hopkins in May — moreover, Rumania was an important precedent, indicating to Stalin how he could succeed elsewhere.

But was Poland an even better "test case"? It did not turn out to

be so; Anders, for example, had no doubts about Poland's future misfortunes. He denounced Yalta before his Army; he saw Churchill on
February 20. The latter was moved, yet he stuck to his argument:
had the Poles accepted the Curzon Line in 1943, the Russians could
not have intervened. On February 24 Anders met Mikolajczyk, who
thought that something could still be done with the help of Britain
and America; Anders remained unconvinced. He even considered
withdrawing the Polish Army in Italy from the front in a gesture of
protest: why should Polish blood be shed for a cause which was now
wholly alien? But then he overcame his emotions and the Army-in-
Exile continued to fight in the front lines, gathering new glories with
a bitter heart. On February 26 Anders was appointed Polish Commander-in-Chief; this met with British disapproval. Next day Winston Churchill delivered his not very convincing report on Yalta in the
House of Commons; a debate followed, in the course of which interesting questions were asked and a critical amendment introduced;
the House divided and the amendment was rejected by 395 to 27. (*3*)

Tired and ill, President Roosevelt presented a generally optimistic
account of the Crimean Conference to Congress on March 1. At least,
he did not speak of the Polish deal in glowing words; he called it a
not too favorable but necessary compromise. That in Moscow it was
not thought of as a compromise became clear on the following day
when an anxious telegram arrived from Harriman; it stated that
Molotov wanted the Polish government to be based exclusively on
the Communists and that the Russians did not wish Mikolajczyk to
participate.

[*The extremities: Greece, Turkey, Finland.*]   Thus in Poland and
Rumania there was now open Allied-Russian controversy; the trend
of events was disturbing elsewhere also. On March 5 the so-called
"Regents" were sworn in in Belgrade; Subasič resigned, and Tito
formed a new government on March 6. (*4*) The Yugoslav and Albanian governments now began to assail the "reactionary" Greek
régime, and although on March 1 the Turkish declaration of war was
in effect against Germany, on March 19 the Russians declared that
they would renounce the Soviet-Turkish Treaty of 1925 unless the
Turkish government acceded to a Soviet wish to revise the Montreux
Convention about the status of the Straits. Only in Finland were
there relatively free elections: the Communist-led front gained but
did not win. The Ministry of the Interior was given to the Com-

munists; leaders in the war period were to be brought to trial. Finland, however, continued her curious twilight existence: completely at Stalin's mercy, her political institutions and internal independence nevertheless were allowed to function.

[*Impact of the Allied advance: Russian suspicions.*]   Meanwhile military events of great significance had developed. Hitler, who felt confident for awhile that his armies could hold the Rhine line in the west and the Oder line in the east, decided on a counteroffensive in a sector where the Soviet advance was furthest from the Reich centers: in Hungary. The Sixth SS Panzer Army could not reach Buda but achieved some success in breaking through southwest of there and temporarily reached the Danube. Yet it was a wasteful operation. By March 10 the German bulge was eliminated, and Malinowski and Tolbukhin could now without greater efforts push through the thin German lines. On March 22 they launched their offensive toward Bratislava and Vienna.

Thus the inevitable fate of Hungary and the almost inevitable fate of Czechoslovakia matured quickly. On March 15, upon Russian orders and with the assistance of the Russian military, the Hungarian government in Debrecen passed a radical and sweeping land-reform decree. The Russians insisted that it be executed with utmost swiftness; one wonders why. (5) On March 17 Beneš flew to Moscow from London; he stayed in the Russian capital for two weeks; he wished to return to Prague via Moscow.

The final phase of the Battle of Germany now opened new vistas and brought new consequences.

In the north the Russian sweep, which reached the Oder with unexpected speed in February, slowed down, and early in March the eastern frontline stabilized along the Oder line; although Küstrin was taken on March 9, the line did not advance further. (6) But on the other side of Germany, the Allies were turning the corner; Montgomery's Twenty-First Army broke into the Ruhr, and the daring capture of the Remagen Bridge on March 7 enabled the Americans to make a magnificent dash into central Germany. The Oder line still held, but the Rhine line had collapsed. All this evoked new and unexpected chances for the Allies. (7)

[*Anglo-American reactions.*]   Stalin was now nervous. On March 11 the German commander in Italy secretly contacted the

Allies in Berne and offered his surrender; although the Anglo-American representatives loyally told the Germans that no separate agreement could be made without consulting the Russians, Stalin, with his suspicious nature, did not want to believe that they had done so: in a bitter message to Roosevelt he complained of the Allied military's permitting the Germans to switch their forces to the eastern front to hold the Russians there while the former were opening the gates of the Anglo-American advance into Germany. Roosevelt was extremely irked by this message and wrote an energetic answer to Stalin, calling his charges "vile misrepresentations." Stalin now remained silent on this issue. Not so with Poland. Harriman on March 17 telegraphed for "firmness" with Russia, in view of Molotov's "arrogant language" and "domineering attitude." Next morning the British Ambassador asked Leahy to urge Roosevelt's approval of a message to Moscow regarding Poland which Halifax had drafted together with the State Department. Leahy agreed, though not without reluctance. On March 22 Churchill cabled Roosevelt, asking him to intervene with Stalin in face of the dangerous trend of events in the Balkans, in Hungary, and especially in Rumania and Poland. Roosevelt answered Churchill on the 27th: he agreed and said that he watched "with anxiety and concern the Soviet attitude" and that he was "acutely aware of the danger inherent in the present course of events."

On the same day the Russians lured the remaining leaders of the Polish democratic underground into a devilishly planned trap: a Russian General Ivanov sent a message to these leaders asking them to come to his quarters for political talks. The Deputy Premier of the exiled government, the Chairman of the recently dissolved National Council, (*8*) the last commander of the Home Army, and thirteen other Poles arrived. They were at once arrested and whisked to Moscow.

On April 1 Roosevelt and Churchill sent two separate messages to Stalin, expressing their dissatisfaction with his handling of the Polish issues; Roosevelt also mentioned the case of Rumania. Here was the first concrete diplomatic action of the English-speaking Powers acting in concert against the eastern European projects of Stalin. A week passed before Stalin answered; in the meantime events favored Russia again. On April 4 Bratislava fell; the whole of Hungary was now in Russian hands and the Second and Third Ukrainian Army Groups entered Austrian territory: on April 5 Tito and Subasič arrived in Moscow; on April 6 the slow Partisan advance against the Germans captured its first prize since early December: Sarajevo fell in Bosnia. On April 7 a new Czechoslovak cabinet was installed, with the pro-Communist (officially Social Democrat) Fierlinger as Premier and Jan Masaryk as Foreign Minister.

Stalin's answer of April 7 was written with his usual clumsiness: brief, disconnected sentences carried countercharges. However, he seemed to retreat in the face of the firmness showed by Roosevelt and Churchill. To the latter he answered that Mikolajczyk's presence in the Polish government was now acceptable to him, provided that Mikolajczyk committed himself to the Yalta frontier formula. This was, at any rate, a concession. To Roosevelt Stalin was somewhat bolder: he again charged that the British and Americans wished to interfere in the internal affairs of Poland. The President felt now that firmness was inevitable in dealings with the Soviet Union. (*9*) He instructed the State Department to draft a joint answer to Stalin which was to be sent simultaneously with Churchill's. Here was, at last, resolution and determination and Anglo-American unity against the Soviets. On April 12 the draft to Stalin was ready and Roosevelt cabled Churchill: "We must be firm . . ."

Within a few hours he was dead.

I shall digress now from the main story for a moment. There is a rising and almost mystical belief among anti-Communists and anti-Russians that Roosevelt was the great villain, who lightheartedly gambled half of Europe (and China) away; some even say that he and his entourage were making a cruelly selfish, underhand deal with Stalin.

It is easy to be under the spell of such appearances for awhile: I have often been tempted myself. This book tries often to point out the fantastic naïveté of the American President during the war years and some of his mistaken actions. Nevertheless it must be evident to the student of the American war scene that Roosevelt was not a lone and prime villain; if he was mistaken in his judgments, so were many others: Hopkins, Marshall, Stimson, Stettinius, for example, whose direct decisions and propositions put before the President were often more decisive than Roosevelt's actions. Also there were very few, if any, among the late and present critics of the President who at any time between 1942 and early 1945 had formulated an alternate plan of action for American foreign policies: their criticism was suspicious rather than constructive, emotional but not realistic, general but not practical. Finally it must be said that about a month after

Yalta Roosevelt began to realize the dangers of the mistaken Russo-phile policies. Within the United States many people admired Franklin Delano Roosevelt for qualities which he did not have; other people hated him for qualities which they did not have. This tendency is now shared by different groups of Europeans, and unfortunately so; for, while it is true that his actions directly led to the tragedy of central-eastern Europe, even more blame rests with the immaturely conceived American "internationalism" of the war years and with the not less immature isolationist criticism which Roosevelt — stooping from aristocratic statesmanship to democratic politicking — could not dismiss from his mind. He was a great friend of Europe and its culture and thus should be respected by all Europeans, central, eastern, northern, western alike: after all, such things should be seen from a truly continental standpoint. But while the ideals of the much narrower Wilson were at least faultily and partly realized, fate did not permit Roosevelt to attempt or witness the correction of a frightful situation to which he, however unwittingly, had contributed.

.   .   .   .

[*Last attempts: Ribbentrop.*]   The nearing collapse of Germany was now of first importance. That the rapid advance of the Allies had Stalin worried and suspicious, the Germans knew. While Field-Marshal Kesselring talked armistice with the Allies in Berne, agents of Ribbentrop planted rumors with the Russians about an impending Western armistice and proposed a Russo-German separate peace. Especially Göbbels and Ribbentrop were behind such plans. The latter's envoy extraordinary, Rahn, called on Mussolini on April 10; the ailing Duce was asked to intervene urgently with Hitler in favor of a Russian separate peace. (*10*) But Mussolini, once the arch-proponent of such plans, thought it useless now:

> Important would be to survive until the end of this war, because to-day every kind of alliance [*combinazione*] could be constructed on the basis of the unique menace which the Soviet advance constitutes for Europe. In every sense, the interest of Hitler is to find which side . . . offers him better conditions. . . . But will he succeed in obtaining these?

Other German agents contacted American diplomats through Spain. But while Hitler in his eerie bunker headquarters wove unfinished dreams of a great political coup in the manner of Frederick the Great, all this was in vain. General Patton was racing through Swabia and Bavaria; Montgomery sealed off the Ruhr and moved quickly toward the Elbe; the Russians captured Vienna and readied themselves on the Oder Front for the last great jump to Berlin. (*11*)

[*Last attempts: Churchill.*]   It was now Churchill again who wanted to redress the balance:

> It is not possible in a major war to divide military from political affairs. At the summit they are one. . . . much of the literature of this tragic century is biased by the idea that in war only military considerations count and that soldiers are obstructed in their clear, professional view by the intrusion of politicians, who for personal or party advantage tilt the dread balances of battle.

These words were written in 1941. Now, in 1945, with the Russians breaking the Yalta agreements, why should the Allies be bound by the purely technical military zone delimitations agreed upon by advisory commissions and military missions? Churchill wanted the Allies to get to Berlin first.

But he again faced the stolid misunderstanding of the American military. On March 28 General Eisenhower sent a message to Moscow outlining the plans of the Allied advance in Germany, suggesting that preparations be made for the meeting of the Anglo-Americans and the Russians at pre-arranged points. Churchill vainly protested against the message; then he brought all kinds of pressure upon the American military: he succeeded in convincing some of the highly-placed Americans and he was not too far from convincing the President shortly before the latter's death. On April 10 the aide of Eisenhower noted: "At the moment the only abnormal pressure [on Eisenhower] is to combat the desire of those who wish him to rush our forces to Berlin." This was very possible: the Russian Oder offensive had not yet begun, and German resistance was crumbling in the center. Patton was moving rapidly eastward and on the evening of April 17 reached the westernmost tip of Czechoslovakia. On that day and the next Churchill vainly argued with Eisenhower to advance to Berlin on his own; but the new American President was told by the Joint Chiefs of Staff to let the Russians take the German capital.

The Russian offensive for Berlin had now begun: Stalin, seeing the rapid advance of the Allies, wanted to prevent their breakthrough to

Berlin by all means. He now assumed better manners: while shortly before the death of Roosevelt it had been announced that Molotov would not attend the San Francisco Conference (scheduled to open on April 25), on April 13 Stalin told Harriman that in spite of the previously invoked "urgent business," Molotov would go. On April 18 the new American President and Churchill sent him the rather firm American-British answer to his April 7 message, an answer which had been drafted while Roosevelt was alive (*12*); to please the Anglo-Americans, Stalin announced through his diplomats on that day that the Allies were invited to send representatives to Vienna, despite the yet unsolved controversies within the European Advisory Commission regarding the administration, the zones of, and the access to that city.

On April 21, after the American spearheads were halted at the Elbe, the Zhukov army reached the outskirts of Berlin, and General Eisenhower said at the conference of the Chiefs of Staff: "Berlin does not have military significance any more." True; but how about the political significance! (Thus Churchill lost his last battle.) Although, as Captain Butcher stated, ". . . every GI wanted to keep going to Berlin and resented being ordered to stop at the Elbe," Berlin was ultimately taken by the Russians. On April 25 another great political opportunity — perhaps a whole country — was forfeited by a military decision taken upon Russian requests. General Antonov of the Russian General Staff asked Eisenhower to stop the advance of the Patton army in Czechoslovakia: an exchange about mutual clarifications and delimitations of operations followed, and Eisenhower instructed Patton not to advance beyond the Karlovy Vary-Plzen-Budejovice (*13*) line in western Czechoslovakia.

[*Poland and the San Francisco agenda.*] Meanwhile the Polish question came to the fore again, as the San Francisco conference was opening. The new American President did not know much about the tortuous and delicate American handling of the Polish issue; some of his cabinet and other advisers did not present the case of Poland to him in its true perspective; Stimson, for example, wrote:

> I believed in firmness [with Russia] on the minor matters where we had been yielding in the past, but this [Polish] problem was too big a question to take chances on . . .

a typically mistaken rationalization. On April 21 it was announced that the Soviet Union and the Warsaw Government had signed a twenty-year Alliance and Friendship Pact. Where were the chances to be taken? (The desperate Polish government in London now issued a declaration, stating that it was willing to come to terms with the Soviets; south of the Alps the Second Polish Brigade had taken Bologna that day.) When the question of legality and free elections occupied the forefront of discussions on Poland (Molotov arrived in Washington on April 22 and spent three days there before going to San Francisco), Stimson said superciliously on April 23: anyhow, "there are no nations in the world except the United States and Britain which have a real idea of what an independent free ballot is . . ."

On April 25 American and Russian soldiers met at Torgau on the Elbe; American and Russian diplomats met at San Francisco. Before the conference opened, Truman, Stettinius, and the Chiefs of Staff conferred on what position American diplomacy should take at San Francisco in view of the Russian violations of Yalta and the problems flowing therefrom; it was again the military who pleaded for patience with the Russians; they wanted Russian friendship preserved, as they wanted to assure Russia's participation in the war against Japan.

[*Hitler and Mussolini: the last days.*]   That afternoon Mussolini was pacing the Italian lake gardens with a Cabinet "Minister" friend, Pellegrini-Giampietro: "Suppose you had to choose what Italy's fate should be: a colony of England or a Soviet republic," asked Mussolini. Pellegrini-Giampietro was startled and said that he could not think in such alternatives: after all, it was Mussolini around whom he and his friends were grouped for the chance of a truly independent Italy. "But if they pointed a pistol at you and made you choose?" insisted Mussolini. And before the other could have answered, Mussolini said: "I would choose the Soviet republic."

Hitler, in his cellar, bombarded by Russian planes and artillery, still commanded imaginary armies on imaginary German battlefields, and on April 27 sent this last message to Mussolini:

> The fight for our existence reached its climax. Employing great masses and materials, Bolshevism and Judaism allied themselves to join their destructive forces in German territory in order to precipitate chaos in our continent.

He still called the force of Britain and America "Judaism"; in their last peril both he and Mussolini showed that within their frustrated hearts they hated the West and the English-speaking world perhaps more than they did the Asiatic East; thus it is difficult to see in them what they wanted to see in themselves and what they wanted their followers to see: great Europeans.

Now Stockholm informed the world that Himmler had offered the surrender of all German forces to the Western Allies. In certain parts of Bavaria, Italy, and Holland German armed resistance ceased.

But now the problems between East and West arose at once and in various instances.

The Americans and British did not invite the legal Polish government to San Francisco from London; yet, they also refused the Russian request to issue an invitation to the Warsaw régime. Here was a definite source of Western-Soviet differences at San Francisco. The British pressed for a more energetic stand, but the Americans were more hesitant. Eden queried the Russians about the fate of the sixteen trapped men in Poland, unsuccessfully for awhile, until Molotov casually turned to him at a cocktail party: "By the way, those Poles, we have arrested them. They have been guilty of undemocratic activities and further information will be given when they are found guilty." "When, not if?" asked Eden. Molotov did not reply. Eden and the Americans got together to issue a communiqué about the Russian handling of the Poles; the advisers (Hiss was in charge of general planning at San Francisco) and Stettinius were cautious, they were against a strong communiqué and asked Eden: "Should we call this a 'grave situation'?" Eden retorted: "No, let's call it a bloody situation." The American-British communiqué was issued on May 5, causing considerable interest at San Francisco. But elsewhere the gigantic spectre of the German collapse occupied all attention.

[*Austrian uncertainties.*] There were now definite areas of friction in the middle of Europe. The Americans and British were unclear about what the Russians were doing in Vienna, from which city the old Socialist Renner wrote a comradely letter to Stalin; the Russians helped him to set up a coalition "Austrian Government" on April 29; on April 30 Washington hurriedly announced that it refused to recognize it. Ultimately, the Renner government turned out to be definitely anti-Communist in Austria, where the Russians never tried to or could impose their régime, given the fact that they were to occupy but one-third of that country. But this the Americans did not yet know, especially as the first of their officers were not permitted to enter Vienna until May 18.

[*The Trieste crisis.*] Further to the south Tito forces, bypass-
ing Zagreb and the major cities of Croatia — still held by the Germans
— concentrated upon the Italian-Yugoslav frontier zone. (*14*) The
Partisan offensive which began on April 20 in the Fiume area moved
forward with the support of some light artillery pieces left behind by
the Germans. On April 30 the "ivth Yugoslav Army" broke into
Trieste. Some fighting continued there until May 3, and the Yugoslav partisans exercised cruel and extreme terror; they threw the
Italian resistance forces and liberation committee out of control; the
situation was not relieved until May 4 when a New Zealand division
of the British Eighth Army, moving up from the Venice area, reached
Trieste. But the Yugoslavs controlled the outskirts of the city and the
whole of Istria. The New Zealanders and the Yugoslav partisans thus
stood facing each other at gunpoint in the days when Germany was
about to surrender — a dark omen for the future. This acute tension
and Tito's terror in the Trieste area lasted for six more weeks; it then
lapsed, only to be renewed again later. (*15*)

Hitler killed himself on April 30, and the Flensburg "government"
of Dönitz was announced on May 1. All the other German quisling-
type "régimes" were mopped up in the mountains of Bavaria and
Austria by eager American special counterintelligence units: Logothetopoulos, Lyotič, Tsankov, Sima, Szálasi, Tiso and their entou-
rages were thus captured. (Some of the hardier types, Pavelič for
example, succeeded in escaping to Argentina.) The gates of Dachau
and Mauthausen opened and the tens of thousands of surviving political prisoners came out, starved and sick. Most of their brethren did
not live to see the day of liberation; some of them, central-eastern
Europeans, thought it better not to go home and face the perils of
other, new concentration camps.

[*Prague and the Russians.*] On May 1 the Russian General
Staff was officially informed of the American acceptance of the
Karlovy Vary-Plzen-Budejovice line in Czechoslovakia; on the 3rd
Czech patriots under General Viest rose in Prague. They were
relatively weak, and the bulk of the German Sixteenth Army was
concentrated around Prague, still well-equipped and easily capable
of quelling any revolt, but the disintegration of this army group had
already begun: thousands were crossing the mountains in the west to
surrender to the Americans. Nevertheless, as the Russians were still
laboring around the defences of Brno and Moravska-Ostrava, eighty

miles to the east, the Czech insurgents' messages, requests for help, reached Eisenhower. Therefore on May 4th the Allied Supreme Commander sent a message to General Antonov in Moscow, proposing to continue the American advance into Czechoslovakia to the "west banks of the Vltava (Moldau) and Elbe rivers." Antonov reacted violently. He immediately informed Eisenhower of Russian opposition and demanded the cancellation of the plan. Thus Eisenhower had to leave the Prague insurrection alone: Patton did not advance into Prague, just as Montgomery did not advance into Berlin — just as Alexander or Eisenhower had not advanced in 1943 or 1944 into Tirana and Belgrade and Zagreb and Budapest and Vienna. It was the Russians who "liberated" Prague when their tanks rolled into the already free city on May 9. (*16*)

[*The European war ends.*] This was V–E Day, whose announcement the Russians delayed by more than a day to profit from the time-limit. Units of the German Sixteenth Army continued to move to the west, and in certain northern Czechoslovak and eastern German areas fighting continued until about May 15. The trapped remnants of the last German Baltic army did not surrender until about May 12. (*17*) On that day the last German soldiers delivered the last islands of the Dodecanese to Allied-Greek landing parties.

V–E Day: in the evening Winston Churchill and Harry S. Truman spoke on the radio. The British Premier warned his people and Europe of grave problems to come; the American President was less colorful and more optimistic. As so often, an eighteenth-century tone rang in Churchill's last words: "Advance, Britannia!" The American President spoke in the Millsian vein of the superficially optimistic nineteenth century: "The flags of freedom fly all over Europe." But in central-eastern Europe the sad truths of the twentieth century prevailed: the flags which flew were red, and Britannia did not advance.

The Russian era begins: III. The end of European continentality. The summer of 1945

[*May 1945: Hopkins' mission.*] The meeting at Torgau cut Germany in two, and subsequently not only Germany but the whole European continent became divided and has remained so ever since. Immediately after the military surrender the political battle for Germany was resumed by the Russians, and the first gun was fired a mere six days after their announced V–E Day. On May 15 a significant article signed by Alexandrov, head of the Propaganda Department of the Communist-Bolshevik Party of the Soviet Union, was published in the German-language newspaper of the Red Army in Berlin: Alexandrov attacked the writings and thesis of Ilya Ehrenburg, who had lambasted the German people scathingly, without mercy or exception, throughout the war. The first Russian-sponsored local administrations in eastern Germany were springing up already. The dull spectacle of San Francisco artificially glittered on the other side of the globe, an assembly drafting meaningless declarations. But the Polish problem was still acute; President Truman decided to send Hopkins for a last personal mission to Moscow. He flew willingly and arrived there on May 25. How he represented Poland there can be seen from his own papers:

> Poland *per se* was not so important as the fact that it had become a symbol of our ability to work out problems with the Soviet Union.

And:

> . . . as far as the American government was concerned, we had no interest in seeing anyone connected with the present Polish government in London involved in the new Provisional Government of Poland.

He repeated this several times and nodded understandingly when Stalin cited the devious British desire to re-create a *cordon sanitaire* on the western borders of Russia. Hopkins made an ill-conceived suggestion to the detriment of Britain when he intimated that it was "obviously desirable" for the United States and the Soviet Union "to talk alone." Stalin enjoyed the fact that the brief show of Anglo-American common determination, inaugurated in the dying Roosevelt's last days, had faded again. He said: "Whether the United States wished it or not, [it was] a world-wide power and would have to accept world-wide responsibilities"; and, complimenting America on the war effort against Germany, he concluded that "the history of the last thirty years shows that the United States has more reason to be a world power than any other state"; he, Stalin, "therefore recognized [the American] right to participate in the Polish question." It must be said for Hopkins that he was not altogether fooled by compliments; yet he left Moscow charmed, and conveyed his optimism to Truman. This was the mission of which Byrnes wrote that "Hopkins had served his government well on many occasions, but the record of this mission does him special credit."

[*A State Department view: the Warsaw régime recognized.*] To Hopkins, Stalin conceded the entry of Mikolajczyk into the Warsaw cabinet; thus the legal Polish government finally broke apart. Within a month Moscow announced that the sixteen captured leaders of underground Poland had been tried and convicted. And when the Polish Ambassador in Washington begged the United States to intervene, one of the chief American diplomats, the head of the State Department's Eastern European Section, answered him thus:

> Mr. Ambassador, you appear to have an exaggerated opinion of the power of the United States. You are wrong. America is not sufficiently powerful to impose her will on Soviet Russia.

Later the same official admitted that, to Washington, the whole Polish complex constituted an "intolerable headache." Such were the results of the new American "internationalism." . . . Yet American intelligence was now aware of the situation within Poland. The Polish "government" was reorganized on June 21, and an OSS analysis stated correctly that this "reorganization" brought about a government "no less friendly to the USSR and considerably stronger than its predecessor. Far from being altered, both the foreign and the domestic policies of this new government can be expected to be the more firmly set." (*1*) On July 5 the Communist-dominated "Provisional Polish Government" was recognized by London and Washington and the exile government thus lost its international legal standing. The recognition (decided upon before his assumption of office) was the first official act of the new American Secretary of State, James F. Byrnes; two days later he sailed from Newport News for Potsdam.

[*Davies and Churchill.*] In late May the former Ambassador to Moscow, Davies, again came to the fore; Truman now sent him on a mission to London (later Davies appeared at Potsdam). He reported on his talks with Churchill, who seemed tired and was extremely pessimistic about the Russians and the Balkan situation, and about Tito; in Davies' words:

> I said that frankly, as I had listened to him inveigh so violently against the threat of Soviet domination and the spread of Communism in

Europe, and disclose such a lack of confidence in the professions of good faith in Soviet leadership, I had wondered whether he, the Prime Minister, was now willing to declare to the world that he and Britain had made a mistake in not supporting Hitler, for as I understood him, he was now expressing the doctrine which Hitler and Goebbels had been proclaiming and reiterating for the past four years in an effort to break up allied unity and "divide and conquer." Exactly the same conditions which he described and the same deductions were drawn from them as he now appeared to assert. (2)

Churchill nodded: he might have used unduly strong expressions; but he insisted that it would be "terrible" if the United States withdrew her troops from Europe. He also insisted that the Anglo-American troops should not be withdrawn from their forward positions in central Germany (beyond the EAC demarcation line), which positions could be used for bargaining. This suggestion horrified Davies. He asked Churchill's opinion about the possibility of Truman and Stalin meeting alone before Potsdam, which query, in turn, upset Churchill. Davies' suggestion to Truman was significant: he advised a Truman-Stalin *tête-à-tête*, with Churchill excluded. Davies' conclusion was illuminating: Churchill "was basically more concerned over preserving England's position in Europe than in preserving peace . . ." To this Leahy agreed: "This was consistent with our staff estimate of Churchill's attitude throughout the war."

.   .   .   .

[*Tito and Trieste.*] Stalin's haste to establish and secure his sphere still met with considerable obstacles, especially where his armies were not dominant over local or other forces. Thus the origins of the Tito-Stalin split developed as early as May–June 1945. In the Trieste area morose Yugoslav Partisans rifled and harassed the Italian population and tried to provoke the British and Imperial troops into leaving the city. (3) Local controversies flared when Stalin cooled Tito's zeal: he understood the difficulty of the situation, Stalin telegraphed, but "a few incidents cannot be generalized." And later he admitted Russian weakness: the Trieste issue cannot be pushed; "since all other means are exhausted," said he, only war remained and in its present condition, the Soviet Union could not enter another one. Around May 15 the situation became critical; on May 19 Field-Marshal Alexander sent a strong protest to Tito: "The world is still

too near to the memories of the methods of Hitler and Mussolini."
True, the Americans were hesitating again; Truman asked Churchill
and Stalin to intervene, and Marshall, according to Leahy, believed
"that every effort should be made to avoid a military clash." Troops
were sent to the area, however, and Tito understood the portents of
British determination: on May 20 his troops withdrew from Austrian
Carinthia, on June 12 from Trieste; and on June 20 the Partisan General Yovanovič grudgingly signed an agreement with the British
General Morgan establishing a demarcation line between the two
occupation zones of the Trieste area.

[*Tito and the Russians.*]   But Tito was not happy with the
Russians either, and the Russians were not happy with him. His
lieutenant Djilas was overheard making critical statements on the
behavior of the Russian soldiery in Yugoslavia; Tito himself had to
explain the issue and excuse Djilas before Stalin. Two Partisan liaison
officers with the British, Velebit and the "diplomat" Lentič, were
accused by the Russians of being British spies; on the other hand, a
Russian Colonel Stepanov was caught recruiting Yugoslav secret
policemen for the Russian MVD. While Stepanov condescendingly
remarked, "for the present, Marshal Tito works as he should," Tito
wondered. He knew now that the Bulgar Communists were told by
the Russians to evade any renewed Yugoslav-Bulgar alliance or federation suggestions. True, the capitalist and imperialist British and
American press now attacked his new Yugoslav republic. But could
he count on the curious and cunning Stalin? In May Tito spoke in
recently liberated Ljubljana, attacking the Italian "Fascists" and the
Trieste deadlock. He also said:

> We don't want to pay for others, we do not want to be used as a
> bribe in international bargaining; we do not want to be involved in
> any policy of spheres of interest.

Obviously, belated reports of "50–50" had reached Tito's ears.
Other ears were perking up in Moscow. On June 5 the Russian Ambassador, Sadchikov, officially protested against the Tito speech; the
subsequent explanation given by Kardelj was deemed unsatisfactory
by Stalin; Moscow stated that if the rambunctious Tito did such things
once again, the Soviets would "expose him." Not quite three years
later Stalin, wishing to drive a wedge between Tito and Kardelj,

quoted the alleged statement of the latter to the Soviet Ambassador in June 1945: "[Kardelj] agreed that the Soviet Union could no longer tolerate similar statements." Whether Kardelj said this or not is almost irrelevant; more important is that Kardelj wanted to please Sadchikov by stating that Yugoslavia could be a constituent part of the Soviet Union "in the near future," whereupon the Soviet Ambassador answered — this is the Soviet version of 1948! — no, at present Yugoslavia should be independent. (*4*)

[*Stalin: territorial gains.*] The Soviet Union was, of course, busily incorporating its gains. On June 29 Beneš ceded the Carpatho-Ukraine to Stalin ("Generalissimo" since June 25). The Czechoslovak President lightheartedly agreed to the establishment of the Muscovite colossus on the separating crest of the Carpathians for the first time in history. Now all Ukrainians, Carpatho- or Polish-, were living within the confines of the Soviet Union. In the north, Königsberg and the northeastern corner of East Prussia were to become Kaliningrad, and while its utmost military-naval importance made this an area of full isolation from the rest of Poland and Russia, administratively it became but a mere *oblast* (province) of the Byelorussian SSR. In the south the Soviets turned on the Turks with harsh demands and unveiled threats: they demanded frontier rectification on "historic" grounds in the Caucasus and revision and bases in the Dardanelles. Molotov officially communicated these demands to the Turkish envoy, Sarper, on June 7. But Turkey was courageous and held fast. In a few days a friendly Soviet request was made to the monarchist, anti-Communist Greek government of Admiral Voulgaris for permission to establish temporary or permanent Soviet bases in the Dodecanese. The Greeks refused the Soviet suggestion: soon afterwards Moscow began to stake new cards again on the underground Greek Communists. (*5*)

Between September 1939 and June 1945 the Soviet Union annexed about 300,000 square miles in the west, while Germany, Poland, Czechoslovakia, Hungary, Italy, Rumania, and Finland were reduced, crippled, depleted, and swarming with millions of refugees from the east. (*6*) But the earth-gods of the sparse Russian plains were hungry and demanded more earth, again more earth for their human masses, masses never pressed together but alone, huddling in millions of solitary specks of communities far apart, with great, bleak fields in between, on the plain Russian landscape under the plain Russian sky.

According to the previous demarcation agreements, the American armies evacuated Thuringia and Saxony in July, withdrawing to the previously fixed zone boundaries. Again Russia moved forward.

[*Vienna.*] In Austria the Allied representatives were allowed to enter Vienna on May 19 but were strictly confined to the city limits, and on June 10–11 they were suddenly requested to leave the city at once: one of the inscrutable and infuriating Russian decisions. The European Advisory Commission was entangled in difficult controversies concerning the administration of Austria and Vienna; although on June 25 the official Four-Power announcement of the Austrian occupation zones was made, difficult discussions concerning Allied access to Vienna continued, and the Soviets gave in only when on July 6 Lord Hood, the British delegate, threatened to walk out of the EAC. Agreement was reached then on July 9 and the Russians yielded: an airport was allotted to the United States, another one to the British and the French; the inner city was to form an international zone. American, British and French troops entered Vienna on July 30.

*   *   *   *   *

[*The Potsdam conference.*] Truman and Stalin met at Potsdam for the first and for the last time. Churchill was there, but only for a week: he and Attlee went home for a day to learn that the British people had voted a great and unexpected majority for Labor. Churchill did not return, and the quiet, colorless Clement Attlee was the voice of Britain at Potsdam for the last eight days. It was not a strong voice. Thus, suddenly, Stalin became the only remaining member of the original Big Three: but the Strange Alliance was breaking up anyhow.

From July 17 to August 2 the American and British representatives attempted to commit the Russians on the peace treaties with Italy, Finland, and the three Danubian states; the Anglo-American approach was that these treaties should precede the German peace treaty and the Austrian state treaty. Ultimately, this again was to work in favor of the Soviets. Stalin deliberately postponed the peace treaty with Germany and Austria for many reasons; one of these was his desire to keep Russian troops in his new satellites (first on the pretext of "guarding" communication lines to his zones in Austria and

Germany) until these satellites were "organized" and all opposition annihilated. Stalin knew that, in contrast with Nazi-type and Fascist-type states all over the earth, where the existence of the German, Italian, and Japanese armed forces was not the necessary prerequisite of the establishment of such dictatorships, the Communist world movement throughout three decades had singularly failed to establish a stable and permanent Communistic state anywhere without the previous existence or the strategic domination of Russian armies in those territories.

The American delegation then stated that the Soviet Union was not fulfilling its Yalta obligations regarding politics within the Danubian states, and Byrnes suggested that the holding of "free and unfettered" elections be internationally supervised. Long hours of semantic wrangling came out of this, while interesting revelations were made by Stalin himself. He still seemed to consider everything on the basis of spheres of influence; at the moment Churchill raised objections to the Soviets' handling of affairs and internal politics in Rumania, Bulgaria, and Yugoslavia ("an iron fence" was thrown around the British representatives in Bucharest, stated Churchill angrily), Stalin presented a *quid pro quo* argument and criticized the internal affairs of Greece. (7) Churchill wanted to discuss Yugoslavia; Stalin said that in this case Tito should be invited; an argument developed in which Churchill wished to push the Balkans into the center of the discussions. (8) But now Truman, inadvertently enough, intervened as the typical American mediator: "I have come here to discuss matters upon which we three chiefs of Government can agree. I have no intention of taking part in any court before which complaints of all kinds may be brought, investigated or adjusted. If we hear Tito, we must hear Franco, DeGaulle, and so on."

"Action on Yugoslavia was postponed."

Stalin also mentioned the Russian desire for "some territory of the defeated states" (Italian colonies in North Africa intrigued him); also the Dardanelles and bases there were brought up. When it came to Poland's frontiers, Stalin suddenly said that the Soviet Union was not bound by the Oder-Neisse Line, "the western frontier question [of Poland] is open." (The Western Allies avoided making a commitment about the Polish-German frontier line and merely declared that they would support the transfer of the Königsberg region to the Soviet Union.) Churchill made a courageous defense of the Polish Army in Britain, (9) which Stalin had censured; the Russians then withdrew this argument and concentrated on Poland's external assets instead. But in a few days Churchill was gone and there remained no one to make a similar spirited defense of Poland; Leahy noted that Bevin, the new British Foreign Secretary, was not even familiar with the map of Poland. Two general statements only were agreed upon, one dealing with an important issue (diplomatic recognition of and peace treaties for the Danubian states) very vaguely, the other dealing more concretely with a less important issue (freedom of Allied press representatives to travel in the former satellites and report from there). Some changes were also made in the procedure of the Allied Control Commissions in these countries. Most of the Potsdam talks, however, dealt with Germany and German reparations (here the great mistake was made by Edwin Pauley of not specifying what constituted "German assets" in the satellites and Austria; from this lack of precision again Russia profited, expropriating a fantastic amount of assets in these countries). Again no specific and decisive agreement was reached.

The sharpening differences between the Western and Russian concepts were thus restricted to the conference and not aired to the world: and Europe got another superficial impression that Big Three unity prevailed. Byrnes' words reflect the same naïveté and lack of political perception as do Stettinius' recollections of Yalta. "We considered the conference a success. We firmly believed that the agreements reached would provide a basis for the early restoration of stability to Europe. The agreements did make the conference a success but the violation of those agreements has turned success into failure," wrote Byrnes in 1947. "The trouble was not the Yalta formula but the fact that the Soviet Union later failed to live up to the terms of agreement," wrote Stettinius in 1949. (*10*)

[*Potsdam: the consequences.*] The Potsdam "agreements," again unwittingly, thus allowed the Soviet Union to proceed largely unhindered with its consolidation of its "sphere of influence"; had the British and American opposition to the Russians' satellite projects (which opposition did, although unorganized, appear at Potsdam) been revealed to the world, the pro-democratic forces within central-eastern Europe would have gathered new strength. But they were now sacrificed for the sake of non-specific, vague, general, and somewhat trite expressions of Big Three friendship and unity which sounded wooden and empty. Only in mid-August did the new British Foreign

Secretary, Ernest Bevin, make a speech in which he protested against Soviet actions in the Balkans; Byrnes followed suit with a less energetic statement two weeks later.

In the meantime the atomic bomb was dropped on Hiroshima on August 6 and Japan surrendered a week later; but nothing was done to exploit the awe-inspiring picture of America's great power for the sake of a stable peace; instead, dreary conferences with Molotov in the "Council of Foreign Ministers" were to follow with bleak regularity, lasting well into 1948. The United States did not admit the existence of the so-called "cold war" until then; even afterwards, its formulated and announced goal was but the "containment" of the Soviet Union. Central-eastern Europe was thus, to all intents and purposes, written off by the West, and although this abandonment was never officially admitted by Britain or the United States, this truth sank deeper and deeper into Western minds; and the memory of the years when Warsaw, Budapest, Prague, Riga were a part of Europe also sank deeper and deeper into oblivion.

MR. CHURCHILL

&

THE BALKAN

INVASION

DEBATE

Perhaps the most important controversy about the history of the Second World War is that which concerns the prospects of an Anglo-American invasion of the Balkans in 1943–44. The thesis — which I have presented and, I hope, somewhat advanced in this book — is that Churchill had wished to put Anglo-American forces into the Balkans; that he had made about half a dozen futile attempts to convince his Allies but that a number of circumstances, foremost among them the opposition and mistrust of President Roosevelt and of the American Joint Chiefs of Staff, prevented the Prime Minister from doing so. This thesis has of late been unreasonably slighted or has received wide challenge from a number of American historians, publicists, and journalists. Consequently it is important to trace the outlines of this historical debate:

It was early in 1946, after the famous "iron curtain" speech by Churchill in Fulton, Missouri, that for the first time references appeared in the British and European press and in a few American publications to the wartime determination of the Prime Minister to invade the Balkans in order to forestall the Russians. Evidence was further provided by American war memoirs, the first batch of which (those by Captain Butcher, Elliott Roosevelt, Sherwood-Hopkins) cited various instances when Churchill had argued for and insisted on plans for a Balkan campaign: vainly, however, for it was emphasized that such sinuous designs were thwarted by forthright American determination: the United States was unwilling to pull British chestnuts from the fire and to bypass the Soviet ally. It is interesting to note how this kind of interpretation coincided, how-

678

ever unwittingly, with the general line of Soviet diplomacy, which until 1947 regarded Britain and not the United States as the main opponent of Russia and of her satellites.

Then in 1947 the direct American-Russian conflict over Europe began to develop. During the next thirty months the main addition to the Balkan invasion controversy consisted of further American and British memoirs which began to reflect some hindsight caution about Stalin's wartime ambitions; also German recollections and fragments of papers now began to be published, wherefrom it clearly transpired that the Allies had not realized how great their chances in the Balkans had been. This disclosure, however, passed generally unnoticed.

Early in 1950 Hanson W. Baldwin presented a concise summary in two articles in the *Atlantic Monthly* in which he stated that the failure of the Western Allies to mount a Balkan invasion had been one of the gravest mistakes of the war. This argument was received in ill grace by many critics. During the next months a minor debate developed in which the critics of a Balkan invasion argued for the following points:

A Balkan invasion had hardly been feasible. Moreover, it would not have been politically propitious. For, even if we suppose that it would have succeeded and that today the Western Allies would have been in Vienna, Belgrade, and Budapest, the Russians, having swept through the North German plains, would control northwestern Europe.

These are weak points. A brief summary of the case against them may be put as follows: From various military revelations it is now evident that the Allies could have sent troops into the Balkans without necessarily depleting their offensive power in Western Europe. Not much more would have been re-

quired for a Balkan campaign than what had actually been expended in Italy and in the Western Mediterranean. And the whole record of Soviet diplomacy and the traditions and caution of Stalin render it very improbable that the Russians would have expected to reach Antwerp, Brussels, Rotterdam, Bremen and to have installed themselves there to organize and incorporate northwestern Europe in their realm. (It is also possible that in view of the appearance of the Western Powers in the Balkans the German opposition against Hitler might have been more successful, for the senselessness of continuing a total war against the West might have dawned with more force and clarity on many German generals.)

The debate on the wartime fortunes of the Balkans suddenly flared up in the autumn of 1951 when the defenders of Roosevelt and of the Joint Chiefs of Staff received an unexpected and veritable godsend from no less an authority than Winston Churchill himself. In the fifth volume of his war memoirs, *Closing the Ring*, he issued a warning. From his printed telegrams and minutes, the Prime Minister stated, the reader should "not be misled by a chance phrase here and there into thinking (a) that I wanted to abandon 'Overlord' [Normandy]; (b) that I wanted to deprive 'Overlord' of vital forces; or (c) that I contemplated a campaign by armies operating in the Balkan peninsula. These are legends." And later: "It has become a legend in America that I strove to prevent the cross-Channel enterprise called 'Overlord,' and that I tried vainly to lure the Allies into some mass invasion of the Balkans." He calls this "nonsense." And the fact that these words came from the pen of such a commanding authority and massive figure gave more than relief to the defenders of American strategy in World War II. Forthwith the critics' arguments became once again reversed: not only would a Balkan invasion have been foolish but it had not even been contemplated by Churchill himself.

Such criticism greeted the book of Chester Wilmot, *The Struggle for Europe*, in early 1952, a part of which book was devoted to a discussion of the basic differences between wartime British and American strategy. While the stylistic ability and research efforts of Wilmot were recognized, it was pointed out that Churchill's statements refuted his contentions about Balkan invasion plans. I intend, however, to refute in turn this criticism, which intimates that the Balkan invasion debate should be considered as definitely closed.

The statements in Churchill's memoirs have by no means put an end to the argument. Their careful reading (and their collating with his own minutes, memoranda, and other evidence) indicate that what the Prime Minister wished to state for the historical record was that 1. he had not wished to construct operations in the Eastern Mediterranean at the expense of the Western European invasion — and we have much evidence to the effect that he believed the two could be mounted independently, without harming each other — 2. that he had not planned to throw mass armies into the Balkans. But, of course, this would not have been necessary. In October 1944 the British occupied Greece with virtually token forces; the presence of this Allied force, which, even after considerable reinforcement, by no stretch of the imagination could have been called an army, was the decisive factor in saving Greece from a Communist fate. There is no doubt that, at least so far as Austria, Yugoslavia, and Hungary were concerned, similar political considerations had been in Churchill's mind and that

his military proposals in the Mediterranean were geared thereto.

There is, however, an important dividing date here: and that is May 1944. For there is no doubt that from this time on he became deeply preoccupied with the problem of the Russians in southeastern Europe. From this preoccupation arose his two minutes to Eden on May 4 ("Broadly speaking, the issue is, Are we going to acquiesce in the Communisation of the Balkans and perhaps of Italy?" and ". . . evidently we are approaching a showdown with the Russians . . ."); from this preoccupation his sphere of influence proposal to Russia on May 19 resulted; and all subsequent British proposals to exploit the Italian campaign northwestward were based on the clearest and most unmistakeable political considerations. It is thus entirely possible that Churchill's argument in the 1943 volume of his war memoirs — an argument he emphatically confirmed in a conversation with Chester Wilmot late in 1952 — does not refer to the period after May 1944 (and that the Prime Minister in the last volume of his war memoirs, will not insist — for he cannot — that he did not wish to forestall the Russians in the Balkans.)

The unique character of this historical controversy is due to the somewhat unusual reluctance of Churchill to reveal the political motives of his Balkan plans to the Americans. Instead, he constantly argued on military grounds. He was seemingly very much obsessed with the fear that an open argument about political plans would weaken the Anglo-American alliance and impair his position. It is not the duty of the historian to impute motives to other authors: yet it is possible that, when writing in 1951, Winston Churchill, before whom the immediate chance of a second Prime Ministry rose, did not wish to jeopardize his diplomatic prospects by rubbing the salt of the historical "I told you so" argument into American wounds, nor did he wish to revive Russian suspicion and sensitivity in regard to himself. But neither the considerably inconsistent arguments of the Balkan invasion critics, nor the available records, nor Churchill's qualifying statements obscure the truth that in 1944 he had contemplated, planned, plotted, and abandoned only in dismay the prospect of putting Anglo-American troops into the western and southern Balkans, an operation with definite postwar political portents.

. 6 .

E P I L O G U E

1946–1952

The task of the contemporary historian is most formidable and ungrateful: for, while he is literally buried by the avalanche of new accounts, articles, memoirs, revelations, notes, an undiluted stream of papers, ever increasing in quantity and scope and seemingly without end, most of these "materials" are also unreliable; there are but fragments of primary sources; only a most superficial documentation is possible and the historian's best effort is not sufficient to enable him to reach even remotely for that illusion of finality for which his colleagues of more detached ages strive with so much more reward and ease. Yet our century which produces these most unreasonable literary conditions also produces a spirit in readership which clamors with understandable anxiety and with less understandable impatience for the story to be carried up to date, however slight and ephemeral the conclusions may seem. And so I am obliged to carry on with this book and extend the story for five more years, dropping, however, the tools of the researcher and trying to assume the more detached view of the essayist.

It can be safely stated that the fate of central-eastern Europe was sealed in 1944–45 and that whatever has happened since to the unfortunate nations there was but the logical consequence of the division of Europe which occurred with the Western and Eastern armies meeting in the center of the continent. The tragic element here was that the Russians regarded this division as permanent and self-explanatory, whereas the Americans originally thought it to be not much more than a temporary demarcation line based on momentary military expediencies. This was a costly misunderstanding. The Russians at once proceeded with the gradual but swift incorporation of central-eastern Europe into their orbit, and this process, presently nearing completion, encompasses the history of central-eastern Europe from 1945 onward. The direct international repercussions of this historical process were altogether surprisingly slight.

However oriental and brutal the Russian methods of incorporation were, some elements of compromise were perceptible: their whole procedure was gradual. There were several reasons behind this relative lack of dispatch. Russians, unlike Germans, are not methodical people, and seldom feel pressed for time. For more than a decade after the 1917 revolution vestiges of the capitalist order, eye-sores to any good Marxist, had lingered on in Russia; similarly, the sovietization of central-eastern Europe was not unduly hurried and in the beginning the Communists were careful lest they create unnecessary obstacles by undue doctrinaire zeal. In the beginning the Russians also took it for granted that their rule over central-eastern Europe would meet with American, if not British, acquiescence, and Stalin did not wish to unnecessarily arouse Western tempers with early and radical measures. He had reasons for such policies. American diplomacy and the British Labor government hoped that central-eastern Europe would develop into an ideological and economic bridge between West and East, that the nations there would form governments incontestably friendly with the Soviets, yet maintaining at the same time important economic and cultural contacts with the West. These naïve dreams lingered on until early 1948, when the disappearance of the last traces of Czechoslovak independence — that state had always been regarded as the typical "bridge"-nation — finally dissolved them.

The accounts of the refugees and of the Western journalists (until 1948 the Russians had permitted visits and departures; even the illegal crossing of the borders westward was generally overlooked) have covered in detail the techniques of sovietization in central-eastern Europe. These were similar everywhere. First, the control of the nerve-centers of the state through "National Committees" was safely secured: the police, the army, the key ministries and administrative points, and the trade unions were grasped by trustworthy Communist hands. In the second phase the Communists brilliantly succeeded in splitting the political parties — that is, the parties, which the Russians originally had permitted to operate; the Communists turned these parties against each other, forced them to join "national fronts"

under Communist leadership, and eliminated the few die-hard resisters. The structure was finally completed through drastic cultural
and economic measures: here occurred the gradually increasing, brutal persecution of the independent Churches, above all of the Roman
Catholic Church. The whole process was gradual, sometimes smooth,
sometimes moving ahead with a sudden, explosive flash which momentarily revealed something of the eastern darkness to the West. Russia's
new satellites were moving with various speeds and with but slightly
varying techniques on the road to sovietization, and it is perhaps
instructive to compare their relative standings, ranging from least incorporated to most sovietized:

Early 1946	Early 1948	Early 1951
Hungary	Czechoslovakia	(Yugoslavia; 30 months after
Czechoslovakia	Hungary	the Tito-Stalin Split)
East Germany	East Germany	East Germany
Rumania	Poland	Poland
Bulgaria	Rumania	Czechoslovakia
Poland	Bulgaria	Hungary
Albania	Yugoslavia	Rumania
Yugoslavia	Albania	Bulgaria
		Albania

A closer look at this relative tabulation may prove of some value.
First, there is considerable fluctuation in the position which the respective states occupy on this scale, for there were considerable differences among the satellites: in 1946 life in Belgrade, for example,
differed at least as much from life in Budapest as did life in Warsaw
and Paris in the corresponding period. The differences have shrunk
greatly since, but there is still considerable variation between Tirana
and Dresden or between present Belgrade and Sofia. The tabulation
also reveals a certain trend toward regional groups: Bulgaria and
Rumania, for example, were put under strict Russian control very
early and did not enjoy many of the "democratic" show-window
privileges which Hungary and Czechoslovakia had had in the twilight, 1945–47 period; Russian anxiety concerning the strategically
crucial Polish and East German area may also be detected from the
relative caution of their policies there.

In viewing this gradual process of sovietization, curious and interesting relics meet the observers' eyes: Rumania, practically a Soviet

colony since 1945, remained a Monarchy until December 1947; American and British Military Missions were in existence in the former satellites until the signing of their peace treaties in 1947, and sometimes one could see more American and British than Russian uniforms along the formerly elegant thoroughfares of Budapest and Bucharest; in Czechoslovakia and Hungary reasonably free elections were held in 1945–46, and while in the former the Communists were the victors (though falling short of an absolute majority), in Hungary the originally conservative Small Holders' Party gained an absolute victory and the Communists got less than 18 per cent of the vote (even in the rigged Hungarian election of 1947, before which they had succeeded in splitting the opposition into various competing minuscule parties, the Communists "polled" not more than 22 per cent).

All this, however, did not have much significance. The non-Communist parties were honeycombed with Soviet agents in key posts; they were further split, one by one, by personal intrigues and Russian promises; and whenever a truly important, independent development was to come about, the Russians either intervened directly or told the Communists to go ahead with a *coup d'état*. Thus when in February 1947 the leadership within the Hungarian Small Holders' Party seemed to fall to the staunch anti-Communist wing, the Russians themselves acted and arrested the leader, Béla Kovács, on the pretext of a "military conspiracy"; and when the Czech Social Democrats, who held a key position on the political scene, finally were to turn anti-Communist in February 1948, this was the signal for the Communist coup which, partially aided by Beneš' weakness, established full Communist control over Czechoslovakia. The process was somewhat easier elsewhere, as fraudulent "elections" in Poland (1947), Rumania (1947), Bulgaria (1945–46), and Albania (1945) assured Communist control without much need for excessive constitutional maneuvers. By the end of 1947 the main political process had been completed, and the more ruthless and doctrinaire period of sovietization (also from the viewpoint of national economics the 1946–48 period could be considered the NEP era of the satellites) began with its brutal measures, especially in the cultural and military field: through the oppression of religion, through elimination of the last shreds of civic liberties, through rearmament, youth indoctrination, and forced industrialization the Soviets speedily proceeded in order to build a Russian glacis and armory in eastern Europe.

Two nations, on eastern Europe's fringe, escaped this fate. Greece and Finland are outside the Russian sphere: each of them had peculiar fortunes. Presumably on Soviet instructions, the Greek civil war broke out again in 1946, and in a few months guerrilla warfare reached critical proportions. Then, in December, the British government turned to the United States. It was explained that because of the depletion of her economic strength, Britain was now unable to afford further financial and military aid for Greece: could not the United States assume the burden and come to Greece's aid? The American government reacted with commendable dispatch and courage: on March 12, 1947, President Truman sent a message to Congress and announced the immediate extension of American military aid to Greece and Turkey in face of Communist aggression from within and Soviet threats from without. This measure, named later the "Truman Doctrine," was probably the most important milestone in American foreign policy since 1941. Forthwith, American military missions were sent to Greece and Turkey; military equipment was shipped in generous quantities. The Greek military situation was very difficult throughout 1947: in 1948 the scales began to turn, and the defection of Tito from the Soviet *bloc* sealed the fate of the Greek guerrillas (the Tito-Stalin split had appreciable effects on the guerrilla leaders: the legendary "General" Markos was killed under mysterious circumstances). By March 1949 the Greek Communists were beaten and the crack Greek Army had largely regained the state frontiers in the north. In 1950 Greek-Yugoslav relations were normalized and, after two years of unnecessary delay, in 1951–52 Greece and Turkey were admitted as full members of the North Atlantic Treaty Organization.

More curious was the position of Finland. Definitely within the grip of the Russian bear, she nevertheless preserved her freedom: and perhaps the Finnish example may prove the point that the, at least, temporary presence of Russian troops in a country is the inevitable prerequisite of the existence of a Communist régime. The Finns' tenacious wartime record and American sympathies saved Finland in 1944 from being occupied by Russian troops; except for the ceded territories (and these were strategically important, especially the Porkkala-Udd peninsula off Helsinki) and for a Russian Military Mission (there was also a small British one), no Russian soldier trod Finnish soil. In March 1945 the Finnish Communist front — DFFF — failed to gain a majority in Parliament; the Finnish "war crimes" trials were relatively lenient, and although Russia at times seemed to be on the verge of direct intervention (her economic reparation demands could have nearly crippled Finnish life), Finland remained free; the Communists' strength decreased; most of the condemned wartime leaders have been released from prison, and Finland is rapidly nearing the completion of her reparations' payments at the time of this writing. Except for being subject to the usual Soviet threats and occasional propaganda bursts through radio and press, Finnish life functioned freely. In 1948 Russia demanded the signature of a military pact with Finland: after some critical hesitation and after having ascertained that the treaty would not necessarily mean that Finland was now to fall unreservedly into the Soviet *bloc*, the Finnish government consented to sign.

There is reason to believe that the decision to leave Finland free was Stalin's personal one: but what could his motives have been? Beyond doubt he was aware how Finland, for a variety of reasons, enjoyed widespread sympathy in the United States: he possibly felt that the incorporation of Finland into his sphere might so much arouse American public opinion that it would not be worth the net result of a fully captured Finland. He, like many other Russians, was also duly impressed by Finnish military virtues; and throughout history, the Russians always regarded Finland in a somewhat different light than, for example, they did their Bessarabian or Galician border provinces. Finally, Stalin was reasonably certain that even if he allowed the Finns considerable liberties, this fact would not necessarily influence their foreign policy: a Finland outside of the Russian sphere did not necessarily mean a Finland inside the American one: a very important point, and one on which Stalin seemed proven right in 1949 when the main factor behind Sweden's refusal to join the North Atlantic Treaty nations was the understanding that this would lead to the immediate incorporation of Finland into the Soviet orbit and the subsequent advance of Russian military outposts to the long and crucial Swedish-Finnish frontier. Finland thus enjoyed an alternative which in Stalin's suspicious mind simply did not exist with his other central-eastern European satellites; there he took it for granted that unless his satraps and key men had complete, "three hundred per cent" control, the result would be the immediate installment of pro-British and pro-American governments and ultimately the formation of Western advance bastions against the southwestern flank of the Russian Empire.

.   .   .   .

When the wartime "One World" illusions faded to nothing, in December 1946, shortly after my arrival in America, I wrote: "In some respects the One World dogma *has* become a reality. America's basic interests today are along the Danube and on the outskirts of Mongolia, in Budapest and in Changchun. And the fate of Poles, Hungarians and Albanians is dangerously dependent on how the people of Minnesota vote and how men in Oklahoma think." Behind my words, then, loomed another illusion: that American determination and active interest could still reverse the gradual sovietization of the satellites. But today the whole revealed record of the Soviet diplomatic and military advance from 1942 onward points to the contrary: notwithstanding Western speeches, statements, general indignation, Yalta or no, eastern Europe lay in the Russian sphere, and without a Balkan invasion nothing could have significantly altered this picture.

Nevertheless there is some evidence that perhaps even after 1945 an energetic American foreign policy could have effected some changes in the status of eastern Europe. American protests in Bulgaria had delayed a rigged election in 1945. American determination made the Yugoslavs recoil at Trieste and again in 1946 when Tito's air force shot down an American airplane. Western awareness and interest stopped the Russians from unduly tampering with the Hungarian elections in 1945. Perhaps in 1945–46 a determined Western diplomacy in the Balkans could have delayed, if not altogether stopped the Soviet machine. For Stalin seemed cautious: as so often after 1942, he did not quite realize how full and uncontested was his grasp of his new domains. From the published correspondence of the Soviet and Yugoslav Communist Parties in 1948 it transpires that in 1945–46 it was the Russians who counseled caution to the Yugoslav (and, presumably, also to other eastern European) Communists; the Russians well-nigh confessed that they were exhausted, not ready for a third world war, and unwilling to run immediate risks for Trieste and other relatively minor points. However, it soon became apparent that a paradox existed in American policy. While on the one hand anti-Communist tendency within the United States began to grow swiftly and American diplomatic resistance against Russia stiffened and American public opinion and diplomacy increased its tone of protest, so far as practice was concerned, eastern Europe was apparently "written off." A typical example of this process may be found in the letter in which the American Minister to Hungary answered a plea from Cardinal Mindszenty in December 1946, a letter which was subsequently produced at the "trial" of the Cardinal in 1948. The American Minister stated: "It is noted that your letters of December 12 and December 16, touching on internal political problems of Hungary . . . requested the assistance of the United States Government in altering certain conditions which Your Eminence deplores. In this connection you are of course aware of my Government's long-standing policy of noninterference in the internal affairs of other nations. . . . It will be clear to Your Eminence that it necessarily precludes action by this Legation which could properly be construed as interference in Hungarian domestic affairs or which lies outside the normal functions of diplomatic missions."

There is no doubt that in due course Moscow became aware of this sterility of American policy in eastern Europe; soon afterwards, as the Kovács and Maniu crises in Hungary and Rumania proved, the strongest Allied protests were no longer able to deflect Soviet ruthlessness. Here, perhaps, lies the clue to the question which I put earlier: why Stalin permitted the twilight period of "democratic" window-dressing in certain eastern European countries in 1945–1947. He wished to make a rather satisfactory impression on Western public opinion (in this he succeeded for a while) in order to prevent Allied interference in eastern Europe during the crucial period when Russian power, while seemingly ubiquitous, was in reality worn and considerably exhausted and his armies underwent a process of relative demobilization from their wartime strength. In 1947, then, Stalin could go ahead in eastern Europe with his final schedule relatively unimpeded, notwithstanding the mounting wave of anti-Communist sentiment in America and the construction of American defenses — in western and southern Europe.

A phase of this 1945–47 policy was also the Russian desire to expedite the Western recognition of the satellite governments, and surprising temporary concessions were often made to achieve this recognition; after 1947, however, all Russian efforts were aimed at the practical severance of normal diplomatic relations between the western Powers and the satellites. For diplomatic recognition before 1947 had facilitated the conclusion of the satellite peace treaties, and whereas the Allies thought that the swift conclusion of these treaties might eventually bring about the lessening of Soviet control in the satellites, the opposite was true. With recognized governments, the Soviets could cast aside all Allied protests against the violation of the civil rights clauses of the satellite peace treaties as "interference" in the internal affairs of the states involved; the restricted and largely inactive but nevertheless symbolically significant American and British Military Missions went home; a network of defense and alliance Pacts between the newly "sovereign" states and, in turn, between these states and the Soviet Union could be concluded; and in accordance with the peace treaty terms, Russian troops remained in Hungary and Rumania to "guard communication lines" until the signing of the Austrian state treaty, the conclusion of which the Russians had hitherto succeeded in delaying.

As stated above, Russian rule in eastern Europe was incontestable and secure by 1947. It was in this year, however, that the United States reshaped her policy and took her first definite countermeasures. There was the "Truman Doctrine" concerning Greece and Turkey; there arose a few months later the "Marshall Plan," underlying which was the American policy of "containment," a concept formulated and explained by George F. Kennan of the State Department in a now famous article in the July 1947 issue of *Foreign Affairs*. It was now clear that the United States had recognized the innate expansionism of the Bolshevist system. Ideological awareness became acute. Soon generous and broad steps were taken to support the economically harassed Western European governments: the French and Italian régimes were particularly bolstered by abundant material aid. Consequently Communist influence began to be eliminated from the French government; in the 1948 elections the Christian Democrats won over the Communists in Italy, and the first hesitant steps were taken to integrate Western Germany into the rest of remaining free Europe.

The question, however, arises whether the "containment" policy had gauged Stalin's contemporary ambitions well enough. It was formulated at a date when the Russian absorption of central-eastern Europe emerged in all its naked brutality. Around the edge of the new Russian empire conditions were fluid and uncertain: the Red froth bubbled in northern Greece; France and Italy seemed withering under the dire strains of postwar economic crisis. It was of the utmost urgency to halt what was considered "the Red flood" before it could trickle and flow into Italy, France, and other crucial states. But was this analysis sufficiently profound? For there is no particular evidence that Stalin in 1947–48 had planned to advance into France and Italy or that he had contemplated the imminent victory of the Communist parties in those countries; indeed the fragments of evidence point to the contrary. All Russian actions were aimed at consolidating, in some cases with frantic haste, the new imperial realms in eastern Europe, and it is not at all impossible that the anxious American preoccupation with Western Europe from 1947 onwards may have suited the purposes of the Kremlin well: for thus American attention was diverted from Eastern Europe.

Perhaps it would be well to put ourselves into Stalin's position in 1947. He regarded Eastern Europe as his; he also felt considerably justified in this possession. Russia had won the war against the German invaders. Her cities were devastated, her armies bled white; with age-old Russian suspicion, Stalin was anyhow prone to underestimate the Allied contribution to the victory over Germany. Russia had carried the main brunt of the war, and the United States, with relatively the least exertion and practically without wounds incurred, had emerged as the greatest and most powerful nation of the earth. Now Stalin did not particularly try to contest American power: he did not challenge America's sphere; did it not seem to him, however, that the Americans were beginning to challenge *his* sphere? Did not the American diplomatic and military missions in eastern Europe slowly begin extending support to anti-Communist elements? Was not this intervention far outranking the efforts which Russian diplomatic and military missions in the capitals of Western Europe made to aid the respective Communist parties there? Stalin did not really compete with the Americans over Western Europe: the financial assistance which Moscow had furnished the Italian Communist Party was less than the effort which Americans poured into Italy before the 1948 elections. He did not really challenge what in his curiously distorted view amounted to the American domination of Western Europe; why, then, the American meddling in eastern Europe? Had they not won enough in the war? all of the Pacific and the Atlantic basins, plus western and southern Europe? With his narrow, Russian eyes peering westward from the Byzantine windows of the Kremlin, Stalin may have reasoned thus.

And thus the strange phenomenon arose in which America was anxiously girding itself to prevent the Russian-Communist conquest of France, Italy, and Western Germany, while this conquest may not have been at all contemplated by Russia: instead, Stalin spent most of his efforts in the corresponding period on organizing and incorporating eastern Europe within the maximum limits of safety and certainty. Another, curious paradox was the corollary of all this: Stalin, with his pragmatic and military mind, and with his Russian fears and suspicions, saw in every American effort to build up Western Europe the first steps toward an American eastward push aimed at his new empire, which he jealously guarded from incursions, whereas such policy was not even being contemplated by the United States. That he actually was extremely fearful of such incursions could be detected from his *quid-pro-quo* tactics. Already at Potsdam, when Churchill brought up what seemed to be the violations of those general statements and platitudes, falsely characterized as Yalta "agreements," in the cases of Yugoslavia and Rumania, Stalin at once retorted by pushing issues concerning Greece or Italy onto the agenda; similar were the Russian negotiation tactics in the United Nations and in the Four-Power ministerial conferences. When he detected the gradual Anglo-American abandonment of what he had considered clear-cut sphere of interest arrangements, Stalin in February 1946 announced a new Five-Year-Plan replete with military expenditures. A month later Churchill in an unofficial speech at Fulton, Missouri, assailed the Russian empire-building in eastern Europe; soon afterwards Moscow renewed the civil war in Greece. And there may be some significance in the fact that the multiple alliances which the Soviet satellites began concluding among themselves and with Russia in 1948 were not extended to Albania after the Yugoslav secession occurred: Stalin may have feared the reduction of Albania by a potentially hostile Yugoslavia and Greece; again, he may not have wished to run the risk of a third world war through unnecessarily entangling alliances. Yet — mainly due to American counsel — a Yugoslav-Greek challenge of Communist and isolated Albania never materialized.

Several decades hence an amused historian may well establish that the first half-decade of the Russian-American crisis over Europe might have been due to a fundamental, mutual misunderstanding: Washington had presupposed that the immediate Russian aim was to upset and conquer Western Europe, which was not the case; Moscow had presupposed that the American aim was to upset and conquer Eastern Europe, which also was not the case.

   .   .   .   .   .   .

But in the fear-dictated measures with which they pushed the incorporation of eastern Europe, the Russians made two very great mistakes. Impatient and overly anxious, in their exaggerated zeal they provoked tension and misunderstanding with Tito's Yugoslavia.

In March 1948 the Soviet Union withdrew her military and civilian missions from Yugoslavia, but neither such gestures nor the acid ideological correspondence between the Central Committees of the Soviet and Yugoslav Communist Parties seemed to have appreciably weakened Tito's position. Indeed, Tito saw that in 1947–1948 the Russians had decisively succeeded in torpedoing the Yugoslav-sponsored plan for Yugoslav-Bulgarian customs' union or later federation: in January 1948 Dimitrov, the famous Bulgarian Communist, was himself being rebuked by *Pravda* because of his occasional advocacy of a Communist Balkan federation. On June 28, 1948, the "Cominform" members — in 1947 a "Communist Information Center" in Warsaw had officially renewed the Communist International in this more limited form — openly condemned Tito. There followed a period of uncertainty; a Danube navigation conference met in Belgrade in August at which the Yugoslav delegates still sided with the Soviets against the hapless Western representatives. But soon the crude Russian threats were joined by the shrill outcry of the minor satellites, and Yugoslav national pride as well as British and American comprehension made Tito stand firm; although important ideological concessions to the West were not made, Tito's national Communism survived; also, "Titoism" — the epithet may, of course, prove ephemeral — had appreciable effects among the Greek Communists (a fact which Tito must have originally sensed, as in the early ideological debates of 1948 the Yugoslav Communists did not extend their attacks to the Greek Party).

Another Russian blunder was that of the Berlin blockade. It also grew out of the tendency of the territorially-minded Russians clearly and irrevocably to delimit the spheres in 1947–48. Although the Kremlin's German policy was never unduly conditioned by illusions (Stalin to Mikolajczyk in 1944: "Communism fits the Germans as a saddle fits a cow"), but rather by a certain caution (on March 10, 1947, the day before the Truman Doctrine was announced, Stalin said to Secretary of State Marshall in Moscow that American-Russian differences in Germany were only the first "clashes of reconnaissance troops," skirmishes), the Soviets tried to incorporate Berlin, geographically in the logical center of zone, into eastern Germany, especially after the close ties between "Trizonia"-Germany and the West, the development of the Greek fighting, and the affair with Tito had set the Kremlin conspicuously aback in mid-1948. The blockade was imposed on Berlin with typical Soviet technique, gradually but swiftly:

for a moment General Clay wished to break through the blockade with a military demonstration, but Washington advised him not to do so. Still, with the unprecedented and heart-warming achievement of the airlift, the Berlin blockade failed and the Russians suffered a setback in Germany. However, their main card, the appeal to German nationalist aspirations, especially concerning the issue of the Polish-German frontier, has not yet been played out and is evidently still being kept in reserve when these lines are being written.

At the same time American foreign policy moved ahead, somewhat wearily, on the road of containment. Along the road it dropped many of the muddled Liberal illusions of the earlier 1940's; yet a considerable quantity of these veritable deadweights remained (cf. the remark of the wartime director of the OWI at the time of the "Truman Doctrine": "Once again the United States aligned itself with a notoriously rotten and reactionary government to gain a tactical success"). American foreign policy was also burdened by some justifiable popular impatience with the faulty illusions perpetuated by American wartime diplomacy; this impatience, however, often demonstrated itself in senseless and crude isolationism (cf. Joseph P. Kennedy in 1947: the United States "should permit Communism to have its trial outside the Soviet Union if that shall be the fate or will of certain peoples. In most of these countries a few years will demonstrate the inability of Communism to achieve its promises, while through this period the disillusioned experimenters will be observing the benefits of the American way of life, and most of them will seek to emulate it").

As the "Marshall Plan" and the containment policy began to crystallize, their inadequacies slowly became apparent. The case could be put glibly and could easily be somewhat oversimplified; as Woodhouse wrote in 1948: "American opinion still has to make up its mind what it is *for* in foreign affairs, instead of only what it is *against*. Anti-Communism, unqualified by positive character had been one of the best allies of the Third International abroad. In viewing the prospects of a conflict between the USSR and the USA, Stalin might well rest satisfied in the conviction that the latter would run out of dollars before the former ran out of doctrine." But, on the other hand, it did become more and more clear that the steadily mounting American preoccupation with the Communist ideological menace was not enough and that something had to be done to forge military ties and build bases against the Russians' geographical and military preponderance in Europe. Thus early in 1949 the North Atlantic Treaty

Organization was born. Yet the North Atlantic Treaty area did not directly border on the Russian sphere, and for more than a year it seemed that American diplomacy was silently striving to create a neutral, "Third Power" buffer zone between what could have been considered the actual Russian and Atlantic spheres. Sweden (and Finland) were not within the Atlantic Treaty Organization. Neither were Germany and Austria; and Greece and Turkey, although defended by the "Truman Doctrine," were also within this vaguely projected buffer area between the American and Russian security spheres; this zone slowly extended further into the Middle East.

The effects upon Europe of the Korean War considerably changed this situation. On one hand Russian nervousness increased; industrialization and rearmament of the satellites were feverishly speeded; purges within their respective Communist Parties showed the desire of the Kremlin to pare leadership down to the most essential and trustworthy agents of Russia; deportations from Hungary and certain other areas pointed up the Soviet intention to ruthlessly eliminate even the weakest, torn remnants of the bourgeoisie from strategically important areas; a Russian defense line began to be constructed along the Russian-Polish, Russian-Czechoslovak, and Russian-Hungarian borders; notwithstanding the rapid incorporation of the satellites, the second iron curtain, which separates the Soviet Union from these satellites, was not in the least lifted; the frontiers, save for occasional visitors and missions, were left hermetically closed. On the other hand the policy of "containment" admittedly evolved into a policy aiming at the creation of "situations of strength," of which more effective Western rearmament, the formation of an American-European command under General Eisenhower, and the efforts toward the definite inclusion of Western Germany into Western Europe were outward signs. While the ominous emergence of German ultranationalist feeling and Russian political maneuvering had hitherto effectively barred the full political-military integration of Western Germany into the Atlantic defense sphere, the American government continued to make it clear that the Atlantic Alliance was purely defensive in character. While the Alliance was presently extended to the southern flank, to Greece and Turkey, American diplomacy continued to intimate that as long as the Soviets did not plan to advance aggressively beyond their present sphere, the United States would not offensively challenge the eastern European *status quo*. Although after the outbreak of the Korean War it was realized that the central-eastern European satellites constituted a weak point in the Soviet system, positive steps (aside from one general statement, Secretary of State Acheson's speech at Berkeley, and the diffusion of "Free Europe" broadcasts from privately constructed and conducted stations) were not taken. But even the critics of the Truman Administration did not observe this omission; during the developing great foreign policy debate of 1950–51 they failed to challenge the prevailing practical, if not diplomatic American acquiescence in the status of eastern Europe. Not until September 1952 did this issue receive public airing, when during the presidential election campaign speeches of the two candidates and of John Foster Dulles debated the future of eastern Europe.

Perhaps the general trend of events in the immediate past may convince the reader that the fate of Europe is one: without eastern Europe, western Europe cannot be even remotely safe; on the other hand only the magnetic force of a rejuvenated, remade, and truly united Western Europe, one that has recovered the erstwhile spiritual greatness of that Christian continent, can eventually develop enough attraction to penetrate the steely barriers separating the West from eastern Europe's modern police states. But without this spiritual rejuvenation and political unity (which, due to British insularity and rapidly rising German anti-Western feeling, seems at the time of this writing to be, alas, too remote), a change in the present sorry state of central-eastern Europe can hardly be expected.

. . . .

The fate of Europe is indeed one; with the partition of Europe in 1945, the international significance of most of central-eastern Europe's national histories ceases to exist; and certain European chronicles become Asiatic epics. For the West can interpret the West; it can but describe the East. And it can interpret even the West only if it goes beyond facts and appearances, sounds the literary flute with imagination, and lures to the fore the non-rational elements so deep within the substance of culture and civilization, intimating sentiments, harmonies, associations known but to Western men who are innately aware of them. The East can only be described: and eastern Europe becomes the East in certain instances from 1938 on; all-out so after 1945. The barbaric events in eastern Europe now lose reality for the Western chronicler, as they can be explained no longer in the framework of Western thought, Western passions, and Western actions.

They can only be analyzed by appearances: clumsily, painfully, incorrectly. Within a wholly different framework are the fantastic lives and passions of the cramped displaced persons, the ten million expellees, their huddling despair and desire for revenge; the new, awful hatreds between Czechs and Germans, Poles and Germans, Croats and Serbs and Ukrainians and Rumanians and Russians; the dull, spiritless moves of the peasants, the new mechanical society of the workers; the fate of the eastern European languages and eastern European culture; the dominance of fear, and of guilt, the fate of the churches; the purges; the origins, motives, actions of the new élite classes and those of the new men: wild and nomadic Ukrainian guerrillas, Bulgarian peasant Communists, national-Bolshevist underground leaders. All this is incomprehensible and fully alien to the West; it is within another framework, in which nothing but relative power in its narrow and totally naked oriental form predominates and is the only point of reference.

As the ramparts of Europe become a part of the great Asiatic plain, the West sees but a few spires breaking through the fog: symbols. These are monuments to a few men, the martyrs of the West in the East. But these spires do not move; they stand like rigid, silent symbols, and in the end they are hardly seen. After a time these old, erect towers are under the eastern fog and behind the eastern walls, losing their meaning to Europe and to the West; ". . . for the martyr without publicity," in Edward Crankshaw's phrase, "dies the death of the sparrow, which may be recorded in heaven but which is certainly not recorded elsewhere."

EXPLANATORY

NOTES:

REFERENCES

(The following abbreviations are used; *BD Documents on British Foreign Policy*; *CD* Ciano, *Diario 1937–38*; *CLD* Ciano, *L'Europa verso la catastrofe*; *GD Documents of German Foreign Policy*; *IMT International Military Tribunal Documents*)

THE DIPLOMATIC REVOLUTION (*1934–1938*)

The Diplomatic Revolution: Phase I

1 — A. François-Poncet, *Souvenirs d'une ambassade à Berlin* (Paris, 1947), Ernest Flammarion, p. 138. Published in the United States as *The Fateful Years*, Harcourt Brace and Company.

2 — Churchill: "This was one of the awful periods which recur in our history, when the noble British nation seems to fall from its high estate, loses all trace of sense or purpose, and appears to cower from the menace of foreign peril, frothing pious platitudes while foemen forge their arms." *The Gathering Storm* (New York, 1948), p. 85. And the biographer of Chamberlain: "Using the exasperating voice of Palmerston and John Russell, without the striking force that had been in their aristocratic hands, British democracy vainly entreated, lectured and hectored other countries to keep the way of peace, and seemed to think they could keep France loyal to the League without defending French interests. Our constitutional mode had thus protested against every German measure, against an army of 300,000, aircraft or shipbuilding, and then always accepted the accom-

plished fact. This process of evacuation had by 1935 brought us to the beaches." K. Feiling, *The Life of Neville Chamberlain* (London, 1947), Macmillan & Co., Ltd., pp. 262–3.

3 — Gamelin, *Servir* (Paris, 1947), II, 25. On the obscure preliminaries to the German-Polish Pact see François-Poncet, *op. cit.*, pp. 161–2; J. Beck, *Dernier rapport: politique polonaise*, 1926–1939 (Neuchâtel, 1951); J. Szembek, *Journal*, 1933–1939 (Paris, 1951); L. Noël, *L'agression allemande contre la Pologne* (Paris, 1947); N. Comnen, *I responsibili* (Bologna, 1948); compare with Beneš and Lipski versions in L. B. Namier, *Europe in Decay* (London, 1950).

4 — J. W. Wheeler-Bennett, *Munich, Prologue to Tragedy* (New York, 1948), pp. 240–1. There is a small error here. Barthou was Foreign Minister not for ten but for eight months (February-October).

5 — Wheeler-Bennett reports having seen a Nazi document in which Alexander and Barthou were scheduled for liquidation as soon as was feasible.

6 — There was some kind of a secret agreement between Mussolini and certain groups of the Spanish Right (Goicochea), dating back to February 1934, yet the value of related documents is debatable.

7 — *Servir* (Paris, 1947), Librairie Plon, II, 131. Even after 1933 "a German-Russian collusion" was not impossible. There were still commercial and military contacts between the two countries and the secret military mission of the German Army, in existence since 1920–22, terminated its activities in Russia only at the end of 1934. In April 1934 the Soviet Union asked Germany for a renewal of commercial credits. In May 1934 Litvinov offered Neurath a mutual guarantee for the Baltic nations and later interrupted his trip from Geneva to Moscow, stopping in Berlin and inviting Germany to adhere to the Eastern Mutual Assistance Pact. The General Staff, Schleicher, and Nadolny, the German Ambassador to Moscow, advocated closest German-Russian collaboration; Nadolny presented his views to Hitler in a memorandum which the latter rejected, and thereafter Nadolny resigned. On June 20, 1934, the Rumanian Minister in Berlin reported to his government that a German-Russian *entente* was not impossible. The chargé d'affaires in Moscow, von Twardowski, continued to be the representative of the Russophile school of thought and he, together with the mysterious Colonel Niedermeyer who acted as middleman between the General Staff and the Russians, traveled to and fro between Moscow and Berlin until 1936. According to Kordt: "Litvinov and the Soviet leaders often made it known to the German chargé d'affaires in Moscow how difficult it is for them to have reasonable relations with petty-bourgeois French and greedy Anglo-Saxons . . ." Kordt, *Wahn und Wirklichkeit* (Stuttgart, 1947), p. 71. And Barthou told his British conversants in the summer of 1934 that Russia, if disappointed, could become a partner of Germany.

8 — On Yugoslav support to Austrian Nazis see *International Military Tribunal Document* (*IMT* further), 2385–PS.

9 — *Munich, Prologue to Tragedy* (London, 1948), Macmillan, p. 285. By permission of Duell, Sloan & Pearce for United States circulation.

10 — It seems, however, that some authors (Schuschnigg, Beloff) put too much emphasis on the reverberations of the Studnicki "thesis" in Polish official circles.

11 — The assassin, Černozemski, was a member of the IMRO, acting in collaboration with Croatian terrorists.

12 — ". . . but it is certainly true that Pierre Laval was more attuned than his predecessor to the general line of British policy." Wheeler-Bennett, *op. cit.*, p. 243.

13 — Seton-Watson, *Eastern Europe 1917–1941* (Cambridge, 1946), p. 378. In handling Hungary there existed considerable disagreement between the moderate Yugoslav Premier Jeftič and the militarist General Zivkovič.

14 — Turkey's mediation helped to convince King Carol in 1934 that the Soviets should be recognized. Yugoslav-Soviet negotiations to establish diplomatic relations had taken place in 1924, but were not successful.

15 — Memel in German — Klaipeda in Lithuanian.

16 — Wilnó in Polish — Vilnyus in Lithuanian — Vilna in German and Russian.

17 — The not quite clear terms of the Italian-French accords were as follows: they were to consult together to pre-

serve Austrian independence; a multi-lateral accord of central European nations was suggested; France guaranteed the status of Italian nationals in Tunisia for 30 years; France ceded a strip of territory to Italy on the borders of Eritrea and French Somaliland, a small island in the Red Sea, and 44,500 square miles on the Tunisian-Libyan frontier and gave Italy privileges in the French-owned Djibouti-Addis Ababa Railway; Mussolini promised to consult with France in any European problem.

According to M. Donosti, *Mussolini e l'Europa* (Rome, 1945), there exists a letter which Laval wrote to Mussolini after he ceased to be French Premier, establishing that in Rome no word was said about any Italian military action in Abyssinia.

18 — The controversial interpretation of Pilsudski's reaction is described in Namier, *Diplomatic Prelude* (London, 1948), pp. 33–4 and 434–67; see also Szembek and Noël, *op. cit.*

19 — For the interesting background and sidelights of this journey see P. Schmidt, *Statist auf diplomatischer Bühne* (Bonn, 1949), chapter 15.

20 — At the end of the Simon-Eden talks a luncheon was given at the British Embassy, where in the reception room the children of Sir Eric Phipps raised their arms in the Nazi fashion and uttered a faint *Heil Hitler* salute. *Ibid.*, p. 301.

21 — Churchill on 1935: "Mussolini, like Hitler, regarded Britannia as a frightened, flabby old woman, who at the worst would only bluster and was, anyhow, incapable of making war. Lord Lloyd, who was on friendly terms with him, noted how he had been struck by the sad Resolution of the Oxford undergraduates in 1933 refusing to 'fight for King and Country.'" *The Gathering Storm*, p. 168.

22 — It was on this occasion that Laval asked Stalin to be lenient to Catholics in Russia; after all, the Vatican is a world power. Whereupon Stalin replied: "How many divisions has the Pope?" Somewhat later Laval said to the Yugoslav envoy in Paris: "I wish I could cut off the hand that signed the Franco-Russian Pact."

23 — M. Beloff, *The Foreign Policy of Soviet Russia, 1929–41* (New York, 1947), Oxford University Press, I, 162. See also the appraisal by Bullitt, then American Ambassador to the Soviet Union, on July 19, 1935: "The Soviet Union genuinely desires peace on all fronts at the present time but this peace is looked upon merely as a happy respite in which future wars may be prepared . . . The fundamental cause of the desire of the Soviet Government to conclude [the Franco-Russian] Treaty was the fear that France might welcome reconciliation with Germany. . . . The leaders of the Soviet Union believe . . . that within ten years the defense position of the Soviet Union will be absolutely impregnable and that within fifteen years the offensive power of the Soviet Union will be sufficient to enable it to consolidate by its assistance any Communist government which may be set up in Europe." Department of State, *The Soviet Union 1933–1939* (Washington, 1952), pp. 225–7.

24 — Even Chamberlain saw the trend; in a letter on July 6, 1935, he wrote that it was unlikely Laval would turn against Mussolini. "Yet if the latter goes on, he will torpedo the League, and the small States in Europe will just race one another to Berlin." Feiling, *op. cit.*, p. 265.

25 — A description of the political manoeuvrings during the Pilsudski funeral ceremonies is very well given in Schmidt, *op. cit.*, pp. 307 ff.

26 — According to a story told to Ciano by Mussolini in 1937, the Hoare-Laval plan failed because Baldwin spent a weekend in 1935 reading a thriller instead of opening the envelope of the Foreign Office which was sent after him to the country and which contained the Hoare-Laval complex. Ciano, *Diario 1937–38* (*CD* further) (Bologna, 1948), p. 12.

27 — Compare the situation with Britain and Russia in 1920. Churchill to Lord Curzon, May 20, 1920: "There is something to be said for making peace with the Bolsheviks. There is also something to be said for making war upon them. There is nothing to be said for a policy of doing all we can to help to strengthen them, to add to their influence and prestige. . . . I must absolutely decline to continue to share responsibility for a policy of mere bluff."
Although few of the document collections now available refer to the period before 1937, it is nevertheless possible to correct some generally held notions about international relations during the Abyssinian War. It is clear, for example, that Germany pursued a pro-British policy in the beginning and expressed her neutrality in more than one way. Cf. Szembek, *op. cit.*, p. 51, for example. The Soviet Union, on the other hand, tended to be pro-Italian in the beginning, notwithstanding Communist propaganda generally in favor of Abyssinia. In Geneva Beck told Eden that in his view Italy should not be unduly weakened, for the moment the Italian counterweight in central Europe would lighten, the influences of Berlin and Moscow automatically would begin to weigh heavier.

28 — In 1935 the British naval attaché in Belgrade told Stoyadinović that the British fleet could hardly do well against the Italians because of fear of the Italian navy's air suicide squadrons. Stoyadinović told this to Ciano in December 1937. Ciano, *L'Europa verso la catastrofe* (*CLD* further) (Milan, 1948), p. 230.
While the British naval attaché's eventual fears were without basis, it is still an awful truth that as early as 1935 Germany, Italy, and Japan could have defeated France and Britain in a joint effort.

29 — Messersmith affidavit, *IMT*, 2385-PS. Yet, it is interesting that as late as the winter of 1935–36 there were private conversations concerning eventual Italian-French military coöperation against Germany between Chiefs of Staff Badoglio and Gamelin and between the French and Italian air chiefs, Denain and Vallin. After March 1936 these conversations ceased.

The Diplomatic Revolution and Austria

1 — Papen revealed the German timetable to G. F. Messersmith, American Minister to Vienna, as early as 1934. See Messersmith's Nuremberg testimony, *IMT*, 1760-PS.

2 — The intellectual and spiritual climate of these years is excellently portrayed in E. Hantos, *Die Neuordnung des Donauraumes* (Vienna, 1935).

3 — Brno in Czech — Brünn in German.

4 — Even in February 1935 Bauer incited the Austrian working class to revolt against any attempts at a Habsburg restoration.

5 — Ljubljana in Serbo-Croat — Laibach in German — Lubiana in Italian.

6 — See Schuschnigg, *Austrian Requiem* (New York, 1947). The Schuschnigg memoirs must be pieced together; they bear the impression of having been hurriedly written. Schuschnigg refutes Ciano on the subject of Italian military intervention. See *Austrian Requiem*, pp. 128–9.

7 — The German General Staff in 1935 advised Hitler not to support Italy, whose army, in its opinion, was very poor. And Germany often exploited the difficulties of Italy in 1935-36 by taking economic advantage of Italy's position. See Donosti, *op. cit.*, p. 75.

8 — On September 9, 1935, Austria and Hungary signed an Agreement providing for mutual consultations but without stipulations for mutual assistance.

9 — Bratislava in Czech and Slovak — Pozsony in Hungarian — Pressburg in German.
Gulick, *Austria from Habsburg to Hitler* (Berkeley, 1948), p. 1693, writes thus about Schuschnigg's rearmament decision: "The reoccupation of the Rhineland provided a possible opportunity to realize [Schuschnigg's] general objectives and to offset the Nazi propaganda by showing that he, like Hitler, was strong enough to tear up a section of a treaty." This interpretation is very close in its thinking to the blind stand which the Bratislava conference took. (A few months later, the conference reversed its stand on a *de facto* basis.)

10 — See *Documents of German Foreign Policy*, Series D (*GD* further) (Washington, 1949), I, 356-9.

11 — *CLD*, p. 70.

12 — The Papal Nuncio in Vienna, the ascetic and defiantly anti-Nazi Monsignor Sybilla, was the greatest obstacle in the eyes of Papen and Hitler at that time. See Papen's testimony, *IMT*, supplement B, 3300-PS.

13 — See *IMT*, 2247-PS. At that time Papen thought that a Starhemberg Regency in the Horthy manner would open the road to a Habsburg restoration. See also *IMT* — 2831-PS.

14 — *IMT*, 150-L.

15 — *CLD*, pp. 30-1.

16 — The provisions and confidential text of the German-Austrian Agreement are given in *GD*, I, 278-81. See also the interesting comments of the unscrupulous Papen, especially that of July 28, *GD*, I, 290 ff., and the report of Hassell, then German Ambassador to Rome, pp. 283-4.

17 — *CLD*, p. 24.

18 — Schuschnigg did not make an altogether bad impression on Göring, who did not like Schmidt. Göring said to Schuschnigg then that if Austria was to restore the Monarchy, Germany would march in with troops. "Germany cannot permit a Habsburg restoration, if only because in the agreement he [Göring] concluded with Yugoslavia [!] he had promised Yugoslavia that he would do so." *GD*, I, 381.

19 — Hitler to Schmidt on November 19: "Central Europe is seriously menaced by Bolshevism and I have been trying to convince the countries of Central Europe again and again that we have no aggressive intentions, but only that of warding off Bolshevism. In this connection two problems arise: Czechoslovakia and Hungary. As to Czechoslovakia, I have tried repeatedly to establish satisfactory relations with her. In vain, unfortunately . . . I do not consider it opportune if Budapest now raises claims for revision in every direction. . . . Rumania and Yugoslavia are more important to me as outposts against Bolshevism than if they were weakened by war or threats of war. Hungary cannot count on Germany's aid in such ventures." *GD*, I, 340.

20 — Papen to Hitler, *GD*, I, 348-9.

21 — It is interesting to note that the Germans then accused Schuschnigg of being "authoritarian" and "undemocratic." E.g., von Stein of the German Legation in Vienna: "How Schuschnigg pictures the relationship between his authoritarian government and the people appears from a remark which he made to some officials of the Fatherland Front in the Tyrol. He declared: 'The people are nothing! If I have 300 devoted officials, men like you in every province of Austria, Austria will belong to the Fatherland Front.'" *GD*, I, 351–2.

22 — When Mussolini and Göring met again on January 23, both of them calumnied the English in a well-nigh fantastic manner, after which Göring turned to the Habsburg question and asked Mussolini to exert influence. Mussolini said that he and the Italian people were against restoration and he had told that to Wiesner. *CLD*, p. 140 ff. Göring also played the anti-Bolshevik record and accused Austria of permitting the transit of Russian officers and certain shipments to Spain — a wholly ridiculous assertion. See Hassell's report on the Göring visit, *GD*, I, 376 ff. About the doubts of Göring see *ibid.*, pp. 384–5.

23 — Schuschnigg, however anti-Nazi, always had a reverence for German arms and German accomplishments. His prison diary reflects great admiration for the feats of the German armies during World War II.

24 — *CLD*, p. 183. Yet at the same time in Budapest the Hungarian Premier, Darányi, told Ciano that he did not trust Kánya fully anymore — a strange statement from a Prime Minister!

25 — Schmidt records that Bavarians and Austrians were not too enthusiastic seeing Mussolini's triumphal train pass through, and Munich was almost cool. "The people of Munich cannot stand the spaghetti-eaters," a Bavarian said to Schmidt. *Op. cit.*, p. 365.

26 — Schuschnigg tried to be as correct with Germany as possible; in 1935, before the July Agreement, he prohibited the activities of German émigrés in Austrian territory and suppressed their writings. Needless to say, all this failed to impress Hitler.

27 — The Austrian churchmen were divided. Bishop Hudal (it is perhaps significant that he was a Carinthian), the Rector of the German-Austrian cultural foundation in Rome, was pro-German, and Cardinal Innitzer (of Sudeten origin) was more on Hudal's side than on the side of the anti-Nazi Monsignor Sybilla and the Prince Bishop of Salzburg, Waitz.

28 — On pro-German feeling in Austria see the report of one of the notorious Nazi agents, Megerle, in August 1936. *GD*, I, 294–5. On letters exchanged between Austrian Nazis (Seyss-Inquart, Keppler, Jury) and Germans in 1937 see *IMT*, 3390, 3392, 3395, 3396, 3397–PS.

29 — *GD*, I, 366 ff.

30 — *Ibid.*, pp. 399–400.

31 — The Hungarian chargé in Vienna was recalled to Budapest in April 1937 because of his unusually friendly relations with Papen.

32 — The documents in Papen's possession were these: A Ballhausplatz instruction to the Austrian Minister to London, Baron von Franckenstein, dated April 14: "The Federal Government states very emphatically that Austria is dependent upon Italy for the preservation and guaranteeing of her political independence and territorial integrity. Austria must absolutely reckon with this fact as long as the principle of *collective security* proclaimed by the League of Nations and the organization of *general European* peace do not have real validity in international law.

A recognition only in principle of Austrian independence by Great Britain and France, without effective guarantees from both of said Powers prevents Austria from adapting its foreign policy to that of London and Paris even to the modest degree consistent with a strict observance of the obligations arising out of the League of Nations' Covenant. The Federal Government is, however, fully aware that it could seriously consider closer adherence of Austria to Great Britain, France and the Little Entente only if all the above Powers, but above all, Great Britain and France, were in a position to give *effective* guarantees for the political independence and territorial integrity of Austria."

Instructions to Rome went on the next day, wherein the Austrian government expressed its regret at seeing growing differences between Austria and Germany in spite of the scrupulous observing of the July 11 agreement and that "the Federal Government finds itself compelled to call the attention of the Royal and Imperial Government to the possibility of a denunciation of the said Agreement with the German Reich. . . ." Austria cannot participate in Germany's policy against Czechoslovakia, and the Austrian Government "notes with astonishment that the attitude of the Royal and Imperial Italian Government toward the problem of Czechoslovakia and toward the problems of a policy affecting the Danube area shows extensive deviations from the principles of the Rome Protocols of 1934 and 1936. . . . The Federal Government must absolutely insist that the Royal and Imperial Italian Government decide to disassociate itself unequivocally from the political objectives of German National Socialism with regard to the Danube area. . . ." *GD*, I, 416 ff.

33 — See *GD*, "E. Schuschnigg Isolated, June–October 1937," p. 427 ff. and "F. Divided Nazi Counsels, October 1937–January 1938," p. 464 ff. During the first period Captain Leopold, leader of the Nazis in the field, and the official Nazi newspaper, *Österreichischer Beobachter*, attacked Papen; in return, Papen called some of their people "political gangsters."

34 — Papen to Hitler, May 26, 1937, *GD*, I, 422–4.

35 — See Schmidt-Weizsäcker talks, July 7, *GD*, I, 438–9. On Schmidt and his connections see *Der Hochverratsprozess gegen Dr. Guido Schmidt vor dem Wiener Volksgericht; die gerichtlichen Protokolle . . . veröffentlichte Dokumente, etc.* (Vienna, 1947). Although on October 10, 1936, Göring met Schmidt and disliked him, a memorandum found in Göring's office dated a month later considers Schmidt pro-German and also pro-National Socialist. See *IMT*, 3062–PS.

36 — *IMT*, 175–C.

37 — *GD*, I, 456–8.

38 — Hassell reported from Rome on November 5 that Austria was trying again to bring about an Austrian-Hungarian-Czechoslovak accord, with Poland and Yugoslavia joining in if possible, as Italy failed to protect Austria adequately.

39 — This was the so-called "Hoszbach Conference." *IMT*, 386–PS. See also Hoszbach, *Zwischen Wehrmacht und Hitler* (Wolfenbüttel, 1949) and the memorandum in *GD*, I, 29 ff. Hitler's statement: "The question for Germany ran: where could she achieve the greatest gain at the lowest cost. German policy had to reckon with two hate-inspired antagonists, Britain and France, to whom a German colossus in the center of Europe was a thorn in the flesh . . .'"

The Diplomatic Revolution: Phase II

1 — Gamelin, *op. cit.*, p. 201; see also pp. 194–239 and 275–87.

2 — Laval confessed his anti-British sentiments to his military committee (Haut Comité Militaire) on November 21, 1935. See Gamelin's most interesting account. *Ibid.*, pp. 177–82.

3 — Boothby, *I Fight to Live* (London, 1947), Gollancz, pp. 136–7.

4 — Prime Minister Baldwin said to Flandin in London that if the French proposal of a limited "police operation" risked even one per cent of war, then Britain could not agree.

Feiling on Flandin: "Flandin, so physically significant and politically so much the reverse." p. 278. Churchill: "Nothing, however, can relieve the French Government of their prime responsibility. Clemenceau or Poincaré would have left Mr. Baldwin no option." *The Gathering Storm*, p. 198.

5 — Joseph Barthélémy developed this argument in 1938 to its logical conclusion thus: "France is not obliged to go to war for the Sudeten territories."

6 — The French literally emptied their reserves to give this credit to the Poles — this was the one and only acknowledgment they could offer of the value of the French alliance.

7 — The memorandum of Beneš to Gamelin and Gamelin's answer through General Faucher, the French military attaché to Prague (a staunch friend of the Czechs who resigned during the Munich crisis, thus protesting against the French treatment of Czechoslovakia), is to be found in Gamelin, *op. cit.*, pp. 235–8. Some interesting highlights of the memorandum:

"During the Mutual Assistance Treaty negotiations with the Soviet Union, Czechoslovakia had expressed its refusal of a Soviet guarantee concerning Poland. M. Beneš then stated that Czechoslovakia firmly resolved to arrange all problems arising between herself and Poland, that there was no need for any guarantee in regard to that matter and that [Czechoslovakia] would not participate in any arrangement with the neighbors of Poland, to be directed against the latter.

"Czechoslovakia has therefore no political or military convention with the Soviet Union which touches upon Poland . . . also, the Czechoslovak government has never had any conversations or arrangements with Germany touching Poland directly or indirectly. Since the year 1933, the Czechoslovak government has three times proposed negotiations to the Polish government in regard to a treaty of enduring friendship between Poland and Czechoslovakia . . ." *Servir* (Paris, 1947), Librairie Plon, II, 235–8.

8 — A secret Wehrmacht directive touching indirectly upon these matters and envisaging "sanctions against Germany" was issued as early as October 25, 1935. See *IMT*, 140-C.

On October 11, 1936, Germany offered a vague Non-Aggression Pact to Czechoslovakia. The Czech counter-proposals given to Berlin next January mentioned a pact on the Locarno model and did not receive a German answer.

9 — Papen to Hitler, January 12, 1937: "Polish policy considers it the greatest success of the past year that the pro-Russian policy of Rumania has finally been buried . . ." *GD*, I, 371. Hitler in 1936 told Horthy of his anti-Czech feelings, of which Schuschnigg also knew.

10 — Comnen, *Preludi del grande dramma* (Rome, 1947). See also his *I responsa-*

bili; Anfuso, *Roma, Berlino, Salò* (Milan, 1950); *CD*, 1937–8 and *CLD, op. cit.*

11 — Ciano, Schmidt, and Kánya met in Vienna between November 8 and 12, 1936; it was merely a periodic meeting of the Rome Protocol foreign ministers and without significance. Ciano then went to Budapest. His reception in Vienna was cool; in Budapest most friendly.

12 — *CLD, op. cit.*, p. 102 ff. Thus it was the Hungarian, Kánya, who was more concerned about the perils of the Czechs than was Italy!

13 — Hitler to Ciano, October 21, 1936: "The English judge two nations to be led by adventurers today: Germany and Italy. But England once was led by adventurers when she made her Empire. Today she is instead being governed by inept people." "In 1939 Germany will be ready," Hitler said, "in 1940 more ready, in 1941, then even better." He asked Ciano to consider Italian-Yugoslav friendship seriously and direct Hungarian revisionism toward Czechoslovakia only. *CLD*, p. 97.

Grandi, the Italian Ambassador to London, secured a *dossier* of thirty-two documents, compiled and arranged by Eden, which presented the German danger to England in starkest colors. Grandi sent it to Mussolini on September 3. Mussolini was just in the right mood; on September 23 he criticized the Catholic Church and the British. He told the future "Governor" of Poland, Frank, that Britain was "a nation which thinks with its arse." *CD*, p. 18; see also *CLD*, pp. 80–1. The whole picture was strangely colored with the rivalry between Neurath and Ribbentrop. Neurath said to Ciano on October 20: "Ribbentrop will learn fast that in London it is easier to say 'yes' for a champagne salesman than to say 'no' for a representative of the Reich government."

CLD, p. 98. That Neurath was not always the moderate Conservative which he portrayed himself at Nuremberg and later may be seen from his conversation with Ciano the next day: he was happy that Hitler got the Eden *dossier* from Mussolini, for now at least the Führer won't be deceived by Ribbentrop's illusions, according to which Britain was filled with amicable feeling for Germany. *CLD*, p. 88. Ribbentrop was angry in 1938 that Neurath was proven right.

14 — Feiling, *op. cit.*, p. 329.

15 — Chamberlain invited Grandi to see him in July 1937, and although Eden knew of this meeting, he was not present. Grandi counseled Chamberlain to write a personal letter to Mussolini which was sent then without Eden's having seen it. This was but the first step in Chamberlain's unfortunate personal diplomacy, the effects of which he thought so much of. He did not know that all this further degraded him and his nation in Mussolini's eyes; neither did he know that the Italians had a well-placed spy in the British Embassy in Rome in 1936–7 photographing documents.

It is interesting to observe that at the time British public opinion was more anti-Italian than anti-German, which the British Ambassador in Rome himself admitted. See Hassell report, *GD*, I, 18.

16 — During the days of the Coronation, Hodža in London told Chamberlain to increase the volume and scope of British economic activities in southeastern Europe, improve Anglo-Italian relations further, and not to provoke Germany, "which might give her the pretext for an adventure." Feiling, p. 302.

17 — There was also the Germans' advantage of their diplomats having clear aims and consistent purpose. There were, of course, rather acrid differences between Neurath and Ribbentrop and Hassell, but not much of this transpired to the outer world. This situation should be contrasted with the lack of unity between envoys such as the Germanophile Nevile Henderson in Berlin and the Germanophobe Selby in Vienna; between men like Bonnet in Paris and François-Poncet in Berlin; the American envoys Kennedy in London and Messerschmitt in Vienna, etc. The initial disadvantage of democratic foreign policy showed itself again and again. And then there were the personal inclinations of men such as Horace Wilson, Henderson, and Chamberlain. Hassell, who served in Belgrade in 1930, knew Nevile Henderson from there, and the two worked in 1937 for a German-British friendship, not caring for the moment whether it would come out to the detriment of Italy. This Ciano knew and he disliked Hassell: "unpleasant and disloyal," and from early 1937 on, Ciano and Mussolini pushed Ribbentrop and his dynamic policies with all their means, as it was now evident that Ribbentrop, frustrated in London, was the real radical and anti-British spirit in Berlin. Hassell was removed from his Rome post in late 1937. And Henderson dined with Papen in May 1937, when Papen could report that Henderson "entirely agreed with the Führer that the first and greatest danger to the existence of Europe was Bolshevism, and all other viewpoints had to be subordinated to this view . . . he said he was convinced that England fully understood the historical need for a solution of the [Austrian] question in the Reich-German sense from the standpoint of historical perspective alone." Papen told Henderson that the British Minister in Vienna, Sir Walford Selby, had different ideas, and Henderson "admitted that he was cognizant of these views of Sir Walford Selby. . . . But I am of an entirely

different opinion and am convinced that my view will prevail in London, only you [should] not rush the solution of this problem. . . . But please . . . do not betray to my Vienna colleague that I entertain this opinion." *GD*, I, 428–9. A few weeks later Sir Walford Selby was quietly removed from his post.

18 — From Ciano, *L'Europa Verso La Catastrofe* (Milan, 1948), pp. 152–60, Arnoldo Mondadori, editore. Other statements of Stoyadinović: an interesting analysis of Communist forces in Yugoslavia; his determination to seek some ties with Hungary; his pleasure that Titulescu, whom he considered a corrupt man, was thrown out of Bucharest. He did not think much of the Rumanians' military value, but Rumania was a rich country: wheat, oil. "Either Rumania will become a part of our system and thus we shall have the wheat and oil at our disposal; or she will be against us and in a short time we shall have the same." Thus an ally.

There are certain vague indications that in March 1937 Mussolini turned a willing ear to France once more, but Blum could not make himself ally with Italy because of his Socialists. See Caillaux, *Mémoires* (Paris, 1947), III, 241–2.

On August 28, 1937, Ciano, through Anfuso, sent to Stoyadinović intercepted documentary proof of French-Czech plans to oust the latter. See *CD*, p. 8.

19 — See *Documents secrets du ministère des affaires étrangères de l'Allemagne — Espagne (III)* 1936–1943 (Paris, 1947), pp. 19–21. This is the French translation of the first Soviet document collection — very haphazardly arranged — relating to German policy in the second world war.

Mussolini about England: ". . . England . . . had become extraordinarily satiated, and satiated people did not like to risk anything." Also: ". . . after Spain, Germany and Italy would have to get hold of one country after another . . ." (In his third conversation with Hitler.) *GD*, II, 5. It was at that meeting that Mussolini tried to bring up the Catholic question in Germany, but the Germans generally avoided discussing this with him. Here for the first time Mussolini indicated his desire to "solve the Jewish problem" of Italy. How Chamberlain was fooled is also clear from the instructions which the German Foreign Ministry sent abroad to German diplomatic posts: "The visit of the Head of the Italian Government went off splendidly and in fullest harmony in every respect. . . . For your information: The foregoing assures that if one of the partners should seek closer rapprochement with Britain than heretofore, the other partner would benefit to the same extent." *GD*, I, 1 ff.

Ribbentrop in Rome on October 22 finally admitted that his dreams and his "mission" in Britain was unsuccessful. *CLD, op. cit.*, p. 216.

20 — News about the Halifax journey was first published on November 10 by the *Evening Standard*. On November 15 Halifax talked with Ribbentrop, then German Ambassador, and mentioned that he would discuss Austria and Czechoslovakia with Hitler; he "stressed that England and Germany ought not to oppose each other. A conflict between the two countries, whatever the outcome, would mean the end of civilization." *GD*, I, 46–7. A Mr. Stewart, press chief of Chamberlain, had very close connections with the Germans and informed them that Chamberlain was extremely angry at British newspaper criticism and speculations concerning the Halifax journey; also, that Chamberlain favored direct contact between Halifax and the Führer particularly. *GD*, I, 52–4.

21 — On the same day Ciano expressed his dissatisfaction with Austria to Hassell and informed the German Ambassador of Stoyadinovič' assurances: Yugoslavia would never fight for Czechoslovakia if Germany attacked the latter. Thus did Italy want to show at the time of the British-German talks that she was most valuable to Germany. It is also interesting that the conservative and later leading anti-Nazi Hassell worked as feverishly for *Anschluss* at that time as anybody else. See *CD*, pp. 46–7. Again, on the same day, the Italian Ambassador in Berlin let it be known that Ciano refused to meet Eden at Brussels (where an international Eastern conference was to assemble). The Germans retorted that Neurath was asked to meet Eden at Brussels as early as October, but then Germany decided not to be present. On December 1 Grandi and Eden had a conversation, the contents of which Ciano confidentially communicated to the Germans. *CD*, pp. 73–4. (It was then for the first time that Britain envisaged difficulties in Czechoslovakia and Eden told Grandi that Britain would welcome settlement of the Sudeten problem by some kind of an autonomy. Naturally, Berlin perked up after learning of such British attitudes.)

22 — *Documents and Materials Relating to the Eve of the Second World War* (Moscow, 1948), vol. I, November 1937– November 1938.

23 — Since then, the published *GD*, vol. I, gives additional documentation. There are three accounts in the German documents. See p. 55, n. 27.

The memorandum which the German Foreign Ministry (Weizsäcker) prepared for Hitler for the Halifax talk said:

"For a long time to come, we cannot consider engaging in a war with England as our opponent. What we want from England we cannot obtain by force, but must obtain by negotiation."

"From England we want colonies and freedom of action in the East, from us England wants military quiescence, particularly in the West. These wishes are not completely irreconcilable. A point of departure for negotiations can be found, and concrete results are of less importance to begin with than the goal of preventing the anti-German front in London from solidifying." *GD*, I, 40.

24 — Feiling, *op. cit.*, p. 333. But Churchill knew differently, and his knowledge was based not merely on opinion but also on experience. He met Ribbentrop at a dinner in London and Ribbentrop explained shortly the German desire for *Lebensraum*, hinting that if Germany could not obtain it peacefully, she was all ready to go to war for it.

25 — Nevile Henderson said to the Austrian Minister in Berlin in the summer of 1937 that he personally never understood why Austria wanted to be so independent.

26 — *Survey of International Affairs, 1937* (London, 1938), Oxford University Press, Royal Institute of International Affairs, I, 339. Lord Halifax, then Lord Irwin, was Viceroy of India in 1931 and made himself understood with Mr. Gandhi better than had been expected.

27 — Churchill on the Halifax-Hitler meeting: "Nothing came of all this but chatter and bewilderment." *The Gathering Storm*, p. 249.

28 — Göring said to an Austrian visitor, Revertera, at the time of the Halifax trip (November 17, 1937) that the foreign situation was such that Germany would be able to take Austria in whatever form and whenever she wanted to do so.

29 — From the minutes of the November 5 "Hoszbach" conference: "Actually, the Führer believed that almost certainly Britain, and probably France as well, had already tacitly written off the Czechs and were reconciled to the fact that this question would be cleared up in due course by Germany."

30 — Eden, probably so instructed by Chamberlain, informed Ribbentrop of the British-French talks and added that "the question of Austria was of much greater interest to Italy than to England." Ribbentrop in turn informed the Italians of what Eden said but carefully omitted this sentence.

31 — *GD*, I, 147–8. But Ribbentrop wrote on the margin of the Weizsäcker memorandum: "And not eliminating the present areas of friction . . . too quickly."

Papen was in Paris in November 1937 (coinciding with "Hoszbach") and had a very interesting talk with Georges Bonnet, who was Finance Minister then, also with Chautemps. The pro-German appeasement line was evident already. Papen: "I . . . was amazed to note that, like M. Bonnet, the Premier [Chautemps] considered a reorientation of French policy in Central Europe as entirely open to discussion — always under the condition, naturally, that Germany's ultimate aims in Central Europe were known. At any rate, he, too, had no objection to a marked extension of German influence in Austria obtained through evolutionary means. He answered emphatically in the negative when I asked whether France still considered the idea of a Habsburg restoration open to discussion and worth supporting." After a long talk Chautemps embraced Papen. . . . *GD*,

I, 41 ff. And before New Year's Day, 1938, Sir Robert Vansittart was side-tracked by Chamberlain and "demoted upwards" — another move toward the fall of Eden. Soon afterwards the predominant influence of Sir Horace Wilson — Chamberlain's Harry Hopkins — made itself apparent. Of him the German Embassy in London reported in February 1938: "It is well known that Sir Horace Wilson is decidedly pro-German but he keeps himself completely in the background." *GD*, I, 224–5.

32 — *IMT*, 75–TC. See also *GD*, I, 162 ff. The document clearly marks the influence of Ribbentrop, who concluded it with the significant statement that during his Ambassadorship in London he thought that a German-British understanding could have come about because of the sympathies of Edward VIII. "Today I no longer have faith in any understanding." He intimated that the abdication of Edward VIII might have been due to the ruler's then pro-German sympathies. The last sentence: "Henceforth — regardless of what tactical interludes of conciliation may be attempted with regard to us — every day that our political calculations are not actuated by the fundamental idea that England is our most dangerous enemy would be a gain for our enemies."

Ribbentrop obviously regarded his opinions in this memorandum as sacrosanct; he requested that "no marginal notations be made" thereon, and the Weizsäcker note on January 13 curtly stated to its august readers: "As nothing can be said against the conclusions contained in the report, a detailed consideration of the rest of it can probably be dispensed with, too." Weizsäcker memorandum, *GD*, I, 175.

The stupidity of Ribbentrop seems even more terrifying, as we know today that the British government was seriously thinking about the award of colonies to Germany at that time, and not even necessarily on a *quid pro quo* basis. See *Documents on British Foreign Policy*, ed. Woodward and Butler (London, 1948), His Majesty's Stationery Office, series III, vol. I (further *BD*, I), and *GD*, I, 22–3, for example, on the Union of South Africa whose "statesmen are evidently of the opinion that they could somehow play the part of the honest broker between us and the British Government."

But on November 5, 1937, Hitler established that after the period 1943–45 "only a change for the worse, from our point of view, could be expected." Truly, it happened so.

Other international developments

1 — How the Vatican saw through the anti-Bolshevik bogey propaganda is evident from the Papal message which the Secretary of State, Cardinal Pacelli, sent to the German Ambassador on April 30, 1937. (*GD*, I, 956 ff.)

"The note of Your Excellency of the 12th asserts that the encyclical *Mit brennender Sorge* has 'destroyed the effect of the papal encyclical against Communism issued just previously, and dealt a dangerous blow to the defense front against the world menace of Bolshevism, so very desirable for the Catholic Church in particular.' This thinking, too, represents a deplorable error of judgment. The Holy See does not fail to recognize the great importance of the formation of inherently sound and vigorous defensive political fronts against the danger of atheistic Bolshevism. The efforts of the Holy See to conquer these errors proceed from concern for the salvation of souls and work with spiritual means, and therefore have their own laws and directions. The Holy See realizes, however, the important mission and task of the political power which stands on the side of order in face of the illegal use of power which is the purpose of both open and secret revolutionary plotting, as well as the systematic mobilization of that political power so that it may be used to advantage against the Bolshevist danger. At a time when those who are now vociferous opponents of Bolshevism were consciously or unconsciously its pacemakers, the Holy See revealed with unflagging zeal the cultural and social, as well as the religious dangers of that system. Similarly, and up to the present moment, the Holy See has let no opportunity go by to strengthen and expand the spiritual defensive front of the faithful against atheistic Bolshevism. The Holy Father owes it to the dignity and essential impartiality of his Supreme Pontificate, however, while condemning the Bolshevistic system of delusion and revolution, not to close his eyes to errors that are beginning to insinuate themselves into other political and ideological movements and are pressing for supremacy. The fact that such errors are also found within political defensive fronts which have a general anti-Bolshevist orientation cannot constitute a justification for tolerating or ignoring them on the part of the highest authority on religious teaching. Such partiality, not justifiable to the Christian conscience, would, in the last analysis, also work to the detriment of those who today, as in the case of the German note, in shortsighted self-deception demand such an attitude from the Church and, when it is not forthcoming, choose to call it an anti-German act. . . . Viewed in this light, the assertion in the German note that the encyclical *Mit brennender Sorge* has 'dealt a dangerous blow to the defensive front against the world menace of Bolshevism' shows a misunderstanding of the facts and a self-deception which, in the interests of the German nation, one can only hope will soon yield to a just and dispassionate appreciation."

On May 18, 1937, the American Cardinal Mundelein spoke of Hitler as a "paperhanger, and a poor one at that . . ." The German protest at the Holy See was rejected. *Ibid.*, pp. 969–71. On July 17 Pope Pius XI praised Cardinal Mundelein to a group of visiting Spanish Sisters and American pilgrims. Cardinal Pacelli then tried to smooth these controversies out and Hitler abated some of his anti-Catholic zeal in legislation.

2 — Hungary and Austria did not grant *de jure* recognition to the Burgos government until January 1938, although Mussolini pressed them to do so.

3 — According to Beneš, and accepted by Churchill in that part of the memoirs which were written before the Communist *coup* of February 1948 in Czechoslovakia, Stalin was indebted to Beneš, who had notified Moscow of the discovery of anti-Soviet negotiations in the Prague Soviet Embassy and in Ukrainian and White Russian circles in Czechoslovakia, the latter acting as mediators between anti-Stalinists in Russia and the Germans. But this hypothesis is difficult to accept in view of George F. Kennan's memorandum of March 12, 1938, quoted in *The Soviet Union 1933–1939*, p. 519 *n.* See also his excellent analysis of the purges in *idem*, pp. 362–9.

4 — General Seeckt in 1933 foresaw that if Germany attacked Russia, Poland would advance her frontiers to the Oder. Niedermeyer in his *Wehrgeographische Betrachtung der Sowjetuni on:* "Russia needs our political and technical help for her internal reconstruction and we need Russian help and friendship in the struggle against Versailles." In the spring of 1934, a number of German generals sent a memorandum to Hindenburg protesting against Hitler's policy of sabotaging their contacts with Russia. These contacts continued to exist until early 1935.

5 — See *The Polish White Book, Les relations polono-allemandes et polono-sovietiques au cours de la periode 1933–39* (Paris, 1940), pp. 60–61. This translation of collected documents is somewhat more accurate than the English edition. In 1935, at a German Embassy reception, Tukhachevsky made a remark to the effect that it was too bad "that the politicians were disturbing German-Soviet relations." *The Soviet Union 1933–1939*, p. 384.

See also C. Dyrssen, *Die Botschaft des Ostens: Faschismus, Nationalsozialismus und Preussentum* (Breslau, 1934), expounding the need for a German-Russian alliance against the "decadent, africanized, Roman-Latin, Catholic powers of Europe"; also C. F. Melville, *The Russian Face of Germany* (London, 1932); Kordt, *op. cit.*

6 — Comnen, *op. cit.* Loy W. Henderson, the American chargé in Moscow, wrote to Hull on November 16, 1936: "There can be no doubt that if a mutual desire for understanding exists, it is easier for countries with dictatorial forms of Government, even though the Government may be of a so-called fascist nature, to maintain good relations with the Soviet Union than it is for countries possessing democratic forms of Government." *The Soviet Union 1933–1939*, p. 308. During the Abyssinian War the Soviets made significant diplomatic gestures toward Italy, presumably to facilitate a Russo-Italian understanding to counterbalance an Anglo-German *bloc*. Significant Soviet oil shipments were sent to Italy, in silent defiance of the sanctions.

7 — CD, *op. cit.*, pp. 8, 15.

8 — But the German Foreign Service was by no means sold on the Japanese alliance. See the highly interesting documents in *GD*, I, 743 ff. A few excerpts: German F. O. to German Embassy in Japan on July 28, 1937: "The Japanese have recently been carrying on radio propaganda in Germany, beamed to Germany, in which they constantly try to represent the war against China as a struggle against Communism and to force at least moral participation upon us. We do not welcome this propaganda." (p. 743.)

On August 13 Raumer of the *Dienststelle Ribbentrop* held talks with the top Japanese of the Embassy in Berlin on drawing other states, for example, Poland, into the German-Japanese Pacts. (pp. 750–1.) There was a German military mission with Chiang Kai-Shek, fully unwilling to leave, and Neurath was equally unwilling to recall the able German Ambassador from Nanking; see the latter's dispatch of October 11. (p. 763.) Mussolini was then much more pro-Japanese than the Germans. Ribbentrop played Blomberg against Neurath, who acidly answered their proddings: it was far more in the interest of Germany to see the German General von Falkenhausen than a Soviet general on Chiang's side. On December 3 the German Ambassador to Japan: "For well-known reasons Germany is interested in an early cessation of hostilities (friendly to both countries), has large economic interests in both, and desires no weakening or pinning down of Japan in view of her mission against Russia." (p. 791.)

On December 2 Chiang formulated his viewpoints re: a negotiated peace. The Japanese demands seemed acceptable and so did Germany's mediation. (p. 795.) But the Japanese demands grew, and China, unwillingly, turned more and more towards Russia instead of Germany. Japan was too greedy. Mackensen of the German F. O., writing to the Embassy in Japan on December 29: "The common interest of Germany and Japan directed against the Comintern requires that normal conditions in China be restored as soon as possible, even if all this could be done only by peace terms which did not meet all the Japanese aspirations. The lessons derived from the history of the Treaty of Versailles should be pondered by Japan." (p. 811.)

9 — *GD*, I, 27–8.

10 — On July 21, 1937, the new Soviet Ambassador to Berlin, Yurenev, presented his credentials to Hitler, who unexpectedly received him in a friendly manner. The Soviet exile, Barmine, intimates that Stalin's Georgian friends were numerous in Berlin and had Ribbentrop's ear. At the New Year's reception of 1938 Hitler spoke lengthily and sympathetically to Yurenev.

11 — *GD*, I, 83.

12 — Two unimportant meetings of the Little Entente Foreign Ministers took place in Belgrade and Sinaia in April and August 1937; the three Premiers met in June on board a Danube steamer for rather ineffective and useless talks.

13 — Brawls during international soccer games, together with the unavoidable catcalls, often caused serious headaches to the Austrian Foreign Office; in 1937 there were various scandals which broke out during the engagements of Italian and Austrian teams. These were often misinterpreted by certain foreign correspondents in Vienna as spontaneous demonstrations of the Socialist workers of Austria against the "Fascist alliance." The German Legation reported these anti-Italian outbreaks with great industry.

Sporting events as political factors were well appreciated and widely used. Ciano in March 1938 proposed in view of the Albanian enthusiasm for learning good soccer that the team of Tirana enter in one of the minor Italian leagues and thereby illustrate as well as facilitate the union of Albania with Italy.

14 — And on December 22, Ciano wrote of the widow of Austen Chamberlain in Rome: "Lady Chamberlain wears the Fascist party emblem. I am too much of a patriot to appreciate an Englishwoman who makes such a gesture in such times." *CD*, p. 72.

15 — Chamberlain's reflections on the "quarantine" speech: "I read Roosevelt's speech with mixed feelings . . . seeing that patients suffering from epidemic diseases do not usually go about fully armed . . . something lacking in his analogy. . . . When I asked USA to make a joint *démarche* at the very beginning of the dispute, they refused. . . ." And later: "it is always best and safest to count on nothing from the Americans but words." Feiling, *op. cit.*, p. 325.

16 — The German Ambassador from Washington reported that the speech was directed mainly against Japan. See Dieckhoff reports, *GD*, I, 633–6. "Meanwhile, as I reported by wire, the Chicago fanfare has turned into a call to retreat. The reception in the country was overwhelmingly negative; the war cry which was immediately sounded by some groups, caused considerable reaction and meanwhile things have become rather quiet." But Dieckhoff added that ultimately the United States would be involved in a war on the side of Britain.

The Germans had various and contradictory reports from America. Hitler in October 1937 read with great interest a "treatise" by a Californian, Baron von Reichenberg, "Roosevelt — America — A Danger!" and requested his propaganda organs to look into the "facts" presented therein. It turned out that the author was a very dubious character. On November 22 Dieckhoff reported from Washington that the American Catholic Church was becoming more and more anti-German; he detected Vatican influence. On December 7 he wrote a memorandum: "American foreign policy: Isolation or action? . . . for the present, at any rate, the majority of the American people are opposed to any foreign entanglement, even though I would not go so far as an English observer who has traveled all over the country during recent months and who told me a few days ago that he estimated 85 per cent of the population to be isolationist." On December 9 Mr. Ickes attacked the "nightshirt nations"; Berlin asked the German Embassy to protest; Dieckhoff cleverly said that all these loud blasts by internationally unimportant figures were nothing to be bothered about. Princess S. Hohenlohe told Dieckhoff in November 1937 that Ralph Ingersoll, Vice-President and general manager of *Time, Life, Fortune*, was now favorable to National Socialism, but then the January 1938 issue of the "March of Time" was strongly anti-German.

The American Ambassador to Germany, the pragmatic and fully undiplomatic, fundamentalist Dodd, delivered an anti-Hitler speech in August on his return to the United States and the Germans protested. Dodd excused himself to the German Ambassador in a miserable manner. And Hull said to Dieckhoff: "Dodd's pet hobby was known to be ideal Jeffersonian democracy and world peace; on this subject Dodd was 'somewhat insane.' " *GD*, I, 627. Dodd was then recalled and from January 1, 1938 on, Hugh R. Wilson was Ambassador to Germany.

It was no wonder that some Germans, Hitler for example, ventured to draw

fantastic conclusions out of this maze of American contradictions.

17 — Mussolini to Ribbentrop in October 1937: "The American threats are always inconsistent: they seem to be mountains and are mere mice." *CLD*, p. 220.

Other internal events

1 — The German-Czechoslovak crisis is covered in *GD*, II, 1 ff. (the Henlein-Hodža talks).

2 — It is interesting that in Memel and the adjacent regions there were a lot of Lutheran, Prussian-type Lithuanians who were Nazis and pro-Germans because of their sociological desires and religion. A clever exposition of this prototype can be found in Kolarz, *Myths and Realities in Eastern Europe* (London, 1946), p. 19.

3 — The reader is warned to take note of the difference between the traditional Polish Socialist Party — a nationalistic and democratic movement, and the so-called Polish Social Democratic Party which for long years was the disguised name for the Polish CP, originally organized by Rosa Luxemburg.

4 — Laval in his *Notes et mémoires* (Geneva, 1948) devotes an entire chapter to the problem of the Bor mines, a problem which came up again in 1940–41.

5 — In December 1937 Ciano found out that the Greek Minister to Rome once spoke disparagingly of him. The Greeks "shall pay dearly for this," noted Ciano.

6 — The Hungarian Minister to Prague, Wettstein, informed the German chargé there in October 1937 that if the Sudeten Germans revolted against the Czechs without direct German military intervention from the outside, it was questionable whether France would come to the Czechs' assistance. This was exactly what the Czechs wished to ascertain. Eisenlohr agreed with this interpretation on November 6. *GD*, II, 28.

7 — *GD*, I, 122–3. See also the memorandum of G. S. Messersmith, then Assistant Secretary of State, on January 3, 1938: "We at least know what the objectives and in a measure the policies of Berlin and Rome are. We do not know this of Moscow. The English have sent Halifax to Berlin to endeavor to determine more definitely German objectives and policy when we all know what they are. No similar effort seems to have been made by England or France to establish this direct contact or to exchange information with Stalin and his immediate associates in Russia." *The Soviet Union 1933–1939,* pp. 504–5.

8 — In this last phase of the purges we may detect a certain coincidence. Stalin's eyes were opening and his foreign policy was slowly changing. In Prague, probably under instructions dispatched to him after witnessing Delbos in Warsaw, the Soviet envoy, Alexandrov, was very reticent during the Delbos visit. Another indication that it was then that Stalin began to revise his central-eastern European policies lies in the fact that from late 1937 onwards most of the Russian envoys in central-eastern Europe were purged: Begzadian in Budapest, Davtian in Warsaw, Ostrovski in Bucharest, Podolski in Kaunas, Ustinov in Tallinn were all good diplomats in the thirties, but by 1938 they had disappeared and were never heard from again.

The Rumanian dictatorship and its meaning

1 — The origin of these was the Iorga-Cuza Anti-Semitic National-Democratic Party of 1910.

2 — See *IMT*, 007–PS.

3 — A. De Monzie, *Ci-devant* (Paris, 1942), p. 112.

4 — On the next day, Mussolini remarked to Ciano that he now favored the complete nazification of Austria. "What is not fully done, remains doubtful: see the Rumanian example." *CD*, p. 110.

5 — The change of times was reflected in the behavior of the leaders of the small Rumanian Social-Democratic Party. While their leader, Petrescu, remained untainted with any semblance of opportunism, two union chiefs and political leaders, Mirescu and Flueras, took up positions which the Goga government offered; two others, Radâceanu and Grigorovici, joined the Front of National Rebirth in 1938.

6 — Paul-Boncour on the other hand maintains that Titulescu spoke to him of a secret oral agreement he had with Litvinov, permitting the eventual passage under certain circumstances. Regent Paul also confirmed this. See Paul-Boncour, *Entre deux guerres* (Paris, 1946); also N. P. Comnen, *Preludi del grande dramma* (Rome, 1947) and *I responsabili, op. cit.*

7 — This was said on December 7, 1937. See *GD*, I, 107–8.

8 — It is interesting to observe that Italy and her press applauded Goga more than the official German organs (except the Nazi party papers) did, as Neurath obviously feared that excessive jubilation and friendship would alienate Hungary too much and would be a gamble on temporary ideological sympathies. Rosenberg and Ribbentrop did not share this view; they disliked the Hungarians and were all for Goga. To Neurath, Rumania was a step further away, and as Austria and Czechoslovakia were the direct objects of German foreign policy, Hungary was needed.

First two months of a terrible year

1 — *IMT*, 386–PS. Thus, as Hitler was interested "in the keeping up of the tension in the Mediterranean . . . a 100 per cent victory for Franco was not desirable . . . from the German point of view," to which Göring added that Germany should "consider liquidating [her] military undertakings in Spain."

2 — This, however, is Beneš' own version. That Beneš was staunch, neither a principled nor moral statesman, is clear from the compliments he showered upon the German envoy whom he invited to a private breakfast on November 9. He praised the Germans and said that "he had drunk from the fountains of German knowledge and German philosophy in Prague, for, owing to their centuries-old cultural fellowship, Czechs and Germans understood one another much better than, for instance, Czechs and French." *GD*, II, 38. This was Beneš' idea of diplomacy. Of course, he was playing for time. But he was reasonable now, and Eisenlohr, in a summary of the year 1937 sent to Berlin next January 12, spoke with a certain respect of the new Czech attitude and counseled moderation to Berlin.

3 — *Documents secrets du ministère des affaires étrangères de l'Allemagne*, II, *Hongrie* (Paris, 1946), 20–4.

4 — Stoyadinović was paid off for his confidences with a temporarily pro-Serb policy of Rome. In December 1937, Croatian emigrés residing in Italy were bitter to learn that Mussolini did not grant them interviews; their movements were obstructed, financial subsidies were cut. Mussolini, in a spasm of friendliness and loyalty, even proposed to Stoyadinović that the latter send a Yugoslav police official to work with the Italian government in supervising the Croats' activities in Italy.

5 — See *CLD*, pp. 241–2; also *CD*, p. 79. Ciano on the occasion of the Bethlen visit: "The Hungarians accept from us all benefices, somewhat with the air of a fallen *grand seigneur*, but they do not know enough of our power and have a sentimental inclination toward London, determined by two potent factors: Judaism and snobism. I told Bethlen that the democracies won't give to the Hungarians anything more than nice words."

6 — *CD*, p. 97. The official communiqué stated that Austria and Italy "watched with great interest the development of relations between Hungary and Rumania." Kánya was unwilling to displease Paris and London and tried unsuccessfully to evade the issue of Franco's *de jure* recognition.

7 — See *Documents . . . Hongrie, op. cit.;* see also *IMT*, 2786–PS.

8 — Csáky, who became Foreign Minister in 1938, was clumsy, unintelligent and stupid; one wonders how clever men like Kánya and later Count Teleki could entrust him with such a high position. He came to have the unusual reputation of being disliked by practically everybody who came to know him because of his extremely garrulous nature; whatever he said had no certainty behind it. To make statements lacking foundations and to contradict himself seemed to him to be the very nature of diplomacy. This was well known by the French and British Ministers to Hungary, by Ribbentrop, by Beck, Ciano, and Montgomery, the American Minister; the latter four confirmed this in writing.

9 — *CD*, p. 106. The British Consul in Vienna thought that the news of an Anglo-Italian rapprochement made Hitler act in Austria.

10 — *CLD*, p. 249 ff. After the conversation ended, Chamberlain sent Ball to the

Italian Embassy secretly that evening — Ball and Grandi met in a taxi — and conveyed his thanks for Grandi's "coöperation." Chamberlain humiliated Eden just as Lloyd George had liked to do with Lord Curzon. But the situation then was less tragic; also, Curzon had better nerves. Lloyd George had a social inferiority complex in regard to Curzon; and Eden was more refined than Chamberlain. The clever Grandi sensed this tension: ". . . the old Chamberlain undoubtedly showed that he had the same tough hide which his cobbler ancestors had had in Birmingham."

11 — CD, p. 117. On what preceded the Eden resignation see also a slightly different record from *CLD* in *CD*; Churchill; *BD*, I; and also Grandi's picture of the various factions within the British cabinet which he gave to the German chargé in London on February 11, *GD*, I, 198–9. On February 24 Grandi asked the German Embassy in London to make "Chamberlain's position easier. Otherwise Eden would make a triumphant comeback after a few months." Two days later Woermann reported: "Eden, of course, had not eliminated himself from British political life because of his more or less voluntary exit. . . . he is naturally waiting for the time when the Chamberlain policy may perhaps suffer a serious failure. We ought not to assist him in this." *GD*, I, 223.

This was the Italians' viewpoint; they even told the Spaniards not to make Chamberlain's position difficult, and for awhile Italian naval support to Franco in exposed areas was withdrawn. To what extent Chamberlain had been ready to go in order to please Mussolini could be seen from this extraordinary episode: On April 7, 1938, copies of the *News Review* were quietly banned from London newsstands upon action of the London Wholesale News Dealers, as that issue

of *News Review* contained a critical article on Mussolini by the American Professor Gaudens Megaro. About this episode see also the New York *Times* of April 9, 1938.

12 — GD, I, 212–4.

13 — Ribbentrop, who disliked Hungarians, was yet reticent.

14 — At the same time, interesting things were developing in German-Japanese relations also, always affecting the Soviet Union. Hitler, in the wake of the pleasantly quiet British reaction to Berchtesgaden, seemed to be convinced of the correctness of his original British-Japanese line against Russia and China, and on February 17 said that he decided to recognize the Japanese satellite state, Manchukuo. This he announced in his February 20 speech. However, the German Ambassador to China protested against this German policy. Chiang Kai-shek, who in December 1937 sent a confidant to Moscow, after having been abandoned by the Germans, obtained nothing in Moscow; Sun Fo was not even received by Stalin, although he was the son of Sun Yat-sen. Also, Soviet attacks against Japan were somewhat toned down from January onwards. Trautmann fought to the last against a German China policy which would drive China to Russia's side. See *GD*, I, 863 ff.

15 — GD, I, 508–9. And Grandi reporting on a talk with Chamberlain on February 22: "Nothing was further from [Chamberlain's] thoughts than an intention to weaken [the] Axis. It was a pillar of European peace. He was more than ever convinced of this today."

16 — The Osuský report is Document No. 4 in the scanty Soviet document collection: *Documents and Materials Relating to the Eve of the Second World War,*

(Moscow, 1948), vol. I, November 1937–November 1938.

17 — That is: *mort le pacte franco-tchéco-slovaque.* Many people think that the 1938–42 attitude of the French Right (De Monzie, etc.), the anti-Czech, and the *munichois*, stemmed from a Latin, dogmatic passion for Fascism. Nothing could be further from the truth. Theirs was the rational view, so typically French, figuring out coolly how the French positions in central-eastern Europe were untenable, how the new position of Britain was fraught with dangers for the French, how, rather, in the Talleyrand manner, France could be saved by rectifying the situation in central-eastern Europe in consort with the dictators; for otherwise. . . . (As a friend of mine once said of Descartes' *Cogito, ergo sum:* "they put Descartes before the horse.")

18 — Henderson requested an interview with Hitler on March 1. He was entrusted with a personal message from Chamberlain, who was about to make a positive offer to Germany concerning African colonies and wished in exchange "to obtain some *quid pro quo.*" *GD*, I, 228. The Germans wanted to conceal the fact of the Henderson-Hitler-Ribbentrop conversation, but the British government went only so far as to avoid discussion of the subject of the talks. As to the memorandum of the talk, see *GD*, I, 240 ff; also Henderson, *op. cit.* Henderson started with saying that the conversation was regarded as strictly confidential by the British government. "No information would be given to the French . . ." This was very unfair. Hitler harped cleverly and successfully on the anti-Bolshevik theme: Germany had to arm, but only because of Russia.

Anschluss *and its consequences*

1 — It is true that Papen suggested to Schuschnigg already in January that he meet with Hitler, yet the wide-spread belief that on February 10 he conveyed an ultimatum to the Chancellor, hinting that if Schuschnigg did not go, Hitler would assail him and Austria in his speech on the twentieth, is erroneous. The topic of the speech first came up during the Berchtesgaden "visit."

2 — See *Documents and Materials . . . op. cit.,* no. 2.

Schuschnigg did not have an especially bad conscience in regard to Hitler. For example, there existed intelligence collaboration between the German and Austrian armed services from 1937 onwards. See *IMT*, Affidavit A, of the star witness, Lahousen, who was a lieutenant-colonel in the Austrian Army and the first intelligence planner of Austria in the late thirties. He was the top man, coordinating certain Austrian and German Army intelligence activities. "This was primarily directed against Czechoslovakia," said Lahousen at Nuremberg.

3 — The Berchtesgaden meeting is also very well described in Schmidt, *Statist auf diplomatischer Bühne* (Bonn, 1949), pp. 394 ff.

4 — Schuschnigg, *Austrian Requiem* (New York, 1947), p. 24. The British Consul-General's later report: "A gloomy lunch followed, which lasted twelve minutes, and at which Herr Hitler only ate spinach." *BD*, I, 129.

5 — *IMT*, 1775–PS.

6 — "The Reich . . . shall no more permit the suppression of ten million Germans across its borders. . . . I am glad to report, however, that the Austrian Chancellor has shown insight and a satisfactory agreement has been reached with Austria."

7 — See *IMT*, 3526–PS (Veesenmeyer-Keppler); 4004–PS, 4005–PS (Rainer, SS leader, later Salzburg Gauleiter);

3254–PS, 3697–PS (Neumeyer-Miklas and Leopold-Schuschnigg conversations). Keppler asked Göring already on February 18 to see to it that Berlin cease negotiations with Vienna completely. See also *IMT*, 1544–PS.

8 — Labor, with characteristic, irresponsible mass-man opportunism, was going over to the other side. This swaying of public opinion was decisive with Schuschnigg. Seyss-Inquart reported to Berlin on February 28: "It was especially encouraging during the last few days to note to what an unexpected degree Labor has come over to our side. Even in the Alpine Mining Company, where the board of directors assumed 70 per cent to be Communists, some two-thirds of the workmen are said to have marched on our side." *GD*, I, 550. Sir Nevile Henderson's contemporary estimate of Austrian popular feeling was essentially correct: 25 per cent for the Nazis, 25 per cent for the Government, the remaining 50 "will surely vote for the winning side." *BD*, I, 43. It should be noted that there is some evidence to the effect that Hitler as late as February 26 seemed to prefer evolutionary absorption and that the Nazi movement and internal developments in this Austria influenced him decisively thereafter.

9 — Schuschnigg, *op. cit.*, p. 39. The final decision to hold the plebiscite was reached in a closed conference during the night of the 8th. See Zernatto, *Die Wahrheit über Österreich* (New York-Toronto, 1938); also *IMT* 2949–PS and the report of the German chargé, *GD*, I, 566 ff. Ciano acknowledged to the German chargé in Rome that Schuschnigg informed them of the plebiscite idea but Mussolini "had flatly advised against the plebiscite." The Italians also rebuked the French when they wanted to discuss Austria.

10 — *Documents and Materials, op. cit.*, no. 3. Yet back in 1934 Chamberlain ex-

pressed himself with greatest indignation when Dollfuss was assassinated.

11 — Gamelin, *op. cit.*, pp. 312–5; see also the French documents found by the Germans at La Charité in 1940 and published in the German White Book No. 5.

12 — There were three reasons why Schuschnigg notified Seyss-Inquart about the plebiscite twelve hours before its announcement. First, Seyss-Inquart was minister of Public Security; it was practically impossible to exclude him from plans which a few hours later all branches and parts of the executive organs were to know. Second, Schuschnigg did not want to open himself to an attack on the grounds of intergovernment disloyalty by leaving Seyss-Inquart uninformed. Third, Schuschnigg had a certain confidence in Seyss, as the latter was a practising Catholic. Therefore he took the latter's word that he would keep the news to himself until its announcement. See also *IMT*, 3254–PS.

13 — *IMT*, 1780–PS. Henderson in a later report (April 21) described to Halifax what Göbbels told him about Hitler's hearing the news of Schuschnigg's Innsbruck announcement: "With long strides, the Führer paced the room, and on his face were god-like wrath and holy indignation." *BD*, I, 179.

14 — According to Donosti, *op. cit.*, p. 79, in February Ciano told the Germans' personal envoy, Prince Philip of Hesse, that Italy continued to be opposed to *Anschluss*. *CD* and *CLD* do not bear this out.

It is interesting that Beck was in Rome on March 8–9. He told Ciano that Poland did not regard her French alliance valid in the case of a Czechoslovak conflict. "In regard to the *Anschluss*, [Beck] showed such disinterest which does not seem to me to be in proportion with what this problem should mean to Poland," noted Ciano. *CD*, p. 128. (Next day, Ciano: "The Duchess of Piedmont, who sat next to me, did not like the Polish Minister: she finds that he has a stealthy face and his looks would qualify him to be photographed in French magazines as a criminal attacker of little girls. Perhaps she exaggerates. But one should not easily dismiss the instincts of women.")

15 — BD, I, 3. A day later, from another telegram: "Schuschnigg's action, as seen from this post, seems precipitous and unwise." *Ibid.*, p. 8. Halifax reprimanded Henderson for his "Schuschnigg's folly" statement.

16 — On the luncheon and talks see Halifax to Henderson, *BD*, I, 21-3. Originally Ribbentrop wanted to have the plebiscite cancelled and wanted Halifax to intervene in this matter, which the British Foreign Secretary refused to do. See the records of their talks in *BD*, and *GD*, I, 253-61. It is extremely instructive to compare the record of Ribbentrop given in *GD*, pp. 264-9.

On the same day, Kordt of the German Embassy had a talk with Sir Horace Wilson. Kordt quoting Wilson: "Some time ago the Führer had compared England and Germany to two pillars upon which the European social order could rest. This comparison had particularly pleased the Prime Minister. . . . [Halifax] hoped very much that we would succeed as much as possible vis-à-vis Czechoslovakia and Austria without the use of force. The prerequisite for this was, of course, that the other side also played 'fair.' " "When I [Kordt] interrupted to say that the plebiscite plan of the Austrian government did not seem to me to be 'fair,' Sir Horace replied that in his opinion, too, this plan created difficulties. . . . 'The impression that would be created in the economic field by

an understanding between Germany, England and Italy (he did not mention France — probably unintentionally) could scarcely be overestimated. Russia ought to be left out entirely at the present time.' In his opinion the system there was bound 'to melt away' some day." *GD*, I, 269-72.

17 — On the exact sequence of events during this confusing day see note 16 in *GD*, I, 580. The telephone conversations of Göring, Ribbentrop, Keppler, Muff, Seyss-Inquart, etc., on that day are given in *IMT*, 2949-PS.

18 — IMT, 102-C.

19 — On that evening Henderson sent a note to Neurath: "I should be extremely grateful if you . . . would use your influence toward the settlement of the question on the basis of Dr. Schuschnigg's offer to go back on his decision to hold the plebiscite." On the margin of this note Weizsäcker then noted: "no reply is necessary." *GD*, I, 577.

20 — IMT, 103-C. The promise given to the Italian Embassy in Berlin that the German Army would halt at Innsbruck and not appear on the Brenner was not kept, and the German Officer who appeared leading the detachment to the Brenner was Colonel (later General) Schörner, who fought at Caporetto in 1917.

21 — During his farewell talk with Ciano, the Austrian Minister to Rome remarked on March 14 that Italy could not have intervened: "If a single Italian soldier would have entered, the Austrian people, including the Jews, would have fired at [them]." *CD*, p. 133.

Only after the masses gave a fantastic ovation to Hitler in Linz, did the latter abandon the original plans for a German-Austrian personal union or some kind of a satellite status for Austria and decide to go ahead with a full incorporation. See H. Holldack, *Wie es wirklich geschah* (Göttingen, 1949), pp. 78–80.

22 — In South Tyrol rumors spread that Italy would cede that region to Germany and then, after March 13, disillusionment set in. Attolico to Ribbentrop on March 17: "Everything is all right, but allow me to tell you that a definite statement — intended for German hearers — about the Brenner is, under the circumstances, absolutely essential."

23 — See *IMT*, 27–TC. See also Comnen, *op. cit.*, p. 7, on the evaluation of the situation which an official of the Hungarian Foreign Ministry gave to the Rumanian envoy to Hungary.

On March 13 certain German planes violated the Czech frontier and after this followed Göring's second reassurance to Mastny. Mastny also was told by the German military on March 12 that German troops were ordered to stay away from the Czechoslovak frontier at a distance of 15 to 30 kilometers.

24 — It was obviously Chamberlain's policy not to talk of Austria with Italy as he saw during the last Eden-Grandi-Chamberlain interview what an obstacle a discussion on Austria might be in dealing with Italy. This was catastrophic diplomacy. When on February 22 Lord Perth transmitted to Ciano the agenda of the forthcoming British-Italian conversations, Austria and central Europe did not figure therein! On the March 12 talk see *CLD*, pp. 292–4. Ciano to Perth: "There is nothing to do. What can we do, we cannot force the people to be independent if they do not wish to be so." Also *BD*, I, 28.

On March 13 the British Minister to Vienna complained of Henderson's ill-placed criticism of Schuschnigg; see *ibid.*, p. 38.

25 — Dieckhoff thought the remark so typical that he inserted it in English in his report to Berlin. *GD*, I, 616.

26 — *Ibid.* Dieckhoff noted that the Italian Ambassador to Washington, Suvich, whose previous post had been Vienna, was very aloof during the *Anschluss* days.

27 — Chiang Kai-shek also warmly congratulated the German Ambassador. So did the Presidents of Brazil and Switzerland.

28 — Previously, Innitzer had rebuked the Jesuit Father Muckermann, a Vatican exponent of anti-Nazism in Austria.

29 — On March 27, the Austrian Bishops came out for a pro-German vote in the engineered plebiscite which was to be held on April 10; on April 1, however, the *Osservatore Romano* declared that the Austrian Episcopate acted on its own initiative and the Holy See was not consulted "either beforehand or subsequently."

30 — See *IMT*, 903–D, also 680–PS.

31 — Later, during the war, some of the best regiments of the German Army were Austrian, and, although the majority of the Austrian people became bitterly resentful of the German régime, such SS henchmen as Kaltenbrunner, Veesenmeyer, and Eichmann were former Austrian Nazis.

32 — *IMT*, 142–R.

33 — *GD*, II, 131–2.

34 — The classic words of Bertrand de Jouvenel: "The constant ambition of reactionaries is to appear as revolutionaries."

35 — *Carnets secrets de Jean Zay* (Paris, 1941), p. 13.

36 — The report of Mr. Mack, British Consul-General in Vienna, to Lord Halifax on April 8, 1938, is excellent. It begins with a tone of resignation: ("Before this mission closes and the diplomatic representation of His Majesty in Vienna, which has extended over centuries, finally ceases . . .") and it ends on a fine note comparable with the best traditions of British diplomacy:

"It seems possible from this time that the German authorities will wish to maintain something of the distinctive character of Vienna and perhaps the Austrian countryside. For the moment, however, it must be said that the spire of St. Stephen's towers over a city which has become germanised almost in a night, and that the city which served as the bulwark of civilisation against the Turks in 1683 has been converted into the eastern bulwark of a country dominated by a race whose cultural and philosophical outlook is the negation of many of the principles for which civilisation stands." *Documents in British Foreign Policy, 1919–1939*, Series III, vol. I, 126 ff. and 136–7. By permission of the Controller of Her Britannic Majesty's Stationery Office.

The Polish-Lithuanian crisis

1 — During these days Paul-Boncour, who was Foreign Minister for a short time, saw the Soviet Ambassador and praised Soviet reticence in the Polish-Lithuanian dispute. Joseph Davies, in *Mission to Moscow*, mentions that he thought a German-Polish secret agreement existed in regard to Lithuania. Neither the Soviets' non-committal reaction nor later evidence bears this out.

2 — The German and Polish "White Books" are "significantly reticent" dealing with the spring and summer of 1938. See Namier, *op. cit.*, p. 33. In the German White Book, eleven pages out of 459, in the Polish volume four of 142 are devoted to that period. See also *IMT*, 388–PS. Lately, however, we have the Szembek papers which fill in many gaps. The German High Command in June 1938 stated that "independent of *Case Green*" (attack on Czechoslovakia) Germany would occupy Memel by a lightning stroke in case of a Polish-Lithuanian armed conflict.

Western doubts

1 — *IMT*, 388–PS. On German military estimates of Czechoslovakia after *Anschluss* see Jodl's 1943 recapitulation, *IMT*, 172–L.

2 — For example, Henderson to his Czech colleague in Berlin on February 23: "If there is another change and Eden returns, you will have Eden but also war."

3 — Feiling, *op. cit.* When on March 20 Chamberlain rejected Churchill's Grand Alliance idea, presented to him privately a few days before, with the argument that it was not practical, Churchill was distressed: "It surely did not take much thought from the chiefs of Staff and F. O. experts to tell the Prime Minister that the British Navy and the French Army could not be deployed on the Bohemian mountain front to stand between the Czech Republic and Hitler's invading army. This was indeed evident from the map. But the certainty that the crossing of the Bohemian frontier line would have involved a general European war might well even at that date have deterred or delayed Hitler's next assault." Churchill, *The Gathering Storm* (Boston, 1948), Houghton Mifflin, p. 275.

Eisenlohr to the German Foreign Office on March 23: "Hodža told me today that he had no illusions regarding British guarantee to Czechoslovakia. British foreign policy would still be guided by the same considerations as in the past." *GD*, II, 185. Hodža also told the German envoy that he was no friend of Russia, but the Soviet pact was needed by his country.

4 — Wheeler-Bennett, *Munich, Prologue to Tragedy*, *op. cit.*, p. 36. See also the memorandum of Halifax to Phipps for use with the French on March 22, essentially reaffirming what was said to Chautemps and Delbos in London in November, 1937. ". . . His Majesty's Government could certainly not go so far as to state what their action might be in the event of an attack upon Czechoslovakia by Germany. They are accordingly not in a position to undertake obligations in advance to render military assistance to France in cases and circumstances not covered by the Treaty of Locarno." *BD*, I, 85.

5 — The German Embassy report on the Chamberlain speech pointed out the specific lack of a British commitment on the side of France, although warning Berlin that if France was involved in a war, British intervention was probable. *GD*, II, 192–3.

6 — *Documents in British Foreign Policy, 1919–1939*, Series III, vol. I, 97–100. By permission of the Controller of Her Britannic Majesty's Stationery Office.

7 — On February 17, 1937, the Soviet Ambassador in Paris, Potemkin, declared to Blum that Russian intervention in the case of a German attack on Czechoslovakia or France depended on the permission of passage on the part of Rumania and of Poland — and, if, for "incomprehensible reasons" these nations refused such permission, the assistance of the Soviet Union "would be forcibly limited." Blum, otherwise a profound thinker, was obviously not versed enough in eastern European geography, because he asked Potemkin why a Soviet passage through Lithuania could not be undertaken. He seemed to forget that the Soviet Union and Lithuania had no common frontier; a passage through Polish or Latvian territory would have been necessary first. Although this technical problem could have been cited, the Russian Ambassador did not cite it and instead transmitted the non-committal answer of the Soviet General Staff: "Passage through states friendly with France has been envisaged. Should there be other alternatives, it is the task of France to explore these in accord with the Soviet Union."

8 — As only Bucharest and Brussels were mentioned, it is evident that Polish assistance was practically written off at that date.

9 — On a juridical study stating that there were no French obligations to Czechoslovakia see De Monzie, *op. cit.*, pp. 23–9.

10 — This was the case with Americans also. Joseph Kennedy, the new American Ambassador to Britain, arrived there in March. Bullitt in Paris was his exact opposite.

Yet Dieckhoff warned Berlin on March 22: "As I wrote you months ago — and I believe that you agree with me — the key to the American attitude is in London. If England remains calm and accepts our increased strength and expansion, even if some circles are not pleased here, no action will be taken; after all, one cannot be more Catholic than the Pope. But if England decides to oppose us, and it comes to war, the United States will not hesitate very long to range itself on the British side." *GD*, I, 696–7. See also the Dieckhoff report on the American attitude after the *Anschluss*, pp. 615 ff.

11 — Although men like the British Consul-General in Munich wrote thus: "A doubt must, however, arise as to the ability of modern Germany to negotiate — undue exercise of strength in the past may have brought impotence in that respect in its train, and other methods have been shown to be highly efficacious and incomparably speedier." *BD*, I, 120. Henderson to Halifax on April 1 wrote very optimistically of long-range German policy when that country was satisfied in Europe. *Ibid.*, pp. 108 ff., and on April 2 he spoke with Ribbentrop, again mentioning the colonial offer.

12 — *Documents in British Foreign Policy, 1919–1939*, Series III, vol. I, 55. By permission of the Controller of Her Britannic Majesty's Stationery Office.

13 — *IMT*, 3060–PS.

14 — *Documents and Materials, op. cit.*, no. 9; also *BD*, I.

15 — Cadogan also voiced the belief that the Czech-Austrian aristocracy, Czech financial circles, and Czech industry were favoring a settlement and were opposed to many of Beneš' policies; this Masaryk denied, adding in his report: "Cadogan is a real aristocrat, dignified but modest, Nevile Henderson is a big snob and our Mr. Newton is a petty snob."

16 — Newton himself doubted the German sincerity in righting their wrongs and expressed this to Halifax on May 16: "Those who have studied *Mein Kampf* in detail assert that it also provides for vassal States of alien population, and they believe that that may well be what the Reich has in mind for the Czechs . . . I believe, *in fine*, that broadly speaking, the Peace Conference was right in thinking that Bohemia forms a natural region, and I am doubtful whether any attempt to divide it up would provide a perma-

nent solution." *Documents in British Foreign Policy, 1919–1939*, Series III, vol. I, 303. By permission of the Controller of Her Britannic Majesty's Stationery Office.

17 — On April 15 the Yugoslav Minister to Rome told Ciano that Yugoslavia would do what Italy would; Belgrade intended to harmonize her actions with Rome. *CLD*, pp. 301–3.

18 — *GD*, I, 1101. Typical of Mussolini's fluctuations was this period. On April 24 he said to Ciano in regard to the South Tyrol: "If the Germans behave well and are respectful Italian subjects, I could favor their culture and their language. But if they think to extort a single meter of land from our frontier . . . this will not be done without the hardest possible war in which I shall bring the whole world together in a coalition against the Germans. And we will put Germany down for at least two centuries." *CD*, p. 164. And the same Mussolini in 1943 timidly acquiesced in the practical annexation of Trieste and Venezia Giulia by German Gauleiters. On May 2 Ciano spoke to Mussolini of the "undesirable growth of German prestige due to the *Anschluss*" and said that Italy should counterbalance it in the Balkans. But such hesitations were not reflected in the Italian press and propaganda. The result was that when Mussolini spoke at Genoa on May 14, the people yelled and booed when he mentioned France and laughed ironically when he mentioned the accord with Britain. Mussolini then changed his speech on the spot and lashed out strongly against France and Britain. Ciano remarked: "The mass [sentiment] carried him." *CD*, p. 173.

19 — *GD*, I, 1092–3.

The Czechoslovak crisis: Phase I

1 — Three years later he confessed in a speech on March 4, 1941, in Vienna:

"In order to protect ourselves against Czechoslovak influence, we were compelled to lie and deny our allegiance to the National Socialist cause. We should have preferred advocating National Socialism openly. However, it is doubtful whether, in doing so, we would have been able to perform the task of destroying Czechoslovakia . . ." See also *IMT*, 2788, 2789, 3061, 998-PS, and *Documents and Materials . . . op. cit.*, no. 8.

2 — The main source for these reports and papers is *GD*, II, especially pp. 173 ff.

3 — See especially in *BD*, I, the wise observations and reports of Mr. Pares, Consul at Liberec (Reichenau).

4 — This is the recollection of Bonnet, in *De Washington au Quai d'Orsay*. On the detailed minutes see *BD*, I, 198 ff.

5 — He also made a very interesting remark: "Doubtless the best thing would be if the three kindred nations, Germany, Britain and the United States, could unite in joint work for peace." France was also necessary, but "Germany and Britain to a certain degree were the protagonists whose task it was to encourage the others." *GD*, II, 246–7.

6 — Feiling, *op. cit.*, p. 353.

7 — *Documents on British Foreign Policy, 1919–1939*, Series III, vol. I, 626–7. By permission of the Controller of Her Britannic Majesty's Stationery Office.

8 — *Documents and Materials, op. cit.*, vol. II, *The Dirksen Papers*, no. 1.

9 — François-Poncet in Berlin early in May: "it was time Europe revised its opinion of M. Beneš." *BD*, I, 274.

10 — See *IMT*, 1780-PS on the timing; also 388-PS.

11 — *BD*, I, 299, n. 2. Also on May 10, at an informal luncheon given by Lady Astor, Chamberlain allegedly made remarks before American journalists in which he stated that the Czechoslovak state was out-of-date and the Sudeten region would have to go to Germany in any case. He later denied these statements, the accurate reporting of which was questionable.

12 — There were several instances in this period when, to prove his diplomatic value, Ciano hurried to tell the German Ambassador the confidences of the British envoy. See for example *CLD*, p. 345.

13 — The Italian Ambassador, Attolico, complained from Berlin on May 31 about German intrigues in Sofia and Tirana against Italy.

14 — Early in June Prince Philip Hesse, presumably on the instructions of Hitler, who was slightly worried seeing Italy's yet neutral intentions, tried to stir up some intrigue between Italy and Greece and spread rumors of anti-Italian remarks by the "feeble-minded" King of Greece. But not much came out of this. Exactly two years later the Italians were to provoke a Greek war and it was Hitler who tried to avoid it.

15 — See Noël, *op. cit.* The Polish envoy in London told Halifax nevertheless on May 4 that Poland was "anxious to improve relations with Czechoslovakia." *BD*, I, 247. Henderson wrote Halifax on May 6 that he was informed that if German soldiers moved into Czechoslovakia, undoubtedly Poland would also march, "not so much out of hostility to Czechoslovakia or because of the Polish minority, which was unimportant, but to prevent Germany seizing all the loot. There would be no previous arrangement with the German Government but the latter

would perforce acquiesce in the Polish action." *Ibid.*, p. 247. Kennard from Warsaw agreed with this view.

16 — See *Documents and Materials . . . op. cit.*, no. 11. See also the British Ambassador's estimates on sentiment within Poland, *BD*, I, 429–31. The controversial issue here is the vague Polish statement to France on May 24 about Polish resolution to stand by her French alliance actively, if needed — Lukasiewicz' reference was to a similar vague statement of March 1936. The records of Szembek, referring to both, do not quite bear out the scathing words of Namier, referring to the undoubtedly tailored version of the Polish offer in Bonnet's memoirs: "The Polish offer, for what it was worth, was first torpedoed by Bonnet the statesman, and next obliterated by Bonnet the historian." *In the Nazi Era* (New York, 1952), Appendix.

17 — At Sinaia the Little Entente foreign ministers met in May, at which time the Czech Krofta was told that Rumania and Yugoslavia would help the Czechs if Hungary attacked them, otherwise not. Rumanian court circles informed the German Minister to Bucharest thereof on May 23.

18 — According to Comnen, Bonnet errs in his memoirs: he talked with him first (on the 9th) and only then with Litvinov. But the essential contents of these talks has been correctly related by Bonnet, says Comnen. On May 27 Bonnet asked Lukasiewicz to ask his government to improve relations with Russia. Bonnet's previous statement that the French government had decided to "put the Franco-Soviet Pact to sleep" was confidentially reported to the German Embassy in Paris. And on May 23 Daladier spoke to the German Ambassador, Count Welczeck: he saw the destruction of Europe if war came. "Into the battle zones, devastated and denuded of men, Cos-

sack and Mongol hordes would then pour, bringing to Europe a new 'culture.' "

19 — The Czech General Staff misinterpreted the situation: an informant told Newton on the 20th that it was the German General Staff which forced Hitler to be aggressive with the Czechs (*BD*, I, 327). This was nonsense. Henderson, of course, could exploit this situation by telling Halifax how stupid the Czechs were: it was in Prague, not in Berlin, that the key to war lay, he wrote.

20 — At midnight Halifax telegraphed a serious plea for restraint to both Prague and Berlin; at the same time he instructed Phipps in Paris to remind the French that there was no guarantee that Britain would help them if they were involved now. Bonnet at the same time intimated that France might release herself of her treaty bonds, if the Czechs were "really unreasonable." It is noteworthy that the idea of British mediation which appears in a Foreign Office document first on April 30 gained official status in the Halifax message to Henderson late on the 22nd.

21 — The final directive for *Green* was issued on the 30th: "It is my unalterable decision to smash Czechoslovakia by military action in the near future. It is the business of the political leadership to await or bring about the suitable moment from a political and military point of view. . . . The following are necessary prerequisites for the intended attack: (a) A convenient apparent excuse and, with it, (b) Adequate political justification, (c) Action not expected by the enemy, which [action] will find him in the least possible state of readiness. . . ."

It was then that the mediation idea assumed shape. Bucharest tried to mediate between Berlin and Prague:

a lightweight attempt. While, in a dispatch on the 25th, even Henderson was somewhat critical of the German methods, Bonnet in Paris praised Germany's "dignified calm, restraint" to Heaven when he spoke to Welczeck, adding that "if the Czechoslovak Government continued unyielding, the French Government would inform them that under these circumstances they would be obliged to submit their obligations under the alliance to revision." On the same day a Foreign Office emissary, Mr. Strang, arrived in Prague, where he sized the situation up with great intelligence. Newton to him: "There are limits to the extent to which we can go in saying one thing in Prague and another in Berlin." Noting the developing idea of mediation, the Czech envoy in London told the German Ambassador there of the extreme Czech readiness to negotiate on all matters, including his country's relationship with Russia. That the British idea of mediation was the new and perhaps dominant factor in the whole Czech affair was noted in Berlin by Weizsäcker on the 27th.

The Czechoslovak crisis: Phase II

1 — There were now intrigues among the Sudeten when Krebs and Frank tried to torpedo Henlein's leadership; but the latter was upheld by Berlin, especially after an editorial of the London *Times* on June 4 praised him. On June 8 the Sudeten Party presented a memorandum to Hodᵛa which, in its essence, demanded the complete separation of the Sudeten regions from Czechoslovakia: this the Czechs could not accept.

2 — One of the ablest Czech diplomats was Osuský in Paris. De Brinon and other elements began to assail him subtly; in early June, Phipps reported such intrigues to Halifax, and the somewhat credulous Hugh Wilson, American Ambassador to Germany, dropped some unflattering remarks to the Germans about Osuský.

3 — On the whole German-American complex of those days, see *GD*, I, 701–23 and *BD*, I, 290.

4 — The Kennedy-Dirksen conversation is a classic example of the "new diplomacy." Kennedy said that Roosevelt "was not anti-German. . . . However, there was no one who had come from Europe and had spoken a friendly word to him regarding present-day Germany and her Government. . . . Most of them were afraid of the Jews and did not dare to say anything good about Germany. . . . Although he [Kennedy] did not know Germany, he had learned from the most varied sources that the present Government had done great things for Germany and that the Germans were satisfied and enjoyed good living conditions. . . . Lindbergh, who had spoken very favorably of Germany, made a strong impression upon [Kennedy]. . . . When he spoke favorably of Germany, people would have absolute confidence in his statements, because he was a Catholic. . . . The Jewish question . . . was naturally of great importance to German-American relations. In this connection it was not so much the fact that [the Germans] wanted to get rid of the Jews that was so harmful to us, but rather the loud clamor with which [they] accompanied this purpose. He himself understood [the Germans'] Jewish policy completely. . . . The overwhelming majority of the American people wanted peace and friendly relations with Germany. The Americans took a very simple view of problems of foreign policy; there were only $3\frac{1}{2}$ million Jews in the United States all told, and the overwhelming majority of them lived on the east coast. Elsewhere, however, the anti-German sentiment was — as mentioned above — by no means widespread; neither did the average citizen of the United States have any particular liking for England; regarding England he only knew that she had not paid her war debts, and that she had deposed her King because he wanted to marry an American; he had no prejudice against Germany." (These are startling statements from an Ambassador accredited to Britain! It would be interesting to know whether Ambassador Kennedy's report in the State Department files tallies with that of Dirksen . . .)

Dirksen then showed him pictures from a German magazine "which showed the war preparations of the Czechs very clearly. Mr. Kennedy was obviously impressed by this. . . . In the course of the conversation Ambassador Kennedy repeatedly expressed his conviction that in economic matters Germany had to have a free hand in the East as well as in the Southeast. He took a very pessimistic view of the situation in the Soviet Union." Kennedy's views in retrospect are given in Langer-Gleason, *A Challenge to Isolation* (New York, 1952), p. 76. Kennedy states that, like Chamberlain, he wished to deflect Hitler eastward where he would exhaust himself in a war with Stalin. But this smacks of unduly much hindsight. And there is certainly reason to suppose that Moscow and Berlin would have seen through this not very sophisticated scheme. It seems that Kennedy would rather have preferred an Anglo-German alliance.

5 — It is an exciting and rewarding endeavor to compare Henderson's telegrams in *BD* with *GD*, II; especially *BD*, pp. 584 ff. and *GD*, pp. 403 ff.

6 — *BD*, I, 592–8 and 610. On the next day Henderson wrote to Cadogan fully echoing the German party line against Jews, Communists, etc., stirring up trouble and stating that there

could never be peace in Europe as long as Czechoslovakia was outside of what he called the German economic orbit. This he called inexorable logic. *Ibid.*, pp. 616–8. At the same time he informed Halifax that the American Ambassador to Berlin was in favor of a plebiscite: "he has so informed State Department though he said the latter refused to exercise any pressure on Prague on ground that it would not lend itself to bullying of small by a big nation." Here was, at any rate, a somewhat naive, but typically honest and American approach. Yet, as Harold Nicolson wrote once: "Intellectual, as distinct from practical honesty is not among our British virtues. . . . Our passion for compromise is so acute that we prefer a compromise even when a logical definition is both offered and advantageous."

7 — *GD*, II, 523. Henderson to Halifax two days earlier: "*Cui bono* is not a bad basis for argument in policy as well as detective stories. War would doubtless serve the purposes of all the Jews, communists and doctrinaires in the world for whom Nazism is anathema, but it would be a terrible risk today for Germany herself and particularly for the new Nazi Government which Hitler has built up in the past five years. . . . It is, unfortunately, a fact and when . . . one realises the strength of the forces in every country which are praying for war as the only remedy for anti-communism, anti-Judaism and against a strong Germany one must remain nervous. If it comes, it will not be Hitler or the mass of the Germans who have sought it, this year at any rate. They will be, of course, blamed for it. Unjustly, in my opinion; but by my contemporaries my opinion will be regarded as worthless . . ." *Documents in British Foreign Policy, 1919–1939*, Series III, vol. II, 11. By permission of the Controller of Her Britannic Majesty's Stationery Office.

8 — GD, II, 439.

9 — IMT, 76–TC.

10 — GD, II, 403 ff.; also I, 1153 ff. "Among the broad masses of the British people the desire for a settlement with Germany exists and is popular. . . . The present British cabinet is the first one since the war to make a settlement with Germany one of the most important points on its program; it thus shows the greatest understanding for Germany that is possible in any group of British political leaders of Cabinet caliber . . ." See also Welczeck's reports from Paris, especially that of July 30, GD, I, 1165.

11 — See GD, II, 504, 526; also 593–4, 602. A strange trio, this, in Berlin who worked for peace: all for different reasons and guided by different principles but with grains of honesty: Attolico, Henderson, Weizsäcker. The German doubts and divergences of those days are given in Kordt, *op. cit.;* also in Dirksen, *Moskau-Tokio-London* (Bonn, 1949).

12 — German intelligence was very good: the Germans even had people go to London and exact information while posing as anti-Nazi military men. See BD, II, Appendix; the same man reporting on his conversation with Churchill in GD, II, 706.

13 — The British envoys now began to be more preoccupied with the actual war chances; Newton in July proposed the neutralisation of Czechoslovakia: on one hand he feared the loss of British prestige, on the other he wisely said that if a stand against the *Drang nach Osten* had to be made, Czechoslovakia was the "least favourable place" for that. Henderson to Halifax, August 6: "I believe that if we really showed our teeth Hitler would not dare to make war today. Nevertheless, in my opinion that would be the greatest tragedy of all. It would be a Pyrrhic victory which, though it might be acclaimed as final, in fact would merely mean postponing the evil day. . . . Just as I was always convinced and years ago that Austria must inevitably come into Germany sooner or later, so I am convinced that the Sudeten must also do in the end. The faint possibility to the contrary I estimate at 5 per cent. Yet even that is worth trying. . . . One may be sorry for the Czechs. . . . One may hate to see Germany encouraged: yet the moral principle is in the end of far far greater importance." *Documents on British Foreign Policy, 1919–1939,* Series III, vol. II. By permission of the Controller of Her Britannic Majesty's Stationery Office.

On August 12 he ridiculed the slogan which, in his phrasing, is "the chivalrous defense of the little dog against the big. Little dogs have also their obligations and cannot presume on their littleness. If we wish to impose law on the strong, we must also impose it on the weak, however unpopular it may be." About four days later Henderson began to suggest that a "surgical operation," the complete cession of the Sudeten region would be necessary. He asked Halifax to keep this from the French, concerning whom he showed evident distrust throughout the whole crisis. On August 19: "In my opinion the chief danger of war lies not in Herr Hitler himself who would be risking more than anyone else but in the forces working for war, namely German and Czech extremists, communists and other influences and the universal hatred abroad of Nazism. I believe if we saw any utility in war, now would be the moment to make it rather than later."

14 — GD, II, 620–2. Stewart asked his German conversant, a Baron Hahn, not to give his name in any report of this conversation: a pledge which the German, of course, broke at once.

15 — *GD*, II, 662–3; 664–6, and *IMT*, 76–TC.

16 — A revealing remark of Halifax to Newton, June 18: "The kind of expert I have in mind would be someone with practical experience of administration and of minority problems, such as an ex-Governor of an Indian province. . . ." Newton counseled him not to: " . . . however foolishly, the connexion might be considered derogatory by both sides." *BD*, I, 505.

17 — The German chargé in London on Sir Horace Wilson: "He is an embodiment of Moltke's idea: 'To be more than you appear to be.' "

18 — An illustration taken from the German Foreign Ministry archives suffices to indicate with what rapidity the appetites of Sudeten politicians increased. Around July 10 a Dr. Kier stated to the German Legation in Prague: "Present Czech bills . . . contain . . . at the best only 20 per cent of safeguard demanded for equality of status." This same man to the German Foreign Office on August 13 (after Runciman's arrival): ". . . even with a 100 per cent fulfillment of the eight demands laid down by Henlein at Karlsbad, there still remain sufficient points of tension between the Czechs and Germans to serve as a pretext for a settlement by force at any time if necessity should so demand." *GD*, pp. 487 and 756–7.

19 — Strang on July 30 wrote from London to Henderson against the idea of Italy at the conference without Russia: this "would be the thin end of the German wedge for keeping [Russia] out of Europe altogether, and this is clearly not an aspect of a policy which we wish to encourage." *BD*, I, 614, n. 3.

20 — Runciman to Halifax on August 10: "Where are we going? The answer can be given as well by you as by me. Success depends on whether or not the Führer wants to go to war. If he does the excuse will be found easily. In any case I can only continue my labours and hope for the best in good faith. It is a pathetic side of the present crisis that the common people here, and, I am told, elsewhere, are looking to me and my mission as the only hope for an established peace. Alas, they do not realise how weak are our sanctions, and I dread the moment when they find that nothing can save them. It will be a terrible disillusionment . . ." *Documents in British Foreign Policy, 1919–1939*, Series III, vol. II. By permission of the Controller of Her Britannic Majesty's Stationery Office.

21 — The Henderson-Wilson policy was revealed with shocking clarity to Th. Kordt, the German chargé (otherwise an anti-Nazi) in the house of Mr. Conwell-Evans, a noted Germanophile. (*GD*, II, 607.) Sir Horace completely agreed on the present "unnatural and absurd position of Czechoslovakia. . . . The Führer had used the simile . . . that European culture rested on two pillars which must be linked by a powerful arch: Great Britain and Germany. Great Britain and Germany were in fact the two countries where the greatest order reigned and which were the best governed. . . . He himself was not one of those who held the view that Germany wanted to organize southeastern Europe and then use its resources for the annihilation of the British Empire . . ."

22 — See *Documents Secrets . . . Hongrie, op. cit.*, no. 18. In order to allay German suspicions, Attolico, referring to Italian sources of information, told Ribbentrop on July 15 that it was indeed doubtful whether France would fight. See *IMT*, 2860–PS. On July 25 Franzoni, the Italian Minister to Prague, was invited to a cordial talk with Beneš, but there was no hope that Italy would mediate between Czechs and Germans. To reassure the Germans, Italy a week later rejected a Czech request to purchase airplanes and motors from Italy.

23 — *GD*, II, 573–4. The opinion at the German Foreign Office tallied with this estimate, as a memorandum of August 18 shows: it would be extremely advantageous for Germany to avoid Hungary's co-belligerence against the Czechs, as thus Rumania would keep out: "Hungarian help, which would bring new opponents to our group, would be no gain for us." *Ibid.*, pp. 583–5. Yet a few days later Hitler attacked the Hungarians for being lukewarm in their war preparations.

24 — He made nasty remarks at the French again: "The times are over when a telephone call from Paris determined Yugoslav politics." On July 20 Henderson reported a conversation with the Yugoslav Ambassador in Berlin, who told him that Yugoslavia would not go against Germany even if the Germans marched through Hungary. Henderson had contacts with the Yugoslav royal house, as in the early thirties he was British envoy to Belgrade. On July 30 the Court Minister there confidentially informed the British chargé of the Yugoslav dislike of Beneš.

25 — See *CD*, p. 211–3; *CLD*, pp. 351 ff. and *Documents Secrets . . . Hongrie*, nos. 19–24. Ciano was also discontented with the Hungarians. Only the simple-minded Csáky (making remarks behind Kánya's back) made irresponsible statements on Hungarian public opinion and Polish eventualities.

26 — See Kordt, Schmidt, *op. cit.*; also *IMT*, 2796– and 2797–PS. At one instance, Hitler to Horthy: "be quiet!" Horthy was ready to walk out. "I am, after all, a head of a state and cannot be spoken to in such a manner."

27 — Imrédy, after hesitations, consented to Göring's wish to erect a German aerial navigation control station in Hungary, but no landing grounds for German aircraft were granted. On Horthy's return the German Minister in Budapest reported: "The Regent . . . spoke with enthusiasm of the impression received on his visit to Germany [but] the extraordinary situation had arisen that he, who for years had desired nothing more ardently than a speedy realization of Hungarian revisionist aims, was now forced to sound a warning note owing to the international political situation." *GD*, II, 651.

28 — The German circular warning notes to Czechoslovakia's allies and neighbors around August 15 were not presented to Moscow.

29 — *GD*, II, 602, 633.

30 — *BD*, II, 219. It was now that the rôle of the United States almost imperceptibly quickened. On the same day Kennedy was instructed to inform Chamberlain of President Roosevelt's support for his mediation attempts. Krofta was planning for an anniversary visit to America in August, but then the pressing events made this trip impossible.

31 — On the evening of that day Maisky called on Churchill at his country home, informing him of what occurred between Litvinov and Payart, adding that Litvinov also asked for Soviet-French-Czech staff talks. Churchill, impressed, intervened with Halifax to exploit this occasion but his efforts went unheeded. However, it is most likely that Stalin already at that time thought it better not to intervene in Czechoslovakia but to profit by entering later as the arbiter of the continent, securing the incontestable domination of central-eastern Europe.

It is very interesting to note that in the summer of 1939 it was the Western Powers who in their negotiations with Russia proposed to choose the same Article 16 of the League of Nations' Covenant for defining aggression which Litvinov evoked to Payart. But Molotov then refused it as impractical! On the whole Russo-Rumanian complex see Appendix IV of Bonnet, *Fin d'une Europe* (Geneva, 1948) (*L'opposition de vues russe-roumaine, 1938: Deux documents*). Also Chapter 12 in his *De Washington au Quai d'Orsay* and Comnen, *Preludi del grande dramma*. I also wish to refer the reader to the historical analogies and striking observations about a number of constant factors in Russian foreign policy presented in J. Kucharzewski, *The Origins of Modern Russia* (New York, 1947), especially pp. 8–13.

Phase III: Berchtesgaden, Godesberg, Munich

1 — Wheeler-Bennett's account of Beneš' dramatic offer (*op. cit.*, p. 91) is not quite substantiated by subsequent evidence: it is probable that his source was the exaggerating Beneš himself; see for example Newton's account in *BD*, II, 332. Nevertheless at a secretive talk between Sudeten and German officials at the German Legation in Prague on the 8th, it was generally stated that the Czech terms were acceptable, "since . . . there can be no doubt that, by reaching an agreement, there would be adequate opportunities of demonstrating to the Czechs the non-observance of their pledges . . . by skillful carrying out of this policy by the Sudeten German Party . . . the power of the State can be completely undermined from within." *GD*, II, 718.

2 — On September 6 the French newspaper *La République* presented a similar editorial thesis. Maisky asked Halifax about the denial on the 8th and received a very noncommittal answer.

It must be said that all Commonwealth members agreed with Chamberlain's policy, he received telegrams from Mackenzie King, General Hertzog, etc. See especially Feiling, pp. 349, 357, 360. Chamberlain cited Canning in these days: ". . . you should never menace unless you are in a position to carry out your threats . . ."

3 — Yet Kennedy two days later to a German diplomat: "Feeling in America had never yet been as anti-German as was the case at present, and in his personal opinion very wrongly so, for Hitler had done wonders in Germany." On the same day an intelligent report from the German chargé in Washington: ". . . in America, as everywhere else, the shadow of Soviet Russia looms in the background. With the exception of outspoken communist and liberal circles, no American relishes the thought that in a future world war in which America participates, he will have the pleasure of an alliance with Moscow. It is clear to many Americans, including responsible members of the State Department, that Russia is only waiting for the opportunity to set the democratic states against the totalitarian states, and to light the torch of communist world revolution at the ensuing conflagration." *GD*, I, 726–32.

4 — *BD*, II, 287, also Noël, *op. cit.* A German military man told Henderson four days later: "The Poles were sitting like vultures on the fence nearby and merely wished to ensure for themselves the possibility of a large share of prey . . ." *GD*, II, 770.

5 — *Documents on British Foreign Policy, 1919–1939*, Series III, vol. II, 303. By permission of the Controller of Her Britannic Majesty's Stationery Office. See also Bonnet. The Halifax statement classically reveals the difference in French and British national character, so admirably explained by

Madariaga. "Undoubtedly France will still have frequent cause for anxiety when the dreaded realism of the British again and again casts doubt upon mutual decisions which France would like to consider final. Undoubtedly England, too, will often enough be embittered by the French tendency to wish to settle everything legally and finally. Decisive, however, is the fact that the two Governments are fully resolved to reach — regardless of all differences of opinion — a unified course of action in every case." Churchill on these days: "If M. Bonnet was seeking for an excuse for leaving the Czechs to their fate, it must be admitted that his search had met with some success . . ."

6 — It is both revealing and rewarding to study Henderson's psychology at Nuremberg. Compare his own report in *BD*, II, 651 ff. (which begins: "I shall not forget Nuremberg 1938 in a hurry . . .") with the memorandum of the SS officer, Baumann, who was delegated to accompany him during the Party Congress, in *GD*, II, 765 ff.

"[Henderson] expressed his regret that the weather was not better for the poor young fellows [of the National Socialist Labor Service], who must surely have been afoot since early morning. . . . He himself was, however (in contrast to many Britishers) convinced of the Führer's peaceful intentions toward Great Britain . . . the compulsory Labor Service was the best thing in the National Socialist program (and added that he would like to see it introduced in Britain too) . . . [Baumann:] To my question whether [Henderson] had understood the excellent words of the songs and party songs of the Labor Service . . . he said, yes, and remarked that Field-Marshal Göring had drawn his attention to several characteristic passages. [Early in the morning Conwell-Evans visited Henderson, whose outlook, Henderson told his SS com-

panion] was more German than British. [Henderson] personally had no sympathy at all with the Czechs. . . . He expressed his aversion to the Czechs in very strong terms. . . . In accordance with [Henderson's] tastes I had arranged . . . an inspection of the latest German Youth Hostel . . . [Henderson] emphasized that on his private visit to Nuremberg he would certainly take advantage [of the Youth Hostel], since he much preferred these attractive quarters to hotel accommodation. [In Britain, said Henderson] the aristocratic ruling class was at present on the defensive against the broad masses of the popular front . . . the English too, being a virile Germanic race, preferred to be led by hunting and shooting men and not their opposites."

Henderson and his German friends took then an automobile excursion and the member of the "hunting aristocratic race," in true petty bourgeois fashion, sent a picture postcard mailed to Halifax at the Foreign Office and made Göring sign it. In the evening the idyll continued: "Business was brisk in the *Nassauer Keller* when we entered. Every single place was occupied by SA, SS, and political leaders and there was a very gay atmosphere. The band was playing popular tunes, among others, Rhenish carnival songs. Sir Nevile Henderson felt thoroughly at home in the surroundings and inquired with great interest about the history and rank of the individual men going up and down the steep staircase which was directly opposite us. As he had already done at last year's Party Congress, [Henderson] showed a marked interest in the various German racial types. . . . When we left about midnight the first morning papers were being delivered. When [Henderson] saw the headlines . . . he merely remarked: "'Oh, these blasted Czechs.'"

Henderson on the last days of the Congress: "It would be tragic if . . . it should come to a conflict between the two great Germanic nations, the Anglo-Saxons and the Teutons. That would be a conflict in which Great Britain had no real war aims . . ." And later: "Sir Nevile Henderson then asked me about *Reichsführer* Himmler, for whom he seemed to have some regard. I informed him of the *Reichsführer's* interest in prehistoric times and folklore . . ."

7 — This meant a slightly new turn, as in October 1937 the French military concurred to extend the interpretation of the Czech alliance to the case of "internal aggression." On German High Command instructions to the Sudeten Free Corps see *IMT*, 366-1-EC.

8 — There is today a lot of unorganized evidence supporting the view that the news of Chamberlain's journey thwarted the only serious and potential German attempt to overthrow Hitler. Shortly after Berchtesgaden, Weizsäcker expressed fears that ultimately Chamberlain would come over to talk with Hitler: this would be bad, for a strong-fisted military man was needed to impress the fanatic Führer. On September 16 he said to Hassell that Chamberlain was definitely not strong enough; there was no British determination shown. According to Hassell, in those days even Göbbels seemed to side with the "moderates," as he feared that Hitler's and Ribbentrop's fanaticism would ruin Germany's chances. To the Polish Ambassador Hitler said five days later that he was surprised at Chamberlain's flight: he expected Chamberlain to tell him that any occupation attempt by force meant war with Britain. Instead, he almost heard the contrary. Daladier told the British Ambassador that he was disappointed: he, who was in favor of a Three-Power Conference, had had several occasions to meet Hitler but never wanted to do so without the British involved. And Mussolini hearing the news: "There

will be no war. But this is the end of British prestige."

Whether because of the British infidelities or the impressions which the visiting Lindbergh made on Bonnet, he broke down on that September 15. Phipps sent two extraordinary telegrams dealing with this unexpected French turn: "[Bonnet] seems completely to have lost his nerve and to be ready for any solution to avoid war." "M. Bonnet's collapse seems to me so sudden and so extraordinary that I am asking for an interview with M. Daladier."

9 — The German Embassy reported the great joy and relief with which Britain greeted the journey. On Chamberlain's flattery see *GD*, II, 786 ff. in the Berchtesgaden memorandum. Collate with Chamberlain's own notes and the German translator's, *BD*, II, 342 ff.; the notes of Sir Horace Wilson, p. 351, are instructive. Chamberlain upon his return: "They were very kind! I had a great time!" To his elder sister on the 19th: he saw "a side of Hitler that would surprise many people in this country" and: "I felt quite fresh and was delighted with the enthusiastic welcome of the crowds who were waiting in the rain, and who gave me the Nazi salute and shouted 'Heil!' at the tops of their voices all the way to the station." Keitel he called a "youngish, pleasant-faced, smart-looking soldier." Feiling, pp. 364–6.

10 — The Hungarian stand was not quite clear. On his own, the Hungarian War Minister secretly granted some airfield facilities for German aircraft, yet Göring protested to Sztójay on the 16th: "Hungary was not doing enough in the present crisis. The Hungarian press was keeping comparatively quiet. There was complete calm prevailing in the Hungarian minority districts in Czechoslovakia in contrast to the Sudeten ones. . . ." *GD*, II, 816.

11 — *GD*, II, 568; also another report by Heeren, the German envoy, on September 12, *ibid.*, pp. 747 ff. The Yugoslavs asked for British advice in September from Henderson. Such advice could only confirm Stoyadinovič' calculations.

12 — See *CLD*, p. 358 and *GD*, II, 803–5. On the same day Lord de la Warr of the British delegation at Geneva talked with Comnen, who said that Russia might pass through Rumania under certain conditions but there could be no definite agreement; anyhow, transport difficulties were immense. Poland and Yugoslavia were the countries to whose policy Rumania had to measure her own; especially Poland. He feared and distrusted Russia. *BD*, II, 354.

13 — Moravska-Ostrava in Czech — Mährisch-Ostrau in German.

14 — Appendix J in Wheeler-Bennett, *op. cit.*, compares the September 19 Anglo-French Plan, the later Godesberg demands, Czechoslovak comments, and the Munich terms.

15 — *Carnets secrets de Jean Zay* (Paris, 1942); also *BD*, II, 372–417. There was now a minor incident between London and Berlin: Hitler and Ribbentrop did not want to give Chamberlain a copy of the Berchtesgaden stenographic minutes: Hitler did not want to be committed to his then stated demands, nor to his statement that that was his last wish; no Polish Corridor, no Danzig. Henderson to Halifax on the 19th: "Public opinion under the influence of press reports seems now convinced that England and France will agree to plebiscite but that the Czechs will resist. In the circumstances fear and dislike of war have almost disappeared. Indeed in some circles prospect of punitive expedition against the Czechs seems to be looked forward to with pleasurable anticipation."

16 — Yet Henderson to Halifax on the 20th: ". . . I regard delay as dangerous . . . and I would rather the two great men [sic!] were together to deal with the situation which may arise . . . [Beneš] still clings to the hope of dragging us all down in his ruin. Folly or resentment, perhaps both." *BD*, II, 654–5. At that time Colonel Gauché, head of the French military intelligence office: "Of course there will be no European war, since we are not going to fight." Berlin learned of this statement.

17 — On this see the article by Táborsky, "Beneš and the Soviets," in *Foreign Affairs* (January 1949). Newton proposed that Britain and, if possible, the United States also should commend the Czechs when they accept: "If Czechoslovak public were made to realise that great Anglo-Saxon democracies thought decision a wise one in Czechoslovakia's own interest, it might make all the difference . . ."

18 — *IMT*, 1780–PS. The Germans had many diplomatic informants in Prague in the Bulgarian and Hungarian Legations; also the Rumanian military attaché was theirs.

19 — The Godesberg conversations are given in *GD*, II, 870 ff. and *BD*, II, 499 ff. In the afternoon of the 23rd tension was so great that Halifax instructed his Under-Secretary to contact Litvinov and find out about the Soviets' stand; at 6:00 P.M. he asked Phipps whether the French knew anything new. At Godesberg the often repeated device of Third Reich diplomacy came up with Ribbentrop suddenly entering the conference room and announcing dramatically that the Czechs had ordered general mobilization. Hitler let Attolico know — answering the Italian question of August 23 after a month's delay — that he would march on the 28th.

20 — *Ibid.*, p. 895. On the same day Wilson, the American envoy, to Under-Secretary Woermann of the German Foreign Office: "for his part, he greatly disapproved of the attitude of the [American] press. The United States was not in danger in any way and it did not become the American press to throw oil on the fire. He was requesting that the whole conversation should be strictly confidential." *Ibid.*, p. 893.

21 — Subsequently, on the 24th, the German Foreign Ministry asked Eisenlohr to mark on a map which districts he would like to be exempted from the blanket aerial bombardment of Prague. Yet on the same day the Director of the European Division of the Czechoslovak Foreign Ministry told the German chargé that in his opinion Beneš and the Sýrový government were ready to cede, if only Germany left the rest of Czechoslovakia alone to live as an independent state. *GD*, II, 921.

22 — There was a stiff British note to Budapest and Warsaw on the 22nd, requesting these governments to be more moderate with their insistences. Kánya promised to take the British wish into consideration; Beck did not. Villani, the Hungarian Minister to Rome, informed Ciano on the same day that Hungary would not leave her minorities and would go even so far as to provoke incidents in Slovakia for a *casus foederis*. All right, said Ciano, but Hungary should watch lest Yugoslavia and Rumania have cause to intervene. Villani said that she would naturally do so.

23 — *CD*, p. 244; *CLD*, p. 364. Zamfirescu also told Ciano that in a Polish-Russian war Rumania would side with Poland at once. Comnen, traversing Yugoslav territory coming back from Geneva, said essentially the same to Stoyadinovič on the 25th.

24 — On the 22nd the Prague government suspended the Czech Communist newspaper, and arrested a few Communists, fearing a rising. On the same day the members of the Spanish Republican colony (all Communists) left Prague for Moscow: a sign obviously not encouraging to those who counted on Russian military intervention.

25 — See Bonnet, Noël, *Documents and Materials . . . op. cit.* French intervention was followed by a British one on the 26th, informing Poland that if she would give a "guarantee of benevolent neutrality" toward Czechoslovakia, the cession of Teschen could be arranged. *BD*, II, 545. Namier shows documents and a detailed treatment of Czech-Polish relations from September 21 to 30, p. 285 ff. Titulescu, Noël, and other sources often hinted at the possibility of a secret Beck-Hitler agreement, a supplement to the 1934 Pact, and concerning an eventual partition of Czechoslovakia; but there is no evidence of this.

On the other hand, Hungary showed a certain restraint in these days. On January 16, 1939, Hitler received Csáky and assailed Kánya: "an enemy of Germany . . . Hungary slept at Munich. . . . If Hungary, at the opportune time would have acted in concert with him [Hitler], he could have laughed in the face of Chamberlain." (*Documents Secrets . . . Hongrie*) Mussolini to Ciano on January 16, 1939: "These Hungarians . . . didn't have the courage to act when they could have acted, and now they carry on like Jesuits."

26 — Gamelin, *op. cit.*, p. 357. He in 1936 asked the Polish and Czech General Staffs to consider a double-flanked attack upon Silesia. See his letter to General Faucher, military attaché to Prague and a great friend of the Czechs.

27 — He also spoke on that day of the "small but noisy corrupt war group" in Paris, whereafter Halifax rebuked him. See *BD*, II, 510, 544.

28 — The September 25 talks are recorded in *BD*, II, 520 ff.; the 26th, pp. 536 ff.

29 — Independent observers, among them Henderson, observed that the following incident on September 25 had a great effect on Hitler: an armored division passed through Berlin streets; Hitler watched it from the balcony of the Chancellery and noticed with evident anxiety the apathetic behavior of the Berlin population toward the soldiers in battledress.

30 — The Wilson-Hitler talks in *BD*, II, 554 ff. Berlin set the date for the announcement of total mobilization for 2:00 P.M. September 28; "X-Day" was advanced tentatively to the 30th.

31 — The anti-war partisans in Paris immediately sprang into action: Flandin, for one, had a manifesto printed which sporadically appeared on the walls of Paris.

32 — *GD*, II, 963 ff. At the end, Wilson told Hitler, alone, "I will still try to make these Czechs sensible."

33 — Henderson, *Failure of a Mission* (London, 1939), p. 19, and Wheeler-Bennett, p. 151. It is an open question why Hitler envisaged Monday (October 3) when before he had announced that he would attack on the 1st.

34 — *BD*, II, 562. The exact sequence of what happened in Rome is laid down in a subsequent summary telegram of Perth on the 30th, *ibid.*, pp. 641 ff.

35 — The German chargé in Moscow correctly remarked: "Thereby the Soviet endeavor to enter into the negotiations of the European Great Powers once again became manifest."

36 — The Czechoslovak Foreign Ministrys' record on Munich is given in *Documents and Materials, op. cit.*, nos. 34, 36, 37. The most reliable stenographic minute is in *BD*, II, 1003 ff. On the plebiscite idea and the sequence of events see *ibid.*, p. 1005, n. 10 and 1011 ff. See also the account of Th. Kordt in *GD*, IV, 293 ff.

37 — Polish national sentiment ran so high over Teschen that even the half-exiled Paderewski and the opposition Socialists approved the subsequent rapid occupation of that area. But it had a bad impression elsewhere: even in Rome one heard of "Polish greediness." On the day of Munich, however, Beck informed Brussels confidentially (Polish-Belgian relations were very good and close throughout the crisis) that, in his view, Munich set a very bad precedent.

On the 29th the Slovaks bombarded Hitler with telegrams: "Mr. Chancellor, we believe in you."

Indirect effects of the Czechoslovak crisis

1 — Having carefully assessed the cautious Russian behavior during the crisis, it was in the Baltic area and in Bulgaria where, notwithstanding the ideological dog-fights of the German and Soviet radio and press, it was envisaged that a future German-Russian agreement over eastern Europe would be indeed feasible.

2 — *GD*, II, 571.

3 — On Italy's plans and wishful thinking regarding the Balkans, see an informant's memorandum to the German Ambassador to Rome, *GD*, I, 1121–4; also *CD, CLD*.

4 — Previously, in 1937, the French ceded the Sanjak of Hatay (Alexandrette) to Turkey in order to put an end to minor but chronic disagreement between the two states.

5 — Typical Balkan disturbances continued to occur sporadically during 1938. On July 30, a minor Venizelist revolution of the Greek Navy broke out, but was quickly suppressed. On October 10, IMRO murdered the Bulgarian General Peëv.

BETWEEN GERMAN HAMMER AND RUSSIAN ANVIL
(*1939–1941*)

The results of Munich

1 — The October 1938 to March 1939 period is covered in Chapter II of *GD*, IV; also in *BD*, III–IV.

2 — In 1918 it caused wide surprise that the Carpatho-Ukraine came to be part of Czechoslovakia; on October 18, 1918, in Philadelphia, Masaryk and a Carpatho-Ukrainian "leader," Zatkovič, agreed that it would form a completely autonomous unit.

3 — Komarno in Czech and Slovak — Komárom in Hungarian — Komorn in German.

4 — Ipolyság in Hungarian — Sahý in Czech and Slovak.

5 — Sátoraljaujhely "kisállomás" in Hungarian — S. Nové Mesto in Czech and Slovak.

6 — As were many continentals, Bárdossy, Ribbentrop, Darlan and others, Chvalkovsky was anti-English because of his experience with snobbery and provincialism when in England. He told Ciano that he had studied in London and at a party there had been given a violin to play — for he was a Czech and the English confounded Bohemians with Gypsies.

On the other hand, when a strong British protest was handed to Kánya on October 8, the Hungarian Foreign Minister asked the British Minister why his Government used such language only with Hungary, why not with Germany or Poland, the greater powers?

And on October 26 a Foreign Office note to Paris and Rome stated that Britain would be "happy to see the Czechoslovak and Hungarian governments to settle their differences by reference to arbitration by the Italian and German Goverments."

7 — *CD*, p. 280; *CLD*, p. 374. Next day Villani intimated that the Duke of Aosta might, under certain circumstances, ascend the throne of Hungary. Ribbentrop was very badly informed on the issues, and Ciano was comforted. In Vienna, Ciano remarked to him: "The way you defend Czech interests, you may get an order from the Czech President." On the first outline map, pencil lines were drawn for the new frontier. First Ciano drew a line; then Ribbentrop drew one underneath; then Ciano again. There was a lot of erasing and re-drawing, and, according to the interpreter Schmidt, "the pencils got duller and duller and the frontier lines thicker and thicker."

The record of the conference which Göring had with Slovak leaders on October 16 very much weakens the case of those who argue for the honesty and decency of the Slovak Nationalists in 1938. Cf. *GD*, IV, 82–3.

8 — The partition of Czechoslovakia took these proportions:

Germany received the Sudetenland and other contiguous minor German-speaking territories, 28,200 square kilometers, approximately 3.6 million inhabitants;

Poland received the Teschen (Olza) territory and certain frontier areas in the Tatra mountains, 1,050 square kilometers, approximately 0.3 million inhabitants;

Hungary received a stretch of southern Slovakia and of southern Carpatho-Ukraine, 12,400 square kilometers, approximately 1.05 million inhabitants.

9 — See *IMT*, 136–C; also 138–C. An additional directive was issued on December 12: "preparations . . . are to be continued on the assumption that no resistance worth mentioning is to be expected."

10 — *Documents and Materials . . . op. cit.,* no. 43.

11 — Ribbentrop on November 20 asked Ciano to have Rome intervene with the Hungarians, accusing them of anti-Axis plans. François-Poncet, now Ambassador to Rome, warned his Hungarian colleague not to confide too much in Italy, which had abandoned one of her allies already. Villani did not agree and told this to Ciano.

12 — *IMT*, 2906–PS.

13 — Of course, this was not the idea of a Beck-Imrédy-Stoyadinovic *bloc,* but rather that of the conservatives around Moscicki and Smigly-Rydz, Admiral Horthy and Prince Paul. Rumania objected, rather narrow-mindedly. Even Ciano did not understand the Rumanians' wrangling against the Polish-Hungarian common frontier idea: "It would be a barrier in their favor," he said. "In our situation, we cannot tell this to them." On October 8 Weizsäcker remonstrated with the Hungarian Minister and threatened Hungary with harsh words. The Ger-

manophile Sztójay was intimidated to such extent that he begged Weizsäcker to consider their conversation as not having taken place. *GD,* IV, 434.

On October 14 the volatile Csáky was dispatched to Rome, where he complained against the Germans; Mussolini ordered Ciano to let the Germans know this, as he himself was not in favor of the Polish-Hungarian frontier idea. Ciano did so, but with a sorry heart. *CD,* pp. 269–70. On the same day, October 15, Rome intervened with Prague for the lives of the captured Hungarian free-troopers, whom the Czechs then let go, knowing that their execution would menace the position of the relatively still moderate Imrédy government in Hungary.

14 — *IMT*, 3638–PS. also *GD,* IV, 40. See also the memorandum of the Political Department of the Foreign Office to Hitler on October 7, examining Slovak and Carpatho-Ukrainian alternatives: "An independent Slovakia would be weak constitutionally and would therefore best further the German need for penetration and settlement in the east. Point of least resistance in the east." German-language enclaves to be left there, "as they are of value as a nucleus for further development in the east." Summary: "From [all] this results a rejection of the Hungarian or Polish solution for Slovakia as well as for Carpatho-Ukraine. In rejecting the demands of both these powers we would have a good slogan in the phrase 'self-determination.' For the outside world no anti-Hungarian or anti-Polish slogans are to be issued. . . . Steps can be taken to influence leading persons in Slovakia and in the Carpatho-Ukraine in favor of our solution. Preparations for this are already on foot." *GD,* IV, 46 ff.

15 — The German White Book No. 1 (published in the winter of 1939) gave

minutes of the Ribbentrop-Lipski talk, omitting Ribbentrop's proposal for a joint German-Polish front against the Soviets.

16 — See *Documents and Materials . . . op. cit.*, no. 44. Raczynski's report to Beck is an excellent account of British trends in public opinion during the winter months of 1938–39.

17 — Polish government newspapers, for example, seemed to approve Italian claims voiced against France in December.

18 — It was often intimated that Bonnet promised a free hand in eastern Europe to Ribbentrop during an unscheduled and unguarded visit to the Louvre. "No one will know their secret," says "Pertinax" (*The Gravediggers of France*, New York, 1944). Today we have the German memorandum of the Ribbentrop-Bonnet conversations (*GD*, IV, 471 ff.). The misunderstandings might have occurred also because Ribbentrop spoke German and French alternately. Bonnet's reference was to French disinterest in Czechoslovakia, but Ribbentrop understood the whole of East Europe instead, including Poland. See n. 1 in *GD*, IV, 471; also p. 494. Bonnet in his memoirs maintains that he had scarcely the chance to be alone with Ribbentrop, as he had to rush to greet Prince Paul who was passing through Paris on that afternoon. Moreover, Ribbentrop had not yet settled down after his return to Berlin when on December 10 Coulondre was instructed to ask the German Foreign Office whether rumors concerning a German occupation of Memel were true. On the other hand, according to Schmidt, p. 424, Bonnet actually did say on December 6 that France was now disinterested in eastern Europe; the then relatively unknown Georges Bidault wrote in the Catholic *L'Aube* that there was reason to believe "our frontier is now recognized and guaranteed so that other frontiers in Europe may be destroyed." And Bonnet said to Lukasiewicz on December 17 that he "regretted the remaining eastern alliances of France."

19 — The Lahousen Affidavit (*IMT*-Affidavit A) reveals that a special purpose squadron of the German Armed Forces ("Rowahls") was operating from late 1938 on; aerial reconnaissance was performed over London and Leningrad during the winter of 1938–39; German fliers in mufti operated from airfields in Hungary with the silent permission of the German-born General Werth, Hungarian Chief-of-Staff, acting behind the back of the Hungarian government. From these fields they undertook reconnaissance flights in the Balkans and in Southern Russia.

20 — A high Soviet functionary told the Italian Ambassador early in October 1938 of the possibility of a Russo-German agreement against Poland.

21 — The story of Imrédy is a strange and significant one. An erstwhile Anglophile and conservative, he was impressed by Axis might and solidarity in the summer. Back from Berlin, in early September he made an extremely pro-German speech. The opposition leader, Eckhardt, just back from his summer vacation, rushed to him with surprise. What had happened? "You can't deal with the British," said the bitter Imrédy; "they have written us off to Germany"; he then told the following story: Upon his return from Germany, a correspondent of the London *Daily Telegraph*, strongly recommended to him by British diplomats, called and asked whether Hungary was now going to follow the Hitler road without reservations. Not at all, said Imrédy, and emphasized very strongly his country's political and spiritual independence; so strongly indeed, that he requested his conversant, who clearly had diplomatic connections, to keep this talk confidential. A week later the German Minister called on him and requested information on alleged anti-German statements which Imrédy made to the British. Upon the latter's denial, the German produced a memorandum, citing Imrédy's exact words and threatened to turn the paper over to the Prime Minister's native Nazi opposition. There is some evidence that a copy of the British report of the conversation between Imrédy and the London journalist was sent to Henderson in Berlin, who in turn informed the Germans.

On January 18, 1939, Ciano expressed his satisfaction to Mackensen that Csáky had succeeded Kánya, whose "Ballhausplatz mentality" had made "many things impossible."

22 — Munkács in Hungarian, Mukačevo in Czech, Slovak and Carpatho-Ukrainian.

Hitler's fatal step: the occupation of Prague. — Memel

1 — Later, in August, when the British determination to fight became evident, he accused Ribbentrop because of his advice to deal with the Czechs first and only then with Poland.

2 — *GD*, IV, 494–5 on Coulondre; *IMT*, 2795–PS on the Hitler-Tuka-Karmasin conference.

3 — On the same day Chamberlain wrote of "the thrush singing in the garden, of spring being near. All the information I get seems to point in the direction of peace." Feiling, p. 396.

4 — Engerau in German — Petržalka in Czech and Slovak — Pozsonyligetfalu in Hungarian. This village belonged

to Hungary before 1920, and certain anti-German Hungarian nationalist organs made political capital out of its incorporation into Germany in November 1938. This was one of the reasons why Hitler assailed Hungary during the Csáky visit.

5 — See *IMT*, 2802–PS on the Hitler-Tiso "conference." Flying back to Bratislava next morning, he bought the text of a Slovak independence proclamation which, according to a number of sources, was drafted partly by Ribbentrop. Tiso, of course, was but a narrow-minded patriot: "When Tiso wanted to reach something for his Slovakia, he would surely go to the devil himself." Schmidt, *op. cit.*, p. 540. See also the report of the German chargé in Prague on March 7 about the Slovak tactics. Slovak Nationalists had expressed fear that, "under pressure from the Vatican, the Slovak government will in the end reach agreement with Prague." *GD*, IV, 226–7.

6 — *IMT*, 2816–PS.

7 — The procedure which Hitler followed with Hácha was similar to that which he followed with Schuschnigg in Berchtesgaden in February, 1938 (the threats, etc.), and to that with Horthy in March 1944 (keeping his "guest" with him until the German troops marched in, thus paralyzing all chances of potential armed resistance). See *IMT*, 2798–PS on the Hitler-Hácha "conference," 3842–PS on the German occupation, 2826–PS on the rôle of the SS on March 15.

8 — On the Slovak Protection Treaty and the Secret Protocol see *IMT*, 1439–PS, 2793–PS. On April 23 the *Frankfurter Zeitung* attempted to excuse the German incorporation of the Protectorate with these words: "Facts of geography, history and political realities play today an equal rôle with the

principle of national self-determina-tion." But by April 23 it was too late; moreover, the *Frankfurter Zeitung* did not necessarily express the official German attitude.

9 — Slovak-Hungarian frontier incidents continued; on March 25, the "Slovak Air Force" bombed the Hungarian city of Rozsnyó. By the end of that month a joint agreement established the new frontier.

10 — On March 15–16, Monsignor Volo-sin, the "President" of Carpatho-Ukraine, offered to hand his country over to Rumania, but Bucharest did not take advantage of the offer, being preoccupied with the danger of a possible joint German-Hungarian pres-sure. Volosin then repaired to Berlin, while Revaj, his "Premier," went to Bucharest.

11 — Chamberlain's biographer does not say that the Birmingham speech was due to Halifax's intervention. On March 18 the King wrote to Cham-berlain approving of the Birmingham speech. The speech pleasantly sur-prised Churchill and unpleasantly the Germans; the influential *Deutsche Allgemeine Zeitung* wrote on the 18th: "Does or does not Britain wish to recognize Germany's continental posi-tion in Europe? . . ."

12 — However, the German pressure for a German-Rumanian economic treaty was neither in the character of an ultimatum nor was it precipitated by the mid-March events. Tilea was reprimanded by Gafencu. (Later, he was the first Rumanian diplomat to go into exile.)

13 — On March 28, a Soviet declaration was given to Latvia to the effect that Soviet Russia wished to see the con-tinued and complete independence of that country.

Mussolini's Albanian venture

1 — See L. Mondini, *Prologo del conflitto italo-greco* (Rome, 1946); also *CLD* and *The Ciano Diaries* (New York, 1946) (*CD*–NY further).

2 — Two years later, in 1941, Germany tried to lure the Yugoslavs with the same bait of Salonika, again unsuc-cessfully.

3 — Chamberlain at the same time (Jan-uary 15): "I found [Mussolini] straightforward and considerate in his behaviour to us and moreover he has a sense of humour which is quite attractive . . ." Feiling, *op. cit.*, p. 393.

4 — Referring to the anti-French demon-strations in the Italian Chamber a month before, when a "spontaneous" demonstration took place: for Corsica, Tunis, Nice!

5 — See M. Toscano, *Le origini del patto d'acciaio* (Florence, 1948), pp. 98–9, n. 112; also *CD*–NY, Donosti.

6 — Göring related a similar story to Ciano a month later. See *CLD*, p. 420; also *IMT*, 1874–PS.

7 — The wife of Zog, Queen Geraldine, was expecting a baby. Ciano: "I cannot imagine Geraldine running around fighting through the mountains of Unthi or of Mirdizu in her ninth month of pregnancy . . ."

8 — According to Donosti, the Yugoslav Minister asked on the 5th if Yugo-slavia might occupy a part of northern Albania; he was told, no, for in the next few days Italy should occupy all. The Yugoslavs did not insist, and this surprised Mussolini and Ciano. The record in *CLD* does not quite bear this out. It is a fact, nevertheless, that on April 4 Ciano instructed all Italian diplomatic posts abroad to give a slight anti-German slant to the occupation of Albania. (See Toscano, p. 110.) The German Ambassador was not informed by Rome until the morning of the 6th; on the 15th Ciano informed certain Italian diplomatic missions that the Albanian action was taken to countermand the growing German interest in the Adriatic.

9 — An Albanian delegation, headed by Bey Verlaci, came to Rome on April 16 to offer the Albanian crown to King Victor Emmanuel. Ciano noted their uneasiness and "depressed" look. A comic episode occurred when the Albanian Minister to Sofia telegraphed that he recognized the Italian occupation of his country, whereupon he was informed that he should be Albanian Foreign Minister; then, within a few hours Ciano decided that Italian-Albania would have no Foreign Minister at all.

10 — Halifax was pressed by certain people in London to occupy Corfu to counterbalance Italy's naval gains with Albania; when Grandi asked him about such rumors, the Foreign Secretary answered that this was "not the sort of thing we did." Feiling, p. 404.

11 — *CD*, p. 63–4.

The origins of the Moscow Pact

1 — See the Dirksen Papers (*Documents and Materials . . . op. cit.*, vol. II) also his *Moskau-Tokio-London* (Stuttgart, 1949).

2 — See Comnen, *op. cit.*, and the letters of Papée, the Polish Minister in Prague to him. On October 20, Beck and King Carol met at Galatz but they did not come to a full agreement. Yet Beck, returning to Warsaw, instructed the Polish press to hint at the conclusion of an agreement. He desired to bring the consent of Bucharest to the Polish-Hungarian partition of

Carpatho-Ukraine, of which the southeastern part (Apsa), partly Rumanian-inhabited, was promised to Rumania. The latter refused. After Galatz, Carol met Regent Paul on November 8 (a week after the Vienna Award), again concentrating on Hungary instead of discussing a broader Danubian plan of anti-German resistance. Then Carol went to London, and he and Comnen listened to the noncommittal British; at Paris, his reception was somewhat more successful, at least on the surface: Bonnet decided to elevate the French diplomatic representation in Rumania from Legation to Embassy rank. Carol met Hitler on his way back from Paris; this was an unscheduled and friendly meeting, at which both agreed on opposing the Polish-Hungarian common frontier. Encouraged by the friendly talks with Hitler, Carol gave orders to "liquidate" Codreanu and his staff, which liquidation took place on November 30 at Jilava. Here Carol's calculations misfired again: Hitler would never forgive him the Codreanu murder.

3 — See Göbbels, *Tagebücher* (Zurich, 1948). Göbbels on October 23, 1925: "And if it comes to an end, let us rather go down together with Bolshevism than tightly enchained by Capitalism . . ." On January 31, 1926: "I find it horrible that the communists and we are cracking each other's heads . . . where could we once get together with leading Communists?" On February 15, 1926, after a Hitler speech: "I am browbeaten. Hitler [speaks] about Italian and British alliances. . . . My heart aches so . . . I would like to cry."

4 — Chamberlain himself said this to Comnen.

5 — This fantastic information was given to Hitler by Oshima on January 31, 1939. See *IMT*, 2195–PS. In 1938, a wholesale purge in the Crimea resulted

in the almost complete liquidation of the Greek ethnic group in that region.

6 — Langer-Gleason, *op. cit.*, pp. 174–5. Perhaps this is somewhat exaggerated. Cf. the article of Rosso in the *Rivista di studi politici internazionali* (1946), p. 9.

7 — Cf. *BD*, Series III, vol. IV, Appendix III; also the Seeds telegram, pp. 188–9. It is clear that, contrary to the generally held view (a view advanced as late as 1949 by Professor Namier), the onus of not having explored closely enough the possibilities of a Western-Soviet alliance in March 1939 does not necessarily fall on British shoulders. A close look at Russian attitudes casts grave doubts on the seriousness of any general proposal emanating from Maisky and Litvinov.

Ribbentrop raised his point about Japan with the alleged attention of easing Japan's military position and making her come into a military alliance. See Toscano, p. 70.

8 — In spite of the complete reversal of Britain, Moscow was still not convinced of the sincerity of Halifax. (The British *de facto* "acquiesced in" if not "recognized" the German occupation of Czechoslovakia by applying for the consular *exequatur* in Berlin instead of Prague.)

9 — Preliminary phase: April 17 to May 30. Tentative phase: May 30 to August 14. Final phase: August 14 to 21. Conclusion: August 21–22. Enlargement and final delimitation: September 3 to 29.

On April 18 Davies suddenly cabled Roosevelt and Hull and made the rather unusual and dramatic proposal that he, who had gotten along so well with Stalin, might be sent to Moscow to expedite a British-Russian Pact. The State Department advised against this proposal. Cf. *The Soviet Union 1933–1939*, p. 756.

10 — *Nazi-Soviet Relations* (Washington, 1948) (further *NSR*), pp. 12 ff.

11 — Gafencu: *The Last Days of Europe* (New Haven, 1949), p. 188. Both Potemkin and Halifax asked Gafencu about the meaning of the Polish-Rumanian Pact: was it against any aggressor, or operative only if the Soviet attacked one of the signatories. The latter was the case. For having granted asylum to the Polish leaders in September, the latter released Bucharest from her treaty obligations after the Soviet attack on Poland: but Rumania would not have fought anyhow.

12 — On that day, Mussolini gave these directives to Ciano, departing for Germany: "Politics with Russia? — To avoid the Russian adherence to the [Western] *bloc*, yes; but otherwise no, as such a policy, clearly contrary to our present attitude would not be understood by the Axis nations and would weaken their ties. . . . General attitude: To speak of peace and prepare for war." Toscano, p. 143. Already on May 5 Rosso analyzed the Russian position very well in a telegram to Ciano.

13 — Note the first use of the word "antitotalitarian" (e.g., *including* Russia with the Axis and Japan).

14 — See *CLD*, *op. cit.* The following were discussed in Milan: *Bulgaria* (her joining a Balkan Pact should be prevented); *Military pact between the Axis powers* (signed sixteen days later — "steel pact"); *South Tyrol problems of the German minority; Greece:* Ribbentrop considered Greece unimportant for the time being and insisted that the King (pro-British) be removed somehow, while the Crown Prince had allegedly strong Germanophile sym-

pathies; *Yugoslavia:* its *status quo* should be maintained; *Poland:* the Poles are "hysterical," said Ribbentrop. Upon Ciano's prodding, he agreed that Italy would need four to five years to be prepared. The German did not reveal his war plans for another four months; only on August 12, at Salzburg, did he say to Ciano the fatal words: "We want war!"

15 — Herr "X" was Herr Bömer of the Wilhelmstrasse, who had the reputation of speaking too much when consuming alcohol. He was later arrested. (General Bodenschatz of the *Luftwaffe* confirmed what Bömer said; and on July 4 the French Consul in Hamburg gave detailed information on German-Russian talks.) On May 17, Davies reported to Washington the possibility of German-Russian contacts, noting all kinds of rumors. See also the opinions of Erich Koch, Gauleiter of East Prussia, reproduced by Renzetti — a cold-blooded analysis of the propitious (and anti-Polish) chances of Nazi-Soviet collaboration. It is reprinted in Toscano, *L'Italia e gli accordi tedesco-sovietici dell' agosto 1939* (Firenze, 1952), p. 29, n. 34-bis.

16 — See *IMT*, 79–L. "We shall not repeat the Czech affair. There will be war."

17 — There is some evidence from a document first cited in A. Rossi, *Deux ans d'alliance germano-soviétique* (Paris, 1949), that the German directives for a far-reaching agreement with Russia were laid down some time between May 23 and 26. The Italian Ambassador reported from Moscow on the 24th that a Russo-German deal was indeed possible and would mean a fourth partition of Poland. See Rosso's article in the *Rivista di studi politici internazionali*, vol. I, 1946. This registered with Mussolini, who on May 30 wrote to Hitler: "1. War between the plutocratic, thus egotistically conservative nations and the populous poor nations

is inevitable. Given this premise, we have to prepare ourselves." On May 26, however, the cautious Attolico suggested from Berlin that instead of a rapprochement with Russia, stronger ties with Japan seemed to be preferable. Ribbentrop was not impressed with this argument. Cf. Toscano, *L'Italia e gli [accordi, op. cit.,* whence it transpires that Attolico had generally been prone to underestimate the chances of a thorough Russo-German agreement.

Development of the Polish crisis

1 — Meanwhile, anti-German student demonstrations in Warsaw gave a strange color to Ciano's visit; the latter recorded cool, drab, pallid impressions of Poland which he carried over to his Diaries and Memoranda: "The Poles are more interested in our art than in our way of living. They know our monuments better than our history. Too many [artists] have represented Italy in Poland in the past, and continue to represent us with the inevitable servility of the artist who, in distant lands, finds a foreign Maecenas." *CD–NY*, p. 34.

2 — On March 23, a German-Rumanian agreement providing for extended commercial relations was signed. Although it contained possibilities of wide German economic penetration of Rumania, it was yet not such a great German advance as was anticipated by Tilea and alarmists.

3 — Churchill, *The Gathering Storm* (Boston, 1948), Houghton Mifflin, p. 347.

4 — Namier, *Diplomatic Prelude* (London, 1946), pp. xiii–xiv.

5 — IMT, 120–C; 126–C.

6 — Beck in London also expressed his distrust of Russia, and Chamberlain understood him: "I confess I very much agree with him, for I regard

Russia as a very unreliable friend . . . with an enormous irritative power on others." Feiling, p. 408. Cf. Beck, *Dernier rapport: politique polonaise 1926–1939* (Neuchâtel, 1951). Beck, because of Hungary, also rejected the idea of a Polish-Rumanian military alliance.

7 — Gafencu, *The Last Days of Europe* (New Haven, 1948), p. 17.

8 — It is doubtful whether such an offer was made; there is no record thereof. But Hitler might have been toying with the idea. On March 25 it was recorded by Brauchitsch (*IMT*, 100–R) "How long the Führer considers himself to be bound by the treaty concluded with Slovakia is open to doubt." (The "Protection Treaty" was signed two days before!) "The Führer [will] free himself of this obligation when the time comes, and . . . he will use Slovakia as an asset for bargaining between himself, Poland, and Hungary. For the time being, however, brakes should be put on Hungary."

9 — He again had Italian hopes, not wholly without reason. Ciano informed Warsaw on May 12 that Rome wished to see a German-Polish reconciliation, although he added that Poland should not nurture illusions, for Italy would stand by Germany if a European war resulted. See Toscano, p. 166, n. 215.

10 — Miroszlav Arciszewski, not to be confounded with Tomasz Arciszewski, later Premier-in-Exile and leader of the Polish Socialist Party.

11 — *IMT*, 79–L. Another evidence that Hitler wanted to go to war as early as September 1938.

Broadening of the Polish crisis: the international scene

1 — In March Litvinov again proposed the lease of Suursari and other islands in the Finnish gulf; in return, he offered a Soviet consent to the Aalands' remilitarization. A Soviet diplomat, Stein, appeared in Helsinki in early April to sound the Finnish government out on this issue and left with empty hands on the 6th.

2 — Hugh Dalton, *Hitler's War — Before and After* (London, 1940), p. 114, quoted in Namier, *op. cit.*

3 — German White Book; *Auswärtiges Amt No. 3 — Polnische Dokumente zur Vorgeschichte des Krieges* (Berlin, 1939).

4 — Poland was not mentioned by Maisky; the British inserted Poland in their draft.

5 — Churchill maintains in his memoirs that notwithstanding the Soviets' designs and obstacles, the Western Powers should have made the alliance with them in the summer of 1939; difficulties would have been ironed out later, if it came to war. But this is a very hypothetical, questionable argument.

Professor Namier's conclusion (*In The Nazi Era*, p. 171) is interesting: "The conclusion which emerges from Coulondre's survey is that those who, from a loathing of the Bolsheviks or from of fear of displeasing Hitler, refused to play the Russian card against him, cannot cite the present world position (1952) for their justification. The card they threw away was picked up by Hitler, and enabled him to bring on the war from which either the Nazis or the Bolsheviks were bound to emerge preponderant, no longer counterbalancing each other." There is much truth in this, though not the entire truth. For in view of the Munich evidence the question arises (and the papers in the forthcoming *BD*, vol. V, dealing with the 1939 Anglo-Russian negotiations, seem to justify the raising of the question): was there a real

Russian card to be thrown away?
Was it in the deck?

6 — That his offer of a triple Slovak "condominium" which he mentioned at
Wilhelmshaven was never real could
be seen from his references to Hungary.
The military directive of April 3
stated that Hungary could not be considered as a certain ally; to Gafencu,
Hitler expressed his view: "a greater
Hungary might be embarrassing to the
Reich." The Teleki government again
made one step forward and another
back; to impress Germany, Csáky
announced on April 11 that Hungary
left the League of Nations (she continued to maintain her seat at the
International Labour Office and the
Hague Court). At the end of April,
Csáky and Teleki visited Hitler; then,
when the Hungarian elections in May
showed a surprising gain in the popularity of the Arrow-Cross movement,
Teleki and his energetic Minister of
Interior, Keresztes-Fischer, cracked
down on Germany's internal allies
strongly.

7 — The Yugoslavs tried in vain to play
the two Axis partners against each
other when the new Yugoslav Foreign
Minister, Tsintsar-Markovič, visited
Hitler in April.

8 — Rumanian-Italian relations were good;
Gafencu was asked by Paris in early
May to convey French goodwill to
Rome; he executed this unfruitful
mission with skill. Also, Ciano seemed
to have liked him personally.

9 — Ribbentrop asked Ciano at Milan to
prevent Bulgaria's joining a Balkan
bloc with Turkey, and Ciano instructed his envoy to Sofia in this sense
on May 30, adding that if Bulgaria
stayed in close relationship with Italy,
"she might get something for herself."
At the same time the Ciano Diaries:
"Mussolini thinks more and more of
attacking Greece at the first suitable
opportunity." (The exact same expression: "first suitable opportunity"
is used in the German military directive against Poland — an interesting
coincidence.)

10 — De Monzie, *op. cit.*, p. 124. Schulen-
berg on June 5 ventured the opinion
that Potemkin was sent to Ankara to
prevent the Turks from signing with
England in a hurry.

11 — Namier: "To sum up: to gain Russia's
cooperation the Western Powers would
have had to convince her [among
others] ... of their readiness to acknowledge Russia's primacy in Eastern
Europe and to acquiesce in the use
which she would make of it; altogether
of a *bienveillance* which she had no
right to expect, nor herself any reason
to feel." *Europe in Decay* (London,
1950), p. 244. On June 11 even the
Italian Minister to Afghanistan reported his opinions about the possibilities of a German-Russian agreement.

12 — Perhaps for the sake of planting false
impressions, the Soviet Ambassador
was absent from Berlin throughout the
whole summer of 1939.

13 — *NSR*, pp. 20–1. (Italics mine.) It is,
however, clear that even before the
Astakhov-Draganov contacts, Schulenburg had progressed to the point where
he could begin clarifying the question
of "political conditions" mentioned
by Molotov and Mikoyan. See the
analysis of Toscano, *op. cit.*, p. 50.
It is also possible that through their
master spy, Sorge, in Tokyo, the
Russians were being informed of
Hitler's sincere inclination to make an
arrangement with them. On June 14
even Göring told the Italian Renzetti,
who had recently arrived in Berlin
from Moscow, that Germany would
profit far more from a Russian than
from a Japanese alliance.

14 — During the Wohltat-Wilson conversations there was even talk of an Anglo-
German Non-Aggression Pact. "The

underlying principle of this treaty was to make it possible for the British gradually to disembarrass themselves of their commitments toward Poland. . . . In addition, a pact of non-intervention was to be signed, which was to be in a way a wrapper for a delimitation of the spheres of interest of the Great Powers." *Documents and Materials, op. cit.*, vol. II, The Dirksen Papers. According to his biographer, Chamberlain in July again toyed with the idea of mediation, now between Germany and Poland: all he asked for was patience from Hitler. He was ready, through Mussolini, to propose a year's truce. But when the United States Senate rejected Roosevelt's proposal to amend the Neutrality Act in July, he wrote to Lord Tweedsmuir: "this . . . is enough to make one weep."

15 — On August 19, 1939, Dirksen sent a summary memorandum to Ribbentrop on Britain's position. Ten days later — after he asked Ribbentrop in vain to receive him — he made a written survey of his ambassadorship. It is not impossible that his pride was hurt by Ribbentrop's evasion and hence he was wont to overestimate these British gestures: that there is not too much evidence of a British-German "collusion" in the summer of 1939 might be deduced from the fact that the Soviet government, which published the Dirksen Papers, included such inconsequential documents as a report of Ow-Wachendorf, the German Minister in Cairo, dated May 3, to Dirksen and reproducing the minister's conversation with a Mrs. Smart: ". . . it is a pity that you did not move into Prague at the same time you entered Vienna," said this Mrs. Smart.

16 — See Gaus Affidavit at Nuremberg, *IMT* — Supplement B. The French Consul in Hamburg on July 4 reported to Paris an almost complete and precise draft of the German-Soviet Non-Aggression Treaty.

17 — Procopé, *op. cit.* On July 18 Bullitt reported from Paris his views about Russia. These were very pessimistic; also Daladier had remarked to him that, after a war, the European Powers, having "torn each other thoroughly to pieces, the Russians might advance and conquer all Europe in the interest of Bolshevism." Langer-Gleason, pp. 123–4. Also Halifax in retrospect, on December 5, 1939, in the Commons: "I think that events have shown that the judgment and instincts of the British Government in refusing agreement with the Soviet Government covering cases of indirect aggression on the Baltic States were right, for it is now claimed that these formulas might have been the cloak of ulterior designs, and I have little doubt that the people of this country would prefer to face difficulties and embarrassments rather than feel that we had compromised the honour of this country and the Commonwealth." Hansard, *Commons Debates*. By permission of the Controller of Her Britannic Majesty's Stationery Office.

18 — On German economic policies and pressure in the summer of 1939 concerning deliveries to the Balkans see for example *IMT*, 133–R.

19 — See the report of the British Consul in Danzig; *IMT*, 71–C; also the Polish White Book. But there were some Polish atrocities, of course.

20 — On the Salzburg talks see *CD–NY, CLD*, Donosti, *op. cit.;* also *IMT*, 77–TC, 1871–PS. Ribbentrop: British armed intervention may be excluded. He claimed that he knew "British psychology." This did not influence Ciano very much, who noted that during their talks Ribbentrop was apt to confound Slovenia with Slovakia. (See Hassell, *op. cit.* Attolico also warned Dirksen on the 15th that in his opinion Britain would fight.) Ribbentrop invited Italy to take advantage of the Polish conflict, attack "untrustworthy" Yugoslavia, and "liquidate its game with Yugoslavia in Croatia and Dalmatia." The last possible date of the German attack on Poland: the last of August. He was obviously still smarting from wounds to his pride: if for no other reason, he said, Italy and Germany would have to fight the West one day "to liquidate the prejudice of moral superiority which animates France and England in front of Italy and Germany."

21 — Another psychological element might enter here. Hitler knew that Burckhardt was not unfriendly to the "new" Germany; various members of the German government between 1939 and 1943 often used the Swiss professor as a mediator between British Conservatives and the Nazi hierarchy in order to bring about a German-British peace at the expense of Russia. It is therefore not impossible that Hitler also nurtured a guilt complex before his Rightist and "western" visitor and wanted to hide by all means his contacts with the Bolshevik "easterners."

22 — Thus it is untrue that the Russian concurrence was timed so that Ribbentrop could dramatically brandish it during his meeting with Ciano. See Toscano, p. 159, n. 202, elaborating on two Rosso telegrams to Ciano. On the other hand another telegram, which on August 12 reached Ribbentrop, might have been decisive: a telegram from Tokyo, which stated that the present Japanese government would definitely not adhere to a *military* alliance with the Axis.

Of the western diplomats in Moscow, Naggiar was a rather poor observer. Payart was more of a realist.

Conclusion of the Nazi-Soviet Pact — the last ten days

1 — *NSR*, pp. 50–2.

2 — Molotov left it to the German government to decide whether a Non-Aggression Pact or the reaffirmation of the 1926 Treaty of Berlin would be more desirable. "In either case there must follow the conclusion of a protocol in which, *among other things*, the German statements of August 15 would be included." *Ibid.*, p. 60. (Italics mine.) On August 16 Magistrati, the Italian chargé in Berlin, reported that the Soviet chargé had visited him and suggested that German-Russian relations were developing very satisfactorily.

3 — General Fritsch allegedly recorded on August 18 that General Brauchitsch told Hitler he could attack Poland only if Russian neutrality was assured.

4 — *NSR*, pp. 66–9. It is interesting to note that Ribbentrop's instructions to Schulenburg with the Hitler letter as well as with his August 14 telegram were to deliver these to Molotov in writing, on a sheet of paper without letterhead. Obviously, care and diffidence still lingered in Berlin.

5 — Even then, the wording of the proposed Polish declaration was extremely cautious; it was rather a statement envisaging eventualities than an invitation to military cooperation.

6 — When the news of the German-Russian Pact broke, Voroshilov turned to the British-French mission members: "I presume the gentlemen are tired." See G. Thimm, *Die letzten Tage in Moskau, Die Gegenwart* (September 1947).

7 — So did Maisky in London, who expressed his opinion to Beneš on August 24 that there would be a second Munich.

8 — Grzybowski in Moscow did a typical piece of Polish rationalization when, after hearing of Ribbentrop's journey,

he told his French colleague in Moscow that in his opinion this trip indicated the desperate situation Germany was in.

9 — The "new proletarians," Iron Guardists, Hungarian Arrow Cross leaders were enjoying the picture as much as, for example, the Greek Communists were; it was a defeat of the effete forces of the Western liberals-bourgeois, their newspapers said; as early as August 24, a Hungarian Nazi paper published a veritable hero's biography of Voroshilov — the same paper which three days before concluded a series of feature articles on the "Jewish-Bolshevik" leaders of Soviet Russia. For a few days, the Soviet radio continued its "anti-Fascist" propaganda; only about the 25th–26th was a gradual change perceptible in its tone.

10 — See the memorandum of Ribbentrop to Hitler a year later, *NSR*, pp. 157–8. Also the excellent description of the journey in Schmidt, *op. cit.*, pp. 442 ff.

11 — See the Gaus Affidavit, *IMT* — Supplement B, pp. 138–142; and *NSR*, p. 78 (Secret Additional Protocol). On the question of the "escape clause" of the Non-Aggression Pact see the discussion of Langer-Gleason, p. 180.

12 — Stalin raised a claim to Liepaja and Ventspils (Libau and Windau) in Latvia, and insisted very strongly. Ribbentrop called Hitler on the telephone and thus obtained his agreement. It is interesting that Baltic statesmen, among them Ryti in Finland, were in one way or another aware of the Secret Protocol with considerable exactitude. During his trial in 1945 (which was held before Gaus in Nuremberg revealed the Protocol) Ryti said that he knew of its existence.

13 — Another evidence of his dissatisfaction with Munich.

14 — August 26 was X-Day, 4:40 A.M. was Y-time.

15 — See *IMT* — 2751–PS (Naujocks Affidavit) on Heydrich's orders to simulate an attack in fake Polish uniforms on Gleiwitz. Also 2479–PS (those participating in the "attack" to be decorated with the War Service Cross, Second Class. This was confirmed by the Lahousen Affidavit [Aff. A] also).

16 — He obviously had not heard from Moscow yet; otherwise he must have known that Reval [Tallinn] fell to Stalin. Kaschau in German — Kassa in Hungarian — Košice in Czech and Slovak.

17 — *IMT* — L–3.

18 — The Anglo-Polish Treaty also had a secret protocol enumerating possibilities of German aggression upon which the Treaty would be automatically invoked. In the House of Commons debate after Yalta, in 1945, Eden maintained that the Protocol covered only an attack by Germany but not by Russia.

19 — On August 28, Naggiar was also told that the French-Soviet Pact of 1935 was "automatically" rendered void by the conclusion of the Franco-German Non-Aggression Pact of December 6, 1938; if so, why did not Molotov mention this fact to the Western diplomats throughout the summer negotiations?

20 — See the Göring testimony, *IMT* — TC–90; also *IMT* — C–126; the time: 4:45 A.M. on September 1. Hitler still had hopes in the anti-war forces of France and Britain: "the German land frontier in the West is not to be crossed at any point without my express consent."

In the earlier German diplomatic memoirs it was stated that Mussolini's communication brought about the

August 26 postponement. From the German military papers it seems that it was rather due to the announcement of the Anglo-Polish alliance. A moot point.

21 — At that time, he wanted war even more badly than Hitler did. The words of Winston Churchill are scathing: "He need not have fretted himself. He received all the war he wanted."

22 — L. Mondini, *Prologo del conflitto italo-greco* (Rome, 1945).

23 — Metaxas was in Rome for a short visit on July 5. See the *Greek White Book* (London, 1942). There is evidence, however, that the documents of the Greek White Book — to wit, that of the Mondini-Papagos conversation, have been heavily edited. See Mondini, *op. cit.*

24 — See *Les lettres secrètes échangées par Hitler et Mussolini* (Paris, 1947); also L. Simoni, *Berlino, ambasciata d'Italia* (Rome, 1946).

25 — There were incidents with local Nazis which Mastromattei, the Italian prefect, could hardly control. By January, 1940, 185,000 of 210,000 German-speaking people had opted for Germany.

26 — It is interesting to note the surprise and reaction in Rome which greeted Ribbentrop's journey: a moment of stunned silence after which Mussolini immediately began to cerebrate about how to extract some territorial profit from this new situation.

That Hungary, anxious to be untouched by the gathering storm, relied very much on Italian help in those days, and that there were certain talks about a strong Hungarian-Yugoslav-Italian alliance and thoughts about offering the Hungarian crown to the Duke of Aosta also weighed in the balance against Mussolini's going to war.

27 — *IMT*, 1889–PS. I am not including here the diplomatic story of these last days, Ribbentrop's famous "16 points," etc. All this has been covered amply by a spate of texts, White, Blue, Yellow Books, memoirs.

The Polish War and central-eastern European repercussions

1 — There was also the Swedish Dahlerus, a friend of Göring's, "an interloper in diplomacy." See Namier, *op. cit.*

2 — The "symbolic withdrawal" was the idea of the Italophiles in Paris. See De Monzie, *op. cit.*

3 — See *IMT*, 3469–PS.

4 — General Sosnkowski, the later Polish Premier-in-exile, halted the SS Armored Division "Germania" there.

5 — It is small comfort to say that, had they attacked, Poland would not have been saved either, for by the time a Franco-British offensive would have necessitated the withdrawal of German forces from the eastern theatre, Poland would have been, at best, defending her last provinces, with Russia stepping in to take the rest.

6 — The *BBC* began to organize her European services in order to bolster anti-German resistance and propaganda from the autumn of 1938 on; by September 1939 the whole immense apparatus was working, and the voice of London ("Here is London") became a password in central-eastern Europe. Radio Strasbourg and Paris beamed programs also, but their propaganda was less able than that of London. London broadcast on extensive short-wave lengths, and it took some time before the Germans began to jam these. Not until the middle of 1941 did the voice of America reach central-eastern Europe. Throughout the war, London was regarded as the most reliable of the Allied broadcasts; the quality and correctness of its programs — with notable exceptions, e.g., Yugoslavia — made it far superior to any of the other Allied nations' services.

7 — Leonardo Simoni reports a conversation between Hitler and Magistrati on February 2, 1940, in which Hitler said that on September 7–8, 1939, certain Polish personalities from Lublin tried to approach Germany with a peace proposal. According to Hitler, it was the British Ambassador who then convinced these people to go on fighting. While his story is as yet unsubstantiated by other sources, it is not impossible that it influenced Hitler, who, in an act of emotion, ordered the Army on September 8 to present arms at Pilsudski's grave in Cracow.

8 — As early as September 2, a liquidation conference assembled in Berlin established the timetable concerning who should be eliminated in Poland first: the aristocracy, the clergy, the Jews and the intelligentsia. See *IMT* — Lahousen Affidavit A (Suppl. A). A few other documents of the early period of German occupation: 2233–1–PS (Frank Diary). Frank was the Governor-General of Poland, who said in January 1940: "My relationship with the Poles is like the relationship between ant and plant louse"; 419–D on the establishment of "Warthegau" (incorporated Corridor territories); 1665–PS: "Order concerning treatment of property of nationals of the former Polish state" September 17, 1939, etc.

9 — In Krzemieniec on September 14 the Soviet Ambassador, perhaps unaware of Moscow's decision to invade Poland two days later, said to Noël and Beck: "the Soviets do not desire to have a common frontier with totalitarian states." It is interesting to observe that a Soviet-Japanese truce on the Manchurian border was signed on September 16, immediately preceding the Russian attack on eastern Poland.

The Russian intervention and the Baltic area

1 — *NSR*, pp. 86 *et passim.*

2 — There was a minor frontier incident between Hungarian frontier guards assisting the remnants of Polish troops around the frontier village of Sianki.

3 — See *NSR*, p. 101 *et passim;* also Kordt, *op. cit.*, p. 217. Skvartsev, the Soviet Ambassador, accompanied Ribbentrop. When their plane touched down in Königsberg, Koch, the Gauleiter of East Prussia, came to greet them. Ribbentrop introduced Koch as a long-standing "antiWestern" and advocate of GermanSoviet collaboration. Skvartsev: "I am glad to meet somebody who thought reasonably for a long time . . ."

4 — See E. Kulischer, *Europe on the Move* (New York, 1947); also J. Schechtman, *European Population Transfers 1939–1945* (New York, 1947).

5 — Another evidence that Stalin thought of a second Munich rather than a European war at that time. See also the conversation between the Soviet Ambassador to Belgium and Davies in *Mission to Moscow.*

6 — Beck remained in Rumania and was subsequently interned. He died there in 1944. The nucleus of the laterestablished Polish Army in France and Britain was formed by thousands who made their way to France and the Near East, silently assisted by certain Rumanian and Hungarian authorities. Meanwhile the unfortunate Poles were dejected to see that there was a complete lack of military activity on the Western front — where, for example, the first British war fatality did not occur until December. See De Monzie

writing at the end of September:
"The Ambassador of Poland . . .
haunts the ante-rooms, complains of
our military inertia . . . trembles . . ."
op. cit., p. 167.

7 — That England was worried and tired
could be seen from the fact that in
those days, after the fall of Poland,
Chamberlain got 2,450 letters, 1,860
of them asking him "to stop the war."
Feiling, p. 424. Chamberlain on
September 10 in a private letter about
Hitler: "With such an extraordinary
creature one can only speculate. But
I believe he did seriously contemplate
an agreement with us. . . . But what
I hope for is not a military victory — I
very much doubt the feasibility of that
— but a collapse of the German home
front." *Ibid.*, pp. 416–8. In October
Göring's friend, Dahlerus, appeared
in England again. See also the extracts
of A. A. Berle's diary, quoted by
Langer-Gleason, p. 203, which estimated American prospects in September, 1939.

8 — See *NSR*, pp. 267–8.

9 — See *IMT*, 170–C (File on German-
Russian relations found in the papers
of the High Command of the German
Navy).

10 — In December 1868 Bismarck wrote
to Prince Reuss: the German government wished no political contacts with
the Baltic Germans, for this would
displease the Russians.

11 — Dagö in German — Hiiumaa in
Estonian; Ösel in German — Saa-
remaa in Estonian; Baltischport in
German — Paldiski in Estonian —
Baltiiski Port in Russian. It is inter-
esting to note that Peter the Great
once designated this place to be one
of the greatest naval bases of the world.
However, Paldiski remained a village.
Now Stalin demanded it again.

12 — Secret annexes to these Pacts provided
that the Russian garrisons should consist of about 25,000 men each. (It is
interesting to note that certain members of the Latvian cabinet for a moment considered requesting Germany
to take over Latvia as a protectorate.)

*Efforts toward a Balkan consolidation and the
uncertain position of Italy*

1 — On August 28, Mussolini to Hitler:
"Whatever can be done from the
psychological viewpoint to emphasize
Italian-German solidarity will be intensified through the press, radio,
screen and minute propaganda." Compare this with an Italian official press
directive of September 1: "Abandon
the motive of English responsibility,
also in headlines." Mussolini to Hitler,
August 29, 1939, 4:30 P.M.: The
English mediation proposals seemed to
him to contain some reason. See
*Hitler e Mussolini, Lettere e Documenti,
op. cit.*, pp. 18, 33, 39. And Grandi to
Chamberlain, September 2: "I wish
to tell you how happy I am on this
very day because of the decision taken
by my country. . . . All that I have
striven for during seven years of my
mission in England and during these
last momentous weeks in Rome has
been saved." Feiling, p. 422.

2 — Hitler's minimum objectives in forming a residual Polish state were: 1. such
frontiers as will permit the total incorporation of German-inhabited territories into the Reich *even where these
are strongly mixed among the Slav elements.*
2. The Polish state cannot be permitted
to eventually develop an independent
propaganda of its own and intrigue
against Germany. 3. It cannot represent an obstacle in the way of German-
Russian collaboration. *CLD, op. cit.*

Obviously this last point alone sufficed
to render the residual Polish state impossible. The Germans were also irked
because of the continued existence and

activities of the Polish Embassy in Rome.

3 — Stalin kept a keen eye on the Balkans: in Moscow he asked Ribbentrop whether he did not think that Italy got Albania with a second thought in mind about Greece. Professor Langer states that the Soviets opposed the Germans in the Balkans already in 1939 and that the Kremlin was playing for a position where Russia could "derive satisfaction from Turkey's opposition to German penetration of the peninsula." *Op. cit.*, p. 318. I do not think this to have been the case.

4 — *NSR*, pp. 85–8.

5 — Nevertheless, on November 1, 1939, the Turkish General Orbay was told that Britain, "upon Turkish invitation and in certain circumstances [was] to come to the aid of Turkey with naval forces superior to those of Russia in the Black Sea." Churchill, *op. cit.*, p. 703. And sporadic and secret talks with Greece were going on about an eventual British-French bridgehead in Salonika. See German White Book No. 6 (Berlin, 1941). On the other hand, a tired Chamberlain wrote the Archbishop of Canterbury at Christmas: "I find war more hateful than ever." And Regent Paul to A. Bliss Lane on December 30, 1939: "The Allies must be crazy to form an eastern front which would provoke an invasion of the Balkans by the Germans." Langer-Gleason, p. 387, n. 25.

6 — See Gafencu, *Vorspiel zum Krieg im Osten* (Berne, 1944). However, there existed a British-Turkish understanding that their alliance was not to be evoked in the case of a sole Russian attack on Bessarabia.

7 — See Mondini, *op. cit.* The Greeks made political capital of the Italian proposal, however: it was subtly intimated in Athens that the "Hellenic determination," i.e., their partial mobiliza-

tion, made Rome withdraw her aggressive plans. As with the Czechs in May 1939 and with the Poles in August 1939, this reached dictatorial ears and engendered undue repercussions.

8 — See *IMT*, 170–C (opinion that the Black Sea be excluded as an operational area of the German Navy).

9 — The Italian Consul in Prague — evidently a Germanophobe — gave very accurate reports of the internal situation in the Protectorate. Having read in November one of his reports, the momentarily impressed Mussolini said to Ciano: "Advise the Bohemians to side with the Communists; this will make German repression harder and will accentuate the causes for disagreement between Moscow and Berlin." Curious advice.

Somewhat later Dr. Pfitzner, the German Acting Mayor of Prague, delivered an anti-Italian speech which caused energetic Italian protests in Berlin. A similar speech was delivered by the Gauleiter in Dresden.

10 — Ciano to his Ambassador in Tokyo: encourage the impression of Italy's new anti-German attitude. See Toscano, p. 198, n. 254.

11 — The name-index of the *Ciano Diaries* might mislead the reader that the visitor was Ion Antonescu or Mihai. But they were to appear on the Rumanian scene only a year later; Victor A. was no relation to either. (A similar error is to be found in Namier, *In the Nazi Era*, Index.)

It is interesting to note that Bulgaria abstained from voting against the Soviet Union when in December the League of Nations expelled the latter from its members.

12 — The busybody Csáky, afraid that the Venice meeting would not please the

Germans, published a "denial" communiqué on January 14, stating that his meeting with Ciano was not of an anti-Soviet character.

13 — Polish personalities continued to exercise a certain influence in Rome; for example King Victor Emmanuel III intervened with Stalin for the release of the old Prince Radziwill, whom the Soviets imprisoned when they invaded eastern Poland. Radziwill was set free in December 1939 and went to Rome.

14 — Hassell, on Attolico at that time: "He looked ill and miserable and in his luxurious green gown was like a sick Pope in a Vatican baldachined bed." Upon Hitler's express wish, Attolico was recalled from Berlin in April.

15 — Quoted from Acikalin's article in *International Affairs* (October 1949).

The Finnish War and central-eastern Europe

1 — On October 14 the first Russian proposal would have ceded some of Eastern Karelia in exchange. On October 23 Stalin said to the Finnish negotiators that for the defense of Leningrad against external attacks, he needed Finnish lands in the Karelian Isthmus. Who would attack Leningrad? asked the Finns. Stalin mentioned France and Britain several times; once even Germany.

The American mediation was partly the result of the insistence of Procopé, the Finnish Minister to Washington, partly due to the requests of the Swedish envoy. Hull was still noncommittal, while Berle was stronger in his suggestions. Cf. Langer-Gleason, p. 322, and also the contemporary remarks by Berle: "It is a curious fact that the United States, which bolts like a frightened rabbit from even

remote contact with Europe, will enthusiastically take a step which might very well be a material day's march on the road to a Far Eastern War." See here the sub-chapter "American Aid to Finland" in Langer-Gleason, pp. 335 ff.

2 — These allegations of Ryti who, as his 1945 testimony shows, was extremely well-informed of the Secret Protocol (when the Nuremberg and since revealed documents were still unavailable) did not hitherto receive other support; neither the Nuremberg papers nor *Nazi-Soviet Relations* contains such a detailed agreement on Finland. Yet there is some evidence to substantiate what Ryti said. That Hitler could inform the Swedish emissary around October 15 in such detail about the "modest" Soviet claims indicates that he knew of them in advance; direct Russo-Finnish negotiations were just beginning at that time. An entry in the German Naval High Command Diary on October 26 establishes that from that day on, "at the suggestion of Molotov," German economic warfare in the Baltic was to be restricted to waters west of 20° E. This might have been the western Finnish line previously agreed upon, for 20° E just about cuts past the Aalands, leaving them within those same waters where the German Navy could continue to operate. It was about October 26 that Molotov dropped his Aaland demilitarization claims during the Moscow negotiations, requesting nevertheless that the islands remain manned by Finnish troops *only*. On April 30, 1940, at a time when Sweden and Germany were discussing the latters' demands for troop transit through the territory of the former, Maisky said to the Swedish Minister in London that Russia would object to an eventual German occupation of the islands. A few months later, at the end of September, 1940, certain German units debarked in western

Finnish ports, a move against which the Soviet government protested. Did she protest because she regarded Finland as totally within her "sphere of interest," or, did she protest against a violation of the territorial limitations which Ryti cites and which in that case provided for a "neutral" Finland east of the Moscow Treaty line? The fact that the Russians, after their military victory, did not push deeper into Finland and conquer that country but instead preferred negotiating on the basis of their pre-war demands providing for limited territorial changes, also indicates that the Soviets had certain reasons not to go further west but to stop at a certain line, for a further penetration might have had consequences in the Aalands and perhaps in western Finland.

3 — It remains for future historians who have access to such documents to inquire whether there was a parallel between the German-Russian agreement concerning Finland as stated by Ryti and an agreement between Russia and the United States in 1944 — if such existed at all. Is it possible that the Russians in 1944 made an armistice and did not advance beyond a certain line for the same reasons they did in 1940? Was there an agreement, secret or oral, between Roosevelt and Stalin to that effect? The position occupied by the United States in 1943–44 in regard to the Finnish-Russian war was almost exactly parallel to that of Germany in 1939–40. At any rate, it is interesting that *NSR* does not publish any Soviet-German documents from December 11, 1939 to March 28, 1940, with the exception of one memorandum dealing with economic matters, dated February 26.

4 — On November 29, *Pravda* published a Stalin statement to the effect that France and Britain, but not Germany, were responsible for the European war.

5 — Ryti became Prime Minister on December 1, 1939, and was elected to the Presidency on December 19, 1940.

6 — Early in November, Göring, Raeder, and Keitel, independently of each other, complained about the inquisitiveness of the Russian military missions in Germany; on November 23, Hitler spoke to his generals: ". . . we can oppose Russia only when we are free in the West." (*IMT*, 789–PS); on December 31 the Naval Diary records the opinion of the German General Staff: "The Russians are no match for an army with modern equipment and superior leadership." (*IMT*, to 170–C.) A beautiful example of technical friction coming from ideological parallel resulted in December, when the German Army complained of difficulties at the Russian frontier created by the expulsion of Polish Jews from German territory, whom the Russians pushed back into no-man's-land.

7 — Holsti, the former Foreign Minister, was the Finnish delegate to the League of Nations. The Baltic States (together with Bulgaria, Switzerland, and China) abstained from voting in the League Assembly.

8 — The Finnish War also provided the fallacy of the Douhet theory of air supremacy: the Soviet Air Force had virtually full control of the air, which fact had nevertheless very limited influence on the outcome of the war. Churchill himself was deeply impressed by what he called "the military incapacity" of the Red Army.

9 — Just as with the Austrian Minister in Berlin at the time of *Anschluss*, sympathy was wasted on this miserable individual also, who, in spite of his Soviet experiences, turned out to be one of the arch-Communist stooges in post-war Czechoslovakia.

10 — On January 8, 1940, Hitler said to Attolico that Finland was fighting Russia only because of encouragement from Britain. "The requests of such a great empire as Russia were not exorbitant and should have induced [Finland] to budge!" Attolico: "But Finland is a sovereign state. She has the right to exist . . ." Hitler [shaking his head emphatically]: "Yes, she has the right to exist as long as she conforms to the interests of the Great Powers on whom the direction of European order depends . . ." Simoni, *op. cit.*

11 — After the publication of the La Charité documents in July, 1940, Ankara vehemently denied that such talks took place in the winter.

12 — In December 1939 British intelligence noted possibilities of a Russian attack on Norway. (According to the German White Book, the British began exploring the Narvik situation as early as December 1939–January 1940.)

13 — Procopé, *Sowjetjustiz über Finland* (Zurich, 1947), Thomas Verlag, p. 125.

14 — These French-British documents are given in the Swedish White Book; an indispensable source: *Handlingar rörande Sveriges politik under andra världskriget — Förspelet till det tyska angreppet på Danmark och Norge den 9 april 1940* (Stockholm, 1947). Tanner, in *Finlands Väg* (Helsinki, 1951), claims that the Swedish stand was so rigid that the Swedish government once even raised the spectre of Swedish and Russian troops side by side, fighting the Allies.

It is interesting to note that the standard Soviet high-school historical atlas (*Atlas Istorii SSSR*, vol. III., Moscow, 1950) marks, with arrows, the projected "invasion routes" of the Anglo-French "imperialists" to Finland in the Winter War.

15 — It is rather possible that Roosevelt sensed what Chamberlain had in mind and American-British relations suffered somewhat. Churchill at that time: "The United States was cooler than in any other period. I persevered in my correspondence with the President, but with little response." That ideological trends were involved could be seen from a Chamberlain note in March: "I would rather have Halifax succeed me than Winston. . . ." See Feiling, p. 422, Churchill, p. 501, also the article by H. Koht, "Mr. Winston Churchill and the Norwegian Question [in 1940]" in *Norseman*, no. 2 (1950).

16 — Welles proposed, in vain, a Mussolini-Roosevelt meeting in the Azores. At that time Göring also sent some kind of an obscure message to Prince Paul of Yugoslavia, hinting that he, instead of Hitler, could offer a negotiated peace on the basis of Germany's 1914 boundaries, plus Austria and the Sudetens.

President Roosevelt raised his idea of a great European peace conference in December and communicated it subsequently to the neutrals. These countries were very sceptical, especially Spain, Portugal, Hungary, Yugoslavia and Greece. Berle also had noted the lack of realism of this approach: ". . . all this . . . sounded a little like Huxley." Langer-Gleason, p. 344.

17 — The Wallenberg family played a significant rôle in the diplomatic history of World War II. Marcus Wallenberg was in contact with the German opposition leader, Goerdeler, in March. He also mediated between Russia and Finland in 1943–44. Raoul Wallenberg saved the lives of approximately 100,000 Hungarian Jews in late 1944 under unparalleled circumstances.

18 — Viipuri in Finnish — Viborg in German and Russian; Fisher Peninsula —

Rybachi Peninsula in Russian; Pet-samo in Finnish — Pechenga in Russian.

The American Ambassador, Steinhardt, confided to the Finnish Minister to Turkey, Yrjö-Koskinen, that in his opinion the new frontier was drawn by the Russians in order to make the strategic defense of Finland practically impossible. See Wuorinen, *Finland in World War II* (New York, 1947). It was due to the failure to impede the conclusion of the Moscow Peace Treaty that on March 21, Daladier fell and a new French government was installed with Reynaud as Premier.

Russia, central-eastern Europe and the German victory in the West

1 — See *IMT*, 2233–B–PS (Frank Diary); see also *NSR*, pp. 131 *et passim*. The Soviets also requested participation in the established commissions dealing with Danube navigation; but the Germans wished to keep them out of the Balkans. Only when the incorporation of Bessarabia brought Russia down to the Danube Delta was she invited to participate in discussions about the reorganization of the international fluvial authority. This then proved to be one of the points where a collision of German and Russian interests showed itself in the fall of 1940.

In Chungking, Sir Stafford Cripps had a surprisingly friendly talk with the Soviet envoy in mid-January; in February Cripps passed through Moscow and spoke briefly with Molotov.

2 — *IMT*, 2353–PS. (General Thomas-Göring.) The new directive of August 14: "The Führer desires punctual delivery to Russia only till the spring of 1941."

3 — The minutes of the Allied Supreme Council are reproduced in The Swedish

White Book, "Bilaga F :" and *Norseman* (March–April, 1946). Cf. *Die Geheimakten des französischen Generalstabes* (Berlin, 1940). On March 28 Norway asked the United States to intervene with Britain and halt the extension of the war to the Scandinavian area. Not before April 23 did the Supreme War Council of the Allies finally shelve the Scandinavian invasion plans.

4 — Beloff, *op. cit.*, interprets the fact that Molotov spoke of the new Finnish frontier ensuring the "safety of Leningrad, Murmansk, and the Murmansk Railway" as a reassuring symptom for the West; Murmansk was a port predominantly destined for Western traffic and the Murmansk Railway was the line where in case of a war with Germany, the Western Powers could aid Russia — an interesting interpretation. But I do not think that Molotov's argument went beyond the standard Russian usage of "safety" as a pretext for territorial claims and adjustments.

5 — That General Jodl's war diary on May 24 showed some concern for Russian troop movements toward Bessarabia (*IMT*, 1809–PS) might have been due to inadequate information on the Secret Protocol.

6 — In spite of the fact that formal diplomatic relations between Yugoslavia and the Soviet Union did not exist, there was much cordiality between the two. Yugoslavia had given aid to the Soviets during the Russian famine of 1921–22; in 1924 formal diplomatic relations were almost resumed; in 1927 the Soviet Red Cross had sent aid to the victims of the Dalmatian earthquake, etc.

Italy, central-eastern Europe and the victory of Germany in the West

1 — From a version given to me by a confidant of Teleki. It coincides almost verbatim with that found in *CD*-NY. It should be contrasted with the attitude of Mussolini as reflected by a notation of Ciano's on March 30: "Mussolini is irritated for the *n*th time at Catholicism, which is to blame for having made Italy universal, hence preventing it from becoming national. When a country is universal it belongs to everybody but itself."

2 — He nevertheless let Ciano inform the Rumanians. They rushed to convince the Axis of their sincerity, and Mussolini, writing to Hitler on the 11th, told him how the Rumanians were exercising fluvial control on the Danube against British plans and boats.

3 — On the German acquisition of shares of important foreign enterprises in southeastern Europe during the spring and early summer of 1940 see *IMT*, 43–EC. After the victory in France, Germany tried to get at the French-owned very important copper mines of Bor in eastern Serbia. See *Le Procès Laval* (Paris, 1946) and Pierre Laval, *Notes et Mémoires, op. cit.*

In the early spring of 1940, a British commercial enterprise was formed to counteract German economic influence in the Balkans. This United Kingdom Commercial Corporation expired after the French defeat.

4 — On the same day, Salazar in Lisbon told the Italian envoy: Italy should not enter the war, for otherwise Russia would be the only winner afterwards. Italy's rôle was to build a neutral, Mediterranean-continental *bloc*. See R. Bova Scoppa, *Colloqui con due dittatori* (Rome, 1949), p. 17.

5 — Also Mussolini to Hitler on May 30 and June 1: "Not to extend the conflict to the Danubian-Balkan basin." On May 20 Bullitt from Paris suggested to Roosevelt that units of the Atlantic Fleet of the United States be sent to Greece, a demonstration which might have an effect on Italy. Langer-Gleason, p. 459.

6 — That ignorance breeds many things, among them hatred, was proven by sad phenomena in central-eastern Europe after June 1940. The common people, misinformed by the press, did not understand the position of Britain. In Slovakia, Hungary, Rumania, Bulgaria, the word "British" soon became synonymous with "Jewish," due to extremist propaganda. The French-British tentatives during May when concessions were offered to Italy (see Reynaud, DeMonzie, Ciano and Churchill, etc.) to bribe her into remaining neutral were misunderstood. The clear-sighted Teleki himself committed a slip when, speaking in the Hungarian Parliament, he hinted at a forthcoming negotiated peace, saying that the end of the war was within immediate sight. The "proud rejection" of French offers and of Churchill's May 16 letter by Mussolini was gloriously trumpeted out in all central-eastern European capitals by the Italian representatives there. After Fascist Italy joined National-Bolshevist Germany on June 10, and "Liberal-Democratic-Free Mason" France fell, the Hungarian, Rumanian, Slovak, and Bulgar Nazi press was read by more and more; the scurrilous phrases of these sheets presented Britain as a decayed, mercenary, ugly old maid, kept in invisible bonds of prostitution by the Jews. Indeed, the tone of the attacks in some of these papers surpassed even that of the German Nazi press.

Ignorance of the real values and of the real forces involved in the war blinded people to such extremes that even in traditionally democratic, anti-totalitarian, and Catholic parts of central-eastern Europe (for example, in Slovakia and Croatia), Britain — and later, America — were laughed at, despised, and cast off. The propaganda of the German minority there of course was eminent in furthering these sentiments. (It is a sad fact that the anti-British theme song of the German war machine, "*Wir fahren gegen Engelland*", originated with Tyrolean troops!) On the mighty pervasiveness of that propaganda, volumes remain to be written. Unfortunately, it continued to serve the totalitarian rulers also after 1944, when the Bolshevik invasion came. The fact cannot be discarded therefore that in most of central-eastern Europe the youth were subject to an uninterrupted stream of abuse against the English-speaking nations — which continuous propaganda is now within its second decade.

7 — *NSR*, pp. 144–8 *et passim.*

8 — After May 10, the Soviets were again somewhat more cautious in their relations with Germany. The Soviet papers failed to comment on the war in the West; although, as Schulenburg noted, there seemed to be not the slightest sign of Moscow being disturbed by the great German victories. On May 22, Molotov announced that the Soviet Union was willing to trade with all belligerents on the basis of equality; also, the new British Ambassador, Sir Stafford Cripps, left for Moscow on May 27.

9 — *CD*–NY, p. 209. The reader may remember how the Russian attack on eastern Poland was preceded by the frontier truce between Russia and Japan on September 16, 1939. On June 10, 1940, when Italy entered the war, another, more important Russo-Japanese frontier agreement was signed; next day the Japanese Foreign Ministry sent notes to the British, French and Italian Ambassadors requesting the withdrawal of their concessionary troops and warships from China. These are significant connexions.

Summer 1940: I. The Soviet occupation of the Baltics and the quandaries of Finland

1 — The Lithuanian Government first suggested that the Foreign Minister should go; but Moscow demanded that the Premier come in person.

2 — See *NSR*, pp. 146–54.

3 — It is interesting to note that from 1917 to 1922 it was the United States which refused to recognize a change in the then *status quo*, i.e., the separation of the Baltic states from the Russian Empire.

4 — 95.5% in Lithuania, 94.7% in Latvia, and, interestingly enough, only 81.6% in Estonia.

5 — In the summer of 1940, Ivanov, the Russian chargé in Paris, excused himself to a Lithuanian thus: "If we had left Lithuania on the other side of the fence, Germany would have seized her."

6 — *NSR*, pp. 164–5; also *NSR*, pp. 154, 156–7. Haste and greed could have been avoided to Russia's later benefit this time also. It is an interesting question how the German-Russian War would have developed, had Russia maintained the 1939–40 status of the Baltic countries. The latter were bound to be scrupulously neutral; their War Ministers went so far as to announce on occasion that they would fight, with Russian assistance, against any foreign invader. Consequently the Germans might never have reached even the outskirts of Leningrad . . .

7 — Concerning this issue, Schnurre and Schulenburg disagreed: the Ambassador requested that the Soviet standpoint be honored. See *NSR*, pp. 183–4.

8 — His famous Executive Order No. 0054, dated November 1940, giving the entire liquidational orders, was published in Arthur Koestler's *The Yogi and the Commissar* (Soviet Myth and Reality) and in the *Lithuanian Bulletin*, 1947 volume.

9 — The remaining Germans in the Baltic states were exchanged in the second phase of the carrying out of the all-round German-Russian population exchange settlement in January 1941.

10 — See the *Finnish Blue-White Book* (*Finland reveals her secret documents*) (New York, 1941).

11 — On evidence of Russian aggressive intentions (instructions to Soviet agents captured, etc.,) see Procopé, *op. cit.*, pp. 131–2.

12 — A full description of the transit negotiations and their international implications is given in the second Swedish White Book: *Transiteringsfrågan, April–Juni, Juni–December 1940* (Stockholm, 1947).

13 — That this Society served subversive ends could be seen from the fact that leading intellectual members of parallel societies, organized in the three Baltic republics after October 1939, provided most of the cabinet members in the Communistic regimes installed by the Russians in June 1940. The pattern of "cultural societies" was used throughout the Balkans, Hungary, Czechoslovakia, and Poland in and after 1945. To assure the Russians of the Finnish desire to extend true cultural relations, the Finnish Minister of Culture and Education offered several times during 1940 to go to Moscow and discuss such matters, but the Soviets frowned on such plans.

14 — When in October 1940 the Germans requested some Finnish military data, Ryti considered that the Germans might convey such information to Russia, as at that time both Germany and Russia were impatient with the Swedish-Finnish Union plans.

15 — See Ryti's testimony in Procopé, *op. cit.*

16 — For example, the Finns caught Vishinsky in a lie. The latter insisted that Cripps in Moscow implied that Britain would forego eventually the concession rights. When Vereker, the British Minister in Helsinki, asked the Foreign Office and, indirectly, Cripps, Vishinsky was fully disavowed.

Summer 1940: II. Rumania, Hungary, Bulgaria

1 — *NSR*, pp. 155 *et passim.*

2 — Hitler asked Ribbentrop to help refresh his memory for a memorandum giving the text and interpretation of the Secret Protocol. Ribbentrop assured him that Bessarabia was included.

3 — *NSR*, pp. 160–1 (italics mine); see also pp. 155–65 in general.

4 — When the ultimatum was handed over to Davidescu, it turned out that Molotov also insisted on the cession of a small area around the town of Herta on the railroad line connecting Bessarabia with Lwów — another territorial addition. It was reported later that drawing the new frontier, Molotov used a thick pencil which traced a line whose width corresponded to about six or seven miles on the scale of the map used; thus many minor frontier questions resulted, of which the Russians always took advantage later.

5 — Molotov to the Hungarian envoy, Kristóffy, on July 1: Russia does not have ambitions in Hungary but would rather support Hungary's own ambitions.

6 — See *CLD*, *CD-NY*; also Kordt, *op. cit.*, p. 253: "Hitler never had many sympathies for Hungary."

7 — On the German *Auslandsorganisation*'s intelligence and espionage activities in Rumania see *IMT*, 3796–PS.

Leca and Devaux were two young French government secretaries who fled through Spain after the French collapse. The police there discovered that their valise contained a very large amount of gold, bonds, money, and important material smuggled out from France for their own purposes. Among other things, plans containing full instructions on how to destroy the Ploesti oil wells in Rumania to prevent their falling into German hands were found and taken from them. See "Pertinax", *Les Fossoyeurs* (New York, 1944).

8 — On July 28 Churchill on the Rumanians: "... we have been treated odiously by these people." *Their Finest Hour*, p. 650.

9 — Brasov in Rumanian — Brassó in Hungarian — Kronstadt in German.

10 — At that time, obviously acting upon German instructions, the Hungarian Arrow-Cross movement, abandoning its ultra-nationalist program, suddenly advocated the transformation of Hungary into a state of various nationalities, a nebulous concept similar to the Radicals' "cantonal" idea of 1917–18. This plan aroused much resentment in Hungary. Later in the year, plans for an attempt to kidnap Horthy were also discovered.

11 — A TASS communiqué denied that the Soviets were offering to be Rumania's protector at the time of the Vienna Award. See also *NSR*, pp. 178–87 and 189–94.

12 — Kolozsvár in Hungarian — Cluj in Rumanian — Klausenburg in German; Nagyvárad in Hungarian — Oradea in Rumanian — Grosswardein in German.

13 — A similar situation existed in 1915–17. But, as Stalin obviously knew, Churchill's Dardanelles Campaign in 1915 also had distinct political aims. In 1943–44, then, Churchill could not forestall the Russians except in Greece. Stalin must have felt in 1940 that Germany would be less inimical toward his Balkan aims than Britain would be. He was subsequently proven wrong in 1941; but how pleasant must his surprise have been in 1944 when he saw that the United States and Britain were practically writing the Balkans off, (with the exception of Greece and Turkey)!

Early autumn 1940: the impasse in German-Russian relations

1 — Langer-Gleason, pp. 644–5. The Soviet Ambassadress in Stockholm, Madame Kollontay, was reported in June to have said that the German danger was common to all Europe. *NSR*, p. 147.

2 — A few hours before this typical piece of Stalinist diplomacy was performed, Molotov asked Schulenburg to convey to Berlin Stalin's request that Germany should agree to the abandonment of the Kalvarija strip. The diary of General Halder mentions how Hitler was irked because of the Soviet insistence on the Mariampole-Kalvarija territory. See also Kordt, *op. cit.; NSR*, pp. 166–8. It is not impossible that Stalin presented Hitler with the text of the Cripps talks to compensate for German acquiescence in Kalvarija's remaining within Lithuania, at that time *de facto* within the Soviet Union. It may seem that such a grave diplomatic gesture was an exorbitant price for Kalvarija; yet such was Stalin's land-hunger that six months later he paid seven and a half million gold dollars for those few square miles which were in his possession anyhow.

3 — Or, rather, neither knew Churchill. For there is Feiling's record of June

1940: "... and there were figures of repute, defeatist at heart, who might be ready to form, or support, an alternative government." He later mentions Chamberlain's contemporary diary entries "of bloodcurdling rumour." Even Churchill evoked the possibility of a British defeat (although obviously for reasons of expediency), in a letter to Roosevelt on June 14.

4 — Probably from these experiences originates Stalin's so often expressed dislike of the French. He thought more of Pétain than of De Gaulle throughout the whole war. He was known to have made critical remarks on the racial qualities of the French (and also of the Italians). At Yalta, he fought against including France as a Fifth Great Power, despite the fact that De Gaulle signed a pact with him in Moscow in December 1944. In 1947, he said to Szakasits, the Hungarian Socialist stooge of the Communists, when the latter was unctuously paying him verbal homage: "Do not speak to me like this, I am not a Frenchman."

5 — See Enquête commissie, *Verslag betreffende de uitkonsten van het underzoek*, Vol. IIB., *Neutraliteitspolitiek* (The Hague, 1949).

6 — There were also disagreements between émigré Czechs and Poles in London. The Czechs leaned towards Russia. Yet in June 1940 the Polish Premier-in-exile proposed to Churchill that Russia be approached concerning the creation of a Polish army-in-exile from among the Polish deportees in Russia. Late in 1940, Stalin began forming a Polish Corps, but for his own purposes.

7 — The Hungarian statesman Eckhardt forecast to Bova Scoppa, the Italian envoy to Portugal, in July 1940: ultimately the United States would further Russian imperialism against Hitler. "This might seem to be a

fantastic project today, but if you consider carefully all elements of the world situation, you will admit that it is less absurd than it seems." Bova Scoppa, *op. cit.*, p. 22.

8 — *IMT*, 3014–PS; also 1229–PS. See the Halder Diaries, quoted by Langer-Gleason, p. 649, n. 2; also p. 651. It is interesting that toward the end of his nervous statement Hitler showed much concern about the Baltic and did not mention the Balkans at all. "A second great power on the Baltic is impossible." He did not speak about Communism, nor did he point at the total eradication of the Soviet state: "Objective: annihilation of Russia's power."

It is rather clear now — in contrast to generally held views, among them those held by "revisionist" historians — that Hitler's decision to turn on Russia was not motivated primarily by his fears of a Russian attack. Rather, he thought that he could beat Britain through Russia. Jodl repeated Hitler's words to General Warlimont on July 29: "due to the defeat of Russia it is expected that Great Britain would incline towards making peace." H. Greiner, *Die oberste Wehrmachtsführung 1939–1943* (Wiesbaden, 1951), pp. 288–9. See also p. 292: "(Hitler's) main motive undoubtedly lay in the supposition that Britain would be ready for peace after her last eventual continental (hope) would be cancelled through the decisive defeat of Soviet Russia."

9 — Mussolini to Hitler on August 27: "everything possible should be done to better relations between Japan and the Soviet Union and to make relations difficult between the Soviet Union and the United States." Yet, "Washington had not shared the hopes of the British that the Soviet Government, after Hitler's astounding victories in the West, might gradually loosen the ties of the Nazi-Soviet Pact and even-

tually support Britain in the effort to check the expansion of German power." Langer-Gleason, p. 723.

10 — Shkvartsev was Soviet Ambassador in Berlin from September 1939 to November 1940. He succeeded Merekalov and was in turn succeeded by Dekanosov after the Molotov visit.

11 — See Gafencu, p. 95. *NSR* does not include documents relating to the Danube commission negotiations.

The Soviets had obviously noted the Italian failure to follow up the previous attempts at a jointly planned Russian-Italian policy in the Balkans; hence their temporary opposition to Italy; also, the Italian stand on Rumania displeased them.

12 — *IMT*, 53–C, 170–C.

13 — The Soviets maintained, among other things, that the Germans had "promised" their support to the Soviet claims to Southern Bukovina. This argument was taken up again by Molotov in Berlin. See *NSR*, pp. 189–94.

14 — *NSR*, p. 195 *et passim*.

15 — On November 2 Mikoyan complained to Schnurre that Germany did not deliver military material to Russia punctually enough, while German war deliveries to Finland were running smoothly. This was the first Soviet complaint regarding German armaments sent to Finland. At that time Hitler was even considering forestalling a Soviet move on Petsamo.

16 — An interesting remark of Hitler's — it is certain that his talk with Pétain impressed him — "I will never permit Pétain to fall into the hands of the Russians." [?]

Molotov in Berlin

1 — *NSR* gives the minutes of the first Molotov-Ribbentrop talk on pp. 217–

26; the first Hitler-Molotov talk on pp. 226–34; the second Hitler-Molotov talk on pp. 234–47; the final Molotov-Ribbentrop talk on pp. 247–55; the Soviet counter-draft of November 26 on pp. 258–9.

2 — Ribbentrop a few days later to the Spanish Serrano Suñer: if Russia were ruled by a Grand Duke, she might go over to the British side, but not with a Stalin. But, if it should come to a war, it will be a parade march to Moscow. R. Serrano Suñer, *Entre Hendaya y Gibraltar* (Madrid, 1947).

3 — Finland, Sweden, Switzerland, and Spain, whose eventual signature of the Pact was discussed in October, were finally not asked to join.

4 — See *IMT*, 3775–PS. In December the Russians demanded the elimination of Tanner, Kivimäki, Mannerheim, and Svinhufvud from the list of presidential candidates. When Paasikivi objected that this was a purely domestic affair, Molotov conceded that Paasikivi was right: "but we have the right to draw our own conclusions."

5 — *IMT*, 1799–PS; 376–PS.

6 — *NSR*, pp. 160–264 and *IMT*, 446–47–PS.

7 — An interesting sequel was a letter from Rosso to Alfieri, written around January 16, in which he bitterly complained that for the second time he was put into an impossible situation with the Russians because Rome had neglected either to inform Berlin previously, or to tell him that Berlin was left uninformed. See Simoni, *op. cit.*; Rosso, *loc. cit.* CD–NY indicates that Ciano decided to inform Ribbentrop only after the first Molotov-Rosso talks took place.

The Greek War and central-eastern Europe

1 — Simoni reports a list of Italian territorial claims ("*Elenco di aspira-*

zioni") which Ciano brought to Berlin on July 7. This document mentions a "settlement" with Greece, which country was to get Cyprus from Britain and cede in exchange Corfu and the Čamuria region on the Albanian border to Italy.

2 — Simoni, *op. cit.* On the other hand it was intimated by the none too objective Mondini that there existed some clandestine Greek-British naval collaboration at that time, to which perhaps the sinking of the Italian warship *Colleoni* could be attributed.

3 — It is therefore questionable how Mondini, the military attaché in Athens, could write in 1945 about "numerically inferior" Italian forces.

4 — The review article by G. Salvemini in the *Journal of Modern History* (December 1949), "Pietro Badoglio's Rôle in the Second World War," is somewhat unfair to Badoglio. See also Mondini; Badoglio's own account, *L'Italia nella seconda guerra mondiale* (Milan, 1946); Mussolini, *Storia di un anno* (Milan, 1945). The original aims were Salonika and certain Ionian and Aegean islands. Jacomoni, Ciano, Visconti-Prasca insisted that the Greeks were not a people who would fight. Jacomoni: "I can arrange some frontier incidents." Visconti-Prasca: "We have prepared firearms and bombs of French manufacture to arrange a feint attack." Mussolini: "Nobody would believe this; yet, for a justification of metaphysical character one could then say that it was necessary . . ." Ciano: "When do you want the incident to take place?" Mussolini: "On the 24th." Ciano: "The incidents will take place on the 24th." Badoglio thought that 20 divisions were necessary for the occupation of all of Greece, while only 10 were available.

5 — That Hitler did not know of the impending Italian action is interesting,

for German counter-intelligence knew the Italian code. General Roatta, the Assistant Italian Chief-of-Staff, informed the German military attaché in Rome on October 23, however. Due to Hitler's journey to France, this proved to be a very late date.

6 — Of course, Hitler was not consistent. Nine months later, on August 25, 1941, he praised Mussolini for his "foresight" in Greece. Seventeen months later, on April 29, 1942, he told Mussolini at Salzburg: "I believe in Providence. The Greek campaign of yours was a sign of Providence, for if the Balkan tumor would not have been opened, awful disasters and menaces would loom for us in this stage of the war . . ." Yet, in the dark end, on December 22, 1944, Hitler implied in a letter to Mussolini that the Greek War was a mistake, for without it Spain would have come in and the war have been won.

7 — According to Kneževič (see *International Affairs*, January 1951) Mussolini deliberately had Bitolj bombed, as he was informed about secret negotiations between Yugoslavia and Germany concerning a Yugoslav occupation of Salonika. This seems very doubtful. There is more evidence that after the Bitolj incident, General Nedič (who in 1941 assumed the task of being "Serbian" Premier during the German occupation) planned an attack against the Italians in Albania to eliminate the Italian bridgehead in the Balkans before the Germans could intervene there.

8 — Part of a Hitler directive to the Army on November 12 reads: "Political talks with Russia introduced. . . . Make preparations to occupy Greece north of the Aegean, through Bulgaria." *IMT*, 444–PS. Two weeks later he told Antonescu that a German attack on Salonika was necessary. Antonescu agreed.

9 — On December 23, Churchill wrote to Australian Premier Menzies: "... we are making out of Suda Bay [in Crete] a second Scapa Flow." Churchill, *op. cit.*, p. 704. Alas, Suda Bay fell too easily five months later.

The Germans in Bulgaria

1 — On December 3, 1940, the Bulgarian Foreign Minister Popov affirmed in a speech that relations between Bulgaria and Soviet Russia were particularly good.

2 — There was also a considerable split among the very important German minority groups in Rumania. The previously extreme Nazi, Roth, turned out to be pro-Antonescu against a young Nazi leader, Andreas Schmidt. Schmidt turned the German Lutheran Church in Rumania into a complete Nazi bulwark (Schmidt called himself a Teutonic pagan-Christian: *"ein Thüringer deutscher Christ"*) and he sided with the Legionnaires. During the Iron Guard revolution, however, Himmler and Schmidt were overruled and Antonescu won with German acquiescence. But on January 29, the German Minister to Bucharest, Fabricius, was removed (ostensibly because of his failure to have averted the civil war), and the SS-supported Killinger succeeded him. Ultimately Schmidt, with Killinger's support, won out over Roth.

3 — It is also interesting that the Axis press — including Rumanian government organs — subsequently called the Iron Guard rebellion "Communist-instigated."

4 — That Moscow thought seriously of the deal with Italy also transpires from these two fragments: 1. When Italy invaded Greece, the Greek Communist leader, Zachariades, instructed the Greek Communists to fight against the Italians on the side of the Greek Government. But the Greek Communist party line suddenly changed in early January, denouncing the Greek crossing into Albania, calling it "an invasion," and asking the party members to sabotage it. 2. Some Soviet suggestions were given to Bulgaria late in December 1940 that if she made a Mutual Assistance Pact with the Soviets, Bulgaria might join in the Italian attack against Greece and gain parts of Western Thrace for herself.

5 — An identical note was given to Schulenburg by Molotov on the same day. See *NSR*, pp. 268 *et passim.* Interestingly, Molotov took the occasion to request an answer to the Soviet Government's Quadripartite Pact draft of November 25. Ribbentrop then answered that he could not answer before having fully consulted Italy and Japan on the subject. Thus the issue was kept in abeyance and never taken up again.

6 — On January 12, Hitler had told the visiting Hungarian War Minister Bartha, "I am only afraid of what would happen if Stalin dies."

7 — Churchill, *The Grand Alliance*, pp. 10–1. See also, pp. 19 and 33–5.

8 — The pro-Communist Louis Adamic maintained that his books had influenced President and Mrs. Roosevelt deeply; of course, this may not be quite so. See L. Adamic, *Dinner at the White House* (New York, 1946) — typical of the views of the Titoist American Left.

9 — *IMT*, 872–PS. About previous *Marita* plans see *IMT*, 448–PS: also 134–C. Technical measures included "no more camouflage in industry" and explanation of troop movements as a feint of *Sealion.* The movements of Russian civilians and diplomats throughout eastern Germany were restricted.

10 — At Bordighera, on February 12, Mussolini said to Franco: "England's hope is perhaps Russia. But Russia is not playing (*fuori giuoco*); Stalin is very shrewd and shall not let himself be influenced by the Jews . . . anyhow there are 85 German divisions along the eastern frontier. . . . Germany will not permit attacks on her flanks against Finland or Rumania." Mussolini thus repeated the exact arguments which Hitler voiced to him on January 20.

11 — According to an undocumented story, Terentiev and Papen called on the Turkish Foreign Minister together in early February. Terentiev is supposed to have requested that Turkey should not ask for British help nor attack Bulgaria, even if the latter would adhere to the Tripartite Pact. Within a few hours, Terentiev (or Vinogradov?) returned alone and said to Sarajoglu exactly the contrary: Turkey should assist Bulgaria and Russia would then furnish Turkey with military material.

12 — Finnish Blue-White Book, *op. cit.* The German Naval High Command on February 5 (see the above cited *IMT*, 33–C) noted "close collaboration" established with the Finnish Navy: also, "support of *B-Dienst* (Naval Intelligence Service) against Russia through the Finnish News Service units as was already practiced up to 1939."

13 — The Bulgarian Communists later derived much advantage from the fact that, due to the Russian hostility against the German's Bulgarian plans, the Communist movement there resisted the Germans from early 1941 onwards — elsewhere the Communist parties turned against Germany only after June 22, 1941.

14 — General Halder in his Nuremberg testimony (*IMT*, Affidavit H) stated that Hitler gave the German Army Chiefs the detailed reasons for his resolution to attack Russia in March 1941 for the first time, while such an important member of the German hierarchy as Funk said that he did not know of the Russian war project until the end of April (*IMT*, 3952–PS).

15 — General Papagos was later forced to modify his battle-order; Churchill in *The Grand Alliance*, p. 94 ("The Greeks had departed in so many ways from the terms of the Athens Agreement that we could, had we so wished, have asked for release from it"), somewhat high-handedly deals with these events. Papagos and the Greek General Staff answered in an extensive statement, issued on March 4, 1950. Papagos insists that he agreed to the Aliakhmon River line only if Yugoslavian cooperation was won. This statement tallies well with the message Eden sent to Churchill on February 24, 1941 (Churchill, p. 75); there is but little discrepancy, a fact which renders British criticism of the Greeks somewhat unwarranted.

16 — Churchill, *The Grand Alliance* (Boston, 1950), Houghton Mifflin, pp. 101–3.

The Yugoslav Revolution

1 — The regent of Yugoslavia was a silent, good-looking man, Anglophile in his manners and general demeanor; once, in the early thirties, King Boris remarked to Alexander I: "Tu sais, toi et moi, nous sommes beaucoup plus balkaniques que Paul." He was cool but only in a silently dignified manner, aloof without being supercilious. Why did he compromise with Hitler then? Paul's sympathies were not pro-German; he wanted the victory of Britain as much as any other decent Balkan statesman did. But he did not want to sacrifice Yugoslavia for the sake of a gallant gesture; he wanted to win time and see what happened. Also, he feared the Soviets and the

Communists. That his pre-war British relations were mostly with those segments of Britain's ruling classes who were toying at that time with pro-German sentiments (Nevile Henderson was British Minister to Yugoslavia in the early thirties and had developed an intimate friendship with Prince Paul) had also a decisive influence on his bearing. Paul was no traitor and no coward; he found compromise necessary, nay, inevitable.

Here the question must be raised: was the Yugoslav Revolution worthwhile, after all? Some Yugoslav statesmen, Tsvetkovič among them, argued after the war that the Tripartite Pact might have saved Yugoslavia from the terrible German occupation, from dismemberment, from the horrors of more than four years of civil war and of later Bolshevization; it would also have provided the chances for a potential southern bridgehead and Allied front against Hitler. There is much to this argument. On the other hand it is indeed questionable whether a victorious Hitler in 1941–42 (or Stalin, when victorious later) would have honored the limitations of Yugoslav participation in the Tripartite Pact.

2 — Churchill knew this. He wrote Eden on March 1: "Your main appeal should now be made to Yugoslavia. A sudden move by Yugoslavia would produce an Italian disaster of the first magnitude, possibly decisive on [the] whole Balkan situation." It was evident that "the defense of Salonika would depend on Yugoslavia's attitude."

3 — He thanked Roosevelt for Donovan's efforts: "he has carried with him an animating, heart-warming flame." To the visiting Hopkins, Churchill wrote off a successful Greek resistance as early as January. See Sherwood, *Roosevelt and Hopkins* (New York, 1948), p. 237. During the meeting of Hopkins

with Churchill in January, Eden expressed his belief that Russia feared the Germans and that Stalin would keep out of the war. This analysis was remarkably correct at that time and at variance with American over-optimistic predictions.

4 — The British Minister in Belgrade was told by Yugoslav officials as early as March 18 — while Paul was in Berchtesgaden — that Yugoslavia would join the Tripartite Pact, as Germany did not demand the right of passage from her. See Cordell Hull, *Memoirs* (New York, 1948), p. 932. See also the controversial articles by Tsvetkovič in *Le Figaro*, April 4, 1950 and R. L. Kneževic in *International Affairs* (January 1951).

5 — The Grand Alliance (Boston, 1950), Houghton Mifflin, p. 160. These were indeed the lowest days of Rumania. The Rumanian Legation in Egypt served German spies. See Churchill to Eden on March 9, *op. cit.*, p. 107.

6 — Ulrich von Hassell made a trip in the Balkans between March 19 and 28; his diary gives a very interesting account of the people in those dramatic days. See Hassell, *op. cit.*

7 — Churchill to Campbell on March 26: "Do not let any gap grow up between you and Prince Paul or Ministers. Continue to pester, nag and bite. Demand audiences. Don't take *NO* for an answer. Cling to them . . . This is no time for reproaches or dignified farewells . . ."

8 — The story of the Yugoslav revolution is another proof that "revolutions" of the twentieth century are always *coups d'état* and have to be organized from above, even if the cause of the insurrectionists is overwhelmingly supported by public opinion.

9 — The chant of the demonstrators was illuminating: "Better War Than Pact."

According to a story, on March 28 Darlan had received Purič, the Yugoslav envoy to Vichy, and asked how many divisions the Yugoslavs had. Purič allegedly answered: "That question we Yugoslavs don't ask; we fight first and count afterwards."

10 — There were a few trampled swastikas and a few stones thrown against the window exhibits of the German and Italian tourist offices. But there were no "unbearable and continuous" attacks against German diplomats or civilians, as the Germans charged.

11 — Yet, if we include Turkey in the whole eastern Mediterranean theatre, there were about 70 British, Greek, Yugoslav, and Turkish divisions against about 30 German. See Churchill, p. 169.

12 — The Italian Minister, Mameli, when he telephoned Rome in those days used a Sardinian dialect to evade detection through tapping of the wires: another *opera buffa* episode in wartime Italian diplomacy.

13 — Fiume was brandished by Hitler obviously to influence the "naval-minded" Horthy. The Italians were, of course, not asked about Hitler's generous "offer."

14 — And in the Yugoslav army on January 1, 1940, there were 162 Serbian, 3 Croat and 1 Slovene general.

15 — Mussolini recommended Pavelič to Hitler on March 28; the Italians readied the Croat in his exile in Pisa. See Anfuso, *Roma, Berlino, Salò* (Rome, 1950), p. 186. "It is difficult to Tuscanize Croatia."

16 — Medjemurje in Serbo-Croat—Muraköz in Hungarian. Bačka in Serbo-Croat — Bácska in Hungarian.
On the German military directives see *IMT*, 1195–PS, 1746–PS, 1835–PS, 95–R, 3031–PS.

17 — Moscow, for example, seemed to favor the Bulgarian Communists. Sarlo-Satorov, leader of the Macedonian Communists, leaned toward the Bulgarian party line rather than to the Yugoslav Communist Party and against an independent Macedonia.

18 — A careful examination of the clumsy Russian style of the "denial" may lead to the conclusion that it might have been drafted by Stalin himself.

19 — Another footnote to history: the Croat Kvaternik's grandfather in 1859–61 courted Paris for support of an independent Croatia. His grandson was supported by Hitler.

The Balkan campaign and the mysteries of Soviet diplomacy

1 — And Rommel defeated the British in Libya, the psychological effects of which event were clear to Churchill: "Far more important than the loss of ground is the idea that we cannot face the Germans and that their appearance is enough to drive us back many scores of miles. This may react most evilly throughout [the] Balkans and Turkey."

2 — There must be some reason why the *Ciano Diaries* do not contain entries between January and April, 1941; also, Simoni's anti-Fascist account of his days in the Berlin Embassy is interrupted on March 30 — the next entry is April 23. Conscience troubles? Careful editing?

3 — The river Mura was crossed, however: a tributary of the Drava, forming the northern limits of the Medjemurje.

4 — Just as Miss Elizabeth Wiskemann wisely stated in her *Rome-Berlin Axis* (New York, 1949), the Balkan peasant erroneously thought so often that it was Russia which was the guardian of his independence. What did he know about Disraeli, Salisbury, Palmerston!

5 — See Churchill, pp. 356–9. On Stalin's reaction and admitted lack of recognition of Churchill's message see Churchill, *The Hinge of Fate*, p. 493.

6 — Many remembered 1915 when the Bulgarian Commander-in-Chief exhorted his soldiers to follow in the steps of that "great Bulgarian, Alexander the Great." See W. Kolarz, *Myths and Realities in Eastern Europe* (London, 1946), p. 33.

7 — General Glaise-Horstenau, the former Austrian pro-Nazi statesman was appointed Reich Commissioner in these territories. He had constant troubles with the SS plenipotentiaries, Veesenmeyer, and the SA "envoy," Kasche, in Zagreb.

8 — The *Südgau* idea (a great German colony on the lower Danube formed by the German-inhabited districts of Tolna in Hungary, the Bačka, and the Banat) was advanced by F. Naumann in his famous *Mitteleuropa* thesis (1915). In 1941 a powerful German radio transmitter in Belgrade and an important German daily, the *Donauzeitung*, were two *Südgau* bulwarks. Partisan warfare, political difficulties with Hungary and Rumania, and the staunch and courageous behavior of certain German Catholic elements in the Bačka (who published an anti-Nazi German newspaper *Die Donau* there until 1944) made then the formation of the Südgau inopportune. Yet the Banat territory remained under rigid German military and civilian control.

9 — Ljubljana in Serbo-Croat — Lubiana in Italian.

10 — The idea of Montenegrin "independence" originated in Rome, partly due to the ties of the Queen of Italy with the former Montenegrin dynasty.

11 — *NSR*, p. 331. Yet compare this statement with what he said to Mussolini four months later: Hitler was grateful that Mussolini started the Greek affair, which saved him from later difficulties. See above, p. 768, note 6.

12 — During the whole campaign the Italians had cause enough to be disturbed. A German division marched into Ioannina to get there before the Italians; the Italians were not consulted in most of the local armistices; a German attempt to occupy Kotor and Ragusa failed only because the Italians forestalled them there. See the report of Alfieri on May 1, Alfieri, *Due dittatori di fronte* (Milan, 1948), pp. 159–60. (Alfieri's memoirs are of not much value otherwise; for example, he fails to remember correctly the name of his Soviet colleague in Berlin: he calls him "De Kasanov.")

13 — It is very interesting to note, however, that in 1941 the German non-Nazi and anti-Nazi conservatives were desperately against the Russian war, while Hitler and some of his Nazis were for it. Even Weizsäcker, ever cautious, ever adaptable, wrote a memorandum on Ribbentrop's request, on April 28, in which he supported Schulenburg's views; Russia should not be attacked, for the attack would only help England. Raeder, even Hassell, thought along similar lines. In other words, they considered the defeat of Britain as the primary task, while Hitler regarded the Soviets as the primary target and main enemy — an interesting symptom which should not be forgotten. See also n. 1, p. 218 of my article in *Current History* (April 1951). On the other hand, distinction should be made between these men and the great number of Germany's anti-Nazi conservatives. (Weizsäcker continued to serve, although full of

doubts, until the very end; while Schulenburg went into opposition, willing to serve the cause of a separate peace — though with Russia.)

14 — Two weeks later, however, the Soviet Ambassador to Vichy hinted to Bergéry that Russia would hardly agree to build a new Europe together with the present Germany.

15 — On April 27 the Finnish Minister to Rumania reported that German troops were near the Bessarabian border and some evacuation of the civilian population was going on.

Beginnings of the central-eastern European resistance movements

1 — This relative order remained approximately the same until March 1944, the date of the German coup in Hungary. From that time until August-September 1944 (the Bulgarian and Rumanian armistices) the order was this: Bulgaria, Rumania, Hungary.

2 — This chapter does not deal with the internal resistance movements of the territories incorporated into the Soviet Union between 1939 and 1941. The Soviet system of political control made every kind of resistance virtually impossible in eastern Poland, the ceded Finnish territories, Bessarabia, and northern Bukovina. There was some resistance in the Baltic states in 1940–41. As Austria became a gau of the German Reich, the examination of the Austrian resistance movement falls outside the scope of this book. Suffice it to say that the *Anschluss* joy of the masses was followed by a real hangover. Glaise-Horstenau admitted that as early as 1939 not more than ten per cent of the Austrians favored the union with Germany.

3 — Hitler to Mussolini on June 18, 1940: "Poland is steppe. My administrators

. . . would prefer to govern Negroes instead of Poles." Between 1939 and 1941 Mussolini, in his letters to Hitler, mentioned three times the desirability of creating a Polish state under German supervision, but Hitler was unmoved.

4 — See, among others, the following *IMT* documents: 864–PS, 2537–PS, on Polish-German relations in and after October 1939, 2916–PS on Polish segregation and population policies, 92–R on transfer of Polish property to Germans, 96–R on seizure of Jewish property, 139–R on the German adaptation of civil law in the eastern territories, 141–R on the regulation with the Germans' intercourse with Poles, 148–R on the treatment of Polish workers.

5 — Italy withdrew her recognition from the Polish government on June 10, 1940. Hungary, Rumania, Bulgaria and also Finland broke relations with the Poles during 1941. An official state of war, however, did not exist between Poland and Italy, nor between Poland and the German satellites.

6 — Flandin in his *Politique française* (Paris, 1948), criticizes very unjustly the rôle of the Polish forces in the defense of France; but Flandin had a steady prejudice againt Poles and Czechs.

7 — The Polish merchant marine, Polish submarines, and minor naval craft took an active part in the Battle of the Atlantic. On October 20, 1940, Churchill wrote: "I am concerned by the very low state of equipment of the Polish troops, whose military qualities have proven so high . . ." *Their Finest Hour*, p. 680. See also Sikorski's offer to give a Polish Brigade to the Greek campaign in his touching talk with Churchill in *The Grand Alliance*, p. 108.

8 — The United States recognized this government on October 26, 1942. This delay, however, was merely automatic and had no diplomatic significance.

9 — Ley said to Ciano and Mussolini in December 1939 that the Skoda and Vitkovice works were producing as never before. From this he deduced a mistaken conclusion of "Slav inactivity," pointing that there were as yet no Polish or Czech rebellions. See also the following *IMT* documents: 3869–PS, 3862–PS (Neurath letters), 3857–PS (on the treatment of Czech workers), 959–D on SS atrocities, 739–D, etc.

10 — A Churchill minute on January 5, 1941: "I certainly intend to talk rather more about the Nazis and rather less about the Germans. We must not let our vision be darkened by hatred or obscured by sentiment. A much more fruitful line is to try to separate the Prussians from the South Germans . . ."

11 — Harold Nicolson's book, *Why Britain Is At War*, published in London in November 1939, reflected British conservative opinion on war aims. This eminent and wise diplomatic historian pointed at the difference between Preliminary Treaties and a Final Treaty, the latter preferably in a neutral capital. He also came out for some kind of a European United States.

The State Department in the spring of 1940 played with the idea of a conference of neutrals. Upon the recommendation of Roosevelt, post-war planning was introduced as early as that time. One of these blueprints planned for three *blocs* in central-eastern Europe: 1. The Baltic states and Poland; 2. the Danubian states: Bohemia-Moravia, Slovakia, Hungary, Yugoslavia; 3. the Balkan states: Rumania, Bulgaria, Greece. (Notice

that the status of Czechoslovakia and of Albania was not supposed to change in these plans.) See *Post-War Foreign Policy Preparations* (further, *PWP*) (Washington, 1950). See also above, p. 760, note 16.

12 — Roosevelt intimated to the Hungarian statesman Eckhardt in 1940 that he favored Otto Habsburg, federations, no return to the Congress of Paris peace treaties and that he was not averse to constitutional monarchies. A Churchill minute to the Foreign Office on March 15, 1941: "Being a strong monarchist, I am in principle in favour of constitutional monarchies as a barrier against dictatorships, and for many other reasons. It would be a mistake for Great Britain to try to force her systems on other countries, and this would only create prejudice and opposition. The main policy of the Foreign Office should however be to view with a benevolent eye neutral movements among the populations of different countries toward monarchies. Certainly we should not hinder them, if we cannot help." *The Grand Alliance* (Boston, 1949), Houghton Mifflin, pp. 476–7.

Compare this with Ribbentrop's statement to Mussolini on May 2, 1938: "The only good thing done by German social democracy was to liquidate the monarchy for good." *CD*, p. 167.

13 — See the letters exchanged between the Central Committee of the Communist Party of Yugoslavia and the Central Committee of the Communist Party of the Soviet Union (Bolshevik) in 1948, when the Tito-Stalin feud erupted, in *The Soviet-Yugoslav Dispute* (London, 1948). The CPY letter corrected erroneous CPSU(B) assertions concerning the date, and the number of those elected.

14 — It is interesting to observe that throughout the war it was the Monarchists who were considered the primary enemies of the Austrian and Hungarian Nazis. The same attitude was taken by the Communists. In March 1940 Mussolini found it necessary to please Ribbentrop by ridiculing Otto Habsburg at a time when Sumner Welles' European trip engendered speculations.

15 — Anti-Italian resistance in Albania again came from the conservative side. Jacomoni and Ciano were often forced to take the wishes of the conservative chiefs into consideration. When the Greeks occupied Koritsa, in January 1940 an anti-Italian "liberation" group of Albanian intellectuals assembled there. (Ciano often hid his displeasure with the Albanian resistance by citing the inferior civility of the Albanians. For example, when the Italian King visited Tirana in May 1941, Ciano wrote that forks and silver cutlery were conspicuously missing after the state dinner there.) A young Albanian attempted to kill the visiting Victor Emmanuel III in 1941, but the assassination attempt had no political significance; the man was a poet whose literary product had been rejected by the judges of a poetic contest.

The external arm of the Albanian resistance was hampered by King Zog's lack of popularity among the few Albanians living abroad, especially among those in the United States.

The last phase of Nazi-Soviet peace

1 — This is one of the very few authentic samples of confidential Soviet diplomatic documents which are available to the outside world. *NSR*, p. 339; also see *ibid.*, *passim*.

2 — Especially General Milch of the German Air Force was against a Russian War. See also *IMT*, 35–C. (Objections to the war against Russia.)

3 — Schulenburg said to Stalin in March 1941 — did he foresee the journey? — that Hess was "crazy." On what Hess said about the Russian War after his arrival in England, see *IMT*, 614–D, 116–M, 117–M, 118–M, 119–M. Yet even in 1944, Stalin pestered Churchill with the tale that Hess discussed with the British a German-British alliance.

4 — *IMT*, 873–PS. This document contradicts former hypotheses about the attack in Russia having been scheduled for June 14 but postponed by eight days because of the weather conditions or the hesitations of Hungary. On *Barbarossa* planning see also 872–PS, 1156–PS, 1157–PS, 2718–PS; 37–C, 38–C, 39–C, 170–C, 54–C, 150–C; also 1866–PS on this Ribbentrop visit.

5 — Churchill to General Smuts on May 16: "It looks as if Hitler is massing against Russia." The massing of German divisions against Russia proceeded quickly: in December there were 34 divisions in the eastern theatre; in May, 87; on June 21 there were 120, with 6 Rumanian ones and about 24 reserves.

6 — Also Slovakia, whose northeastern corner, although not directly bordering the Soviet Union, almost touched the Soviet frontier in the Carpathians. The Bratislava "government" also declared war on the Soviet Union on June 22.

7 — Bárdossy visited Rome on June 4–5, according to Ciano, in "a classically useless visit. One recognized in him the classic career diplomat, devourer of cakes at ladies' teas, frequenter of South American Legations and salons of unknown countesses."

8 — Buschenhagen was later captured in Russia and became a member of the Paulus group. His testimony concerning these events conflicts with that of Ryti.

9 — Finnish diplomacy still feared a last-minute broad German-Russian agreement, and on May 31 the Finnish Minister to Berlin was told to present Finnish claims in case of a German-Russian settlement, lest Finland be deceived again by Russia and Germany. As the Finns knew that any such agreement would be made due to German pressure, they presented modest demands through their envoy in Berlin.

10 — What did Stalin know? It is, of course, possible that he and his cohorts were "bunglers, simpletons," as Churchill calls them. In 1948 a statement by the chief of the Soviet State Planning Commission seems to confirm that in the spring of 1941 Stalin thought that he could keep out of the war.

11 — On the same day a member of the conversing German conservative opposition asked Hassell to intervene with Mussolini and get the Italian in turn to stop Hitler from a Russian war. Hassell said he could not do this.

12 — Already the June 1 *Barbarossa* timetable had ordered that beginning June 15, Russian ships "should be kept [away] by disguised measures from Kiel and Gdynia."

13 — This was preceded by a remark he dropped to his secretary on June 21: "If Hitler invaded Hell I would make at least a favourable reference to the Devil in the House of Commons."

14 — Göbbels boasted eight months later in his diary in a burst of slang: "Schulenburg had got no wind of the

launching of *Barbarossa*." Göbbels, *Tagebücher* (Zurich, 1948) — entry of February 14, 1942. He adds as a necessary conclusion: diplomats should be kept as uninformed as Schulenburg was. Compare this with Ribbentrop's opinion on Schulenburg and Köstring: "Diplomats and military attachés in Moscow are the worst informed people in the world."

15 — According to Gafencu, the meeting took place at 6 P.M. See also *NSR*, pp. 353–7.

16 — Schmidt, *op. cit.*, p. 538: "Never before have I seen Ribbentrop as excited as in those five minutes before Dekanosov's arrival." Ribbentrop spoke aloud to convince himself that the attack on Russia was a good move.

17 — We do not have a full record of the Schulenburg-Molotov talk. According to Gafencu, Molotov was pale and anxious. He said: "This is war. Your air force has just bombarded ten open cities. Do you believe we deserved that?"

18 — Churchill's comment: "Thus the ravings of hatred against Britain and the United States which the Soviet propaganda machine cast upon the midnight air were overwhelmed at dawn by the German cannonade. The wicked are not always clever, nor are dictators always right."

19 — Beloff, *The Foreign Policy of Soviet Russia*, vol. II, 1929–1941 (London, 1949). Hitler to Alfieri on June 22: the Russian problem had caused him sleepless nights, "I examined all eventualities."

THE WAR OF WARS (*1941–1944*)

The Russian War, the "satellites" and Finland — 1941

1 — Orlov supposedly explained to members of the American Legation in Finland on June 27 that he had heard before the Finnish declaration of war

that the Soviet Government had cut off the Finnish Legation in Moscow from the outer world and therefore he, Orlov, had advised Moscow to start with the military operations. Procopé, *op. cit.* Also, the Soviet Consul in the Aaland Islands asked permission from the governor there to leave for Helsinki as early as the 23rd. It is also interesting to observe that while the German Embassy in Moscow was completely surrounded and isolated from June 22 on, the Finnish, Italian, Rumanian, and Hungarian Legations enjoyed relative freedom for almost a week.

2 — In March 1944 Molotov in a conversation conceded to the Finnish peace delegates, Paasikivi and Enckell, that the Soviet Union had attacked first in 1941. See a similar confession to Gafencu about 1940, above, p. 418.

3 — A. Ullein-Reviczky, *Guerre Allemande-Paix Russe* (Neuchâtel, 1947). Horthy, for example, did not know about the existence of the Molotov-Kristóffy conversations until 1944. It seems that the Hungarian government in 1941 had nonetheless waited with its decision until Finland, the "sister nation" had made up her mind. But this reliance on Finland was as pathetic as that of three years later: in September 1944, the Hungarian Premier General Lakatos said in a radio address that the Finnish example had exhorted Hungary to go on fighting. Next day the Finnish armistice was announced.

4 — Munkács in Hungarian — Mukačevo in Czech, Slovak and Ruthenian.

5 — Early in 1942, CSIR became ARMIR (Armata Italiana in Russia).

6 — There was, however, a small Finnish SS organized by the Germans. It had ceased to exist by 1943.

7 — Petrozavodsk in Russian — Asaunislinna in Finnish.

8 — See these *IMT* documents: 1058–PS, 37–C; on the situation and German

plans in the Baltics 1189–PS, 1519–PS, 1520–PS, 411–D, 841–D, 347–PS, 2952–PS, 2953–PS, 221–C, 180–L; in the Ukraine 197–PS, 294–PS, 695–PS, 1017–PS. In Lithuania some of the former "Iron Wolves," in Estonia some of the former "Liberators" were accepted for auxiliary police work by the Germans; local SS legions were formed. The Germans also encouraged "native anti-Semitic forces," who in Lithuania according to an SS report (see *IMT*, 841–D, 347–PS) killed 3800 Jews in two days, while the Latvian "cleaning action" could show only 400 victims and the Estonians killed none. A few of the Lithuanian and Latvian SS recruits were sent to Poland, where they did ghetto policing together with some brutal and inhuman Ukrainians.

9 — According to General Blumentritt, Chief of Staff of the Fourth German Army, in November 1940 a Lithuanian colonel was planted in the Soviet Army by German intelligence and gave information on Russian troop dispositions. The former Lithuanian Minister to Berlin, Skirpa, and the politician Kublilunas had some influence with the Rosenberg group, but a Lithuanian "government" formed by the conservative Ambrozivicius was not recognized; indeed, some of its members were put into concentration camps.

The international position of the central-eastern European states — 1941

1 — A psychologist might find interest in an involuntary slip of the tongue by Ribbentrop, who, at the early press conference on June 22 announcing the Russian War, mentioned "documents found during the occupation of Great Britain" (*Grossbritannien* instead of *Jugoslawien*). See Simoni, *op. cit.*

2 — After 1942 these lines of thought changed:

Nazis and extreme pro-Germans: Germany would stop the Russian counteroffensive and negotiate a favorable separate peace. Germany and Russia, together with Japan, would form a worldwide proletarian alliance against the English-speaking nations.

Conservatives (pro-German): Germany and Britain would arrive at a compromise. The Russians would be kept out of Europe. Most of central-eastern Europe would continue to belong to a German sphere of interest.

Conservatives (pro-British) and Liberals: The coming invasion, whether in the West or in the South of Europe, would crush Hitler, and Germany would sue for peace before the Russians could arrive in central-eastern Europe.

Radical Democrats; the Left: Russia and Britain would be equal factors in defeating the Axis. Central-eastern Europe after the war would undergo radical social changes, constituting a bridge between East and West, a healthy territory of compromise between western European individualist and eastern collectivist ideas, but by no means under communistic influences. These developments would come irrespective of what Power would liberate central-eastern Europe in the last phase of the anti-Axis war.

The *Communists'* position and their expectations were, of course, unchanged.

3 — Were not, in the first ten days of the Russian War, some hopes left with Stalin of reaching a *modus vivendi* with Hitler at the price of concessions? The almost conciliatory manner with which Molotov treated the departing Axis diplomats, the Russian silence in regard to Britain, the fact that not until July 3 did Stalin find it necessary to address the peoples of the Soviet Union in a nationwide broadcast might point to such a hypothesis.

4 — Strangely, it was now Matsuoka who championed a Japanese attack on Russia. He had to resign in July. Yet Hitler to Raeder on August 22: "I am convinced that Japan will attack Vladivostok as soon as her forces have been assembled."

5 — Admiral Leahy to President Roosevelt on May 26, 1941: in Vichy, Frenchmen told him that the experience of Poland, Norway, Greece "had convinced them beyond the possibility of change that British promises of assistance had no value." However, these people looked differently at America.

6 — See J. Ciechanowski, *Defeat in Victory* (New York, 1947). Sikorski expounded the ideas and plans of a central-eastern European federation to President Roosevelt. The President was very receptive. He even spoke about the Baltics, indicating that he did not accept the Soviet view that the incorporation of the three republics could not be altered. This is especially interesting, as about the same time (March–April 1941), the Soviet Ambassador in London stated to Eden that the first condition of any successful British-Russian contact would be the official British recognition of the Soviets' incorporation of the Baltics.

7 — Here some pre-1938 émigrés of central-eastern Europe, who were by 1941 United States citizens — many of them of extreme Leftist leanings — played destructive rôles. Personal friendships and literary contacts, above all, their command of the English language put them at an immeasurable advantage over the post-1938 and 1939 émigrés, whose social insecurity and lack of experience contributed to the fact that their predecessors had a disproportionately important rôle in the evaluating of central-eastern European policies and persons. Such influences were, unfortunately, strong at the White House also.

8 — The Soviet Union perceived this American sympathy. She asked the United States to protect Russian interests at Vichy when that government broke off relations with the Soviet Union on June 30. Harry Truman, Senator from Missouri in 1941, reflected a rather sensible American attitude when he said at the outbreak of the German-Russian war that, in his opinion, Russia should be helped if the Germans seemed to be winning; Germany should be helped if the Russians seemed to be winning. He added that Hitler should not be allowed to win in any case.

9 — On that day, a British official statement in the House of Commons still insisted: "At present we are maintaining relations with Finland." A favorable statement was made in the House of Lords also. It seems that there was a divergence of opinion between Ryti and Tanner in handling the problem of British relations. (Tanner entered the cabinet early in July.)

10 — *The Grand Alliance* (Boston, 1950), Houghton Mifflin, p. 534.

11 — See Bova Scoppa, *op. cit.*, pp. 28–9, 39. The German SS envoy, Killinger, hated his Italian colleague and intrigued against him.

12 — See *Documents secrets du ministère des affaires étrangères de l'Allemagne*-III-*Turquie* (Paris, 1946). There is some evidence that, at least in 1940, some of the Turkish "pan-Turanians" were in contact with a few Polish "Prometheans," both envisaging a territorial division of certain southern territories of the Soviet Union.

13 — This attitude lasted for exactly two years. In 1944 it began to change and early in 1945 the Soviets raised their demands for Kars and Ardahan.

14 — A Polish daily newspaper was also published in Budapest. Later, the Polish colony there became a center of British intelligence activities.

15 — The British Government accepted the Bulgarian declaration only on December 26. While the departure of the British diplomats from Sofia, Bucharest, and Budapest in the spring of 1941 took place in a bleak atmosphere (in Bulgaria, a bomb was planted in the diplomats' luggage, killing and injuring some of the diplomatic personnel), the American diplomats, especially in Budapest, were treated with exceptional courtesy and given considerable freedom of movement.

16 — The Churchill directives are given in *The Grand Alliance*, Appendix D. See also *ibid.*, pp. 457 *et passim.*

17 — Hassell, *op. cit.;* see also R. Rahn, *Ruheloses Leben* (Düsseldorf, 1949). Stalin during the whole war was keenly aware of the truth established by Clausewitz that military operations and political actions are intertwined, indeed, essentially of the same character. During the retreat in the summer and autumn of 1941 the only front where the Russian armed forces engaged in sporadic offensive operations was in the Black Sea area, where Russia strove to give the impression that she held the initiative. Constanta was shelled by the Black Sea Fleet, and in the worst days of the Ukrainian and Smolensk battles the Soviet Air Force could spare a handful of planes to undertake a symbolic bombardment of Bucharest.

18 — See Sherwood, *Roosevelt and Hopkins* (New York, 1948). It can be detected that Stalin was more solicitous toward Harriman than to the British, and did not fail to make a remarkable impression on the Americans. Churchill had no particular desire to be apologetic. See Churchill, pp. 468, 472–4. On October 28 he telegraphed Cripps: all

Soviet reproaches "leave me quite cold. If they harbour suspicions of us, it is only because of the guilt and self-reproach in their own hearts." On October 20 Churchill to Roosevelt: "The Russians much disturb Persia by their presence, their theories and their behaviour . . ." At that time Churchill pondered the stakes of amphibious landings in Norway and Sicily but a few weeks later these plans were abandoned.

19 — See his 1942 New Year's Report in *Documents Secrets . . . Turquie, op. cit.*

20 — Secret Anglo-American staff discussion in Washington had already established in January 1941 that the United States would give priority to the Atlantic-European theatre under any circumstances.

21 — On March 28, 1942, the American government transmitted a "last-minute" note to Hungary, Bulgaria, and Rumania through Switzerland, warning them to cease active participation in the war.

Britain, Poland, and Russia — 1941

1 — Ciechanowski, *Defeat in Victory*, pp. 28–9.

2 — *The Grand Alliance* (Boston, 1950), Houghton Mifflin, p. 391.

3 — At the same time Polish troops fought with undaunted valor in every theatre with the British Empire; for example, a "Carpathian" Brigade excelled at Tobruk. Throughout 1941 Churchill's minutes bristle with references to and requests for more arms and consideration for the Polish troops. See for example his minute to Sir Alan Brooke, *op. cit.*, pp. 840–1.

4 — The disorganization of the Polish army in September 1939 made the Russians collect tens of thousands of civilians into their camps as "prisoners-of-war."

5 — The Polish National Council, formed in France in the winter of 1939–40, was dissolved. Sosnkowski was later Liaison Minister between the government and the underground in Poland. In 1944 he became Premier.

6 — Ciechanowski, *op. cit.* In November, Roosevelt instructed Harriman to telegraph Stalin again on that matter.

7 — It could not be expected, of course, that when the Russian Army was to surge later victoriously westward, Stalin would have stuck to his "little" frontier requests. But, had Stalin committed himself in December 1941, it would have been infinitely easier for the Polish government to secure the support of Britain and the United States for the maintenance of a Polish-Soviet territorial agreement.

8 — Disturbing symptoms continued to appear during the Sikorski visit. On December 1 the Polish Embassy was informed by Soviet authorities that they regarded the Ukrainian, White Russian and Jewish people of eastern Poland — that is, in the territory which the Ribbentrop-Molotov line allotted to the Soviet Union — as "citizens of the Soviet Union."

On December 3, two noted Polish Jewish Socialists, Alter and Ehrlich, who were busy in creating an anti-German organization of Polish Jews within the Soviet Union, were suddenly arrested in Kuybishev and later executed on the pretext of "conspiracy with the Fascists."

9 — *PWP*, p. 62. See also *The Grand Alliance*, pp. 628–31, and Hull, *op. cit.*

10 — It is interesting to note that, about the same time, Papen offered the same rectification in Bulgaria to the Turks.

Did he know of the Stalin-Eden talks, or did the Russians know of Papen's offers?

11 — Nevertheless Churchill showed some understanding for Russian territorial aims and mentioned to Eden that some revision of the 1939 Finnish frontier around Leningrad seemed reasonable to him in view of recent experiences. His general disdain of Russian arguments, however, continued. From his 1942 war plans: "If it is true, as Stalin asserts, that [the Japanese] have, in addition to their own air force fifteen hundred German airplanes (and he would have opportunities of knowing how they got there) . . ." *Ibid.*, p. 652.

12 — *The Grand Alliance* (Boston, 1950), Houghton Mifflin, p. 630.

The national resistance movements during 1941 and 1942

1 — See here the following *IMT* documents: 50–, 51–, 52–C, 389–PS, 81–UK, 2746–PS, 165–, 170–L, 1019–, 1024–, 1030–, 1034–, 1039–, 1056–, 1058–, 1061–PS. Also the documents gradually declassified since 1948 of the Office of Intelligence Research, U. S. Department of State (the predecessor organizations of which were the Office of the Coordinator of Information and the Research and Analysis Branch of the OSS), — R&A further: R&A 607, 1756, 878.2, 1905.

2 — Early in 1942 an SS directive concerning the prisoner-of-war and concentration camp of Oranienburg established with some German meticulousness that volunteering Polish or Russian prisoners willing to kill their own countrymen — international disputes and all-round spying and corruption were consciously furthered by the administration of these camps and some broken inmates and semi-bestial criminals were provided with picks

and knives and unusually sharp shovels for such tasks — would receive three cigarettes for each individual execution instead of the previous "compensation" of three Reichsmarks. *IMT*, 569–D.

3 — About that time a "Kossuth Radio" carried similar programs for Hungary, and parallel "clandestine" Yugoslav, Rumanian, Bulgar, and Greek programs were broadcast from Soviet territory.

4 — On the epicurean life of Frank and his interesting neo-renaissance philosophy see C. Malaparte, *Kaputt* (New York, 1946) and also the Gestapo's secret report on Frank, *IMT*, 3815–PS. Forster, the former Gauleiter of Danzig, and Lohse in Riga also changed somewhat for the better during 1943.

5 — On Bormann's views on Poland and the *Ostland*, see *IMT*, 36–R. Also *IMT*, 910–PS on the "germanization" of the Góral, Lemke, Hucul groups in Poland, and the "germanization" of the three cities Lublin, Zamósc, and Cracow. By that time Lodz was Litzmannstadt and Gdynia Gotenhafen.

6 — Oswiecim in Polish — Auschwitz in German.

7 — See here *IMT*, 1972–, 2118–, 2773–PS. A similar and less known Lidice occurred in the Greek village of Kalavrytas (and the French Oradour).

The liquidation of the Czech Jews went on according to plan, although some of the victims fared relatively better than their unfortunate Polish brethren: a so-called "sample" ghetto city, named Theresienstadt, was erected in central "Czechia," where death had, of course, its bountiful pickings, but it was not yet such an organized slaughterhouse as were Oswiecim,

Majdanek, or some of the German camps. Yet only a minority of Czechoslovakia's Jews could share in the relative fortunes of the Theresienstadt inhabitants, as by the end of 1942, only twenty per cent remained within the Protectorate — the other eighty had been transported to Poland. The Germans also organized the extermination of the central-eastern European Gypsies.

8 — See W. Kolarz, *Myths and Realities in Eastern Europe* (London, 1946). There was sporadic and limited Communist activity in the traditionally pro-Russian Carpatho-Ukraine, beginning late in 1942.

9 — See *IMT*, 204–, 347–, 2280–, 3040–PS; 170–L.

10 — In 1942 Pavelič stated in an article: "Great deeds were done by Germans and Croats together. We can proudly say that we succeeded in breaking the Serb nation, which, after the English, is the most thick-headed, the most stubborn and the most stupid."

11 — Medjemurje in Serbo-Croat — Muraköz in Hungarian.

12 — From 1941 on, it was Hitler's policy not to send trained diplomats but SS and SA leaders to diplomatic posts in the Balkans, Hungary, and Slovakia. By 1942 there were SA Ministers in Bratislava, Zagreb, Budapest, and Sofia. Killinger in Bucharest was an SS man. In 1943 an SS plenipotentiary was sent to Zagreb and the relatively easygoing Jagow was succeeded by the SS Veesenmeyer after the German coup in Hungary in March 1944.

13 — He was extradited by the Western Allies to Tito in 1945: before his "trial," he committed suicide in September 1945 by jumping from the fourth floor of the prison building.

14 — Only one Mihailovič commander, the unscrupulous and brutal Pečanač, deserted in December to the Germans. Conflicts arose now in Macedonia, where Mihailov, the leader of IMRO, the Macedonian terrorist organization, sought support from Sofia and Zagreb. (See R&A 764; also E. Barker, *Macedonia*, London, 1950.) There was also a perceptible difference between the Yugoslav and Bulgar Communists concerning Macedonia, which difference was a meager forerunner of the Tito-Stalin conflict. In 1941 the Macedonian Communists refused to heed Yugoslav Communist directives. In July Tito wrote the Bulgarian Communist Party to stop their anti-Yugoslav propaganda in Macedonia and ultimately turned to Moscow for a ruling which, according to the Yugoslav Communists, was made in their favor. But in September Macedonian Communists called Tito "an Anglophile." In October Moscow, resuscitating Pan-Slavism, called an All-Slav Congress at which an old professor from Leningrad, Derzhavin, surprisingly appeared; Derzhavin in 1916 had written a book praising Bulgaria and commending a Bulgarian Macedonia.

15 — Novi Sad in Serbo-Croat — Ujvidék in Hungarian.

16 — See K. Fotitch, *The War We Lost* (New York, 1948). A Churchill minute to the Chiefs of Staff on November 28: "Everything in human power should be done to help the Yugoslav guerrillas."

17 — Churchill became aware of these complications and on June 2, 1942, asked for a summary report from the Director of Military Intelligence on the relative position of the Yugoslav resistance forces. See Churchill, *The Hinge of Fate*, p. 867.

18 — For example, the BBC attributed resistance feats done by the Mihailovič forces to the Partisans. See F. A. Voigt, *Pax Britannica* (London, 1948), pp. 271 ff.: "The inconceivable was happening: the voice of Britain was speaking falsely while the voice of Germany spoke the truth." Except for the *Manchester Guardian*, the British newspapers gave almost exclusive space to Tito.

19 — The note was revealed by the Yugoslavs in 1949. See A. B. Ulam's article in the *Review of Politics* (January 1951).

20 — In March the British Foreign Office surprisingly requested the Yugoslavs not to negotiate a new treaty with Moscow. The British reasoned that a treaty not fully conforming with Soviet desires would not be accepted by Moscow; on the other hand, any treaty acceptable to Stalin would leave, at best, a wide leeway for various interpretations which sooner or later would reveal themselves and furnish the pretext for an open break between the Soviets and the Yugoslav exile government. Three years later a Soviet-Yugoslav Treaty of Friendship, Non-Aggression, and Mutual Assistance was signed between Tito and Stalin on April 11, 1945, which proved to be the model of the later treaties which the Soviet Union concluded with her postwar satellites between 1946 and 1949. The April 1945 treaty was then denounced by the Soviet Government in August 1949.

21 — The designation EDES was first assumed by a secret republican democratic organization, headed in Athens by General Plastiras in September 1941. A Rightist resistance group, PEAN, was organized in early 1942; it partly merged with EDES, partly continued as "Organization X" under Zervas. The leader of KKE, the Greek Communist Party, Zakhariades, was in a German concentration camp; the political leaders were now Siantos and

the guerrilla chief, "Ares"-Velukhiotis. SNOF was EAM's equivalent among the Macedonian Slavs and Greeks. See Woodhouse, *Apple of Discord* (London, 1948); also R&A 872 here. The Germans attempted to reorganize EEE, the former Greek Fascist movement, but with little success.

22 — See Woodhouse on Athens: "From everything that follows, there is one initial exception: the common people of Athens. Others abide our question; they are free. They are not to be criticised, or even named except on bended knee. They are exempt firstly because their rôle was politically passive; secondly because such decisions as they made collectively came not from the head but from the heart. One should never again think of Greece without thinking first of the women who seized the brooms from the hands of British prisoners scavenging the streets, to do their work for them; of the street-urchins who flung the cigarettes with which they earned their living into lorries loaded with British prisoners as they passed; of the families that died in Khaidhari prison-camp for helping British prisoners to escape. When the common people does such things, it too is influencing the history of human relations, but not in the way that politicians do so, not for their reasons. The men and women of Athens were not guided by reason, but by emotion and instinct. What they did under the impulse of those emotions has no place in a political survey; for under the impulse of another emotion, they could easily do something entirely different. It was, for instance, a girl belonging to the same heritage who returned from a Communist demonstration in October 1944, exclaiming: 'What crowds! What enthusiasm! What a marvel! What popular democracy! Just think what it will be like when the King comes back!' " From *Apple of Discord* by C. M. Woodhouse (1948), by permission of Hutchinson & Co. (Publishers) Limited, London, p. 26.

23 — In Hungary no decree was passed against listening to foreign radio stations, although local authorities sporadically confiscated radios when listening to enemy stations was reported by a jealous or spiteful neighbor or by that cornerstone of civic order in the central and eastern European police states, the janitor.

In Rumania, Bulgaria, and Hungary restrictions against the Jews continued to be enacted; yet, except in Bulgaria, where a number of them were confined to concentration camps by the pro-Nazi Minister of the Interior, and in Rumanian-occupied Bessarabia, where a few formidable massacres occurred, the lives of the Jews in these three countries were not yet imperiled. Especially to Hungary thousands of Slovak and Polish Jews flocked clandestinely between 1940 and 1944 in order to save their lives.

24 — *Documents Secrets . . . Hongrie, op. cit.* See also *CLD, CD.* Ciano also visited Horthy's main adviser, the anti-German conservative and former Premier, Count Bethlen, who categorically denied hearsay that he, Bethlen, was an Anglophile: on the contrary, he feared that an English victory would result in the Bolshevization of most of central-eastern Europe and an automatic and rigid re-creation of the ill-famed Little Entente.

25 — Compared with Killinger and the others, Jagow was a nineteenth-century diplomat. Killinger, for example, casually remarked to Hassell during the latter's visit in 1942 that Bucharest was a "filthy pigsty."

26 — It should not be forgotten that under the impact of terrific propaganda, the average Hungarian, Rumanian, and Bulgarian was virtually unable to visualize an Allied victory in the future. The "resistance parties" were a distinct minority; in Rumania and Hungary they were effective almost exclusively in urban areas. Optimistic sociologists would do well to note that in these countries it was the relatively small, compact, educated and organized industrial workers' class which was most receptive to the Nazi (and after 1944–45, Communist) ideas and which was most violently anti-Ally.

27 — *IMT*, 3319–PS. See also 1517–PS.

28 — Sibiu in Rumanian, — Hermannstadt in German, — Nagyszeben in Hungarian.

29 — On April 13, 1942, plans of the German Naval High Command to mine the Crimean coasts "had to be dropped temporarily because the necessary Rumanian naval forces were refused. The Führer orders that none of the German batteries be given either to Bulgaria or Rumania." On October 28 Hitler and Keitel angrily disparaged the quality of Rumanian troops.

The Hungarian-Rumanian crisis of 1942: the "new Little Entente" idea

1 — All this shows how groundless was a statement made by Beneš in December 1942 that Hungary and Slovakia were discussing post-war union plans.

2 — At that meeting Hitler said to Mussolini that he was somewhat dissatisfied with the Japanese; he disliked Horthy and Mihai Antonescu and even his sympathies for Ion Antonescu had diminished somewhat lately.

3 — See *Documents Secrets . . . Hongrie, op. cit.;* also Bova Scoppa, with whom Mihai Antonescu again raised the "Latin Entente" idea in May.

4 — Himmler was for awhile against Horia Sima, and in December 1942 he asked the Italian government to extradite him. Horia Sima was to have a short half-year of lonely personal glory when after the Rumanian armistice in August 1944 he became the head of the Iron Guardist "government" set up in Germany.

5 — Twice, but for a few days only, the Little Entente idea was to flare up again: in January 1943 when Pavelič clashed with Hungary over the Medjemurje frontier and in March 1944 when Germany occupied Hungary. In 1942–43 there was also sporadic collaboration between Zagreb and Sofia, a collaboration of a clearly anti-Serb character.

Russian developments — 1942

1 — *The Grand Alliance* (Boston, 1950), Houghton Mifflin, pp. 695–6. Roosevelt tried to insist with Litvinov that the issue of complete religious freedom be inserted into the United Nations Declaration. On the other hand the American President was swayed by his conviction that his personal diplomacy could be most effective. Concerning the antecedents of Roosevelt's personal diplomacy with Russia as early as 1933 see *The Soviet Union 1933–1939, op. cit.*

2 — See *PWP, op. cit.*, pp. 89, 143. Which conclusion, of course, shows a tragic misunderstanding of the nature of international politics. As Churchill put it about the same time: "The concern of the Americans with the strategy of a world war was bringing them into touch with political issues on which they had strong opinions and little experience." *The Hinge of Fate*, p. 209. On the legalistic approach practiced by American diplomacy cf. George F. Kennan, *American Diplomacy 1900–1950* (Chicago, 1951); also Langer-Gleason, p. 7: "Mr. Hull was a man of the people and as such easily moved to that moral in-

dignation characteristic of the American people when confronted by the iniquities of foreigners. With much vigor and in highly picturesque language he would lecture and at times berate foreign diplomats, without necessarily making progress toward the solution of existing issues."

3 — *Ibid.*, p. 327. Churchill about this: "My opinions about the Baltic States were, and are, unaltered, but I felt that I could not carry them farther forward at this time."

4 — According to Hull, this suggestion was mainly due to Sumner Welles. But Churchill's original influence seems of greater importance. (Hull's dislike of Welles was well known.) On April 23 Admiral Standley, the American Ambassador in Moscow, asked Stalin to meet with Roosevelt but Stalin excused himself, as he was very much occupied with the military situation.

5 — Especially the Joint Chiefs of Staff urged Roosevelt to go soft with the Russians, as "whatever advantages might theoretically be gained by trying to settle political and territorial problems during the war, these future assets must be regarded as offset by the immediate dangers of awakening controversies with Russia." Sumner Welles, "Two Roosevelt Decisions, One Debit, One Credit," *Foreign Affairs* (January 1951).

6 — A. B. Ulam rightly raises the question which occurs to him while examining Yugoslav accounts of their civil war: In 1942, the Russians' "military situation was as yet precarious and they may have had . . . an exaggerated opinion of the political intelligence and motivation of the West . . . it was conceivable that a political bargain, postwar Yugoslavia being one of the items in it, would have to be struck with the Western Allies. . . . Was Soviet domination of Eastern Europe

... predestined by the course of events during the war, or was it the result of a policy improvised by the USSR when confronted with the unexpected submissiveness of the Western Allies on this issue?" In the *Review of Politics* (January 1951).

7 — See *IMT*, 1381–PS, which cited the English example of colonization as commendable. "Every proclamation of an aim that repulses those who are of the best use for us in the eastern area today, which makes them resent the German leadership is, from a soldier's point-of-view, a mistake which has to be continually rectified by the commitment of German blood." See also the complaints of the Chairman of the "Ukrainian National Committee" to Frank, 1526–PS, 1997–PS.

8 — Papen to Berlin on February 16: "Menemenčoglu (and Sarajoglu) did not let their English friends entertain any doubts . . . that Turkey desired to see the Soviets beaten." *Documents Secrets . . . Turquie, op. cit.* On February 21 the Turkish Ambassador in Berlin told Alfieri that Turkey would probably enter the war when German victory seemed assured in the Caucasus. But such a juncture never came. On August 28 the Turkish Ambassador painted a somewhat unduly dark picture of his country's position in a conversation with Churchill.

9 — This British decision was entirely due to military reasons: the only political factor which entered was the knowledge of how catastrophic and well-nigh fatal the world-wide political repercussions of a defeated Anglo-American invasion attempt would be. The desire to employ the bulk of the Allied offensive in southern and southeastern Europe because of the one Churchillian eye cast upon Russia — on political grounds — appeared only later.

10 — To a later question, Eden replied that he hoped Poles and Czechs would jointly find an equitable solution in the former Teschen controversy.

11 — Edmund Burke in the *Annual Register*, 1772, on Poland: "It has been at all times the language of a voluptuous and frivolous age, that while a state is flourishing within itself, and suffers no immediate injury from others, it has no concern in the quarrels, interests, or misfortunes of its neighbors."

12 — One example: When Churchill thanked Stalin for forty American light bombers (Bostons), originally destined for Russia, which Stalin consented to divert to the badly needed Egyptian front, Stalin said: "Those were American aircraft. It will be time enough to thank us when we give you some of our Russian bombers." Sherwood, *op. cit.;* see also *The Hinge of Fate*, pp. 472–503.

To Churchill and Harriman Stalin also said: ". . . apparently the Germans have found a way to make the Hungarians and Rumanians fight more like Germans." H. Butcher, *My Three Years with Eisenhower* (New York, 1948).

13 — A Soviet film-writer in 1947 put these words into the mouth of Stalin at the Moscow Conference, who reprimanded Churchill on the screen: "All is clear. A campaign in Africa, Italy. They simply want to be the first in reaching the Balkans. . . . Nothing will come out of this!" An indication that Stalin, if perhaps in retrospect, saw himself keenly aware of the political implications of a Mediterranean campaign in 1942. Virta, *Stalingradskaya Bitva*, quoted in I. Deutscher, *Stalin — A Political Biography* (New York, 1950).

14 — On September 5 the Soviet Consulate at Varna was raided. The Soviet government protested, while TASS

denied that Russian planes were flying over Bulgaria.

15 — The Italians in Berlin again noted rumors of Russo-German peace soundings at that time.

16 — *The Hinge of Fate* (Boston, 1950), Houghton Mifflin, p. 562; also 581.

17 — From *Apple of Discord* by C. M. Woodhouse (1948), by permission of Hutchinson & Co (Publishers) Limited, p. 49.

18 — He repeated this urging on the 18th, again on December 3. See *The Hinge of Fate*, pp. 651–6.

19 — Experts of the American Army Air Force even believed that strategic bombing alone could beat Germany — a pathetic fallacy.

20 — See especially his instructive chapter, pp. 146–52, "The American interest in the European settlement." There were but few American and British periodicals (The *Nineteenth Century and After* was one) which argued for caution with Russia and battled for a just peace. See also the State Department's Polish study of January 12, 1943, in *PWP*, pp. 492–513. On the other hand, Churchill to Eden on December 13: "Of course it would be a very good thing to have an Austrian unit if it could be managed without too much trouble. I am extremely interested in Austria and hope that Vienna may become the capital of a great Confederation of the Danube. It is perfectly true that Europe left Austria to her fate in a pusillanimous manner in 1938. The separation of the Austrians and Southern Germans from the Prussians is essential to the harmonious reconstitution of Europe." *The Hinge of Fate*, p. 914.

Efforts toward a Finnish-Russian separate peace — Phase II

1 — This stemmed from the 1920's and Finland's "unique record" of having paid her war debts. On the singularly curious American popular overemphasis of the Finnish war debt issue see the remarks of Professor Bailey in his *The Man in the Street* (New York, 1948).

2 — In the words of Professor Wuorinen: "When one considers how ruthless and shameless German ways of doing things were in countries that were occupied by or allied with Germany, their attitude to Finland was quite exceptional. It must be frankly admitted that the Germans' behavior in Finland was correct throughout, and that they respected the Finnish social and legal system and avoided all needless interference. In spite of that, the relations between the Finns and the Germans never became close or cordial. That was partly due to the general antipathy toward National Socialism, and partly to the helplessness which at the beginning of the war became obvious in the activity of the German forces. The Finns seemed to expect too much of their new brothers-in-arms and felt disappointed when the Germans failed to deliver under the conditions that prevail in the North where individual fitness and initiative, not dependent on technical equipment, decide the issue. The Finns soon began to treat the Germans with patronizing condescension and the term 'brother-in-arms' acquired an ironical implication. The German army staff in Finland took care of their responsibilities without interfering with Finnish internal affairs. It must be stated, for instance, that claims of Gestapo infiltration into Finnish governmental organizations is completely without foundation. Only the chief of the Finnish police seems to have been too ready to agree to some of the proposals made by the German Gestapo. Finally, it must be stated that the position of those Jews who were Finnish citizens did not suffer the slightest change during the war, nor did the Germans make any demands in this respect because they knew in advance that they would have been firmly refused." *Finland and World War II* — John H. Wuorinen, Ed., Copyright 1948, The Ronald Press Company, pp. 122–3. See also W. Erfurth, *Der finnische Krieg*, 1941–4. (Wiesbaden, 1950.) To this it may be added that the German attitude was also dictated by expediency; for they knew that German pressure on Finland would rapidly expedite a Finnish separate peace.

3 — Procopé, *op. cit.* It seems that the Ryti retort was reasonable, as the charge of having deliberately let the Yartsev "offer" lapse was not held against him in the final summation of the prosecution.

4 — Somewhat later another, direct attempt was made to reach a Finnish-British agreement when the Finnish Trade Union leader Vuori went to Stockholm to meet the British Deakin there.

5 — Procopé, *op. cit.* Also Finnish-Danish relations were very good and an interview given by the Finnish Fagerholm to a Danish conservative newspaper in February stated that Finland was a democracy; she fought no ideological war; indeed, her operations since December 1941 were confined to "guarding and patrolling." See Wuorinen, *op. cit.* (It is interesting to consider why and how a Danish newspaper could print this interview under German occupation.)

6 — On April 22 the Americans came surprisingly near to indicating that the United States was about to break off diplomatic relations with Finland; within two days, however, the situation turned back to normal. According to Professor Wuorinen, "Two items in the newspapers just at this time might have influenced the American decision: one of them was the German radio's jubilation over the erroneous reports that the United States had already broken off diplomatic relations with Finland. The second [was] . . . the much-publicized Katyn affair. . . . It may be assumed that both of these incidents caused restraints in the United States' Finnish policy." *Op. cit.*, p. 154.

The returning prestige of the West

1 — By the end of 1943 Steinbeck and Hemingway volumes were translated; a Hungarian edition of *Mrs. Miniver* appeared; and the great Révai publishing house was preparing a Hungarian edition of Eric Knight's *This Above All* when the German occupation of Hungary in March 1944 put an end to these cultural endeavors. Shakespeare and Molière were played on the stages of Budapest, Bucharest, and Sofia; in Budapest a daring group of actors staged very thinly veiled anti-German demonstrations, and even two openly anti-German plays appeared. In the bookshops, German translations of American wartime books, including Willkie's *One World*, were purchaseable in paper-bound Swiss and Swedish editions. Books in Hungarian appeared on the American system of presidential election, the Beveridge Plan, and similar matters. The Russians shared also. Tolstoy's *War and Peace* reached new editions and even Soviet writers like the historian Tarlé, the popular writers, Ilf and Petrov, and the novelist Solochov were translated and their books published in Budapest, some of them in Sofia.

2 — On the ideological appreciation of these common destinies and the future of the European idea and the small states, see especially the appendices in Gafencu, *op. cit.*, first of all his answer to Professor Carr and his correspondence with René Payot, editor of the *Journal de Genève*.

3 — Central-eastern Europeans in exile could see more clearly, of course; the suicide of two central-eastern European intellectuals of Jewish origin in exile during 1942–43 was indicative: one was the Viennese novelist, Zweig, an erstwhile freethinker who grew more and more conservative in his later years, who saved his life and fortune but felt he could not survive what he saw to be the definite end of the old order (*The World of Yesterday* was the title of his penultimate volume). A Polish Jewish Socialist, Zygielbojm, killed himself in London, foreseeing what he called an awful future; in F. A. Voigt's words. "Zygielbojm was deeply disillusioned by the indifference of the once so chivalrous English Left."

The strange spring of 1943: I. — Rome, Budapest, Bucharest

1 — This desire of Mussolini prevailed until his very death. Such were his sentiments. In 1942, while Mussolini veered towards radicalism (and an Axis-Soviet alliance), many leading Fascists leaned toward a new kind of Fascist neo-conservatism. In December 1942 two important Fascist periodicals, *Rivoluzione Fascista* and *Gerarchia* (the editor of the former was the Duce's nephew, Vito Mussolini) published articles emphasizing the Christian character of Europe, an attitude which could be understood as indirectly anti-National Socialist. (In December 1942 Göbbels thought that Italy wilfully spared her fleet from major activities in order to keep it as a trump card for later negotiations.)

2 — Ciano and Cavallero asked the Germans' opinion whether occasional agreements with the Chetniks could be entered into. Ribbentrop angrily refused: no, the Chetniks were conspirators. See *CD*; also *IMT*, 735–D.

3 — See Bova Scoppa, *op. cit.*, pp. 54–6, 72 *et passim*. When the Antonescus visited

Hitler in September 1942, Mihai Antonescu told the Italian envoy on his return that he spoke up very energetically for a new Axis policy. But much of what Mihai Antonescu said could be discounted. Queen Helena got into close contact with Bova Scoppa in October and had an important talk with him on November 10. (She and King Mihai used to talk English at the dinner table, which irked Ion Antonescu considerably.)

4 — He even said that he was willing to consider a reconciliation with Hungary. Contrast this with Antonescu's 1940 opinions, when he said that the future belonged to large states only — this was one of his arguments against the partition of Transylvania.

5 — See P. Monelli, *Roma 1943* (Rome, 1946); also *CD*. Grandi read the Bova Scoppa-Antonescu memorandum and told Ciano it was "the most interesting and most important diplomatic document" he had lately read; "it has decisive, capital importance." Bova Scoppa, p. 80.

6 — On February 22 Hitler wrote a letter to Mussolini in which he said that the withdrawals on the Russian front were due to the defections and poor fighting qualities of the Italian, Hungarian, and Rumanian troops. Ribbentrop carried this letter to Rome with him.

7 — See Anfuso, *op. cit.*, pp. 299 ff. Filippo Anfuso was among those few high-ranking Italian diplomats who followed the neo-Fascist regime after September 1943 to the very end. He became then Ambassador to Germany and in March 1945 Mussolini named him Under-Secretary of Foreign Affairs in the Salò "government."

8 — Such was the atmosphere that when in December 1942 Count Dampierre, the French Minister to Hungary, resigned from the diplomatic service of Vichy, the Hungarian government refused to heed German demands to curtail his personal activities.

9 — The Germans also demanded that the SS be granted rights to recruit soldiers from among the German minority in Hungary, albeit Hungarian citizens. This was also refused.

10 — IMT, 705–PS; see also Kordt, Göbbels, Rahn, *op. cit.*, Weizsäcker, *Erinnerungen* (Munich, 1950).

11 — The Germans tried to obstruct the Antonescu visit to Italy, and even Mussolini hesitated once, delaying Antonescu's departure for a few more days. See Bova Scoppa, *op. cit.*, especially pp. 112 ff.; also Monelli.

12 — After the Fascist Grand Council meeting and four hours before his arrest, Mussolini received the Japanese Ambassador and told him to inform the Japanese government that next week he, Mussolini, would take an energetic step with Hitler to stop the Russian war and make a separate peace with Russia.

The strange spring of 1943: II. — Berlin, Washington, London, Moscow

1 — Bydgoszcz in Polish — Bromberg in German.

2 — IMT — Ribbentrop testimony. This Foreign Minister's memory, as so often, slipped in regard to the most important dates, e.g., "After [the Anglo-American] landing in Africa in *1941* . . ."

3 — The Soviets tried to prove that the Western Allies intended to talk peace with Germany at that time. See the Soviet-published *Falsifiers of History* (New York, 1948), which refers to two contacts. Evidence concerning these is either too scanty or contradictory to support the Soviet thesis.

4 — See *Hitler e Mussolini, Lettere e Documenti, op. cit.*, also Simoni, *op. cit.* Mussolini's original draft contained a pale remonstration with Hitler for having left Mussolini uninformed about the invasion of Russia until the German troops had already crossed the Soviet frontiers. Then the hesitating Duce deleted this passage.

5 — From March 14 to May 8, 1943, the Göbbels Diaries contain significant items: they reveal sharp differences between Göbbels and his Propaganda Ministry on one side, and the Foreign Ministry on the other. There is a cryptic note on March 16, a complaint that the Foreign Ministry made "enormous difficulties" in regard to Göbbels' foreign propaganda, especially concerning Russia; intervention was fruitless; Ribbentrop was not available. On March 17 Göbbels noted that Hitler had adopted a middle position between Ribbentrop and himself concerning the propaganda policy in the eastern territories and toward the Soviet Union. Similar difficulties existed between Göbbels and the Army; on March 14 he complained about these difficulties, but an elaboration of the differences is not given. When Mussolini again wrote Hitler, pleading energetically for a separate peace with Russia, on the same day, March 25, the conservative Kircher, editor of the *Frankfurter Zeitung*, wrote an editorial which, carefully analyzed, could be understood as a further exposition of the "common danger of the West" theme, an editorial well-nigh stretching a hand toward England. The Kircher article incensed Hitler and later, upon his personal orders, the *Frankfurter Zeitung*, on the pretext of the wartime paper economy, was liquidated.

Kordt, for example, knew of Russian-German negotiations in 1943. Hitler had a special "line" connecting him with Ribbentrop, and their conversations were recorded in a special file which was not found in 1945; it may have fallen into Russian hands.

6 — See Schmidt, p. 575; also Kordt, *op. cit.;* especially M. Mourin, *Les complots contre Hitler* (Paris, 1947) and his *Les tentatives de paix séparée pendant la deuxième guerre mondiale* (Paris, 1949). Of course, there were deep inclinations on both sides. "It is clear, this one thing: Germany needs us even more than we think, and not for a momentary political alliance, but for an eternal union . . . our two great nations are destined to change the face of the whole world. This is no fantasy, no proposal of human ambition: this is the course of the world." Thus the orthodox Dostoievsky in 1877 (*Journal of an Author*). On December 14, 1942, Kleist and Clauss made their contacts: they were said to be informed by the Soviet side that on the basis of the 1939 frontiers a Russian-German peace could be immediately concluded. Cf. P. Kleist, *Zwischen Hitler und Stalin* (Bonn, 1950). Clauss died in Stockholm in April 1946, just before the British were to bring him to Germany to be interrogated.

7 — Simoni on Katyn: ". . . horrified before those tragic graves, we do not subscribe to the shameful speculations of Göbbels with these corpses. Poland is Europe's noblest martyr. To stand on her side, against those who butchered her: this is a sentiment worthy of every true European." These are noble words.

8 — See Göbbels, *op. cit.* Anfuso, while in prison four years later, wrote about this period: "But if there is one thing I want to read in this accursed postwar period, so full of useless printed paper, it is the telegrams of Oshima [the Japanese Ambassador in Berlin] to Tokyo."

9 — *Documents Secrets . . . Turquie, op. cit.*

10 — Here Ciechanowski was mistaken: the Baltic states were the first victims.

11 — The Anders-Sikorski controversy lasted until May 1943 when the two met in the Middle East. See the letter of Sikorski on June 2 quoted in Anders, *op. cit.*

12 — There is strong evidence that the Katyn massacre was committed by the Russians (although Göbbels was worried in May 1943 when German ammunition was found in the Katyn grave). In January 1944, after the reoccupation of the Smolensk area, the Russians conducted their own examination of Katyn and "established" that the murderers were Germans, yet the Soviet government consistently refused permission for an international commission to examine Katyn. The latest refusal was dated November 1949 when Vishinsky did not answer a letter of Arthur Bliss Lane addressed him on that matter.

13 — *PWP*, pp. 492–513; also 545–52. See also Hull, "At the beginning of 1943 Russia was a complete sphinx to all the other nations of the world except that she stood there fighting heroically." William C. Bullitt in the spring of 1943 expressed some criticism of the organization and handling of peace preparations within the State Department. See also the comment on the wartime editorial policies of the *Atlantic Monthly* by W. H. Chamberlain in *America's Second Crusade* (Chicago, 1950), pp. 246–8.

14 — G. F. Hudson in the stately *International Affairs* (April 1950), a journal seldom critical of the Foreign Office: "In 1943 the behaviour of the British and American governments, albeit in extenuating circumstances, amounted to what is called in criminal law conspiracy to defeat the ends of justice."

Churchill to General Ismay on July 13, 1943: "The time has come to bring the Polish troops from Persia onto the Mediterranean theatre. Politically this is highly desirable, as the men wish to fight, and once engaged, will worry less about their own affairs, which are tragic." *Closing the Ring*, p. 653.

15 — Roosevelt respected Churchill. But toward the British Empire, in the words of Voigt, the President had "a Jacobinical distrust . . . his ideas about the British Empire might have been gathered from reading the works of Professor Laski."

16 — At that time even Stalin agreed with Churchill that Turkey should be brought into the war on the Allied side. See his letter of November 28 in *The Hinge of Fate*.

17 — *Documents Secrets . . . Turquie, op. cit.* The date of this document is misprinted as September 9.

18 — See *The Hinge of Fate*, pp. 696–714; also Hull, *op. cit.*

19 — See Sherwood, *op. cit.* But it is not quite clear how the Hopkins papers were edited. It is interesting to note, for example, that except for occasional utterances, President Roosevelt is scarcely quoted during this most important talk, while Hopkins is quoted even less.

A note from Roosevelt to Churchill on March 17: "Anthony has spent three evenings with me. He is a grand fellow, and we are talking everything, from Ruthenia to the production of peanuts! It is an interesting fact that we seem to agree on about 95 per cent of all the subjects — not a bad average." *The Hinge of Fate*, p. 738.

20 — It was also remarked that the name of a Lend-Lease warship given to the Poles, the *Lwów* (to which Hopkins refers as *Lemburg*) might create diplomatic misunderstandings with the Russians.

21 — *The Hinge of Fate* (Boston, 1950), Houghton Mifflin, p. 943.

22 — Leahy was narrowly anti-British. On April 14 Roosevelt agreed to Churchill's request that General Alexander be the Chief of the Allied Military Government in Italian territory. Leahy tried to influence the President against such appointments; in his own words, written in 1950, "I felt that this was a British effort to gain position in the peace talks, whenever they might begin." See Leahy, *I Was There* (New York, 1950). At his military conference on May 19, Hitler told his generals that he considered the Balkans more dangerous and crucial than Italy.

23 — On May 23 he argued with Roosevelt over Europe. "It was important to re-create a strong France, for the prospect of having no strong country on the map between England and Russia was not attractive." He spoke of a Danubian federation, with Bavaria, if possible; a Balkan federation, Prussia divided but not dissected, Poland, Czechoslovakia "neutral," friendly with Russia, a European Regional Council. He said that he thought much of Count Coudenhove-Kalergi's ideas (which were advanced in the late 1920's) of European unification.

24 — Butcher, *My Three Years with Eisenhower* (New York, 1946), Simon and Schuster, p. 316.

25 — Simoni, *op. cit.* On July 19 Hitler said to Mussolini at Feltre that the invasion of the Italian mainland might be imminent.

26 — Butcher, *op. cit.* There were, however, points where Churchill's political vision also failed. He spoke to Fitzroy MacLean on the night of July 25–26 at Chequers. MacLean, his Yugoslav adventurer-envoy, asked the Premier about Tito's future. "Politics must be a secondary consideration," answered

Churchill. See F. MacLean, *Eastern Approaches* (London, 1950), p. 281. Yet Churchill received such intelligence estimates from the Chiefs of Staff as that of June 6 which stated that Mihailović seemed "hopelessly compromised in [his] relations with the Axis in Herzegovina and Montenegro."

Effects of the Italian armistice: the Great Powers

1 — On August 2 strategic bombing of Balkan points began with the raid of the American Ninth Air Force (later to be renamed the Fifteenth) on the Ploesti oil fields. Many planes were lost; the price of this raid turned out to be too high. A few days later a message from Marshall to Eisenhower requested the withdrawal of American bombers from the Mediterranean theatre to England, for the strategic bombing of Germany was not only regarded as more important than tactical operations in the Mediterranean-Balkan theatre, but it was mistakenly considered to decide the war. See Sherwood, p. 781, n. 18.

2 — Sherwood, *Roosevelt and Hopkins* (New York, 1948), Harper & Brothers, p. 748.

3 — His efforts having been frustrated in Quebec, Churchill now concentrated on the theme of postwar American-British unity as the main factor of the peace. He addressed Congress in this vein: "The price of greatness is responsibility."

4 — Yet two reports of the American Office of Strategic Services in August noted with restrained concern the propaganda potentialities of the Soviets' Free Germany Committee in Moscow (See R&A 1033, 1593); as in these months the Russian "soft-line" radio and press methods toward Germany reached perhaps the acme of subtlety, (this line actually started with Stalin's

speech on November 6, 1942, and continued until the Moscow Conference of October 1943), emphasizing that the Soviet Union did not wage a war against the German people and especially not against "honorable" German soldiers and officers, but only against the "Hitlerite-Fascist clique" on the top — what a difference between this and the "unconditional surrender" line! Simoni noted in Berlin on August 31: "Voices particularly insistent, coming from Tokyo and Ankara, indicate that Germany would be now negotiating an armistice with Russia. It is rumored that Ribbentrop went personally to Moscow. Rome is very excited . . ."

On August 17 a State Department committee report on the future partition of Germany was filed (*PWP*, pp. 554 ff.); on September 23 a much more reasonable paper was drafted "on the political future of Germany." *Ibid.*, pp. 558–99. State Department study committees on certain central-eastern European countries were established in September. A "Unit of Biographical Analysis," to study "the background of current and emerging leadership in all enemy-occupied countries of Europe" also appeared.

5 — In the Trieste area, for example, the German commander admitted that he could not hold the coast against the smallest invasion attempt even for hours; until September 18–20 this situation prevailed and similar was the case in other coastal sectors.

6 — Wiskemann, *op. cit.* See also the excellent summary of the Italian General Favagrossa, *Perchè perdemmo la guerra* (Milan, 1946), pp. 202–4, of how the Allies failed to exploit the military chances rendered by the Italian armistice.

7 — Wiskemann, *op. cit.* In addition, the smaller Allied governments were neither consulted nor informed in advance of the Italian armistice terms — thus the Yugoslav and especially the Greek governments-in-exile were justly angry.

8 — T. Kase, *Journey to the Missouri* (New Haven, 1950), p. 163. Russia informed the United States of the Japanese offer. By that time (September 11) the Western Allies agreed to send their Foreign Secretaries to Moscow in October for a Foreign Ministers' Conference.

9 — The British were probably well aware of the separate peace attempts, for Churchill's speech and Eden's statements in Parliament on September 22 contained three significant items: 1. Churchill spoke not only against National Socialism but said that no Prussian clique of Junkers would be allowed to assume the rôle of an eventual successor to the Nazi government in Germany; 2. The Italian front was the third, and not the second, front — the latter already existed, as many German divisions were in the West, standing guard against the coming invasion; 3. Unexpectedly, Eden gave a detailed statement on the Hess story of two years before, disproving rumors that Britain ever had considered negotiating with Hitler's Germany. It is possible that these items were meant to soothe Stalin and turn him away from considering a separate peace.

10 — On September 26 the formidable Vishinsky arrived in Italy to assume his position as the Soviet representative on the Inter-Allied Mediterranean Commission.

11 — Donald Nelson, the American War Production chief, staked so much hope on the strategic bombing of Germany that by October 5 he informed Eisenhower that in his opinion "if weather had permitted the continua-

tion of the bombing two days more, the Germans would have given in," a fantastic estimate which Eisenhower did not share.

Effects of the Italian armistice within central-eastern Europe

1 — At that time Mihailović fought the Germans and also Tito, the Germans' enemy; he was on working terms with the Italians, the Germans' allies; Italian officers occasionally encountered British and American officers in Mihailović' mountain camps.

2 — An agreement between the Greek and Bulgar Communists, Ioannides and Daskalov, was made in July 1943. The Ioannides-Daskalov agreement envisaged, among other things, an independent Soviet republic consisting of Macedonia, Salonika, Western Thrace, and the Dardanelles.

3 — Split in Serbo-Croat — Spalato in Italian. The Partisan rule in Split was earmarked by a series of indiscriminate murders.

4 — See the very informative chapter VI in B. Coceani, *Mussolini, Hitler, Tito alle porte orientali d'Italia* (Bologna, 1948). In Trieste the Germans played the Slovenes against the Italians and there was some talk of a "Liburnian autonomous republic" in the Fiume-Laurana-Susak area. From all this Tito ultimately profited.

5 — The relatively fewer EDES troops behaved differently. The text of the Pinerolo armistice agreement is given in Appendix D of Woodhouse, *op. cit.*

6 — Mussolini weakly protested with Hitler against the South Tyrol and Triestine seizures; he even nominated a Prefect for Zara in a symbolic act. Hitler answered that these were no annexations, only steps taken due to military exigencies. Mussolini once again protested in 1944.

7 — After the formation of the Neo-Fascist Republic of the North, the Croat Minister in Berlin told the Fascist representative there that the Croat condition of re-establishing diplomatic relations with "Italy" (that is, the Republic) was that the latter should renounce all claims to Italian Slovenia and to the Croat-Dalmatian territories. The republican Embassy rejected this "condition," stating that this was neither the time nor the occasion to discuss such a matter. The Italians asked the Wilhelmstrasse to intervene and the Minister of Croatia agreed to "postpone" such discussions.

8 — Pro-Western spiritual tendencies grew in Hungary and Rumania. In Budapest a pamphlet by the famous novelist, Márai, criticized the German system of education and culture: in Bucharest the increasing flexibility of the government censorship enabled certain columnists to intimate and suggest between the lines. The circulation of the Social Democrat daily, *Népszava*, doubled in Hungary and the Liberal-conservative *Magyar Nemzet* began to issue certificates with a national-color border to its subscribers; everybody knew that such certificates would prove very valuable when the Allies won.

9 — The anti-Jewish measures were also slightly relaxed, partly due to the stern warnings which the Vatican sent to the corpulent Tiso.

10 — This quotation and subsequent documents concerning the secret Hungarian negotiations were put at my disposal by the kind consent of Their Excellencies Kállay and Eckhardt and His Royal Highness Otto Habsburg.

11 — Bova Scoppa, p. 117; see also R. W. Markham, *Rumania Under the Soviet Yoke* (Boston, 1949) and *Mémorial Antonesco* (Paris, 1950).

12 — Villari, *Affari esteri* (Rome, 1948) gives very interesting details of these unusual diplomatic events from a Neo-Fascist angle. Odenigo played a rôle on the fringes of central-eastern European history twenty years earlier. A follower of D'Annunzio, a *Carnarista*, he was "Foreign Minister" in the Fiume Republic of 1919–21.

13 — The British answer to the Rumanian approach was given on October 17; similar to the note to Hungary, perhaps slightly more sceptical. One thing must be said here, however. I have tried to collect and present all evidence that "jumping off" by Hungary, Rumania, and Bulgaria was planned as early as the summer of 1943. The Anglo-Americans failed to exploit their opportunities and when the Russians appeared in the Balkans in late August, 1944, the three jumped in quick succession: because of their geographic situation, Bulgaria and Rumania succeeded well, Hungary very badly.

All this would have been, however, done much better and easier, had these three countries collaborated, coordinated their plans, and faced Germany with a united remonstration, declaring their withdrawal from the war. They could have acted in concert and possibly won the military collaboration of Greek guerrillas, Turkey, and Mihailovič, as well. Yet, the whole stealthy diplomatic procedure which was going on since early 1943 was slowed down and impeded because each country had one eye cast upon its neighbors: Rumania was jealous of Hungary, Bulgaria of Rumania, and vice versa. There is no doubt that once again nationalism contributed to the failure of a great opportunity in the history of central-eastern Europe.

On the other hand, it is true that 1943 was not the time when these respective nationalisms could have been overcome and the differences patched up;

the roots of these mutual jealousies went back to 1940, 1919, 1912, 1848, far back on the road of history. Thus these milestones, however distant, could not be erased from the memories of nations; this fact was to serve, again, Germany and, ultimately, Russia.

The resistance movements at the end of 1943

1 — See Kordt, *op. cit.;* also R&A 1342, 1756, 1564; *IMT,* 940–D, 3443–PS. This was especially evident in regard to the Jewish situation in 1943. Only in Bulgaria, Hungary and Rumania were the Jews outside of SS "jurisdiction"; in these countries their lives were largely safe. The Jewish question brought about a parliamentary crisis in Bulgaria in March 1943, when the opposition and Peshev, the second vice-president of the Bulgarian Parliament, protested against the deportations of the Jews from Sofia; a vote of confidence showed that one out of every three deputies stood with the opposition. Although twelve thousand Jews had been already deported to Germany and Poland from the Bulgarian occupation zones, Boris III forced the extreme Interior Minister Gabrovski to stop deportation. 45,000 Bulgarian Jews were not deported; the only forced dislodgement affected the Sofia Jews, who during the year were quietly transferred to the provinces. The Bulgarian population in general was friendly toward the persecuted. With the exception of the Bessarabians, no Rumanian Jew lost his life or was deported in 1942–43; except for those young Hungarian Jews who perished in forced labor batallions on the Russian front during this period, Hungarian Jewry was also unharmed and, relatively, surprisingly well off. But where the SS ruled, the gas-chambers were stoked with the flesh and bones of hundreds of thousands of Latvian, Lithuanian, Estonian, Polish, Czech, Croatian, Serbian, some Greek, and a few Slovak Jews. And the temporary fortune of the Hungarian and some of the Slovak Jews did not last long, for a special SS organization under Eichmann, Kaltenbrunner, and Wisliceny in 1943 began to prepare for the "liquidation of the Jewish problem" in these countries. This, then, affected 600,000 Jews in 1944 (this *Kommando* had already "liquidated" about 40,000 Slovak, Bulgarian and Greek Jews in 1943. Some of the latter were evacuated, due to the assistance which the Franco regime granted to some Sephardic Jews of Salonika of Spanish origin, investing them with Spanish citizenship). The other deported Greek Jews were, according to the carefully kept accounts of the SS *Kommando:* "exterminated because of their poor quality." See *IMT,* Affidavit C; also 2615–PS, 3311–PS, 18–L, 3943–PS and the wartime accounts of the Swiss *Israelitisches Wochenblatt.* Before, under Italian rule in Greece, the treatment of the Jews there was much better. In May 1943 the Italian military authorities in Western Thrace protested against the German deportation of Jews. The Italian military often abetted the flight and concealment of Jews; the Germans often accused the Italians for such complaisance and leniency with the Jews.

2 — SD and SS forces executed a number of Latvian patriots in Audrini and Morduki.

3 — A secret meeting held by Serb leaders in the Bačka decided for Mihailovič in November 1943.

4 — From *Apple of Discord* by C. M. Woodhouse (1948) by permission of Hutchinson & Co. (Publishers) Limited, London, pp. 102–3.

5 — Zervas' nationalist guerrillas also arranged for some kind of armistice with the Germans in the Corfu area in October 1943; at that time, with the help of the then Mayor of Athens, a British officer and a German intelligence officer also met. See Woodhouse, p. 168. Most confusing was the Macedonian situation, where the Greek Communists made an agreement with the Bulgarian Communist Party about the creation of an autonomous Macedonia after the war; they also silently collaborated against Yugoslav plans in Macedonia. Now only Tsaous and Filiates, two Greek Macedonian nationalists, fought with equal fervor against Germans and Bulgarians there. In 1944 an agreement was made between Greek Communists, Germans, and Bulgarians at Mount Kaimaxillar (the text of which is given in Woodhouse, pp. 295–7). The first rift between Tito and the other Balkan Communists was now evident. The Yugoslav Communist Party and the KKE had hardly any contacts during the war, and later, in 1944, when ELAS began to fight the British Tito did not give them any aid. On August 2, 1943, the Central Committee of the "Macedonian Communist Party" met, and Vukmanović, Tito's lieutenant, controlled the scene, a control against which the Bulgarian Communist Party protested. Yet on the other hand, the Greek Communist Party had no close contacts with the Russians; it was strongly Greek in tendency. In the summer of 1943 the first "political" EAM–ELAS conference was held in the mountains, and although practically all Balkan Communist organizations were represented in one way or another, there were no Russians present; Russian prisoners-of-war whom ELAS liberated from the Germans were forced to join the guerrilla ranks; some of these Russians complained that ELAS treated them worse than the Germans did. Because of the outrages of the civil war, anti-Communist sentiment in Greece grew and Rhallis organized "Security Battalions" to fight the guerrillas in the villages. These, like Nedić' Guards,

were permitted by the Germans but were by no means pro-German in sentiment.

6 — November 22, 1943, was a turning point when a Ukrainian-language German broadcast for the first time spoke of the Ukrainian "Liberation Army" and of German-Ukrainian comradeship in arms. See R&A 1756; also 878.3 and 878.4.

7 — By the end of 1943 Germans recruited Baltic "volunteers" and granted certain liberties all through the eastern territories, except in Poland. In certain Russian cities, for example in Odessa, they installed Russian mayors for the first time. In Estonia and Latvia also half-hearted concessions were made.

8 — At the end of 1943 the short-wave broadcasts of Radio Moscow were of the following duration to the following peoples:

to Germans more than 11 hours
to Czechs 4 hours 10 minutes
to Hungarians 3 hours 40 minutes
to Italians 3 hours 30 minutes
to Poles 3 hours 30 minutes
to Bulgars 2 hours 40 minutes
to Finns 2 hours 40 minutes
to Greeks 2 hours 5 minutes
to Rumanians 1 hour 35 minutes
to Slovaks 1 hour 35 minutes
to Serbs 1 hour 5 minutes
to Croats 1 hour 5 minutes
to Slovenes 1 hour.

It is interesting that there was no broadcast to Austria nor to Albania; equal time was allotted to Poland and to Italy.

9 — He should not be mistaken for Colonel McLean, who was a British intelligence officer operating in Albania.

10 — "The conflict that divides the world so deeply today was reflected in Yugoslavia. Just as the Spanish Civil War was an adumbration of what was to

come, so the Yugoslav Civil War was the adumbration of what is upon us now." Thus Voigt in 1948. A Gestapo colonel, Fuchs, stated in his trial in Belgrade in 1946 that the Germans regarded Mihailović their most dangerous enemy in the Balkans.

11 — Wallace Carroll, *Persuade or Perish* (Boston, 1947), Houghton Mifflin, p. 182. See also Woodhouse: "Disasters to the civilian population and political troubles in the future were, if anything, welcome to the Communist Parties of the Balkans, since a suffering and discontented population was a potential reinforcement of Communism. Considerations based merely on the war effort against the Germans were indifferent to Balkan Communists, since the Germans were certain to be evicted in any case. . . . It was a mistake to perpetuate the myth that the Balkan guerrillas still contributed indispensable aid to the war effort; having decided in Yugoslavia that backing Mihailović was no longer worth while, the correct inference should have been that no guerrillas were worth while, not that Tito was worth adopting in his place." From *Apple of Discord* by C. M. Woodhouse (1948) by permission of Hutchinson & Co. (Publishers) Limited, London, p. 173.

12 — "That Tito and all those around him might in course of time evolve into something more than mere Soviet puppets seemed too remote a possibility to serve as a basis for our calculations. But it was nevertheless an eventuality which seemed worth bearing in mind. Much, I wrote in a report which I sent to Mr. Churchill, will depend on Tito and whether he sees himself in his former rôle of Comintern agent or as the potential ruler of an independent Jugoslav state." Fitzroy Maclean, *Eastern Approaches* (London, 1950), Jonathan Cape. Published in the United States as *Escape to Adventure* (Boston, 1950), Little Brown.

13 — This American dislike of commitments was evident everywhere, including Poland. See Leahy's diary of September 27, 1943, when the Polish military attaché in Washington asked for more help to the Home Army. The spirit of paper memoranda prevailed. Leahy: "Poland, located between Russia and Germany and wanted by both, was in an apparently hopeless position. I advised Colonel Mitkiewicz to present his request to the Combined Chiefs in a formal written communication."

Moscow, Cairo, Teheran: central-eastern Europe and world strategy

1 — The Polish suggestion concerning Slovakia obviously aimed at maintaining an independent Slovakia after the war as well; it was also meant to counterbalance Beneš' Soviet orientation. The Polish government-in-exile was very well informed of conditions in the so-called "satellites" and had valuable clandestine contacts with the many thousands of Polish refugees there.

2 — It is remarkably significant of the spirit of those times that Major-General Deane, who was appointed American Military Attaché and Head of the American Military Mission to the Soviet Union, received a particular instruction from General Marshall to abstain from the general duties of a military attaché, to "avoid seeking information about the Russians." Deane, *The Strange Alliance* (New York, 1947). At that time Roosevelt told Bullitt that in his opinion Stalin wanted nothing but security, "and I think," continued the President, "that if I give him everything I possibly can and ask nothing from him in return, *noblesse oblige*, he won't try to annex anything and will work for a world of security and peace."

3 — *Closing the Ring* (Boston, 1951), Houghton Mifflin, p. 286.

4 — See the interesting article by E. C. Erickson, "The Zoning of Austria," *Annals of the American Academy of Political and Social Sciences* (January 1950).

5 — Ciechanowski, p. 243. Harold Nicolson's classic remarks written a decade before Moscow were totally disregarded in these wartime meetings: "*Diplomacy by conference* . . . such occasions are exceptional and dangerous. Such conferences should be entered into only after careful preparation, on the basis of a programme elaborated and accepted in advance, against a background of acute public criticism and with full realisation that many months of discussion will be required. The subjects for debate should moreover be rigidly curtailed to those requiring a decision of policy, and all secondary issues, entailing negotiation only, should be left in expert hands." *Curzon: The Last Phase* (New York, 1939), Harcourt, Brace, p. 398.

6 — Ciechanowski described Stettinius well: "As time went on and my close friendly relations with Stettinius developed, I saw that he did not appear to realize how much he could achieve by initiating real collaboration among the United Nations.

"He appeared to me to regard foreign relations as a mixture of publicity and propaganda rather than as an art of cultivating delicate plants of thought and policy which had to be nursed and sheltered from the crude rays of spotlights and publicity until they were strong enough to stand them.

"As I observed his very sincere efforts during the time he was Undersecretary of State, and especially when he became Secretary of State, it seemed to me that his pursuit of efficiency was mostly aimed at streamlining, while as concerned the merits of international problems, he acted partly as

showman, partly as would a chairman of a big board of shareholders.

"He did not seem to see the difference between running a meeting of shareholders and an association of nations. He appeared to regard even superficial unanimity as more essential than the merits of the solution. He seemed to think that it was possible to buy unity, sometimes even by sacrificing fundamental principles, without appearing to realize that only on the basis of fundamental principles could such unity be sincere and durable in a United Nations association.

"He seemed to forget that at a shareholders' meeting, although some members held enormous quantities of stock and others only a few, one could safely press for 'unity above all other considerations' because all of these shareholders held stock in the same concern, which made their interests coincide; individual nations, in an association embracing the globe, had only some identical interests and many very divergent ones." *Defeat in Victory* (New York, 1947), p. 227.

7 — Nicolson: "*Imprecision.* The essence of a good foreign policy is certitude. An uncertain policy is always bad.

"On the other hand, parliamentary and press opposition is less likely to concentrate against an elastic foreign policy than against one which is precise. It is thus a grave temptation for a Foreign Minister under the democratic system to prefer an idealistic formula, which raises only intellectual criticism, to a concrete formula which is open to popular attack. This temptation is one which should be resisted. Nor merely does it promote in Foreign Secretaries a habit of complacent, unctuous and empty rectitude, but it diminishes the credit of international contract." Curzon: *The Last Phase* (New York, 1939), Harcourt, Brace, p. 394.

8 — Deane, *op. cit.* Deane felt a few days later that he had committed a mistake by having caused "considerable unnecessary apprehension" to the U. S. Chiefs of Staff, "because when they met the Soviet representatives in Teheran the subject of increasing the intensity of our Italian operations or starting new ventures in Southern Europe was scarcely mentioned and certainly not urged by our Soviet friends."

9 — Stalin excused himself from Cairo with the argument that he did not want to arouse Japan unnecessarily by meeting with Chiang.

10 — Butcher, *My Three Years with Eisenhower* (New York, 1946), Simon & Schuster, pp. 448–9.

11 — Leahy, *op. cit.*, p. 201. The only American in Cairo supporting Churchill was the hard-headed American Ambassador to Turkey, Laurence Steinhardt.

12 — It must be noted, however, that Roosevelt turned to Churchill before the conference assembled: "Winston, I hope you won't be sore at me for what I am going to do." F. Perkins, *The Roosevelt I Knew* (New York, 1947). There was, of course, the Sword of Stalingrad, with which Churchill thought to lure forth the warm flow of human pride from beneath the icy crust of Bolshevik *ratio* over Stalin's heart.

13 — Deane, *The Strange Alliance* (New York, 1947), Viking Press, p. 43.

14 — It is interesting to note how Teheran coincided with important Balkan events. On November 29 the Jajce Assembly took place. On November 30 British destroyers forayed into the Adriatic and shelled Durazzo in Albania; it is possible that Churchill ordered the increased activity of his sea and air forces in the eastern Mediterranean after the bitter pill of Cairo.

15 — Sherwood, p. 780. There was another Balkan plan, presented by Churchill, the one already mentioned at Cairo: through the Po Valley and the Ljubljana Gap. Three full sessions and four sessions of the Chiefs of Staff took place at Teheran.

16 — Discussions at Teheran about Finland furnish interesting insights into the different approaches. Roosevelt spoke with the voice of a radical ideologist when he stated that the "present Finnish leaders were pro-German," and Stalin, the conservative realist, answered: "Maybe so," but he "did not object even to Ryti. Anyone, even the Devil, might come." He was "not afraid of Devils." He informed the conference of the Boheman-Kollontay talks. Churchill defended the Finns, "There is still ringing in my ears the famous slogan, 'No annexations and no indemnities.' Perhaps Marshal Stalin will not be pleased with me for saying that." "Stalin, with a broad grin, replied: 'I have told you that I am becoming a Conservative.' " Churchill, *Closing the Ring*, p. 398. The Hopkins papers mention that due to a translator's error (such errors were frequent in Teheran and Moscow), Stalin misunderstood Roosevelt when the latter spoke about the desirability of freedom of the Baltic Sea. Stalin understood Baltic States and said that he would not discuss this topic.

17 — Deutscher: "The intricate game over Poland was not yet played out."

On October 6 Churchill had instructed Eden that he should remember that the agreement about the western frontiers of Russia had been "sheered off" and the Twenty Years Treaty substituted because of "the perfectly clear menace of very considerable division of opinion in the House of Commons." There was no reason to believe that such opposition might not show up again, maybe stronger. "At a Peace Conference . . . adjustments in one direction [may be] balanced by those in another. There is therefore the greatest need to reserve territorial questions for the general settlement. This is even more true of the United States' position, especially in an election year." The American attitude should be "clearly deployed" before Britain took up "a new position in advance of the Twenty Years Treaty. 2. I think we should do everything in our power to persuade the Poles to agree with the Russians about their eastern frontier, in return for gains in East Prussia and Silesia. We could certainly promise to use our influence in this respect." Churchill, p. 667. Then, at Teheran, Stalin asked Churchill whether the Premier was authorized to draw frontier lines. The Russian was continually curious, in the words of Churchill, whether "we thought he was going to swallow Poland up. Eden said he did not know how much the Russians were going to eat. How much would they leave undigested? Stalin said the Russians did not want anything belonging to other people, although they might have a bite at Germany." This was a reference to Königsberg. It was not specified, however, whether the proposed western frontier of Poland would continue along the East or the West Neisse.

At Teheran it seemed that not only Austria but also Yugoslavia would fall into a sphere where Britain would at least equally share her influence with Russia. In the minutes quoted by Churchill: "The Soviet Government nevertheless agreed to send a mission to Tito *as a result of Mr. Eden's initiative.* They also wished to keep contact with Mihailović" (Italics mine).

18 — The optimism of Roosevelt was reflected in his message to Congress on January 11, 1944: "In the last war such discussions, such meetings did not begin until the shooting had stopped and the delegates begun to assemble at the peace tables. There have been no previous opportunities for man-to-man discussions which lead to meetings of minds. The result was a peace which was not a peace. That was a mistake which we are not repeating in this war."

19 — But perhaps for the better, for there are views that in the long run — this is the opinion voiced by Knatchbull-Hugessen in his memoirs — it was to the advantage of Turkey and perhaps also to the Allies' postwar position in the eastern Mediterranean that she did not enter.

20 — See R. Moyzisch, *Operation Cicero* (New York, 1950). Kordt, pp. 370–2, gives a well-based deductive analysis of Teheran, in spite of the fact that at the time of his writing the only source he had was some general knowledge of the *Cicero* reports and the book of Elliott Roosevelt.

The official communiqué of Teheran was non-specific and was regarded in diplomatic circles as unnecessarily vague and obscure.

21 — The evacuation of Sofia was ordered then. The diplomatic corps and many government offices moved to the summer resort of Tsamkuria.

22 — Beneš told Fotitch in March 1943 that he felt he had to align himself closely with Russia: "I have to believe in them whether I believe in them or not." See E. A. Mowrer, *The Nightmare of American Foreign Policy* (New York, 1949), p. 271, n. 34. Visiting Churchill at Marrakesh on January 6, 1944, Beneš boasted of Stalin's friendship and his own ability to reconcile Russia with Poland. He produced a map, "with pencil marks by Uncle Joe," giving Poland Lomza and Bialystok in the north but not Lwów in the south, nor the Oder line.

23 — The Carpatho-Ukraine was not the only territorial commitment made in Moscow. There Stalin promised the Glatz frontier region to the Czechs, who in 1945 were unpleasantly surprised by the Soviet support of the Polish occupation of that area.

24 — Deeply pessimistic over the fate of Poland, the American Ambassador to the Polish Government, Anthony J. Drexel Biddle, resigned from his post in December 1943. In September 1944 the post was filled again by another great friend of Poland, Arthur Bliss Lane — but the appointment then was connected with attempts to please the Polish-Americans before the Presidential election of 1944. See also the article by F. A. Voigt in *Nineteenth Century and After* (February 1944).

25 — In regard to Yugoslavia it was Churchill who showed undue high-handedness and superficiality: he met Fitzroy MacLean in Cairo. The latter showed some concern about the Communist future of Yugoslavia. Churchill to MacLean: "Do you intend to make your home there after the war?" MacLean: "No, Sir." Churchill: "Neither do I. And, that being so, the less you and I worry about the form of Government they set up, the better. That is for them to decide. What interests us is, which of them is doing most harm to the Germans." MacLean, pp. 402–3. On December 21 a Soviet note to Britain established the Russian desire to bring about a compromise between Mihailovič and Tito. Yet the British Ambassador to the Yugoslav exile government unequivocally supported Tito. And on December 30 Churchill wrote Eden: "There is no possibility now of getting

Tito to accept King Peter as a *quid pro quo* for repudiating Mihailovič. Once Mihailovič is gone, the King's chances will be greatly improved and we can plead his case at Tito's Headquarters."

26 — Before and during Teheran the Hungarian secret armistice negotiations continued. Early in October 1943 Archduke Otto dined with President Roosevelt, who offered the use of the American Navy code to facilitate the sending of Otto's and Eckhardt's messages to Lisbon. (The President also indicated that, unlike Russian allusions made to Rumania, the United States and Britain would eventually support Hungary's retaining some parts of Transylvania.) On November 26 another Kállay message was sent to the British: ". . . it may be further reminded that the Hungarian Government is constantly flooded by German protests and recriminations because of their liberal policy and the tendency of the Hungarian Press."

The answer was, however: "The British Foreign Office is dissatisfied with your recent message. They cannot accept the present position and if the Hungarian Government really means business it must make a better offer. . . . With regard to Otto's claims about his contacts with United Nations' statesmen, HMG is always willing to listen to any anti-German proposals when made by Hapsburgs or others. British policy gives no support to Hapsburg scheme in Austria or Hungary and we should be surprised if American policy were different . . ." This was disillusioning. On November 28 Kállay ordered the Hungarian Minister to Portugal to get into contact with Archduke Otto at once if and when contact with Budapest would be interrupted or broken. The Minister was also instructed to tell Otto of Kállay's and Horthy's thanks for his intervention and that the Archduke be asked to try to avoid by any means a Russian occupation of Hungary. The Hungarian government was also intensely preoccupied with Beneš: news from America showed that he and his circle were violently anti-Hungarian, ready to sabotage any secret Hungarian secession efforts; Eckhardt and Otto indicated that the Czechs might inform the Russians and the Russians might let the Germans know indirectly. In case of necessity, a direct Hungarian approach to the Soviets was preferred to Hungarian-Czech contacts.

The Hungarian government statement reached Otto on January 12, 1944; on January 15 it was handed to President Roosevelt. The memorandum again reiterated willingness to surrender to the Allies and said that the occupation of Hungary by Russian armies should be avoided, while American, British, and Polish troops would be most welcome. The brother of the Archduke now flew to Lisbon to be liaison man at the receiving end of the code messages, whose transmission Roosevelt personally had facilitated.

This indicated that Roosevelt at that time was fully unaware of the implications of the 1944 military plans; he did not expect to see Russian satellites in the Balkans, even less in Hungary. There were other significant and secret developments at the end of 1943 which indicated more realism, however. Certain American diplomats pondered whether the United States should not declare war on Finland so that American troops would be there at the end of the war. Certain German resistance circles were informed through Switzerland by people close to Churchill that the British belief in a separate peace with a conservative Germany was now tempered; for Churchill was said to have believed that even in a one-front war, the German army could not stop the Russians, and he wished to avoid by all means that the Russian Army arrive in Germany alone. Franco and the Spanish Foreign Minister, Jordana, also tried to influence Churchill to make a separate peace with Germany (see their interesting memoranda in Templewood, *Complacent Dictator* (New York, 1946) and Doussinague, *España tenia razón* (Madrid, 1950)). This was at least one of the reasons why Churchill left the somewhat unrealistic Spanish proposals unheeded.

THE RUSSIAN ERA BEGINS (*1944–1945*)

Preliminaries to the Russian era: the ominous spring (January–June) of 1944

1 — Neither did all leading officials of the State Department understand the trends and issues involved. On December 23, 1943, a high official said to the Yugoslav Ambassador: in Washington's opinion British policy in the Balkans, and in Yugoslavia in particular, was not understandable.

2 — *IMT*, 2233–PS–BB. It is interesting to note that no particular change took place in Germany's policies in Lithuania.

3 — Yet the well-informed Voigt had it from highest British authorities that in 1944 a Russo-German separate peace "was but a hypothetical contingency which did not weigh much with the British War Cabinet." Voigt, p. 316 and n. 1 of same.

4 — It is, of course, possible that, had the Poles immediately accepted Churchill's proposals and offer, Polish independence would have been saved and Yalta would not have turned into such a complete failure. But this is by no means certain. First, who knows what Washington would have done had a British-Russian rift occurred over the composition of the Polish government. Then, even if Britain had had her way, the Russians would have had a trump card in their dealings with postwar Germany, which they undoubtedly would have used.

5 — At that time the State Department had already begun searching for a formula to find Poles "acceptable to Russia" among the exiled people; see the R&A 3180 report on certain members of the Polish government-in-exile.

6 — Six days earlier, Montgomery, who by now saw the issues involved, requested Eisenhower to consider abandoning *Anvil-Dragoon*.

7 — Earlier in February Churchill communicated a proposal coming from Stalin to Mikolajczyk, and asked for a prompt reply. But Mikolajczyk delayed his answer and sought a compromise formula of his own. This was given on February 17, when he proposed to call the Curzon Line a "temporary line of Polish-Russian demarcation" and insisted that the final frontier question and the fate of Wilnó and Lwów be dealt with during the peace conference.

8 — Yet it was clear that Churchill was preoccupied with the future Polish government. Of the Communist Polish Committee he said: "I do not know what misfortunes will attend such a development." The South African Field-Marshal Smuts, however, wrote Churchill on August 20, 1943 with profound foresight: "We may have a wave of disorder and wholesale Communism set going all over those parts of Europe . . . certainly in Greece and the Balkans. . . . The Bolshevisation of a broken and ruined Europe remains a definite possibility, to be

guarded against by supply of food and work and interim Allied control."

9 — Early in February the Polish paper *Wiadomosci Polskie* was suppressed upon British request, as it was "sowing discord among the Allies." About this period, Umiastowski wrote:

"Paid by Catherine the Second, Voltaire had lauded her partition of the Polish Commonwealth; and now, once again, a class of paid intellectuals in the countries of the United Nations were, under the name of 'true democrats,' conniving with the Russians for the destruction of the Polish republic." These are bitter words. It should, however, be remembered that in Poland millions of Poles were killed during the German occupation; the Polish fighters in exile lost about 60,000 men in Allied uniform, men who had participated in the battles and sieges of Tobruk, Libya, Cassino, Pescara, Ancona, Arnhem, Breda, Bologna. By V–E Day the Polish army-in-exile numbered about 240,000 men.

10 — Wuorinen, *op. cit.* Russia did not demand that Finland declare war on Germany. The relatively more lenient armistice (and later peace) terms were due to various factors; see Epilogue.

11 — Or, if we can believe Nano (see his most interesting article in the *Journal of Central European Affairs*, October 1952), it was rather the Russians who contacted him. He had arrived in Stockholm in September 1943. "My mission was to ascertain whether there existed any disposition on the part of the Allies to discuss terms on which Roumania could surrender unconditionally." An oversimplified statement which, however, contains the outlines of truth. Yet later: "But by the summer of 1943 it had become clear that the Axis armies would be unable to defeat Russia, at any rate

without the connivance of the Western Powers. Of this, however, there were no signs. Just the opposite!" Such reference to such illusions, from the retrospect of 1952, reflects the somewhat crude naïveté of M. Nano and of the Antonescus.

In November 1943 Nano contacted H. W. Johnson, the American envoy to Sweden, but their meeting was fruitless. Presently, on December 21, there came a shady Bulgarian, offering Soviet contacts. (It is interesting to note this standard Soviet practice of using Bulgarians as intermediaries.) "Having sold me the idea of dealing with the Russians, Mr. Goranoff apparently decided I was an easy man and rather unexpectedly produced a collection of second-hand jewelry which, he assured me, I could have for a song."

12 — At that time Bulgarian Communist partisan activity appeared. Some Bulgarian gendarmerie units, noted for their cruelty, joined the Tito forces in Macedonia: soon a Communist "Hristo Botev" battalion was formed among them.

13 — Public opinion grew more conservative. The Primate repudiated Nazi doctrines in a speech in November 1943 and censured the anti-Semitic and Germanophile Father Nyisztor in January 1944. See also R&A 2026.

14 — *IMT*, 679-D, 908-D. It was just on March 15 that an agreement had been made to receive an American Military Mission in Hungary, with which reception the second phase of the Hungarian secession attempt would have begun.

15 — In the opinion of Woodhouse (the Plaka Agreement is given in his Appendices), PEEA was set up in March, as the Greek Communists expected the Allies to land in April. London was better informed of the Greek situation, on the other hand, than of Yugoslav events and their portents. Churchill stood for the Greek monarchy, a stand which, for complex and often incomprehensible reasons, he did not extend to Yugoslavia. On April 9 he instructed his Ambassador to the Greek government: "Our relations are definitely established with the lawfully constituted Greek Government headed by the King, who is the ally of Britain and cannot be discarded to suit a momentary surge of appetite among ambitious *émigré* nonentities. Neither can Greece find constitutional expression in particular sets of guerrillas, in many cases indistinguishable from banditti, who are masquerading as the saviours of their country while living on the local villagers. If necessary, I shall denounce these elements and tendencies publicly . . ."

16 — That the Balkan situation was deemed to have entered its decisive phase transpired from an interview which Count Sforza thought necessary to give to the New York *Times* on March 5 about Italy's peace aims: Italy should renounce the Dodecanese, Fiume, Albania, should make a compromise over Zara, and Trieste should become a free port. Tito naturally ranted against such modest concessions.

17 — Voigt on Tito: "[Tito] would have been worse than a fool had he not responded to the marvellously favourable opportunities which Mr. Churchill offered to him. If Paris *valait bien une messe*, Belgrade was well worth a little flattery, a few kind words to the British Prime Minister in his illness, a few assurances of political moderation, and a few promises to be broken at the earliest opportunity." Churchill also received congratulations from Franco. In a message to Roosevelt on December 30, 1943: "I received on the same day congratulations on my recovery from Franco and Tito. So what?" Roosevelt on December 31: "I suggest that on New Year's Day you invite the two gentlemen who congratulated you, then lock them in the top on the tower where we saw the sunset, and tell them you will stay at the bottom to see whether the black or the red throws the other one over the battlements." Churchill on January 1: "I have not yet been able to arrange the contest in the tower. The Red is in better training than the Black." (*Closing the Ring, op. cit.*) See also same, for several Churchill-Tito telegrams in early 1944.

Voigt on Churchill, concerning Yugoslavia: "He lacked the deep scepticism, the scepticism of a Richelieu or a Bismarck — which is essential to greatest statesmanship." Voigt on British propaganda, etc.: "And there were, in London, Cairo and Bari, a number of persons employed in the *Intelligence* (a British intelligence handbook issued in 1944 almost unilaterally reiterated pro-Tito views) and other services who perpetrated that kind of perfidy, which, whether unconscious or semi-conscious, is peculiar to the tribe of *Fellow Travellers.*" See also MacLean, p. 418, on the Chequers meeting when Churchill, hearing British officers with both Tito and Mihailovič, felt that there was but little disagreement and that his pro-Tito policy was right.

18 — Jagow knew what this meant. He, in spite of being a former SA-man, was relatively lenient and tried to play the rôle of a diplomat instead of a satrap. (The challenge of relatively peaceful Budapest and its epicurean society was too strong for him. This Hitler and Ribbentrop knew.)

19 — Ribbentrop during his Nuremberg testimony denied that Hitler wanted to arrest Horthy. See also *IMT*, Affidavit XIV of Nicholas Horthy, Jr. and Ullein-Reviczky, *op. cit.; also*

G. A. Skousès, *Les Huns et les autres* (n. pl., 1949); Schmidt: "the gangster-tricks which Hitler, in his proletarian wrath, put against the old aristocrat."

20 — It is interesting to note how these bombings were joyously greeted by the Hungarian Nazi press. A psychologist could draw interesting parallels with primitive desires from how these newspapers commented upon the bombings with such joy: "At last we are really in the war! We are bombed!"

21 — One might ask why, in order to save Hungary's future, Horthy did not resign on March 19. Actually this question was asked by a Hungarian statesman, conversing with Horthy during the summer of 1944. This statesman brought up the example of the Danish King. Horthy angrily rose from his chair: "I do not insist on sitting in this seat, I can go. But I cannot permit that Szálasi or Archduke Albrecht [of well-known Nazi connections] should occupy my place."

22 — Lincoln MacVeagh became American Ambassador to Greece after the war. On March 19 the State Department asked for the opinion of the Joint Chiefs of Staff "toward a proposal made in Cairo by a Mr. [sic!] Stirbei," as Leahy recorded it.

23 — The next Three-Power Declaration, on May 11, included Finland for the first time among the "satellites," obviously due to the breakdown of her separate peace negotiations.

24 — The Russian proposals for "minimum conditions of an armistice with Rumania" were handed to Stirbey by Novikov on April 12. See p. 251 in the article by Cretzianu in the *Journal of Central European Affairs*, October 1951. In these proposals Rumanian territory was not to be occupied by Soviet troops during the armistice,

"though the Russians were to be allowed to operate there." Markham,
op. cit., p. 173. The more authoritative
Cretzianu account reaffirms this. The
hesitations of Manise were due to the
lack of a clear-cut Russian guarantee
of political nonintervention. Ion Antonescu was also more optimistic, as
the Finnish peace terms seemed to be
reasonable.

25 — It is interesting to note that Ciechanowski, who was thoroughly disturbed
by the trend of American foreign
policy, noted with anxiety in April
1944 a growing American sympathy
for the Germans.

26 — See Schmidt, p. 575; Anfuso, p. 472.
And in Tokyo, Marquis Kido in
January 1944: "We [Japan] had better
seek the termination of hostilities by
aligning ourselves with the Soviet
Union and China who are oriental in
their outlook." See T. Kase, *Journey to
the Missouri*, p. 131 (New Haven,
1950).

27 — On April 12 a German decree sig-
nificantly abolished all discrimination
against Russian workers in Germany.
Around the 15th "a prominent
American politician" conversed with
Procopé and told the Finnish envoy
confidentially that he heard from Hull
and "another high official" of the
State Department that the United
States could not help Finland and that
American-Finnish relations were "fully
dependent on United States relations
with the Soviet Union, where the
United States could not alienate
Russia, especially in view of a possible
Soviet-Japanese rapprochement which
would be of greatest danger to the
United States." Procopé, p. 205.

28 — Erickson, *loc. cit.* At that time both
the United States and Britain counted
on the Russian occupation of Berlin.
The American proposal of March,
however, placed the boundaries of the

American zone nearer to Berlin than
the British did. See also the article of
P. Mosely in *Foreign Affairs*, (April
1950).

29 — *Closing the Ring* (Boston, 1951),
Houghton Mifflin, p. 708.

30 — See Eisenhower, *Crusade in Europe*
(New York, 1948), pp. 783–4. Elliott
Roosevelt said to Captain Butcher on
May 23, 1944: "Stalin was a stickler
for keeping his word."

31 — "In one place we support a King, in
another a Communist. . . . There is
no attempt by us to enforce particular
ideologies . . ." It was meant also as
an indirect invitation to the anti-
Hitler resistance in Germany, indicating that unconditional surrender
meant not much more than slogans
usually do. Churchill also had a few
good words for Franco Spain in this
speech.

32 — On the same day Hull met Gromyko
and Halifax to inform them that the
United States was "ready to proceed"
with conversations in the postwar
international organization. Obviously,
such idealistic topics pleased him more
than obscure dealings with obscure
spheres of interest in the obscure
Balkans.

Deutscher, who by no means may be
called unfriendly to Roosevelt, writes
about the American position in regard
to the British sphere of influence idea:
"[Roosevelt] refused in fact to face the
consequences of his own attitude at
Teheran, which helped the Russian
army to become the sole master of the
Balkans, while Churchill was now
drawing the conclusions from his
defeat at Teheran and doing his utmost
to keep Greece out of Russian reach.
But Roosevelt raised no explicit objection, and so Stalin took it for granted
that under the agreement of June 1944
Britain and the United States had

assigned the greater part of the Balkans to Russia." Deutscher, *Stalin: A Political Biography* (New York, 1949), Oxford University Press. p. 515.

In the meantime the Soviets informed the British that they were willing to deal with Antonescu and on May 30 — after the Churchill sphere of influence proposal — they even suggested to Nano in Stockholm that perhaps King Carol might be brought back to Bucharest. All this shows how, unlike the Western Allies, ideological considerations were not likely in the least to hamper Russian diplomacy.

33 — Mikolajczyk, just then in Washington, impressed him with difficulties which were to be expected with Russia; this impression was somewhat tempered by the excitement concerning D-Day.

34 — An obsession not unlike that of the State Department with the so-called "non-Communist Left," a "concept" emerging in 1948 which was so profusely dealt with in interdepartmental correspondence that it began to be referred to as "NCL."

35 — W. M. McNeill, *The Greek Dilemma — War and Aftermath* (Chicago, 1947), p. 123: "In general, British officials in Cairo were more dubious than was the King's political position than was the Foreign Office in London, and, as a result, British policy was lacking in clarity and fluctuated between lukewarm support of the Greek King and an uneasy neutrality on the question." And Woodhouse, p. 319: "[The Greek Communist Party] had a policy but no principles; the British authorities had principles but no policy." One of the healthy consequences of the revolt was that the Greek government organized a strong-armed local unit, the so-called "Third Brigade," which excelled itself on two occasions: it took Rimini on the Italian front and stamped out many a Communist nest

in the Greek Civil War in the winter of 1944-45. Meanwhile for a few months a Greek wireless station beamed Communist propaganda to Greece, surprisingly enough, from British-controlled Palestine.

36 — How strange all this was: Scottish officers drinking Serb plum brandy in Partisan headquarters; Tito walking under St. Peter's arcades in Rome.

37 — Others remembered the affair. When in 1948 the Stalin-Tito break developed, the Central Committee of the Communist Party of the Soviet Union wrote to the Yugoslav Party that all the postwar success of the Yugoslav Communist Party was due to the fact that after the destruction of Partisan Headquarters by German paratroopers the Russian Army came to help and saved Tito.

38 — An emissary of Mihailović, the Social Democrat Topalović, was not admitted to Britain in May 1944. German propaganda was now very clever. It told the Serbs that Britain had abandoned Mihailović; it printed leaflets with Churchill's statements criticizing Mihailović and ceased jamming the Yugoslav broadcasts of the BBC. See Voigt, p. 289, n. 1. The *Times* cast a slur on the General's rôle even during his tragic 1946 trial.

39 — On June 12, Mao Tse-tung declared that he would support Chiang Kai-shek.

40 — Sir M. Peterson, *Both Sides of the Curtain* (London, 1950), pp. 251-2. His description of a hapless "Danube Force," of ambitious Britons and Americans, who thought that they would be permitted to enter Bulgaria and Rumania after the Russian occupation of these countries, is excellent.

41 — Thus they had to witness the roundup of about three hundred thousand Jews in the Hungarian provinces by the Nazi-controlled Hungarian field gendarmerie and German SS troops. By mid-June only the 250,000 Jews of Budapest remained within the country, the rest from the provinces having been deported to the death-camps, in which eventually about ten per cent survived.

42 — It is interesting that the Germans distrusted the development of contacts between their satellites and the Neo-Fascist Republic. In March 1944, economic negotiations took place in Vienna between Germany and Slovakia, where the Germans insisted (this among other issues) that the Slovaks should not make direct deals with the Italian Republic. In April Mussolini asked Hitler in vain to allow a symbolic Italian return to Zara. Even the Croat Minister Lorkovič plotted in June to go over to the Allies; he was then found out and executed.

43 — Lange, among others, recounted to Mikolajczyk what Stalin had said to him about the Polish frontier question: "I must take into consideration the feelings of my Ukrainian people." See Mikolajczyk, *The Rape of Poland* (New York, 1948), p. 62. *Pater familias*, indeed!

The decisive months of Russian victory: the climactic summer (June–October) of 1944

1 — How did Steinhardt know this? If there were such an agreement between Roosevelt and Stalin, no one has up to now mentioned it.

2 — From the testimony of Ryti in Helsinki, September 1945: this part was not permitted to be read during the trial. See Procopé, *op. cit.;* also R&A 2127.

3 — Deane, p. 119. The first shuttle-bombing operation was made against Debrecen. On June 10 the bombing boundary was voided, as the Russians

realized that its existence essentially helped the Germans. On June 21, after a German plane trailed the American bombers into Russia, a night bombing attack by the Luftwaffe wrought great havoc at the Poltava base.

The American Air Force heavily bombed Belgrade on Easter Sunday 1944; there were many civilian casualties and the population bitterly remembered the senseless air attack by the Germans on the same feast day three years before.

4 — "Later criticisms will gain point if they are read not as criticisms of British or American policy [in the Balkans] as the case may be, but as criticisms of Anglo-American policy; the chief defect of which was that it did not exist. Not until 1946 did the two Governments set about contriving an Anglo-American Balkan policy into which an Anglo-American Greek policy could be integrated. The next year the whole burden passed to the USA; 1947 was too late for integration between Britain and the USA as equal partners." From *Apple of Discord* by C. M. Woodhouse (1948), by permission of Hutchinson & Co.(Publishers) Limited, London, p. 106.

5 — Some of these are interesting; they are reprinted in *PWP*, pp. 595–6.

6 — In July even the French General Giraud presented a paper to the Allies which argued for their advance into Austria.

7 — This appalling American naiveté was on the other hand accompanied by admirable manifestations of American humanitarianism. As early as July 6, 1944, the State Department had prepared a paper on assuaging the European "Displaced Persons" problem after the war. See *PWP*, pp. 641–4. (It is probable that the expression "DP" originated there.)

8 — There were many complex and interesting episodes. Badoglio in Italy ran into trouble with the Russian Ambassador, Kostilev, who protested against the residence of "terrorist, Fascist" — i.e., non-Tito — Yugoslavs in Bari and elsewhere. A few Mihailović planes flew with the U. S. 15th Air Force in 1944. In June Mihailović again tried to cooperate with Zervas and sent two of his officers to Greece, but the British told Zervas to decline. Royalist Serbs in Trieste approached the Italian and German authorities in June to try to mount a common fight against the Tito partisan forces in that area but they were refused. On the other hand a local Partisan armistice with the Germans was made on July 3 in the Gorizia area, also elsewhere sporadically: thus the argument fails that Tito alone refused to make any deals with the Germans.

9 — Bova Scoppa records how great an effect the fall of Rome had on Bucharest: immediately correspondence was addressed to him as "Minister of His Royal Majesty, King of Italy." Mihai Antonescu was more confused than ever: the British were not to deal with him, but allegedly Hayes in Madrid let him know that he was acceptable: Hayes was said to have promised that the Americans would stop air attacks on Bucharest; yet on June 28 a mass air raid came. The Orthodox Patriarch of Rumania got a friendly letter from the Archbishop of Canterbury, requesting that Rumania try to get out of the war (Mihai Antonescu told several people that the letter was addressed to him). On July 10 the King received a secret message from President Roosevelt, who asked that he do something concrete about the Rumanian secession.

10 — Mussolini knew it too; he seemed to be involved in an obscure affair which perhaps should be recounted here. Even in his northern Italian captivity, tired, moody and sick, he thought that under certain circumstances he could intervene in the great moulding of global affairs again. Through the Japanese Ambassador, Hidaka, he expressed his wish to bring about a Japanese-Russian-German alignment and it seems that these suggestions got to Moscow. Around July 13 Mussolini secretly disappeared from his residence: there are some who claim that he went to meet with four British agents around Brescia who had come from Switzerland. On July 15 he returned to his headquarters and went directly to Hitler. Did he have a message to give? Did he have an idea, a formula to solve the two-front war? Whom did he approach and by whom was he approached? We do not know. Some claim that he was in contact with Churchill; some people claim that he was in contact with Stalin. There are some who believe that the purpose of the short journey of Churchill to Como in June 1945 was to obtain the documents in connection with these most secret talks; but this, of course, cannot be substantiated. See the articles by Lanfranchi in the *Corriere della Sera* (April 17–20, 1951).

11 — Although the leaders of the aristocratic conspiracy planned for a separate peace with the Soviet Union, the possibility cannot be excluded that Russian intelligence was instrumental in sabotaging the *coup*: one of the conspirators, a German Communist, was a Gestapo spy and revealed much of the plans.

It is sad and instructive to read the fantastic and unbalanced comments of the New York *Herald Tribune* and of the New York *Times* on the failure of the conspirators. See also the article of R. W. Ingrim in *Thought* (March 1947) and H. Rothfels, *The German Opposition Against Hitler* (Hinsdale, 1948), pp. 160–1.

12 — The Turkish government declared war on Germany only on March 1, 1945.

13 — *The Second World War* (New York, 1949), Duell, Sloan & Pearce, p. 324.

14 — There he met the Polish Socialist leader Arciszewski, just flown out from the underground in Poland.

15 — I do not agree with the interpretation of Chester Wilmot in *The Struggle for Europe* that it was because of logistic and economic difficulties that the Russian armies were halted in Poland from August 1944 to January 1945.

16 — Woodhouse, p. 197. Also: "ELAS . . . found Colonel Popov unable even to supply his own party with vodka, let alone ELAS with gold, arms and ammunition. . . . the Soviet Mission, which had expected to find an army of at least the same kind, if not the same magnitude, as Tito's partisans, found a rabble thinly veiled by an elaborately centralised command," pp. 198–9. The British Mediterranean Command in June considered an eventual declaration of war on ELAS, denouncing it as "an enemy of the Allied cause." ELAS–KKE knew about this consideration and in 1946 the Greek Communist press published documents pertaining to these plans.

The United States steadfastly declined to send troops into Greece, and as the civil war flared up in July, the Germans tried to exploit it. The captured intelligence summary of the German 22nd Mountain Corps confirmed the earlier observation that in certain coastal sectors the Germans deliberately did not interfere with British supplies shipped ashore to Zervas' forces. In other sectors the Germans indirectly aided the Communists, as, for example, the Mount Kaimaxillar Agreement indicated; in the north, aware that ELAS would fight the legitimate Greek government and the British, the Germans left vast supplies of weapons deliberately within the EDES regions. Woodhouse calls

this a "masterstroke. . . . So well did [the Germans] calculate their plan that one ammunition dump was left within a few hundred yards of the boundary between [ELAS and EDES], with the certainty that ELAS would reach it first. These stocks played a part in bringing the [Communist] revolution of December 1944 near to success."

17 — These Bulgarian statements also alluded to the hope that Bulgaria might "discuss" the problem of western Thrace during the future peace conference.

18 — Even Churchill was momentarily optimistic. On August 18 he sent a "glowing message" to Eisenhower: "the results of all the Allied efforts may eclipse the Russian victories." Butcher, p. 647.

19 — Appealing to nationalistic sentiment, the King proclaimed that the Rumanian Army would now "liberate Transylvania."

20 — At that time the Russians had already passed through two Carpathian passes in Rumania. Tolbukhin occupied Varna already on September 8, despite the Bulgarian requests for a march on Sofia. There are some indications that Stalin even at that time feared an Allied landing in the Black Sea-northeastern Aegean area, a landing he wanted to avoid; hence this rapid advance on the Black Sea coast.

21 — In the North there was some fighting, as the Germans held on to Lapland; indeed, not until April 25, 1945, did the last German detachments leave Finnish soil in the desolated regions of the Finnish-Norwegian border.

280,000 Finns left Finnish Karelia before the Russians. (In the Winter War there were 420,000 evacuees, 250,000 of whom returned to their former homesteads between 1941–43.)

See R&A 2665; also J. Schechtman, *European Population Transfers 1939–1945* (New York, 1947).

22 — The special order to arrest Horthy was given to Skorzeny, who had liberated Mussolini. The SS General von dem Bach sent the greatest siege gun in the world, the 600-mm. (24 inch) *Thor* to be used for an eventual attack on Budapest.

23 — The Poles continued to fight extremely well in Italy, notwithstanding the looming tragedy of their homeland. The Germans established a clever Polish-speaking *Radio Wanda* on the Italian front, the propaganda of which was aimed to appeal to Polish frustrations. Yet this had no effect whatsoever, while droves of Poles inducted in the German army or in the Todt labor forces deserted to the Allies.

24 — When the SS in August herded most of the civilian population of the German-controlled part of Warsaw into concentration camps, Frank sent a strong protest to Himmler, who then forbade further deportations.

25 — The attitude of certain British circles and the newspapers, especially that of the *Times*, was certainly enough to provoke Polish rancor and bitterness: they were noncommittal, eulogized the Russian war effort, and tendentiously played down the rôle of the London Poles, even going so far as to underemphasize the communiqués and stories of the Warsaw uprising.

26 — Previously in France, Polish armored troops captured a journal of German High Command telephone conversations around and after D–Day, a most important document, enabling the Allies to examine the procedure of German field intelligence. In July pieces of the experimental V–2 rockets were smuggled out from Poland to England with the help of the Polish underground.

27 — See a *commedia dell'arte* illustration of émigré committees and general obscurity about the future of Austria in R&A 2355 concerning the doings of Austrian émigrés after the liberation of Rome.

28 — Erickson, *loc. cit.* The aura of the day was well reflected in Mrs. Roosevelt's words at Quebec: "Mrs. Roosevelt argued with conviction that peace can best be maintained by improving the living conditions of people in all countries. Churchill, on the contrary, said that his only hope for a durable peace was an agreement between Great Britain and the United States to prevent international war by the use of their combined forces if necessary." Leahy, p. 265.

29 — Leahy: "The complete agreement of our British colleagues at Quebec represented, *we hoped*, the final abandonment of the project of an early recapture of the Island of Rhodes." (Italics mine.)

30 — Yet here was a moment of all-Slav solidarity. Pavelič' envoy to Vichy (after two of his predecessors had already spirited away to Switzerland) burst out suddenly during lunch with some French politicians: "All the same, the time has come to give the Slavs their place in the sun!" A. Mousset, *The World of the Slavs* (New York, 1951), p. 91.

A small American mission remained with Mihailovič; its primary task was to expedite the escape of American pilots shot down over Yugoslavia. In such aid, collection, sheltering, and ferrying out the pilots, the Mihailovič people did an admirable job; however, on higher orders, news of their activities was suppressed by American military censorship.

31 — Voigt, p. 410. One of the basic factors had been that the British Mission to Tito was considerably impressed with him, which was not the case in Greece (partly due perhaps to traditional British condescension toward Greeks).

32 — It is very interesting to observe that in 1944 the Russians came back to Estonia and Latvia with a certain guilt complex. There were clandestine propaganda announcements before their arrival, and certain official statements, even afterwards, declared that the character of the Russian policies had changed, that things were going to be different from 1940–41. In 1944 most of the Soviet troops did not behave too badly in Estonia (worse in Latvia and far worse in Lithuania). For example, they made the non-Communist Professor Kruus "Foreign Minister" in the Estonian Soviet Government. There were no deportations. In October 1944 even a number of British and American correspondents were allowed to enter Tallinn for a short visit. After V–E Day in 1945 much of this attitude changed; for example, Soviet soldiery indulged in a prolonged nightmare of shooting, rape, robbery throughout the countryside.

Chaadayev, the Russian philosopher, pessimistic and dejected about Russian culture and Russian national character, wrote in 1829: "To call attention to ourselves, we would have to expand from the Bering Straits to the Oder."

33 — There is no evidence of the Germans having intercepted it and, of course, it is not impossible that due to certain influences in the White House, it was never sent.

34 — These officers arrived in Sofia upon the invitation of General Velchev, the Bulgarian War Minister; they even discussed measures against the Greek Communists in Macedonia. (Bulgarian nationalism was not extinct: the last Bulgarian troops left Thrace only on October 25.) This indicates how many opportunities the Western Allies still

had to influence Balkan affairs. As E. A. Mowrer states: "There was probably a period when a single American brigade on the Yugoslav coast of Dalmatia could have given General Mihailovič a new lease on life. One American batallion — and a firm political attitude — in Bulgaria at the time of the first Bulgarian armistice agreement (which the Soviet Union swept aside) might have altered that picture." *The Nightmare of American Foreign Policy* (New York, 1949). But the Allies did not act accordingly, and men like Velchev were duly impressed; he, for one, to ingratiate himself with the Russians, soon became their very ambitious stooge.

35 — Sherwood, *Roosevelt and Hopkins* (New York, 1948), Harper & Brothers, p. 833. It must be stated that there was, alas, practically no intelligent opposition to criticize Roosevelt's foreign policy in these months. There was a "civil war complex" concerning western Europe: Bullitt, Leahy (and Salazar) expressed fears that the Communists might plunge France and other regions into civil war; their views were instrumental in the American hostility toward De Gaulle. There were, of course, troubles in France, Belgium, Italy. But it was not seen that Communism was dangerous primarily where it was established and maintained by Russian armies.

36 — This shows how, as late as October 1944, Churchill still hoped in Tito.

At that time the Germans were evacuating the Bačka and the Vojvodina, traditionally Serb-Royalist provinces. Between the German evacuation and the arrival of the Tito forces, local Serb national administrations were set up in villages and towns. They were quickly dissolved by the Partisans. A few weeks later the wholesale herding of the local German population (notwithstanding their previous political affiliations) into concentration camps began.

37 — The Macedonian controversy nevertheless continued; in it now the Soviets were involved. They ordered the Bulgarians to withdraw from Macedonia and seemed to favor the Yugoslav view there. The Macedonian Communist movement was allowed "to maintain its refusal to serve under ELAS, and to revert to the command of Tito's lieutenant, Tempo (Vukmanovič) in Yugoslavia. The frontiers of Greece and her neighbours were temporarily tidied up." Woodhouse, p. 209. All this pointed to the fact that Stalin wished to adhere to the rigid zones of influence, which seemed to satisfy him then.

At this point it is significant to notice that, as in many other instances, it was Stalin who proved most cautious in his advice: he suggested that Tito keep the monarchy and King Peter for good, which advice Tito successfully disregarded in 1945.

38 — At the end of September Horthy himself installed a secret radio transmitter in his country home; later another one in the Buda palace, through which a British Lieutenant-Colonel and certain Poles, later also Nicholas Horthy, Jr., kept contact with the Allies.

39 — Rahn writes that he asked Horthy: "have you any hopes that three Anglo-American airborne divisions would occupy Budapest instead of the Russians? Only then will I agree that you have been right." Horthy refused this argument also. See R. Rahn, *Ruheloses Leben* (Düsseldorf, 1949), pp. 262 ff.; also Ullein-Reviczky, Kordt, Montgomery, *op. cit.;* D. Sulyok, *Zwei Nächte Ohne Tag* (Zurich, 1948); I. Kovàcs, *Im Schatten der Sowjets* (Zurich, 1948); also R&A 2628, 2543-S (this latter shows the

strong influence of Leftist Hungarian émigré opinions in Washington).

40 — Stalin always had some respect for honest anti-Communists with a strong past; probably remembering the defeat of the Communists in Hungary in 1919, he felt a certain respect for Horthy and for Bethlen. Bethlen, hiding in his country estate from the Germans, was the only leading Hungarian statesman whom the Russians immediately deported to Russia. He was reported to have been kept in relative comfort around Moscow, where he died in 1949.

41 — It is rather significant that when the armistice delegates of the Soviet-sponsored Hungarian government arrived in Moscow on December 30, 1944, they were not permitted to establish contact with the previous delegation, which was then held incommunicado.

From Moscow to Yalta: a winter of chaos

1 — Winant remarked in April of these Polish-Americans that they were "fine people but very intense." Mikolajczyk, *op. cit.*

2 — The German offer of surrender was communicated to Colonel McDowell of the American Mission with the Mihailović forces by Stärker, an emissary of Neubacher. At the same time Tito forces were attacking Chetnik strongholds; concentrating on this task, they often neglected to fight the retreating Germans.

An article by Tito's Foreign Minister, Smodlaka, in a Yugoslav paper in October repudiated the Italian-Yugoslav Treaty of 1924 and stated that Trieste, Gorizia, and Istria belonged to Yugoslavia. A controversy developed in which Italian liberals, Salvemini and Sforza, vainly offered compromise solutions in the American press.

At Pola, Fiume and the surrounding islands, the Tenth Italian Motorboat Flotilla (which served with the Neo-Fascist Republic of the North) was continuously engaged in bitter fighting with the Partisans.

3 — Voigt, writing in 1948 (p. 379): "The Greeks are not ideologues. . . . A Spaniard may kill a man because that man, against whom he may have nothing personally, embodies or represents an idea. A Greek may kill a man for personal reasons (the vendetta in Greece is personal, rather than political), but he will not kill a man in the belief that he is killing an idea. Even today, when . . . the liberties of the Greek people . . . are menaced by the *Comintern*, discussion of the Communist idea is singularly free and tolerant."

4 — The "Tudor Vladimirescu," named after a 19th century Rumanian "people's democrat."

5 — The Russians also began to plan for the vital Danube navigation issue. Already in October, an informal Danube conference was held in Bucharest with Russians, Rumanians, Bulgers, and Yugoslavs participating; and while the Russian command had the effrontery to ask the cooperation of the British Naval Mission to assist them in the task of sweeping the lower Danube of mines, the Western Powers were to be totally excluded from Danube sailing and shipping. See OSS, R&A 2267.1; also Peterson *op. cit.*, p. 253. An exclusive Soviet-Rumanian navigation and shipping agreement was signed on May 8, 1945 (V–E Day); the Soviet-Hungarian one was signed in August. (According to the popular story, these agreements were not so bad, said one citizen to another, for they provided for the creation of 50–50 percentage companies. Not so bad! retorted the other: it means that we are going to sail across the Danube,

while the Russians are to sail lengthwise.) The Russian-sponsored new Danube charter was finally presented and accepted by the satellites and Yugoslavia at the Belgrade conference of 1948.

6 — Even such a clever man as Bova Scoppa thought in Bucharest in November 1944 that if the Rumanian government behaved in the right manner, the Soviets would not reduce Rumania to a full satellite. See his memoranda in Bova Scoppa, *op. cit.*, pp. 180 ff.

7 — Within Budapest, a fantastic adventure repeated itself day by day, night by night: a young Swedish volunteer humanitarian, Raoul Wallenberg, Jr., by his personal intervention saved at least half of the remaining 200,000 Jews of Budapest from death. (Wallenberg was, in all probability, killed by Russian soldiers after the siege of Pest.)

8 — On the same day the hero of the Hungarian resistance, the Magyar De-Gaulle, Bajcsy-Zsilinszky, was hanged by the Szálasi government in the military prison of Sopron-Köhida, near the Austrian border. Had Bajcsy-Zsilinszky survived (as the Communist Rajk of the resistance did, due to the fact that his brother was a prominant Arrow-Cross leader) in Budapest or elsewhere to be present at the time of the "liberation," he surely would not have been able to be the Hungarian counterpart of the great Frenchman for long, but would have shared the fate of Mihailović or Petkov, or, at best, that of Mikolajczyk.

9 — E. Barker, *Macedonia — Its Place in Balkan Power Politics* (London, 1950). The words of Kolarz (*Myths and Realities in Eastern Europe*, London, 1946, Drummond, pp. 29–30) are especially applicable here: "In the present day there is still a conflict between the earlier territorial and the modern ethnic conceptions of a 'nation.' The peoples and States of Eastern and south-eastern Europe are inclined to invoke one or other criterion of a nation, according as it appears to further their particular interests or their prestige. In areas where some of the people hold to the territorial and others to the ethnic conception, there is a constant change of allegiance from one nation to another and membership of a nation has hardly more significance for them than membership of a party."

10 — In this the Germans still hoped. For example, in October at one of Hitler's situation conferences Dönitz did not "expect British action in Northern Norway, as this would obviously be directed against Russia" and Hitler disagreed: "England can only prevent Russia's advance into Norway, e.g., the Narvik region, by occupying that territory herself."

11 — *The Strange Alliance* (New York, 1947), Viking Press, p. 138.

12 — EAC agreed in the exact demarcation of the German zones and the Berlin sectors (lines which largely favored the Russians) on November 14. See the comment of General Lucius D. Clay, in *Decision in Germany* (New York, 1950), p. 85.

13 — The typical shortsightedness of the American military, even if non-isolationist and anti-Communist, transpires from notes in Admiral Leahy's diary at the end of 1944: "Men such as Hanson Baldwin, a writer for the New York *Times*, who had a considerable following among the reading public, expressed to me a conviction that it was necessary for the United States to interest itself in the governments that were to be established in the areas from which the Nazis had been or would be expelled. I told him that, in my opinion, involvement of America

in European politics would inevitably bring us into another European war. He took an exactly opposite view . . . From such information as was then available, it seemed to me that the interests and future safety of America pointed to the necessity of this Government's going on record with a public announcement that we were committed and devoted to concerted action by the Allied Nations which would be intended to prevent international war, but that we did not intend to sacrifice American soldiers in order to impose any government on any people, or to adjust political differences in Europe or Asia, except when it should be necessary to act against an aggressor with the purpose of preventing international war." *I Was There*, p. 284.

A few weeks later Leahy and General Hurley inveighed against "British-Dutch-French imperialist propaganda in China" as against America's "unification and democracy" efforts. Hurley (who was goaded into this by Stalin) "summarized the purpose of the British-French-Dutch propaganda at that time as follows: 1. To condemn America's effort to unite Chinese military forces as interference in the Chinese government, 2. To keep China divided against itself, 3. To use Chinese and American forces and American lend-lease equipment for reconquest of their colonial empire, 4. To justify imperialism as opposed to democracy." (Leahy, pp. 288–9.) Indeed, to Mao Tse-tung's democracy! Hurley also spoke of British, Dutch and French "underhand tactics."

14 — *The Nineteenth Century and After*, 1944.

15 — Churchill was indeed angry and said that if the Greeks did not succeed "in laying democratic foundations which are satisfactory and inspire confidence it will probably be necessary that you be placed temporarily under inter-

national trusteeship of some form."
McNeill, p. 188. Was this the same
Churchill who on April 12, 1941,
deeply moved, spoke to gaunt and
phlegmatic Anglo-Saxons, his own
kith and kin, on the day after the
bombardment of Bristol: "That you
should gather in this way is a mark of
fortitude and phlegm of a courage and
detachment from material affairs,
worthy of all that we have learned to
believe of ancient Rome *and modern
Greece.*" (Italics mine.)

16 — This government was supplanted on
April 7 by a more conservative-
Royalist one presided over by Admiral
Voulgaris. Sophianopoulos remained
Foreign Minister.

17 — As in the Polish case, the *Times* was,
curiously, more critical of the Athens
government (and less critical of the
Communists) than some British Liberal and Labor organs were. As to the
United States, some Communist demonstrators on December 3 appeared
on Constitution Square with American
flags and cheered Roosevelt; such was
their belief in American justice and
American friendship for the Greek
common people.

18 — *British White Book, Documents Regarding the Situation in Greece.* By permission
of the Controller of Her Britannic
Majesty's Stationery Office.

19 — The Anglophobe sentiments of Admiral King were such that he went so
far as to prepare orders to the commander of the American naval forces
in the Mediterranean to immediately
withhold American naval and landing-
craft used in the ferrying of British
troops and supplies to Greece.

Before the outbreak, EAM published
a political magazine, *Nea Ellada,* containing articles about the internal and
foreign policy of their desired post-war
Greece; it reflected the Communist
tactics which were the order of the day

throughout Europe and Asia: most of
the writers were not clear-cut Communists but fellow-travellers, cooperation with the legal government was
stressed, renunciation of the dictatorship of the proletariat idea emphasized;
in foreign policy it was stated that
EAM strove for a Greece friendly not
only with the Soviet Union but also
with the other Great Powers. All
this did not fail to impress even those
officers whose duty it was to analyze
the political situation in detail, as the
OSS report R&A 2821 indicates. Its
tone suggests that the analysts fell into
the Soviet-inspired ideological trap.

20 — Later, from 1947–48 onwards, when
they turned to "investigate" Communism, a number of Republicans began
to interview Kravchenko and other
exiled Russians. But why had they
never interviewed people like Ciechanowski in 1942–45?

21 — The official title of these dwellings
was *Luxusquartier für Deutschlandstreue
und von ihrer Heimat einstweilig entfernte
Regierungshäupte.*

— On the epicurean flight of Frank and
his entourage from Poland see the
confidential SS document, *IMT,*
3814–PS.

23 — See *IMT,* 2520–PS. Collate this
official German account of foreign
workers within the Reich with OSS,
R&A 2887 and 2887.a on population
displacement estimates in Europe on
January 1, 1945. The situation was
further complicated by the volunteer
and displaced Russians. In January
1945 General Vlassov's Russian "Committee of Liberation" announced its
first "Congress" in Prague. Old
Russian White Guardists fought against
Tito in Serbia under General Steiffon,
and a Cossack cavalry brigade operated in Croatia. Another Cossack unit,
under Domanov, was active in the
Istria-Trieste area.

24 — Hitler promised Szálasi during the latter's visit in early December that he would defend Budapest to the last — thereafter Szálasi gave orders to dynamite all the Budapest bridges, making a Stalingrad out of Budapest; on December 30 his soldiers murdered three Russian soldiers acting as parliamentarians communicating to the garrison commander the offer to capitulate, while Szálasi and his crowd motored out of the capital days before the siege. It is true, however, that Hitler in January 1945 ordered the 6th SS Panzer Army from the western front to Hungary instead of sending it to western Poland where it was so badly needed.

25 — Piyade recounted these negotiations in *Borba*, March 1949; see also the account given in the London magazine, *European Affairs* (March 1950).

26 — Poznan in Polish — Posen in German; Bydgoszcz in Polish — Bromberg in German; Torun in Polish — Thorn in German.

The Russian era begins: I. Acknowledgment at Yalta

1 — Ciechanowski, pp. 573-4.

2 — On December 6, 1944, Churchill proposed that the Combined Chiefs of Staff meet in London before the Three-Power Conference, but the Americans rejected the idea.

3 — Alger Hiss was a top political adviser. He ranked very high among the American delegation; for example, his telephone number was No. 4 (Roosevelt's was No. 1). The chief diplomatic advisers-analysts were Charles F. Bohlen and H. Freeman Matthews, then far more optimistic about the chances of Russian-American cooperation than the British were. On the other hand, there were minor differences between Churchill and Eden on certain issues.

4 — Perhaps Alger Hiss was the adviser? This volume, bearing the officious title of *Postwar Foreign Policy Preparations* (1950), does not refer to any specific areas in its recapitulation of the Crimean Conference. Poland, for example, this most important item at Yalta, which occupied at least half of the time of the conference's plenary session, is left entirely unmentioned in this State Department account for posterity.

5 — Again the middle ground! See also Leahy: "I was agreeably surprised at the Russian attitude on the Polish Government questions and on the United Nations Organization. It seemed to me . . . that Roosevelt was handling the frequent arguments between Churchill and Stalin with great skill . . ."

6 — The list of the suggested invitations was most interesting. It contained none of the Polish military leaders nor diplomats and only a few loyal, pro-London Poles. (The list included: Bierut, Osóbka-Morawski, Archbishop Sapieha, Vincenty Witós, Zurlowski, Buyak, Kutrzeba.) Who proposed this list? It strongly indicates Leftist suggestions and influences.

7 — He evidently thought as Burke did in 1791 (in the *Annual Register*): "The present violent dismemberment and partition of Poland without the pretence of war or even the colour of right is to be regarded as the first very great breach in the modern political system of Europe." From the Stettinius and Hopkins records it is clear that on that day President Roosevelt still had his pledges to the Polish-Americans strongly in mind. But already on the evening of February 6 Roosevelt sent a note to Stalin. Therein he stated his opposition to the Lublin régime but added that "the United States will never lend its support in any way to any provisional government in Poland which would be inimical to your interests." Wilmot wisely remarks: "Although he regarded his letter as an act of mediation, Roosevelt compromised his independence by telling Stalin, I am determined there shall be no breach between ourselves and the Soviet Union. With that statement he admitted that, if Stalin made an issue of Poland, the United States would give way." *The Struggle for Europe*, p. 649.

And later Hopkins noted to Roosevelt: "Mr. President, the Russians have given in so much at this conference that I do not think we should let them down. Let the British disagree if they want to — and continue their disagreement at Moscow."

8 — Later Molotov suddenly popped up, agreeing that "Yugoslavia was in an unstable situation"; he seemed to concur in the British proposal that in the final declaration it should be stated that the Three Powers wished to see the Subasič-Tito agreement truly executed. In the afternoon of February 9 Eden proposed two amendments to the Subasič-Tito agreement which were opposed by Stalin, who then added again that he had "complete confidence in the British policy in Greece"; he said "it would have been exceedingly dangerous" had Churchill allowed other than British forces to go into Greece.

9 — Only shortly before Yalta did the State Department agree to continued British demands that France be reintroduced among the Great Powers. Leahy: "I felt that conferring that status on defeated France was an extravagant stretch of the English language." Thus a former American Ambassador to France. Stalin, more wisely, foresaw that ultimately France would be a Western factor, against Russian interests. In a faint resurgence of French sentiment to reconstruct her traditional eastern European ties,

Paul-Boncour was named French Minister to Bucharest in early 1945, but the Russian authorities withheld his entry visa for several months.

10 — It was also agreed that the Russians would permit the United States Air Force Strategic Bombing Survey to investigate the effects of American bombing in the Balkans: this was another agreement never implemented, due to Russian obstacles and evasion.

11 — Three propositions in Harold Nicolson's classic essay on diplomacy are indeed pertinent here:

". . . error of diagnosis is a common feature in all democratic diplomacy. The central and original cause of illness is too painful to admit or even to contemplate. The manifestations and symptoms of that illness are thus dealt with as if they were the illness itself. And great indignation is expressed when the patient refuses to respond to treatment."

And: "The main distinction, therefore, between the methods of the new and those of the old diplomacy is that the former aims at satisfying the *IMMEDIATE* wishes of the electorate, whereas the latter was concerned only with the *ULTIMATE* interests of the nation . . ." From Curzon: *The Last Phase* (New York, 1939).

12 — MacLean on Belgrade (p. 528): ". . . we waited for the thunder to issue from the Crimean Olympus. In due course the combined oracles spoke. There was the traditional show of these adornments, reference to democratic principles. . . . the utterance amounted to an exhortation to Tito and Subasič to get on with it. There was no mention of King Peter."

The Russian era begins: II. The consequences. From Yalta to the German surrender

1 — Probably due to 80:20 and Greece. (Churchill and Eden stopped in

Athens to "check" on their way back from the Crimea.)

2 — Harriman insisted that no one-party régime should be installed in Rumania. The Soviets quickly agreed, for they could get around such commitments by studding the government with crypto-Communists, Left-wingers, and even a few unimportant anti-Communists. Actually, the Communists were in a minority in practically all of the initial satellite governments in central-eastern Europe. (Until 1950, most of these governments still had nominal non-Communists heading them.)

3 — It was clear that Churchill foresaw the inevitable in Poland, for he had already announced that Polish soldiers with the Exile Army would be granted British citizenship if they so desired.

4 — Subasič and the remaining Democrats were quickly put aside. Grol had to resign in August, Subasič in November 1945, when the communization of Yugoslav political life was completed.

5 — An interesting opinion is voiced by Stalin's biographer which deserves to be quoted fully. I do not fully concur with Deutscher's view, but I agree with him that Stalin himself did not believe that all of eastern Europe was now really his:

"The question must be asked whether Stalin, while he was bargaining for his zone of influence, already contemplated putting it under exclusive Communist control. Had the scheme of revolution been in his mind at the time of Teheran or Yalta? Had it finally taken shape at the time of Potsdam? His detractors as well as his apologists concur on this point, for both want us to see an extremely shrewd and far-sighted design behind his actions. Yet Stalin's actions show many strange and striking contradic-

tions which do not indicate that he had any revolutionary master-plan. They suggest, on the contrary, that he had none. Here are a few of the most glaring contradictions. If Stalin consistently prepared to install a Communist government in Warsaw, why did he so stubbornly refuse to make any concessions to the Poles over their eastern frontier? Would it not have been all the same to him whether, say Lvov, that Polish-Ukrainian city, was ruled from Communist Kiev or from Communist Warsaw? Yet such a concession would have enormously strengthened the hand of the Polish Left. Similarly, if he had beforehand planned revolution for eastern Germany, why did he detach from Germany and incorporate in Poland *all* the German provinces east of the Neisse and the Oder, of the acquisition of which even the Poles themselves had not dreamt? Why did he insist on the expulsion of the whole German population from those lands, an act that could not but further embitter the German people not only against the Poles but also against Russia and communism. His claim for reparations to be paid by Germany, Austria, Hungary, Rumania, Bulgaria and Finland, understandable as it was in view of the devastation of the Ukraine and other Soviet lands, could not but have the same damaging effect on the Communist cause in those countries. This was even truer of Stalin's demand for the liquidation of the bulk of German industry. Already at Teheran, if not earlier, he had given notice that he would raise that demand; at Yalta he proposed that 80 per cent of German industry should be dismantled within two years after the cease fire; and he did not abate that demand at Potsdam. He could not have been unaware that his scheme, as chimerical as ruthless, if it had been carried out, would have entailed the dispersal of the German working class, the main, if not the only, social force to which communism could have appealed and whose support it might have enlisted. Not a single one of these policies can by any stretch of the imagination be described as a stepping stone towards revolution. On the contrary, in every one of these moves, Stalin himself was laboriously erecting formidable barriers to revolution. This alone seems to warrant the conclusion that even at the close of the war his intentions were still extremely self-contradictory to say the least." *Stalin: A Political Biography* (New York, 1949), Oxford University Press, p. 508.

The hurried Hungarian land reform and its Russian-made, lightning-like execution also points to the possibility that Stalin had thought he might have but limited time to deal freely in certain parts of central-eastern Europe. Churchill protested against the manner of Russian intervention in Hungary, while Leftist influences could be discerned from the American phrasing of the intelligence report on the Land Reform Decree, R&A 3087, speaking of "the present land reform, with its peaceful liquidation of feudalism" and the like.

6 — It is significant to note how many encircled forts the Russians left behind in their rapid drive westward: Poznan, Bydgoszcz (Bromberg), Breslau, Glogau, Königsberg, etc.; Breslau, for example, did not fall until after the German surrender.

7 — The record of the March 10 Führer Conference is illuminating. All present feared a British landing in the Adriatic "or in the German Bight." Dönitz: "the British seem to be trying to spare their strength in view of the overall political situation." Hitler agreed: "the British inaction in Yugoslavia, where even a few troops could have caused us great difficulties, can be explained only by the fact that the British are intentionally trying to save their forces."

Alas, Hitler and Dönitz again overestimated Allied imagination.

General Bradley himself admitted his suspicion of British "inclinations to complicate·the war with political foresight and non-military objectives." And Eisenhower on April 7: "I am the first to admit that war is waged in pursuance of political aims, and, if the Combined Chiefs of Staff should decide that the Allied effort to take Berlin outweighs purely military considerations in this theater, I would cheerfully readjust my plans and my thinking so as to carry out such an operation." Cordell Hull in his *Memoirs* states that Roosevelt never consulted the State Department about the routes of the invasion and movements of American armies in Europe.

8 — Raczkiewicz dissolved it on March 21. See R&A 2991, 2494. It is, however, remarkable that the subsequent trial of the sixteen Poles in Moscow resulted in relatively light prison sentences, according to Russian standards. See the instructive S. Stypulkowski, *Invitation to Moscow* (New York, 1951).

9 — At that time Roosevelt knew of the Russian circumvention of the agreement made at Yalta about the temporary establishment of American air bases near Budapest; also, the Russians still did not permit American war prisoners' missions to operate behind their lines in Poland, Hungary, and the Balkans.

Seeing the growing difficulties between the United States and the Soviet Union, Stalin directed the international Communist movement to gradually disassociate itself from the pro-American, "united front" policies of 1941–44. See the scathing attack on "Earl Browderism" by the French Communist, Duclos, in April 1945.

While in 1944 he was not averse to try to gain the eventual confidence of the

Vatican (this was partly behind the Orlemanski affair), in January 1945 the Soviet press and radio began to attack the Papacy and Rome.

10 — See Rahn, *op. cit.*: also Anfuso, p. 571. Göbbels, before his suicide, contacted Zhukov's headquarters.

11 — It should be noted — indeed, it casts some doubts on Tito's military legends — that as late as April 15 most of Croatia and Slovenia were still German-occupied.

12 — In his first message to Churchill, President Truman stated that he would collaborate with him on the Polish issue in the spirit of Roosevelt.

13 — In German: Karlsbad, Pilsen, Budweis.

14 — Ljubljana did not fall until May 5; Zagreb not until May 8. Tito repeated Stalin's tactics; he left important military areas behind and concentrated instead on occupying areas whose political future was doubtful and which were in the range of the British-American forces.

15 — See Coceani, *op. cit.*: "La quarantena titina." On May 5 an "Assembly of Slovenes" was announced with Tito's confidant, Kidrič, as its president. The agreements between the Italian resistance committees and the Partisans were crudely flouted by the latter.

16 — Beneš on May 5 exhorted the Prague population with the war cry: "Death to the Germans!" A number of outrages followed in the spirit of revenge against individual Germans and captured German soldiers. This generated much hatred and awful consequences. (Jaksch, the Sudeten German Social Democrat, participated in the Czechoslovak exile cabinet until 1944, when Beneš and his group began to be obsessed with the plan for the total expulsion of the Sudeten German population.)

Units of the Russian "volunteer army" of General Vlassov had an ambiguous rôle in the Prague uprising; in the last two days they sided with the Czech insurgents against the Germans, possibly because of considerations of last-minute expediency, or hope in the arrival of the Americans.

17 — Many of these had previously escaped by sea to northern Germany, among them Latvian volunteers in the German army and the Germans' Latvian appointee, General Dankers.

The Russian era begins: III. The end of European continentality. The summer of 1945

1 — See R&A 3180. Yet the ignorance of leading Americans regarding central-eastern European issues continued. Admiral Leahy, the same man who harbored the darkest suspicions about DeGaulle in France, called the formation of this crypto-Communist Polish government "a happy omen." Concerning this period there are a few illuminating entries in the *Forrestal Diaries* (New York, 1951) and in S. Hillman, ed. *Mr. President* (New York, 1952).

2 — Leahy, p. 378.

3 — Nicolson's remarks on the Anatolian situation in 1920 were rather applicable here: ". . . from every area in the Middle East [the British] were rapidly withdrawing their troops: only a few unhappy Majors remained scattered throughout Anatolia, relying solely upon their red tabs, their excellent manners and their confidence in the clean-fighting Turk. Kemal quickly realised that these amiable officers could be ignored and even insulted.

He was much encouraged by this realisation. . . ."

4 — See *The Soviet-Yugoslav Dispute* (Royal
Institute of International Affairs,
London, 1948). According to the
letter of the Communist Party of the
Soviet Union, Kardelj was supposed
to have contrasted this own wish of
his with Tito, who was "inclined to see
Yugoslavia as a self-sufficient unit outside the general development of the
proletarian revolution and socialism."

5 — At San Francisco the Greek delegate
voted with Russia against Britain and
the United States on some occasions;
thus did the Greek Government wish
to manifest its sincere friendliness
toward the Soviet Union. Yet on
V-E Day the congratulatory telegram
of the Greek Government to Stalin
remained unanswered.

6 — UNRRA was extended in generous
quantities to the victor states of central-
eastern Europe: Poland, Yugoslavia,
Greece, Czechoslovakia.

7 — It is significant of the ideological trends
of 1944–45 that Stalin, in order to
support his charges, constantly and exclusively quoted certain American
and British press organs which wrote
of the "reactionary" tendencies of the
Greek Government.

8 — During Potsdam, Tito and Hoxha
signed a Yugoslav-Albanian Mutual
Assistance Treaty, the first in the post-
war Soviet-sphere alliance series.

9 — Churchill also spoke of religious freedom for Poland's Catholics; whereupon Stalin: "How many divisions has
the Pope?" (Ten years before he said
the same thing to Laval.) At that
time he had made some promises.

10 — This mistaken American perception
of Potsdam curiously survived; President Truman, as late as May 27, 1950,
greeted the Secretary of State returning from London "on a most successful
meeting — the most successful one, I
think, since Potsdam."

BIBLIOGRAPHICAL

NOTE

The difficulties which confront the historian of the very modern or contemporary period are necessarily repeated when it comes to the composition of a bibliography which, by necessity, cannot be exhaustive. There is also a further restriction: that of space, a limitation arising from the tremendous quantity and extraordinary range in the quality of source materials. Because of lack of space, this Bibliographical Note cannot claim the title of a critical and annotated bibliography: I try to enumerate, classify, group, but comment very little. I have tried to enumerate most books whose contents, however slightly, have some bearing on the history of central-eastern Europe and the Great Powers from 1917 onwards: books (and articles) written in the English, French, German, Italian, Spanish, and Swedish languages. This restriction alone might well provide ammunition to bibliographical critics. Yet a closer examination of this issue may be warranted; it may ultimately absolve me from the sin of undue omission or of a bias in favor of Western languages. Concerning the topic of this book there are very few articles, books, or documentary materials available exclusively in eastern European languages; we have not had access to eastern European archives; yet "facts" important or significant enough for historical record do, by and large, filter through to the West and subsequently become known to and recorded by Western writers and scholars. (The two remaining free nations, Greece and Finland, fall naturally into a different category.) And those who may censure me for not having made more use of Russian diplomatic material, I refer to the penetrating article of Alfred Vagts on the documentatory techniques of Soviet diplomatic historiography, in the October 1949 issue of *World Politics*.

·   ·   ·   ·   ·   ·

[*Bibliographies; reference works.*] There are few general and useful bibliographies of the central-eastern European area. L. Savadjian, *Bibliographie balkanique*, Paris, 1926, is necessarily incomplete. Extensive and discriminating are the two *Foreign Affairs' Bibliography* volumes: *1922–1932*, W. L. Langer and H. F. Armstrong, eds.; *1932–1942*, R. G. Woolbert, ed. I hope that a 1942–1952 volume may soon follow; see also M. Toscano, *Fonti documentarie e memorialistiche per la storia diplomatica della seconda guerra mondiale*, Milan, 1952; the article by E. Wiskemann in the London *Times Literary Supplement*, October 3, 1952; also L. J. Ragatz, *Bibliography for Study of European History 1815–1939*, New York, 1941, and supplements thereof, C. Bloch-P. Renouvin, *Guide de l'étudiant en histoire moderne et contemporaine*, Paris, 1949, and the two bibliographies of recent eastern European materials compiled by the Office of Intelligence Research, External Research Division of the Department of State, Washington, 1952. Primary and secondary materials of interest, and extensive book review sections may be found in the following journals: *American Historical Review, American Political Science Review, American Slavic and East European Review, Baltic Review* (Stockholm), *East Europe* (London), *Foreign Affairs, International Affairs* (London), *Journal of Central European Affairs, Journal of Modern History, Political Science Quarterly, Review of Politics, Russian Review, Slavonic and East European Review* (London), *The Eastern Quarterly* (London), *Soviet Studies* (Glasgow), *World Politics*. Of European journals especially the *Revue historique, Historische Zeitschrift, Revue d'histoire contemporaine, Rivista di studi politici internazionali,* the new *Revue historique de la deuxième guerre mondiale, Osteuropa* and the *Vierteljahrshefte für Zeitgeschichte* publish relevant and extensive bibliographies and reviews. Works published by the Royal Institute of International Affairs are notable for their useful bibliographies. Recent and relevant bibliographical articles are those of Stavrianos and Panagopoulos in the *Journal of Modern History* (June, 1948); Vuchinich in *idem* (March, 1951); Toscano in the *Rivista Storica Italiana* (January, 1948); Ravà-Spini in *idem;* Baumont in *Foreign Affairs* (July, 1947); Renouvin in the *Revue historique* (April, 1951). See also the discussion by Toscano on the problems of diplomatic bibliography dealing with World War II in the *Rivista di studi politici internazionali* (July, 1950).

Diplomatic historians are indebted to the unusual and commendable decision of the British Foreign Office to reveal material in its archives concerning the immediate origins of the last war, and *Documents on British Foreign Policy, 1919–1939,* edited by E. L. Woodward and R. Butler has, at the time of this writing, published four volumes within its Third Series, dealing with the Czechoslovak crisis of 1938 and its aftermath, in addition to the First Series, beginning with the year 1919 and the Second, beginning

with 1930. *Documents on German Foreign Policy 1918–1945* is the result of the fortunate capture of about ninety per cent of the Wilhelmstrasse archives by the United States Army in April 1945 and the subsequent joint publication policy of the American, British, and French Governments. There are presently five volumes in print, all within Series D, dealing with the 1936–1939 period. The policy followed in publishing these documents is outlined in the Introduction chapters of the volumes (the reader may also be interested in the technical dispute between G. L. Weinberg and B. E. Schmitt in the March and September, 1951 issues of the *Journal of Modern History* and the critical comment by Weinberg in the *Journal of Central European Affairs,* April, 1952.) The general American policy observing a seventeen-year restriction brings the available records of American diplomacy to the year 1935. The Italian Foreign Ministry is presently printing admirably edited document collections of which Series VIII, under the able direction of Professor Toscano, embraces the 1935–1939 period. In this *I documenti diplomatici italiani,* Series VIII, vol. XII (May 23–August 11, 1939) has already appeared. Series IX will cover the years 1939–1943.

An important general reference series is the yearly *Survey of International Affairs, 1923–38,* edited by Arnold J. Toynbee; see also the *Survey for 1938,* vol. II, edited by R. G. D. Laffan, London, 1951, with the complementary *Documents on International Affairs,* published yearly by the Royal Institute of International Affairs. Much material may be found in the fourteen volumes and appendices of the Nuremberg transcript, International Military Tribunal, *Nazi Conspiracy and Aggression,* Washington, 1947 and in volumes 12, 13, 14 of the subsequent *Trials of War Criminals Before the Nuremberg Military Tribunals,* Washington, 1949–, 15 volumes. (See also the relevant review article by W. C. Askew in the October, 1951 issue of the *Journal of Central European Affairs.*) A helpful reference work is J. Degras, ed., *A Calendar of Soviet Documents,* London, 1948; also her *Soviet*

Documents on Foreign Relations, vols. I–III, London, 1947–53. Works of general interest are O. Halecki, *Borderlands of Western Civilization,* New York, 1952; G. Stadtmüller, *Geschichte Südost-Europas,* Munich, 1950; the second half of A. Mousset, *Le monde slave,* Paris, 1947; the revised English edition, New York, 1951 is translated most abominably. Of background importance are F. Schevill, *A History of the Balkan Peninsula from the Earliest Times to the Present Day,* New York, 1933; J. A. R. Marriott, *The Eastern Question — A Historical Study in European Diplomacy,* New York, 1938; D. Tomasic, *Personality and Culture in Eastern European Politics,* New York, 1948; W. Kolarz, *Myths and Realities in Eastern Europe,* London, 1946. Two studies on migration and population changes are S. Kulischer, *Europe on the Move,* New York, 1948; J. Schechtman, *European Population Transfers 1939–1945,* New York, 1947.

[*I. The illusion of independence: 1917–1934.*] On the diplomatic background and secret agreements of the First World War which affected central-eastern Europe see three works by M. Toscano, *Gli accordi di San Giovanni di Moriana,* Milan, 1936; *Il patto di Londra,* Bologna, 1934; *La Serbia e l'intervento in guerra dell'Italia,* Milan, 1935. A general account is given in the useful chapter by E. C. Helmreich in J. Roucek, ed., *Central-Eastern Europe,* New York, 1946. See also L. Aldrovandi Marescotti, *Guerra diplomatica 1914–19,* Rome, 1949 and P. H. Michel, *La question de l'Adriatique: 1914–18,* Paris, 1938. On the Russian front and its background: M. v. Hoffmann, *Der Krieg der versäumten Gelegenheiten,* Munich, 1924; M. I. Florinsky, *The End of the Russian Empire,* New Haven, 1931; Winston Churchill, *The Unknown War,* New York, 1931; P. R. Mancuso, *Tipi strategici delle campagne sul fronte orientale 1914–1917,* Lanciano, 1938; C. Reisoli, *La grande guerra sul fronte orientale dal Baltico al Mar Nero,* Bologna, 1939. On Brest-Litovsk see J. W. Wheeler-Bennett, *The Forgotten Peace — Brest-Litovsk,* New York, 1931, and J. L. Magnes, *Russians and Germans at Brest-Litovsk: A Documentary History of Peace Negotiations,* New York, 1919.

Two classic surveys of the Paris Peace Conferences are H. W. V. Temperley, *A History of the Peace Conference,* London, 1924, vols. I–VI, and H. Nicolson, *Peacemaking, 1919,* New York, 1933. General histories with perspective are L. v. Muralt, *From Versailles to Potsdam,* Hinsdale, Ill., 1948; É Giraud, *La nullité de la politique internationale des grandes démocraties,* Paris, 1949; M. Baumont, *La faillite de la paix,* Paris, 1947, vol. I; L. Genêt, *Cinquante ans d'histoire, 1900–1950,* Paris, 1950, vol. II; and A. Wolfers, *Britain and France Between Two World Wars,* New Haven, 1940; see also G. A. Craig-F. Gilbert, eds. *The Diplomats, 1919–1939,* Princeton, 1953.

General works on the immediate postwar period include: M. H. H. Macartney, *Five Years of European Chaos,* New York, 1924; E. Nitti, *The Wreck of Europe,* Indianapolis, 1922; T. Masaryk, *Das neue Europa,* Berlin, 1922; H. Ronde, *Von Versailles bis Lausanne,* Stuttgart, 1950; and H. Nicolson, *Curzon — The Last Phase,* New York, 1939. Political analyses of interest are A. J. Zurcher, *The Experiment with Democracy in Central Europe,* New York, 1933; A. Nowak, *The Collapse of Central Europe,* New York, 1924; J. Kornis, *L'homme d'état — analyse d'esprit politique,* Paris, 1938; H. Kohn, *Revolutions and Dictatorships — Essays in Contemporary History,* Cambridge, 1939; J. Ancel, *Slaves et Germains,* Paris, 1945; R. Michels, *Umschichtungen in den herrschenden Klassen nach dem Kriege,* Stuttgart, 1934. The survey of H. Seton-Watson, *Eastern Europe 1917–1941,* revised edition, Cambridge, 1946, is well-nigh indispensable. Other, more limited surveys are M. W. Graham, *New Governments of Eastern Europe,* New York, 1927; J. Roucek, ed., *Central-Eastern Europe,* New York, 1946; W. Lemberg, *Osteuropa und die Sowjetunion,* Stuttgart, 1951. Economic problems of the postwar era are discussed in D. Mitrany, *The Effect of the War in Southeastern Europe,* New Haven, 1936; L. Pasvolsky, *Economic Nationalism of the Danubian States,* Washington, 1928; O. S. Morgan, *Agricultural Systems of Middle Europe,* New York, 1943; J. Taylor, *The Economic Development of Poland,* New York, 1952.

The crucial issue of Soviet foreign policy and especially Russo-German relations are covered in E. H. Carr, *German-Soviet Relations Between the Two World Wars, 1919–1939*, Baltimore, 1951; C. F. Melville, *The Russian Face of Germany*, London, 1932; Lord D'Abernon, *Diary*, London, 1926; parts of *Documents on British Foreign Policy*, Series II; M. Beloff, *The Foreign Policy of Soviet Russia, 1929–1941*, London, 1947, vol. I; R. Fischer, *Stalin and German Communism*, New York, 1948; E. v. Rabenau, *Seeckt*, Leipzig, 1940; H. Berndorff, *General zwischen Ost und West. Aus den Geheimnissen der deutschen Republik*, Bonn, 1951; W. v. Hartlieb, *Das politische Vertragssystem der Sowjetunion 1920–1935*, Leipzig, 1936; C. Dyrssen, *Die Botschaft des Ostens: Faschismus, Nationalsozialismus und Preussentum*, Breslau, 1934; H. v. Dirksen, *Moskau-Tokio-London*, Stuttgart, 1949; W. v. Blücher, *Deutschlands Weg nach Rapallo*, Bonn, 1951. See also the articles of M. Beloff in *Soviet Studies* (October, 1950), J. Fraenkel in the *Review of Politics* (February, 1940), G. Hallgarten in the *Journal of Modern History* (March, 1949), P. Kluke in *Historische Zeitschrift* (May, 1950), H. Speidel in *Vierteljahrshefte für Zeitgeschichte* (January, 1953), and the standard source of Russian diplomacy in the twenties, L. Fischer, *The Soviets in World Affairs*, revised edition, Princeton, 1951, vols. I–II.

The early history of the independent Baltic republics is well covered in the Royal Institute of International Affairs' volume, *The Baltic States*, London, 1938; see also A. Mousset, *Aux confins septentrionaux de l'Europe*, Paris, 1929; H. de Montfort, *Les nouveaux états de la Baltique*, Paris, 1933; C. Grimm, *Jahre deutscher Entscheidung im Baltikum 1918–1919*, Essen, 1939; and A. Nissell, *L'évacuation des pays baltiques par les allemandes — une contribution à l'étude du mentalité allemande*, Paris, 1936. On Finland see J. O. Hannula, *Finland's War of Independence*, London, 1939; J. Sihvo, *Sturmfahrten für Finnlands Freiheit*, Essen, 1939; J. L. Perret, *La Finlande*, Paris, 1936; R. Delavoix, *Essai historique sur la séparation de la Finlande et de la Russie*, Paris, 1932; and J. H. Wuorinen, *Nationalism in Modern Finland*, New York, 1931. On Estonia: H. de Chambon, *La république d'Estonie*, Paris, 1936; L. Villecourt, *L'Estonie*, Paris, 1932; A. Pullerits, *Estonia*, Tallin, 1935; H. Kruus, *Histoire d'Esthonie*, Paris, 1935. On Latvia: A. Bilmanis, *A History of Latvia*, Princeton, 1951; and his *Latvia in the Making*, Riga, 1928; A. Spekke, *History of Latvia: An Outline*, Stockholm, 1951; H. de Chambon, *Origines et histoire de la Lettonie*, Lille, 1933; H. Dopkewitsch, *Die Entwicklung des lettlandischen Staatsgedankens bis 1918*, Berlin, 1925; A. Schwabe, *Grundriss der Agrargeschichte Lettlands*, Riga, 1928; W. Wachtsmuth, *Von deutscher Arbeit in Lettland 1918–1934*, Tübingen, 1951, vols. I–III. On Lithuania: J. Jakulis, *La Lithuanie restaurée*, Louvain, 1932; M. Turchi, *La Lituania nella storia e nel presente*, Rome, 1933; A. Bossin, *La Lithuanie*, Paris, 1933; H. de Chambon, *La Lithuanie moderne*, Paris, 1933.

Six general histories of Poland which deal in detail with the rebirth and early crises of that nation after 1918 are O. Halecki, *History of Poland*, New York, 1943; *The Cambridge History of Poland*, New York, 1941; B. Schmitt, ed., *Poland*, Berkeley, 1945; R. Machray, *Poland 1914–1931*, London, 1932; R. Dyboski, *Poland*, London, 1933; and W. J. Rose, *The Rise of Polish Democracy*, London, 1944. See also M. Handelsman, *La Pologne: sa vie économique et sociale pendant la guerre*, New Haven, 1938; S. Filasiewicz, *La question polonaise pendant la guerre mondiale*, Paris, 1920; M. Handelsman, *Les idées françaises et la mentalité politique en Pologne*, Paris, 1927. The crucial 1919–21 period is covered by Count Skrzynski, *How Poland Fought*, London, 1923; Joseph Pilsudski, *1920*, Warsaw, 1933; I. Donnedieu, *La lutte des aigles aux marches orientales*, Paris, 1939; see also C. A. Manning, *Twentieth-Century Ukraine*, New York, 1951 and the article of M. K. Dziewanowski in the *American Slavic and East European Review* (February, 1951). On the birth and early fortunes of Czechoslovakia: E. Strauss, *Die Entstehung der tschechoslowakischen Republik*, Prague, 1934; T. G. Masaryk, *The Making of a State*, New York, 1927; see also F. J. Vondracek, *The Foreign Policy of Czechoslovakia, 1918–1935*, New York, 1935; R. J.

Kerner, ed., *Czechoslovakia: A Record of Two Decades*, Berkeley, 1940; H. Münch, *Böhmische Tragödie: das Schicksal Mitteleuropas im Lichte der tschechischen Frage*, Braunschweig, 1950; and S. H. Thomson, *Czechoslovakia in European History*, Princeton, 1943.

There is much valuable literature on the dismemberment of the Austro-Hungarian Empire and its consequences. The main accounts, ranging from the memoirs of an Imperial Minister to the story presented by the leader of the Austrian Socialists' radical wing, are these: Count S. Burian, *Austria in Dissolution*, New York, 1925; E. Glaise-Horstenau, *The Collapse of the Austro-Hungarian Empire*, London, 1930; V. Bibl, *Die Tragödie Österreichs*, Leipzig, 1937; F. Kleinwächter, *Der Untergang der österreich-ungarischen Monarchie*, Leipzig, 1921; O. Jászi, *The Dissolution of the Habsburg Monarchy*, Chicago, 1924; O. Bauer, *Die österreichische Revolution*, Vienna, 1923. R. H. Lutz-G. Almond, *The Treaty of St. Germain*, Stanford, 1935, is an objective study of the 1919 peace contract.

General histories dealing with the first fifteen years of the Austrian republic are P. Charmatz, *Vom Kaiserreich zur Republik: Österreichs Kampf um die Demokratie*, Vienna, 1947; A. Buschbeck, *Austria*, New York, 1950; and V. Bibl, *Geschichte Österreichs im 20. Jahrhundert*, Leipzig, 1933. More detailed accounts are F. Tremmel, *Die erste Republik 1918–1938*, Graz, 1946; A. Winkler, *Geschichte Österreichs 1918–45*, Vienna, 1946; P. T. Lux, *La leçon de l'Autriche, 1919–37*, Neuchâtel, 1937; I. Kunschak, *Österreich, 1918–1934*, Vienna, 1934; M. MacDonald, *The Republic of Austria 1918–1934: A Study in the Failure of Democratic Government*, New York, 1948; and K. W. Rothschild, *Austria's Economic Development Between the Two Wars*, London, 1947. C. Gulick, *Austria from Habsburg to Hitler*, Berkeley, 1948, vols. I–II, reflects a strong pro-Socialist bias. On German-Austrian relations see A. Ciller, *Vorläufer des Nazionalsozialismus*, Vienna, 1932; M. M. Ball, *Post-War German-Austrian Relations*, Stanford, 1936; the valuable memoir of H. Curtius, *Bemühungen um Österreich: das Scheitern des Zollunionsplan um 1931*, Heidel-

berg, 1947; and the thoughtful R. Pannwitz, *Die deutsche Idee Europa*, Munich, 1931; and the articles of E. v. Kuehnelt-Lehddin in the *Journal of the History of Ideas* (July, 1948) and of P. R. Sweet in the *Journal of Modern History* (December, 1947).

Two standard works on Hungary are F. Deak, *Hungary at the Paris Peace Conference*, New York, 1942; and C. A. Macartney, *Hungary and Her Successors*, London, 1937. See also the interesting revelations of M. Toscano, *L'accordo revisionista franco-ungherese del 1920*, Rome, 1942. The Hungarian Foreign Ministry has published two English volumes of materials from its archives concerning Hungarian diplomacy during and after the Paris Peace Conference, but unfortunately very few copies are extant.

Five general works dealing with the creation and the early fortunes of Greater Rumania are R. W. Seton-Watson, *A History of the Roumanians*, New York, 1934; D. Mitrany, *The Land and Peasant in Rumania*, New Haven, 1930; H. L. Roberts, *Rumania: Political Problems of an Agrarian State*, New Haven, 1951; G. C. Logio, *Rumania, Its History, Politics and Economics*, Manchester, 1932; and J. Roucek, *Contemporary Rumania*, Stanford, 1928. The early history of the Yugoslav Kingdom is discussed in G. v. der Maur, *Die Jugoslawen einst und jetzt*, Vienna, 1935; C. Beard-Radin, *The Balkan Pivot: Jugoslavia*, New York, 1929; B. P. B. Baerlein, *The Birth of Yugoslavia*, London, 1922; H. Wendel, *Der Kampf der Südslawen um Freiheit und Einheit*, Frankfurt, 1925; É. Haumant, *La formation de la Yougoslavie*, Paris, 1930; in R. Kerner, ed., *Yugoslavia*, Berkeley, 1949, see especially the chapter by H. N. Howard. See also S. Graham, *Alexander of Yugoslavia*, New Haven, 1939; parts of R. West, *Black Lamb and Gray Falcon*, New York, 1941, and the article of C. Galli in *Mondo Europeo* (Jan.–Feb., 1946). Two books touching upon Yugoslav diplomatic history in the early 1930's are N. Henderson, *Water Under the Bridges*, London, 1945, and J. F. Montgomery, *Hungary, the Unwilling Satellite*, New York, 1947. On Albania and her frontier problems see C. Umiltà, *Jugoslavia e Albania — memorie d'un diploma-*

tico, Rome, 1947; R. Albrecht-Carrié, *Italy at the Peace Conference*, New York, 1938; A. Mousset, *L'Albanie devant l'Europe*, *1912–1930*, Paris, 1930; R. Bernard, *Essai sur l'histoire de l'Albanie moderne*, Paris, 1935; V. Robinson, *Albania's Road to Freedom*, New York, 1942; also C. Sforza, *Fifty Years of War and Diplomacy in the Balkans*, New York, 1940. Bulgaria and the Macedonian quarrels are discussed in H. Prost, *La Bulgarie de 1912–1930*, Paris, 1932; G. T. Danailov, *Les effets de la guerre en Bulgarie*, New Haven, 1932; J. Buchan, ed., *Bulgaria: Problems and Politics*, London, 1919; J. Swire, *Bulgarian Conspiracy*, London, 1937; Molloff, ed., *Die sozialökonomische Struktur der bulgarischen Landwirtschaft*, Leipzig, 1936; S. P. Ladas, *The Exchange of Minorities Between Greece, Bulgaria and Turkey*, New York, 1930; H. N. Howard, *The Partition of Turkey, 1913–1923: A Study in Diplomatic History*, Norman, Oklahoma, 1931; E. Barker, *Macedonia — Its Place in Balkan Power Politics*, London, 1950. On Balkan federation or union attempts see the earliest article by G. Stephanove in *Current History* (April, 1922); the books of G. Stavrianos, *Balkan Federation: A History of the Movement toward Balkan Unity in Modern Times*, Northhampton, Mass., 1942; R. Kerner and H. N. Howard, *The Balkan Conferences and the Balkan Entente 1930–1935*, Berkeley, 1936; T. Geshkoff, *Balkan Union*, New York, 1940; also K. Todorov, *Balkan Firebrand*, Chicago, 1943. On Greece see G. F. Abbott, *Greece and the Allies, 1914–1922*, London, 1922; E. v. Thadden-Schramm, *Griechenland und die Grossen Mächte 1913–1923*, Göttingen, 1933; E. A. Adamov, ed., *Die europäischen Mächte und Griechenland während des Weltkrieges*, Dresden, 1932; A. J. Toynbee, *The Western Question in Greece and Turkey*, London, 1922; J. Mavrogordato, *Modern Greece*, London, 1931; S. Ronart, *Griechenland von Heute*, Amsterdam, 1935; D. Alastos, *Venizelos*, London, 1942.

[*II. The diplomatic revolution. 1934–1938.*]
Of the important document collections concerning the Diplomatic Revolution of 1934–1937, *Documents on German Foreign Policy*, Series D, Washington, 1949–, vols. I

(From Neurath to Ribbentrop), II (Germany and Czechoslovakia), III (Germany and the Spanish Civil War) and V (Germany and the Minor Powers) are of immediate interest here, together with *Documents on British Foreign Policy, 1919–1939*, London, 1948–, vols. I–III in the Second Series, and vols. I–II in the Third. The special volume, *The Soviet Union 1933–1939*, in the Foreign Relations of the United States series, Washington, 1952, contains some relevant and interesting materials. See also the French Yellow Book, *Le livre jaune — documents diplomatiques*, Paris, 1939; the forthcoming *Documenti diplomatici italiani*, Series VII and VIII; the German White Book No. 1, New York, 1940; also the essay of L. B. Namier on the "colored books" in his *Diplomatic Prelude*, London, 1948; and the article of Toscano in *Rassegna Italiana* (July, 1940). The three volumes of Ciano papers dealing with the latter phase of the Diplomatic Revolution are G. Ciano, *Diario 1937–1938*, Bologna, 1948; *Lettere e documenti*, Milan, 1948; and *L'Europa verso la catastrofe*, Milan, 1948.

There is an abundance of French memoir literature concerning these years: P. Laval, *Notes et mémoires*, Geneva, 1948; J. Paul-Boncour, *Entre deux guerres*, Paris, 1946, vols. I–III; G. Bonnet, *De Washington au Quai d'Orsay*, Geneva, 1947; A. François-Poncet, *Souvenirs d'une ambassade*, Paris, 1947; M. Gamelin, *Servir*, Paris, 1947, vol. II; P. Reynaud, *La France a sauvé l'Europe*, Paris, 1947; G. Réquin, *D'une guerre à l'autre, 1919–39, souvenirs*, Paris, 1949. See also the French parliamentary *Rapport fait au nom de la commission chargée d'enquêter sur les événements survenus en France de 1933 à 1945: I. Les événements du 7 mars 1936*, Paris, 1951; and the reminiscences of the Belgian Ambassador, J. D'Avignon, *Berlin, 1936–1940*, Paris, 1951. The most detailed account of Poland's position is given by L. Noël in, *L'aggression allemande contre la Pologne*, Paris, 1947; interesting are the posthumous memoirs of J. Beck, *Dernier rapport: politique polonaise 1926–1939*, Neuchâtel, 1951 and of Count J. Szembek, *Journal 1933–1939*, Paris, 1951. N. Comnen, *I responsabili*, Milan, 1949, has some relevant details; see also the material reproduced in the article of W. J. Rose in the *Journal of Central European Affairs* (July, 1951) and the article of di San Savino in the *Rivista di studi politici internazionali* (January, 1951). Critiques of what is termed the French "Right" in this period include E. A. Cameron, *Prologue to Appeasement — A Study in French Foreign Policy*, Washington, 1942; A. Werth, *The Twilight of France, 1933–1940*, London, 1942; Pertinax (pseud., A. Géraud), *The Gravediggers of France*, New York, 1944; and C. A. Micaud, *The French Right and Nazi Germany, 1933–39*, Durham, N.C., 1943. Post-war German revelations and memoirs are these: E. Kordt, *Wahn und Wirklichkeit*, Stuttgart, 1947, and his *Nicht aus den Akten*, Stuttgart, 1950; A. Hoszbach, *Zwischen Wehrmacht und Hitler*, Wolfenbüttel, 1949; P. Schmidt, *Statist auf diplomatischer Bühne*, Bonn, 1950; H. Holldack, *Was wirklich geschah — die diplomatische Hintergründe der deutschen Kriegspolitik*, Munich, 1949; G. v. Schweppenburg, *Erinnerungen eines Militärattachés, London 1933–37*, Stuttgart, 1950. Contemporary observations of some value were E. Hantos, *Die Neuordnung des Donauraumes*, Vienna, 1935; G. Schacher, *Central Europe and the Western World*, London, 1936. Three rather journalistic accounts are L. Fodor, *Plot and Counterplot in Central Europe*, Boston, 1936; G. Schacher, *Germany Pushes South-East*, London, 1937; L. Einzig, *Bloodless Invasion — German Economic Penetration into the Danubian States and the Balkans*, London, 1938; see also L. Jócsik, *German Economic Penetration in the Danube Valley*, Budapest, 1946; and S. Graur, *Les relations entre la Roumanie et l'URSS depuis le traité de Versailles*, Paris, 1938.

Books with more historical perspective are these: É. Giraud, *La nullité de la politique internationale des grandes démocraties*, Paris, 1949; E. Wiskemann, *The Rome-Berlin Axis*, New York, 1949: Winston Churchill, *The Gathering Storm*, New York, 1948; M. Baumont, *La faillite de la paix*, Paris, 1947, vol. II; M. Beloff, *The Foreign Policy of Soviet Russia*, London, 1949, vol. II; L. B. Namier, *Europe in Decay*, London, 1950; and J. Menkin, ed., *The World at War*, London, 1951, vol. I.

The tragedy of Austria has been abundantly covered by literature, much of which received mention in Part I of this bibliography. Further memoirs and accounts of interest are these: K. v. Schuschnigg, *My Austria*, New York, 1938, and his *Austrian Requiem*, New York, 1947; J. Basdevant, *La condition internationale de l'Autriche*, Paris, 1935; G. Zernatto, *Die Wahrheit über Österreich*, Toronto, 1938; P. Chaillot, *L'Autriche souffrante*, Paris, 1938; R. Ingrim, *Der Griff nach Österreich*, Zurich, 1938; B. Skottsberg, *Der österreichische Parlamentarismus*, Stockholm, 1940; H. Hubner, *Österreich 1933–38: der Abwehrkampf eines Volkes*, Vienna, 1949; R. P. Rambaud, O. P., *Dollfuss — le grand petit chancellier*, Paris, 1948; Brandis, *Österreichs historische Mission in Europa*, Zurich, 1946; G. E. R. Gedye, *Betrayal in Central Europe*, New York, 1939, and his *Fallen Bastions*, London, 1938; D. M. Tuminetti, *La mia missione segreta in Austria, 1937–8*, Milan, 1946; E. R. v. Starhemberg, *Between Hitler and Mussolini*, New York, 1942; G. v. Franckenstein, *Diplomat of Destiny*, New York, 1940; H. Heinl, *Über ein halbes Jahrhundert: Zeit und Wirtschaft*, Vienna, 1949; F. Borkenau, *Austria and After*, London, 1938; and P. T. Lux, *Österreich 1918–1938, eine Demokratie — Betrachtungen eines Neutralen*, Graz, 1946. Three works reflecting Socialist views are Pertinax (pseud., O. Leichter), *Österreich 1934*, Zurich, 1935; J. Braunthal, *The Tragedy of Austria*, London, 1948; W. Boehm, *Februar 1934: ein Akt der österreichischen Tragödie*, Vienna, 1948. Three Nazi accounts are W. v. Hartlieb, *Parole: Das Reich*, Vienna, 1939; H. Bleyer-Härtl, *Ringen um Reich und Recht: Zwei Jahrzehnte politischer Anwalt in Österreich*, Berlin, 1939, and H. v. Fritsch, *Die Gewaltherrschaft in Österreich, 1933 bis 1938*, Leipzig, 1938. Interesting documents are to be found in *Der Hochverratprozess gegen Dr. Guido Schmidt vor dem Wiener Volksgericht: die gerichtlichen Protokolle . . . veröffentlichte Dokumente, etc.*, Vienna, 1947; and *Rot-Weiss-Rot Buch*, Vienna, 1946; see also Papen's memoirs, *Der Wahrheit eine Gasse*, Munich, 1952. A few interesting dispatches from Vienna and Berlin are to be found in the volume of

Papers Relating to the Foreign Relations of the United States series which covers the year 1934, Washington, 1951; see also the relevant Nuremberg documents, *IMT*, 1760–, 2994–, 2995–, 2996–, 3254–, 3425–, 3697–PS, and especially the Messersmith and Papen affidavits, 3300–PS and 2931–PS; also the article and bibliography of P. R. Sweet in the *Journal of Modern History* (March, 1950).

The standard diplomatic sources of the Munich period are *Documents on German Foreign Policy*, Series D, vols. I, II, V, and *Documents on British Foreign Policy*, Third Series, vols. I–III. Other documentary materials are *Documents and Materials Relating to the Eve of the Second World War*, vol. I, *November 1937–November 1938*, Moscow, 1948; another Russian publication is *Falsifiers of History*, Moscow and New York, 1948. The *State Department Bulletin* during the year 1946 published interesting extracts from the captured German papers. See also F. Berber, *Europäische Politik 1933–38 im Spiegel der Prager Akten*, Berlin, 1942, and Appendix IV in G. Bonnet, *Fin d'une Europe*, Geneva, 1948. Comments and relevant articles include C. Bloch in the *Bulletin de la société française d'histoire moderne* (March, 1947); M. Baumont in *Foreign Affairs* (July, 1947); O. Odložilik in the *Journal of Central European Affairs* (January, 1949); E. Táborsky in *Foreign Affairs* (January, 1949); G. A. Craig in the *Political Science Quarterly* (March, 1950); E. H. Carr in *Soviet Studies* (June and October, 1949); M. Beloff in *idem* (October, 1950); M. Vaussard in the *Revue historique de la deuxième guerre mondiale* (October, 1951); and P. Audiat in *Figaro littéraire* (March 17, 1951).

The early standard narrative of the Munich period is J. W. Wheeler-Bennett, *Munich — Prologue to Tragedy*, New York, 1947, presently supplemented with material culled from the since opened archives by R. G. D. Laffan, in his *Survey of International Affairs 1938*, London, 1951, vol. II. The standard background study of the Sudeten ethnic dispute is E. Wiskemann, *Czechs and Germans*, London, 1937. Memoirs and accounts of substantial interest concerning the Czechoslovak crisis are K. Feiling, *The*

Life of Neville Chamberlain, London, 1946; N. Henderson, *Failure of a Mission*, London, 1940, and his *Water Under the Bridges*, London, 1945; Viscount Maugham, *The Truth About the Munich Crisis*, London, 1944 (the first "revisionist" view on Munich); E. v. Weizsäcker, *Erinnerungen*, Munich, 1950. Beneš' memoirs, *Pameti*, Prague, 1946, vol. II, were scrutinized in the above-cited articles by Odložilik and Táborsky; see also the articles by V. L. Tapié in the *Revue historique* (Jan.–Mar., 1952) and by Sir B. Lockhart in *Foreign Affairs* (July, 1948). There is also an account by Henlein, an article in *Die Verwaltungsakademie — Ein Handbuch für den Beamten im nationalsozialistischen Staat* (Heft 20, 1941). The Czech national view is expressed by H. Ripka, *Munich — Before and After*, London, 1939; see also the less reliable J. Hanc, *Tornado Over Eastern Europe*, New York, 1942. Of the previously cited memoirs, those of Bonnet, Gamelin, Reynaud, Churchill, Kordt, Schmidt, and Ciano are of most interest. Other French memoirs with specific relevance for this period are E. Flandin, *Politique française*, Paris, 1948; J. Caillaux, *Mémoires*, Paris, 1947, vol. III; A. de Monzie, *Ci-devant*, Paris, 1942. Fragments of information may be found in two ambassadorial memoirs, N. Comnen, *Preludi del grande dramma*, Rome, 1948, and E. Labougle, *Misión en Berlín*, Buenos Aires, 1946; see also H. B. Gisevius, *Bis zum bitteren Ende*, Zurich, 1946, to be taken with reservation. S. Grant-Duff, *Europe and the Czechs*, London, 1938, contains contemporary reflexions; see also the little unpublished paper of Sister M. Alberta, S.S.J., *Public Opinion in Great Britain and France between Godesberg and Munich* (in my possession) and the article by R. G. D. Laffan in the London *Tablet*, September 27, 1952.

The history of the rest of central-eastern Europe during the Diplomatic Revolution is covered by the two Royal Institute volumes, *South-eastern Europe*, London, 1938 and *The Baltic States*, London, 1938, as well as by H. Seton-Watson, *Eastern Europe 1918–1941*, revised edition, Cambridge, 1946. A Soviet publication, *Documents secrets du ministère des affaires étrangères d'Allemagne, Hongrie*, vol. II, Paris, 1946, contains surprisingly much interesting material. Other volumes include L. Noël, *L'aggression allemande contre la Pologne*, Paris, 1947; J. Beck, *Dernier rapport*, Neuchâtel, 1951; J. F. Montgomery, *Hungary — The Unwilling Satellite*, New York, 1947; see also B. Kosatov, *La Bulgarie et le pacte balkanique*, Paris, 1938; A. Bilmanis, *Latvijas Werdegang*, Leipzig, 1934; K. Gloger, *Baltikum*, Berlin, 1938; A. Tamborra, *L'intesa baltica*, Milan, 1937; J. H. Jackson, *Finland*, London, 1938; J. Cathala, *Portrait de l'Estonie*, Paris, 1937; and H. de Chambon, *Aspects de la Finlande*, Paris, 1938.

[*III. Between German hammer and Russian anvil. 1938–1941.*] Documentary materials here include *Documents on German Foreign Policy*, Series D, vol. IV; *Documents on British Foreign Policy*, Third Series, vols. III–V; the *Documenti diplomatici italiani* vols. XII–XIII of Series VIII and the forthcoming Series IX; the French *Livre jaune* and the German White Books, especially No. III; the important *Nazi-Soviet Relations*, Washington, 1948; the Greek White Book, London, 1942; the Polish White Book, London, 1940 (its French version, *Les relations polono-allemandes et polono-soviétiques au cours de la période 1933–39*, Paris, 1940, is more precise); the Swedish White Books, especially those concerning the Finnish War and early 1940: *Handlingar rörande Sveriges politik under andra världskriget — Förspelet till det tyska angreppet på Danmark och Norge*, Stockholm, 1947 and *Transiteringsfrågan*, Stockholm, 1948, vols. I–II; the Finnish Blue Book, New York, 1940, concerning the first Winter War and the Blue-White Book, New York, 1942, concerning 1940–41; *Documents and Materials Relating to the Eve of the Second World War, II. The Dirksen Papers*, Moscow, 1948; the 1939–43 *Ciano Diaries*, New York, 1946 (the American edition should be handled with a certain caution: see the note of G. Megaro in the *American Historical Review* (October, 1948), and also p. xvii in the introduction to the earlier *Diario, 1937–1938*); also *Hitler e Mussolini — lettere e documenti*, Milan, 1946; and E. Re, *Storia di un archivio:*

le carte di Mussolini, Rome, 1946. See also the *Survey of International Affairs 1938*, vol. III., R. G. D. Laffan, ed., dealing with the post-Munich period. *The World in March 1939*, New York, 1952. Toynbee–Ashton–Gwatkin, eds., is the first in the *Survey of International Affairs 1939–46* series.

On the origins and development of the German-Russian Pact period, *Nazi-Soviet Relations* is indispensable. Other related volumes are these: M. da Buranca (pseud., M. Lanza), *Russia e Germania, 20 anni di storia diplomatica*, Milan, 1942, extremely rare; R. Coulondre, *De Staline à Hitler, souvenirs de deux ambassades, 1936–1939*, Paris, 1950; A. Rossi, (pseud., A. Tasca), *The Russo-German Alliance August 1939–June 1941*, Boston, 1951; H.–G. Seraphim, *Die deutsch-russische Beziehungen 1939–1941*, Hamburg, 1949; A. Seidl, ed., *Die Beziehungen zwischen Deutschland und der Sowjetunion 1939–1941*, Tübingen, 1949; P. Kleist, *Zwischen Hitler und Stalin*, Bonn, 1950; D. Dallin, *Soviet Foreign Policy 1939–1942*, New Haven, 1942; B. Newman, *The Captured Archives*, London, 1948; J. Davies, *Mission to Moscow*, New York, 1941; the pro-Soviet book of W. P. and Z. K. Coates, *A History of Anglo-Soviet Relations*, London, 1943; and G. Gafencu's brilliant work, *Préliminaires à la guerre de l'est*, Lausanne, 1943, German edition, Berne, 1944, English edition, London, 1945. See also pp. 602–37 in *Documents on German Foreign Policy*, Series, D, vol. IV; parts of vol. V; pp. 731–1013 in *The Soviet Union, 1933–1939*; the above cited memoirs of Bonnet, Kordt, and Noël; the chapter on Anglo-French-Russian negotiations in L. B. Namier, *Diplomatic Prelude*, London, 1948; the paper of G. Doumenc in *Documents of International Affairs, 1939–1946*, London, 1951, vol. I; the articles of H. C. Deutsch in *The Historian* (Spring, 1947); E. H. Carr in *Soviet Studies* (October, 1949); G. Thimm in *Die Gegenwart* (September, 1947); A. Rosso in the *Rivista dei studi politici internazionali* (1946); M. Toscano in *idem* (September, 1950); see also his article in the *Revue historique de la deuxième guerre mondiale* (April, 1952).

The summer crisis of 1939 and the diplomatic fortunes of Poland are covered in the "colored books" and in most of the previously cited memoirs, especially those of Beck, Noël, Szembek, Bonnet, Reynaud, Henderson, Ciano, Dirksen, Kordt, Weizsäcker, and Schmidt. Of special interest here are *Documents and materials. . . . II. The Dirksen Papers;* vol. XII of Series VIII in *I documenti diplomatici italiani,* and the forthcoming vol. VII in *Documents on British Foreign Policy,* Third Series. See also M. Toscano, *Le origini del patto d'acciaio,* Bologna, 1948; M. Toscano, *L'Italia e gli accordi tedesco-sovietici dell'agosto 1939,* Firenze, 1952; G. Gafencu, *The Last Days of Europe,* New Haven, 1949; L. Simoni (pseud., M. Lanza), *Berlino, Ambasciata d'Italia,* Rome, 1946; M. Donosti (pseud., M. Luciolli), *Mussolini e l'Europa,* Rome, 1945; Sir L. Namier, *In the Nazi Era,* New York, 1952; the chapter by S. Possony in F. A. Cave, ed., *Origins and Consequences of World War II,* New York, 1948; *Carnets secrets de Jean Zay,* Paris, 1941; G. Suarez-Laborde, *L'agonie de la paix,* Paris, 1942; J. Scott, *Duel for Europe,* Boston, 1942; S. Mackiewicz, *Colonel Beck and His Policy,* London, 1944; Count E. Raczynski, *The British-Polish Alliance, Its Origins and Meaning,* London, n.d.; R. L. Buell, *Poland — Key to Europe,* New York, 1939; H. L. Leonhard, *The Nazi Conquest of Danzig,* Chicago, 1942; K. Assmann, *Deutsche Schicksalsjahre,* Wiesbaden, 1950; and H. Nicolson, *Why Britain is at War,* London, 1939. See also the articles of G. Doumenc in *Carrefour* (May 21, 1947); A. Dallin in the *Journal of Central European Affairs* (April, 1950); J. Lukasiewicz in *Dziennik Polski* (1946); M. Magistrati in the *Rivista di studi politici internazionali* (October, 1949). Military treatises of the Polish campaign are to be found in the most valuable H. Greiner, *Die oberste Wehrmachtsführung 1939–1943,* Wiesbaden, 1951; in the first part of H. Bidou, *La bataille de France,* Geneva, 1941; R. Jars, *La campagne de Pologne,* Paris, 1948; M. N. Neugebauer, *The Defense of Poland* London, 1942; see also parts of J. F. C. Fuller, *The Second World War,* New York, 1949, and W. Görlitz, *Der zweite Weltkrieg 1939–1945,* Stuttgart, 1951.

The Finnish-Russian war of 1939–40 and the accompanying diplomatic events are illuminated by the previously cited Finnish and Swedish document collections; see also J. H. Wuorinen, *Finland in World War II,* New York, 1947. This standard account is supplemented by the valuable memoirs of V. Tanner, *Finlands Väg 1939–40,* Stockholm, 1951; see also The Royal Institute of International Affairs, *The Scandinavian States and Finland,* London, 1951; H. Danjou, *L'héroique Finlande,* Paris, 1940; Minart, P. C. Vincennes, *Secteur 4,* Paris, 1945; H. B. Elliston, *Finland Fights,* London, 1940; and the March–April, 1946, November–December, 1950, and November–December, 1951 issues of *The Norseman;* see also the articles of Jakobson in the *Manchester Guardian Weekly* (February 22 and March 1, 1951). Here the European diplomacy of the United States begins to assume importance for central-eastern Europe, a subject which receives extensive treatment in W. L. Langer and S. E. Gleason, *The Challenge to Isolation, 1937–1940,* New York, 1952; see also J. Alsop and R. Kintner, *American White Papers,* New York, 1940; Sumner Welles, *The Time for Decision,* New York, 1944; W. H. Chamberlain, *America's Second Crusade,* Chicago, 1950, and the revisionist C. C. Tansill, *Back Door to War,* Chicago, 1952. On the end of Baltic independence see A. Bilmanis, ed., *Latvian White Book,* Washington, 1942; *Latvia 1939–1942,* Washington, 1943; and *The Baltic States and the Baltic Sea,* Washington, 1943; W. F. Reddaway, *Problems of the Baltic,* New York, 1940; J. H. Jackson, *Estonia,* London, 1948; K. R. Pusta, *The Soviet Union and the Baltic States,* New York, 1942; A. Oras, *Baltic Eclipse,* London, 1947; R. Suduvis, *Ein kleines Volk wird ausgelöscht,* Zurich, 1948. On the Carpatho-Ukrainian issue of 1939 see M. Winch, *Republic for a Day,* London, 1939. A Rumanian view on the Dobrudja problem is that of R. Vulpe, *La Dobrudja travers les siècles: evolutions historiques et considérations géopolitiques,* Bucharest, 1939. Two contemporary Balkan descriptions are J. Blainy, *Crépuscule danubien,* Paris, 1946, and S. Pribichevich, *World Without End,* New York, 1939. The historical question of Turkey and Allied plans in 1939–40 is partly covered in M. Sokolnicki,

The Turkish Straits, Beirut, 1950; the memoirs of Sir H. Knatchbull-Hugessen, *Diplomat in Peace and War*, London, 1949; and in one of the German official publications, *Die Geheimakten des französischen Generalstabes*, Berlin, 1940. The Yugoslav quandary and resistance in 1941 is dealt with by K. Fotitch, *The War We Lost*, New York, 1948; *Le procès Laval*, Paris, 1946, contains a section about the wartime fate of the French-owned Bor mines in Yugoslavia; on the controversial months of October–November, 1940 and March, 1941, see the very extensive account and revelations in Greiner, cited above; see also the debated articles of D. Tsvetkovic in *Le Figaro* (April 4, 1950) and J. Knezevic in *International Affairs* (January, 1951), Tsvetkovic replying in *idem* (October, 1951); also A. Acikalin in *idem* (October, 1949). Some interesting diplomatic details of the summer of 1940 are given in R. Serrano Suñer, *Entre Hendaya y Gibraltar*, Madrid, 1947, and in Enquêtecommissie Regeringsbeleid 1940–45, *Verslag betreffende uitkonsten van het underzoek*, vol. 2b, *Neutraliteitspolitiek*, The Hague, 1949. The origins of the Italian attack on Greece are discussed by Ciano, Hitler-Mussolini, Greek White Book, cited above; also E. Grazzi, *Il principio della fine*, Rome, 1946; L. Mondini, *Prologo del conflitto italo-greco*, Rome, 1945; P. Badoglio, *L'Italia nella seconda guerra mondiale*, Milan, 1946 (see also the somewhat unfair review article of G. Salvemini in the *Journal of Modern History* (December, 1949)); G. Visconti-Prasca, *Io ho aggredito la Grecia*, Rome, 1946; F. Pricolo, *Ignavia contro eroismo — l'avventura italo-greca 1940–41*, Rome, 1946; and M. Roatta, *Otto millioni di baionette*, Milan, 1946. Two very philhellene views are those found in S. Casson, *Greece Against the Axis*, London, 1942, and in the first part of C. M. Woodhouse, *Apple of Discord*, London, 1948; see also A. Papagos, *La Grecia in guerra*, Milan, 1950; and the books of two German witnesses: E. v. Rintelen, *Mussolini als Bundesgenosse*, Tübingen, 1951; E. F. Moellhausen, *Die gebrochene Achse*, 1949; also the article of Vogel in *Europa-Archiv* (October, 1950).

Early stories of reisistance movements include the *Black Book of Poland*, New York, 1942; S. Grant-Duff, *A German Protectorate*, London, 1942; *Czechoslovakia Fights Back*, Washington, 1943; B. Kalnins, *De baltiska staterna frihetskamp*, Stockholm, 1950; A. Bilmanis, *Latvia Under German Occupation*, Washington, 1943. M. Hodza, *Federation in Central Europe — Reflections and Reminiscences*, London, 1942, was written from a higher viewpoint; parts of it, as well as the Finnish Blue-White Book and the Baltic accounts, were early but futile warnings against the imminent danger of Russian imperialism.

[*IV. The war of wars. 1941–1944.*] The United States Government began declassifying the wartime intelligence papers of the Office of Strategic Services in 1948: the *OSS*, Research & Analysis Branch papers threw some light on the intelligence material behind American wartime policies. There is also a wealth of interesting little fragments in the opened papers of Franklin D. Roosevelt. The State Department publication, *Post-war Foreign Policy Preparations*, Washington, 1950, contains a few documents of interest. Other primary sources for this period include the *Correspondence Between President Roosevelt and Pope Pius XII*, New York, 1947 and *Documents secrets du ministère des affaires étrangères d'Allemagne*, III — *Turquie*, Paris, 1946. Official and personal papers are reprinted in the Churchill memoirs which deal with 1941–44, *The Grand Alliance*, *The Hinge of Fate*, *Closing the Ring*, New York, 1949–51. Wartime books preoccupied with postwar planning are Walter Lippmann, *U. S. Foreign Policy — Shield of the Republic*, New York, 1943, and E. H. Carr, *Conditions of Peace*, London, 1942; see also the answer by G. Gafencu in the Appendix of his *Préliminaires à la guerre de l'est*, Lausanne, 1943; the reflexions of G. F. Kennan in his *American Diplomacy 1900–1950*, Chicago, 1951; M. Hodza, *Federation in Central Europe — Reflections and Reminiscences*, London, 1942; and R. Schlesinger, *Federalism in Central and Eastern Europe*, London, 1945 (the latter with a strong pro-Russian bias). There were a host of premature and illusion-ridden articles about the future of central-eastern Europe in British and American periodicals between 1942 and 1945; interesting is the comparison of two of these, that of Otto Habsburg and that of Edvard Beneš in *Foreign Affairs* (1942).

Certain works dealing with the military aspect of the war have some value for the student of wartime diplomacy; among these are Greiner, cited above; R. de Belot, *The Struggle for the Mediterranean 1939–45*, Princeton, 1951; H. Picker, *Hitlers Tischgespräche im Führerhauptquartier 1941–42*, Bonn, 1951; A. Valori, *La campagna di Russia*, Rome, 1950; C. Léderrey, *La défaite allemande à l'Est*, Paris, 1951; and A. Guillaume, *La guerre germano-soviétique*, Paris, 1949; see also my review in the *American Slavic and East European Review* (December, 1951); C. Wilmot, *The Struggle for Europe*, London, 1952; and the article by Hanson W. Baldwin in the *Atlantic Monthly* (January, 1950).

Concerning this period American memoirs abound, including many, sometimes unwitting, revelations. Such memoirs are Henry L. Stimson-McGeorge Bundy, *On Active Service in War and Peace*, Boston, 1947; J. Winant, *Letter from Grosvenor Square*, New York, 1948; H. Butcher, *My Three Years with Eisenhower*, New York, 1946; W. L. Leahy, *I Was There*, New York, 1950; R. Sherwood, *Roosevelt and Hopkins*, New York, 1948; Cordell Hull, *Memoirs*, Boston, 1948; Elliott Roosevelt, *As He Saw It*, New York, 1946, rather unreliable; W. Carroll, *Persuade or Perish*, Boston, 1948; Sumner Welles, *Seven Decisions That Shaped History*, New York, 1951. Two very valuable accounts by military figures are J. Deane, *The Strange Alliance*, New York, 1947; M. W. Clark, *Calculated Risk*, New York, 1950.

Fragments about intricacies of wartime Axis diplomacy and separate peace attempts come to light in Ciano and Simoni, cited above; see also Josef Göbbels, *Tagebücher*, Zurich, 1948; Papen and Kordt cited above; D. Alfieri, *Due dittatori di fronte*, Milan, 1949; R. Guariglia, *Memorie*, Rome, 1950; F. Anfuso, *Roma, Berlino, Salo*, Rome, 1950; U. v. Hassell, *Vom andern Deutschland*, Zurich, 1946; R. Rahn, *Ruheloses Leben*, Dusseldorf, 1949; T. Kase,

Journey to the Missouri, New Haven, 1950; M. Mourin, *Les complots contre Hitler*, Paris, 1947, and his *Les tentatives de paix séparée pendant la deuxième guerre mondiale*, Paris, 1949; G. Bottai, *Vent'anni e un giorno*, Rome, 1949; P. Kleist, *Zwischen Hitler und Stalin*, Bonn, 1950; R. Moyzisch, *Operation Cicero*, New York, 1950; and the only partially reliable J. M. Doussinague, *España tenía razón*, Madrid, 1950.

The wartime fortunes of Finland are described in J. H. Wuorinen, *Finland in World War II*, New York, 1947; W. Erfurth, *Der finnische Krieg 1941–44*, Wiesbaden, 1950; W. v. Blücher, *Gesandter zwischen Diktatur und Demokratie*, Wiesbaden, 1951; H. J. Procopé, *Sowjetjustiz über Finnland*, Zurich, 1947; A. Tosti, *Mannerheim e il dramma della Finlandia*, Bologna, 1952; D. de Roussillon, *Vérités sur la Finlande*, Paris, 1946. Many Finnish memoirs have been published lately, among them Mannerheim, *Minnen*, Stockholm, 1951 and Tanner, *Finlands Väg*, Stockholm, 1951; see also the article by G. Hafström in *Svensk Tidskrift*, 1952(5); J. Kolehmainen carefully records this literature in the *Journal of Modern History*.

I. Deutscher, *Stalin — A Political Biography*, New York, 1950, presents a sweeping panorama of wartime Soviet foreign policy, parts of which are of interest here. The crucial problem of Polish-Russian relations is dealt with in R. Umiastowski, *Poland, Russia and Great Britain 1941–45 — A Study of Evidence*, London, 1946; also in his *Russia and the Polish Republic*, London, 1946; J. Jedrzejewicz, *Poland in the British Parliament*, London, 1947; J. Ciechanowski, *Defeat in Victory*, New York, 1947; A. Zoltowski, *Borders of Europe: A Study of the Polish Eastern Provinces*, London, 1950; W. J. Rose, *Poland — Old and New*, London, 1948; B. Kusnierz, *Stalin and the Poles*, London, 1949; S. Mikolajczyk, *The Rape of Poland*, New York, 1948; J. Shotwell and M. Laserson, *Russia and Poland 1939–45;* and many articles, among them that of R. Kulski in *Foreign Affairs* (July, 1947). On the German occupation and Polish resistance see the relevant IMT documents: Bühler, *Das Generalgouvernement, seine Verwaltung und seine Wirtschaft*, Berlin, 1942, an official Nazi account; L. Frascati, *Il destino passa per Varsavia*, Bologna, 1949; J. Karski, *Story of a Secret State*, Boston, 1944; W. Anders, *An Army in Exile*, New York, 1950; T. Bór-Komorowski, *The Secret Army*, New York, 1951; see also J. Tenenbaum, *Underground*, New York, 1952. On Katyn and Russian cruelties see J. Mackiewicz, *Katyn — ungesühntes Verbrechen*, Zurich, 1950; *Amtliches Material zum Massenmord um Katyn*, Berlin, 1943, the German account; anon., *The Dark Side of the Moon*, London, 1946; E. Dangerfield, *Behind the Urals*, London, 1946; J. Gliksman, *Tell the West*, New York, 1948; W. Anders, *Katyn*, Paris, 1949; see also the article of F. Hudson in *International Affairs* (April, 1950).

The quandaries of satellite diplomacy are portrayed by H. Seton-Watson in his extensive *The East European Revolution*, London, 1950. Concerning Hungary, see Schmidt, Kordt, Weizsäcker, Montgomery, cited above; also A. Ullein-Reviczky, *Guerre allemande — paix russe*, Neuchâtel, 1947; G. A. Skousès, *Les Huns et les autres*, n. pl., 1949; the articles of S. Kertész in the *Review of Politics* (January, 1949) and G. Paikert in the *American Slavic and East European Review* (February, 1952). About the Italian-Danubian bloc and secession attempts in 1943 see Simoni, Alfieri, Anfuso, Guariglia, cited above; also L. Villari, *Affari esteri 1943-1945*, Rome, 1948; P. Monelli, *Roma, 1943*, Rome, 1946; A. Mellini Ponce de Leon, *Guerra diplomatica a Salò*, Bologna, 1952; A. Tamaro, *Due anni di storia*, vols. I–III, Rome, 1949–50. R. Bova Scoppa, *Colloqui con due dittatori*, Rome, 1949, has much interesting material concerning Rumania; see also Roberts, cited above; the interesting articles of A. Cretzianu and F. C. Nano in the October 1951 and October 1952 issues of the *Journal of Central European Affairs; Mémorial Antonesco — le troisième homme de l'Axe*, Paris, 1950; R. Markham, *Rumania Under the Soviet Yoke*, Boston, 1949; and A. G. Lee, *Crown Against Sickle: The Story of King Michael of Rumania*, London, 1950.

Yugoslavia's fate is discussed by K. Fotitch, *The War We Lost*, New York, 1948; see also F. A. Voigt, *Pax Britannica*, London,

1948; F. MacLean, *Eastern Approaches*, London, 1950, and his article in *Foreign Affairs* (January, 1950); and the interesting article of B. Raditsa in the *New American Mercury* (December, 1951) about L. Adamic and the latter's *Dinner at the White House*, New York, 1946. Some highly colorful sidelights on Croatia are given in C. Malaparte, *Kaputt*, New York, 1946. Italian-Yugoslav contacts and the effects of the Italian armistice are described by D. Pariset, *Roatta e il retroscena del S.I.M.*, Rome, 1949; see also B. Coceani, *Mussolini, Hitler, Tito alle porte orientali d'Italia*, Bologna, 1948; P. A. Quarantotti-Gambini, *Primavera a Trieste: vicendi del '45*, Milan, 1945; Minister degli Esteri, *Note relative all'occupazione italiana in Jugoslavia*, Rome, 1945; and the article of Rocco in *Nuova Antologia*, 1947. On guerrilla warfare see also J. Amery, *Sons of the Eagle — A Study in Guerrilla Warfare*, London, 1949, especially concerned with Albania; and C. Lawrence, *Irregular Adventure*, London, 1945. V. Dedijer, *With Tito Through the War: A Partisan Diary 1941-44*, London, 1951, is a partisan's partisan account; see also his official biography, *Tito*, New York, 1953; and S. Clissold, *Whirlwind*, London, 1949; B. Davidson, *Partisan Picture*, London, 1947; S. Rootham, *Missfire*, London, 1945; and M. Bassi, *Due anni fra le bande di Tito*, Bologna, 1950. The first signs of the later Russian-Yugoslav dispute are observed and explained by E. Barker in *Macedonia*, London, 1950; see also A. B. Ulam, *Titoism and the Cominform*, Cambridge, 1952, and his article in the *Review of Politics* (January, 1951).

There is much material about wartime Greece and a preliminary bibliography by Stavrianos and Panagopoulos in the *Journal of Modern History* (June, 1948). The standard account is the excellent book of C. M. Woodhouse, *Apple of Discord — A Study of Greek Politics in Their International Setting*, London, 1948; see also W. H. McNeill, *The Greek Dilemma: War and Aftermath*, Chicago, 1947; F. A. Voigt, *The Greek Sedition*, London, 1949; A. W. Gomme, *Greece*, London, 1945; W. Byford-Jones, *The Greek Triology*, London, 1945;

E. L. Dzelepy, *Le drame de la résistance grecque*, Paris, 1946. On the betrayal of the armistice agreement and the tragedy of the Italian troops on Cephalonia see Ministerio Difesa, Ufficio Storico, *Cefalonia*, Rome, 1947; Triarius (pseud.), *La tragedia di C.*, Rome, 1945; R. Formato, *L'eccidio di C.*, Rome, 1946; see also V. Spigai, *Lero*, Leghorn, 1949. A pro-Communist argument and account is given in the book by Sarafis, *Greek Resistance Army: The Story of ELAS*, London, 1951; also in the essay by L. S. Stavrianos in D. E. Lee and G. E. McReynolds, eds., *Essays in History and International Relations in Honor of George H. Blakeslee*, Worcester, Mass., 1949; see also his articles in the *American Slavic and East European Review* (December, 1950) and in the *Journal of Modern History* (March, 1952).

[*V. The Russian era begins. 1944–1945.*] The degeneration of Greek strife into civil war is further described by L. Marc (Marcandonatos), *Les heures douloureuses de la Grèce libérée: journal d'un témoin*, Paris, 1947; the good accounts of Woodhouse and McNeill carry the story to 1947; the British government published a few interesting *Documents Regarding the Situation in Greece* in 1945, and an unofficial "EAM White Book," "documenting" the Communists' cause was privately published by certain Greek-American circles later in that year in New York. The debate was renewed in the articles of L. S. Stavrianos and W. H. McNeill, in the *American Slavic and East European Review* (December, 1949). See also the memoirs of the former British Ambassador, Sir R. W. A. Leeper, *When Greek Meets Greek*, London, 1950; Delvanis and Cleveland, *Greek Monetary Developments 1939–48*, Bloomington, Ind., 1949, is a valuable study of the unique Greek inflation.

Signs of some friction between Tito and Stalin are apparent in the collection of party correspondence in the Royal Institute of International Affairs' *The Soviet-Yugoslav Dispute*, London, 1948; see also the treatise of H. F. Armstrong, *Tito and Goliath*, New York, 1951. Mihailovič'

tragedy is covered in B. Lazitch, *The Tragedy of General Mihailovitch*, London, 1946; D. Martin, *Ally Betrayed*, New York, 1946; R. Markham, *Tito's Imperial Communism*, Chapel Hill, 1947; and J. Korbel, *An Ambassador's Report on Tito's Communism*, Denver, 1951; also the articles of A. B. Ulam, cited above and of M. Piyade in *European Affairs* (March, 1950). Two partisan views on the Macedonian issue are Macedonicus (pseud.), *Stalin and the Macedonian Question*, St. Louis, 1948; I. Mihailoff, *Macedonia: A Switzerland of the Balkans*, St. Louis, 1950. More indispensable is the excellent work of H. R. Wilkinson, *Maps and Politics: A Review of the Ethnographic Cartography of Macedonia*, Liverpool, 1951.

Anglo-American foreign policy leading to the Yalta and Potsdam declarations will undoubtedly be further explained in the forthcoming vol. VI of Churchill's war memoirs. In addition to the memoirs cited in Part IV, the following, largely personal, accounts are of some value: Sir M. Peterson, *Both Sides of the Curtain*, London, 1950; Sir G. Martel, *The Russian Outlook*, London, 1948; W. L. Leahy, *I Was There*, New York, 1950; J. F. Byrnes, *Speaking Frankly*, New York, 1947; E. Stettinius, *Roosevelt and the Russians*, New York, 1949; and the early part of the W. Millis, ed., *The Forrestal Diaries*, New York, 1951. See also R. Aron, *Le grand schisme*, Paris, 1948; E. A. Mowrer, *The Nightmare of American Foreign Policy*, New York, 1948; and R. Ingrim, *After Hitler, Stalin?*, New York, 1946; also the article of J. Amery in the *Nineteenth Century and After* (January, 1950). See also Horthy's interesting letter to Churchill, dated July 5, 1945, in Papen, cited above, pp. 619–21. The origins of the Stettin-Trieste line and the zoning of Germany and Austria are touched upon in Dwight D. Eisenhower, *Crusade in Europe*, New York, 1948; and in Lucius D. Clay, *Decision in Germany*, New York, 1950. See also J. Thorwald, *Es begann an der Weichsel* and his *Das Ende an der Elbe*, Stuttgart, 1950. The subject is somewhat more closely examined in the article by Erickson in the *Annals of the American Academy of Political and Social Sciences* (January, 1950) about the Austrian zoning; and by Mosely in *Foreign Affairs* (April, 1950) about the German zoning; see also the article by F. C. Pogue in *World Politics* (April, 1952).

Contemporary accounts of the early, national consequences of central-eastern Europe's abandonment to the Soviet sphere consist mostly of eastern European personal memoirs, some of which had been cited in Part IV. Memoirs in addition to these are: A. Bliss Lane, *I Saw Poland Betrayed*, New York, 1948; J. Stypulkowski, *Invitation to Moscow*, London, 1951; D. Sulyok, *Zwei Nächte ohne Tag*, Zurich, 1948; I. Kovács, *Im Schatten der Sowjets*, Zurich, 1948; see also A. Georgescu-Cosmovici, *Au commencement était la fin*, Paris, 1951; H. Ripka, *Le coup de Prague: une révolution préfabriquée*, Paris, 1949; J. Brown (pseud.), *Who's Next? the Lesson of Czechoslovakia*, London, 1951; O. Friedman, *The Break-Up of Czech Democracy*, London, 1950; and J. Stransky, *East Wind Over Prague*, London, 1950.

Of considerable value are the chapters of P. A. Mosely and S. Kertész in W.

Gurian, ed., *The Soviet Union: Background, Ideology, Reality*, Notre Dame, 1951, and the standard account of H. Seton-Watson, *The East European Revolution*, New York, 1951. Other works of general character are R. Betts, ed., *Central and South-East Europe 1945–48*, London, 1950; F. Hertz, *The Economic Problem of the Danubian States*, London, 1947; E. Kareda, *Technique of Economic Sovietization*, London, 1947. E. Kulischer, *Europe on the Move*, New York, 1948; and J. Schechtman, *European Population Transfers 1939–1945*, New York, 1947, deal with the extraordinary population displacement in central-eastern Europe during and after the last phase of the war; see also the broad study of OSS, R & A 2587, on this theme and the article by J. Schechtman in the *Journal of Central European Affairs* (October, 1949). S. Skrzypek, *The Problem of Eastern Galicia*, London, 1948, is a regional study; the tragedy of the German expellees is examined in Lember-Lothar, ed., *Die Entstehung eines neuen Volkes aus Binnendeutschen und Ostvertriebenen: Untersuchungen . . .*, Marburg, 1950.

GERMANY, RUSSIA AND EASTERN EUROPE

1914: BALANCE OF POWER

1921: THE MIDDLE TIER

1940: PARTITION

1948

[/////] PARTIALLY GERMAN-OCCUPIED   [▦] RUSSIAN-OCCUPIED

THE DIPLOMATIC REVOLUTION 1934 – 1937

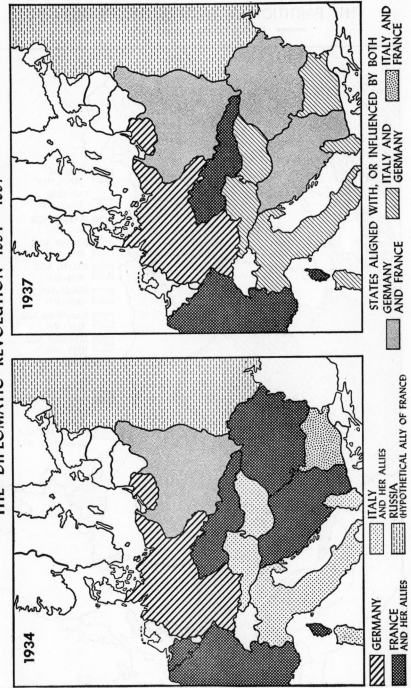

1934

GERMANY
AND HER ALLIES

ITALY
AND HER ALLIES

FRANCE
AND HER ALLIES

RUSSIA
(HYPOTHETICAL ALLY OF FRANCE)

1937

STATES ALIGNED WITH, OR INFLUENCED BY BOTH

GERMANY
AND FRANCE

**ITALY AND
GERMANY**

**ITALY AND
FRANCE**

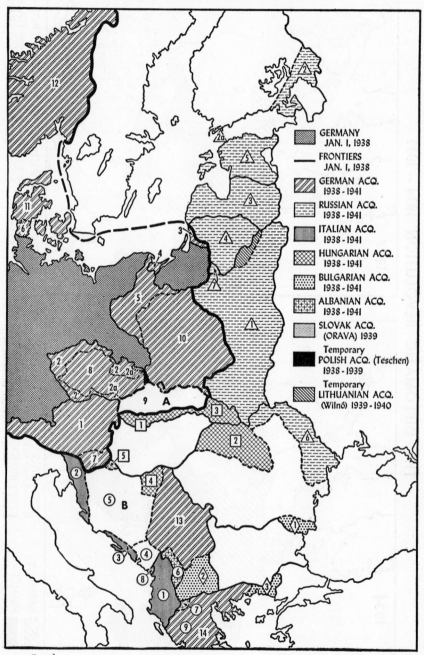

THE PARTITION OF EASTERN EUROPE 1938 - 1941
THE GERMAN EMPIRE JUNE 22, 1941

GERMANY
JAN. 1, 1938

FRONTIERS
JAN. 1, 1938

GERMAN ACQ.
1938 - 1941

RUSSIAN ACQ.
1938 - 1941

ITALIAN ACQ.
1938 - 1941

HUNGARIAN ACQ.
1938 - 1941

BULGARIAN ACQ.
1938 - 1941

ALBANIAN ACQ.
1938 - 1941

SLOVAK ACQ.
(ORAVA) 1939

Temporary
POLISH ACQ. (Teschen)
1938 - 1939

Temporary
LITHUANIAN ACQ.
(Wilnô) 1939 - 1940

THE PARTITION OF EASTERN EUROPE, 1938–1941

Legend of Acquisitions

GERMANY

Annexations

1 Austria — March 1938
2 Sudetenland — October 1938
2a Frontier adjustment with Czecho-Slovakia — November 1938
3 Memel — March 1939
4 Danzig — September 1939
5 W. Poland — October 1939
6 N. Schleswig— April 1940
7 S. Carinthia — April 1941, June 1942

Protectorates

8 Bohemia & Moravia — March 1939
9 Slovakia — March 1939

Occupied Territories

10 Polish "Generalgouvernement" — October 1939
11 Denmark — April 1940
12 Norway — May–June 1940
13 Serbia (and Banat) — April 1941, June 1942
14 Greece — April 1941

RUSSIA

Annexations (incorporated)

⟨1⟩ E. Poland — October 1939
⟨2⟩ E. Karelia (and Petsamo) — March 1940
⟨3⟩ Latvia — July 1940
⟨4⟩ Lithuania — July 1940
⟨5⟩ Estonia — July 1940
⟨6⟩ Bessarabia & NW. Bukovina — June 1940

Leased for occupation

⟨2a⟩ Hangö peninsula — March 1940

Purchased

⟨7⟩ Suwalki triangle — January 1941

ITALY

Annexations

① Albania — April 1939

② NW. Slovenia — June 1941
③ Dalmatian Zone — June 1941

Protectorates

④ Montenegro — June 1941
⑤ Croatia — May 1941–August 1943

Annexations to ALBANIA

⑥ From erstwhile Yugoslavia — June 1941, 1942
⑦ From erstwhile Greece — June 1941, 1942

Occupied Territories

⑧ Zone of Kotor — June 1941
⑨ Greece (jointly with Germany) — April 1941

HUNGARY

Annexations by international award

☐1 N. Hungary–S. Slovakia — November 1938
☐2 N. Transylvania — August 1940

Military annexations

☐3 Carpatho-Ukraine — March 1939
☐4 Bachka — April 1941

Occupied Territories

☐5 Medjomurje (Muraköz) — May 1941

BULGARIA

Annexations

◇1 S. Dobrudja — September 1940

Occupied Territories

◇2 Macedonia & SE. Serbia — May 1941, June 1942
◇3 W. Central Thrace, Greek Macedonia — May 1941

ALBANIA (see ITALY)

NEWLY CREATED STATES, 1938–1941

A Slovakia
B Croatia

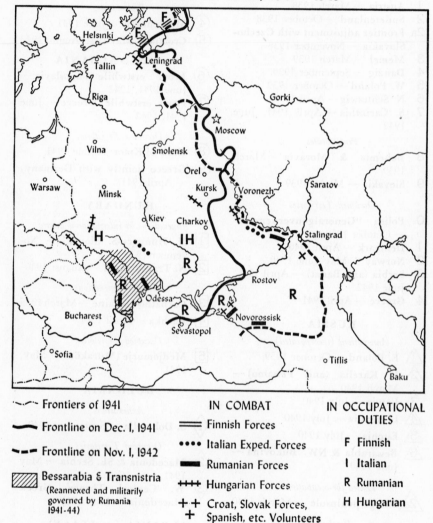

EMPLOYMENT OF GERMANY'S ALLIES
IN THE RUSSIAN WAR, 1941 – 1943

Helsinki

Tallin

Leningrad

Riga

Gorki

Moscow

Vilna

Smolensk

Orel

Kursk

Voronezh

Saratov

Warsaw

Minsk

Kiev

Charkov

Stalingrad

H

IH

R

R'

Rostov

R

Odessa

Bucharest

R

R

Novorossisk

Sevastopol

Sofia

Tiflis

Baku

IN COMBAT	IN OCCUPATIONAL DUTIES

〰️ Frontiers of 1941

▬ Frontline on Dec. 1, 1941

▬▬ Frontline on Nov. 1, 1942

▨ Bessarabia & Transnistria
(Reannexed and militarily
governed by Rumania
1941-44)

IN COMBAT

═══ Finnish Forces

•••• Italian Exped. Forces

▬▬ Rumanian Forces

+++ Hungarian Forces

++ Croat, Slovak Forces,
+ Spanish, etc. Volunteers

**IN OCCUPATIONAL
DUTIES**

F Finnish

I Italian

R Rumanian

H Hungarian

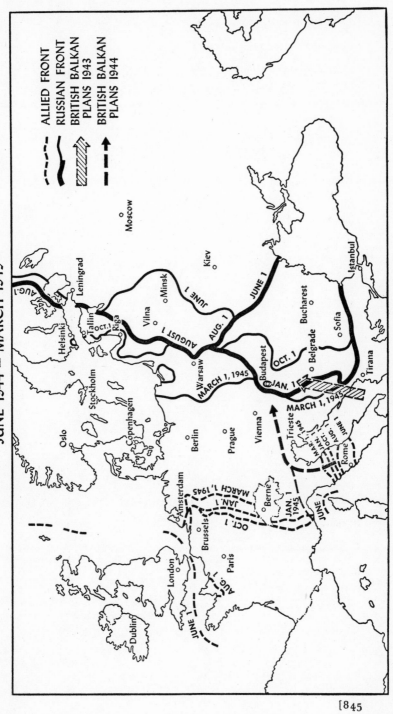

THE MILITARY ROAD TO THE DIVISION OF EUROPE
JUNE 1944 – MARCH 1945

ALLIED FRONT
RUSSIAN FRONT
BRITISH BALKAN PLANS 1943
BRITISH BALKAN PLANS 1944

Moscow

Leningrad
Kiev
Helsinki
Minsk
Tallin
Riga
Vilna
Warsaw
Stockholm
Oslo
Copenhagen
Berlin
Prague
Vienna
Amsterdam
Brussels
London
Paris
Dublin
Budapest
Bucharest
Belgrade
Sofia
Tirana
Istanbul
Trieste
Rome
Berne

JUNE 1
AUG. 1
OCT. 1
AUGUST 1
MARCH 1, 1945
JAN. 1
OCT. 1
MARCH 1, 1945

INDEX